University Economics

Elements of Inquiry

Third Edition

Armen A. Alchian
University of California, Los Angeles

William R. Allen
Texas A&M

Wadsworth Publishing Company, Inc.
Belmont, California

© 1972 by Wadsworth Publishing Company, Inc.
© 1964, 1967 by Wadsworth Publishing Company, Inc., Belmont,
California 94002. All rights reserved. No part of this book may
be reproduced, stored in a retrieval system, or transcribed, in any
form or by any means, electronic, mechanical, photocopying, recording,
or otherwise, without the prior written permission of the publisher.

ISBN–0–534–00030–4

L. C. Cat. Card. No. 70–173499

Printed in the United States of America

1   2   3   4   5   6   7   8   9   10---76   75   74   73   72

Foreword

This edition of *University Economics* is subtitled *Elements of Inquiry* to emphasize that economics enables a more accurate inquiry into how our economy works and how our behavior is influenced by the kind of economic system we have. This version is based on the earlier editions and on *Exchange and Production,* a paperback version of the first portions of *University Economics.* Still, economics, like any substantial body of analysis and information, is not something to be acquired by mere reading, any more than is chemistry, biology, or physics. Careful study and exercise are essential. The book is not intended to train professional economists. It is directed to the student who is interested in learning about economics in a one-semester or one-year course. The simplest fundamentals are adequate for that purpose.

A test of any theory or science is its ability to explain reality consistently. Economics passes that test. This book is an introductory exposition of economic analysis, with emphasis on its usefulness and validity. Students can easily learn the concepts and theorems, but application to real events and to their interpretation is difficult to master. It has often been said, "They can parrot the theory, but they can't apply it to problems." To provide analytical competence, this text emphasizes applications of the basic theorems.

The appropriateness of stressing the fundamentals of analysis is evidenced by the statement of an economist, Alain A. Enthoven, who had filled a government position of great responsibility:

> . . . the tools of analysis that we . . . use are the simplest, most fundamental concepts of economic theory, combined with the simplest quantitative methods. The requirements for success in this line of work are a thorough understanding of and, if you like, belief in the relevance of such concepts as marginal products and costs in complex situations, combined with a good quantitative sense. The economic theory we are using is the theory most of us learned as sophomores. The reason Ph.D.'s are required is that many economists do not believe what they have learned until they have gone through graduate school and acquired a vested interest in the analysis. ("Economic Analysis in the Department of Defense," *American Economic Review,* 53 (May 1963), 422.)

In this edition, the theory covering choice, demand, exchange, and supply has been extended beyond the narrow, private-property, wealth-maximizing behavior. The analysis of cost and its relation to various dimensions of output has been modernized to include mass-production economies. The startling advances provided by the role of information and transaction costs have been integrated into the analysis, explaining much behavior as well as laying a foundation for analysis of fluctuations in national income and employment and personal income.

The instructor who is familiar with earlier editions will note that the consequences of costs of acquiring information about marketing opportunities and costs of negotiating transactions and enforcing contracts are analyzed with more attention. The use of time in purchasing and consumption is also given more recognition. The chapter on costs and outputs (the cost curves) has been lightened in detail and depth. The treatment of national income fluctuations has been modified to reflect recent advances in monetary theory and evidence about monetary forces. So-called pollution problems—which are really nothing more than problems of getting costs to be heeded and hence influential in what is done—are even more extensively covered than in earlier editions. What had been in the earlier editions a final chapter on growth has been distributed throughout the text rather than being left as a special topic following international trade, for it is in fact an inherent aspect of all economic activity, rather than a wholly separate issue.

Study questions are referred to at appropriate places in the text so that the student will at that point read the questions and try to answer them as an exercise in applying the material. Instead of being cocktail conversation questions, they (1) reinforce the learning of concepts and principles, (2) develop a familiarity and ease in applying economic theory, (3) test the student's progress, and (4) stimulate exploration in slightly more advanced aspects not covered in the text. Most novel to economics, though not to texts in other sciences, is the inclusion of answers to half of the questions. (In the question sections, *answered questions have a boldface number.*) Answers serve two purposes: to guide and give the student confidence in his progress and to demonstrate that economic problems can have testable answers. Of course, questions that ask for one's preferences or beliefs admit of no uniquely correct answers. Answerable questions not answered in the text are answered in the Instructor's Manual.

Beginning the text as Chapter 0 is "A Note on Simple Analytics." The arithmetic and geometry there applied to some standard economic exercises should help to dispel the feeling—still quite common among college students—that even the elementary mathematics used in this book is an art form that requires a strange sort of genius for mastery.

Many examples and assertions in the text are not documented. In the Instructor's Manual, references are given to articles presenting applications of economic theory with factual and evidential material. These will enable the instructor to give more detail in classroom discussion. Acknowledgment of aid to specific persons was made in earlier editions. But now so many have aided in so many ways that the list would be too long to print here. We express our apologies for not listing them and our genuine gratitude for their aid—and make the usual disclaimer of attributing blame to them for any errors.

A Study Guide for *University Economics,* enabling the student to reinforce his learning, check his comprehension, and become acquainted with some extensions of the analysis, has been prepared by Richard Newcomb of Pennsylvania State University and David Ramsey of the University of Missouri.

Contents

0   **A Note on Simple Analytics**

1   **Scarcity, Competitive Behavior, and Economics**

Our Economic Activities   5
Three Attributes of Economic Analysis   6

2   **Competition**

Competition   11
Competitive Criteria and Survival Traits   13
Scarcity, Productive Activity, and Culture   14

3   **Some Behavior Postulates**

The Unit of Analysis Is the Individual   19
Behavioral Postulates   20
Meaning of Value—Input Value versus Output Value   23
Rational People versus Rational Analysis   24
Meaning of Self-Interest   24
Utility-Maximizing Behavior   25
Functional Analysis in Economics   25
Appendix: Preference Maps and Utility Lines   27

4   **Basis of Exchange**

Mutually Advantageous Trade and the Middleman   35
Diminishing Personal Values   39
Open Markets, Costs of Exchange, and Profit Reduction   41
Constrained Markets   41
A Few Implications of Exchange Analysis   43
Freedom: As You Like It   45
Criticisms of Methodology   45
Appendix: The Edgeworth Exchange Box   47

5 Demand and the Laws of Demand

Money 55
Markets 56
The Money-Price Quantity Demand Function 57
The Demand Function 57
Price and Value at the Margin—Not of Total Stock 58
The First Fundamental Law of Demand 60
The Second Fundamental Law of Demand 63
Some Illustrations of the Laws of Demand 64
Needs versus Demand 67
Alleged Exceptions to the Laws of Demand 67
Price Effects on Income and Substitution 68
Direct Evidence of Validity 70
Indirect Evidence of Validity 70
Income and Demand 71

6 Market Demand, Allocation, and Equilibrium Price

Market Demand in a Society 79
Markets as Economizers on Costs of Collecting Information 81
Market Supply and Demand: Graphic Interpretation 82
Purpose of Demand and Supply Concepts 86
Appendix 88

7 Applications of Demand Analysis to Market Pricing and Allocation

The Cost-Push Illusion 95
Rental and Allocation 97
Prices of Common Stock 99
Pricing and Discrimination 100
Price Controls as a Restriction on Market Exchange 100
Popularity of Price Controls 104
Economic Rent 105

8 Price-Takers' and Price-Searchers' Markets

Price-Takers' Markets: Virtually Horizontal Demand Facing Individual Seller 111
Price-Searchers' Markets: Sellers Face Negatively Sloped Demand 114
Why Price-Searchers? 118
Oligopoly 120
Multipart Pricing 123

Price Discrimination   125
Wealth versus Utility Maximization   127
Producer or Consumer Sovereignty?   128

9 Nonclearing Market Prices

(1) Costs of Information about Prices and Exchange Opportunities   137
Actions that Economize Information and Adjustment Costs and Increase Price Predictability   139
(2) Costs of Negotiating Exchanges and (3) Enforcing Property Rights   141
(4) Allocation under Rights Other Than "Private Property": Nonprofit Institutions   144
(5) Public Goods   147
Conclusion   154

10 Allocation of Consumable Goods over Time: Speculation

The Risk-Taker in Commodity Markets   161
Allocation of Risks in Futures Markets   167
Speculative Markets under Different Economic Systems   168

11 Capital Values, Interest Rates, and Wealth

Rate of Interest   176
Future Amounts Corresponding to Given Present Values   180
Present Capital Value for Series of Future Amounts   182
Illustrative Applications of Capitalization Principles   185
Wealth, Income, Consumption, Savings, Profits   189
Capital Values, Property, and Care of Wealth   190
Human Capital   191
Some Confusions about Interest Rates   193

12 Production, Exchange, Specialization, and Efficiency

Production and Exchange   200
Specialization and Enlarged Output   201
Achievement of Efficient Production by Market Exchanges   208
Gains from Trade and the Size of the Market   210
Are Specialization and Efficient Production Good?   211

13 Production in Various Market Conditions

Measure of Costs   219
Production-Possibility Boundary as Supply Schedule   220

Production Controls under Private-Property, Open-Market
System   223
Productive Efficiency and Wealth Maximizing   228
Productive and Utility Efficiency   230
Actual Attainment of Productive and Utility Efficiency?   231

14 Market Restrictions, Pollution, Property Enforcement Costs, and Public Goods

Restricted Market Access: A Source of Production
Inefficiency   237
Pollution and Property Costs   239
Public Goods Production   245
Appendix: Closed Market Inefficiency   251

15 Costs and Production

Preview   255
Costs of Acquisition, Continuing Possession, and Operation   256
"Size" of Output Programs   258
Proportionate Increases in Both Rate and Volume   262
Timing of Production: Long Run and Short Run   265
Costs Relevant to Entry and to Shut-down Decisions   268
To Continue or Not to Continue Production   268
Joint Products with Common Costs   269
Depreciation, Obsolescence, and Resource Uses   271
Appendix: Example of Cost Calculation of a Specific Output
Program   276

16 The Business Firm and Profits

Why Do Business Firms Exist?   281
The Formal Legal Structure of Business Firms   283
Profits and Business Firms   287

17 Production by Firms in Price-Takers' Open Markets

Influence of Demand Changes on Output   311
Market Supply: Aggregated Supplies of All Firms   316
Supply Response by Entry of New Firms: Long-Run
Response   318
How Resource Values Direct Resource Uses   320
Consequence of Basing Output on Wealth Maximizing   322
Adjustments without Full Information   322
Timing of Supply Responses   323

Summary of Output Response   323
Illustrative Analysis: Effects of a Tax   324

18 Production and Pricing in Price-Searchers' Open Markets

Two Types of Monopolies   333
Price and Output for Price-Searchers in Open Markets with Full Knowledge of Demand and Cost   335
The Search for Wealth-Maximizing Price and Output with Incomplete Information   336
New Capacity and Entry of New Firms in Response to Demand Changes   339
Response of Producers to Anticipated Demand   340
Desirability of Directing Output by Wealth-Maximization for Price-Searchers   343
Some Confusions about Price-Searchers' Markets   343

19 Sellers' Tactics for Changing Market Conditions

Methods for Changing Market Competition   353
Ethics or Desirability of Collusion   357
Price Discrimination?   363
Protection of Consumers   364
Protection of Producers   368
Public Utilities   372
Monopoly Rents: Creation and Disposition   374

20 Derived Demand for Productive Resources

Labor and Capital as Standard Names of Resources   387
Variety of Productive Techniques   388
The Law of Diminishing Marginal Returns   391
The Derived Demand for Productive Resources   394
Position of Derived Demand   396
Generality of Marginal-Productivity Theory   397
The Circle Closed   400

21 Wages and Employment in Open Markets

Labor Service Is a Commodity   407
Demand for Labor   410
Supply for Labor   410
Open-Market Wage Rates   411
Wage Differences   413
Effect of Technological Progress on Job Allocation and Wages   419

22 Restrictions on Open Markets for Labor

Employee-Employer Bargaining Power   427
Labor Unions   428
Unions and Wage Rates   433
How to Raise Wage Rates   433
Legal Restrictions on Open Markets for Labor   438
Closed Monopsony: Buyers Close a Market to Other Buyers   442

23 Interest, Saving, and Investing

Means of Converting Current Income into Wealth   456
Net Productivity of Investment Activity   458
Demand for Investment: The Most Profitable Rate of Investment   459
Savings Supply   461
Coordinating Investing and Saving Decisions   461
The Meanings of the Interest Rate   464
Stipulated Explicit Interest Rate and the Implied Effective Interest Yield   465
Effect of Quantity of Money versus Effect of *Increasing* the Quantity of Money   467
The Money and the Real Rates of Interest   467
Specialization of Borrowers and Lenders   468
Negotiability of Bonds   469
Legal Restraints on Access to Loan Market   470
Personal Investment Principles   473

24 Growth and Distribution of Wealth

Sources of Greater Wealth   487
Sources of Wealth   490
Greater Availability of Wealth?   490
Growth, Property Rights, Pollution, and Conservation   491
Personal Income and Wealth Differences   493
The Poor   496
Group Differences in Income and Wealth   500
Some Ghetto Economics   502
National Differences in Per Capita Income and Growth   503
The Dismal Mathematics of Growth   503
Epilogue and Preview   505

25 Unemployment and Economic Fluctuations

The Magnitude of Employment and Unemployment   513
Unemployment   514

Some Sources and Kinds of Unemployment   515
Structural Demand and Aggregate Demand Decreases   517
General Aggregate Demand Decrease   520
Dispassionate Analysis and Compassionate Policy   525
Determination of Aggregate Demand   525

26 National Income: Measurement and Meaning

Gross National Product (GNP)   529
Domestic Current Output   530
GNP and Changes in Quantities and Prices   531
Net National Product   533
National Income   534
National Income, Output, Employment, and Prices   534
National Income or Wealth   537

27 National-Income Theory: The Basic Model

Income Creation and Income Disposal   541
The Consumption Demand Function   544
Arithmetic-Tabular Determination of Income   547
Graphic Determination of Income   548
Money and Income   548
Income Determination in an Investment and Consumption Model   550
Arithmetic-Tabular Determination of Equilibrium Income   551
Graphic Determination of Equilibrium Income   552
Money versus Investment Goods versus Consumption Goods   552
Changes in National Income   554
An Interpretation of the Process of Income Changes   556
Autonomous Change in Consumption Function: Alleged Paradox of Thrift   559
The Multiplier   560
Income or Interest Rate as Adjusting Variable   562
Investment Volatility: The Accelerator   563

28 Money and Income

Money   571
The Demand for Money   573
Preview of Effects of Changes in Quantity of Money Supplied   575
Money versus Investment   576
The Quantity Equation and the Quantity Theorem   577

29 Money Supply and Commercial Banks

Commercial Bank Money: Supply Transactions   585
Expansion of Demand Deposits in the Single Bank   593
Expansion of Demand Deposits in the Banking System   595
Supply and Demand for Commercial Bank Money   598
Supply (Lending) and Demand (Borrowing) of Deposits   598
Conclusion   601

30 Money Supply: Determinants and Techniques of Control

Bank Reserves and the Monetary Base   607
Federal Reserve Bank Techniques for Control of Reserves   610
Appendix: Sources and Forms of Reserves and the Monetary Base   615

31 Government Finances

Government Expenditures and Receipts   629
Efficiency of Government Services   636
Redistribution of Wealth and Income   639
Deficits and Debt   639

32 Fiscal Policy Impacts on Income

Equilibrium Income with Government Spending and Taxing   646
Fiscal Policy and Variations on a Theme   650
Route 1: Increase Government Spending with Constant Tax Rate   651
Route 2: Unchanged Government Expenditure with Reduced Tax Rate   653
Route 3: Increase Government Spending and Reduce Tax Rate   655
Route 4: Increase Government Spending and Tax Rate with Budget Balanced   655
Route 5: Increase Government Spending and Tax Rate with Budget Deficit   659
Route 6: Increase Government Spending and Tax Rate with Budget Surplus   659
Route 7: Decrease Government Spending and Tax Rate with Budget Deficit   660
Which Route?   660
Limits to Expansion of Income   661
A Different Problem: Revised Allocation of Income to Guns or Butter   662

Appendix: Algebra in the Analysis of Income Determination 664

33 Inflation

What Is Inflation? 671
The Meaning of the Effects of Inflation 673
Wealth-Transfer Effects of Unanticipated Inflation 674
The Wage-Lag Doctrine: An Exercise in Debunking 681
The Causes of Inflation 682
Personal Protection from Inflation 685
Quantity of Money and Inflation: Some Historical Episodes 685
Anticipated Inflation 687
Anti-Inflation Monetary Reforms 692

34 Stabilization or Destabilization Policy?

Inflation, Low Employment, and Wage and Price Controls 702
Political and Economic Problems in Discretionary Policy 706
The Stabilization Record of the Federal Reserve 709
Discretionary Monetary Policy and Stabilization Possibilities 713
Automatic Stabilizers 716
Full-Employment Income Budget Balance 718

35 Imports and the "Gain from Trade"

The Gold Bug, Foreign Aid, and National Income 724
International Payments and Exchange Arbitrage 727

36 International Trade Theory

The Output-Price Theory 733
The Single-Input Theory 741
The Multiple-Input, Factor-Endowment Theory 746

37 Resource Allocation, Terms of Trade, and Tariffs

Trade and Resource Allocation 757
Reciprocal Demand and the Terms of Trade 759
Tariffs and Trade 763
What Do the Terms of Trade Measure? 767
Customs Unions and Trade 769

38 The Balance of Payments and Its Interpretation

Balance-of-Payments Accounting   777
Interpretations of "Imbalance"   780
The Dollar, the Deficit, and International Liquidity   784

39 Balance-of-Payments Adjustment

Adjustment and Absorption   792
The Adjustment Alternatives   793
Adjustment and the I.M.F.   803
Answers   809
Index   845

A Note on Simple Analytics

O **How Much Mathematics and Graphs?**   xvii

"How much mathematics must I know to understand economics?" Only arithmetic, but one must also be able to read charts and graphs. It is not arithmetic or graph reading that causes confusion so much as it is *interpretation* of quantitative relationships between economic magnitudes. Therefore, this Appendix presents interpretations along with the arithmetic and chart reading. If you can follow it, you are adequately prepared. The arithmetic, chart reading, and interpretation are presented by simple examples in imaginary economic contexts. Numbers are chosen primarily to make computations and relationships easy to see, rather than to reflect reality.

Imagine we are producing "tees" for golf balls—little wooden devices on which the ball is placed prior to striking it 250 yards down the middle of the fairway. To make one tee costs, we assume, $1.00, counting all material, labor, etc. Costs of producing 2, 3, 4, etc., tees per day are in Table A-1. The more tees produced in a day, the greater the costs of that day's output. Two tees cost $1.90, and three cost $2.70. "Total costs" and "tees produced" both change in the same direction. The change of two magnitudes in the same direction is called a *positive* relationship. Another example would be daily caloric intake and one's weight—usually assumed to be positive, for more of one means more of the other. (Nothing is assumed about *causal* connection in saying a relationship exists. Whether or not any causality runs either way from one magnitude to the other is presently of no concern.)

An example of a *negative* relationship is age and strength for people over about 30 years. However, for younger people, the relationship is positive; a youth gets stronger as he grows, but after some age interval strength ceases to grow and then decreases with age. Thus over the *entire* range of age, the relationship with strength is at first posi-

TABLE A–1. Output of Tees and Costs

Tees Produced Daily	Total Costs
1	$1.00
2	1.90
3	2.70
4	3.40
5	4.00
6	4.70
7	5.50
8	6.40
9	7.40
10	8.60

tive, then possibly zero (indicating no change in strength as age increases), and then negative.

We can picture relationships with graphs. Figure A–1 portrays that assumed between costs and number of tees. The height of each bar indicates *total costs* of the number of tees to which it corresponds. Each bar has an upper shaded section showing simply how much higher it is than the neighboring bar for one less unit of output. The shaded part of the bar portrays the *increment* to total costs consequent to producing one more. We could draw a smooth line along the tops of the bars to indicate total costs without showing a lot of bars; this is done in Figure A–2 to make a cleaner looking chart. You will see that the line passes through several dots, each representing a combination of an integral (i.e., no fractions) number of tees and total costs. You may interpret the *line* between the dots as guiding the eye from point to point, or the line may represent the costs of producing fractional amounts. For example, if three tees are produced in two days, this is 1.5 tees per day. So fractional amounts of even non-divisible things do make sense, if interpreted as a *rate* of production per day. Even though only discrete or "integral" amounts of some good can be produced, we can still speak of fractional amounts per some unit of time.

So far in interpreting a chart, we have taken a point on the horizontal axis and then read up to the line to find the value of the corresponding variable in which we were interested. We first found 5 units of tees on the horizontal axis, and then by reading up directly above that point we saw the cost was $4. Usually the graph can also be read the other way. Suppose you were told that $4 could be spent on producing tees. How many could be produced? To answer, find $4 on the vertical scale, then go horizontally across the chart to the curve and drop straight down to the horizontal axis to an output of 5 tees.

We now direct attention to three different aspects of costs as different outputs of tees are considered. Three different, important concepts, "total, average, and marginal," must be understood. The *total* costs of Table A–1 are again shown in Table A–2, along with *average cost* per tee and *marginal cost* of tees. The *average* cost is the total cost per day divided by the number of tees per day. For two tees, the total cost per day, $1.90 divided by 2, is $.95 per tee. And for 5 tees the average cost is $.80. Compute the average cost of 5 and of 6 tees. If you agree with the numbers shown, proceed; if not, give up.

The continuing scholars should next look at the *marginal* costs column of Table A–2. These are the *differences* in the *total* costs of producing two different quantities of tees

TABLE A-2. Costs and Output of Tees

Tees Produced Daily	Costs		
	Total	Average (Dollars)	Marginal
1	$1.00	$1.000	$1.00
2	1.90	.950	.90
3	2.70	.900	.80
4	3.40	.850	.70
5	4.00	.800	.60
6	4.70	.783	.70
7	5.50	.785	.80
8	6.40	.800	.90
9	7.40	.825	1.00
10	8.60	.860	1.20

Total costs increase with number of tees produced daily. Average costs are total costs divided by number of tees produced daily. Marginal cost is increase in total costs for *one* unit increased output.

—those differing by *one* tee. For 5 tees a day the total cost is $4.00, and for 6 tees is $4.70; the difference, called the *marginal cost,* is $.70. This is shown in Figure A–1 as the shaded section of the bar for 6 units.

This simple concept of change, difference, or increment in cost associated with *one* unit larger output is *"marginal* cost." It is the *change* in one variable (here, total cost) associated with a *one* unit change in the other (in this case, output of tees). This could have been called the "incremental cost when 6 are produced rather than 5," or the "marginal cost of producing 6 rather than 5," but it is in fact called the *"marginal* cost of 6." Note carefully that it is not the total cost of producing 6, for that is $4.70, and it is not the average cost of producing 6, for that is $.78 per unit. It is the *increase* in total cost of six over the cost of 5.

We shall use these interpretations extensively. Unless you *always* keep these three *concepts*—(1) total, (2) average and (3) marginal—clearly separated, you will almost certainly not acquire a good grasp of economic principles. Hint: Never use the term "cost" by itself; always modify or identify it with "total," "average," or "marginal," so that you won't confuse one with the others. Let's test your ability to *interpret* and apply these concepts. Someone asks the question, "What is the cost of the sixth tee?" If you try to answer that question as it stands, you have just missed the boat. What cost? Total, average, or marginal? Each is different. But there lurks still another potential ambiguity. What is meant by the "marginal cost of the sixth tee?" It means, as we have said, how much more total costs are than if only 5 are to be produced. In the present example that seems clear enough. But to see how things can get muddied up in other contexts, we give you the following example.

Imagine a retail store with 4 clerks. Total sales are $2000 per day for the total of all four clerks—with some selling more than the $500 average and some less. Add a fifth clerk, Mr. E., to the sales force, and sales increase by $200 to $2200. Now it is *erroneous,* but tempting, to infer that Mr. E. is not a very good salesman or not as productive as the first four. Yet if you were to look at the details you would discover that he had $800

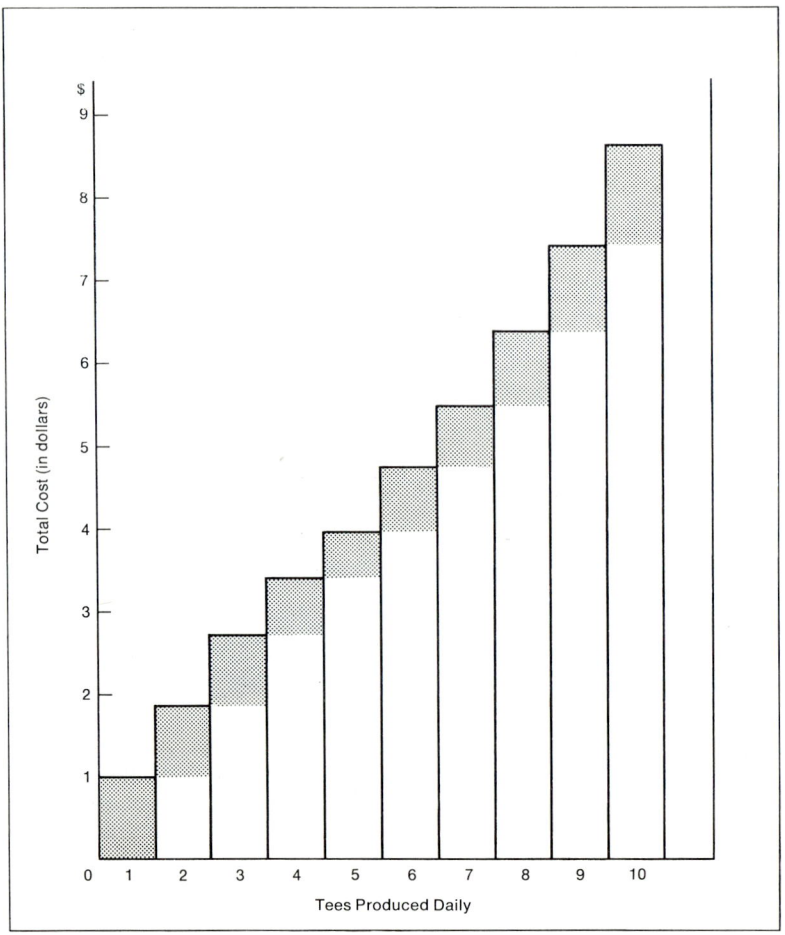

FIGURE A–1. Bar Chart of Total-Cost–Output-of-Tees Relationship

Shaded sections denote how much costs increase with each unit increase in daily output. Relationship between total cost and tees produced is *positive,* for both increase (or decrease) together.

of sales, which is more than for any other clerk. His presence enabled the store to sell $200 more by getting customers who otherwise would have decided not to buy, but he also managed to attract customers away from the other clerks, because of his superior looks and personality. *His* sales were $800, but that is not called his marginal sales or the marginal sales of the fifth person. The marginal sales with a fifth person were $200. Average sales were $440 with 5 people ($2200/5). And what about his $800? Is that *necessarily* comprised of $600 of sales taken from other clerks plus $200 of new customers? Not necessarily. All of the $800 may have been from old customers attracted from other clerks, while the other clerks scrounged around to get the extra $200 in sales. As we use the term, "marginal sales with a fifth person" is *not* to be interpreted as what *a* particular person or any other one did, but only as the *change* in the *total* results of having a *team* of 5 clerks rather than a team of 4. "Marginal sales" or "marginal costs"

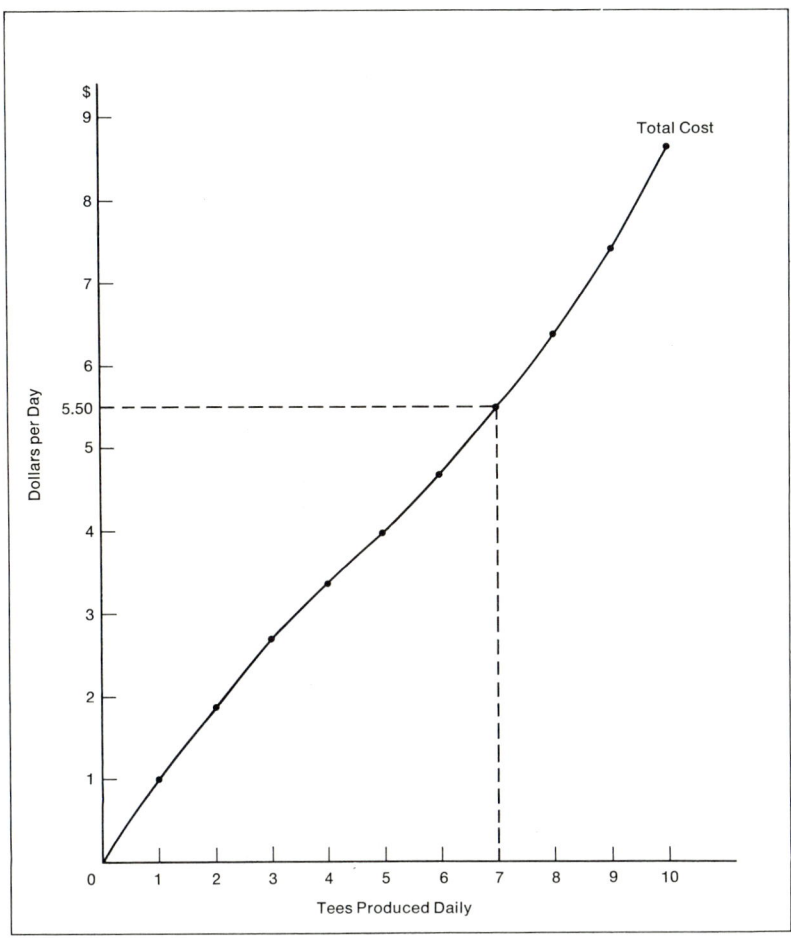

FIGURE A–2. Line Chart of Total-Cost–Output Relationship

Line chart shows more clearly how total cost varies with daily output of tees. Height of line at each output measures daily total cost. Upward slope, called positive slope, indicates positive relationship.

or "marginal whatever" will always be interpreted that way—as the *change in total* of one variable consequent to having *one* more of the other variable.

We do not give any name to the $800 of sales of the fifth person. In fact, often it cannot even be detected or conceived. For example, you have a team of four men rowing a boat with a trailing net to catch fish. You add a fifth man to row or help tend the net. How can you make any meaning of what the fifth man himself caught? You can't. The only possibility is the meaning we have given—the change in the *total* consequent to having 5 rather than 4. (If you think the *average* per man is interesting you may use it, too—but it has a clear name, the average.)

Turn your attention to the possible quantitative *behavior* of these magnitudes. Looking in Table A–2 at larger outputs of tees, you will notice marginal costs *increase* after their earlier initial decreases at smaller outputs of tees. Taking the total costs as the correct initial data, check the average cost and marginal costs calculations.

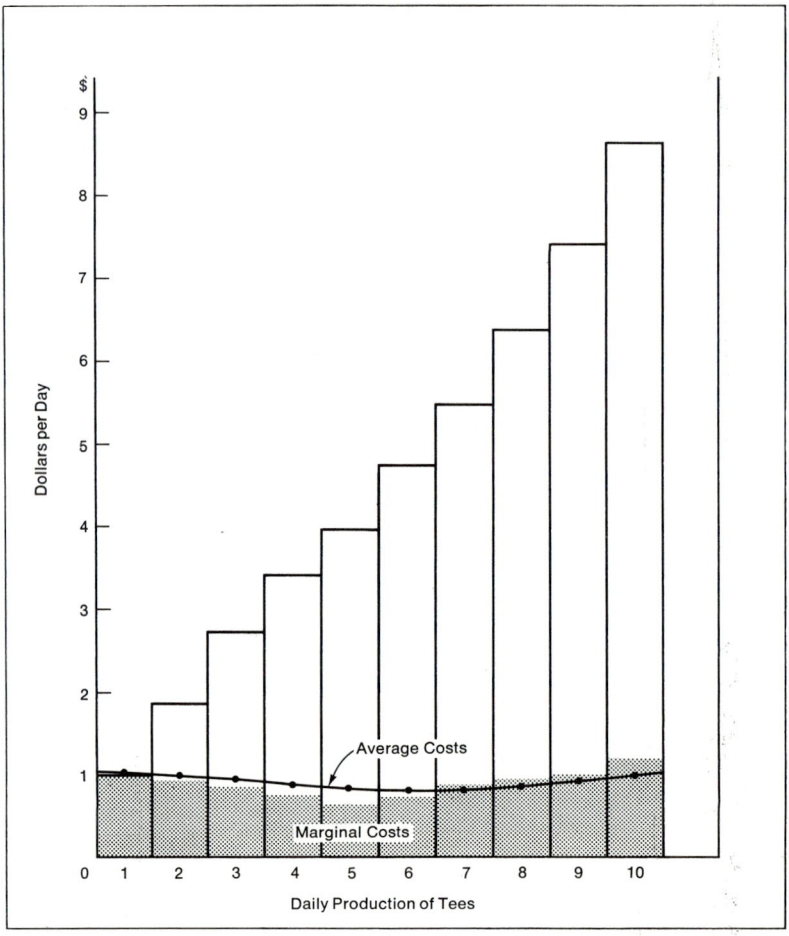

FIGURE A–3. Bar Chart of Total and Marginal Cost–Output Relationship

Shaded sections show marginal costs. Average costs are shown by line through dots, to avoid cluttering graph. Average costs fall when marginal costs are less than average cost; and rise when marginal cost exceeds average cost.

To exercise your arithmetic talents a bit more, consider how "averages" *must* behave relative to "marginals." Suppose as you increase output by one unit, from 8 to 9, the total cost *increase* (the marginal cost) is greater than the average cost at 8. What will be the average cost of 9? To see what is meant by the question, look at the output of 8 tees. For that output, average cost is $.80. Now the question is, "What will happen to the average cost of output, *if* you know that when you expand output from 8 to 9, the *increase* in total cost, $.90 (i.e., the *marginal* cost), is greater than the average cost ($.80) at 8?" Isn't this exactly like asking what will happen to your average test score if the points earned on your next test are higher than your present average? Won't it raise your average? And if one more test adds *fewer* points than your existing average, the average will be pulled down. We repeat, if the marginal exceeds the average, the average will rise;

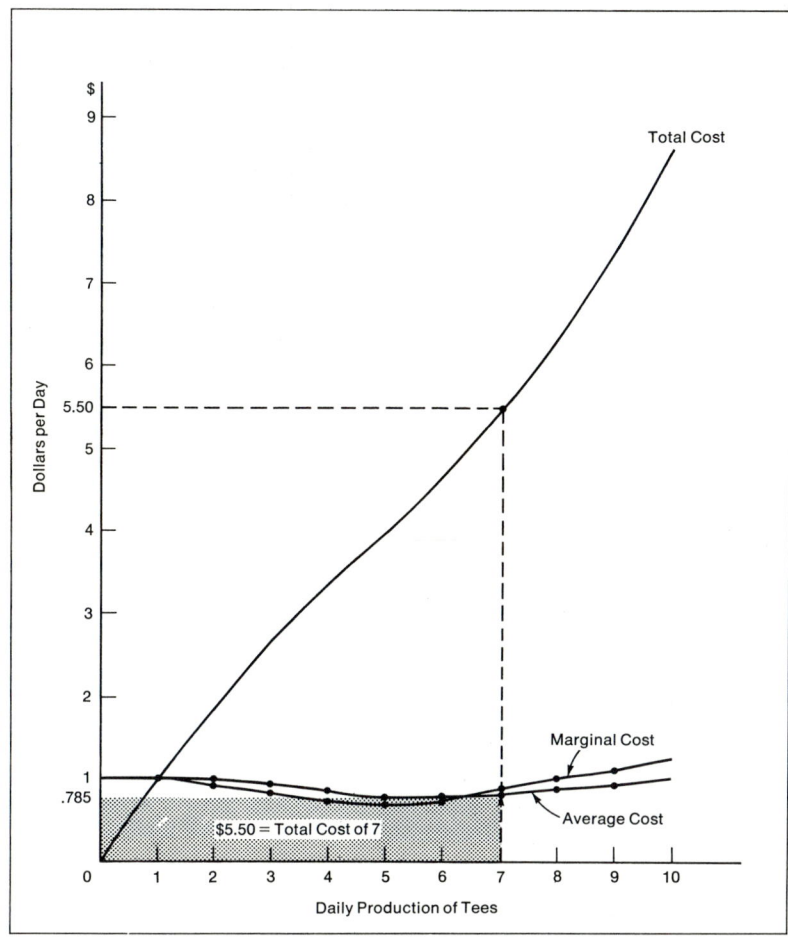

FIGURE A–4. Line Chart of Total, Average, and Marginal Cost Relationship with Output Rate

Rectangular area with height at average cost and base at output rate is measure of total cost. Area under marginal cost curve is also measure of total cost.

and if it is less than the current average, the average will go down. Hence the answer to the question is, "The average will be rising if the marginal is greater than the average." To verify this, look at the marginal costs for tees ranging from 7 to 10. For all those, the marginal cost is greater than the average, and the average cost rises in that output range.

If you examine all the marginal costs for tees of 1–6 you will see that the marginal cost is less than the average, so the average falls with increases in outputs. Always, where the marginal value exceeds the average value, the average must be increasing. And if the marginal value of the variable is less than its average, the average must be decreasing. Only if the marginal value equals the average will the average remain unchanged. If you look at the table and compare the average with marginal costs you will see that this is true.

To familiarize yourself with graphic presentation and analysis, examine Figure A–3, which shows bars for total costs; superimposed are the marginal costs, this time at the bottom of each bar. The marginal cost bars are exactly the same as the shaded sections at the top of the total cost bars in Figure A–2. We quickly see that the marginal costs at first decrease and then increase. Note also that the *sum* of all the marginal costs up through 7 tees is the total cost of 7 units. This general equality between the sum of marginal costs and the total cost is true for every output, by definition. Also shown are average costs per unit of each output, as dots connected by a smoothed line. You can see that average costs decrease so long as marginal costs are less than average costs, and when marginal costs have risen above average costs, the average costs rise.

The same figure is repeated as Figure A–4 but with lines rather than bars. The total cost of 7 units of output is shown in three ways. (1) It is measured by the *height* of the total cost line at 7. (2) It is measured by the *area* under the marginal cost line from the first through the seventh: it is the sum of the marginal costs. (3) Total cost is measured also by the shaded area of a rectangular box whose base is the horizontal axis from 0 through 7 and whose height is the average cost of 7. The average cost of 7 ($.785), shown by the height at 7, multiplied by 7 will be the total cost ($5.50, rounded to 3 figures). If you see that both the area *under the marginal cost curve* and the *rectangular area* formed by the average cost curve height at 7 units represent the total cost, then you have passed the hardest arithmetic and graphic interpretation test.

As evidence of your talents, examine the new data in Table A–3. The first two columns show prices and the number of "tees" that can be sold. The lower the price, the more that can be sold at any price. Complete the empty columns labeled "total receipts," "marginal receipts," and "average receipts"—which you will see is the same as price, because each unit is sold at the same price. Do not be surprised to get some *negative* marginal receipts. And in any event do the arithmetic without worrying much about why the relationship is shown as it is.

TABLE A–3. Sales Price and Number of Tees Sold Daily

Tees Sold	Price of Tee	Sales Receipts or Revenue (Dollars)		
		Total	Marginal	Average
1	$10	$10	+10	10
2	9	18	+8	9
3	8	24	+6	8
4	7	28	+4	7
5	6	30	+2	6
6	5	30	0	5
7	4	28	−2	4
8	3	24	−4	3
9	2	18	−6	2
10	1	10	−8	1

Complete the table and plot the results in Figure A–6. Negative marginal sales receipts indicate total sales proceeds diminish at lower price despite increased number sold. Sales proceeds are typically called "revenue."

On the partially completed graph in Figure A–5, on which some of the points have already been placed, put in the rest of the dots for the average receipts and for the marginal receipts and connect the points in each set with a smooth line. Then draw in the *two* alternative areas representing total receipts for 4 tees at a price of $7. Do the same for 8 tees at a price of $3. Which has the larger area?

We have some algebra! You should know that 1.10 times 1.10 can be written as $(1.10)^2$. And we require that if you see the expression, $4X = 20$, you can solve it for the value of X that satisfies that relationship. Even more, it is desirable that if you see the expression $C = .5Y + 10$ and are told that Y is assumed to have a value of 100, you can compute that C must be 60.

And finally we ask for some analytic geometry! Can you verify, by testing at a couple of values of Y, that the associated values of C and Y implicit in that relationship, $C = .5Y + 10$, are shown by the line labeled CC in Figure A–6 and by no other line? If so, fine!

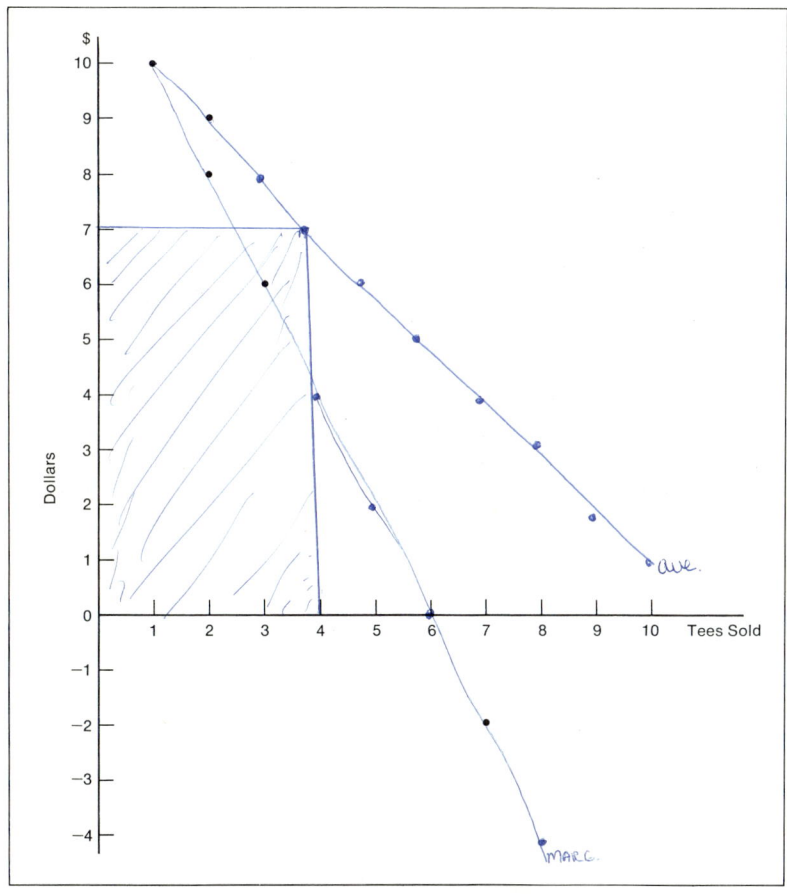

FIGURE A–5. Exercise Graph for Receipts–Units-Sold Relationship

You are to complete set of dots and draw lines of average costs and marginal costs. Relationship of price and units sold is negative. Is relationship between total sales receipts positive, negative, or both?

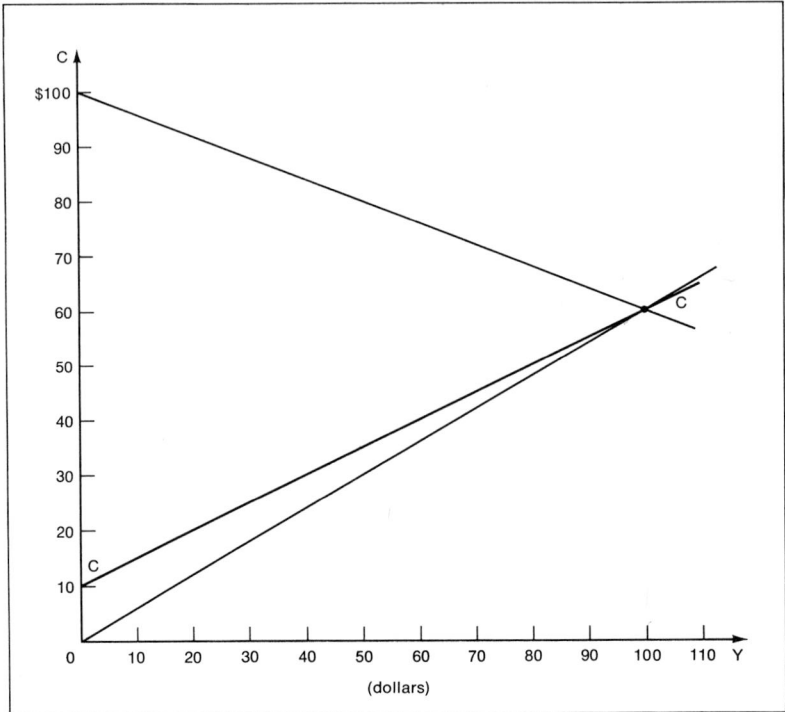

FIGURE A-6. *CC* Line Represents Pairs of Values of *C* and *Y* That Satisfy Relation $C = .5Y + 10$.

Test assertion in title by computing C for $Y = 100$, 50, and 0. Relationship —or *function*—between C and Y is positive. What is *marginal* value of C at $Y = 100$? Do you agree it is $.50? And that it is $.50 at every value of Y? It is.

You have demonstrated adequate knowledge of arithmetic, graphics, algebra, and analytic geometry. If some of the concepts are a little unfamiliar, don't worry. So long as you understand it, later exercises will make it familiar and easy. It really is, or will be, easy, if you'll just give a try. You will probably find that your instructor will help make it easy and will cleverly take you on to more mathematics with no trouble at all.

$\frac{50.5}{.25}$

$\frac{100.5}{\frac{5.0}{60}} \cdot 49 \frac{5}{\frac{19.5}{10.5}} \frac{5}{.5}$

$\frac{60.00}{-59.50}$
$.50$

$.5 \frac{100.0}{5.0.0}$

$\frac{50}{10}$

$.5 \frac{100.0}{5.0.0}$ $e = 60$

$\frac{90}{.5} \frac{5}{\frac{450}{00.35}}$

Scarcity, Competitive Behavior, and Economics

1

EVER since the fiasco in the Garden of Eden, most of what we get is by sweat, strain, and anxiety. Two villains—nature and other people—prevent us from having all we want. Nature is niggardly: it provides fewer resources than we could use, and much of what is available is made useful only by hard work. As for other people, the problem stems not from malevolence: their wants and ours simply exceed what is available. Do not suppose that if they were less greedy, more would be within our grasp. Greed impels them to produce more, not only for themselves, but, miraculously, more for us, too—provided that productivity-inducing arrangements exist.

Man wants more than there is any prospect of obtaining. Some assert we *could* satisfy our "needs" if only we were more efficient or worked harder. As a former government official put it: "We have not had enough of anything, because we have not used fully the fantastic productive power which could provide us with enough of everything." "Enough" of *everything?* To satisfy *every* conceivable whim and desire? Of *every* person? It is a frustrating fact that the world is a poor place. Despite religious and philosophical exhortations to abandon natural desires for "more," our wants evidently are boundless: as soon as we have more of this, we want still more of it and more of that . . . and that. To say that we always want more is to say that man lives, even in the most affluent societies, in a state of *scarcity.*

An alternative contention is that we *do* produce "enough" in the aggregate, but—because of selfishness, inept planning, and poor taste—we turn out the wrong things: silly gadgets, cosmetics, and over-large and too frequently remodeled automobiles instead of more symphony orchestras, better housing, art museums, and lunar explorations. But this expresses merely a preference for one collection of output *instead of* another.

Planning would not prevent scarcity. Indeed, in the blissful absence of scarcity, there would be no occasion to plan; with nonscarce resources, there would be no necessity to decide if productive services should be shifted from "silly" to "wholesome" output.

A simple diagram dealing with two commodities, "guns" and "butter," can illustrate some features of scarcity. In Figure 1–1, society could produce a maximum quantity, G, of guns if all available resources were directed to that end; alternatively, B of butter could be produced if guns were not; and any combination of the two could be produced along line GB. Society can achieve a production point *on* or *inside* the GB boundary line but not *outside* that boundary, which denotes its present productive powers and tastes for leisure. (1) A problem to be solved, somehow, by the socioeconomic organization is at what *point* to be on that boundary—that is, the output *mix*. Point I has more guns; II, more butter. Which will be chosen? (2) Will society produce as much as feasible? Or will it underproduce at a point *inside* the bounded area? Being inside may be the result of two kinds of inefficiency: (a) unnecessarily idle, unused resources or (b) misdirected, though fully employed, resources. (3) Growth is indicated in Figure 1–2 by an outward

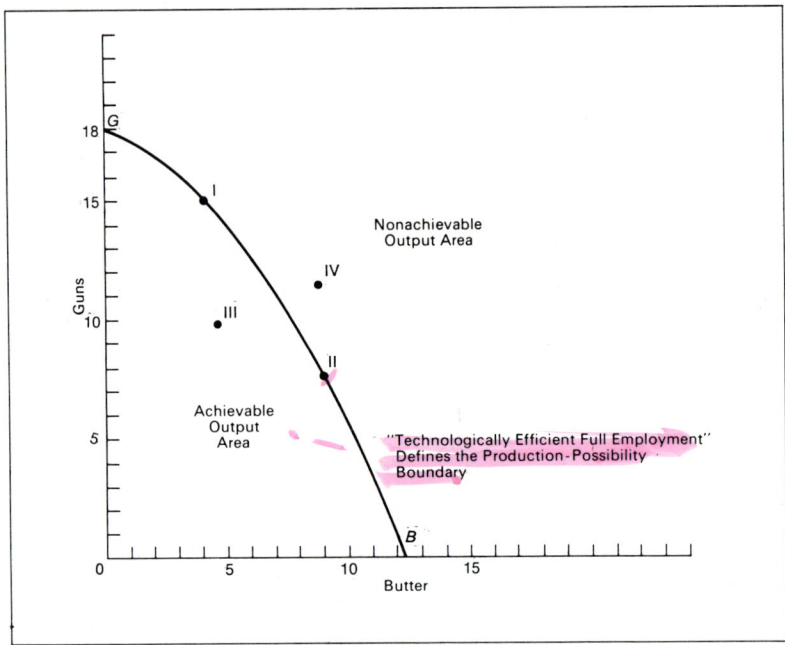

FIGURE 1–1. Scarcity, Efficiency, and Choice Illustrated by Production-Possibility Boundary

The curved line portrays largest combinations of amounts of guns and butter producible in the economy. Any point on the line (e.g., I or II) can be produced. No combination of guns and butter outside the curved line (e.g., point IV) can be achieved by the economy given its productive powers and preference for leisure. Less would be produced if the productive resources were unemployed or used inefficiently—as, for example, at point III. In some manner society selects a point on the boundary or inside it. Productive efficiency means that the economy is on the production boundary. We shall be studying the means for determining what pushes the economy to that line *and* to what point on that line. Why the curve has the shape shown here will be discussed later.

shift of the production-possibility boundary. This means society becomes richer by acquiring improved technology or by more resources or both.

Even more is involved in the response to scarcity. What determines how much *each* person produces and gets of that total? And what determines the particular *mix* of goods *he* consumes? These and more subtle issues, to be elaborated later, constitute the area of economic study.

1, 2*

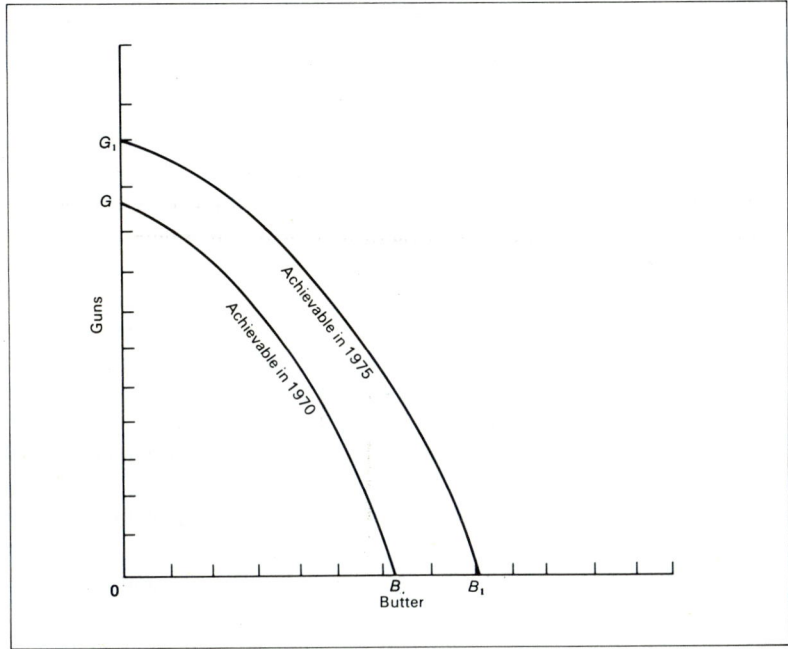

FIGURE 1–2. Growth of Economic Productive Powers of the Economy

A richer, more productive economy is represented by a production-possibility boundary that is higher and more to the right, as for 1975 compared to 1970. Growth can occur in several ways. A greater production-possibility boundary is usually induced by a larger labor force. (But does the output per person increase? That cannot be indicated by this diagram, which gives only the social totals.) Moving the frontier outward involves restricting current consumption by saving either to create more productive goods or to invest in knowledge and inventions. (Problem: Suppose the two boundaries intersected. Which would represent greater productive power?)

Our Economic Activities

Consider the awesome dimensions of the American community: a population exceeding 200,000,000 includes a labor force of 80,000,000 (one-third of whom are women) and, through 11,000,000 business units (including 9,000,000 single proprietorships, 1,000,-

---

* These numbers direct you to the questions at the end of the chapter. You should refer to these questions when their numbers appear in the text—and to the selected answers, at the end of the book. Boldface numbers indicate at the end of the chapter the questions that are answered.

000 partnerships, and 1,000,000 corporations), annually produces goods and services worth more than $1,000,000,000,000—some 30 percent of the world total. Who or what directs this vast production-and-distribution system? In small and intimate matters, willy-nilly individual decision making may be tolerable, but to resolve the vital, over-all, aggregate problems, it seems that someone must be in charge.

But American economic activity is *not* directed, planned, or controlled by any economic czar—governmental or private. No person or group poses detailed questions of how the community is to use its resources, and no one imposes comprehensive answers to the questions. Yet such problems—large and small—somehow *are* solved daily. No agency is appointed to ensure that adequate food reaches every city and is allocated among competing claimants—and yet the people eat. No "big brother" oversees the multitudinous operations of the economy and ensures that the essential functions are performed. The alternative to "big brother" evidently is not chaos and anarchy. An economic order does exist; some sort of control and direction does operate. Moreover, this mysterious system allows individuals and businesses to be essentially autonomous—and self-interested—agents (subject to the constraints that define property arrangements) and, at the same time, yields a viable and enviable degree of economic efficiency.

The individual, far from wrestling with grandiose problems of the universe, decides how much of his own wealth and income to expend for this or that and what kind of work to do. No farmer adds up the total demands for food in a city, comparing the total with the amount being shipped to the city, to make sure (because of his compassion) that adequate supplies will be available. Instead, with his individual interest and perspective, he asks, "Would I personally be richer or poorer if I shipped *and exchanged* more or less?" Millions of us make *exchange* decisions on our own "little pictures."

Although many of us solve our personal problems, we may still be grossly ignorant about how our actions and laws affect the rest of society. Comprehension of these larger effects requires economic theory, even if virtually none is required for individual decisions. We can be sure, as we shall see later, that economic analysis is ignored when the following incorrect assertions are proposed: the rationale of the capitalistic system requires a "harmony of interests"; customers must take what producers offer them; minimum-wage laws help the unskilled; discrimination can be stopped; pollution of air and water unquestionably should be stopped; automation reduces available jobs; tariffs protect domestic wage earners from foreign labor; our otherwise unlimited productive capacity is curtailed by monopolistic capitalists who arbitrarily set prices high; unions protect workers from greedy employers; inflation hurts the wage earner and benefits the employer; private firms serve private interests while publicly owned agencies serve public interests; used-book markets must reduce the royalties of textbook authors; social conscience and civic sensitivity are or should be the guides to business corporate behavior; unemployment occurs because not enough jobs are available or because some people are shiftless and lazy; or American agriculture produces a surplus of wheat because it is so productive. And that is only a tiny sample!

Three Attributes of Economic Analysis

To help understand what economics is, three methodological attributes should be clarified.

1. Economic theory is "positive" or "non-normative." It gives no generally accepted criteria for determining which consequence or type of behavior or economic policy is good—any more than physics tells whether gases are "better" than solids, or any more

than medicine can tell whether you "ought" not to smoke and drink. Economics can tell only the consequences of certain conditions, policies, or choices. It is no more proper for the economist than for any other person to sit on Mt. Olympus and decree what is desirable, though everyone may in fact make such pronouncements.

2. Economics explains what conditions will lead to what consequences. Economics yields conditional "if-A-then-B" propositions; it does not forecast that the A will occur—although some *economists* (as opposed to economics) may hazard such forecasts. It says a lower price of cars will sell more cars, but it doesn't say car prices *will* be lowered.

3. Valid economic theory exists and is applicable to *all* economic systems and countries. There is *not* a special economic theory for capitalism and another for communism, although significant differences exist in the institutions and legal frameworks to which the theory is applied. For the present, it is sufficiently accurate to define capitalism as a system of exchangeable private-property rights in goods and services, with the central government protecting these rights. Private-property rights, in turn, can be defined as the rights of owners to choose the use of their goods and resources (including labor and time) as they see fit. If a rock is said to be my property and a piece of glass is yours, I have control over only the rock, and you over only the glass; for me to throw my rock through your glass without your permission would exceed my rights to use only my goods as I wish because it would usurp your rights to use only your property as you see fit. In socialism, rights to the uses of a good are not assigned to specified individuals but instead are divided among various people in government agencies, who decide about uses and consequences to be borne. This is a system of "government ownership."

Market exchange of property rights is applicable to a wider class of activity in a "capitalistic" private-property economy than it is in a socialistic society. The extent of and reliance on interpersonal market exchange is greater in a capitalistic system. In a socialist system, political power and exchange of *non*private rights are used more widely to solve the economic questions. If we were to devote primary attention to socialist systems, we would investigate much more fully political exchange, political decision making, and political competition. Although applicable to all economic systems, economic theory has been more extensively and fruitfully applied to the analysis of capitalistic than of socialistic systems. However, some applications to noncapitalistic organizations are given in this book.

In sum, economics studies the competitive and cooperative behavior of people in resolving conflicts of interest that arise because wants exceed what is available.

Introductory comments cannot adequately reveal all that economics is or the richness of applications of economic theory. Only a study of economics can do that. Societies and open markets *have* grown and prospered in the face of almost universal illiteracy about economic theory, so there *are* limits to the significance and usefulness of the formal study of economics. But give it a fair try, anyway. Economics does deal with important things. Unless you fight it assiduously, it may well even be quite interesting.

Summary

A cautionary note: do not use these summaries as quick learning devices for examinations. Instead treat them as listing in capsule, cryptic form the major ideas of the chapters. The statements do not always reveal the full content and significance of each idea.

1. Given the limitations of nature and the unlimited desires of man, scarcity is inevitable and pervasive.

2. Efficient productive activity exists if an increase in the output of any good requires a reduction of some other good.

3. Economic theory is explanatory and amoral, not moral or prescriptive.

Questions

Questions at the end of each chapter are a basic element in this book. Read each question, ponder it, and then read the selected answers at the end of the book. Answers have been supplied for questions numbered in bold type. Do not skip the questions and answers; they contain some important ideas, applications, and interpretations you will find nowhere else in the book.

1. A recent book states (in essence): "We are trapped by the 'dismal science'—economics, which is dominated by the belief that the achievement of abundance is impossible and that the economic problem is still the distribution of scarce resources. This is nonsense. Abundance has arrived! The United States can produce so much that the basic problems are to see that the potential production is realized and distributed fairly and equitably." Are you inclined to agree or disagree? Why?

2. What is nonsensical about the proposition, "A good economic system maximizes the welfare of the maximum number of people"?

3. When a group of Russian officials touring American farms persistently asked who told the farmers how much to produce in order to supply the appropriate amounts of goods, the farmers said that no one told them. But the Russians were convinced the farmers were concealing something. What would you have told the Russians?

4. Try to give a definition of "efficient" production, "scarcity," "shortage," "surplus," "needs." (Later, compare your definitions with those given in subsequent chapters.)

5. What is meant by specialization? Do you know anyone who does not specialize? Why do people specialize?

6. "The economy of the United States is directed by the capitalists concentrated in Wall Street." Evaluate this assertion now, and again when you have completed this course.

7. "Food is grown, harvested, sorted, processed, packed, transported, assembled in appropriately small bundles, and offered to consumers every day by individuals pursuing personal interests. No authority is responsible for seeing that these functions are performed and that the right amount of food is produced. Yet food is available every day. On the other hand, especially appointed authorities are responsible for seeing that such things as water, education, and electricity are made available. Is it not paradoxical that in the very areas where we consciously plan and control social output, we often find shortages and failure of service? References to classroom and water shortages are rife; but who has heard of a shortage of restaurants, churches, furniture, beer, shoes, or paper? Even further, is it not surprising that privately owned businesses, operating for the private gain of the owners, provide as good, if not better, service to patrons and customers as do the post office, schools, and other publicly owned enterprises? Furthermore, wouldn't you expect public agencies to be less discriminating according to race and creed than privately owned business? Yet the fact is that they are not." How do you explain these paradoxes?

8 The *Statistical Abstract of the United States,* published annually by the U. S. Department of Commerce, Bureau of the Census, is a standard summary of statistics on the social, political, and economic organization of the United States. Every college library has a copy. You are urged to spend half an hour or so scanning the volume. For example, on page 125 of the 1969 edition you will find some data about faculty salaries. Do you think your instructor is underpaid or overpaid? After thinking about that for three minutes, compare faculty salaries with the information on pages 227–230 of that same edition about earnings in other industries.

9 What is meant by (a) the logical validity of a theory? (b) the empirical validity? (c) Does either imply the other?

Competition

2

COMPETITION is inevitable with scarcity. Scarcity forces a choice among limited options, and we compete for those options. Hence, in a society of more than one person, *scarcity implies competition.* There is only one way to avoid competition: according to the renowned practical philosopher, Arnold Palmer, "If you aren't competing, you're dead." And conversely.

You may have heard: "The free-enterprise, private-property system, because it is competitive, promotes antisocial, jungle behavior. It induces cheating, conformity, discrimination, and the dominance of the lowest quality, while discouraging humane behavior." But *competition*—whether it does, or must, yield dire consequences—is not unique to the free-enterprise, private-property system. *Competition exists in every social system.* It is a result of conflicts of interest in a world of scarcity—not of the social, cultural, or economic system within which we live. However, there are many forms of competition. We have some choice, even as individuals, about which form to rely on more heavily.

Violence as a Form of Competition

Violence is an exceptionally important mode of competition—that is, of resolving interpersonal conflicts of interests. Before rejecting or condemning violence, observe that it is highly respected and widely practiced—at least when applied successfully on a nation-wide scale. When Caesar conquered Egypt, he was praised and honored by the Romans; had he instead roughed up a few people in Rome, he might have been damned as a ruffian and thief. When Alexander conquered the Near East, he was not regarded by the

West as a gangster; neither was Charlemagne after he conquered Europe. The white man acquired America from the native inhabitants by force. Lenin and his successors are not universally regarded in Russia as a line of gangsters. Nor is Franco regarded by all in Spain as merely a successful usurper who seized power by force. Nor Castro in Cuba nor Gowon in Nigeria.

So effective is successful application of violence or force that it is a jealously guarded necessary monopoly of the national government. We shall see that even in certain areas of activity within a nation, violence or force is an accepted method of eliminating competitors—always, of course, for the good of the people as a whole, according to those who use it. Street demonstrations and riots are sometimes regarded—even by college students—as appropriate competition for access to political power and economic goods.

Violence and its threat are, and have been, powerful in all human society. Reservation of violence or force to the government in fact defines, for all practical purposes, what is the government. A general dispersion (not disappearance) of violence or force negates the government and implies anarchy. The issue is, "For the defense of what kinds of permissible behavior should violence be threatened or be used?" Our legal and judicial system obtains acceptance of most of its decisions, but relies ultimately on force for those who do not accept them. Anyone who resorts to force (not sanctioned as part of the government's action) is literally revolting against the government.

These simple facts do not constitute a defense of every existing government; they constitute nonromantic statements about the role of violence and its threat. To what purpose and in what manner force, or its threat, is to be put is the crucial issue. One can debate these purposes and modes of force. But to deny that it should ever be used or its threat made believable is to ignore not only a central characteristic of life from time immemorial but an inevitable characteristic of any society and its government. Hence, those who advocate nonviolence are either accepting its continued monopoly by the existing government or are advocating anarchy if they suggest that not even government should use physical force or confinement.

Offers of Exchange as a Form of Competition

As an alternative to violence, mutual exchange is available (even though it, too, is sometimes classed as improper). A free-enterprise economic system—in which the bulk of property is privately owned and assets typically can be freely traded—is a commonly used basis of competition. But let Adam Smith, the eighteenth-century British economist, comment:

Man has almost constant occasion for the help of his brethren, and it is in vain for him to expect it from their benevolence only. He will be more likely to prevail if he can interest their self-love in his favor, and show them that it is for their own advantage to do for him what he requires of them. Whoever offers to another a bargain of any kind, proposes to do this: Give me that which I want, and you shall have this which you want, is the meaning of every such offer; and it is in this manner that we obtain from one another the far greater part of those good offices which we stand in need of. It is not from the benevolence of the butcher, the brewer, or the baker, that we expect our dinner, but from their regard to their own interest. We address ourselves not to their humanity but to their self-love.

We will investigate this kind of competition in great detail, but we will investigate others, too, with possibly surprising implications.

Other Types of Competition

Violence (i.e., physical force) and exchange are two of an enormous variety of interpersonal competitive techniques that can be suggested by examples.

Suppose you had to distribute 200 tickets to the Rose Bowl football game without selling them to the highest bidders. What forms of competition would you use in assigning priorities for deciding to whom to award the tickets? That is, what system of rationing or allocation would you use? If the authors of this book could set the rules, we would ask all applicants to send pictures, the subjects preferably in bathing suits. (Males need not apply.) We would select the prettiest 300—using our own standards—and ask them to appear in our offices for interviews. Of these we would then select the most personable 200—using our own standards.

Certainly this pleasant system is discriminatory. *All* competition is discriminatory. That, indeed, is its reason: to discriminate among claimants in deciding who gets what. Beauty and personality as competitive, discriminatory factors are generally accepted and applied widely every day. Men and women select mates, in part, according to beauty and personality. You and I allocate money to the prettiest women for letting us see them perform in the movies. In fact, it is difficult to find situations in which beauty is not a competitive advantage.

If you think beauty is an improper criterion, you might use the "first come, first served" method. For instance, all the applicants could run a race with the tickets going to the first 200 to arrive at the finish line. Sounds silly. If you replace the words "finish line" by "box office at the Rose Bowl" (or registration desks for popular college classes), it is realistic, but is it less silly? The only difference is that for Rose Bowl tickets there is no uniform starting time or place, so that some people start out earlier and then camp right at the finish line. In any case, economic theory does *not* say what form of competition is silly, nor what is fair. That depends on what you mean by "fair"—it depends on the kind of competition *you* prefer. If you think "fair" means giving everyone an equal chance, would you want to give everyone an equal chance to operate on you for appendicitis, or sing for you, or teach you, or be your wife, or be the person you had to hire in your restaurant—or to whom you give Rose Bowl tickets? An equal chance could be provided by putting everyone's name (even those who did not take the time to apply for a ticket) on cards, then drawing 200 at random. That would be as equal a chance as possible, and nondiscriminatory. But, again, do you want to pick your mate that way? Do you want men selected for the armed forces that way?

Note a difficulty. After the goods (Rose Bowl tickets in our example) are initially distributed, what is to stop your selected recipients from handing the tickets on to other people, according to other preferred criteria? What is to prevent the prettiest girls from handing the tickets to the handsomest boys? It is extremely difficult to ensure that one's competitive selective criterion will in fact be the only criterion followed. Of course, you *might* tell all persons to whom you initially give the tickets that they must go to the game themselves and not re-allocate the tickets in exchange for money or love. How you enforce that condition we leave to you.

1, 2, 3, 4

Competitive Criteria and Survival Traits

Nothing in economic theory suggests which forms of competition are "absurd." That evaluation rests on cultural and personal preferences. The first-come, first-served race to the box-office window, if used to parcel out food, would mean that the people best able to camp out or withstand the rigors of waiting in line would have the best prospects. In accordance with the classic theory of selective survival of the fittest, that type of person would prevail. And the institution of "camping out" would be characteristic of the economy. Instead, if food were parceled out to the tallest people, with short people getting the least, the average height of the population would increase over time. And, alternatively, if beauty were rewarded, the beauty of women would increase—because women would make deliberate, conscious efforts to improve their beauty, and because the more beautiful would be more likely to survive. Or one might propose to allocate goods on the basis of forensics and personality, somewhat as we compete for political office. Under that system, the society would become noted for its articulate and personable people. Or resources could be given to those with the most talent for deception and misrepresentation; the reader can imagine the mores and dominant types that would evolve in that society. Or resources could go mainly to those who are best able to create goods and services. In that kind of society the more productive would be the wealthier and the dominant group.

In the wide gamut of economic problems of every society, there is, then, a pervasive, inescapable, inevitable pair: *scarcity and competition.* That is the starting point of our analysis, and behavioral consequences stemming directly or indirectly from it are our subject matter.

Scarcity, Productive Activity, and Culture

Since we cannot have *all* of *everything* we want, we must *choose* how to use available resources. What things shall we make and in what proportions? Under what institutions and laws? How and with what resources? Who will consume which goods and how much? How much shall we direct from current to future consumption?

These questions leave open the matter of precisely *who* is to make the decisions of what and how much to produce, how the production is to be done, and what goods to allocate to each person. To say simply that "we" do so does not identify who makes those detailed decisions, under what circumstances, and in response to what incentives and penalties. How is the diverse information about every person, his capabilities and preferences, to be collected and coordinated into decisions guiding *each* person? Is it to be done under the direction of an all-powerful economic czar with central planning? Is there any feasible alternative?

Not all systems for organizing production lead to equally productive results. What are the characteristics of "appropriate" production (or efficient production, as it is called in economic jargon)? What institutional arrangements encourage that kind of productive activity? Kinds of property rights, rights of access to markets and rights to exchange goods and services, kind of money system used—all these are influential.

Whatever societal organization is used, what kinds of social and cultural behavior will it foster in people? Not many know much about these questions. A former President of the United States admitted he felt unable to evaluate and refute charges that the private-property, open-market exchange (capitalist) system for organizing production and distribution was not only inefficient, but also bred more materialistic, less humanitarian, and inferior cultural traits than did socialism.

Summary

1. People's desire for more goods leads to activity to resolve conflicts of interest (competition). Scarcity and competition are inseparable.

2. Instead of futilely complaining about the *existence* of competition, devote attention to the *alternative modes* of competition. Different types of competition imply differing methods of ordering society or regulating the way people behave. It is not pertinent to ask, "How can we *eliminate* or *reduce* competition?" Ask instead: "What *kinds* of competition—or controls—are 'desirable' or 'undesirable'? What will make 'desirable' competition more viable, pervasive, and powerful; and what will make 'undesirable' competition ineffective?"

3. The preceding question involves three phases: (a) understanding the effects of different kinds of competitive behavior; (b) choosing—on some basis not derivable from economics—a criterion of "desirability"; (c) knowing what laws or institutions will affect the prevalence and effectiveness of each type of competition.

Questions

1. "If people were reasonable and acted with justice and good faith, there would be no strikes, no economic problems, and no wars." Do you agree? If so, why? If not, why not?

2. "Government monopolizes coercive violence." "Government is a social agency for resolving interpersonal conflict."
   a. Are those two propositions correct and compatible statements of fact?
   b. What evidence can you cite for your answer?

3. Name three honored statesmen who obtained their status by successfully competing in ability to use violence and who, had they failed, would have been punished for treason or crimes against mankind.

4. "Scarcity, competition, and discrimination are inextricably tied together. Any one implies the other two. Furthermore, to think of a society without these is to be a romantic dreamer." Do you agree? If so, why? If not, why not?

5. "A more equal distribution of wealth is socially preferred to a less equal distribution."
   a. Explain why you agree or disagree.
   b. What is meant by "socially preferred," as contrasted to "individually preferred"?

6. **a.** If you had the power to decide, what kinds of competition would you declare illegal?
   b. What kinds of competition are made illegal by laws establishing price ceilings, minimum wages, fair-employment practices, pure food and drug standards, private-property rights, and by socialism?

7. Defend competition for admission to colleges on the basis of mental ability, athletic ability, good looks, residence, willingness to pay, alumni status of parents, color, sex, religious belief. All are used to some extent. Why?

8. **a.** What kinds of competition that are permissible in seeking political office are not permissible in private business?
   b. What kinds of competition are permissible in seeking admission to college but not permissible in competition for grades in this course?

c. What kinds of competition are approved for business but not for admission to fraternities? Explain why.

9. What do you think is meant by a fair share? Do you think other people agree with your interpretation? How does your interpretation compare with the idea of students getting "fair" grades?

10. Evaluate the statement: "When property rights conflict with human rights, property rights must give way."

11. a. What does "equality of opportunity" mean?
    b. How could you determine whether it exists?
    c. Is there equality of opportunity to get an *A* in this course?
    d. How would you make it equal, if it is not?
    e. What is the difference between *increasing* opportunity and *equalizing* it?

12. As a group, which people do you think are most honest—politicians, businessmen, or teachers? What is your evidence? Can you think of any reasons why dishonesty would be more surely punished in one of these professions? Is there any reason to suspect that dishonesty, if successful, would be more rewarding in one rather than the others?

13. "Under socialism, cooperation will replace competition."
    a. Do you believe the quoted proposition is correct?
    b. What evidence can you cite to support your answer?
    c. What is the difference between cooperation and competition?
    d. Is there any difference between cooperation and coordination?

14. The economic ideals of the Middle Ages were influenced by Christianity and by Aristotle's doctrines. Among those ideals were the following:

    "(1) The purpose of economic activity is to provide goods and services for the community and to enable each member of society to live in security and freedom from want. Its purpose is not to furnish opportunity for the few to get rich at the expense of the many. Men who engage in business with the object of making as much money as possible are no better than pirates or robbers.

    "(2) Every commodity has its 'just price,' which is equal to its cost of production. No merchant has a right to sell any article for more than this price plus a small charge for the service he renders in making goods available to the community. To take advantage of scarcity to boost the price or to charge all that the traffic will bear is to commit a mortal sin.

    "(3) No man is entitled to any larger share of this world's goods than is necessary for his reasonable needs. Any surplus that may come into his possession is not rightfully his but belongs to Society. St. Thomas Aquinas, the greatest of all medieval philosophers, taught that if a rich man refuses to share his wealth with the poor, it is entirely justifiable that his surplus should be taken from him.

    "(4) No man has a right to financial reward unless he engages in useful labor or incurs some actual risk in an economic venture. The taking of interest on loans where no genuine risk is involved constitutes the sin of usury.

    "It would be foolish, of course, to suppose that these lofty ideals of an economic system largely devoid of the profit motive were ever carried out to perfection." (E. M. Burns, *Western Civilizations, Their History and Culture,* 5th ed. New York: W. W. Norton, 1958.)

    What do you think of these ideals? Do you approve of them? Which ones? If you disagree with any, how would you express your ideal? After completing this course, answer these questions again.

15 The economic system is alleged to have an effect on the social and cultural characteristics that will be viable in a society. Among these characteristics are the patterns of speech, expression, religion, travel, marriage, divorce, inheritance, education, legal trials, art, literature, and music.
   a. Do you believe that these characteristics are in any way different under capitalism than under socialism? Why?
   b. Can you cite evidence for your answer?

16 "The free-enterprise, capitalist system is free in the sense that it involves no imposition of force or compulsion." Do you agree? Why?

Some Behavior Postulates

3 SOME of the concepts and postulates characterizing human nature are presented in this chapter. These delineate behavior patterns of people, not necessarily their thought processes. There is nothing presumptuous or absurd in basing analysis of human behavior on a few idealized concepts. Indeed, there is no alternative. This approach is the essence of science. But first we make a specification about the method of analysis and an observation about foresight.

The Unit of Analysis Is the Individual

The actions of groups, organizations, communities, nations, and societies can best be understood by focusing attention on the incentives and actions of members. When we speak of the goals and actions of the United States, we are really referring to the goals and actions of the *individuals* in the United States. A business, union, or family may be formed to further some common interest of the constituents, but group actions are still the results of decisions of individuals. Therefore, do not ask, "Why does the U. S. government, or General Motors, or some union, behave as it does?" Ask instead, "Why does the decision maker decide as he does?" Economics analyzes behavior by assuming a person adapts to environmental changes so as more fully to satisfy his preferences or goals. Economics studies also how his response changes the environment.

No Man Can See the Future Perfectly

Not all future events or outcomes of current actions are totally unpredictable, yet perfect foreknowledge escapes our ken. A changing, imperfectly predictable future means that the usefulness or value of resources will change in unforeseen ways. Unavoidably and unpredictably, some resources will become more, and some less, valuable. As a tornado or earthquake destroys some resources, so psychological variables such as tastes and fashions, or biological factors such as age and health, destroy or create values in unexpected places and things. These profits and losses cannot be eliminated; they are thrust on somebody. If a city grows in one area and decays in another, who suffers the loss in usefulness (value) of the declining areas, and who reaps the gains in the growing areas? Upon whom *should* the profits and losses be thrust? The first question is one that economic theory can answer. The second is one that theory can help to answer by discerning (but not judging) some consequences of various methods of determining who will bear the unforeseen losses or gains. As long as uncertainty exists, the first question will persist and will receive some answer. The second may never be answered.

Behavioral Postulates

Postulate 1. Each Person Desires a Multitude of Goods[1]

A "good" is any desired entity or goal. If having some of an entity is preferred to having none, the entity is a "good." Your "goods" may differ from other people's. Maybe you think that cigarettes are not "goods" and that others would really be "better off" without them. Despite this possible difference of opinion, the term "good" means no more than that some person—as *he* judges his situation—prefers to have some. All this is compactly summarized by saying that a good gives *utility* to someone.

It is useful to classify goods into *free* and *economic* goods. Economic good is the technical name for a *scarce good*. A good is scarce if, and only if, one prefers to have *more* than he has. Fresh chicken eggs are more plentiful than stale eggs; but fresh eggs are scarce, while stale eggs are not. If a good, however desirable, is so abundant that one does not want *more* of it, it is for him a *free* good. Both free goods and economic goods provide utility, of course. But by definition *more* of a free good does not *add* utility. More of an economic good does. The classic case of a free good, to most of us most of the time, is air: we simply inhale, and there it is, without our sacrificing anything to obtain it. Usually, for each of us, *more* air would be of no value—that is, it would not *add* utility. However, air is an economic good to the astronaut and the deep-sea diver; and so is fresh air to the city resident on a smoggy day. Hereafter, almost invariably when we use the word "good," we mean "economic good."

Beware of confusing another usage of "free good." Often it denotes an *economic* good *distributed* at a *zero price,* even though the good is scarce, e.g., education, streets, or books at the "free" public library. Just because a good distributed at a zero price to the recipient is called "free," it is not thereby so plentiful as to be a noneconomic good in our formal sense. And to compound confusion, as we shall see later, distributing economic goods for "free" (at a zero price) paradoxically makes their scarcity *seem* even greater.

Often, economics is incorrectly alleged to presume an "economic man," whose sole interest is making more money or getting wealthier. Not so! Economics does *not* assume

---

[1] The Appendix to this chapter presents a graphic interpretation of these postulates, sometimes also called "preference" postulates.

men are motivated solely, or even primarily, by the desire to accumulate wealth. Instead, economic theory assumes that man—in Karachi, Canton, or Kalamazoo—has many goods or goals: prestige, power, friends, other people's welfare, love, respect, self-expression, talent, liberty, knowledge, beauty, leisure. Day to day, economic theory is usually applied to the production, sale, and consumption of goods with money expenditures via the market place. But economic theory does not ignore, let alone deny, that man is motivated by cultural and intellectual goods or goals, and even by an interest in the welfare of other people—as we shall see.

Postulate 2. For Each Person, Some Goods Are Scarce

Despite work, we are unable to produce enough to satisfy *all* the wants of *all* people *all* the time. Desires for more goods exceed known bounds. People prefer more. Even affluent America is a society of scarcity. *Choices* among opportunities are still required: better hi-fi equipment, wall-to-wall carpeting, walnut paneling, longer vacations. There are conflicting demands for more missiles, airplanes, hospitals, schools, highways, and houses—and for more foreign aid to buy peace and influence and to foster foreign economic growth. Nature simply has not provided enough to satiate desires of every living being—not merely people, but animals and plants, for they, too, are busily claiming all the earth.

3, 4, 5, 6, 7

Postulate 3. Substitution: A Person Is Willing to Sacrifice *Some* of Any Good to Obtain *More* of Other Goods

Man does not wait until he has obtained some specific level of food before he wants clothes or shelter or freedom. He simultaneously wants *some* of *all* these things. Even in the poorest primitive societies, a good deal of effort is devoted to art, music, play, self-expression, and status, as well as to food and shelter. Man does sacrifice *some* food for the sake of *more* leisure or friendship or prestige or art. A *bit* of friendship or prestige or love will in turn be forsaken for *some more* wealth or artistic accomplishment. *There is no hierarchy of goods or of goals.*

The substitutability postulate can be stated more precisely: "For *some more* of any good, a person is willing to sacrifice *some* of any one, or group, of other goods." Or, in reverse, "A person is willing to sacrifice *some bit* of any good he has if he can obtain a *sufficient increase* in the amount of some other desired goods." It does not mean that he would sacrifice *all* of a good; but he will sacrifice *some* of a good for *more* of other goods.

Economics has a special measure of substitutability. The *maximum* reduction of some good that a person is willing to incur to get *one unit more* of some other specified good can be expressed as a ratio, or rate, of substitution. If someone were willing to sacrifice up to two bottles of Coke per month to get one *more* pack of cigarettes per month, his "subjective marginal consumption-substitution ratio" between Cokes and cigarettes is

$$\frac{2 \text{ bottles } fewer \text{ of Coke per month}}{1 \text{ pack } more \text{ of cigarettes per month}} = 2 \text{ Cokes per pack of cigarettes.}$$

He may have twenty Cokes and twenty packs of cigarettes for the coming month. Given that amount of each, if he is indifferent to a substitution of *one more* pack for *two fewer* Cokes, his substitution ratio is 2/1—placing the *decrement* in the *numerator* and the *increment* in the *denominator*. A pack more of cigarettes is worth two Cokes in his *personal* valuation. Eighteen Cokes and twenty-one cigarette packs then are a combination that has the same utility to him as twenty of each. This ratio is the amount which one would have been just *willing* to pay for one more pack per month.

If he did make an exchange at that rate, he would *not* reach a *preferred* situation, because the sacrifice of the two Cokes is just large enough exactly to offset the gain of one pack of cigarettes.

Some special notation is helpful for avoiding confusion. So we shall let ΔC denote that largest acceptable *change* in the number of Cokes and ΔG the change in cigarettes. Then the ratio $\Delta C/\Delta G$ denotes and measures the subjective rate of consumption-substitution between Cokes and cigarettes. For the proposed increase in cigarettes (ΔG), the decrease in Cokes (ΔC) is that which is just exactly large enough to make one *indifferent* about the exchange. This ratio is also called the "indifference rate of substitution."[2] Remember, this is a ratio of two *changes*: a *decrement* of one good and an *increment* of another. It is *not* the ratio between the *total* amount of Cokes and of cigarettes that the person happens to have.

To emphasize that we are dealing with a ratio between *small* changes, this "indifference ratio" is labeled the "*marginal* rate of substitution" between Cokes and cigarettes.

The ratio indicates a *subjective*, or *personal*, valuation (in terms of Cokes) of cigarettes. Placing the good being valued downstairs in the denominator and the good being paid up in the numerator, we say that the subjective value of one more Coke is one-half pack of cigarettes: $\Delta G/\Delta C = 1/2$.

Resist the temptation to say, "Mr. A likes cigarettes less than Mr. B." There simply is no basis for comparing *intensity* of likes of two people for *one* good. Neither economics nor psychology has yet discovered a way validly to compare "absolute" likes of different people for a good on some psychic scale. Mr. A may put a value of two Cokes on one cigarette, and Mr. B's indifference ratio may be three Cokes for one cigarette. A puts a smaller *Coke* valuation on cigarettes than does B. But we have no way of knowing how much A and B like cigarettes without Cokes (or some other good) for reference. For all we know, A tingles at the mere thought of a cigarette (but he likes Cokes so well that he would give up only two Cokes to obtain one more cigarette) while B could easily swear off cigarettes (but Cokes make him burp, so he is willing to sacrifice as many as three of them for one more cigarette).

Though the postulates have been expressed in Cokes and cigarettes, they hold for *every* person for *every* pair of *all* economic goods.

Value (in economic analysis) of any good is measured in terms of an amount of *some other economic good*. Value is not measured in terms of some psychic, psychological, or moral goodness or satisfaction. The *value* of a good to a person *is the substitution* rate, between that good and some other, at which he would be *indifferent* whether the exchange is made.

Because we buy or sell goods for *money*, the personal substitution value is expressed

---

[2] "Personal," "internal," or "subjective" values are synonymous expressions for this indifference rate of substitution in consumption. Do not presume the *name* of something is also a *definition*. Many names poorly connote the concept given that name—a Ford Thunderbird is not a bird of Mr. Ford's which thunders.

Postulate 4. An Individual's Personal Substitution Valuation of Any Good Depends upon the Amount He Has of That Good; the More He Has, the Lower His Personal Value of the Good

The personal substitution value a person places on goods is not entirely random or unpredictable. While it depends upon many things—such as past experience, education, general preference, and psychological traits—it depends in a predictable way upon the amounts of the goods he has. Since little can be said about how other factors affect his personal substitution valuation, we shall concentrate on the effect of the amounts possessed. In rough terms, the larger the amount of any good at his command, the lower its *personal* substitution value to him—that is, the lower the value of still another unit of that good. If my amount of X were increased, my personal substitution valuation of an additional unit of X would decrease. I would be willing to give up only smaller amounts (ΔY) of any other good, Y, for an increment (ΔX) in X, the more of X at my command. That is, as the ratio $\Delta Y/\Delta X$ at which I am willing to acquire more X decreases, the larger is the amount of X that I have. This is sometimes called the law of *diminishing* value.

Postulate 5. Not All People Have Identical Preference Patterns

Although everyone's nature corresponds to the first four postulates, no two people are exactly alike in all characteristics. Diversity extends beyond talents, personality, initiative, responsibility, and appearance. One man's tastes are another man's prejudices; one's selectivity is another's discrimination. One person might value one more cigarette at two Cokes, while a second, even with the same amounts of various goods, might value it at three Cokes. This means that at the same given combination or "endowment" of various goods for each person, some people place a higher value on cigarettes relative to Cokes than do others. Or turning it around, the first person places a lower value on Cokes relative to cigarettes than does a second person.

Meaning of Value—Input Value versus Output Value

The expression "personal substitution value" does not mean an inherent value of the services of these goods. Instead we mean simply its *substitution* value as an input to a person's situation. The personal substitution value of good A is the amount of some other input or good (and is *measured* by that amount) that a unit of A would substitute for in yielding the person a situation that is just as preferred as the original. The amount of some other good for which a unit of A is a substitute is what is meant by value as used *here*. We could have called it the "personal input value placed on a unit change of the good." However, conventionally, economic analysis uses the technical term "marginal rate of substitution in consumption," which in turn is often abbreviated to "marginal rate of substitution." Whatever the term, be wary of misinterpretation. It is not a value of an increased welfare added to the person by having one more unit of the good. It refers only to the *amount of some other input* for which one unit of this good is a substitute in providing whatever level of personal welfare (utility) is available under the initial conditions.

Rational People versus Rational Analysis

If these observations and postulates seem trite, so much the better, for they form the bases of the rational, logical *analysis* used in deriving "explanations" of observed behavior. None of the postulates requires that people be *aware* of them, any more than parents are necessarily aware of the laws of genetics or sexual attraction. The postulates assert simply that people display certain consistent and predictable patterns of response to changes in their environment. Stones and rocks are not rational; they do not know the laws of gravity and physics, yet they conform to them. Does that mean physics assumes that rocks and stones are rational? No, just the *analysis* of their behavior is rational; i.e., it is a logically consistent analytic theory which enables one to derive implied forms of behavior which, if in fact they are observed, make that rational theory an *empirically valid* theory. Absolutely nothing in economic theory rests on any premise that *people* are rational or logically consistent in their thought processes. Nothing is said about people's mental processes. A rational, logical economic *theory* will be empirically valid if it does imply behavior that *is* observed in the real world. If it did not, there would be little point in learning it.

For example, the second postulate says that people prefer more to less goods. But so do many animals. In animals it is called the acquisitive *instinct*. In man we may call it rationality. In fact, it may be instinctive in both. Or possibly millions of centuries ago, very early in the evolutionary stream, some species of pre-man manifested acquisitive behavior: collecting sticks, bones, food, or areas of land from which it kept out potential invaders. It may not have had any conscious reason for doing so, but nevertheless that behavior had high survival characteristics. Storing up food and territory enabled it to live longer and breed more prolifically. The survival aid of that trait to the individual and to his species in the evolutionary selective process may have been a factor in the subsequent dominance of acquisitive species. Alternatively, you may believe that the acquisitive urge was instilled by God as punishment for man's fall from grace—a part of his original sinfulness. Man, by that acquisitive drive, is condemned to greed, work, and conflict. Or you may believe that since man has the capacity to think and foresee consequences, he has consciously decided that acquiring more goods is "better."

At any rate, economic theory does not imply that these drives or traits are taught and subtly imbued by particular types of economic systems and institutions. These characteristics exist whether the society is capitalist, communist, or anarchist.

Meaning of Self-Interest

Where in the preceding postulates is the assumption that man is interested only in his own wealth or welfare? It isn't there, and properly so. We did assume that man is greedy—meaning solely that he wants *command over* the decision about uses of more rather than less goods. But a man may want control over more goods in order charitably to help others. It is not assumed that he is oblivious to other people or unsolicitous of other people's welfare. If these assumptions had been made, the resultant theory would be immediately falsified by the fact that people do engage in charity, are solicitous of other people, do consider the effects of their behavior on other people, and do sacrifice marketable wealth for leisure, knowledge, and contemplation.

What *is* meant by "selfish" man is that one of his "economic goods" is the right to choose among options that will affect ensuing affairs. In short, the *right to make choices* about the future is a desired thing, an "economic good." However, like all other goods, raise the cost of that right, and less choice will be retained. Lower it, and more will be retained. Raise my salary enough, and I'll let you determine what kind of clothes I wear to work, or where I work, or how my retirement fund is invested.

Utility-Maximizing Behavior

The preceding set of postulates is often called the "utility-maximizing" theory of human nature. This may suggest that there is something called "utility"—something like weight, height, wealth, or happiness—that people are trying to maximize. The name originated during the early history of economic analysis. At that time it was popular to think that goods provided utility or usefulness in some measurable psychological sense. But although that misleading psychological conception has been abandoned, the name "utility" has stuck. It is now simply an *indicator* for ranking options in accord with one's preferences.

Saying that a person "maximizes" utility may seem an elaborate camouflage of our ignorance; for whatever a person does, could he not be said to be "maximizing his utility"? Yes, if we were unable to specify what entities are goods and goals and if we could not classify some situations according to higher or lower costs of acquiring goods. But we *can* make specifications of goods and relative costs and therefore can provide meaningful, refutable theorems. And we shall give several in this book. For the moment, consider an example. Saving lives may be a good. But consider two different situations. In one, he can save a life by jumping into a pond and pulling out a child; in the other, he must jump into a raging torrent with .99 probability of drowning himself. Now, what does our theory tell us? The probability with which people will jump into ponds is higher than for jumping into torrents.

Another example is a trade off between income and leisure. Both income and leisure contribute to a higher utility. The person will choose a mixture of income and leisure so as to maximize his utility rather than maximize his income. No one maximizes his income at the sacrifice of all leisure, nor does everyone work at the highest paying job regardless of the working conditions. People trade income for more pleasant surroundings.

23, 24, 25, 26

Functional Analysis in Economics

A great deal of analysis in economics—and in other areas—uses the "function." A *function* is a *relationship* between two or more entities. A functional relationship is said to exist between caloric intake and weight, between force and speed, between height and weight, between age and baldness, between smoking and incidence of cardiovascular disease, and between wealth and higher education. Sometimes one entity is related to a *group* of other entities. Weight can be related to height and to girth and thus can be called a function of height and girth.

It is customary also to refer to one set of the variables as the explanatory or *independent* variables and the remaining one as the explained or *dependent* variables. This does not mean that the dependent or explained variable is causally dependent. Thus, one could regard education as a variable dependent on wealth in the sense that we can estimate more accurately the extent of one's formal education if his wealth is known; it does not have to mean that the extent of his wealth determined how much education he did obtain. The extent of his education may, in fact, have determined how much wealth he later earned. Regardless of whether the causation works in one direction or the other or even in both or in neither direction, to call one of the variables the independent, or explanatory, variable means only that a knowledge of the magnitude of that variable enables one to know the other variable with a greater degree of precision.

A relationship between the explained variable and an explanatory variable is said to be *positive* if an increase (decrease) in one is accompanied by an increase (decrease) in the other; it is a *negative* function if larger magnitudes of one are associated with smaller magnitudes of the other.

Finally, use of a functional relationship between *two* variables does not mean that the explanatory variable is the *only* or even the best variable to use to explain the other, or that other unspecified variables are assumed absent. An increase in caloric intake implies a gain in weight, even though an increase in caloric intake accompanied by increased physical activity may result in a weight decrease. There is still a positive relationship between caloric intake and weight, because—regardless of other factors—the weight will be greater than it would have been if caloric intake had not been increased. The expression "other things being the same" is merely a crude way of *concentrating attention* on the relationship between two particular variables, even though other explanatory variables may be pertinent and changing in magnitude. Take the assertion "If I give you $10, you will be richer—other things being the same." This is not falsified if other things change. For instance, if you lose $100 elsewhere, you are richer than if I had not given you the $10.

Summary

This chapter presented some postulates about certain features of human "nature" that are at the foundations of economic theory. These are not an exhaustive catalog, but they are particularly significant for present purposes.

Observations

1   The unit of analysis is the individual.

2   No man can foresee the future perfectly.

Postulates

1   Each person desires a multitude of goods.

2   For each person, some goods are scarce.

3   A person is willing to sacrifice some of any good in order to obtain more of some other good.

4   The more one has of any good, the lower his personal, marginal substitution valuation of it.

5   Not all people have identical patterns of preferences.

Some Behavior Postulates

Rationality in analysis should not be taken to mean that the people being analyzed are animate calculating machines. Self-interest is the desire to have the right to make those choices that will affect one's circumstances. Utility-maximizing behavior is a name for behavior in accord with the postulates. Functional analysis does not require cause and effect, nor does it mean that the identified and analyzed factors are assumed to be the only entities that affect or are related to each other.

Appendix: Preference Maps and Utility Lines

The postulates characterizing the economically relevant attributes of human behavior can be described by graphs called preference maps.

In Figure 3–1, point A denotes a combination of two goods, X and Y. The amount of X is measured by the horizontal distance to the right from the vertical axis, and the amount of Y by the vertical distance upward from the horizontal axis. Point B denotes a different combination of goods X and Y. It contains more X, but no more Y, than does combination A: it lies directly to the right of point A. On the other hand, combination C contains more Y than point A, but no more X.

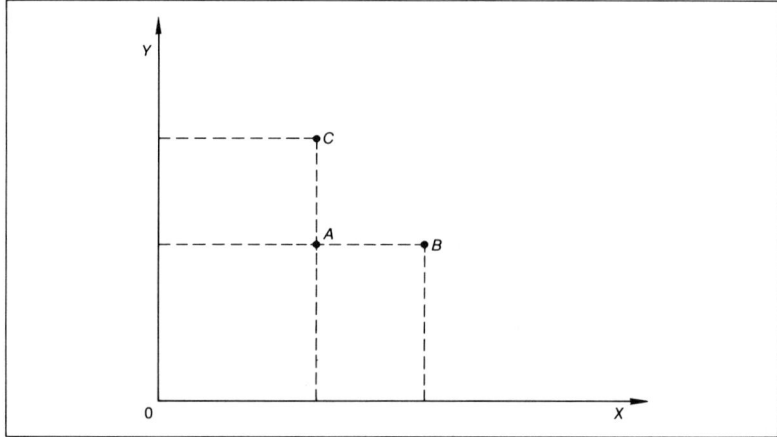

FIGURE 3–1. Combination of Goods X and Y

Points A, B, C denote different combinations of X and Y. The combination denoted by B has more X and the same amount of Y as the combination at A. C has more of Y. If point B is preferred to A, X is an economic good. Similarly, if point C is preferred to A, Y is an economic good. (Why?) If B is not preferred to A, X is either a free good or a "bad" (rather than a "good"). But we have defined X and Y to be goods and, in particular, economic goods. How could you portray diagrammatically the personal value of a unit of X at point A? Would it be greater or less than at B? At C? (See Figure 3–2 for the answers.)

According to our postulates, the combination denoted by point B is preferred to that of point A; also, point C is preferred to point A. We mean that, if offered a choice between options A and B, our person would choose B, since it has more X and no less Y.

The preference of *B* over *A* means that *X* is an economic good. Similarly we assert he would choose *C* over *A*, which means that *Y* is an economic good.

To indicate his preference pattern or ordering, we could arbitrarily assign some number to point *B*, say 76, and assign a smaller number to point *A*, say 49. A point assigned a higher number is preferred to a point assigned a lower number. We shall *arbitrarily* attach the name "utility" to that preference indicator. Perhaps the name "preference" or "choice index" would be better, but the convention of economics dictates the name "utility."

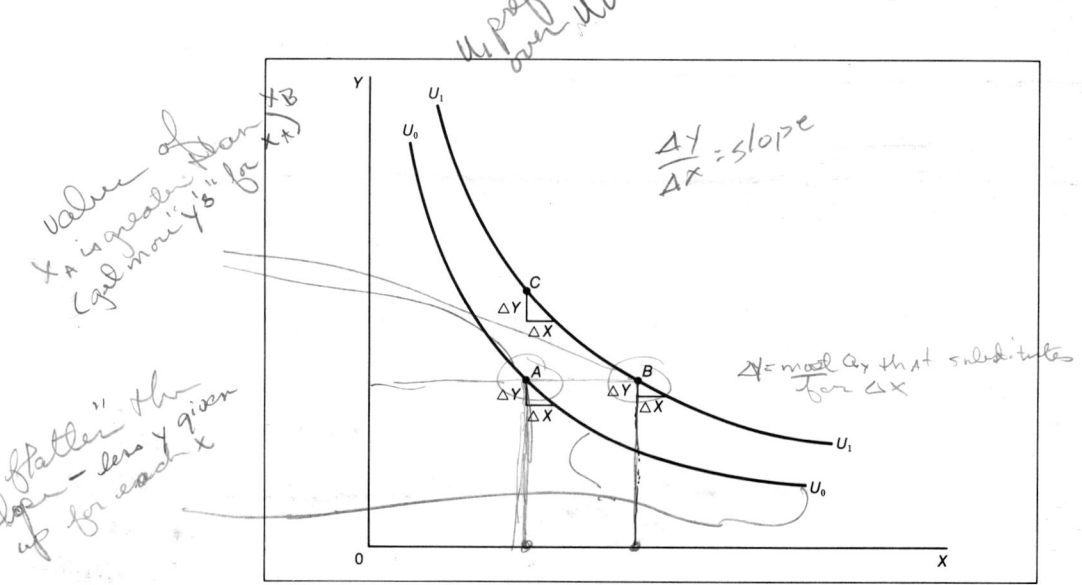

FIGURE 3-2. Convex Constant Utility Curves for Some Person

Any point on $U_1 U_1$ is preferred to any point on $U_0 U_0$. At each point, the slope of the curve measures, by ΔY, this person's valuation of ΔX, a uniform increment of *X*. Slope at *B* is less than at *A*; and at *A* is less than at *C*. Also, slope of a curve diminishes along curve as one moves from upper left to lower right. That is, personal substitution valuation of *X* decreases as one moves from much *Y* and little *X* to less *Y* and more *X*.

Now consider Figure 3-2. A curved line labeled $U_1 U_1$ runs through point *B*. At point *B* is a little "triangle," the length of whose vertical side measures the decrement of *Y*, ΔY, that would be the *most* our person would be willing to sacrifice to get the small increment (horizontal side) of *X*, ΔX, with the person initially at combination *B*. The ratio of ΔY to ΔX, $\Delta Y/\Delta X$, is indicated by the *slope* of the hypotenuse of that triangle; that slope *is* the slope of the curved line $U_1 U_1$ at *B*. The flatter that slope, the less is the decrement, ΔY, that our person is willing to sacrifice for the increment ΔX of *X*. The less is $\Delta Y/\Delta X$, the less is the substitution value of an *X* (in terms of *Y*) and the greater is the substitution value of a *Y* (in terms of *X*). Remember that the personal substitution value of a unit of any good *is* the amount of his "equally preferred" change of some other good. The slope at point *A* is steeper than at *B* (with reference to the *X* axis). This means the value of an *X* at combination *A* is greater than the value of an *X* at *B*.

The slope of the line through point *C* is steeper than at *A*. The value of a unit of *X* is greater (in terms of Y) at C than at A. Our person has more Y, and the more he has of a good (the amounts of other goods being unchanged), the less its personal value. That steeper *slope* indicates a reduced personal substitution value of a unit of Y relative to X: it takes more of an increment in Y to offset the unit change in X. Remember that the larger ΔY is for a unit change in X, the *lower* the personal substitution value of Y (and the greater the personal substitution value of X).

Line $U_1 U_1$ marks combinations of X and Y, all of which are equally preferred (i.e., equally desired, have the same utility) with point C or B. All combinations of X and Y through which $U_1 U_1$ goes are equally desirable. In terms of our preference indicator, utility, all points on $U_1 U_1$ have the same utility index.

Every point above and to the right of line $U_1 U_1$ is preferred to any point on that line, since every point above it represents a bigger combination than any point directly below or to the left of it. Every point below the line is less preferred than any point on the line. A curve, $U_0 U_0$, drawn through A, shows all combinations indifferent to A. And every point on $U_0 U_0$ is less preferred than any point on the line $U_1 U_1$. (Be sure you see why!)

How does a convex sloped constant-utility line describe the postulates? First, it has two dimensions—two goods—not just one, which reflects postulate number 1. Second, any basket with a larger amount of either good (lying to the right or above) will be on a constant-utility curve with a greater index of utility—which means that more of X (or of Y) is preferred. This is postulate number 2. Some goods (here, X and Y) are scarce. Third, the $U_1 U_1$ line's constant-utility, or indifference, curves have *negative slopes*—which means that some increment of X will make up for some loss of Y, and vice versa. That negative slope expresses our third substitutability postulate. Fourth, the slopes of the successive indifference curves that one crosses, from left to right, get flatter. At each point the *slope*, which is the personal substitution valuation of X, decreases the more X one has. This is postulate number 4. Also, as one moves up vertically—indicating more Y for a *fixed* amount of X—slopes of successive indifference curves get steeper, which means his personal substitution value of X increases as Y is increased. But this is the same thing as saying that his personal substitution value of Y decreases as Y is increased.

The personal substitution value of good X is measured by the slope of the indifference curve at any point. It is *not* measured by how much the utility of the person increases as he gets one more unit of the good X. Why not? Because we define the personal substitution value to be that slope, and, anyway, it so happens that as yet no one has discovered a generally acceptable, objective method of measuring increases in utility so as to make them comparable among different people. Lacking any such interpersonal comparability of a measure of utility, we must not pretend one exists—unless we want to get into all sorts of errors in comparing measures that simply cannot be compared.

Questions

1 "The college football team has a goal."
   a. Is it the social goal of the "team," or is it the common individual goal of each member of the team?
   b. Are you sure that each member has only that goal and not also one of playing more of the game himself?
   c. Is it helpful to talk of one goal's being preferred over another?

2 In trying to understand some policy enforced at your college, why is it misleading to ask why the college adopts that policy?

3 "People want wealth, power, and prestige." What is wealth? Power? Prestige?

4 Are the words "scarcity" and "shortage" synonyms? If not, what is the difference?

5 If you don't smoke, is tobacco a good? Are purchase and sale necessary for an entity to be considered a "good"?

6 "A free good is an inconsistency of concepts, because no one wants what is free; otherwise it wouldn't be free. And if no one wants it, it can't be a "good." Evaluate.

7 Suppose it were claimed that a denial of college facilities for the purpose of exercising free speech is a denial of the right of free speech. Show how that argument confuses free resources with free speech.

8 Explain or criticize the following statements and questions about the substitution postulate:
a. "Every student substitutes romance for grades when he dates rather than studies as much as he otherwise could have." Criticize.
b. "The substitution postulate says that a student does not seek the highest possible grades." Explain.
c. Does the substitution postulate deny that water, food, and clothing are more basic than music, art, and travel? Explain.
d. "There is no hierarchy of wants." What does that mean? Can you disprove it?
e. Is travel in Europe a substitute for formal academic education? For some food? For a bigger house or new clothes or medical care? For what would it not be a substitute?
f. "I'd like to play poker with you again tomorrow night, but I don't think my wife would like it." Is this consistent with the substitution postulate? Is the wife's utility being compared with the husband's? Explain.

9 In testing a person's preference between two known options, it has been suggested that if a person agrees to let some unknown second party choose between the two options for him, then he is indifferent between the two options. Do you think that is consistent with the postulates listed in the text?

10 A recently published book was entitled *Social Needs and Private Wants*. Would the title have suggested something different if it had been *Social Wants and Private Needs*? Why do you suppose the first title was chosen?

11 Suppose that I am indifferent if given an option among the following three combinations of steaks and artichokes:

		Steaks	pounds per year	Artichokes
	A	100	and	30
Options	B	105	and	29
	C	111	and	28

a. What is my personal value of steak (between options A and B)?
b. What has the greater utility to me, A or B?
c. What is my personal value of artichokes (between B and C)?
d. If the amount of meat in A were doubled to 200, what do you think might be the amount of meat required in B to make it of equal utility to A?

e. Using your answer to (d), compute my personal valuations between the new A and the new B. Is your result consistent with the fourth postulate?

12 The following are combinations of X and Y, all of which are equally preferred by Mr. A.

Equal Utility Combinations	X	Goods	Y
A	9	and	50
B	10	and	40
C	11	and	34
D	12	and	30
E	14	and	26
F	17	and	21
G	21	and	17
H	26	and	13
I	33	and	10
J	40	and	9
K	47	and	8
L	57	and	7

a. Plot each of these combinations as points on graph paper (Y on vertical axis and X on horizontal). The Appendix discussion will have made this question easy.
b. Connect the points with a smoothed line.
c. What postulate is expressed by the fact that there is more than one combination of the same utility to Mr. A?
d. Do these combinations conform to the postulates?
e. What postulate is expressed by the negative slope of the line connecting these combinations (the iso-utility line—sometimes called an indifference curve, to connote that the person is indifferent among the combinations on this line)?
f. What postulate is reflected in the curvature (not the slope) of the iso-utility line?

13 If I regard each of the following combinations as equally preferable, do I conform to the postulates of economic theory? If not, which postulate is denied?

		X	Goods	Y
	A	100	and	70
Options	B	105	and	69
	C	110	and	68
	D	115	and	67

14 Suppose that Mr. A is indifferent between options A and C of the following combinations.

		X	Y
	A	100	and 200
Options	B	110	and 180
	C	120	and 160

If he is given a choice among the three options, prove that, according to the postulates, he will choose option B over either A or C. (The proof is easy—but it is *not* easy to discover that proof.)

15 What refutable proposition is suggested by the statement, "*A* has more utility than *B* for me"?

16 Explain why the following statements are or are not consistent with the postulates.
 a. Diminishing personal substitution value means that the more a person has of something, the less satisfaction he gets.
 b. Diminishing personal substitution value means that, as a person consumes some good, he gradually gets less satisfaction.
 c. Diminishing personal substitution value means that as a person acquires more of a good, he begins to value other goods more than this one.

17 How could you show graphically, on the diagram you drew for question 12, the meaning of postulate 3?

18 Explain the difference between the statements, "People act in accord with certain fundamental propositions" and "People consult or refer to such propositions for guidance in choosing their behavior." Does either interpretation assume "free will" or independence from other people's behavior or tastes?

19 "All goods or goals are incompatible. And at the same time they are compatible." Can you make sense of that?

20 Many, if not all, of the postulates do not apply to some people. What happens to those people? Why?

21 Four postulates were used to characterize some aspects of human nature and behavior.
 a. Do you think any of them are also applicable to nonhuman animal life? For example, which of the postulates would give valid characterizations of behavior of monkeys, ants, bees, tigers, and birds?
 b. Which postulates, if any, do you think serve to distinguish human from nonhuman behavior?
 c. What evidence can you cite to support your answers?

22 Do you think the human race would survive if it lost the attribute described by postulate 3 while some animals retained it?

23 "Economic theory is rational and logical, but man is not necessarily that way." What is the difference between a rational man and a rational theory?

24 "Don't be selfish, Jane," said Mother. What did Mother mean?

25 Would man be better off if he weren't selfish? How do you know?

26 Why is it that economic theory—in using the principle of utility maximization—does not assume that man is maximizing some psychological entity?

27 Answer the following questions concerning applications of functional analysis.
 a. "Air density diminishes as altitude increases." If this is true, is density a positive or a negative function of altitude?
 b. Do you think one's rate of gasoline usage is a positive or a negative function of his wealth? Of his family's size? Of his age?
 c. In the relationship between gasoline consumption and wealth, which is the explanatory, predicting, or independent variable; and which is the explained, predicted, or dependent variable? Can you suggest a situation for which the direction of explanation between these two variables is reversed?
 d. In the functional relationship between the amount of a person's smoking and the state of his nervousness, which is the independent and which the dependent variable?

28 "Older people have more wealth than young people. Wealthier people eat more candy than poorer people. Therefore, older people eat more candy than younger people." What is the hidden assumption in that line of argument?

29 "Smoking shortens one's life." Does this mean that smoking is the only cause of death? That smoking is the only cause of a shorter life? That smoking is undesirable? That everyone who has ever smoked will surely die earlier than he otherwise would? That advertisements for tobacco should be prohibited?

Basis of Exchange

4

A MAJOR implication of the postulates is their interpretation of *trade,* or *exchange.* To expose that implication easily, we shall at first use "toy" problems, devoid of unessential, cluttering details. Real-world applications will be made in succeeding chapters.

Mutually Advantageous Trade and the Middleman

Cuban and Hungarian Refugee Camp

Imagine a refugee camp with Cubans and Hungarians. Weekly, each person is given a parcel of twenty bars of chocolate candy and twenty cigarettes. Into this camp a new refugee, for whom there are no parcels, arrives from an unknown country. Clever and knowledgeable about human nature, he suggests the possibility of a favor—he could arrange for the Cuban to have thirty candy bars and thirteen cigarettes instead of twenty each. "Merely give me seven of your twenty cigarettes," he says, "and I will give you ten bars of candy." The Cuban considers and accepts; his acceptance reveals that to him ten extra candy bars are worth *more than* seven of his cigarettes. He may even think he is taking advantage of the newcomer, because, while he would have been willing to forsake as many as eight cigarettes for ten more bars of candy, he was asked to give only seven.

Table 4–1 gives the composition of three different consumption-combination "baskets": A, B_1, and B_2. The Cuban started with A and voluntarily accepted a move to B_2. But basket B_1 has the *same* utility as basket A; although it is different in composition from A, it is no better or worse. In B_1, the reduction in cigarettes, eight, exactly offsets the increase of ten candy bars—which is another way of saying that ten more candy bars are as valuable to the Cuban as eight cigarettes, given his initial circumstances. So B_1 is equally desired as A, and since B_2 is bigger than B_1 (more cigarettes and the same amount of candy), B_2 is a better basket than B_1 or A. He achieves a more desired combination with B_2.

TABLE 4–1. Equivalent and Preferred Baskets for Cuban

		Candy	Cigarettes
	Basket A	20	20
		(+10)	(−8)
Equivalent:	Basket B_1	30	12
		(+10)	(−7)
Preferred:	Basket B_2	30	13

Personal substitution values. The ratio of eight cigarettes to ten candy bars, 8/10, is our old friend the marginal consumption-substitution ratio between candy and cigarettes. It is the individual's *personal substitution value* of candy relative to cigarettes, his *indifference ratio* between candy and cigarettes. It is that ratio of exchange which leaves him at the same level of utility.

indifference ratio = same level of utility

Choice: value and cost. When the Cuban is faced with a choice between options (twenty each of candy and cigarettes versus thirty candy and thirteen cigarettes), whichever combination he chooses means that he will have sacrificed the other. *Choice*, by definition, involves *cost*. His personal substitution valuation of the selected option presumably exceeds his personal substitution valuation of the best of all the rejected options. The value of the selected option exceeds its cost—*cost* being the *highest-valued rejected option*. All choice involves substitutability, values, and cost.[1]

Exchange and personal substitution values. How do we know whether the opportunity rate of exchange presented to a person is in fact less or greater than his personal value? We rarely know; but by assumption, "A person chooses to accept an opportunity only if he feels it will put him in a preferred position—whatever may be the factors that he regards as relevant." We need not know his personal valuation at each possible situation. We need to know only that the person has accepted some of these opportunities and refused others. For the moment, we assume that we know the exchange rates at which he would and would not trade—simply to help expose the underlying concepts.

[1] Substitutability among alternatives is involved. The most preferred option will be taken, by definition. The word "cost" is assigned to the value of the best option *not* chosen—the highest valued of the options that had to be rejected in order to get the one that was chosen. The scope and power of the concept of cost will not be evident at this point. Later it will be shown to encompass such features as freshness of air, purity of water, health, social amenities, recreation, comfort, leisure, privacy, and many other aspects of a desirable life. Economics is not so blind as to assume costs are comprised only of sacrificed material things.

Warning: Hereafter, for convenience and by convention, we shall usually omit the adjective "substitution" from "personal substitution value."

Where does the newcomer acquire candy for the Cuban? From some other refugee—say, a Hungarian. To the Hungarian he offers five cigarettes for ten candy bars; the Hungarian accepts. The Hungarian's *personal value* of cigarettes relative to candy is (as we can see in Table 4–2) 10/4 or 2.5, but he is offered cigarettes at a cost of only two candies. His personal value of cigarettes (in units of candy), 2.5 candy bars, exceeds the cost of getting more cigarettes.

The Hungarian in effect trades his basket A for basket B_2. Basket B_2 is superior to B_1, for it contains more cigarettes and as much candy; and since basket B_1 is assumed to be exactly as desirable as basket A, the Hungarian has moved to a more preferred consumption basket, B_2, as shown in Table 4–2.

And so—by the newcomer's transferring some candy from a Hungarian to a Cuban and some cigarettes to the Hungarian from the Cuban—*both* the Cuban and the Hungarian have moved to improved situations. They both hope that the newcomer will repeat his offer next week, after the new gift parcels arrive.

TABLE 4–2. Equivalent and Preferred Baskets for Hungarian

		Candy	Cigarettes
	Basket A	20	20
		(−10)	(+4)
Equivalent:	Basket B_1	10	24
		(−10)	(+5)
Preferred:	Basket B_2	10	25

Gain from trade. We now have an amazing situation. The newcomer has two cigarettes left over for his own use. He has taken two cigarettes from the total stock of forty cigarettes previously divided between the Cuban and Hungarian. Yet—although they have less goods in total—both say they are better off. How can they be better off with *fewer* goods? Has the newcomer exploited them, when all the time they thought they were being benefited? Suppose the Hungarian and Cuban get together and find they have, between them, lost two cigarettes? Could the newcomer explain or defend this odd result? Using our postulates, he could, as follows:

"You have not been cheated. In fact, you both have been made better off. Although, of course, you both could use all the candy and cigarettes that you formerly had, each of you preferred a slightly different combination. I made it possible for you to shift to preferred combinations. The cigarettes can be considered a payment for my helpful services. To be sure, I did not do all this with the sole intention of helping you. I helped you revise your baskets because I was interested in myself. And—admit it—each of you thought you were outwitting me, because you were prepared to give up more (or receive less) than you did. Certainly you would have been even more benefited if I had kept fewer than two cigarettes, but there is no denying that each of you is now better off than initially because of the revised proportions of candy and cigarettes. None of us has been foolish."[2]

[2] For an alternative, more powerful explanation of the principles of exchange, see the Appendix to this chapter, where the Edgeworth Box is utilized.

Conditions for gains from trade. To isolate the essential condition in which people gain from (that is, prefer to) trade, even if they have to pay middlemen, compare the initial personal valuations of the Cuban and the Hungarian. Table 4–3 shows the Cuban's personal value of candy was .8 (in cigarette units), while the Hungarian's personal value of candy was .4 (in cigarettes). To each, his personal value of candy indicates the price below which he would buy candy and above which he would sell candy. The Cuban would buy more candy if the price of candy were lower than .8 cigarettes; but he would sell and hence consume less candy, if the price were over .8. The Hungarian, whose initial personal value of candy is .4 cigarettes, would buy more candy at any price below .4 cigarettes but would sell if the exchange rate were over .4. The direction of trade will always be such that *commodity X moves from the person with the lower personal value of X to the person with the higher personal value of X*. Candy, in our example, moves from the Hungarian to the Cuban. In summary, *in any situation in which personal values differ, an opportunity exists wherein appropriate exchange will result in a more preferred position for each person.*

TABLE 4–3. Results of Trade

		Cuban		Hungarian	
		Candy	Cigarettes	Candy	Cigarettes
	Basket A	20	20	20	20
		(+10)	(−8)	(−10)	(+4)
Equivalent:	Basket B₁	30	12	10	24
			(−7)		(+5)
Preferred:	Basket after exchange	30	13	10	25

This exchange proposition is one of the most important in economics. An *inequality of personal substitution rates* (*or values*) is a condition of "inefficient," and hence improvable, allocation. It will be applied again later in numerous different contexts: production, specialization of labor, bearing of risks, and interregional trade.

Warning: Do not confuse efficiency with equity. The preceding proposition refers to efficiency in re-allocation of goods *given an initial allotment*. When no further revision would increase the utility (i.e., attain a more preferred situation) of each person, we have achieved an efficient extent of exchange. But it may not be equitable. The initial allotment from which each person started in our toy problem was "equal," at least in terms of amounts of each good. But that may or may not be equitable. Equity is not necessarily equality—and, indeed, after the mutually beneficial trade, the Cuban and the Hungarian do not have equal amounts of either commodity. "Equitable" is a matter of personal judgment. I may think it equitable for brown-eyed people to be born smarter, to inherit more, and to be taxed less, while someone else may think the opposite or whatever he likes. Economic analysis contributes nothing to the judgment of an "equitable" situation. All we have analyzed is efficiency of exchange, whatever the initial allotment was.

Obviously, this "toy" example abstracts from many details, but that is precisely its purpose: to reveal the crucial explanation of trade in bold, uncluttered fashion. For example, we did not ask whether the Cuban likes candy more than the Hungarian likes candy. As explained in our discussion of postulate 5 in the preceding chapter, no interpersonal comparison of absolute psychological level of desire for each good is involved. The Cuban may regard candy and cigarettes as barely desirable goods, while the Hungarian drools and pants for both.

In this example, the middleman seems to serve only a small role that could have been performed by the Cuban and Hungarian themselves. But we cannot ignore the costs of collecting, transporting, and displaying merchandise and of searching out offers and bids of potential buyers and sellers. The service of the middleman in "making a market" is no trivial task, as anyone will discover who attempts to sell his own used car to some other car user directly rather than via a dealer. It has even been argued that such examples show how capitalistic middlemen exploit the ignorance of the consumer. Indeed, that is true, in exactly the same way a teacher exploits the ignorance of students, doctors the ignorance of patients, and authors the ignorance of their readers. (Never confuse ignorance with stupidity or carelessness.) An economic way to behave is *not* to try to learn everything, but to specialize and exchange information for other information or goods. Of course, it is more passionately spectacular to call this "exploitation." 1, 2, 3, 4, 5, 6

Diminishing Personal Values

We have learned *why* trade occurs and in what *direction* it occurs. We have not yet discerned the *extent* to which people will revise their consumption patterns. How much will the Cuban, for example, revise his consumption pattern by trading cigarettes for more candy before he says, "Stop; I have reached a most preferred combination of candy and cigarettes"? The answer requires the application of our fourth postulate, which states how personal values of goods depend upon the combinations of the goods available.

Our newcomer (middleman) has just completed his first trade. Why not buy still more candy from the Hungarian to sell to the Cuban for an extra gain of .2 cigarettes per bar of candy sold per week? But when the trader tries to buy additional candy from the Hungarian, he discovers he cannot get more at the old price. Although the Hungarian happily gave up the first ten bars of candy for five cigarettes *when he had twenty of each*, he is not willing to give up another bar for the same old price of .5 cigarettes for a candy bar. As he puts it, "When I have less candy and more cigarettes than formerly, cigarettes become less valuable relative to candy. More than .5 cigarettes is now required to compensate me for a further reduction in candy." In economic terms, his personal value of candy has risen (relative to cigarettes). Only at a higher price of candy would he revise his consumption toward even less candy. Conversely, the middleman will have to offer to the Cuban more candy than before for cigarettes. The middleman is experiencing postulate 4. One's personal valuation of any good is higher the less he has of that good (with constant or greater amounts of other goods). In sum, if the middleman wants to expand the amount of weekly exchange between the Cuban and the Hungarian, he will have to pay a higher price to buy candy from the Hungarian and accept a lower price for the candy he seeks to sell to the Cuban. The middleman must determine how much candy, in total, he should sell each week to the Cuban and buy from the Hungarian, and conversely for cigarettes, so as to yield for himself the maximum profits, *assuming that he is the only middleman*.

Competition between Middlemen

Before the first middleman discovers how much to revise prices, his wonderful world of profits is shattered by the appearance of another wily refugee. An old hand at the art of trading, this new dealer offers better terms to the Cuban: ten units of candy at a price of only six and a half, rather than seven, cigarettes. The Cuban accepts, happy to buy candy at a lower price, and (what is the same thing) to sell cigarettes at a higher price.

To the Hungarian, the new middleman offers five and a half, rather than only five, cigarettes for ten bars of candy. This, too, is a better offer than that of the first established middleman—who argues that the new middleman is an unreliable fly-by-night who will not deliver; or, if he does, will deliver stale candy or dry, wrinkled cigarettes, and will not give service with a smile, and in any event cannot possibly cover costs of good service with such prices. But the Hungarian takes his chances and buys from the new trader. Both the Cuban and Hungarian prefer the new prices. The price at which the Cuban can now buy one candy bar is down to .65 (from .70) cigarette. The selling price available to the Hungarian from the middleman is up to .55 (from .50) cigarette for each bar of candy. Buyers like lower prices, and sellers like higher prices. If bigger baskets are better than smaller ones, the Cuban and the Hungarian are better off, since each has .5 cigarettes more than when trading via the first middleman, as shown in Table 4–4.

TABLE 4–4. Consumption Baskets before and after Competition among Middlemen

	Cuban	
	Candy	Cigarettes
Before Trade	20	20
After trade via First middleman	30	13
		(+.5)
After trade via Second middleman	30	13.5

	Hungarian	
	Candy	Cigarettes
Before Trade	20	20
After trade via First middleman	10	25
		(+.5)
After trade via Second middleman	10	25.5

Competition between middlemen has reduced the spread between buying and selling prices. The consumer now pays a lower price and receives a higher price for what he sells. The spread between the buying and selling price for candy is narrowed from .2 to .1 cigarette per candy, and the gain to the middleman is now one instead of two cigarettes.

Competition between middlemen reduces the buying-selling price spread to the "costs" of providing the service at the quality wanted by the consumers. If the spread were larger, more middlemen would be attracted; and they would shave the margin in order to get business. If the profits were negative, some middlemen would not survive as middlemen; only those who could produce the middleman's service at lowest costs would be left in the business. The competition that reduces profits is the competition of middleman against middleman, *not* consumer (or seller) against the middlemen. Middlemen do not compete with consumers; they compete with other middlemen.

7, 8, 9

Open Markets, Costs of Exchange, and Profit Reduction

The smaller spread between buying and selling prices is a consequence of open-entry market competition, or, as we shall call it, *open markets. Open markets mean that access to markets is open to all people without legal or arbitrary barriers*—not that there are no costs involved in providing exchange-facilitating services.

When there are no artificial barriers to exchange, the price spread is competed down to just the covering of costs (the middleman's services). A difference between the price at which the middleman buys candy from the Hungarian and the price at which he sells it to the Cuban does not necessarily indicate "profits." There are costs of conducting exchange. These include rent for space in which transactions can be conducted and goods can be stored for inspection and immediate delivery; costs of record keeping; the cost of inventory, advertising, light, heat, and insurance. In part, lower-cost discount houses permit the consumer directly to bear part of the costs of exchange—for example, collecting information about the item, return privileges, credit buying, delivery service, convenience of shopping conditions and location, speed of service by salesmen. All of these can be substantial portions of the total cost.

Exchange costs could be reduced to zero only if *everyone* knew (without incurring any costs) *all* the characteristics of what *everyone* else was willing to sell or buy, at what time, and at what price. And in this extreme case, the personal values of every person for any good would be equated among everyone. Any difference between two people's personal values for a good would mean that trade would be profitable. Trade would occur until everyone's personal value moved to equality with each other's, as the initially disparate personal values of the Cuban and Hungarian converged toward each other with the execution of trade and revision of the combinations of goods possessed by each party. In reality, if there are costs of negotiating and conducting trade, the buying and selling price spread will reflect those costs and prevent complete equality of everyone's personal value for the particular good. (But if the values of such services are included, then there will be equality of values for "goods plus services of negotiating exchanges.") 10, 11, 12

Constrained Markets

An open market is not a universal condition. Constraints *are* interposed—often at the urging of those already in the business, in order to protect or increase their wealth. A brief scenario of a possible episode in the refugee camp will illustrate some common constraints; in later chapters we analyze the constraints in more realistic settings.

Threat of Violence

The original middleman thinks: "The gains to the Cuban and to the Hungarian (and my profit) were the result of *my* acuteness but someone has stolen my discovery." To protect his interest, he therefore warns the new trader that any poaching will cost him his teeth. But if the Cuban and the Hungarian promise to protect the new trader, the first trader must turn to other tactics.

Control of Business Hours

The original trader notes that the refugees are trading with the new trader at unheard of hours of the day, at nights, and even on Sundays. Arguing that it is improper to work at night or on Sundays, he suggests that trading be permitted only from 8 to 5 on weekdays. The camp manager agrees, thinking that this will be conducive to order and genteel life in the camp. Unfortunately, the new trader is so busy with other, more productive tasks during the hours of 8 to 5 that he is then unable to offer his services so conveniently as a middleman. Furthermore, for some refugees it is inconvenient to negotiate with middlemen during the designated hours. Some who formerly dealt with the new trader after working hours are now restricted to dealing with the old trader, whose prices are less favorable. However, difficulties of enforcing this 8 to 5 restriction soon lead to its abandonment.

Coalition by Merger or Collusion

Cunningly, the old trader approaches the new and offers to merge businesses. He points out that both have been forced to lower their selling prices and raise their buying prices to a very narrow spread. Through agreement, they might restore the price spread to two cigarettes per candy (with one going to the new trader and one to the old). This proposal appeals to the new trader, for it will give him a one-cigarette margin on *all* the candy trades at the new prices instead of one cigarette on only those exchanges that he himself would have conducted at the previous prices; the old trader will get the same benefit. But the profitability of this coalition will attract new middlemen, who either have to be bought off or let in on the group profits. In either case the attempt to maintain high profits for the two middlemen will fail as profits are spread over more and more new middlemen, until the net gains per middleman over and above costs of exchanges are brought back to zero—a result achieved not by reducing prices to consumers but by raising costs of exchange because of the excess number of middlemen.

Compulsory Licensing and Self-Regulation

A means of preserving the profitability of the collusive group is the prohibition of new entrants. To this end, the two middlemen persuade the camp manager to permit only "approved" (that is, duly licensed, properly trained, ethical) traders. The camp manager naturally agrees that the best judges of "proper training, competence, and ethics" are those already in the business (who automatically get licenses). They, of course, determine when "public necessity and convenience" calls for additional licensed middlemen. This arrangement, called *self-regulation,* is supposed to protect the unwary, unsophisticated customers from unscrupulous, incompetent, quack middlemen. As expected, the "standards" are so high and concern for consumer welfare is so great that no more licenses are issued. So the price spread is maintained at a level sufficient for a *few* respectable, qualified middlemen to enjoy the standard of living they think they deserve.

To make life easier for the "self-regulating" middlemen, the cartel (a group with the right to exclude newcomers from the market) permits trade only between the hours of 9 and 3, weekdays. The traders say longer hours would serve no purpose, since they can take care of everyone during that time. Customer convenience is somehow forgotten.

Yet, all is not tranquil. Every licensed member has an overwhelming temptation to get more customers by special services, gifts, and advertising. Thus, pains and costs must be incurred to prevent such mutually damaging competition. Costs must be incurred to hire spies and agents to detect secret price cutting or rendering of special services by members of the cartel.

Franchise Fees

Not long after initiation of the self-regulating, licensing scheme, the camp manager realizes that he can capture part of the dealers' enhanced wealth by charging a "fee" for the right to be licensed. He calls it a license or franchise fee. This fee happens almost to equal the value of the anticipated future profits earned by the licensees in excess of what they would have earned if there were an open market. Or he could levy a special "tax" on them. In either way, the camp manager transfers to himself the present and future monopoly-protected profit.

13, 14, 15

A Few Implications of Exchange Analysis

We can more fully appreciate the problems of maintaining constraints, or recognize the forces that operate in their absence, if we investigate real markets, wherein millions of people are involved with uncounted numbers of goods and services and money. We start on that task in the next chapter, but before doing so, a few other implications should be elaborated.

Exchange Directed by Personal Values of Goods, Not by Importance of the Users

The feasibility of exchange arose because people had combinations of goods to which they assigned different personal, subjective values. Neither the Cuban nor the Hungarian had to tell what he was going to do with the goods or to determine who had the more important function to perform with his goods. Interpersonal comparison of importance was totally irrelevant . . . for exchange. But it is necessary for deciding how *large* a basket to give each person *initially*.

An excellent demonstration that comparison of importance of use is irrelevant is provided by the Army and the Navy. We might decide the Army should have twice the total budget or amount of goods that the Navy should. That would depend upon how much a larger batch of goods devoted to the Army would provide in the form of defense capability compared to the same batch if given to the Navy. But once that decision was made and the Army and Navy were given resources, might both their defense potentials be increased if they could *exchange* or redistribute goods with each other? Perhaps the Army would trade *some* men for *more* nuclear material.

For that nothing must be known about the ultimate importance or value of Army relative to Navy services. That is relevant *only* in deciding how *big* a batch of goods, or budget, to give each. All we have to know is the Army's own internal value of nuclear materials in terms of men and the Navy's own valuation of nuclear material in terms of men. Each service branch could compute its own internal valuation. The one that places a higher internal value on more nuclear material (in terms of men) will find it advantageous to trade some men for some more nuclear material, and the other branch will find it advantageous to give up some of its nuclear material for those men. To see why, go back and change names from Cuban and Hungarian to Army and Navy, and the candy and cigarettes to men and nuclear material.

Yet until about 1960 such calculations and exchanges between the military services were not systematically performed. Subsequently, however, the services have begun to make intra-service valuations and negotiate revisions in their resources. Simple economics can have enormous benefits.

Reasons for Trade

Trade between two people is sometimes said to rest on the fact that one has a "surplus" to dispose of. Even social scientists have held this fallacious notion: "The development of cities rests ultimately on food surpluses of agricultural producers above their own requirements." But nowhere in the preceding was there any "surplus" of cigarettes or candy. Surplus has nothing whatever to do with the possibility of exchange.

Productivity of Exchange

Our analysis also shows that trade is productive. Middlemen (retailers, salesmen, brokers, wholesalers, transporters) are productive in the only sense in which the word "production" has economic meaning. Production means an act that increases utility. A productive act improves the shape, place, or even the time of availability of something. Profit-making middlemen are not "parasitical intermediaries." By performing those intermediary tasks more economically than each of us could for ourselves, they enable us more easily to reach preferred mixtures of goods.

Ethics and Free Trade

Economics does not demonstrate that exchange makes people *better off* in some moral or objective sense. It does not even show they *should* trade. If you believe it is "good" for a person to get what he thinks he will prefer, you can conclude that trade contributes to "goodness." However, a new chosen position may not be as nice as he imagined it would be. Information before the exchange is sometimes inaccurate and inadequate; the assumption that the trader preferred to get what he actually did get is then open to doubt. Could someone else make a better choice for the individual? One may hear that individuals know "well enough" what the consequences are. Or that although other people may know more about consequences, their inferior knowledge of individual preferences more than offsets knowledge of consequences. Or that you can't trust other people to act in your interest. Or that people, as a moral duty, *ought* to make their own choices because this will produce the responsibility and self-reliance of the "good" society. Some believe that whether or not people *ought* to, they *do* in fact want the right to make their own choices. It is wrong, they say, to prohibit the exchanges other people mutually agree upon, even if what they do doesn't accord with what we think is "for their own good."

Some humanitarian persons believe that some people are not capable of proper understanding and therefore should be influenced or controlled "for their own good," much as with children. In many instances—for medical care, food, education—adults are prohibited from entering into mutually agreeable exchanges with whomever they please to exchange whatever they please.

The critics of open market exchange probably attach more weight to the regrettable consequences for those who make unfortunate choices than to (1) the forsaken gains removed from those who would otherwise have made fortunate choices and (2) the desirability of individual choice *per se*. Those who favor enlarging the range of individual choice of exchanges probably make exactly the opposite evaluation. Neither group is necessarily more humanitarian or socially conscious than the other.

Still different are those who contend that other people's tastes and preferences are simply wrong or improper and that they should learn the right kinds of tastes and preferences. People *ought* to prefer classical music to jazz and modern music; realistic to abstract art; decent to immoral, decadent literature; wine to beer; opera and theater to TV and movies; compact, severe cars to chromium-splashed cars; adult education to bridge and poker; and study to football. These critics would reduce the scope of the free-exchange market (because access to that market enables people to realize their "idiosyncratic, cruder" preferences and odd tastes, just as the Cuban chose more fatness and the Hungarian more cigarette cough); or they might try to change tastes and preferences by educating, informing, persuading, or propagandizing.

Freedom: As You Like It

This evaluation of the right to voluntary exchange of goods in the open market is part of the clash between the capitalist and socialist cultures. We have been careful not to express the matter as "free versus unfree" or "democratic versus undemocratic." The socialist could say that people are freer in Russia, because they are free from the task or risk of making uninformed choices. They are freed from the danger of making certain kinds of later-regretted choices, just as you and I are "freed" (prevented) from the risk of hiring a quack to perform an operation or advise us about our illnesses, or from the possibility of buying whole milk with too low a cream content, or from all sorts of possibilities of acquiring inferior things—substandard food, substandard airplane flights, substandard houses. We are supposedly protected from our own folly; we are "freed" from doing or acquiring things that someone thinks we *really* do not want. This may seem an unusual meaning of "free," but it is a widely accepted meaning in Russian *and* American life. It is easy to allege that one's proposed restrictions on other people are those that really give them "more freedom," promote "good" and prevent "bad" consequences. Restraint from doing what is "bad" is, some of us think, no restraint on "true" freedom. But different individuals have different notions of what is good and what is bad. Thus, to use the term "freedom" is to beg questions.

Nor do we speak of democratic versus undemocratic economic rights. Democracy is a way of allocating political power, not a criterion of what is done with it. A dictatorship which is undemocratic could enforce economic and legal rules that are conducive to what some might call a desirable society. A democracy can, by majority revision of various economic and legal rules, produce an "undesirable" society. It is *not* perfectly self-evident to all that democracy as such is more conducive than *any* other system to the emergence or continuance of a society that many would call "free," "open," or "desirable."

Criticisms of Methodology

A misconceived objection to the economic analysis of exchange contends it assumes an unwarranted degree of rational, calculating behavior. Economic theorems, as pointed out earlier, are formulated only for observed behavior. Economics describes how people behave in exchange. People are not necessarily aware of the principles of economics when they exchange. Sticks, stones, and birds behave according to the law of gravity, even though they do not know what it is; human beings obey this same law before they have learned anything about it—and their behavior conforms to the economic postulates in the same way.

Of course, people *do* calculate, and even "habit" is a form of purposeful behavior. If a person discovers that habitual or conventional purchase patterns are less useful than other patterns, he forms a new habit or customary pattern. Habits are economic ways of avoiding unnecessary mental effort. Thinking, comparing, calculating, and deciding are difficult and costly activities. They take time from other, more pleasant activities—as every college student knows.

A partially effective criticism of the preceding analysis of exchange is that one party to a potential exchange may dislike the other or fear his motives and refuse to trade because a gain to the second party may be turned against the first. Witness our restrictions on trading with communist countries: we fear their consequent gain in economic strength may ultimately be used against us. In our analysis, we did not assume that each person's utility is independent of what other people have. More generally, we assume that each person can regard a more preferred position for the other person as desirable in itself, as we do explicitly in Chapter 9. If we were to consider motivations of envy or fear, then the analysis is even more complex.

Another criticism notes that some days a person eats candy, and on others he may smoke. He varies his daily consumption mixture. Hence, the preceding concentration on a particular mixture that is supposed to be preferred over some other mixture is "artificial." Not at all. We said only that a person can in the course of a week consume candy and cigarettes. He is at liberty to eat all the candy at once or spread it out over time, any way he wants.

Summary

1 As long as there is a *revealed* disparity between the *personal values* of goods for any two persons, the allocation of these goods can be revised by trade so that each person moves to a more preferred situation, *provided the costs of discovering the people whose values are unequal and negotiating the exchange contracts and transporting goods* are not prohibitory.

2 Every choice has a cost—the highest valued option forsaken.

3 Each party shifts toward *more* of the particular goods for which his personal value exceeds the market-exchange rate (price). Trade moves goods toward the higher personal values.

4 Each party will increase (reduce) his stock of a good, relative to other goods, until the personal value he places on increments of it is reduced (increased) to equality with market price.

5 At equilibrium, each party has the same personal value of a good as every other party—a value that is also equaled by the market price at which exchange is available.

6 Every seller in the market has an incentive to try to keep out other sellers. In the absence of arbitrary obstacles or legal restrictions, the prospect of profits will entice new sellers into the market. Existing sellers have incentives to reach agreements to avoid cutting price. The enticement to violate the agreements increases with the size of the gain from the collusion. The government will be appealed to as a means of keeping out new competi-

tors—that is, restricting the open market in order to maintain a larger buying-selling price spread, under the guise of protecting the consumer from unscrupulous sellers, who would undermine the quality of the product. The legally protected "profits" often are taken by the government.

7. The importance of what a person does with his goods is not relevant for determining either the direction of trade or the final combination of goods held by that person.

8. Exchange rates do not measure a value of the *total amount* of some good; they measure only the value of an *increment*.

9. Trade is not a result of a "surplus" of some good to one party while another has an "insufficiency" of that good.

10. Economics does not imply that trade is a good thing, in any sense other than that people, if given the opportunity, will engage in trade. The right to trade may put some people in a regretted position—when they discover that the new combination was not as desirable as they anticipated.

Appendix: The Edgeworth Exchange Box

The Edgeworth Exchange Box is a powerful method for explaining the principles of trade.

The Edgeworth Box is named for Francis Ysidro Edgeworth, who first suggested it in his *Mathematical Psychics* (1881). The box consists of a combination of two utility or preference maps (explained in the Appendix to the preceding chapter) for two people, here called Cuban and Hungarian, between whom there will be trade (without a middleman).

To construct an Edgeworth Box, the utility or preference map of the Cuban and the map of the Hungarian are superimposed as in Figure 4–1, *after* rotating one of them 180 degrees so that it appears upside down, with the conventional left-hand scale on the right side running from *top* to bottom. Here the Hungarian's map has been rotated so that *his* zero point, 0_h, is in the *upper-right* corner. The length of each side of the box represents the *total* amount of X and Y available to these two people. The total amount of X is measured on the horizontal axis and is allocated with $0_c X_c$ to the Cuban as his initial amount of X; $0_h X_h$ (shown at the top of the box) is the remainder and is the amount of X initially held by the Hungarian. Note that the distance $0_c X_c$ plus the distance $0_h X_h$ exactly equals the width of the box, denoting the entire existing amount of X.

Similarly the initial division of Y between the two people shows that the Cuban has the amount $0_c Y_c$, measured vertically up from the lower-left origin, 0_c, for the Cuban; and the Hungarian has $0_h Y_h$ of Y, measured down from the upper-right origin, 0_h, for the Hungarian. The distance $0_c Y_c$ plus $0_h Y_h$ equals the vertical height of the box, and denotes the total amount of Y.

Point Q in the box denotes the *initial* allocations of X and Y to the Cuban and Hungarian, with the horizontal distance of the point measuring the amounts of X available to the Cuban (on the left) and to the Hungarian (measured from the right). The vertical height to the point Q indicates the amount available initially to the Cuban, and the vertical distance down from the top side indicates the amount of Y initially available to the Hungarian.

The curved solid lines are utility isoquants, or indifference curves, of the Cuban. The dashed curved lines are utility isoquants for the Hungarian; these may at first sight

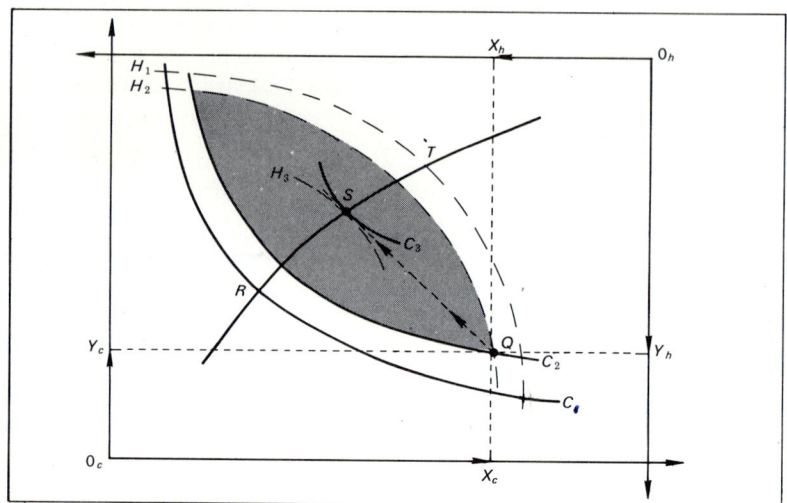

FIGURE 4-1. Edgeworth Exchange Box

appear to be curved in the wrong direction, but remember that his map is turned upside down so that its origin is in the upper right, at 0_h.

Point Q is on the utility isoquant, C_2, for the Cuban. Line C_1 is another of his indifference curves, but with lower utility, while C_3 is a higher indifference curve. Similarly point Q, measured with reference to the origin, 0_h, is on an indifference curve, H_2, for the Hungarian. Turning the book around, you will see that the curves H_1 and H_2 are lower and higher indifference curves, respectively.

The *slope* of the indifference curve, C_2, as explained in the Appendix to the preceding chapter, shows the Cuban's personal values of the commodities, or marginal rate of substitution between X and Y in consumption at point Q. If he could trade *some X* for *some Y*, at a rate of exchange indicated by the slope of the dashed, arrowed "trading" line emanating from point Q, he could move to higher utility on C_3, at point S. If at the same time the Hungarian were to get what the Cuban gave up—i.e., if the Hungarian and the Cuban were trading with each other—then the Hungarian would also be revising his combination of goods from Q along the dashed line to S. He, too, would be moved to *higher* utility, H_3. So long as they trade with each other along some dashed line that moves each to higher indifference curves, trade can be mutually agreeable. And any dashed trading line that starts from a point like Q and runs inward into a football-shaped shaded area, bounded by the two indifference curves through point Q, will move both the Cuban's and the Hungarian's resultant mixture of goods to preferred combinations, i.e., to higher utility lines for each person.

In general, so long as the dashed straight trading line (whose *slope measures the price for X, and Y,* at which the Cuban and Hungarian might trade) *cuts* the utility curves of both the Cuban and the Hungarian at point Q, it will pay each to move on that trading line in the direction that moves both to higher utility curves. The dashed trade line at point Q has a slope *between* that of (1) the Cuban's indifference curve slope through point Q and (2) the Hungarian's indifference curve through the point Q; this means that the proposed buying (and selling) prices of X (in terms of Y units) differ from the personal values placed on X relative to Y. Such a trading price will enable both parties to reach combinations with higher utilities.

Through every point on the diagram there is an indifference curve for C, and there is also one for H. Wherever a curve of one man cuts a curve of the other man, some trade would improve each person's utility. Only for a special series of points do the utility curves of one person not *intersect* those of the other person. Instead, the curves are *tangent*. These special points form the "contract curve," indicated by the thick line, labeled RST. This "contract curve" line indicates *all* the combinations of goods X and Y for each person at which the indifference curve for the Cuban for that combination is *tangent* to the indifference curve for the Hungarian. At that point of tangency, the curves have the same slope. Any initial allocation of X and Y between the Cuban and Hungarian (except those on the line RST) can be improved by trade along a trading line toward RST. In our diagrammed example, the straight trading line from Q to S extends into the football-shaped enclosure bounded by the initial situation's two indifference curves. This is a line along which they could move by trading with each other, until they came to point S. If they moved along their trading line past S, they would each be moving to lower indifference curves (i.e., to less preferred positions). Once they have reached the RST line, they have exhausted the possibilities of *mutual* gain from trade with each other, no matter from where they started. The line RST is called the contract curve, because it is to some point on this curve that their contracts for trade will take them. This tangency of the two indifference curves and the trading price line means that the price between X and Y equals the personal values placed on X relative to Y by both the two trading parties.

Once they have *reached* the contract curve, no further *mutually* acceptable revision of consumption patterns is possible. Moving *along* the contract curve means that one party gives up some of *both* goods to the other. That would be a transfer of wealth from one party to the other, not an exchange.

If we accept the premise that each party should be the judge of his own interests, then any distribution of goods between the two parties represented by a point *off* the contract curve is *economically inefficient*: things could be improved for everyone by trading and moving to a point *on* the contract curve at which no *jointly* beneficial revision is feasible. Hence any point on the contract curve is *economically efficient* in the sense that it is impossible to make a change that would improve the position of *both* parties. Economically efficient allocations of goods are those from which there is no possibility of improving the situation of someone without reducing the utility of someone else. (We say *economic* efficiency, because later we shall identify a more restricted concept: *technical* efficiency.)

Econ. efficient = no transaction possible that is mutually helpful.

Questions

1. The left half of the table below shows three combinations of vegetables and meat among which Linus would have revealed indifference if he had been offered a choice; that is, all three are equally desirable to him. The right half shows three combinations among which Charlie would have revealed indifference.

	Linus				Charlie		
Options	Vegetables		Meat	Options	Vegetables		Meat
A	10	and	14	A	40	and	16
B	13	and	13	B	45	and	15
C	17	and	12	C	52	and	14

a. If Linus has combination B, between what limits is his consumption-substitution ratio between vegetables and meat?
b. If Charlie has combination B, approximately what is his personal value for vegetables?
c. In what sense it it impossible to say who likes vegetables more, Linus or Charlie? In what sense is it possible?
d. If Linus and Charlie each have their combinations designated B, does any possible trade exist whereby each could reach a preferred combination? If so, give an example.
e. State the necessary consumption-substitution exchange-rate conditions if exchange between two people is to move them to preferred positions, even though part of their goods might be lost in the process.

2 Suppose that Charlie and Linus have the following initial indifference consumption-substitution ratios:

$$\text{Charlie: } 7 \text{ meat} = 1 \text{ fruit}$$
$$\text{Linus: } 3 \text{ meat} = 1 \text{ fruit}$$

a. Compared to Linus, is Charlie more fond of fruit or meat?
b. If the government makes it illegal to trade fruit for meat, always assuming that the law is obeyed, who gains and who loses? Why?
c. Now, the government relents and allows trade, but makes it illegal for anyone to trade at any exchange ratio other than one meat for one fruit. Explain the likely consequences of this new ruling.
d. Next, suppose the government relents still more, but—in order to protect the "little people" who consume fruit—a price ceiling is put on fruit. The maximum price of one unit of fruit is set at four meats. Who is likely to gain, and who is likely to lose by this price control? Explain.
e. Finally, imagine that the government takes off all restrictions on the trade of meat and fruit. Introduce a middleman who conducts the trade between Charlie and Linus. What is the *maximum* cut the middleman can take in the form of meat? Or of fruit?

3 "The postulates of economics imply that to permit trade is better than to prohibit trade." Do they? Explain.

4 Your college allots some parking space for your car while a friend is alloted a desk in the library stacks. Suppose that you and he would each be better off if you were to trade your parking space for his desk space.
a. This kind of trading is almost invariably prohibited by the college authorities. Why?
b. If you were the college president, why would you prohibit it?
c. Would you consider solving the whole problem by simply selling parking space to one and all at the market-clearing price, like a downtown parking garage? Why?

5 "Trade between the Mediterranean and the Baltic developed when each area produced a surplus of some good."
a. What do you think this quotation, from a widely used history text, means?
b. Can you propose an alternative explanation?

6 A parent gives each of his two children some milk and meat. The two children then exchange with each other, one drinking most of the milk and the other eating most of the meat. If the parent does not permit them to make that exchange, which of the postulates (if any) is he denying? Or does the explanation rest on some new postulate not made explicit in the text?

7 "Economic theory is built on an idealization of man: that he has tremendous computational power, a detailed knowledge of his desires and needs, a thorough understanding of his environment and its causal relationships, a resistance to acting on impulse or by habit.

It is difficult to bridge the gap between that model of economic man and the groping uncertain man of the real world." Does this statement correctly characterize the state of economic theory? Explain.

8 "Competition is never 'buyer against seller' but always seller against other sellers and buyers against other buyers."
   a. Is this true for you when you buy food? Automobiles? Shoes? Sell your labor?
   b. Can you cite a case in which it is not true?

9 According to economic principles of competition, which tactic would be more likely to get you a lower price on a new car: going to just one dealer and acting like a tough and aggressive bargainer; or going to several dealers and mildly asking for their selling price while letting it be known that you really intended to buy a car? Explain why. Can you cite any evidence?

10 It is estimated that 25 percent of the price a housewife pays for a head of lettuce goes to the farmer, while the remaining portion is for middlemen and distribution costs.
   a. Would you, as a farmer, necessarily prefer to have your percentage raised? Explain why not.
   b. Would you, as a consumer, prefer to see his percentage raised? Explain.

11 "Middlemen and the do-it-yourself principle are incompatible." Explain.

12 Some discount stores advertise that they can sell for less because they buy directly from the manufacturer and sell to the consumer, thus eliminating many middlemen. What is the flaw in this reasoning?

13 Which of the following are compatible with open (or free) markets:
   a. A lawyer must get permission of present lawyers before he can engage in that trade.
   b. Medical doctors must pass a state examination before being allowed to sell medical services.
   c. Banks must first obtain a license from the state before being allowed to operate—and not everyone can get a license merely for the asking.
   d. Selling is prohibited on Sunday.
   e. Pure food and drug laws restrict the sale of "impure" foods and drugs.
   f. Consumption, manufacture, or sale of alcoholic beverages is prohibited.
   g. Dealers and agents must be certified by the U.S. Securities and Exchange Commission before they can act as middlemen in buying and selling stocks and bonds, that is, before they can be security dealers.

14 Suppose you succeed in leading an army of liberation to rid Cuba of Castro Communists. Upon taking office as new dictator, you abolish all existing monopoly rights.
   a. Would you then grant new monopoly rights?
   b. If you did, how could you benefit the government (you)?
   c. If you didn't think of doing that, who would suggest it to you?

15 You are campaigning for mayor or councilman in your home town, in which the taxi service (or, for that matter, garbage service, milk delivery, electric power, water, gas, etc.) is provided by anyone who wants to operate a taxi business or drive his own cab. In other words, the taxi service is provided by an open market. You campaign for more government control of taxi drivers in order to ensure better quality of service.
   a. If elected, would you initiate a system of giving just one company the right to perform the service? Why?
   b. If so, how would you decide which company?
   c. Do you think that company would be one of your campaign financiers?
   d. In California the right to sell liquor is restricted by the state government to a number

far below that which would prevail otherwise. Would you be surprised to learn that the liquor dealers are a strong political "lobby" and source of "power" in state politics? Why?

e. What generalization does this suggest about a source of political power?

16 "It is well to remind ourselves from time to time of the benefits we derive from a free-market system. The system rests on freedom of consumer choice, the profit motive, and vigorous competition for the buyer's dollar. By relying on these spontaneous economic forces, we secure these benefits: (a) Our system tends automatically to produce the kinds of goods that consumers want in the relative quantities in which people want them. (b) The system tends automatically to minimize waste. If one producer is making a product inefficiently, another will see an opportunity for profit by making the product at a lower cost. (c) The system encourages innovation and technological change . . . . I regard the preservation and strengthening of the free market as a cardinal objective of this or any Administration's policies." (President J. F. Kennedy, September 1962, speaking to business magazine and newspaper publishers.)

Is it not surprising and confusing that while espousing the virtues of an open competitive economic system, businessmen and politicians restrict markets—for example, by controlling allowable imports of sugar so as to maintain sugar prices in the United States at about twice the open-market level—in order to maintain larger wealth for incumbent businessmen and their employees? A confusion between freedom *of* competition and freedom *from* competition is suggested. What explains this espousal of the virtues of a system of private property and open markets with simultaneous attempts to suppress it?

17 Can you explain how what is often called "impulse" buying is consistent with the postulates of choice? Can you explain why habitual buying is also consistent with the postulates of choice? Can you suggest some behavior that would not be consistent with the postulates?

Demand and the Laws of Demand

5

DO markets with thousands of people operate consistently with the principles of the preceding chapters? After all, we rarely trade candy for Cokes with other consumers. We buy and sell goods and services for *money* from producers and middlemen in a market place. By spending less money for candy and more for Cokes, you do, in effect, trade candy for Cokes; you revise your consumption pattern toward one good and away from another by the way you select your purchases. We don't all get gift rations, but instead, in one way or another, have a money income to spend for goods. If I spend less for candy and more for Cokes, more candy and fewer Cokes are left for other people. Each of us is trading with the rest of the world by spending the intermediary good, money, in a market place. In reality then we have two new institutions to consider: money and markets.

Money

Common Medium of Exchange

When we buy shoes, we pay money. When we sell labor services or a used car, we are paid money. We buy with money and sell for money, because it is more economical and convenient. Imagine the problem of carrying around a sample of various goods to exchange for other goods. We would have to guess what goods people with whom we might trade would want at the time we considered an exchange. We would tie up a larger portion of our wealth (and time and energy) in various goods for trading purposes than if there were a common medium of exchange. A common medium of exchange—money—makes search over the population for mutually advantageous exchange less costly and releases productive resources. In other words, money, as such, enhances our social productive power. For now, it is not necessary to inquire which good will serve as money. It suffices to understand that the existence of money, as a common medium of exchange, reduces the costs of exchange, and hence enables more production. The cost-reducing property of money is generally described as "lower transaction costs." Sometimes this attribute of money is called "liquidity."[1]

The Common Measure of Values

Imagine the difficulty one would have in deciding upon his purchases if, when he went to the market, he found the price of shoes expressed in pounds of cotton, the price of shirts in pounds of iron, and the price of meat in pounds of wool. Imagine his even greater confusion if different sellers used different commodities as the basis for the price of meat—for example, if one seller used cotton as his basis, another used pounds of iron, and still another used gallons of gasoline. Money is a convenient common denominator for expressing exchange rates *and* facilitating comparisons of values of various commodities.

1, 2, 3

Markets

Without a marketplace, trading would be more expensive. When considering the possibility of securing more of one good in exchange for some of another, would you sample people at random, testing if he and you could agree on some barter? Imagine the required time and effort. But suppose there is a particular place where a person can compare his personal valuations with all other people. This is precisely the purpose of marketplaces. To facilitate market activity, people resort to advertising—publicly informing other people—to help find potential buyers or sellers. And that, despite all the criticism of advertising, is its major role: to call attention to the fact that one is prepared to exchange certain described items. This way of identifying sellers and buyers reduces the cost of searching for information of exchange opportunities. Another information-economizing activity is provided by retailers, brokers, or specialized trading agents who establish a meeting place for potential buyers and sellers and furnish cheap access to information about particular goods and prices. Because a pooling of information generally means cheaper information, buyers and sellers tend to go into one larger market rather than many dispersed exchange locations. A market is a place or device enabling people to negotiate exchanges. Usually markets are concentrated in well-defined geographical areas and times. A city or village is basically a market—a group of people living near each other to facilitate exchange of goods (as well as of productive services). So widely recognized are advantages of a market that "primitive" tribes have truces on market days. In the Bronx of New York City on a certain street at a certain day of the week there assemble people interested in

---

[1] Though money is an excellent facilitator of exchange, it also is a buffer that prevents reduced demand for some goods from being offset by increased demand for other goods. For example, if investors should view future investment prospects more hesitantly and less profitably, they will reduce expenditures on investment goods; and instead of shifting to more purchases of consumer-type goods, which would induce increased production of such goods, they will seek to hold larger money stocks. As a result, depressions can be created. Also, rapid decreases in the stock of money available to the community can have depressing effects as people are forced to revise prices downward. Analyses of these events and corrective policies are given later.

Demand and the Laws of Demand

buying and selling bakeries. In medieval times, some political leaders amassed fortunes by fostering marketplaces (fairs) in their favorite cities and permitting foreigners to enter the market—for a modest fee. Even today, Hong Kong provides an example. Cheap telephonic and other means of communication and transportation have made markets more efficient. Yet, at the same time, people have continued to restrict access of their competitors to the market, by devices and rationales mentioned in the last chapter and which we shall investigate later in more detail.

The Money-Price Quantity Demand Function

When a person buys some goods, he gives up money—and ultimately, of course, some other goods that he might otherwise have had. The rate of consumption or purchase of any good depends upon its price as well as many other things: the person's wealth, time involved in buying or consuming the good, age, sex, education, fashions, etc. We first focus on the effect of the role of price, without denying the great importance of the others. A relationship between price and quantity demanded is called the *demand function*—Table 5–1 shows one such possible relationship. At each possible price the amount demanded is shown. At a price of $1, one egg is consumed weekly. It is assumed that at each possible price the market will supply him the amount he chooses (given his wealth and other factors), indicated in the demand schedule.

The Demand Function

TABLE 5–1.   Demand Schedule

Price	Eggs Demanded per Week
$1.00	1
.90	2
.80	3
.70	4
.60	5
.50	6
.40	7
.30	8
.20	9
.10	10

One a week is worth $1.00 to this consumer, while two a week is worth $1.90 so that a second is worth $.90 more than just one. A third per week is worth $.80 more than two per week; so the worth of three per week is $2.70 ($1.00 + $.90 + $.80). Continuing, a fourth is worth $.70 more than only three, giving a value of $3.40 for 4 per week. Clearly, the first column shows how much unit increments to consumption are worth. As a last example, we see that the worth added by a ninth egg is $.20. And the total to the consumer of 9 eggs per week is $5.40 (= $1.00 + $.90 + $.80 + $.70 + $.60 + $.50 + $.40 + $.30 + $.20) while the cost would be only $1.80 if he could buy 9 eggs at $.20 each.

In fact, the market usually presents a consumer with a given price and permits him to decide how many to buy at that price. If the market price of eggs were $.70, according to the data in Table 5–1 he would consume 4 eggs weekly. He would not consume more because a fifth is worth only $.60. At whatever price he faces he will buy up to that amount beyond which an *increment* would be worth less than its price. At $.70 per egg he would buy 4 weekly. Each egg costs him $.70 ($2.80 for the four eggs), even though the first is worth $1.00, the second is worth $.90, and so on, to a total of $3.40 for the four eggs. The opportunity to buy as many eggs as he wants at a constant market price gives him a "consumer's surplus"—the difference between what the eggs are worth to him ($3.40) and what he pays for them ($2.80).

This distinction between (a) worth and (b) cost is important. We can see that if we wanted to know what 9 eggs were worth to the consumer as compared to 4 eggs, we would not take the *market* costs or sales value as the measure. Certainly, more eggs are worth more to consumers than less, even though the sales proceeds and price per egg may be smaller.

Price and Value at the Margin—Not of Total Stock

This explains a puzzle that for a long time disturbed some people. Diamonds are more expensive and valuable per gram than are eggs, yet who would say diamonds are more valuable than eggs? Obviously it's all a question of "what value of what?" The value to consumers of *one more* of any good is revealed by market price: that is what price can measure. But the value to consumers of the *entire stock* of diamonds or the entire stock of eggs is not indicated by "price times the number of units." As we saw in preceding paragraphs, for the *entire stock* the value to consumers exceeds the total purchase cost and the difference is called "consumer's surplus." Probably the value to consumers of all the eggs exceeds that of *all* diamonds, but we can't be sure since we don't have the necessary data. What we can measure is the value of *one more* unit to the existing stock and the *sales proceeds* of that stock. And as we have seen, sales proceeds can vary in the opposite direction from total value to consumers (as when we moved from 4 to 9 eggs when the price was lowered from $.70 to $.20).

Changes in Amount Demanded versus Shift in Demand

The changes in *amount demanded* are shown by moving up or down the columns in Table 5–1 or sliding along the unchanged demand line in Figure 5–1. Changes in the amount demanded, in response to changes in *price*, are called changes in the *amount demanded;* they are not called changes in "demand." A *change in demand* is the response to factors *other* than price. For example, if a person's wealth or family should increase, the amounts of eggs demanded would increase for every specified price as illustrated in Table 5–2. At any price, more is demanded than formerly. This is an increase in *demand* (in response to factors other than the price of this good) and is indicated graphically by shifting the demand line to right, as in Figure 5–1. *An increase in demand* means that *at each price more is demanded than formerly; it does not refer to the effect of lowering the price.* A change in price of a good changes the *amount*

Demand and the Laws of Demand

TABLE 5–2. Increase in Demand

Price	Old Demand	New Demand
$1.00	1	2.0
.90	2	4.2
.80	3	6.4
.70	4	8.6
.60	5	10.8
.50	6	13.0
.40	7	15.2
.30	8	17.4
.20	9	19.6
.10	10	21.8

demanded, but it does not change or shift the demand schedule—called "demand" for short. Only a change in factors other than the price of a good will change or shift the "demand." This distinction between changes in amount demanded by a movement *along* a demand schedule (as the price changes) and a *shift* in the whole demand schedule (as other factors than price change) is crucial to error-free economic analysis, as we shall see later.

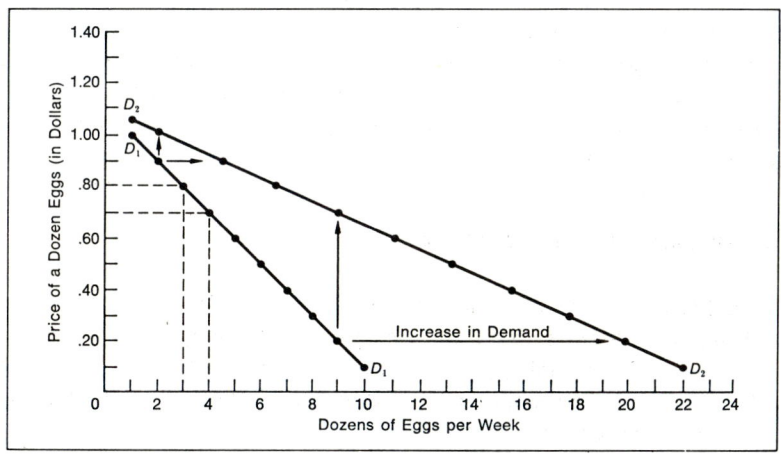

FIGURE 5–1. Demand Curves

Two different demand schedules, or demand curves, are shown (they are called curves even if straight, as in this illustration). If state of demand shown by D_1D_1 prevails, at price of 80 cents, three eggs per week are purchased for consumption. If price falls to 70 cents, rate of consumption increases to four. This is not called an increase in demand; it is a change in *amount demanded.* Increase in demand curve (that is, a change in state of demand) is shown by a shift in the demand curve to the right, as to D_2D_2, where at price of 80 cents the consumption rate would increase to 6.4 per week. We slide along a curve when the price of the good changes. We shift the curve when factors other than the price change the demand.

Meaning of a Change in Price and of a Change in Quantity

A change in price means a change in price of a good *relative* to prices of other goods. If the price of eggs falls from $1 a dozen to 90 cents, and if other prices are unchanged, the egg price has fallen relative to other prices. This is a fall in both the nominal (money) and the relative price of eggs (relative to prices of other goods). However, if the nominal (money) price of milk had also fallen from 20 cents a quart to 18 cents, then the price of eggs and the price of milk both are lower by the same percentage so that neither has fallen relative to the other. Hereafter, we shall usually be referring to a price change that is both a nominal change and a *relative* change in the price of a good.

The measure of the amount demanded. In Table 5–1, the quantity column gives *rates* of consumption per week. It does not mean that a person buys or consumes that quantity at one instant. People do their shopping sporadically or at irregular intervals and do not consume goods at the moment of purchase. This causes no difficulty in the analysis, even if it creates inventory problems for retailers and manufacturers. "Durable" goods (automobiles, houses, pianos, appliances) do not create a problem in interpretation of the demand curve. If most people have only one house and automobile, how can a person consume more than one car if he owns only one at a time? He can replace it more frequently, or use it more intensely, or he can buy a more awesome car, or two cars. Whether the quantity refers to amount owned, rate of consumption, rate of purchase, frequency of replacement, or size of item, the principles of demand, to be presented shortly, will hold true.

Consider one last point about the measuring unit of the quantity. The amount shown in Table 5–1 at 90 cents is two. This means he demands eggs at the *rate* of two per week *or* at the *rate* of 104 per year *or* at the *rate* of about eight per month. All these are measures of exactly the same rate.[2]

4, 5, 6, 7, 8

The First Fundamental Law of Demand

A fundamental law of demand can now be restated: "The higher the price, the lower the rate of consumption." More elaborately: "Whatever the quantity of any good consumed at any particular price, a sufficiently higher price will induce any person to consume less." Or: "Any person's consumption rate for any good will be increased (decreased) if the price is lowered (raised) sufficiently."

---

[2] As a test of our understanding of the demand schedule, try a few interpretations. A person faced with a price of $1 per egg will—according to Table 5–1—purchase about one per week. Suppose that she has just purchased some; while going home, she notices the price at a neighboring store is 80 cents. According to her demand—which we assume we miraculously know—at this price she will buy and consume about three per week. Does she immediately go in and buy more? She might, but need not. She will probably keep the lower price in mind and consume the eggs at a faster rate (three per week), knowing she can replace them at the lower price of 80 cents. Bygones are bygones, and the price *now* is 80 cents; so she increases consumption, in accordance with the new price. *Assuming the state of demand as characterized by the demand schedule remains unchanged,* her *rates of consumption* and purchase rise when she can buy eggs at a lower price.

Similarly, if she discovers the price is higher, will she try to sell back some of the eggs? No. She will consume them at a slower rate, purchase at a slower rate, and keep a smaller stock on the average.

Demand and the Laws of Demand

Whence comes this proposition? It is an invention to describe the observed behavior of people. This present proposition of demand is a law simply because it describes a general, verified truth about peoples' consumption and market behavior.

Elasticity of Demand and Total Expenditure

The responsiveness of the quantity demanded to a change in the price (*with the demand schedule unchanged*) is called the *elasticity* of demand. More generally, the ratio of (1) the percentage change in quantity consequent to (2) a small percentage change in price is the elasticity of demand. The price change is taken to be a small percentage change (because the *ratio* may vary with the size of the price change). The demand schedule is said to be "elastic" where the percentage change in quantity demanded is numerically greater (and "inelastic" where the percentage change in quantity is less) than the percentage change in price.[3]

As the price of a good is reduced, more is sold, but will the increase in the number sold offset the effect of the lower price on total expenditures? Table 5–3 presents, in addition to the same data as Table 5–1, the *total* sales proceeds (or *receipts* or expenditures) for this good at several prices.

TABLE 5–3. Demand Schedule, Total Receipts, and Elasticity

Price	Amount Demanded	Total Receipts	
$1.00	1	$1.00	
.90	2	1.80	
.80	3	2.40	Elastic demand in this range of price
.70	4	2.80	
.60	5	3.00	
.50	6	3.00	← Unit elasticity between prices of $.60 and $.50
.40	7	2.80	
.30	8	2.40	Inelastic demand in this range of price
.20	9	1.80	
.10	10	1.00	

At prices above 60 cents, the demand is elastic. This means that between any pair of prices above 60 cents, if we were to *reduce* the price, the total receipts would be *increased*. Total receipts increase with lower prices down to 60 cents. At any price below 50 cents, a reduction in price results in *smaller* receipts; the percentage increase in amount purchased is smaller than the percentage cut in price. We can summarize as follows:

1. "A price *reduction* gives an increase (decrease) in total receipts" means that the demand is elastic (inelastic) at those prices.

---

[3] In mathematical terms, point elasticity for continuous functions is defined as $dx/x \div dp/p$ of the demand function $x = f(p)$, while $\Delta x/x \div \Delta p/p$ is called arc elasticity. Point elasticity is the limit of arc elasticity as $\Delta p \to 0$.

2. "A price *increase* gives a decrease (increase) in total receipts" means that the demand is elastic (inelastic) at those prices.

3. "A price *change*—fall or rise—leaves total receipts *unchanged*" means the demand has "unit" elasticity at those prices.

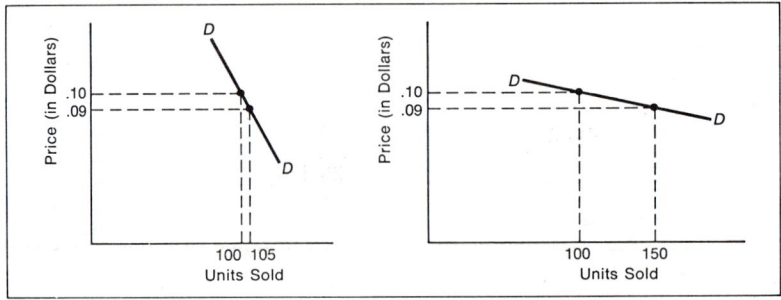

FIGURE 5–2. Inelastic and Elastic Demand

Left demand curve is inelastic between prices of 10 and 9 cents. Right curve is elastic between these prices. With left curve, total sales revenue falls from $10.00 to $9.45. On right curve, it increases to $13.50. Price cut on original 100 units reduces income $1.00 (1¢ × 100), but sales value of extra fifty units sold at 9 cents is $4.50. On left curve, the $1.00 loss of sales revenue on original 100 units is offset to extent of only $.45 from extra five units sold at 9 cents, giving a net loss of sales revenue. On right curve, amount demanded increases 50 percent with a price cut of 10 percent, whereas on left curve amount demanded increases only 5 percent, which is less than the 10 percent cut in price. (What is the quantity that must be demanded at price of 9 cents if the left curve is to have unitary elasticity between 10 and 9 cents?) Areas of rectangles at each price for each curve measure total revenue at each price. For right-hand demand curve, note larger area of rectangle at price of 9 cents compared with area of rectangle at price of 10 cents. And note reverse relationship with left demand curve.

Estimates of Demand Elasticities

Statistical studies suggest that cigarettes have an inelastic demand in the area of current price. The total community demand for beer and wine appears to be elastic in the range of current prices. However, classification of commodities by elasticities is difficult; furthermore, the classification would depend upon the particular prices at which the elasticity was being measured. As yet, there are no known general characteristics of goods from which economics can deduce the elasticity of any good in the real world. What is the elasticity of demand for salt at the current price? For ice cream? For chocolate ice cream? We can only conjecture. But all is not lost. In the first place, the closer the substitutes available, the greater is the elasticity of the demand schedule for a good at any specified price. If practically the same good can be purchased around the corner, any change in price by one seller would have a big effect on his sales. Later we shall see how this important proposition can be used to analyze effects of attempts to raise wages or prices.

The Second Fundamental Law of Demand

A second law of demand says something about elasticities: *"The longer any price change persists, the greater the elasticity."* Although a price change may have an immediate effect on the rate of consumption, the adjustment will be greater after a week and still greater after a month, until eventually the full adjustment will be effective. Elasticity of demand is greater in the longer run than in the shorter run. Why? In the first place, more people will learn about the price change. Second, the cost of revising consumption patterns or activities is less if done with less haste and with more economical side adjustments. For example, if the price of water were to be increased by 100 percent, the immediate rate of consumption would decrease—but it would decrease a great deal more within a few months, after people had made adjustments in associated activity and in water-using equipment.

Diagrammatically, the increased elasticity with persistence of a new price is illustrated in Figure 5–3. Let the price fall from p_1 to p_2. The different demand curves (1, 2, 3, etc.) show the greater amounts for the lower price at succeeding moments after the price change, with the ultimate rate indicated by the curve labeled n. After one "day" the rate is up to X_1, after two days it is X_2, etc., until at most it ultimately reaches X_n on the nth day. The more time available, the flatter the curve (whether the price moves up or down from initial level)—up to some limiting demand when full consumption adjustment to the new price will have occurred (or until price changes again, in which event the analysis starts over from the newly changed price).

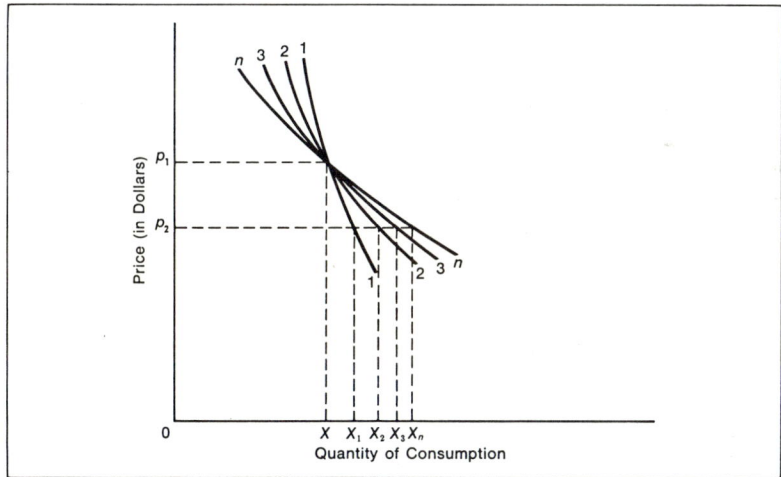

FIGURE 5–3. Effect of Time on Price-Elasticity of Demand

The longer the time after a price change, the greater the effect of that price change on the amount consumed—shown by the flatter curves for more elapsed time after a price change.

"Demand," then, really refers to a host of demands, each applicable to a different lapse of time subsequent to any price change. If it were necessary to know all these curves and their exactly paired price-quantities, we would be lost. Fortunately, because we know that these curves, whatever their location, are (1) negatively sloped with respect to price and (2) even flatter for longer-persisting price changes, we can draw some important explanations or implications about economic activity.

Some Illustrations of the Laws of Demand

Demand for Food

A higher price of meat will induce people to economize on it—to shift their pattern of expenditure, buying less meat and more of other things. Alternative sources of protein—eggs, fish, cheese, milk—are fairly obvious. Vegetables and even candy substitute for meat. So do some drinks. Even more distantly, since some of us eat for both nutrition and pleasure, we can reduce this source of pleasure and substitute more recreation, reading, or entertainment.

We should not speak of the demand for "food" as such, since no one buys "food." He buys particular commodities, each of which is a part of his "food." For each of these, his total consumption is affected by its price. But even if one insists on talking of the "demand for food," the law of demand asserts that the amount of food consumed is affected by the price of food. To deny this is to assert that one is *completely unconcerned* about what he could have if he gave up a little food, or that all he wants in life is food and no amount of other goods and services, *no matter how large*, would induce him to consume a little less food. (Remember the postulates?)

Demand for Wood

The law of demand applies to wood, too. If its price rises, we substitute more plaster, plastics, steel, aluminum, copper, glass, paper, coal, oil, and electricity; so, less wood will be demanded at the higher price. You and I may think we do not respond very much, if, at all, to a 10 percent rise in the price of wood. But since industrial engineers, product designers, and businessmen will shift in varying degrees to substitutes, the things we buy will have less wood in them and more of other things. Furthermore, since wooden furniture will rise in cost relative to metal or plastic furniture, some of us will shift in some degree to the latter. It is not necessary that every person revise his purchase habits. There are *some* people on the margin of choice between one and the other; and, as prices change, these marginal choices shift.

Demand for Water

An especially powerful example is water. Surely, people cannot live without it; no one will reduce his use of water just because its price goes up. As a matter of fact, however, water is not an exceptional commodity. The amount that people use depends upon its price. We could all use more water than we do now, and we could all use less. The reason that people in the arid regions use less water is not that they couldn't use more but that they don't *want* more, given the *high* price of getting more water (say, by pumping it thousands of miles). Because the price is high, they choose to consume less and to use for other, more desired, purposes the resources that would otherwise have been used in making more water available to that area.

In the United States the average per capita daily purchase of water varies among cities from, for example, 230 gallons in Chicago to 150 in New York and Los Angeles, to 120 in San Diego and 110 in Boston. The quantities reflect, for one thing, differences in industrial uses. Chicago has steel- and oil-refining industries, which use a great deal of water; New York City businesses—finance, retail, apparel—are light water users.

The law of demand shows that *one* way to reduce consumption is to raise its price. If water prices rise, water will be more worth saving. Reduction of waste is not costless and will be done more the higher the price of water. In New York City, 10 percent of the total water consumption is estimated to be from leakages in street mains. As costs of water rise, it will pay to spend more money to reduce that loss. For example, water meters, which make people pay according to use, are not universally used in New York City! If they were installed, people would have stronger incentives to waste less water (by repair and modification of faucets and water-using equipment). The New York water shortage could then be eliminated by raising the price of water consumed, assuming the cost of installing meters was not prohibitive.

Some waste-reducing activities are less obvious and occur in indirect ways. With higher water prices, residential areas will have smaller gardens and lawns. Sprinkler systems will be used more because they waste less water. Gardeners will sweep, rather than wash off, lawns and sidewalks. Rock gardens, paved yard areas, and brick patios will become more common. Automobiles will be washed less often. Water will be softened to conserve it; already several cities partially soften the water to make it more effective. In sum, it has been estimated in studies of domestic water consumption that a doubling of water prices would within a year reduce domestic household water consumption by about 30 to 50 percent.

TABLE 5–4. Variations among Firms and Products in Industrial Consumption of Water, per Unit of Output

Product or User and Unit	Draft (in gallons)		
	Maximum	Typical	Minimum
Steam-electric power (kw-h)	170	80	1.3
Petroleum refining (gallon of crude oil)	44	18	1.7
Steel (finished ton)	65,000	40,000	1,400
Soaps, edible oils (pound)	7	. . .	1.5
Carbon black (pound)	14	4	0.25
Natural rubber (pound)	6	. . .	2.5
Butadiene (pound)	305	160	13
Glass containers (ton)	670	. . .	120
Automobiles (per car)	16,000	. . .	12,000
Trucks, buses (per unit)	20,000	. . .	15,000

Source: H. E. Hudson and Janet Abu-Lughod, "Water Requirements," in Jack B. Graham and Meredith F. Burrill (eds.), *Water for Industry* (Washington, D. C.: American Association for the Advancement of Science, 1956), Publication No. 45, pp. 19–21.

Still more ways of conserving water exist. Industrial users take about half the water in many cities. They are probably more responsive to price than are domestic users. As shown in Table 5–4, there are great differences in the use of water even within the same industry. The figures in the "maximum" column represent the amounts used in the most profligate plants in each industry, while the "minimum" column shows the least amount used per unit of output produced. Note the tremendous range in the first three industries, which happen also to be the heaviest industrial water users. Many industrial firms use large amounts of water for cooling purposes on a once-through basis without recirculation through cooling units. Some steel mills use 65,000 gallons of water per ton produced, but the Kaiser steel mill (in the Los Angeles area) has reduced it to 1,600 gallons. One soap plant in the same area has installed recirculatory cooling towers to reduce water consumption from about six million to less than half a million gallons per day. At higher water prices, the value of the water saved, appearing as savings to the firm, would make the cost of recycling worthwhile. Clearly, the amount of water "needed" is a variable depending upon various factors, one of which is price.

There are still other ways to adjust the uses of water in response to price. The largest user of water in Southern California is agriculture, which accounts for approximately 80 percent of the water usage. Water is sold to farmers for irrigation at prices much lower than those at which it is sold to urban dwellers, even after allowance for distribution and purification costs. What would the farmers do if the price of water were allowed to rise to reflect its higher value in city uses? Some would go out of business—a blunt way of saying that some of the water used by farmers is *worth more in other uses* than in agriculture and is being transferred there. The community communicates this fact via the impersonal indicator—water prices. Higher prices for water would indicate that some water now used to grow watermelons, lettuce, and celery, for example, is more useful elsewhere. Less of these products would be grown in Southern California; they may be grown elsewhere, where production is cheaper, and shipped to Southern California, because that is cheaper than shipping in the water with which to grow them. Some areas or towns would decline as people find it preferable to move to places where water is cheaper or to tasks that use less water. That is, after all, the reason that the Western deserts are sparsely populated.

How do consumers discover how to use less when the price rises? Some people make a living by giving just such advice and information. Business is constantly sought by industrial engineers, architects, home-economics consultants, and commercial *salesmen* of water-recycling equipment, water softeners, automatic faucets, fertilizers, irrigation and sprinkling equipment, air-conditioning machinery, hard-top patios, chemicals that reduce evaporation, washing machines that use less water, steam generators, etc. Every rise in water costs provides them with more business prospects. Salesmen make it their business to detect situations in which their equipment is economical to use and to convey that information by advertising and personal solicitation. As students and teachers we may think that all worthwhile education and knowledge comes from schools, teachers, and books. But a very large amount of information and knowledge of practical matters is provided by salesmen—not because they are interested in us, but because it is to their personal interest to see that potential customers are educated to particular facts. We slurringly call this "advertising and propaganda," and indeed it is; but that does not change its educational value, assuming it is truthful. Even though no one can now precisely know how the use of water, rubber, wheat, sugar, steel, or gasoline would respond to a change in price, the users of those goods would soon be swamped with information about new uses or substitutes if the price changed.

We can classify these effects of price changes on quantity. Suppose that price falls. First, more of the item will be used in *current uses*. Second, *new uses* will be observed— uses that are valued too low to justify paying the former higher price. Third, *new users* will appear—people whose tastes were different or whose incomes were too low. And the reverse holds for higher prices. As long as we think only of the first possibility (that is, using more or using less in the same old customary ways), we will underrate demand elasticity.

Needs versus Demand

The law of demand is a denial of the idea of "needs." People often say that they need more water. What do they mean? That less than the "needed" amount would be absolutely intolerable? That even more would be useless? Of course not. Less water (not *none*) could be tolerated (although clearly less is not desirable). Statements that certain areas or people have water "requirements" suggest that they simply *must* have *that* amount of water. And to get that water it is often proposed that water committees or boards be set up to assure that there is no "unjustified" competition for water and that all areas have their "needs" satisfied—regardless of cost, presumably. But when they refer to "needs," people forget that the market price of water affects the amount used (the law of demand). They are talking nonsense.

It is said that we "need" more highways. Does this mean that we should have them regardless of the cost—that is, despite the forsaken alternatives? If someone says that we "need" more teachers, does he mean that, if *he* had to pay the costs of getting more teachers, he would hire more? When someone says there is a "need" for something, he should always be asked, "In order to achieve what, at what cost of other goods or 'needs,' and at whose cost?"

If he says, "We need something," for whom is he speaking? When my wife says, "We need a new car" or "We need a larger house," if I want to object, I "agree" by saying, "Of course we need it. What shall we give up to get it? What do we need less?"

We know of no more common denial of the law of demand than the repeated talk about "vital needs." At best, such talk is the result of ignorance that goods are scarce. At worst, it is a calculated attempt to confuse the reader or listener into paying the costs of what the speaker wants. Yet, do not conclude that you should never speak of *your* "critical, urgent, crying needs." As a matter of practical, good advice, you may find it worthwhile to speak that way in a self-serving attempt to con others into paying for what you want. But do not confuse yourself with your own language or be confused by others who talk of "critical needs."

Alleged Exceptions to the Laws of Demand

Some people think that they know of counter-examples to the laws of demand. The first law of demand asserts that people buy *less* in response to the higher price. Someone might object by pointing out that people *could* conceivably be insensitive to price or that they *could* buy more of some things when the price rises. Indeed, they *conceivably* could; but the law of demand says that *actually* they do not. Possibility or conceivability, therefore, cannot be regarded as an exception; it is the *actuality* of such behavior that the law of demand denies. The pertinent question is "Does such denied, but conceivable, behavior actually occur?" Three cases bear examination.

An exception to the law of demand is alleged to occur when the price of, say, wheat falls and the buyers think to themselves, "Price is falling. It will fall further. If I wait, I can later buy more cheaply. Therefore, I will withdraw current orders to buy." This appears to mean that a lower price has resulted in less, not more, purchases. But has the price fallen? It is lower now than it was earlier. However, the relevant fact is that future prices are expected to be even lower. Therefore, relative to expected future prices, the present price has *increased*. People who have the alternatives of buying now or buying later transfer their purchases from relatively high-price times to relatively low-price times—exactly as implied by the law of demand. Remember, it is relative prices that count.

Another alleged case is that of "prestige" goods—like Mumms champagne, Cavanaugh hats, Rolls Royce cars, Orrefors crystal, Harvard degrees, or whatever you aspire to. Presumably, people are motivated to buy high-price goods because possession of such goods sheds prestige on the buyer. But prestige goods do *not* produce a demand curve that is *positively* sloped with respect to price; let the price of the "prestige" good be still higher, and less of it will be bought. Otherwise, what would prevent the price from rising without limit? Perhaps the advocates of the prestige-good case have in mind the so-called "fashion" goods—items that experience violent fashion swings. But fashions mean simply that demand *schedules* shift in response to a shift in tastes. The new, higher demand curve still has a negative slope. Mink stoles would be even more common if the price were lower. The pursuit of discriminatory distinctiveness is not inconsistent with the laws of demand.

And there is the case in which a person offers to sell at a higher price to make the buyer believe the item is better. Similarly, anyone who proposes to sell something at far below its current market price will immediately stir doubts about the genuineness of the item being offered. But this attitude results from the fact that price is an index of quality in open markets. If I offer to sell my new Plymouth for $1,000, a potential buyer will probably hesitate, suspecting that I don't really own the car or that it isn't in good condition. If he can satisfy himself that the lower price is not the result of lower quality, he will buy the car more readily than if I asked $4,000. Normally, an inferior-quality good is sold at a lower price because only then will anyone buy it; at the same prices, everyone would prefer the better item. Fundamentally, then, inferior goods sell at lower prices. The public's association of higher price with higher quality is a consequence, not a refutation, of the law of demand.

Showing the error in these alleged exceptions does not prove the laws correct (we call them "propositions" until the evidence is overwhelming). We shall very briefly hint at some of the evidence—both direct and indirect—for the validity. (A qualification, in principle at least, is discussed next.)

Price Effects on Income and Substitution

The remainder of this book will be based on valid applications of the laws of demand. Are there any possibly invalid applications?

There can be, if we completely neglect factors other than price that affect the quantity demanded. So far, we have restricted our attention to price by analytically holding the other elements constant. Changes in income or wealth will change (shift) the demand function. A larger income will induce a person to buy more of some goods: transportation, food, housing, medical care, education, travel, champagne, and "prestige" goods as suggested earlier. However it is not easy to construct a *long* list of goods that *decrease* as income or wealth increases. Candidates might be rump roasts, "soul food," and hamburger. Probably these would be characterized as "low quality goods"—such as regular grade gasoline or cheap golf balls. Figure 5–4 shows how some services increase in demand at higher incomes. The term given to goods for which demand increases with incomes is "superior" goods; when demand decreases with increases in income, the term "inferior" goods is applied. These terms are suggestive of high and low quality goods (though not in some ethical or moral sense). It is conceivable that a very poor person would buy more of some things with gains in income and yet buy less of these same

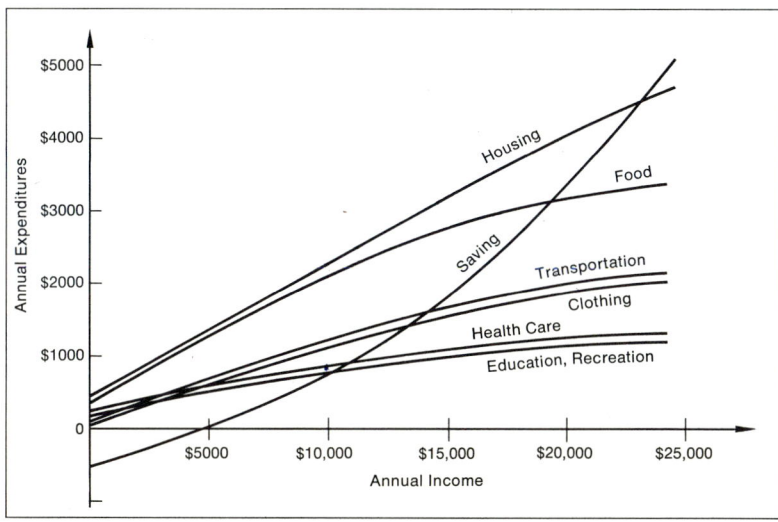

FIGURE 5-4. Income Effect on Demand for Services

The lines show that expenditure rates on general classes of goods and services are related to income—increasing with income but at a lower proportionate rate. Amounts demanded are clearly related to *income* and therefore not only to price. Of course, a combination of a price change and income change can affect the amount demanded, possibly in opposite directions if the lower price is for some good that is a significant part of the goods a person produces and sells in getting his income.

The variation of saving, from negative rates at low incomes to highest rates at high incomes, is deceptive if you think it shows that people whose annual incomes over the years average about $5000 or less do not save. Because incomes fluctuate not unexpectedly over the years and because a person tends to consume according to his longer-run income average, savings will show large residual fluctuations as income fluctuates transiently from year to year.

things if his income were to increase to substantially still higher levels. Now, with these concepts we are ready to see how invalid interpretations of the law of demand can occur.

Sometimes changes in both income and price occur simultaneously. One case is that in which a price changes for some good that is part of the source of a person's income. For example, if an owner of a natural-gas well experiences a big rise in the price of the gas he sells, his higher income will induce him to have a larger house in which he consumes more gas for air conditioning. Despite the higher price he must pay for gas, that higher price has also increased his income sufficiently to *shift* his demand upward to more than offset the effect of a higher price. Figure 5–5 shows a pair of demands for gas, the higher one associated with a larger income caused by a higher price of the gas from which a person has income. He is now so rich that even when pushed back up along his new demand curve to the higher price, he still consumes more gas. Here the higher price creates *both* an "income" effect and a "substitution" effect. The latter makes him slide back up the new higher demand curve. In the present illustration the increased price of a good *serving as a source of his income* has had two effects—an income effect (shifting his demand curve) and a "substitution" effect (*sliding* up the new demand curve). When the two effects are combined, *in this example,* not enough substitution occurs away from gas in response to the higher price to offset the income effect. So, at a higher price he consumes more because of the income-effect dominance.

Unless we are careful to separate and detect these two effects of a price rise, we shall erroneously keep a demand function unchanged when it really has shifted because of price-change effects on a person's wealth.

As a matter of fact, any price change is accompanied by an income effect—even if the good is not a source of income—but usually of such a small magnitude as to be negligible for present purposes.

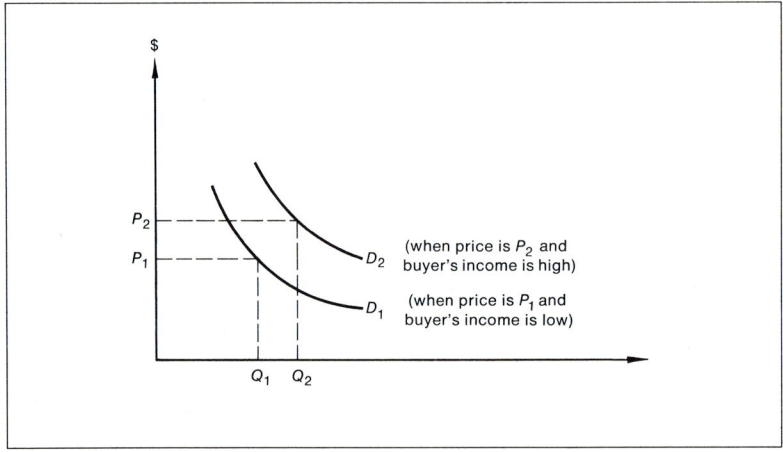

FIGURE 5–5. Price Effects on Income Can Offset Price Effects on Amount Demanded by Shifting Demand Curve

D_1 is demand when price is low and therefore consumer whose income is heavily dependent on this good has low income. At higher price, P_2, consumer's income is enough larger to increase *demand* curve more than enough to offset simply higher price effect on amount demanded.

Direct Evidence of Validity

Do merchants advertise by announcing that they are temporarily raising prices? Have you noticed that prices of fruits and vegetables are lower when the crop is in season? The greater amount can be sold only at a lower price. If prices did not change with seasons of perishable crops, the law of demand would not be true. If poorer-quality goods sold for the same price as better-quality goods (where everyone agrees in ranking of quality), the first law of demand would not be true. Can you see why? Even more, there would be no point in charging prices to collect more from those who buy more, for that would have no effect on how much they buy, if amount demanded does not respond to price.

Indirect Evidence of Validity

Usually, it is in the corroboration of less direct, hidden implications that the power of a law is made strikingly evident. For example, how does one explain the larger *proportion* of *good* quality relative to poor quality oranges or grapes sold in New York than in California? Why is a larger proportion of the good, rather than bad, shipped to New

York? Is it because New York's population is richer or more discriminating? Possibly; but then why are the oranges and grapes sold even in the poor districts of New York better than those sold in California? The question can be posed for other goods: Why do Asians import disproportionately more expensive American cars rather than cheaper models? Why are "luxuries" disproportionately represented in international trade? Why do young parents go to expensive plays rather than movies *relatively* more often than do young couples without children? Why are "seconds" more heavily consumed near the place of manufacture than farther away? Why must a tourist be more careful in buying leather goods in Italy than in buying Italian leather goods in the United States? Why is most meat shipped to Alaska "deboned"? The answers are implications of the law of demand. Let us see why.

Suppose that grapes grown in California cost 5 cents a pound to ship to New York, whether the grapes are "choice" or "standard" (poorer), that the production of grapes is 50 percent "choice" and 50 percent "standard," and that in California the "choice" grapes sell for 10 cents a pound and the "standard" for 5 cents a pound (in California 2 pounds of "standard" and 1 pound of "choice" grapes sell for the same price). If grapes are shipped to New York, the shipping costs will raise the cost of "choice" grapes to 15 cents and of "standard" grapes to 10 cents. In New York, then, the price of "choice" grapes is lower, *relative* to "standard" grapes (1.5 to 1), than in California (2 to 1). To buy 1 pound of "choice" grapes in New York would mean a sacrifice of 1.5 pounds of "standard," whereas in California it would cost 2 pounds of "standard." According to our first law of demand, New Yorkers, faced with a lower price of "choice" relative to "standard," will consume *relatively* more "choice" grapes than Californians. In California, where "standard" grapes are cheaper relative to "choice" grapes, a larger fraction of "standard" grapes should be consumed. And it is so.

Try this analysis on choice versus commercial grades of meat in Alaska and Texas, or French wines in New York and France. A transport cost is added—a cost that is almost the same for the two classes of items; the cost of the better item, *relative* to the poorer item, is lower after shipment than at the place of manufacture. Because the *relative* price of the higher-quality good is lower at more distant places than at the place of origin, more distant consumers purchase a larger proportion of superior (to second-grade) items than consumers nearer the place of manufacture. For instance, Italian producers export more of their better items; lower-quality goods are left at home, so tourists have a greater chance of finding inferior Italian goods in Italy than in countries to which Italy exports.

What about parents of young children? If they hire baby sitters at, say, $1 an hour and are out for four hours, it will cost $4 just to leave the house. Now, add the cost of two movie tickets at $1 each, and compare that total cost with the cost of going to the theater (at $4 per ticket). The theater costs a total of $12, and movies cost $6. The theater, then, costs twice what a movie costs. But if a couple has no children and can avoid the baby-sitter fee, the movie will cost $2 and the theater $8—a ratio of 4 to 1: the theater is relatively more expensive. In our original question, we did not assume parents will go to the theater *more* than people who have no children; we said, *when* young parents go out, they will go to the theater a *larger fraction* of the time than will childless couples. QED.

27, 28, 29

Income and Demand

In this chapter we have concentrated attention on the effect of price on the amount of a good demanded, and we have called the relationship between market price and amount

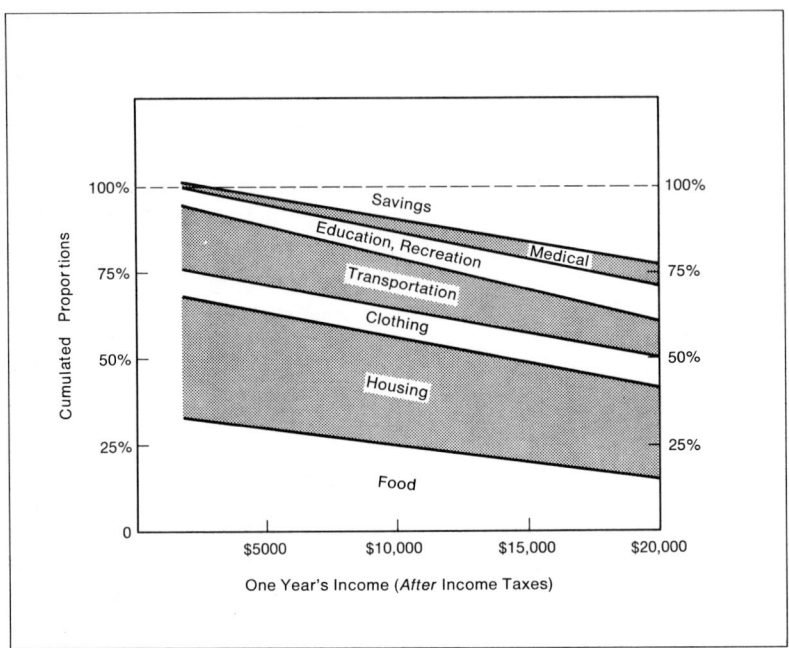

FIGURE 5–6. Fraction of One Year's Income (After Income Taxes) Spent for Various Consumption Purposes

As incomes increase, the proportion spent for food decreases, as it does also slightly for housing. For clothing and transportation, the proportion shows no great change, while for education, recreation, and medical care an increase is observed. Savings show the greatest increase. However, beware of a very serious measurement bias which distorts the interpretation. The incomes are for just one particular year and not the average, more stable income over a longer period to which people appear really to gear their expenditures. Thus a person (businessman) whose annual incomes vary, say, from $5,000 in one year to $15,000 in the next with expectations it will fall to about $10,000 or will fluctuate around $10,000 over the longer run will gear his spending rate in any year to about $10,000 of income. Thus he will save a lot of the temporarily high year's income and dissave in the low years. But if a person's income were relatively steady over several years at about $5,000 or $15,000, the savings each year would be about the same fraction each year *and also about the same* for the $5,000 long-run income person as the $15,000 long-run average income person. The different savings ratios for high- and low-income people shown in the table reflect in part the transient fluctuating-income effect rather than only the true effect of higher income levels versus lower income levels.

For expenditures on consumption, it follows that those commodities which show a relatively constant or decreased ratio relative to the transient fluctuating incomes can have an increased ratio of the higher longer-period incomes spent for those commodities. This follows because the expenditures on consumption are less sensitive to temporary fluctuations in income (with the temporary adjustments being made in savings). And for those goods showing an increased ratio of temporarily high incomes, an even higher ratio of permanent longer-run income levels will be spent (medicine, education, recreation). (The chart does not show allocations in percentage terms for near-zero incomes, because percentage of near-zero incomes approaches "infinity." Also, less data are available.)

Source: Bureau of Labor Statistics.

demanded *the demand function*. Though we shall devote primary attention to this relationship in the first part of this book, another important, obvious factor affecting amount demanded is the income or wealth of the person. (Below, on page 88, we will indicate something about income effects.) At the moment, rather than completely ignore the direct income effect on amount demanded, we interject Figure 5–6, which shows not only that the amount demanded increases with incomes, but also that the ratio of income devoted to various goods may decrease or increase. In other words, a one percent increase in income may be accompanied by a less-than-one-percent increase in the amount spent on any particular good. And, to no one's surprise, this would be called an *income* elasticity of less than one, while if the percent of income spent on a good increased with an increase in income, the elasticity of income demand would be greater than one. In particular, the percentage change in amount spent on a good (or the percentage increase in amount of the good bought, which, since price is constant, is the same percentage of amount spent for the good) divided by the percentage change in income (giving rise to that change in expenditure) is called the *income* elasticity of demand. To avoid the common error of inferring from the chart more than can validly be inferred, read its caption carefully. (The source of confusion or bias referred to there will again be pertinent in the discussion of national income determination in the second half of this book.)

Summary

1. Markets reduce the costs of obtaining information about exchange possibilities.

2. Money is the common medium of exchange and the common denominator of value. It economizes on information costs about other people's demands by reducing transaction costs.

3. The demand function or schedule, often called "demand" for short, is a relationship between price and amount demanded. Keep distinct the "demand" and the "amount demanded." The latter is the amount *at a specified price*.

4. "A change in price" of a good means a change relative to prices of other goods.

5. The first fundamental law of demand states, "The demand for any good is a negative relationship between price and amount demanded." Or: "Whatever the quantity demanded at any price, there is a higher price that will induce a reduction in the amount demanded."

6. The elasticity of demand with respect to prices is a measure of the responsiveness of amount demanded to changes in price. In general the ratio of the relative (percentage) response in amount demanded to the relative (small percentage) change in price is the measure of elasticity near that price. An elasticity greater than "one" implies that a reduction in price increases the total receipts, in the neighborhood of that price.

7. The second fundamental law of demand asserts the elasticity of demand is greater in the longer than in the shorter run.

8. At lower prices, more of the item will be used in current uses, new uses will be observed as they become economical, and more people will use the good.

9. "Need" is a word often used to conceal the cost of what is desired.

10. Incomes affect demand.

11. Price changes induce a substitution and an income effect.

Questions

1 What properties of a good will enhance its chances of being used as money? To what extent are these properties attributes of gold, bricks, cigarettes, chewing gum, seashells, pearls, cattle, matches, diamonds, platinum?

2 If one pair of shoes can be exchanged for four shirts, and one shirt trades for two pairs of socks, and if one pair of shoes trades for six pairs of socks, what series of trades could you make to get steadily richer? (This is known as "arbitraging" among markets for different goods.)

3 What are prices? Can there be prices without money?

4 To say that a person purchases and consumes water at a *rate* of 50 gallons per day, or 350 per week, is to say the same thing in two ways. What is the equivalent statement in terms of rate per year?

5 The following questions are intended to reveal clearly the difference between a *stock* and a *rate*. (Thus, they ignore the argument of the woman who told the traffic policeman that she couldn't have been driving 60 miles per hour, since she had been traveling only ten minutes.)
   a. How many eggs does a person eat in one week at the *rate* of 365 per year?
   b. How many miles does a person walk in seven hours at a *rate* of 24 miles per day? At the rate of 1 mile an hour?

6 Mr. *A* currently uses water at a rate of 3,650 gallons per year at the present price. Suppose that his demand doubles, so that his rate increases to 7,300 gallons per year. How many more *gallons* of water will he consume during the first week of higher demand?

7 If the price of candy rises from $1 to $1.25 a pound while the price of ice cream rises from 50 cents to 75 cents a gallon, in what sense is that a *fall* in the price of candy?

8 Can Table 5–1 be read as follows: "A person sees a price of $1, and he therefore buys one egg. The next day he sees that the price has fallen to 80 cents; so he dashes out and buys three. A couple of days later, the price rises to 90 cents; so he buys two." If it can't be interpreted that way—and it can't—how is it to be interpreted?

9 a. Because we represent a demand curve with precise numbers, does that mean that people have these numerical schedules in their minds?
   b. What essential property illustrated by the demand-schedule data does characterize their behavior?

10 "According to the law of demand, the lower the price of vacations, the more vacations I should take. Yet I take only one per year. Obviously the law of demand must be wrong." Is it?

11 Do you think the demand for children obeys the fundamental theorem of demand? The demand by immigrants for entry to the United States? The demand for divorces? The demand for pianos? The demand for beautiful women? The demand for a winning college football team? The demand for "*A*'s" in this course? The demand for appendectomies?

12 "Elasticity is a measure of the percentage increase in demand for a one-cent change in price." There are two errors in that statement. Rewrite it correctly.

13 Are the following statements correct or incorrect? Explain your answers.
   a. "A 1 percent rise in price that induces a 3 percent decrease in amount taken indicates elasticity of less than one."

b. "A 1 percent fall in price that induces a 3 percent increase in amount purchased indicates an elasticity of greater than one."

c. What is wrong with asking whether a 1 percent rise in price induces a 3 percent decrease in demand?

14 An increase in demand is shown graphically by a demand curve (to the right of) (above) (below) (to the left of) the old demand curve. Select correct options.

15 A person purchases and consumes eggs at a rate equivalent to seven per week if the price of eggs is 5 cents each. Another person purchases and consumes eggs at the rate of 365 per year when the price of eggs is 4 cents. Who reflects a greater demand?

16 Sometimes luxuries are defined as goods that have an elastic demand, while necessities are those with an inelastic demand. Evaluate the usefulness of those designations. How would you define a luxury and a necessity? For what problems is it useful to attempt the distinction?

17 "If the price of gasoline fell by 10 percent, the average person would not change his rate of consumption." Explain why this does not refute the law of demand.

18 The demand schedule of Table 5–1 shows that at a price of $1, the weekly consumption is 1 unit. At a price of 90 cents, the weekly consumption is 2 units.
a. Can it be said that this person wants *each* one of those 2 units more than he wants 90 cents' worth of weekly expenditures on any other goods?
b. Note that at the price of $1, he spent weekly $1.00 on this good; whereas, at a price of 90 cents, he spent $1.80 or 80 cents more than previously. Do you still say he values the extra unit at approximately 90 cents, even though he spends only 80 cents more?
c. Explain why. In doing so, explain clearly what is meant by "value."

19 In 1966 the Governor of California asserted that the reduction of Mexican labor in California did no harm, because the total value of the crop harvested was larger than before. Evaluate the relevance of that criterion.

20 In the graph below, which of the three demand curves has the greatest elasticity at price p_1? At price p_2? Does the elasticity change as the price changes?

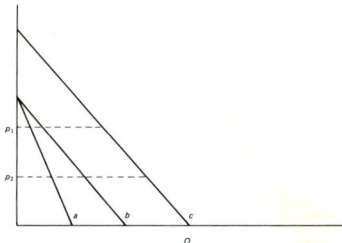

21 a. If the price of gasoline were 30 percent lower, would automobile manufacturers be induced to make changes in the designs or operating characteristics of automobiles?
b. What effect would they have on gasoline consumption?
c. Would the effect be more extensive at the end of three months or at the end of three years?

22 Which of the following do you think would increase a woman's demand for wigs?
a. A raise in her husband's salary.
b. Higher price of hats.
c. Having a swimming pool.

d. Rise in cost of hair care.
   e. Getting divorced.
   f. Number of other women who wear wigs.
   g. Lower price of wigs.

23 Which "needs" do you think are more important: urgent, critical, crying, vital, basic, minimum, social, or private needs?

24 Explain wherein each of these is a denial of the law of demand and the basic postulates of economics:
   a. "The budget of the Department of Defense covers only our basic needs and nothing more."
   b. "Our children need better schools."
   c. "Nothing is too good when it comes to education."
   d. "America needs the atomic bomb."

25 Diagnose and evaluate the following news report from the *Los Angeles Times*: "Los Angeles needs 24 more golf courses, according to a report submitted to the City Recreation and Park Department by the National Golf Foundation. The survey discovered that there are 160,000 golfers in the Los Angeles area, and many of them do not play as often as they would like because of the lack of courses." How does this differ from the situation of filet mignon steaks, champagne, and autos?

26 Does a prestige good *give* prestige or *reflect* one's prestige?

27 Let p_1 and p_2 be the domestic prices of two goods. Let T_1 and T_2 be the transport costs of these goods to a "foreign" market. Show that if $T_1/T_2 < p_1/p_2$, then *relatively* more of good "1" will be shipped; if the inequality is reversed, relatively more of good "2" will be shipped. "Relative" to what? In your answer, what do you assume about demand conditions in domestic and in "foreign" markets?

28 Economics asserts that people prefer more goods to less. Yet there are waiting lists of people seeking small apartments in slum areas while bigger, better apartments do not have a list of applicants. How can people want smaller, less luxurious apartments rather than bigger apartments, without violating our postulates about people's preferring more economic goods?

29 A competitor to this text publishes a *Study Guide* as a supplement and asserts it is "invaluable." Does that sound consistent with economic analysis?

Market Demand, Allocation, and Equilibrium Price

IN this chapter, we use the market-demand concept to begin our study of how market pricing and exchange affect the allocation of goods among people.

Market Demand in a Society

Start with a society of four people, *A, B, C,* and *D,* with the demands for automobiles given in Table 6–1; all automobiles are alike. The schedules for each person and for the group conform to our first law of demand: greater amounts are demanded at lower prices and lesser amounts at higher prices.

At first glance, one might guess *A* is richer than *B.* In fact, *B* might be a wealthy old man who rather regrets the invention of the internal-combustion engine; and *A* might be the head of a poor family, with everyone in the family commuting to work. We may reasonably suppose that a person's demand for automobiles will increase with income, but the fact that *one* person's demand is greater than *another* person's demand is not proof that the first person is wealthier.

Re-allocation of Cars

Suppose there are seven cars in this community; three are owned by *A,* one by *B,* one by *C,* and two by *D.* It happens, as seen in Table 6–1, that this distribution of present ownership is the same as the pattern of amounts *demanded* at a price of $500. With the community holding seven cars and demanding seven cars, the *equilibrium price* is $500:

TABLE 6–1. Car Ownership Demands of A, B, C, and D

	Quantity of Automobiles				
Price	A	B	C	D	Total Market
$1,000	2	0	1	1	4
900	2	0	1	1	4
800	2	0	1	2	5
700	2	0	1	2	5
600	3	0	1	2	6
500	3	1	1	2	7
400	3	1	2	2	8
300	3	1	2	3	9
200	3	1	2	4	10
100	4	2	2	4	12

no one would pay more than $500 to get another, and no one would sell a car for less. The market is cleared. This is called an *equilibrium distribution*.

But an initial distribution needn't be an equilibrium distribution. Suppose all seven cars were owned by *A*. (And suppose, for expository simplicity, that a person's wealth and demand schedule are not changed perceptibly by the particular sequence of trades in reaching an equilibrium.) The following is one possible scenario of exchanges leading to an equilibrium. *A* would sell some cars even if he could get only $100 per car. (Query: How many?) *C* and *D* each offer to buy a car for $900. *A* will sell. Then *B* offers $400 for a car; again, *A* sells. (We shall assume for simplicity that $100 is the minimum possible price change.) These exchanges leave *A* four cars, and *B, C,* and *D* one car each. *C* buys another car from *A* at $300; *A* sold because he would rather have $300 than a fourth car. Though *D* is prepared to offer up to $800 for a second car, he now offers *A* only $300 for a second car, but *A* says that he doesn't have any cars to "spare" now that he has only three. However, he has a car to spare if *D* will pay $700. By this time, *B,* alert to the market, offers his car for $600, even though he just bought it. But *C,* who values his second car at only $400, will undercut *B*'s price by offering to sell at $500. At $500, neither *A* nor *B* would sell. Only *C* would sell, and *D* is willing to pay that price. So *D* pays $500 to *C* for a car; thereafter everyone is content with his *pattern* of goods, given his preferences and *wealth*.

An Equilibrium Allocation and Price

The cars are now distributed as follows: *A* has three, *B* has one, *C* has one, and *D* has two. And, during every stage of the exchange process, each buyer and seller moved to a position he preferred. Several alternative possible sequences of trade could be conjured from the illustrative data. All lead to the same equilibrium pattern of distribution of goods, and in each sequence the equilibrium price is $500.[1] The equilibrium price (1)

---

[1] Depending upon the sequence of exchanges and interim prices, each person's wealth will change and affect his demand for cars. However, here we have ignored these wealth-change effects and have kept individual demands unchanged. Were we to take these into account, we would have to trace a sequence of prices gradually converging to some equilibrating price, slightly different from the one reached here. Our convergence to a unique equilibrium is permissible analytically in this kind of

makes the total amount demanded equal to the total available stock, *and* (2) it will also equate the number of cars that people wanted to buy (in addition to what they already had) with the number that other people wanted to sell from their holdings.

With this final equilibrium allocation, *no further revision would be mutually acceptable. This is a "market-clearing" situation.* In order to improve his situation further, a person would now have to take away some cars from someone else—that is, without mutually acceptable exchange. We have here simply shown *how* various goods are allocated, not whether this is the best possible distribution or whether there should be more or less equality.

The play of demand and supply is important not simply because it sets a price but because, in the process, it reveals relative subjective values; it sets a price that enables people to exchange so that they each achieve a preferred combination of goods. Although we imagined a four-person society, the principles are applicable to a million-person economy, with middlemen to economize on the costs of search for exchange opportunities.

Demand Functions Need Not Be Known

It may be objected that no one knows demand schedules with the accuracy specified here. But we have *not* assumed that anyone knows the demand schedules. No one need know even his own demand schedule in the sense that he can write it out for you. All we require is that when faced with the opportunity to buy or sell, *he can make a decision.* To this we add our first law of demand: At a higher price he will buy less than at a lower price. Precisely *what* that larger or smaller amount is for each and every price is not necessary information. Our use of explicit numbers merely makes it easier to follow the analysis. We see that market-price bidding and negotiations reveal to each person whether there are any possible exchanges that will bring him to what he regards as a preferred pattern of goods. The process of bidding higher or asking lower prices, in accord with each person's attempts to improve his situation as he sees it, is the essence of the operation of demand in the market.

1, 2, 3, 4

Markets as Economizers on Costs of Collecting Information

It is convenient that each person can simply look at a market price and then decide how many to buy or sell. That is how markets appear to operate for most of us for many goods. But if there were no formal market place or its location were unknown, we would incur greater costs scurrying around to discover at what prices all other people in the community were willing to buy or sell. Clearly, the less well that markets are organized, or the more difficult it is to communicate, the more time that will be spent discovering and comparing offers of potential sellers and buyers to arrange the best possible ex-

---

exchange problem, but for more advanced analyses concerning determination of *production* and *employment* as well as exchange of produced products, more general and complex considerations must be introduced. Then the convergence may be sufficiently slow to cause serious income and employment effects.

These matters are the subject of general employment and national income theory (usually called "macroeconomics"), dealt with later.

changes. As we shall see much later, "unemployment" (of people and of nonhuman goods) is in no small part a result of the high cost of discovering the demands of all other people and of communicating with them to learn more about the particular attributes of goods or services they might want to "sell" or "buy."

Market Supply and Demand: Graphic Interpretation

An analysis of pricing and allocation is facilitated by diagrams of demand and supply curves.

In Figure 6–1 the individual demand curves, *AA, BB, CC, DD,* indicating demand to own cars, are added *horizontally* to get the total demand, *TT*. The available supply, seven units, is shown by a supply line, *SS*; it is vertical because, regardless of price, the stock of cars is fixed at seven. The *total* demand and supply curves intersect at $500; at that price the number of cars demanded by *A, B, C,* and *D* is three, one, one, and two, respectively, for a total of seven. Only the *final* equilibrium outcome is revealed. The *process of adjustment* is not, but the net change from initial to final pattern for each person can be deduced.

Inspection of Figure 6–1 suggests that at a price of $800 the community number demanded would be less than the number it actually has. Eight hundred dollars is greater than the equilibrium price. A law might stipulate that cars can be sold only for $800. There would then be a *surplus* of cars. At the legal price of $800, people would want to own only five, but they have seven. In particular, *A* and *B* would claim that they have a surplus of one car each; each would prefer $800 to the car.

On the other hand, the surplus would instantly become a *shortage* if the permissible

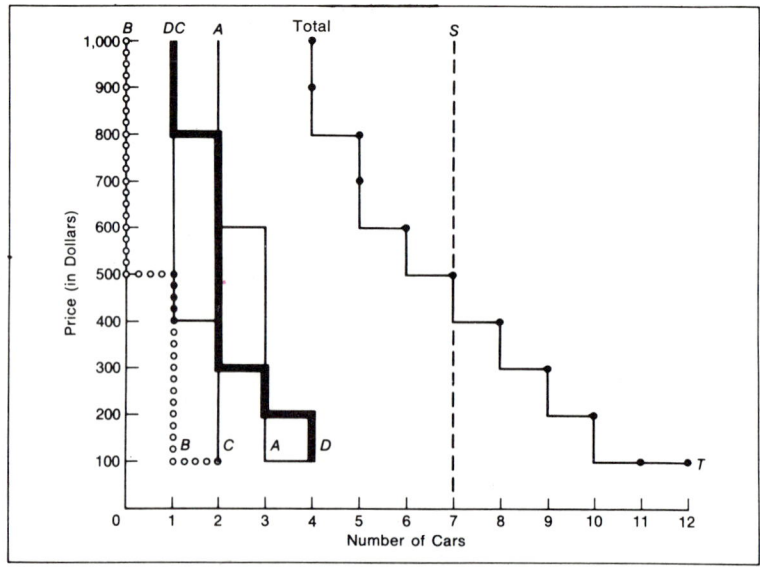

FIGURE 6–1

Individual and total community demand curves with existing stock of automobiles as the supply. The total demand curve, *TT*, is the sum of the horizontal distances of each of the individual demand curves at each price.

price somehow were set at $200, below the equilibrium price. Everyone wants more cars at $200 than at $800. *At the price* of $200, more cars are demanded than are available. A says that the car he "needs" would be used by his daughter in going to college. Currently she has no car and uses taxis and buses to come home. She "needs" a car. Of course, when the price of a car was $800, that "need" was less urgent than the "need" for what else one could get with the $800. Or, in more scientific language, "At $200, A finds a car preferable to $200 worth of other things." And the same goes for everyone else.

How could "surpluses" or "shortages" be eliminated? A price of $500 would eliminate them. At that price, the amount that individuals want (or say they "need"), as reflected in the desired patterns of various goods, matches the total available. This is what the intersection of the demand and supply curves means. This equilibrium price is *market-clearing*. There remain no unexploited exchange possibilities, no shortage and no surplus.

Adjustments to Changes in Supply

What happens if total supply changes? Suppose a car belonging to A is destroyed by fire. Even if no one else knows of the loss, everyone will be affected. The total supply has decreased to six, as is shown by shifting the supply curve leftward to six on the horizontal axis in Figure 6–2. The intersection of demand and supply is now at $600. This

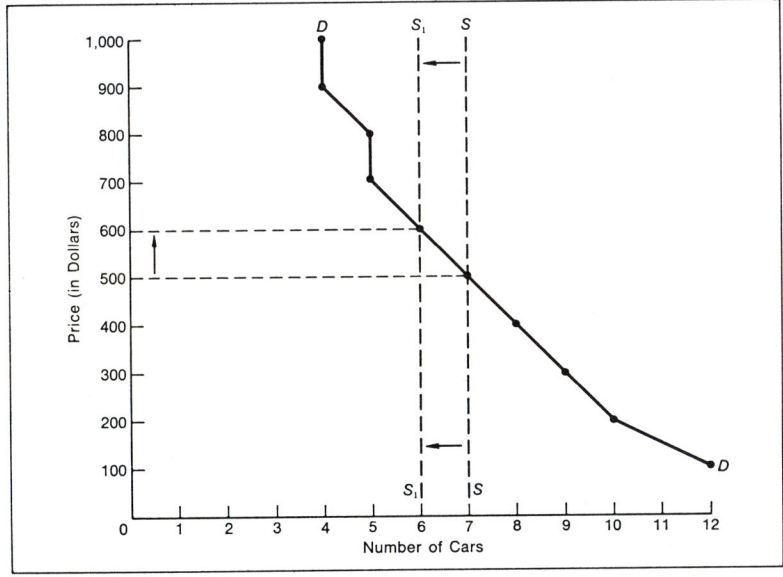

FIGURE 6–2

Reduction in supply is shown by a shift of the supply curve to the left. With a *fixed* number of cars available regardless of price, the supply curve is a vertical line. The rise in price from $500 to $600 facilitates a redistribution of cars from those who value a car less than $600 to those who value a car at least at $600. Without the option of bidding higher prices in response to a reduction in supply, cars would not be re-allocated according to relative personal valuations. The total market demand line, hereafter called *DD*, is smoothed for ease of reading.

suggests that the price will rise. How does a higher price come to pass? And what function does the higher price fulfill?

The reduced supply *is* an increased scarcity of cars. Who suffers? *A* has lost some wealth—his car. If that loss is not great enough to affect his demand for cars perceptibly (as we assume in this example), *A* will try to buy another car at the old price of $500. But no one wants to sell a car at $500. There is a "shortage of supply" or, to put it in different words, an "excessive demand" at that price. Everyone prefers his car to an additional $500. *A* prefers a third car even to $600; he will, if he finds *B*, get a car, because *B* would rather have the $600. Initially, *A* was pushed to a less preferred position *by the burning of the car,* but he has now moved to a more preferred level, although not so high as before the fire. Inducing trade by offering a higher price enabled *A* to reach a position preferred to the one he was put in by the fire.

The fire brought a benefit to *B* as he judges his position. It may seem "unfair" that someone else gains because of *A*'s loss. But under the system of private property, this can happen.[2] However, don't overlook that the gain to *B* occurred as he helped *A* to recoup his situation. And reciprocally, by offering to improve *B*'s situation, *A* was also able to improve his own—as judged by *A* and *B* themselves. Whether it was *A* or *B* or the reduced supply that raised the price is impossible to say and *irrelevant*.

One way to prevent a mutually agreeable change—*given* the disaster, about which nothing can be done now—is to limit the price at which cars may be sold to the pre-disaster price of $500. *B* is prevented from "gouging" *A* or, as it is sometimes said, "profiteering from *A*'s misfortune." We might think we were doing *A* a favor by preventing him from buying cars at over $500. But he *cannot* get any cars at that price. A *shortage* has been created—not by the burning of a car, which increased the *scarcity,* but by the prohibition of higher prices. In *A*'s opinion, is he helped or hurt by a price ceiling at $500 if the price ceiling prohibits full exploitation of mutually preferred exchanges?

Adjustments to Changes in Demand

Suppose with the original situation of seven cars, a newcomer, *E,* joins the community. His demand and the new market demand are in Table 6–2.

TABLE 6–2. Car-Ownership Demand Schedules of *A, B, C, D,* and *E*

Price	Quantity Demanded		
	A,B,C,D	E	Total
$1,000	4	0	4
900	4	1	5
800	5	1	6
700	5	1	6
600	6	1	7
500	7	1	8
400	8	1	9
300	9	2	11
200	10	2	12
100	12	3	15

[2] Voluntary insurance is a method for distributing the loss over all co-insurers, rather than concentrating it on one person.

E prefers a car to $500 but is unable to get one at that price. According to Figure 6–3 the equilibrium price is higher (in this case, $600) when demand increases—and lower when demand decreases. More pertinent is an understanding of what function is served when higher offers are permitted in the markets to push actual price to the new equilibrium. A *re-allocation* of goods occurs. Each person can reach what *he* regards as a preferred pattern of consumption or combination of assets. *E* prefers a car to any amount of money up to $900. An offer of $600 would attract a car from *B*, who prefers $600 to a car. Exploration and discovery of opportunities are possible if *E* is allowed to offer whatever amount he chooses in the market.

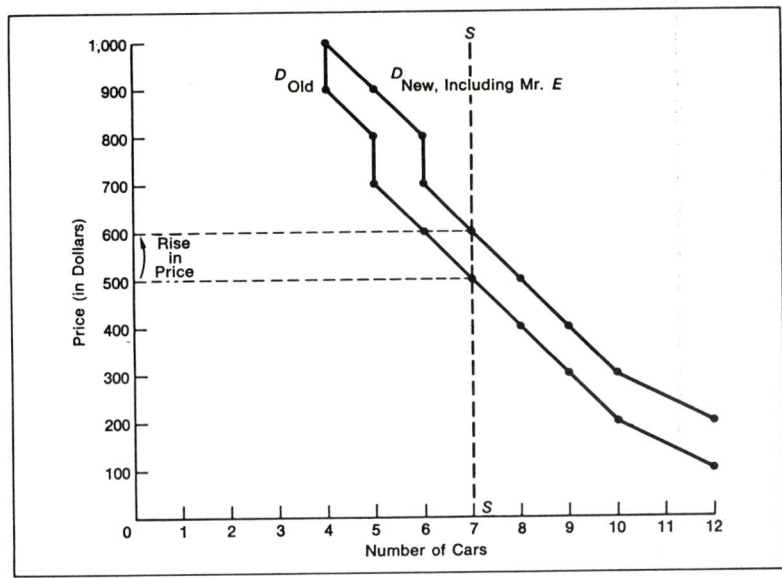

FIGURE 6–3

Higher-price effect of increased demand. Important conclusion is not merely that price is increased, but that the higher price permits a re-allocation of an automobile to *E* from *B*, who prefers $600 to an automobile.

This equilibrium price is *defined* by the intersection of the new demand and supply. If price is pushed to that equilibrium value, the resulting distribution of goods will give each person the pattern he prefers at that price. No further revision of the *pattern* of consumption of goods would be acceptable to *any* two persons (it takes two to trade), given the distribution of the total stock of all goods. (However, still more wealth would be preferred.)

Cost-Economizing, Exchange-Facilitating Intermediaries

If the exchange of cars had been conducted with intermediaries (used-car dealers), the buyers would probably complain that middlemen had unscrupulously hoisted prices. In truth, used-car dealers do raise prices scrupulously when demand increases—and they must also raise their buying prices to replenish their inventories. They attract more cars from the rest of the public who prefer the greater amount of money to cars. And the reason the used-car dealers *can* offer more for cars (*and* still stay in business) is that the consumer-demanders of more cars are offering more to get cars from other people. It makes no difference whether the higher bids *first* come from the potential buyer or a used-car dealer. The willingness of some people to pay more to get a car, combined with unchanged willingness of the rest of the public to sell cars, will result in a higher price—even without the used-car dealers as intermediaries. One thing dealers do is make it cheaper for the buyers to communicate (indirectly) with other car owners and negotiate exchanges.

Used-car dealers are not responsible for the higher equilibrium price. They buy and sell only at the "offer" and "asking" prices of the public. The price spread provides for their services in economizing on costs of communication between all potential buyers and sellers. As people's demands change, the dealers must move both selling and buying prices; otherwise, used-car lots will either overflow or empty. To let changing demands be reflected by changing prices, even when the supply is fixed and non-increasable, is *not* a matter of tolerating higher or lower prices for their own sakes. Instead, it is a matter of facilitating revisions in people's consumption patterns to what they consider preferred patterns.

Purpose of Demand and Supply Concepts

What is the point of all this demand and supply apparatus? It attempts (1) to explain how markets enable people more cheaply to revise their consumption patterns to suit their tastes; (2) to show how interpersonal competition for existing goods is resolved in the marketplace; (3) to explain how price adjustment or price negotiation aids reallocation of goods; (4) to see how the market and market prices economize on the search activities that people would otherwise engage in at much greater cost and loss of time; and (5) to prepare ourselves for comparing this system of allocating goods with systems with restrictions against negotiated prices that would be mutually acceptable to both parties.

Interdependent Demands and Prices

The amount of butter demanded depends on the price of butter and also on the prices of margarine, peanut butter, cheese, milk, and bread. The amount of gasoline demanded depends on the prices of tires, automobiles, bus fares, and taxi rates, in addition to its own price. For almost every good, prices of other goods also enter demand.[3]

A more explicit formulation is achieved by showing, for example, that the amount of butter demanded depends (1) on the price of butter, i.e., its own price, *and* (2) on the price of margarine, i.e., the price of other goods. This is done by *shifting* the demand

---

[3] Those prices and events that affect, but are largely unaffected by, prices and events in a particular market are called "exogenous" factors. Those that affect, and also are in turn affected by, prices and events in a particular market are called "endogenous."

curve for butter when the price of margarine changes—that is, for each price of margarine there is a different demand *curve* for butter. Figure 6–4 shows two demand curves for butter, the lower one for a margarine price of 30 cents per pound and the upper one for a price of 60 cents. This means that butter and margarine are *substitutes*.[4] If the price of margarine is increased, people will shift from margarine to butter, increasing the amount of butter demanded at each possible price of butter. If the supply of butter were BB in Figure 6–4, the price of butter would be p_2 when the margarine price is 60 cents and p_1, a lower price, when the price of margarine is 30 cents.

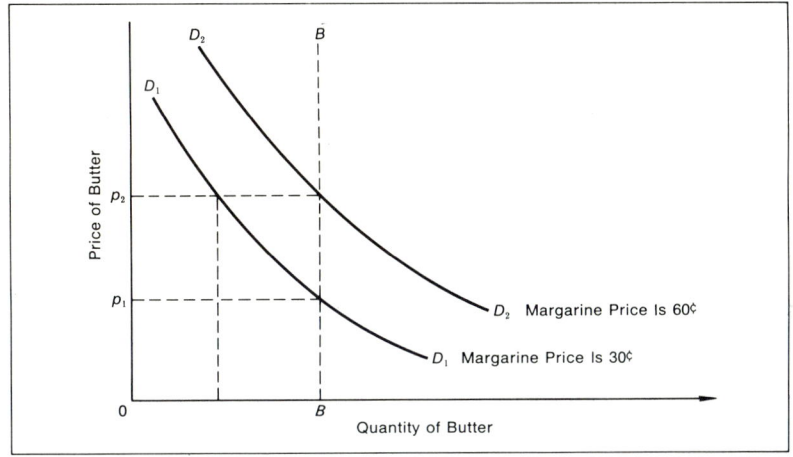

FIGURE 6–4. Shift of Demand for Butter with Change in Price of Margarine

This portrays dependence of demand for and price of butter on price of margarine. This diagram does *not* give equilibrium price of butter or of margarine. Because prices are interdependent, price of p_2 for butter may not be consistent with margarine equilibrium price of 60 cents. The equilibrium pair of butter and margarine prices can be derived only with more complex, multidimensional analysis.

But after we recognize that the price of margarine is itself *dependent* on what happens to the price of butter, we must make a complete demand-and-supply analysis of both markets simultaneously. As a result of the simultaneous, joint analysis, we can derive an implied process of clearing the markets for both butter and margarine by interdependent changes in both prices rather than only one. In brief, an increase in demand for butter will raise the price of butter, which will increase the demand schedule for margarine, thereby raising the price of margarine. Since the demand schedule for butter depends in part on the price of margarine, a higher price of margarine will increase the demand schedule for butter—pushing butter prices still higher, which will again raise margarine prices, and on and on. Where will the process end? The prices rise and *converge* toward an equilibrium pair of prices. That analysis is beyond the elementary level. It is sufficient

---

[4] If a higher price of one good lowered the demand curve of another good, the two goods would be called *complements*. Examples are gasoline and tires, golf balls and golf clubs. (What about ham and eggs? Why can't you be sure?)

for present purposes to note that attempts to legally constrain one price will necessitate attempts to control other prices as well. The interrelationship among demands for different commodities, and hence their prices, is so pervasive that attempts to control prices of some goods lead one into a much wider range of price controls.

The range can be appreciated by tracing some effects of a reduction in the supply of gasoline. The rise in price would restrict the amounts demanded to that available; a rise to double (say) the former price would induce people to walk a bit more on short errands, to travel more by group transportation. Motels would experience a reduced demand. Some motels and service stations would lose employees to other jobs, some to public transportation and some to TV and entertainment serving as substitutes for "joy rides." Automobiles would be reduced in size, with less powerful engines. Trucks would be less widely utilized, while railroads expanded. Farms closer to the city would be advantaged because transportation costs would be more effective in determining profitability. The demand for housing near places of work would increase. Shopping centers would be smaller as more neighborhood retail stores reduced transport costs.

5, 6, 7, 8

Appendix

Other Kinds of Demand and Supply Concepts

Demand can be expressed as either (1) the total amounts people want to *have* on hand or (2) the amounts they want to *acquire* by current purchase (or dispose of) in order to adjust the stock they have to the desired level. The first concept is often called the *reservation* demand, indicating the amount, at each price, that a person wants to reserve for himself. The second indicates amounts of new *acquisition* by *purchase* (or

TABLE 6–3. Current Purchase Demand and Sales Supply

| | Individuals | | | | Aggregated | |
	A	B	C	D	D_p	S_p*
$1,000	0	0	−1	−2	0	3
900	0	0	−1	−2	0	3
800	0	0	−1	−1	0	2
700	0	0	−1	−1	0	2
600	1	0	−1	−1	1	2
500	1	1	−1	−1	2	2
400	1	1	0	−1	2	1
300	1	1	0	0	2	0
200	1	1	0	1	3	0
100	2	2	0	1	5	0
Current holdings	2	0	2	3		

Price at which aggregated demand to buy D_p and supply to sell S_p are equal ($500) is the price that would permit all mutually advantageous exchange or re-allocation of cars. At a higher price a "surplus" of cars would exist, since some would prefer to sell more cars at that price than others wish. And at a lower price a "shortage" would exist, for those who prefer the money to cars are offering fewer cars than others seek to buy. The "surplus" and the "shortage" indicate potential mutually advantageous, but unexploited, exchange opportunities. (*Minus sign omitted.)

Market Demand, Allocation, and Equilibrium Price

sale) to adjust the amount of the good possessed to that desired (reservation) amount.

Errors of analysis can result from failure to see the logical mathematical tie between the two. Consider the first, the demands-to-own for our initial four-person community (discussed on pages 79–84). Suppose the cars initially held are two by *A*, none by *B*, two by *C*, and three by *D*. The differences between the amount each person *has* and the amounts he could *demand* to have at different prices (given in Table 6–1) are the second concept, the amounts *demanded* to *purchase* (or *supply for sale*) at each price in order to bring home what he wants. In the schedule for *D* in Table 6–1, at a price of $300 he wants three, which is what he has. At a higher price, say $500, he wants fewer and therefore would offer to sell one (−1), while at a lower price, say $200, he wants one more and hence would demand to buy some (+1). The amounts each person would demand to *buy* (to increase his holdings) and supply for *sale* at each price (to reduce his holdings) are shown in Table 6–3.

At each price, add all the *positive* amounts, to obtain the demand for *purchase* by those who would like more. Adding, *at each price*, negative quantities, we get the schedule of amounts offered as the supply for *sale* by those who have more than they want. These quantities in the last two columns constitute the schedule of quantities demanded for *purchase* (D_p) and the schedule of quantities supplied for *selling* (S_p). Figure 6–5

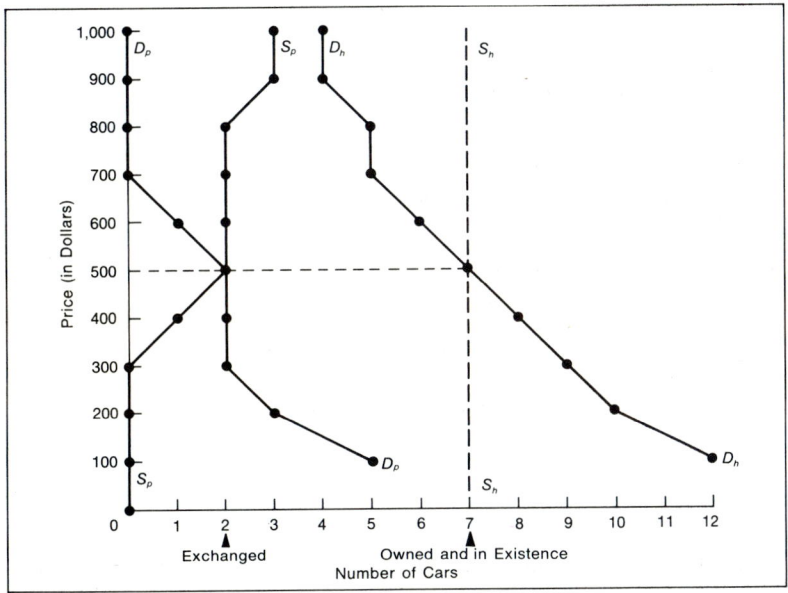

FIGURE 6–5

Demand-to-buy (D_p) and supply-to-sell (S_p) curves are shown with demand-to-own (D_h) and supply-in-existence (S_h) curves. The horizontal distance between one coordinated pair is, at a stipulated price, equal to the horizontal distance between the other coordinated pair. Either pair can be used to ascertain effects of changes in demand or supply on determination of price. Do not use demand curve from one pair with the supply of the other.

graphs these purchase-sell schedules, intersecting at $500, at a quantity of two. Two items will be sold (one each from C and D, to A and B). Then every person will have the amount demanded by him at that price.

The lines, D_h and S_h, on the right side of the figure, depict the schedules of *reservation demand* and *supply in existence*. These lines also intersect at $500.

Both pairs of matched demand and supply curves give the same equilibrating price. They must, because the two pairs of schedules are logically related. How? The difference between the amounts demanded for purchase and the amounts offered for sale at any price (say, one unit at price $400) *is* the excess that people demand to own over the supply amount in existence. That is, $D_p - S_p = D_h - S_h$.

At the equilibrium price, people with excess amounts will sell to those with deficiencies. After the exchanges, everyone will have the quantity he wants at that price. The D_p and S_p will have shifted leftward to give an intersection with no remaining exchanges at the equilibrium price, $500. Price will stay there until there is a subsequent shift in the state of demand or supply. If a good is durable, currently held in large stocks, and subject to resale (like cars, corporation common stocks and bonds, houses, paintings, land, buildings, etc.), the demand and supply are usually conveniently expressed in terms of demand to *hold* and the stock in *existence*. This is sometimes called a "stock" demand and supply approach.[5]

Summary

1. The demands of people can be aggregated into a total market demand by summing at each price the amount demanded by each person.

2. An equilibrium price in the market is one at which all possible mutually acceptable exchanges can occur. At that price, each person can have exactly the amount of each good that he would like, given his total wealth.

3. By looking at the one market price, and using intermediaries, each person is saved the trouble, cost, and time of inquiring of everyone else what their subjective, personal values are for a good; people can thereby more cheaply ascertain the exchanges they can make.

4. Suppressing access to the market or to mutually negotiated prices raises the costs (and reduces the extent) of mutually acceptable exchanges.

5. The amount demanded of a good depends on other prices, as well as its own price. This makes prices and demands interdependent.

---

[5] In the foregoing, the supply was an existing durable stock without any new production being considered. If, however, the existing stock is negligible and the supply consists of new production—say because the goods are highly perishable (without resale among consumers), like bananas and food—the demand and supply quantities are different from either of the two just discussed. Then the supply will be the *production flow* of *new* products from producers. But this will be explained later when production is discussed.

Market Demand, Allocation, and Equilibrium Price

Questions

1 The demands to own by *A* and by *B* for good *X* are:

Price	A's Demand	B's Demand	Market Demand
10	0	0 ~~2~~	0 2
9	1	0 ~~2~~	1 3
8	2	0 ~~2~~	2 4
7	3	1 ~~3~~	4 6
6	4	2 ~~4~~	6 8
5	5	3 ~~5~~	8 10
4	6	3 ~~5~~	9 11
3	7	4 ~~6~~	11 13
2	8	5 ~~7~~	13 15
1	9	6 ~~8~~	15 17

a. What is the market demand by *A* and *B*?
b. If six units of *X* are available, what allocation will there be between *A* and *B* if open-market exchange is used? *4 to A, 2 to B*
c. With six units available, if price were legally imposed at 4, would there be a shortage, a surplus, or an exchange equilibrium? *shortage*
d. If the price were legally imposed at $9, would there be a shortage, a surplus, or exchange equilibrium? *surplus*
e. How can there be a change from a shortage to a surplus without any change in supply or demand?

2 In problem 1 above, increase the amounts demanded by *B* uniformly by two more units at each price.
a. What will be the new open-market price?
b. What will be the allocation between *A* and *B*?
c. If the price is held at the old level by law, will there be a surplus or a shortage?
d. How can that surplus or shortage be eliminated?

3 The following is characteristic of Mr. *A*'s market demand for shoes. Each price is associated with the number of pairs of shoes he demands to own.

Price	Quantity	Total Revenue
10	1	$10
9	2	18
8	3	24
7	4	28
6	5	30
5	6	30
4	7	28
3	8	24
2	9	18
1	10	10

a. Complete the total revenue.

b. At a price of $6 Mr. *A* would own five. At a price of $5 he would own six. At each of these two prices, he would have a total of $30 in shoes. Does this mean that he attaches no value to a sixth one? What value does he attach to a sixth one?

4 Using the demand-schedule data for Mr. *A* in problem 1, suppose that these refer to shares of common stock in a corporation and that he now owns four units of *X*.

a. How many units of *X* would he buy or sell at each possible price?

b. If the exchange-equilibrium price in the market turned out to be $3, how many would he want to buy or sell and how many would he then own?

5 The demands for tires and gasoline are interrelated, somewhat in the sense that butter and margarine were related.

a. Make a demand-and-supply graph to show the effects of a reduced supply of gasoline on the prices and quantities of tires and gasoline. (Hint: use two demand curves for tires: the demand before and after a gasoline-price increase.)

b. In what sense are butter and margarine substitutes whereas tires and gasoline are "complements"? (Hint: see footnote on page 87.)

6 Consumption is a rate concept, even though the good being consumed may be held as a stock or finite amount of goods. True or false?

7 For goods like shoes, a rise in price will reduce the number of pairs of shoes a person will want. Since the price at which he can sell used shoes is low relative to the new-shoe price, he will not sell some shoes in order to reduce his stock of shoes. How does he adjust his stock of shoes to the new, lasting, higher cost of shoes? (Hint: How does a person adjust his stock of clothes to his new demand after experiencing a reduction in demand consequent to a reduction of his income?)

8 There are *three measures* of the amount demanded: (1) The *rate* of consumption; (2) the quantity a person wants to buy in order to increase his current stock; (3) the quantity a person wants to own. As an example of each: (1) a person may consume eggs at the rate of 6/7 per day (which does not necessarily mean he eats a fraction of an egg each day); (2) and on Saturday he buys a half-dozen eggs; (3) he may have an average of three eggs in his refrigerator. Normally, explicit distinctions between rates of purchase and rates of consumption are not necessary since they are so highly related. Which of these three measures must be expressed as a rate of activity and which as a "stock"?

9 "The community's demand to own houses may remain unchanged; yet the market demand to *purchase* and to sell houses may change enormously." Explain how the demand to hold houses (in a two-person community) could be unchanged, while the demand to *purchase* and sell houses increased.

Applications of Demand Analysis to Market Pricing and Allocation

7 HAVING learned the laws of market demand and exchange, we now apply them to some real situations to see how open markets and prices ration existing supply by discriminating among claimants.

The Cost-Push Illusion

The avenue from increased demand to higher exchange-equilibrium prices often is concealed by *inventories* in the distribution chain from producer to consumer. As a result, many prices appear to be set by costs of production instead of competition among consumers. The cause of this widespread illusion is illustrated in the following example of an increased demand for meat.

To start, for some reason people's desire for meat increases. Housewives express their increased desire for meat by increasing their market demand. Market demands reflect what people do in the marketplace, not simply something they dream of doing later. Housewives reveal an increased demand by buying more than formerly. Retail butchers have inventories adequate for a day or two at usual rates of sale. As sales increase, inventory is depleted more rapidly than expected. No butcher knows that the demand has risen for the community as a whole. No butcher knows that he could raise his price and still make no fewer sales than earlier. All he knows is that *he* has sold more meat at the existing price. But the increased demand takes its toll of inventories. Whether or not a butcher believes that the increased rate of sale is a temporary fluctuation, he will buy more meat than usual the next day in order to restore his inventory from its abnormally low level; and he will buy even more than that if he believes the increase in sales will persist. If the demand for meat does increase so that one butcher's increased sales is not merely some other butcher's loss, the purchases by the aggregate of butchers from the packers will increase.

Why does he have an inventory large enough to take care of *more* than the normal expected daily sales? To accommodate transient increases in daily demand without having to raise price late on those days when his inventory approaches depletion. Stable, predictable prices are convenient to housewives in their planning what to buy and where to buy it—rather than incurring the extra costs of shopping around and making last-minute revisions in their shopping in response to unexpectedly and temporarily high or low prices. Hence inventories are held to increase the efficiency of the market system, by assuring immediate supply as well as more predictable prices. (Highly predictable prices can be assured by legally controlling prices, but that would result in a facade of price stability, while reducing or destroying the market's effectiveness in assuring supply at that price. Such *imposed* stability is obtained only by destroying the function of the price system in providing convenience and assuring supply to consumers.)

Just as butchers use inventories, so their meat suppliers—packers—also rely on inventories as a buffer to their sales fluctuations. We assume that the first day's change in demand was within that inventory limit and was met without a price increase by depleting inventories.

Packers restore inventories by instructing their cattle buyers (who travel among cattle raisers and fatteners and to the stockyards where cattlemen ship the steers for sale) to buy more than usual. But with all the packers restoring their inventories in this manner, the cattle available for sale each day are inadequate to meet the increased amount demanded *at the old price*. There are not sufficient cattle in existence to take care of this increased demand. Either some buyers for packers must report that they cannot get the amount requested, or they must boost their offer prices to persuade cattlemen to sell steers to them instead of other packers.

Rather than go without any increase in stocks, some buyers raise their offers. This rise in offer prices may occur nearly simultaneously among the buyers, as if there were collusion among the cattlemen or buyers. The cattlemen simply let the buyers bid against each other until the price rises to a point where the packers will not want to buy more meat than they did at the old lower price; that is, the packers are induced by the higher price not to buy more than is available.

In terms of our demand-and-supply apparatus, the supply curve of cattle is vertical. An increased demand by packers for cattle (a demand *derived* from ultimate consumer demand for meat) implies an intersection at a higher price but at the same quantity. Each packer is therefore forced to move back up his new increased demand curve to a higher price, at which point he buys less than he had planned at the old price. The total amount purchased is no greater than before, but the price of cattle is higher. At this high price, the amount wanted on the new demand curve equals the constant amount supplied. Each packer must pay a higher price for cattle to avoid getting less than before. Competition among the packers has raised the price during the immediate period when cattle production cannot be increased.

Cattle raisers bask in the glow of higher selling prices. But to the packers this appears as *a rise in costs*. Why did their costs rise? The costs of raising cattle did not increase. Nor did the costs of getting cattle to market, nor of slaughtering, nor of distributing meat. The price paid by wholesaler-slaughterers to cattlemen rose in response fundamentally to the increased demand by consumers—the housewives. Their demand, from retail meat stores through slaughterers, was first met by depleting inventories. But the cattlemen did not have inventories that they could deplete and then restore quickly. Therefore, they simply let the buyers bid for the available amount (rather than allocating the cattle among slaughterers on some other principle).

Whether or not anyone is aware of the law of demand and supply, which says that a *higher demand will permit higher prices,* and whether or not they are aware that demand has increased, the higher price of cattle (higher *costs* to the packers) will mean that the packers must charge a higher price to retail butchers *if* they are to continue as profitable meat packers. And they will be *able* to charge a higher price in response to higher costs without any loss in sales only because demand had increased first. In sum, a higher price occurs because the demand for meat has increased. Retail butchers, in turn, post higher prices to housewives. When housewives complain about the higher price, the butcher in all innocence, honesty, and correctness says that it isn't his fault. The cost of meat has gone up. Cost, to him, is the cost of getting meat. The butcher can say, "I never raise prices until my costs go up." And the packers can honestly say the same thing. If the housewife wants to know who is to blame for the higher prices of meat, she can look in the mirror behind the butcher's counter and see her face and those of all her neighbors. She might then turn to each of them and say, "If you didn't want more meat, I could have more." But that observation and tactless behavior is neither useful nor fostered by the competitive exchange system. The exchange system tends to conceal this facet of competition and makes it appear as if the higher price of meat were caused by butchers' or packers' or farmers' greedy behavior—not that of ourselves or our neighbors.

The consumers' increased demand for meat, then, brought about a rise in the price of meat to consumers. This rise *appeared* to be the result of a rise in costs because the first price effect of the increased demand occurred at the cattle raisers' end of the line. The demand increase pulled up the price in the first stages of the production and distribution channels. The first rise in price could have occurred in the butcher shops and then have been transmitted back step by step to the farmers. But butchers' inventories are usually adequate to cushion the changes in demand temporarily until the impact of increased sales goes all the way through the productive processes. This explains the common illusion that increases in costs are responsible for higher prices.

This example accurately describes a period of inflation. An increase in the money stock increases everyone's demand for all goods including meat. Total available manpower, equipment and other resources limit the ability to expand output, but the attempt to increase output by each producer raises costs and makes it look as if each must raise prices because his costs have risen. Actually it is the increased aggregate monetary market demand that is at last running up against the fact of limited resources that produces inflation—a topic reserved for more complete analytical discussion in a later chapter.

1, 2

Rental and Allocation

Demand-and-supply analysis can be applied to rentals as well as to purchases of goods. A person renting a house will feel the effect of increased demand by other people for housing space when the price (rent) rises. At the higher price he will tend to rent smaller or poorer quality housing, which is to say that he has been induced to release some housing to those whose demands have increased. Since the renter does not own the house, he will not capture the higher value of the house.

This can be analyzed graphically. We shall use the "housing demand" curve plotted against the total stock in existence, because we want to compare holdings of housing space before and after the demand change. In Figure 7–1, curve $D_a + D_b$ represents the community's total demand for housing space *before* the increase in demand. D_a represents the demand for space by those whose demand is unchanged, and D_b is the initial demand by those whose demand later increases. Initially, rental price was p_1, and the space was rented, with OX_a held by group A and OX_b by group B. Group B's new, increased demand curve is shown by D'_b. The total demand, formed by summing the demands D_a and D'_b, is $D_a + D'_b$. This demand intersects the existing housing supply at price p_2, greater than p_1.

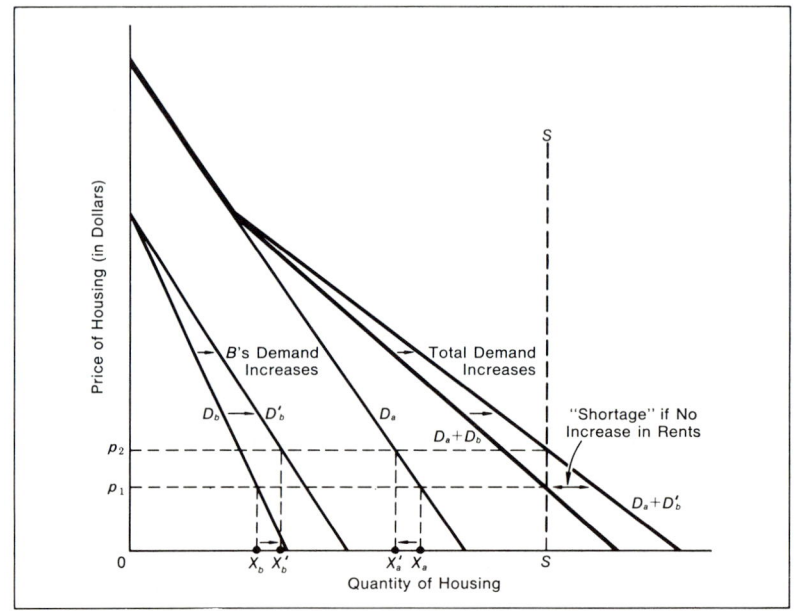

FIGURE 7–1

Change in price of housing enables re-allocation of housing space among competing demanders, from *A* to *B*.

If rents do not rise from p_1 to p_2, the amount of housing space demanded will exceed the amount available, shown by the distance between the supply line and new demand curve at all prices less than p_2. This excess demand is commonly called a shortage; rarely is it called excess demand. At prices below p_2 there simply is not enough to satisfy amounts of housing demanded or, as it is misleadingly called, "housing needs." With open-market bidding for the available housing, the price will be pushed up, toward p_2, as frustrated demanders make higher offers to get more housing. The market for housing would be called "tight" or "strong" or a "seller's" market. Vacancy rates that normally exist to facilitate the flow of movers, just as stores maintain inventories, will diminish.

When rents rise from p_1 to p_2, as group B seeks more housing by trying to outbid other people, what happens to the housing allocation? Group B obtains the larger amount OX'_b instead of only OX_b. Members of group A end up with only OX'_a. The decrease, $X_a - X'_a$, to those whose demand did not increase is the increase to group B.

(At the present stage of analysis, we are leaving the effect on production or supply for later; however, any increase in housing production as a result of a price increase would offset part of the decrease imposed on group A and also reduce the price rise.)

As the price rises in response to the increased demand (represented by the shift to the right of the market-demand curve), claimants for housing space will reduce the amount demanded—the higher price moves them, figuratively, back up along their demand schedules to smaller amounts demanded. Their demands have not decreased.

House owners get more rent; their houses are worth more. The members of the A group, whose demand did not increase, pay higher prices and use less housing space. The members of group B present a more complex result. Those whose demands increased most get more space than they were getting at the lower price. Other members of group B, those whose demands may have increased by only a very little, may end up paying higher rents and getting very little more or even less space than originally. The A's and the B's blame the owners for raising rents. But what enabled the owners to get higher prices? The *increased demand* by tenants in group B pushed up the rent. Had their demand not increased and had they not offered to pay more, the owners would not have raised rents. The owners simply echoed the higher bids by the B people. The owners, in effect, told the A people to meet the competition of the B's. Maybe the B's and A's are friends and neighbors who complain to each other about the higher "exorbitant" rentals that the landlords are charging—never thinking to blame their own competition for the higher price.

Objections to the higher prices are objections to the competitive superiority of other people in providing more favorable offers to the owners than formerly. If anyone wants to gain from the possibility of trade, he must be prepared to face the fact that the *terms* of trade and the realizable *gains* from trade will vary from day to day. To put it differently, trade can, under commonly found circumstances, enable each party to move to a situation preferred to *no* trade at all; but the gains from *today's* available trade may be larger or smaller than the gains from *yesterday's* trade. Economics does *not* say that with *every* change in demand *everyone* moves from one exchange equilibrium to still more preferred positions. It implies only that, with fully exploitable trade opportunities, any person can reach the most preferred of all the *possible* patterns, and these possibilities may expand *or contract* as conditions change.

Prices of Common Stock

Some 500,000,000 shares of American Telephone and Telegraph stock are owned by 2,500,000 people. Yet on any typical day only about 500,000 shares (1/10 of 1 percent of the total owned) are bought and sold by 1,000 people (less than 1/20 of 1 percent of the owners). From these figures, it is sometimes concluded that only a small portion of the owners of the stock affect or determine its price. Similar statements are made about many other markets, like that for used cars, suggesting that used-car prices are unaffected by the mass of car owners.

Shares of A.T.&T. common stock are exchanged daily on the New York Stock Exchange, because people's personal situations change from day to day. While some decide to sell shares at its current price, in order to buy something else, others may have just received an increase in wealth or wish to hold more of their wealth in the form of ownership in A.T.&T. Thus, the demands of some people to own shares have increased (the demand curve shifts to the right) and for others have fallen, but not necessarily by exactly offsetting amounts. These changes in demand schedules will initiate an exchange of shares among the various holders (just as the housing space in the preceding example was reallocated).

If those whose demand (curves) have fallen exceed the demand (curve) increase by those whose demands have increased, there will be a net downward force on price. Those people whose demands (curves) did not change will affect the extent of the price change, because as price changes they—or some of them—will be induced to buy if the price falls, or sell if the price rises, thus restricting the extent of the price and hence its ultimate market clearing value. This is exactly what happens for any durable good—be it houses, automobiles, land, or stock. Every owner has an impact on price—not only those whose demands have shifted, but also those whose demands have not shifted. Even those who do not own any but are ready to buy some at a lower price will affect the price. In sum, those whose demands shift initiate price changes or fluctuations while the rest of the public attenuates its extent.

Pricing and Discrimination

These examples show how pricing in the open market enables exchange of goods. It is an analysis of discrimination among competing claimants. The discrimination, or competitive, criterion is heavily weighted by the amount of money (that is, claims to other goods) offered. Pricing and exchange is a distributive, discriminatory process. So is *every* allocative system. Our interest in pricing is not in whether prices are high or low, or good or bad, but instead in how they influence who gets what.

The analysis does not say that this system of competition or discrimination among claimants is good or bad. It is misleading to say, as some have said, that the private-property (price) system puts goods where the *most* dollar votes are. Rather, it puts *more* goods where there are *more* dollar votes. More akin to proportional representation than to majority rule, the exchange system puts goods *wherever* there are some dollar votes for the good. A poorer person can, if he wishes, by bidding for a proportionally smaller amount, get *some* of the goods. For example, no one has to be rich to have some services of a big expensive jet plane.

Sometimes it is said that the system permits rich people to feed dogs while poor children have too little milk. The system is permitting people to do what they want with their wealth. One might then object either to people's being allowed to be rich or to feed dogs while children still want milk. You may seek either a different distribution of wealth or a different pattern of tastes in utilizing wealth. But do not think it likely you can find a feasible system or mechansim which will result in a wealth distribution *and* a taste pattern which conform to your ideas of a better world of 3 billion people.

We are not saying the price-exchange system is desirable or undesirable—only that we should not misinterpret it. This discussion suggests the desirability of investigating what determines how much wealth each person has, and we shall do that later. For the present, we are accepting the distribution of wealth as given—but not ordained as "naturally proper."

3, 4, 5,
6, 7, 8

Price Controls as a Restriction on Market Exchange

We can better understand how a free-market pricing system allocates goods if we try to get along without it for a while. Our analysis of the market pricing system suggests that everyone can buy all he chooses of any good, given his wealth, and can sell all he chooses at the going market price. According to our preceding analysis, there should not be queues or waiting lines or shortages. But at the going, current market prices, you may find there *is* a long waiting list for some goods. In other situations, sellers find that at the market price, there are *no* buyers. What has gone wrong with our analysis? (Do not ask, "What has gone wrong with the world?") One answer is that we failed to recognize legal or customary restrictions on permissible market prices. We assumed, not entirely correctly, that potential buyers and sellers could negotiate exchanges with each other at whatever prices they chose. If, as is sometimes the case, prices are restricted or controlled, we must modify our analysis. However, our laws of demand are not changed. We must not use them solely for open markets, which are markets in which everyone is allowed to buy and sell whatever they wish at mutually agreeable prices. In many parts of the world—and for many goods, the negotiable terms of trade are restricted by law or social ostracism. In New York City, the rents you can pay for old apartments are limited by law; in most cities, taxi rates are set by law, and taxis cannot legally collect higher fares during rain or snow or rush hours. All these cases are characterized by "shortages," queues, or waiting lists.

To analyze what happens when price controls are effective, suppose that demand for, say, housing space increases and that rents or house prices were not allowed to rise.[1] The total amount demanded exceeds the available supply at the old, legal-limit price. A shortage, or, what is the same thing, an "excessive demand" develops.[2]

This situation can be analyzed with the demand and supply graphs of Figure 7–2, a diagram basically the same as Figure 7–1. The demand lines of A and B are shown as they were before a demand increase by B and also as they are after his increase in demand. At the old price, p_1, the total amount demanded exceeds the amount supplied, S. As long as the price is restricted to p_1, B will want more housing space; he complains of a shortage since he can't get as much space as he "demands" (or as he is likely to say, "needs"). Two other effects will occur also: a wealth transfer and an increase in nonprice competitive discrimination.

Wealth Transfer

The potential wealth transfer (increased market value of housing) is easy to discern. Suppose a tenant were allowed to sublease to others at uncontrolled prices, while the rent paid to the landlord is restricted to p_1. With his new demand, B wants more housing space higher than at p_1. It would pay him to rent more $(X_a - X'_a)$ space from A and pay a price of p_2 per unit of space, all of which space will go to B, as $X'_b - X_b$. A prefers this because he would rather have the extra money income than the space, and B prefers the extra space to the money. The greater market value of housing services would be captured by the old tenants. The part of the increased value kept by B would be $(p_2 - p_1) X_b$, and the part to A would be $(p_2 - p_1) X_a$.

This market-value increment occurs whether or not subleasing side-deals like those contemplated in the preceding paragraph are permitted. If permitted, they enable a re-

---

[1] In a later chapter, we shall investigate the effects of legally imposed *minimum* prices.

[2] Although the legal maximum price of housing is deemed "fair," some demands are not met at that price. Any person caught in that situation could ask, "What is the meaning of a price at which I *can't* buy?"

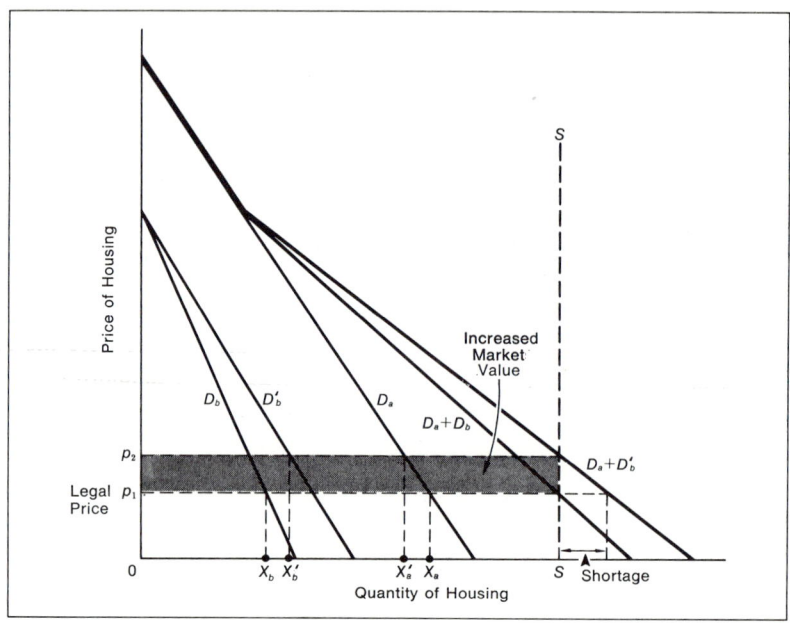

FIGURE 7-2

Effect of rent control. Shortages are created by rent controls, resulting in transferral of wealth.

allocation of housing space to help both *B* and *A* reach mutually preferred positions, but with no transfer of the increased market value of housing to the housing owner. If not permitted, the housing space is not re-allocated so effectively, but the higher value is still retained by the tenants. Under rent controls, with or without uncontrolled subleasing, the increased income that would belong to the owners is "taken" from the owners by the legal rent limit, and the original tenants get that wealth from the owners. Hardly anyone has proposed that under rent controls tenants really be allowed to sublease at market-clearing prices—despite the gains that would accrue to tenants. Is it because this would make the whole element of wealth redistribution too transparent to be acceptable politically?

Under rent controls, *without* subleasing at market prices, the same amount of wealth is being taken from the house owners. Since there is no open-market exchange-equilibrium value being openly expressed, wealth is transferred to the tenants, but not so obviously and not so efficiently.

We say "not so efficiently" because when tenants cannot sublease at higher rents, they gain only insofar as they have the greater wealth *in the form of housing space*. It is a gift, given on the condition they use it for their personal living space instead of being allowed to exchange it for other, more preferred goods. The issue comes down to whether the apartment-house owners "deserve" the right to the value of housing space or whether that should be transferred to the renters under the doctrine that wealth should be taken from the apartment-house owners and given to the tenants. The ethics of such a purposeful wealth transfer lies beyond the scope of economics, which can indicate only the circumstances under which the wealth transfer occurs and some of its effects. And there is another effect of price controls to consider—the change in discriminatory, competitive criteria.

Discrimination under Nonmoney Competition

As we have seen, suppression of open-market pricing and exchange implies that (1) more of the good is wanted than is available at the suppressed, controlled price; (2) the extent of re-allocation is reduced. And (3) we add now, other criteria will be used for discriminating among claimants for the available good. As the authors discovered during World War II, when meat prices were restricted below market-clearing prices, their wives' extraordinary beauty suddenly began to count more heavily in the butcher's eyes when he decided to which customers to give the amount of meat demanded and which to disappoint. The butchers favored our wives, while old, homely women became vegetarians. Similarly, with controlled housing rentals, our beautiful wives were the ones sent to apply for an apartment that was to be vacated. As long as the landlord couldn't get a higher price from less desirable people, why should he ignore the virtues of delightful tenants? While rentals and meat prices were *un*controlled, the money offers from the "less desirable" types made it more costly for the butchers and landlords to exercise their preferences for beautiful women as customers and tenants. *When not allowed to offer higher prices, handicapped people, rich or poor, are less able to compensate others to tolerate their "undesirable" features.* One can more cheaply overcome a handicap when he is free to use *all* his competitive powers, including price competition.

A difference between personal-characteristic competition and wealth-bidding competition is that a dollar of resources bid for one good necessarily means the bidder then has a dollar less for other goods. The amount of his biddable claims is some fixed total at any moment—given by the monetary value of his wealth. But the competition of "personal-characteristic wealth" does not necessarily involve this same degree of limitation on one's bids for various goods. More "beauty" offered to get more meat does not mean that that much less beauty is available for vegetables. Competition by personal characteristics has elements of an all-or-nothing system, whereas competition by money-exchange inducements is a sharing or pro rata division.

Since scarcity, competition, and discrimination are inseparable, the basic economic question "For whom?" is merely a polite way of asking, "What will be the criteria for discriminating among the competing claimants?" With open-market prices to restrict the amount demanded to the amount available, less (not necessarily *no*) weight will be given to nonmonetary characteristics of the competing customers. Whatever your pecuniary wealth, you will get still less if you are poorer in the nonmonetary desirable characteristics—for example, if you are a foreigner or a less-advantaged or a homely person. Price controls reduce the ability to counteract these "undesirable" personal attributes by pecuniary price offers—whatever your pecuniary wealth. Your nonmonetary, personal, disadvantageous traits become more important in determining what you get. Of course, if you are beautiful but poor, you may prefer price controls for some goods, for then the homely rich will find they are restricted in their legal ability to offset homeliness with higher monetary offers.

This should be kept in mind by "unpopular" people who believe that price controls will necessarily help them in comparison with people who are richer in money. These "unpopular" people forget that the *other* forms of competitive power become more relevant. The disadvantageous personal characteristics, which they could more effectively make up for by a willingness to pay a higher money price, are no longer so effectively overcome.

The connection between rent controls and manifestation of greater discrimination by personal characteristics is exemplified in New York City, almost the only American city still imposing rent controls. Perhaps no city is so beset with complaints of shortages, racial discrimination, personal favors, and rundown conditions in rent-controlled apartments and publicly subsidized housing—all involving rentals at less than exchange-equilibrium rates.

It is not clear which competitive systems give greater *equality* of distribution of all goods. If people's economic wealth were more disparate than their personal characteristics, it would not follow that the disparity of their share of goods would increase—because money bids help to offset the all-or-nothing feature of personal characteristics. The actual comparative outcome depends upon the degree to which people with inferior personal characteristics are also relatively inferior in other competitive characteristics, and upon their diversity of preference patterns and the society's attitudes toward personal characteristics. Little is known about this complex of factors. All we can conclude is that if you want to give more importance to race, creed, religion, and other personal characteristics in allocating goods, you should seek to reduce the effectiveness of the money offer in the market.

Rationing

A perceptive student might ask, "Why not avoid nonmonetary personal discrimination by *rationing* the available stock—either giving equal portions to everyone or allocating to each the same amount he got before?" Either procedure will eliminate discrimination, nonmonetary and personal. But each recipient will still be seeking to obtain a more preferred *recombination* of goods by further exchange re-allocation with other people, exactly as were the Cuban and Hungarian in our refugee camp. Rationing schemes *with* price controls restrict the realization of these more preferred combinations arrived at by exchanging the rationed goods: take your allotted share and no swapping.

Popularity of Price Controls

Students persistently conjecture that the exchange restriction effects should make price controls unpopular. However, the popularity of price controls, or of any other devices that keep prices below the exchange-equilibrium level, can be attributed to several factors.[3] First, as we have seen, *some* wealth is transferred from owners of the price-controlled resource to *some* users (renters or buyers). Those who expect to receive sufficient amounts of the good at that price will be inclined to want price controls.[4]

---

[3] This is not a complete analysis of price controls. *Production* effects have been ignored in order to concentrate the analysis on interpersonal allocation and exchange of existing goods. We warn you, in addition, that wage and price controls do not serve to prevent inflation—i.e., the deterioration in purchasing power of the dollar. Those controls, in fact, even more effectively reduce the purchasing power of the dollar—simply by legally restricting your right to use dollars to bid for goods. The wage-price controls themselves destroy some of the value of the dollar—thus giving the illusion that inflation has been avoided. If this blunt preview is surprising and too assertive rather than explanatory, expect to have matters explained in Chapters 33–34.

[4] Resist mightily the temptation to reason erroneously as follows: "Labor unions in the steel industry successfully struck for higher wages. It is realistic to assume that other unions in other industries also would be spurred to successful efforts to get higher wages. So a number of industries are forced to grant wage increases, which when translated into higher costs and consumer prices means that in time there has been a general rise in prices. Price and wage controls help to restrain higher prices in other parts of the economy, thus restraining the inflationary spiral of costs." If this line of reasoning seems plausible to you, you can gain from a study of economics! Inflation is analyzed in Chapter 33.

Furthermore, price controls are imposed by a political process; if tenants far outnumber the owners, rent controls are more likely. And in New York City, where tenants enormously outnumber owners, rent controls have continued since 1941 (and in Paris since 1914). Second, some paternalistic life-arrangers think others should be restricted in their choice of consumption. If I wanted people to eat a specific amount of a certain kind of food or hear a certain amount of highbrow music, I would seek to keep the prices so low that everyone would want at least as much of that food or music as I thought proper. When the shortage developed, I would ration these goods. And then to keep people from re-exchanging rights to those goods among themselves, as they would if allowed to compare their different subjective values via open-market price offers, I would prohibit transfers. Private property—which implies the right to buy and sell at any mutually agreeable prices—makes it harder for third parties to restrict the consumption patterns of people who have private-property rights in goods.

Third, price controls are popular because they are an alleged antidote for inflation. However, the price controls merely suppress exchange and production, not the general increase in demand nor the reduction in the value of money.

From the preceding, we discern three results of effective restrictions on open-market pricing—ignoring production effects.

1. The distribution of goods and services depends more upon other (nonmoney), personal-characteristic preferences.

2. The realized extent of mutually advantageous exchange is reduced.

3. Wealth is transferred from the owners of price-controlled goods in part to some who get the goods, and is consumed in part as costs of new forms of competitive activity or terms of trade.

13, 14, 15, 16, 17, 18, 19

Economic Rent

A misconception often arises in situations in which the supply of a durable good is *not augmentable*. It is complained that an increased demand and higher price lead only to unjust enrichment of current owners without increased production. Therefore, it is argued, higher prices should be prevented, for they serve no useful function. Holding in abeyance the question of "unjust" enrichment, we state it is not true that higher prices serve no function. As we have seen, the higher price, like it or not, does serve the function of deciding who will get how much. If the price were not allowed to rise, some other technique would have to serve.

To avoid confusion between two functions of market pricing—the *allocation* of the existing supply and the control of *production* of goods—the concept of economic rent has been developed. Although "rent" connotes a payment for housing space, the term here has a different meaning. "Economic rent" of any good is the portion of the price that does not influence the amount of that good in existence. In our earlier automobile example, the number of cars was fixed and unchanging, regardless of price. The entire price or value of each car would be "economic rent." There is a persuasive reason for not calling this a "surplus." It is not a surplus because it allocates the good to the highest-valued competing uses. Any lower valuation would fail to do so. Economists have long realized that prices, although not always affecting the amount in existence, did affect their *particular uses*. From the point of view of the current *existence* of the good, the payment may be an ineffective surplus; but for another purpose—that of allocating to highest-valued uses—it is effective. Hence, it is called a rent rather than a surplus.

Economic rent serves a rationing function. From the point of view of any individual user, the payment made to get that resource away from some other use is a cost. The willingness to pay at least that price to get some of the good is his competitive way of (1) asserting that the use he will make of the good yields greater value than other uses and (2) actually getting that good assigned to him for his use. The classic example of this kind of rent is the value of a piece of land. The value of the land (or the rent paid for its use) is far in excess of the amount necessary to keep that land in *existence*. Yet to decide the *use* of that land, the rent value is crucial. Any renter or subsequent purchaser must pay that rent to bid the land away from other competing claimants.

Quasi-Rent

Economic "rent" does not affect the *present* amount. A tough-minded logician could push us into a corner by asking, "Even for those goods that are produced every day, the currently available supply *is now* in existence no matter what its current price may be. Therefore, does it not follow that any payment for any existing good is an economic rent, in that it does not affect the current amount?" The answer is "Yes, but only momentarily."

The present price has an effect on future supplies, because expectations of future prices are not independent of current prices. Furthermore, very few goods are indestructible. To emphasize the impact on the *later production* of goods, economics has developed the concept "quasi-rent." A quasi-rent is a payment that has no effect on the amount of the good in *existence now*, but which does affect the *current or future rate of production* and hence the amount that will exist in the *future*. Payments for existing goods that will wear out are quasi-rents, for the current rate of production and the current rate of maintenance will depend upon current price.

Some goods that people think indestructible are really not. Land, for example, is surprisingly perishable. Its attributes include levelness, and absence of rocks, trees, and bushes if it is to be used for agricultural purposes. But any farmer can tell you these are perishable; he labors against erosion, loss of fertility, and growth of unwanted bushes and trees. Economic goods that require no maintenance are rare indeed—so rare that we cannot find one example.

Land Rent—A Taxable Surplus?

Some people, believing that the payments for some goods seem to be unnecessary to create either the existing or the future supply, conclude that its value is economic rent and should be taxed from those who get it. Prominent are the "single-taxers"—followers of Henry George, a nineteenth-century novelist and reformer, who believed that land rent is an economic rent and should be taxed away. (Somehow he overlooked an equally "pure" economic rent on another resource—beautiful women.)

Other doctrinaire advocates of taxing, or nationalizing, land rents are the socialists. The English Labour party theorists argue that landsite values reflect the actions of society as a whole and not the owners of a particular parcel of land. Therefore, the site rent should belong to all the people. This sounds plausible, if you are interested only in sounds. It fails to explain why every person in the society should have to bear the consequences of changes in value of every parcel of land—even those he will never see or have any effect on. Some people might not want to carry the risks of gains or losses to some particular parcels of land and instead might want to trade their share of those goods for risks of value changes of other goods instead. We can then re-allocate and specialize in bearing the risks of value changes from various goods among ourselves just as we now re-allocate ordinary consumption goods among ourselves to conform more to our personal differences in tastes. To do this would require private-property rights. But the socialist cannot permit private-property rights in productive resources. The socialists imply it is better that everyone have the same pro-rata nontransferable share in the value consequences of certain goods—hence those goods are socialized.

It has been argued that even if the land ownership were socialized so that the land rent went to the government, the *use* of the land would be unaffected, since the government would rent the land to the highest-bidding user. This could be correct if it were not for the difference in incentives. The incentive for a private owner to incur the expenses, risks, and trouble of discovering or creating the highest-valued uses is different from that of a government employee in charge of the socialized land. Further, the penalties for failure to find the highest use value are different. The government employee is less likely to put the land to its highest market-valued use. Whether this be good or bad depends in part (and only in part) on whether you think the highest-valued use as judged by individuals competing in the market, and reflected by market prices, is a good or bad criterion. It is a little early to hazard judgments about that. Many other differences between socialized ownership and private property remain to be investigated; for example, effects on ability to be different in beliefs, ideas, and behavior; willingness to produce new, varied goods; cultural mores; attitudes about personal responsibility; distribution of wealth; ability to communicate ideas with other people; costs of disagreeing with wealthy or politically powerful people; and discrimination by race, origin, or creed.

20, 21

Summary

1 Prices are demand determined, even though they appear to be changed with changes in costs.

2 Shortages of goods are implied by price controls. The resulting allocation of goods and services depends more heavily on nonpecuniary attributes of demanders and tastes of sellers—for example, preferences reflecting race, religion, family size, and personality. Some potential exchanges are prevented.

3 Prices (payments) not required for the current supply of a good (that is, rents) are important in directing the use of the good.

Questions

1 "Higher prices cause higher costs." Explain why.

2 "Allowing the prices of goods to rise in periods when none of the good is being produced is immoral, because the higher prices do not induce a larger output. They merely give unwarranted profits to those who are lucky enough to own the goods. Either prices

should be prevented from rising, or the government should take over ownership in order to prevent unjust enrichment." Do you agree with this analysis? If so, why? If not, why not?

3 When prices on the stock market fall, the financial pages report a surge to sell stock; yet every share sold is bought by someone. Why don't they refer to a surge to buy?

4 "Demand and supply is not simply a classification that is applicable only to private-property market exchange. Demand and supply is a categorization that is applicable to any problem of allocating scarce resources among competing uses. In any given possible use, the usefulness of the resource in that use is what is meant by its demand, while its usefulness in all alternative uses (against which this particular use must compete) is the supply." Do you agree? Explain.

5 The Council of Economic Advisers (to the President of the United States) once argued that keeping down the price of cattle could keep down the price of meat to the consumer. Explain how the application of economic analysis given in this chapter rejects that argument.

6 A distinguished professor of law has said: "Some people believe that every resource which is scarce should be controlled by the market. And since, in their view, all resources except free goods are scarce, all resources—even rights to radiate radio signals—should be so controlled. But surely some resources are 'scarcer' than others, and thereby possibly merit different treatment. It doesn't advance the argument very much to place a label of 'scarcity' on everything." Do you think economics should be studied by professors of law? Why?

7 "In the capitalistic system, only money or market values count in allocating productive resources." Evaluate.

8 "In capitalism, commercialism dominates and suppresses social, artistic, and cultural values." Evaluate.

9 When both are the same price, you choose a color television set over a black-and-white set; but when a black-and-white set costs half as much as a color set, you choose the black and white. In which case are you "discriminating"?

10 Which of the following choices involve discrimination? (a) Cadillac versus Chrysler, (b) Van Gogh versus Gauguin, (c) blondes versus brunettes, (d) beautiful versus homely women, (e) Negroes versus whites, (f) Japanese versus Koreans, (g) filet mignon versus hamburger.

11 "Under open-market, private-property pricing, a person is allowed to make any kind of appeal to a seller to get some of the good—even offering him money as a common medium of exchange for other goods. Under price controls, the buyer is told that there is one particular kind of appeal he cannot use—i.e., offer of a larger amount of other goods." True or false?

12 "With open-market pricing, housing units are scarce or expensive, whereas with rent control the housing market is characterized by shortages." Explain.

13 Do you think rent controls would be good or bad for each of the following: (a) Middle-aged couple who do not contemplate moving, (b) young married couple with two children moving to a new town, (c) Negro moving to a new town, (d) young person receiving a raise in salary, (e) old person in retirement, (f) person who likes to drink and smoke, (g) beautiful young woman, (h) homely immigrant, (i) Mormon in a Jewish community, (j) Jew in a Mormon community, (k) excellent handyman who likes to work around the

house and care for gardens, (1) old couple who have saved wealth and invested in apartment house.

14. "Price controls are used in order to give adequate housing to those in the lower-income levels who would otherwise not be able to afford it." Subject this proposition to economic analysis.

15. In Figure 7-2 (page 102), showing the demand for X by A and by B and the total demand, let price be held at p_1 by some legal authority. Suppose that one-half the supply is sold to A and the other half to B at the legal price. Show that A would prefer to buy some more from B. How much would A be prepared to pay, and would B find this a desirable trade—if it weren't for the legal prohibition against sales at a price above p_1? What legal inducements do you think A and B could construct to consummate a sale at the legal price p_1?

16. The military draft of the U. S. government involves price control—in which the maximum price that can be paid by the military services is set by law. As a result, the number of personnel demanded exceeds the supply *at that price*; but the buyers, instead of letting the sellers provide the amount they are willing to provide at that proffered price, resort to a compulsory draft to satisfy their "excess" of demand. Graphically, in Figure 7-2 (page 102), the price, military wages, is limited to p_1, at which the excess demand is obtained by the draft. Who gains what by this system of price controls? (Before presuming that military personnel could not be obtained by a wage system, note that the permanent military officers, the leaders, are obtained by a voluntary open-market wage system. So are policemen and firemen.)

17. News item (July 15, 1963): "Seoul, Korea (AP). The city government ordered the capital's 1,500 restaurants not to sell any meal containing rice during lunch hours. The measure is designed to encourage the customers to take other food. South Korea is experiencing a serious food shortage because of a poor rice crop." Would open-market prices achieve the same result? How effective will this measure be?

18. It has been argued that politicians tend to gain from price controls and hence they advocate them. What line of reasoning would support that argument?

19. Prices (tuition fee) for colleges are kept below the market clearing price in many colleges. Without inquiring why, explain how we know the price is that low. Applying the principles of competition when prices are kept below market clearing levels, indicate the kinds of non-price competitive payments or behavior (of competing student applicants) that acquire added influence. To whom are these other enhanced forms of competition for admission advantageous? Indicate (or conjecture) who captures the value of the excess of the market clearing price over the controlled price of the services of the colleges.

20. Which of the following do you think contain some economic rent? Insofar as any of them contains rent, for what is that rent unnecessary? For what is it necessary?
    a. The wealth of those who owned land in Palm Springs, California, from 1940 through 1960, when land values boomed.
    b. Elizabeth Taylor's income.
    c. The income of a genius.
    d. The income of smart students.
    e. The salary of the President of the United States.

21. "The rent for land in New York City is not a payment that is necessary to produce that land. It is a necessary payment to obtain use of the land. From the first point of view, it is an economic rent; from the latter point of view, it is a cost." Do you agree? If so, why? If not, why not?

Price-Takers' and Price-Searchers' Markets

8 THE analysis in Chapter 6 suggested there is a price for each good at which every buyer can buy as much as he chooses and every seller can sell all he wishes. That price is reached by open-market competition among many buyers and sellers, and is represented by the price at the intersection of the demand and supply curves. At that price, there would be no shortages, no surpluses, no queues of waiting buyers or sellers. There would be no sellers' advertisements; no seller would keep inventories awaiting customers. The facts of the world fly in the face of all these implications. What is deficient in that analysis? We can begin to overcome some of these defects if we categorize markets according to demand conditions facing a seller.

Price-Takers' Markets: Virtually Horizontal Demand Facing Individual Seller

A useful conception we have ignored so far can be framed in terms of the demand conditions seen by an individual seller. Consider first a seller who provides so insignificant a part of the total market supply of some homogeneous good that if he raised his asking price, his sales would drop to practically zero, or to zero in the extreme case. And if he withheld all his supply from the market, the effect on market price would be practically undetectable. If he lowered his price, the increased amount demanded would swamp his available supply. For all intents and purposes, the demand curve he sees facing him for his products is virtually a horizontal line at the prevailing market price. A slightly higher price would reduce his sales to zero while a slightly lower price would increase the amount demanded beyond the amount he can supply. In jargon, the

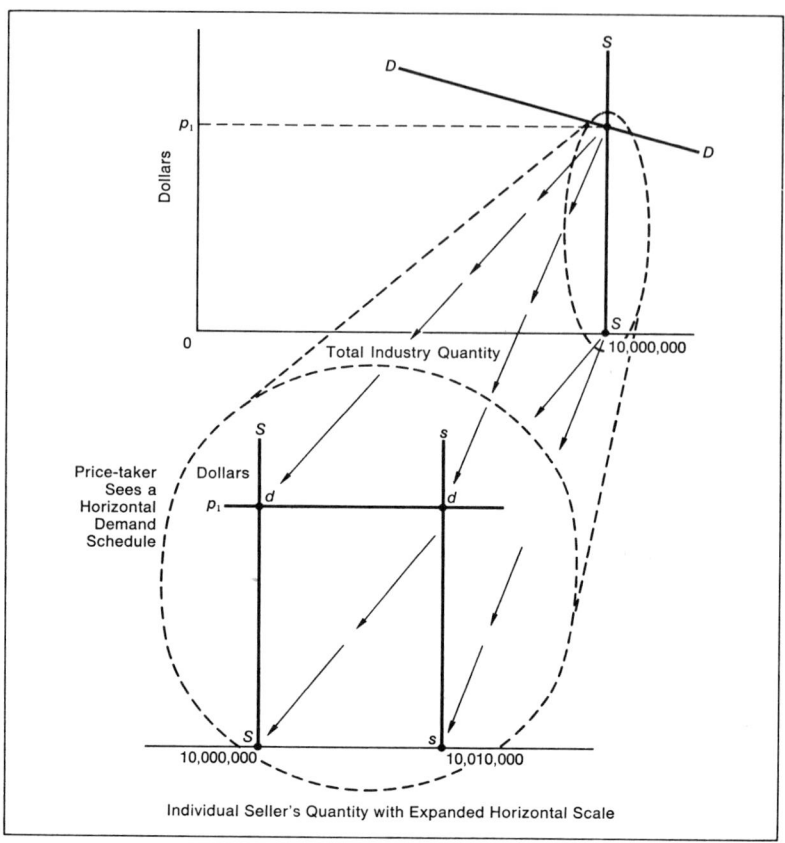

FIGURE 8-1. Price-Takers' View of Market Demand

Curves *DD* and *SS* are the market demand and supply totaled over *all* demanders and suppliers. Curve *SS* is a vertical line indicating an unchanging stock of the good regardless of current price. Each supplier accepts the market price given by the market demand and supply. The supply from any *one* supplier, shown by *ss* and measured from *SS*, not from the origin, is so small that even if it were withheld from the market the shift in the total supply along the total demand curve would have an insignificant effect on price. Therefore, any one supplier can sell all he has at the market price—a condition portrayed by a *horizontal* demand curve, *dd*, at the price p_1 for his product. This is the market demand for *his product*, not the demand by him for the product. The demand curve shown here is flat, at least until beyond the range of his supply. In saying that the demand line facing a price-taker seller is a *horizontal line at the existing market price*, we mean that the line is so close to being horizontal that a literally horizontal line captures all relevant features of the situation. The demand seen by the seller still conforms to the law of demand: raising the price sufficiently (and here the slightest rise is sufficient) will reduce (to zero) the amount demanded. The elasticity of demand facing him is essentially "infinite," because the slightest increase in price will result in a loss of virtually *all* his sales. The reduction in amount supplied in order to raise price by a tiny bit would constitute a large fraction (practically 100 percent) of any one supplier, but only a trivial fraction of the industry supply.

Price-Takers' and Price-Searchers' Markets

elasticity of demand facing him is infinite. A seller facing an infinitely elastic demand is called a price-taker.[1] This is also sometimes described as an atomistic market. For this kind of market situation, the price facing a seller is the market price, and he has no choice but to take that price as his selling price if he wants to sell any of his product. The situation is portrayed in Figure 8–1.

Market-Equilibrium Price

If the total community demand for a good should fall (meaning that the total amount that people want to have at any price is less than before), the equilibrium price will fall—as indicated by the intersection of the new lower demand and same supply at a lower price. In Figure 8–2, the demand has fallen from D_1D_1 to D_2D_2; and at the price p_1, which prevailed with demand D_1D_1, the amount of goods $X_1 - X_2$ would be unsold. Some suppliers have the choice of selling very little or nothing at the old price or of lowering the offering price to p_2, where enough buyers can be induced to buy the existing supply. The price-cutters can be thought of superficially as setting the lower price. Basically, however, the *reduced demand* lowers the market price at which the entire supply can be sold. The frustrated sellers *reveal*, rather than determine, the new market-equilibrium price. Price will fall to the intersection of the new lower demand and

FIGURE 8–2

Equilibrium Pricing, with Market Demand and Supply for Price-Takers' Markets

[1] In the literature of economics, this market situation—where each seller is faced with an essentially infinitely elastic demand for his output—has been given special names: "pure competition" and "perfect competition." These names are misleading, since this market situation is neither more nor less competitive than many others. We use the term "price-takers' markets" to describe a class of markets where every supplier (and also every demander) provides so small a portion of the supply (or demand) that his output (or demand) has no significant effect on price; hence, he "takes" the market price as if it were given by outside forces. The name "price-taker" apparently was first used by T. Scitovsky in his advanced textbook, *Welfare and Competition* (Homewood, Ill.: Richard D. Irwin, Inc., 1951).

supply curves, at which price every seller can sell all he wants and each buyer can buy all he wants. There is no pressure to lower price further.[2]

Efficiency of Extent of Exchange

In open *price-takers'* markets, with price equating amounts demanded and supplied, the personal value between any two goods is made equal for all individuals. If anyone values cigarettes more, relative to Cokes, he purchases more cigarettes and fewer Cokes per week so that the increased stock of cigarettes relative to Cokes in his consumption pattern reduces his personal valuation of cigarettes relative to Cokes. At the market-equilibrium price, for all persons with access to the market, no unexploited opportunity of trade remains to enable any person to reach still more preferred situations by revision of the allocation of goods.

Price-Searchers' Markets: Sellers Face Negatively Sloped Demand

In many markets the sellers are each sufficiently large suppliers relative to total amount demanded that each can set his selling price higher (and sell less), or lower (and sell more). We shall call these markets *price-searchers'* markets to emphasize that sellers must constantly search for the best price at which to sell. By "best" we mean the price that maximizes the income, wealth, or profits of the seller.

If a seller were faced with the demand schedule of Table 8–1, and each day had a supply of ten units available *at no cost whatsoever,* what price would maximize his

TABLE 8–1. Illustrative Demand Schedule with Marginal-Revenue Data

Price	Daily Quantity Demanded	Total Daily Revenue	Marginal Daily Revenue
$10	1	$10	$10
9	2	18	+8
8	3	24	+6
7	4	28	+4
6	5	30	+2
5	6	30	0
4	7	28	−2
3	8	24	−4
2	9	18	−6
1	10	10	−8

[2] We repeat an earlier warning. What is important is not merely that a change in demand indicates a changed intersection price in the demand and supply diagram, but that price will change *in order* to permit individuals to find and exploit mutually preferred exchange opportunities. If for some reason price were not allowed to change—because of legal or moral restraints on price changes—some buyers and sellers would be unable to discover feasible, mutually preferred exchanges. This does not mean that price *should* be allowed to change to permit those exchanges to occur. That depends upon whether or not one "likes" the consequences of an individual-choice, voluntary-exchange system. And many of these consequences still remain to be more fully revealed.

Price-Takers' and Price-Searchers' Markets

wealth? At a price of $6 per unit he will sell five, and at $5 he will sell six. Either way his total daily revenue is $30. No other single price for each unit gives so much. The price that maximizes his wealth is either $5 or $6, the equilibrium prices.

Marginal Revenue

The demand "curve" facing him is a negatively sloping demand "curve" with respect to price. To show the full consequence of the negative slope, we use the concept of *marginal revenue*—the *addition to total revenue* when *price is reduced just enough to sell one more unit*. In Table 8–1 a price of $10 per unit induces daily sales of one unit. Alternately, a price of $9 sells two units. Total daily revenue changes from $10 to $18, an increase of +$8, when two units instead of one are sold daily. The *increase* in total revenue, $8, is *not* the *price* of the extra unit sold. The $9 of the second unit is in part offset by the $1 reduction of price on the other one.

The fourth column in Table 8–1 shows the *changes* in total revenue between prices that are just enough different to increase the daily sales rate *by one unit*. For example, the marginal revenue for a sales increase from five to six per day is zero. This is expressed as a zero marginal revenue for six units (not for *the sixth*). Marginal revenue is −$2 when sales are at a level of seven, even though the seventh unit itself sells for $4. The data of Table 8–1 are plotted in Figure 8–3.

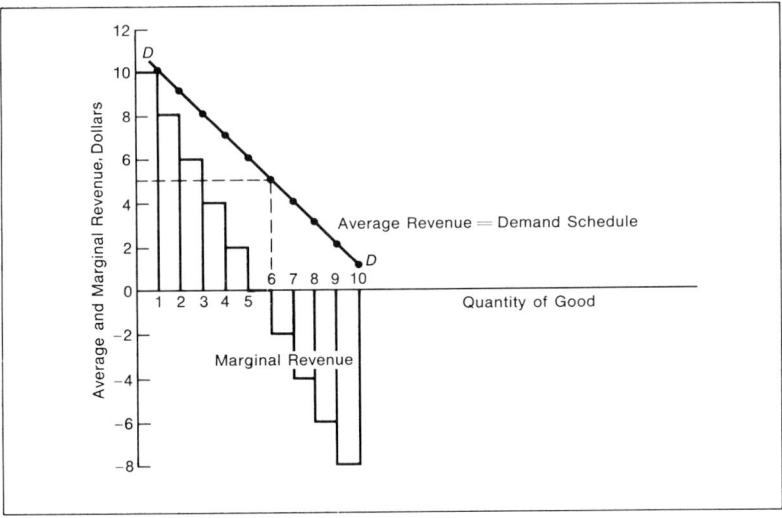

FIGURE 8–3. Average Revenue (Demand Schedule) and Marginal Revenue Seen by Price-Searcher

At a given rate of sales (for example, 6), all units sell at the same price ($5); marginal revenue is zero. The *area* of the rectangle, based on the quantity sold and the price (the average revenue), depicts the total revenue. If the price were *lower* by just enough to sell one unit *more* per day, the new rectangle's area may be larger or smaller than the old rectangle. If it is larger, total revenue is larger and marginal revenue is positive: the *increase in units sold at the lower price* brought enough additional revenue to more than compensate for the *lower price* on all the units.

The area within the marginal-revenue vertical rectangles from the vertical axis out to a stated rate of sales measures the total revenue. For example, at daily sales of six units, the total area of the marginal-revenue rectangles ($10 + $8 + $4 + $2) gives a total value of $30. This is also equal to the area of the dashed rectangle, one corner of which touches the demand curve at the five-unit, $6 price.

For the price-searcher, marginal revenue is *less* than average revenue (price). But for the price-taker, who can sell all he wants at the market price, the marginal revenue line is essentially identical to the average revenue line—the demand line facing him. If the price-taker sells one more unit at the existing price, his total receipts increase by the value of that increased unit of sale; there is not significant reduction in price on any of the units sold. Marginal revenue, which measures the change in total revenue, is virtually equal to the price of the extra unit sold. This is summarized in Figure 8–4. The concept of marginal revenue and its distinction from the concept of price is extremely important for much of the ensuing analysis. Learn it well.

5, 6, 7, 8

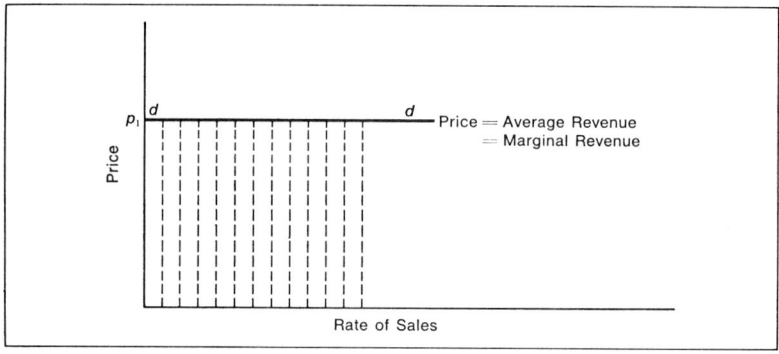

FIGURE 8–4. Demand Line as Seen by Price-Taker

Price-taker can sell all he has without noticeably affecting price, p_1. Hence each unit sold adds that unit's price to his revenue, because there is no noticeable reduction in receipts from the other units sold.

Elasticities of Demand Facing Price-Taker and Price-Searcher

The difference in demands facing a price-taker and a price-searcher can be expressed by the elasticity of demand. The demand for the price-taker's goods is almost infinitely elastic at the market price common to all the other sellers of that good. He can sell more without *any* significant reduction in price; and his sales would drop to zero with a rise in price. On the other hand, the price-searcher faces a much less elastic demand for his goods. The demand for his goods may be less than unity.[3]

---

[3] Review the meaning and measure of elasticity given in Chapter 5. Warning: only with *zero* costs of production would he seek to maximize total *receipts*—for only with no costs are receipts and profits the same.

Effect of Difference between Marginal Revenue and Price on Seller's Pricing Behavior

A significant difference between marginal revenue and price of each unit sold implies a difference between price-takers' and price-searchers' pricing tactics. Suppose the existing supply of some fine drinking water comes from ten wells owned by ten different owners, each of whom gets one gallon a day, with no costs of producing or bottling the water. A total of ten gallons is available every day. What will be the equilibrium price of water? If we knew the market demand we could tell what the price would be in a price-takers' market. Assume that the schedule in Table 8–1 is the demand for this water. With ten different sellers competing for buyers, the price will be $1 a gallon. At that price the amount demanded equals the amount supplied. Total receipts of the *group* of ten owners are $10 per day.

To contrast this with a price-searchers' market, let all the wells be controlled by a single agency representing all the owners (leaving for later a discussion of how this might be accomplished). Holding part of the water from the market, the single controlling agency could obtain a total daily revenue of $30 a day by raising the price to $5 (or $6) and selling only six (or five) gallons a day. Each owner would get $3 a day, even though only half the water were sold. Any other price would bring in smaller net receipts for the *group as a whole* (remembering that costs are zero). The agency would be delighted to sell more water *at the set price,* but no more is demanded. Rather than cut price to sell more water and thereby reduce net revenue to the group, the unsold water is wasted. A lower price would indeed sell more water, but the receipts from the extra water sold would be more than offset by the reduced receipts from the initial amount of water sold each day.

This example shows the potential wealth gain available *if* one could convert a price-takers' market into a price-searchers' market by coordinating or organizing all the price-takers into one agency or firm. (But beware of jumping to conclusions. It does not follow that all price-searchers are more profitable than price-takers.) The difference between price-takers and price-searchers is fundamentally a difference in the wealth-maximizing *output and price program,* not in the *amount of profit.* (It is true that in the *present* example there is a difference in profits, but we shall later see why the profits rest on another feature. For the moment we study the pricing process as a facilitator of exchange.)

In a price-searchers' market, less water is sold than in a price-takers' market—if the basic sources of water are the same. The equilibrium price is higher, and *the equilibrium extent of exchange is less.* If we define as inefficient any situation in which resource use could be revised to increase the utility of some people without reducing that of anyone else, then price-searchers' markets can result in inefficient exchange. Here the inefficiency is the nonexchange (nonuse) of half the water.

One warning: Although a price-takers' market was changed to a price-searchers' market by concentrating ownership of supply (which made the one gross supplier so large, relative to the market, that he operated along a significantly large range of the demand curve), it does not follow that the only, or even the most important, source of price-searchers' markets is concentration of ownership. Even if it were, one could not justifiably recommend, on the basis of anything investigated so far, a policy of enforced dispersal of ownership in order to create price-takers' markets as a means of achieving market-exchange efficiency.

Though you might be surprised, many people advocate laws to prevent exchange "efficiency." For example, compulsory licensing of doctors, required prescription of drugs, prohibition of alcoholic beverages, non-enforcement of contracts by minors, control of hours of business—all are examples of laws that restrict the extent to which exchange potentialities are achieved. Perhaps, after all, exchange efficiency is not "good," especially if it means that people will be more able to trade and consume some goods or services (marijuana, tobacco, alcohol) which *you* think, for their own good, they should not.

Another reason we cannot conclude that dispersal of ownership should be forcefully introduced is that the means of enforcing dispersal involves ancillary effects that should be known before concluding that dispersal to achieve efficiency is worth the costs. We are not yet in a position to do that.

How Price-Takers' and Price-Searchers' Market Behavior Differs

We have accomplished our first objective of this chapter—to explain behavior inconsistent with price-takers' markets where price is at the intersection of demand and supply schedules. (1) Not every seller sells all he would choose to sell at the current market price. And he refuses to lower price to sell more. (The price-taker seller could sell all his supplies at the price at which he could sell any.) (2) Unsold water is kept as an inventory he will happily sell if the amount demanded *at the current price* should increase. (The price-taker had no inventory for potential sales at the existing price.) (3) It will occur to the price-searcher that some advertising might increase demand for his product so he could sell more of the available water. (The price-taker, who could sell all at the existing market price, would not gain sales by advertising or get a higher price.) (4) Finally, the price to the price-searcher is not determined for him as if by some impersonal market mechanism. Instead he must search out the optimal (wealth-maximizing) price. And, not knowing the demand schedule exactly, he will have to resort to trial-and-error search processes. No demand-and-supply intersection principle determines his price, although the demand (and, as we shall see later, the costs of production) plays a crucial role in determining his prices. Finding the wealth-maximizing price is costly and risky. A revised price may take him away from that price. The costs of learning where his demand is and what his costs are may exceed the expected gain, if any, in profits. And even worse, as we shall see later, if the person in charge is not the owner of the enterprise, he will deliberately set price too low.

9, 10, 11, 12

Why Price-Searchers?

Having analyzed some elementary differences in pricing and exchange activities between price-taker and price-searcher markets, we can now add a few remarks about the *sources* of these different kinds of markets. This discussion will be incomplete, however, because some of the conditions are results of costs and production conditions, yet to be analyzed.

General Motors, a giant assembling almost half the cars in the United States, is a price searcher. So are U.S. Steel, Du Pont, Alcoa, and Boeing. And so is the tiny drugstore catering to its small neighborhood, as is every retail store. What attribute makes a price-searcher? His supply must constitute a significant portion of the total supply of the product in the market in which he is selling. The local grocer is a larger seller *relative* to the demand in his neighborhood. He can raise the price of his beans above that of neighborhood rivals and still sell some beans, although not as much as at a lower price. The local gas station can charge a higher price than its nearby rivals, and still sell some gasoline. Distinctiveness of product or seller's services means that there are separate though interdependent demands. These close, but differentiated, substitutes—such as brands of cigarettes, soap, gasoline, oil, cars, shirts, stockings—are not exactly alike in every respect. Customers discriminate among the myriad major and minor details of the product, associated service, and location.

Product Differentiation

Some people think that most product differentiation is silly. Are Chesterfields not the same as Lucky Strikes, Cokes not the same as Pepsis, and Palmolive not the same as Lux? All men are created equal; yet women are disconcertingly choosy. The difference between mink and rabbit fur is "slight," except perhaps to minks and rabbits. Yet the public's preference between them is enormous, even if it is all a matter of looks and feel. The difference between two gasoline stations may be merely in their location, some hundred feet apart. Yet that is enough to give one a preference. Ridiculous? Not in the eyes of the customer. The attendant may be more pleasant and cordial. Irrelevant? Not in the opinion of people. How many marital mates are chosen on more substantial grounds? Differences that do not matter to us will matter to others—and *they* may think that what matters to *us* is of no matter. You may think it really is of no matter whether you eat pork rather than beef, or meat rather than vegetables, or worship this deity rather than that one, or rest or work on Sunday; but many people do and have killed over such "trivial" issues. You could declare them prejudiced, ignorant, or discriminatory, but all you mean is that their tastes or preferences differ. And this should give us reason to pause before confidently asserting that buyers who discriminate among brands of cigarettes, aspirin, paper tissues, soap, corn flakes, or canned milk do so only because they are irrational, uninformed, or lazy.

The difference between two cola drinks, Coke and Pepsi, is minor, but real, in my opinion; at the same price I would always choose Cokes. If the former were priced 25 percent higher, I would still take Coke. But at a 100 percent difference in price, Pepsi would capture a dominant if not entire portion of my cola purchase. The smaller the difference between prices of goods, the greater is the influence of any other difference on the purchase decision. This is, of course, merely an application of our old friend, the law of demand.

Much product differentiation is "natural," and no one else, try as hard as he can, can duplicate the product or service. Racquel Welch, Johnny Carson, Bob Hope, and Arnold Palmer have attributes no other person can duplicate. Each is a price-searcher for the service he renders. Carson can raise his fees and still perform, even if less frequently. There is no legal restriction against anyone else's trying to copy Carson, but the consumer can tell the differences even without trademarks or copyrights.

Some preferences may result from ignorance (not stupidity). Sears' portable electric typewriter is the Smith-Corona typewriter, except for the exterior shell. The prices for the two are different, if you don't shop around for special sales or discounts. Some people do not know this, and hence they pay a higher price for the "identical" item (assuming that the value of the superficial design difference is less than the price difference). However, to point out that such behavior reflects ignorance is to say nothing useful, since everything we do reflects a lack of perfect knowledge. To say that buying behavior is based on ignorance would be more meaningful if one meant that it is based on the high cost of acquiring more information—because usually the extra cost is expected to exceed the value of the extra information. Why do I buy gasoline from the local distributor when it happens to be selling today at a lower price three blocks farther down the street? You may know it, but how am I supposed to know that if I drive around those three blocks I'll find a station selling gasoline at a cheaper price—ignoring considerations of convenience and quality of service.

Brand Names

For many goods the buyer never knows exactly what he gets until he has purchased and used the good. Not even the seller knows exactly how his product will perform in the hands of each buyer, because it is prohibitively costly to produce only goods that are so thoroughly tested—be they shoes or cars—that performance qualities are perfectly predictable. There is an appropriate degree of testing; the buyer and seller share risks of eventualities. Contracts can allocate all the risk to the seller, thereby raising the purchase price, or to the buyer, thereby lowering the purchase price. Or a combination can be achieved with some gross failure risks borne by the seller and the many minor risks borne by the buyer. Warranties, guarantees, return and exchange privileges, maintenance contracts, are some examples. Consider also the variety available when purchasing a TV set—or the variety of ways to get automobile services—leasing, renting, or buying.

The seller's reputation for standing by his product or for producing reliable products is another very important factor. High-reliability sellers normally get higher prices for their goods, not only because of high quality, but also high reliability of getting what was expected. Seller's reputations are built by proven reliability of performance. Even though a newcomer says his product is just as good, and even if it really is, how can the buyer be sure? How can the seller? Such information or proof or evidence is costly to establish and distribute. Brand names—the seller's mark—Kodak, American Express, Holiday Inn—represent verified, reliable standards of quality. The buyer is less uncertain of what he is getting than with less well-established brands. People who buy by brands are not silly people who with a little intelligent analysis should change their behavior. They are using economically efficient sources of information about product performance expectations.

The brand name is an indicator of reliability of future performance and saves the costs of obtaining information from other more expensive means.

You have only to imagine moving to a new community or country and trying to make purchases without knowledge of the brand-name reputations. We can see why established brand-name products sell better at equivalent prices or command slightly higher prices. In fact, one can argue with much merit that a major asset of the established companies with established reputations is exactly that established reputation.

When you select a marriage mate the family name tells you more than a little about the probable future consequences of the marriage.

Oligopoly

When the number of sellers of even an *un*differentiated, homogeneous product is so small that any action by one will induce the *other sellers to react in a way that the first seller must take into account,* the situation is called "oligopoly," meaning a few sellers (from Greek *oligi* for "few" and *polein* for "sell"). "Few" means sufficiently few that one has an effect on prices of *other* sellers and not merely his own prices. If the first party could ignore other sellers' price or service *responses* to his actions, the situation would be called "monopoly" or "price-takers." The cases called "price-searchers" include both the cases where competitor's *responses* to one's initial acts can *and* where they cannot be ignored. Oligopoly is a special subclass of price-searchers. This is presumably true for steel, copper, autos, nad aluminum. If U.S. Steel reduced output or raised price, the impact on sales of other firms (by shifting the demand curve facing those firms) would be sufficient to induce them to respond with a price change, which the first party would have anticipated. U.S. Steel would be aware of this response of other steel producers while considering its initial possible action.

Price-searchers, then, can be comprised of the many sellers of slightly differentiated products and also of the *few sellers of one product*. In this latter case, the sellers (1) are faced with negatively sloped demand curves and also (2) give heed to potential responses of other sellers: oligopoly.

Thus, although steel is produced by over one hundred companies in the United States, many are big enough so that if any cut production in half, the output of the industry would be reduced enough to cause a rise in price to its competitors—even if all firms did produce identical steel and sold it under identical sales conditions (as they do not). U.S. Steel Corporation certainly has the power to raise the price of steel for all steel producers if it is willing to reduce its output and income.

A question we *cannot* answer is "Why are some goods produced under conditions of oligopoly?" Except for laws that may prohibit entry of new firms, we can give no satisfactory explanation other than the question-begging remark that it depends upon the technological characteristics of the product or its production process.

Monopoly

A monopolist is sometimes said to be the only seller of a good, as if he faced no competition from close or distant substitutes. But the telephone company faces the mails, telegraph, microwave radio, or even personal travel. The electric company faces the competition of gas and oil and diesel generators for power and heat. The bus company faces taxis, private autos, rented autos, and walking. All goods are substitutable to some degree. But degrees are important. We shall therefore refer to the "monopolist" as the case in which a seller faces a negatively sloped demand curve but has no significant *reaction* from any other sellers in response to his pricing or output programs. Unlike other price-searchers, who also have negatively sloping demand curves, he is free of other seller reaction effects—as is a price-taker. But unlike the price-*taker,* who is free of reactions of other sellers, he does not face a horizontal demand at a going market price.

The distinction we have used between price-takers and price-searchers has hinged upon the demand conditions facing the seller. We have given relatively little attention to the reaction of other sellers, because for the moment we are interested in explaining why the behavior of market price cannot be typically categorized as one in which price is set at the intersection of a demand and supply curve—with no shortages, surpluses, queues, advertising, inventories, and conscious price administration by sellers. The negatively sloped demand facing each seller is sufficient to explain all these. The *interdependence* effect explains still more activities (i.e., oligopolistic behavior), but we shall postpone our consideration of that.

In using the word "monopoly," we have opened the door to confusions. To bar that door, we note that "monopoly" is often used in two different ways. (1) Historically, it means a grant of exclusive right to sell some good. The state would prohibit other sellers from access to the market. The market was closed to all except those given the monopoly franchise or license. Elizabeth I granted to Essex a monopoly on the importation and sale of French white wines, and to Raleigh the monopoly for sale of playing cards. These grants were rewards for special service to the Crown. The French state retained the monopoly of salt sales. Today, many governments retain monopolies in television, radio, telephone, and railroads. In most large cities, taxi owners constitute a legal monopoly in that no other people are allowed to enter the taxi business. The market is closed. This kind of monopoly we shall call *closed monopoly,* a shorter expression than "closed-market monopoly."

Sometimes the original seller can get laws passed prohibiting his customers from reselling. In many states milk cannot legally be resold by a customer. The ostensible reason is to protect purchasers from buying "impure" milk from intermediate customers (who, it is alleged, will "water" the milk to make an even greater gain). Power and gas are sold more cheaply to larger users, who by law cannot resell the power or gas to smaller users who pay higher prices charged by the power company to the smaller customers. Nor can one family purchase telephone service and then resell some service to a neighbor—say, by running an extension over to his house. In Chapter 19 we shall investigate some of the reasons advanced for these legally enforced restrictions on resale. Closure may not be absolute but only severely retricted. (We shall discuss that in more detail in Chapter 19.) (2) "Monopoly," in modern technical economics, also means a seller faced with a negatively sloping demand line for his product, *whether or not* the market is open or closed to other sellers. Both kinds of monopolists are called price-searchers, because the term describes pricing activity of sellers faced with a negatively sloped demand (whether or not in closed or open markets). But price-searchers in closed markets behave differently from those in open markets. Possibly it would be better to refer to "open monopolies" (open-market price-searchers) and "closed monopolies" (price-searchers in closed markets).

TABLE 8–2. Market Seller Classification Criteria

	Degree of Legal Restraint or Closure of Access to Market for Sellers	
	No restriction	Closed
Price-takers (Horizontal demand curves)	Open-market price-takers	Closed-monopoly price-takers
Price-searchers (Negatively sloped demand curves)	Open-market price-searchers or Open monopolists (Oligopolists, differentiated product sellers, monopolistic competitors, imperfect competition)	Closed-market Price-searchers or Closed monopolists (Cartel)

TABLE 8–3. Classification of Sellers and Markets

			Range of Entry	
			Open	Closed
Range of Elasticity of Demand Facing Seller	Infinite	Price-takers	Cattle growers, truck farmers, common laborers	Producers of wheat, oranges, cotton, tobacco, oats, lemons, milk Physicians, lawyers, longshoremen
	Less Elastic	Price-searchers	Retailers, movie stars, artists, most manufactured goods	Patented goods, taxis, local airlines, public utilities

Multipart Pricing

Price searchers' markets explain more than the defects we earlier noted with price-takers' market analyses. Price-searchers' markets help to explain the rationale of some relatively unusual pricing and selling tactics. Our price-searcher water-selling agency will not necessarily let part of the water be unused. There *are* tactics for selling that water and avoiding waste, even short of converting the price-searcher to a price-taker.

Sellers do not always permit the buyer to buy *whatever amount* he wants at a particular price; yet that was the only kind of offer considered in the preceding discussion. The seller might post a *sliding scale* of prices, with prices depending upon the amount taken. This procedure can get more income to the seller (while also increasing the amount of water sold). Imagine him to be faced with the simple demand schedule characterized by the data in Table 8–1. The seller has ten units available for sale each day, and it costs him nothing to produce them. (This last assumption enables us again to isolate selling policy from production problems.) How can he maximize his daily income? We know a flat price of $5 (or $6) will bring in total receipts of $30 daily, with sales of six (or five) units. And the remaining unsold units are wasted (unexploited exchange opportunities).

Our clever seller might tell the buyer that the price is $5 a unit only *for the first six units*. After purchasing the first six units, the buyer may, as a quantity discount, buy more at $3 each. The buyer will buy six at $5 each (paying $30) and then buy two more at $3 each. How do we know?[4] According to his demand schedule, he would have bought eight per day if the price had been $3 for every unit. From this it can be deduced that he will, after buying six at $5, demand about two more units if they are available at that price. Note that only two units are now left unsold—that is, the extent of exchange is increased, and waste is reduced.[5]

An even more clever seller can set up a more detailed schedule of discount prices and get still greater daily income from the sale of the water. If he knows the demand

---

[4] Review pages 57–60, if necessary.

[5] We are comparing two alternative cases: (a) buy eight units at $3 each—which is indicated in the demand schedule; and (b) buy eight units, six of them at $5 and two at $3. Certainly, the alternatives are not identical: total expenditure in the first case is $24, and it is $36 in the second. In the first case, in which all units at the same price of $3, the eighth unit is worth $3 to the buyer; but in the second case, in which he is $12 poorer, the eighth unit may be worth slightly less than $3. And the reason for this possible modification of demand may be labeled the "income (or wealth) effect." We shall discuss it further in the next footnote.

schedule for his water, the seller knows the buyer regards having one unit per day as worth $10 more than having none. Furthermore, if we continue to assume a negligible effect on wealth, the buyer would rather pay $9 more to get a second one daily than be confined to only one daily at $10. How do we know? The schedule shows he would buy two at $9 each rather than just one; therefore, a second one daily must be worth to him at least $9, given his current total wealth and state of preferences. This means we could induce him to buy two units daily in either of two different ways: (1) offer him all he wants at $9 each, or (2) offer him one for $10 and then a second one for $9.[6]

As a seller, you could offer the great bargain of "$10 for one or two for $19"—which is precisely the same thing as $10 for the first one and $9 for the second one. The buyer may think you are doing him a favor, and you are—compared to charging a price of $10. As a seller, you are interested in doing favors for other people insofar as the favor also improves your situation.

Why not offer the buyer three for $27? Then he can buy three at a cost of only $8 more than for two. According to the demand schedule, he will prefer to buy three for $27 rather than only two for $19. There are two ways of expressing your sale offer: (1) "One for $10, 2 for $19, or 3 for $27." (2) "Ten dollars for the first one, $9 for the second, and $8 for the third one." Either way, you will sell three and get $27 daily.

If you now offer the buyer a fourth one for $7 ("or four for $34"), he'll accept, because he would rather have a fourth one than $7. You now have total daily receipts of $34. Continue the process. Offer the buyer a fifth one daily for $6 (after he buys the first four on the preceding terms) or offer him a package of "five for $40." He'll take the offers. So extending the logic, offer him a sixth for $5 (or a package of six for $45); a seventh for $4 (or a package of seven for $49); an eighth for $3 (or eight for $52); a ninth for $2 (or nine for $54); and ultimately a tenth for $1 (or a package of ten for $55); at most, he would buy ten per day for a total outlay of $55.

You have made offers to the buyer that are just sufficient to squeeze from him approximately all they are worth to him. He gets no "consumer's surplus."

Before seeing where this kind of pricing is actually used, notice that it is equivalent, in extreme form, to what appears to be a still different pricing system. Suppose that, as the seller, you announce a fat daily *fee* of slightly less than $55, which entitles the buyer to have all he wants each day. He will take ten. (An eleventh is worth zero, so he is indifferent about whether or not he gets it.) The buyer pays almost $55 each day as a fee and then gets all the daily service he wants free (at no subsequent cost). This is precisely the same kind of offer as the earlier graduated sliding scale of prices.

We have used an extreme case of complete information to the seller (and we have ignored other sellers who might underprice him). This extreme example merely exposes the basis for multipart, or fixed-fee, pricing. If this theory is valid, we should observe this kind of pricing. And we do, though usually in much cruder form.

[6] What he pays for the first one is *almost* irrelevant in his demand for a second one. If he pays $10 instead of $9 for the first one, that would not reduce the value of the second one to him by $1, even though the effect of the $10 price for the first unit is to reduce by $1 his income available for *all* other things. This reduced-wealth effect will be spread over *all* his purchases. In fact, there *will* be a small effect on his demand for this article; and the amount he would be willing to pay for a second one, if he paid $10 for the first one, would be not $9 but, say, $8.90. A price of $10 for the first item and a price of $8.90 for the second would get two items sold for a total daily income of $18.90, compared with $18 for two units at a flat price of $9 each. As before, in order to avoid these minor adjustments, we continue as if the demand schedule stays unchanged, so that the seller can sell the first one for $10 and a second for $9.

Examples of Multipart Pricing

At the grocery, some goods are marked "15 cents, two for 25 cents." You may take the cynical view that quantity discounts make the price higher to those who buy only a few, or you may view them as a special favor to the customer who buys more. But this does not mean the seller must think of the device; the *buyer* can suggest it. The buyer, seeing unsold units, may suggest that the seller offer a volume discount. The arrangement can be viewed as a scheme whereby the seller squeezes most of the exchange advantage from the buyer, or a scheme whereby the buyer gains over the one-price system. In either event, the amount sold can, by multipart prices, be extended so that less is unused.

Electricity, water, and gas are almost always sold on multipart-pricing schedules, where the unit price depends upon how much customers buy. Telephone service and sometimes water are sold for a fixed total fee of so much per month, with the buyer taking all he wants. Social, recreation, and golf club membership fees are often flat "dues" per month. This kind of pricing will be viable provided certain conditions are satisfied, as we shall see in the next section.

Price Discrimination

In the preceding examples of pricing, the seller was charging a scale of prices to a given buyer, rather than a single price at which the buyer could purchase all he demanded. Now we inquire into tactics for charging *different* prices to *different* customers, with each being charged a price—though different from the other customers—at which he can purchase all he demands. Your campus book store probably sells to faculty at a lower price than to students. Airlines charge less to a wife or dependent under the family than to a nondependent for the same seat. Hotels charge different prices to commercial patrons than to vacationing travelers. This kind of pricing is called price discrimination—for the same good different prices are charged different customers. (Caution: the difference is not only an adjustment for differences in quality or attendant services.) What is the rationale and under what circumstances can it be successfully employed?[7]

It is necessary that customers differ in their demands for this seller's good—in particular the demand elasticities must differ among the customers. That is, the relative responsiveness in rate of purchase to a change in price must differ among the customers. Some must change their amounts purchased by a small fraction in response to a change in price, while others change their rate of purchase by a large fraction in response to a price change. In terms of marginal revenue (see pages 61–62), the marginal revenue from the former (small fraction changers or low-elasticity demanders) is lower than the marginal revenue of the latter (large fraction changers or high-elasticity demanders) at the price common to both sets of customers.

A lower marginal revenue from one class than another implies that if some output were transferred from the lower-marginal revenue customers and instead sold to the higher marginal revenue customers, the net increase between those marginal revenues would increase profits. How can a seller do this? Very simply. Induce less to be bought by the customers from whom the marginal revenue is low by raising the price to them. They will buy less but the reduction in receipts (the marginal revenue lost) will be less than the gain in receipts (the marginal revenue gained) from the other customers to

---

[7] You will find question 14 helpful in understanding the analysis.

whom price is lowered in order to persuade them to buy more. Therefore, charging appropriately different prices according to the elasticities of demand of the different customers enables units to be sold where the "last" unit sold in each adds as much to total receipts from one class of customers as from the other. In the final adjustment the marginal revenues from each class will be equal and no further revision in prices or of sales among the two classes is necessary. Prices will differ, but marginal revenues will be equal.

If the different classes of customers lived in areas sufficiently far apart a seller might set different prices, because the communication and transport costs between customers would be prohibitive to resale among customers. If one seller tried price discrimination it would pay some new seller to enter the high-priced district and by competition bring prices back to uniformity. So we have at least four requisites: (1) The seller must have some monopoly (negative-sloped demand) power, i.e., he must be sufficiently different from any other seller who might enter and try to provide the "same" services. (2) The seller must have customers with different elasticities. (3) Resale among customer classes must be prohibitively expensive. (4) The seller must be able to ascertain which customers have high and which have low elasticities.

These are not easy to fulfill, but they are sometimes possible. Take the first. Many sellers are so unique in reputation or talent or some quality that customers now regard no other actual or potential seller as being his equal in quality or reliability. Customers may have more confidence in the brand name, or maker, known as GE, GM, RCA, than in other sellers. Or a particular location or personality may not be reproducible by other potential producers. Such distinctions by buyers among sellers is not a result of irrationality or stupidity, as we have attempted to explain in a preceding section.

Take the second condition. If the various buyers have different degrees of confidence in the brand name, or if they have different personal costs of searching for qualities and prices of other sellers, or if their tastes for the particular seller's goods/services differ, or if the availability of near substitutes differs among the customers, they will have different elasticities of demand.

Take the third condition. Resale from lower-price to higher-price customers is not simple in the case of automobiles, or even groceries. And lastly, the fourth of these conditions. Can the seller tell which customer is which? Is it not apparent that on the campus the faculty has a more elastic demand for books—given its ability to buy more leisurely directly from the publishers? Is the demand by the wife to travel with her husband as little elastic as her husband's demand for business purposes? Hotels in resort areas typically give lower rates to residents than vacationers. Can you now conjecture why? In many cases it is relatively cheap to tell which customer is which. But if it is not, price discrimination will fail—as it will if any other one of the conditions is prohibitively costly to achieve.

You might think, correctly, it would pay to devise means of distinguishing among the customers with different elasticities. Then one could use or sell his schemes to merchants who would gladly pay for the opportunity. This has been done in many ways. Green stamps—as the stamps given out at many retail stores are typically called—is a fine example of this effect.[8]

---

[8] Yes, green stamps result in higher prices to inelastic-demand customers and lower prices to elastic-demand customers—if the stamp value *to* the customer is highly correlated with his elasticity of demand for the store's services. Housewives have high elasticity of demand because of ability to shop around, etc., while other buyers with inelastic demands have a high value on their time *and*

In this chapter, three kinds of pricing have been investigated. First, every buyer could buy *all he demanded at the market price* in price-takers' markets and also in many price-searchers' markets. Second, in some price-searchers' markets, a buyer was faced not with a single price at which he could buy all he demanded, but instead with a multiprice arrangement. The *"price" he paid for one more depended upon how many he would buy.* Third, the seller discriminated among his many buyers by charging *different unit prices to different customers*—with each being permitted to buy all he demanded at the price announced to him. Different prices to different buyers of the same good is called "price discrimination." For a further twist, contemplate a seller who could combine the second and third forms—separate his customers according to their demand elasticities to discriminate in the prices he charged and *also* use multipart pricing with each customer. We have not discussed examples of that, but it happens again that public utilities or monopolies relying on legal power to keep out competitors and to prevent customer resale appear to be the locale of this double discrimination.

Many people have asserted the normative proposition that price discrimination and multipart pricing are undesirable or socially wrong. We know of no objective basis for that judgment. The circumstances that permit that pricing should be investigated. Even if it turns out that laws like licensing, franchising, or patents restrict entry to the market and permit that kind of pricing, one must ascertain why those laws were instituted. It behooves an economist to assume that economic analysis provides a basis for a superior moral judgment about the laws that should prevail.

15

Wealth versus Utility Maximization

Have we been a little careless? How did *wealth*, or income, slip in to replace utility maximization when describing our sellers? The explanation is simple. One way to increase your utility is by increasing your wealth. You could work sixteen hours a day and get more money wealth than if you worked ten hours a day. But you would be sacrificing other sources of utility such as health, leisure, and recreation—losing more utility than the utility gained from money wealth.

In some situations these effects on other sources of utility are trivial. Suppose we are analyzing a businessman's pricing policy. If we assume that his decision to set a high or a low price involves no other factors affecting his utility, then we can concentrate solely on the wealth-maximizing effect of his pricing decision. Whether he sets a high or a low price, he will have to go through the same analysis and take just as much time and trouble. Therefore, he will pick the price that maximizes his wealth. In such cases we can simply assume he is a wealth maximizer—for that is now a special subcase of a utility maximizer. In other problems we shall not want to be so limited in our perspective, and we will then treat wealth as only one of the components that affect his decisions.

Some people honestly say they run a business for the fun of it, as is sometimes con-

---

are those who do not regard stamps as worth much to them. They do not bother to take them or save them. This separates the buyers into the two classes. If they don't take stamps, the retailer clearly gets a *net* higher price by not having to give stamps for which he has paid. If any customers do not save for later redemption, the purchase cost of the stamps to the merchants who give them out will be less. In either case, though not to the same extent in each, by first raising the price to all customers upon adopting stamps, and then giving stamps to customers, the effective price—or net price—including stamp value is reduced to the high-elasticity customers who tend to save the stamps, but not to the low-elasticity customers who do not take, save, or redeem stamps, because of the higher costs to them of doing so.

tended by owners of racing stables and professional athletic teams. Still, the higher the costs of that activity in terms of losses of wealth, the less likely will that hobby be sustained. Ultimately, utility maximization is the objective, but, as we have said, if some of its component sources, such as marketable wealth, can be increased without any decrease in other component sources, we can use wealth maximization as the proximate criterion.

Producer or Consumer Sovereignty?

"Consumer sovereignty" is often called a characteristic of the capitalistic open market, because ultimately the salability to a consumer determines a product's market value and hence profitability of continued production. Producers may decide what goods to proffer, but consumers decide which to prefer. Anyone can proffer a product, but he can't assure its profitability. Producers won't continue to produce goods salable at prices below costs—unless they do not care to maintain their wealth or are supported with funds from sources other than market sales receipts, such as tax-financed subsidies. To the extent the producer's wealth is less dependent on his production (e.g., absence of private-property rights in producers' equipment or closure of markets to other potential producers)—to that extent he is able to escape the force of consumer demand. So long as private-property rights exist in consumers' *and* in producers' goods, the consumers' market-revealed demand will control the viable, profitable output.

As we shall see in the next chapter, there are many situations in which a producer's personal wealth situation is less affected by the forces of the market in which he sells goods—e.g., as in firms that are not privately owned or are "not-for-profit." It should come as no surprise that market prices and consumers' preferences then play a reduced role. Whether that reduction is "good" or "bad" is a subject of moral, philosophical, and ethical debate.

On the other hand, though consumers may demand some good, if it is too costly or unpleasant for someone to produce, consumers won't get it. People's preferences for kinds of work—as producers—are equally important, as we shall see later.

16, 17, 18

Summary

1 Price-takers face a horizontal demand for their goods at the market price. Their marginal revenue equals price. For price-takers' markets, buyers and sellers can buy and sell all they wish at the prevailing price. Market price is accepted and not subject to change by an individual seller's supply situation.

2 Price-searchers face a negatively sloped demand for their goods. Marginal revenue is less than price. Price-searchers must search out and test the market demand to try to find the equilibrating (wealth-maximizing) price. With uncertainty and incomplete knowledge about the demand facing him, no seller can be positive he has found the wealth-maximizing price.

3 In price-searchers' markets, the disparity between price and marginal revenue can lead to an underexploitation of exchange opportunities. Pricing and selling tactics that increase the fulfillment of exchange opportunities include multipart pricing. Multipart pricing involves a sliding scale of prices rather than unit prices. For multipart pricing to be successful, subsequent exchanges by buyers must be prevented.

4 Markets can be distinguished by the degree of entry restraint. Sellers can be distinguished by the elasticity of demand facing them. A monopoly exists either where there is a legal restriction against new sellers who might enter the market, or where sellers have negatively sloped demand curves for their goods. "Pure competition" denotes open, price-takers' markets. Pure "monopoly" usually denotes closed, price-searchers' markets. Price-searchers in open markets are often called monopolistic competitors, imperfect competitors, or, if there are only a few interdependent sellers, oligopolists.

Questions

1 This question is designed to explain the demand situation facing an individual seller in atomistic, price-takers' markets. The community demand for wheat is shown below, in the vicinity of the market price, $2 per bushel. (Conventionally, wheat prices are expressed to the nearest eighth of a cent per bushel.)

Demand Function

Price	Quantity
$2.01	9,986,000
$2.00\frac{7}{8}$	9,987,000
$2.00\frac{6}{8}$	9,988,000
$2.00\frac{5}{8}$	9,990,000
$2.00\frac{4}{8}$	9,992,000
$2.00\frac{3}{8}$	9,994,000
$2.00\frac{2}{8}$	9,996,000
$2.00\frac{1}{8}$	9,998,000
2.00	10,000,000
$1.99\frac{7}{8}$	10,002,000
$1.99\frac{6}{8}$	10,004,000
$1.99\frac{5}{8}$	10,006,000

a. You have 1,000 bushels. The rest of the suppliers provide the remaining 9,999,000 bushels. Could you detectably affect the market price by withholding all or any of your supply from the market?
b. If you tried to sell at $\$2.00\frac{1}{8}$ while the market price was $2, would anyone buy wheat from you?
c. What does the demand curve for your wheat look like?

2 Suppose you had 6,000 of the 10,000,000 bushels provided by all the farmers.
a. Could you sell *any* wheat at a higher price than the market price of $2? How much would you sell if you asked $\$2.00\frac{1}{8}$? If you asked $\$2.00\frac{2}{8}$? $\$2.00\frac{3}{8}$?
b. Would it pay you to ask for a price of $\$2.00\frac{1}{8}$ in view of the effect on the sales revenue? What is your marginal revenue?
c. What does the demand curve facing you look like? Would you agree that it is, for all practical purposes, essentially regarded as a horizontal line at the market price?
d. Suppose you owned 1,000,000 bushels of the 10,000,000 bushels of wheat. Could you now affect the market price to a significant extent?

3 In a price-takers' market, does the marginal revenue of each seller approximate the average revenue (price)? Why?

4 If price is set by demand and supply in an open market, then which of the following will not be observed in price-takers' markets? (a) Rationing by waiting lists, (b) sellers who would like to sell more of their available supply at current prices, (c) buyers who want more at current prices than are supplied to them, (d) queues, (e) buyers forced to buy at least a certain quantity to get any at all, (f) tie-in sales, wherein to get one good you must buy some of another, (g) advertising, (h) inventories.

5 In a price-searchers' market, is each seller's marginal revenue approximately equal to price?

6 You own 1,000 shares of General Electric common stock. If you try to sell some, you find you can get a price of $61½ per share for all 1,000 shares. If you offer only 500 shares, you can get a price of $61⅝—12½ cents more per share. By reducing your amount sold by a half, you can get a price that is higher by about $\frac{1}{500}$. And if you sought a price of $61¾, you would sell nothing. This is an insignificant rise in price for you, but effective in reducing amount demanded as a result of withholding one's supply. Is this a price-takers' market? Compute your marginal revenues as best you can with the given data. Is the elasticity of demand for your shares high or low?

7 At a price-takers' market-equilibrium price, every buyer can get all he wants at the price; and every seller can sell all he wants to at that price.
   a. Do you know of any firms that do sell in price-takers' markets?
   b. Try tentatively to classify the following as price-takers or as price-searchers: (1) egg producers, (2) chicken farmers, (3) tomato growers, (4) crude-oil producers, (5) corner drug store, (6) local service station, (7) medical doctors, (8) music teachers.

8 Answer the following questions concerning the demand schedule below.
   a. Complete the total-revenue, marginal-revenue, and average-revenue data.

		Revenue		
Price	Quantity	Total	Marginal	Average
20	2	40		20
			+17	
19	3	57		19
			+15	
18	4	72		18
17	5	—	—	—
16	6	—	—	—
15	7	—	—	—
14	8	—	—	—
13	9	—	—	—
12	10	—	—	—
11	11	—	—	—
10	12	—	—	—
9	13	—	—	—

   b. What happens to the difference between selling price and marginal revenue?
   c. How many units would you want to produce and sell if you could produce as many as you wanted at an average cost of $8 per unit and if you want to maximize your net receipts (revenue minus costs)?
   d. What price would you charge?
   e. Could you charge $18 if you wanted to? What would be the consequences?
   f. What are the consequences of charging $14?

Price-Takers' and Price-Searchers' Markets

9 **a.** How can a price-searcher be searching for a price, when in fact there is available a wide range of prices—any of which he can charge?
   b. What happens if he is not good at finding what he is searching for?

10 Most elementary arithmetic books contain the following type of question: "Mr. Black, the grocer, can buy bread for 15 cents. What price should he charge to make a profit of 50 percent?" Without worrying why Mr. Black should be content with 50 instead of 500 percent profit, wherein does this question ignore a basic economic fact of life? Suggest a formulation of the problem that will enable students to learn how to manipulate percentage calculations without being taught erroneous economics.

11 Let the demand schedule of Table 8–1 (page 114) represent the characteristics of the demand for your services as a gardener, and suppose you sell in a price-searchers' market.
   a. What price should you charge per garden to maximize your daily net receipts if the "cost" of caring for a garden is zero?
   b. If your time is worth the equivalent of $3 per garden maintained, what price would you charge?
   c. Is this the "highest" price the traffic will bear, the highest price possible, the lowest price possible, or a "reasonable" price?

12 "A price-searcher does not have a supply curve, i.e., there is no schedule of amounts that he would offer at alternative possible prices, and which can be juxtaposed on a demand schedule." Explain why this is a correct statement.

13 You are buying trees to landscape your new home. The following demand schedule characterizes your behavior as a buyer:

Price of Trees	Quantity Demanded
$10	1
9	2
8	3
7	4
6	5
5	6
4	7
3	8
2	9
1	10

The price is quoted at $6. Accordingly, you buy five trees. Then *after* you buy the five trees, the seller offers to sell you one more for only $5.
a. Do you take it?
b. Suppose, strange as it may seem, he then offers you an opportunity to buy more trees (*after* you have already agreed to purchase five at $6 each and one more for $5) at the price of $3. How many more do you buy?
c. If the price had been $3 initially, would you have bought more than eight trees?
d. Suppose you had to pay a membership fee of $5 to buy at this nursery, after which you could buy all the trees you wanted for your own garden at $3 each. How many would you buy? (Assume price at other nurseries is $4, with no membership fee.)
e. If you could buy trees at $3 each from some other store without a membership fee, would you still buy only eight trees—saving the $5 for use on *all* your consumption activities?

f. Now explain why, according to the demand schedule, your purchase of eight trees at $3 each, at a total cost of $24, is a consistent alternative to your purchase of eight trees under the former sequential offers, in which you pay a total of $41 (five at $6, one at $5, and two at $3). (In this example we assume we can slide down an *unmodified* demand curve, because the required modification by the change in wealth is slight.)

14 In the text, two kinds of pricing by a price-searcher were discussed: (1) uniform prices to all buyers, at which each *buyer* can buy all he wants; (2) multipart pricing, in which a buyer cannot buy all he wants at one price; instead the prices depend upon how many he buys. We now consider briefly a third type of pricing policy by a price-searcher: he charges *different* prices to *different* customers—called "price discrimination." Within this third category there are two subcases: (a) "simple discrimination," where each buyer can buy all he wants at a price that is *different* from the price to other buyers; (b) "multipart price discrimination," where multipart pricing is applied to *each* customer, with different sets of prices to each buyer. We shall, with a series of questions, explore these.

a. First, we see how simple price discrimination among different customers can give greater revenue to the seller than uniform prices. Suppose you are a gardener and are faced with the following aggregate demand for your services from eight garden owners:

Price per Garden	Homeowners Demanding Garden Services
$10	1
9	2
8	3
7	4
6	5
5	6
4	7
3	8

If one customer cannot sell your gardening services to another customer, can you think of some pricing technique that would maximize your daily income without increasing your work, assuming that it always costs you $3 in time and effort to care for a garden? What prices are involved and what would be your income?

b. An obstacle to *discriminatory* pricing is that other gardeners will find it profitable to underbid your higher prices. They would offer to sell to your high-price customers at a slightly lower price than you charge. Several gardeners would, by competing, be led to a single price. You must prevent other gardeners from undercutting your higher-priced sales. But with open access to the market, there is no way to prevent them. (We shall later investigate some cases where markets are "closed" by government action to all except a particular class of sellers.)

c. Still assuming customers can be separated and other gardeners outlawed, we assume the *amount* of services demanded by each of two buyers is different and responds differently to price changes. Such a case is illustrated by the following two demand schedules of two separate customers.

Suppose you, the seller, have seven units of this good available. At any price you ask of *A* you must let him buy all he wants, and you must permit *B* to have all he wants at the price you ask of *B*; but the price asked of *A* and *B* can be different.

(1) What price should you charge *A*, and what should you charge *B*, if you want to maximize your revenue?

Price-Takers' and Price-Searchers' Markets

	Hours of Garden Service Demanded by		Marginal Revenue	
Price	A	B	A	B
$10	1	0	8	0
9	2	0	6	8
8	3	1	4	6
7	4	2	2	4
6	5	3	0	2
5	6	4	−2	0
4	7	5	−4	−2
3	8	6	−6	−4
2	9	7	−8	−6
1	10	8		

(2) If you charge the same price to both buyers, what is your best price and revenue?

(3) Suppose you can produce this good at a cost of $4 for each unit you make. How many should you make, and what price should you charge to A and what to B in order to maximize your net earnings? How many will A buy, and how many will B buy? What will be your net earnings?

(4) Construct an example of *multipart pricing* with *different sets* of prices to each buyer, so as to get still more revenue than with the preceding policy. Why do you think this kind of multipart plus discriminatory pricing is relatively uncommon? Can you give some examples of it? (Hint: Check the water, telephone, gas, and electric rates charged in your community; what prevents new sellers or customers from reselling to each other in all these cases?)

15 Consider another ingenious pricing policy: suppose that you are a movie producer and have made two movies: A, a social-problem-oriented drama, and B, a horror movie. You rent your pictures to various exhibitors, two of whom are "Roxy" and "Drivein." You know the amounts that Roxy and Drivein would pay for each movie rather than not get them.

	Maximum Values to Exhibitors	
	Movie	
	A	B
Roxy	$100	$70
Drivein	60	80

We now investigate three alternative price tactics.

a. Set a price on A, with Roxy and Drivein each being allowed to rent at that same price; and set another price on B, with each being allowed to rent B at that price. Under this arrangement the revenue-maximizing prices are $60 for A and $70 for B. Your revenue is $260.

b. Set a price on A for Roxy and a different price on A for Drivein. Also set different prices on B for Roxy and for Drivein. You may have four prices. What is the revenue-maximizing set of prices, and what is that revenue? ($310 is the total revenue.)

c. We come to the third alternative and the purpose of this problem. Suppose that you are *not* legally allowed to charge different prices to Roxy and Drivein. However, you do discover that you can engage in "block booking," whereby an exhibitor must take both pictures if he is to take any from you. What price (*same to both exhibitors*) would you set for the *pair* of pictures as one "block book," if you wish to maximize your revenue? What is the maximum revenue you can get this way? (Answer: $280.)

Explain how you determined the best block-booking prices. (Answer: For each exhibitor compute the sum of the highest amounts that would be offered by each exhibitor for each picture. Charge the lowest of these two sums as the price of the "block." As a seller, it pays to engage in block booking only if your customers assign different relative values to the various products in the block. To show this, try to get a gain—over uniform prices for separate pictures—by block booking when both exhibitors value the various pictures in the same relative way. Remember, in block booking you charge the *same package price* to all exhibitors. You will see that block booking gives no advantage to the seller, and no disadvantage either relative to the pricing tactic explained in b.)

d. The exhibitors Roxy and Drivein, who would prefer to prohibit block booking and discriminatory pricing, force you to sell the pictures at the same price to Roxy and Drivein, although permitting a different price for picture A from that for B. (In this case, as we have seen in part a, the most you could get is $260.) In an effort to keep down their costs, Roxy and Drivein complain to the government that under block booking you, the producer, really are "tying" B, the poor picture, to A, the better picture, in order to get rid of your inferior picture. They complain they do not have freedom to buy what they want and that you are an unfair monopolist. Explain why the complaint is in error. Is the producer forcing the exhibitors to buy goods they do not want? Explain why or why not.

e. What open-market forces reduce your power to engage in block booking? (Block-booking is used by TV networks.)

16 The market for economics professors in most colleges is completely open. No legal requirements about training or prior experience exist as a condition of teaching. A majority of the profession has opposed certification—under which a certification board, consisting of professors, would administer standards of competence. Consider the following:

a. If all present college professors were automatically certified (under a kind of exception called a "grandfather clause"), but all new entrants had to obtain certification by passing certain tests, would the market be open or restricted?

b. If the number of professors admitted were controlled by the board of college professors, which is what would happen, do you think they would restrict entry to the "needed" numbers and would keep out inadequately trained people in order to protect students? Would this have any effect on wages of college professors? What would be the effect on the number of professors?

c. Similar systems of certification (or admission or licensing or self-policing) are used by doctors, lawyers, pharmacists, architects, dentists, morticians, butchers, longshoremen, psychiatrists, barbers, and realtors, to name a few. What do you think it implies about the wages in these professions relative to wages in an open market? What does it imply about the quality of those who actually practice the professions? About the quality and quantity of services provided the community? Is there a difference between quality of competence of those certified and the quantity of service obtained by the public as a whole?

17 "Retail grocery stores are monopolies." In what sense is that correct and in what sense is it false? "The medical profession is a monopoly." In what sense is that true and in what sense false? Which kind of monopoly implies a higher price?

18 On a television interview a prominent theatrical producer expressed delight that tickets for his play had been sold out for the next four months. Explain why he might have cause to be very sad, rather than happy.

Nonclearing Market Prices

9 WITH an instantly adjusting market-clearing price, consumers can always buy all they want, given their incomes and tastes. No queues, waiting lists, reservations, or shortages exist. However, even a casual look at the world reveals queues, shortages, surpluses, unemployment, and inventories of goods awaiting buyers. Not all of these are explicable by statutory maximum or minimum price controls or even by price-searchers' markets. Clearly we must relax some more simplifying assumptions in our preceding analysis.

So far we have assumed that costs were zero (1) for obtaining information about potential bids and offers in the process of negotiating exchanges, (2) for using a money exchange system, and (3) for negotiating and enforcing contracts and property rights. (4) We assumed private-property rights in all goods and firms. We assumed (5) no public goods and (6) no philanthropic activity. We now relax all these assumptions, one by one.

(1) Costs of Information about Prices and Exchange Opportunities

Some observers of the economic scene who forget that information about potential bids and offers and attributes of various goods is not *instantly* available at *zero* cost to everyone regard markets as "imperfect." But we know that information is costly, as is the production of steel and wheat. If markets operate in ways not accounted for by our theory, the theory is imperfect.

If information about everyone's offer and asking prices and their potential buying and selling plans were instantly and costlessly available to everyone else, then indeed we would be hard put to explain the phenomena of slowly responding prices, "unemployment," and "idle" resources. Recognizing that information is costly and obtainable only with effort and expenditure of time, we should expect to see substantial resources devoted to collecting information about exchange possibilities. And we do. Real-estate agents, retailers, salesmen, brokers, and wholesalers act not only as sellers of goods but also as providers of information about goods and services and potential buyers and sellers. Housewives devote substantial time to comparison shopping and inspection of goods—that is, to collecting information about purchase possibilities. That a retail store provides information about goods as well as the goods themselves is made painfully obvious to those who try to buy only by mail order.

The graduating student looking for a job quickly discovers the cost of collecting information about the details of working conditions and wages of various potential employers. He spends hours and money learning about and comparing different employers. Information about more distant employers is so costly that often he doesn't try to get it. Similarly, employers devote large sums of money to telling students about working conditions and discovering the attributes of potential employees. Look, for example, at the advertisements of employers seeking employees.

If complete information about all job possibilities, all workers, and all goods were free and instantly available, there would be no point to shopping or seeking better offers. One would instead instantly take the best one. But information is neither free nor complete, despite the existence of markets which certainly do help to lower the costs. Consequently, people will devote resources to collecting more information so as to make better purchase and sale decisions. A failure to grasp this has led to much confusion and misinterpretation of the role of certain kinds of economic activity—especially much of that which is called "idleness" or "unemployment."

Before investigating some of the actions consequent to the cost of information collecting, we state four central propositions. (1) *Information is not free.* (2) *The more rapidly it is obtained, the greater the cost of information.* Making the search less hastily is less costly per unit of new information obtained. Production and acquisition of information, as with any other good, conform to the general laws of production. More rapid acquisition may or may not be worth the extra cost, as we shall see. (3) *Adjustment of resources to new uses or customers is costly, and the more rapidly a move is made the more costly it is.* Again, moving from one place to another or from one job to another uses up productive effort and resources. As with other production, "moves" are not free. (4) *Information about attributes of goods and about potential offers is sometimes cheaper to obtain with inventories of "unemployed" goods.* Inspection of goods is easier and cheaper if inventories are on display. It would be costlier to have to inspect items already being used by consumers prior to the order of similar items.

Given these inescapable costs of information, about potential buyers and attributes of goods, and about transfers of resources, how do people react to changes in demand for their goods and services? How do they collect information about the changes? What use activity is economical in the face of the costs of getting information? The behavior implied by the answers often gives rise to what are called "unemployment" and "idle" resources—with a consequent misinterpretation of the purpose being served by this apparently undesirable state of affairs. *This does not mean that all forms of behavior that are called unemployment are merely economic adjustments to the higher costs of acquiring information more rapidly; nevertheless we will see that many forms of it are.* Even in mass unemployment during depression, uncertainty and the cost of acquiring information play a vital role. But before we can conveniently apply economic analysis to mass unemployment during depressions, we must see how people react to the aforementioned costs.

Actions that Economize Information and Adjustment Costs and Increase Price Predictability

Buffer Stocks: Inventories

In the presence of uncertainty of foresight and recognition of information-collecting costs, stocks of goods are held in inventory, even though these may appear to be "idle" or "unemployed." They are more accurately identified as economical "information-collecting" uses of resources. Consider, as a simple example, the problem facing a newsboy who expects to sell at a stated price an average of one hundred copies of each edition of a local paper—but not exactly one hundred each day. He has several options: (1) spend money to find out who was going to buy copies each day; (2) stock fewer than one hundred and rarely have any unsold copies; (3) stock more and have copies left over; (4) stock one copy, and each time he sold one order another, getting special-delivery service. The first and last options are very costly. The more accurately he tries to predict or the more quickly he tries to adjust to demand fluctuations, the more expensive the process. Customers prefer to have him stock an excessive number on the average in order to have instant availability out of inventories, despite a slightly higher cost of the newspaper (implied by each seller's ending up with extra copies). The higher cost to customers need not appear as a higher money price; it may appear as a smaller newspaper or as fewer retailers. But this will be less costly than if the newspaper sellers attempted to obtain *complete* information or make *instantaneous* adjustments in the number of papers.

An apartment owner builds more apartments than he expects on the average to have occupied. It pays him to build more apartments in order to satisfy the unpredictable vagaries of demand rather than relying on instant fluctuations in rents to clear the market. The apartment-house owner could keep the apartments fully rented at a lower rental; or at a higher rental he can have some vacancies part of the time. In providing vacancies, he is catering to renters' desires to move when they want rather than making plans and reservations far in advance. The situation is exactly analogous to a person's building a home with enough bathrooms and dining space to seat more visitors than he will ordinarily have. To say he has "surplus," "idle," or "unemployed" bathroom or dining-room capacity is to consider only the cost of extra capacity and to misunderstand its value and to overlook the higher costs of alternative ways of obtaining equally high convenience or utility.

Empty apartments *per se* are not waste. They are a method of production to economize on the high costs of predicting the future and also of the high costs of *immediately* producing whatever a person wants. By producing in advance at a less hasty, more economical rate and holding resources available for contingent demands, we economize in having more housing services at a cost that is worth incurring, taking into account the value of being able to move without long, advance, "reservation-type" planning and higher search costs. We could reduce costs of housing *per se* by more advance planning of people's activities and refusals to allow them to change their minds, but this would also reduce housing services and convenience and raise other adjustment costs. There will also be an "extra supply" of service stations, barber shops, dress shops, real-estate agencies, insurance salesmen, and car dealers. The "extra" supply is an inspection supply or a convenience supply. Imagine what it would be like trying to move in a community that had as many apartments as families and every apartment was now rented. "Costs" would be imposed on tenants who wanted to move. Vacant apartments are "waste" only in an imaginary world of perfect predictability and full information at zero cost or in a world where instant production to every moment's demand is no more costly or troublesome than is advance preparation.

Buildings have fire escapes and residential areas have fire hydrants; first-aid kits are in homes and fire extinguishers in strategic places in buildings. Such provisions would be wasteful if information about the future were free and available immediately. Everyone could know early enough how to avoid catastrophes. Or if information were not free, but it were just as cheap to make instant physical adjustments as slow ones, then upon word of fire the building could immediately be altered to have fire escapes. Water lines could be laid to the site of the fire. This is fantasy; it denies higher costs for more rapid acquisition of information and more rapid subsequent physical adjustments. If "instant production" could be achieved at no more cost than less hasty production, if instant information were as cheap as less rapidly obtained answers, there would be no "idle," "excess," "unemployed" resources. But instant adjustments *do* cost more than less hasty adjustments. We therefore expect to observe what might foolishly be called "idle" resources.

Earlier chapters indicated that prices serve to re-allocate goods among competing claimants. How rapidly do prices respond to changes in demands? How rapidly and accurately are new alternatives revealed? Information about changing purchase demands and supplies is not free. An essential function of the market is to make that information more readily (cheaply) accessible. But it does not become "free."

Price Predictability and Stability in Face of Transient, Unpredicted Demand Fluctuations

Higher search costs imply more price stability in the face of transient, temporary, unpredictable fluctuations in purchase demand. A seller might instantly and temporarily vary the price upward or downward as inventories fell or rose so as always to clear the market to customers without their waiting in line. But imagine a restaurant in which the price of food varied instantly to newcomers to avoid their waiting in line. The greater the unpredictability of prices, the more would customers devote resources ahead of time to looking for sellers with lower prices at that moment. But persistently looking for places with lower prices is costly, and the higher the costs of search, the more people will prefer to stand in a line a bit. Some seller could set a predictably stable, slightly higher price (to cover inventory buffer costs), and customers would still prefer to patronize him because of their cheaper knowledge of the price they will face. Given these considerations, it will pay some sellers to provide inventories as a buffer to shorten queues and to reduce customers' waiting and search costs, especially where search costs are relatively high. For example, in the organized stock market, where costs of finding other sellers of a common stock like American Telephone and Telegraph are very low, prices will fluctuate more transiently and sensitively to transient purchase demands than in most other markets.

Imperfectly predictable transient shifts in demand and the costs of adjusting price instantly—costs both to the seller and imposed on the buyer by the unpredictability of price—imply a queue with some modest amount of waiting, which along with price will be an economical means of rationing demand. Our standing in line is not the only way that time enters into the rationing process. Some goods require more time in the act of purchase or consumption than do others. Getting a haircut may cost $3 but it also takes about half an hour, whereas one can buy $3 worth of gasoline in about 3 minutes. The total cost of a haircut is greater than the total costs of an equivalent *money*-valued purchase of gasoline. A round of golf may cost $5 and 4 hours, while $5 of nightclub entertainment will take only 15 minutes. The costs of some activity include not only the money price paid the seller but also the opportunities forsaken by the buyer— in this case measured by the time involved in acquisition of the good. The existing stock of any good or service is rationed among competing claimants partly by the money price and partly by the amounts of time involved in its acquisition; in addition, a price that is too low will create a line whose length will indicate the time costs which along with the money price clears the market.

Hence we observe various goods sold not only at different prices but also at different "time-costs" of purchase. Producers seek ways to reduce the time required for purchase as well as the money costs to the buyer. Some restaurants or stores give quicker service at a higher price, with a "total lower price" to the buyer. The money cost of a trip to Europe by air may exceed the boat price, yet the total cost may be less by air because of the smaller loss of opportunities for other activities by our not being confined to a boat for 5 days. As you would expect, those whose wages per hour are higher would have a greater demand for quicker service than those of equal income derived not from wages but from stocks and bonds. The conclusion from all this is that while we have in the beginning concentrated attention on the money price as the rationing, market-demand clearing variable, there is another important item—time cost for purchase. We shall not in this book devote as much attention to the influence of time costs or ways in which time costs are varied or adjusted to ration goods, other than to point out that they do. Our reason is twofold. First, the time cost to the purchaser is not "paid to" the seller as fully and directly as is a money price and hence has less impact on the producer's decisions, and, second, the analysis has not been so well worked out yet.

(2) Costs of Negotiating Exchanges and (3) Enforcing Property Rights

For market prices to guide allocation of goods, there must be an incentive for people to express and to respond to offers. If it is costly to reveal bids and offers and to negotiate and make exchanges, the gains from exchange might be offset. If each person speaks a different language, if thievery is rampant, or if contracts are likely to be dishonored, then negotiation, transaction, and policing costs will be so high that fewer market exchanges will occur. If *property rights* in goods are weaker, ill defined, or vague, their reallocation is likely to be guided by lower offers and bids. Who would offer as much for a coat likely to be stolen?

The higher market value attaching to goods with strong ownership rights spurs individuals to seek laws that would strengthen private-property rights. However, not all jurists and politicians have viewed with uniform sympathy the tendency to secure private-property rights. To the extent that private-property rights exist, the power of government officials to control uses of goods decreases; a major alternative to private property is government property. History is a long story of fluctuations and variations in this development. At times, private-property rights have dominated; at others they have been weakened and replaced by socialism, government ownership, or communal or tribal ownership.

Authority to Use Resources

Property rights of a person are the expectations a person has that his decision about the uses of certain resources will be effective. The greater the probability those expectations will be upheld in one way or another (custom, social ostracism, or government punishment of violators), the stronger are the property rights. Private-property rights in goods constitute the exclusive rights of the owners to use their goods, *and only their goods,* in any way they see fit, including the right to transfer these rights to other people. If, in using my goods, I affect your goods, then I am violating your rights to the use of your property. However, I can legally throw a rock through your window or tear down your house and occupy your land if, and only if, I obtain your permission or buy the rights from you. Exclusivity of control constitutes a basic component of the private-property economic system. We emphasize that property rights are *not* rights *of property*; they are rights *of people* to use of goods. In sum, two basic elements of private property are *exclusivity* of rights and *voluntary transferability* or exchangeability of rights.

It is silly to speak of a contrast or conflict between human rights and property rights. Property rights *are* human rights to the use of economic goods. Furthermore, a presumed conflict between human rights to use property and civil rights is equally vacuous. However civil rights may be specified, they do not conflict with human rights to use goods. A *genuine* difficulty arises from the differences afforded people in the protection of their rights. To protect property and the political rights of some people more than of other people is a source of much discontent and open conflict. But this real conflict does not pose any conflict of property versus human or civil rights—it poses an *interpersonal* conflict about whose, if anyone's, rights are to be more thoroughly respected and enforced. Minority groups, poor people, and the less educated are often said to get poorer enforcement service.

Transferability of Rights

Transferability is the right to exchange property rights with other people at terms that only the buyer and seller need approve. No third party can impose the terms. In a weaker sense, transferability could exist even if exchanges were permitted only at prices set by a third party. We do not exchange goods *per se*; we exchange *rights* over goods. Physical possession is not the essence of property rights; at best, physical possession is a means of asserting or giving evidence of rights.

A series of United States Supreme Court decisions vacillates between strong and weak transferability. Early in the nineteenth century, imposition of legal limits on prices was declared not to be a denial of private-property rights; but about fifty years later the decision was reversed. Subsequently, the Supreme Court again reversed itself and declared that price controls are not invasions of private-property rights as defined in the Constitution.

Exclusivity of Rights

If all the costs of use of a good are borne solely by the owner, there is said to be an identity of private and social costs; the owner does not inflict some of the cost on the rest of society. However, rights to control every physical attribute of goods are not always clearly assigned to particular people or owners. If I burn refuse or operate a factory so as to emit smoke, ashes, smells, soot, and airborne acids on and over your land, I am using my goods in ways that harmfully change "your" goods without your permission. When a neighbor walks his dog for its nightly relief, my property is damaged. When I drive my scooter with a blaring exhaust that sends sound vibrations across his property, I momentarily change its physical attributes for the worse. These actions change the characteristics of the goods other people are said to own—except that here the owner does not so effectively "own" rights to those affected attributes.

The costs of transactions comprise the costs of finding other people to buy the rights, to transport the goods to the market, to write up a contract of sale, to make the cash payment, and to assure the new possessor protection of the transferred rights. Millenniums ago man learned geometry and trigonometry and how to demarcate specific plots of land. Identification and, hence, sale and resale of land became cheaper and more prevalent. Today we are learning how to exchange and police rights over radio "waves," just as we do land rights. Airlines are learning how to keep track of planes with sufficient accuracy to measure, police, and exchange rights to moving cocoons of airspace. Water is still a relatively expensive item to control in its natural state, though not after it has been captured in reservoirs, canals, or pipes. Water meters are cheap enough to be used extensively in almost all cities. Therefore, pricing of water is used to ration and allocate water among most residential and industrial users, though not so commonly to agricultural users. "Shortages" of water are less likely to occur where meters are used since the price of the water can make the amount demanded equal to the amount supplied.

Undoubtedly the future will bring new, more economical metering, policing, or contracting devices for the control of water, streets, airspace, radio-TV, and the ocean floor. As radar ranges increase and boats become faster and use longer-range guns, greater distances from the shore can be policed and will therefore be worth claiming by the nearest country—as has already been done for oil rights hundreds of miles into the North Sea. Peru is selling rights to fish "her" ocean 200 miles out from the shore; this gives Peru an incentive to conserve the ocean resources rather than wastefully exploit them.

Exchanging Enforceable Rights

We now investigate examples of the effects of negotiation and property-enforcement costs on the prevalence of queues, waiting lists, and other (nonmarket-clearing price) means of allocating goods. If it costs a landowner more to collect the price and police the transactions for a parking space than the value of the parking space, he has no incentive to rent the space for parking. He either gives away parking rights "free" or lets no one park, depending upon the side effects. Formal market exchange and prices will be used only if devices are invented (for example, parking meters with police enforcement) to lower the costs of exchange (or if the demand rises sufficiently to raise the value above the costs of policing contracts). In European countries where labor is cheaper relative to land values than in the United States, the cost of using parking attendants to collect fees and police the space is lower relative to the value of the space. Therefore, we observe a greater use of such attendants than in the United States.

The variety of prices of theater seats is affected by the cost of ushers to enforce multiple-sectioned seating. If ushers' wages are high relative to admission prices, fewer ushers will be used; this will make it more difficult to ensure that those who pay premium prices are the only ones in the premium seats. In Europe, because of the lower wage rates *relative* to values of theater seats, there will be a greater variety of price classes than in the United States. Various seats within the theater will be priced more closely to the price that equilibrates demand with supply. There will be less incentive to come early to stand in line to get a "good" seat; good seats are not then allocated on a first-come, first-served basis. Otherwise, the better space is rationed by the cost of standing in line—which is a cost to be borne by the standees. This means it cannot be asserted that a lower than market-clearing price lets people get goods at a lower *cost*. If the buyer must wait in line, he must include the waiting as part of the cost. The longer the line, the greater the "standing" costs. It is "time and standing" that now clear the market.

Parking meters permit cheaper metering of street parking, so more of the spaces can be allocated by money prices. Why don't market prices control the allocation of *traffic lanes*? As yet no one has devised an economical way for drivers who want to use the parking lane for a traveling lane to bid away that space from those who want to park. The cost of negotiating these exchanges far exceeds the value to one buyer.

Similarly—partly because of the high costs of negotiating exchanges—the market exchange system has not been used for allocating radio and television programs to listeners. In the past, it was simply too costly to provide an electronic device whereby a receiver could pick up a program only if he had paid for it. Economical cables have now been developed, but the U. S. government has restricted their use. In 1970, restrictions were relaxed so pay TV appears on the verge of enormous expansion.

Another example of economical market-exchange operations is the coin vending machine. Telescopes at viewpoints operate with coin-controlled machines; some airport waiting rooms have coin-operated turnstiles to allocate seats in which patrons can view airport operations; coin-operated devices control access to dormitory rooms and restrooms for travelers between flights. We have coin-operated rental typewriters at libraries and pay telephones. (Why not "pay" drinking fountains?)

A capitalist system is aided by cheap transferability and exclusivity of rights. When these rights do not prevail, or are "expensive" to define or exchange, the market exchange system fails. Other forms of competition for determining uses of goods dominate. Examples are plentiful. (1) The western states fight each other in the courts over use of water from various watersheds, but they don't fight about the use of forest timber, oil, iron ore, coal, or other "natural" resources—because rights to water are not transferable as are those for oil and lumber. Government agencies allocate water, whereas no agencies are required for wood or oil. (2) Traffic conditions on streets and behavior on public beaches are examples of rights-claiming competitive behavior with "fleeting, insecure, undefined, nonexchangeable" rights to road space. (3) Sewage provides another example of unusual competition: cities upstream dump sewage, and cities downstream bear the consequences; so each city is tempted to build a pipeline farther upstream nearer the source to catch purer water.[1] *Excessive* pollution arises because of expensive or ill-defined or ill-enforced property rights to the resource being polluted.

(4) Allocation under Rights Other Than "Private Property": Nonprofit Institutions

The preceding analysis of pricing and exchange referred to private property. Let us examine behavior under forms of property rights that are not what we ordinarily call private-property rights. We shall consider nonprofit institutions and state- and city-owned property.

In a *nonprofit* corporation, there is no group of "owners" who can decide to distribute

---

[1] A more complete investigation of the effects of costs of enforcing private-property rights on production is given in Chapter 23.

the net gains to themselves as their own wealth, as can be done in a for-profit corporation. Funds must be spent in the enterprise to further the purposes of that enterprise. Most private colleges are nonprofit institutions, and resources must be devoted to the educational aims of the institution, although precious few colleges cover their costs by tuitions. Most charitable foundations—for example, the Ford and Carnegie Foundations—are nonprofit organizations; all their income is to be used not for the benefit of the trustees but to further the stated aims of the foundation. The Rose Festival Association, the Metropolitan Opera Association, and almost all religious and fraternal organizations are nonprofit institutions.

Remember, the discovery of the *best* selling price of your product is no simple matter. You have to incur time and trouble doing research to estimate and search for that price. And you never can be sure you've found it. But for every dollar's worth of time or cost devoted to getting a better estimate of that price, what would you get for yourself if the proceeds went to some other people who themselves could not treat the proceeds as "theirs"? Who will reward you to the extent you would if you owned the business, or if you were working for someone who did? No one. Hence, your incentive as the person responsible for searching for the profit-maximizing price, is reduced. Not only that, you will be induced to set it too low! Look at a sample case, the Rose Festival Association, to see why queues, shortages, and "low" prices are likely to occur.

Rose Festival Association

Each New Year's Day, for the Rose Bowl football game in Pasadena, California, sure as fate, more tickets are wanted than are available at the price set by the Association. Some buyers offer higher prices to get seats; and yet the Rose Festival Association and the associated colleges refuse to accept those offers and persist in selling at a lower price to students, alumni, and Rose Festival Association affiliates (and to 2,000 winners of a race to get to the Rose Bowl box office for a special "public" sale). Furthermore, the Association and the universities declare it illegal for anyone to resell his ticket to some other person at a price higher than he originally paid for it. (The authors, from personal experience, know that many tickets *are* resold at $40 premiums.)

Why does the Rose Bowl Association refuse higher offers from frustrated buyers? Why does it refuse greater wealth? The Rose Festival Association is not *privately owned* in the conventional sense. One-third of the gate receipts are used to finance its activities, such as providing the game, the Rose Parade, and other civic affairs. One-third of the receipts goes to each of the participating universities and their athletic conferences. But no person can claim any *pro rata* part of the proceeds as being "his"; no one can spend the net proceeds in the way he could spend his privately owned wealth. In these circumstances, will the operator-members of this association—those who set its policies and determine the specific activities—behave as they would if they owned the association?

Forget that there is a large association, and assume one person (call him the manager) makes the decisions. At what price shall tickets to the football game be sold? The answer, in accordance with our familiar principle, will be "at the price that maximizes the decider's utility." He could set too low a price, so that more seats are demanded than are available. He might then, by virtue of his position, secure tickets and resell some at market-clearing prices, thereby unethically diverting wealth to himself. Being a moral person, he eschews *this* line of "gain." He can still gain utility by this "too low" price policy. First, by under-pricing the tickets, he can buy tickets for himself more cheaply, thus releasing a bit of his own private wealth for other uses. Second, the excess demand for tickets enables him to extend favors to selected applicants for tickets. This means that the "right" people can get tickets at a price less than they *and others* are willing to pay. In return, his prestige is increased: he is invited to the best places, clubs, and circles; and even when he buys a car or furniture, past favors are fondly and effectively recalled. Third, too high a price would leave empty seats—which would look bad—though this maximized receipts because of inelastic demand. This price policy will cost the association some income. Although smaller receipts for the association reduce the manager's own utility, he must weigh this reduction against utility increase from being able to distribute tickets cheaply to favored people.

But if the association were a privately owned corporation with private-property rights residing in the stockholders, the *owners* (stockholders) will have a stronger incentive to fire him or place him on a commission basis, to reduce the discrepancy between realizable and realized income.

Let's strain the analysis a bit further. If there are several kinds of seats, which seats will be underpriced? Primarily the kind that the manager and the association members would want. These are the best seats. Market-clearing prices should more likely be charged for the inferior seats that go to people who are neither students nor alumni, and the facts agree.

There is still more to the situation, for the universities surely should want maximum receipts and therefore should oppose underpriced tickets. But the "universities" also are nonprofit, nonprivate-property institutions, and so the *individuals* who make the decisions on this matter are also acting in the absence of private-property rights. The university administration of athletic affairs is like the Rose Bowl administrator. Thus, the same story is repeated.

Other Nonprofit Associations

Nonprofit corporations under research contracts to the federal government (for example, RAND Corporation, Aerospace, Franklin Institute) will allocate their available resources with a weaker incentive to maximize wealth. They will have incentive to provide services in a more expensive manner, with smaller profits. Why? Because no one could claim the sacrificed potential savings in the same sense that a privately owned, for-profit organization's owners could. Costs to the managers of exercising their idiosyncratic tastes are lower. Managers like pretty women, so they will have prettier secretaries, even if they ask higher wages than less attractive secretaries. If the managers prefer whites to equally productive but lower-priced Negroes, the managers will hire fewer Negroes and more whites. Furniture and equipment will be more luxurious than for employees doing the same quality of work in private, for-profit businesses. Such are the implications of economic analysis. And data being collected are slowly providing corroboration.

The foregoing considerations may be interpreted as favorable or unfavorable to the private-property system, depending upon whether one prefers that allocation respond to the wealth influence of other people via the marketplace. The analysis is simply an indirect application of the law of demand in alternative property-rights contexts: "The lower the cost, the more of a good that is demanded." The cost to the manager of a nonprofit association of engaging in activities costly to the organization is lower than for the manager of a privately owned organization. Why? In the latter, the cost (forsaken wealth) to the organization is more fully imposed on people who could have had that forsaken wealth: The forsaken wealth is more effectively impressed on the manager as a cost that he must bear in a lower salary or a higher probability of losing his job. In strict logic, the analysis implies that only with private property will market prices behave as equilibrium prices. However, notice that the *law of demand* holds, no matter what the form of property right and regardless of the extent to which formal market exchange is used.

7, 8, 9, 10, 11, 12, 13

(5) Public Goods

So far we have dealt only with goods for which (1) the utility a person gets depends upon how much of that good he has *and* (2) the more he has of that good the less someone else *must* have. The hot dog I eat is one no one else will enjoy. Only my utility depends upon the amount of hot dogs *I* get. However, for some kinds of goods, the amount I consume does not reduce the amount you can consume. I can view a television program *and* you can too. My viewing is not at the cost of your viewing (*once the program is put on*). The same holds for some forms of national defense, which means more for me with as much for you, unless it is a kind of local antimissile defense for your town rather than mine. "Public" (or "collective") goods are those for which *the extent of consumption or use by one person does not diminish the amount available for other people* (*once the goods are produced*). For "private" goods, more for one person means less for someone else. Some goods have mixtures of private- and public-good attributes. A band concert has both attributes. The space around the band is limited, and a better space for some of us means a poorer space for others.

Some examples of goods almost exclusively composed of public-goods attributes are mathematical theorems, TV and radio programs, songs, poems, technology, ideas, and knowledge. One person's use of an idea does not prevent anyone else from using it. One viewer of a TV program does not displace another.[2] For pure public goods there seems no point in requiring someone to give up some other goods in exchange since (once the pure public good is created) any person can have as large a part of the available amount as he chooses without anyone else having less. No rationing price is necessary, for *there is no rationing problem for the existing amount of the pure public good*. There is no reason to have the existing public-good service moved toward users with the higher personal valuation for the good, as for hot dogs in a private-goods system, because everyone can simultaneously use all that exists.

Be careful of jumping to incorrect conclusions. Some have concluded that it is wrong to permit pay-television, because the price charged for looking at a program would wastefully dissuade some viewers without making more available to others. This is correct *so far as it goes,* but it doesn't face all the inescapable issues. Allocation or utilization of the service *once it is created* is only part of the problem. The decision of how much and what kind of public goods to produce also must be faced in a world of scarcity. Public goods are not "free" goods; they are scarce. Those who advocate pay-TV are concentrating their attention on bringing to bear viewer's direct influence on what and how much shall be *produced* and who should bear the costs.

Although pure public goods pose no *rationing* problem, there is the problem of determining how much and which public goods to *produce*. Production is not costless. If no price is charged, how can its value to society be determined relative to other goods? Potential users of new public goods are tempted to conceal their valuations so someone else can be inveigled into paying, then those who do not pay can, *once the good is*

---

[2] However, teaching it to one person does not automatically teach it to everyone else. So knowledge is not a pure public good, because more for me will mean less for you—since resources are used to teach me rather than you.

produced, use all that is available without having borne its production costs. Concealing one's demand for a good could be prevented if the provider of the public good could exclude that user unless he paid a price to have the public good. The provider would have to know what price the user would be willing to pay for the amount available or at least charge a price not in excess of that value. For some public goods, it may be impossible to exclude nonpayers; we shall call those special public goods "collective goods," to indicate that though the consumption or use of that public good by one person does not reduce the amount available to any others in the community, it is also impossible (or too expensive) to exclude any user who does not pay something for the service obtained.

Some amounts of services with some goods with public-goods attributes are produced outside the normal market-exchange private-property system. Often they are produced by government and financed by taxes or fees for the services, as in England where radio and some television are provided by the government and financed by a tax on every receiver. In the United States, national defense is provided by government and financed by taxes. And if you don't pay taxes you'll be excluded! In cities and towns, police protection is financed by taxes, although in some cities private police forces are bought by those desiring more police protection.

A few more remarks are appropriate. If there are two potential users of a unit of a public good, one valuing it at $10 and the other at $20, and since *both* can enjoy its services, that unit of service would be worth $30, not merely the $20 of the single highest-valuing user. The value of another unit of such services is the public's *summed* value of $30 since *both* people get their individual values. Another unit of the public good would be produced if it cost up to $30 and if the *sum* of the individual private valuations were *brought to bear as an inducement to production.* If the users do not or cannot express the *sum* of their values, there would be too little produced, according to users' valuations.

It is not demonstrable that the solution to the problem of determining how much of which public goods to produce can best be solved by government or socialist methods. Similarly, it is no solution to say, without recognition of differentiating attributes, that public goods should be produced and distributed just like private goods. Each method involves "undesirable features." To analyze this further, we must know some principles of production and its control. Then later, in Chapter 13, we shall return to study some techniques of distributing, producing, and financing public and collective goods.

(6) Philanthropy

Charity or philanthropy totals to billions of dollars annually. Charitable foundations and colleges are two prime examples—not to mention religious groups and individual gifts. Musical concerts, museums, libraries, and art galleries are open to the public at prices far below those that would clear the market, precisely because the sponsor wants to be charitable. The Ford, Gulbenkian, Mellon, and Rockefeller Foundations, to name but a few of the largest, are supposed to give wealth—not sell it. Almost every college provides services at less than costs, because they are supported by people who want to give educational opportunities to (*smart*) young people. In all these cases of charity, because the price is zero, a long list of applicants must be screened on some other competitive, discriminatory basis. How do the results differ from those of market-price competition? Economic analysis will shed light on that question—perhaps with some surprises.

Nonclearing Market Prices

The *economics* of charity or gifts may seem contradictory. If, according to economic theory, people seek to increase their utility, how then can they give gifts? Are these acts to be set aside from economics as unexplainable behavior? Not at all. I may believe that other people should consume certain goods, and I may so value their doing so that I am prepared to pay. Thus I pay to have milk and food for my children. I may so value other people's reading of good literature that I am willing to pay to make it available to them. For this kind of situation, we see people engaging in charity or philanthropy.

The postulates of economic theory do not say that man is concerned only about himself. He can be concerned about other people's situations also.

From my point of view, I would rather you were richer than poorer, even if it cost me something. It is even possible that a $1 decrease in my wealth could reduce my utility by *less* than a $1 increase in *your* wealth would increase *my* utility. Then I would contribute wealth to you. That is irrefutable, by definition. But the likelihood of this happening is greater if my wealth is large and yours is small. And that is a refutable proposition. As my wealth increases relative to yours, my willingness to contribute to you will increase, just as an increasing amount of candy increases my willingness to give up candy for Cokes. (This is postulate 4.) Furthermore, a *matching grant* would induce me to give still more, because now I know that each dollar I give up gets you more than $1. This implies that matching grants should be commonly observed in charity. And they are.[3]

Who Gains What from a Gift

A gift (unintentional or intentional) can be defined as an allocation at a price set below the open-market price by those "giving away" the goods. Suppose I own a house that would rent for $100 monthly in the open market; however, I offer it to you for only $40 as a favor. Suppose you would not have paid $100 for this particular house, but would have been prepared to pay $80 for it. We now have three valuations: A—the market rent of the house ($100), B—the price at which you *would* have been willing to rent the house ($80), and D—the actual price of the house to you ($40). We want one more item of information: How much would you have spent on housing if I hadn't made you this special offer? Your answer we shall suppose to be $65, denoted by C; that is, you would have chosen a smaller or inferior house than the $100 one I offered for $40. The following new concepts can now be specified. The difference between A and D (i.e., $A - D$) is the total wealth transferred *from* me, the donor. The house is worth $100, and I get only $40 for it. In this transfer of $60 of wealth from me, what did you get?

First, compare what you did pay, $40, with what you would have paid for some house ($65) had I not provided you with this unusual opportunity. This difference $(C - D)$ is ($65 - $40) $25, a measure of how much *money* you can release every month from housing purchases and use in any way you like. We call this an increase in your "money" wealth, a gift of $25 to you. The quantity $(C - D)$ *could* be negative, indicating that the recipient would have spent less on this kind of good than if the subsidy had not been offered.

Second, compare the cost of whatever housing you would have bought had this special offer not been made with what the house that I made available is worth to *you*. This difference $(B - C)$ is, in our example, $80 - $65 = $15. You now have $15 more of wealth in the *specific* form of housing than you otherwise would have had.

Of the $60 wealth transfer, we have accounted for $40: $25 $(C - D)$ as a *general*

---

[3] Income-tax reductions for gifts are another way to reduce the donor's costs of giving money to other people—by making other taxpayers pay more to offset my reduced tax payments.

(money) wealth increase to you and $15 ($B - C$) more of a *specific* resource, housing; that leaves $20 ($A - B$) unaccounted for. As far as *you* are concerned, that extra $20 is simply wasted: you have acquired for $40 a house that you value not at $100 but at only $80. Although I have borne a cost of $60, the gift is worth only $40 to you. From your point of view, if I had given you $60 in money to spend as you wished, you would have been better off by $20. This "waste" (from your point of view) of $20 is the third component of the $60 gift.

Don't forget *my* (the donor's) point of view. Is there a waste of $20? If I am fully aware of these implications, and nevertheless choose to make the particular gift that I do, then from my point of view it is worth $60 to me to give you the gain of $25 in cash and $15 in superior housing. It is worth more than $20 to *me* to induce you to live in a house that costs $100 (but which you think is worth only $80). I put you in an environment that I prefer for you.

For *every* instance in which goods are transferred (from me to you) at less than the free-market exchange-equilibrium price, we can summarize the analysis succinctly if we let

A be the market value of the transferred goods.
B be the hypothetical price which, if existing, would have induced you to buy the good.
C be the money you would have paid for whatever amount of the transferred good you otherwise would have purchased.
D be the amount actually paid by you.

Then,

($A - D$) is the net total cost to me of the resources transferred to you which can be subdivided into the following three components:
($A - B$) is the waste, from your (the receiver's) point of view, but not necessarily from mine (the giver's);
($B - C$) is the value to *you* of the extra specific resources made available to you;
($C - D$) is the general-purchasing-power wealth transfer to you.

We have ignored the impact that opportunities to capture subsidies or gifts will have on the behavior of potential receivers in their attempts to qualify for the subsidies. Prospects of competitive applicants can be improved if they spend money or direct their activities so as to reach a more advantageous position, as judged by the allocative criteria used by the donor. Each applicant will be induced to spend an amount, at the most, equal to the value of the subsidy as valued by the potential recipient. This is an extra waste not included in the prior concepts—and sometimes an important source of livelihood for those who can help applicants qualify for these gifts. Examples are lawyers and public relations experts.

Business Dinner Dance for Employees

To illustrate the consequences of a gift, let us apply the analysis to an employees' dinner dance sponsored by a business firm. Suppose the cost of the dinner is $14 per person, but the company sells tickets to employees for only $6. Question: Who gets what by this company gift? The quantity A is $14, the market value or cost of the service being sold for $6, which is denoted D (using the letters in the earlier example). We now consider employee I, who we ascertain would have spent $14 on a dinner dance anyway, even without this subsidy. His C is $14. We also learn that he would have been willing to buy this particular dinner-dance ticket even if the price had been the full $14. His B is also $14. Now we can carry through the computations. The company is spending $8 per ticket as a subsidy $(A - D) = (\$14 - \$6) = \$8$. Employee I gets a cash gain of $8 $(C - D) = (\$14 - \$6) = \$8$. His gain in *specific kind* of goods is zero, for $(B - C) = \$14 - \$14 = 0$. From his point of view there is no waste, for $(A - C) = \$14 - \$14 = 0$. The subsidy has given him simply a cash release of the full amount of the $8 subsidy, to spend however he wishes.

Consider employee II, who does less dinner dancing and would have spent only $7 for dinner dancing in the absence of this particular party. His C is $7. Suppose further that he would have been willing to pay $9 for this particularly elaborate party if the price had been that high, but he would have refused this particular party if the price had been higher. His B is $9. For him, $C - D = (\$7 - \$6) = \$1$; he gets $1 cash gain. His $(B - C) = (\$9 - \$7) = \$2$, which means he gets $2 (as he values it) more of dinner dancing than he otherwise would. And the third component $(A - B) = \$14 - \$9 = \$5$ is a measure of the waste of company money. The company spent $14 for something worth only $9 to *him*. Of the total $8 net cost to the company, $5 was a waste and $2 went to give employee II more dinner dancing than he otherwise would have had, and $1 was his cash gain.

And then there is employee III, who doesn't think the dinner dance is worth even $6. He buys no ticket and gets no gain of any kind.

Question: If you were the owner of the company, what would you think of partially subsidized dinner dances as a scheme to aid the employees to have a good time? Which employees?

Reconsider employee II, who would have paid $9 for a dinner-dance ticket. Why doesn't he play it smart? Why doesn't he buy a ticket for $6 and sell it to some outsider for $14, thereby gaining $8? This is better for him than the alternative gain of $1 in money and $2 more of dinner-dance activity. But the company prohibits him from doing so, probably because the managers don't want outsiders at the dance. Then why doesn't he resell the ticket to some other employee? There are two cases to consider. On the one hand, the supply of tickets at $6 may be large enough to provide all that the employees want at that price. But if the supply of tickets is not large enough at $6, the lucky employees who first get tickets could resell them at a higher price and take their gift entirely as generalized money gains, rather than as less-valued dinner-dance activity.

Would reselling to a fellow employee thwart the intent of the company managers? Did they want to encourage dinner dancing by employees? If so, allowing employees to resell will not reduce the number who attend. If the management wants more dinner dancing, it has to subsidize more tickets. The effect of permitting resale is to break the connection between dinner dancing and gifts, allowing some gift to those who don't dinner dance.

To make this analysis strike home, inquire if on your campus the faculty have special parking rights not granted to students. If so, apply the above analysis to discern what gains the faculty get and what would be the gains if they could sell the parking rights to students. Also apply it to student admission procedures at your college.

Foreign Aid

The United States government grants aid (gifts) to some foreign governments, ostensibly for specific purposes. If the U. S. government gives $10,000,000 to the Egyptian government to build a dam, what has Egypt gained? What would the Egyptians have done without the gift of aid? Suppose they intended to build the dam anyway, financing it by domestic saving. To that extent, a gift for the dam releases wealth of the Egyptian government for other things. The gift purportedly "for a dam" is actually for general purposes—the Egyptian government now simply has $10,000,000 more than it otherwise would have. Conceivably it could lower taxes—thus giving the Egyptians that much more income for general consumption—or the government itself will spend the extra funds.

Why, then, do we give the money "for a dam"? One possible answer is that otherwise they would not have built the dam, so that the gift does provide one more dam. The embarrassing implication of this answer is that this particular use of the money for the dam is so unproductive that the Egyptian government itself wouldn't have paid for the dam. Or, if they were too poor to have done so, a simple gift of $10,000,000 to the Egyptians with no strings on its use would have enabled the Egyptians themselves to decide what were the most valuable uses of the extra $10,000,000 of wealth made available. Of course, government officials of both the United States and Egypt understand all this, and the "conditional" form of the grant is employed primarily to try to induce the Egyptian government to behave more in accord with the interest of the U. S. government.

Free School Transportation

Children in some public-school districts are given free bus rides to school. From this gift (subsidy) of bus rides to school children, who gains what? The answer should now be easy. The parents of the children must be classed according to those who would have provided transportation for their children and those who would have made their children walk. The first group receive all the subsidy as a general increase in their wealth. They can buy more of all things with the wealth which otherwise would have paid for their children's transportation. The other parents get no gain in general wealth, but take it all in the specific form of better transportation for the children. "Free bus rides" for school children turn out then to be composites of gifts of wealth to parents and of better transportation for children, with some families getting all of it in general wealth, some in mixtures, and some exclusively in more transportation.

The corollary of our general proposition is that gifts might as well be resalable or given as money by the donors to the extent that the recipients already possess or use the services or resources given to them. If I am given a case of Coca-Cola each month by some kind-hearted person who thinks he is inducing me to drink more Cokes, he should note that already my family consumes a case a month. Therefore, I shall temporarily stop buying Cokes from the store and use the released wealth for other purposes. Whether he gives Cokes (whether or not he lets me sell them) or money is essentially irrelevant.

Unintentional Charity

Intentional and unintentional gifts cannot always be distinguished. Nor, as we shall see, can we conclude that every allocation of resources made at less than a market-clearing price, even at a price as low as zero, involves a gain to the recipient. Fortunately, intent is not necessarily to discern what happens.

Currently, anyone wanting to operate a new television station must first obtain permission of the Federal Communications Commission (FCC). Rights to operate a station are valuable, and many applicants appeal to the FCC for authorization.[4] Each will try to show why he is the proper person. How? In sales of government-owned forests and oil lands, the "right" person is the one who will bid the most, with the proceeds going to the public treasuries. But the law creating the FCC forbids it to allocate channels on the basis of competitive money bids. Nor is "first come, first served" the rule (although it was for radio in the early 1920s). Instead, the commission in some unspecified manner chooses among applicants.

The applicant is asked to show why the community "needs" another station—over protestations of the existing station owner, whose television station's value would fall. Because there is no money-price competition of the open-marketplace variety, other competition in terms of applicants' attributes takes on more significance. Money that would have been paid to the government under price competition for that right or "property" will instead be devoted, at least in part, to competition for the commissioners' support. Since something worth millions is at stake, duplicative millions are spent seeking the license.

On what criteria do commissioners select the winner? That is what the various applicants would like to know. They do know that the applicant should be a man of respectability, good moral standing, public service, and high education. A newspaper publisher or a radio-station operator has an advantage, for he is experienced in news collecting and dissemination. If he doesn't put on religious programs, if he plays only jazz and Western shows and intends to present few if any "cultural" programs, he will lose competitive rank. He must detect the preferences, tastes, and kinds of shows that commissioners think the public ought to be shown; then he must suggest that he will present those programs. He must be careful not to offer explicit, detectable bribes to the commissioners. On the other hand, if in the past he hired some of the FCC technical staff to operate his other radio or television stations, or if he is an ex-congressman, or if he employs an ex-congressman as a legal counsel to advocate his case to the FCC, this indicates that he recognizes able people, and he therefore could successfully operate a television station. All the value of the rights to broadcast accrues neither to the federal taxpayers nor to the winning applicant; instead, part is consumed in legal fees, costs of publicity, production of kinds of programs the FCC prefers, and other expenses to win the license. Thus, even though the nominal price of the license is zero, the costs of getting it are substantial—not to mention the costs of the losers' efforts.

The magnitude of the gift is revealed by the jump in the stock prices of companies that receive a license. Fortunately for the station owners, this wealth gain *is* transferable; they can sell that station to other people instead of keeping the gift in the form of a television station. Was it the intention of the government to make a gift? The *motivation* of this rationing procedure is to "safeguard" the public and to provide to the public what is "good." The preceding illustration does not imply that the Federal Communications Commission acts irresponsibly. The commissioners act just as anyone else would in the same situation.

More examples could be presented. Competitive prices are not used initially to allocate

---

[4] The number of channels that could be used at one time is not a technologically fixed constant. It depends upon the kind of receiving and transmitting equipment. With more expensive and sensitive receivers and transmitters, the number of available channels could be greatly increased. And the possibilities with cable are enormous.

licenses to operate (a) scheduled passenger airplanes, (b) liquor stores (in many states), (c) taxis (most cities), (d) banks (most states), and (e) sugar beet and tobacco farms in the United States. But these rights are salable once they have been awarded. For example, the right to operate one taxi in New York City sells for about $25,000.

Nontransferable Gifts

There is a class of possibly unintended gifts where the allocated goods *cannot* be re-allocated or resold after they are initially allocated. Rights to enter college, obtain a medical training, enter the United States, join some unions, adopt a child, play golf on a publicly owned golf course, camp in a national park—these rights often are allocated at zero prices or at prices below those that would clear the market. (Consequently, there are "shortages" and allocation by methods discussed in the earlier examples.) Whether or not the allocated item is subsequently resalable does not destroy the fact of gift. However, that affects the extent to which the gift can be realized as an increase in the recipient's general wealth, instead of only as a gain in a particular kind of good. For example, when a municipally owned golf course underprices its services and has a waiting list and "shortage" of playing space, those "lucky" enough to get access receive a particularized gain—if they haven't had to pay other costs to get on the reservation list.

Nothing in economic analysis warrants a judgment about which allocative procedures are good or bad. That judgment must be based on criteria derived from other sources.

Conclusion

This chapter completes our analytical survey of various modes of allocating *existing* goods among competing consumers. That analysis helps to discern effects of various modes of allocation, but it does not provide a *criterion* for evaluating them. Evaluation is a matter of personal ethics. Probably it is safe to say that no one believes that fully utilized exchange opportunities for all goods for all people are desirable (children, slavery, opium?) or, on the other hand, that no exchange should be allowed. We conjecture that most disputes about the desirability of various allocation methods reflect difference in (1) attitudes toward individual responsibility, etc., and (2) in understanding how different allocative markets and systems operate. This second source of dispute, we hope, has been reduced by the preceding analysis, which attempted to clarify how things do operate, not how the world ought to be.

Summary

1 The extent of mutually preferred revision of goods among consumers is affected by the costs of obtaining information about bids and offers for goods or their uses, by the costs of negotiating a binding exchange, by the costs of policing the contract, and by the kinds of property rights people have to the goods. The higher those costs or the more weakened are private-property rights, the less will mutually preferred re-allocation of goods occur.

Noncleaning Market Prices

2 High market-exchange costs and weak private-property rights will induce both greater use of nonmarket exchange and prices below the highest personal valuation of the goods. Nonmonetary attributes will have an enhanced weight in determining allocation. Nonprofit (that is, nonprivate-property) institutions provide weaker incentives to decision makers to utilize market-clearing prices.

3 For private goods, the amount of service a person gets from the good affects how much others can have; in particular, the more one person has, the less others can have. For public goods, the amount of service one person can have from a good does not reduce the amount others can have, once the good is created.

4 A positive (greater than zero) price for a public good is not necessary for rationing purposes, since anyone can have as much as is available, without reducing the amount available to others. Prices could be charged for a public good, so long as the price did not reduce the amount any one person wanted below the amount available; any price in excess of that would unnecessarily reduce his consumption. Prices for a public good would have to be different for each consumer if no one is to be restricted to less than total amount available. Charging a price, while not necessary for the rationing task (since there is no rationing problem), would serve as a guide to production of more or less of the public good. The price relevant for this valuation is the *sum* of the individual prices charged various users.

5 Philanthropic and charitable behavior is consistent with the economic laws of demand and supply.

6 Charity involves some combination of (a) gifts in kinds, (b) gifts of general purchasing power, and (c) waste from the recipient's point of view, though not necessarily waste from the donor's point of view. The recipient does not necessarily get net gain over market-clearing prices, since he may pay in equally costly activity to obtain priority for the nonmarket-allocated goods.

7 To the extent to which gifts are marketable by the recipient, he can convert his gains, if any, into monetary equivalents, rather than necessarily taking them in the particular "kind" of good in which the gift was granted.

Questions

1 Distinguish between the law of demand and the law of price that says price equates the amount supplied to the amount demanded. Which holds more generally?

2 It has been estimated that carrying a spare tire on automobiles costs the public about $150,000,000 or about $5 per year per car. Is this a wasted, idle resource? What do you think it would cost if that figure were cut to zero by not carrying spare tires at all? Do you think it would be cheaper to make tires more durable and to devote more resources to handling emergency "flats"? What evidence can you cite?

3 You are planning to build an apartment with eight units. You are told you can add a ninth unit for an extra cost of $10,000; and, if the extra unit is occupied all the time, it will be worth $15,000. If occupied three-fourths of the time, it will be a breakeven proposition.
   a. Would you then consider building more apartments than you could expect to keep always rented?
   b. Would you consider that apartment to be unemployed when not occupied?

c. Would you consider every unemployed person as a "waste"?
d. Why?
e. Is there any distinction between unfortunate and wasteful?

4 a. Can you make an estimate of the fraction of your wealth tied up in resources designed to ease the consequence of your own unforeseeable changing demands or circumstances?
   b. How about the amount of money you hold; items in the medicine cabinet; waiting time for a haircut in the barber shop; food kept at home in the refrigerator, freezer, and in canned goods? Are these idle, unemployed resources?

5 If a cheap enough method could be invented for metering the extent to which each motorist uses a street, would use of streets be rationed more with a price system? Do you know of any such cases now in use? Name two.

6 Shopping centers often provide free parking spaces. In effect, the shopping-center merchants provide free parking for some nonshoppers so that their customers will find adequate space. Some allege that the number of parking spaces is excessive (that is, more resources go into the provision of parking space than should) where the space that "should" be available is the amount that would clear the market when a charge is levied to cover the construction and maintenance cost of the parking space. However, policing "pay" parking space involves a cost of estimating charges, collecting fees, and prosecuting violators. Does the fact of that cost mean that it might be "better" to provide "too much" parking space than to provide the "right" amount with a price rationing system? Explain.

7 Churches are typically nonprofit institutions. Can you think of a problem in allocation of church facilities that is solved without use of the price system?

8 The college you now attend is almost certainly a not-for-profit institution. Are any of its resources allocated at less than market-clearing prices? (Hint: Library facilities? Athletic facilities? Counseling? Course admission? Campus space?) Who gains by the power to select admissible students?

9 "To the extent that nonprofit private institutions do not use the price-exchange system to allocate resources, they are operated inefficiently." True or false? Explain.

10 Camping fees in almost all state and national parks are so low that people want more space than is available.
   a. Why is the market price not at a market-clearing level?
   b. How much space would people want at a market-clearing price?

11 In Los Angeles two closely situated golf courses, one privately owned and one publicly owned, are both open to the public.
   a. Which do you think charges the higher price, and which do you think requires less or no advance reservation? Give your reasons.
   b. Who is benefited in what respects by each course's policy?
   c. As land values rise around the course, which one do you think will be converted to housing or business first? Why?

12 "Californians are crazy. Near a beautiful California beach, there is a luxurious motel and a state-owned camping area. Despite the greater luxury of the motel facilities, scores of cars are lined up for hours each morning seeking camping sites, whereas at the motel there is hardly a day the rooms are all taken. This shows that Californians prefer outdoor, dusty camps to the luxuries of a motel with pool, TV, room service, and private bath." Do you agree? Explain.

13 "Economic theory is applicable only to a capitalist society." Evaluate.

14 Public goods are those for which (choose the correct statement): (a) several people can simultaneously enjoy the good; (b) it is impossible to exclude some consumers; (c) no consumer reduces the amount of the good available to others by his act of consuming the good; (d) prices should not be charged; (e) the government should provide the goods.

15 A theater performance with several simultaneous viewers is not a public good. Why?

16 A melody is a public good. Why? What is the best way to induce people to produce melodies?

17 "More of a public good can be produced without the production of other goods being curtailed." Evaluate.

18 "Even if it were costless to exclude nonpayers from enjoying a public good, it does not follow that nonpayers should be excluded." Explain why.

19 "When a pretty girl wears beautiful clothes, the people who see her get a public good—for which they do not pay. Therefore the standards of dress for pretty girls should be regulated by law in order to induce sufficient amounts of well-dressed girls." Evaluate.

20 "Financing public goods by taxes is a means of excluding nonpayers, for nontaxpayers will be put in jail." True or false?

21 Name three goods that are partly public and private.

22 There are reputed to be over 100,000 voluntary health and welfare organizations soliciting contributions from the general public, in addition to hundreds of individual hospital-support groups, as well as about 100,000 fraternal, civic, and veteran's organizations and 300,000 churches which sponsor a variety of charitable activities, not to mention individual charities or gifts. A professor of public-health administration says, "It should not take over 100,000 voluntary agencies to provide private health and welfare services in the U. S." How many do you think it should take? Why?

23 The *New York Times* sponsors a charity appeal each Christmas and gives cash to selected poor families. The *Los Angeles Times* sponsors a charity appeal each summer to send children of poor families to summer camp. Given your choice, to which of these forms of charity would you contribute more? Why? Do you think people who choose the other way are mistaken?

24 In 1950 many public-welfare and charitable aid organizations refused to help families that owned a television set—no matter how poor the family might be. The welfare workers claimed they were not supposed to finance luxury. What would have been your policy if you were dispensing the aid?

25 Suppose you are running a university and the faculty is asking for higher salaries, some of which you will have to grant at the sacrifice of buildings and activities. Now, the Ford Foundation gives you $1,000,000, the income of which is to be allocated exclusively to faculty salaries. Who gains what?

26 Let your current college education involve a true annual cost of $2,000, of which you are required to pay $300, and for which you would have been willing to pay $1,200. If you had to pay the full costs of $2,000, you would not have purchased your present level of education; instead, you would have purchased a lower level of training costing $800.
  a. What do you gain by being able to get the $2,000 education for $200?
  b. If the above quantities ($300 or $200) refer to the amount your parents are willing to spend for your tuition, who gains what?

27 A parent spends 50 cents for his child's school lunch. Subsequently, the school initiates a low-cost subsidized school lunch program, so that now the parent spends only 40 cents for the same lunch.
a. Who gains what?
b. Suppose the new lunch is a better one that costs 60 cents but is provided at a subsidized price of 40 cents. Who gains what?
c. Suppose the school lunch is still better and costs 75 cents and is sold to students for 55 cents, so that the parent who formerly spent 50 cents now gives his child 55 cents to buy the bigger lunch. Who gains what?

28 Some colleges charge high tuitions, but at the same time they give a large number of tuition fellowships ranging from full tuition payment down to practically nothing. If you apply the principles of discriminatory-pricing techniques of an earlier chapter, can you show that tuition grants are a form of discriminatory pricing of education? Does that make them undesirable?

29 The faculty of many colleges are given free parking space even in areas where parking space is not a "free good."
a. Who gains what?
b. What would be the effect if the faculty could sell their space to students?

30 The state of Washington permits a person to collect twenty-four razor clams a day from its beaches.
a. Why is the right to collect clams given free, and why does the state limit the number to twenty-four instead of permitting more if a higher fee is paid?
b. Who gains what under the present system?

31 Immigration-quota rights to the United States are priced at "zero" instead of being sold at a market-clearing price to "acceptable" types of people. Who gains what? Why are these rights not sold at the highest price to acceptable people?

32 In 1963 the right of Northeast Airlines to offer commercial air service between New York City and Miami was rescinded by decision of the Civil Aeronautics Board, the U. S. government agency that allocates such rights.
a. What do you think happened to the value of the stock of Northeast Airlines upon news of that decision?
b. At the same time, the price of the common stock of two other airlines remaining in service on that route, Eastern and National Airlines, jumped about 25 percent. Why was Northeast Airlines not allowed to sell its right to that route to National and to Eastern instead of having the right taken away from it?
c. Who gained what by the decision to take that right away from Northeast Airlines and let National and Eastern remain as the two carriers?
d. As a final twist, after losing that right, Northeast Airlines reverted to the status of a "local-regional" airline, serving only the New England area. As such, it is entitled to federal subsidies. Who lost what by the transfer of flight rights by authority rather than by sale to other airlines?

33 Some state governments, when disposing of property, sell at auction to the highest bidder. The right to form and operate a bank, a liquor store, a race track, or a savings and loan bank is not sold at auction to the highest bidder among a set of "acceptable" businessmen. Instead, the "winner" is selected by a board, much as judges choose the winner in a beauty contest.
a. What is your explanation for not letting the highest bidder win?
b. Who gains what?
c. Which system do you think increases the wealth of lawyers? Of politicians?

d. Explain why a system of controlled entry is conducive to strong political lobbying groups.

34 The U. S. Congress has agreed with governments of foreign countries producing coffee to prohibit the import into the United States of more than a specified amount of coffee, thereby raising the price in the United States and increasing the total proceeds to foreign countries. (What is the elasticity of demand for coffee in the United States assumed to be?) Why would Congress agree to a law that raised costs of coffee to American consumers? Explain how this could be considered a form of foreign aid that does not appear in the federal government's budget record of taxes and expenditures.

Allocation of Consumable Goods over Time: Speculation

10

WHAT we eat today, we cannot eat tomorrow. We must allocate between *today* and *tomorrow*. After the summer's harvest of wheat, how much should we eat in the fall, winter, and next spring? Must a central planning agency set consumption quotas for each month until the next harvest? If not, how do we avoid famine in midwinter? In the United States no agency is responsible for seeing that we don't consume too much now. But some people, without delegated responsibility, devote their major activity to this task. In a capitalist system these individuals are acting in the interests of their own wealth; yet, in some mysterious way, their decisions influence the allocation of consumable goods over the year. In this chapter we shall study the way these actions affect that allocation. The example of the conservation of wheat between harvests will bring out the essential details. Although we discuss only harvests, the principles here apply to *all* goods, whether agricultural or manufactured.

The Risk-Taker in Commodity Markets

The wheat crop (assuming only one type of wheat) has been harvested. Must the farmers store it, gradually selling a bit each month until the next harvest? Farmers do not want to keep so much of their wealth in the form of wheat. They prefer to sell the wheat when harvested, letting someone else store it and bear the risks of changes in value of the wheat stock and decide how much to sell to consumers each month. Who buys the harvested wheat? The millers, who grind the wheat grain into flour, don't want to store a year's supply of wheat in advance. Even the housewives refuse to take on this duty, because they do not want to make commitments so far ahead. But there is a very simple device to induce someone to store the wheat. If people refuse to store the harvested wheat, the price of wheat falls. There is an increased prospect of profit in buying wheat at the lower price, storing it, and selling it later at a higher price after some of the wheat is consumed. In a capitalist open-market system, anyone may buy wheat at harvest time in a self-serving endeavor to make a profit by selling it *later at a higher price*. This is known as speculation.

Without *professional speculators,* the price would fall still lower until the less venturesome, less perceptive people were induced to buy the wheat. For at a *sufficiently* low price of wheat, millers (and even housewives) could be induced to buy a year's stock of wheat, because prospects for profits before the next harvest would then look so good. Differences among people in the willingness to bear risk, in their talents and facilities for storing wheat, in the profit prospects that will induce them to risk buying wheat—all determine how low the price of wheat will be after the harvest.

Permitting *any* or all persons to buy stocks of wheat for speculative purposes keeps the price from falling so far, thereby giving farmers a higher price than if some of these buyers were not allowed to buy for speculation. And speculators' actually realized profits, if any, will be smaller. In the United States, anyone can buy and store wheat by telephoning a commodity-market broker who will arrange to have wheat purchased, stored in rented facilities, and insured against theft or spoilage.

The market for these transactions is the *futures* market. That market is characterized in folklore as a place where antisocial, money-mad speculators gamble on the price of wheat, corn, etc., causing prices to fluctuate even more as they are pushed down when farmers sell and pushed up when consumers buy.

We conjecture that this folklore about futures markets reflects the fact that many people do not understand the special character of a "futures" contract. An illustration will reveal the crux. You are a flour miller converting wheat grain to flour. You want your income to depend on efficient milling operations, not on a changing price of unmilled wheat grain. A drop in the price of wheat grain, after you have bought the grain, could ruin you. You can isolate your business income from that risk in three ways.

1. Don't buy any wheat in advance of your milling operation. Buy it only after you have an order to mill some grain into flour. But this is expensive and does not allow a smooth flow of production. You won't survive with this system.

2. Find someone else to own the wheat and store it in your place of business while you buy it from him as you mill the wheat. In this way any fluctuations in the value of the stock of wheat are borne by the other person. This is expensive to do, as you will see if you try to find someone to do it.

3. You can buy the wheat yourself before receiving any orders for the flour you will make from the wheat, at the same time placing a side contract with someone else, so that if the price of the wheat goes *up* (giving you a gain in wealth) you will give the gain to *him,* but he will compensate *you* for a *drop* in value of the wheat you are holding. You are *hedging* by "betting" with him on the value of wheat. In either event, your wealth is unaffected whether the wheat price rises or falls. This means of insulating your wealth from contingent events is called *hedging.* This is one thing the futures contract does. It is the cheapest known way of separating ownership of the wheat by the miller from his bearing the risk of fluctuations in wheat value. It also enables wheat millers to conduct their purchases of wheat more efficiently—but we shall not here elaborate on this important feature.

Allocation of Consumable Goods over Time: Speculation

All three methods involve risk bearing. They differ in who bears it and in how that is arranged. They do not eliminate gambling or speculation or risk of loss or gain in value from holding wheat. That risk is inevitable when the wheat is kept unconsumed. Perhaps the reason futures contracts are so widely regarded as sheer gambling is that they separate the risk-bearing element so cleanly, efficiently, and *openly* from the *use* of the wheat, and therefore appear to be only devices to satisfy hungry speculators, bent on profiting from unanticipated changes in supplies or demands.

Control of the Rate of Consumption out of Stocks

What determines the *rate* at which the harvested stock of wheat is consumed? Who tells speculators how much wheat to sell each month for consumption? No one. Some *thing* does, and that thing is the current price of wheat relative to expected future prices.

Past experience, that prime source of knowledge, provides the basis for *expectations* of what the price of wheat will do between harvests. And the closer the current price is to future price expectations, the more will speculators be willing to sell currently, because profit prospects of holding wheat are diminished.

The present (*spot*) price of wheat is affected by the consumption demand and the supply of wheat coming into consumption channels from storage. If current consumption demand should increase, the *current* spot price of wheat will rise and reduce prospects of profits from storing wheat, thus inducing storers of wheat to sell more wheat to consumption channels. *The relationship between the current "spot" price for wheat and the price that is expected in the future affects the rate at which wheat will be released from storage into consumption.* And the prices (*futures* prices) of current contracts for future deliveries of wheat reflect beliefs and predictions about the future price. Why? People make contracts to deliver or to accept delivery in the *future* and will pay or be paid in the future at *presently* agreed-upon prices. This means that the prices now agreed upon for future delivery are predictions of what the price will be in the future; no one would purchase and store wheat today at a price higher than he thought the price would be in six months. Nor would anyone sell wheat *forward* (that is, contract to make future delivery) if the price were less than he thought it would be in the future.

"Futures" Prices and "Spot" Prices

Suppose it is now September, and you can buy wheat (in 5,000-bushel lots) for $2 a bushel for delivery immediately—on the "spot." Today's *spot* price of wheat is $2. Today, you also can make a *futures* contract for delivery of wheat upon payment of $2.10 per bushel *next May*. The price of $2.10 agreed to now, but to be paid in May, is called the *May futures price* (formed in September of the prior year). The difference between the two prices (spot and futures) usually just covers storage, insurance, and interest costs of holding wheat in the interim, because of competition among speculators.

Markets for Futures Prices

Prices in the commodity *futures* markets are reported in the financial sections of major newspapers. You will find (in September of 1972) something like the following for the wheat futures market (Chicago is the location of the market).

"Futures Price" of Wheat

September 1972 (harvest)	$2.00
December 1972	2.04
March 1973	2.07
May 1973	2.10
September 1973 (harvest)	2.02
December 1973	2.06

The interval extends from one harvest beyond the next. Unless next year's harvest is anticipated to be a failure, the September (after-harvest) 1973 futures price presumably will be lower than the May 1973 (pre-harvest) price. May is the last month before the new crop harvesting begins. The September harvest cannot be used in the *preceding* May to increase the amount available for consumption; if it could, the May price would be pushed down and the September price raised.[1]

These *futures prices* in today's futures markets provide predictions of what the spot price will be in the future. If anyone can make a better prediction of next May's spot price of wheat (that is, one that in fact turns out to be a more accurate prediction), he can quickly reap a fortune. For example, suppose the present (in September 1972) futures price for May 1973 is $2.10, a price lower than he believes will actually exist in May of 1973. He could place a bet in this futures market that the presently quoted *May futures* price is too low and that next May's spot prices will be higher. The process for placing this bet is to buy now a *futures contract* for, say, 5,000 bushels of May 1973 wheat at $2.10 a bushel—to be delivered to him and paid for next May. He agrees to this contract now in September at the presently quoted *May futures price* of $2.10 per bushel. Then he nervously waits until May; *if* the spot price next May is higher than $2.10, he can take delivery of the wheat and resell at the then higher price, reaping the difference as a profit. If the price is lower, he suffers a loss.

An important consequence of this activity is that increased current demand for wheat for delivery in the future pushes up the current "futures price" of future (that is, May) wheat from $2.10 toward that predicted May price. In this way, beliefs that the current "futures" price of future wheat is too low will increase the current "futures" price and *reveal to the world* the new expectations of future spot prices.

Of course, for every buyer of a contract for future wheat, there must be a seller who promises to deliver wheat in the future. That other person may believe the spot price in the future will be lower than the current futures price, and, if *he* is correct, *later* he can buy wheat at the lower spot price in the future and deliver it to the buyer for the currently agreed-to higher futures price. Or that other person may be a *hedger*.

If the demand for current consumption increases so that the present price of wheat rises, continued storage will be less profitable unless it is also expected that the price in the future will be correspondingly higher. A faster rate of consumption will leave smaller stocks and higher prices in the future. Currently, therefore, *futures* prices in the futures markets will be pushed up. What will push them up? First, the knowledge of the faster rate of consumption of current stocks of wheat will induce speculators to anticipate higher prices in the future, and they will act accordingly by demanding more futures contracts. Second, there is a sort of automatic force in the sense that this force does not

---

[1] There is some downward pressure on May prices, for consumers will reduce current consumption in the expectation of buying and consuming more wheat at a lower price after the new crop is harvested.

require any general knowledge of a faster rate of reduction of the stock of wheat. This second force is the result of *hedging*. The larger the inventories of wheat, the more wheat that will be hedged by selling "futures contracts." The increased supply of futures contracts (reflecting large stocks) lowers the futures prices.

We are now in a position to see how a higher demand, higher spot price, and consequent faster rate of consumption out of inventories has an effect on futures prices. As the hedging inventory holders sell their wheat for the current consumption at a more rapid rate, they have less wheat to hedge, so that they want to cancel (buy back) their commitments to speculators to deliver wheat in the future. The increased demand to buy back futures contracts, as hedgers reduce their inventories, raises futures prices, which restrains their willingness to sell so much current wheat.

We have an answer to our question of who bears the risk of value changes of the wheat between harvests. Under the incentive of increased wealth (buying low and selling later at a higher price) anyone can shoulder this task—not because he *intends* to perform some socially useful function (rationing wheat from harvest to harvest). Private interest motivates this method—a method not consciously designed or motivated by the social storage purpose but one discovered by a trial-and-error selective process and not widely understood by the members of society, not even by many of the speculators and farmers.

1, 2, 3,
4, 5, 6,
7

Illustrative Application: Coffee Futures Markets

To illustrate the interrelationships of prices, stocks, and speculative decisions, we shall use a "scenario" of public reaction to price movements of coffee futures. The scenario is only semi-imaginary, being based on recent actual events.[2]

The rumor spreads that the next coffee crop now blossoming in Brazil has been nipped by unseasonably cold weather. During these snaps, no one really knows how much the buds are affected, but there is an increased probability that next year's yield will be reduced. This implies greater (or surer prospects of) profits for those who own coffee today and who store it for next year's prospective higher prices. Immediately, the flow of coffee out of current stocks to consumption is reduced. Therefore, the current price of coffee to consumers will rise as less coffee is released for current consumption.

There is, of course, just as much coffee as there was before the news about a potential smaller crop. And yet the present (spot) price has risen. With the rise in price, congressmen, responding to housewives' protests, begin publicly to demand investigations. Sure enough, there is just as much coffee in existence *now* as before the rise, and greedy, antisocial speculators have driven up the price.

If you were a speculator—and they're people of all types: dentists, carpenters, students, salesmen—what would you tell complaining congressmen? What, according to economic analysis, were the source and the effects of the current price rise? Could you defend yourself by saying that you deserve not censure but a medal for having benefited *all* mankind; or were you working against the interest of other people? Your defense might run something like this:

[2] In addition to the coffee market, today there are organized open futures markets for at least the following goods: wheat, soybeans, oats, corn, cotton, barley, sorghum, sugar, cottonseed oil, soybean oil, hides, lard, eggs (frozen, powdered, and shell), potatoes, frozen chickens and turkeys, silver, tin, rubber, cocoa, platinum, pepper, flaxseed, copper, lead, zinc, wool, pork-bellies, and orange juice. One for Scotch whisky may open soon. One for onions was outlawed!

"It is true that news of the cold weather suggested the coffee buds would be nipped and the coffee harvest reduced. This would mean higher prices *next* year. I believed that if I bought some of this year's currently stored crop at present spot prices, I could later sell it at next year's higher prices at a tidy profit. Fortunately, I was one of the first who believed the crop damage was severe and was able to buy claims to coffee from people who did not believe the future supply looked smaller. I was not alone; many people were competing for current stocks of coffee. Soon, those who had coffee were not willing to sell at the former prices. They, too, looked forward to selling the coffee next year rather than this year. Less coffee was released from stocks for consumption. No one would sell existing stocks at a price less than he could get by holding until next year (allowing for the costs of storage, insurance, and interest). The current price, therefore, rose almost to the expected future prices as reflected in 'futures prices' of coffee. This higher current price was necessary to attract some coffee out of storage and to induce consumers to decrease consumption to match the smaller flow of coffee out of storage. All this is summarized in the first fundamental law of demand, which states that less will be consumed as price increases.

"I bought coffee as a speculator. However, quite incidentally and unintentionally, my action—like those of the many other similarly motivated, foresighted, more informed persons—augmented the supply of coffee for next year, by adding part of this year's stored stocks to next year's reduced harvest. The consumer next year will have more coffee to consume and at prices lower than if we speculators had not carried more coffee from this year over to next year. For that, the consumers should thank us—not condemn us!

"We speculators did not cause the reduced supply of coffee next year. Nature did that. There simply *is* going to be *less* coffee next year. The choice facing people therefore is: 'Shall we continue to consume coffee today *as if* there were not going to be less next year, and then reduce consumption next year by the full reduction in the harvest? Or, shall we reduce consumption this year in order not to have to reduce it so much next year?' The choice is *not* more coffee rather than less, nor is it lower prices rather than higher prices. It is 'when shall the available coffee be consumed?'

"If I must *defend* my actions rather than merely *explain* them, I would say that, like the middlemen in the refugee camp, we speculators enabled people to obtain greater levels of utility than they otherwise would have obtained, despite their protestations about the currently higher price of coffee. From the fact that prices are predicted to be higher next year than now, I know that people *prefer* to give up a pound now in order to have one more next year. This is precisely what the higher futures price for next year's coffee means, relative to the present price this year. And if we are right in that forecast, we will make a profit; if wrong, a loss. The profitability of our activity is an acid test that people did want some coffee shifted to the future.

"As speculators, we have immediately relayed to people our prediction of less coffee relative to other goods next year. We are not responsible for that *bad event,* but we are responsible for anticipating the effects of impending unfavorable events so that people can more cheaply adjust to them—so as to keep their utility greater than if the news of the coming crop failure were hidden until even more of the current crop was eaten up. We speculators are blamed for bad events because people either confuse *news* of the event with the *event,* or because they sometimes think that news of bad future events is worse than not knowing about it.

"You say, 'But what if your predictions were wrong? Suppose only a few buds on each tree were damaged, while the hardier undamaged buds produced even bigger coffee beans—more than enough to compensate for the reduced number, so that the crop next year was going to be even larger! Or suppose the cold snap did no damage at all. Or maybe the news about cold weather was simply false. After all, South American governments have been known to issue false bad news about an impending coffee crop precisely to drive up the price of coffee now, so that they could sell some of their existing stock at higher prices. What then?'

"The answer is simple. If speculators are wrong and if anyone else thinks he can predict better, all he has to do is out-predict the present speculators, and his fortune is made. Moreover, if speculators or people who store coffee make *perverse* mistakes in foresight, they will lose wealth, which, in part, pays the rest of the community for the error. Speculators will have paid more for the coffee than they will get when they sell it.

"I will not go so far as to say that any damage done to other people by our *erroneous* forecasts is made up to them by the losses we incur—a transfer of some of our wealth to the rest of society. In part this is correct, but our perverse forecasts do more damage than our loss of wealth to the rest of society can offset. They do damage in the sense that if our forecasts had been more correct, everyone could have achieved a more desirable adjustment in his consumption patterns over time than he did achieve. Obviously, the more accurate our forecasts, the better for us and for everyone else. The less accurate they are, the worse for us, and the worse for everyone else. However, and this is crucially important, the results are not as bad for everyone else as they would be if everyone had to do his own forecasting and storing of stocks for his own consumption, thereby bearing the full consequences of his own forecasts—right or wrong.

"Clearly, then, the issue is not whether the forecasts of speculators are correct or incorrect. The issues are instead: (a) What systems exist for making and acting on better forecasts? (b) What systems exist for allocating coffee among people over time *and* for allocating the risks and consequences of the erroneous forecasts? Any system will have erroneous forecasts. Which one will have fewer erroneous forecasts? Who will bear the major burden of the consequences of erroneous forecasts?"

And so our scenario ends. While it answered one question, it ended up by posing new ones, to which we turn.

Allocation of Risks in Futures Markets

Do the speculative markets, to which everyone has access, predict future prices more accurately than some other possible scheme? The organized futures market in onions was abolished by federal law in 1959. Among those who wanted the markets closed were firms that specialize in assembling, storing, sorting, and distributing onions to retailers. Without an open futures market, information about onion conditions is less widely dispersed; insiders, such as these processors, can benefit by their more exclusive access to information and opportunity to buy and sell onions. How they managed to induce enough congressmen to vote for that legislation is a question for your professor of political science. However, as it happens, this prohibition provided a fine opportunity to compare the behavior of prices of onions—with and without futures markets. The record is clear. With the organized futures markets for onions, the forecasts were more accurate than when they were closed. In particular, spot consumers' prices varied less between crops with open speculative markets than without them. In other words, the forecasts of future prices—the futures prices—influenced spot prices more accurately toward what was going to happen, avoiding large fluctuations when spot price responds to unforeseen events.

How should consequences of forecasting errors be borne? It has been contended that only experts should be allowed to make speculative decisions; this would avoid the errors made by less-informed people. To this there are several comments. First, if experts are now better informed than the consensus of the markets, they could easily get wealthy very rapidly by speculating. Furthermore, experts' superior information would help move the present spot and futures prices in the "correct" directions. Second, there is the problem of finding experts. When the government employs a group of specialists in this matter, the specialists are not automatically superior forecasters. The predictions of "experts" differ. If, despite these inherent difficulties, a group of experts were responsible for making forecasts and controlling the storage rates, who bears the losses when the forecasts are erroneous? In other words, how are the consequences of ignorance about future events to be allocated among people? Shall we require that all people, whether they individually want to or not, shall bear, in proportion to their taxes, the changing wealth values of the stocks of stored commodities? If the speculative activity were a voluntary arrangement with open futures markets, those who want to bear more of the risk can hold more of their wealth in the form of goods to be stored, and those who want to be relieved of those risks can own other forms of wealth. This points up one fundamental attribute of a capitalist system: It permits individuals to adjust their patterns of risk bearing, as well as their pattern of consumption goods. If you wish to avoid the wealth changes of certain goods, you can choose to own some other goods. You can concentrate your risks on a few particular goods or on a large class of goods, by appropriate patterns of ownership of goods. Complete avoidance of risks is not possible, but selectivity and choice of types of risks are possible with open markets and private-property rights. But whether that is desirable, economics cannot say.

Speculative holding of goods is inevitable. People differ in attitudes or willingness to bear the risks of losses of wealth consequent to emerging prices. Given these differences, each individual can move to a preferred position, as he sees it, if he will let the risks be borne by those who are more confident about a price rise, or more willing to bear risks inherent in the uncertainty of futures prices. Of course, he will have to pay them to bear those risks, but if they regard carrying such risks as less burdensome than he does, the cost will be less than if he bore the risks. Abolishing futures markets raises the costs of performing the storage function, because it prevents those who are more willing to bear these risks from doing so, and forces the less willing persons to bear these risks.

Having chosen not to bear the risk of wealth changes of a certain good, a person should not complain later if its price rises. His complaints would amount to the assertion that "hindsight is wonderful" and that insurance is wasted if the insured-against disaster doesn't happen! (In this case, by not holding stocks in advance of use, he has insured against decreases in their value.)

Sometimes it is mistakenly believed that speculation can be avoided by legally imposing fixed prices on commodities. This is identical to painting the thermometer to avoid a fever. Price controls do not prevent shifts in demand or supply. They reduce the opportunity of people to adjust by exchange to differences in interpersonal values among goods as well as among risks.

Speculative Markets under Different Economic Systems

Who will bear the profits and who the losses is an issue in all societies, and it cannot be evaded by abandoning a capitalist system. Only the method of allocation changes. In a capitalist system, individuals can negotiate among themselves, offering to exchange "this" risk of loss or gain for "that" risk. Just as people negotiate for the particular pattern of consumption goods they shall have, so they can negotiate about the pattern of risks they shall bear. Although the option of bearing no risk at all is open to *no* man, in a capitalist society risks may be exchanged for risks on other kinds of wealth. In a socialist system, the risks of value changes, for state-owned goods—or those owned by the people as a whole—are borne by everyone in accord with tax liabilities and access to state services. The risk patterns are not individually negotiable with other people.

If you believe a person should have less choice of risk patterns and if you think risks should be separated from the people who control the use of goods, you will prefer to reduce the scope of private property. But if you prefer a wider choice of risk patterns and a closer correlation between risk bearing and control of use, you will prefer a greater range of private property.

Summary

1 Allocation of goods between harvests is affected by present prices relative to prices expected to prevail in the future. A drop of spot prices immediately upon harvest induces some people to buy the crop and hold some of it in the expectation of a profit.

2 Futures markets are markets in which contracts are made in terms of future prices. Current "futures" prices negotiated in a futures contract—which is essentially a contractual agreement to compensate or be compensated for a price change—are predictions of what price will be in the future of the good.

3 Not everyone has to carry his own consumption supply through the interharvest period. People who are more willing to bear the risks of wealth fluctuations in the good will be the formal "speculators." People who use large stocks of the good in their business can shift the major portion of risks of price changes to speculators by futures contracts. Without hedgers seeking to have speculators bear the risks of price changes, the futures markets would not survive.

4 Concurrent increases in the "futures" prices and in the present (spot) price of a good may reflect, not a smaller current stock on hand, but an anticipated smaller future stock or larger future demand. More of the current stock will be carried over to the future, by releasing less for current consumption, which raises current prices.

5 Higher predicted (futures prices) values for the future will attract goods from the present (by reducing present consumption), whereas lower expected future values will increase present rates of consumption of existing stocks, leaving less for the future. (Future goods cannot shift to the present; instead, less of presently available goods are shifted to the future.)

6 Economic systems differ in the determination of who will bear which risks of the changing values of existing goods. In capitalism, they are individually negotiable or pooled. In socialism, they are pooled and borne by people more in accord with their tax liabilities and their access to state services.

Questions

1. The following was reported in the *New York Times* on April 23, 1970:

   Prices of Wheat Futures (Chicago)

May	1970	$1.49
July	1970	1.40
September	1970	1.41
December	1970	1.45
March	1971	1.47

   a. In what months does it appear that the new crop is harvested?
   b. Explain the basis of your answer.
   c. Approximately how much does it cost to store a bushel of wheat for one month?

2. Does storage from one crop season to the next season occur because people are farsighted and contemplate their own future demands, or is it done because people think they can make a profit?

3. Which good will have a greater fall in its price as the crop is more fully harvested: one that will store readily or one that is more perishable? Why?

4. What is the difference between a "futures" price and a "future" price?

5. Today you can buy 100 bushels of wheat to be delivered today and paid for today. Does this involve a spot or a futures price?

6. In May, what is the September futures price an estimate of?

7. In what sense is insurance a one-sided hedge?

8. "That speculators push up the price of a good is evidenced by the fact that the price often rises before there is any change either in the rate of consumption or the existing supply." Do you agree? If so, why? If not, why not?

9. A soybean processor buys in March 50,000 pounds of soybeans at $2.35 per 100 pounds. He expects to crush the beans and sell the soybean oil in about two months. He sells "futures" in soybeans at the same time he buys soybeans, hoping to obtain some protection from wealth changes resulting from changes in the price of soybeans and soybean oil. He sells futures in soybeans—say, May futures—to the extent of 50,000 pounds. Suppose the price of soybeans falls to $2 per 100 pounds in the interim, and therefore the price of soybean oil also falls. How will this enable the processor partially to avoid wealth changes caused by fluctuations in soybean prices?

10. "If forecasts are correct, some speculators will reap a profit. Also, they will have pushed up present prices, which will reduce current consumption and give a larger carryover to next season, so that prices in the future will be lower than they otherwise would be; but current prices are higher than they would have been had foresight been less perfect." In what sense can it be argued that this is "preferable" to a higher price later and lower price now?

11. "When speculators' foresight is good, they make a profit and perform a service to society. When it is bad, they incur losses and thus compensate the rest of society for the maldistribution of goods they induced." Do you agree? If so, why? If not, why not?

12. News item dated August 5, 1963: "The New York Sugar Exchange, where sugar futures prices soared and then dived in May 1963, will have to be placed under government supervision according to Rep. Leonor K. Sullivan (Democrat, Missouri), chairman of the Consumer Affairs subcommittee of the House of Representatives. Her report said in part, 'It was excessive speculation in futures, rather than manipulation, that stimulated the price advance and the subsequent price break. The investigation did not show indications of price manipulation on the part of any individual or groups of traders.' Mrs. Sullivan said the interest of consumers—'who are still paying higher prices for sugar and products containing sugar because of the market behavior'—requires some measures to dampen speculation." What do you think of Representative Sullivan's economic analysis? Explain.

13. I own $1,000, and tomorrow I will own either $2,000 or nothing depending upon whether an oil well I am drilling strikes oil. You own $1,000 in wealth, and it is all in cash. Who bears the greater risk for the next twenty-four hours?

14. Explain how markets in which people can bet with each other can result in (a) exchanges of risk, (b) reductions in risk, or (c) increases in risk. If such a market increases risk, is it bad? Why or why not?

15. The Los Angeles Dodgers and New York Mets are tied for the National League baseball title. They are to have a play-off game in a neutral stadium. The winning team will then be host for the World Series, with consequent receipts to the owners of neighboring parking lots. I own a parking lot near the Dodgers' stadium, and you own one near the Mets' stadium. If the Mets win the play-off, you gain; if the Dodgers win, I gain.
   a. Into what kind of contract can we enter to reduce the risk each of us bears?
   b. Have we exchanged or reduced risk? Can you construct a kind of "futures contract" that would accomplish the same effect?

16. There are no speculative futures markets in some countries. Does that mean there is no speculation? Explain.

17. "If the speculative commodity markets were closed, there would be less speculation and smaller fluctuations in the prices of goods. Farmers could more reliably know what their crop would be worth, and consumers would be spared the price swings that are initiated in the speculative futures markets." Do you agree? If so, why? If not, why not? Can you cite any evidence?

18. In 1963 a U. S. Senate Agriculture Committee recommended the prohibition of futures trading in potatoes in formal speculative markets.
   a. Would such a prohibition stop speculation in potatoes?
   b. What would be its effect?
   c. Why do you think congressmen were induced to advocate the prohibition of futures markets in potatoes?

19. "Short selling" consists of selling promises to deliver at a specified date in the future some goods that the seller does not now own. Newspapers sell short when they take subscriptions with advance payment. A house buyer sells short when he borrows money, for he is promising to pay money in the future—money that he does not now have. A college that charges tuition and room and board in advance is engaged in short selling; it sells something it has yet to produce. I sell short if I sell a promise to deliver 1,000 bushels of wheat to you next year for a price currently agreed upon and in receipt for payment now from you. Why is short selling often regarded as immoral, improper, or bad?

20. The Chairman of the U. S. Securities and Exchange Commission proposed to prohibit or restrict short selling at times when the market prices are under "temporary pressure or distress." The presumption is that short selling destabilizes the market and induces larger

downward swings than are justifiable in times of temporary distress. Suppose you were appointed by the President to decide when to restrict short selling in order to prevent it from pushing prices down lower.
a. How would you decide when a drop in prices was temporary and unjustified?
b. Who would decide when a drop in prices was "justified"?

21 Things similar to, but not identical to, futures contracts exist for stocks and bonds. These are known as "Puts" and "Calls." A "Call" is a right to purchase a stock within the next six months at a prespecified price, regardless of how high the price of that stock may rise in the next six months. A Call is guaranteed or sold by a party who, in effect, has sold "short." He is betting that the stock price will fall in the interim. If it does, he will not have to fulfill his promise to sell at the higher specified price, since the buyer of the Call can buy more cheaply on the market. If the stock rises, the guarantor of the Call will have to buy the stock on the market at the higher price and deliver it to the holder of the Call for the lower contract price in the "Call" contract.

The buyer of a "Put" buys the right to sell a stock at a prespecified price within some agreed-upon period of time regardless of how low the price may have fallen in that interval. The other party to the agreement (the seller of the Put) agrees to buy later at the specified price. Thus, a person owning A.T.&T. common stock can guarantee himself against a serious decline in the value by purchasing a Put. If it falls, he exercises his right to sell to the seller of the Put.

On August 1, 1966 you could have purchased a Call for Uniroyal stock giving you a guaranteed price of $44 per share, at which price the seller of the Call would have sold 100 shares of Uniroyal stock to you at any time during the following ten months. That Call would have cost you $600. How far would Uniroyal stock have to rise for you to have made money by purchasing that Call? If the price rose $1 per share, would you have exercised your option? Or if the price fell $1?

22 The following was the set of futures prices of wool on August 1, 1966:

October 1966	136.9
December 1966	136.4
March 1967	135.7
May 1967	134.0
July 1967	133.5
October 1967	133.4
December 1967	133.3

What explanation consistent with economic analysis can you give for this "reverse" sequence of future prices?

23 "Open speculative markets are defended on the premise that it is better to be aware of impending events than to be unaware of them. But for events like impending crop disasters, earlier news merely shifts forward the effects and thereby spreads them over a longer interval, to no one's benefit. People might prefer to experience a short, intense period of less coffee in the future rather than have an earlier, longer-lasting though less intense reduction in consumption." What does economic theory say about this?

24 There are no organized speculative exchanges or futures markets for wine, raisins, dried peaches, coal, oil, gasoline, whiskey, or olive oil.
a. Does that mean there is no speculating in these commodities?
b. Who does the speculating?

Capital Values, Interest Rates, and Wealth

11 MANY goods are durable; they provide future services. All those future services have values summed into the present price of the durable good, called its capital value. We must understand how these present prices or capital values are determined. To do that we must understand the "rate of interest," an extremely important concept.

Both present and future consumption are *goods*, and, as with all goods, a person is willing to substitute among them. He is willing to give up *some* present consumption for *more* wealth or more future income. This kind of trade is called "saving." The reverse direction of substitution, known as "dissaving," involves "borrowing" or consumption of wealth so that a person consumes more today and less tomorrow. Just as we analyzed exchange of present goods, we can analyze exchange of rights to present and future income. In the earlier-discussed exchange of goods, each person had a subjective personal value (marginal rate of substitution in consumption) of one current good for another. Now we have a subjective value (marginal rate of substitution) between present and future consumption. Instead of asking how much candy a person would give up *now* for one more cigarette *now,* we ask how much candy a person would give up now for one more candy to be received, say, a month *later.*

At first one might think, "Candy is candy; therefore, I would give up one candy now for the right to one candy a month from now." But second thoughts suggest if you give up candy now you also will have given up the right to eat or otherwise use the candy any time during the next month. The candy you will get at the *end* of the month will not give back the right to use or eat candy *during* the month. You will have accepted a reduced range of possible actions—and you will have obtained nothing in return. On the principle that more is preferred to less, you are not willing to accept such an exchange. Candy now is preferred to candy available only at a later date: candy now and candy available a month from now are simply not the same commodity. The former, in our jargon, has more "utility." *Less*—even if not much less—than one candy now will be traded for one candy a month from now.

Rate of Interest

Suppose you were willing to give up at most 0.9 candy today for the right to one a year from now (with no uncertainty or doubt about the payment). The *present* price of one candy *now* is, of course, one candy, while the *present* price of one candy available in a *year* is 0.9 candy. The relative price or exchange rate between present and future candy can be expressed as a ratio 1/.9, which equals 1.11. A current candy sells for a price premium, or higher price, of 11 percent over the present price of a right to one candy deferred a year. In other words, one year's delay in availability reduces the *present* value of something, by 11 percent in our numerical example. The value of earlier availability is 11 percent for one year; the *rate of interest* is 11 percent per year.

Express this generally in money. If you were to ask me, "How much money would you give up today for the right to get $1 a year from now?" my reply would be, "I would today pay 90 cents." I would give up 90 cents now for the right to $1 a year later; I regard the loss of one year's availability of opportunity to use goods as equal to 11 percent of the present value of current goods. For every good I can buy with money, earlier availability of that (and all) goods is worth 11 percent per year.[1]

Because money is the commonly used medium of exchange, it is customary to speak of the rate of interest on current and future *money* rather than commodities.

Although interest rates are expressed almost exclusively in terms of money *loans*, they represent the value (price) of earlier rather than later availability of nonmoney commodities, just as *money prices* for ordinary exchanges reveal the value of alternative commodities that must be forsaken. Nor does the fact that interest rates usually apply to *money* loans mean that interest is a monetary, financial distortion or exaction that financiers and bankers impose on ordinary people. Some people often believe that the rate of interest on loans for financing building projects should be ignored in order to get at the "real" costs. That error amounts to saying there is no preference for earlier over later availability—a proposition that no one would defend once he realized what he was saying.

Economics does not say that people prefer to have something now rather than later because they are impatient or shortsighted. They may or may not be. It is not necessary for deducing a lower present value for deferred relative to nondeferred goods.

Some other considerations imply a lower present value of deferred goods. The certainty of death—the certainty that we shall some day *not* be able to enjoy some postponed goods may make us unwilling to give up 1 gallon of gasoline (or anything) today for just 1 gallon in the future. Another, and probably most important, factor is the productivity of capital—even if you don't die during the period in question, you could be using the unconsumed income to earn more income.[2]

The rate of interest, then, reflects: (1) convenience of earlier availability, (2) preference for assured consumption over contingent consumption, and (3) ability to use income to increase total output. *Any* society—capitalist, communist, advanced, primi-

---

[1] This is not because of inflation; this holds for constant price levels over time.
[2] The "productivity of capital" will be discussed later in Chapter 23.

tive, industrial, agrarian, democratic, totalitarian—in which these elements are present will have a *positive rate of interest*—that is, a rate greater than zero. Some of these societies have an official dogma which denies or conceals this fact—but it is, nevertheless, present in all of them.

So far, we have stated that (1) earlier availability has a value; (2) this higher value of earlier availability, expressible as a percentage of the present value of a future good, is called the "interest rate"; and finally, (3) the interest rate applies to *all* goods as well as to money.

Methods of Expressing or Measuring Rate of Interest

There are several ways to express or measure the rate of interest; all are really the same thing in different guises.

1. Suppose you can lend 90 cents today and get $1 a year later. We say that the rate of interest is 11 percent, because 90 cents today "grew" into $1, or required a repayment of 11 percent more than was initially lent. "If I lend 90 cents today, I can get back $1 in a year—I get 11 percent interest per year." Or, "I can today purchase for 90 cents a $1 payment deferred one year." Or, "Since I pay the 90 cents (lend it) for your promissory note as evidence of the right to a deferred payment of $1, I have bought today for 90 cents your promissory note for $1 to be paid a year hence." That promissory note may say that you will pay me 90 cents plus 11 percent interest per year, or simply that you will pay me $1 in a year with no explicit reference to interest. That makes no difference —except possibly in the eyes of the law, which is sometimes blind to certain economic facts of life. But the total repayment is composed of repayment of the money loaned, plus interest.

This way of interpreting the rate of interest is

$$P_1(1 + r) = A,$$

which is to say that the present payment, P_1, will grow in one year at the annual rate of interest, r, to A, the future amount. In our present example, 90 cents, P_1, will grow at 11.1 percent per year (r) to $1 ($A$).

$$\$.90(1 + .111) = \$.999 = \$1.$$

Rearranging the equation, we get

$$\frac{(A - P_1)}{P_1} = r = \text{annual rate of interest.}$$

For example, if A represents $1 to be obtained in one year, and if 90 cents is P_1, the *present price* of that future dollar is 90 cents, the rate of interest works out to

$$(\$1 - \$0.90)/\$0.90 = 0.11 = 11\%.$$

This can be expressed in terms of the goods one can buy with money. If the price of a gallon of gasoline *available today* is 30 cents, and if you could make an agreement to pay 27 cents today and get a gallon *one year later* (presumably selling at that future time for 30 cents), then the annual rate of interest implied is

$$(\$.30 - \$.27)/\$.27 = 11\%.$$

Few of us ever have occasion to make this kind of arrangement, because we find it cheaper and more convenient to make commitments for money rather than for specific goods; barter is less convenient for exchanges involving the present and future just as it is less convenient for exchange of current goods. So we shall persistently use rates of interest on money, even though underlying the use of money are the specific goods and services.

The rate of interest can be interpreted—in fact, defined—as the relative premium of the *present* price of *present* goods over the present price of the same goods *deferred* a year. For example, if the present price of a gallon of gasoline to be delivered now is 30 cents, and if the present price to be paid now for a gallon to be delivered a year from now is 27 cents, then the annual rate of interest is 11.1 percent, from the expression

$$\frac{\$.30 - \$.27}{\$.27} = .111 = 11.1\%.$$

Consider a more common illustration. Almost every week the U. S. government seeks to borrow money for short periods—say, one year. It does so by selling its promissory notes (called "Treasury bills") to pay $1,000 in one year to the buyer at a *zero* interest rate. Thus, no interest rate is explicitly specified. These notes are then sold to the highest bidders. Suppose the highest bidder offers only $900 for one of these notes. What is the implicit rate of interest? By what percent of $900 will the $1,000 repayment exceed the amount actually loaned (paid for the note) to the U. S. government? The $100 difference is 11.1 percent of $900. Therefore, the annual interest rate is 11.1 percent. (The price for the last several years for such notes has been around $950–960, implying an interest rate of about 4–5 percent.) Even though no interest rate is *stated* on the note, there is actually a positive rate as long as the present price or amount borrowed is less than the amount to be repaid. This is a legal and orthodox arrangement; it is a convenient way to find the best possible terms at which the government can borrow.

2. The present price, P_1, of something deferred a year is sometimes known as a *discounted* value. The term "discounting" is suggested by the fact that, at positive rates of interest, $1 due in a year (deferred for a year) has a *present* value less than $1. The *lower* present price of a future amount due is the "discounted" value of the future amount due. This way of looking at the problem means simply that we solve the basic equation for P_1 as the key variable, in which case we get

$$P_1 = \frac{A}{(1+r)}.$$

If A is $1 and the rate of interest is 11 percent,

$$\$.90 = \frac{\$1.00}{(1+.11)}.$$

So the amount deferred one year is now worth 0.90 of that amount, at 11 percent interest. Or, 90 cents, at the annual rate of interest of 11 percent will grow to $1 in one year. Or, if $1 deferred one year has a price now of 90 cents, the implied rate of interest is 11 percent. These three different ways of saying the same thing correspond to the three alternative equations in the preceding paragraphs.

All of this analysis is independent of any assumed inflation. Inflation is not necessary for interest rates or differences between prices of present and future dollars.

Interest—The Price of Money?

The interest rate is often called the price of money. This "nickname" is misleading, for the price of $1 right now is, of course, simply $1. More accurately, the rate of interest is the price of earlier rather than later *availability*—sometimes also carelessly referred to as the price of time. The term "price of money" has become popular because people usually borrow or lend money rather than specific goods. Lenders buy future money in exchange for present money; they pay less now than the future amount to be received. That excess *future* amount (interest) is the future *price* paid for earlier money; the emphasis is on the *time* element. Rigorously speaking, interest is the price of earlier availability, rather than later availability, of rights to use goods.

To digress momentarily, our purpose in this chapter is not to see how interest rates are determined by the demand for present relative to future goods. We shall take that up later. Here we are concerned with the implications of the facts that (1) people evaluate and exchange present for *future* goods and services (that is, there *is* a rate of interest); and (2) future goods are less valuable now than the same amount of goods and services available now (that is, the rate of interest is *positive*).

We observe in the real world that people lend money only if they can get a positive rate of interest in one form or another. Just try to borrow money at a zero rate of interest! True, in some areas and in some times, there have been laws against "usury"—another word for interest. The Catholic Church long considered interest as improper, unjust, and unsanctioned. Similarly, Communist doctrine regards interest as a capitalist tool of exploitation (although *recent* Communist economists have "rediscovered" the presence and role of the interest rate). And when William the Conqueror ruled England, interest was illegal—except if collected by Jews—a convenience to William, who allowed Jews to live in England so that people (especially William and his nobles) could borrow from them. It is impossible to give a satisfactory economic reason for the Christian and Communist opposition to interest—when one understands that interest is merely a manifestation of individuals' preferences for earlier rather than later availability. We can only conjecture that perhaps the stricture against interest reflects the doctrine that people *should not* be the way they are; they *should* be neutral as between earlier and later availability. Why did the Communists object to this fact of life? Perhaps its facade of objection is a carry-over of Marxian confusions about economic fundamentals. But now they do recognize interest, if you judge by their actions rather than their words. The Russian government borrows money and pays a premium, and its investment policy recognizes the advantage of early over later availability. Instead of the term "interest rate," Russia uses "efficiency index," which, when you consider it, seems a better name.

The Farther in the Future, the Lower the Present Value

The *more distant* the deferred service (or income, or goods), the *lower* its present price. At an interest rate of 6 percent, the current price of $1 deferred a year is 94 cents—the amount that will grow at 6 percent in one year to $1. This is given by the formula

$$P_1 = \frac{A}{(1+r)} = \frac{\$1.00}{(1+.06)} = \$.943.$$

To get the present price for $1 deferred *two* years, simply repeat the above operation. If $1 deferred one year is now worth 94 cents, then deferring the dollar an additional year again reduces its present value by the same proportion. For two years, this is .943 × .943 = .890. A dollar due in two years is worth 89 cents today.

This can be expressed by noting that at 6 percent per year 89 cents will grow in one year to 94 cents, and then in the second year the 94 cents will grow to exactly $1. This can be written in algebraic form

$$P_2(1+r)(1+r) = A,$$

where P_2 represents the price now that will in two years grow at the 6 percent annual rate of interest to the amount A. Solving for P_2, we get

$$P_2 = \frac{A}{(1+r)(1+r)} = \frac{A}{(1+r)^2} = \frac{\$1.00}{(1.06)^2} = \$.890.$$

Two years' discounting is measured by the factor $1/(1.06)^2 = .890$; three years of discounting is obtained by multiplying the future amount due in three years by $1/(1.06)^3 = .839$. The present value of $1 deferred t years from today is obtained by use of the "present value factor" $1/(1.06)^t$. Multiplying an amount due at the end of t years by this present-value factor gives the present value (or present price, or discounted value) of the deferred amount, A, due in t years. A set of these present-value factors is given in Table 11–1 for various rates of interest and years of deferment. The present-value factor decreases as t is larger; the farther into the future an amount is deferred, the lower is its *present* value. This is in no way dependent upon an assumption of inflation of prices.

Future Amounts Corresponding to Given Present Values

Instead of working from future amounts to present values, we can derive for any annual rate of interest the future amount that will be purchasable for any present value. How much will $1 paid now purchase if the future amount is due in one year, or in two years, or in three years? At 15 percent per year, $1 will be worth $1.15 in one year. And at 15 percent for the next year, that $1.15 will in turn grow to $1.32. Hence, $1 today is the present price or value of $1.32 in two years. In terms of our formula, this can be expressed

$$P_2(1+r)(1+r) = A,$$

$$\$1(1.15)(1.15) = \$1(1.32) = \$1.32.$$

If the future amount is deferred three years, the term (1.15) enters three times, and if deferred t years, it enters t times. For three years, the quantity (1.15) is multiplied together three times, denoted $(1.15)^3$, and equals 1.52. Therefore, in three years $1 will grow to $1.52. In general, the formula is

$$P_t(1+r)^t = A$$

for any present payment, P_t, that is paid for an amount A available t years later. The multiplicative factor $(1+r)^t$ is called the *future-value* (or *amount*) *factor*. Values of this future-amount factor for different combinations of t and r are given in Table 11–2.

Capital Values, Interest Rates, and Wealth

TABLE 11-1. Present Value of a Future $1: What a Dollar at End of Specified Future Year Is Worth Today

Year	3%	4%	5%	6%	7%	8%	10%	12%	15%	20%	Year
1	.971	.962	.952	.943	.935	.926	.909	.893	.870	.833	1
2	.943	.925	.907	.890	.873	.857	.826	.797	.756	.694	2
3	.915	.890	.864	.839	.816	.794	.751	.711	.658	.578	3
4	.889	.855	.823	.792	.763	.735	.683	.636	.572	.482	4
5	.863	.823	.784	.747	.713	.681	.620	.567	.497	.402	5
6	.838	.790	.746	.705	.666	.630	.564	.507	.432	.335	6
7	.813	.760	.711	.665	.623	.583	.513	.452	.376	.279	7
8	.789	.731	.677	.627	.582	.540	.466	.404	.326	.233	8
9	.766	.703	.645	.591	.544	.500	.424	.360	.284	.194	9
10	.744	.676	.614	.558	.508	.463	.385	.322	.247	.162	10
11	.722	.650	.585	.526	.475	.429	.350	.287	.215	.134	11
12	.701	.625	.557	.497	.444	.397	.318	.257	.187	.112	12
13	.681	.601	.530	.468	.415	.368	.289	.229	.162	.0935	13
14	.661	.577	.505	.442	.388	.340	.263	.204	.141	.0779	14
15	.642	.555	.481	.417	.362	.315	.239	.183	.122	.0649	15
16	.623	.534	.458	.393	.339	.292	.217	.163	.107	.0541	16
17	.605	.513	.436	.371	.317	.270	.197	.146	.093	.0451	17
18	.587	.494	.416	.350	.296	.250	.179	.130	.0808	.0376	18
19	.570	.475	.396	.330	.277	.232	.163	.116	.0703	.0313	19
20	.554	.456	.377	.311	.258	.215	.148	.104	.0611	.0261	20
25	.478	.375	.295	.232	.184	.146	.0923	.0588	.0304	.0105	25
30	.412	.308	.231	.174	.131	.0994	.0573	.0334	.0151	.00421	30
40	.307	.208	.142	.0972	.067	.0460	.0221	.0107	.00373	.000680	40
50	.228	.141	.087	.0543	.034	.0213	.00852	.00346	.000922	.000109	50

Each column lists how much a dollar received at the end of various years in the future is worth today. For example, at 6 percent per year a dollar to be received ten years hence is equivalent in value to $.558 now. In other words, $.558 invested now at 6 percent, with interest compounded annually, would grow to $1.00 in ten years. Note that $1.00 to be received at the end of fifty years is, at 6 percent, worth today just about a nickel. And at 10 percent it is worth only about .8 of one cent, which is to say that 8 mills (.8 of a cent) invested now would grow, at 10 percent interest compounded annually, to $1.00 in fifty years. Similarly $1,000 in fifty years is worth today $8.52, and $10,000 is worth today $85—all at 10 percent rate of interest. *Forty* years from now (when you are about 65) $10,000 would cost you now, at 10 percent rate of growth per year, about $221. (See the entry in the column headed 10 percent and in the row for forty years.) Why not make that investment? Formula for entry in table is $1/(1 + r)^t$. (No inflation is involved in this table.)

For example, at 6 percent in five years, the future-amount factor is 1.34, which means that a present payment of $1 will buy, or grow to, the future amount $1.34 at the end of five years. Notice that the entries in Table 11–2 are simply the reciprocals of the entries in Table 11–1.[3]

In a later chapter we shall see why such growth is possible. At the moment we are investigating its complications, not its causes.

[3] The "rule of 72" is an ancient, quite accurate, and convenient financial rule. "The number 72 divided by the annual rate of interest yields the number of years required for a present sum of money to *double* at compounded interest." An investment that increases at 8 percent a year, for instance, will double every nine years—because 72 divided by 8 equals 9; or if it doubles in nine years, the interest rate must be 8 percent. (Test the rule in Table 11–2.)

TABLE 11–2. Compound Amount of $1: Amount to Which $1 Now Will Grow by End of Specified Year at Compounded Interest

Year	3%	4%	5%	6%	7%	8%	10%	12%	15%	20%	Year
1	1.03	1.04	1.05	1.06	1.07	1.08	1.10	1.12	1.15	1.20	1
2	1.06	1.08	1.10	1.12	1.14	1.17	1.21	1.25	1.32	1.44	2
3	1.09	1.12	1.16	1.19	1.23	1.26	1.33	1.40	1.52	1.73	3
4	1.13	1.17	1.22	1.26	1.31	1.36	1.46	1.57	1.74	2.07	4
5	1.16	1.22	1.28	1.34	1.40	1.47	1.61	1.76	2.01	2.49	5
6	1.19	1.27	1.34	1.41	1.50	1.59	1.77	1.97	2.31	2.99	6
7	1.23	1.32	1.41	1.50	1.61	1.71	1.94	2.21	2.66	3.58	7
8	1.27	1.37	1.48	1.59	1.72	1.85	2.14	2.48	3.05	4.30	8
9	1.30	1.42	1.55	1.68	1.84	2.00	2.35	2.77	3.52	5.16	9
10	1.34	1.48	1.63	1.79	1.97	2.16	2.59	3.11	4.05	6.19	10
11	1.38	1.54	1.71	1.89	2.10	2.33	2.85	3.48	4.66	7.43	11
12	1.43	1.60	1.80	2.01	2.25	2.52	3.13	3.90	5.30	8.92	12
13	1.47	1.67	1.89	2.13	2.41	2.72	3.45	4.36	6.10	10.7	13
14	1.51	1.73	1.98	2.26	2.58	2.94	3.79	4.89	7.00	12.8	14
15	1.56	1.80	2.08	2.39	2.76	3.17	4.17	5.47	8.13	15.4	15
16	1.60	1.87	2.18	2.54	2.95	3.43	4.59	6.13	9.40	18.5	16
17	1.65	1.95	2.29	2.69	3.16	3.70	5.05	6.87	10.6	22.2	17
18	1.70	2.03	2.41	2.85	3.38	4.00	5.55	7.70	12.5	26.6	18
19	1.75	2.11	2.53	3.02	3.62	4.32	6.11	8.61	14.0	31.9	19
20	1.81	2.19	2.65	3.20	3.87	4.66	6.72	9.65	16.1	38.3	20
25	2.09	2.67	3.39	4.29	5.43	6.85	10.8	17.0	32.9	95.4	25
30	2.43	3.24	4.32	5.74	7.61	10.0	17.4	30.0	66.2	237	30
40	3.26	4.80	7.04	10.3	15.0	21.7	45.3	93.1	267.0	1470	40
50	4.38	7.11	11.5	18.4	29.5	46.9	117	289	1080	9100	50

This table shows to what amounts $1.00 invested now will grow at the end of various years, at different rates of growth compounded annually. For example, $1.00 invested now will grow in thirty years to $5.74 at 6 percent. In other words, $5.74 due thirty years hence is worth now exactly $1.00 at a 6 percent rate of interest per year. If you invest $100 now at 10 percent, you will have $1,740 in thirty years. Isn't that worth it? The entries in this table are the reciprocals of the entries in Table 11–1; that is, they are the entries of Table 11–1 divided into 1. You really don't "need" this extra table, but having it saves some calculations. Formula for entries in table is $1(1+r)^t$.

Present Capital Value for Series of Future Amounts

For a *sequence* of amounts due at future times, we can find a present value. Just as we add up the costs of individual items in a market basket of groceries, we add the present values of each of the future amounts due. That sum is the present value of the whole series of amounts due at various future dates.

This series might be compared with an oil well that each year on December 31 spurts out one gallon of oil that sells for $1. To simplify the problem, let's first suppose that the series of dollars (spurts of oil) continues for only two years. If the interest rate is 6 percent, the present value of $1 deferred one year is 94 cents (see Table 11–1, column of .06 rate of interest for one year); and the present value of $1 due in two years is 89.0 cents (see the same table, same column, but now read the entry for year 2). The sum of the present capital values of both amounts due is the sum of 94.3 cents and 89.0 cents, which is $1.83. To say that the rate of interest is 6 percent per year is equivalent to saying that you can exchange $1.83 today for the right to receive $1 in one year *and* another dollar in two years.

Suppose the sequence is to last three years, with three $1 receipts. The aggregate present value is augmented by the present value of the dollar due in the third year. At a 6 percent rate of interest, this third dollar has a present value of 83.9 cents (see Table 11–1). Therefore, the present value of the three-year series is $2.67 (given in Table 11–3). The present value of a series of amounts due is called the *capital value* of the future receipts. Capital value is the current *price* of the rights to the stream (series) of receipts.

Some technical jargon will be convenient for subsequent analyses. The sequence of future amounts due is called an *annuity,* a word that suggests *annual* amounts. A two-year sequence is a two-year annuity. A person who has purchased the right to a stream of future annuities or amounts due—for example, his pension benefits—is sometimes called an *annuitant.*

What is the present capital value of a four-year annuity? The fourth year's $1 has a present value of 79.2 cents, which, when added to the present value of a three-year

TABLE 11–3. Present Value of Annuity of $1, Received at End of Each Year

Year	3%	4%	5%	6%	7%	8%	10%	12%	15%	20%	Year
1	0.971	0.960	0.952	0.943	0.935	0.926	0.909	0.890	0.870	0.833	1
2	1.91	1.89	1.86	1.83	1.81	1.78	1.73	1.69	1.63	1.53	2
3	2.83	2.78	2.72	2.67	2.62	2.58	2.48	2.40	2.28	2.11	3
4	3.72	3.63	3.55	3.46	3.39	3.31	3.16	3.04	2.86	2.59	4
5	4.58	4.45	4.33	4.21	4.10	3.99	3.79	3.60	3.35	2.99	5
6	5.42	5.24	5.08	4.91	4.77	4.62	4.35	4.11	3.78	3.33	6
7	6.23	6.00	5.79	5.58	5.39	5.21	4.86	4.56	4.16	3.60	7
8	7.02	6.73	6.46	6.20	5.97	5.75	5.33	4.97	4.49	3.84	8
9	7.79	7.44	7.11	6.80	6.52	6.25	5.75	5.33	4.78	4.03	9
10	8.53	8.11	7.72	7.36	7.02	6.71	6.14	5.65	5.02	4.19	10
11	9.25	8.76	8.31	7.88	7.50	7.14	6.49	5.94	5.23	4.33	11
12	9.95	9.39	8.86	8.38	7.94	7.54	6.81	6.19	5.41	4.44	12
13	10.6	9.99	9.39	8.85	8.36	7.90	7.10	6.42	5.65	4.53	13
14	11.3	10.6	9.90	9.29	8.75	8.24	7.36	6.63	5.76	4.61	14
15	11.9	11.1	10.4	9.71	9.11	8.56	7.60	6.81	5.87	4.68	15
16	12.6	11.6	10.8	10.1	9.45	8.85	7.82	6.97	5.96	4.73	16
17	13.2	12.2	11.3	10.4	9.76	9.12	8.02	7.12	6.03	4.77	17
18	13.8	12.7	11.7	10.8	10.1	9.37	8.20	7.25	6.10	4.81	18
19	14.3	13.1	12.1	11.1	10.3	9.60	8.36	7.37	6.17	4.84	19
20	14.9	13.6	12.5	11.4	10.6	9.82	8.51	7.47	6.23	4.87	20
25	17.4	15.6	14.1	12.8	11.7	10.7	9.08	7.84	6.46	4.95	25
30	19.6	17.3	15.4	13.8	12.4	11.3	9.43	8.06	6.57	4.98	30
40	23.1	19.8	17.2	15.0	13.3	11.9	9.78	8.24	6.64	5.00	40
50	25.7	21.5	18.3	15.8	13.8	12.2	9.91	8.25	6.66	5.00	50

An annuity is a sequence of annual amounts received at annual intervals. This table shows with each entry how much it takes today to buy an annuity of $1 a year at the rates of interest indicated. For example, an annuity of $1 a year for twenty years at 6 percent interest could be purchased today with $11.40. This amount would, if invested at 6 percent, be sufficient to yield some interest which, along with some depletion of the principal in each year, would enable a payout of exactly $1 a year for twenty years, at which time the fund would be completely depleted. And $1,000 a year for twenty years would, at 6 percent compounded annually, cost today $11,400, which is obviously 1,000 times as much as for an annuity of just $1. Formula for entry is $[1 - (1 + r)^{-t}]/r$.

TABLE 11–4. Uniform Annual Payments Provided at End of Each Year for Annuities of Various Lengths, per $1 of Present Value

Year	3%	4%	5%	6%	7%	8%	10%	12%	15%	20%	Year
1	1.03	1.04	1.05	1.06	1.07	1.08	1.10	1.12	1.15	1.20	1
2	.524	.529	.538	.546	.552	.562	.578	.592	.613	.654	2
3	.353	.360	.368	.375	.381	.388	.403	.417	.439	.474	3
4	.269	.275	.282	.289	.295	.302	.316	.329	.350	.386	4
5	.218	.225	.231	.238	.244	.251	.267	.278	.299	.334	5
6	.185	.191	.197	.204	.210	.216	.230	.243	.265	.300	6
7	.161	.167	.173	.179	.186	.192	.206	.219	.240	.278	7
8	.142	.149	.155	.161	.168	.174	.188	.201	.223	.260	8
9	.128	.134	.141	.147	.153	.160	.174	.188	.209	.248	9
10	.117	.123	.130	.136	.142	.149	.163	.177	.199	.239	10
11	.108	.114	.120	.127	.133	.140	.154	.168	.191	.231	11
12	.101	.106	.113	.119	.126	.133	.147	.162	.185	.225	12
13	.0943	.100	.107	.113	.120	.127	.141	.156	.177	.221	13
14	.0885	.0943	.101	.108	.114	.121	.136	.151	.174	.217	14
15	.0840	.0901	.0982	.103	.110	.117	.132	.147	.170	.214	15
16	.0794	.0862	.0926	.0990	.106	.113	.128	.143	.168	.211	16
17	.0758	.0819	.0885	.0961	.102	.110	.125	.140	.166	.210	17
18	.0725	.0787	.0855	.0925	.0990	.107	.122	.138	.164	.208	18
19	.0699	.0763	.0826	.0901	.0971	.104	.120	.136	.162	.207	19
20	.0671	.0735	.0800	.0877	.0943	.102	.118	.134	.161	.205	20
25	.0575	.0641	.0709	.0781	.0855	.0935	.110	.128	.155	.202	25
30	.0510	.0578	.0649	.0724	.0806	.0885	.106	.124	.152	.201	30
40	.0433	.0505	.0581	.0666	.0752	.0840	.102	.121	.151	.200	40
50	.0389	.0465	.0546	.0632	.0725	.0820	.101	.120	.150	.200	50

An annuity is a sequence of annual amounts received at annual intervals for a specified number of years. The entries in the table give the possible annuities of various lengths, for various interest rates, which have a present value of $1. For example, for $1 present value or cost, at 6 percent interest, one can receive an annuity for *one* year of $1.06, or of 54.6 cents for each of two years, or 37.5 cents for each of three years, or 28.9 cents for each of four years.

Another way to use the data is to treat annuities as payments. For example, a debt of $1 can be paid off, at 6 percent interest, with $1.06 in one year, or 54.6 cents for two years, or 28.9 cents annually for four years, or 10.2 cents annually for twenty years.

annuity of $1 a year, gives $3.46. A five-year annuity would have a present value of $4.21, because the dollar received at the end of the fifth year is now worth 74.7 cents. Proceed to the end of ten years, and you will find (in Table 11–3) that at 6 percent interest the present capital value of a ten-year annuity of $1 each year is $7.36.

If we extended the series to twenty years (still with $1 at the end of each year) at 6 percent per year, the present capital value would increase to $11.40. Notice that the *present* value of the *last half* of that series (the ten amounts due in the eleventh through the twentieth years) is only $4.04 (= 11.40 − 7.36). At a 6 percent interest rate, $4.04 *today* will buy you $1 a year for ten years, beginning at the end of the eleventh year.

Table 11–1 gives the present value of each separate future payment in the annuity. For convenience, Table 11–3 gives the present value of annuities of various lengths, where the payment *at the end* of each year is $1. Look at the entry for two years at 6 percent. It is the sum of .943 and .890, based on the data of Table 11–1. For an annuity lasting fifty years, the entry is $15.8—which says that a fifty-year annuity of $1 per year, with the first payment coming at the end of one year, has a present capital value of only $15.80 (at 6 percent).

Capital Values, Interest Rates, and Wealth

Even an annuity that lasted forever (called a *perpetuity*), or for as long as you and your heirs desire, would have a finite capital value—namely, $16.67 (at 6 percent interest).

A second thought will remove the mystery from the fact that an infinitely long series of $1 amounts due yearly has a finite (limited) price today. To get a perpetual series of payments of $1 every year, all one has to do is keep $16.67 on deposit in a bank, if he can get 6 percent per year. Every year the interest payment of $1 can be taken out, and this can be done forever. In effect you pay $16.67 today to purchase an infinitely long sequence. But (from Table 11–3) you can also see that the first fifty years of receipts (a fifty-year annuity) has a present value of $15.80. Hence, the remaining infinitely long series of $1 receipts, beginning fifty years from now, is worth today only about 87 cents. Distant events have small present values!

Table 11–4 gives the annual annuity payments one could purchase with one dollar now. (The entries are reciprocals of the entries in Table 11–3.) Thus $1 *now* will buy $1.49 annually at the end of each of ten years (at 8 percent interest).

6, 7, 8, 9, 10, 11, 12, 13, 14

Illustrative Applications of Capitalization Principles

1. *Discount or credit?* Two salesmen want to sell you a car with an official "list" price of $2,000. Salesman *A* offers it for $1,900. Salesman *B* sticks with the official price, but he will let you pay him that full amount one year hence. Which offer is "cheaper"—that is, will reduce your wealth least? It depends upon the rate of interest, which we shall suppose is 10 percent per year. To pay salesman *A* costs $1,900 now. To pay salesman *B* takes $2,000 one year hence, equivalent to $1,818 now. Why? Because $1,818 is the present price or present value (to the nearest dollar) that will grow *at 10 percent* to $2,000 in one year. By lending (investing) $1,818 now at 10 percent per year, you will have $2,000 with which to pay salesman *B* at the end of the year. Where did those figures come from? See Table 11–1 for the present values of future amounts. At 10 percent, an amount deferred one year is worth now .909 of that deferred amount; therefore .909 of $2,000 is $1,818, the present capital value of $2,000 deferred one year, at 10 percent per year. Salesman *B* costs you now $82 less than *A* does. If you buy from *B*, you have $82 more current wealth left.

Another way to view this is to consider what you could have done if you had, instead of buying from *A*, invested the $1,900 at 10 percent per year. At the end of the year you would have $1,900 (1.1) = $2,090. Out of that future amount you could pay salesman *B* and have $90 left over for other "goodies." That future amount of $90 is a future measure of how much cheaper salesman *B*'s offer is. In present-value measure, *B* is cheaper by $1,900 − $1,818 = $82, which, expressed as a future amount one year hence, is equivalent to a *future* $90 difference ($2,090 − $2,000). At a 10 percent rate of interest, $82 now is equivalent to $90 one year from now.[4]

But suppose the rate of interest were 4 percent. Then $1,924, the present value of next year's $2,000, exceeds the $1,900 asked by salesman *A*. Salesman *A* is cheaper by $24 in current wealth. Clearly the cheaper option depends upon the rate of interest. If you haven't got the amount of money now, you can borrow it at 4 percent (after all, we

---

[4] If we use greater accuracy in our computations the $1,818 would be $1,818.1818. The present-value difference is $81.8181, and 10 percent of that is $8.1818, which, added to $81.1818, gives $89.9999.

assumed a 4 percent rate of interest in this problem). Borrow the $1,900 now and at the end of the year pay back $1,900 plus 4 percent of $1,900, which is $76. The payment at the end of the year will be precisely $1,976, which in wealth a year hence is $24 less than the $2,000 that salesman *B* asks.[5]

2. *The risk of expropriation.* You own a new building from which you will receive an annual rent of $1,000 after allowing for all expenses of maintenance, insurance, and taxes. At a 10 percent rate of interest that house will, by definition, have a present value or price of $10,000. (Can you see why? With maintenance paid for, as it is, the building will last indefinitely and if it brings in a net of $1,000 for an indefinitely long time, it is like a perpetuity.) But speaking realistically, suppose the building is in a South American country, and you learn it is about to be nationalized with a present payment to you of $4,000. How much would it be worth to you to bribe the government officials to delay the confiscation for eight years during which time you would continue to maintain the building and pay the same expenses as before—if you were naive enough to trust them? (See Table 11–3 for entry under 10 percent rate of interest for eight years. That figure of 5.33 is the present value of an annuity of 1.00 per year for eight years. For $1,000 per year that gives $5,330, to three-figure accuracy. You might risk up to $5,330 trying to delay the confiscation eight years.)

3. *Honor thy father and mother.* Your parents, having reached age 70 with a small fortune of $50,000, plan to retire on that fund. They want to use it up at a rate that permits them to draw out a fixed amount each year for fifteen years. After that, if they are still alive, you will shoulder your moral responsibility. How much can they spend each year for fifteen years? Rephrased, the question is the following: "What fifteen-year annuity has a present value of $50,000?" If you can invest the fund at 10 percent, the answer is in Table 11–3 in the column headed 10 percent. The entry in the fifteen-year line is 7.60. That is the present capital value of a fifteen-year $1 annuity. Since there is now $50,000 in the fund, $50,000/7.60 = $6,570 is the amount of each annual payment for the next fifteen years. (This is an approximation, since $6,570 is really the amount that could be spent at the *end* of each of fifteen years, not during each year, but the difference is slight.)

If they want to use up the fund in ten years, they can get $8,140 (= $50,000/6.14) at the end of each year. If they invest at 4 percent, they will get a fifteen-year annuity of $4,500 (= $50,000/11.1).

Do not be astonished by earning rates around 10 to 15 percent. The stock market gave about 12 percent per year (based on almost *any* thirty-year period taken from the twentieth century, *even after allowing for inflation*). For some thirty-year periods, the market did much better. For some five- to ten-year episodes, it gave less or a great deal more. This average of the performance of all listed stocks is higher than one can get by lending money in bonds, if one will accept a *variable* annuity. For bonds, with less year-to-year variation, the rate has averaged about 5 to 6 percent, but hereafter, with better anticipation of inflation, will average about 8 to 10 percent.

[5] How is it that we got the same saving, $24, in both present and future values? The measure in future values must be larger. What went wrong? Not enough computational accuracy! If we had used more significant digits, the difference would have shown up. Thus the .962 in Table 11–1 under 4 percent for one year is more accurately .9615. Multiplying this by $2,000 gives $1,923 (instead of $1,924). This saving of $23 (not $24) in *present-value measure of wealth is equivalent to $24 in terms of next year's wealth—a difference of 4 per cent. Check!*

4. *The low interest rate gimmick.* If I were trying to sell you a machine that earns $100 at the end of each year for the next thirty years, would I use a high or a low rate of interest to express the present value? If I used 10 percent, it would work out to $942, as can be seen from the data provided in Table 11–3. (Be sure you check this calculation. A purpose of these examples is to give you facility in using the tables.) At 3 percent, it would work out to $1,960. (Again, be sure to check this.) If the machine cost $1,500, I would be tempted to speak in terms of the low rate of interest, for then it would appear to be a profitable purchase.

Always be on the alert to detect incentives to use a "biasing" rate of interest. For example, advocates of the California Feather River water project, an immense state-financed endeavor to supply additional water to Southern California, held it to be an excellent investment—as it may be at interest rates of about 2 percent. But if the rate of interest is higher, as it is, the resources would be more valuable if used for other things in the meantime and the project were postponed for about twenty years. In the public pre-election debate, virtually no attention was given to the question of the appropriate interest rate. The project is now being built.

5. *Eat your cake and have it too.* Consider a more personal application. In some colleges you can borrow money (say $1,000) for tuition and expenses without paying any interest for eight years. Should you borrow? Of course! Put the money in a savings account for at least 5 percent per year. Each year you can draw out the $50 interest and throw a big party. At the end of eight years, you can draw out the $1,000, plus the last year's interest; repay the $1,000; and have $50 for a last party.

Another way to look at this is to see that you are being given free a $50 eight-year annuity beginning in one year. Even at so low a rate as 5 percent, the present value is $50 × 6.73 = $323.60. (See Table 11–3.) The possibility of borrowing $1,000 at *zero* interest for eight years is equivalent to a gift of $323.60 upon entrance to college. Any student who fails to borrow is throwing away a gift.

Question: How many college students who get interest-free or low-interest loans thereby enable parents to withhold money from college expenses and divert it to personal uses? It is no answer to say that no parent *intends* to act that way. The fact that he is *enabled* to do so is sufficient. You can see why low-interest government loans are sought by people who at the same time claim they do not get tax support.

6. *It's "only" 3 percent a year.* Suppose the price level were to creep upward at the rate of 3 percent per year. Today a Coke costs 10 cents. If the price of Cokes moved up with the general price level, what would they sell for in thirty years? At 3 percent per year a present amount would grow to 2.43 times as large an amount in thirty years. (See Table 11–2 thirty-year entry in column for 3 percent.) Cokes would sell for about 25 cents. In forty years, when you are retired, they would sell for almost 40 cents. (See same table, forty-year entry.) At a 5 percent per year price rise, a Coke would sell for about 75 cents, when you retire in 40 years.

7. *The whole is less than one of its parts.* We give now another practical problem that will probably face everyone at one time or another. After ten years of working for one employer, you transfer to a new job. During these few years your employer contributed (that is, he diverted from your wages) $1,000 each year to an account for your retirement (a fringe benefit), and you contributed a matching amount each year. The whole fund was invested at 4 percent during that time; the value of the account now stands at

$24,000. Two options are open. (1) You may leave both contributions in that fund until retirement in thirty years when you will get the future value of this amount at 4 percent per year interest. (2) Your other possibility is to take out the cumulated value of "your" contributions, which is $12,000 (one half of the total of $24,000). You can do as you wish with the money you take out, but the other half will be lost as far as you are concerned. In other words, you can give up $12,000 today for the sake of getting now the other $12,000, with which you may do as you like. Otherwise, you must wait thirty years more to get the accumulated value (at 4 percent interest) of the entire fund. Which shall you choose?

One of the issues upon which the answer depends is the growth rate you can get on your own fund. Suppose you believe you can get 10 percent per year. Should you sacrifice $12,000 now for the opportunity to get 10 percent on the other $12,000 rather than 4 percent on $24,000 for thirty years?

$12,000 invested at 10 percent will grow to $208,800 in thirty years. (See Table 11–2, 10 percent column, thirty years.) If you leave your money in the fund at 4 percent, the $24,000 fund will grow to only $77,000 in thirty years. (See Table 11–2, 4 percent, thirty years.) Shocked?

Only if you failed to earn over 6.7 percent would your $12,000 fund have been smaller at the end of thirty years than the whole $24,000 fund at 4 percent. Today almost all company or union funds credit the accounts with barely 5 percent a year, while the rate of return available on the stock market just by random investing, including interest and profits, exceeded 10 percent a year, for *any* thirty-year period you care to pick in this century.

But suppose you had just twenty years before retiring. Would it pay you to take out your own contribution? Look in Table 11–2 (10 percent column for twenty years). The amount to which $1 will grow is $6.72. And at 4 percent the dollars in the fund will grow in twenty years to $2.19. Each of your own dollars at 10 percent will grow to *more* than twice the amount that the amount credited to you in the fund will grow to at 4 percent. Even for twenty years a 10 percent growth rate will overtake the slower (4 percent) growing fund that is initially twice as large. What rate of interest is the rate that makes the two funds grow to the same amount in twenty years? (Answer: about 7.5 percent for your half, if the total pension fund accumulates interest at 4 percent.)

8. *"But I wouldn't save if I weren't forced to."*   Finally, look at Social Security. Under social security an employee and his employer *must* both pay out of the employee's wages 4.2 percent of the first $6,600 received each year. That is 8.4 percent each year, or $554 annually. At age 65 the employee may retire and receive about $4,000 annually for the rest of his or his widow's life (whoever lives longer). But suppose beginning at age 25 you set that same amount ($554) aside yourself. (The fact that half of social security is set aside by the employer does not change the fact that it is taken out of the employee's wage—by the employer rather than by the employee himself.) To what amount would $554 invested annually accumulate at the end of forty years? At 10 percent per year (a *very modest* and safe rate of return for investments in the stock market) you would have accumulated an amount of $245,000! You could then eat that up at a rate of $25,000 per year for the next twenty years, which is certainly a lot more than you are going to get from social security, no matter how you figure your likely returns from social security. (Incidentally, at 8 percent, which is far *below* the stock-market average of the past seventy years, you would accumulate about $143,000, which would give you over $14,500 annually for twenty years. We have ignored the income tax you would

have to pay—but that would, when applied to the 10 percent growth, bring results close to those for the 8 percent rate.)

Why the great disparity between social security and what you can do privately? Social security (as well as most private insurance companies) credits you with barely 4 percent. At that rate you would accumulate a fund of about $53,000, which would yield an annuity of $3,870 for twenty years. Again note that social security payments promise some life insurance if you should die before age 65 and medical insurance afterwards, but both could be bought on an individual basis and still leave you far ahead. The essential difference arises from the difference in the credited growth rate.

Wealth, Income, Consumption, Saving, Profits

We are now in a position to give rigorous statements relating wealth, income, interest, profits, losses, consumption, saving, and investment.

Wealth. Wealth is the current stock of economic goods. A measure of the market value of wealth is the sum of the values of those goods, each unit of each good being valued at the market price. With 100 units of goods, each selling today for $1, wealth is $100.

Standard Income. If wealth is put to maximum *foreseeable* valued use, the wealth value in exactly one year hence will, we shall suppose, have increased to $110. Wealth is 10 percent larger at the end of a year. The rate of interest, which is here the rate of growth of wealth, is 10 percent per year. It follows that during that year people could have consumed $10 worth of goods while still keeping the original wealth of $100. That rate of consumption is predictable from the current wealth and rate of interest. This predicted (by the market) realizable rate of increase in wealth is the *standard income* available from the wealth of the economy. A person can consume all his income and still end the year with exactly the same amount of wealth he started with. Standard income is defined as the maximum predicted rate of growth in wealth (that is, rate at which wealth can be consumed and still leave the owner with an unreduced wealth).[6]

If wealth is $100 and the rate of interest is 10 percent, then annual income is $10 per year. Income is equal to wealth times the rate of interest: $I = W \times r$, where r is the rate of interest, W is wealth, and I is income. Wealth, the rate of interest, and income are locked together. If any two are known, the other can be determined.

Savings. Why did we say "predicted" realizable rate of increase in wealth when defining standard income? Because there are two different ways for wealth to increase. The first is foreseeable income that can be saved. *Saving* (investing) can, by definition, occur only at a rate that does not exceed the flow of goods and services (income). Hence, at 10 percent interest, wealth of $100 today can yield goods and services during the year which, if saved, would bring the total wealth to $110 in one year.[7] By buying that good

---

[6] The effect of inflation can easily be allowed without upsetting this definition of income.

[7] More accurately, if the standard income flows in at a constant rate all during the year, then the saving during the year will itself be yielding an income during the rest of the year. Allowing for this instantaneous compounding of interest, the wealth at year's end would be about $111.

today for $100, you are buying the claim to the predicted $110 in one year. So wealth can be increased by not consuming all the income—that is, by saving (investing).

Profits. A second way wealth can increase is through *revision in beliefs,* expectations, or anticipations about future yields. The change may occur because people increase their expectations of yields, physical growth, or demand. In other words, present values can change *unpredictably.* Present beliefs about future yields or values of services from current goods can change for an enormous variety of reasons: earthquakes, fire, fashions, population migrations, inventions, and so on. As knowledge about those factors or events becomes surer, current values of goods change to reflect that revised demand for current goods. These *unforeseen* value changes (*profits* or *losses*) reflect changes in knowledge and demands, changes that were not formerly fully anticipated in the market.

If your wealth today is $100, and unexpectedly good news develops about future yields *or* about demands for the services of the goods you own, market prices of the goods will rise, and your wealth will increase to, say, $120. (The interest rate we shall suppose is 10 percent.) Your increase of $20 of wealth may occur in one day. Your unpredicted (by the market) $20 increase in wealth is a *profit* (the interest or income accumulation in one day at 10 percent annual interest is minuscule). In that day you realized a profit of $20. Your rate of income *flow* increased by $2 per year—from $10 to $12 annually. The $20 increase in wealth will give you $2 more income *per year*. Your income flow is now $12, instead of $10 per year. Do not confuse the *wealth* measure of profit with the increased flow of income of $2 per year.

It is tempting, but wrong, to say that you must have decided also to *save* the $20 increase in wealth rather than to consume it. This would be inconsistent with our definition of the term "saving." There is no need to do any saving to get that $20 profit, any more than there is a need to save every day all of one's wealth in order not to consume it. Saving, as defined, is not simply nonconsumption; it is a special kind of nonconsumption. It is nonconsumption of *income*. The nonconsumption of wealth is not an act of saving. If a person consumes none of his income, he saves all of his income, and he can't possibly save more than that. If he consumes all of his income, he saves nothing. And if he consumes more than his income and thereby destroys part of his wealth, he is said to be *dis*saving.

15, 16, 17, 18, 19

Capital Values, Property, and Care of Wealth

Anticipations of future events affect present prices of assets, even without any other changes in the current situation. It is sufficient that expectations change. In the stock exchange these revisions are made especially apparent, for the price of a share of common stock—a share of ownership in a business corporation—is interpreted as the capitalized present worth of the expected future net receipts. A firm may have negative net receipts this year; but if it is expected to have positive net receipts thereafter, its stock price now reflects that entire future flow. If it is suddenly expected that *higher* taxes will be placed on cars, the capital value of General Motors stock will drop now, imposing a loss of wealth on the *current* owners.

Do not miss the implication. Both private-property rights and capital-goods markets, in which ownership of assets can be bought and sold, are essential institutional foundations of the capitalist system. If either is suppressed, the system will lead to actions that appear to be "wasteful or shortsighted," especially in the maintenance of and investment in durable goods with future yields. A houseowner will maintain and repair his house even though the repairs may not give him better housing now. The market price anticipates lower subsequent maintenance expenditures consequent to present repairs. The houseowner may, in fact, sacrifice some current heating and lighting to pay for that repair and maintenance. If, instead, the owner had spent the money for current services—such as a warmer, brighter house—the value of the house would have fallen.

This suggests that a renter-tenant who is responsible for maintenance and repair would divert less funds from current heat and light to maintain and improve the premises than would an owner. However, the owner is not blind to this potential "biased" tenant behavior and, therefore, takes precautionary countermeasures. The rental contract will provide penalties for carelessness by the tenant in maintaining premises.

Another illustration of the differences in effects of types of property rights is provided by the modern business firm. The owner is influenced by all effects—present and future—that change the wealth of his firm. Future developments will be capitalized more into the ownership value of the firm than onto the current employees, who will therefore be motivated more by what happens now and less by what happens to the firm in the more distant future. To direct employees' actions more toward the total range of effects, two kinds of pay systems are sometimes annexed to the wage system. One is a stock-option scheme, in which employees have rights to buy shares of stock at pre-assigned values. Because the long-run effects of their actions will be capitalized in the present value of the shares of stock, employees will pay more heed to the long-run effects than they would without the stock-option scheme. Another scheme—called "profit sharing," in which employees share the annual "earnings" of the firm—misses the mark because "earnings" do not measure the capital-value changes of the firm. The profits are the changes in the capital value of the business revealed by the price of the common stock. The computed current "earnings" are less responsive to the longer-run implications of present events and fail to call as much attention to the wealth-changing factors. Of the two, the stock-option plan is more effective in encouraging decisions according to the wealth-maximizing criterion, because employees with stock options share in the capitalization process, in which future consequences of present actions are capitalized into their present wealth as co-owners.

Human Capital

Capital values exist for people as well as for nonhuman goods. However, we see and measure profits and wealth of a *non*human type much more easily and clearly, because inanimate goods are bought and sold. A person normally sells only his current services as they are performed. Yet, each person represents a quantity of wealth—a future flow of services. Although there is no market sale of "free" people by which that value can be observed, measured, or exchanged for other forms of wealth, there are other indicators of human wealth.

One measure of human wealth is life insurance. People earning only $10,000 per year may take out insurance for $50,000 to insure themselves against a future loss of wealth, from death or disability. The amount of insurance a person buys is correlated with his human wealth.

If a person could literally sell his future services now, he could hold other forms of wealth. As it is, he must keep his wealth tied up in the form of his own labor services. This is a disadvantage for "free" people. They must continue to bear the risks of unforeseen developments that may change the value of their human wealth—whether they want to bear that risk or not.

Occasionally, however, people do manage to sell some rights to their future labor services. Classic examples are athletes who receive "bonuses" for signing with some ball team to play exclusively for that team. Nearly half a million dollars was paid to a college athlete, J. Namath, for the exclusive ownership of his future football services. He sold the risk on his future services to the person who now "owns" them. Mr. Namath has sold some of his liberties. Other athletes (probably thousands) have received bonuses for part of their future playing services. That they will also receive annual salaries does not affect the fact that they have sold part of their future services.

Star entertainers make exclusive service contracts for many years at specified minimum salaries. Although they cannot be forced to render specific performance, they cannot legally work for anyone else, and can be sued for damages if they do. These contracts help the employee to exchange his long-run service value for other wealth. Long-term contracts enable the employee to borrow *larger* amounts of money now with which to buy a house and other present goods. Their wealth (future services) is more exchangeable for current services or other goods.

Borrowing has advantages that its critics often fail to see. These advantages may best be explained in terms of one group of people who find it difficult, even today, to borrow against their human wealth—college students. If students could offer lenders iron-clad rights to collect parts of their future earnings, many people would be more willing to make loans to them. After all, a young man now entering college represents a wealth on the average of about $100,000–$150,000. When the average man asks his best girl to marry him, he is offering her at least $50,000 in wealth. If that seems large, compute the present value (at say, 8 percent) of an annual stream of wages of about $10,000 for the next forty years—which is probably an *under*estimation of the average for college graduates.

If, after a few years of work, your earnings prove to be much higher than anyone expected, your wealth will jump—except that you won't see it recorded in some marketplace. Will you call that unexpected increase "profits"? You should. If you had formed a business firm to sell your services, the firm would have become much more valuable. Its profit is your earnings capitalized into the present wealth measure. But almost no one goes through that formality; so we confusingly do not speak of profits to labor—only to owners of inanimate goods. And if you should unexpectedly learn that your current job will end in six months, your wealth at this very moment will have fallen, even though there is no market to register the fact. You will not wait until your wages fall before you readjust your consumption. You will adjust it immediately. Your behavior will reflect that loss of wealth.

Since human capital has no market-revealed capital value, as it would if people were bought and sold, the concept of human wealth and income to labor is difficult to measure. Consequently, "income" to labor is typically considered to be the current rate of earnings. For income-tax purposes, current earnings are treated as "income." The various connotations and interpretations of the word "income" are troublesome if one does not guess the correct one. Occasionally, "measured current income" is used in economics to refer to this *current-earnings* rate, while "permanent" or "equalized" income refers to some long-run life-time average of earnings, as a sort of proxy flow measure of human wealth. Sometimes current "measured" income is called "transitory" income, because it may fluctuate temporarily around some long-run average trend—the so-called "permanent" averaged income. A change in permanent income would result

Capital Values, Interest Rates, and Wealth

from some unforeseen change that induced one to revise his beliefs about that long-term average. Not every fluctuation in current measured income is unexpected, hence not every change in current income induces a change in "permanent" income or in behavior.

Some Confusions about Interest Rates

If we are to be financial geniuses, we must avoid a common confusion about the relationship between inflation and the rate of interest. While we will analyze it later, a useful understanding of the relationship can be indicated here by an example. You lend $100 for a long time, say 30 years, at a rate of interest of 5 percent per year. The $5 interest paid to you annually will rise or fall in purchasing power depending upon whether or not the general price level of various goods and services falls or rises. If the price level should increase during the first year by 3 percent, this means that of the 5 percent interest ($5 each year) about 5 percentage points (or $3 in real terms) is eroded away by the higher prices you must pay for goods and services. In effect, in real terms you have gotten only about 2 percent interest on your $100 loan.[8] (For simplicity of exposition, we ignore the fact that the $100 to be repaid will also have lost purchasing power if the price level is higher when the principal is repaid some 30 years later.) If, however, you and most other people *correctly anticipated* that the price level would rise in that first year, you would not have been willing to lend at so low a nominal rate, and the borrower would have been more willing to pay a higher rate. As a result, the nominal interest rate on the loan would have been higher, say 8 percent per annum, allowing 3 percentage points for the anticipated price level rise and 5 percent for interest in real purchasing power terms. In all the exposition earlier in this chapter, we were assuming no inflation and that the lenders and borrowers correctly anticipated there would be no change in the price level. Of course, if they anticipated incorrectly and there were a subsequent unanticipated inflation, the initial negotiated nominal interest rate would have remained at 5 percent and the lenders would have suffered a loss in real purchasing power of the interest received, while the borrowers who repay in diminished purchasing power would have gained. (But we shall analyze the inflation effects more fully in Chapter 32, after we have acquired some requisite knowledge of the monetary processes.) Roughly speaking, you can see that the *nominal* (as we shall call it) interest rate indicating the number of dollars to be paid annually per dollar of principal value of the loan will reflect two considerations—(a) the *basic* rate of interest (the rate of interest that would exist in the absence of any inflation anticipations) and (b) the adjustment for the anticipated percentage rate of rise of the price level. As this is written in 1971, the *monetary* rate of interest being negotiated on first class (AAA) long-term industrial bonds is about 8 percent. (In the financial community, the best bonds are given the rating AAA (triple A), with less secure bonds being rated with letters down through AA, A, and B.) It is widely believed (if we judge from financial newspapers and other evidence) that the public anticipates that inflation will continue at about 3–6 percent per annum; it has been occurring at that rate for the past five years. If we accept the premise that inflation of 3–6 percent per annum is anticipated and, therefore, that currently negotiated *monetary* (or, as they are also called, *nominal*) interest rates incorporate that

---

[8] The more exact relationship between the "real" interest rate, r, in money units for a stable price level, and the nominal market interest rate, R, in money units, if the price level is *known* to be changing at the rate of p percent a year, is $R = (1 + r)(1 + p) - 1$.

anticipation, then the rate of interest implied (or paid in real terms) is about 2 to 5 percent—not an unusual rate, judging from the past century of experience.

To complete a catalogue of terminology, suppose the inflation, as we initially assumed, had *not* been anticipated at all. The *promised nominal* (*monetary*) rate on the $100 loan was 5 percent, the *basic* rate was 5 percent, the anticipated inflation rate was zero, the *realized nominal* rate was 5 percent, but the realized rate in *real* terms was only 2 percent. The terms "realized" and "real" are so similar that the two very different meanings are often confused. There is a realized nominal monetary (dollar) rate and there is realized rate in real purchasing power terms. For example, as explained earlier, if the promise to pay $5 a year is not fully honored and only $4 is paid despite the promised nominal rate of 5 percent, the realized monetary rate would be only 4 percent (even without inflation). If there had also been an inflation of 3 percent during that first year, the realized real rate would have been only 1 percent. So keep the terms distinct: monetary rate, realized monetary rate, realized real rate, and basic rate.

Let's move to the brink of our present analytical skills. We have not yet analyzed the determinants of the *basic* rate of interest. Nor have we explained what causes inflations, affects their rates, or induces anticipations about inflations. But it is clear, we hope, that to bring down the *monetary* nominal interest rate from the present 9 percent on loans, two separate tactics would be necessary. One would operate on the rate of inflation in order to bring down anticipations of inflation to anticipations of less or no inflation. The other would have to bring down or prevent a rise of the basic rate of interest. As it happens, these are influenced by separate, yet correlated, factors. To anticipate later analyses, large governmental deficits financed by increased borrowing will push up the basic rate. On the other hand, large increases in the national stock of money will enhance anticipations of inflation. As we shall see, ability to control the stock of money to avoid inflation and its anticipations is not entirely divorced from the size of government deficit that is financed by borrowing. Submission to public or political outcry insisting on a lower rate of interest (which one—the *nominal* or the *basic* or the *real*?), by permitting a more rapid increase in the money stock, will lead to inflation and anticipations of more inflation with an even higher nominal rate of interest being negotiated on bonds. The confusion between the basic and the nominal expressed rate (which *includes* anticipations of inflation) becomes a source of political mischief and newspaper- and television-commentator nonsense. Avoid it, if you can. Please bear with us until later when we shall analyze the factors and forces affecting the basic rate and the anticipated rate of inflation—and thus the nominal rate.

Summary

1 Capital goods can be used at more than one moment in time. Present prices, or capital values, exist for and reflect beliefs about a sequence or series of future services. By means of present capital values, different future sequences of future amounts can be made comparable.

2 Earlier availability is more valuable than later availability—that is, the rate of interest is positive. The rate of interest is: (a) a measure of the relationship between present amounts of a good and the amounts of future goods for which they can be traded; (b) a measure of the maximal rate of growth of wealth; (c) a measure of the price of earlier availability of a good; and (d) the time premium paid for borrowed wealth.

3 Failing to allow for interest—that is, assuming a zero rate of interest—will produce erroneous analysis. The higher the rate of interest, the lower is the present price of any future service.

4 $P(1 + r)^t = A$ summarizes the relationship among r, P, A, and t.

5 Standard income is the predicted maximum rate of consumption that can be maintained without reducing wealth. It is equal to the product of wealth and the rate of interest. Saving and investment are both defined as the unconsumed portion of standard income.

6 Profit (or loss) is the unpredicted (by the market) change in wealth.

7 Under the influence of a capital market with private property, decisions will be affected by the fact that future consequences of present decisions are capitalized in wealth.

8 People have wealth values, but they are not readily measured in the marketplace, because people are not bought and sold.

9 Nominal interest rate is approximately basic interest plus anticipated inflation rate.

Questions

1 You invest $350 today. At the end of one year, you get back $370. What is the implied or effective rate of interest?

2 To how much will $250 grow at 7 percent compounded annually in three years? (How long will it take to double? Use the rule of 72.)

3 At the end of a year you will get $220. At 10 percent interest rate, what is the present amount that will grow to that amount? In other words, what is the present value of $220 deferred one year, at 10 percent?

4 In what sense is interest the price of money? In what sense is it not the price of money?

5 What is the present value of $2,500 due in five years at 4 percent?

6 What present amount is equivalent to $1,000 paid at the end of each of the next three years, at 6 percent interest?

7 If you can borrow money from college at a zero interest rate for six years, and if you borrow $1,000 now, what is the present value of the "gift" to you, at 5 percent rate of interest? (Hint: Each year you earn $50 interest by investing that money now at 5 percent. What is the present value of that six-year annuity of $50?) Which would you rather have—an outright gift of $250 or that loan?

8 You borrow $1,000 today and agree to pay the loan in five annual equal installments at 6 percent interest rate. Using Table 11–3, determine amount of each payment, the first due in one year.

9 You buy a house by borrowing the full price of the house, $20,000. Your annual installments in repaying the loan are $1,754 for twenty years at 6 percent. (Do you agree?)
a. At the end of the first year, how much of the house's value is yours—what is your equity? (Hint: On $20,000, the interest for one year at 6 percent is $1,200. You paid $1,754 at the end of the first year.)
b. At the end of the second year, what is your equity?
c. At the end of twenty years, assuming the house is still worth $20,000, what is your equity?

10 You are a building contractor. The rate of interest rises.
   a. What happens to the value of buildings that you may build?
   b. What do you suppose the effect will be on your business?

11 If the value of your buildings or common stock should fall, how can you tell whether there has been a rise in the rate of interest or a fall in anticipated future net receipts? (Hint: Look at the bond market. How will this help give an answer?)

12 You own a building worth $10,000. You receive word that the value of your building has fallen to $5,000. One possibility is that the interest rate has risen to twice its former level. A second possibility is that the building has been damaged by a fire. In either event your wealth is now $5,000. Do you care which factor caused a decrease in your wealth? Why?

13 Mr. *A* has an income of $10,000 per year. At Christmas his rich uncle unexpectedly gives him $5,000 in cash.
   a. What is his income during that year?
   b. Is the $5,000 gift a part of his income?
   c. How much is his annual rate of income increased as a result of the gift of $5,000 (at interest rates of 10 percent)?

14 Which do you think will have a bigger influence in revising your consumption rate over the future—an unexpected gift of $1,000 or an unexpected salary increase of $50 per month? (Hint: What is the present value of each at, say, 6 percent per year?)

15 Your wealth today is $1,000. At 10 percent interest rate, what is your standard income?

16 If your income from nonbusiness wealth is $500 a year, what is your wealth, at a 10 percent interest rate?

17 If you consume none of your income for two years, what will be your wealth at the end of two years, if it is $1,000 now with 5 percent interest?

18 If you announce today that you intend to save all your income for the next year, what will happen to the value of your wealth now? In one year?

Production, Exchange, Specialization, and Efficiency

12

UNTIL this chapter, production of goods has been ignored. What determines which goods are to be produced, how they are to be produced, and who will produce them?

As with the task of rationing existing goods, there are many ways to resolve these questions: a dictator can direct slaves; people can work cooperatively in a communal-ownership society; they can act within a private-property market system—to mention a few.

We have concentrated on a system characterized by private property in goods and services, in which the owner has the right to decide how those goods shall be used or to whom he will pass the title (right to use). A person's right to his labor services was included in his own private property. To the extent that a person's rights are restricted by threats of violence, anarchy intrudes. To the extent that the government enforces legal restrictions on the choice by individuals of use or of exchange of goods, socialism replaces private-property systems. Socialism is a system in which decisions about the use of economic goods and services are exercised via governmental political processes. Every society is a mixture of private property and socialism; furthermore, the composition of the mixture varies over time, partly in response to changing attitudes toward risk, degrees of tolerance for idiosyncratic behavior, and ease with which competing groups can acquire government power.

Regardless of the systems, certain tasks are involved, and certain concepts are essential to analysis—for example, *production, efficiency, comparative advantage,* and *specialization.* After explaining and relating these concepts, we shall apply economic analysis to see how production is controlled in a private-property society; that is, the "production logic" of that system will be derived. We concentrate on that system because it is the dominant system for controlling production in the United States—not because it can be shown to be the "best" system. If one feels he must make judgments, the analysis permits a more informed judgment.

Production and Exchange

In the broadest sense, production is the act of increasing one's utility. *Exchange* of existing goods is *productive* because, as we have seen, it increases one's utility. Production also can occur when the physical attributes of resources—including their time of availability, place, or form—are changed. Moving water from a well into a house is productive; carrying coal from the mine to the furnace is productive; tilling the soil, planting seeds, or caring for the crop is productive; so is harvesting, cleaning, grading, transporting, preserving, and distributing the crop to retail stores; so is advertising, wrapping, and delivery to the consumer's home. Production consists also of play and of entertainment. Any activity that I offer to pay a person to do (to increase my utility) is productive from *my* point of view. If he accepts my offer, the activity is productive from *his* point of view.

Economic theory analyzes ways in which given amounts of technical knowledge, effort, and resources can be coordinated so that production can be achieved. Economics implies that production of goods will increase when people appropriately "exchange" their productive activity. Adam Smith, in his famous book *An Inquiry into the Nature and Causes of the Wealth of Nations,* called this last principle "division of labor" or "specialization"; it is now generally labeled "comparative advantage."[1]

In the same way that *exchange for consumption* was numerically illustrated earlier, we will show how *specialization and exchange in production* can yield a greater physical output than if no exchange in production were permitted. Then we shall investigate some methods for inducing that specialization—one method relying on the free marketplace with individual incentives and private-property rights.

The existence of corporations, labor unions, credit buying, suburban shopping centers, trading stamps, discount houses, factories, and all the other institutions through which economic activity is conducted obscures the basic principles that underlie the organization of production in a private enterprise society. A television set is a complicated mechanism; yet it is built up with a chain of relatively simple principles. Once these principles are grasped, the method by which a set operates is said to be understood. On the surface, the system looks enormously complicated and confusing. And, without a theory, it is. But if one has a valid theory, bewilderment is replaced by confidence, complexity by sequences of simplicity, and confusion by order. So, in this and the next chapter, do not think the expository simplicity means the principles developed are not applicable to the real world. They are, and like all theory and analysis, their ability to be expressed in, and based on, such simple form is a virtue. This enhances the understanding of the way the economic constellation operates. It is not a disordered collection of uncoordinated activities.

---

[1] Had Smith lived today, he might have called it the *"Don't*-do-it-yourself" principle. It is interesting that Smith's book did not contain a logically correct exposition; instead it contained a masterfully persuasive statement of the results of free exchange. It was Robert Torrens, who some forty years after the idea had been "sold," demonstrated its logical validity. Possibly, had Smith tried to give a logically air-tight demonstration, instead of a suggestive plausible interpretation, he would never have made his "point" popular.

What assurance do you have that the economic analysis to be presented is valid? At the present moment, you have none—just as you have none when you take a physics or chemistry course. Experiments in a physics course *illustrate* the principles in special experimental circumstances. In precisely the same way, the principles stated in economics can *here* be illustrated. How does one know that these principles will apply to the rest of the world, which the student cannot yet observe? He doesn't know; and he doesn't know that the principles of physics will always work, either. He simply has to wait until he has had time to observe real events; in that way he tests, observes, and decides for himself whether to continue to believe in these principles and act accordingly. At present, we do tell the reader that overwhelming evidence supports the validity of the economic principles. With this prologue, we present in this chapter the principles of specialization in production, in the context of a simple two-man society with two alternative producible goods. Then in Chapter 13 we shall investigate the effects of enlarging the society; we also expand a bit to consider the effects of price-takers' and price-searchers' markets on the response of production to consumer demands. In Chapter 14 we go into institutional features: (a) closed or restricted access to markets, (b) how private-property rights make one heed effects of his actions and thus influence his productive behavior, (c) the effects of costs of information about potential transactions, and (d) the problem of production of goods heavily loaded with "public-goods attributes." This will prepare us for analysis of further principles of production that are dependent upon still other institutional idiosyncratic features—large business corporations, labor unions, extensive durable goods, credit buying, advertising—that modify in one way or another some of these basic propositions about production.

1

Specialization and Enlarged Output

Upon entering our two-person society, we first meet Mr. A, whose currently relevant distinguishing attribute is not his sex, color, age, religion, height, weight, marital status, eye color, blood type, political affiliation, or personality, but is instead his *production-possibility set* for two goods, here called X and Y.

The production-possibility boundary. Suppose Mr. A can, with a given amount of time and energy, produce daily six units of X, *or* three units of Y, *or* any linearly interpolated combination of X and Y. If he devoted half a day to X and the other half to Y, he could produce daily three units of X and one and a half units of Y. Or he could produce three Y and no X. Table 12–1 shows part of the set of possible daily output combinations of X and Y. For a unit increment of X, he must forsake production of $.5Y$ (or, conversely, for each extra Y he must forsake $2X$). His ratio of the *change* in output of X consequent to a unit *change* in output of Y is always $2X = 1Y$, or $.5Y = 1X$. This ratio is his *production marginal rate of transformation* between X and Y. This can be expressed also by the statement that his marginal cost of producing Y is $2X$. "Marginal cost of Y" is the amount of the other goods that must be forsaken to produce a unit increment of Y.

Mr. A's production-possibility set can be easily graphed. In Figure 12–1, all his possible output combinations are represented by the straight line; if he produces less than is possible, his production is represented by a point inside the triangular area bounded by that line and the axes. The daily rate of production of X is measured along the horizontal axis and the daily rate of production of Y along the vertical axis. The extreme upper-left point

TABLE 12–1. Some Daily Combinations from Mr. A's Production-Possibility Set

X and Y
6 and 0
5 " 0.5
4 " 1.0
3 " 1.5
2 " 2.0
1 " 2.5
0 " 3.0

In one day Mr. A can produce any of the listed combinations of output of X and Y. He could produce 6X and zero Y, or he could produce 5X and .5Y, and so on. To increase his daily output rate of Y by 1 unit costs him 2X per day. Thus his marginal cost of a Y is 2X. To produce, on the other hand, one more X costs him the sacrifice of .5Y; hence, his marginal cost of X is .5Y.

on the production-possibility boundary denotes an output of all $Y(3)$ and no X, while the lower-right-hand extreme point denotes the maximum possible output of $6X$. Point I denotes an output combination of $2X$ and $2Y$. Point II denotes $4X$ and $1Y$. Mr. A's production technique will be called *efficient* if he is producing outputs *on* the production-possibility boundary at points like I or II, but not III *inside* the boundary. A production

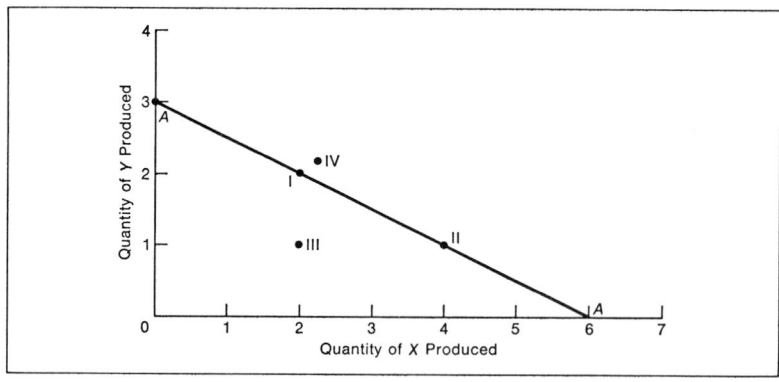

FIGURE 12–1. Mr. *A*'s Efficient Production-Possibility Boundary

Mr. *A* can produce any combination of X and Y indicated by any point on or inside the area bounded by the line AA and the two axes. To produce the combination denoted by III would be inefficient, because with no greater available resources he could produce more of X and Y (any point on the line between I and II). The combination denoted by point IV is not producible by Mr. *A*. It lies outside his possibility. All points on the line AA denote efficient outputs because at any point on that line, Mr. *A* cannot produce more Y without having to produce less X (or more X without having to give up some output of Y). The *slope* of the line measures marginal cost.

technique is "efficient," by definition, as long as the output of *both* X and Y cannot be increased. To be efficient means that the only way he can increase the output of any product, X, is by giving up some output, Y (or conversely). Every point on his production-possibility boundary is an efficient *production* combination.

An impossible output of 2.25 of X and 2.25 of Y is portrayed by Point IV *outside* his production frontier. If he produces the same number of X's as Y's, the best he can do is 2 of X and of Y. Unless Mr. A sacrifices leisure, gets extra productive resources, or learns better methods of production, he cannot be outside the production-possibility boundary, AA.

The *best* of all the efficient points (that is, the one that gives him the greatest utility) cannot be detected from just these data. That depends upon his demand conditions. For the moment, we will arbitrarily suppose that for Mr. A the best is two units of X and two units of Y per day. He is self-sufficiently producing and consuming that output.

TABLE 12–2. Some Daily Combinations from Mr. B's Production-Possibility Set

X and Y
3 and 0
2.5 " 0.5
2.0 " 1.0
1.5 " 1.5
1.0 " 2.0
0.5 " 2.5
0 " 3.0

Mr. B can produce any of these combinations in one day. To produce one more Y costs him 1X; hence, his marginal cost of Y is 1X.

Mr. B has his production-possibility set indicated in Table 12–2 and Figure 12–2. If he wants an *equal* number of X and Y, he can produce 1.5 of each. He could produce 2X and 1Y, giving up .5Y in order to get .5 more X. His marginal cost of producing Y is 1X, differing from Mr. A's marginal cost of Y, which is 2X. We shall see that this difference in marginal costs—portrayed by the differences in the *slopes* of the two production boundary lines, AA and BB—is a crucially important feature. Mr. B's line, BB, has a slope of "minus one": with every increase of one unit in output of X, he has a decrease of one unit in Y. Mr. A's slope is minus ½, because for every increase of one unit in X, he sacrifices a half unit of Y. A steeper slope of the production-possibility boundary shows a greater marginal cost of X, because the greater is the amount of Y that must be sacrificed to get an increase of one unit in X. Mr. B has the steeper slope; i.e., he has higher marginal costs for producing X. Conversely, he must be the lower marginal-cost producer of Y.

A *straight-line* production-possibility boundary for each person means the marginal cost of production for each person is *constant* regardless of the rates of production of X and Y. (Later we shall investigate a less artificial case, in which the marginal cost increases as a person produces a good at a higher rate. For the moment we are using this artificial case to show just the gain from specialization, rather than also the equilibrium rate of production of each good.)

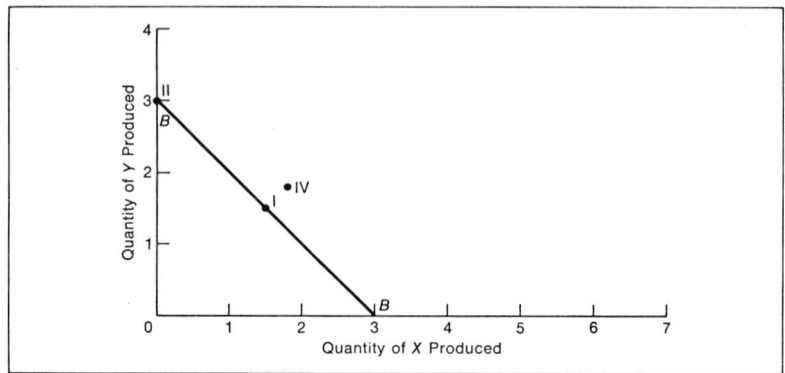

FIGURE 12-2. Mr. *B*'s Efficient Production-Possibility Boundary

Mr. *B* can produce any output on the line *BB* (or any output beneath it—but all beneath it are inefficient). Point IV is beyond his production capabilities. The slope of the line, "minus 1," tells us that the marginal cost to Mr. *B* of producing one more *X* is the loss (minus) of 1 unit of *Y*. His marginal cost of *X* is one *Y*. Contrast this with the slope of Mr. *A*'s line in the preceding diagram, where the marginal cost of an *X* to Mr. *A* is .5*Y*.

Production and exchange. Temporarily, suppose that Mr. *A* prefers a consumption mix such that for each *X* he has one *Y*. Also assume Mr. *B* wants the same ratio of *X* to *Y*. In this event, Mr. *A* would be producing and consuming 2*X* and 2*Y*, while Mr. *B* would be producing and consuming 1.5 of each—each combination being portrayed by points "I" on the respective graphs of the production possibilities. Both persons are self-sufficient.

The top half of Table 12–3 shows that the *total* "national" output of *X* is 3.5, and the total "national" output of *Y* is also 3.5. At best, *A* can have 2*X* and 2*Y*; Mr. *B* can have 1.5 of each—*if we prohibit production specialization*. But if specialization (and exchange) is allowed, then—*while still staying on each person's production-possibility boundary*—it *is* possible to get an output of *more* than 3.5*X* and 3.5*Y* to be allocated between Mr. *A* and Mr. *B*. This means each person can consume amounts *above* his production-possibility boundary. How can this "magical" synergistic increase in total output be achieved? Answer: By use of the principle of *specialization,* which rests on the fact of *comparative advantage*—a name for differences in marginal costs of production. To show how this principle of production leads to a *larger* output of *both X* and *Y*, we shall resort to a parable.

In the community we are visiting, a dictator is responsible for all production control. By a clever reassignment of tasks, the dictator can get a bigger total output. The dictator tells Mr. *A* to reduce his output of *Y* by one unit and increase his output of *X* by two units. His output mix changes from 2*X* and 2*Y* to 1*Y* and 4*X* (represented by point II *on* his production-feasibility frontier of Figure 12–1). At the same time, the dictator orders Mr. *B* to reduce his output of *X* by 1.5 units, down to zero, and to increase his production of *Y* by 1.5 units to three units. This moves him from point I to point II *on* his production-feasibility frontier (Figure 12–2).

The "national" output is four units of *X* (4*X* from Mr. *A*) and four units of *Y* (1*Y* from Mr. *A* and 3*Y* from Mr. *B*). The national output has "miraculously" increased from 3.5 units to four units for both *X* and *Y*! Before "explaining" how this miracle

TABLE 12-3. Before Specialization: Production (and Consumption)

	X	Y
Mr. A	2 (2)	2 (2)
Mr. B	1.5 (1.5)	1.5 (1.5)
	3.5 (3.5)	3.5 (3.5)

After Specialization and Exchange: Production (and Consumption)

	X	Y
Mr. A	4 (2.25)	1 (2.25)
Mr. B	0 (1.75)	3 (1.75)
	4 (4.0)	4 (4.0)

Mr. A can without specialization produce 2X and 2Y and he can consume those 2X and 2Y each day. With specialization he can produce 4X and 1Y, and then by exchange with B be able to consume 2.25 of X and of Y each, exactly .25 more of each than without exchange. Similarly, Mr. B can obtain an increase in his consumption potential from 1.5X to 1.75X, and a similar increase for Y. The increased output and the increased consumption with only the added work of engaging in exchange is the synergistic gain from trade (specialization).

occurred, we note from the bottom half of Table 12–3 that for Mr. *A* and Mr. *B each* to have *more X* and *Y* than before, the dictator may take 1.75 units of *X* (or anything less than two units and more than 1.5) from Mr. *A* and give them to Mr. *B* in return for 1.25 units of *Y* (or any amount less than 1.5 units and more than one) which he transfers from Mr. *B* to Mr. *A*. This will leave Mr. *A* with 2.25 units of *X and* also 2.25 of *Y*, which is exactly .25 units more of *X* and of *Y* than he was able to produce alone without the dictator's instructions. On the other side, Mr. *B* will have 1.75 units of *X* and of *Y,* or .25 more of each than he is able to produce. Several other combinations of total output and of its division could be selected, but we have chosen the one that makes the increase in output stand out in boldest, simplest numbers.

Efficient specialization. What has happened can be summarized by saying that Mr. *A specializes* in the production of *X,* while Mr. *B specializes* in the production of *Y.* To specialize means that a person *produces more of some commodity than he consumes*. It does *not* mean he produces only *one* thing; rather, he produces *more* of some things, and less of others, than *he* consumes. It most certainly does *not* imply "surplus" production of *X* by Mr. *A,* nor of *Y* by Mr. *B.* Except for the work involved in the dictator's instructions and actions, neither *A* nor *B* works any harder than before. Both were working on their production possibility before the revision; they were *individually* efficient. Now neither person has violated his production-possibility boundary—yet the total output has increased. Although each was *individually* efficient in his production, there was "inefficient" *social* production.

As long as the marginal costs of production of X and Y for Mr. A are different from those for Mr. B, it will always pay them to specialize. Mr. A can produce one more X at a cost of .5Y, while Mr. B can reduce his X by one unit and produce 1Y, which is 5Y more than Mr. A has to give up to produce an X. If Mr. A were to produce two more X, he would sacrifice 1Y, but that 1Y could be produced by Mr. B at a cost of only 1X, leaving a net gain of 1X (with no decrease in Y). Mr. A can produce one more X at a "cost" of only .5Y, but Mr. B can produce one more X only at a higher cost of 1Y. Mr. A is the lower-cost producer of X. Who is the lower-cost producer of Y? Mr. B. He can produce another Y at a cost of only 1X, whereas Mr. A has to sacrifice 2X. Table 12–4 shows the new production possibilities. This represents the output potential from the most efficient production assignments of Mr. A and Mr. B. It is impossible to get more X (or more Y), with each indicated amount of Y (or X), than given in this table. Try to beat it. (We safely offer $1,000 to every person who can.)

TABLE 12–4. Total Daily Production Possibility of X and Y by Mr. A and B

Output X and Y
9 and 0
8 " 1
7 " 2
6 " 3
5 " 3.5
4 " 4
3 " 4.5
2 " 5
1 " 5.5
0 " 6

The production potentials of Mr. A and Mr. B can with efficient coordination result in any of the listed output combinations. At the output combination of 8X and 1Y, who will be producing how much of X and of Y? (Do you agree that Mr. B will be producing 1Y with none from Mr. A? Check it.) Who will be producing how much of X and of Y at the combination of 2X and 5Y? Be sure you can answer this question.

The principle for efficient production is simple. Efficient production of X is obtained if it is produced by those with the lower marginal cost in production of X, while resources with higher marginal costs in production of X should be used in production of non-X.[2]

---

[2] A proof of the logical validity of this proposition requires a bit more complicated mathematics than our simple arithmetic example. For those who have had at least a year of calculus, this proposition is a verbal translation of some of the conditions (marginal equalities or inequalities) for a constrained maximum—that is, for a specified output of Y, maximize the output of X, subject to the constraints of all the individual production-possibility conditions.

Other Rules of Production Control

Results of some other production assignments of Mr. *A* and Mr. *B* can be illustrated by Figure 12–3. In that figure are plotted the production-possibility boundaries of Mr. *A* and Mr. *B* individually, and the *total* national-output boundaries for three different rules of production control.

I. Let both Mr. *A* and Mr. *B* produce *Y*, and then if any *X* is wanted, first have Mr. *B*, the *higher*-marginal-cost producer of *X*, divert some resources toward producing the desired amount of *X*. If more *X* is wanted than Mr. *B* can produce, let the next highest marginal cost producer of *X* also produce *X*. Line I gives the total set of production possibilities yielded when Mr. *A* and Mr. *B* are assigned to production of *X* and *Y* according to this pattern. It doesn't look like the best system.

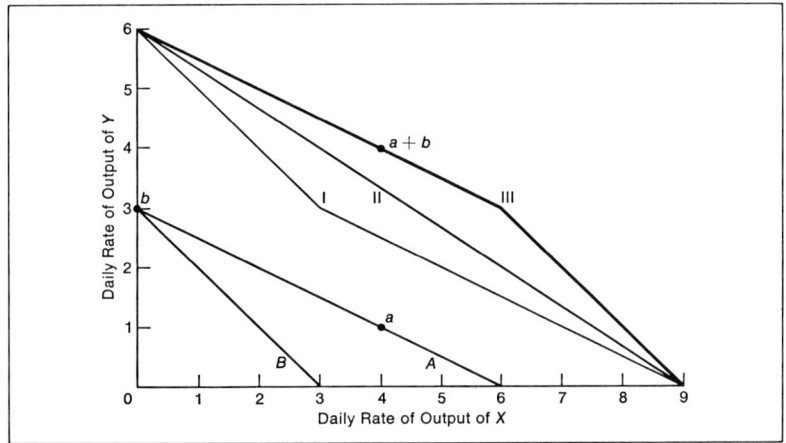

FIGURE 12–3. Production Possibilities for Different Production Rules

Line III denotes achievable combinations of X and Y that can be produced by A and B together. For example, if A produces at point a on his line, AA, and B produces at point b on his line, BB, the sum of the outputs of X and Y from A and B is given by the point a + b on line III. It is impossible to get more X and Y from A and B than that indicated by point a + b. They could get more X, but only with less Y; this would slide them down the line III. If A and B do not coordinate their outputs in an efficient way, they will end up with amounts of X and Y less than those on line III— the efficient production-mix boundary. Lines II and I denote two *in*efficient output boundaries which would be achieved if inefficient rules for coordinating production were followed. Line II results from A and B's devoting *equal proportions* of resources to X and Y. Line I results from reversing the lowest-marginal-cost rule for controlling production (the rule that gives boundary III). Which of the lines—I, II, or III—plots the outputs given in Table 12–4?

II. Line II is obtained by telling Mr. *A* and Mr. *B* always to produce *X* and *Y* in the same proportion as each other. If more *X* is wanted, everyone is told to increase his output of *X* by that desired percentage, and decrease *Y*. It doesn't look best either.

III. Line III is the achievable set of outputs if the rule for line I is reversed. Let both

Mr. *A* and Mr. *B* produce *Y* if only *Y* is wanted; but if some *X* is wanted, assign first to its production the lower-marginal-cost producer. If more *X* is wanted than Mr. *A* can produce, assign the next higher-marginal-cost producer, Mr. *B*. The resulting set of production possibilities is indicated by line III, the outermost, and hence the most efficient, boundary. This is a graph of the unbeatable data in Table 12–4.

In effect, we first move down along Mr. *A*'s production-possibility boundary from all *Y* toward more *X*, while keeping *B* fixed at all *Y* and no *X*; and we move down *B*'s boundary only after *A* has moved to the point of all *X* and no *Y*. Illustrating the earlier numerical example: Point $a + b$ on boundary III is obtained by assigning Mr. *B* to production of *Y* only (represented by his being at the upper-left-hand point, *b*, where his production line cuts the *Y* axis) and by assigning Mr. *A* to the point *a* on his boundary. The sum of the outputs of *Y* from Mr. *A* and *B* is represented by the height of the point $a + b$, while the sum of their outputs of *X* gives the horizontal position of the point $a + b$.

3, 4

Achievement of Efficient Production by Market Exchanges

If the output decisions are made by an all-wise dictator who knows all the production possibilities of each person, presumably efficiency can be achieved—ignoring questions of how the dictator will get his orders enforced and how he will distribute the resulting product.

But in the event of a successful revolt against the dictator, how can people know what to produce? What induces them to do so? One possibility is that after the revolt a system of private property is instituted in each person's rights to his labor services. He is a "free man"; he can work where and at what he wishes. He can sell his goods or services to others if both parties can find a mutually acceptable price (wage). In such a private-property capitalist system, the new "dictator" is the rule of law of private property if the government enforces that rule against all people, even those who do not like private-property systems.

What will each person do? Suppose, at first, each subsists on his own production; each is self-sufficient. He will produce whatever mixture of *X* and *Y* he most prefers of those he can produce. If Mr. *A* is producing a mixture such that he personally (subjectively) values one more *X* as equal to 1*Y*, he will note that he can produce one more *X* if he forsakes only .5*Y*. Therefore, he will shift production toward more *X* and away from *Y*, for he is *willing* to forego (in consumption) as much as 1*Y* to obtain one more *X*, whereas he *must* (in production) sacrifice only .5*Y*. He will continue to shift toward more *X* until he values one more *X* as equivalent to only .5*Y*. In this way he is led to a consumption pattern at which he personally values 1*Y* at .5*Y*, the same as his marginal cost of producing 1*X*. His *personal valuation* of another *X* is *equated* to his *marginal cost* of producing (getting) an *X*. Let us arbitrarily suppose this situation is reached when he produces 2*X* and 2*Y* per day.

Compare this with Mr. *B*. His marginal cost of *X* is 1*Y* (instead of .5*Y* as it is for Mr. *A*). Mr. *B* adjusts his production output until he has a consumption mixture such that he personally values one more *X* at 1*Y*. Now his personal valuation of another *X* is equated to his marginal cost of producing (getting) *X*. Suppose that this occurs at the output mixture of 1.5*X* and 1.5*Y*.

Each person is a subsistence producer. He subsists on what *he* produces. He does not specialize, he engages in no exchange, he is independent, he is his own boss. But as we shall see, each is poorer than if he were not self-sufficient. We have just learned that production is efficiently organized if those who produce X have lower marginal costs of X than those who do not produce X. But here we have Mr. B producing X when his marginal cost of X ($1Y$) is *greater* than Mr. A's ($.5Y$), and Mr. A is producing Y when his marginal cost of $1Y$ ($2X$) is *greater* than Mr. B's ($1X$). (If at this point you feel a bit swamped with comparisons, carefully recheck the numbers in Tables 12–1 and 12–2 once more, because the hard part is over.)

We shall now see how exchange between these two people, each seeking to improve his own situation as he sees it, will lead to an efficient reorganization of production, just as under an all-wise dictator. The end results will be exactly the same as those shown in Table 12–3, and reference to that table will help you follow the discussion. Since we have already investigated how a middleman facilitates exchange, we shall omit him and let Mr. A and Mr. B deal directly with each other—and be their own (unrealistically costless) middlemen.

We know that Mr. B would prefer to buy X at any price below $1Y$, since it costs him that to make X's for himself. (See Table 12–2.) Mr. A can produce them at a marginal cost of $.5Y$ (Table 12–1). Therefore, Mr. A could profit by producing more X to sell to Mr. B for any price over $.5Y$. We shall *arbitrarily* assume he gets a price of $.71Y$ from Mr. B.[3] Each X sold to Mr. B gives Mr. A a net gain of $.21Y$. Mr. B gets a gain of $.29Y$ by being able to buy an X for $.71Y$ instead of producing it himself at a cost of $1Y$.

The next question is how many X's Mr. B buys from Mr. A. To answer would require knowing each person's relative demands for X and Y. To avoid having to bring in, at this time, that extra analysis, we assume that the equilibrium amount of trade is such that Mr. A sells $1.75X$ to Mr. B at a price of $.71Y$ for each X. Mr. A receives $1.25Y$ from Mr. B. Each day they exchange those amounts of X and Y.

How much does each person consume each day? If you check, you will see that Mr. A produces $4X$ and $1Y$; he sells $1.75X$ and gets $1.25Y$, which leaves him with $2.25X$ and $2.25Y$, exactly $.25$ more of each X and Y than he had before trade and specialization (as in Table 12–3).

Mr. B is producing no X and $3Y$, buying $1.75X$ in exchange for 1.25 of his $3Y$, which leaves him with 1.75 of X and Y. The situation is precisely as it was before, under the all-wise, benevolent dictator, shown in Table 12–3. The national output is $4X$ and $4Y$, instead of 3.5 of each as it was before exchange and specialization. And each person, after exchange, gets more of both X and Y than before exchange. What is more, it is impossible to rearrange the assignments of production and trade to give each person a still bigger consumption.

Each is specializing on his product of comparative advantage, *without a dictator*. Such specialization was induced by the compulsion, desire, or drive of each person to benefit himself by getting more goods, and a chance to negotiate acceptable exchange with other people. Even though this driving force is not imposed by other people, it is a pervasive, persistent, and powerful response to the compulsive desire for more.

Profits and Lower Cost of Living

The increased output of $.5$ units of X and of Y is distributed in the form of (1) profits and (2) reduced consumers' prices. Mr. A produced more X's and sold them at a price ($.71Y$) above his costs ($.50Y$). And in turn Mr. B bought X's more cheaply (for only

---

[3] With this assumption we are *implicitly* specifying the demand conditions which are buried in this solution.

.71Y, instead of 1Y). Reducing the cost of X to the consumer and inceasing the producer's profits are ways of distributing the increased output of X to A and B. (A similar division can be made for product Y.) Profits are part of the increases in product, *not* a result of exploitation of consumers.

The Unseen Hand and Laissez-Faire

Production resources (human or physical) can be guided toward an efficient allocation as if by an "Unseen Hand." The "Hand" is (1) the desire of each person to achieve a more preferred situation, in this case via increased profits and lower costs of getting goods; (2) open access to the right to exchanges; and (3) private-property rights in goods and services. This is often called a capitalist, *laissez-faire* ("let-it-do" by itself) system, because no one has to intervene to guide people, *assuming* in the first place a system of private-property enforcement and a marketplace where exchanges can be negotiated at mutually agreed upon prices. Compared to a subsistence or self-sufficiency system, appropriate specialization yields a larger aggregate output. Restrictions that prevent Mr. A or Mr. B from producing and exchanging goods will reduce the force toward efficient production by specialization. In our current example, if Mr. A could not produce any of product X—because production and sale of X is reserved exclusively for Mr. B as a legal monopoly—then the aggregate feasible output in our example could *not* be achieved. The smaller output is a result of "monopoly restraints," restrictions on "open markets" or "free enterprise." This is why it is said that "legal monopoly" or "closed" markets or "entry restrictions" are bad. They are not bad for those who are protected by the restrictions; they have a larger wealth as a result, but a smaller gain than the loss imposed on the rest of society.

Although this toy example speaks of Mr. A and Mr. B, it applies to America and Britain—and thus provides an explanation of international trade; or Albany and Buffalo, implying interregional trade; or Aluminum Company of America and Bulova, implying specialization by business firms. The essence of all market exchange among producers is captured by this simple "two person" example.

5, 6, 7, 8, 9, 10, 11

Gains from Trade and the Size of the Market

A proposition of major importance can now be presented. *In general, addition of another person with different talents will provide the rest of the community with increased total consumption potential.* Into the community of A and B comes another person, C, with talents different from those of A and B, say with the ability to produce $2Y$ or $1X$ daily (or linearly interpolated combinations of Y and X.) If C specializes and trades with A and B, he will be able to realize consumption above his own production possibility. A and B will also be able *jointly* to realize a still higher consumption than without C's presence. Before we illustrate this, a few preliminary remarks orient the analysis.

Not necessarily every person in the rest of the community prior to the newcomer will in fact benefit, nor will anyone necessarily lose. It depends upon how the increased product is distributed among them, and that depends upon who is producing how much of what. The increase goes primarily to members of the community who do not compete in production with the newcomer. For example, if C enters the community he will be a competitor primarily of B in the production of Y. If you refer back to pages 202–203, you will see that C can produce Y at a lower marginal cost (.5X) than can B, whose marginal cost of producing Y is 1X. The resulting increased output of Y by C and lower price of Y will benefit A and hurt B. Present producers of Y will suffer from the lower price of Y while consumers will gain. The results can be illustrated with the data in Table 12–5, which is based on the data presented earlier in Table 12–3. The amount produced and consumed by each person is shown in the top third of Table 12–5, where A and B trade with each other while self-sufficient C produces solely for himself, prior to his entering the community. The total output is 4.67 each of X and Y.

TABLE 12–5. Production and Consumption before and after C Enters the Community of A and B

Before Trade with C

	X	Y
Mr. A	4(2.25)	1(2.25)
Mr. B	0(1.75)	3(1.75)
Mr. C	.67(.67)	.67(.67)
	4.67(4.67)	4.67(4.67)

After C Enters and Trades

	X	Y
Mr. A	6(3.3)	0(2.45)
Mr. B	0(1.6)	3(1.55)
Mr. C	0(1.1)	2(1.0)
	6(6)	5(5)

By entering the community, C increases the consumption potential for A and B and for himself. With specialization he can produce no X and 2Y; with exchange at a rate of 1.1X for 1Y, for example, he can sell 1Y for 1.1X, giving him more than if he did not specialize. Similarly A can buy 2.45Y by paying 2.7X. A can buy 1Y from C and 1.45Y from B, giving C 1.1X and B 1.6X. This, however, leaves B worse off than formerly.

If we place a tax on C of .25X and .25Y and give the total proceeds to B, we achieve the results shown below. Everyone then has more than prior to entry of C. (We could tax A instead; obviously, there are many possibilities.)

After Tax Compensation to B from C

	X	Y
Mr. A	3.3	2.45
Mr. B	1.85(1.6 + .25)	1.80(1.55 + .25)
Mr. C	.85(1.1 − .25)	.75(1 − .25)
	6.0	5.0

If C now trades with A and B, he will find it best to shift production to Y, while A will find it best (in the sense of getting the highest income) to shift completely out of Y to all X (6X and no Y). C, the new lowest-cost producer, displaces A as a producer of Y. B will continue to produce Y even though he is now poorer (with the lower selling price of Y). The output for each person is shown in the second portion of the table; the total output is 6X and 5Y (instead of 4.67 of each). The resulting consumption distribution is shown in parentheses for each person. A consumes more of Y and X; C consumes more of each than when he was self-sufficient; B, the former major producer of Y, is poorer and consumes less. He has lost income to A and C. The legend in Table 12–5 explains with numerical detail just how this happens.

The entry of C as a competitor primarily of B has lowered the price of Y and hence B's income. A and C benefit. The gains to A are in part the result of the lost buying power of B, now partially transferred to A via lower prices for buying Y. The other source of gain to A is the increased total output. Also, part of B's former income is transferred away to C.

The increased output to the community consequent to C's entry is large enough so that even if B were more than compensated for his lost income, everyone else would still have a gain from C's entry. See the bottom of Table 12–5 for an illustration of a tax on C that accomplishes this. (Part of the tax could have been on A also.) Actually, such compensation by taxes and payments to those who lose from new entrants is rare. More common is a law preventing entry of C!

This analysis of distribution of income effects sheds light on a related phenomenon. A person newly graduated from school enters the community with specialized talents. His entry and greater productivity contribute gains to many people in the rest of the community. These are a mixture of net productive gains and income transfers as in the former illustration. Some people mistakenly leap to the conclusion that since education contributes to other people's welfare, they ought to pay for a student's education. Such reasoning would suggest that everyone else ought to pay for every new investment or productive equipment or subsidize every new immigrant. The error is in failing to distinguish between (a) the gains from *increased productivity* and (b) *income transfers* to those who buy products at lower prices from those who are competed against by the newly trained entrants. That is why it is not possible to deduce who should pay for whose education—even when there are net gains to the rest of society. The joint presence of productive gains and transfers explains the conflict about immigration policies and tuition fees for education.

Are Specialization and Efficient Production Good?

The more cheaply people can communicate, negotiate, and exchange, and the greater the possibilities of discerning and exploiting differences among their productive abilities and tastes, the greater will be the specialization and wealth in the society. In the words of Adam Smith, the gains from specialization depend upon the "extent of the market" and so does the degree of specialization. In small markets, you will find less specialization in medical services, and in types of auto, or TV, or watch repair services. Even bakeries will be less specialized.

Disadvantages of Specialization

Monotony and tedium are said to be more likely—though rewarded by a greater wealth—for those who specialize. Apparently the monotony and tedium are worth bearing, for anyone who wants to forsake wealth can be more self-sufficient and poorer. It would be nice if there were some way to get all that increased output without specialization and exchange. But it hasn't yet been discovered.

Specialists' wealth depends heavily upon other people's tastes and activities. To specialize more effectively involves making advance investments in specific goods and kinds of training. Specialization seems to increase risks, because if other people's demands or willingness to work in certain tasks should change, some specialists will lose much of the value of their investment in goods and training. They will end up poorer than if they had specialized in something else, or possibly with even less than if they had been more self-sufficient like olden-day farmers. But do not make too much of this point, for the losses of overinvestment in certain goods and skill are not the consequence of specialization. They are the consequence of imperfect foresight. People know that their forecasts are fallible, and they correspondingly make smaller long-term investments in riskier trades. In part this reduces the possible losses and the extent of specialization. But even a self-sufficient nonspecialist will make long-term investments to get products for his own use. And does he know his own future demands any better?

Is Efficient Production for Market Demand Good?

"Efficiency in production" is desirable in the sense that more economic goods are preferred to less. But are you sure the demanded good is a "good" economic good? For example, the authors do not allow their minor children unrestricted access to the market, because children buy goods we believe they should not. We don't accept their judgment of what is a "good." If someone believes other people do not know what is good for themselves—as evidenced by differences of opinion about the use of tobacco, alcohol, opium, heroin, gambling, low-brow television programs, comic books, lewd literature—he may seek to prohibit their production. Many highly educated, socially conscious people do so. To them, the standard of efficiency is useful only insofar as the "right" goods are wanted by others. However, doing the "wrong" thing efficiently is *not* necessarily undesirable, because whatever the amount of the "bad" produced, it permits more "goods" to be produced. Economics is neutral or amoral; it does not say what is "good" or "bad."

Socialism, Specialization, and Marxist Alienation

Karl Marx asserted that specialization of production with market exchange "alienated" producers from understanding their social role and interrelationships with other people. Each producer was said to feel he was producing solely for some impersonal marketplace in response to impersonal market prices, rather than to human wants and values (as if the prices were unrelated to such human desires or as if the producers thought the prices had no relationship to human values). Marx said that since it is primarily through exchange of their products that producers come into social contact with one another, "The persons exist for one another merely as representatives of, and therefore as owners of, commodities" (*Capital,* Vol. I, Modern Library Edition, Random House, 1959, p. 97). Social relations are said to be transformed into relationships among commodities and money. Marx went on to assert "the process of production has the mastery over man instead of being controlled by him" (*Capital,* p. 93). To eliminate that alleged "mastery of production processes over man," he proposed that men should consciously control production and distribution by centralized directives in accord with a preconceived settled plan, as if the workers of the society were in a single, huge factory. Hence, Marx called for socialism, i.e., government ownership of all the productive resources, believing this would eliminate "alienation."

A second interpretation of the roots of socialism in Marxist thought suggests that socialized production and centralized control would facilitate the ability of politicians in the government to control society and retain office. A still more recent interpretation is that centralized government control of productive resources and production according to a conscious plan is more efficient and gives a more rapid growth of output. The first of these is a well founded interpretation of the Marxist precepts. The second may be a convenient fact of life for the ruling political group. The third is completely unsubstantiated, and the authors believe it is thoroughly falsified by historical evidence; you may believe what you wish.

13, 14

Summary

1. Specialization is the production of more of some and less of other goods than a person consumes himself. Production is efficiently organized if for specified rates of production of all goods except one, that one is maximized, or, if it is impossible to increase the output rate of any good without reducing that of some other.

2. Specialization in an open market leads toward efficiently organized production. A central planning and directive agency is not necessary to achieve efficient organization of production and consumption.

3. The production marginal rate of transformation (substitution among goods by production) between X and Y is the minimum reduction of output of Y that must occur if the output rate of X is to be enlarged by one unit. This is also called the marginal cost of production of X (in units of Y sacrificed). The principle of efficient organization of production requires that each good be produced by the lower marginal-cost producers of that good.

4. The gains from specialization are distributed as lower buying prices to consumers and profits to producers. The latter are competed away via lower prices to consumers and larger payments to the productive resources.

5. Specialization has undesirable features—for example, tedium and interdependence. Efficiency is neither morally good nor bad. It depends upon whether you think the goods produced more cheaply and in larger amounts are "good."

6. The larger the market in numbers of people with diverse talents, the greater the gains to its members from specialization and trade.

7. The gains from exchange that result from a larger market are mixed with income transfers among the members of the community. Gains that are income transfers *within* the group should not, in principle, be confused with gains that are increases in real output. The gains from new entrants are large enough to compensate fully any who might have lost income and still leave a net gain for the rest of the group. But the feasibility of determining the mix of such gains and transfers is an issue on which nothing constructive can be said with present knowledge.

Questions

1. A steals from B successfully.
   a. Is that "production"? Why?
   b. If you say "No, because someone is hurt," what would you say about the case in which a new invention displaces some other producers?
   c. Are there some kinds of production which you think should not be allowed?

2. Smith's production possibilities are indicated by the following table:

Production, Exchange, Specialization, and Efficiency

Alternative Daily Production Possibilities by Smith

Oats		Soybeans
10	and	0
9	and	.2
8	and	.4
7	and	——
6	"	——
5	"	——
4	"	——
3	"	——
2	"	——
1	"	——
0	"	2

a. Compute the missing data, assuming linear interpolation gives his production possibilities.
b. For each increment of oats, he incurs a uniform sacrifice of an amount of soybeans. The ratio between these two changes is called the marginal rate of transformation between oats and soybeans. This rate also yields his marginal cost of oats (in terms of soybeans). What is the marginal cost of a bushel of oats?
c. Of a bushel of soybeans?
d. If that marginal cost is constant at all combinations, then production is said to involve constant costs. Does this example reveal constant costs?
e. Graph Smith's production possibility, with oats on the horizontal scale.
f. On the graph, label, as point I, the output that has an equal number of bushels of oats and soybeans.
g. What is the number of bushels of each?
h. Which is the larger output—1.67 bushels of each, or 5 bushels of oats and 1 of soybeans?

3 On the graph of the preceding question, plot the production possibility of Mr. B (call him Black) taken from Table 12–2. Let X denote oats and Y denote soybeans.
  a. Label this line BB and mark the point of equal numbers of bushels of oats and soybeans (that is, 1.5 of each).
  b. What is the maximum amount of oats that Mr. Smith and Mr. Black jointly can produce if they produce only oats?
  c. Only soybeans?
  d. What is the maximum amount of soybeans and oats they can produce if each person produces as many bushels of oats as he does of soybeans?
  e. What is the total output of each if they divide their time and resources equally between oats and soybeans?
  f. Which output is larger—the one where (i) each divides his time equally among the two products or (ii) where each produces as many bushels of oats as of soybeans?
  g. Which output is better?
  h. Would it be efficient for them to produce either of these two combinations?

4 On the graph for question 2, plot the outputs of soybeans and oats that represent the "efficient" total production-possibility set for Smith and Black.
  a. Plot also the set of possible outputs obtained if Smith and Black use identical ratios when dividing their time between oats and soybeans.
  b. Does this give the same production-possibility set as the preceding question?

5 a. If the price of a bushel of soybeans is $1 and the price of a bushel of oats is 50 cents, which good should Smith produce if he wants to maximize his wealth? Which should Black produce?
   b. If the price of a bushel of oats rises above $1 while soybeans stay at $1, what should Black do if he wants to maximize his wealth?
   c. At what ratio of prices would Smith be induced to produce soybeans?

6 What is meant by efficient production? Give two different versions of the definition.

7 What is meant by a subsistence, self-sufficient economy as contrasted to a specialized, interdependent economy?

8 Increased output resulting from more efficient specialization is distributed via what two means in a capitalist open-market system?

9 An open-market system presumes enforcement of certain institutions or rules. What are they?

10 "It's wrong to profit from someone else's misfortune."
   a. Explain why, if that were taken literally, we would *all* be poorer.
   b. Does the doctor profit from your illness? The farmer from your hunger? The shoemaker from your tender feet? The teacher from your ignorance? The preacher from your sinfulness?
   c. How are their earnings different from those of the liquor producer, the race-track owner, the burlesque strip-teaser, and the dope peddler?

11 The following remark is commonly made about some rich people: "He is an independently wealthy man." From what is he independent? Does his wealth not depend upon other people's demands?

12 a. Do you think specialization will be carried to greater extent in a large city or a small one?
   b. Why?
   c. Give examples of what you mean by greater specialization.

13 A premier or prime minister of a new "emerging" country bragged that he was going to make his country self-sufficient and independent of foreigners. Do the principles of this chapter suggest anything about how you as a native of that country might be affected? Explain.

14 "Laissez-faire means the government should do nothing." Evaluate.

Production in Various Market Conditions

Money Measure of Costs

13

INHERENT in the *allocation* of productive resources among competing uses is the concept of *costs*. Costs are values of alternative forsaken uses. In choosing between A and anything else, we ask what is the value of A and what is the value of the highest valued of the alternative possibilities that would otherwise have been realized; the highest valued forsaken opportunity is called the cost of A. And it follows that A should be chosen if and only if its value exceeds its cost.

None of the preceding makes reference to "labor, toil, trouble, and pain" as costs. Costs are *not* defined as the *undesirable,* or *painful,* consequences of some act, even though it may engender "undesirable consequences" that are weighed when one evaluates that act. For example, a swimming pool yields the pleasures of swimming and keeping cool, but it also involves the undesirable consequences of neighbors' children splashing the yard. The desirable and undesirable are taken into account in assigning a *valuation,* but not in determining the *costs,* of having a pool. Cost is the best alternative set of consequences that could have been realized with a different use of the resources. Exactly how labor, toil, and trouble do enter into valuation is something we shall take up later, after hinting here only that they have some effect on the amounts of goods produced.

At present, we emphasize two important matters: (1) the meaning of cost and its components and (2) the means whereby costs are revealed and more fully heeded by decision makers. First, cost is *not* the sum of the bad things consequent to some action—though the term is often used loosely in that way. The *measure* of cost is a measure of the *value* of the *totality* of the *best* option necessarily *forsaken.* Every option will include good and bad elements, all of which are weighed in one's personal

1, 2, 3

valuation scale for a judgment of the most desirable of all the options. Cost includes, indeed *is*, the loss of all the features of the next best state of the world that could otherwise have been had. The conception of cost includes as its component features not only such things as sacrificed material goods, but cultural, social, political, and personal amenities, and all the desirable features of the state of the world that are forsaken. Any *choice* means, by definition, a *cost* will be incurred.

Many think cost refers only to those material sacrifices of things that are normally bought and sold in the market. Cost includes everything of the next best option. Some components of cost do get into the market calculus via explicit purchase and sale prices, while some do not. Economics seeks to explain why some components of cost are not fully reflected in market prices and how such omissions affect the decisions made. Those components that somehow escape full revelation and measurement via the market are less heeded by decision makers, to the intense annoyance of those who bear the costs. Avoid the error of assuming that costs are defined in economic analysis to include only those components that are revealed via the market or heeded by the decision makers. Economic analysis strives instead to explain why such components of costs are not communicated and assigned via the market. It also suggests how costs might be communicated and made more influential, by bringing them more fully into the market purchase and sale nexus or possibly by having political forces exert influence on the decision makers who otherwise would be unheedful of the full costs.

Production-Possibility Boundary as Supply Schedule

Table 13-1 gives the production possibilities of five people, Messrs. *A, B, C, D,* and *E*. *A, B,* and *C* are the people in the preceding chapter.

Mr. *C* is the least productive person of all, on an *absolute* scale. Maybe he is lazy, slow-witted, physically weak, poor in productive resources, very young or very old, or just doesn't want to work much. Mr. *D* and Mr. *E* are more productive. Mr. *D* can produce more *X* daily than anyone else, while nobody can outproduce Mr. *E* at *Y*.

Who will (not necessarily "should") produce what? At what rates? How are they

TABLE 13-1. Daily Production-Possibility Functions and Marginal Transformation Rates in Production

Person	Goods X or Y			Marginal Transformation Rates by Production	Marginal Cost of Y in $X
A	6 or	3	or all linear combinations	$2X = 1Y$	$2.0
B	3 "	3	" " " "	$1X = 1Y$	1.0
C	1 "	2	" " " "	$.5X = 1Y$	.5
D	9 "	6	" " " "	$1.5X = 1Y$	1.5
E	6 "	10	" " " "	$.6X = 1Y$	.6

Mr. *A* can produce $6 of *X* or 3 units of *Y* in one day. Or he can produce other combinations of *X* and *Y*, but for each extra *Y*, he must forsake output of 2*X*, as indicated by his marginal transformation rates. This means that his marginal cost of a *Y* is 2*X* or $2 (valuing, as we shall, each *X* as worth $1). Mr. *E* has a marginal cost of 60 cents for production of *Y*. (Do you agree that Mr. *E* could produce 3*X* and 5*Y* in one day? He can. Or that he could produce 9*Y* and .6*X*?)

induced to do so? One possible set of answers to these questions is the following. Let each person's production possibilities be reported to a dictator. If only X is desired, A, B, C, D, and E are told to produce only X, for a total of $25 worth of X. On the other hand, if only Y is wanted, then all will produce Y, for a total of 24 units.

Now make the dictator's task a little harder. If he wants precisely one of Y and as many X's as possible, whom should he order to produce the Y? At first sight, it appears that E is the man. He can produce daily more Y than can anyone else. In just one tenth of a day, he can produce $1Y$, whereas poor C requires half a day. E is "absolutely" the most productive producer of Y, while C is "absolutely" the poorest producer of Y. Yet the truth is that the dictator should reverse the assignments! Absolute productivity is completely irrelevant for determining efficient production allocations.

Poor little C is the person to assign first to the production of Y! E is the *second* person to put to work on Y. And the reason is simply that C is the *lowest-marginal-cost* producer of Y. Cost is *not the amount of labor or time* it takes to produce a Y; cost, as we have seen, is what is sacrificed when labor or time is used to produce a Y. No one can "save" time; it is used, like marriage, for better or for worse. What *can* be saved is sacrificed output. C sacrifices only $.5X$ when he devotes half a day to producing a Y. C's marginal cost is $.5X$ for $1Y$, while E's is $.6X$ for $1Y$. With C producing $1Y$, and the rest of the people producing X's, total output is $1Y$ and $24.5X$. But if E had produced the $1Y$, total output would be $1Y$ and only $24.4X$. (Which person would have been the worst to assign to Y? Had he been assigned, the total output would have been $1Y$ and only $23X$.)

If the dictator desires more than two units of Y, E is the next worker, after C, to assign to Y. If the dictator wants more than twelve units of Y (two from C and ten from E), he will assign B, whose marginal cost of Y is $1X$. If C, E, and B produce Y, and D and A produce X, the total output will be $15Y$ and $15X$. No other assignment can produce more than $15X$ on days that $15Y$ are produced; other assignments will result in *less* than $15X$ being produced. (We again offer $1,000 to any student who can get more than 15 of each.)

We can summarize the principle of efficient allocation. Workers, or productive resources, should be ranked according to their *marginal* costs. Assign first those workers who have the lowest *marginal* cost for the particular good and then, as a larger output rate is desired, gradually divert to that task those with successively higher *marginal* costs. This principle holds for *all* economic systems, be they capitalist, socialist, communal, or whatever.

The community's efficient total production-possibility frontier is listed in Table 13–2. (When a man's name appears as a producer of both X and Y, he is producing some of each.) It is impossible to get more Y for any stated X or more X with a stipulated Y. Other assignments would eliminate efficiency.

Graphs of every person's production-possibility boundary are superimposed in Figure 13–1. Lying beyond all these lines is the community's total or aggregate implied production-possibility boundary. Note that the community's production-possibility boundary starts at the upper left with the flattest slope (the same as that of A's boundary line) and then moves downward to the right along lines that are successively steeper. The slope of the boundary line with respect to the horizontal axis is a measure of the marginal cost of producing X (and the slope with respect to the vertical axis is the marginal cost of Y). Failure to follow the principle of assignment according to increasing marginal cost to produce more of a good will give a boundary that lies inside the portrayed "efficient" boundary. The flattest boundary line (least loss of X for producing Y) is C's; the next is

TABLE 13–2. Community's Total Production Possibility

Producers of X	Feasible Production		Producers of Y	Marginal Cost of Y in Terms of X
	X	and Y		
ABCDE	25.0	0	–	.5
ABCDE	24.5	1	C	.5
AB DE	24.0	2	C	.5
AB DE	23.4	3	C E	.6
AB DE	22.8	4	C E	.6
AB DE	22.2	5	C E	.6
AB DE	21.6	6	C E	.6
AB DE	21.0	7	C E	.6
AB DE	20.4	8	C E	.6
AB DE	19.8	9	C E	.6
AB DE	19.2	10	C E	.6
AB DE	18.6	11	C E	.6
AB D	18.0	12	C E	.6
AB D	17.0	13	BC E	1.0
AB D	16.0	14	BC E	1.0
A D	15.0	15	BC E	1.0
A D	13.5	16	BCDE	1.5
A D	12.0	17	BCDE	1.5
A D	10.5	18	BCDE	1.5
A D	9.0	19	BCDE	1.5
A D	7.5	20	BCDE	1.5
A	6.0	21	BCDE	1.5
A	4.0	22	ABCDE	2.0
A	2.0	23	ABCDE	2.0
–	0	24	ABCDE	2.0

This table shows the feasible daily combinations of X and Y producible by all five people. At the output of 22.8X and 4Y, X is being produced by A, B, D, and E (part time), and Y by C and E (part time).

E's; and so on, until at last there is brought into the production of Y the producer with the highest cost or least *relative* productivity of Y—namely A.

On each straight-line segment is the name of a person. When the point of production (showing the combination of X and Y produced by the whole economy) is on a given segment—say, E's segment—each of the other workers is producing a single good; C is producing 2Y; and A, B, and D are producing only X. E also produces solely one good if the production point is at one end or the other of his segment; he is producing X if the point is at the lower end and Y if it is at the upper end. If the point of production is at some intermediate position of E's segment, he is producing both commodities.

In the far right column of Table 13–2 are the marginal costs of producing Y, starting at .5X and increasing to 2X at higher production rates. These are the marginal costs of the last person reassigned. Implied in this efficient allocation is the principle of *increasing* marginal costs at faster (or larger) rates or speed of output. As the daily-output rate of any good is increased, marginal costs increase—if production is efficient. If we can interpret X *as the dollar value of all sacrificed outputs* necessary to produce Y, the marginal costs of producing Y increase from 50 cents at an output rate of 1Y per day, up

Production in Various Market Conditions

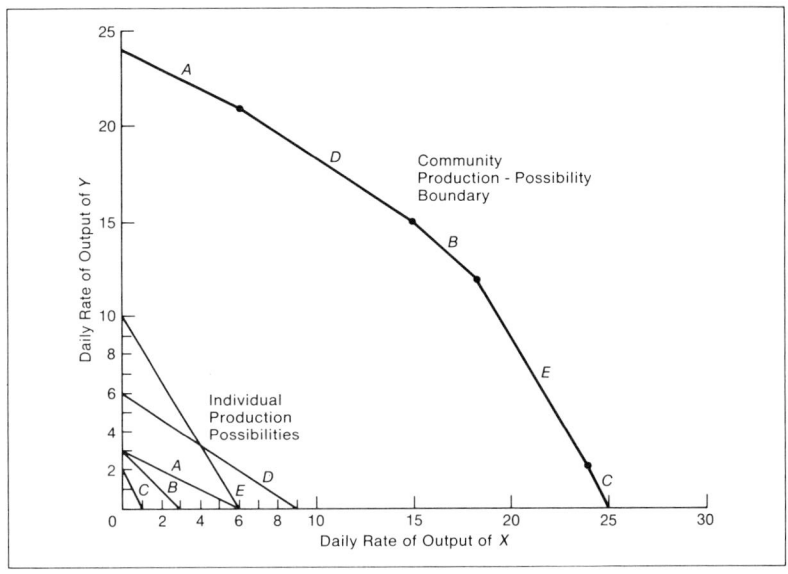

FIGURE 13-1. Total Production Possibility of Community and of Each Person Alone

On the community production-possibility boundary, each segment is identified with the name of the person who in that interval switches from one product to some of the other. Reading from lower right to upper left, the sequence of letters indicates sequence with which people enter into production of Y if more Y is to be produced.

to $2 at an output rate of $24Y$ per day. Figure 13–2 shows marginal costs for each output rate. This marginal cost line, MC, is also the supply schedule of Y for the community if each producer acts like a price-taker, which we shall elaborate later. The more resources available of various types the longer the horizontal axis and the smoother the upward path of the marginal cost line.

Production Controls under Private-Property, Open-Market System

Here we trace out *market* means for *achieving* production assignments to X and Y. We shall assume that the people feel that working at X is just as unpleasant as working at Y. (Later we shall see that differences in attitudes and willingness to work at different tasks can be taken into account.)

Incentives to Production Efficiency

When everyone is producing X and no Y, let Mr. B decide that he would like some Y, even if it does cost him $1X$ to produce it himself. If he *reveals* to others that $1Y$ is worth up to $1X$ to him, as he can by expressing a willingness to pay $1 for $1Y$ (remember, we now assume an X is worth $1), some people will be induced to switch to production of

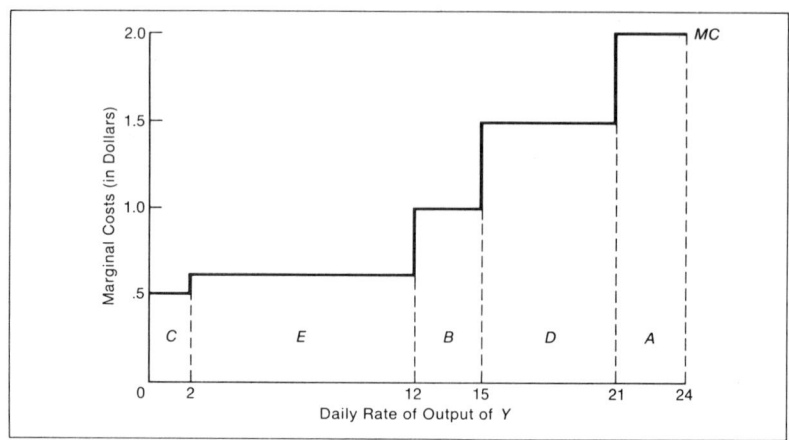

FIGURE 13-2. Daily Marginal Costs as Function of Rate of Daily Output of Y, with Efficient Production

As output of Y per day is increased, marginal costs increase as individuals with successively higher marginal costs are brought into production of Y. As a result of efficient allocation of resources, *marginal* cost rises while daily rate of output of Y is increased.

Y. One of these is Mr. E, who can produce a Y for only .6X (60 cents) and sell the Y to Mr. B for, say, .9X (90 cents). This transaction leaves Mr. B with $2.10 of X for the day and 1Y, which is a bigger basket than if Mr. B produced the 1Y himself. (B would have had $2 of X and 1Y.) Mr. E ends the day with $6.30 instead of the $6 of X he had formerly, for he produced the Y at a cost of 60 cents and sold it for 90 cents.

Other people are allowed access to the marketplace. If Mr. C discovers that Mr. B is paying 90 cents for a Y, it may occur to him that he can produce a Y and sell it for, say, 80 cents (taking business away from Mr. E) and earn a net gain of 30 cents.

Only Mr. E and Mr. C can produce a Y, sell it for as little as 80 cents (.8X), and make a gain. If Mr. A and Mr. D think *they* are lower-cost producers than C and E in the production of Y and test their belief, they will incur losses.

The test is now between Mr. E and Mr. C. Rather than lose all the business to Mr. C, Mr. E can cut his price below 80 cents, even as far as 61 cents if necessary. And it is necessary, because Mr. C can gain by producing some Y as long as he can get anything over 50 cents for 1Y. The result is clear. Mr. C will drive Mr. E out of the business of producing Y. Only Mr. C, lowest marginal-cost producer of 1Y, will specialize in Y if the community wants just 1Y or 2Y. And the price that Mr. C gets is at most 60 cents. (Why? Mr. E!) The right to buy and sell in a market provides this result.

Free competition (that is, open markets) for Mr. B's business has resulted in only Mr. C's specializing in the production of Y. "Greed," which induced Mr. C and Mr. E to make competitive offers in the marketplace, resulted in an increase of utility for Mr. B—although neither Mr. C nor Mr. E entered the market with that motivation. With Mr. C's survival in production of Y, the total output is 1Y and $24.50 (24.50X)—precisely as large as under an all-wise planner. Apparently, central planning can be replaced by the capitalist private-property, open-market system.

If anyone wants more Y, he will have to offer the independent, private-resource owners a price at least equal to what they could get from producing other things. And that, of course, is measured by the marginal costs of producing more Y. The marginal costs of Y *rise* as the daily *rate* or speed of output of Y is increased by efficient production assignments; this phenomenon is the *law of increasing marginal costs with higher or faster output rates.* Not only does the *total* cost of Y increase as the output rate increases, but the total daily cost increases by larger *increments*: the larger the output rate of Y, the greater the *marginal* cost. This is a consequence of productive efficiency in resource allocation.

10, 11, 12, 13

Control of Production Rate with Price-Takers

At what rate will Y be produced and sold in the market? To get a numerical answer, let us use the arbitrarily assumed demand schedule for Y given in Table 13–3. According to this table, the daily sale of Y is one if the price is $2.00; it is two per day at a price of $1.50; and so on. It will be profitable for Mr. C to produce all the Y he can ($2Y$) and for Mr. E to produce $3Y$ daily. This total of five per day can be sold at 70 cents each, and it would not be more profitable for Mr. E to produce a fourth one each day (because that would cost him 60 cents, and he could sell it only if the price were dropped to 50 cents). Our equilibrium result is that, with this demand, five units of Y (2 by Mr. C and 3 by Mr. E) will be produced and sold daily at an open-market price of 70 cents.

Notice that we are assuming each person acts like a price-taker. He acts as though his output would have no effect on price. This may seem absurd given the small quantities we have assumed. However, we could imagine that these five people were just five of 500 producers, 100 each like A, B, etc. And we could have imagined the demand to be so large that the few items produced by each person had no noticeable effect on the selling price. Then the solution would be $2Y$ by each of 100 producers like Mr. C and $3Y$ by each of 100 producers like Mr. E. In any event, we shall assume for the moment that the situation is a price-takers' market; then the equilibrium is $5Y$ (2 by Mr. C and 3 by Mr. E) at an open-market price of 70 cents. (We are still assuming the price of X to be $1.00 regardless of its rate of production, an assumption made solely for computational convenience. In reality, that price should change too; however, the *principles* would not change, and the arithmetic would become unbearably complicated and tedious.)

TABLE 13–3. Daily Community Demand for Y

Price in $	Y
$2.00	1
1.50	2
1.10	3
.90	4
.70	5
.50	6
.40	7
.30	8

This is an arbitrarily assumed demand schedule for Y by the five-man community. Is the elasticity less, or more, than 1 at a price of $1.50? As a further review, what is the marginal revenue when the quantity sold is 4Y? 7Y? (30 cents and −20 cents.)

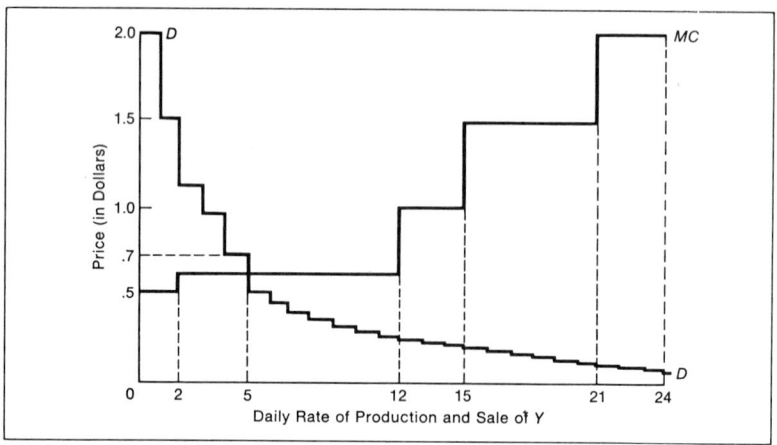

FIGURE 13-3. Community Demand and Supply for Y

If we assume each seller acts as if he were a price-taker and has no power to alter the price by his offerings of Y, the marginal-cost schedule for various daily output rates of Y by the community is called the supply schedule of Y for the community. The price that would clear the market is at the intersection of the demand and supply schedules—a price of about 70 cents. Actually, if Mr. E produced one more than the three he is producing, price would fall to 50 cents (and would rise to 90 cents if he produced only two (which with Mr. C's two units would give a total of four)). We temporarily assume that Mr. E is unaware of this.

Figure 13-3 shows the analysis. It is obtained by combining the demand curve with the graph of the marginal costs for producing Y (Figure 13-2). The curves intersect at an output of five units of Y per day, with an open-market price of 70 cents. Our community's *supply* schedule has turned out to be the *marginal-costs* schedule for all the members of the community added together where all act as price-takers. We have a demand-and-supply-curve intersection like that used in the first chapters—except that the supply curve, instead of being vertical, slopes from lower left (low prices and low daily rate of output) to the upper right (higher prices and higher daily rates of output). Higher prices on the market will elicit a higher daily rate of output, while lower market prices will reduce the daily rate. At last, we have derived the supply curve.

Check our subsequent statements and calculations as we go along to be sure you understand our procedures. The arithmetic is easy, though a bit tedious. The principles explained are important, so work carefully and slowly. If you do, one of the things you might see is that a different equilibrium output is possible. The one we just arrived at with 5Y being produced and sold at a price of 70 cents assumed that each seller acted as a price-taker. Each seller of Y acted as though the amount he offered for sale had no effect on the price of Y. Everyone took the market price as beyond his control. As a result, the group output mix is 5Y and 22.2X.

14, 15,
16, 17

Output Control with Price-Searchers

Suppose Mr. E realizes it would be in his interest to act as a *price-searcher*. How much Y should he produce to maximize his wealth? In Table 13-4 we list the revenue and

TABLE 13-4. Revenue and Costs for Mr. E as a Price-Searcher in Sale of Y

Production of Y by E	Price of Y	Total Revenue from Y	Marginal Revenue from Y	Production Value of X	Marginal Cost of Producing Y	Total Income
0	$1.50	$0.00	–	$6.00	–	$6.00
1	1.10	1.10	$1.10	5.40	$.60	6.50
2	.90	1.80	.70	4.80	.60	6.60*
3	.70	2.10	.30	4.20	.60	6.30
4	.50	2.00	–.10	3.60	.60	5.60
5	.40	2.00	.00	3.00	.60	5.00
6	.30	1.80	–.20	2.40	.60	4.20

As a price-searcher, Mr. E is now assumed to recognize that his production and sale of Y have a significant effect on the market price. Assuming the same demand schedule as given in Table 13-3, *with* Mr. C producing and selling the first two units of Y, Mr. E's demand schedule is given by the first two columns. The output rate that maximized Mr. E's wealth is 2Y per day (in addition to the 2Y produced by Mr. C), at a selling price of 90 cents per unit. The consequence of price-searcher behavior is to reduce the quantity of Y sold from five to four, and to increase the quantity of X sold from 22.2 to 22.8. The total community output remains on the community production-possibility boundary (of Figure 13-1)—only a different combination of X and Y is selected. (*Maximum income production combination for Mr. E is 2Y and 4.8X.)

costs for the different possible outputs he can produce. If he produces no Y, and all X, the market price of Y will be $1.50; we know this because the demand for Y, given in Table 13-3, shows a price of $1.50 if two are produced in the community (and Mr. C is producing 2Y). If Mr. E produces 1Y, the total community rate will be three and the market price will have to be $1.10. His earnings are $1.10 from Y and $5.40 from the 5.4X, a total of $6.50. If Mr. E produces 2Y, the community total will be 4Y with a price of 90 cents. Mr. E's revenue from the 2Y would be $1.80. This 70-cent increase of earnings from Y is called his marginal revenue of producing 2Y daily.

By producing that second Y each day, Mr. E incurs a cost increase of 60 cents, the marginal cost, because the value of his output of X falls from $5.40 to $4.80. His income would increase by the difference between the marginal revenue and the marginal cost at 2Y, a gain of 10 cents. His total income is $6.60. If he produces and sells 3Y daily at the lower price of 70 cents, his receipts from Y will be $2.10, instead of $1.80, giving him a marginal revenue of 30 cents for 3Y. The marginal cost of 3Y is 60 cents. The negative difference between marginal revenue and marginal cost means he would incur a reduced net income of 30 cents. His total income would be $6.30 (= $2.10 + $4.20). To maximize his wealth as a price-searcher he would produce and sell just 2Y, rather than the 3Y he would have produced in a *price-takers'* market (as we saw in the preceding section). The total community output in a price-searchers' market for Y is 4Y and 22.8X, which is less Y and more X than a price-takers' market.

Although the output combination for the community is different with a price-searchers' market, the assignment or allocation of producers to various outputs is still efficient. It is impossible to produce more than 22.8X with an output of 4Y. Productive efficiency remains. What has changed is the particular output combination. See Table 13-5 and Figure 13-4 for a summary of results.

In Figure 13-4, the output mixture with price-takers' markets is at point T. With price-searchers' open markets the output (still on the production-possibility boundary)[1] is at

---

[1] P_{om} indicates all combinations of production efficiency in a *technological* productive sense in open markets.

TABLE 13–5. Effect of Price-Searchers' Open Market on Output Combination

Open-Market Situation	Production of X and Y
Price-takers Actual	22.2 and 5
(Achievable)	(22.2 and 5)
Price-searchers Actual	22.8 and 4
(Achievable)	(22.8 and 4)

In price-searchers' markets, output combination is shifted, in this example from 22.2X to 22.8X and from 5Y to 4Y. Less of Y and more of X is produced. Y was assumed to be sold in a price-searchers' market. Effect is to shift output from price-searchers' markets to more of good sold in price-takers' markets. Nevertheless, while output mixture is changed, no potential output is lost for no productive inefficiency occurs; it is impossible to produce more than 22.8X given that 4Y is to be produced.

point S, which though *productively* efficient is not an efficient combination in the sense of *utility* efficiency.[2] In Figure 13–4 utility inefficiency (as we shall explain on page 230) exists at any point S if at that point the *slope* of the production-possibility boundary, a measure of the marginal costs of producing Y and X, is not equal to the ratio of the selling prices of Y and X. In the present instance, we know Y's are valued more highly relative to X than the cost of producing another Y. Though this inequality is not revealed, the figure shows the difference in the two outputs.[3]

Productive Efficiency and Wealth Maximizing

Wealth or income maximizing gives an efficient *production* assignment of producers to various outputs, *given* the market prices or demands. This holds true in both a price-takers' and a price-searchers' open market (whether or not the *output mixture* is *utility* efficient). The price-takers' market for Y yielded an output mixture of $5Y$ and $22.2X$.

A check of each person's wealth situation in Table 13–2 will show that no other production pattern will earn him a larger wealth, given the prices of X and Y that induced the mixture of $5Y$ and $22.2X$. The price of X is $1.00, and the price of Y is 70 cents. By referring to Table 13–1, we see that in one day Mr. A can earn $6 if he produces $6X$, or $2.10 if he produces only Y. His maximum-valued output is obtained

---

[2] Everyone could be better off if the following were done. Everyone could agree to contribute toward paying Mr. E a total of 65 cents for producing a third Y which is worth 70 cents to them. They would agree also to continue to buy the first four units in the market at 90 cents (from Mr. C and Mr. E). Mr. E would accept since he would collect 65 cents more for producing the third Y (and no less on the first two) at a marginal cost of only 60 cents.

This would make everyone better off (than staying at $4Y$ and $22.8X$) as each individually judges his situation. With output back at $5Y$ and $22.2X$, the distortion is gone. The trouble is in getting people together to make this agreement. There are other possibilities, too, which we shall discuss much later.

[3] The Edgeworth Box presented earlier (pages 47–49) could be utilized in conjunction with the production-possibility frontier to show graphically this utility inefficiency.

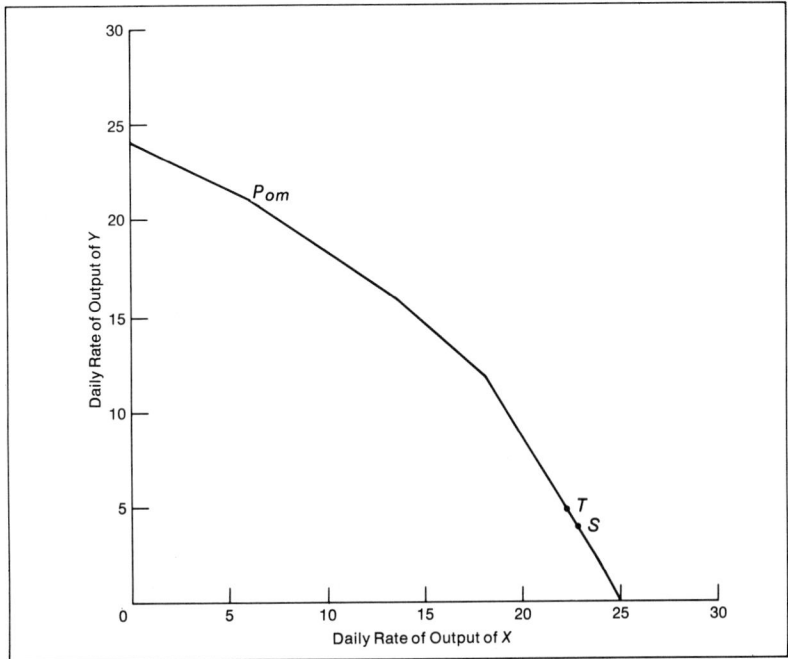

FIGURE 13–4. Socially Determined Combinations of Output in Price-Takers' and in Price-Searchers' Markets

On the community production-possibility boundary, the output choice is T if price-takers' open markets prevail and S in price-searchers' open markets. S does not achieve efficiency in the utility sense—in that some people could be better off (and no one worse off) by moving production from S to T with appropriate side payments. Price-searchers cannot be eliminated by law; they result from technological facts. Only a system of wealth transfers or subsidies could in principle be effective. But what is possible in principle is not necessarily possible in fact, because of political and institutional factors.

by specializing entirely in X. And that matches the efficient assignment of his productive resources for an output of $5Y$ and $22.2X$ (see Table 13–2). Similarly, B will maximize his wealth if he produces only X—which gives him $3. (Check our calculations.) Mr. C earns $1.40 if he produces Y, whereas he earns only $1 if he concentrates on X. Thus, Mr. C produces 2 of the $5Y$. Mr. D—who earns $9 from producing X, compared to $4.20 if he produces Y—will maximize his earnings by concentrating on X. Mr. E can earn $6 if he produces only X, whereas he can earn $7 if he produces and sells only Y. But the most Y he can sell at the market price of 70 cents, according to our demand schedule, is three; therefore (assuming he acts like a price-taker) he will produce that many and devote the rest of his resources to producing X. His daily earnings would be the value of the $3Y$ at 70 cents each, plus $4.2X$ at $1 each—a total value of $6.30.

If the demand for Y increases and its price rises relative to that of other goods, some producers will be induced to produce more Y and less X to maximize their wealth. For example, if the demand for Y increases so that it will support a sales rate of $14Y$ per day at a price of $1.10 (with $1X$ equaling $1), you should be able to show that individual wealths will be maximized if Messrs. A and D concentrate on X, with Messrs. C, B, and E concentrating on Y. Also note that this allocation is efficient, in addition to being the result of each person's efforts to maximize his wealth. Thus, a private-property, open-market system is in this use conducive to efficient production and resource allocation in a price-takers' open market.

The equilibrium price is 90 cents in the *price-searchers'* market. Why? Again it will turn out that each person is maximizing his wealth under efficient production allocation. (Work out the calculations. For example, Mr. A's income will be maximized at $6 if he produces only X. Any output of Y by him will yield him a smaller income.) Both in a price-searchers' and a price-takers' market the outputs are produced efficiently. The difference is in the equilibrium output *combination* of goods.

Productive and Utility Efficiency

Although production organization is efficient in both kinds of markets, in the sense that for any specified amount of Y produced the largest possible amount of X is being produced, is the particular output combination a most *preferred* one? (Most preferred by whom?) Is this economy producing the "right" or "wrong" output mixture efficiently? To be specific, under a price-takers' market, the output mixture is $5Y$ and $22.2X$, while under the price-searchers' market it is $4Y$ and $22.8X$. Are these two alternative combinations equally "good"? That depends upon whether *you* think it is better for society to have more X or more Y. But no one is in a position to establish right and wrong for society. We can show, however, that from one point of view a price-searchers' market "distorts" the output mixture—in the sense that personal values of goods exceed the costs of producing more of the goods sold in price-searchers' markets. To see why, first examine Table 13–3, in which it is evident that if $5Y$ were produced and sold, the price would be 70 cents, which tells us that the buyers personally value a fifth Y at 70 cents.

If Mr. E were to produce a third Y (for a total on the market of five), he would sell his three at 70 cents, for a total of $2.10, instead of $1.80 when he sold just two at 90 cents each. (See Table 13–4.) His marginal revenue would be only 30 cents, although the price is 70 cents. *He has his eye on his marginal revenue, not the price of Y.* Since his marginal cost is 60 cents, he refuses to produce a third Y, even though everyone else values one more Y at 70 cents. They prefer one more Y (worth 70 cents) to the extra $.6X$ (worth 60 cents) now being produced. In other words, they prefer a mix of $5Y$ and $22.2X$, but they get a mix of $4Y$ and $22.8X$. Although each mix is efficiently produced, the price-searchers' mixture is the less preferred, hence is not efficient in the *utility* sense.

Distortion is caused by producers of Y being guided by a marginal revenue that is less than the price of Y. It is sometimes called "inefficiency (in output mix) or price-searchers' or monopoly markets."

The principle of having output at that rate at which marginal cost just equals *price* rather than marginal revenue is a necessary but not *sufficient* condition for utility efficiency in all economic systems—capitalist, socialist, or whatever—but the systems differ in the probability with which this condition may be achieved. As we have seen, price-takers' markets appear to be more conducive to it than monopoly markets. And nonmarket-controlled production in socialist economies seems even less likely to approach it, if we judge by their system of incentives and their attempts to introduce free-market pricing.⁴

Actual Attainment of Productive and Utility Efficiency?

Nothing *guarantees* that the lowest-marginal-cost producer of Y will actually produce Y let alone doing so at the rate at which marginal cost equals price. If any of a host of things sufficiently interferes with his opportunity or willingness to risk wealth in the hope of greater wealth by producing Y, inefficient organization of production will continue. Efficient (that is, cheaper) producers will be discovered more easily if access to the market is not restricted, if more people desire wealth, and if the people are willing to take a chance for wealth. And this, as we have seen, depends, in part, on the kinds of property rights. The trial-and-error costs incurred by hopeful but overconfident people are great.

Which dominates: over-entry into activities in which people lose wealth, or under-entry into activities in which they would have increased their wealth? The answer is not known. For example, I *believe* that my costs would far exceed my market value as a professional in the following capacities: professional football player, musician, steel welder, farmer, doctor, lawyer, and so on. I may be wrong. But rather than run the risks and costs of an experiment to find out, I prefer to continue as a teacher—simply because the "discovery" costs are too high to induce me to try the experiment. Therefore, as a teacher, I allocate my productive efforts inefficiently, and my wealth is smaller. That smaller wealth reflects the reduction in total output resulting from my misallocation of productive resources. Too many resources (mine) are in teaching instead of elsewhere. Despite my unwillingness to switch, the laws of production still hold. If the earnings elsewhere should rise high enough relative to the wages of teaching, I shall switch. But I doubt that I shall see that ratio in the real market.

The pertinent questions are: (1) Is the dispersed knowledge utilized efficiently? (2) Is there incentive for a person to increase his knowledge of what he can do? To both, the answer is: Wider access to the market increases the likelihood of a "yes" answer. The market-exchange system, with its prices, provides more than a place to exchange goods. It is a place where information is collated and compared. A restriction on property rights and on price and exchange information would restrict the exchange of existing goods and also the transfer of productive resources to higher-value uses.

It is easy to see why. First, market prices reflect consumers' demands, or values, of goods and services. They also reflect producers' costs of production. Each potential and actual producer, by looking at the selling prices, indirectly compares his estimated and realized costs with those of other producers, and with the values that consumers place on his product. If his (marginal) costs exceed prices, he will reduce or eliminate his production and move to something else unless he is willing to lose wealth. The fact that his marginal costs are greater than prices indicates that other people can produce this good more cheaply than he can, and that consumers value his product less than other things he could do.

⁴ Another necessary condition of "utility" efficiency is that the output be allocated among people such that no further interpersonal *exchange* is desired.

Second, specialization in production is in large part specialization and coordination of knowledge. Specialization of production does not mean simply that one person produces a pencil while someone else produces paper. It means also that different people produce the various component parts of goods and that different people perform the various special tasks in making goods. In fact, in a modern society *no one* knows how to produce all of any one thing. A pencil represents the culmination of the joint efforts and knowledge of millions of people. One person knows something about the paint; others about the graphite—how it is mined, transported, processed, shaped, and inserted in a pencil; others are knowledgeable in growing timber, cutting it, shaping the wood, and painting it; others make the steel holder for the eraser; and still others are involved in making the rubber eraser. Activities of thousands or possibly millions of people are coordinated to produce pencils at lower costs.

Warning: From our simplified expository example we abstracted many details which have no effect on the principles involved. Nevertheless, there is one simplification that might be misleading. We assumed that each person, A, B, C, D, and E, could produce various mixtures of goods, but no matter what mixture he produced, the marginal cost of production was a *constant*; it did not depend upon the rate of production. Normally when a person increases his net production of a good, his marginal cost increases. No one person is a completely homogeneous resource; if he tries to concentrate more heavily on one product, the loss of some other product increases for each extra unit. In other words, just as the five-man economy shows this phenomenon of increasing marginal costs as the rate of production of one good is increased by transferring resources from other products, so for one person the same phenomenon occurs. This would mean that the graphs of the production-possibility lines for each person are not straight but are curved and bowed outward just as the community's production frontier is.

Incorporating this effect would lead us to conclude that producers could be simultaneously producing several different goods rather than producing essentially just one. However, they would be selling some of the goods and buying others. For example, a farmer or a business firm may produce several different products, rather than one as in our example. But he would still be specializing, in that he produced amounts different from his consumption, and for the same reasons explained in the text. This modification in consumption does not upset the explanation for gains from specialization; it alters the number of goods or services from each producer.

18, 19, 20, 21

Summary

1 Specialization enhances output and enables individuals to attain more preferred situations than do "do-it-yourself" or "self-sufficiency." Specialization yields more efficient production if increases in the output rate of any good are provided by the lowest-cost producers. Specialization relies on relative, not absolute, productivity. A person does not need to understand the principle of specialization to act in accord with that principle.

2 Because people are not identical in relative productive ability, *every* person will *always* find some goods or services for which his marginal costs are less than or equal to the market price; he can therefore produce these goods or services as a means of increasing his wealth (and utility) above what it would have been had he acted self-sufficiently— unless his access to the market is prohibited.

3 The cheaper the cost of access to the market, the greater the extent of specialization. Cost of a specified output is defined as the *highest* valued of the alternative forsaken opportunities. The measure of that cost is the market-exchange value of the forsaken output.

4 Human rights to property and access to a market in which mutually acceptable opportunities can be exploited provide incentives and means to produce efficiently.

5 The increase of output brought by increased efficiency is distributed via (a) profits to the owners of the productive resources and (b) lower prices to consumers.

6 As market demand for any good increases, and as the market price of that good rises, higher-cost producers will switch to that product.

7 Individual wealth-maximizing behavior in the face of market-equilibrating prices is conducive to productive efficiency.

8 Productive efficiency is not disrupted by price-searchers, but the output mixture is affected. Insofar as marginal revenue is less than price for price-searchers, the output mixture tends to be underweighted with products from price-searchers and is not utility efficient.

9 No economic system guarantees continuous realization of productive efficiency.

Questions

1 "Cost is an opportunity concept." Explain.

2 Are costs the same thing as the undesirable consequences of some action? Explain why not.

3 a. If there is more than one opportunity to be forsaken, which forsaken opportunity is the cost?
   b. How are opportunities made comparable so that one can determine which one is the cost?
   c. Can there be production without costs?

4 A lower-cost producer can produce more than a higher-cost producer. Do you agree? If so, why? If not, why not?

5 "The slope of the production-possibility curve is a measure of costs." Explain.

6 "An implication of efficient production is that marginal costs increase as the rate of output becomes larger." Explain.

7 Why are costs not measured in terms of labor hours?

8 The production-possibility schedules are:

Mr. A			Mr. B		
X	and	Y	X	and	Y
5		0	3		0
4		1.5	2		1
3		2.9	1		2
2		3.8	0		3
1		4.5			
0		5			

a. Add these two production possibilities together for the efficient, combined production possibility. (Hint: Notice that Mr. A's production possibilities involve *increasing,* rather than constant, marginal cost of X. Use the condition that must hold between each person's marginal cost at an efficient allocation of productive inputs.)

b. Who would be the first to produce profitably some X at a low price of X? Who would be last?

c. Who would be first to produce profitably some Y at a low price of Y?

d. Why is the answer to (b) and (c) the same?

e. At what ratio of the price of X to price of Y would Mr. B switch from production of X to production of Y?

9 Think of the five men A, B, C, D, E as being the five employees in a manufacturing company.

a. Can you think of any reason why the output data could be different if the five men were to work together as a team rather than specialize separately with exchange of individual products? Do you think the output would be larger or smaller?

b. Why?

10 In the discussion on pages 223–225, let Mr. C be a resident of Japan, while the others are residents of the United States. Mr. E is a tuna-boat owner and fisherman; A, B, and D are American workers in other American industries. Let Y be "tuna" and X be "other products." Mr. E persuades his congressman to induce other congressmen to pass a law prohibiting the importing of Japanese tuna—product Y produced by Mr. C. Who gains and who loses by a tariff or embargo on Japanese tuna? (This example captures the essence of the purposes and effects of tariffs and embargoes.)

11 The five-person problem in this chapter can also be interpreted as a case in which all producers of Y must be members of an organization, and Mr. C is denied membership in this organization. Who gains and who loses? Can you give some actual examples of this situation in the real world?

12 The five-person problem can also be interpreted as a case in which admission to the market for sale of one's production of Y requires a license from the state, and this license is given only if the current output from those now in the production of Y is deemed "inadequate to meet current demands." Who gains and who loses? Can you give some real examples of this situation?

13 Would the problem also serve as an example of the effect of apprenticeship laws that prohibit a person from acting as a "qualified" carpenter, meat cutter, etc., until he has served a specified number of years as an apprentice? Explain.

14 A and B can produce according to the following:

	Daily Rate of Output of X or Y	
Mr. A	10 or 15	(or any linearly interpolated combination)
Mr. B	5 or 10	(or any linearly interpolated combination)

a. Who can profitably produce Y at the lowest cost and price of Y?

b. Who can profitably produce X at the lowest cost and price of X?

c. If Mr. C is allowed to trade with Mr. A and B and if C's production possibilities are $4X$ or $4Y$ (or any linearly interpolated combination), who now is the lowest-cost producer of X? Of Y?

d. Who is not the lowest-cost producer of either X or Y? Does this mean he will have nothing to gain by specializing and trade? Explain.

Production in Various Market Conditions

15 The following questions involve the production data of the five people given in Tables 13–1 and 13–2.
   a. If the selling price of an X were $1 and the selling price of a Y were also $1, what should each person produce in order to maximize his wealth?
   b. Would the resulting assignment of tasks be an efficient one?
   c. What should each person produce in order to maximize his wealth if the selling price of an X is $1 and the selling price of a Y is $1.60?
   d. Is the resulting job allocation an efficient one?
   e. If the price of an X is $3 and the price of a Y is $3.20, what should each produce in order to maximize his wealth?
   f. If the price of an X falls to $2 and the price of a Y is still $3.20, what should each produce to maximize his wealth?
   g. Is the allocation of labor efficient?
   h. Is it absolute prices or relative prices of X and Y that guide allocation?

16 The following questions are based on data in Table 13–3.
   a. If all the prices in the table were to be doubled (as a means of expressing an increased demand), what would happen to output, if the price had initially been 70 cents?
   b. Is this the result of an increased demand for Y or of a reduced demand for X?
   c. Suppose a tax were to be collected from each producer of Y—a tax of 50 cents for each unit of Y produced. If, before the tax, the prices of an X and of a Y were both $1, what effect would this tax have on job allocation and output?

17 The following questions are based on data in Tables 13–1 and 13–2.
   a. What are the dimensions of the output of X and Y? That is, are they measured in units of total output or in rate (speed) of output?
   b. If the output is 15 per day, does this mean that 15 will be produced? (Hint: What if price changes at midday?)
   c. What would be the total volume of output of X in five days if C and E produced Y exclusively and the other three specialized in X?
   d. What would be the rate of output per hour for a ten-hour day?

18 Open markets with price-searchers (or open monopolies) change the output pattern from that of open markets with price-takers. In what direction is the output pattern changed?

19 "The increased output of increased specialization is distributed as profits and as a lower price to consumers." What determines the portion of each?

20 "Every profit represents the gain from moving resources to higher-valued uses." Do you agree? If so, why? If not, why not?

21 Evidence of the very extent of specialization of knowledge is provided by Albert Einstein's assertion just prior to his death (*Socialist International Information*): "The economic anarchy of capitalist society as it exists today is in my view the main cause of our evils. Production is carried on for profit, not for use." Give evidence of your superiority over Einstein by exposing his error in economic analysis.

22 Does efficient production assume that perfect knowledge exists? Explain.

23 "Someone always has a comparative advantage in the production of some good." Explain.

Market Restrictions, Pollution, Property Enforcement Costs, and Public Goods

14

THE principles of production, specialization, and exchange have been explained in a private-property, open-market context. Also, we have assumed implicitly that private property is enforced at essentially zero cost. However, markets are not open to all people and goods, nor are private-property rights costless to establish and enforce, nor are these the only kinds of rights that exist.[1] It is necessary for valid analysis to consider the effects of market closure and significant costs of establishing and enforcing property rights.

The exposition can be illustrated in Figure 14–1. Two production-possibility boundaries are shown, P_{om} and P_{cm}. The one slightly inside is labeled P_{cm} and results from closing the market for Y to, say, Mr. C. The loss of production possibilities, shown by the line P_{cm} being inside the other, is a result of inefficient selection of production techniques (wrong producers), in this case caused by market closure to some of the members of the community. But the difference between the selected mixtures of output T and S depends upon another factor—the presence of price-takers' or price-searchers' markets, as we saw in the last chapter.

Restricted Market Access: A Source of Production Inefficiency

Not every activity designed to increase one's wealth will lead to efficiency. Thievery, violence, and restricted market access for one's competitors will obstruct efficiency. Although few capitalists would encourage theft and violence, many people who have

---

[1] Read pages 141–147.

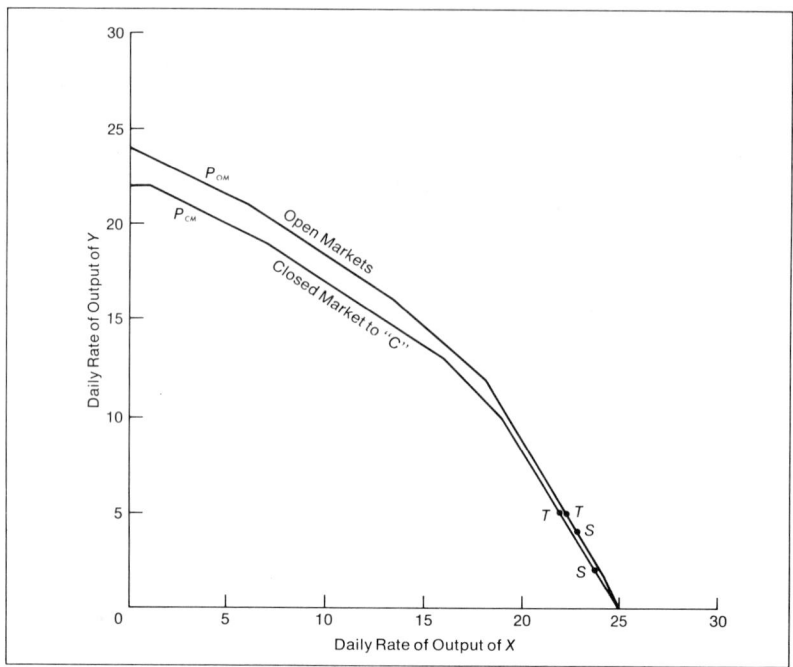

FIGURE 14-1. Production-Possibility Boundary Made Inferior by Market Closures and Restrictions

The interior boundary, labeled P_{cm}, is for economies with market closures to some potential producers. In the present instance, it shows effect of closing market for Y to Mr. C. Also shown are selected output mixtures with price-takers' and price-searchers' markets, T and S, respectively. In each case, T is the utility-efficient mixture for each boundary of production. It is possible to move from interior to exterior line by abandoning market restrictions.

benefited from capitalism advocate socialism and mercantilist restrictions on access to the market—not necessarily because they like socialism or mercantilism and dislike capitalism, but simply because their own wealth will be increased.[2] A common example is the legally instituted and enforced restriction on rights of access to the market. Such restrictions are mercantilistic. Mercantilism refers to an economy in which, though there is private ownership of goods, the right to buy and sell them or their services in the marketplace is reserved by law to a restricted set of people. The privileged groups are denoted by franchises, licenses, monopolies, or guilds—all enforced by law.

Examples of mercantilistic restrictions include laws controlling hours of business, Sunday closing, quality standards, apprenticeship, prices, interest rates, minimum wages, and professional licensing, to name but a very few. Support for such restrictions can be found among many successful businessmen; it is not confined to so-called callous, unscrupulous people. Some of our most thoughtful humanitarians advocate them. Some

---

[2] In our own time, this has been increasingly associated with the euphemism "self-regulation" (by *existing* sellers).

justices of the Supreme Court of the United States deem them not only constitutional but desirable. The medical profession and many labor unions regard them as essential. Obviously, their support does not reflect an anticapitalist bias *per se,* but something else.

Every time someone manages to close out competitors, he gets a gain, but only at a greater loss to society.[3] That loss will be borne by all buyers of this product—even those who are protected in sales of their products. As more people achieve protection for their own sales, the losses to society as a whole increase. It will always pay any *one* person (for the moment) to get *more* protection for *himself,* but it would pay everyone else to prevent that if they could overcome costs of getting together to exert offsetting political pressure.

Ideal policy for a person interested in his wealth is to get the government to close his market to present and potential competitors, and at the same time to espouse the cause of free-enterprise, open-market capitalism when *others* seek to restrict open markets in which he buys.

Do laws restricting entry of competitors to the market involve political chicanery and immorality or bribery, considering that the protected parties pay part of their monopoly gains to the powers that be? No. The most noble monarchs of England have accepted these "taxes." Most of our states and cities in the United States do, too. The modern way is not to reward a particular official by paying him personally, but rather to be willing to "accept" a larger tax burden or pay a larger license fee for the privilege of being a monopolist or, as it is euphemistically put, a public utility—for example, water, light, power, gas, or taxi companies that have obtained operating franchises that eliminate competitors or raise the costs of getting into the market.

Various techniques for passing laws that restrict entry are moral, politically encouraged, and openly utilized. Later we shall examine some. For the moment, it suffices to indicate that laws can deny free access as well as protect it. For example, the government can help to *ensure* access by protecting entrants from private threats of violence and physical harm; it can *restrict* access by failing to grant such protection and by enforcing laws that keep "outsiders" from the market.

Pollution and Property Costs

Costs of Safeguarding Property Rights

The more expensive is protection against theft, the more common is thievery. Suppose that thievery of coats were relatively easy. People would be willing to pay only a lower price for coats. The lower market price of coats will understate the value of coats, for it will not include the value to the thief. If the thief were induced to rent or purchase a used coat, the price of coats would more correctly represent their value to society. It follows that the cheaper the policing costs, the greater the efficiency with which values of various uses of resources are revealed. The more likely something is to be stolen, the less of it that will be produced. People seldom plant apple trees where passers-by can easily take apples even if the value of the apples to society would exceed the costs.

---

[3] See the Appendix to this chapter for a numerical example for a price-taker and for a price-searcher.

Costs of Defining and Exchanging Property Rights

Defining and sanctioning private-property rights for some goods may be more costly than it is worth. The cost of protecting a person's rights to property from *all* noise produced by other people may exceed the costs imposed on the people whose "rights" are attenuated by the noise. Similarly, the costs of disposing of old leaves by other than burning may be so high that people may prefer to burn them even though there is mutual contamination of each other's property. The costs of subduing some "torts" or "nuisances," as the law calls these denials of rights to exclusivity of use, may be greater than the damage done. For example, the cost of eliminating all smog-creating exhausts is greater than the cost imposed by smog itself, but new inventions are changing the situation.

If property rights are cheap enough to define and enforce, we could compensate other people for any invasion of their property. The payment must, of course, be lower than the cost of other alternatives. I would rather pay a neighbor $50 for the right to dump refuse on his property than pay $200 to cart it elsewhere. If I build a shopping center near your house and change the physical attributes (via noise and bright lights) of your property so that you cannot enjoy it as formerly, I could pay you $100 a year for the right to do so, if you prefer $100 to no such "nuisance." But if the courts are sufficiently inept in defining property rights, I can create the "nuisance" without paying you anything.

Land-use rights are enforced because we can survey the land, detect trespassers, or "squatters," and apprehend and punish them at a sufficiently small cost to make that worthwhile. On the other hand, it is claimed, we cannot, when property is despoiled, detect dogs and identify their owners at a sufficiently low cost to make it worthwhile.

Effect upon Maximum-Value Use of Resources

The great significance of the costs of negotiating contracts and policing property rights—called *transactions* costs—can be seen by imagining a world in which these costs were absent. There would be no difficulties in knowing everyone else's preferences and values for all goods and activities. Everyone would know, at no cost of time or resources, what everyone else wants. (A major function of the market is to reduce costs of such information.) There would be no costs of policing contracts and enforcing agreements and property rights. In that fantasy world, (1) all the harmful and beneficial effects of any action would be brought to bear on the person authorizing that action, the property owner; (2) property (resources) would be used efficiently, in the sense that all exchange opportunities of mutual benefit would be realized and all production would be efficiently performed; (3) the uses of resources and the output produced with various goods would depend only upon the demand patterns and *not* upon who owns rights to goods.

All this can be made evident with a surprising example. A new product is contemplated. If produced, it will attract customers from other goods. The producers of old goods will lose wealth. In this context, consider two alternative initial assignments of property rights: (A) Producers have the right to sell new products without compensating old producers for their loss of sales. (B) The old producers are assigned rights to their customers, who cannot shift to a new product without the permission of the old producers. What difference would assumption of one alternative instead of the other make to the production of goods (use of resources)? None!

Under either alternative, existing producers would bear losses, but under A, they can try to retain customers by paying the new producer to abstain from production, offering an amount up to that of the loss they would have suffered, *or* they could cut the prices on their product to retain customers. If the cost this imposes on the old producers exceeds the gains proffered to customers by the new product, the old producers will be able to forestall production of the new good. But if the gain to the customers of the new good exceeds the loss to the old producers, the new producers could not be bought off.

Now consider alternative B in which the new producer would have to buy from old producers the rights to sell to customers. He would have to pay the old producers at least the loss of wealth they would suffer by loss of their sales (the same as the maximum the old producers would give up in the first alternative). Again, if the new producers would exceed the losses to the old, the new product would be produced; otherwise, the product would not be produced.

The important conclusion is that *if transactions costs are absent,* then under either assignment of *clearly specified rights,* the same production outcome is obtained: resources are put to their highest values. In sum, it makes no difference who has what rights, so long as the rights are *specified and enforced and exchangeable at zero transactions costs.* Exchanges will shift the uses of various goods to the highest valued uses.

In the real world, however, transactions costs do exist. They range from the trivial to the prohibitive. If the costs to the houseowner of detecting the driver of a noisy scooter and persuading him by a contract to stop are excessively large relative to the loss of value imposed by the noise or the value of being able to drive in noisy fashion, then noise will be made even though it inflicts a greater loss on one houseowner than the value to the scooter rider. And remember, there may be a hundred houseowners who suffer from the noise.

In Chapter 9 we analyzed the effects of "high" transactions costs on the allocation of produced goods. We saw that the higher the contracting costs, the more the market-exchange process was displaced by other rationing criteria. But there is more than a rationing problem; there is also the problem of producing the *appropriate* amounts of goods—the amounts that would be most desired *if* the costs of revealing demands were zero. If these demands cannot be cheaply revealed, an important incentive to producers is lacking. Too few of these goods are produced—because of the excessively high costs of discovering demand and negotiating a contract that can be effectively enforced. As in the case of the noisy scooter, *privately perceived* gains and costs do not reflect accurately the total gains and costs, so there are too few quiet scooters.

When transactions costs are excessive, resources are used in a way so strikingly at variance with what would be done if social benefits and costs were accurately recognized that people demand some kind of correction. Their first temptation is to ask for government action to either prohibit or require specified actions.

2, 3, 4, 5

Allocative Effects of Indefinite Property Rights

Even when transactions costs are not excessive, rights may be so ambiguous that no one knows who has what rights. If the case is taken to higher authority, the courts or the legislature may decide the rights belong to the government and not to any individuals. If an unambiguous specification of exchangeable property rights is made, the disputing parties can work out an exchange. No doubt, the initial assignment will determine that one party will be *richer,* but once that is settled, subsequent negotiation and contracting will reshuffle those rights in conformity with the principles of maximum-value use of resources.

Radio and TV. As a first example of the absence of clearly specified rights, we cite our use of radio and TV frequencies. In the 1920s, anyone could set up a radio transmitter and broadcast on any frequency he chose, regardless of who else might be broadcasting on the same or adjacent frequencies. Chaos resulted. The courts began to specify that the first broadcaster on a frequency owned the right, and subsequent parties would have to buy it from him—just as for early land. This would have stopped the chaos. Before this system of rights assignment could be completed, Congress, at the urging of the Navy (which wanted all the rights) and the Secretary of Commerce, decreed that the rights belonged to no one; the government would appropriate them and decide who could broadcast on what frequency, much as other governments have appropriated land. (The higher valued uses of radio and TV cannot be achieved, because direct sale of programs to viewers—the consumers of the radio spectrum—is not generally permitted.)

In contrast, land can be rented by private individuals and put to highest valued uses by offering present owners sufficient payment for the rights to the land. For radio and TV, private exchangeable rights are not allowed—that is, pay-TV by wireless transmission is prohibited. In other words, transaction costs are made "prohibitive" simply by declaring any such payment or exchange to be illegal. Since the values and costs do not impinge on any persons as private benefits and costs, more valuable programs are not produced. This is an example of the disparity between social and private benefits and costs (because of prohibitive transactions costs). This disparity occurs only partly because of some naturally present transaction costs, but they are made prohibitively expensive *by law*.

The problem of "unsatisfactory" performance by radio and TV is basically a result of our legal structure which denies salability of information by radio frequencies. The Federal Communications Commission, appointed to *define and police* radio-frequency rights, has become a *control* agency determining permissible programming and uses of radio and TV—much as if we had no private exchangeable rights to land and therefore created a Federal Land Commission to decide how and for what each piece of land could be used.

Water. Property rights in water also are weakly defined, probably because of the problems of surveying and monitoring the water (underground reservoirs, for example). More extensive property rights in the more valuable commodity oil, however, have been defined by subsurface pooling laws.

Airport noise. If an airport were to be used by noisy jet planes, the planes' owners, or the airport owner, could compensate nearby landowners for the noise nuisance, or, in effect, buy rights to particular uses of the land. Instead, one of the following extremes is usually taken: (1) There is no compensation for the noise damage. (2) The planes are prohibited. (3) The neighboring land is bought and left *empty* as people are prohibited from living there—even though many would prefer to live there despite the noise, *if* they could buy the land at a low enough price, and thereby be compensated for the noise. The extreme policies are based on a false assumption that it is impossible to buy the rights to "dump" noise on land.

Smog. A much more difficult problem arises from smog-producing processes. To eliminate smog completely would require prohibition of gasoline engines; and *that* now costs more than the gain from smog elimination. The other extreme is to permit unrestricted smog pollution. In between is some degree of legal restriction or incurring of costs to reduce smog. As yet, however, no one knows of an enforceable system of exchangeable property rights in clean air that would protect people from "excessive" air pollution.

Creation versus operation of private property. One confusion about the meaning of a private-property system has arisen from the various ways in which private-property rights are created. The way in which private-property rights are *created* and initially allocated is different from the way that system *operates* once it is in existence. An excellent example is provided by the Enclosure Movement in England about 500 years ago. People had rights to *use* particular portions of land in common with other people but could not sell this right. If the rights had been legally salable, it would have paid a person to sell his use rights to the person who could make the most valuable use of the land. One would think that the law would have been modified, so that each holder of a right to use could be identified and allowed to sell his right to someone. If transferability by sale were authorized, all the use-right holders would have been compensated for their rights. However, the common-use-right holders were not allowed to sell their rights; they simply had their rights expropriated, and some lucky (politically powerful) person was declared to be in control of the sole right. This method of *creating* private property has no bearing on how the system will operate thereafter, but to the people of the time, the *operation* of a system of private property (capitalism) was identified with this particular method of *creation* of new property rights—expropriation of common-use rights. Tenants who lost their rights regarded private property as theft.

Imagine how you as a student would feel if your admission to attend your present college were revoked and given to new students, who in turn could resell those rights. You would feel cheated. But if your current "rights" to attend were converted to a "private-property" right that *you* could sell to other people, you would not lose anything. (Of course, the university administration, including the faculty, would lose part of its cherished rights to decide who was admitted to college.) 6, 7, 8, 9

Interpersonal Dependence: External Consequences

The term *private* property suggests that *private consequences to the owner* of a good dominate his decisions about the use of privately owned goods. Yet, the way we use our resources very generally has consequences for others, too. When you wear clean, good-looking clothes, or cultivate a pretty garden, or even read the kinds of books that I think you ought to read, my utility is increased, i.e., I prefer that you do so. This kind of interdependence or external social effect was not ruled out in the preceding chapters; nor is it inconsistent with that analysis. Exchange, which is a use of goods, provides, as we saw, benefits to the other person, too. Still, there are actions you can take that would benefit other people, but which you do not take because you are not offered adequate inducements to take those actions.

Beneficial effects for other people that are *induced* by those who benefit are called *induced* external benefits. The gains from exchange and specialization analyzed in earlier chapters are "external" effects that have been induced by the reward of the *quid-pro-quo* exchange—a reward that reflects the value of the external service provided. The ability to sell or transfer goods or their services means that other people can influence the use of goods, no matter who owns them. Social effects are not all left without influence on the decision about how goods shall be used. Every home owner takes into account the effect of his uses of his house on the sale value of the house. The use everyone makes of his own marketable goods depends on the preferences and desires of other people. When one uses goods, he must reckon with the gains he otherwise could have. Sometimes this inducement feedback is called "internalizing the external effect." In essence, much of economic theory concerns the allocation of the uses of economic goods by *internalizing* external effects.

However, it is difficult to make the use of some goods respond to external effects. A public fireworks display at a Fourth of July celebration would benefit many viewers. An extra dollar's cost of display provides possibly 90 cents more utility to one person, 80 cents more to another, and 40 cents more to another. The extra cost is $1; yet the sum of the independent marginal values is $2.10. The extra dollar of use is not worth that much to any one person; yet, because it provides utility to several people simultaneously the sum of the marginal values over all the beneficiaries exceeds the extra $1 of cost. Still, no one, unless he could be excluded, will offer to pay the $1, if the service is provided.

Costs and Incentives for Excluding Nonpayers

We must, however, be careful. The single fact that several people benefit jointly is not crucial. At a theater, everyone pays; his contribution is only a small part of the total cost of the performance. Jointness of beneficiaries does not upset the ability of market exchange to get desired services performed. Flood-control projects, national defense, sanitary campaigns—all are identical with theatrical presentations and football games insofar as *commonality and simultaneity* of benefit are concerned. A crucial element is in the *costs of exclusion of nonpayers,* i.e., of "free riders." For some goods and services, nonpayers are "naturally" excluded; consumption of food by one person naturally excludes other people. For other goods the cost of excluding nonpayers is prohibitive.

If there were a cheap way to exclude nonpayers from enjoyment of the service, the external effects would be "internalized." As we have noted, it may not be possible or desirable to internalize the benefits if the costs of doing so exceed the value of service. But there are some techniques for doing so without excessive costs.

For example, a golf course provides benefits to the neighboring property owners, who benefit without paying. A golf-course builder could buy enough land to build a course with surrounding houses. When he sells or rents the surrounding property, he captures the higher value stemming from proximity to the golf course. Those external benefits have been "internalized" as inducements to build the golf course.

Another example is provided by the apartment-house owner who includes maintenance of the gardens and exterior appearance of each apartment in the rental price, rather than having the tenant provide it. Similarly, the purchase price of a cemetery plot usually includes the costs of maintaining the cemetery rather than permitting each owner to choose the degree of maintenance—again, because of the neighborhood external effect.

A most important institution to internalize external benefits is the partnership or corporation. These enable larger ventures to be undertaken so that more of the benefited resources can be owned by those who produce the benefits. If all the land of a suburban shopping center is owned by one enterprise, there can be a more complete response to the total effect of the shopping center on neighboring land values. A department store with all the departments in one building owned by one firm is another example of how the neighborhood effects of each department are "internalized" upon the others.

Another adaptation can be cited. A business firm that locates in a new area knows that it will provide a benefit to other firms that spring up in its neighborhood. Presumably, the initial firm would have to expect to capture the value of external benefits to other people in order for its decision to be influenced by those external effects. Yet the owner may instead "bet" that while his action provides external benefits to other firms that locate near him, he will get reciprocal external effects from other new firms that spring up. An anticipated exchange of external effects is an inducement, even though a formal contractual exchange agreement is not involved. Shopping districts spring up without formal advance contractual agreements among all who eventually open a business. Each businessman gambles on the mutual-benefit effect. A factory owner, when relocating his factory, "bets" that others will open nearby restaurants, apartments, housing tracts, and appurtenant services. House owners who cultivate gardens to beautify their homes "bet" that others will also do so with mutual external benefits. "Keeping up with the Joneses" is not always a silly social code.

One of the principal means for internalizing externalities and handling some public-goods cases is by ownership of a large piece of land on which a shopping center or entire residential community exists.[4] The landowner, heedful of the effects of each person's action on the willingness of others to continue as tenants, will restrict undesirable external effects and increase the extent of desirable ones—to enhance the rental value of the land in the entire complex.

We can see that neither the existence nor the extent of so-called "non-influential" external benefits is determined by "technological" conditions alone. The scope of non-inducing benefits is affected by the ownership arrangements, which are often adapted and modified so as to capture previously uncaptured benefits. People are ingenious. They use television cable so that only those who pay will get a picture. Fences are built around athletic arenas and high walls around theaters. Colleges keep out students by instructing professors to exclude *nonpaying students*.

Finally, we note that the existence of social external benefits to other people does not in itself prove that more of the responsible action should be taken nor that it should be subsidized. The extent of the responsible action may already be so great that extra action may not *add* to the social effect. The marginal effect is important, not the total existing effect.

10, 11, 12, 13, 14, 15

Public Goods Production

Even if it were costless to exclude nonpayers, it does not follow that nonpayers should always be excluded! There is a class of goods known as "public goods," wherein the amount of use of the good or service by one person does not reduce the amount

---

[4] Trailer courts, apartments, condominiums, hotels, shopping centers, large business buildings, department stores—all are examples of groups of people living in conditions where the external effects of their actions and the "public goods" provided by the complex are responsive to values totaled over all members.

available to others *if* the good has been produced.⁵ Classic examples are melodies, poems, ideas, and theories. Anyone can use them without in any way reducing someone else's supply. If I hum a new tune, you can hum it too. *Once the good is produced,* any restriction on its use by some person, say by charging a price for each use, would be "inefficient"—in the sense that the restriction reduces the total utility of the members of the community. Someone has less utility and *no one* else thereby gets more. (It is not a *free* good once it is produced, for even more of it might be desired; but it is a public good in the sense that no actual or potential user supplants some other possible user.)

Exclusion of any potential user would be undesirable if we accept the ethical criterion that more for some people, if it does not mean less for anyone else, is certainly desirable. However, accepting this criterion creates a conflict of goals. We want to encourage the invention of new ideas, melodies, and literature, and we want them fully used. But to charge for their use in order to provide incentive for development and invention will restrict their use. How can we induce people to create public goods if we prohibit charging for their use?

Examine the example of a lighthouse. All shipowners benefit, and they would like more light. If the lighthouse builder were able to control the light rays so that any nonpaying shipowner could not see the light, beneficiaries could induce him to provide as much more of the service as it was worth. Barring this possibility, some shipowners will not voluntarily pay for their value of service received—pro-rated share (say, $100) of the light they otherwise would get free, plus an amount (say, $10) to cover the cost of a larger light that they each might prefer. They would have to share payment for all the light ($110), but the worth of the additional light they get by cooperating is only the marginal increment ($10). As far as any one user is concerned, the choice is between paying the pro-rata share of the total cost of $110 to get a $10 gain in value of light, or paying nothing and still getting some (or hoping others will provide) lighthouse service. Obviously, it will benefit him not to pay at all. And almost everyone will hope to get a "free ride." Too few lighthouses would be built too late. The consequence arises from the "unwillingness" of the nonexcludable beneficiaries to induce the provider of the service to provide more. Yet, *once the lighthouse is built,* exclusion of anyone could be wasteful (except that it is a very reliable means of ascertaining the value of the service for guiding production).

The landlubber counterpart is television. If all who wanted the program were to pay, the program would be available, but no one person is willing to bear the full cost of an "optimum" amount of service if he can view for nothing. Each person holds back in the hope that someone else will act.

If, fancifully, there were a way to measure the benefit obtained by each user and then have each pay not more than that amount to the producer, the problem would be solved. The user would pay a nonrestrictive lump sum, and all who paid could use as much of the public good as was available. The lump-sum payment is not restrictive, because it is not a price for more use of the public good. It is an entry fee that one pays, once and for all, and thereby does not restrict his use of the public good.

How to determine for each person what the appropriate lump-sum payment is and how to collect it? Everyone would want to conceal the value to him while someone else paid to get the good produced. An excellent current example is the community television antenna for relatively isolated towns. Once the antenna is installed everyone can tap it

---

⁵ Review the earlier discussion of "public good" attributes on pages 147–148.

with no loss of signal to anyone else. So why should anyone pay? And to prohibit its use by nonpayers is to restrict needlessly the extent of viewing—needlessly, in the sense of maximizing total utility *once the antenna is installed*. But if, in the absence of pricing and restricting, the antenna were not constructed (not enough volunteer to cover the costs), then pricing may be desirable to *get* the antenna *constructed*. Is it better not to restrict (and have no antenna) or to restrict and have an antenna? Clearly, the latter is superior.

But there is another alternative. Let the government tax everyone on a lump-sum basis and, with the proceeds, build the antenna. Then do not restrict the number who use it. But this solution also has flaws. (1) The tax is compulsory even on those who do not want an antenna. (2) It, too, is exclusionary, for failure to pay taxes will "exclude" you. (3) Who decides what ideas and programs shall be produced by the tax proceeds? Without a price per unit of use, viewers have no means of directly rewarding producers of more desirable programs. The control of production passes to the political arena and is more controlled by group political competition than decentralized, market competition. For those who are strong in political competitive power, this may seem desirable. The choice is not determinable by any known ethical criterion.

Another alternative to government is voluntary group action. The church is a prime example. In the United States, churches are not supported by taxes paid for support of the church, although they are in some other countries (Scandinavia). In Scandinavian countries, the number of churches per person is lower than in areas with voluntary contributions to church support. Are there too many in one system or too few in the other? We cannot tell.

The problem of public goods is a relatively new one in economic analysis. Perhaps in a few more decades, more definitive analyses can be accomplished and rigorous implications perceived. The problem is covered here to warn against blind carryover of principles from private goods to public goods as if there were no difference.

We can summarize the problem of "external effects." Some potential uses of resources also benefit people other than the current owners. Those "external" benefits can be made influential by paying the resource controller to adjust his use of the good. "External effects are thus internalized, or social effects are made private." For some goods this is prohibitively expensive; there then exists a disparity between social and private benefits and costs. For any good heavily loaded with the "public goods" characteristic, *once the good is produced*, there is no allocating or rationing problem, since no one user will deprive any other user. Hence, charging a price for its use would restrict use unnecessarily. But a means of defraying the costs of production and of discovering how much to produce is necessary. The conflicting objectives for "public" goods are (1) to induce beneficiaries to reveal their values of services and to pay for the production of the service and (2) the "unnecessary" restriction on use if any fee restricts use. Various devices were mentioned that have been adopted to meet partially both objectives of inducing appropriate production and of not restricting use once production has occurred. Some involve group action via private markets and some via government taxing or production.

16, 17, 18

Summary

1 Productive efficiency is disrupted if markets are closed or restricted to potential entrants.

2 The private-property system specifies exclusive decision over use and transferability of specified resources.

3 For a large class of goods the private consequences of use to the owner are the entire set of consequences; the uses of many other goods have external effects. When the external effects are not taken into account by the decision maker, more harmful effects or less beneficial effects will be provided. Externalities are more influential (a) the more explicitly property rights are known, (b) the more economically and surely they are enforced, and (c) the lower are the costs of negotiating rearrangement of rights.

4 If costs of negotiating exchanges were zero, and if enforcement and policing of rights were costless, it would make no difference (so far as how goods are used) who initially had what rights to what goods. The exchanges of rights to use various goods would give more goods to those who would put them to the highest market-valued uses. Radio, television, water, and roads are resources for which use rights have not been specified and made transferable; as a result, their uses do not approach the highest market-valued uses.

5 Public goods are those for which one person's consumption does not reduce any other person's consumption. Beneficiaries of public goods prefer not to reveal the value of the goods to them, because they can realize the benefits without paying. To exclude nonpayers is to reduce social total of benefit; there would be no offsetting gain to anyone else.

6 "Externality" inducement is partially provided by ownership of enough neighboring land to capture benefits of such services via higher rental.

7 If externalities are not sufficiently internalized and if goods have heavily public aspects, the government will probably provide or control such services.

Questions

1 Closed markets (price-takers or price-searchers) imply a reduced output compared to open markets. Yet no increase in unemployment or idle resources is involved. Explain why the output is smaller and why there are no idle resources.

2 What is meant by an equality between private and social costs?

3 "Privately owned goods are those which a person has the right to use however he wishes." Explain why it is not necessary to add the clause "subject to not destroying other people's property." Explain why that first statement does not give an owner the right to hit you on the head with his hammer or to dump his garbage on your property.

4 The City of Palm Springs prohibits construction of any building whose shadow will fall on some other person's land between 9 A.M. and 3 P.M. Is that a restriction of private property or a strengthening of it? Explain.

5 A restaurant opens near an apartment. The cooking smells annoy the apartment tenants. The apartment owner sues for invasion of property rights.
   a. You are on the jury. Would you find in favor of the restaurant or the apartment owner?
   b. Would your decision depend upon whether or not the apartment owner lived in the affected apartments?
   c. Do you know what decisions have actually been rendered in similar cases?

6 A owns a hillside lot with a beautiful view. B, owner of the lot just below, plants trees that grow up to 50 feet in height and block A's view. A asks him to trim the tops. B refuses. A offers to pay for the trimming. B refuses. A offers $300 in addition. B refuses; B asks for $2,000. A sues for $5,000 damages to the marketable value of his property.

a. As the judge, how would you rule?
b. If, earlier, *A* had sued to force the person to trim the trees, how would you have ruled?
c. What will our courts really decide today in such suits?

7. *A* owns and lives in a home near an area in which it is announced a series of twenty-story apartments will be built. This will have only trivial effect on a view, since the land is all flat. *A* sues to prevent the construction on the contention that it will create extra traffic hazards and congestion. In court, *A* proves to the judge's satisfaction that his allegation is correct. As the judge, how would you rule? Why?

8. In Mexico, landless people are invading large farms and settling on the land as "squatters." The government has not acted to maintain the property rights of existing owners. The new occupants are not claiming the right to sell the land to others. They claim only the right to the use and fruits of the land, called usufruct rights, which at law is the right to enjoy all the benefits of a thing without the right to sell it. Rights of usufruct often pass by inheritance or by occupancy.
a. What effect will this development have on the sale value of the land?
b. How will it affect the willingness of the owner to invest in the land?
c. If the usufruct rights and sale rights were assigned (owned) by the land owner, would that increase or decrease the incentive to invest in the land? Explain why.

9. You are asked by the government officials of a new "emerging" nation whether occupants should have private-property rights in land or whether only usufruct rights should be allowed.
a. What would you recommend? Why?
b. You are then asked whether occupants should have the right to mortgage the land; some concern is expressed that the occupants might borrow against the land and then simply let the creditor have it. What do you recommend and why?
c. Would you permit tenant farming—whereby the land is rented from the owner by a farmer? (If so, you are permitting absentee ownership, which is widely held in disrepute.)

10. A city passed a zoning ordinance prohibiting the owner of a large parcel of land from constructing homes on it because of a fear that the noise of a nearby airport owned by the city would be so disturbing to the new tenants that airport operations would have to be curtailed.
a. Whose rights were being curtailed by the zoning ordinance?
b. Under the definition of private-property rights, were the landowner's rights being taken from him?
c. Can you suggest some other solution to the problem?
d. If you were a taxpayer in that town and did not live near the airport, what solution would you have voted for?
e. If you owned vacant land near the airport, what solution would you advocate? If your vote is different in each case, do you think you are denying the morality of decisions by voting? Why?

11. "When property rights interfere with human rights, property rights have to give in." This statement is reported to have been made by a lieutenant governor of California. What do you think it means?

12. If I don't reciprocate in social invitations with my friends, I find they stop inviting me to their social functions. If I am impolite to other people, they are impolite to me. Much of our social etiquette is a matter of formal, though nonmarket, exchange, with the exception that when I host a party I do not obtain a contract from my guests promising to

invite me as a guest to one of their parties. Would it thereby follow that there are too few parties and too few guests invited? Why?

13 "The fact that some airplanes collide is evidence that there is too little air traffic control." Evaluate. (Hint: What would it cost to avoid all risk of air collision?)

14 a. Non-inducible externalities are one reason for government economic activity. Free libraries are often justified on that ground. Look up the history of free libraries to see how they were started.
b. Subsidized education is also justified on that ground. Look up the early stages of subsidized or free education to see how it started.
c. Religion is not financed by government activity. Is that because it has no non-inducible external effects? Is there too little wealth devoted to religion? What evidence can you cite?
d. Name the ten best universities or colleges. How many of them are "private"? How do you explain that?
e. Do the preceding four problems imply that government does either too much or too little in these areas?

15 "Social ostracism is a form of social control and is often a substitute for some government action." Evaluate.

16 "National defense is shared by everyone. More of it for one person does not mean less for someone else. Therefore, it is a public good and should be provided via government taxes and operation."
a. Does greater anti-missile defense for New York City mean greater defense for Houston, Texas?
b. Do more public concerts on the west side of town mean more on the east side?
c. Does it follow that public goods—those that give benefits to several people without less to anyone else—really do not exist?
d. Do external benefits mean that more than one person benefits, or that a nonowner benefits, or that those who benefit do so without any less of the service to someone else?

17 "The imbalance between governmentally and privately provided services is evidenced by the fact that the family that vacations in its air-conditioned, power-braked, power-steered car passes through cities over dirty, badly paved, congested streets, not to mention the billboards obstructing the beauties of the countryside. When the family picnics with excellent food provided by private business, they must sit by a polluted stream and then spend the night in a public park that is a menace to health and morals and littered with decaying refuse. Private abundance and public poverty are facts that assail every observant person. A plentiful supply of privately produced goods and a shortage of publicly provided services is inescapable testimony to the lack of a social balance between private and governmentally provided services."

Without trying to prove that there ought to be less or ought to be more governmentally provided services, tell why the arguments, taken from a popular book advocating more governmentally provided services, are faulty and do not indicate anything at all about whether there is too little of governmentally provided services. (Hint: Note the use of the term "shortage"; what does it suggest? How are governmentally provided services rationed?)

18 The following is orthodox Chinese Communist (Marxist) economic doctrine: "The goal of socialist production is not profit but the satisfaction of social needs. Goods must be produced as long as they are needed by society, even if a loss is incurred. Not profits, but the calculation of assigned target goals and their fulfillment is the most important consideration. This follows from the Marxist-Leninist tenet that, contrary to capitalism which

Market Restrictions, Pollution, Property Enforcement Costs, and Public Goods

seeks maximum profits, the objective of socialism is the maximum satisfaction of the material and cultural requirements of society. This fact gives the Communist Party, as representative of society, the right to determine society's requirements and what the economy should produce." However, in 1962 the Chinese Communists permitted some Chinese economists to publish the following ideas: "Profits should not be set against the goal satisfying social needs. The profit level is the best measure of the effectiveness of management. This would mean that no enterprise would operate at a loss because the output would be curtailed unless the state valued its product sufficiently to raise its prices, and no enterprise would try to exceed the output plan at the expense of profits. There would be less need for political participation in enterprise management decisions, if prices were more realistic, in reflecting either market values or costs. The capitalist evil connotations of profits are not present in socialism, because under socialism profit takes on an entirely different character, where it is a good thing."

But still later in 1962, the Communist Party authorities reaffirmed their initial orthodox doctrine and did so both directly and by indirection with an attack on "revisionist" ideas as exemplified by Yugoslavia, which engaged in what the Chinese Communists regard as backsliding policies—like adopting market pricing (permitting more prices to be set in the open market, decentralizing state enterprises and permitting more private property in farming and handicraft activities). In reaffirming their orthodox Marxist tenets, the Chinese Communists directed factory managers to adopt political and economic means to raise labor productivity and to overfulfill specified targets of gross value of outputs whenever possible.

In order to understand why the issues of "proper" pricing, the use of the market, and kinds of incentives are so crucial to the Communists, it is pertinent to understand the effects on the power position of the Communist Party politicians if the economists' 1962 proposal were adopted. What would those effects be? Explain why.

19 Ralph Nader, currently a popular exposer of defects, complains that a person who relieves himself in the Detroit River is fined, but industries that pollute the same river are not. He says also that muggers are punished but smoggers are not. These he cites as illustrating the inequities and irrationalities of our society and economy in its attitude toward big corporations. What has Nader overlooked in his condemnation?

Appendix: Closed Market Inefficiency
Price-Takers

Suppose that Mr. E gets a law passed preventing Mr. C from selling Y. The results are shown in Table 14–1. In a price-takers' market Mr. E would then produce and sell all $5Y$ at the market price of 70 cents per Y. He gets $3.50 from sale of the Y and $3.00 from the X he makes with the rest of his time, for a total of $6.50 (20 cents more per day than with open markets as can be seen by reviewing page 224). If this happens, the total community output is $5Y$ and $22X$ instead of $5Y$ and $22.2X$ as it was with open markets and price-takers (check it!). Because of restricted rights to the market, the total social loss is $.2X$ or 20 cents per day. Excluded producers, therefore, must use their resources in less valuable and less productive ways than if they could sell in the market.

The "national" income has fallen from $25.70 ($22.20 of X and $3.50 of Y) to $25.50 ($22.00 of X and $3.50 of Y). But Mr. E's share is up to $6.50, from $6.30, while the rest of the population has $19 instead of $19.40 (check it). The upshot is that

TABLE 14–1. Production of X and Y in Open or Closed and in Price-Takers' or Price-Searchers' Markets

Marketing Situation	Production of X and Y
Open:	
Price-takers	22.2 and 5
Achievable	(22.2 and 5)
Price-searchers for Y	22.8 and 4
Achievable	(22.8 and 4)
Closed:	
Price-takers for Y	22.0 and 5
Achievable	(22.2 and 5)
Price-searchers for Y	23.8 and 2
Achievable	(24 and 2)

In closed markets, achieved production is less than achievable production. Achieved output is now on the inside community production-possibility boundary (of Figure 14–1), not because of any idle resource, but rather because of inefficiency ("misdirected" producers) resulting from restriction against resources entering markets where their uses are of highest value.

for Mr. E to gain 20 cents, the rest of the total population has to suffer a loss of 40 cents. The net social loss of 20 cents is the reduction in the output of X, caused by inefficiency. Clearly it would have paid everyone else to prevent such a market-restriction law from being passed. Why didn't they?

Price-Searchers

In the closed market situation just discussed, we assumed sellers were price-takers. We now suppose that Mr. E is a price-searcher; he acts in awareness that his output affects price. Since he is the sole, privileged seller of Y, the demand schedule in Table 13–3 faces him. He sees that the marginal revenue of selling $1Y$ at $2.00 is $2.00; the marginal revenue of selling $2Y$ is $1.00 (the difference between selling $1Y$ at $2.00 and $2Y$ at $1.50 each); and the marginal revenue of 3 is 30 cents. However, the marginal cost of a third Y is 60 cents; so producing and selling $3Y$ would reduce his net income by 30 cents, the difference between the marginal revenue and marginal cost at $3Y$. It is not the selling price with which he compares marginal cost, but the marginal revenue. Since marginal revenue to a price-searcher is less than price—the value of another Y to buyers—he will produce only $2Y$, and he devotes the rest of his resources to making $4.80 worth of X per day.

The national output is $2Y$ and $23.8X$. The results of the different cases (1) with and without open markets and (2) with price-takers' or price-searchers' markets can be readily compared in Table 14–1. *Closing other sellers'* (except Mr. E's) *access* to the market for Y resulted in smaller output. This loss reflects an inefficient organization of productive resources. A bigger output of *both* X and Y is possible by a different allocation of productive resources. The community output without closed markets could have been $22.2X$ (instead of $22X$) and $5Y$ for price-takers' markets; it could have been

$24X$ (instead of $23.8X$) and $2Y$ for price-searchers' markets. These losses reveal the inefficiency of closed markets. The extent of the loss depends upon who is excluded and who is allowed to produce and sell in the market. If Messrs. C and E were excluded, and only B were allowed, the loss would be even greater. (You can check this as an exercise.)

Costs and Production

Preview

15 THIS chapter explains some quantitative relationships between costs and outputs. Students who take only one course in economics will not find this chapter as valuable as will those who plan to take economics as a major field of study. To accommodate the first group of students, we present at the outset what should be an adequate summary statement of the main propositions. Those who plan to be economics majors will want to read the chapter with care; for them the brief summary at the beginning should serve as a helpful guide to the chapter: (1) The behavior of cost already enunciated and explained in the preceding chapters related costs of production to the speed or rate at which the product was produced. The higher the rate of production the greater the average and the marginal costs. (2) Now we present a second proposition that most people are already familiar with in everyday experience: the greater the volume to be produced, the lower the average and marginal costs, at any given speed of production—known as the law of the economies of mass production. For example, if ten automobiles of a given model are to be produced, each will cost more than if 100,000 of that model are made. Custom-made items are more costly than mass-produced items of the same quality. (It is this second law that some students have in mind when balking at acceptance of the first law in earlier chapters.) But the two entirely different propositions are consistent with each other. (3) When different output programs are compared in a special way, we get another proposition. We compare output programs, *all* lasting one year, but differing in their rates and volumes as follows. If the output *rate* is twice as large, the total volume produced in the year is also doubled. The total time-length of the production run is not changed—just the *rate* of production, and with it necessarily the total volume produced. If the rate is increased for a given interval of time, the volume produced in that interval will increase in the same proportion. If we compare the costs of this series of alternative potential output programs, all starting at any given moment and lasting the same length of time, average cost per unit can fall with increasing output at the smaller scales, but as one moves to the very high rate-volume programs the average cost of output rises. Why is there this U-shaped relation between average cost and size of output program? The fact is that the volume effect in reducing average costs loses force at very large volumes, whereas the cost increasing effect of higher *rates* gets stronger at the very high rates. So if potential output programs are arranged according to the scale of the output program, where the scale is measured in terms of *both* (i) the speed (or rate) of production and (ii) the total volume to be produced in the given interval, we get average cost (and marginal) curves like that shown in Figure 15–3.

That summarizes the main cost-output relationships. The chapter explains them with specific numerical examples and graphs in order to make the propositions more familiar and easier to use. In the course of the discussion a few other related ideas are explained. We indicate different stages in a production program and the ways the costs of each can be measured; the meanings of short-run and long-run output programs; joint production; and depreciation, obsolescence, and replacement of equipment.

To avoid getting bogged down in a variety of costs that can be confusing, we suggest that you not try to retain each one in mind as you proceed. Instead, look for the meaning of each action and see how its cost is computed. Only a few will be used in our subsequent analysis, but they can be more precisely understood later if the variants are initially distinguished. Read pages 257, 258 to see how costs are computed for some steps in an output program. Then in pages 259–265 we shall see how costs depend on the size or dimensions of an output program.

Costs of Acquisition, Continuing Possession, and Operation

Normally, we speak of the purchase price as the cost—when the resale price is typically zero, as for bread, shoes, or socks. But for many long-lived capital goods, the resale price is far from zero. With an ordinary new car, it may be 85 to 90 percent of the initial purchase price. If you buy a car for $2,000 and then immediately resell it for $2,000, the cost was zero. If you had resold it for $1,800, the cost you incurred would have been $200. The longer you keep possession of the car, the less will be the resale value. That subsequent depreciation in resale value is the cost of *continuing* possession, whereas the initial, immediate turn-around, purchase-resale price differential is a cost of *acquisition*. To make the example concrete, suppose the initial purchase price is $2,000, with an immediate resale value of $1,800, and with a subsequent $1-a-day depreciation in resale value. (1) The acquisition cost is $200, the difference between price and current resale value. (2) The cost of continuing possession of the car is $1 per day. The cost of *acquiring* ownership of a car and *keeping* it for one week is $207.[1] (3) The cost of driving it 1,000 miles in a week, assuming the operation costs are 6 cents a mile, is $60. The total costs thereby incurred are $60 for the gasoline, $7 for the depreciation—a total of $67 for *operating and continuing possession* of the car. On the other hand, if I do not yet have the car, the total cost of *acquiring, continuing possession, and operating it for one week* would be $267.

[1] The cost of keeping it for another week—*given* that I have already acquired it—is $7.

Fixed and variable costs. You might think these costs would normally be called (1) acquisition (or entry) cost, (2) continued possession cost, and (3) operating cost. But conventionally they have been called almost everything except those names. Sometimes, (1) is called "fixed" (or "sunk") cost, to suggest that once you acquire the item this cost is "fixed" upon you and irrevocable. For *any subsequent* decision this "cost" is totally irrelevant and can be forgotten. When "fixed" is applied to this first cost, the term "variable" is applied to the *sum* of (2) and (3) costs, in the sense that you could vary them by *shutting down and selling out* or varying the output plan.[2] (3) is called out-of-pocket costs.

Before we go to a detailed explanation of why the preceding distinctions are made, and how costs depend upon output, a few subsidiary points should be noted. First, do not confuse all expenditure with cost. Expenditure may be an exchange of one form of wealth for another—usually money for nonmoney goods. *Cost* of an *action* is the associated *reduction* in *total wealth*. Second, a cost of $200 *incurred now* by some action does not mean that one must reduce his *consumption* now. He may continue to consume at the same rate, deferring the reduced consumption till later. And there is nothing wrong or irrational with deferring the consumption sacrifice. Many young people do this by buying on installment plans. Third, to incur a cost does not mean one is worse off. When you buy the car and lose, say $200 in wealth, it means only that you could not now go back (by a market exchange) to your original set of resources. But if you knew that the cost of acquiring the car was going to be $200 (difference between the purchase and the immediate resale price) we presume you decided that having the car was worth that cost, and also worth the sacrifice of other services you could have had instead.

1, 2, 3

Per-Unit-of-Service Measures of Costs

Costs can be expressed per units of output, in particular as costs per mile of service. For example, for a two-year, 20,000 mile program, which we assumed in the preceding chapter, we simply divide the total costs by 20,000 miles to get the average (per mile) cost. The results are in the extreme right column of Table 15–1: $1,678.90/20,000 = \$.084$, a little more than 8 cents per mile. You can cover that cost with revenue if you rent your car for 8.4 cents per mile—but you must *collect the receipts in advance*. If you wait until the mileage occurs, interest should be included, since the measure used for cost is a *present*-value measure. If you were to be paid by credit-card at the end of each year, how much should you demand from the renter of the car? Or, what uniform two-year annuity (payments at the end of a first year and a second year) will have a present value of $1,678.90? Using Table 11–3, we get (at 10 percent) $969, due at the end of each of the two years (9.69 cents per mile paid when transport service is provided).[3]

The average *present* value cost of 8.4 cents per mile can be partitioned into operating (variable) costs and a remainder (which does not depend upon the mileage) here called the "possession" or "fixed" cost. $644.40/20,000 = 3.2$ cents per mile, the per-mile

---

[2] Just to confuse things, apparently, economists use the expression "fixed" cost to refer to the first two costs, with "variable" for just the third one.

[3] Since the receipts are to be spread over a two-year period, with interest at 10 percent each year, the payment due at time of mileage is delayed on the average about 1.5 years. At 10 percent per year, that is about 15 percent interest per 1.5 years. As expected, 9.69 cents is about 15 percent larger than 8.4 cents. Hereafter, to simplify computations, we shall express all costs, whether for the total program or a unit of mileage basis, in terms of the present-value measure.

TABLE 15–1. Total Cost (Present Capital Value) Dependence on Volume (Miles of Service) at *Constant* Rate of 10,000 Miles per Year

Distance (Miles)	Total Cost	Incremental Cost	Average Cost
5,000	$ 750	$750	$.150
10,000	1,100	350	.110
15,000	1,400	300	.093
20,000	1,679	279	.084
25,000	1,940	261	.078
30,000	2,200	260	.074
35,000	2,420	220	.067
40,000	2,600	180	.065
45,000	2,760	160	.061
50,000	2,900	140	.058

average *direct operating,* or variable, costs—excluding the initial acquisition *and* subsequent continued possession costs. The per-mile "fixed" possession cost is ($1,678.90 − $644.40)/20,000 or 5.2 cents. (Remember, this is merely the fixed cost spread over the 20,000 miles. The greater the mileage provided in those two years, the lower will be the per-mile average measure of that "fixed" cost.)

Let us compute one more average cost. What is the cost of the program minus *only* the ($200) initial acquisition cost? If the *already acquired* car is kept and used for 20,000 miles in two years, $1,478.90 in costs will be incurred. On a per-mile basis over 20,000 miles that is 7.4 cents per mile, excluding only the initial acquisition cost. This is an "average variable" or avoidable (if operations ceased) cost.

4, 5, 6

"Size" of Output Programs

There are several dimensions of "size" of an output program. One is the *volume,* or amount, of the good to be produced. A second is the *rate,* or speed, at which that volume is produced once it is under way. Finally, there are the *dates* of the output (for example, dates it is to be started and completed). In making refrigerators, the manufacturer can plan a volume of 150,000 refrigerators at the rate of 15,000 per month (for ten months), with the first completed item to appear six months from the date of decision to produce. The *volume* is 150,000 items, the *rate* is 15,000 per month, and the *date* is six to sixteen months hence. In the rest of this chapter, we will discuss how these three components of "size" affect cost.

Cost Effect of Volume

A larger volume (mileage or distance, in our current example) for some given initial date and constant rate of output will cost more than a smaller volume. More resources are required. In our automobile example, mileage is the volume. If mileage is to be 40,000 miles in *four* years rather than 20,000 in two years (constant *rate* of 10,000 miles per year), the total cost will be greater. But although the volume (40,000 miles) is twice as large, the total cost will not necessarily be doubled. *Generally the cost increase will be less than in proportion to the increase in the volume* (keeping the *rate* unchanged). The average cost per mile falls as the volume (mileage) increases. This is an economy of large or "mass" production.

The *volume* effect is important in reducing average and marginal cost for mass-produced, large-volume-of-output goods, like automobiles, radios, typewriters, electric motors, refrigerators, and tires.

If you ask a printer to print some personal letterheads or circulars, you will be told that the price *per unit* is lower, the more you buy. Aircraft companies know that the average cost of a jet plane is cheaper if they can produce one hundred than if they produce only ten. Ford knows that the average cost of a car is lower for half a million than for one hundred. Polaroid cameras are cheaper if several thousand are produced rather than a hundred.

If larger-volume production is cheaper *per unit* than small-volume production, *standardization* of products is implied. People who want individually styled or custom-built goods will face higher prices. We should expect to see many people using standardized goods, as they in fact do with automobiles, shirts, shoes, watches, airplanes, etc., because of the cost-reducing effect of a larger volume. A country with a large population can take greater advantage of this cost-reducing effect since it can produce in larger *volume*. This effect of a large market in reducing costs is one of the major advantages of the United States over smaller countries. Larger markets permit greater specialization and mass-production economies.[4]

Annual changes in automobile models prevent costs from falling for *particular* models. Then why change models every year, if that is more expensive than keeping the same model for a larger scheduled volume? There are two reasons: (1) The percentage decrease in average cost is related to the *percentage* change in output volume; therefore, the cost reductions are very small for increases of an already very large volume. A 10,000-unit increase over 100,000 is only a 10 percent increase, whereas it is a 100 percent increase over 10,000. American producers therefore change models more frequently than is done in smaller countries. (2) Tastes change, new ideas occur, improvements in technique must be incorporated if a producer is to continue to have a profitable business.

Exceptions to the average cost-reducing effect of larger volume: exhaustion of raw materials. Not for every good does a larger volume yield lower unit costs. Sometimes as a larger volume is contemplated, more cheaply available raw materials are used up, and resort must be had to more expensive ores and raw materials. For example, the production of oil is now characterized by deeper drilling, in more remote areas. Fortunately, however, technological progress and growth of our wealth have more than offset that exhaustion of easily available raw materials—because men were induced to use the

---

[4] Yet the *amount* produced is not a simple concept; for example—with an airline, is the amount of the service the number of passengers carried in a year, the number of plane flights per day, the number of seats per flight, the speed of a flight, or the number of years of service? Obviously, it comprises all of these. Or take a hospital; is the output the number of patients, the number of beds available, the number of patient-days of service, the number of operations, the number of cures? For cars, is it the quantity of any one model, the number of models, the speed with which the cars are produced? It is all of these. Any well-specified production program must stipulate several characteristics that constitute the product and its "amount."

easily available materials first. Had they instead been worried only about "conservation," they would have used resources at a lower rate, with the result that income would have been lower; and hence not so much could have been devoted to investment, technology, and research.

The advance in technology and supply of capital goods has meant that, despite the relative decrease in existing amounts of some raw materials (iron ore, coal, wood), many goods are producible at lower costs than formerly, when "cheaper" sources but poorer technology and less wealth were available. Perhaps man has been lucky so far in the race between technological knowledge and depletion of natural resources, but, whatever the reason, the fact remains that technology and growth of capital from saving and investment have more than offset the increased difficulty of obtaining some raw materials and have increased the stock of existing man-made wealth by a more than offsetting amount. It is profitable *investment*—rather than conservation of natural resources—that increases the wealth of future generations. Conservation, as we shall see more clearly later, can mean less *income,* not more saving.

8, 9, 10, 11, 12

Speed of Production and Cost

The faster a *given* volume must be produced, the greater the total, the average, and the marginal costs. This was illustrated in our earlier examples of a five-person, two-goods world. A larger *rate* of output of Y involved a greater rate of sacrificed X. One might have thought that since the same volume of output is being produced, the same stock of materials will be used up, whether it be produced quickly or slowly. However, a higher rate of production uses more resources *at the same time,* thus requiring resort to relatively less efficient resources.[5] Furthermore, the resources insist on higher pay for overtime because the sacrifice of leisure is increased. This is called "increasing costs" with higher rates or speed of production.

Effect of different rates of output. The relationship between costs and output in Chapters 12 and 13 showed a *rising,* not a falling, marginal and average cost as output was increased. Can this be reconciled with the present decreasing marginal and average costs as output increases? Yes, and the answer lies in the ambiguity of the word "output." In earlier chapters we were increasing the daily *rate* or speed of output. Here, we have been increasing the *volume* while holding the daily rate constant. But we can change the rate. One can produce one thousand houses in one year or in ten years; in each case, volume is the same, but the rates differ. And one can produce one house in three months or ten in thirty months; here, the rate of production is constant, but the volumes differ.

The way total cost changes with changes in the projected volume can be made clearer by a graph. In Figure 15-1, the curve *MC* indicates the *addition* to total cost for unit increases in volume. This is a graph of the "marginal cost of extra units of volume." If it were a horizontal line, it would mean that a unit increase in the volume raises total cost by a constant amount. But a *downward*-sloping line indicates that unit increments of volume can be produced at decreasing increments to total cost.

The *average* cost per unit of volume for different programs is also shown. For larger

---

[5] Remember the analysis of Chapters 12 and 13 and the reason given there for the rising marginal costs of higher rates of output.

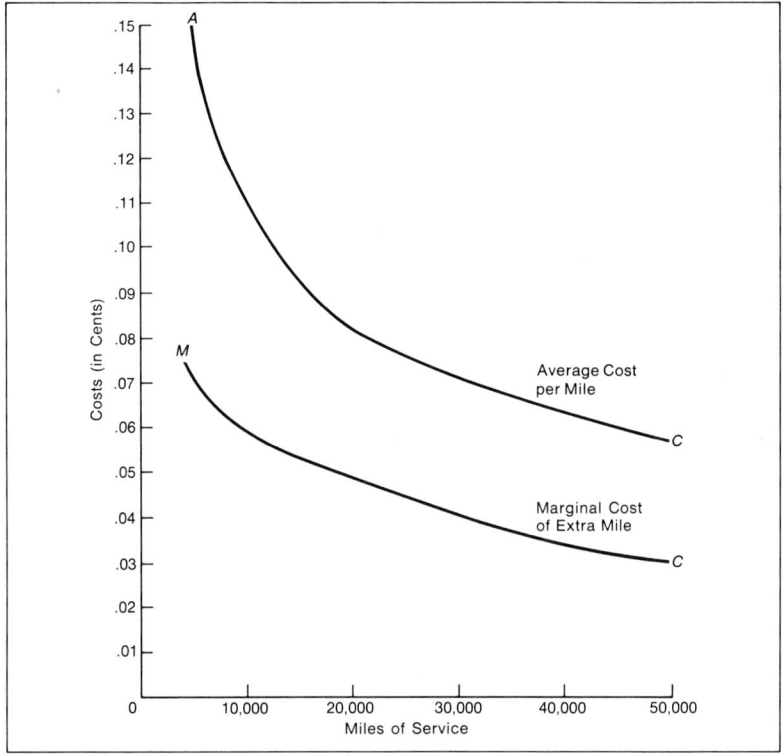

FIGURE 15–1. Marginal and Average Cost per Mile of Service (at Constant 10,000 Miles per Year Rate of Service)

A greater volume of output (in miles) results in a lower cost per mile. An increase in programmed miles of services results in cost increase, but extra cost decreases with increased mileage. These costs are valid if rate of speed of performance is not increased; increased mileage is obtained by using equipment over longer periods of time.

volumes the cost per unit decreases, possibly to some ultimate lowest value. This is, as said earlier, the *economy of mass* or *volume production*. The increase in volume is obtained by lengthening the run of production while holding the rate of production constant.

Why average costs fall with larger volume. (1) Variety of Techniques. If we now recognize that it is impossible to divide some complicated machines into miniatures that would produce just one item, we can see that what can be used economically for larger volume may not be economical for small volume. On the other hand, what is possible with small volumes can be replicated (at the same *rate*) to get the bigger volume. But we can't miniaturize or subdivide in the opposite direction. Thus, if any technique results in lower costs for some large volume, there is not necessarily a way to use this technique at lower volumes too.

A case in point is the "initial setup" cost. For a large volume, this can be very large; if that same technique were used for only a small output, the costs would be catastrophically high. Therefore, large initial or investment cost will be observed only with large volumes. An example is the transport of oil from wells to refineries. If the well owner believes the well will produce about 100,000 gallons before exhaustion, he might ship the oil by truck—shipping, say, 1,000 gallons a day for one hundred days. But if he thinks he will get 1,000,000 gallons, at the same rate of 1,000 per day, he will use either truck or pipeline. Suppose the pipeline is cheaper for 1,000 days (at the rate of 1,000 gallons per day) but more expensive than a truck for only one hundred days. Depending upon the volume (not the daily rate) of oil to be transported, the selected method will be different, with the larger volume having less cost per gallon transported.

(2) Learning. Another possible explanation is called the "learning" factor. Improvement by experience is evident in managerial functions, production scheduling, job layouts, material-flow control, on-the-job learning, and physical skills. The rate of learning may be greatest at first and then reach a plateau; but, in any event, the larger the volume of output, the more opportunity for learning and hence the lower the unit costs of larger outputs.

If one is *allowed* longer time to do something, it will not cost him more to do it—and usually it will cost less. If he wishes, he can do it as early as is most economical. By obstinately (and inefficiently) delaying his production, or starting it too early, he could incur various storage costs. But the proposition here is that allowing more time *within* which to efficiently perform some task or produce some output will result in costs that certainly are *not* higher, and most likely lower. The less time he is allowed, the smaller is his range of options and the less he can utilize any available cheaper means of production.

13, 14, 15, 16, 17, 18, 19, 20, 21, 22, 23, 24, 25, 26, 27

Proportionate Increases in Both Rate and Volume

For many goods, a common feature of production is a joint change—indeed, proportional change—in *both* the rate and volume of an output program. For example, *if the length of the production run is constant*, say one year, then a higher rate in that period will also mean proportionally larger volume. An automobile manufacturer can contemplate *rates* of output from 1,000 a month to 50,000 a month for one year. If any of these rates persists for a full year, the range of volumes implied is from 12,000 to 600,000 cars. In these cases, one can speak either of the annual rate (*lasting for a year*) or of the volume of a program, since both increase proportionally. Hereafter, unless specified to the contrary, we shall assume this to be the case.

Higher rates of output and larger volumes both increase *total* costs, but by different amounts: they have *opposite* effects on *average* cost per unit of volume of output. Larger volumes reduce average costs, while higher rates raise average costs per unit of any volume produced. Which effect dominates when both the rate and the volume increase in the same proportion—that is, when the total volume is increased but is produced in the same interval of time? The average cost may fall as both the rate and volume of output are increased at lower output ranges, but larger rates of output, even though accompanied by a proportionate increase in the volume, will ultimately dominate and cause higher average costs.

Table 15–2 shows how total costs vary for different output programs in which the volume *and* the rate of production differ in the same proportion. The data are graphed in Figure 15–2. For example, at point *A* the *volume* is 5,000 miles at a *rate* of 2,500 miles per year; the total cost is $500. At *B* the volume is 10,000 miles and the rate is 5,000

TABLE 15–2. Costs of Alternative (Two-Year) Ouput Programs

	Output (Miles)	Rate per Year	Costs Total	Costs Average	Costs Marginal
A	5,000	2,500	$ 500	10.0¢	9.0¢
B	10,000	5,000	900	9.0	7.7
C	15,000	7,500	1,200	8.0	7.0
D	20,000	10,000	1,600	8.4	9.0
E	25,000	12,500	2,200	8.8	11.0
F	30,000	15,000	2,800	9.3	13.0
G	40,000	20,000	4,200	10.5	16.0

Output is miles of distance at rates of miles per year such that distance is yielded in exactly two years. Both distance and rate increase proportionally from A through G. Total costs are plotted in Figure 15–2, and average and marginal costs are in Figure 15–3. The output increase of 5,000 miles, from 5,000 to 10,000, raises total costs by $400. Dividing this increase by 5,000 miles gives 8 cents a mile—a crude approximation to the marginal cost for one mile of service in that interval. The tabled numbers are correctly computed marginal cost from more detailed information and are centered on the 5,000th mile, the 10,000th mile, etc. You could estimate the marginal costs around 30,000 miles by getting the increase in cost from 25,000 to 30,000 miles and dividing by 5,000 miles (which gives 12 cents), or by dividing the increase in costs between 30,000 and 40,000 by 10,000 miles (which gives 14 cents). The marginal cost at 30,000 miles is 13 cents.

miles per year—both twice as big as at *A*. The total cost is $900, not quite twice as large. And at *G* the costs are for an output program with volume of 40,000 miles at the rate of 20,000 miles per year, each of which is eight times larger than for program *A*. The total cost of that bigger program is $4,200, more than eight times as large; now the rate effect has dominated the volume effect.

The marginal cost curve, *MC*, in Figure 15–3 shows (by its *height*) the increase in total cost between two output programs differing by one mile of distance (volume) and 1 mile an hour of speed of production per two years. For example, the marginal cost at 20,000 miles of service is 9 cents. This means that if we were to produce 20,000 miles in two years at a rate of 10,000 miles per year, the total cost would be greater by 9 cents than for a program of 19,999 miles in two years (at the rate of 9,999.5 miles per year).

Converted to average cost per mile of service, the costs are shown by the *AC* curve in Figure 15–3 for different output programs. The total cost of 5,000 miles (at 2,500 miles per year for two years) is $500, which gives an average cost per mile of 10 cents, shown as point *A*. The total costs of 20,000 miles in two years is $1,680, which gives a per-mile cost of 8.4 cents. For 40,000 miles in two years the total cost is $4,200, with an average per-mile cost of 10.5 cents. These per-unit costs are pulled down by the effect of large volume production, but they are pushed up by the effect of higher rates. The average cost per unit of output (mile) curve for different possible output programs will be roughly U-shaped, with a falling segment followed by a flatter, possibly horizontal, section and ultimately rising more and more sharply.

Figure 15–3 is a useful analytical diagram and should be thoroughly understood. The shape and position of the curves are for our present automobile example. Obviously the diagram will differ for other situations. Which features will persist? For generality, we show the curve as U-shaped—with nothing implied about the *length* of the downward,

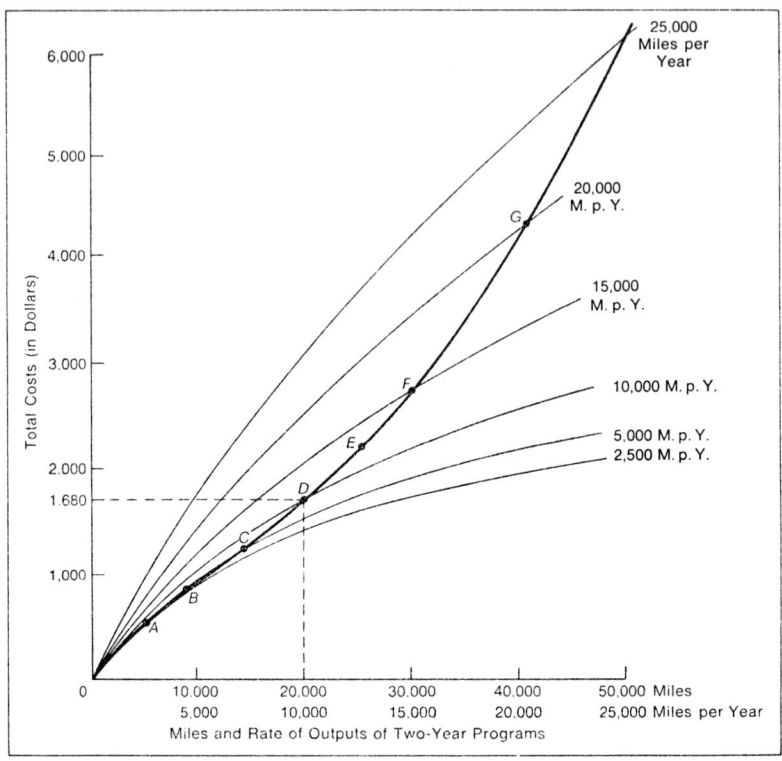

FIGURE 15-2. Total Costs of Two-Year Programs, with Proportional Increases in Both Volume and Rate

Rising curve shows how total costs increase with *proportionate* increases in rate and volume of output. Increase in total cost is always "positive" but increase diminishes at first till about point C, and then increases in total cost with each increment as output becomes greater and greater (shown by increasing slope of line). Light lines in background are curves showing behavior of costs for increases in mileage but at constant rate (speed) of output during production.

flat, and rising segments. There may not always be a falling segment for small outputs. But an ultimately rising segment always will occur for the larger outputs (for the effect of faster speeds of production will dominate any volume effects for larger joint rates and volumes). Thus the average cost curves of all production situations with joint proportional changes in volumes and rates have at least this one property in common: for sufficiently large outputs they will rise and rise with increasing rapidity.

The *marginal* cost curve always cuts through the minimum point of the average cost curve. If you remember what marginal costs are, you will see why. Marginal costs are the increment in costs for a unit increment of output. If that increment of cost is greater than the average cost of production, that will increase costs by more than the average. Since more is added (to the total) than the current average cost, the average cost is pulled up. Like taking another test—if your marginal score (the score on this new test) is higher than your average, it will pull up the average. And if it is lower, it will pull the average down.

Costs and Production

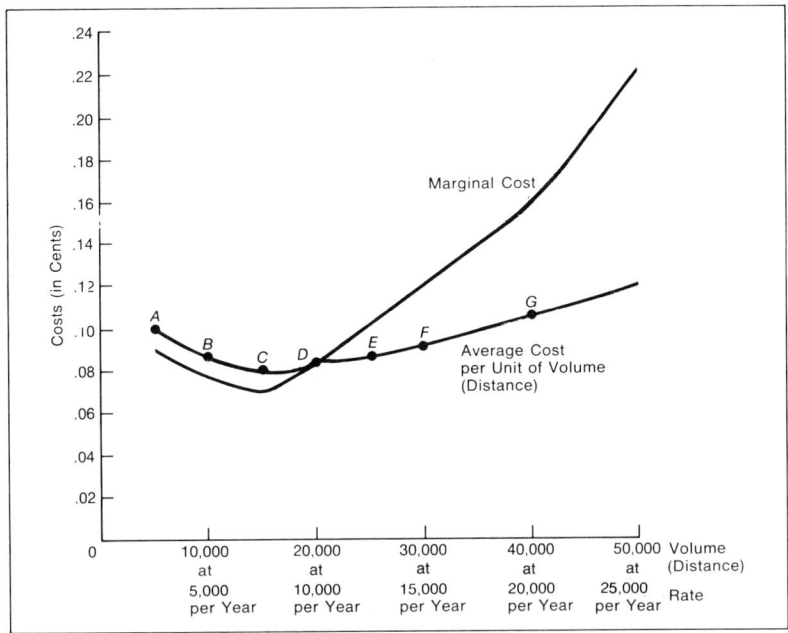

FIGURE 15-3. Average and Marginal Cost of Two-Year Program with Joint Volume and Rate Increases

Total costs of Figure 15-2 have been converted to average costs per mile of service and plotted as average cost per unit of volume (distance in miles). Points on total cost curve of Figure 15-2 are shown here as corresponding points, lettered A, B, C, etc. Notice that average costs at first fall for smaller outputs and then begin to increase for larger outputs. Marginal cost curve shows increase in total cost with each increase in output of one mile by increasing speed just enough to get out one more mile in the two year period. For example, at 30,000 miles of service at rate of 15,000 miles per year, the cost per mile is shown by point F and is about 9 cents per mile. But an increase in the number of miles from 30,000 to 30,001 by increasing speed sufficiently will increase total cost about 13 cents (depicted by height of marginal cost curve above 30,000 mile point on horizontal axis).

Though marginal cost may be decreasing at small outputs (where volume effect dominates the speed) it will, possibly after a long flat portion, certainly rise at large joint speed and volume of output. This behavior is similar to the shape of the average cost curve. If the marginal cost curve, starting out from zero output, *always* rises—the average cost curve will be below the marginal cost curve and rising. (Can you see why? Recall the analogy of your test scores.)

Timing of Production: Long Run and Short Run

Still another dimension of the program affects costs—the date or time at which the output is to be provided. Hasty (though not reckless) output adjustments, whether made with existing equipment or with newly acquired equipment, are more expensive because revisions of equipment are more expensive the faster they are made. In other words, for a specified cost, the inputs are less variable in a shorter than in a longer interval. Turned around, this means the physical constraints are more binding for immediate adjustment.

Deferred output programs cost less than those initiated more hastily with existing equipment, unless the existing equipment just happens to be optimally suited to the proposed output, in which case the cost is no greater. Figure 15–4 shows two average-cost curves, a short-run curve giving the costs for the output to be produced shortly and a long-run curve for the later output. For all outputs except the one for which the existing equipment happens to be optimal, the long-run curve lies below the short-run curve.

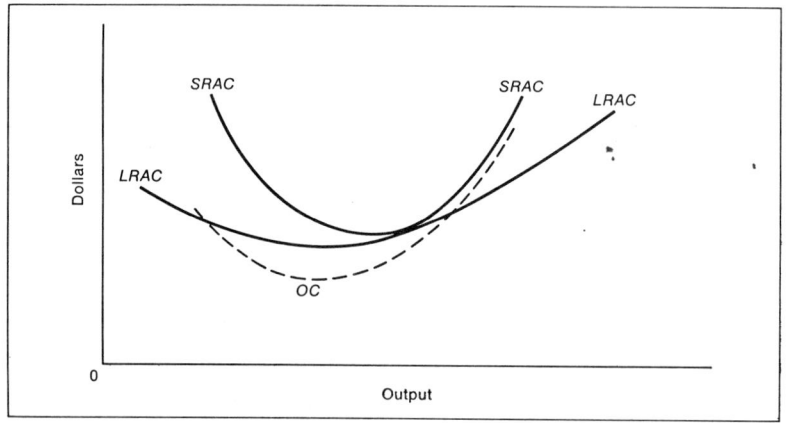

FIGURE 15–4. Long-Run and Short-Run Costs

Curves show average costs of long-run output program and of short-run output program, the former being the lower limit of costs achieved by deferring the output program. Output at which both curves are tangent is output for which existing equipment is optimal. For any other output, a different set of equipment would be more economical, as shown by fact that the long-run cost curve lies below the short-run cost curve for all other outputs. Curve labeled *OC* shows average per-unit operating costs with existing equipment; it excludes from *SRAC* all the costs (per unit) that would be incurred if possession were continued and if no output were produced. (See pages 256–257.)

There is a limit to how low costs can be made by deferring the output; that lower limit is called the *long-run cost*. Here we shall show just the two extreme cases, the immediate (called the short run) and the long run. Intermediate cases are ignored for present expository purposes.

Carefully note that two curves do not mean there are two costs for a given program, a short-run cost and a long-run cost. Rather there are two different programs, a short-run program and a long-run program, each with its own cost.

Why a long- and a short-run cost distinction? Because we must allow for the fact that the responses of production to changes in demand and market price usually extend over time, and the more deferred response usually comes at a lower cost (and is larger).

Marginal costs of short and of long run. The short-run and the long-run *marginal* cost curves are shown in Figure 15–5, which is otherwise the same as Figure 15–4. These curves, you will recall, show by their height the increment in cost for producing a larger output (by one mile in the two-year period). The short-run marginal cost rises more rapidly, which reflects the inappropriateness of existing equipment for output programs substantially different from that for which the equipment was intended.

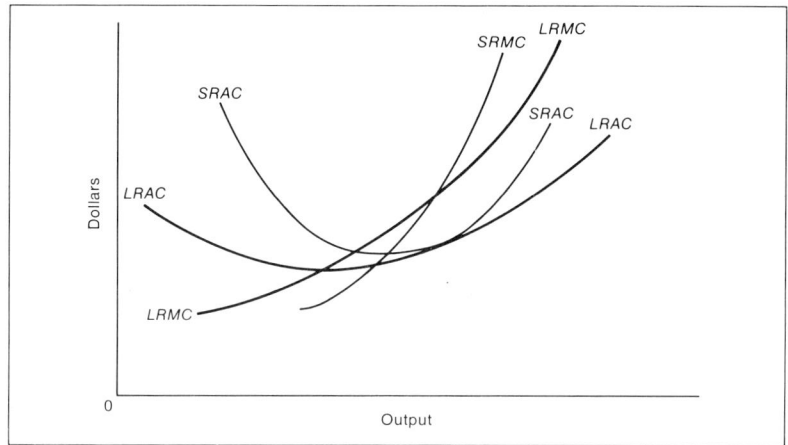

FIGURE 15–5. Marginal Costs of Short-Run and Long-Run Output Programs

This is basically the same as Figure 15–4, with marginal cost curves added (and *OC* omitted). Although short-run average costs (for a short-run program) are always larger than for a long-run program, marginal costs of short-run output program changes can be less than for long-run output changes.

Short-period, short-run, long-period, and long-run outputs. "Short period" means a short-*lived* run of production—not a short time until production started. If we could create conventions, we would call one the short-period output (*lasting* for a short time) and the other the short-run output (*beginning* after a short time). But convention is too strong; both cases are called the short-*run*. So from the context you must discern which is meant. A short-period output can have a per unit cost that is lower than for short-run outputs and even less than for the long run—since it is a cost of an output different not only in timing but in length of output. (Since it is short lived, we can ignore the costs of some of the activities that would have to be met if production continued for a longer interval—for example, *acquisition* costs of new equipment.)

Another convention bears noticing. Usually in elementary texts the "short run" is used also to refer to an output produced under conditions in which not all the inputs can be adjusted, i.e., in which one is fixed and invariant. Changes in output, in that case, can, by definition, be achieved only by varying *some* (not all) of the inputs, which implies higher costs than if *all* the inputs could be adjusted.

In fact, *all* inputs *can* be varied in any interval, but the costs of varying some inputs immediately increase so much more rapidly than for delayed variations that almost certainly they will not be varied quickly. For example, a new factory building could be constructed or purchased in a few weeks, but it would cost a lot less if done in a few months. On the other hand, there is not so much difference in the costs of getting more labor or raw materials in a few weeks instead of a few months. Thus, rarely will it be economical to increase all inputs at the same rate. Factory space or equipment will usually be increased less rapidly than labor. At an extreme, as a limiting case, we may assume it won't be changed at all, i.e., is "fixed."

Hence if your instructor refers to short-run *intervals* as those in which some inputs are fixed, remember this limiting assumption is an expository simplification to avoid more complex features that may usually be ignored in elementary courses. For students who progress to more advanced work, the correct, more general interpretation must be used.

Costs Relevant to Entry and to Shut-down Decisions

Long-Run Entry Cost

What is the minimum amount of revenue in present-value measure that you must receive to make it worthwhile to produce the output program—20,000 miles of service over a two-year interval? The answer is $1,678.90 or 8.39 cents per mile. You would not consider entering this business unless you expected at least 8.39 cents per mile for the rent of your car. That is called the *long-run* minimum per-mile cost of that complete program.

To Continue or Not to Continue Production

If the price received for a mile of your car's services stays above 8.4 cents, you will cover your costs. But if the price is lower, your business will have lost wealth, and you may decide on some changes.

1. Should you stop operations temporarily, awaiting a return to better times?
2. Should you continue operating temporarily at least, making the best of the situation?
3. Should you immediately get out of business?
4. Or should you change the scale of your operations?

This last question will be discussed in the next chapter. For the present, consider the first three. Since we assume you entered business to enhance your wealth, you should do whatever will preserve your wealth, now that the former hopeful expectations are replaced by the less favorable price.

1. If you continue, instead of shutting down immediately, costs will be incurred at the rate 7.4 cents per mile; this excludes the cost of *acquiring* the car, since you already have incurred the initial $200 cost (between the $2,000 purchase and the immediate $1,800 resale price which amounted to 1 cent per mile for the projected 20,000 program). Any amount over 7.4 cents per mile would bring in more than it would cost for the next two years. Your initial entry cost, which is past history, is at least being partly covered if you

get anything over 7.4 cents a mile. When the time came to get a new car, you might get out. So, if price is above 7.4 cents per mile, continue to operate for up to two years; do not shut down immediately.

2. But if price fell below 7.4 cents, and you thought it was a *short-lived* dip, you might temporarily stop operating the car, awaiting the return shortly to better times. Only if price doesn't fall below 3.2 cents a mile, would it pay to continue to operate the car for a while. Why? Because any amount over 3.2 cents would cover the costs of *operating* the car, *given that you are going to keep it for better times*. Just keeping the car is costly—costs of storage, depreciation, taxes, insurance, and license will occur. Whether we operate or not (while keeping the car), we will incur those costs, and they are assumed to be 4.2 cents a mile of the forsaken miles if we don't use the car. So the cost of *operating* the car, *given* that we are going to keep it, is 3.2 cents per mile—the difference between 7.4 and 4.2 cents per mile. That 3.2 cents is the operating cost per mile of service—above or net of the costs of keeping it.[6]

3. If price falls below 3.2 cents, shut down immediately. Whether you do so permanently or temporarily depends upon how long you expect the price to stay low.

4. The preceding discussion ignored the determination of the output size; we simply assumed 10,000 miles per year for two years. We did so purely for an expository purpose, i.e., to indicate some of the decisions other than changing the output that must be constantly weighed. Probably the decision most frequently assessed is the determination of the quantity of output. To see how this decision depends upon market price and costs, we must know how costs depend upon the quantity of output.

Joint Products with Common Costs

"Joint and variable" outputs. Production processes do not all yield only one product. Many give several *joint* products. Beef and hides are joint products of cattle. Cotton and cottonseed oil; kerosene, fuel oil, and gasoline; butter and milk—these are joint products. They are interdependent in supply; generally, more of one involves more (or less) of the other. More beef also yields more hides. More cotton yields more cottonseed oil; a higher price for one of the outputs will, by inducing a larger output of cotton, also lead to an increased output of the joint good. Thus, the supply of a good is dependent upon not only its own price, but that of other goods—especially of joint-product goods.

Yet we mustn't overdo this jointness; even for these joint products, more of one can mean less of the other. Beef and hides, although joint products, are substitutes in that there are different breeds of cattle, yielding different ratios of beef to hides. One could increase the ratio and, in fact, get more hide and less meat, by selecting different breeds and slaughtering ages. These propositions hold for gasoline, kerosene, and fuel oil—all of which are obtained by refining crude oil. Different refining methods yield different ratios of output. Cotton and cottonseed are also variable, though joint, products. Depending upon which of the joint products one is interested in, the other is often called the by-product.

---

[6] As a matter of fact, if price fell below 3.2 cents per mile, it might also pay to continue to operate temporarily. If the service is provided at a lower rate than at 10,000 miles per year, the costs will be lower. If we anticipate the principles to be explained in the next sections, it can be shown that the costs per mile of service would be as low as 2 cents for a lower rate of output, given the existing equipment. Operating less intensely means slightly lower direct operating costs so that the costs can be shaved down to as low as, say, 2 cents per mile for temporary operation.

Impossibility of allocation of common costs. If two products are produced jointly from a "common" input, how does one allocate the costs of the common resource to each of the joint products? If, for example, hides and meat are produced from one steer, and if the feed and care of the steer is a common input or a common cost to both products, what portion is the cost of the hide and what portion is the cost of the meat? If an airplane carries passengers and freight cargo, what portion of the common costs of gasoline, labor, and facilities is assigned to each? Can a "common" cost be allocated among joint products?

Depending upon which product is treated as a residual or by-product, a different allocation of costs may be obtained. In effect, by calling one product the by-product, one is implicitly assigning all the "common costs" to the other, the "basic," product. But this, of course, is merely an arbitrary allocation, depending upon which product one calls the basic product. If costs can't be allocated, how can one tell what prices to charge? How can a producer tell whether he is making a profit on each item? How can he tell how much to produce? Things seem to fall apart at the joints. In fact, however, the presence of costs which cannot be allocated uniquely to the joint products does not upset anything (except possibly some accountants).

Pricing and output decisions are independent of assignment of common costs. One purpose of market prices is to allocate the existing supply of product among the competing claimants, and another is to induce production. Both tasks can be performed by the same market price, even if common costs cannot be allocated. The "rationing" price, as we have seen, does not depend upon how costs are apportioned; it depends upon demand and supply. What about the second function—that of inducing production of goods? There is no necessity to allocate the common costs to the joint products. All that is necessary is a comparison of the total costs of the whole *set* of joint products with the total revenue from their sale. If the total revenue does not cover the total costs, some producers will be induced, by a loss of wealth, to stop production, leaving a smaller output and resultant higher prices of the various joint products, until the price is high enough to cover the total costs of the entire set of joint products.

Still unsolved is the question of the rates of each of the joint outputs by those firms that are profitable. The producer still does *not* have any use for an average cost of each joint product based on some allocation of the common costs. He requires instead a measure of *marginal* costs for each of the joint products. If he expands the output rate of any of the joint products, either singly or jointly, how much do total costs increase? If that marginal cost is observed to be less than the marginal revenue from that extra output, that output will be expanded, assuming the producer wants to increase his wealth. Otherwise, the output will be contracted. In other words, the wealth-maximizing output decision does not require any allocation of common costs to the component products. Only total costs and total revenue effects need be discerned. None of these decisions—pricing or output, or even combinations of inputs—depend upon separability or bookkeeping allocation of the cost of any input shared by the joint products. This is a crucial point. Pricing and output decisions can be made even though one cannot assign portions of costs of a common production input to the products that are jointly produced. Nothing is lost, except an answer to a pointless question: "What is *the* cost of production of *one* of the joint products?" To say that the question is pointless doesn't mean it won't frequently be asked.

Depreciation, Obsolescence, and Resource Uses

Depreciation is the predictable reduction in the value of an asset caused by physical deterioration and wear and anticipated improvements in new competing goods. (Sometimes the depreciation which reflects the *anticipated* new improved competing products is called obsolescence.) In contrast to depreciation are the reductions in value caused by *unanticipated* developments. Those unexpected falls in the value of an asset occur when the hitherto-unexpected event becomes anticipated, whether it be physical damage or a new superior product. That fall is a *"loss,"* a negative profit. How does that unexpected event affect the use of existing assets?

If buyers anticipated future developments when considering the purchase of a machine, they would offer a price low enough to discount or allow for the loss of value. If purchasers do not anticipate that future development, the asset is not necessarily idled. Instead, the reduction in value is just sufficient to permit successful use or sale of the old machines in the face of competition with the newcomer. This is why today propeller airliners are still flying, despite the existence of superior jet aircraft. Not until the value of the old falls to zero will it be idled. The old machine will be abandoned only when the present capital value of the reduction in operating and possession costs (or gains in revenue) for a new one exceeds the acquisition cost of a new one.

For example, suppose some machine is now available at a price of $100 and will produce 1,000 units of X before it "falls apart." Suppose further that the machine's value will decline in proportion to its use—that is, at the rate of 10 cents per unit. This means the machine *depreciates* at the rate of 10 cents per unit produced by the machine. Suppose also that there are associated costs for materials and labor of 20 cents per unit; the total cost per unit is 30 cents. Finally, suppose the product sells for 30 cents per unit. The receipts just cover the cost.

Soon after purchase of the machine, as luck would have it, a new machine is unexpectedly introduced for the same price. The new machine will produce 1,000 units before it falls apart, but the associated costs are only 16 cents per unit, instead of 20 cents as with the old machine; so total costs are 26 cents per unit.

The old machine will not be left idle. It will be used until the price of the product falls below 20 cents per unit, under the impact of an increased supply as the new machine is more commonly used. However, the *value* of the old machine will fall. The value imputed to the old machine reflects the difference between the price of the item produced and its costs of producing the item, 20 cents. At a price of 30 cents the machine can be used for 1,000 items; therefore, the machine's value would be $100 (equal to 1,000 units times the difference between 30 cents and 20 cents). When the price of the product falls *to* 20 cents, that difference is wiped out; the old machine is then worthless. The machine will be retired from use if the price of its products falls *below* 20 cents. This decrease in value of the machine because of the unforeseen reduced price of the product is a *loss*.

29, 30, 31, 32, 33, 34

Summary

1 Expenditures on capital goods are not costs.

2 Costs are not concurrent with reductions in consumption. Incurring a cost does not make a person worse off, necessarily.

3 Depreciation is the predictable reduction in value of assets. Obsolescence is the unpredicted reduction in value of equipment. It is a loss.

4 Decisions to enter into some output program involve "long-run" costs. Decisions to continue with production, given that production equipment has been obtained, involve "short-run" costs.

5 Decisions to shut down immediately or to continue use of equipment until replacement depend on the direct operating costs.

6 Average per-unit costs decrease with larger volume, rate held constant. Average cost per unit increases with larger rate, volume held constant. With both rate and volume increasing in proportion, average cost per unit first falls, and then, after an interval of near constant average costs, begins to increase as a function of size of output program.

7 Reduced unit costs with larger volume imply standardization of goods.

8 Increased average costs as a function of speed of production imply that goods are not produced instantly.

9 Marginal costs ultimately increase with programs proportionally larger in both volume and rate. (They rise up through the average variable cost at the latter's minimum cost point, by logical necessity.)

10 Short-run average and marginal costs for outputs larger than that for which the existing equipment is most appropriate increase more than do long-run average costs.

11 The cost of producing any given output can be reduced by postponing production.

12 Joint and unallocable common costs do not prevent market rationing of jointly produced goods or the determination of wealth-maximizing output combinations of the jointly produced goods.

Questions

1 "The expression 'to incur a cost' is equivalent to saying that one has committed certain acts that sacrifice an opportunity." Do you agree? If so, why? If not, why not?

2 Why are capital values used as a measure of costs?

3 Why cannot money expenditures be identified with costs?

4 A house can be purchased for $20,000. At the end of a year it could be resold for $21,000 if you had also spent $1,000 for a concrete fence, $300 for landscaping, $800 for air conditioning, and $1,200 for carpeting; otherwise, the house could have been resold for $19,000. Taxes of $300 must be paid in any event. Assume that all these expenditures—except for the taxes, which are to be paid at the end of a year—are paid at the moment you buy the house. The interest rate is 10 percent.
a. What is the cost of owning a house for one year—if you do not install fence, landscaping, airconditioning, and carpeting?
b. What is the cost of owning the house if you do install those improvements?
c. What is the year's depreciation on the house without the proposed improvements?
d. Express this cost of ownership of the improved house for one year, as a constant two-year annuity.
e. Express the cost as a perpetuity.

Costs and Production

    f. Express the cost as a five-year annuity.
    g. Which of these is the correct way to express cost?

5 You operate a cleaning establishment. A new cleaning machine has a price of $5,000. You estimate its resale value at the end of the first year to be $3,000 and $1,500 at the end of the second year. The rate of interest is 10 percent.
    a. What will it cost to purchase and own the machine for one year?
    b. For two years?
    c. What is the present value measure of the depreciation on the machine in the first year?
    d. In the second year?
    e. If you use the machine, you will incur expenses during the first year of $6,000 for labor, power, and repairs; and the machine will still have a resale value of $3,000 at the end of the first year. The same expenses will be involved in the second year, and the resale value will be $1,500 at the end of the second year. Assume that all expenditures are payable at the end of the year in which they are experienced. What is the cost of having and using the machine for one year?
    f. For two years?
    g. What is the cost of the second year of possession and operation?
    h. If, immediately after buying the machine, you should reconsider and decide to sell it, the resale value would be $4,000. What cost would the purchase of the machine "fix" upon you? This is called "fixed," "sunk," or irrecoverable cost.
    i. After purchasing the machine, you can either keep it idle or use it with the attendant expenditures indicated earlier, in (e) above. As between these two alternative actions, what is the fixed cost?
    j. What are the variable costs; that is, the costs incurred over and above the "fixed" costs?

6 "Don't buy your business cars. Lease them from the A and A Leasing Company. You can lease a Chevy for $60 a month. Avoid the loss of depreciation and necessity of tying up capital funds in the purchase of capital items." This is an accurate paraphrase of leasing advertising. What errors of analysis does it contain? Would the reasons given provide any advantage to a businessman? Explain why not.

7 What happens to total cost of production for larger volumes of planned output?

8 Output has at least two dimensions. What two have a bearing on total costs of some output programs?

9 A firm plans to produce 2,000,000 cameras in the next six months. What is the volume and what is the rate of output?

10 If that rate in question 9 is continued for one year, what will be the volume?

11 Do you know of any products that have become more expensive over the past several decades or centuries because of the exhaustion of cheaper ores or resources from which that product is obtained? (One answer is "oysters.") Is it true for copper, iron, oil, tin, diamonds, coal?

12 Give some examples of how the selected technique of production will depend upon the *volume* to be produced. For example, what about methods of producing letterheads, cookies, holes for fence posts, dresses, airplanes?

13 What happens to total cost as the rate or speed of output is made larger, while the volume is kept constant?

14 What happens to average cost per unit of volume for larger planned volumes with unchanged rates of output?

15   What happens to average cost per unit of volume for larger rates of output with constant volume?

16   What is the behavior of marginal cost as a function of volume (for a fixed rate of output)?

17   What is the behavior of marginal cost as a function of rate of output for a fixed volume of output?

18   Are the answers to the preceding questions implied by comparative advantage and efficient means of production?

19   One of the first things an economist learns is to distinguish between total, average, and marginal cost. What are the differences?

20   If it were illegal to sell automobiles outside the state in which they were made, would cars be cheaper or more expensive in the United States? Give two reasons for your answer.

21   Why do manufacturers produce a few standardized models rather than a much larger variety of custom-made, custom-designed models?

22   Give some examples, if you can, of average costs being lower with large-volume production. Can you cite from personal memory the price history of television sets, transistor radios, surfboards, aluminum, penicillin, Polaroid cameras, ball-point pens?

23   Telephone a local printing company and ask the price for 100 letterheads on bond paper. Also get a price for 10,000 letterheads. Which has the lower cost per unit? Ask for the expected delivery date. Then ask how much it would cost to get the letterheads in half that time—even if it means setting up a night shift and overtime work. What do you expect will happen to the quoted price?

24   Ask a local building contractor to build a garage at your residence. After getting his price, see what he charges if you insist on getting it in half the promised time. Also ask how much he would charge if you want five garages. Do you predict it will be five times as much?

25   The British Aircraft Corporation manufactures a two-engined jet plane for intermediate-distance flights. Airlines are quoted a price of $2,500,000 with delivery in one year. What do you predict the price would be if you requested to have one delivered in six months? Do you think there would be any connection between the price of quicker delivery and the price you would have to pay to buy such a plane from someone who already has one —for example, from Braniff Air Lines?

26   If a business firm finds its selling price and output so related that larger output is associated with lower selling price, is this an indication that it has lower costs with larger volume or that the demand is such that more can be sold only if the price is lower?

27   Give some examples of goods for which you think the selected technique of production will depend upon the *rate* at which items are produced—for fixed volume.

28   "The price of a new organic chemical depends on how badly it is wanted—precisely as conceived by classical economic theory, except for reversal of direction. The bigger the demand, the lower the price. A 1000-lb-per-day process operates more efficiently than a 1000-lb-per-month process—which is obvious to you but wasn't to Adam Smith. Old Adam set down the rules for our game in ignorance of elementary chemical engineering and advanced advertising." Quote from an advertisement for Eastman Kodak Co., *Scien-*

Costs and Production

tific American, May 1964, page 57. Explain wherein apparently even the ad writers for Eastman Kodak are doubly confused—on both the demand- and the supply-function side.

29 "New business firms can underprice older firms, because the newer firms can buy the latest equipment and are not burdened with the older, less economical equipment which older firms must retire before they can economically adopt the new. This is why continued technological progress contributes to maintaining a competitive economic system." Explain the errors in both sentences.

30 Your car will depreciate by $500, we shall assume, regardless of whether you use it for recreation or business, and regardless of whether you drive it 5,000 or 10,000 miles. Each mile you drive it, you will also pay 8 cents for gasoline, oil, tires, repair, etc. (not counting the depreciation). If you drive the car 10,000 miles, the depreciation cost amounts to $500/10,000 = 5 cents per mile. If you drive it 5,000 miles, the depreciation cost is 10 cents a mile. Suppose you drive it 5,000 miles for recreation and 5,000 miles for business.
   a. What is the cost for the recreation mileage, and what is the cost for the business mileage?
   b. Should you allocate half of the depreciation to the recreation?

31 Why did some airlines continue flying propeller planes long after more economical and better-performing jet-driven planes were available? Because of lack of competition among airlines?

32 Heat and light are joint products of an electric light bulb that uses electric power at the rate of 1,000 watts. In one hour the cost of the power is 5 cents.
   a. How much does the light cost? How much does the heat cost? How much do the light and the heat together cost?
   b. If you were selling the heat to someone, how much would you charge him? And if, at the same time, you were selling the light to someone else, how much would you charge him?
   c. Suppose that you are getting 4 cents for the light and 2 cents for the heat. You discover a new light bulb that gives more light and less heat, but this costs 6 cents per hour to operate. You can sell the extra light for 3 cents more, but you get a total of only 1 cent for the available heat. Should you use the new device? (Forget the cost of the new bulb—to simplify the arithmetic.)
   d. But now the *light* buyer complains that you are charging him a total of 7 cents, which is more than enough to cover all the costs, while formerly you charged him only 4 cents, which did not cover the whole costs. He contends that the price should be lower and that the buyer of heat should pay part of the costs. What is your reply?
   e. Having told him to take it or leave it, you find he leaves it! Why? (Answer: Because someone else can duplicate your service and charge him a lower price to get his business. The price will, with open markets, be cut to the point that total receipts from the joint products are just sufficient to cover the cost of production. And the total amount produced will be of such size that another joint increment would not bring in quite enough new receipts to cover the marginal cost of producing that joint increment of output.)

33 Meat, wool, and hides are joint products of sheep.
   a. What assurance do you have that the prices paid for meat, for wool, and for sheepskin are just adequate to cover their cost of production?
   b. What assurance do you have that meat users are not paying a disproportionate share of the common costs?

34 Gasoline price "wars" are not uncommon in cities near refineries. Why are these price changes more common near the sites of refineries? (Hint: gasoline, kerosene, fuel oil,

and other distillates are obtained by refining crude oil. Although the proportions in which these joint products are yielded are not constant, it is relatively expensive to alter the proportions significantly or to store gasoline at refineries. Suppose the demand for fuel oil increases and that more crude oil is refined to meet the demand. What happens to the output of the other joint products? To their prices? Who will store the extra gasoline?)

Appendix: Example of Cost Calculation of a Specific Output Program

Acquisition Cost

You contemplate buying a Ford at a purchase price of $2,000. Table 15–3 (top half) lists all the pertinent expenditure data, which we shall explain. The immediate resale value is $1,800. If you kept the car for two years (without using it) the resale value at the end of two years would be $1,400. If you use the car at the rate of, say, 10,000 miles of travel per year, the resale value will be only $1,300 in two years. What is the cost of acquiring the car? It is $200, the difference between the price and the *immediate* resale value. Once the car is acquired, this is a "fixed" or "sunk" cost.

TABLE 15–3. Expenditures and Costs for Acquisition, Possession, and Operation of Car for Two Years

	Expenditures			
	Now	End of First Year	End of Second Year	Present Value
Purchase price	$2,000	—	—	$2,000
Resale Value				
Not driven	(1,800)	—	1,400	1,156.40
Driven 20,000 miles	—	—	1,300	1,073.80
Tax and insurance	100	100	—	190.90
Gas, tires, repairs	—	300	350	561.80

	Costs	
1. Acquisition:	$2,000	
	−1,800	
	$200	
2. Possession for two years; zero mileage—that is, without operation.		
Current resale	$1,800	
Final resale	−1,156.40	
Depreciation	643.60	
Tax and insurance	190.90	
Possession for two years		$834.50
Acquisition and continued possession without operation:		$1,034.50
3. Operation (20,000 miles in two years)		
(Extra depreciation	$1,156.40	
because of mileage)	1,073.80	
	82.60	
Gasoline, oil, tires, etc.	561.80	
Operation		$644.40
Total costs of acquisition, possession, and operation		$1,678.90

Continuing Possession

Given that the car is acquired, what is the cost just of continuing its possession for two years? It is the difference in the value of the car now and the *present value* of its resale value in two years. Do not subtract $1,400 from $1,800! They are values as of *different* dates. If you learned your lesson well in Chapter 11, you will know that the two figures must be compared in contemporaneous values. Therefore, convert the $1,400 of two years hence to a present value. At 10 percent annual rate of interest, the present value of $1,400 deferred *two* years is .826 × $1,400 = $1,156.40 (use Table 10–1). Subtracting this from $1,800 gives $643.60 as the cost of two years' possession, *given* that the car has already been acquired. The cost ($200) of acquiring *and* continuing possession for two years is $200 + $643.60 = $843.60. $643.60 is depreciation, the present-value measure of the predictable reduction in the resale value of the car.[1]

To add more realism, assume taxes and insurance must be paid if the car is possessed. At the *beginning* of each year $100 is due for the year's tax and insurance, whether or not the car is operated. Converting these two payments to present values gives $100 + (.909)$100 = $190.90, the present value of taxes and insurance if the car is possessed for two years. The cost of two years' continuing possession, *given that the car is already acquired,* is $643.60 + $190.90 = $843.50. The cost of *acquiring* and *keeping* (but not using) the car for two years is ($200 + $643.60 + $190.90) = $1,034.50.

Operating Cost

But you are not managing a museum of cars; you want to use the Ford. Other outlays, listed in Table 15–3, will be made for repairs, gasoline, etc., and will be paid at the *end* of each year, as if they accumulated on a credit card. (Note that we call them expenditures and outlays—not costs.) Since we cannot properly add outlays now to outlays a year later, without adjusting for interest, we convert all outlays to present values. They sum to $561.80.[2] (See Table 15–3.) The resale value of the car will depreciate more if the car is used. We assume it will decrease to $1,300 at the end of two years rather than to the "non-use" $1,400. The extra depreciation over the two-year interval is $100, which has a present value of $82.60 (at 10 percent rate of interest). Adding this $82.60 to $561.80 gives $644.40 as the present value measure of costs of *operations*.

$644.40 is the cost that could be avoided if operations were stopped (but the car were kept). Depending upon the actual use of the car the figure of $644.40 would vary. (We assumed 10,000 miles per year.) You can see why this figure is sometimes called the *variable* cost. It is the cost that will depend on the actually performed service. The other cost, $1,034.50, is independent of the mileage performed, and is therefore also commonly called "fixed" (which gives us a second concept of a "fixed" cost). The sum of $644.40 and $1,034.50 is $1,678.90, the total cost in capital value measure, for acquisition, continued possession, and provision of 20,000 miles of service in two years. These distinctions are important for answering such questions as (1) whether to enter the

---

[1] Although, in strict rigor, depreciation is the *present value* of the implied decrease in wealth, $643.60, it is very common practice to subtract $1,400 from $1,800 and call the difference, $400, depreciation. Of course, this understates the true depreciation, $643.60; it doesn't allow for differences in *times* of the initial and resale values.

[2] ($300 × .909) + ($350 × .826) = $561.80.

business and (2), once one has entered the business, whether to get out of business if receipts fall short of expectations or to shut down temporarily until conditions improve.

We now have the following classification of costs for the two-year, 20,000-mile output program:

Cost of acquisition, possession, and operation = $1,678.90 or 8.39 cents/mile.
($200) + ($834.50) + ($644.40)
Cost of operation = $644.40 or 3.22 cents/mile.
Cost of possession and operation = $1,478.90 or 7.39 cents/mile.

Each of these costs has several different names and keeping them all straight is a tedious task. We list their most common names:

Acquisition cost ($200): fixed; sunk.
Possession cost ($834.50): overhead.
Operation cost ($644.40): direct; operating; out of pocket.
Possession plus operation cost ($1,478.90): short-run total; variable.

Especially ambiguous are the terms "fixed" and "variable," which are used in several conceptual senses. The above list of names is not exhaustive. You will simply have to deduce from the context what specific cost is meant if you hear one of these, or some other term, used. Or else ask the user.

The Business Firm and Profits

16

PRODUCTION is organized and controlled through the medium of the business firm. An owner or manager tells employees what to do; he monitors their performance; he decides what to produce and how and in what amounts. In this chapter, we investigate the business firm, its reason for existence, its formal structure, and means of assessing how well it accomplishes its purposes.

None of the realistic business elements introduced in this chapter changes the preceding analysis. Businesses are basically means of economizing on contractual, exchange, and communication costs. They do not constitute a different system of production control. Unless one can see through this organizational facade, he may confound specific means of communication and contracting with the general underlying principles of control of production.

Why Do Business Firms Exist?

Business firms are the agencies used to organize resources to produce in response to competitive market guides. In a market economy, they respond to market prices and demands and produce the kinds of products that the public deems more valuable than others that could have been produced. Every society relies on business firms; economies differ in how it is decided which firms can exist, which people will have what roles in the firm, what incentives will be used to reward and guide each member of the firm, and what signals and information will guide production.

Is the existence of a business firm really consistent with market-exchange principles outlined earlier? Why don't people in the firm individually engage in direct market exchange? If resources are directed and coordinated by prices and market exchange without conscious direction, then why are centrally directed organizations—business firms with employers and employees—in existence? Why are there "islands of conscious power in this ocean of unconscious cooperation like lumps of butter coagulating in a pail of buttermilk"?[1]

Team Production and Discipline

There are technological advantages in *team production*. Two people working together as a team to catch fish, one rowing and one netting, will do better than if each catches fish separately. Two men working a two-man saw can fell more trees than working with separate saws on separate trees. Essentially, in team activity, several people work together in such a way that there is no separate product of any individual which can be totalled into the group's marketable output. But if it is difficult to detect each party's effect on the total output, then each member of the team would be able to shirk and make other members share in the consequences of shirking; he would not bear its full cost. In markets, competition by potential substitutes normally punishes those who cheat and thereby reduces the extent of cheating. Various means for metering contributions are used to make payments to producers accord with product delivered. In team production, some costs must be incurred to watch each other's performance, because it is not possible to look only at the total output changes and decide who is responsible. Yet, even though team production may involve higher metering or monitoring costs of *each* member's performance, the greater productive potential of team activity may exceed the higher costs.

The business firm is a means of organizing and monitoring team production. In this sense it is a substitute for competition in markets. The disciplinary effects of competition are carried on within the firm. Monitors, or "supervisors," watch the team members at work and direct them (by contractual agreement) to perform in ways that will reduce the possibility of shirking. Managing the ways the team members are used serves as a substitute in team production for metering the individual's contribution to the team's output. But who will monitor the monitors? One check is competition of other potential monitors who will offer to replace shirking monitors in so far as they can be detected. Another force can be imposed on the monitor; he can be paid a residual from the product of the team, *after* prespecified payments to the other team members. He gets the "profits or losses." The less he shirks, the bigger will be the net he can claim.

The monitor will perform his tasks not only by passively watching the other team members, but also by disciplining them by the right to fire or hire members or renegotiate new contracted wages or rentals. He will be the party common to all the contracts of all the team members. As the common party to all contracts, he can terminate or hire anyone, but no other team member can do that to anyone else in the team. The *contractual* structure among members involved in team production characterizes the essence of the "firm." A *central* (common party to all contracts) *monitor* is induced to be efficient by self-monitoring because of his claims to the *residual*. He is called the "profit or loss" recipient, i.e., the owner of the firm. He may delegate some of his rights, but the subordinate is responsible to (i.e., has a contract with) the owner and not with the other team members.

---

[1] D. H. Robertson, *Control of Industry* (Cambridge: Nisbet & Co., 1923), p. 85.

The firm, then, is a supplement or substitute for the market. Within it, all members have entered into voluntary contracts with a common party. In the market, there is ordinarily no single party central to all the exchange contracts. The contractual rights given to the central agent constitute what is called a business firm in the free-enterprise economy.

In socialist enterprises also the advantages of team production have to be offset against the incentive to shirk. But in the socialist economy the laws restrict this kind of common centralized-agent contract with residual claims assigned to the central agent. How can one really agree to bear the profits and losses if he has no private wealth to draw on in the event of losses? And if profits cannot be kept by him if they occur, the incentive to self-monitoring is attenuated. The manager-director-monitor-supervisor has less self-discipline than if his own wealth is at stake to back the losses or to capture profits that may occur. This problem is the difficulty facing socialist enterprises and government enterprises when they seek good discipline of management and supervision. Various devices are used to try to give the director bonuses or penalties depending upon team performance, as substitutes for the self-discipline effect of bearing profits or losses. The *contractual organization* within the team differs in socialist and free-enterprise economies; but in both economies the technical physical productivity advantages of team production are sought, providing the metering and detecting of team-member performance can be made sufficiently cheap and effective.

The classic free-enterprise employer-employee type of contract with residual share going to the employer as director and manager is one means to make team production more efficient. Notice how this contrasts with the exploitation-of-employees-by-employers interpretation so dear to superficial but "concerned" observers. A little analysis goes a long way. You could reverse the contention and claim the employees are exploiting the employers by making the former do all the guaranteeing and risk-bearing because employers will not act as self-disciplined monitors unless they are "forced" to bear those unpredictable gains and losses. But both these moralistic interpretations only substitute emotional words for useful cognition.

The Formal Legal Structure of Business Firms

Business firms commonly take one of three legal forms: individual proprietorship, partnership, or corporation. A proprietorship is owned by one person, who is also responsible for all debts of the firm to the full extent of whatever wealth he owns—that is, he has *unlimited liability*. A partnership is a joint proprietorship of two or more people, each of whom has unlimited liability for the entire firm and can individually make contracts binding the other partners. A corporation is a form of ownership usually with limited liability—that is, limited to each owner's existing financial investment in the firm. Very often several people share the ownership of a corporation. One might have 30 percent of the ownership; his legal title would be evidenced by ownership of 30 percent of the shares of "common stock"—each share denoting a minimal unit share of ownership. Corporate owners are called stockholders.

Features of Corporations

One might think that by mutual agreement a group of individuals could organize a corporation, issue common stock as evidence of owners' shares, and engage in business

—just as one can with a proprietorship or partnership. But historically the state has not recognized an inherent right of people to form a corporate contract with others. In the United States, incorporation must first be authorized by state officials. In some instances, approval is pro forma; in others, substantial fees and conditions are imposed.

What are some of the distinctive features of corporations?

Limited liability. Only the wealth expressly invested in the corporation can be held as security or for payment of corporation debts. Other wealth of the owners cannot be legally attached for payment of any liabilities. In England, the name of the corporation is usually followed by the abbreviation "Ltd." (Simpson, Ltd.), to indicate the limited liability. Because of limited liability, lenders (creditors of the firm) may regard corporations (other things being the same) as higher risks and thus charge them higher rates of interest; but limited liability is so attractive from the investor's standpoint that corporations usually have less difficulty in collecting large sums to finance ventures.

Prior to public sale of corporation stock, approval must be received from a state regulatory agency or a federal agency called the Securities and Exchange Commission, depending upon to whom the stock will be sold. To obtain that approval, the corporation must reveal about its assets and liabilities certain information that might be useful to any prudent investor. But if the regulatory commission thinks the corporation is not "strong enough," it can in some states prohibit existing owners from selling stock to other people.

Continuity. Death or selling out to a new owner by any stockholder does not terminate a corporation's existence, as it does a partnership and proprietorship. Corporate continuity is achieved by the right of the owners to transfer their shares by sale, gift, or legacy without permission of the other current owners; in a partnership, permission must first be obtained. Sales of shares of stock of many large, widely owned corporations are usually negotiated in a stock market, a formal marketplace where shares of many corporations are sold by brokers. For most corporations, shares are sold so infrequently that they are not listed on the formal stock exchanges. These lesser-known corporation shares are bought and sold by private negotiation through a dispersed but close-knit set of independent stock brokers known as the "over-the-counter" market.

Capital accumulation. Relatively large amounts of capital can be accumulated if many individuals each contribute portions of the total investment in some venture. Given limited liability, continuity, and the transferability of shares of ownership, it is not surprising that the corporate form of enterprise thrives as an institution for financing more expensive or riskier production ventures.

Because of these advantages, the corporate form of doing business has thrived despite special burdens imposed by law. For one thing, it is taxed more heavily, probably because corporation taxes do not alienate as many voters as do some other forms of taxation. Nearly one-fourth of the federal tax receipts are from taxes on the corporate form of business; about half of corporate net earnings (over $25,000) is taxed away by a special tax not levied on the earnings of other forms of business.

Ownership and control. Stockholders elect directors on a one-vote-per-share basis. Directors are authorized to make contracts (that is, to conduct the business) in the name of the corporation. Stockholders who own only a small portion of the shares individually have an insignificant effect on the voting outcome. In fact, in many large corporations no single owner owns a majority of stock. Hence, it is said that directors, in effect, control the wealth of the corporation (while stockholders bear the ultimate risk of changes in the value of the corporation). This kind of statement is easy to make but harder to interpret and still harder to substantiate. Is it true that the director-managers run the corporation while the shareholders hold the bag? This has certainly been a common allegation.

A little thought and a few facts may suggest a different interpretation. Many people want to invest wealth in ventures operated by especially skilled persons and to share in the profits. The resources they provide enable skilled managers to operate on a larger scale; in turn, the stockholders bear the value changes in those resources, freeing the managers from those risks. Whether one calls this "holding the bag" or "submitting to control of others" or "being duped by those who use your money" or "investing in resources" is largely a matter of words.

There *are* conflicts of interest within the corporate structure, but this is true for every group. The diffused ownership and the large size of the corporation raises to each stockholder the costs of policing the corporation's internal management as thoroughly and effectively as in a small proprietorship. This is similar to the case of the taxpayer, whose cost of policing government employees relative to the gain he thereby achieves is ludicrously high. But since stockholders are aware of this, the effect of these costs is to change the *form* in which managers are paid. They will receive less monetary income and more corporate ease. However, the corporation shareholder, in contrast to a taxpayer, has a salable right in the capital value, changes in which will thrust upon him more fully the gains or losses of his employees' behavior. The relatively lower price of shares of inefficiently managed corporations is an inducement to replace current inefficient managers with more efficient ones. The subsequent rise in stock values gives an immediate gain to the shareholders. Neither theory nor fact supports the belief that more widely dispersed stock ownership enables managers to act with less regard to stockholder interest.

There are about one million nonfinancial active corporations (nonfinancial means they are not in banking and insurance). The two with the most stockholders are American Telephone (3 million stockholders) and General Motors (1½ million). How unusual these are is indicated by the fact that the next largest has about ¾ million. The numbers fall off rapidly; data suggest that about 7,500 corporations have over 300 stockholders (not a large number of stockholders), while over 200,000 have 10 or fewer stockholders. But more pertinent is the dispersion of the stockholdings. Available data suggest that in most corporations a few stockholders hold a large enough percentage (10 to 20 percent) to exercise direct effective control. The fallacy of judging from the *average* stockholder is probably the root of the belief that stockholders are impotent. Most of them are, but if there is a small group in a corporation that is active in exercising voting power, stockholder interests will not be slighted. That group exercises power in their own interest, which, because they are stockholders, usually conforms to the interest of other stockholders. True, in many cases we hear of directors or managers bilking the company, but there is no evidence that this more likely occurs in large dispersed-ownership corporations than in small ones. The larger cases are simply more sensational. Even if stockholders' interests were widely and uniformly dispersed so that no identifiable group had the power to turn out management at its own discretion, it does not follow that managers could ignore stockholders' interests.

2, 3, 4, 5

There is still another very potent force controlling the behavior of managers so as to make them respond to their stockholders' interests—the force of competition from other employers who might hire the managers. Management is not a monolithic bloc of persons scratching each others' backs and tolerating shirking and inefficiencies. Each person is interested in his own fortune. If he goes along with any such presumed "collusion," he will sacrifice job offers from other corporations. And that is the source of his rapid advancement. Even a faculty member would be careful in his work despite the fact that his employer may be relaxed and inefficient in surveillance of the teacher's performance. Why? To attract offers from other schools. We work for the world at large; our current employer is only one of the intermediaries in the vast constellation of specialized activity. We advance not only by appealing to his interests but to the interests of other potential intermediary employers. Teachers have interests in excelling and in letting others know of their excellence. This holds for management as well.

The force of competition from other people applies to stockholders. If stockholders are lax in exercising control, the value of the stock will be lower, and this will attract other people to buy a sufficiently strong block of the stock to displace the existing management. You will hear of "takeovers" (stock offers by one corporation to exchange its shares for that of the acquired corporation—in order to displace or improve the management in the acquired company), proxy battles for voting rights of the common stock, and tenders (offers to buy a block of stock at a stated price somewhat above the current market price). All these activities, and the threat of them, help to discipline management. The improved management, if so it is, will result in a rise in the stock prices, thereby rewarding all the stockholders. Of course, existing management will not approve of raiders and will be happy to see their efforts frustrated by regulations and laws prohibiting such offers or takeovers. (The Securities and Exchange Commission has promulgated rules that make takeovers more difficult, to whose benefit we leave to your imagination.)

It is the profit-regulated or not-for-profit enterprise that permits more departures from market-value corporate-wealth maximization—and hence from consumer demands, because consumer demands become less influential the less managers are judged by their effects on the profits of the firm.

The corporation, with approximately 65 to 75 percent of the total sales value of production, is by far the dominant form in the United States. Proprietorships account for about 15 to 20 percent. But in numbers of firms, the proportions are almost reversed. Almost half of the five million business firms are in (wholesaling and retailing) proprietorships. If we include agricultural and professional activity, the number of firms would be larger by about another five million, most of which are unincorporated proprietorships. The largest ten corporations have from 100 to 600 thousand employees each. The one hundred largest industrial corporations employ almost six million people, or about 10 percent of all employees. The top fifty each have over a billion dollars in sales annually, with assets of about the same value.[2] Often, when hearing that the size of business firms today is much larger than thirty years ago, we are tempted to conclude that it is harder to organize a new business. However, people are getting wealthier, so that organizing a $50,000 fund of capital for an initial business venture is probably easier than getting $10,000 fifty years ago. Each year for the past fifty years, new firms have been organized at a ratio of about one for each ten existing firms.

---

[2] General Motors has about $20 billion in sales, followed by A.T.&T., Standard Oil (N. J.), Ford, General Electric, Socony Mobil, Chrysler, U. S. Steel, A. and P. Stores, and International Business Machines.

Of new firms, half are terminated in five to ten years. Relatively large size may not *cause* or *assure* success; larger size may be a *result* of efficient operation. Bigger firms are more efficient because efficiency increases the growth rate, while the inefficient are killed off before they can grow large or get old. And small, new firms are not necessarily handicapped compared to big, old firms; newcomers *can* and do effectively compete and grow faster than bigger, older firms, but they will need phenomenal growth rates for a long time to surpass some of the giants.

A few hundred large corporations "produce" nearly half the total value of industrial output. But the significance of that is not entirely clear. General Motors buys from thousands of smaller firms; when all these products are assembled in a Chevrolet, can it be said that General Motors produced the Chevrolet? Thousands of firms were involved in providing parts and equipment to that giant assembly line known as General Motors. If we count only the last assembler, then we can say that General Motors "produces" 50 percent of the cars. If we count all of its suppliers, then over one thousand firms "produce" half of the cars. Does General Motors "dominate" the automobile industry in the sense of setting prices, styles, quality, and employment policies for other producers, or merely in the share of cars produced? Is General Motors less responsive to consumer demands than if there were several firms in place of one General Motors? Does General Motors' "dominance" mean that its employees are paid lower wages? Or that improvements occur less often? Or that General Motors' decisions about its production play a bigger role in affecting the economy than if there were a hundred firms replacing it? The answers to some of these questions will be suggested in the succeeding analysis. For the moment we note that the corporate form of business organization is far and away the major form and that some corporations are of enormous size.

6, 7, 8, 9

Profits and Business Firms

As mentioned earlier, business firms exist primarily as a means of increasing wealth (and thereby utility) by production and exchange. The firm sells its products and obtains receipts. If these exceed costs, the firm is said to have realized an increase in wealth—to have earned income or even made a profit.

Revenues and Profits

I hope to have sales receipts or revenue from the use of a car if I operate it as a taxi for 20,000 miles in two years. The wage I would have earned at some other job is estimated at $4,000 per year. Suppose I believe I shall obtain, in the taxi business, sales of $6,500 in the first year and $5,500 in the second year, with the receipts presumed to come at the end of the year—on a credit-card system.

Compiling estimated expenditure and receipt data in Table 16–1, where each column lists the receipts (+) and expenditures (−) as of January 1, 1970, January 1, 1971, and January 1, 1972, we estimate the aggregate gain over the two years as $2,450 and the *present* value (at 10 percent interest) of the business as $1,833. This is the value of the business enterprise. It is computed as follows.

The cost of the taxi service, *including* the foregone wages, is $8,619—the present value of the two annual $4,000 outlays ($6,940) added to the $1,679 present-value cost of owning and using the car. The present value of the sales receipts, or revenue for each year ($6,500 and $5,500), is $10,452, which exceeds the cost by $1,833 ($10,452 − $8,619). My wealth will be $1,833 larger if I buy and operate the taxi service for the

TABLE 16–1. Receipts and Expenditures of Taxi Business

	1/1/1970	1/1/1971	1/1/1972
Purchase of car	−$2,000		
Tax, insurance	− 100	−$ 100	
Operating and repair		− 300	−$ 350
Wages and salary		− 4,000	− 4,000
Receipts		+ 6,500	+ 5,500
Sale of car			+ 1,300
Net receipts	−$2,100	+$2,100	+$2,450
Present-value factor (10%)	(1.000)	(.909)	(.826)
Profit (capital value) $1,833 =	−$2,100	+$1,909	+$2,024

Expenditures in each year (assumed to be payable at end of each year) are indicated as negative numbers; receipts are indicated by positive numbers. Net expenditures (or receipts) are converted to a present value at 10 percent annual rate of interest by multiplying by discount factor shown in parentheses in next to last line. Sequence of expenditures shown here produces a receipt sequence whose present value exceeds that of the expenditures by $1,833—the profit of this venture.

next two years than if I work for wages of $4,000 per year. My *profits* in the taxi business will be $1,833 *in present-value* (capital value) terms.

We can clarify the deeper meaning of these results by assuming that on the first day of operating the taxi, business is so good that people perceive what a splendid idea I had. Suppose, for reasons we shall investigate later, it will be two years before other people enter competition sufficiently to eliminate subsequent net earnings. But anyone who wants to enter the business immediately can buy the business from me. The total investment in the business the day of opening consists of the car and the prepaid tax and insurance for the rest of the first year; these total $2,100. The present value of all the assets of the business is now $3,933, which is $1,833 greater than the initial investment of $2,100. I have a profit of $1,833 in present (capital) value terms.

If I had incorporated the taxi company and held stock in it, and if I had issued 100 shares of stock for the $2,100 to raise the money to buy a car and pay for the first year's tax and insurance, the cost of each share initially would have been $21. Now, upon perception of what the future promises, the price of each share of the stock rises to $39.33, for a profit of $18.33 per share.[3]

"Paper profits?" When the higher market value is revealed, my wealth is higher. I have at that moment realized a profit. Although people often erroneously call this profit a "paper profit" because I have not yet "cashed" it, it *is* a genuine increase in my wealth. The only question is whether to convert the form of the greater wealth into other assets or whether to keep it in the present form of business assets.

Alternative Measures of Profits: Changes in Wealth and in Income

Very few firms would report their profits as a $183 perpetuity. Instead, they would usually express it as a two-year flow over which the actual net receipts were expected.

---

[3] Tax authorities usually call this a "capital gain or loss," when it is converted to cash by a sale.

The Business Firm and Profits

For example the profit (capital value) increase, $1,833, is the present value of the first year's net receipts over costs plus the second year's net receipts over costs. These, for the present example, were obtained as follows: providing the car service over the two years has a present value of $1,679, which when converted to a uniform two-year annuity is equivalent to $969 each year (at 10 percent rate of interest). This is the rate of cost in each of the two years—for uniform service flows in each of the two years. But if the services of the firm are not the same in each year, the firm would not consider its cost each year to be the same. It would prorate total cost over the two years according to the rate of service performed and upon other factors such as advertising that may not be correlated perfectly with the concurrent rate of service. Consequently the appropriate cost of each year is open to a range of arbitrariness depending upon whether one regards items like advertising as outlays for present sales or for future sales.

But the firm's accountant, however he may apportion the costs, must distribute costs that add up in present value terms to the $1,679 cost of the entire enterprise. Hence, depending upon how the accountants distribute those costs over the life of the enterprise, the reported annual profits in each year can be altered—but their present value *sum* must add to $1,833—the profit in capital value (wealth change) terms.[4]

You are now painfully aware that what we have measured profits both as the *increase in wealth* and as the increase in *income* flow consequent to clever or fortuitously good use of resources that were otherwise initially worth (cost) $8,619 in capital value terms. (Recall from the earlier paragraphs that the aggregate resources, materials and labor services involved in *and owned* by the enterprise were initially valued at $8,619 in capital value terms. See, above, the section under the heading, "Revenues and Profits.") That value of resources owned by the firm is capable of rendering *elsewhere* services having a perpetuity income value of $861.90 annually (at 10 percent rate of interest). In other words the standard income initially available from those owned resources was $861.90 annually. (Note carefully that this is the cost value of the resources owned by the firm; it is the total value of the resources *minus amounts borrowed*.) By our clever use of those resources, we can generate the equivalent of a perpetuity income flow of $1,045.20, which is $183.30 *larger*. Now the strange and confusing terminological feature is that both the $1,045.20 and the $183.33 are called "profits" earnings or net income by different people.

We now have four measures or concepts of profits—(1) the capital-value gain ($1,833); (2) the perpetuity value of that capital-value gain ($183); (3) the somewhat

---

[4] One possibility, for example, is to report profits (in the flow sense) of $1,531 in the first year and $531 in the second year. How? Since the cost of the entire two-year service is $1,679, this can be converted to a two-year *uniform* annuity of $969 annually and this can be called the costs of each year (using 10 percent rate of interest). To that $969 we must add the labor costs of $4,000 each year, giving an annual *rate* of cost of $4,969 per year (in which the service is a uniform 10,000 miles annually). The receipts in the first year from the taxi business (shown in Table 15–1) are $6,500 and $5,500 in the second, giving net earnings over costs of $1,531 in the first year and $531 in the second. (Incidentally, you should be able to verify that the present value of the two-year stream is—at 10 percent interest—equal to $1,833, our wealth measure of profit.)

Business accountants would report, as the profits and net earnings of each period, the amounts of $1,531 and $531, if the events materialized as predicted and if they reckon $4,000 each year as the implicit wages of my own time—as we did in our numerical calculations. However, accountants do not always enter a cost item for the time of the owner. Failing that, the accountant's reported "net earnings" (*not* counting my implicit wages in costs) would be reported as $5,531 and $4,531. This differs from what we call profit or net earnings because it includes the foreseeable imputed value of my labor services.

discretionary allocation over the two years ($1,531 and $531); and (4) the new total standard income of the firm ($1,045 annually at 10% interest on its new $10,452 value of its assets). All these are sometimes called "profits"—a rather confusing state of communication.

The first is what *we* have called profits in the *unforeseen wealth increase* sense. The second and third are annuity equivalents of the first, depending upon the particular pattern of the annuity and its length. The fourth is the new perpetuity income flow annually that is based on the net asset (net of borrowings) value of the firm. This new "income" level from the firm, $1,045, is bigger (by $183) than the income that would have been otherwise available from the value of resources owned by the firm (an income flow of $861.90). After the firm had been created and its performance evaluated, the *income* increased to $1,045, which is the sum of the profit (increased income) flow of $183 plus the formerly otherwise available income of $861. And, as we have called it, the present *capital* (*wealth*) value of that $183 increase—not available prior to the formation of the firm and which is the "second" measure listed here—is $1,833 in *wealth* (our "first" measure) increase—the profits in units of *wealth,* rather than income.[5]

Of these gages of wealth or income changes, only the capital-value (wealth) measure is directly measurable in the market. The price of any resource is its present value. Therefore, if upon opening a taxi firm I were to solicit bids for its sale, the price (above the cost) I could get would measure the wealth value of profits. If other people now appreciate the possibilities and estimate them consistently with our data, the market value of the business will have jumped by $1,833.

If all this leaves you confused, we hope it is confusion in the way terms are used and that you are not confused in understanding how each relates to the other, whatever they may be called by the men "in the street."

Accounting records of earnings. Business accounting is designed to keep a clear record of the company's financial activities, such as the amounts of money spent or committed to future payment, and the goods and services obtained in exchange. A record is kept of actual expenditures and receipts, but *not* of all the foreseen and predictable receipts and expenditures. More accurately, although all past expenditures and receipts are accounted for, only *some* of the future commitments for expenditure and foreseeable future receipts are included in the accounts. Noncontractual future receipts or expenditures are excluded. To see why accountants exclude noncontractual *prospects* of future receipts and expenditures from their valuation processes and data, consider the following example.

With $31,000, I buy land and oil drilling equipment and pay wages to the drill workers. In a year we strike oil. What should our accountant do? Should he record the present value of the oil, which as yet is an unknown amount, uncaptured and unsold? If the market offers me $100,000 for that oil land, then, whether or not I sell, my wealth has increased to $100,000 plus the resale value of the drilling equipment, which we shall assume is now $6,000 (down $4,000 from its assumed initial price of $10,000). My wealth totals to $106,000 and since I have no liabilities, my wealth gain, my profit, is $75,000 ($106,000 − 31,000).

The accounting records say we *lost* $24,000 during the year! (We used up $4,000 of oil-well equipment and $20,000 for wages and related services and have sold no oil.)

---

[5] In addition, words like "earnings," "net earnings," "net income" are also used in a mixture of meanings. You simply have to figure out what is meant in each case.

Why is the accountant unwilling to record a value of the future oil sales? Because it is not yet a legally obligated future receipt.

If the oil reservoir is to be valued, he could say that it cost $24,000 to find it. This $24,000 is the book value of the oil reservoir. As long as we know the convention, we can ignore it when deciding what we think the company is worth. But if we didn't know the convention, we might think the $24,000 represented an estimate of what the oil field is worth on the market. The alternative accounting convention is that of not recording any value at all, or a formal $1, until there is a clear-cut sale of that asset, in which its value can be and *has been* measured by actual sales.

The zero or $1 value procedure is adopted frequently when the asset is not a physical tangible thing but an idea, design, patent, new product, trademark, or personality. A reliable product built the name "Kodak" so much that the name "Kodak" serves as a symbol of reliability, thereby attracting sales. How should that asset, the name "Kodak," be valued? At the advertising costs? At zero? Or at some estimated value? Convention prefers the zero value, false though that figure may be.

Earlier, we commented that in the taxi example the accountant usually ignores the implicit $4,000 annual wages that I, as owner, could have earned if I did not operate the taxi business. You can now see why the accountant does so. How would anyone know that the accountant is reporting an unbiased estimate rather than a figure to make the net earnings look good or bad as suits his whim?

Regardless of what the accountant does, *we* must not take his final figure for "profits or net earnings" to be a measure of the actual change in value of wealth. We must recognize that the prospect of future sales *is* part of the value of a good. Ford has no guarantee that it will sell any cars next year. No retailer or manufacturer has any warranty that the public will continue to buy his product. He has no contract or commitment with consumers in which consumers bind themselves to future purchases. And yet we can be "sure" that sales will occur. To be "sure" means only that we are prepared to "bet" on it. I am prepared to bet that Ford will have lots of sales next year, and I am prepared to back my bet by *buying* some share of ownership (common stock) in that corporation. I pay for (bet on) the *prospect* of successful future operations. In fact, the value of almost *every* good rests on a present bet about *prospects*.

The present price or value rarely rests on a contract for future sales. About the only commodity for which there is legal commitment of that nature is a debt contract (bond) or money which can be so used for the legal payment of debts.

Profits are unpredictable increases. A principal idea of this discussion is that the wealth of a business depends upon the expectations of the future, not simply on how much was paid in the past to create the particular assets. One reason that reports by business firms of annual net earnings or profits are so important is that they serve as an indicator of the extent to which earlier forecasts are being fulfilled. For example, business firms with rapid growth rates, like International Business Machines and Xerox, have a present price of their stock (wealth) that is nearly one hundred times greater than the current annual reported net earnings. The average of most firms is about ten to twenty times current earnings. The market expects the future net earnings to increase rapidly, and the high present price of the stock relative to *current* net earnings reflects that future growth expectation. Those future net earnings are capitalized into current values of assets—that is, stock prices. Other companies (for example, U. S. Steel) have prices for their common stocks only five to fifteen times as great as current annual net earnings. If the reported net earnings for IBM in any year should merely equal the prior year's, instead of being

10 to 25 percent higher, the price of IBM stock will fall. If earnings fail to increase, expectations are disappointed and revised downward. On the other hand, if the net earnings of U. S. Steel are reported as unchanged from a prior year, the price of U. S. Steel stock will not fall—that is, the expectation that U. S. Steel does *not* have substantial growth facing it will not be upset. Evidence for these statements of fact is available from the behavior of stock-market prices.

These examples provide a good opportunity to explain another much misunderstood term, "watered" stock. Suppose that on the day I started my taxi business with the $2,100 investment, I offered to sell you one of the one-hundred shares of stock in the company for $30. At first, you might think I was selling you something worth only $21. You might say I was selling you a share at an inflated value, or that the stock was "watered," or that I was selling you "blue sky."[6] In fact, however, the share of taxi stock is worth more than $30, if the foresight we have is accurate. For this reason, investors often pay more for a share of stock than the costs of the resources in the business. What they are buying is part of the higher value of those resources—the profits. As long as you can get a share of my taxi stock for less than $39.33, you will have made a profit, too—assuming we have forecast future events accurately.

Fundamental Sources of Profits

Because foresight is imperfect, unforeseen changes in market values are inevitable; profits and losses will be realized. Profits and losses occur in all economic systems. A change from a capitalistic to a communist or socialist or feudal society will not even hide them. It will only change the determination of who bears the profits and losses. Only if uncertainty is eliminated will the situation be different; and it is certain that no earthly revolution will remove uncertainty.

It is convenient for exposition to group the sources of uncertainty into two polar classes: extraneous, uncontrollable events and deliberate innovative activity by resource owners.

Extraneous events. Changes in demand are often extraneous, uncontrollable events. And if people shift their preferences unpredictably, values will change unpredictably, with profits or losses as the result. For example, the value and usefulness of a dress or suit of clothes falls because of changes in styles. A dress will still keep the wearer as neat, warm, and modest as ever, but the dress simply does not give all the value it formerly did. It no longer gives a feeling of stylishness, attractiveness, or sense of belonging. And who can say that these are irrelevant, superficial attributes that shouldn't count? The simple fact is that they do. I may say that people so concerned with style are extravagant and that the prices of their clothes, for example, bear little relationship to "real" values. We have every right to *say* that, but we should realize that we are saying we know better than other people what the properly desired things are in this world and, therefore, the market values that reflect *their* preferences are not proper values.

Innovative activity. Another source of profits and losses is deliberate innovative activity, in which owners try to use resources in ways not heretofore evaluated by the

---

[6] Almost all states have "blue sky" laws to control sales of stock in new corporations—sales of which, folklore says, would too often be made to gullible investors if it were not for these laws.

community. Their hope, ambition, or gamble is that their product will be more highly valued by the market after innovation. Anyone who seeks to do this must have some control over some resources, the value changes in which will accrue to him.

If I increase the value of a house by painting it, so that the new value is equal to the former value plus that of the paint and labor, then the change in value is merely the sum of the former values of a changed set of goods. But if the value of some newly combined set of resources is greater than the sum of their former values, there is a profit, an *unexpected increase in value*.

The prospects of profits serve as a motivating force for innovative activity. Yet one man's innovation and resultant profits may cause a loss to another man. For example, the invention of the automobile reduced the value of buggy whips, and the innovation of television reduced the value of theater buildings. The loss in value of the theater building is more than offset by the social gain from television. But the theater owner who bears that loss, if he is not somehow compensated, is no better off than if a fire damaged the theater. When losses are the result of improvement elsewhere, is the bearer of this loss always compensated, even if in principle it is possible to do so? As we shall see, in every social and economic system the answer is "No." Still another question is whether or not one should try to compensate him; but that is a question of normative policy, and we shall postpone it.

Profits, Ownership, and Management

Although an owner may hire a manager to run his business, the owner still owns the resources and still bears profits or losses. The owner may seem to be passive, abiding by the manager's decisions and advice; yet the so-called "passive" owner is the one who has decided to permit this use of his resources. And though the manager makes all the decisions after the owner decides to submit his wealth to the venture, and even though the manager seems to be doing all the work, the owner still bears the market value (wealth) consequences.

If an owner operates his business as his own manager, he counts wages for his labor services. Some owner-managers make the mistake of combining into one total their wages of management and their profit—calling the whole thing "profit" or calling it all "wages." In the earlier taxi example, in which profit was $1,833, wages for driving the cab (and let us assume also for managing the firm) were $4,000. The former is profit, a value change in wealth; the latter is annual wages or payment for labor services. To call *both* either profit or management wages would be to mix two different economic concepts. However, in the language of the layman, you will often find this confusing practice. You will, in each instance, simply have to reinterpret the situation for yourself, if you want to keep your analysis consistent.

Profits of Labor

A distinction between profits and wages of management, or between profits and wages in general, does not mean that labor or personal service is not a source of wealth to a person. Wages are payments or receipts for personal services, while "rent" is the name for the payment to the owner of inanimate goods. Both a flow of wages and of rentals has present values (wealth), reflecting anticipated future receipts. The present value of my future wages may be $200,000. If I have an accident and fracture my skull, I will suffer a reduced prospective future series of receipts; and the present value of my wages will fall, say, to $150,000. The accident will cost me $50,000.

We see and measure profit of nonhuman wealth more clearly because inanimate goods can be bought and sold, whereas a person does not sell himself; he sells only the current services as they are performed. If he could literally sell his future services now, he could convert (or "cash in") his profit to other forms of wealth. But he cannot, and so he must keep more of his wealth in the form of his labor services. Even though there is no marketplace where a person can sell his future services now, he *can* borrow now against his future wages as we saw in Chapter 11.

In a sense, all profits—or values—are values of people rather than of inanimate goods. Goods are valuable only because of the way in which people use them. People with superior talents know how to use resources to make them more valuable. If, for example, General Motors hires a superior designer to design a car of greater value, the increased value shows up as a profit to General Motors. But if we keep our analysis correct, we must recognize that the designer was obtained for a salary less than his worth proved to be to GM. No one *knew,* in advance, just how valuable his services would be. GM had to accept the initially uncertain value of his services. GM's ability to hire him for less than his ultimately revealed worth reflected differences in opinion about that worth among General Motors, other potential employers, and the employee himself. GM cannot continue to purchase his services at less than they are revealed to be worth unless *all* other potential employers remain ignorant of his ability—and he will not let his ability stay hidden. The high value of his services will accrue to him as other employers bid for his work, driving up his wages and raising costs to all who thereafter use him.

None of this means that GM or any other employer makes profits by paying less for resources than they are worth. What resources are paid is what the rest of the market thinks they will be worth *at the time* they are bought or hired. Always, too little is bet on the winner and too much on the losers. If anyone makes a profit, it follows, by definition, that the earlier value placed on the resource was too low. And losses result from earlier overvaluation.

15, 16, 17, 18

Profits, Losses, and Insurance

To avoid the risks of "losses" from physical damage (fire, flood, etc.) or theft, people "insure." Thereby, they modify the pattern of risks and incidence of losses. By joint voluntary insurance, people share losses by spreading them over the group, in the form of premium or insurance fees paid by each member. Out of these fees, compensation is paid to those who suffer the contingent misfortune. This pooling of risk of losses does not necessarily reduce the total social losses. It spreads them over the insurees, as each one pays a fee for the insurance. The aggregate of the fees is (hopefully) enough to cover the losses incurred. In general, the insurance converts the risk of a possible large loss into the certainty of a small loss—the payment of the premium for the insurance.

Even though, as a condition of getting insurance, the insuring group may require that the insured take special precautions, the remaining precautionary incentives are reduced. Without insurance, we may devote more resources and care and anxiety to protection than with it. Nevertheless, even if total losses are greater with insurance than without (as they may well be), the savings in precautionary resource use and anxiety may be greater.

Some losses are not insurable. For example, insurance by a retailer against bad business or loss of customers would mean (if such insurance were somehow available) that the retailer could try less hard to provide consumers with desirable products—relying on the insurance company to indemnify him for his laziness. The resultant claims for indemnifying the insurees against the "losses" will exceed the amount of wealth that the insurance company can get from voluntary insurees as premiums for insurance. For this reason, insurance on business failure because of loss of customers, or on crop failures for farmers, or on unemployment is not actually sound.

There are many other uninsurable hazards. For example, it seems you can't get insurance against having your oil well dry up, or *not* finding gold on your land, or having other people's tastes and demands shift against your services or goods, or against divorce, or against dull children, or against marital infidelity. And yet in a sense you can insure against some of these events. The risk of your oil well's drying up unexpectedly can be transferred to someone else. Just sell the asset to him and hold money. When you sell your oil-well land, you get the present value of that land as judged by other people on an expectational basis (weighing odds that it will dry up against odds that it won't). If the oil well does dry up, the buyer bears the loss.

In this way—by choosing not to hold certain goods—you can escape the hazards of loss of those goods (and chance of profit). In a private-property system, those risks are borne by the owner of the particular goods.

This redistribution of risks of loss is a form of insurance and is available in a private-property system, in which people can exchange ownership and choose which risks to bear. By shifting private-property rights to various goods and buying one kind of good rather than another, people can obtain "insurance" against certain kinds of risks and losses. More precisely, private property is not insurance in the sense that one takes a small but sure loss (premium) in order to avoid a large contingent loss; rather, it is a selective, discretionary, risk-bearing institution.

A rental arrangement is also a risk-shifting system. By renting a house on a month-to-month basis, instead of owning one, you "own" only one month's value of the house and thereby avoid having so much of your wealth in a particular house. A renter will not suffer the entire loss of value of a house if its value changes. By renting goods, a person can diversify his ownership of goods or he can concentrate on one good, independently of his consumption patterns.

It is worth noting that in some countries farmers cannot sell the land they "own." They can use it for themselves or sell the crop for their own wealth, but they cannot sell the land or borrow against it as security. (If they could borrow against the land, they would borrow its current value and then let the lender take the land when they refuse to repay the loan—thus circumventing the intended ban on sale of the land.) This is a modified form of private-property rights, but it does not provide the extent of risk sharing and re-allocation that is provided by a system of full private-property rights. Obviously, the incentive to improve the land is weakened, since the risks of value changes cannot be shifted to those most willing to bear the risks of changes in the value of the land. A person who "owns" land under these restricted conditions will invest more of his wealth in goods with more transferable property rights. An implication of this analysis is that people in backward countries (i.e., with these incomplete property rights) are less willing to invest in land.

Attitudes toward various systems of property rights should, in part, be based on attitudes toward the *way* they determine the *distribution* of profits and losses. Since profits and losses occur regardless of the form of property rights, the issue is not whether one is for or against profits and losses but whether one is for or against this or that system of distributing them over various people. Who shall bear the joy of profits and the despair of losses? Laws might be passed to impose losses on brunettes and profits upon blondes, by an appropriate system of taxes. Profits and losses could be owned by people as a whole, with each person's use rights determined by a lottery or his taxes or his standing in line, as it is with public parks and rights to hunt deer in some states.

Profits and losses could be assigned by the political decision system, in which case the assignments will depend on one's power of affecting political decisions. Socialism is an example of this form of profit-and-loss risk-bearing system. Part of the issue between a capitalist and a socialist system is over the kind of risk-distribution institution used. Under the capitalist private-property system, those who decide about the use of resources are more likely to be the ones to bear the effects of resulting value changes. As a result, under the private-property system the resources are more likely to be used where the market wealth potential is highest. But proponents of socialism believe that market values should not be so influential in determining resource uses and that individuals should not be able to specialize in bearing various kinds of risks.

Profits, Monopoly Rents, and Changes in Monopoly Rights

Not every profit reflects a transfer of resources from lower-valued to higher-valued uses. Suppose I managed to have a law passed preventing other people from producing goods that compete with mine. The reduced supply from a reduced number of competitors will raise the price of my goods, giving me a profit. This kind of profit can be created by the levying of special taxes on my competitors; for example, interstate tariffs on goods produced in other states that compete with mine in domestic sales.

The profit that results when greater restraint is placed on competitors' access to the market is called a "monopoly rent"—*monopoly* because of the legal restriction on market access—*rent* because it is not allowed to induce an increase in supply.

The legal-monopoly restriction on entry will raise the market valuation of assets already in the protected industry. The restriction prevents more resources from being transferred to higher-valued uses from lower-valued uses. The result, from the consumers' point of view, is the same as would occur if costs were higher than they really are. The "privileged" or "licensed" resources earn their owners a higher value, while the excluded resources receive a lower value.

How much of the current value of a resource is "monopoly rent"? This is an interesting, important, but unanswered question. We have some estimates and evidence on tobacco acreage, ranging up to $3,000 for an acre of land on which tobacco can be grown and sold in the market without a special tax. This is nearly 50 percent of the total value of that acre of land. In New York City the monopoly rent of one taxi is over $20,000. In California the monopoly rent of a liquor license ranges from $10,000 to $40,000. In most states the present value of banks, insurance companies, airlines, and all public utilities reflects a monopoly rent of various amounts, depending upon the extent to which entry is restricted. Value also depends on the extent to which the monopoly rent is taxed away by the government, or prices are kept down by law so that the legal monopolists cannot realize the maximum market value of their monopoly situation.

We must be careful not to confuse monopolists in this situation with price-searchers, who are also called "monopolists" in the technical economic literature. Almost all retailers and manufacturers, large and small, are "monopolists" in this technical sense because they face a negative-sloped demand curve for their products. We have in this book used the name "price-searchers" for such sellers who operate in *open* markets, where there are no restraints on entry. The reason for calling them "price-searchers" rather than "monopolists" is to avoid confusion between open and closed markets. There is nothing about price-searchers' markets to suggest monopoly rents resulting from protected competition. In a price-searchers' market, anyone can make a new kind of cornflake, and anyone can open another drugstore, but the fact that they will be facing negatively sloped demand curves for their products does not mean they can produce the product profitably. It is easy to identify many firms that are losing wealth despite a negatively sloping demand curve for their services. Yet folklore about the American economy would have us believe that the price-searcher firms make most of the profits.

Where does the myth arise? Probably from two sources. One is the failure to distinguish between the two types of monopoly. The second is the notion that big firms make bigger profits because they are big, rather than that firms making big profits will become big firms. Being big is in itself no assurance of a higher probability of making profits. That, at least, is what economic theory indicates, and the evidence is consistent. It is easy to think that one can refute this evidence by pointing out a big firm like General Motors, which has earned profits in the capital-value sense during many years (and had losses during many years in that same sense). But some very large firms have lost wealth in many years (Chrysler, Ward's), and some very small firms have had spectacular growth (Litton, International Chemical and Nuclear, Kaufman and Broad, Xerox, Control Data). The total evidence falls into the predicted pattern—namely, the probability that any firm will in the next interval of time experience a profit (unforeseen capital-value gain in its wealth) is the same for big and small firms, for price-takers and price-searchers, and even whether the resources of the firm have free or restricted access to the market. All the foreseeable events have been capitalized into the present valuations; only the unforeseen ones remain to be revealed.

The idea that it is possible to know which firm or class of firms is more likely to earn profits is self-defeating. If they were detectable in advance, it would pay to buy the firms immediately, pushing up their values *now*. Consequently, any statement about which class of firms will in the future experience unusual wealth increases, as profits, is a statement with which the general public (and especially the wealth-holding portion of it) is in disagreement. It is in disagreement because the statement implies that there is today a class of firms whose assets or resources (stock prices) are systematically undervalued. If you know of that class, you have a good road to profits for yourself; but beware, for you are betting against the judgment of the rest of the community.

Other Definitions of Profits

Difference between wholesale and retail price. "Profits" to the ordinary businessman do not always correspond exactly to "profits" as defined here, since no one has a copyright on the term "profit." The term is used for a wide variety of relationships between expenditures and receipts. Sometimes the difference between the price which a retailer pays for goods and the price at which he sells is called "profit." More normally, that difference is called "markup," as an indication of how much above the purchase price the selling price must be if all the other attendant costs are to be met. To ignore those other costs is to forget about space, shelter, management, sales clerks, inventory for display and immediate delivery, record-keeping, safeguarding, insurance, advertising, taxes, light, heat, fixtures, breakage, pilferage, packaging, returns, employee training, and many other costly activities. "Overhead costs" commonly refers to some of those costs. Some ignorantly say that a markup of 100 percent (of the wholesale purchase price, or 50 percent of the retail price) represents a profit of 100 percent—if he sells at that price. Even U.S. congressional reports have said so.

Profits before taxes. Another error is to omit taxes as a cost and calculate "profits before taxes"—although allowing for all other costs. Remarkably, this concept was used by a government agency apparently unaware of its implications, for when it was initially presented no reference was made to profits *after* taxes. Does it not suggest that taxes are really not a part of costs—that they are payments for no service? It is difficult to believe that the government agency would want to suggest that taxes are merely tribute collected from those obtaining profits. One would hardly be more surprised if a labor union published a graph of "profits before wages" as if to assert, falsely, that wages are not a part of costs.

Expected current losses. If you examine the annual reports of business firms, you will find assertions like: "We have started production on a very promising new product and are currently operating at a loss, but we expect that in a year we shall be covering costs and making profits." If that statement were taken literally, one would wonder why they hadn't waited until next year to start operations. In our terms what was meant is: "At the present time the rate of receipts is less than current expenditures, but the present outlays will bring larger future receipts that exceed future outlays. We believe the new product will promise a net flow of actual receipts in the future that will increase our wealth. In fact, the investing public is now of the same opinion, and that is why the market value of our shares of common stock has increased during the current year, so we have really had a profit. Hooray!"

The quick pay-off period. "It takes three years for us to recover our investment before we can start making a profit." This type of statement, implying some "payout" or "cost-recovery" period, means merely that money outlays exceed the money receipts during the first three years and that only in the fourth year do total receipts begin to overtake the total expenditures. But who cares; the important thing is that the *present wealth value* of the receipts should exceed that of the outlays. To worry or be concerned about the length of that period is to be worried about whether or not the expected or hoped-for receipts will really materialize. The virtue of a short "payout" or "recovery" period is that it reduces the time one has to wait to find out whether the new venture really does as well as hoped.

Summary

1 Business firms are groups of people jointly seeking to increase their wealth by jointly producing goods and services for consumption by other people.

2 Within a firm the managers direct and monitor the activities of other people; there is no immediate market for exchange of services.

3   The most desirable specific future services are uncertain, and repeated recontracting for services is costly. The result is single contracts specifying general classes of services to be provided at a constant price—the wage. This is known as an employer-employee contract.

4   Large stocks of capital equipment typically found in business firms are not the essential distinctive characteristic of firms, nor is the form of ownership or risk bearing.

5   A proprietorship has one owner responsible for all liabilities to the full extent of his wealth—that is, he has unlimited liability. Partnerships have more than one owner, each of whom is authorized to act for the partnership, and each of whom has unlimited liability. Corporations can have several or many owners, each with no liability; ownership is divided into "shares," with decisions and contacts being made for the corporation by elected officers. Corporations, in contrast to proprietorships and partnerships, have continued life in the event of the death of an owner or of transfer of ownership.

6   Formation of corporation usually requires, by law, authorization from the state. Limited liability of a corporation facilitates large investment ventures. The corporate form enables investors to specialize in the skills of managers and directors; there is separation of management and ownership. The largest business firms are corporations. Corporations account for over two-thirds of the total value of market output, but they comprise only about one-fifth the total numbers of business enterprises.

7   Close to 1,000,000 business ventures are opened each year; about half do not survive three years.

8   Profits, the unforeseen changes in wealth, can be re-expressed as equivalent-valued annual flows, as they almost always are. Attempts to prorate the profit over the output stream usually are expressed as "net earnings" of the period. Profits, once they occur as an increased value of assets, are capitalized into higher costs of subsequent operations. All assets, human and nonhuman, obtain profits (or losses), but the existence of a market for selling the assets facilitates measurement of the profits (or losses).

9   Insurance, a pooling of risks and sharing of profits or losses, does not in itself change the total of profits or losses.

10 Private property enables risk re-allocation and specialization in risk bearing.

11 Closing or restricting markets enables incumbents (with access to the market) to obtain a larger market value for the services of their assets. This increase is monopoly rent.

12 The term "profits" is commonly used to cover many other concepts distinct from "profits" in economics.

Questions

1   The purpose of this question is to explain how to interpret business financial statements. Most business firms periodically (commonly every three or six months and annually) issue financial reports of their activities and current status. Reproduced below is a slightly modified (for teaching purposes) balance sheet reported for the United Nuclear Corporation for March 31, 1970. A *balance* sheet presents a listing and valuation, according to the company's books, of its assets, liabilities, and ownership structure. Assets, as we know, are the resources owned and used by this corporation. There are always claims held by other people against a business; these claims are called liabilities. The net (of liabilities) value of the owners to these assets is called proprietorship, capital, equity, or net worth.

The basic identity is

$$\text{Assets} - \text{Liabilities} = \text{Equity},$$

which can be rewritten

$$\text{Assets} = \text{Liabilities} + \text{Equity}.$$

The firm's situation is then presented in the form of a balance sheet, with items classified as assets on the left side, with liabilities and equity on the right side. What do the items mean?

United Nuclear Corporation
Balance Sheet, March 31, 1970
(in Thousands of Dollars)

Assets		Liabilities	
Current		*Current*	
Cash	$ 4,469	Accounts payable	$ 4,500
Receivables	9,950	Notes payable	1,088
Reserve for bad debts	−300	Accrued liabilities	11,764
Unbilled costs	3,018	Current liabilities	17,352
Inventories	9,028		
Prepaid expenses	500	*Long-Term*	
Marketable securities	5,867	Long-term debt	37,848
Current assets	32,527	Minority interest	2,869
		Long-Term liabilities	40,717
Long-Term		*Equity*	
Investments	4,690	Preferred, convertible stock,	
Government contracts	3,900	10,000 shares (5%, $100)	1,000
Plant and equipment	50,457	Common stock ($.20 par)	
Less reserve for depreciation	−5,400	5,156,000 issued	1,031
Other assets	22,992	Capital surplus	28,505
Goodwill	100	Retained earnings	20,661
Long-term assets	76,739		51,197
Total assets	$109,266	Liability + equity	$109,266

ASSETS

Cash. The amount of money held, including checking accounts.

Accounts receivable. These are the past sales yet to be paid for by customers for the company's products: charge accounts or credit extended to customers allowing them, usually, thirty days to pay.

Reserve for bad debts. Very likely some customers will fail to pay their debts when due. To express this fact and to estimate the expected amount of receivables that will become "bad," the accountants subtract an amount called a "Reserve for bad debts" or "doubtful accounts." This is called a "reserve" because it expresses a "reservation" or "qualification" about the value of the receivables. Reserves in accounting statements do *not* represent collections of money or particular assets that have been reserved (in the sense of set aside) for some particular purpose. This balance sheet later shows "Reserves for depreciation," which is a way of expressing a reservation about the value of the assets. It represents the total depreciation so far accumulated; it is *not* a fund set aside for new equipment to replace the depreciation. As used in bookkeeping, the word *reserve* almost never denotes a setting aside of cash or actual reserving of assets. It is almost always used to express explicitly a reservation or adjustment in the stated value of some asset or liability.

Unbilled costs. The corporation is making nuclear reactors to custom order; and as a reactor is gradually completed the corporation records the incurred costs as claims accruing against the customer, for which a bill will be submitted upon completion and delivery to the customer.

Inventories. The corporation also refines uranium ores. This is the value of the ore it has removed from its mines and has not yet sold, plus any other unsold products. In general, this records values of products on hand.

Prepaid expenses. The corporation has paid in advance for some goods and services yet to be obtained. These are rights against other people who have contracted to deliver goods and services for which the corporation has already paid. This is an asset. For example, when you prepay a magazine subscription, you would record that asset as a prepaid expense in your personal balance sheet.

Marketable securities. These are typically U. S. government bonds or notes payable in the immediate future, common stocks of other companies or bonds of other companies. In all cases, these securities are saleable on bond or stock exchanges.

Investments. The corporation owns stock in another company. Usually, the particular investment is identified in footnotes that accompany the balance sheet.

Plant and equipment. This is the cost of the physical property—mines, mills, etc.—of the corporation. Sometimes this is recorded as the "cost of replacing" it, especially if there have been drastic changes in costs of this equipment since purchase.

Reserve for depreciation. The property, plant, and equipment have been used and partly worn out. An estimate of the portion of the plant so consumed is called "depreciation." Subtracting depreciation from the initial price gives the "book" value of equipment. (See above: Reserve for bad debts.)

Other assets. There can be almost any kind of asset of the company—from mines, land, buildings, claims against others, patents, or even U. S. government bonds. Usually footnotes attached to the balance sheet will give clues. While this item is usually not large, sometimes it is enormous, especially if there is some temporary unusual holding of assets. In the present case it is larger than usual when compared to past balance sheets for this company.

Goodwill. Patents and trademarks are often given some small or token estimate of value and called goodwill. Sometimes the continued success of a company is attributed to certain intangibles, e.g., its reputation or brand name. This may be recorded as a goodwill item. Usually the *recorded* value is not significantly large, because it is intangible.

LIABILITIES

Liabilities are conventionally categorized into *current* and *long-term* liabilities, with the former usually representing claims that must be paid within a year.

Accounts payable. The corporation has purchased goods and equipment for which it must yet pay. The amount still due is recorded.

Notes payable. The corporation has borrowed for a short period of time, and the amount due is shown. This item may also include any long-term debt that will fall due within a year.

Accrued liabilities. At the present moment (the end of the month), the corporation has accrued obligations to pay taxes or wages at some near future date. For example, if wages are paid on the fifteenth of the month, then at the end of the month it will owe about half a month's wages, to be paid in two weeks.

Long-term debt. The corporation has issued bonds to borrow money. In the present instance, these will run until about 1975.

Minority interest. The corporation is the primary owner of a subsidiary company, the entire value of which has been recorded among the assets. However, since United Nuclear Corporation is not the sole owner, it has recorded here the ownership rights of the other owners of this subsidiary mining company. Usually every balance sheet has an appended list of footnotes or additional information giving further details. In this case the report happens to tell us in a footnote that the subsidiary company, which has a recorded value of about $14,700,000, is all included in United Nuclear's reported property, plant, and equipment ($50,457,000) on the asset side. $2,869,000 of that belongs to other people—the subsidiary company's other owners, the *minority interest*. This recorded minority interest offsets part of the value shown on the asset side. In other words, of the total recorded value of the subsidiary company, $2,869,000 is the share of the other owners.

EQUITY

Many firms include more than just equity under the heading of Equity. Some, as this one does, include also a special form of debt, "preferred convertible stock." We shall first explain what that is and then explain the way the pure *equity* is presented.

The first item shown is *Preferred, convertible stock*. "Preferred stock" is a fancy name for what is simply a debt of the company. It is called preferred stock because the holders of that stock, in the event of bankruptcy, have a preferred claim against the company, prior to that of the common stock holders. This might have been called bonds of $100 denominations paying 5 percent per year—except that preferred stock often differs from a bond in that if the $5 "interest" or "dividend" on the preferred is not paid, the preferred stock holder cannot institute legal foreclosure proceedings against the company. He simply has preference to the earnings, if any, for payment of interest before any dividends can be paid to the common stock holders. Sometimes the preferred stock is "cumulative," which means that any arrears of unpaid dividends (or interest, if you will) accumulate, and until they are paid, the common stock holders cannot take any dividends. And, as in the present instance, the preferred stock may be "convertible," which means that the preferred stock holder has the option to exchange (convert) it into common stock at a preset exchange rate. In the present instance, the exchange rate is ten common for one preferred stock (information usually given in a footnote to the balance sheet). Thus the present preferred convertible stock has a par of $100 with 5 percent, it pays $5 preferred dividends each year (if earned) and may be converted to ten shares of common stock.

A person who buys a share of preferred convertible stock for $100 has some hope the common stock will rise above $10 a share; by converting to ten shares he will then have more than $100. As the price of a common share approaches $10 in the stock market, the selling price of preferred convertible stock will rise above $100, reflecting both the current price and the present values of further future rises in the common stock price. A purchaser of *convertible* preferred common stock is in fact a partial common stock holder or owner. A purchaser of nonconvertible preferred stock is simply a creditor of the company.

Finally, some preferred stock is "callable"; that is, the company has the option to pay it off prior to its due date. A $100 callable preferred stock will usually be callable at some price slightly above $100, but the premium diminishes as the due date approaches. The owner of a "callable, convertible, cumulative, preferred stock" (of $100 par value, at 5 percent, convertible at $10, and callable at $105 within five years) will collect $5 a year dividends, if earned; he may be offered $105 for the stock (which he must take unless he decides to convert); he can convert it to ten shares of common stock (since ten shares of common at $10 per share will equal the $100 par value of the convertible preferred share). As you can see, all sorts of terms are possible in a "preferred stock."

The remaining three items show the equity proper, which usually is expressed in three parts: *common stock, additional paid-in capital,* and *retained earnings* (sometimes the last two are combined and called simply *capital surplus*). We already know that equity, by definition, equals the difference between assets and liabilities (including preferred stock as a liability). In the present instance, if we subtract the liabilities from the assets ($109,266,000 − $58,069,000), we get $51,197,000, which is the *book value* of the common stock holders' equity. How was it attained? Initially there was paid into the company when the stock was issued $29,536,000 (= $28,505,000 + $1,031,000). The figure is recorded for legal and tax purposes as $1,031,000 as the *initial par value* and $28,505,000 as the *additional amount paid* originally for that stock. This division is of no economic significance and reflects some technically legal quirks. We mention it here to avoid any impression that the par value reflects some true economic value.

What has happened to that $29,536,000? It has been spent (along with proceeds of loans) for property, wages, equipment, etc., and at the moment the results of that activity are shown as assets on one side and as incurred obligations on the other.

Retained earnings. The corporation has *invested* $20,661,000 of its net earnings to purchase new equipment and facilities. The corporation may also have paid out some dividends to common stock holders, but we can't tell from the balance-sheet data. (Retained earnings are often called *earned surplus*.)

Such is what the historical balance sheet record of the United Nuclear Corporation indicates. If we divide the recorded *book value* of the ownership, $51,197,000 (= $1,031,000 + $28,505,000 + $20,661,000) by the 5,156,000 shares outstanding, it comes to about $9.94 a share.

It is tempting to conclude that a share of common stock is worth $10; but don't yield to that temptation, or else you are rejecting everything you have learned in this book, and especially in Chapter 11. Why? Because the figures in the balance sheet's asset column are the historical outlays for the equipment (adjusted for depreciation). They do not tell us what the company will be able to do in the future. How do we know that the uranium mine—which *cost,* say, $1,000,000 to find and mine—is not going to yield $100,000,000 in receipts, or maybe nothing?

None of this is revealed by the balance sheet's asset records—unless the corporation directors decide to make a prognosis of that future receipt stream, discount it into a present value, and record it under "goodwill" or "profits." But they don't do this, simply because they know how unreliable that is. Instead, they issue a report of operations and events along with their balance sheets. For example, United Nuclear Corporation reported in its 1963 annual report: "The outlook for widespread civilian and military use of nuclear energy for both power and propulsion improved greatly during the past year. The capability of the industry in the free world countries, based on presently known or reserve information, is estimated to be about 20,000 tons annually. This in the face of a projected annual amount demanded during the early 1970s of 40,000 tons, excluding military purchases." But the directors did not foresee that within a year the decision on a proposal to build another nuclear-powered airplane carrier would be negative. All the directors could do was report what was then known and make some clearly labeled forecasts, which other people can accept, reject, or revise at their volition.

Try to guess the purchase price of a share of common stock in United Nuclear Corporation in April 1970. Probably not less than $10? Actually the price was about $8. The book value is a measure only of the past costs of accumulating the assets—adjusted by a formal depreciation method. It is *not* a measure of what the assets would sell for now if disposed of piecemeal if the company were to be liquidated. Nor is it a measure of the value of the company's future net receipts from its business operations. The present value of its future operating earnings may be far above the costs of the assets it uses . . . as it was in our taxi example. An excess of stock price over book value is an indication of profitable prospects . . . it is not an indication of deception of the stock holders. Nor is a stock price below the book value any evidence that it is a safe investment in the sense that if worst came to worst the company could sell off its assets and collect enough to pay each stock holder the book value. The book value is a measure neither of the piecemeal disposal value nor the value of the going enterprise as a whole. It is instead merely a formalized means of indicating the past costs of the owned assets, adjusted for depreciated use value by some formal method that often bears little if any relation to the future earnings prospects nor the decrease in current market demand for those assets.

In the present instance the demand and price for nuclear material and nuclear reactors had fallen so much that there was not much prospect the future earnings in the near future at least would have a present value that covered the costs of the assets now owned by the company (net of liabilities). However, if future events should change and that demand increase, possibly as environmental effects are more economically controlled, the stock price may rise. It sold in the past for nearly three times its present price. In early 1971 the price had risen to $12, now above the book value. Moral—forget book value for all practical purposes and look deeper into the company's situation.

United Nuclear Corporation
Income Statement, Year Ended March 31, 1970

Sales		$70,759,000
Costs and Expenses		
Costs of goods sold (labor, materials, power)	$54,501,000	
Depreciation of equipment and depletion of ore	6,665,000	
Selling and administrative	4,212,000	
Interest on debt	2,256,000	
Miscellaneous	51,000	67,685,000
Operating net income		$ 3,074,000
Share belonging to minority interest		294,000
Federal Income Tax (No provision for federal income tax because losses from prior years may be carried forward to current year to offset current income.)		
Net earnings		$2,780,000
Earnings per share		$.54

At the time the balance sheet situation is disclosed the company also issues its *Income Statement,* a statement of its receipts and expenditures during the year ending at the date of the balance sheet. United Nuclear reported net earnings of $.54 per share of common stock for the year ending March 31, 1971. That is about 5% per year on the value of a share of stock, hardly a competitive return compared to yields available on secure bonds (about 6%) or on common stocks (around 12%). Why the difference? The current earnings may in the future grow to large earnings. It is the present value of all those future earnings that is reflected in the stock price.

A company with expectations of rapidly rising future earnings will have a high present value on its stock, but low *current* earnings. Stocks with different patterns of future earnings should not be compared by looking at only their current earnings. A company with negative earnings this year but with superb prospects of large positive earnings in the future could be worth more than one with positive earnings this year but no prospects for future earnings growth. The ratio of stock price to current earnings is a highly misleading basis for comparing two stocks—although many people naively use that ratio.

a. What do you think owners' beliefs must be about the future earnings?
b. If reported earnings in the next few years stayed at about the current rate, what do you think would have happened to the price of the stock?
c. Look up the price of this stock now. Get its reports of earnings and latest balance sheet from *Moody's Manuals of Industrials* at your library or any local stockbroker's office and check your answer to "b."

2 "A corporation owned by one person is the same as a proprietorship." Do you agree? If so, why? If not, why not?

3 "Continuity of a corporation means that if any or all of the current owners of the corporation die, the corporation continues as a unit of ownership." Do you agree?

4 Why is the corporation the dominant form of ownership of very large conglomerations of wealth?

5 Is it a disadvantage of the corporation that not every stockholder can make the controlling decisions? That the control is dispersed? That some people who own less than half of the corporation can make controlling decisions?

6 "Business firms exist because some people do not have enough wealth to own the capital equipment and machinery with which they can work more efficiently." Evaluate.

7 A friend of yours, a brilliant engineer and administrator, is operating a business. You propose to bet on his success and offer him some money to expand his operations. A corporation is formed allotting you 40 and him 60 percent of the common stock. You invest $30,000. This is often described as separation of ownership from control, since he now has the majority controlling vote. Would you ever be willing to invest wealth in such a fashion—that is, give up control while retaining ownership in certain property rights? Why?

8 A criticism of the modern corporation is that the management or directors, by virtue of their central position, are able to collect proxies (rights to cast votes of stockholders) from the other stockholders; and as a result the management is in a powerful position and cannot be easily dislodged. It has been said that "the typical small stockholder can do nothing about changing management and that under ordinary circumstances management can count on remaining in office; and often the proxy battle is fought to determine which minority group shall control." Take the assertions as being correct.

a. Does it follow that stability of management in "ordinary circumstances" reveals some kind of weakness of stockholders?

b. Does it follow that a typical small stockholder "should" be able to turn out management?

c. If a minority group succeeds in getting a majority of stock votes, does this mean that a minority controls or that a majority controls through the medium of a minority group? Is this to be interpreted in the same way that political parties consisting of a group of organized politicians have elections to see which minority group shall control the government? Why or why not?

9 a. In analyzing the behavior of corporation management and directors, why is it pertinent to distinguish among nonprofit or publicly regulated, profit-limited corporations on the one hand, and private-property, for-profit business corporations on the other?

b. Which do you think would be more marked by self-perpetuating management and stockholder lethargy? Why?

c. Which do you think would show more discrimination in employment practices according to race and religion? Why?

10 Suppose you operate a cleaning establishment and expect to obtain $8,000 revenue from use of a new cleaning machine during the first year. (Assume you receive all of it by the end of the first year.) Also you expect to receive $15,000 during the second year. (Again assume all revenue is received by the end of that year.) Assume the costs are the same as for the cleaning machine in question 5 of Chapter 15. For convenience, all the data are summarized in the following schedule:

	Beginning of 1st Year	End of 1st Year	End of 2nd Year
Purchase	$5,000	0	0
Expenses	0	$6,000	$ 6,000
Resale	0	0	1,500
Receipts	0	8,000	15,000
Net Receipts	_____	_____	_____
Present Values	_____ +	_____ +	_____ = _____ (Profit)

a. What is the profit implied by your expectations?

b. Suppose that within a month after you have installed the machine, other people form expectations consistent with yours; however, despite their efforts to open similar cleaning establishments, your revenue forecast will still be accurate (since it was in part based on anticipations that other people would soon copy your techniques). At that time the capital value of your business will be revised upward with a profit of $5,491. When do you realize that profit?

11 On July 15, 1964 Chrysler Corporation president announced that earnings for the past quarter year (April–June) were up 20 percent over the preceding quarter and 50 percent over the similar quarter a year before. At the beginning of the quarter reported on April 1, the price of Chrysler common stock was $70. On June 30 it was $65, and on the day this news was reported the stock *fell* from $65 to $60 because investors expected an even bigger earning. Did the owners of the company have any profits during the quarter from April 1 to June 30? Two years later (1966) the price had fallen to $40. Did Chrysler have profits over that two-year period? Did the owners? Is there any difference between profits to Chrysler and profits to Chrysler owners? What is its price now?

12 You buy some stock for $100. A month later it has risen to a high of $150. Another month later it is down to $125. Have you had a profit or a loss?

13 "Very few corporations lose wealth, and still fewer go broke." Do you agree? What evidence can you cite?

14 Joseph Thagworthy has a stable of race horses and a breeding farm. The two, although operated as a business, lose him over $50,000 annually. Yet he continues year after year because he enjoys the activity more than if he spent a similar sum for travel or conventional types of consumption activities.
a. Would it be correct to say that he is maximizing his wealth in that business?
b. Would it be correct to say he is maximizing his utility?
c. Do you think an increase in the losses would induce an increase in that kind of activity? What does economic theory postulate about that?

15 A young college teacher hits upon a sparkling teaching style and is rewarded with a higher salary. Has he had a profit? Explain.

16 An actress, after years in the movies, suddenly hits it big and obtains an enormously larger salary. Has she a profit? Three months later she begins to get fat, and in a year her contracts are canceled. Has she experienced a loss in any sense different from that suffered by Ford when it introduced the Edsel?

17 Estimate the present value of your future earnings. Project your earnings until age 65. Then obtain the present value of that projection, using a 10 percent rate of interest. Can you promise your fiancée that you are now worth over $200,000?

18 "Paper profits and losses are not real profits or losses." Do you agree? If so, why? If not, why not?

19 "Under a socialist system, profits and losses are eliminated." Comment.

20 "Private property permits selective, discretionary risk bearing." Comment.

21 Contrast socialism and private property as means of distributing risks of profits and losses.

22 What is the relationship between the right to buy and sell and the distribution of profits and losses?

23 For what events is the distribution of risk the same in socialist and capitalist systems? (Hint: How about divorce, cancer, baldness, homeliness, having only female children, being left-handed?)

24 Our laws and customs reflect the assignments of risk bearing. A person who owns land as private property must bear the consequences of changes in the value of that land if people move away or no longer value that location so highly. Similarly, if he catches cold or breaks his leg or becomes hard of hearing and can no longer earn so large an income, he must bear the consequences.
a. Would you advocate that people bear the wealth losses to their private property regardless of cause (aside from legal recourse to violators of property rights)?
b. Would you want a homeowner to bear the consequences of a meteorite's falling on his house? Fire from using gasoline in the house? Flood damage to houses near rivers? Income loss from cancer? Blindness?
c. Who do you think should bear the loss if the individual does not?
d. Why would you draw the line differently in different cases? What is the criterion you used?
e. In each case, do you think people's behavior would be affected according to the risk bearing involved?
f. Would you allow people to agree to take on certain risks in exchange for not bearing other risks, if two people could make a mutually agreeable partition and exchange of such risks? How would that differ from a system of private-property rights?

25 "It is better to buy from a firm that is losing money than from one that is making a profit, because the former firm is charging too low a price while the latter is charging more than costs." Evaluate.

26 "I bought some stock at $70 a share. It has fallen to $55, but I'm going to hold it until it rises to $70 so I can avoid taking a loss." What is wrong with that reasoning—even assuming that the stock price does shortly thereafter rise to $75?

27 Suppose it were true that rich people got rich exclusively from profits. Suppose further that those who received the profits were no smarter, no more foresighted, no nicer, no harder working, no more productive than other people. Does this mean that their profits are "undeserved" and that the rich people perform no service? Would you advocate taxing away those profits? Why or why not?

28 A liquor-retailing license in California recently was sold for over $40,000. The seller was the person who initially got the license from the state at a cost of $6,000. Did the subsequent buyer get a profit in the form of a monopoly rent? Did the initial licensee get a profit in the form of a monopoly rent?

29 **a.** Which of the following represent some wealth based on monopoly rents? TV station in Texas, United Air Lines, General Motors, teamsters in Teamsters' Union, General Electric Company, American Telephone and Telegraph Company, Frank Sinatra, beet-sugar farm land owners, local electric company, Aluminum Company of America, savings and loan banks, professional baseball teams.
b. In each case in which you think wealth based on monopoly rent is present, how would you test for its presence? And how would you measure the amount of monopoly rent?
c. In each case where you think it is present, who gets it?

30 International Business Machines common stock sells at a price one hundred times as great as the accountants' reported current annual earnings. The stock of Allegheny Ludlum Corporation, a steel producer, sells at about ten times its accountants' reported "earnings." Assume that the same accounting principles are used in each firm. What do you think will happen to the price of each firm's stock if in the next reporting period each firm reports earnings that are *unchanged* from the preceding period? Explain.

Production by Firms in Price-Takers' Open Markets

17

IN the two preceding chapters we explained in some detail how costs are measured and that production is carried on primarily by business firms seeking profits. In this chapter we investigate the adjustment a price-taker firm makes to its demand situation and also inquire into the total supply adjustment of the *industry* (of the which the firm is but one component). We shall draw some conclusions about the effect of a price change on the output and wealth of a firm, and we shall also characterize the way the industry supply depends on costs and how it affects price and output available to society. Remember that business firms have two types of roles: (1) a personal *purposive* role to increase the wealth of the members of the firm, and (2) a resultant social, and *functional* role to produce goods in response to present and anticipated market demands. The purposive role—wealth increases for the members of the business firm—has the effect (function) of relating the production activities of the team members to society's market demand. To see how this occurs with price-takers is the basic objective of this chapter. (In the next we consider price-searchers in open markets, and then in Chapter 19 we inquire into the effects of restrictions on entry to markets.)

Influence of Demand Changes on Output

A change in demand could mean a change in (1) the *rate* at which the demanders wish to consume or (2) the total *volume* the community demands. For example, an electric-power company may place an order for 120 generators to be delivered five per month for twenty-four months; shortly thereafter it may modify that decision and increase its demand by ordering sixty more to be delivered in a third year at the same rate of five per month. Only the *volume* of demand, not the rate, has increased. At the other extreme, the buyer may increase his *rate* demand from 120 in two years to 120 in one year. Or he may increase his demand for *both* rate and volume—from five per month for two years, to ten per month for two years. We will clarify cost principles by examining a *joint, proportional increase in both rate and volume* over a given period.[1]

We shall not conduct a sequence of analyses, each designed to tell what happens one day, one week, one month, one year, and so on, after an initial disturbance. Instead, for convenience of exposition, the analysis of the supply reaction will first be in terms of the response of *existing* firms. Then, adjustments in the number of firms are introduced.

Initially, we shall assume that each producer knows the costs of his possible programs, that he is already in business with acquired equipment, and that the characteristic relationship between costs and production is shown in Table 17–1. These are the "short-run" costs of various outputs, given that his equipment is that most appropriate for an output of eight or nine units per year. If the firm planned *initially* for one of the other

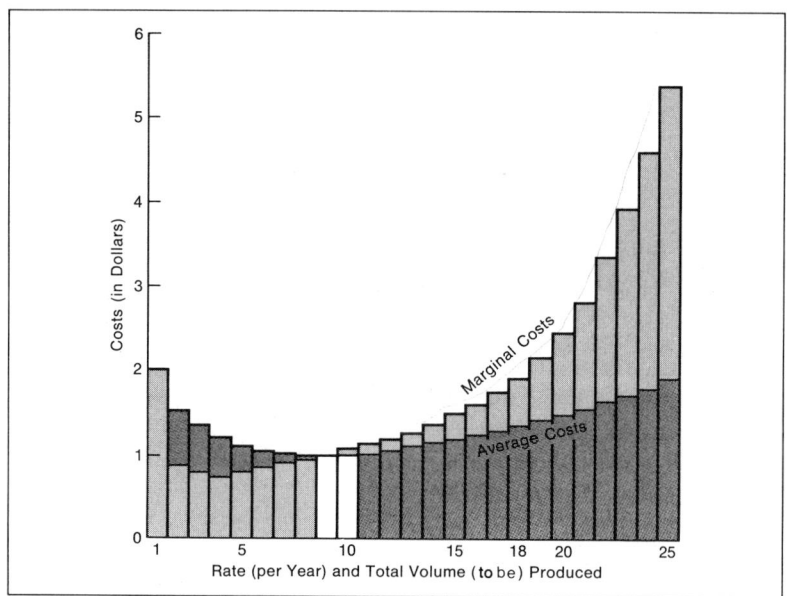

FIGURE 17–1. Marginal, Average Total, and Average Variable Cost for Alternative Output Programs for One Year

This chart plots the data in columns 3, 4, and 5 from Table 17–1. It shows that, with sufficiently large rates of output, marginal costs increase and so do average costs. Average-variable-cost curve is below average total cost by an amount exactly equal to the average acquisition cost (per unit of output). Supply response of this price-taker firm at any market price is given by the output at which the marginal cost rises to the market price (for any price greater than the lowest average variable cost—in this case 85 cents). Output will not continue indefinitely by this firm if price stays below 99 cents.

---

[1] In our earlier discussion of production problems, we could, without causing confusion, treat the increase as an increase in the demand for either the volume or rate or both. But now that production can be changed in at least rate and volume, with different effects on costs, the kind of demand change will have to be made explicit.

possible outputs, it would have selected other equipment and then the costs of these other outputs would differ from those shown in Table 17–1. But as it is, the costs shown here are those that the firm faces given that it now has the equipment that it does.

TABLE 17–1. Costs of One Year's Output (Indicated Rate per Year and Volume for One Year)

(1)	(2)	(3)	(4)	(5)	(6)	(7)	(8)	(9)	(10)	(11)
1	$ 2.00	$2.00	$2.00	$1.00	$ 1.10	$1.10	$ −.90	$2.00	$ 2.00	$ .00
2	2.90	.90	1.45	.95	2.20	1.10	−.70	2.00	4.00	1.10
3	3.70	.80	1.23	.90	3.30	1.10	−.40	2.00	6.00	2.30
4	4.45	.75	1.11	.86	4.40	1.10	−.05	2.00	8.00	3.55
5	5.25	.80	1.05	.85	5.50	1.10	+.25	2.00	10.00	4.75
6	6.10	.85	1.02	.85	6.60	1.10	+.50	2.00	12.00	5.90
7	7.00	.90	1.00	.86	7.70	1.10	+.70	2.00	14.00	7.00
8	7.95	.95	.99	.87	8.80	1.10	+.85	2.00	16.00	8.05
9	8.95	1.00	.99	.88	9.90	1.10	+.95	2.00	18.00	9.05
10	10.00	1.05	1.00	.90	11.00	1.10	+1.00*	2.00	20.00	10.00
11	11.10	1.10	1.01	.92	12.10	1.10	+1.00*	2.00	22.00	10.80
12	12.25	1.15	1.02	.94	13.20	1.10	+.95	2.00	24.00	11.75
13	13.50	1.25	1.04	.96	14.30	1.10	+.80	2.00	26.00	12.50
14	14.85	1.35	1.06	.99	15.40	1.10	+.65	2.00	28.00	13.15
15	16.30	1.45	1.09	1.02	16.50	1.10	+.20	2.00	30.00	13.70
16	17.85	1.55	1.12	1.05	17.60	1.10	−.25	2.00	32.00	14.15
17	19.55	1.70	1.15	1.09	18.70	1.10	−.85	2.00	34.00	14.45
18	21.45	1.90	1.19	1.13	19.80	1.10	−1.65	2.00	36.00	14.55*
19	23.55	2.10	1.23	1.18	20.90	1.10	−2.65	2.00	38.00	14.45
20	25.95	2.40	1.29	1.25	22.00	1.10	−3.95	2.00	40.00	14.05
21	28.75	2.80	1.37	1.32	23.10	1.10	−5.65	2.00	42.00	13.25
22	32.05	3.30	1.46	1.41	24.20	1.10	−7.85	2.00	44.00	11.95
23	35.95	3.90	1.56	1.52	25.30	1.10	−10.65	2.00	46.00	10.05
24	40.55	4.60	1.69	1.65	26.40	1.10	−14.15	2.00	48.00	7.45
25	46.00	5.45	1.83	1.80	27.50	1.10	−18.50	2.00	50.00	4.00

(1) Annual rate *and* volume.
(2) Capital value measure of total cost of which $1 is sunk acquisition cost.
(3) Marginal cost (for one-unit increment in annual rate *and* volume of output).
(4) Cost per unit of output.
(5) Variable or operating cost per unit of output.
(6) Total receipts before demand increase.
(7) Marginal receipts (at price of $1.10).
(8) Profits (at price of $1.10).
(9) Marginal receipts (at price of $2).
(10) Total receipts (at price of $2).
(11) Profits (at price of $2).
 *Maximum-profit programs.

Short-run average costs are divided into two categories: average *total* costs (*including* a fixed, sunk cost of $1) per unit of output (column 4), and the average *variable* costs (excluding that sunk cost) per unit of output (column 5). The remaining columns give demand, revenue, and profit data. This producer is selling in a price-takers' market and can sell all he cares to sell at the going market price of $1.10 per unit. For each output the excess of *total* revenue over total cost is given in column 8; the excess of total revenue over *total variable* cost would be exactly $1 larger for each output (by the $1 of sunk cost).

Which output maximizes the firm's wealth—that is, gives the greatest profit? If the market price is $1.10, the wealth-maximizing output is ten units (or eleven). Total costs are $10. Total revenue is $11. Profit is $1. At all other outputs the profits are smaller, as you can see by looking at column 8.

The characteristic cost conditions can be portrayed more usefully, for subsequent analysis, by the cost *curves* in Figure 17–2. The bars in Figure 17–1 are replaced by the curves. Notice their characteristic shape. They *may* fall at first, *may* have a near-flat portion (possibly over a large range of outputs), and ultimately for larger outputs certainly *will* rise, at a rate that increases until an upper limit to the productive capacity is approached (cost increase becomes practically infinite). Nothing more should be inferred from the particular shapes of the curves.

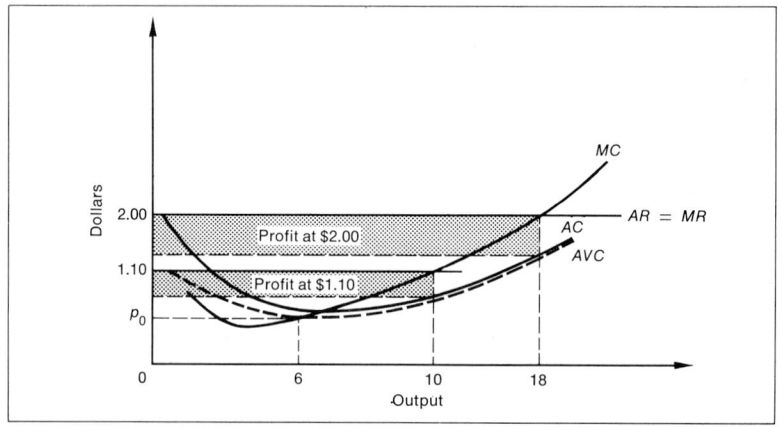

FIGURE 17–2. Cost and Demand Facing Price-Taker

At price of $2, wealth-maximizing output is eighteen units, which exceeds wealth-maximizing output (eleven units) when price is lower ($1.10). Output would cease if price fell below p_0 and was expected to stay below p_0. Dotted curve is short-run average variable cost, AVC. Light area below $2 demand line (average revenue equals marginal revenue) and above dashed line (average cost at output of eighteen units) is a measure of profits. It equals (price minus average cost) multiplied by output, that is ($2 − $1.19) × 18 = $14.58.

Three cost curves are drawn. One is the average (per unit of output) *total* short-run costs curve, *including* the past fixed, sunk cost that this firm would have to cover if it were to be said *in retrospect* that the decision to buy the particular equipment *and produce* had been profitable. The dashed curve, the average short-run *variable* cost, *AVC*, shows the cost per unit of output *after* the firm is *already in business with acquired equipment*. As it continues to produce, equipment will wear out and the cost situation will change.[2]

---

[2] The variable-cost curve *will shift* toward (and ultimately become) a long-run planning cost curve, which shows for each possible output the per-unit costs of production with new equipment that is optimal (least costly) for that particular output. The curve labeled *LRAC* in Figure 15–4 is a long-run average-cost curve. The average *variable* cost curve will shift to and become the total average-cost curve, in the long run.

Production by Firms in Price-Takers' Open Markets   315

Although the meaning of these curves has already been detailed in Chapter 15, for assurance and ready familiarity the student is urged to relate each curve to the appropriate column of Table 17–1.

Wealth-Maximizing Output

On Figure 17–2 (the tops of the bars of Figure 17–1 have been replaced by smooth lines), the horizontal line labeled $AR = MR$ at $1.10 is the demand line facing the producer. He can sell at $1.10 as many as he cares to: the line extends out far beyond his production at that cost. He would sell none if he raised *his* price. If the *market* price were higher, say $2, the demand line for this producer would be at a height of $2 and extend beyond his production capability at that cost.

We now can develop the power of this diagrammatic approach by answering the question, "What affects the profitable output program?" First, the higher the market price, the larger is the output that maximizes his wealth. That wealth-maximizing output is, by definition, the output at which the rising marginal-cost curve intersects the demand line. At any smaller output, an increase of output would augment receipts more than it would total costs. In economic jargon, for any smaller output program the forsaken marginal revenue (given by the horizontal price line) exceeds the marginal cost; at all larger outputs, marginal costs exceed marginal revenue. It is to ascertain the maximum wealth output that we draw the marginal-cost curve and the marginal-revenue line (coinciding with the demand line for every seller in a *price-takers'* market).

But it may validly be objected, we don't know any producer's actual cost curves, so how can we tell what his wealth-maximizing output program really is? We can't. But our purpose is not to tell each producer what to do. Instead, our purpose is to characterize his *output response to demand changes*. The powerful and important generalization suggested by the analysis is that a larger demand and a higher price induces a larger output. The *supply curve* of a *price-taker* producer is given by his *marginal-cost curve*. That curve is a "supply curve" because it identifies for each price the output that the producer would provide. The higher the demand and the price, the greater his output; this is the important implication. *1, 2, 3, 4, 5*

Continue to Produce or Shut Down?

It is now seen why we distinguished between total average costs (including entry acquisition costs) and variable average costs. For each firm, there is a lower limiting price below which it will stop production. That lower limit is the lowest average *variable* (i.e., yet to be incurred) cost of all possible contemplated continued outputs. We show this by the dashed line at p_0 on Figure 17–2.

The portion of the marginal-cost curve above where it intersects the average-variable-cost curve (and it must intersect at the minimum average-variable-cost by logic of defined relationship between the two) indicates the supply schedule of contemplated outputs at each possible price. When price is below the average *total* cost, the producer will say he is losing money—meaning that his past (regretted) decision to enter the business lost him wealth. He will nevertheless continue temporarily to produce even at that low price, since he will not lose as much as he would if he shut down immediately and permanently. So long as he operates at any price over the minimum average *variable* operating cost, this excess will make his loss that much less. Ultimately, his equipment will be run down. But he will not incur new acquisition or substantial repair cost, because at the low price the projected receipts would cover only the subsequent variable operating costs, not new acquisition (or repair) costs. So he quits production.

We can summarize with a second generalization: Price can be less than the average total cost (including *past sunk* cost) without causing a producer *immediately* to stop production. Nothing like this was implied in our production examples of Chapters 12–14. Hence, to make the theory more valid we had to introduce a new element—the existence of durable capital goods for which the initial purchase price and immediate resale price differ. Or in general terms, once you make or buy capital goods you can't *at zero cost* unmake or sell them. Production is not reversible. In Chapters 12–14 we assumed, invalidly, that Mr. C could switch back and forth between production of X and Y at *no* switching or equipment-revision costs, but we have now incorporated that cost and adjusted our analysis.

6, 7

Market Supply: Aggregated Supplies of All Firms

The preceding discussion concentrated on the output adjustment of one firm. However, the market supply of a good is provided by many firms—which make up an *industry*. The proposition that an increased demand induces a larger output from a *firm* is easily converted into an *industry* proposition: The higher the price, the greater the industry output. *For each price, the sum of the outputs of all firms is the industry output.* The schedule of prices and associated industry outputs is the industry supply schedule.

To illustrate, *marginal-cost* data like those of Table 17–1 are shown in Figure 17–3 as a smooth line labeled MC_A, for Firm A. Also in that figure is the marginal-cost schedule (MC_B) for Firm B, which produces less at any given price. The total output of this industry (as if there were only two firms in the industry) is obtained by *adding the output (horizontal distance) of each firm's marginal-cost curve at any specified price (above the lowest average-variable-cost output of that firm)*. The summed curve, SS, is the industry supply curve. The *price-takers'* industry supply curve is the horizontal sum of the marginal-cost curves above each firm's minimum average variable cost. If the price were $2, the maximum-wealth production programs of Firms A and B would be X_A and X_B. At prices below $1.30, Firm B would shut down, while A would not shut down *immediately* unless prices were as low as 85 cents. These lower limits are their respective lowest average variable costs.

Figure 17–4 gives the same information as Figure 17–3, with the addition of a market demand curve, DD, which intersects the *industry* supply curve at the price of $2. According to the price-determination process outlined earlier, the price will be $2. The portions of the total output produced by Firms A and B are indicated by the distances OX_a and OX_b. In earlier chapters, we saw how price rationed the existing stock among the competing claimants; here we see that price also affects the production by each firm. Market price allocates in the sense that it both rations existing output and assigns production.

This demand and supply "intersection" price is the price at which each producer can sell all he wants to produce at that price, and each consumer can buy all he demands at that price. It is an *equilibrium* or *equilibrating* price, because it makes the amount demanded equal the amount of production evoked by that price. A higher price would

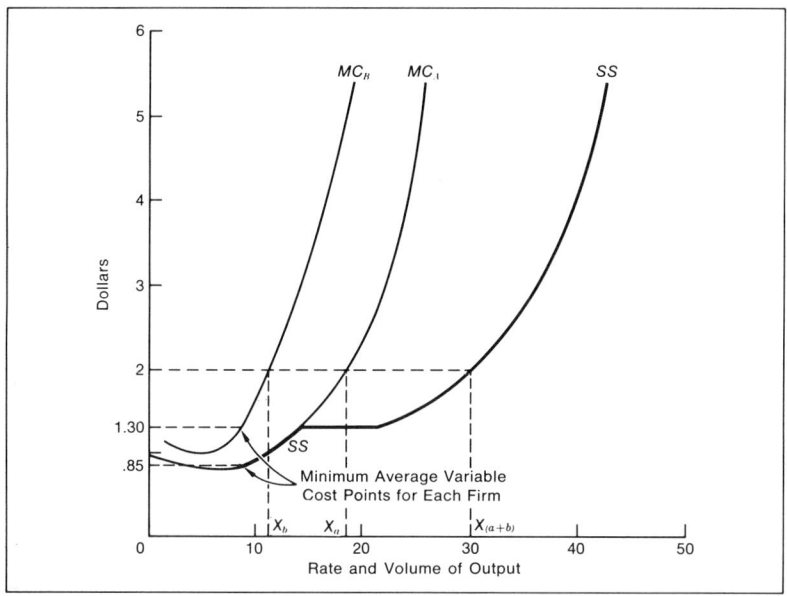

FIGURE 17–3. Marginal-Cost Curves Are Bases of Supply of Industry under Price-Takers' Market Conditions

Marginal-cost curves of two firms, above the minimum average costs (variable in short run, or total costs for long run) are summed horizontally to get output of industry—here shown as just two firms. At any specified market price, the output of the industry is shown by the marginal cost. Main implication is that higher price induces larger output, because at any price each firm will maximize its wealth if it produces that output at which its *marginal cost equals market price.* Firm can sell all of the output it cares to produce without affecting the price in the market.

reduce the amount demanded to less than the larger amount of production induced by that higher price; at a lower price the amount demanded exceeds the amount produced.

If demand increases (that is, if the demand schedule, DD, shifts to the right in Figure 17–4 to D_1D_1), price will be bid up—in the absence of effective laws, customs, or conventions preventing price changes. The higher demand and price induces each producer to increase output—as indicated by the SS curve, which shows larger output at higher prices (and marginal costs). And new producers are attracted, as C. Conversely, a reduced demand would, under the stipulated conditions, yield lower prices and a reduced output.

When demand and, hence, price change, not all firms change output by the same extent, because the *slopes* of their marginal-cost curves differ. For some firms the marginal-cost curves are steep and for some they are flat. As price rises in response to increases in demand, the former firms will not increase their output as much as the latter ones. If price should fall in response to demand decreases, some firms will reduce output and some will shut down before others do, the earlier ones being those with higher minimum average variable costs—*not* those that are poorer, smaller, or have less money on hand. Whether rich or poor, each firm shuts down not when wealth is exhausted but when continued operation at low prices would *reduce* wealth even more than shutting down.

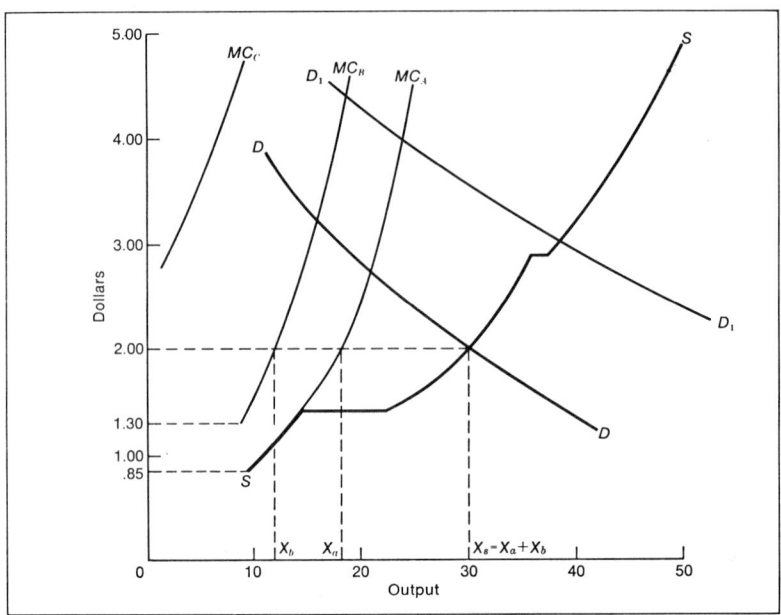

FIGURE 17-4. Demand and Supply and Output Determination in Price-Takers' Markets

As market demand increases, new firms are attracted by higher prices and wealth prospects. At a price of approximately $3, Firm C will be able to produce profitably. Supply of output by industry shows increased output with higher price because of (1) increased output by each firm which increases output to point where marginal costs equal price and (2) increased number of firms as price rises above minimum average costs of new potential firms. SS, the supply line, is the horizontal sums of the three firms' marginal-cost lines, above their minimum average costs.

Supply Response by Entry of New Firms: Long-Run Response

If price rises, new producers will be attracted. Firms that produce *only* when price and demand are high are higher *average*-cost firms; they cannot survive unless price is high. This fact is not indicated by their marginal costs (for every firm adjusts its output until the marginal costs have increased to the higher price so they all have the same marginal cost at their respective output rates). Many will be regarded as "marginal," "fringe" firms,[3] for if demand falls, the lower price will induce them to shut down. Potential firms on the "margin" will appear if demand and price rise sufficiently. If demand stays high, these firms become recognized as "established" firms, and in turn look on still higher-cost firms as constituting the new fringe of marginal, unreliable firms.

This is portrayed graphically in Figure 17-4 by the marginal-cost curve of Firm C, a high average-cost firm in the sense that the lowest price at which it will enter production is higher than for the other two firms shown.

---

[3] Do not confuse the average cost of a marginal firm with marginal cost.

A homely and easily observable example is that of parking-lot operators near a stadium. For big crowds, the parking fees are higher, and there are more high-cost parking lots available as local residents sell parking space in their driveways and yards. These "fly-by-night," fringe, temporary operators are disliked by the "established" operators. They appear when demand and price are high; prices are lower than if they did not appear.

However, the experienced student may note that established firms often do not raise their prices when demand increases temporarily—the fringe sellers seize the opportunity to sell at the higher prices. How do the fringe operators, who do not hesitate to take a higher price, contribute to *lower* prices—if they are the ones who in fact charge the higher price? There are two answers. Remember that "price" or consumer cost includes more than the monetary payment. People who cannot park in the "standard" lots overflow to surrounding areas. The price they must then pay is "walking farther." The cost imposed on the patrons of parking farther away and walking is greater than the parking fee of the fringe operators. How do we know? Simply because some people do prefer to pay more and walk less. Without the services of the fringe operators, the costs (pecuniary and nonpecuniary) imposed on patrons would be even higher—especially on those who do not get to park in the standard established parking lots.

When demand for building or farm products increases, the number of contractors and builders increases, and the number of farmers increases. In Washington, D. C., hundreds of people with full-time jobs elsewhere become taxi operators during "rush" hours. Steel mills operate some blast furnaces only during peak demands. Barber shops have chairs that are "idle" most, but *not* all of the time. The chairs represent high-cost, rather than excessive, capacity. Some firms use second and third shifts when demand warrants it, even though they are higher-cost ways of production. Later, if demand falls, the lower price makes it impossible to maintain so high a rate of production and still cover costs. Therefore, all firms reduce output and some begin to withdraw from that business. The displaced resources regretfully and complainingly revert to their next-best sources of income (which served as a measure of their costs).

"Sick" Industries

Another useful application of this economic analysis is to what are commonly called "sick" industries—"sick" because they allegedly have an "excessive" number of firms; "excessive" because most of the firms do such a small volume of business that most of them lose wealth. And as rapidly as old ones lose out and leave, new ones enter—only to experience a similar fate. There seems to be no long-run adjustment that restores the industry to a profitable or at least a nonloss balance. The more commonly cited examples of "sick" industries are retail groceries, bars, restaurants, night clubs, coal mines, gasoline stations, textile manufacturers, and farming.

People who make this argument usually point to long-term declining demand, foolish gambling, overestimation of one's ability, plain ignorance, or the low cost of entering the business. But upon closer study these explanations fall to the ground. In the first place, all firms in an industry could be losing wealth when demand is falling unexpectedly. There is nothing "sick" about a decreasing demand. In the second place, all firms could be losing wealth if the business provides a sufficiently large amount of nonpecuniary satisfaction, as is said to be the case for horse racing or novel writing or acting or owning baseball clubs. One man grows orchids and makes money and considers it a business; another grows orchids and loses money but regards it as a hobby or consumption activity. Everyone could lose money in some business if the fun of the business operation were great enough to be worth the losses. These considerations help to explain why some industries or occupations always run at a loss and seem never to reach a long-run adjustment to profitable operations.

But there is another consideration. In some industries the profits may be large for only a few winners, with the rest of the members losing money. In acting, writing, painting, and sports only a few seem to make a big success while the vast majority never make enough to justify the effort. Nothing in economic analysis says that an industry in which only a few make vast fortunes should not have a vast number of "failures." These failures (or is it more accurate to call them nonsuccesses?) entered in the hope that they might join the favored few, and they often remain despite years of frustration and disappointment.

There is the contention that an industry is sick because it has excess capacity that is almost never fully utilized (for example, barber shops and service stations). Only a naive observer would believe they should be constantly "fully" utilized. Some barber shops have chairs or barbers that are not utilized most of the time; but when demand hits its peaks, they are utilized, and it is precisely the peak demand that is served by this "apparent" overcapacity. How would you like to live in a community in which there were just enough barbers to cut everyone's hair if the barbers were always "fully" employed? Would you like to have to plan your purchases on some schedule that allowed you no opportunity to adjust to unexpected events? Would anyone argue that Palm Desert or Palm Beach has too many hotel rooms because most of them are empty during the summer and that there are too many ski resorts because they are idle most of the time, or that there are too many churches because all of them are empty almost all the time? If you think there are too many service stations, would you be prepared to let me assert that the one you happen to buy from is the one that should be abolished? Does Sak's Fifth Avenue have too many salesgirls because many or most of them are "idle" most of the time? Would you say two-bathroom houses are uneconomic because neither bathroom is fully utilized at all times? To ask any of these questions is to answer them all.

How Resource Values Direct Resource Uses

Equilibrium in the number of firms and in the industry's production means that the price is at the minimum total cost per unit of output of that firm whose minimum is the highest of any in this industry. An incentive for a new firm to enter would then reflect the belief that it would have lower costs, not that price had risen so as to attract new firms. If all firms had the same cost conditions as in Table 17–1, the price would be 99 cents at the long-run equilibrium. In fact, of course, not all firms have identical costs. Nevertheless, prices and hence costs of *productive resources* used by each firm will be changing so as to make *every* firm's minimum average cost of production equal to the market price of the output. How will this occur?

If we tie the lessons of the chapter on costs and profits and capital values to this chapter, we can see the elements of the process. When market demands change unpredictably (for example, for sports cars, compacts, miniskirts, wigs, polyunsaturated fats), prices of goods used to produce those consumer goods also change. Or the prices may be revised because someone discovers how to use resources in "better" ways than foreseen.

In either event, the earlier value placed on resources proves erroneous. Producers, seeking greater wealth, revise the allocation of their resources. Anyone who ignores the new demands sacrifices the gain or takes a loss of wealth. This higher productive value will increase the demand for the responsible resources. The increased value (profit) results in an *imputation* of that value into higher prices of the responsible resources.

The profit has been amalgamated into higher costs. The revised greater costs are reflections of the higher use values. It is not a contradiction that a profit (a gain in wealth) leads to an increase in cost. Profits are unforeseen gains in wealth, and the higher value of output of the resources means that costs of their use elsewhere are greater once their higher value of output is seen. To say that profits imply higher costs of subsequent production is to say both that the output is of greater value and that the cost of diverting responsible resources to other uses is higher. These increases are the two sides of the imputed "profit."

As an example of this imputation process, suppose I discover oil on my land. I can then sell the land with the oil rights to you and convert my wealth (including the profit) to cash. You will certainly count what you paid for the land and oil rights (and that includes my profit) in your costs of *subsequent* operation. Even if I had not sold my land and oil rights, *I* must count the cost of subsequent operation at the same high figure that *you* would. The costs do not depend upon *who* uses them. If these resources are used for any other purpose, the value will be less than their costs. The value which is actually ultimately realized may depend upon who uses them, but the present cost of using them does not.

The imputation process means that any firm that puts resources to higher-valued uses than any other firm will have to revise the value of those resources. This revaluation appears to the owner of those resources as a profit and to the user (whether or not he is also the owner) as a higher cost of *use*. (And then people will bid more for the goods.) To use the goods now means one uses more valuable goods. Profits and losses not only reveal unforeseen *changes* in value of particular resources but also *direct* those resources to their higher-valued uses (as judged ultimately by the consumers' market).[4] The quicker and more complete the market's revaluation of assets and recalculation of costs, the more quickly will resources be directed in accord with highest-valued uses, whatever may be the value criterion used for this purpose.

The redirection of resources in response to a change in demand extends through a long chain of substitutions. If, for example, as a result of an increased demand, more wheat is to be produced, resources must be released from production of some other goods. Resources are transferred into wheat production as their owners seek greater wealth. Land transferred to wheat is taken from oats, corn, and building sites, and thus their supply will fall and their price increase. Other land will then be used for corn and oats—land formerly used for, say, cotton, barley, grazing land, parks, and potential housing or industrial sites. Not only land but also labor and other resources are diverted

---

[4] In Chapter 13, we defined the cost of a given use of resources by one person as the highest *alternative* sacrificed value of output of those resources, seeming to exclude the value of their *present* use. But we now see that a more general conception of costs consists of imputing to a given resource a market value which reflects its highest possible value in *any* line of activity, including the present one. Costs of resources in a particular occupation stem not only from *alternative uses,* but also from alternative *users.* Even if my land is good only for oil production (i.e., it has no alternative uses) it still has a value, which must be taken into account, because other people are willing to bid for it.

to wheat. Some laborers who would otherwise work as barbers, carpenters, or gasoline-station attendants devote more time to wheat production. And their places are partly filled by resources from still other occupations. The long chain of substitutions and shifting of resources is so broad and extensive that each one of the many effects on output of other final consumers' goods may be so slight as to be hardly noticeable over the perturbation of the many other everyday events. For this reason we are sometimes misled into thinking that some more of a good can be produced without producing less of some other, be it leisure or lingerie.

In sum, if any firm has people or resources that enable it to produce at lower average cost than other firms, the value of that special resource or people will be bid up as others compete for it. Its price will rise (because the profit is imputed to the responsible resource) until at that higher value it no longer yields a lower cost to the firm.

Consequence of Basing Output on Wealth Maximizing

According to the data in Table 17–1, although the wealth-maximizing industry output program at a market price of $2 is eighteen units, this producer could produce twenty-five and still make a profit. But in the interests of his own wealth, he does not. There is a temptation to call this restriction socially wasteful, because there appears to be under-production of this particular product. However, although the price does exceed *average* costs, it does not exceed *marginal* costs. Consequently, if this producer were to expand his output beyond eighteen units, he would use resources worth more than $2 (that is what marginal costs measure), and he would be selling to people who value the extra output at only $2—which is *less* than the costs of the extra output. A larger output would *not* be preferred by consumers. Therefore, the price-taking producer, by holding his output rate to eighteen units per year in order to maximize his wealth, is not "underproducing," even though he could produce more without wiping out all his profit.

Ironically, this implication of wealth-maximizing producers with free access to a price-takers' market was developed by socialists. Socialists asked what "should" be the output, and when they used the criterion that resources should provide the greatest value as judged by individual consumers and producers, they noticed the implication that a private-property system of wealth maximizers with free access to a price-takers' market gave precisely that result. Everyone was embarrassed—the socialists because this provided an "argument" for capitalist markets and the capitalists because, much as they would have liked this "justification" of their activity, not all of them could validly claim to be selling in open markets or even defending open markets. Although some discussion and argumentation about each system hinges on this kind of criterion of productive and allocative efficiency, there are other important considerations: "freedom," culture, and social behavior, which we shall not discuss here.

10, 11

Adjustments without Full Information

With market-revealed values of goods, there is no necessity for anyone to have *full* information about all possible costs of various programs in order for a higher demand and price to induce a greater output in a price-takers' market. There are forces inducing a larger output if demand increases—and a smaller output if demand decreases—in a private-property, open-market economy. We examine some of them now.

In the first place, many producers do keep records and compile data with which to estimate their own costs. They have data to increase the probability of being near the wealth-maximizing output. They know that when demand rises and permits a higher price, an expanded output becomes more profitable. If their output had been less than the wealth-maximizing amount, the incentive to an increased output is now even stronger. If the output had been too large, the incentive is again to increase it. The wealth-maximizing potential output is larger, whether or not each producer knows exactly what that output is. All the forces are now stronger for a larger output.

Second, even for those who may not compute costs in an endeavor to find the wealth-maximizing output, the increase in demand means that the set of profitable output programs is larger than formerly. Even if every firm picked outputs at random, those that picked larger outputs would be more profitable than those that picked smaller output programs. The observed or revealed profits will be greater for the producers of the larger outputs. Imitation of more profitable producers will expand output.

Third, a powerful force toward the wealth-maximizing output is the competitive actions of people. If the demand for wheat should increase, a corn farmer will more probably shift his land into wheat production. This would *not* be done by exhortations or appeals invoking the national or social interest. The prospect of greater personal wealth can be realized either by changing production in the greater wealth direction or by renting or selling his farm land and resources to others who will. Prices of productive resources reflect valuations not merely by current owners but by *other* people, who offer to buy or rent the resources. When other people think the use value of a piece of land has risen in response to higher demands for its potential products, the current owner can capture the presently perceived higher capital value of that future product. The important point is that resources are transferred to higher-valued uses as people seek greater wealth—if the resources are salable as private property.

Timing of Supply Responses

Not all producers make output adjustments at the same time. Some find it economical to delay the adjustment. This deferred output is often referred to as a "longer-run" output—in the sense that the run of time prior to the output is longer.

Lower costs of later action are a direct implication of the fundamental cost proposition that higher rates of production are more expensive. Immediate action requires a higher rate of use of existing resources. Overtime, premium delivery prices, greater use of higher-cost resources to hasten output are only a few of the cost-increasing factors involved. However, to defer indefinitely in order to get lower costs will reduce the value of the output. There is some lower limit of costs, below which they will not be reduced by any practical deferment. These lowest-cost, or long-run output, programs represent the ultimate adjustment of inputs.

Summary of Output Response

The production and market-price effects of an increase in demand can be generalized in summary form. Starting at an initial full-equilibrium price and output position, the rate of output can be quickly increased only at very high costs; with time the output rate can be increased more cheaply. This relationship of costs to time of output can be suggested graphically, by two supply curves: one for the early reaction, and one for the later

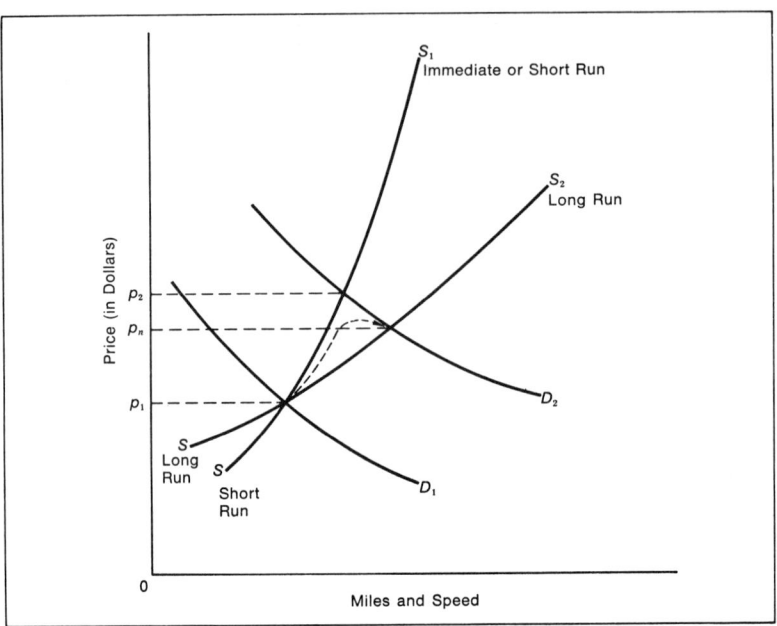

FIGURE 17–5. Supply Curves for Various Adjustment Dates for Various Outputs

Starting at the initial equilibrium situation, with price p_1, as demand increases, its intersection with supply will slide along S_1, the intermediate, or short-run, supply, which shows increased production from existing firms. In time, new firms will be attracted or new productive equipment will be installed by incumbent firms and outputs will be indicated by long-run supply curve, S_2. Short-run supply curve is summation of incumbent firms' marginal-cost curves. Long-run supply curve is sum of amounts firms (including new firms with new equipment) could produce at each price without losses.

extreme limiting response. Figure 17–5 shows "before-and-after" situation. Demand, at D_1 with price at p_1, has increased to D_2. As it did, price rose and then fell along a path suggested by the dotted line as the larger output was forthcoming—to the long-run equilibrium at p_n. We cannot indicate the exact course of the price. All that can be deduced is that, depending upon how much and how rapidly the demand increases, price will move in some fashion toward the long-run equilibrium at p_n, as the output adjustment takes place.

By definition, the long-run equilibrium involves an equality of price and minimum average costs and stable output in terms of industry output and number of firms. There will always be some firms expanding and others contracting (for example, the owner is aging, the firm has lost its special abilities, population is shifting).

Illustrative Analysis: Effects of a Tax

Uses of resources and outputs of consumer goods are affected by many factors other than changes in demand. Technology of production, or supply of productive resources may change. One factor that especially lends itself to instructive analysis is the imposition of a tax on the production or purchase of some good.

Tax on all producers in industry: Price and output effect. Suppose that the producers of playing cards are taxed 50 cents for each deck. This tax increases each firm's marginal costs by 50 cents, and it adds 50 cents to the average cost of each deck. Summing the new higher marginal-cost curves over all the firms of the industry yields a smaller supply curve, as illustrated in Figure 17–6. Before the tax, the price was 75 cents. Each firm, now operating on a higher marginal-cost curve, will be induced to reduce its output *at the initial price* from X_1 to X_2 in Figure 17–6. The reduced *industry* supply to the market will push up price, which will induce each firm to restore *part* of the output—back to X_3. Our first conclusion is that the higher tax raised costs but price rose only *because the supply decreased*. The effect on price is through the effect on industry supply, and only because the higher tax decreased the industry supply did the price rise.

Wealth effect. The price is increased by less than the tax on each deck—namely, by 25 cents (to $1 from 75 cents). Part of the tax is avoided by reducing the rate of output, so that the output is at a lower point on the marginal-cost curve. But this also means that some of the resources used in producing playing cards are no longer as valuable to the firm. This decrease in resource worth reflects the lower net price to the playing card

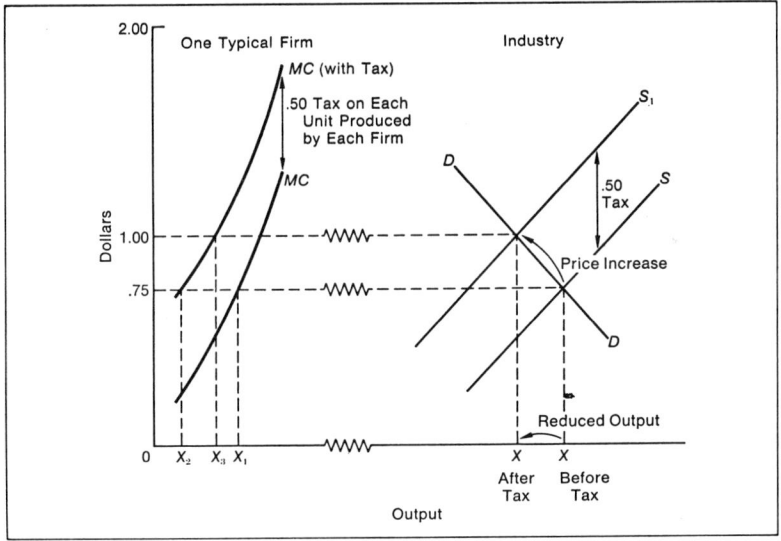

FIGURE 17–6. Price and Output Effect of Tax on Each Unit Produced or Sold

Tax is levied on output of playing cards of all firms in industry. Supply curve shifts upward to incorporate taxes of 50 cents per unit. This reduces output at the old price and the price moves up to $1. Higher price results from the smaller supply function. Unless tax affects supply curve, price cannot be affected. Price rises by less than tax because, at smaller output, marginal and average costs are lower. Part of tax is revealed as a higher price to consumer and a smaller rate of consumption; another part is reflected in reduced wealth value of resources used in production. Tax is borne by consumers and by owners of capital goods and labor services used in this industry.

producer after the tax that must be paid. Thus, we see that the total tax receipts (tax per deck times number now produced) are accounted for in part by a higher price to consumers and in part by a lower value of resources used to manufacture the taxed good. If someone says that taxes are all ultimately borne by the consumer of the taxed good, we can see the error in that statement. Instead, *part* of the tax is borne by consumers in the form of higher prices and fewer decks of cards, and part is borne by the owners of the resources, whose wealth fell at the time the tax was announced. Be careful not to confuse the effect on the wealth of those who own resources useful primarily in card production at the time the tax is announced with that of those who purchase those resources afterward. New buyers will make offers that reflect the lower capital value of the future receipts *net* of the taxes that must be paid for as long as the tax exists, which we assume is for "many" years. This imposes the wealth loss on the owners of these special resources at the time of the announcement of the tax.

But this is not the end of the adjustment. In the long run the stock of resources devoted to card making will be further reduced, and the output will be smaller than the immediate or short-run response, as can be seen in Figure 17–7. The longer-run adjustment in price and output includes the adjustment in all the resources in all the firms making cards. When this final adjustment is achieved, the price of cards will be high enough so that the price net of tax will cover the cost of *replacing* or maintaining the smaller stock of resources. The reduction in output of just cards is not a measure of the total output consequences of the tax; some resources that would have produced cards are now directed to other goods. But these other goods are less valuable, in the opinion of consumers, than that of the "unproduced" cards. We know this because, without the tax, the cards were preferred; that is why they were formerly being produced. However, there are two further considerations. First, it is sometimes argued that taxes are imposed on goods that *should* not be produced so extensively because they have bad side effects. Thus, some people argue for taxes on alcoholic drinks, gambling, night clubs, tobacco, and gasoline engines. Second, it is alleged, the tax proceeds are spent by the government for goods that are "more important." Educators and parents commonly advocate taxes on cigarettes, alcohol, etc., in order to permit more educational expenditure—facilitated by resources released from card production.

This analysis of the response of price, output, and wealth to a tax is very similar to that for a change in the price, unaccompanied by any change of productive power, of some resource used in making cards.

Tax on one firm only. Suppose the tax had been levied on *just one* producer. His wealth-maximizing output rate would be smaller. Could *he* therefore raise his price? No. Without a similar tax on the other producers, the market supply curve of the *industry* does not shift by a perceptible amount. In this case, *his* output and wealth fall more than if the tax had been levied against all producers. And he has no way to recoup part of his wealth by a higher price. If he tried to raise prices, his buyers would simply shift to other sellers.

Passing on higher costs. The tax discussion shows what is erroneous in the common belief that whenever a person's costs are increased he can obtain a matching higher price for his services. This misconception rests on misunderstanding the connection between costs, supply, and demand. Higher costs cannot be passed on to the buyer simply by raising the price. What is necessary is that a sufficient rise in costs must affect a large

14, 15

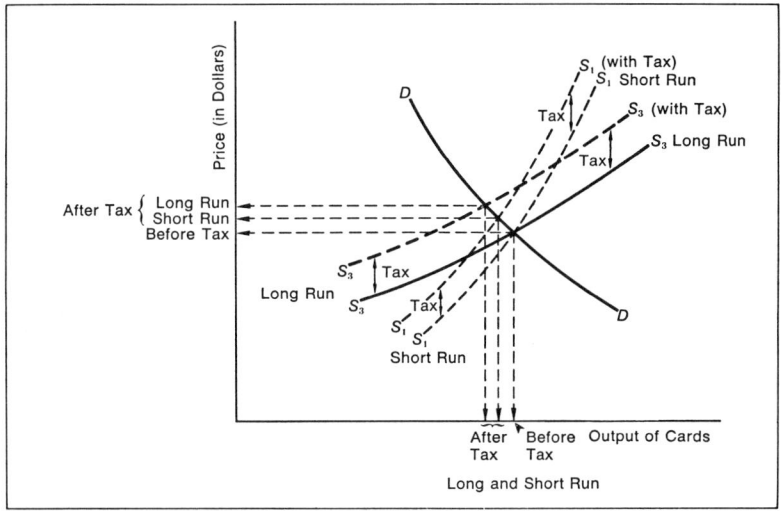

FIGURE 17-7. Price and Output Effects, Long- and Short-Run, of a Per-Unit Tax on Playing Cards

The longer the amount of time allowed after a tax increase the greater the effect on the amount supplied at any price—and the flatter the supply curve (reflecting withdrawal of resources from the industry). The demand curve in the diagram represents both the long and the short run. But if we remember that long-run demand response is more elastic, the demand appropriate for the long-run supply will be flatter than the one for the short-run supply. Draw in a new demand curve with a flatter slope (intersecting the demand curve shown at the pre-tax price and pre-tax output point), and you will see the effect on the new long-run output and price. The output must be smaller, and the price must be lower than that shown in the present diagram as the long-run after-tax price. It might even be lower than the after-tax short-run price, if adjustment in the amount demanded in the long run at a higher price is sufficiently large. In any event, tax results in higher price to consumers, smaller rate of card consumption, and reduced wealth to owners of productive resources used in card production. The diagram shows price and output effects but *not* the *wealth* effects.

enough number of suppliers so that the total amount supplied (by the total number of suppliers) is reduced (whether of labor services or potatoes or automobiles). This reduction in supply will raise price. Note several characteristics of this situation. A rise in costs will reduce market supply the more, the greater the number of suppliers who have their costs increased. To raise the cost of just one supplier who is but a small part of the total supply will affect the total supply by a negligible amount and will have no appreciable effect on the price he can get. But even if every supplier is affected, price will not rise as much as the cost which shifted the supply schedule upward (i.e., to the left, to a smaller supply), because the demand schedule is negatively sloped—less will be sold when price is raised—and because the supply schedule is positively sloped. See Figures 17-6 and 17-7. So, either price is raised by less than the rise in costs, or less is sold, or some of both.

Even if you were the sole provider of the service you would not be able to get an equally higher price unless you are willing to accept a lower rate of sales. You simply cannot add on costs and raise price with no reduction in sales. The fallacious idea that when one's costs have risen he can simply pass them on probably arises from thinking of *inflation* (which increases costs and *also increases market demand* by a matching amount, so that in real terms no net effect has occurred). It is not safe to assume that any increase in *your* cost is accompanied elsewhere in the economy by equal rises in costs *and demands*. That way lies bankruptcy or poverty for you, unless—Aha! There is an unless! The "unless" is to *close the market* to your competing suppliers. If you can exclude competitors (whose supply in the market makes your selling price lower) you can raise price. But there is no point in waiting until your costs rise before excluding competitors.

Summary

1 Increased demands and higher prices induce larger outputs. The supply relationship between price and output of each firm is given by a firm's marginal-cost curve above the minimum average variable (for the short run) costs for existing firms. For entering firms it is the portion above the minimum total per-unit costs.

2 At a firm's wealth-maximizing output, marginal cost is equal to marginal revenue—which is the average revenue or price to a price-taker.

3 Firms will temporarily produce even if price does not cover the total costs including the fixed acquisition cost of already-possessed equipment, which is a sunk, no longer relevant cost. The decision to enter or acquire the equipment for production was a wealth-losing decision, but if production is nevertheless continued temporarily, the loss will be minimized. Then the *minimum* variable per-unit cost is pushed above price as higher maintenance or replacement cost occurs, the firm will shut down.

4 An industry is the collection of firms producing a particular good. The industry short-run supply curve (which excludes new firms) in a price-takers' open market is the sum of the amounts given by each firm's marginal-cost curve at the market price—that is, those portions of each firm's marginal-cost curve above its minimum variable per-unit cost.

5 The long-run supply curve reflecting entry and acquisition of new productive equipment is more elastic.

6 Entry of new firms occurs not only when new enterprises seek to replace or compete with other firms by producing at a lower per-unit cost, but also when price rises in response to demand increases.

7 Industries that have a high turnover of firms are sometimes mislabeled "sick" industries.

8 Profits are imputed, by revised market prices, back to the responsible productive resources. In this way costs of subsequent use of the resources are revised to reflect higher value of the resources. Thereafter, returns to producers just cover the new adjusted revalued costs.

9 Unless resources are directed toward their highest market-revealed value uses, the owner will not maximize his wealth. Wealth-maximizing use of resources to determine outputs is economically more "efficient" the more fully market values reflect the values of all the consequences of each possible use.

Production by Firms in Price-Takers' Open Markets   329

10 A per-unit tax on a good reduces its output (releasing resources for use elsewhere). The tax results in (a) wealth decrements to the productive resource owners at the time of the tax and (b) wealth decrements to consumers of the produce who now pay a somewhat higher price for less of the taxed good and more of some other goods, depending upon use of tax receipts.

11 All responses and actions analyzed in this chapter were of price-takers in open markets. To think that people let open-market forces operate without attempts to interfere or restrain the open-market adjustment process is naive. Many producers or owners of goods seek to prevent the open-market forces from operating. Why they do so has been amply suggested in earlier chapters. How such restrictions or closures of the market can be brought about, and some of the effects, will be the subject of Chapter 19.

12 An increase in costs for a particular seller or for a particular product of some industry cannot be passed entirely to consumers via equivalently higher prices. Output will be reduced and prices will be somewhat higher, depending upon how much the rise in costs affects the market supply of the service under analysis.

Questions

1 Do the data in Table 17–1 yield constant costs for the firm?

2 What is the wealth-maximizing output program if the selling price is $1.50? What is the profit? What is the wealth-maximizing output program if the price is $5?

3 Explain why part of the marginal-cost schedule (that is, for outputs at which marginal costs are at least equal to the average, or variable, costs) is the supply schedule of the firm in a price-takers' market. What is the supply curve for the firm in Table 17–1?

4 A producer with the costs given in Table 17–1 could produce *more* than twenty units at a price of $2.50, but he would be penalized with reduced profits.
   a. In what sense is it good that he does not produce more?
   b. In what sense is it bad that he does not produce more?

5 You are a public employee operating a publicly owned golf course, or swimming pool, or taxi service, or gun factory; and you have the costs indicated by the data of Table 17–1. Furthermore, you are selling the product in a price-takers' market.
   a. At a price of $1.80 you choose to produce not seventeen units but about twenty-five units. Why do we predict you would produce about twenty-five units? (Hint: How do the rewards and punishment meted out to you as an operator of a nonprivate-property firm depend on, or vary with, the selected output program? Compare this with a privately owned business.)
   b. Suppose that you are *told* to maximize profits. Would you? Why?

6 Is there a short-run cost and long-run cost for a given output program, or are there two different contemplated output programs, each with its own cost?

7 "Marginal costs serve as a guide as to how much of a good to produce, while average costs help indicate whether to produce the good at all." Explain.

8 If, in some industry, there were 100 firms exactly like the one whose cost data are given in Table 17–1, what would be the supply schedule—assuming a price-takers' market? Plot that industry's (100 firms) supply curve on graph paper.

9 The following describes the state of market demand in the price-takers' market for the hundred firms assumed in the preceding question.

Demand Schedule

Price	Quantity	Price	Quantity	Price	Quantity
$5.00	450	2.80	810	1.40	1,400
4.50	500	2.60	850	1.20	1,700
4.00	560	2.40	900	1.00	2,100
3.75	610	2.20	950	.90	2,400
3.50	660	2.00	1,000	.80	2,800
3.25	710	1.80	1,100	.70	3,300
3.00	770	1.60	1,200	.60	3,900

a. Draw this demand curve on the diagram of the preceding question.
b. What will be the equilibrium price?
c. What will be the rate of output at that price?
d. At that price what will be observed in the market?
e. To each seller what will appear to be the shape of the demand curve of his products?
f. If price is somehow kept from that equilibrium, what will be observed in the marketplace?
g. At the equilibrium price of the current problem, will new firms be attracted into producing this good?
h. Would the attraction be more pronounced and more effective if the demand were twice as great, with the supply schedule being what it is? Explain why.
i. If new firms can enter this business, each one having the same cost conditions as firms already in the business, to what value will the market price move? (Hint: You must first determine the long-run supply curve, including entry of new firms, in order to get the answer.)
j. When plotted on graph paper, what kind of shape or position will the new supply curve have relative to the older one?
k. As new firms enter, what will happen to the output of the existing firms?
l. What will be the total long-run equilibrium rate of output? (You should be able to read the answer from the chart you have graphed or compute it from the tabled data.)
m. Will all the firms that enter survive in the business? Why?
n. If all the new firms are not identical, in that some have higher minimum average costs, to what level will the long-run equilibrium price move?
o. What will happen to the costs of the firms whose minimum average costs were lower? (Hint: What happens to the profits of those lower-cost firms?)

10 Stradivarius violins are rated as about the best in the world. Yet there is evidence that at the time they were built (1700) other violin makers were making even more costly violins. Those more costly violins did not, at that time, sell for as much as the Stradivarius violins, nor do they even today sell for as much. How can you reconcile this with the statement that prices depend upon, or are affected by, costs? Were the Stradivarius violins really less costly?

11 The average cost of the resources used in producing X is $5, where cost is interpreted as the highest sacrificed use value. On the other hand, if these resources were to be used elsewhere, their sacrificed value of output here, $6, is their cost. What will make these two different "costs" of the same resources converge to the same value?

12 The process whereby secret information is revealed by the stock market is exemplified by the following episode: On March 7, 1954, the *New York Times* reported a test in which a new bomb of enormous force had been exploded on March 1, 1954. On March 31, 1954, Atomic Energy Commissioner Strauss reported publicly for the first time the nature of the new bomb and its dependence on lithium. Weeks prior to his announcement, the price of

the stock of Lithium Corporation of America, one of the producers of lithium, increased substantially. How is this rise in price consistent with the fact that everyone connected with the corporation and the test really kept the secret?

13 "The free-enterprise, capitalist system is a system of consumer sovereignty. Consumer preferences determine what shall be produced and how much shall be produced." Evaluate.

14 A tax of 1 cent is levied on each pound of peanuts grown by farmers.
   a. What effect will this have on the output of peanuts?
   b. How will it induce that effect?
   c. What will happen to the price of peanuts?
   d. Will the land on which peanuts are grown fall in value—in view of the facts (i) that peanuts are grown from plants that must be seeded every year, and (ii) that the land can be used for other crops?
   e. What will happen to the value of *existing* machines used for harvesting, shelling, roasting, packaging, and crushing peanuts? Why?
   f. Explain why these changes in value will not be permanent even though the tax is permanent.
   g. Does the temporary drop in value mean that the wealth-reduction effect of the tax is only temporary? Why or why not?
   h. The proceeds of the peanuts tax is used to finance purchases of this book for free distribution to college students. Who is paying for the books so distributed? (The answer is *not* that those who lost wealth from the revised valuation of existing resources are paying for books. That loss of wealth is not offset as a gain to anyone else.)
   i. Who gains what as a result of the tax and expenditure of the proceeds?

15 Suppose that the tax in the preceding problem is levied against only *one* producer of peanuts.
   a. What will happen to the price of peanuts?
   b. To the output?
   c. To the wealth of the various peanut producers?
   d. Whose wealth will be affected by this tax?

Production and Pricing in Price-Searchers' Open Markets

18 UNLIKE price-takers, price-searchers set prices by various pricing strategies, advertise their goods, and hold inventories. We have seen how a negatively sloped demand for its product would require a firm to search for the wealth-maximizing price (and corresponding output rate) instead of finding it almost ready-made in the market. U. S. Steel announces prices of its steel; Papermate states its selling price for pens. The local restaurant, druggist, and grocer set their prices. Each could set a higher price without losing *all* its sales, and each could have set a lower price to increase the amount demanded (not to increase the demand schedule). It might seem, therefore, that each could set price arbitrarily, without regard to market demand and production conditions. Yet price-searchers cannot survive with *any* price: some prices will yield more wealth than others. Which price will make the most profits for the business, and how can it be found? What restrictions are placed on price and output by demand and costs of production?

Two Types of Monopolies

Price-searchers are often called monopolists because the seller has the power to set price. But we must distinguish between two different situations, both of which are commonly called monopolistic: *closed* monopoly and *open* monopoly.

Closed Monopoly

Historically, monopoly referred to sellers who, by government authority, were granted exclusive access to the market. *Closed* monopolists are sellers who are protected from   *1, 2, 3* open-market competition of new entrants. Examples of closed monopolies are: the medical profession; telephone, gas, electric, and water companies; airlines; taxi services in almost every major city; retail liquor stores; teamsters' and longshoremen's unions; many trade unions (though probably not most); and lawyers. In some of these cases, new sellers can enter only by permission of a government agency; in others, those already in the profession determine who shall be allowed to enter. Thus, closed markets are those with restrictions on who may enter, not just markets in which authorities completely prohibit entry of new sellers. From time immemorial, rights to sell goods have been restricted. Foreigners, and even residents of neighboring towns, have been proscribed from selling in domestic markets. Today residents of one state cannot always sell goods or services in some other state within the United States (doctors, lawyers, and musicians, to name a few). On the buying side, some people are excluded from the market or restricted as buyers (children for tobacco and alcohol, and adults for medicines).

Distinguish between *restrictions* on sellers' access to markets and the *high investment costs* of production. By restrictions on access to the market we mean restrictions imposed on people (consumers or producers) as a condition of engaging in exchange of goods. Examples are special taxes imposed as a condition of doing business in the market; requirements that sellers pass qualifying examinations; special apprenticeship and training laws; legally imposed maximum (or minimum) prices; tariffs that prohibit or tax goods that foreigners would like to sell in our markets; prohibition of sales on certain days or hours; prohibition of sale of certain kinds of goods; necessity of having a certain race, creed, or residence as a condition of buying or selling.

Actually, markets run the range from completely open to completely closed. For some markets or goods, the aspiring seller must first pass an examination about his knowledge of how to make or sell the good he proposes to sell (doctors, lawyers, dentists, morticians, architects, hairdressers); or he must have had some official education in a particular trade (teachers, barbers, butchers); or he must have acquired some experience as a trainee (apprenticeship as a carpenter, electrician, plumber); or his good must be certified as safe and appropriate for sale (drugs, foods, milk, stocks and bonds); or he must meet government criteria on appropriateness of the service (liquor stores, banks, TV and radio stations, gas and electric companies, airlines, railroads, taxis).[1] In some cases, a tax must be paid as a condition of entry which sometimes is so heavy as to be prohibitive.

Completely closed markets are not the only alternative to completely open markets. Nevertheless, we shall refer to open-market and closed-market conditions, always remembering that it is a matter of degree. *Any seller facing a negatively sloped demand curve is called a monopolist,* or as we prefer to call him, *a price-searcher.* He is also called an *open* monopolist or *open* price-searcher if entry to the market is open to all potential sellers.

An open price-searchers' market sometimes is said to have "monopolistic competition." The term "monopolistic" concentrates attention on the uniqueness or single-seller aspect of a differentiated product, and "competition" emphasizes the context of open markets. In this chapter, we study only open markets with price-searchers—that is, open monopolies.

---

[1] The cases cited are illustrative. They vary among cities, states, and countries.

Price and Output for Price-Searchers in Open Markets with Full Knowledge of Demand and Cost

If a price-searcher had full knowledge of the demand for his product and of costs of alternative output programs, he could easily ascertain his maximum-wealth price and production program. To illustrate, we shall assume that a contemplated output program is for one year and that an increase in the output *rate* implies also a proportionate increase in the planned volume with already acquired equipment.

The *costs* of alternative output programs (different annual rates and planned volumes for one year) are assumed to be those given in Table 17–1. The demand conditions are given in Table 18–1. All this is portrayed in Figure 18–1. The average costs and the marginal costs are labeled AC and MC. The demand curve (average revenue) and the marginal-revenue curve are DD and MR. The output that maximizes the firm's wealth is fourteen units. These can be sold at a price of $2.70, with average total cost of $1.06. The profit is $22.95. If a larger output (for instance, fifteen units) were to be sold, the price would have to be lower ($2.60), and the average cost would be greater. The marginal revenue at fifteen units is $1.20, which is less than the marginal cost, $1.55—the extra sale is not enough to compensate for the reduced gain on each unit sold. Marginal revenue falls below marginal cost beyond fourteen units; therefore, the output program of fourteen units is the profit-maximizing output.

The seller could, instead, have set some other price if he were prepared to bear the consequences. At $1.60 he will sell twenty-five units and lose $5. At $3 he can sell eleven

TABLE 18–1. Demand for Price-Searchers' Product

Price	Quantity Purchased in One Year	Total Revenue	Marginal Revenue
$4.00	1	$ 4.00	$4.00
3.90	2	7.80	3.80
3.80	3	11.40	3.60
3.70	4	14.80	3.40
3.60	5	18.00	3.20
3.50	6	21.00	3.00
3.40	7	23.80	2.80
3.30	8	26.40	2.60
3.20	9	28.80	2.40
3.10	10	31.00	2.20
3.00	11	33.00	2.00
2.90	12	34.80	1.80
2.80	13	36.40	1.60
2.70	14	37.80	1.40
2.60	15	39.00	1.20
2.50	16	40.00	1.00
2.40	17	40.80	.80
2.30	18	41.40	.60
2.20	19	41.80	.40
2.10	20	42.00	.20
2.00	21	42.00	.00
1.90	22	41.80	—.20
1.80	23	41.40	—.40
1.70	24	40.80	—.60
1.60	25	40.00	—.80
1.50	26	39.00	—1.00
1.40	27	37.80	—1.20
1.30	28	36.40	—1.40
1.20	29	34.80	—1.60

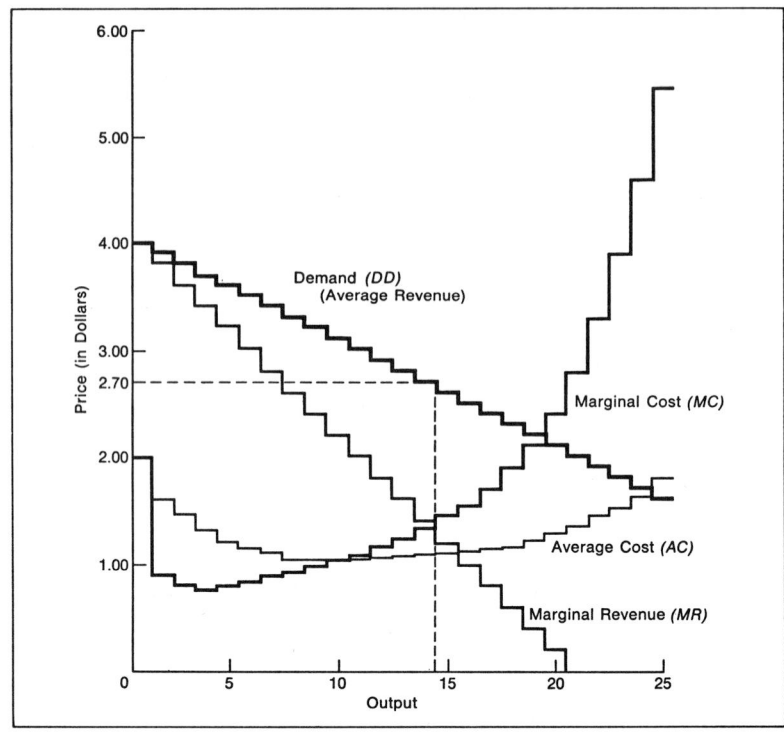

FIGURE 18–1. Demand and Cost Conditions for Price-Searcher, and Profit-Maximizing Output and Price

A price-searcher, faced with the demand function, *DD* (also known as the average-revenue function), will find his profit-maximizing output where marginal revenue falls to equality with the rising marginal-cost curve. At any output less than fourteen, an increase in output would increase revenue (marginal revenue) more than it would increase cost (marginal cost). At any output larger than fourteen, the extra output would increase costs more than revenue. If price is set at $2.70, the firm would be able to sell fourteen units, though it would be happy to sell more units if they were demanded—at least out to twenty-one units. But if it did find itself selling more than fourteen at a price of $2.70, would it continue with that price of $2.70? Why not?

units, but he will gain only $21.90, compared to $22.95 at a price of $2.70. His market demand and cost conditions, along with the desire for more wealth, constrain him toward the price of $2.70.

The Search for Wealth-Maximizing Price and Output with Incomplete Information

4, 5, 6, 7, 8, 9, 10

If businessmen had full knowledge of the demand curve facing them, and *if* they knew what it would be in the future, and *if* they knew their cost conditions for various possible output programs, then the preceding analysis would be sufficient to show how people shift resources toward wealth-maximizing points in response to demand and costs of production.

In fact, however, the search for the price-output programs of greater wealth must be done *without* perfect foresight and without cost or demand data as explicit as those in our numerical examples. People may know all the laws of economics; they may know that an increased demand indicates greater wealth for higher-price–larger-output programs. But how do they know which demand, if any, has really increased and how much? Perhaps an observed increase in sales is merely a transient, random fluctuation. How do businessmen know when they are charging the wealth-maximizing price?

With complete information, it is a trivial task to find the wealth-maximizing price. With incomplete information, the businessman's task is difficult. But the task of the economist or student of economic affairs is slightly different: to predict the direction in which specified changes in demand and cost conditions will modify the preferred price-output programs. The economist can postulate changes in these external conditions; and then, with his principles of demand and cost conditions, he can deduce the direction in which the new wealth-maximizing price-output programs are shifted. But that is not all the economist should do; he should show also *how,* even when there is incomplete knowledge about demand and cost conditions, changes in demand and cost conditions induce new price-output programs in the directions indicated by economic theory.

To see how output responds to market demand and cost conditions, we replace the fiction of free and full knowledge with partial ignorance—which is *not* to be identified with stupidity or irrationality. The price-searcher must feel like a gambler at the racetrack; there is *a* horse that will provide his biggest returns if he bets on it, but *which* one is it? What price will maximize his wealth?

Consider the problem faced by an airplane company. It has just designed a plane which it believes will make a good replacement for the DC-7—the Douglas four-engine piston-prop plane that was the backbone of the air transport industry. What price should it announce, and what scale of production should it plan? This is precisely the kind of question faced by Boeing with its 707 and by Convair with its 880. Only Boeing calculated sufficiently well to get a profit. How close it was to the profit-maximizing price, no one will ever know. The demand for the Boeing 707 did lie above the cost curve for a region that Boeing managed to find, whereas if the demand curve for Convair commercial jets ever did lie above their cost curve, they weren't able to find out. If they had known, they would have saved the stockholders scores of millions of dollars. Apparently Douglas was luckier with its DC-9—a tail-jet plane.

Ford, when deciding to produce the Edsel, misjudged the demand for Edsel cars—to the loss of millions. It guessed right with the Mustang. Packard Bell Electronics also badly misjudged—not on the demand curve for an important electrical item which it offered to produce for the government—but on the costs. Philco Electronics produced a "futuristic model" television set in 1960, for which the directors estimated the demand curve was above the average-cost curve at the planned output program. They were wrong—but they didn't find out until they had lost considerable wealth. Chrysler designed an automobile in 1958 for which the demand curve was under the average-cost curve. Chrysler lost millions, and this was evidenced by the decrease in the value of its stock during that year. We could list thousands of such failures. Not even the alleged consumer manipulators of Madison Avenue could adequately sway the minds of buyers —which should give pause to those who contend consumers are pawns who buy what advertising tells them to buy.

Not only the giants demonstrate uncertainty, ignorance, and fallibility. A corner restaurant must decide what prices to set and types of food to offer, and what volume to plan for. And the same goes for the local gasoline-station operator, the drug store, grocery store, discount house, automobile repair shop. We don't hear much about those who lose wealth. Success breeds fame; failure, obscurity. No glamour publications are called *Death* or *Misfortune*.

Price stability, transient demand fluctuations, and information costs. How are changes in demand for existing goods revealed to existing producers?

Buyers shop sporadically and accumulate goods for subsequent consumption. Sellers know that there is a difference between transient fluctuations in sales and lasting changes in demand around which the sales rates fluctuate. Perhaps they could handle these transient fluctuations by letting price rise or fall at each instant so as to balance out demand with existing supply, much as stock-market prices match momentary demand and supply. However, *it will pay sellers to maintain an inventory of buffer stocks and predictable prices for consumers to meet these transient fluctuations in daily market demands rather than to try to produce to order instantly as buyers are faced with transient, unpredictable price changes.* Inventories stabilize prices and make the *momentary* supply schedule a horizontal line at the selling price, out to the limits of the existing inventory. However, it is only for *transient* demand fluctuations that inventories serve as a buffer stock. Should demand have permanently increased, a continuing higher sales-rate would deplete inventories and induce higher replacement rates to accommodate the continuing larger rates of sales. Output will increase to replenish inventories, even before prices are adjusted.[2]

The higher *rate* of production raises marginal cost, and a higher price will have to be available. The higher price will be *maintainable* because of the increased demand. The sequence of effects from increased demand to inventory depletion, to replenishment of inventories by higher rates of production, and to higher costs and then prices can be identical with that explained in Chapter 7, where we traced the effects of a demand increase on the price of meat.[3] Again, it appears as if prices rise because costs rise—if one confuses timing with causation.

Prices in price-searchers' markets are not "less adaptive" to changed market conditions than are prices in price-takers' markets. Because of inventory availability, price-searchers will provide amounts wanted by demanders during transient fluctuations without having to change prices. This stability is not a reflection of price rigidity or power of seller to control price. It reflects instead the greater ability to provide price predictability by use of price-searchers' inventories.

The preceding adjustment process is applicable to decreases in demand. *Changes* in demand and cost conditions are effective in inducing output changes even though firms do not know instantly the precise demand and cost conditions or the new wealth-maximizing output and price program. A trial-and-learn search process will induce convergence toward that wealth-maximizing program. The farther the actual output program is from the optimal, the smaller are earnings or the greater are losses—either of which will increase the probability of the firm's changing its tactics.

[2] Recall Chapter 7, pages 95–97.

[3] If the larger output is larger in *volume* as well as rate, and *if* unit costs fall sufficiently with larger volume, then prices, which may first have risen before output increase, will again fall, possibly to lower levels than originally. In any event, the increased demand is translated into an increased output.

New Capacity and Entry of New Firms in Response to Demand Changes

The preceding analysis has concentrated on the output and price response of firms already in this "industry." Output of particular goods expands with higher demand, both because existing producers increase output and because new firms enter into production.

Increased wealth of an existing firm cannot be long concealed. Its expansion is visible. If the firm enlarges, if the owners drive more expensive cars and their homes become more expensive, you have telltale indicators. Employees of firms know who is doing well. In various ways, the word gets around. As a result, other firms try to copy this firm. Managers are hired away by competitors. Employees organize their own company, taking part of the company's "know how"; for example, hundreds of firms have been created by former employees of the earliest electronic-computer companies.

Other firms find it profitable to shift production toward closer substitutes for the good whose demand has increased. If the production of Cokes, Fords, or Arrow shirts becomes more profitable, other producers will produce close, if not perfect, substitutes and reduce the profits of the first producer as some customers switch part of their purchases to the substitutes. Goods are substitutable in one degree or another, and a rise in demand for steel can be attenuated by an increased use of wood or brick. Or an increased demand for a certain kind of Ford will within a year bring similar models from General Motors, Chrysler, American Motors, or foreign producers.

The same two competitive open-market pressures that were described for price-takers in the preceding chapter operate on price-searchers: (1) Other producers will enter the market for this and related goods. (2) They will bid away resources. Assemblers, supervisors, designers, production engineers, salesmen, managers, and research staff will respond to competitors' offers. The cost of keeping resources rises. Even the cost of having the owner stay in his business must be valued at a higher figure; the more others are willing to offer for his services, the higher are the costs he must impute to continuing in his own business.

The resulting zero-profit situation is shown graphically in Figure 18–2. The demand curve is tangent to the average-cost curve. A larger or a smaller output would result in costs that exceeded price per unit. There is no incentive for more firms with similar cost situations to enter the business.

If demand falls, the analysis is reversed. A reduced demand implies a lower price and output. The value imputed to resources used to produce that product falls as prices and output are reduced. Resources devoted to this particular good will be shifted to other activities, where they can earn more. Existing producers will reduce output, and in time some will leave the industry.

By selective differential survival, growth, and imitation by competitors, the population of business firms converges toward the maximum-wealth output and price programs. Add the activities of "raiders" who think they know how to run a business better than the present owner and offer to buy the firm. The new owner pays less than he thinks he can earn with the firm, while the old owner gets more than he thinks he could earn. The resources are shifted toward higher-valued uses—if these forecasts or conjectures are correct. If not, the new buyer discovers his error and can sell out, but only by bearing the loss. The more accurate forecasts *yield* higher gains and enable the higher-valued uses to displace less appropriate uses of resources.

The simple facts stated in the preceding paragraphs are full of heartbreak. When demand falls for any good, some people find their current services no longer so valuable.

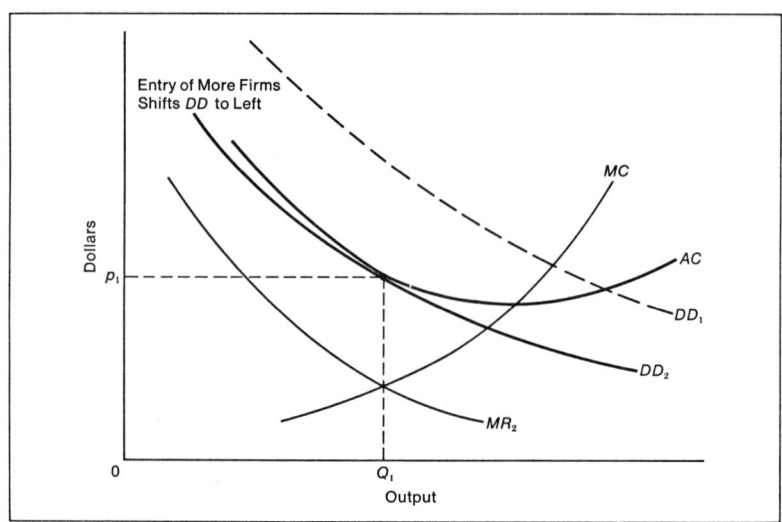

FIGURE 18-2. Zero-Profit Equilibrium for Price-Searcher

Entry of new firms reduces demand for each firm until price is at zero-profit situation. DD_1 is the old demand curve (prior to entry of new firms) with which this firm had positive profits. The new lower demand function, DD_2, is just tangent to average-cost curve. Under new demand function, there is no output at which the firm can make profits. At every output other than Q_1, it will lose wealth. (Marginal revenue for old curve DD_2 is not shown.)

Wage cuts or movements to new jobs are indicated. Business owners experience losses in the value of their plant and equipment.

The fundamental institutional features of the adjustment process are private property and open markets, not price-takers' and price-searchers' markets. In *both* market situations, resource owners bear wealth changes and are induced to revise the uses to which the resources are put. In a nonprivate-property system, there is less specialization and less pressure to make revisions; and resource use is less influenced by people's relative valuations of various goods. The influence is reduced because each person's own wealth is less correlated with the market value of resources. In the last section of this chapter, we shall explore this influence of market values more extensively.

Response of Producers to Anticipated Demand

Some consumers believe they can buy only what open-monopolist price-searchers decide to offer them. To some producers, the opposite seems to be true. Although both contain truths, neither of these positions is correct.

The Problems of Anticipating Demand

Some demands are revealed only by the appearance on the market of new goods. Transistor radios found a market demand although consumers had not induced their production by advance orders. How many of us who now have stereo records "demanded" them before 1955? New products and methods of satisfying consumers are continuously being subjected to market demand: power steering, miniskirts, automatic transmissions, color television, instant coffee, supermarkets, frozen foods, credit cards, electric wrist watches, cordless electric shavers, no-iron fabrics, synthetic fibers, stretch clothes, coin-operated dry-cleaning machines, water-based paints, zippers, etc. In what sense did these represent a response to demand? The hope of increasing wealth provoked someone to invest some of his wealth into producing some new item to test the market demand. The demand need not be demonstrated in advance. It is enough that there are venturesome, greedy, optimistic individuals willing to use some of their wealth to produce new goods for which they hope revealed demand will be great enough to yield profits. Consumers may not give birth to or order new goods, but they decide which shall survive.

Response to Anticipated Consumer Demands

An especially common example of businessmen anticipating market demand for as-yet-unproduced goods is the speculative housing builder and land developer. Future renters and buyers usually do not order the construction of buildings. Yet speculative businessmen build in the expectation that the public does demand these new goods. If correct, they make a profit; if not, a loss. Suburban land developers are often criticized as interested only in a quick dollar—a true charge. But to whose demand are they responding by their efforts to buy the land and construct houses and apartments? The people living far away in other areas who will move to the area—even unborn generations. If you were to ask some of those "unseen" people if they now demand those new buildings, they might deny it. Yet some of them will be moving into the area and will be demanders. Fundamentally, anticipated demand of those unidentified people drives up the land values. The present value of the land is the capitalized value of that latent future demand as judged by the landowners and speculators.

The market valuation will induce the land to be used or reserved for uses in which its value in that use is higher, if the owner has a right to the gains in capital value of the land. Without those rights, the land developer will not respond so fully to the desires of the future. Another way to attenuate responses to capitalized values is to transfer the decision from a market context to nonmarket criteria—voting, for example. If the issue is settled by number of votes, then only those now qualified to vote will be counted. One speculator representing hundreds of future dwellers has only one vote. Furthermore, current landowners of already-developed sites and owners of existing homes and apartments will be likely to vote against an increase in supply of the type of goods they own. Their wealth would be reduced. Some (but not all) zoning ordinances prevent such market-induced change in resource uses in order to protect the wealth of owners of some existing sites and buildings.

In sum, market values expressed by speculative developers reflect demands of many people not visibly present. If gains in wealth cannot be obtained by speculative development, the future and latent demands will be less heeded.

Reactions to New Product

Another example of the way in which market valuations operate is provided by the introduction of a new product by a new producer. The injured competitors, who lose customers and revenue, will be able to bring this loss of wealth to the attention of the new producer by offering to pay for the elimination of his competition. They could, in principle, offer the new producer an amount up to the measure of the damage done them, or they can and do offer this amount to the customers if they will not buy the new product—by lowering prices of the old product. If the gain conferred by the new product is greater than the losses to old producers, the new product cannot be eliminated, either by price cuts to customers or by paying the new producer not to produce. If the losses that would be imposed on the old producers by the entry of the new product exceed potential gains to the new producer, the old injured producers would successfully keep out the new product.

Product Interdependence

Is it true that some goods aren't produced because they must be used jointly with some other as-yet-unproduced good? Congress enacted a law requiring every producer of television sets to sell *only* sets that can receive all 83 television channels, from channel 2 to 84. Presumably that law was passed because there was not enough incentive to make all-channel sets, and until sets were made to receive all 83 channels there would be insufficient incentive to telecast on the higher-channel stations. A "vicious circle" was alleged. What are the analytical implications and empirical evidence about this "vicious circle"?

Historical facts do not support it. Automobile production did not wait for gasoline stations. Did radios wait for radio stations? Did FM receivers fail to be developed because they required transmitters to send FM first? In fact, they developed despite laws restricting FM broadcasting. Did stereo records await stereo record players? Did FM multiplex stereo programs and FM multiplex stereo receivers "bottleneck" each other? Did automobile repair shops and automobiles "bottleneck" each other? Did frozen foods and freezers for home use "bottleneck" each other? Did color television require a law compelling all manufacturers of television sets to include color capabilities?

The examples of FM radio and color television provide direct refutations of the presumed necessity for a law compelling UHF television receivers. No law required radio manufacturers to make only FM-AM combination radios. They could make any kind. As the design technology improved in the 1950s, FM sets became easier to tune and keep tuned, cheaper, and more reliable. The public demand was evident. In color television, for a long time the Federal Communications Commission *prohibited* color broadcasts until it could decide on the "best" kind of color system. And when it decided, it chose wrong. Fortunately, the Korean war forestalled production until the superiority of the electronic scan system became more obvious. Color television did not require a law compelling color transmission or receivers with color capability.

What happened to the alleged vicious circle of new-product interdependence? It never was there in the first place. Specialization of production is the rule in an economy in which exchange and access to the market are permitted. *Specialization implies reliance on other people to produce jointly used products as they seek opportunities to increase their wealth.* Interdependence is *not* ignored in the economic system. The search for greater wealth correlates the production of jointly used products. Only if one forgets the incentives and exchange opportunities in a marketplace will he fail to see the coordinated activity of other people. A visitor from Mars might contend that the real world is a much too complicated place for a decentralized market system to operate in. He would be surprised that exchange prices and narrow specialization in a private-property context are capable of organizing a society as complex and productive as those in Western countries. Specialization does not imply lack of coordination, nor that joint-product profit opportunities will be ignored. In fact, it implies jointly used goods will be more effectively produced if specialization *is* permitted rather than if one person or firm must do the whole task.

In truth, the vicious-circle bottleneck among jointly used products is a delusion arising from the belief that output must be carried out on a large scale initially, that people are unwilling to invest now in anticipation of future receipts, *implying that present capital values are irrelevant.* These suppositions are disproved by events in the real world.

Desirability of Directing Output by Wealth-Maximization for Price-Searchers

This discussion of the impact of capital values is not a justification of private property and open markets. In *some* communist and socialist states, market-revealed values are regarded as undesirable guides to productive-resource uses; hence, maximizing market-value wealth is considered undesirable. However, some socialist states (Yugoslavia, for example) are increasing the role of markets for consumers goods as rationing agencies and as sources of signals as to what to produce. (But incentive to follow those market signals is weaker without private property.) Every society to one degree or another reduces the power of open-market values to direct resources. Examples are provided by all goods whose production or distribution is in any way controlled outside of the marketplace: education, socialized medical care, radio and television, drugs, roadways, and many more.

A charge of inefficiency is commonly made against a system that allows wealth-maximizing to be a controlling force in price-searchers' markets. You may recall that price-searchers can distort production by not carrying output or sales to the rate at which marginal cost equals price.[4] They will produce, instead, to the rate at which marginal cost equals marginal revenue. Hence, it is concluded that a price-searcher's wealth-maximizing outputs are inefficient in that the output mix is one which could be revised so as to benefit some people by more than the loss to others.[5]

Some Confusions about Price-Searchers' Markets

Arbitrary Administration of Prices

A modern myth has grown up around the "facts of life" in price-searchers' markets—the facts that their prices fluctuate less than those of price-takers' markets, the prices of individual firms change at about the same time, and the largest firm usually is a price

---

[4] See Chapter 11.

[5] But recent advances in economic theory indicate that the implication of inefficiency applies more to the *closed-market* monopoly and less to the open-market monopoly. In both cases, the demand function related price to quantity of output for a *given, unchanged* good. But, and this is the crux, if the producer or seller can change the product—by redesigning it, advertising, having several models, and varying his services—then the marginal cost and the marginal revenue are the changes in costs and revenues for quality as well as quantity. In this case, the relationships we perceive among price, marginal revenue, and marginal cost must include the effects of other variables. The two-dimensional (price and quantity) diagrams are not analytically powerful enough for that expanded problem. Suffice it to say that the more powerful analysis recognizing these other variables does not imply that efficiency is necessarily thwarted by open-monopoly price-searchers seeking to maximize their wealth.

Do not be distressed if the supporting logic of the preceding paragraph is not entirely clear. It would take us substantially beyond the appropriate limits of an elementary course to justify the preceding assertions.

leader. These facts have been used to support the myth that dominant firms administer or set prices and that unless they do so with responsible self-restraint, government must intervene to protect the public interest.[6] It has been said that U. S. Steel, General Motors, and large drug companies set the prices of their products by arbitrary administrative decision. Such sellers do, indeed, set their prices. They do not find or take them in the market as wheat sellers do. The Aluminum Company of America announces its price of aluminum; R.C.A. sets the price of its radios and television sets.

Price-setting versus price search. Such price-setting reflects each seller's search for the wealth-maximizing price.[7] But everyone does this, the lettuce farmer, the laborer, and the steel company. It's just easier to find that price in some price-takers' markets.[8] Each price-taker *could* have sold his product at a *lower* price. But his selfish disregard of "public interest" made him "set" the price at which his wealth would be greatest. At a higher price he would sell none. He has a wide range of prices he can set, from zero up to the highest price at which he can sell any. This highest possible price is determined by the market and the total supply of competitors (including other commodities).

That same motive dominates price in *every* market for privately owned goods. The poorest common laborer or retail clerk or employee *could* charge a lower price and be poorer; but because he, too, is greedy and wants more wealth for himself, he charges whatever price will give him the maximum of income. Thus, Du Pont does *not* set the highest possible price at which it could sell *any* of its output; it seeks the wealth-maximizing price appropriate to (but not readily disclosed by) the market. It cannot discover this price as easily as the price-taker can; it has to resort to trial and error, never being sure it has found it. Because of this exploratory charging of prices above or below the "best" price, some think that Du Pont, U. S. Steel, or other sellers have "market power" to *set* or *administer* any price they please in a monopolistic, noncompetitive sense.

What kind of "market power" is that? The price-searcher can raise his price, *but* he suffers a reduction in quantity sold. He cannot raise price at will—if he also "wills" to have more wealth, for higher price can mean smaller wealth and income. Unlike the price-taker (without market power?), who can sell more (by producing more) at the existing price, the seller with so-called market power has no such power. He must lower his price to sell more. Is that a relevant "power"? Although the term "market power" correctly states the seller has the power *in principle* to raise or lower price, in fact the seller is constrained by the powerful drive for more wealth. That kind of market power is about as relevant as the "power" each of us has to give away most of his income.

Whether sellers are described as using their "market power" to "set" prices or merely searching for the best (wealth-maximizing) price in the market is all a matter of semantics. Call them "monopolist-administered prices" if you want to make the seller

---

[6] "Folklore and mythology" is admittedly name-calling and simply is a way of indicating which theory you think best explains observed economic events. Some regard the economic analysis presented here as mythology. What is the truth? As we said at the beginning, that must be judged in the light of both the logical consistency of the whole theory and the conformity of empirical facts with its implications. We believe the evidence provides overwhelming support for the economic theory we present.

[7] To avoid the impression that we are assuming businessmen have no goals other than maximum wealth, reread page 319.

[8] But not in all, as we shall see when looking at the market for labor, for example.

look like a selfish, noncompeting, economic royalist. Otherwise, call them "market-revealed, market-demand-and-supply-determined prices." Neither self-restraint nor concern for interests of other people keeps him from raising prices. It is the effect on his wealth that restrains him; higher prices may lower his net receipts. *All* prices in all markets are administered in the sense that each person decides at what price he shall sell (in the light of market demand). But the parenthetical phrase reminds us that the profitability of prices depends upon consumers' demand and the prices of all other goods. The prices and sales of firms are interdependent. They watch each other closely and, like dogs chasing a rabbit, move together, even in those cases where there is no leader, simply because they seek the same quarry.

Absence of aggressive price competition. Another naive idea is that an industry of a very few sellers, an oligopoly, is characterized by an absence of "aggressive" price competition. Although it is never made clear what is meant by "aggressive" price competition, the context suggests that any one seller is aware that if he cuts price, others will quickly match his price, and everyone's profits will take a beating. So instead the sellers tacitly agree to hold prices at some "reasonable" level.

The argument confuses a price in common with competitors on the one hand and the level of the common price of the few oligopolists. The maintenance of a common price may mean simply that it is not profitable to try to charge a lower price (nor a higher one!) than others are charging—just as for a price-taker. Collusive behavior is not so simple as it may seem at first sight, as we have already suggested and shall again see in the next chapter.

Profits and Concentration

Associated with the preceding misconception is the belief that the more an industry is concentrated in a few firms, the larger the profit rates. Thus, if the industry has (say) over 90 percent of sales in four firms, the profits will be larger than if the four firms had only 20 percent. How do such beliefs develop? Some industries with a few firms are observed to be more profitable than some with a large number of firms . . . a conclusion is suggested.[9] But if all industries are examined, the evidence so far collected either does not support the conclusion or is very tenuous.[10]

Justifiable price changes. Compounding the confusion are the excuses and utterances of price-searchers who seek to justify their actions, as if they had the power to raise prices *and* get more wealth whenever they thought they had a "justifiable" reason—justifiable in the eyes of public opinion rather than in the market-demand and cost conditions. Instructive in this respect is the U. S. Steel price-rise episode of 1962.

Roger Blough, board chairman of the United States Steel Corporation, announced an

---

[9] In the photocopy business, Xerox has made enormous profits. It and a couple of other "copiers" have a very large share of the market. They have a large share because they have developed superior products. Unusually superior products can explain several cases of high concentration and large profits.

[10] J. S. Bain, "Relation of the Profit Rate to Industry Concentration," *Quarterly Journal of Economics,* August 1951, pp. 297–304. G. J. Stigler, *Capital and the Rates of Return to Manufacturing Industries* (Princeton, N. J.: Princeton University Press, 1963), and a review of published evidence by Y. Brozen, *The Antitrust Task Force Deconcentration Recommendation* (Chicago, 1970).

increase in prices, asserting that costs were higher and profits were needed for new investment. In the first place, whether he wanted a fancier office or new steel mills has nothing to do with the ability of U. S. Steel to get more wealth by raising prices. In the second place, the fact that costs had risen does not mean that he could thereby raise prices and get a higher income. If that were true, he could let costs mount without limit and simply raise prices to cover them. What he could have said is that costs of *all* steel producers were rising so that the wealth-maximizing price had changed, and U. S. Steel, in the interest of maximizing its wealth, intended to move to that new price. Other producers concluded that higher prices would not give greater wealth, because market conditions of demand and costs had not changed in that direction. They did not follow the lead of U. S. Steel. That the same firm is usually the first to make a price change which others almost always follow does not mean that the leader dictates prices to other firms, nor does it imply some tacit agreement not to compete with prices. It can attest to the lead firm's greater acuity and knowledge of market conditions. Other firms watch its behavior and then follow, thereby avoiding the costs of maintaining a research staff. If the price change turns out to be a money loser, then "follower" firms will return to the original prices.[11]

Price rigidity. Evidence refutes the charges that price-searchers administer prices regardless of demand and supply—or that the more concentrated is the output of an industry in a few large firms, the more inflexible the price. The number or size of firms in a price-searcher industry has no statistical connection with the frequency or magnitude of price change. Yet to this day, some Congressional committees are misled by the myth that administered prices are rigidly set in industries characterized by high degrees of concentration of output in a few firms. Also it is asserted that output fluctuates more in those rigid-price industries than where prices are not so administered. The myth lives on and on, sometimes buttressed with the same errors of statistical methods applied to more recent data.

What are the data so naively interpreted? Initially, price data were collected for goods like automobiles. The price of automobiles was reported to be stable and invariant because the list—or recommended—price announced by the automobile companies stayed unchanged throughout the year. One of the first things a person learns in shopping for a car is that the list price is the selling price only at the beginning of the new-car season. Immediately thereafter, the salesmen's pencils are sharpened for "special" deals, which are offered to everyone who says he is going to shop around.

The catalogue prices of varieties of steel do not change for many months. Yet the actual transaction price at which steel is sold does vary. Discounts for cash vary; speed of delivery and special services vary from week to week; quantity discounts are common. A steel purchase is a complex transaction. Extensive studies of actual contract prices of steel show that the actual prices are highly variable from week to week, despite constant quoted prices.

The current assessment of the price-rigidity allegation has been summarized characteristically by a president of the American Economic Association:

---

[11] In 1963, a year later, the price of steel was raised immediately after the U. S. Tariff Commission announced it would open hearings to decide whether to impose higher taxes on imports of foreign steel—and to impose them retroactively on all prior imports at prices deemed too low. That simple announcement immediately induced foreigners to reduce shipments to the United States. For some government agents to protest the rise in the market price of steel would have been somewhat awkward, since other government agents had granted domestic steel producers closed monopoly protection from continued foreign imports.

Economists have long struggled to find a rational explanation for prolonged price rigidity, which is in general as inadvisable for profit-maximizing monopolists as it is impossible for "price-taker" industries. Putting aside minor or special circumstances (the cost of a price change; the procedural delays in cartel or public regulation), they have failed to discover any such explanation. It appears that the real world has been equally remiss in supplying the phenomena they were seeking to explain.[12]

15, 16, 17, 18

Excessive Advertising

Price-takers do not advertise their prices or the quality of their products since they can sell all they have available at the current price. Nor would advertising enable them to get a higher price, for other sellers of the identical product in the same market would provide the increased amount demanded. On the other hand, price-searchers are eager to sell more at the current price but will not find it profitable to cut price to sell more. Advertising their product will inform some potential customers of their existence and goods. Information about possible sources of goods is a scarce resource, as anyone knows who enters a strange town and seeks accommodations and restaurants. Often we forget this when we see advertising that tells *us* nothing we didn't already know. We may say that advertising inflicts cost on bystanders who have no interest in buying the advertised product. The advertiser would be delighted to advertise in selective ways not noticed by people who would not possibly be interested in the product. But that is often more expensive than general advertising. Much criticism of advertising reflects failure to take account of the lack of ability (1) to identify in advance each potential buyer and (2) to advertise in ways that will be noticed only by them. If we knew who was going to have flat tires at which times, repair cars would be at the spot ready to give service, and that would be less expensive than carrying around fifth tires. The fire-escape sign is useless on many nights, but should the light be turned off on nights when there will be no fire? Similarly, in school are we not taught several things that some of us will never use again later? Was there a waste of resources in that act of "indiscriminate" teaching? In exactly the same sense, some advertising is "wasteful"—which means only that if we all knew more, we could save resources.

One form of advertising brings forth probably more criticism than any other—that on radio and TV. Economic theory has something to say about that. The amount of advertising on radio and television is the result of the way in which radio and television are paid for. Movie theaters do not show commercials the way television does, because the patron pays directly and guides the producers' future actions. Pay television (which is illegal in most areas) could give the viewer more control over the programs. One can readily imagine the programs in movie theaters if patrons could come in free of charge. Programs appealing to a smaller group would be less common because a minority could not concentrate its "dollar votes" on preferred programs; diversity of preferences yields to majority tastes. If newspapers could not be sold, they would have even more advertising, as is evidenced by the ratio of advertising to news in neighborhood throw-away newspapers. The criticism of advertising on television is a criticism of the system of paying for television and radio programs.

Perhaps, next to radio and TV advertising, billboard and roadside advertising seems to run a close second as an object of criticism. (What about bumper stickers and advertising on cars?) But it is not advertising *per se* that is objected to; rather it is the

---

[12] George J. Stigler, "Administered Prices and Oligopolistic Inflation," *The Journal of Business of the University of Chicago*, Vol. 35, No. 1 (January 1962), p. 8.

thrusting of that advertising upon people in places and circumstances and ways they dislike. The blocking or destruction of scenic views is a prime example. There are two basic reasons for that destruction. First, the scenic view is not owned by anyone, not even the landowner from whose property the view can be had; there is less reward for anyone to take action individually to preserve that view than there is for normally salable or negotiable goods. Second, even if an owner could be assigned to the viewing point, there is a very great cost of negotiating with all the people who might in some way alter that view. The technical problems have been too complex for man to have discovered how to bring that "good" into the rubric of resources controllable by normal market operation of the property system. Failing some such system or politically imposed control, scenic goods, like the apples on the public tree, will be rapidly consumed.

Another complaint is about duplicative mutually cancelling advertising. Camel advertises, and in self-defense Chesterfield advertises. The net effect is alleged to yield no gain except to the advertising people. Is there any other interpretation? When I see people *presumably* being influenced by inane, tasteless, or substantially empty advertising, I am tempted to regard that advertising as wasteful or harmful. However, if I took a less authoritarian attitude, with more recognition of differences in tastes, I might be willing to entertain the possibility that customers prefer—perhaps for reasons which they have never articulated—the cigarette that advertises to one that does not.

Finally, we consider the situation regarded as the clearest use of undesirable advertising: the advertiser deliberately *misleads*. But it is dishonesty that is bad, not advertising. We should not condemn commercial advertising for dishonesty any more than political speeches. People are dishonest in daily conversation, in part, by being excessively tactful. As far as dishonesty is concerned, is it as fruitful in advertising as in private conversation? Open advertisements can be seen by competitors, and dishonest statements will more surely be refuted in open advertisements. And how many people really are fooled?

Fear that advertising will mislead people suggests that political authorities decide what is permissible advertising. We already engage in censorship. We expose our children to censored ideas when we control by authority what public schools teach them. The continuity of a culture requires that it pass on to the younger generations its customs, taboos, and habits. However, this censorship applies to children, and all parents have a large say in it. We censor our children's channels of communication because they are children—and this brings the crux of advertising content control to the fore. Are we to extend the concept to adults? Each of us may differ in our judgment. We may not like the way others behave when exposed to ideas and persuasive thoughts. But authoritarian control of advertising content is censorship of ideas; of that there is no dispute. The dispute is how much of it is good or bad.

19, 20, 21, 22

Summary

1 Inventories, price stability, price-searching activity, and advertising are implied for price-searchers' markets.

2 Price-searchers are monopolists in the technical sense of facing negatively sloping demand functions with respect to price.

3 Transient, fluctuating-demand functions imply inventories for price predictability by price-searchers.

4 Price-searchers seek the price and output at which marginal cost equals marginal revenue, rather than price.

5 Price-searching pricing activity can be explained without collusion.

6 Open-market monopolies have no artificial or arbitrary restrictions on access to the market; closed-market monopolies are those with restricted or closed access to competitors.

7 Production responds to anticipated demands of potential customers via speculative production for profit *via* capital-value gains.

8 Advertising is a form of communication. Like communication at every level—personal, political, social—it contains dishonesty, exaggeration, and ulterior motives. That it contains less of these than any other communication is a defensible proposition. "Excessive" advertising reflects its use as a rationing device and a means of financing some goods distributed at a lower than market-clearing price (as with radio and TV and throw-away newspapers).

Questions

1 "If some firms producing X have unsold output potential that they would like to use to produce more X at current selling prices, if only the market demand were great enough, then the good X is not being sold in a price-takers' market." Explain why that conclusion can be drawn.

2 The difference (for pricing and output behavior) between price-takers' and price-searchers' markets can be characterized by a difference in the demand curve facing each seller. Describe the difference in the demand curve.

3 Market closures need not result in price-searchers' markets, especially if the existing number of sellers is very large. Can you identify or suggest cases where market entry is restricted and yet a price-takers' market exists? (Hint: How about agriculture—wheat, tobacco, milk producers? Teachers?)

4 Tentatively classify the following, on the basis of your present information, as (a) price-takers, (b) closed monopolists, or (c) open monopolists. (Remember, market closure does not necessarily convert a price-takers' to a price-searchers' market.)

    Electric company   Prescription pharmacist
    City bus line   U. S. Steel Corporation
    Airline   Lettuce grower
    General Motors Corporation   Electrician
    Corner drug store   Elizabeth Taylor

5 a. Can you suggest some good for which the differences among various brands are insignificant? (Hint: Sugar, flour, aspirin, tires, dog foods, bread, milk, soap, corn flakes, cigarettes, canned peaches, banks at which you can have a checking account, beer.)
b. Obviously you will not agree that *all* these are examples of goods whose brands are of insignificant differences. Are any? If so, does this mean that when you buy this kind of good, you purchase at random without regard to brand?
c. If not, what do you mean by an insignificant difference?
d. What makes you prefer one brand over another at the same price?
e. Can you name any good and two of its brands for which you believe no one in his right mind could have a "good" reason for preferring one over the other?

6 Change the data in Table 18–1 as follows: From every indicated "quality purchased" at each price, subtract 6. If the new number is negative, simply call it zero.

a Recompute the total and marginal revenue.
b. What is the new wealth-maximizing output for this producer?

7 Suppose a $5 tax is levied on your business—an annual license tax of a flat $5 regardless of how much you produce. Use the cost (only) data of Table 17–1 and revenue data of Table 18–1 to answer the following questions.
   a. What will be your price and output?
   b. What is the amount of your profits?
   c. Suppose a $25 tax is levied. What will be your new price and output?

8 Again using the data of Tables 17–1 and 18–1, suppose that your costs of production are changed by a rise in the cost of materials or labor so that at every output your costs are 30 cents greater per unit of output.
   a. What will this do to the marginal-cost schedule?
   b. What will be your new wealth-maximizing price and output?
   c. What are your profits now?

9 As a superior student you provide a tutoring service. The higher the price you decide to charge, the fewer the hours of work you get.
   a. Are you a price-taker or a price-searcher?
   b. Assume that your time, when you are not tutoring, is worth an equivalent of $2 an hour. The daily demand for your tutor services is not perfectly predictable; it varies at "random" around a mean rate of daily demand which depends on the price you can charge. If, at the price you charge, you find that all your available time is always used, and there are occasional applicants whom you must reject because you are fully booked up, do you think you are charging the wealth-maximizing price? Explain.
   c. If you are charging a price at which you occasionally have idle time, are you charging too low a price?
   d. Given a fluctuating demand, how can you be sure that you have charged the "right" price?

10 In what sense can the marginal-cost curve of a price-searcher be considered a supply curve?

11 You are constructing an apartment building. You can build one with many units and have vacancies sometimes, or you can build a smaller unit and have a no-vacancy sign all the time.
   a. If the latter behavior is profitable, can the procedure of having vacancies sometimes be even more profitable?
   b. Would you interpret an average vacancy rate on apartments of 5 or 10 percent as evidence that they are oversupplied, overpriced, or neither?

12 Are there any products that are not being produced today because complementary, jointly used products are not being produced, so that each is waiting for more of the other—with a resultant underproduction of both items?

13 "General Electric announces a new 11-inch, 12-pound portable television for $99.50." "Parker '45' Pens are sold at an announced price of $5." "Sunbeam appliances are sold at retail prices set by the manufacturer." Explain why the above statements do not imply price setting by the seller. That is, explain why the prices were not all three times as high as they are.

14 A year after the steel-price hassle of 1962, the federal government, in response to complaints from domestic steel producers about low-priced imported foreign steel, initiated hearings to determine whether foreign imports were being provided at less than the foreign costs—with nothing explicit as to what is meant by costs. The hearing determined that imported steel was being sold at prices below cost (below whose cost?), so taxes were

imposed on the imported steel. Within a month, the domestic steel companies began raising the price of steel, in a discreet manner, with only lip-service complaint from politicians.
a. Do you think it likely that the higher prices proved to be more profitable?
b. Why did the government at one time object to higher prices of steel and then within a year take action to reduce the imports of steel, thereby enabling a higher domestic price?

15 Higher costs have induced a firm to reduce output and raise price.
a. Is this to be interpreted as an example of the power of the price-searcher to raise price?
b. If your answer is "No," how do you reconcile your answer with the Council of Economic Advisers, who regarded the attempt of the Aluminum Company of America to raise its prices as an "unjustified" use of the power to set prices?

16 In France, Italy, Spain, Hong Kong, and New York individual bargaining over the price of a good is commonplace.
a. Would you prefer that custom to the more common one in the United States of not bargaining?
b But on second thought, can you name three goods that are commonly purchased in the United States by bargaining?
c. How would you explain the simultaneous presence of two different customs?

17 You are collecting data for a cost-of-living survey. For each of the cases below, which "price" would you report as *the* price? Why?
"List price, $125. Special discount to $90!"
"35¢ box of Kleenex for 29¢."
"One cent sale. First for $1. Second for 1¢."

18 When collecting prices for your cost-of-living survey, you discover that not all customers can buy a good advertised on sale because the limited stock was sold out in the first hour. Continuing with your cost-of-living survey, in New York City the rents are controlled; but at the controlled rents apartments are not available to many who would pay the legal price. Would you use that legal price as the cost of housing? Why?

19 Is it possible for an economy to be one in which everyone is a closed monopolist and a price-taker, and yet everyone is poorer than if there were no restrictions on the open market? Explain.

20 "Advertising by savings banks is wasteful. It doesn't induce any more saving. All it does is attract depositors away from one bank and to another. Since all banks are guaranteed and regulated, there is no difference among the banks. Hence, advertising that merely attracts depositors away from other banks does not a whit of good." Do you agree? If so, why? If not, why not?

21 "Much advertising is deceitful, dishonest, misleading, fraudulent, and disingenuous. Therefore, it should be subjected to government regulation." If you accept that conclusion, would you accept the same conclusion for daily conversation, political talks, lovers' pleadings—which are subject to the same charges? Explain why or why not.

22 Is it true that for some products you prefer one brand over the other if both have the same price, but if there is any price difference between them you will take the lower-priced one?
a. If this is true for some goods, does it suggest something about the basis for or "strength" of your preference?
b. Would you say that you "discriminate" among brands?
c. Is that "justifiable" discrimination?

Sellers' Tactics for Changing Market Conditions

19 WHETHER they be employees, business owners, or politicians, people do not passively submit to open-market competition. They seek to close markets to competitors in three general ways: (1) predatory action against rivals, (2) collusive action with rivals, and (3) statutory legal closures of the market to actual or potential rivals.

In this chapter we shall investigate if and how these objectives can be achieved.

Methods for Changing Market Competition

Predatory Tactics

It is often said that if a firm can destroy its rivals, it can realize larger profits. And so, sales below cost are often regarded as a predatory tactic to bankrupt rivals. But there is another purpose of sales "below cost" (that is, below average operating costs). A firm can sell below cost to inform potential customers of its existence and product quality. This is an investment, just like many other activities that involve greater cost than the *current* rate of receipts. The action is not designed to eliminate existing sellers so that the store can later set the price above current competitive levels.

The attempt to impose losses on competitors in order to achieve a monopoly position with subsequent "above-competitive" prices would be predatory action. A case frequently cited as a predatory action involved Rockefeller's Standard Oil Company in the nineteenth century when Standard's low prices in selected local markets were interpreted as devices to bankrupt smaller refiners. Would this be an intelligent tactic—that is, wealth-maximizing—even if no law prohibited it? Both the predator and prey lose wealth. The bigger firm with more sales will take a bigger absolute loss. The smaller firms can often shut down production of that item and wait out the return to higher prices, letting the predator take the greater losses. But whether or not the prey can take that action, it still is clear that below-cost selling as a predatory tactic is not as smart as it is alleged to be.[1]

If a firm were to gain by driving a competitor to bankruptcy, the prey's productive assets must be retired from production. Bankruptcy does not *destroy* productive resources; they go to someone else, who probably acquired them at a sufficiently low cost to make their continued use profitable. The aggressor, who has been suffering losses to impose losses, would have to continue his predatory tactics as long as required to wear out the other resources, and this would mean larger losses for the predator, too. Even if the predator were wealthier, it does not follow that he would find it sensible to bear greater losses. Careful study of the Standard Oil example has revealed no evidence of predatory tactics; there was substantial evidence that Standard had bought rivals at a handsome price and retired the productive capacity.[2]

Collusion

If what one seller may try to do to another is not profitable, perhaps what they do together can be. Agreement between the parties to cooperate by merger or covert agreement is a possibility. However, the attempt to remove market competition does not eliminate competition. It shifts its form or locale—in the case of collusion, to the conference table, where the competitive issue is the division of the gain—by no means an easy one to resolve. Let's see what problems beset that attempt to collude successfully.

The potential gain from effective collusion, or avoidance of open-market competition, can easily be seen from our earlier water-demand example of Chapter 8, page 122. You may recall that the individual competitive price would have been $1, but if the firms selling the product could agree to charge $6 per gallon, the income for the whole group would be larger. Achieving that control over the *market* supply is extremely difficult.

Whether open or covert, an effective collusion—sometimes called a "cartel"—is faced with a formidable series of hazards, even in the absence of legal prohibitions:

1. Who are your competitors? If you were trying to organize doctors, what would you do about interns, chiropractors, registered nurses, druggists, dentists, and drug companies? All of them are substitutes in one form or another for some medical service. If doctors raise their fees, some people will ask more aid of their druggists and use self-prescribed drugs. Or suppose you are a steel producer. What would you do about aluminum, brass, plastics, wood, and concrete? Would your "collusive" group be able to raise steel prices without intolerable losses of sales to nonsteel products? And what about firms that make their own steel? If you collude and raise prices, they will sell some of their steel output to other steel users; a new producer appears to take away your sales. Excluded firms will profit and grow under the umbrella of restricted output by the cartel members.

---

[1] Warning: What appears to be a predatory policy is often in reality something entirely different. It can be competition by more efficient lower-cost producers. Or when demand falls, producers who cut prices may appear to be "predators" when they are merely adjusting to the new situation by trying to minimize their wealth losses (maximize their wealth at the lower attainable levels).

[2] See J. McGee, "Predatory Price Cutting: The Standard Oil (N. J.) Case," *Journal of Law and Economics,* 1958, p. 137.

2. Suppose, however, that you decide to include only the steel companies and not those who produce aluminum or other substitutes. Of the more than one hundred companies producing steel in the United States, ten produce 90 percent of all the steel, so you plan to get just the big ten together. The rest will not be able to grow rapidly enough to upset your plan too quickly, you hope. Not all ten will agree upon what is the best price. It depends on each firms' cost-output relationship, elasticity of demand, and growth prospects. Lower prices are more advantageous to lower-cost firms than to higher-cost, smaller-output firms. Some collusions never pass this obstacle.

3. Each member is alert to the potential gains from competition in ways not yet prohibited by the cartel. For example, a firm could vary its delivery, credit, trial, and refund privileges. Detecting *all* forms of competition is prohibitively expensive. The airlines have a regulatory agency and a legally enforced cartel, but competition in beauty and personality of airline hostesses, in types of planes, and in fringe benefits to passengers has yet to be controlled.

4. The probability of secret price-setting is very high and is related to product and market characteristics. Secret price-cutting to a large buyer is more profitable than to a small buyer, considering the risk of detection. If all the colluding members *pooled* their output, sold it through a central sales agency, and split the proceeds, secret price-cutting could be controlled. However, how does one determine what share of sales goes to each member? The younger, growing firms want an *increasing* share. An alternative to "pooling" all output for sales via a central agency is to assign each buyer to one seller. This would reduce the incentive for price cutting (though not entirely, for by cutting prices, you would enable your buyers to undersell their competitors and in this way indirectly undermine your fellow conspirators).

An especially common collusion (in *open* markets) is that of sales to the government via sealed bids; a sealed-bid buyer is a "sitting-duck" for collusive sellers.[3] The government solicits bids from several sellers and opens them all at one time. Usually, the lowest bid wins. No rebidding is allowed (in sharp contrast to the purchase of a car by a private party who solicits bids from various sellers *and* giving each a chance to undercut the others). Therefore, the incentive for sellers to engage in collusion is stronger, because the buyer is less able to play one seller against the other. Furthermore, if any colluding sellers do not bid as agreed, the others will find out immediately since all bids are revealed. It does not seem accidental that almost all of the cases of established effective collusion have been on sales to government agencies or government-regulated public utilities.[4]

5. The economic costs of creation of new facilities may dissuade new potential competitors from quickly entering the business. This lag would appear to make short-lived effective collusion more likely; but there is another side to this coin. If expensive facilities are involved, the colluders will lose their own large investment if new entrants

---

[3] Sealed bids are often used by government agencies—for example, schools, regulated public utilities, and federal agencies.

[4] An alternative explanation of the observed predominance of cases of collusion against the government is that the government is more willing to take cases to court, and hence reveal the collusion, whereas a private firm is less willing to resort to court costs. This sounds like a good alternative explanation if we forget that the greater facility of legal prosecution by the government should serve to inhibit attempts to collude against the government.

The notorious electrical-equipment case of 1962 involved sales to *sealed-bid* governmental agencies. Subsequent accusations of collusion against sellers of meat, flour, water, pipe, steel, office furniture, cement, milk, banking services have all involved sealed bids to government.

do appear—an effect that will continue after the effectiveness of the collusion has ended.

Such are some of the inherent contradictions, obstacles, and hazards to *effective* collusion. We emphasize *effective* because many exploratory attempts to collude simply never come to fruition. Proposals are discussed, agreements are reached only to be dashed on the hard realities just mentioned.

Simultaneity of price action or "dominance" by one firm is not evidence *for or against* the existence of *effective* collusive agreements. The number of sellers and the coordinated price-search process, whether it be simultaneous or lagging behind some apparent "price leader," are also irrelevant. What is good evidence? The use of an *enforcement* technique. If costs are being incurred to enforce concurrence in competitors' actions, there is strong evidence that an *effective* collusion exists—one effective enough to make it worth the enforcement of costs. Restrictions on new entry and penalties for noncompliance with the terms of the collusion are enforcement devices. Self-regulation or *legal* self-policing by members of an industry provides a weapon of enforcement. Members who do not comply can be denied the right to do business because licenses or special privileges can be revoked for "unethical" behavior. The privileges include access to special information or research, exemption from special taxes, the right to do business with the government or avoid strikes by unions.

A strong conclusion suggested by the foregoing considerations is that an effective collusion will be associated with some organization in which membership is essential if one is to stay in business. The organization can be one that obtains special privileges (government subsidies, tax favors, pooling of patent rights) or simply one in which membership is a qualification for doing business. Any member who does not conform to conditions of the collusion will be expelled from the organization, and thus legally excluded from the market. For example, the American Medical Association gives its members sufficiently great special privileges (for example, access to surgical hospitals) to enforce observance of its strictures against certain types of competition. Similarly, business firms in Germany prior to World War II were compelled by law to belong to Chambers of Commerce as a condition of the right to engage in business; member firms could then enforce the strictures against types of market competition by expelling from the Chamber any firms that violated conditions and thus excluding them from the market! It is no wonder that Germany was typified by many collusive cartels. In the United States, airlines find it nearly essential to belong to the Air Transport Association, which then serves as a policeman to punish cheaters in the cartel of airlines.

Mergers

A merger superficially appears to be an ideal vehicle for collusive action. Simply merge with your rivals into one big firm and thereby control output so as to get a bigger profit, which can be divided among the merged firms. Again there is the problem of who pays how much to whom. But even supposing this difficult problem can be resolved and a merger arranged, will it be worth the costs? Most firms make more than one kind of product. Is it worth merging with rivals for *one* of these products at the cost of losing productive efficiency in the others? Your superiority in other lines of products is dissipated in the merger.

So far we have ignored a very important handicap of merger. *New firms* with additional productive capacity will enter if existing firms merge and hoist prices above the competitive level. These entrants can be very damaging indeed. The merging firms may make a dollar more per year for say four years, but with new firms attracted the later results will be a smaller earning than otherwise. A dollar gain for four years, with a subsequent income that is 60 cents smaller than if there had been no merger, literally constitutes a *loss* of *present wealth*. The present value of one dollar a year for four years is $3.46 (at 6 percent), but the present value of 60 cents a year for ten years thereafter (the loss) is $3.50, a net *loss* in present wealth.[5]

Probably only a small fraction of mergers have the monopoly situation as an objective or consequence. Many are profitable, because they provide a more efficient combination of resources; others profit because of superior new management of firms that had been operated inefficiently. Mergers and takeovers of other kinds—by stock purchases, exchange of stock, or direct purchases of assets—often represent competition among managers and entrepreneurs in using productive resources. Outsiders rarely know the purpose of a merger or how successfully the purpose is served. On this subject there is much conjecture but very little reliable evidence. It suffices for present purposes to know that mergers reflect several different objectives.

1, 2

Ethics or Desirability of Collusion

Collusions raise an ethical issue. Insofar as they are voluntary, with no compulsion placed on outsiders who do not want to join, what ethical precepts, if any, do they violate?[6] If firms do collude effectively to raise prices and reduce output, they do not differ from any price-searcher, who, faced with a negatively sloped demand curve, charges the wealth-maximizing price. For example, Bob Hope, Arnold Palmer, and Natalie Wood hire agents to sell their services. Each could hire several agents, who would compete with each other. Each of Hope's agents would look only at the amount of services *he* could sell. He would cut the proffered price of Hope's services below the offer of Hope's other agents, driving down Hope's income. To avoid this, Hope hires *one* agent and prevents "ruinous" competition among sellers of his services. No one seems to complain. Similarly, why should one complain if the diamond mines are owned by one person who acts in the same way? Is it that, in the one case, diamonds will be produced in smaller amount? But so would Natalie Wood performances. In each case, from the point of view of the rest of us, a natural talent is not "fully" used. In the Wood case, it is even worse, since the talent ages, whereas diamonds do not.

The fundamental ethical question is whether the rest of the public should require by

---

[5] The 60 cent per-year perpetuity has a present value of $.792 \times \$4.42$, because the stream is deferred four years (which accounts for the .792 factor) while the ten-year annuity of 60 cents has a capital value of $4.42. Check our calculations and reasoning by refreshing yourself on the capital-values principles (Chapter 11). These principles will come in handy for solving practical problems long after you have left college.

[6] If there is something bad about collusion, is there not also something bad whenever people voluntarily pool their private wealth to form a corporation that is big enough to affect the market price by its offerings of some good? Every corporation and partnership uses jointly owned resources in wealth-maximizing ways. Why is effective collusive agreement among several businesses different from merger or new creation of a large business? It isn't. Then why have we devoted the past several pages to a discussion of inter-firm collusion, as if it were different from the formation of a corporation or partnership? To show the obstacles to any group's controlling of market behavior, either by collusion or by buying up firms until only one firm is left—*in the absence* of legal compulsions requiring producers to join a collusion as a condition of access to the market.

law that Wood or Hope or Palmer perform more frequently. Economics gives no judgment about this. The case against effective collusion comes down to the same point raised in connection with price-searchers' markets—"inefficiency" (misdirection) in the allocation of resource uses.[7] Granted for the sake of the argument that there is misdirection, a proposal to prevent voluntary pooling of private wealth is denial of private-property rights. The criterion of "misdirected" or inefficient use of resources is itself dependent on the normative premise that individuals should have the right to make choices about use of goods. Of course, you may feel that private property and individual choice are not desirable; but we hope you make that judgment only in awareness of what their absence implies.[8]

The Law on Collusive Practices

As we have seen, potent forces deter the attainment of extra wealth *via* collusive sellers' arrangements. Nevertheless, not *all* collusions are unsuccessful. The success of collusion in the absence of prohibitory laws is said to be proved by the frequency of cartels and collusive agreements in European nations. However, where successful collusions have been carefully investigated, it has been found that special laws, favors, tax exemptions, or government controls have enabled colluding groups to "police" recalcitrant members and keep out new producers.

There are laws in the United States against collusion and other actions considered to be "restraints on competition." The Sherman Antitrust Act of 1890 prohibited "monopolizing" and "combinations or conspiracies to restrain" trade. Since it did not define "monopoly" or "restraint of trade," the act, as enforced, depends upon ad hoc arguments in individual law suits against companies. At the turn of the century, the Standard Oil Trust, the U. S. Sugar Trust, and the American Tobacco Trust were prosecuted by the U. S. government's antitrust division and were split into smaller companies. It is still a moot point whether these "trusts" did charge higher prices than would have been charged by a larger number of smaller firms and, if they did, whether or not the power to do so was a result of laws denying other competitors the right to enter the market. In any event, the Sherman Antitrust law is intended to dissuade further growth of some firms. For example, in 1961 the Du Pont Company was compelled to divest itself of ownership of a substantial portion of General Motors. Bethlehem and Youngstown steel companies were dissuaded from merging when told by the antitrust division of the Justice Department that the proposed merger would be prosecuted in court as a violation of the Sherman Act. More recently, the Brown Shoe Company was forced by court order to divest itself of ownership of a former competitor. All of these were results of judicial opinion or belief that these mergers "tended to reduce" competition. In fact, the judicial interpretation is even stronger; it is now sufficient to show that competition "might probably" be reduced. No great understanding of economics is required to perceive that the law is ambiguous, vague, and subject to individual interpretation, preference, and opinion. As early as 1914 confusion had reached the stage that the U. S. Supreme Court could seriously declare that only "unreasonable" restraints of trade were illegal.

---

[7] And there is still dispute even about that.

[8] Individual freedom of choice is the ultimate test of value or "proper" direction of resource use in *this* efficiency criterion. This will be evident if you recall that the measure of value is derived from "individual preference" as revealed in choice of use or exchange of goods.

In a futile effort to achieve greater precision in concepts, the Clayton Act of 1914 prohibited both "price discrimination" and mergers "reducing competition" (but exempted labor unions from antimonopoly laws). As we have already seen, price discrimination sometimes increases the efficiency of resource use. Mergers can enhance the competitive status of some firms in the market.

Complaints by some businessmen against their competitors' behavior resulted in passage in 1914 of the Federal Trade Commission Act, which created a commission with power to investigate any business activities alleged to be in violation of various laws, and to dissuade "unfair practices" by issuing "cease and desist" orders. These orders prohibit further violations but do not penalize for past "unfair practices." What is and is not an unfair practice often cannot be determined in advance by the businessman.

In 1938 the Wheeler-Lea Act authorized the Federal Trade Commission to prohibit still other "unfair practices"—those "unfair" to the consumer, such as false advertising. For example, it is illegal to artificially color margarine without saying so on the label (but it is permissible to artificially color butter without so labelling it). Such exceptions are sometimes authorized by legislation that is not always obviously consistent.

During the Depression of the 1930s many (still existing) laws were passed to prohibit price cutting: in fact many encouraged sellers to get together and raise prices, with penalties on those who did not comply. Legislation passed at that time to prevent what was regarded as ruinous competition has done much to thwart open-market competitive forces.

Protection of *or* from *competition?* One of the principal "undesired" effects of business regulation is that it tends to confuse protection *of* competition with protection *from* open-market competition. For example, the Federal Trade Commission relies heavily on complaints of one business against another in deciding which actions to investigate. Complainants will try to protect their wealth from market competition rather than to preserve open-market competition. They complain of "unfair," "de-stabilizing," "disorderly," and "cutthroat" competition—which can mean that one's competitors are more successfully catering to buyers' preferences in open markets. Therefore, you contend that he is driving you out of business and "tending to reduce" competition.

Collusion by Employees

A common successful collusion is that of some sellers of labor. If the employees of a firm or industry form a collusion to agree not to offer their services at less than some wage, they face the usual obstacles of successful collusions. They may strike in order to enforce their collusion. The right to strike and to strike effectively is currently an accepted part of our economic and legal institutions. A strike is an attempt to prevent *other sellers of labor* from offering their services at rates (or working conditions) lower than those sought by the striking employees. Access to the labor market by any other sellers of labor is restrained by the "peaceful" *threat* of violence to the person or property of would-be strikebreakers, including any striker who might be tempted to cheat on the agreement. The market is closed. While the laws do not authorize strikers to physically restrain workers from crossing a picket line, crossing the line incites retaliation. Therefore, to avoid violence at the strikers' picket line, anyone who tries to cross a picket line and thereby provokes violence may be jailed along with the strikers for contribution to a disturbance of the peace. Both the strikebreaker and striker are declared guilty. In few areas will the police sweep aside the strikers and permit strikebreakers free access to the market for work (at lower terms than those sought by the strikers), for that usually leads to violence.

If the preceding sentences seem antilabor, the reader is injecting his own interpretation. They are no more critical or disapproving than the statement that hydrogen is lighter than nitrogen. They do not say that employees ought not to engage in strikes. They do differ from common folklore in their explicit recognition of a fact which strikers sensibly prefer not to publicize; after all, threat of violence is generally disapproved by the public.

That the union acquires legal "closed-monopoly" power when allowed to strike is widely recognized. Our courts decreed this in 1914 when unions were specifically exempted from the Sherman Antitrust law. The Norris-LaGuardia Act of 1932 legalized group picketing and boycotts. The Wagner Act of 1935 required employers to deal with unions and made it legal for employees to form or join the union of their (majority) choice. And the National Labor Relations Board was created to enforce the conditions of those acts.

If the preceding analysis seems incredulous, ask yourself: Is there any reason why the people who seek to collude or to eliminate competitors should be only, for example, businessmen, doctors, teachers, radio and television station owners, rather than ordinary employees like teamsters, carpenters, auto assemblers, retail clerks, or dock workers? If one group can ethically rely on legal tax-supported state police power, it should not be surprising that others resort to some private violence to deny access to the market.

3, 4, 5, 6, 7, 8

Trademarks and Trade Names

Anyone can enter the market with his own goods under his own trademark. But trademarks and trade names cannot be copied. Even though I were to manufacture an item physically identical to Morton salt or Bayer aspirin, I could not legally sell it if I inscribed on it their trademark. Trademark laws prevent someone from trying to pretend a product is made by someone else. Some countries do not recognize trademarks and trade names, and they do not prohibit imitation of trademarks, just as we do not prohibit imitation of the good itself. However, trademarks and trade names are included in the spectrum of property rights in the United States; they are not restrictions on access to sell *their* goods and services. They identify the maker and help predict the quality of the product.

Patents and Copyrights

Patents and copyrights are grants of exclusive rights, in a closed monopoly, to sell certain goods or ideas.[9] A patent is what a statutory *monopoly* used to be called. The principle of Polaroid film is patented; the inventor has exclusive rights to it and can license others to produce and sell that film. The patent is given for a period of years, usually seventeen, and is occasionally renewable for another seventeen years. Patents and copyrights are intended to induce people to discover and reveal useful techniques and

---

[9] Patents do not prevent other people from using some idea or device if they use it for themselves and not to produce something for *sale* to other people; only commercial use is forbidden. Also notice that ideas are "public goods."

knowledge—if a person invents a way to kill flies, show three-dimensional television, or cure the common cold, everyone else could quickly use the idea without paying him anything. Even though many people try to invent or do research without that incentive, the prospect of a gain will attract more people and resources into such activity.

We should not be surprised that the patent holder charges for the use of his idea. (The purpose of the patent or copyright was to reward him for ideas.) But the price he charges restricts the use of the idea. Having given a patent as a monopoly right, we should not be surprised when the patent holder uses that closed right like a *monopolist*.[10]

What is the right amount of reward and inducement for an invention? One might conjecture that the right amount should not exceed the "value" of the resources the invention saves or the gain it gives society. If an invention reduces the costs of production by $1,000,000, then presumably the inventor should be paid something. But who knows how much? And who is to pay the inventor? The absence of a clear-cut criterion for "proper" inducement leaves room for considerable dispute about how long a patent should be protected and what kind of pricing and use of the patent should be allowed.

Several misapprehensions exist about uses and effects of patents.

Suppression of new ideas. Sometimes an inventor discovers a new idea that will make obsolete what he currently owns. If I owned a pay-television system using wires from station to home and then discovered a means to eliminate the wires, would I use the wireless system or suppress it? What I would do depends upon the relative costs. Since the wires are already installed, their ("variable") cost of continued use is low (until they must be replaced). If it would cost me less to produce and install the new equipment than to pay the costs of using the old system, I would immediately abandon the old system. Otherwise I would not use the new system until the old wires had to be replaced or repaired. This delay in introducing a new idea is sometimes regarded as "unjustified," but instead, in fact, it may reflect the lower cost of using up existing equipment first.

Modern folklore has a legend that gasoline producers have discovered a new kind of fuel or carburetor that would enormously reduce the demand for gasoline. In order to protect their wealth, they withhold the device from use. What are the facts? If the invention were not patented, then a person who knew about it could manufacture the device and make an enormous fortune—more than the existing companies would find it worth their while to pay him in order to induce him not to sell the secret. And if the device or idea were patented, it would be public knowledge; but there is no patented evidence or record of any such device.

Nonpatentable research and development. Much research and development is carried on without the incentive of patents or copyrights. Most businessmen who develop new ideas have to rely on being first and being able to make enough profit before competitors come in. For example, the supermarket, the double-pump arrangement in gasoline service stations, drive-in banks, colored soaps, open-all-night stores, discount houses, and a host of other business innovations contribute to cost reductions or quality improvements. Yet they are not subject to copyright or patent. There is no generally accepted, objective rule as to what range of exploratory activity should or should not be given the special protection of patent and copyright monopolies.

---

[10] See pages 121.

The collusive pricing tactics employed by some drug firms are feasible because of patents for new drugs. Congressmen frequently complain about prices of patented drugs. The crucial issues are: How much reward should the patent holder be allowed? What methods of monopolistic pricing *should* he be allowed? Multipart pricing? Fixed fee? All-or-none pricing? Uniform price to all licensees? No clear-cut answer is obtainable from economic analysis. Actual practice finds all sorts of combinations. When you see them, some legal monopoly is probably the basis for enabling that kind of pricing.

Alleged extension of patent monopoly to other goods. There may be "price discrimination" related to the *use* of some patents or copyrights, wherein the licensees of a patent pay different prices for the right to use the patented idea. This pricing tactic has been interpreted by the courts as an attempt to extend one's monopoly (in the patented item) to other kinds of items. For example, the International Business Machines Corporation, which owned the patent to punched-card computer machinery, required users of its machines to buy the *cards* from IBM only. Another example is provided by Christian Dior, who gives retailers the right to sell his dress "creations" (which he can copyright) *only* if they also agree to buy handkerchiefs from him. It might appear that IBM is trying to extend its monopoly into the paper-card areas. Yet there is another interpretation that is more consistent with economic theory and fits the facts more closely.

Recall our water monopolist in Chapter 8, who sells water at the wealth-maximizing *uniform* price.[11] There were two other pricing policies he could have used, under certain circumstances, to get more wealth with less waste of water. In one case, a person buying a certain amount at one price could then have purchased more at a lower price.[12]

The IBM company, as patentee—assuming that it faces a negatively sloping demand curve and that *no one else can legally enter the market*—would like to use a multipart pricing system to get all the wealth it can from its machines. However, to use multipart, discriminatory pricing with *many* different buyers, IBM would have to know each buyer's demand curve and set *different* rates for each.

How can IBM detect each user's demand curve and charge appropriate fees to each user? The number of *cards* the customer uses is related to his demand for the use of the machine. IBM could simply count the cards used and charge a fee for the machines based on that number—say, one cent per card per day. A big user of cards would be charged a higher price than a smaller user of cards. IBM did so by charging a higher price for the purchase of cards than the customer would have to pay if he could have bought the cards from someone else. If a user could buy cards from some other source, IBM would lose its measure of demand and its method for collecting. Therefore, IBM insisted that, as a condition of using the machines, only IBM cards be used (even though their price was higher). By guaranteeing to service and maintain the machines under the

---

[11] See pages 121–126.

[12] Ideally, he was charged a price of $10 for the first unit, with the right then to buy a second one at $9; and then, *given* that he agrees to buy a second one for $9, he is allowed to buy one more at $8, and so on down until he can buy a tenth one at $1. In this way, the water seller collected $55 for the ten units of water, whereas the best he could have gotten with a uniform, constant price per unit—take all you want at that price—was only $30 (having sold six) with four being left unsold. This multipart pricing (wherein the "price" changes for each possible amount) has the "advantage" that inefficiency in use is eliminated. Nothing is wasted. There is no misdirection of resources. And it also gives the water seller a bigger wealth, leaving the consumer with minimal gain from exchange. This kind of "ideal" or complete discrimination is hardly achievable.

rental scheme, IBM could also check to see that its cards were being used. Thus, insistence on tie-in of IBM cards to be bought at higher than competitive price was not intended to *extend* IBM's machine monopoly into the card area. Instead, the tie-in of cards enabled IBM to use the cards as a meter device to charge different total amounts to its machine users. To prevent its customers from buying a machine and thereby ignoring IBM's policy, IBM would only rent the machines, thereby enabling itself to retrieve machines from contract violators.

Federal and state governments and the courts have attacked these tie-in and restrictive arrangements, alleging that they represent attempts to enlarge the range of goods monopolized or restrict competition. However, economic analysis implies that they are really devices to (1) measure each customer's demand conditions to determine and (2) collect the discriminatory price or fee that will enable IBM to obtain more of the value of the patented item.

Other examples of the use of tie-in sales as metering devices to measure demand and collect discriminatory prices are: cans tied to use of can-closing machinery; staples to stapling machines; mimeograph supplies to mimeograph machines; repair parts to automobiles; toilet paper to dispensers; rivets to riveting machines; steel strapping to wrapping machines.

9, 10

Price Discrimination?

One must be careful to state precisely what is meant by discriminatory pricing in any given circumstances. For example, the Robinson-Patman law of 1938 prohibits "price discrimination" where it will tend "to create a monopoly, lessen competition, or injure competitors." One thing we should know by now is that the words "discrimination, monopoly, competition, competitors" are loaded with many possible meanings. We should not be surprised that the confusion created by this law has provided lawyers with higher incomes and business firms with extra costs and uncertainty as to what they can do legally.

One of the classic examples of "discriminatory" prices is that in which a railroad charged more to ship goods from New York to Denver than from New York to San Francisco. Naturally, this seems "unjustly discriminatory" against people in Denver. Why did those rates exist? The railroads from New York to San Francisco compete with transport by water via the Panama Canal. There was no low-cost competition to Denver.

The prices set for rail services to San Francisco and Denver are market-rationing rates, and must meet competition of other sources of services. It seems "unjust" to charge more to Denver, since it certainly costs more to ship to San Francisco by rail than to Denver. Price rations the existing supply, *and*, it is hoped, provides revenue to induce the output. The idea that, for joint products, each one's price "should" cover some equal pro-rata portion of total costs is a fallacy.

The fact that it costs more to ship goods by rail to San Francisco than to Denver from New York neither *justifies* nor *permits* a higher price for rail shipments to San Francisco. What one can get for what he produces depends not upon what it costs, but upon what the supply will sell for when confronted with market demand. The supply of available water and rail transport to San Francisco was much larger than to Denver at any given price.

The source of the "discrimination" is that nature provided a superb harbor at San Francisco, whereas Denver is located in a landlocked area to which transportation is more expensive. To correct this "injustice," the law has compelled the railroads to charge no more to Denver than to San Francisco. So, being unable to raise the San Francisco rail rate (because of the cheaper water transport), the railroads lowered the rate to Denver. Had Denver been the major terminal of most of the freight, the rate would not have been cut. The San Francisco rate would have been raised, since the railroads would prefer to lose that smaller service income rather than the large Denver-service revenue. In that event, fares would still have been "equal," with San Francisco suffering in the cause of "equality."

Sometimes, joint products that cost the same sell for very different prices. Daytime demand for long-distance telephone service is higher than at night. There is no way to allocate the common-facility costs to night and to day service, except in some arbitrary way. There is no point in doing so. Given that the facilities exist, the phone company charges a lower night rate simply because the demand is smaller at night. If the night demand were stronger, the night rates would be higher than the day rates. The relative level of rates depends upon the relative demands which must be rationed.

Is it "fair" that night workers should be able to make long-distance calls more cheaply? That theaters should charge less for matinees than for evening performances? That paintings involving the same costs should sell for different prices? That beautiful girls get richer than homelier girls, even if both spend the same amount in trying to be more beautiful? All these "disparities" arise because of some differences in the demand for the good or service, reflecting differences in availability and convenience or, in the eyes of the demander, in quality.

The person paying a higher price wishes he, too, could buy in the lower-priced market. Then why doesn't he shift to the lower-priced market? Because *to him* the lower-priced market is not worth all the sacrifices he must make in order to do so (like moving to San Francisco from Denver or working nights rather than days in order to save on long-distance calls or learning to ignore superficial beauty).

There is nothing in economic analysis that determines what is fair or not fair. The words "fair," "just," or "reasonable" have no objective content—Aristotle, Aquinas, the Council of Christian Churches, the President of the United States, or anyone else to the contrary notwithstanding. Except, possibly, "The fair price is what I think it should be."

Protection of Consumers

Standards of Sanitation

Laws prohibit sale of foods that the Federal Food and Drug employees deem unfit for human consumption. Consumers use government agencies to enforce some standard of cleanliness; time and resources are saved for them by reducing private costs of collecting information for each buyer. But on reflection, there are some "costs" of this law. Some consumers prefer the right to buy cheaper goods (for example, imported dates), even though they are produced in less sanitary conditions (cleanliness is not a costless "good"). This right may seem silly for anyone to want—if costs are ignored. But consider the fact that the Food and Drug Administration refused to allow the sale of a cheap, high-protein, biologically sterile food made in powdered form, because the Food and Drug employees said it was a filthy food—being made from *whole* fish. Yet people eat whole oysters; pigs and chickens are converters of garbage, insects, and worms. The point is that people who make decisions to restrict certain items do not necessarily have the same preferences as those for whom they are thought to be acting. No one can object to cleanliness, if the *degree* of it is not "excessive" in view of the costs. But a high-priced barbershop that uses a new protective apron for *every* customer will find itself underpriced by one that reuses the apron with a new piece of paper around each customer's neck. The higher-priced shop would do well to insist on higher standards of cleanliness as a means of keeping out lower-cost competitors. Clearly, a requirement that all sellers maintain at least the same high standards is a restriction on those buyers who prefer less sanitary, but cheaper, service—usually the poorer people. Insisting on higher quality means more of the higher-cost quality goods and less of the cheaper lower-quality goods. Which is better for the poor and/or for the rich? For the informed and the uninformed?

Quality Protection

Until about 1950, margarine could not be sold in some states—ostensibly because it was considered a "low-quality" substitute for butter. And in many areas it could be sold only as a *white* spread—even though butter can be artificially colored and flavored. These laws protected milk producers from new competition—as is evidenced by the fact that major milk-producing states had the strongest bans on margarine. Even mayonnaise was at one time similarly protected from competition from the "inferior" (and cheaper) substitute, salad dressing.

Codes in every city control the materials that can be used in buildings. One result is that obsolete methods are preserved; the codes are not revised often enough. New York City's building code was unchanged for over thirty years after the 1930s. The rapid development of mobile trailer homes can be explained partly by the fact that they are not covered by building codes. Now, under pressures from the conventional housing industry, codes are being expanded to include mobile homes.

When television sets were first built, manufacturers who used expensive, high-quality materials and techniques proposed to prohibit lower-quality television sets. Had the law passed, current inferior, cheaper sets would not be available. Speakers would be larger, picture quality better, tuning easier, repairs less frequent. But the set would cost more. Highest-quality sets are so expensive that only a few are produced.

"Bad goods drive out the good. Cheap champagne drives out good champagne. Cheap music drives out good." So go the complaints that arouse people to "save" others from inferior items. A less costly item usually is inferior, in the same sense that cotton is inferior to silk, a Ford to a Rolls-Royce, Macy's to Dior's. But the lower cost more than offsets the lower quality, in the opinion of the buyer. When both quality *and price* are permitted to be determined in open-market competition, we can no longer say that bad drives out good. Instead, *the better drives out the worse*—when price is allowed to adjust.[13]

Often, a seller seeks laws prohibiting consumers from buying lower-quality goods so that he will not be undersold by lower-cost competitors—whose products may be as good or worse but whose prices are enough lower to make them preferred items, just as

---

[13] The old saw known as Gresham's law—bad goods drive out good—was developed for situations in which the prices of both the good and the bad were not allowed to reflect differences in quality. In that case, "too low" prices of higher quality goods reduce incentives to produce those goods and increase incentives of sellers to palm off inferior goods. In the absence of price controls, the better (taking into account cost) drive out the "bad."

Volkswagens are worse cars than Porsches and Sam's Cafe worse than the Hilton Escoffier Room.

The medical profession restricts entry to the market for medical aid by state licensing laws administered by the licensed doctors, to assure higher quality, given the current state of medical knowledge. If a law permitted the sale of only Rolls-Royces, Cadillacs, and Lincolns, we could certainly say we had the best-*quality* automobile service in the world—and the most pedestrians. The medical profession emphasizes that it has brought the United States the highest-quality medical care. But the same cannot be said for the quantity. It can be contended that there would be *fewer* deaths if lower-quality *and* hence more mediocre medical aid were available, because at the present time even worse substitutes are used—nurses, druggists, books, self-medication, faith-healers, friends, hearsay, phone calls instead of personal inspection, not to mention *no* medical attention at all.

It is hard to separate sincerity and duplicity in this desire to protect other people. For example, would you regard the remainder of this paragraph as sincere? Like health, wealth can be ruined by carelessness. If a person breaks his leg, it can be reset. If he breaks his budget, it can't be reset. Wealth, like health, must be protected from personal ignorance. If a person wants to invest $1,000 in some business, how can he be sure that it is a safe investment? If he loses, his family suffers. Therefore, before making *any* investment every person ought to be required to consult a licensed, certified economist, who will prescribe how wealth should be invested. He can then take the prescription to the stockbroker. Without this safeguard millions of people every day make foolish investments and irrevocably lose their wealth and harm their families. Many people follow the advice of economic quacks—stockbrokers, politicians, friends, and tip sheets. They overinvest without consulting economists, who could prevent their going too far into debt or buying in the wrong area or taking the wrong job or the wrong kind of insurance.[14]

11, 12, 13, 14, 15

Protection of Employees, Morals, and Service Standards

Laws prohibiting sales during evenings and Sundays ostensibly are to protect the health of employees, the morals of the community, and the quality of the service. Sunday selling diverts people from rest and violates the Sabbath. The United States Supreme Court says so. However, the facts are that although stores may be open twenty-four hours every day, the employees don't work twenty-four hours. Sunday and evening buying is a convenience to many shoppers. Of course, consumers *could* do all their shopping between 9 and 5 on weekdays. They *could* do it between 3 and 7 on Monday, Wednesday, and Friday only. Any store able to reduce costs enough by such hours could

---

[14] Or are there signs of progress? In 1964, the Securities and Exchange Commission issued a report evaluating the securities and stock-market dealers' practices. In the covering letter written by Mr. Cary, the chairman of the committee, is the following prescient passage: "Under existing Federal law there is a right of free access and unlimited entry into the securities business for anyone, regardless of qualifications, except those excluded on the basis of prior securities violations. The steady growth in the very numbers of investors and participants, according to the report, has made this concept obsolete. . . . Greater emphasis should be given by the Securities and Exchange Commission and the exchanges and associations of security dealers to the concept of suitability of particular securities for particular customers." (Can you imagine what this would do to economists' incomes?)

survive with the business it managed to get from consumers who prefer the lower prices at those days and hours. But there aren't enough people with such preferences, for those hours are exceptional. These laws are often supported by employers rather than by employees. In particular, conventional retail stores are aided by a ban on evening and Sunday shopping. Because conventional retail stores provide more labor service relative to capital than the evening-Sunday discount houses, the extra hours add more to total labor costs for conventional retail department stores.

Protection of Consumer from Unethical Sellers

Commonest of all attempts to restrict entry to the market in the name of consumer welfare are those aimed at "unethical" operators who promise a spectacular bargain, special prices, etc. These competitors take business from the established, better-quality, higher-cost, more reliable sellers. One who buys his new car from the old, well-established pillar of the local chamber of commerce can be surer that squeaks, defects, scratches will be given prompter attention than if he buys from the fast-dealing seller on the edge of town who sells at 10 percent less but can't be counted on to give such service. Yet the 10-percent-lower price may be worth more than the assurance of that "free" service. Laws prohibiting "bargains" provide protection to the unwary, but they impose costs on those who prefer the lower-quality bargains; the cost is the lost opportunity for a buyer to have more of other goods by accepting lower quality or greater risk.

The time spent in acquiring information about purchases costs more for a rich person with high earnings per hour than for a poor person. Hence a rich person is more likely to take his custom to high-quality sellers. Forcing lower-quality sellers out of business by law would hit the poor more severely, since the poor more often find it cheaper to shop around and compare various sellers for the best buys than to rely on the high-quality seller.

16, 17

Advertising Restrictions

Although a person may have a legal right to enter the market, any obstacle to providing information about himself or his offers will protect those sellers already in the market, about whom buyers are better informed. Advertising is primarily a means of informing potential buyers of the presence of a seller and of his goods.

The flow of information from sellers to buyers is important, even though frequently ignored. How should General Motors act with respect to advertising if it wanted to restrain the growth of American Motors (makers of Rambler) or Volkswagen? One way would be to prohibit advertising. Since GM is already well known, a reduction of advertising would make it more difficult for newcomers to call attention to their presence and offerings. And since the newcomer often has yet to demonstrate and establish the quality of his service, a ban on price cutting would be especially helpful to GM. Price cuts enable newcomers to attract customers to try new products. Holiday Inns, a nationally known motel firm, is advantaged by bans on highway advertising. It is interesting to note that the American Medical Association prohibits advertising. Examine the yellow pages of the telephone directory and compare the advertising of various professions. Whatever business you may enter as a young man, would you regard restrictions on advertising as helpful to your ability to attract customers?

The foregoing discussion of laws designed to protect the welfare of other people by restricting entry to the market has been negatively critical. Our judgment is that most people are sufficiently exposed to the well-publicized protective effects of such laws; therefore, we have intentionally emphasized some of the costs to provide a more complete understanding.

Protection of Producers

Orderly Markets

The "orderly market" argument asserts that unless an industry is controlled so as to ensure adequate prices and profits during hard times, some firms will go out of business, and later when demand increases there will not be enough firms. Prices and output will swing like a pendulum. Thus, for highly seasonal products like milk (peak supply comes in June and the low point in November), if price fluctuated from troughs in June to peaks in November, the farmers would be driven out in June and wouldn't be available in November to provide adequate milk. Also, when prices are high, fly-by-night producers will enter and "skim the cream," only to leave when prices and demand fall. The "responsible," year-around producers will not survive. Therefore, controls should be placed on entry so that irresponsible short-term producers cannot undermine the long-term stability of the industry.

Can you spot the holes in these arguments? Any supply is "inadequate" if the price is low enough. For goods with seasonal swings in *production,* a *stable* price over the year implies too large an output at peak periods and too low a supply at low-output months—unless storage costs are low enough that the output can be stored from peak-production to low-production months and thereby allow relative price uniformity. Seasonal variation of prices over a year is predictable; no business will be pushed out by low prices in peak periods if it recognizes the seasonality phenomenon. Retail stores do about half their business in the Christmas season. They are not bankrupted by the summer low-sales months—just as they are not by low Sunday sales. Yet the milk industry has obtained control over entry to the market to assure "adequate" supplies at all seasons—with a uniform year-round price despite prohibitively high storage costs. The "adequate supply" is achieved by maintaining enough cows for periods of low production (per cow) and too many for the rest of the time. Instead of letting price fall during peak-production, milk in excess of the amount wanted as fresh milk at that high, controlled price is diverted into cheese, ice cream, and processed foods. Essentially, what is achieved is a higher income for the milk producers, *less* fresh milk over the year, but more ice cream and cheese, and a prohibition on entry by new farmers.

The argument is also carried over to business fluctuations of a nonseasonal nature. "Producers must be protected during bad times to ensure their survival into good times. Furthermore, during good times too many new firms might enter the business, so that, when demand falls off, all firms will lose money. As a result, there will be extreme variations in output." This argument is internally inconsistent. On the one hand, too few firms will survive the depression, so that the *prosperity* output will be too small because of the fewness of firms. Yet too many new firms will enter during prosperity. Both can't be true. We suspect the "orderly market" argument seeks to deny access to the markets by competitors simply to keep wealth and production more "orderly" for incumbent producers. The "orderly-market" rationale has an almost unlimited number of manifestations. Farm price-support laws, for example, control entry of new producers to the market. Farm marketing boards for grapes, peaches, cantaloupes, oranges, and lemons, to name a few, control the salable output of those crops in the interest of greater wealth for the producers, but in the name of orderly competition. Domestic sugar producers have a law permitting political control of sugar imports, so the domestic price will be high enough to increase the market value of resources in the domestic sugar industry. We shall investigate a few examples in considerable detail—wheat, lemons, cotton, and tobacco.

Agricultural "Surpluses"

When the demand for wheat falls, rather than take their losses and reduce output, distressed wheat producers resort to political procedures they would not normally condone in others. But now "times are not normal," "this is a special case," and besides, "everyone else does it." Their political action has been so successful that much has been said in solemn terms about the "great farm-surplus" problem. The fact of the matter is that prices of many farm goods have, by law, been kept above the market-clearing level; as a result, the public has demanded less than the amount available. There is no truth to the popular allegation that farm production exceeds demand. Demand is not a fixed amount; the amount demanded varies with price—a fact possibly embarrassing or tedious to the reader, but one it is necessary to repeat again and again. The American public (not to count the enormous foreign population) would happily consume all the current farm output if prices of those "surplus" farm goods were not kept up by political controls. The genesis of the political controls is the *relative* decline in demands for food. A consequent decline in price would be normal—if the output were to be purchased and consumed. Rather than submit to the reduced wealth resulting from decreases in demand for their products, the farmers sought to force a higher price. But when prices were kept above free-market levels (by devices we shall investigate in a moment), the amount demanded was reduced. Hence the so-called "surplus." This unwillingness to submit to the market discipline is not unique to the farmers. The "surplus" problem arises because the farmers have successfully obtained sufficient political power to prevent consumers from influencing output via the market.

If these seem like words of condemnation, reread them; there is no suggestion of impropriety by the farmers. We examine the agricultural case simply because it is a particularly instructive example of efforts to protect wealth from the effects of open access to the market.

Holding crop off the market. A specific example is provided by lemon growers, who first sought to keep up prices by voluntarily withholding part of their output from the market. Their hopes were thwarted by the refusal of some producers to reduce output, for it would pay any grower to stay out of the agreement and sell *all* his crop at the higher price while the other producers reduced their offerings. Furthermore, some superior producers preferred not to join because they could make more wealth for themselves if there were no such agreement at all than if there were an effective one. How can they and other producers be induced to join? Perhaps they can be accused of standing in the way of those who are "voluntarily" willing to reduce output and threatened with private violence.

The threat of violence, however, is not as reliable as a law—if it can be passed. The lemon growers, along with many other groups, were able to get laws passed to compel joint action. The industry calls this "self-policing." In 1941, a law was enacted permitting a majority of the lemon growers to compel *all* lemon growers to withhold part of their crop from the market. Any grower who refused to do so could not legally sell *any* fresh lemons in the American market. Thus, state police power was used.

Still, as we know, even 100 percent membership does not solve all the problems facing the sellers. How much of each producer's output is to be sold? Who is to get the lion's share of the sales? Whatever the share, how can the group know that the quota assigned to each producer is observed and that no more is sold? One way to police the "pro-rata quota" scheme is to have a central sales agency through which all lemons are sold. That is known as "pooling" the sales. It determined what part of each producer's output could be sold as fresh fruit in domestic markets and what part would be sold as concentrates or flavorings in domestic and foreign markets. Domestic fresh-lemon prices were raised. But to keep fresh-fruit prices high, the proportion of lemons authorized for sale had to be steadily reduced over the years—from 90 percent of the crop in 1942, when the sales-control scheme went into effect, until now, when over half of the crop is barred from the fresh-fruit market.

Diverting unsold fruit to other markets resulted in lower prices for other lemon products than would have prevailed. Without the scheme, there would have been fewer, but more efficient, producers and a lower price of fresh lemons. In effect, fresh-lemon consumers are subsidizing the output of frozen juices and concentrates. The success in raising prices and incomes to lemon growers has induced a larger output by each grower and attracted new growers into production.

Subsidized production. There are still more weapons in the political arsenal that producers can exploit. For example, let the government buy (out of taxes) whatever part of the crop the consumers refuse to buy voluntarily in the market. This kind of law, which denies *consumers* the right of withdrawal from markets, has been passed for producers of wheat, cotton, tobacco, peanuts, rice, and corn, and it is proposed for more.

We exaggerate slightly. The government, *or* the taxpayers, do not *buy* the unsold crop. They only *lend* money to the farmer, using the crop as security. However, if the farmers don't repay the loan, the government keeps the unsold crop—which is, after all, no different from selling the crop to the government. The farmer is thus assured of a minimum price, but the maximum is open. Unfortunately for appearances, since the government is usually left holding the deteriorating "surplus" product, there will be *visible* signs that this storage scheme is wasteful. In 1965, the total accumulated crops in government-held stocks had cost the taxpayers over $5,500,000,000, including an annual cost of about $1,000,000,000 to keep them stored.

Production controls. An alternative scheme is to produce only as much as can be sold at the desired price.[15] This kind of crop control, if effective, is very tidy and solves the problem in the sense that there will be no "surplus" around to embarrass anyone and no low price to the producers.

One way to obtain effective crop controls or "self-policing management" is to assure each producer who agrees to reduce acreage of a particular crop by at least 20 percent

---

[15] "Parity" price is the common euphemism for the "desired" price.

(obviously he will pick the poorest 20 percent of his land) that he will be guaranteed a sale at the "parity" price for all he produces of that crop, and that he will even be paid something for the released land if he keeps it idle—a payment called a "conservation" payment. Those who do not agree to restrict their acreage probably will not be allowed to sell at the market price. In fact, in the case of tobacco a prohibitive tax of 75 percent of the value is levied on such production.

To get such a program into effect requires a majority vote of the current producers—which usually is not so easy. Under this acreage-control scheme, efficiency in production will *not* be the criterion for deciding which land will be licensed for tobacco (or whatever crop is being "protected"). One procedure is simply to require all existing producers to eliminate the same percentage of land. But percentage of what total amount of land used by each producer? The amount he planned to use this year? Or the amount he used last year? Or five, ten, or twenty years ago? This comical question is indeed a serious one. Acreage in any product is always changing. New areas develop. Cotton production has swept westward to more efficient lands—in the San Joaquin Valley of California, where cotton can be produced at a lower average cost than in the southeastern United States. In no small part, it is because of this new, cheaper source that cotton prices have fallen; the older higher-cost producers are using the government taxing power to help protect them from the new competitors, who are often hurt by the crop-control plan, as we shall see.

Open-market forces toward efficiency are reduced because the use of land is affected by a political voting process. The government authorizes someone (government employees or industry representatives) to decide on the land allocation. A voting majority of the growers must agree, else the whole acreage-reduction scheme will be jeopardized. In cotton, the most efficient lands are in the western United States, and the farms are larger. Therefore, the more efficient producers are outnumbered. A proposal to cut back the use of older, less efficient lands before that of the newer ones is obviously not acceptable to that majority. A proposal to cut everyone back by the same percentage is used instead, and it is ingeniously effective in reducing the newer, more efficient acreage by a bigger percentage than the old. How? Suppose you decide to cut all acreage back to the former amount. Which former amount? Last year's? The farther into the past one goes for his base, the greater the cut for the newly expanding areas. And conversely for older areas that are *declining*. Anticipating this kind of restriction, the newer, more efficient, expanding producers vote against the scheme. While they will get a higher price, it is on such a greatly reduced output that they would have smaller wealth than if they were permitted to produce more for sale at lower prices. The votes of cotton landowners for acreage-restriction schemes fall off dramatically as one moves into the more efficient western lands.[16]

Acreage control, combined with a guaranteed high price of output, promotes larger

---

[16] We interject an ironic note. Although we have been calling the western lands more efficient, some of these lands are more efficient only because the costs of irrigation are not borne by the farm landowners who use that water. Some of the water is provided to the farmers by federal irrigation projects at prices substantially below the costs—the difference being made up by taxes on the rest of the country. Thus, we see farmers in southeastern United States paying taxes to enable water to be sold to cotton growers in the western desert areas at less than cost in order to compete with the cotton from the southeast. And to protect themselves from the consequent lower prices, they appeal for more taxes on the city consumers to finance "loans on unsold cotton"; finally, they appeal for federal regulations restricting production of cotton on those very same western lands for which they have paid taxes to help irrigate at less than cost.

use of fertilizer and other jointly productive resources. Production becomes more intensive; the output per acre skyrockets. Acreage must be cut back more than expected, because farming becomes "surprisingly productive."

Acreage controls have been most effectively and rigorously used in tobacco production. Land licensed for tobacco growing is marked and policed. Unlicensed producers must pay a prohibitive 75 percent tax on the value of the output. No one could afford to produce without a "license"—unless tobacco growing were a hobby. Since the licenses are for so few acres, the untaxed output is small enough to yield a high price. There is no tobacco surplus because the price goes to whatever level will clear the market of the *licensed* (untaxed) output. The type of output control for tobacco has been extolled by recent Presidents as deserving application to other crops.

Public Utilities

If larger rates (and volume) of some good can be produced by a firm with ever decreasing costs *per unit,* the firm is a decreasing-cost firm. Two firms producing identical goods could not reach an equilibrium. One could expand more and eliminate the other. In view of the impossibility of more than one firm's being profitable, two is one too many. But if there is only one, that firm may be able to set prices above free-entry costs for a long time. Either resources are wasted because too many are in the industry, or if there is just one firm, it will be able to charge monopoly prices. That, in essence, is the reasoning behind government regulation of a single authorized firm in this industry—often called a public utility.

But that analysis is incomplete. While it may be true that only one firm should be *producing,* nothing implies that there cannot be competition among many applicants for that *right* to produce. The lowest annual bidder, in terms of prices to be charged the public, could be granted a franchise. Several other techniques have been proposed for permitting competition among potential producers, even though only one is allowed to produce. But none has been used extensively. Instead, the political processes of control have usually endorsed the following: (1) Only one firm is allowed to produce for the market; a legal, closed monopoly is created. (2) The closed-monopoly firm is subjected to political regulation of profits, prices, amount and kind of service, costs it can incur, and many other details. If the utility fails to make money, the stockholders bear the losses. They may then sell at a loss to new buyers who expect to do better; or the service will come to an end (railroad passenger service, street cars) or be subsidized by taxes (city bus lines, subways, local airlines).

Examples of public utilities are electric, gas, water, sewage, telephone, railroad, and airline companies. Other products that are sometimes monopolized by law, but not because of the decreasing-cost technicality, are also called public utilities (taxi, radio, television, and municipal garbage-collection services).

The creation of a legal, closed monopoly imposes some costs on consumers. Prohibiting new entrants does not so fully encourage new products or lower-cost methods of production. It is not that the incumbent firm refuses to use known lower-cost techniques; rather, the incumbent firm does not know everything. Others, with different ideas about how to produce, are blocked out. The incumbent is dilatory in introducing known lower-cost innovations—not because it is a monopolist but because its *profits are limited* by the regulatory commission. Cost-reducing devices would be introduced if the firm could garner the profits; however, if the firm is already making its maximum allowable profits, incentives to reduce costs are blunted. Members of the regulatory commission cannot capture the net gain of lower costs, so they, too, will be less motivated. It's not that regulators are indolent or lazy; it is just that the incentives in the form of rewards for instituting cost-reduction techniques are lower than for those in open markets, where customers can shop among competitors.[17]

Whose "Utility" in Public Utilities?

An especially instructive example of the incentives for and consequences of regulatory agencies is provided by the history of regulation of the railroads. A long list of pricing "abuses" presaged the creation in 1887 of the Interstate Commerce Commission to regulate the railroads in the interests of the consumer. What was the basic problem? Prior to 1880, open-market entry resulted in the overbuilding of railroads. Railroad investors had been too optimistic; many states gave railroads land, the power of eminent domain (legal power to acquire land for rights-of-way), and tax exemptions. (Eventually there were seven tracks between Omaha and Chicago.) The high initial investment acquisition costs of creating a railroad and the low variable (operating) costs (relative to the total costs of having created the railroad) enabled the railroads to cut prices far below the total average costs (including the sunk costs). Rather than shut down if price did not cover "full" costs, some dropped prices to average variable costs of continued operation of existing equipment. The railroads sought to prevent piece-cutting that was self-destructive or involved secret price discounts. Shippers who paid more were at a cost disadvantage. They demanded the government prohibit secret price cuts. Even the railroads wanted to avoid it as a group.

The lower prices of rail service, even without secret price cuts, would have continued for a long time, until some rails and equipment wore out and only the more economic railroads survived. However, the law of 1887 requiring that railroads charge "just and reasonable" rates and publicly post their rates enabled railroads to do what they had sought to do by private collusion—to prevent individually advantageous but mutually disadvantageous price-cutting.

The Interstate Commerce Commission became the vehicle facilitating the maintenance of an effective cartel. Although only three years later (1890) the Sherman Antitrust Act declared all collusive (cartel) activity illegal, the railroads with the aid of the Interstate Commerce Commission continued to act effectively as a collusive cartel until 1948. In that long interim the railroads had legal backup in setting prices (much as if General Motors, Ford, and Chrysler could make it illegal for any of them to secretly sell their cars for less than prices jointly agreed to by themselves). In 1920 the Interstate Commerce Commission acquired the power to set prices and to *control entry* into the railroad business, thus securing the railroads' wealth position even more firmly. Unfortunately for the railroads, new forms of transportation, which developed under the umbrella of high prices for rail service and the "regulated monopolistic service" of railroads, managed to take away many railroad customers. This led to insistence that the new competitors also

20, 21, 22, 23

---

[17] Recall the discussion (on page 355) of the likelihood of successful collusions against governments. The same analysis is applicable here in the case of sales to public utilities, since they are "profit limited" and regulated by the government. Because of the restricted incentives or rewards available to public utilities, collusion among sellers of items bought by public utilities is more viable. In fact, and as an illustration of this implication, the conviction of the major electric-power-equipment companies involved collusion of items sold almost exclusively to regulated public utilities and governments.

be regulated. The conflict of interest among the forms of transportation is still being fought within the Interstate Commerce Commission, the Congress, and to some extent in the market.

The Commission now is authorized to approve rates charged by highway transport, waterways, pipelines, and telephone and communication companies. If companies want to change service or routes of services, they must obtain permission from the Commission. Its extensive authority is used primarily for policing rather than for administering details. Additional federal regulatory commissions deal with other public utilities. The airlines are controlled by the Civil Aeronautics Board, which allocates routes and authorizes rates, types of service, mergers, etc. The Federal Communications Commission controls radio- and television-station entry. All these regulatory boards were set up because Congress reflected the belief that open-market competition was inappropriate for providing such services.

Monopoly Rents: Creation and Disposition

In all the preceding cases wherein legal barriers were placed on market access, the effect, and often the purpose, was to increase the wealth of those who were first in the market. This increase is called *monopoly rent*. Here monopoly refers to *closed* monopoly only. The term *rent* is used to describe wealth in excess of that which would be normal in an open market.

Closed-monopoly rent is achieved by *restricting* entry of resources, so that a difference between value of product and costs is created by restricting output. Closed-monopoly rent is not achieved by transferring resources from lower- to higher-valued uses but, rather, by restrictions on that transfer. The value difference that is created or preserved beyond what it would have been in the absence of such legal restriction is the monopoly rent.

What happens to the monopoly rent that results from the agricultural crop-control scheme? It goes to the *landowners* who owned the land at the time the scheme was first revealed. The higher value of the particular land on which the authorization, or license, to grow tobacco is granted is the value of the crop after all other costs of production (labor, equipment, fertilizer, insecticides, management, taxes, etc.) are subtracted. Suppose that net revenue of a licensed acre is $400 for each crop year. Recall from the earlier capital-value analysis that an annuity of $400 per year would have a value of about $4,000 if the interest rate were about 10 percent. Taking that as a simple assumption, suppose that land of the same kind, without a "license," has a value of $1,000. This difference, $3,000, is the capital-value measure of the monopoly rent resulting from the acreage-licensing scheme in tobacco.[18] As the licensing scheme is revealed, the favored acre rises in value, and anyone who at that time owns it captures the higher income. He can then sell the land (with the "license" for exemption from the crop tax) and use the wealth for other kinds of consumption (vacations in Florida); he can keep the land and the annual higher-income stream; he can rent the land out for the higher annual value.

A *new* purchaser gets no monopoly-rent *gain* since he pays a higher price to get the land. The high monopoly-rent income from tobacco production is equal to a normal competitive return on *his* $4,000 purchase price. The person whose wealth increased by the amount of the monopoly rent is the owner at the time the controls were announced.

---

[18] These are realistic values.

If the license to grow an acre of untaxed tobacco could be sold "naked" separately from an acre of land, it would be profitable and more efficient to have the landowners of less efficient lands transfer their licenses, acre for acre, to the more efficient lands. A bigger crop, or a lesser-cost crop, could be grown; and the owners of more efficient lands would compete among themselves to buy the "naked" licenses from the owners of less efficient lands, who would capture some of the value of the crop which could be grown on the more efficient lands. Regardless of who captures that monopoly-rent gain, the total costs of the produced tobacco would be lower if transfers to better land were legal. This general increase in achieved level of efficiency is not permitted under the law. Why? The total tobacco output would be larger for the same cost of production, and that would involve a lower selling price. An appropriate further restriction of licensed acreage could offset that increase in yield per acre. Some political observers have suggested that the outright sale of these bare licenses would expose the monopoly rents provided to the tobacco landowners—just as they would be exposed in the sale of bare liquor-store licenses, taxi franchises, and radio- and television-station licenses.

The effects of the tobacco price-support program—widely regarded as politically "good" because there is no "surplus"—are (1) reduction of consumption compared to what it would have been had the price been allowed to reflect an open-market demand and supply, (2) wealth gains in the form of monopoly rent to those who were able to get their land licensed, (3) political protection of the wealth of tobacco landowners (as distinct from tobacco growers), (4) inefficiency, (5) reduced range of choice of occupation for producers.

As we saw in Chapter 4, there are ways to make the monopolist pay for the monopoly rent. In some cases, he must pay a price to get that legal monopoly right. Outright bribes, political contributions, higher taxes as a payment for monopoly rights, costs of public-relations men and lawyers to obtain "rights, licenses, franchises, or authorization" are sometimes large enough to match the monopoly rent. If there were restrictions on entry into some business, so that in each year only selected people were admitted, candidates for admission would be prepared to spend money to obtain admission rights. They would each seek to buy whatever qualities the candidate believes the authorities will use in their criterion of admission. For example, a young man setting out to enter the medical profession might find that by the time he had paid the "costs" of being admitted to practice, he would be so old that the high but short-lived income he eventually gets has a smaller capital value, as seen from date of application to medical school, than the average of all college students. In other words, the monopoly rent is consumed by these entry "fees."

In some states, liquor licenses—right to sell bottled liquors at retail—have sold for over $40,000. Tobacco-growing rights are worth about $3,000 an acre. Cotton allotments are worth over $500 per acre—if we judge by the prices paid in certain illegal transfers in Texas in 1962. In many areas, milk farmers must have a license to produce and sell milk. Entry into the savings-and-loan bank business in many states is subject to approval of state officials. The value of permission to open a bank has exceeded $50,000 in California, as evidenced and measured by the immediate rise in price of stock of groups obtaining permission. Radio and television stations are "requested" to provide free coverage of political campaigns, especially at the national level, for the major parties. They are also required to broadcast the kinds of programs that the federal-government authorities think they should broadcast. (Notice the contrast with newspapers, which do not have to apply for a license. Not surprisingly, they act in ways that radio and television cannot.) Part of the "monopoly rent" of radio and television is taken not necessarily in the form of money but by the kinds of programs that the authorities prefer.

Public utilities generally pay higher taxes than other businesses of similar size; these transfer part of their monopoly rent to the government. Employees of public utilities get larger wages or more secure jobs or easier jobs than similar employees in open-market firms. The extra payment to employees is a sharing of the monopoly rent. The owners of a closed monopoly cannot count on capturing all the monopoly rent for themselves. The political processes that can give the monopoly rent can also take it away in one form or another.

25, 26, 27, 28, 29, 30, 31

Summary

1. Reduction of market competition by elimination of rivals or by collusion is potentially profitable.

2. We have been unable to show that predatory tactics are profitable. They impose losses on both contending parties and give no assurance that elimination of one would allow higher prices or larger profits—because of potential entry of new firms.

3. Effective collusion is difficult because rivals find it hard to reach agreement, police the agreement, and keep out new entrants who would be attracted by the higher profit potential.

4. Mergers do not appear to be an important means of achieving collusive action to change market conditions. Rather, many allow efficient managers to take over less efficient firms or provide certain economies of joint production, none of which involves raising prices as a consequence of the merger.

5. Sealed-bid purchases by government agencies encourage collusion, because they make enforcement of secret agreements easy.

6. The argument against collusion is essentially the argument against monopoly inefficiency (explained in Chapter 14).

7. Under the Sherman Act, the Antitrust division of the Department of Justice and the Federal Trade Commission are supposed to prevent "monopolizing tactics" and "unfair" trade practices. Whether these laws have on net protected competitive markets or hindered them is not clear, and the evidence for either position is extremely weak.

8. Some labor unions represent effective collusions by sellers (of labor) to raise wages above the competitive level. Wage cutting and entry is in those cases reduced (though not entirely eliminated).

9. Restrictions on access to the market occur for several, sometimes conflicting, reasons: (a) encouragement of invention; (b) protection to consumers, by saving them each from incurring costs of discerning undesirable features of goods; (c) to prevent uneconomic duplication of resources, as with *some* public utilities; (d) to protect existing producers from products of other potential producers. While the first three are generally, though not universally, applauded, each serves as a facade for the fourth effect. Therein lies the source of objection to many governmental and political controls over people who would buy and sell in the open market. Political authorities can create and obtain monopoly-rent wealth through closed, legal monopolies. This enhances the role of competition for political power.

10. Some market controls are ostensibly intended to protect consumers from their gullibility and sanguineness; others are intended to lower individual information-collection costs.

Sellers' Tactics for Changing Market Conditions

This latter objective implies governmental licensing for "approved" sellers, but *not* exclusion from the market for non-licensed sellers.

11 Some market-entry restrictions are designed primarily to protect existing sellers from competition of new and existing sellers. Almost every agricultural crop-market or production control does this. Although advertising restrictions are intended to protect the buyer from gullibility, they also protect existing producers from new competitors by raising the costs of entry to the market.

12 Closing the markets to new entrants, or to any sellers who would sell below an "approved" price initially provides a closed-monopoly rent to the producer. Hence, many of the crop price-support laws intended to help the poor farmers give a greater gain to the larger, richer landowner.

13 Public utilities are closed monopolies, regulated by the political process, presumably because the product is produced at decreasing cost and more than one seller would be wasteful. That regulated monopoly is superior in its over-all results (introduction of new processes and goods, reductions of price, reliability of service) to unregulated open monopoly is open to serious question.

Questions

1 Suppose there are ten identical producers of the good being sold in the market characterized by the demand schedule given here. Each producer has *zero* costs of production for twenty units; he can produce no more.

Demand Schedule

Price	Quantity Demanded Daily	Dollar Value of Daily Revenue		
		Total	Increment	Marginal (for Unit Increase in Quantity)
$1.00	56.52	$56.52	0	0
.95	62.25	59.14	$2.62	.46
.90	68.39	61.55	2.41	.41
.85	74.65	63.45	1.90	.30
.80	81.36	65.09	1.64	.24
.75	88.17	66.13	1.04	.15
.70	95.45	66.82	.69	.09
.67	100.00	67.00	.18	.03
.65	103.00	66.95	—.05	—.02
.60	110.67	66.40	—.43	—.05
.55	118.60	65.23	—1.17	—.15
.50	127.01	63.51	—1.72	—.18
.45	135.72	61.07	—2.44	—.28
.40	144.48	57.79	—3.28	—.37
.35	153.76	53.81	—3.98	—.43
.30	163.07	48.92	—4.98	—.53
.25	172.92	43.23	—5.69	—.58
.20	182.79	37.16	—6.07	—.61
.15	193.21	28.98	—8.18	—.78
.10	203.92	20.39	—8.59	—.81
.05	214.62	10.70	—9.69	—.91

a. If all are selling in a price-takers' market, what is the price and output?
b. If all sellers could reach an effective agreement to restrict output and raise price, what price should they select?
c. What will be each seller's output and revenue?
d. How much would each seller gain by the effective agreement?
e. How much (money) would it be worth to each seller to seek means of reaching and enforcing that effective agreement?
f. How much would you gain if you as *one* seller succeeded in staying outside the agreement or in secretly breaking it while all others raised the price and reduced their output?

2 Ten concrete-block companies in a certain community were accused by the city attorney of colluding to restrain output and fix the prices of concrete blocks. The accusation stated that the ten producers accounted for 85 percent of the output of concrete blocks in the community. Which do you think was meant by "colluding": Meeting and talking in an effort to reach an agreement? Or reaching an agreement? Or those ten firms restricting output and raising prices? Or all firms raising prices?

3 Assume that all existing firms producing a commodity were successfully and effectively to collude to restrict output and raise prices.
a. What open-market forces would operate to obstruct the effectiveness of the collusion?
b. How can those forces be restrained from operating? Illustrate in the context of the behavior of lemon growers, wheat producers, tobacco growers, longshoremen, carpenters, doctors, retail liquor stores, and steel producers.
c. What devices are used in each instance to keep the supply below the open-market supply?
d. Are these regarded as "proper"?

4 The first case prosecuted under the federal laws against collusion to raise prices involved steel pipe sold to the U. S. government. More recently, an electrical-equipment industry's collusion, which sent some business leaders to jail, was also against the government. What explanations are there for the fact that a majority of prosecuted proven cases involve collusion against the government?

5 The National and the American Baseball Leagues are two separate leagues of ten teams each. Teams are owned by different people. To prevent competition among team owners for *new* players, a draft (similar to that used in the football and basketball leagues) has been adopted, wherein each newcomer from a high school is assigned to a particular team. Under this agreement, or assignment, no other team owner will be allowed to sign that newcomer. Once a player signs a contract, he cannot change "employers" at his own volition; but the employer can trade or sell him to another team owner.
a. Who benefits from this arrangement? Who suffers?
b. Why does this system exist in sports and nowhere else?

6 Almost every team in the two baseball leagues is subsidized by the city governments, which provide stadium facilities. If new leagues cannot be assured of access to those facilities, will this have any effect on the income of the existing teams?

7 What is the difference between collusion, cooperation, and competition? How would you define collusion between two people so as to exclude partnerships and corporate joint ownership from the concept of collusion? Why is collusion considered undesirable?

8 Suppose you could live in a society in which trademarks were not protected by law and anyone could imitate the trademark.
a. As a consumer, would you prefer to live in that world or in one where trademarks were exclusively reserved for a particular manufacturer as part of his property? Why?
b. As a producer, which would you prefer?

9   You invent a photocopy machine. You know that the average cost of making the machine is $1,000 and that its operating costs are 1 cent each time the machine is used. You could sell the machine for, say, $2,000, letting users pay the 1-cent operating costs. On the other hand, if you can discriminate among customers, and charge some a higher price than others, you can make still more money. In order to make discriminatory pricing effective, you must not sell machines to the users, for they could then resell them from the "low-priced" to the "higher-priced" customers, and undermine your attempt to get more revenue. Suppose, however, you rent the machine to each user at a uniform fee but charge 3 cents each time the machine makes a photocopy.
a. Would that achieve your purpose? Explain.
b. Selling at different prices is illegal; 3¢ per copy is legal. Why?
c. Is this kind of "discrimination" good?

10 Charles Pfizer Company, the patent holder of the drug tetracycline, used in various forms as a general antibiotic (Aureomycin is an example), has licensed other firms to produce and sell the drug. In doing so, it has set certain conditions as to price and amounts for each licensed producer. This practice has been attacked by the Federal Trade Commission as "illegal." The patent holder does not have to license other firms at all. Under the patent terms, it could be the only producer of the drug.
a. As a potential consumer of drugs, which arrangement would you prefer to exist?
b. Do you think this kind of licensing would explain why this drug is sold for a lower price in foreign countries than in the United States?
c. Is that kind of price discrimination bad? Why?

11 European countries import inspected frozen fresh meat from Argentina. But the United States limits imports of fresh meat, because some other countries have hoof and mouth disease (a rapidly spreading disease that kills cattle, although it does not endanger human life). Whom does the import limitation benefit and whom does it hurt? How?

12 The stock exchanges, with the sanction of the U. S. Securities and Exchange Commission, occasionally prohibit (suspend) all trading in a certain common stock, especially when some spectacular news about that company suddenly is heard. For example, if the president of a corporation is sued for fraud by some government agency, with a consequent rush of sell orders by common stockholders, the exchange suspends trading to permit time for the full news to be digested and to prevent wild swings in the price of stock. The defense of the suspension is that it protects some stockholders from selling in panic at the developing, but as yet unsubstantiated and unweighed news. These sellers would later find the price had recovered—that they had sold at exceptionally low transient prices.

Does that reasoning—as a defense of suspension of trading of the stock—convince you that it would be better for you to be in a situation in which the exchange could stop trading in common stocks you happened to own? In making your decision, consider the risk that the news will turn out to be accurate and the swing will not be temporary. Consider also the effect on the new potential buyers who are restrained from buying. (Incidentally, trading can always go on elsewhere than in the formal exchange markets—whether or not the exchange suspends its trading.)

13 It is probably safe to say that a majority of the faculty at any college contends that students are not competent to judge the quality of the instruction in various courses and hence should not be relied upon as evaluators of instructor competence.
a. What do you think?
b. At the same time, it is probably safe to say that a majority of the faculty thinks its students have come to that college because the students can tell good colleges from bad. Do you see any inconsistency in this pair of beliefs? Explain.

14 Texas, which has the legal right to subdivide itself into seven states, surprises us by doing so. One of the new states, Texaseven, with no college in its boundaries, decides to give to every high-school student a four-year annual grant of $1,500 to be applied to education costs at the college of his choice anywhere in the world.
a. Would you consider that new state to have the finest or the worst educational system in the world?
b. Why is that method not used more widely, despite its temporary wide use immediately after World War II as an aid to veterans?
c. Why is it opposed by the officials of most state universities?

15 a. Do you know of any instances where inferior goods have driven out superior goods?
b. Would any of the following be such cases: compact versus larger cars; margarine versus butter; salad dressing versus mayonnaise; blended versus straight whiskey; plastic cartons versus milk bottles; frozen versus fresh orange juice; ready-made versus custom clothes; office versus home visits of the doctor. Would you consider any of these to be unfortunate developments? Why?

16 Read the first quotation in footnote 15, page 366.
a. Why has the growth in numbers of investors made open markets for security dealers and for investors an obsolete concept?
b. If you were a Negro, a Jew, or an immigrant, would you find this development to your advantage? Why?

17 Refer to the last passage in footnote 15, page 366.
a. Restate the proposition of that passage in terms analogous to the control of medication by prescriptions from doctors.
b. Do you think economists should campaign for laws to prohibit any person from buying a security, land, or a house without a prescription from an economist certifying the suitability of that particular purchase by the particular person involved? Why or why not?

18 "Capitalism encourages deceitful advertising, dishonesty, and faithlessness." Do you agree? If so, why? If not, why not?

19 European coal producers pool their sales through a central agency.
a. Why is that essential for an effective policing of the collusion agreement among the producers?
b. Why haven't some coal producers stayed out of the agreement and taken advantage of the opportunity to sell more coal at the price maintained by the "cartel," as it is called?

20 Diagnose and explain the various features reported in the following news story: "An attractive brunette seated in a rear row gave an excited whoop when her name was called Wednesday during a drawing at the County Building. She had good reason to be elated. For $6,000 she had picked up an on-sale liquor license with a market value of about $9,500. She was one of 54 persons who had applied for the 25 new on-sale licenses to be issued in the county this year by the Alcoholic Beverage Control Board. A drawing was used to determine who would get the new on-sale licenses, which permit sale of drinks on the premises. An applicant must have had a premise available and must operate the business for two years before he can sell the license."

21 Milk delivery is sometimes called inefficient because when several firms deliver milk to homes, there is duplication of delivery trucks and labor.
a. For standard items such as milk, would you prefer to live in a community with one centralized delivery service controlled by a regulatory commission to ensure low prices and adequate quality, or in one where anyone who wants to deliver milk can enter the market? Why?

b. Apply your analysis of the preceding problem to the case of garbage collecting. Would you feel differently about that?
c. How about mail service? Newspapers? Electric power?
d. If your answers differ, what factor makes you change your preference?

22 Gasoline price "wars" have induced many gasoline-station owners to propose a regulatory agency to establish orderly marketing conditions in gasoline markets. Also, they propose that no service station be allowed to charge a price less than costs, and further that no new stations be opened unless the convenience and necessity of the area warrants more stations.
a. Who would benefit and who would be hurt by these proposals, if carried out?
b. If the proposals were carried out, how should the commission decide who got to open a new service station?
c. What would be your preference about this kind of regulation if you were a Negro, immigrant, or young gasoline-station operator?

23 **a.** Why will a person who has salable property rights in an enterprise for which he is making decisions be more influenced by the longer-run effects of his decisions than if he did not have salable property rights in the enterprise?
b. Does this difference in type of property right induce a systematic difference in the kinds of decisions made by government employees, as contrasted to employees of a privately owned enterprise—even if both are engaged in the same kind of activity (production of power)? Explain why the influence of the salable capital value of property rights will or will not make a difference in decisions.

24 When seeking a replacement for a retiring member of a regulatory board, President Johnson said that he wanted a strong man of action to help strengthen the board, because he had noted that even the regulated industry didn't like weak regulatory boards. Why do you suppose the regulated industry likes a strong regulatory board? (Hint: Who is regulated for whose benefit?)

25 As determined by Congressional action, radio and television networks are not required to give "equal-time" rights to any political parties other than the Republican and Democratic parties.
a. Would you consider this a collusion by the two major political parties against the many smaller political parties? Explain.
b. Why are newspapers not required to give equal-space rights to the two major political parties? (Hint: The answer is *not* that radio space is limited or a natural resource that "belongs to the people.")

26 Why, despite so much political campaigning against "monopolies," do politicians create closed markets or closed monopolies?

27 The judicial council of the American Medical Association recommended that it be considered unethical for a doctor to own a drug store in the area in which he practices medicine. It also recommended similarly for ophthalmologists who dispense eyeglasses for a profit. "Any arrangement by which the physician profits from the remedy he prescribes is unethical," in the opinion of the council.
a. Who do you think would benefit if this recommendation were adopted by the American Medical Association and made effective?
b. If it is unethical for a surgeon to profit from the remedy he prescribes, should any surgeon diagnosing a patient be allowed to perform the recommended operation?
c. Should a building contractor be allowed to have any interest in a lumber company? Should any teacher be allowed to use his own textbook? Should a doctor be allowed to own a hospital? Or own an undertaking business?

d. As a patient, would you prefer to deal with doctors who are prohibited from ownership of drug stores? How would this help you or hurt you?

28 The U. S. Postal system is a monopoly. No one else may institute a competitive system of transporting personal messages for pay.
a. Why do you think it has remained a monopoly?
b. The prices charged are uniform despite vast differences in costs of service to different patrons. Why is this kind of discriminatory pricing practiced for mail but not for food, clothes, or dancing lessons?

29 Why do union officials object to admitting that their power rests on a closed monopoly, while at the same time opposing any legislation that would destroy that monopoly power? Answer the same question when applied to the American Medical Association.

30 Moving companies are regulated by the Interstate Commerce Commission; their rates per pound are legally set. Explain why that would entail prohibition of making binding bids, prior to moving, as to the cost of the move? In what manner will they compete for business?

31 Public utilities often have their rates controlled by a regulatory commission. Explain how this can be used to make one class of customers pay for service to another class. How does this differ from a tax on one group with the proceeds going to the other?

Derived Demand for Productive Resources

20

UNTIL now our interest concentrated on the first two of the following social tasks: (1) allocating consumption goods among competing claimants, (2) determining how much of each good to produce, (3) deciding with what resources goods shall be produced, (4) determining incomes of each person. The first two were investigated primarily as determined in a market system. Now we study the last two. Again the focus will be markets between business firms and households—this time, the householders selling productive services to firms.

We can portray a relationship between households and business firms by the circular-flow diagram of Figure 20-1. The top half represents consumers' goods markets, with money flowing from householders to business firms (left to right) and consumers' goods going in the opposite direction. In the bottom half, money flows from business firms to householders (right to left), while services go in the opposite direction. The bottom half represents the producers' goods market, the market in which households earn income by selling their various productive services.

We have already analyzed the influence of householders' demand for consumption goods on the supply of goods from producers—the top half of the circle. We shall now see how a market system determines which productive goods are used to make which consumers' goods; this is the question the business firm will be solving in deriving their demands for productive services. We shall see also how incomes of people are determined, since the prices and quantities of services they sell determine their income.

The logic of the analysis, in contrast to the pictures, is not circular. It is a simultaneous determination of interdependent outputs of various goods—like the simultaneous solution of a set of equations. Not surprisingly, the analysis will be based on demand for and supply of productive services. In this chapter, we investigate the general

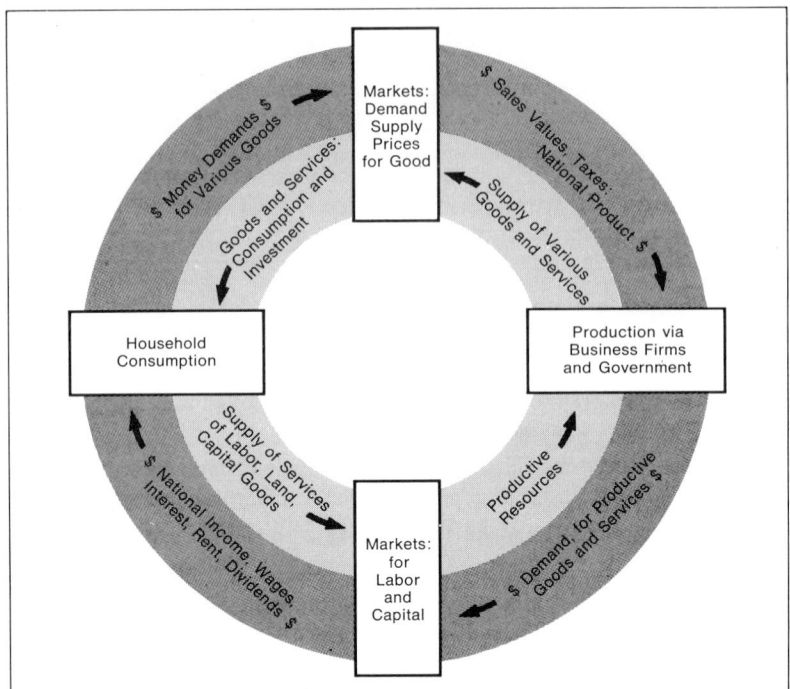

FIGURE 20-1

This chart relates the aggregate flows of goods and incomes with some of the institutions and problems of economics. Chapters 4–10 discussed allocation of existing goods (the upper left quarter of the circle). And Chapters 11–19 covered the amounts of goods produced (upper right portion). Methods of determining how goods shall be produced and by whom and for whom (the bottom half of the circle) are discussed in Chapters 20–24. These chapters will also cover determination of individual incomes and wealth. For each case, in the capitalist market system, the communications and controls are channeled via prices and incomes. Fluctuations in the total flow of services and values "around the whole economy" are problems of aggregate employment and national-income and are covered in Chapters 25–34.

conditions of *derived demand* for productive resources, derived from the value of the consumer goods these services help to produce.

Forms of Distribution of Earnings

The total income produced by the economy's resources and people is somehow apportioned among them. Who gets what share? How is it decided? We know that about 70 to 80 percent of the total income is received in the form of wages and salaries—decidedly toward 80 percent if we count as wages-and-salaries the earnings from labor services of a person running his own business.

Most of the rest is distributed to people in payment for uses of capital goods, paid in the form of rents, interest, or dividends. Dividends usually comprise payments by corporations to the owners of the corporate assets for the services of those assets (hence, they are rental payments) and payments of the residual net earnings of the businesses paid to the owners who bear the risks that the residual will be negative. Usually a portion of what could be distributed to corporate owners is invested in the corporation. Payments for use of capital goods take two forms: rent and interest. If you rented a house to me, I would pay you *rent*. If you lent (i.e., rented) me money, I would pay you *interest*. We give different names to payment for use of wealth—although, as above, either could be called "rent" or "interest" as payment for services of capital goods.

Several resources are jointly or simultaneously used as productive "inputs." How much is produced by each? If I mow a lawn *with* a lawn mower, how much did I produce, and how much did the mower? If three people jointly move a box, how much did each person move? With jointly used productive resources, it is impossible to measure or even define how much of the product is produced by any one of the jointly used inputs.

This question of "what it produces" is a "red herring." You have heard that in the communist society each will be paid according to what he deserves or needs, not according to what he produces. Whatever its emotional worth, that statement is objectively meaningless. And if it is said of the capitalist system that people are paid according to their product, that, too, is a meaningless statement. Instead, we ask, "What determines what it gets—that is, its price?"

Labor and Capital as Standard Names of Resources

In Chapters 11 and 12, we called different resources by names of people, Messrs. *A, B, C, D,* and *E*. For reasons evident later, we have here two classes of resources, "capital" and "labor." Do not let the *name* serve as the *definition*. We can initially think of capital as nonhuman resources and labor as human resources; but in fact both human and nonhuman resources are capital goods, for both are durable and can render services in the future as well as the present. And in a still different, and less fundamental, sense of the term "capital," both human and nonhuman goods are capital: each is usually created by *earlier* activity. For example, earlier labor is used to create machines or rear children or train students, thereby increasing nonhuman goods and also the productive power of human beings. Those earlier productive services are paid at the time of the service—in advance of the ultimate service rendered by the enhanced productive powers thereby created. The people who advance payment and wait for future compensation as the machine or human services are ultimately rendered are "capitalists." The machines and the human talents developed are, respectively, nonhuman and human capital.

Anyone working at that later time with the machine is called labor; labor is said to be working with capital. The use of the machines is often called substitution of capital for labor, since the machine takes the place of some current labor services, releasing those services for work elsewhere. More accurately, earlier labor which made, say, a computer is substituting for the currently released labor and is enabling current human services to produce more. Since human capital cannot be divorced from the person (contracts for advance sales of all of a person's future services are not enforceable by custom or law), capitalists of human resources are the persons themselves.

If this all seems confusing, you are getting the correct impression. The word "capital" has a variety of meanings; (i) the *present value* of a future sequence of receipts, (ii) a capital *good*—i.e., one that can yield services in the future, and (iii) something made from *past services,* even though some capital goods are natural and not manmade, e.g., lakes and springs and flat, arable land. In the present chapter we shall mean by "capital" nonhuman capital goods. The term "labor" denotes current services from people, who have the ability, in common with capital goods, of being able to provide services in the future.

To explain as simply as possible how input prices and quantities are determined, we will work with just two kinds of inputs, even though there really is an infinite variety.

Although we shall investigate sources and valuations of capital goods more fully in Chapter 23, we note here that people are capital—human capital. You students are investing in increasing your productive talents and knowledge. You are also paying teachers to create that capital in you. At graduation, you are akin to a machine that has just been completed. You are a capital good in that you represent a capability of yielding services *now and in the future*. And you happen to be the owner of that human capital.

In the remainder of this chapter we shall elaborate a few basic propositions: (1) There is an unlimited variety of techniques by which any output may be produced. (2) Of these, some are technologically efficient. (3) Of all the technologically efficient ways, one is economically efficient, i.e., has lowest cost. (4) The lower the relative price of an input, the more will its services be used in the economically efficient technique. (5) The demand for a productive input depends in part upon the amounts of other inputs jointly available. (6) Substitution among productive inputs occurs not only by varying the productive technique but also by varying the output mixture. (7) The response in amount demanded of a productive input when price is changed is greater in the longer run.

**1, 2, 3,
4, 5, 6**

Variety of Productive Techniques

Alternative techniques exist for producing every good. Techniques differ in using different proportions of productive inputs. One uses more water and less cooling equipment; another fewer laborers and more equipment. One technique may use more electric power, while another uses more hand power. Houses can be built with varying combinations of power tools, pre-cut lumber, on-the-site assembly, and common-laborer assistants. In the operation of a grocery store, the variety of available techniques is enormous. Fewer butchers can devote their time only to cutting while women clerks sell the cuts of meat to customers. The butchers can be provided with power cutting equipment and elaborate facilities, or these can be eliminated by using more butchers. At the checking stand an expert cash-register operator can concentrate on checking items purchased by the customer, with an automatic machine to deliver "change" to the customer, plus a moving belt to convey the groceries past the checker to the high-school boy who bags and boxes the groceries for the customer. Alternatively, the grocer could use more clerks and less equipment and still sell the same amount of groceries at the same rate (but higher cost).

There is an unlimited variety of ways of doing something. This often escapes our notice simply because we usually see very similar ways used in our own neighborhood of experience. But if you travel to other countries or regions and look for these differences, you will see them. Alert businessmen watch competitors and other producers; trade journals are read for ways to improve production. Equipment salesmen tell of different ways of doing things and seek to show how their ways are better. Employees and labor-union representatives suggest that things are done differently in other firms. Business consultants and employees from other firms are hired to facilitate copying different techniques. A fundamental pervasive property of the "production function"—*the variety of combinations of inputs that can be used to produce a product*—is illustrated by the "toy" data in Table 20–1. The table shows the amounts of outputs and different alternative combinations of two inputs, labor and capital—each considered to be a homogeneous resource.

TABLE 20–1. Production of *X* as Function of Inputs of *L* and *C*

		Output of *X*					
	6	246	304	340	372	395	416
	5	224	277	310	340	360	376
Inputs	4	200	246	277	302	321	333
of	3	171	210	237	259	277	285
Capital	2	141	172	194	214	228	234
	1	100	121	138	152	162	165
		1	2	3	4	5	6
		Inputs of Labor					

For any combination of inputs of capital and of labor indicated along the left-hand and bottom sides, the entry in the table gives the total output of *X*. For example, for four units of capital and three units of labor, output is 277 of *X*. Note that 277 of *X* can also be obtained with three inputs of capital combined with five of labor. (Combinations with fractional amounts are omitted.)

Technological Efficiency

Table 20-1 lists some of the several techniques used to produce, say, 277 units of X. It can be done using $5C$ and $2L$, or $4C$ and $3L$, or $3C$ and $5L$. Other combinations (techniques) are available if C and L are divisible; thus, something like $3.5C$ and $4L$ will produce $277X$. All these combinations are *technologically* efficient; it is impossible to produce $277X$ with less of those inputs. If there were no substitutability among inputs, only one combination of C and L could produce $277X$. However, the fundamental proposition in the preceding paragraph says there always is more than one technologically efficient way to produce any specified output. Which of the many technologically efficient techniques is the *economically* efficient one?

Economic Efficiency

Is the most economic process the simplest, the newest, the most reliable, or the most commonly used? Or is it the technique with large expenditures now but small ones later? Or one that maximizes output per unit of input? (Which input? Raw materials, power, labor, or floor space? Actually, none.)[1]

---

[1] From one point of view, the question of the appropriate combination of inputs may seem pointless. After all, at any moment there is a certain amount of each productive resource in the community and hence a given over-all ratio of inputs. With full use of resources the community can't help but use the resources in that given ratio. That is true for the community *as a whole,* but consistent with that over-all total ratio of inputs is an unlimited set of different sub-combinations of use by the producers of various goods. The task is not, then, to select the average ratio for the economy, but the *specific allocation* for each of the many members of the community competing for those resources.

Society will penalize you for using an inappropriate *criterion*. But what is the appropriate criterion? The appropriate one depends *in part* upon the economic system. In a private-property, free-enterprise, open-market system, owners of productive resources are most rewarded if they achieve the *highest known market value* of the output obtainable with those resources. The farther one is from that goal, the more can other people bid away those resources and put them to higher-valued uses to increase their wealth. Open-market competition for access to resources will make it expensive to persist in using resources inefficiently. You will lose command over productive resources, which will be diverted to users more successful at discerning wealth-maximizing techniques of production. Your personal desire for more rather than less wealth will "force" you to choose the higher-valued, or lower-cost, techniques or let your resources be sold to those who can. Whether you judge that to be a desirable solution depends upon your evaluation of the social, cultural, and economic consequences. At any rate, it is an *accurate* explanation of the incentive system that operates in the private-property *open*-market economy.

Efficient Production Techniques and Relative Prices of Inputs

Returning to our numerical example, Table 20–2 shows three alternative ways to produce 277X: five capital and two labor; or four capital and three labor; or three capital and five labor. All are equally efficient in a *technological* sense, but only one is *economically* efficient. Which one? That is, which one will give 277 units of X per day and the *highest-valued bundle of other goods*? Or in other words, which one is the cheapest-cost method? It depends upon the prices of labor and capital which reflect what they can produce elsewhere. Suppose that a unit of capital costs $35 and a unit of labor costs $30. Then in the middle column we see that the lowest-cost, or economically efficient, method is with four capital and three labor. The cost is (4 × $35) + (3 × $30) = $230. The costs for the other combinations at these prices are $235 or $255.

This table shows also the costs of production at other input prices. Suppose the price

TABLE 20–2. Costs of Producing at Rate of 277 Units of X at Different Prices and Input Combinations of Capital and Labor

				Pairs of Prices of Capital and Labor			
		Capital		$30	$35	$45	
			Labor	$50	$30	$15	
Rates	5	and	2	$250*	$235	$225	
of	4	and	3	270	230*	255	Costs
Inputs	3	and	5	340	255	210*	

At $30 for a unit of capital and $50 for a unit of labor, 277 units of X can be produced at varying costs depending upon the input combinations shown. With five capital and two labor, shown in first row, cost is $250; for four capital and three labor, cost is $270; and it is $340 for three capital and five labor. Minimum cost combinations of capital and labor for producing 277X depend upon prices of labor and capital. For example, at $45 per capital and $15 per labor, minimum cost combination is three capital and five labor, compared with minimum cost combination of four capital and three labor at $35 per capital and $30 per labor. As price of capital is raised (from $30 to $45) and price of labor is lowered, the minimum cost combination of inputs have less capital and more labor. (Minimum cost combinations are indicated by asterisks.)

of capital were higher (say, $45) and the price of labor lower ($15), as in the right-hand column. The economically efficient combination has moved to one with more labor and less capital. This is not surprising, since capital is now more expensive, while labor is cheaper.

Conversely, if the price of labor had increased to $50 and the price of capital had fallen to $30, the costs would be those given in the first column in Table 20–2. This shifts the *economic* technique to five capital and two labor. As would be expected, the lower price of capital moves the efficient technique to a combination with more capital relative to labor. What is the point of this example? Simply that the efficient input combination depends on the input prices *and* that the lower the price of one input relative to others, the more the amount demanded. The law of demand holds also for productive resources.

10, 11, 12, 13, 14, 15, 16, 17

The Law of Diminishing Marginal Returns

Won't a different (than 277) total output rate make the producer's wealth even larger? And how will that new output affect the input combination selected? To answer this, we look at the *marginal-productivities* of each input. The marginal productivity of an input is the *increase* in output consequent to a *unit increase* in one input. The marginal products obey the *law of diminishing marginal returns*. This law states: "As any rate of input is increased by unit amounts, the marginal product, although possibly increasing at first to a maximum (called the point of diminishing marginal returns), *will* thereafter *decrease*." Note that it is the *increase* in rate of output and not the *total* that decreases. This law holds for the *rate,* not volume of production.[2]

For example, examine the output data in Table 20–1 *along one horizontal row;* the row with three units of capital shows increasing output rates of 171, 210, 237, 259, 277, and 285 as *labor* increases. Each *unit increase* of labor used jointly with the fixed amount of capital yields a higher rate of output. The daily output rate increases by 39 from 171 to 210 as a second unit of labor is applied to three units of capital. The *increment* of output with the third unit of labor is 27 units of X (237 − 210). The *increment* of output for the fourth unit of labor is 22 units of X. The *increments* in total output rates are shown in Table 20–3, which must be read along the horizontal *rows*; each *row* is for a fixed amount of capital. The *increments* in output rate with one more unit of labor (capital held constant) are called *marginal* products of labor.

A graph of diminishing marginal products of labor, for capital fixed at three units, is shown in Figure 20–2. Also shown (with dashed lines) is the diminishing marginal product of labor, with capital fixed at *four* units.

Two cautioning remarks against misinterpretations are warranted. First, these increments are obtained by the use of a one-unit-larger rate of input of labor daily with the same amount of capital. In adjusting to this larger rate of input of labor, one can rearrange the capital so that it is most effectively used with the larger amount of labor.

What Is a Marginal Product?

The second remark concerns the meaning of "product." When four units of labor and three of capital are used, the total product is 259 units of X. How much of that is due to

---

[2] This means that a unit of capital could elsewhere add $35 of value and labor could add $30.

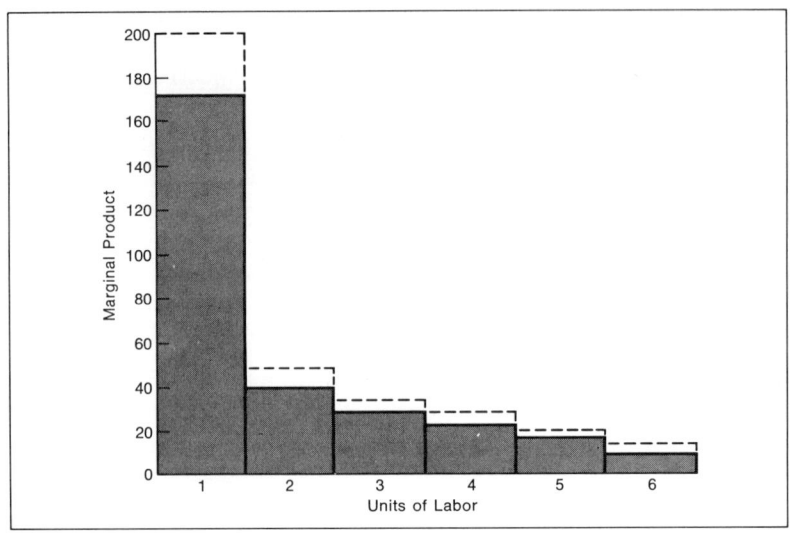

FIGURE 20–2

Marginal product schedule of labor with three units of capital (solid line) and with four units of capital (dashed line). Heights of each bar are entries shown in Table 20–3. Diminishing heights, from left to right, portray diminishing marginal productivity.

the capital and how much to the labor? This is not an answerable question. The marginal-product concept does not answer the question of "how much a unit of input produces." According to Table 20–3, the marginal product of four units of labor (as compared to three units of labor), when used jointly with three units of capital, is twenty-two units of X. Twenty-two units of X are not produced by the fourth unit of labor. Instead, that is the increase in the total product when four units of labor are used instead of three units, along with three units of capital. If a basketball team used six men instead of five, would

TABLE 20–3. Increments in Output Rate for Unit Increments of Labor with Various Fixed Amounts of Capital

		Marginal Products of Labor						
	6	246	58	36	32	23	19	. . . .
Fixed	5	224	53	33	30	20	16	. . . .
Amounts	4	200	46	31	25	19	12	. . . .
of	3	171	39	27	22	18	8	. . . .
Capital	2	141	31	22	20	14	6	. . . .
	1	100	21	17	14	10	3	. . . .
		1	2	3	4	5	6	. . . .
		Rates of Inputs of Labor						

Read this table horizontally along a row. For a stipulated amount of capital, say one unit, as inputs of labor are increased, the *marginal products of labor diminish* from 100, to 21, to 17, etc. Entries in this table are the differences between total output entries in Table 20–1, along a *horizontal row* of that table. (You can construct a table for the marginal products of capital by taking differences along a vertical column of Table 20–1.)

the sixth man say that produced the larger score? Each can validly claim that six of them produce more than do five, and that increase is what is meant by the marginal product for six people. Instead of the marginal product *of the sixth worker,* then, we speak of the marginal product of labor when the number of workers is six.[3]

The marginal products diminish at larger inputs (*with other inputs fixed in amounts*). Table 20-3 illustrates the law of *diminishing marginal* productivity; the data given are all beyond the point of diminishing marginal returns.

Either labor or capital can be the variable input. The law of diminishing marginal returns will hold; that law holds for every productive resource. (You should verify that the data of Table 20-1 conform; they do.)

18, 19, 20, 21, 22

Implication of the Law of Diminishing Marginal Returns

What use would be made of resources if there were increasing, not diminishing, marginal productivity? With a small plot of the best soil, a farmer could, by adding successive increments of labor to that soil, obtain successively larger increments of output until he was able to feed the world and do so with less labor than if he used more land also. He would put no labor on any other equally fertile soil since the marginal product would not be as large there—given *increasing* or nondecreasing marginal productivity of labor on the best soil. And certainly he would not apply any resources to inferior soil. All labor in production of wheat would be concentrated on one small piece of the best land. But in fact we see inferior land being used for every crop. Farmers do so because the greater amount of labor applied to the superior land has moved the farmer down the diminishing marginal-productivity curve of labor to where the marginal product is no greater than that obtained by applying a unit of labor to inferior land. Thus, labor is applied in varying degrees to *all* types of land, not merely to the best, with more on the best land (acre for acre). This is the kind of allocation of resources implied by the presence of diminishing marginal productivity. And this holds for all types of resources. In sum, we see all grades of resources being used, with superior resources used more intensively (that is, with relatively more of other resources)—a phenomenon we would not expect to observe if increasing marginal returns prevailed.[4]

---

[3] Review the analogous marginal revenue concept.

[4] Recognition of *intensive* margins, at which the marginal products of an input are equated by varying the amount of the input, is important because it generalizes the earlier simplified analysis of production (in Chapter 12), which was based on only one unit of each of several different qualities of productive inputs. That chapter explained only the assignment of different *kinds* or qualities of resources on the oversimplified principle that each input had a constant marginal product no matter how much it was used to produce Y rather than X. That assumption appeared as the constant marginal cost of producing X regardless of how much Y the person produced. There we had decreasing marginal products (or increasing marginal costs) *only by bringing in inferior producers,* after first utilizing the lower-cost producers of Y. However, the present law says that there is a diminishing marginal product for applications of increasing amounts of each *homogeneous* input as it is used more intensively with any specified amount of other resources. Therefore, now, for efficient production, an input should be increased wherever its marginal product exceeds its marginal product in other directions of use (where its use should be decreased). We can thereby apply our analysis to the assignments of *amounts* of different, but homogeneous, inputs, as well as to assignments of different kinds of inputs.

The Derived Demand for Productive Resources

In the preceding section, several technologically efficient techniques for producing a given output were illustrated. The economically efficient one depends upon the prices of the resources. If an input's price changes relative to another, it will pay to *substitute* more of the cheapened input for the others. This is possible because any specified rate of output can be produced with a variety of input combinations. Moreover, a lower input price will reduce production costs, permitting more profits at a *larger* output. And so, more of the input will be used, even aside from its substitution for the more expensive inputs at a given output rate. The *substitution* effect is joined with the *output expansion* effect of a change in input prices.

A reduced input lowers the cost of an input below its marginal product for the amount then employed. The wealth of a producer would be increased by hiring another unit of input. A rule is suggested: "Increase the amount of a productive input to the point at which its marginal value-product is brought down to the cost of one more unit of that input." In other words, "Employ that quantity of an input at which its marginal value-product is equal to its price. Do this for all inputs."

The marginal product *schedule* (for example, as shown in Figure 20–2) of each kind of input will depend upon how much of the other inputs are also used. Everything depends upon everything else. A simple expression summarizes some of that relationship. "In a wealth-maximizing situation, the amount of an input used is that at which its marginal value-product (the physical marginal product times the price of a unit of the product) is brought to equality with the price of the input."[5]

These conditions are met (1) if the output level is produced in the cheapest way, and (2) if that output is the most profitable one as judged by market demands. Generally speaking, this means the marginal value-product derived from an extra dollar's worth of each and every input is equal to a dollar. Another dollar's worth of input would give less than a dollar's worth of output; don't spend a dollar for a nickel of product.

Even if there were no substitution between jointly used inputs for a given product, the lower price of some input leads to lower costs of those goods it is used to produce. Consumer goods that use more of the now relatively cheaper inputs will be relatively less costly, and their sales or profits will increase. Therefore, substitution among inputs also occurs via substitution by consumers among the final, produced goods. If the price of plastics falls relative to glass, the supply schedule of plastic containers increases relative to that of glass bottles; the price of plastic containers falls; the consumer buys more plastic containers; and plastics are thereby substituted for glass. This effect, operating through the consumer's substitution of different consumer goods, is called *inter-product* substitution.

Much of the discussion can be summarized by a graph of the *demand for an input* (Figure 20–3). The amounts of the input are assumed divisible, and the curve portrays the relationship between the price of the productive input and the amount that would be demanded for production (with allowance for adjustments in output rate and price and amounts of jointly used inputs). The negative relationship between price and the amount

---

[5] In symbolic, abbreviated form for labor, L:

$$(P) \times (MPL) = P_{L'}$$

where P is the price of the product, MPL is the marginal product of labor, and P_L is the price of labor.

The same holds true for capital:

$$(P) \times (MPC) = P_{c'}$$

and for any kind of input.

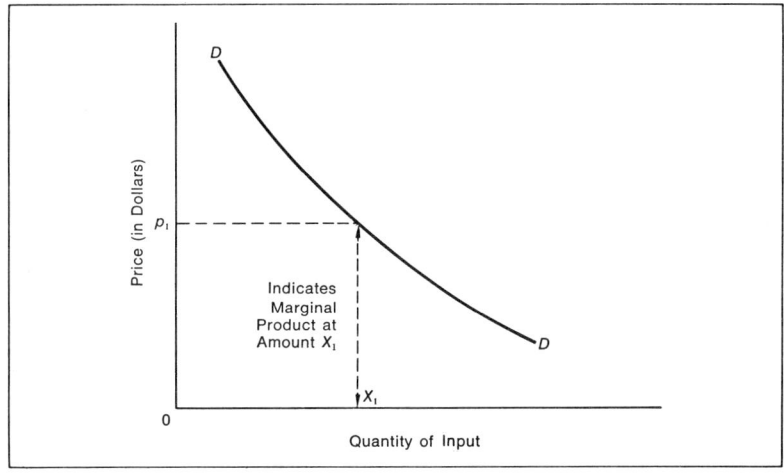

FIGURE 20-3. Demand Curves for Inputs as the Marginal Productivities

At amount of good X_1, the marginal product to the buyer is shown by the height of the curve DD. At price p_1, the amount X_1 would be bought, at which the marketable marginal product obtained by the employer from using X is equal to the price of X. At any larger amount than X, the marketable marginal product would be less than price p_1, and wealth of employer would be decreased.

demanded conforms to the fundamental law of demand for any good. The position and shape of the demand curve depends upon the amounts of other inputs that it is most profitable to use jointly with this input—in other words upon the costs of other inputs.[6]

At any specified price of inputs the amount of the input demanded will be given by the demand function. Since the height of demand for any input reflects the marginal productivity of that good at each different amount of the good, the intersection of a horizontal price line with a demand curve gives the amount of the input employed and also shows an equality between the price and the marginal productivity of the input *for the amount that it is most profitable to employ*.

The italicized phrase is an important condition. Equality of wage or rent for the input to its marginal product may not occur if the firm is restricted in its choice of inputs at given prices or if the firm lacks sufficient information about the marginal productivity of its inputs. Finally, one warning. The productivity of any input may be indirect—it may provide better working conditions for the other inputs so they can be obtained at lower prices, e.g., provision of sanitary and safety facilities. Its marginal productivity is measured by the contribution to lower costs of getting other inputs—rather than to increased physical output, as suggested by our earlier examples of marginal productivity.

Inter-firm Substitution

The demand relationship between the price of an input and the rate of its use is a result of more than any purposive adjustment of each producer. Even if no producer were to

---

[6] This recalls the earlier discussion of the demand curve for butter and for margarine wherein the *demand* (the schedule—not just the amount demanded at some price) depended upon the price of margarine.

substitute a more efficient input combination, each would experience a change in his wealth. Those firms that are nearer the new, more efficient combination will have a greater increase in their wealth than will those firms whose input techniques are now less efficient. Profits and losses will change as a result of the revised price structure, with bigger rewards going to the possibly inadvertently lucky firms that happened to have the input combination nearest the most appropriate. Less lucky firms with less efficient techniques will experience bigger losses or smaller profits and will soon be dominated by the more rapid growth and proliferation of the more efficient combinations.

The changing environment *adopts* the more appropriate existing techniques by rewarding their users with greater profits and growth—whether or not the individual producers themselves *adapt* to the new price situation. Adaptation will occur as productive techniques of the more successful firms are copied. The imitating firm, emulating the successful firm, may not know the marginal productivities of various inputs. All it knows is what techniques succeeded best. Not even the initially successful firm has to know the marginal products. All it has to do is happen to be nearest the "right" combination. Whether it got there by calculating marginal productivities via an extensive research and testing program, with the help of astrologers, by consulting economists, or by sheer luck is irrelevant. The fact of being there is sufficient.

Competition among firms with different productive techniques is a selective survival force, just as is purposive, knowledgeable selection by one producer among alternative available production techniques. Inter-firm market competition adds its force to the intrafirm selectivity of production techniques and consequent response of input use to price.

Position of Derived Demand

The marginal product of any worker is a function not merely of his own talents and education but also of the quality and quantity of other goods with which he can work jointly. To "work jointly" does not mean merely to work hand in hand with other goods, as a carpenter works with a hammer, a seamstress with a needle, or a driver with a truck. It means also to work within the environment provided by the equipment and resources of the whole economy. The transportation system, power costs, the education and technology of other workers, the effectiveness of the market in facilitating specialization and exchange, the amount of theft, the extent to which contracts are honored—all these are examples of "joint cooperative resources." Take all the carpenters in any small city in the United States to India, Morocco, Brazil, or Indonesia. The wages they would get are lower simply because there is less jointly available "capital." A richer country with lots of capital equipment and stable, market-facilitating institutions is a better place for a given amount of labor. While the productivity of the American carpenters would be less in other countries than in the United States, the productivity would be greater than for natives of those countries—a reflection of the greater education of the Americans.[7]

[7] In Table 20–3, the marginal value-product of labor depends upon which row you read. The more capital (the upper rows), the greater the marginal products of labor. The two resources are said to be *complementary*. The opposite effect could have occurred: larger amounts of capital might have caused small marginal products for labor. They then are called *substitutes*. Unfortunately, this is very misleading terminology. The two inputs are substitutes for each other even though they are complements in the sense just indicated. The term "substitutes" has two different meanings: (1) It is possible to produce some specified rate of output with less of one input and more of another. (2) More of one input causes a *lower* marginal product for the existing amount of the *other* resource. It is in the former sense that the term "substitutable" is ordinarily used. A more precise term for the second effect would be "negative cross-marginal productivity," suggesting that the effect of increasing

Speed of Substitution and Adjustment of Production

Making substitutions and *changing* the rates of employment of inputs are costly activities. One doesn't change a production technique by a wave of his hand. He must learn of new ways, administer his decisions, rearrange the inputs, and schedule the arrival of the new inputs to ensure efficient coordination. In other words, the amount of substitution carried out in response to a new price situation depends upon these adjustment costs and upon how much time has elapsed since the price change. The longer the time, the more substitution or revision of employment of inputs will have taken place. Again, as in the consumer's behavior, the demand response for an input is more elastic with respect to a price change, the longer the time since the price change. And it can be portrayed graphically by showing different demand curves for different times after the price changes from that level at which the curves are all shown intersecting each other—as in Figure 5–3.

The relatively inelastic demand for an input in the *immediate* period, when changes can be made only at high adjustment costs, sometimes misleads people into thinking that the price change has no effect on the amount demanded. But in the ensuing days, or weeks, the adjustments can be made at a more economic pace. Since they are made after a substantial interval, the changes often are not identified as consequences of the price change. Of course, the employer need not announce to the inputs that he no longer will buy so much of their services because their price is too high. He simply says that his sales aren't big enough to warrant their employment.

For example, we cite the rise in wages of Chicago elevator boys. Formerly, wages were $1 to $1.25 an hour. There was then imposed a minimum wage of $2.40 an hour for operators in downtown (not suburban) Chicago buildings. Owners of some of those buildings then found it profitable to use automatic elevators, which annually cost about $8,000. With two shifts of operators, the higher wage of $2.40 per hour raised the cost of manually operated elevators to about $10,000 per year. Clearly, it paid the owner to "automate." This process took several months. When the elevator operators were discharged several months later, after having been paid $2.40 an hour for the intervening time, they were not likely to have believed that it was a result of the higher wage, since that was "initiated" a long time ago. They blamed it on "automation." This is not to say that all introduction of automatic equipment is a response to higher wages (as we shall see in the next chapters), nor does it imply that higher than open-market wages are "wrong" or "bad." Nothing in economics establishes "badness" or "goodness."

Generality of Marginal-Productivity Theory

A few side issues may be explored.
1. *Is total product sufficient?* The payment for a unit of a productive input is its price. If we multiply the number of employed units by the marginal product, which also equals

---

one resource "crosses over" to another resource and lowers its marginal product. In Table 20–1, there is positive cross-marginal productivity, and negative *self*-marginal productivity (called the law of *diminishing* marginal returns).

We cannot tell in advance whether, in the interaction between two joint inputs, an increase in the amount of one will raise or lower the marginal productivity of the other. But whatever the effect on the marginal productivity, the implied demand schedule for any input retains its negative slope with respect to its own price.

its price in equilibrium, we get the income to that resource. For example, suppose that in Table 20–1 we were employing three units of labor and one unit of capital, because the price of labor was $17 while the price of capital was $138. We now compute the total payments to capital and labor from our firm. Three units of labor at $17 each is $51 while the one unit of capital gets $138. The total payments to the productive resources are $51 + $138 = $189, an amount that *exceeds* the total value of the output produced, $138. How can a producer continue in this situation? Has something gone wrong with our theory? How can inputs be paid more than the total product? This is not impossible, for awhile at least. The employer of these productive inputs must make up the loss out of his past accumulated wealth. That's one of his functions. But it is not something he can do indefinitely.

Abandoned will be the "loss-resulting" production. Resources will be released from that business and that product. Economy-wide input prices are pushed down and output prices increased. Other employers who were just breaking even or losing money will now be able to get profits or break even by employing the released resources. The situation is saved. No inconsistency is inherent in the open-market equilibrium.

2. *Abstractions and validity*. The present analysis does not require the assumption that there be different sets of internally homogeneous and infinitely divisible resources. They can all be discrete, different items; interpolation such as we used in our example might be impossible; equality between the marginal value-product and prices may not be achievable. Instead of equality of marginal value-product and price, an *in*equality condition suffices; inputs will be employed up to the point beyond which the marginal value-product of the input would be smaller than the marginal cost of the input.

Many assumptions commonly used in marginal-productivity principles of the demand for productive resources are simplifications of reality. Many readers conclude that a theory built on such assumptions must therefore be false in all its implications about observable events. Do not fall into that error. Every theory abstracts from details and considerations, many of which it is not seeking to explain. All theories make overly strong assumptions for ease of logical analysis. They assume away certain idiosyncrasies in the interest of concentrating on basic phenomena. For example, a theory relating caloric intake to body weight can assume, as a means of abstracting from tangential detail, that all people are alike (for a given age and sex); then certain consequences are implied if caloric intake is increased. It is doubtful that you would challenge the validity of that implication by challenging the validity of the assumption that people are alike or the assumption that when caloric intake is increased, no other events impinge on the individuals—such as their getting sick or other coincident causes. Actually, the complexities could be included; but then the theory would be cumbersome in having to use more complex methods of notation, logic, mathematics, etc., in deriving and expressing its results. (Do not presume that one theory is better than another simply because it is more detailed in its premises, assumptions, and number of variables considered in its premises.)

3. *Pecuniary and nonpecuniary productivity and "discrimination."* Is the marginal-productivity principle *of demand* applicable only to capitalist economies? No, the marginal-productivity theory of demand is valid in every economy. In the capitalist economy, the increase in wealth belongs to an identifiable *private* owner, or *private* group of owners. If, however, a property holder were not able to keep the profits (or did not have to pay the losses) of his business, he would more heavily weight other sources affecting his utility. He would be more disposed to employ pretty typists if he weren't able to retain the profits of hiring lower-cost homely girls who were equally productive

of pecuniary value of marketable goods. If the economic rules of surviving in business only mildly penalize people for not increasing wealth when possible, or if the business owners cannot keep the profits, then both they and their employed agents will be less influenced by profits. This is implied by the *generalized* marginal-productivity theory of demand. (See Figure 20–4.) The lower the price of *any* source of utility, the more it will be used. Marketable wealth is only one of the "products" yielded by inputs.

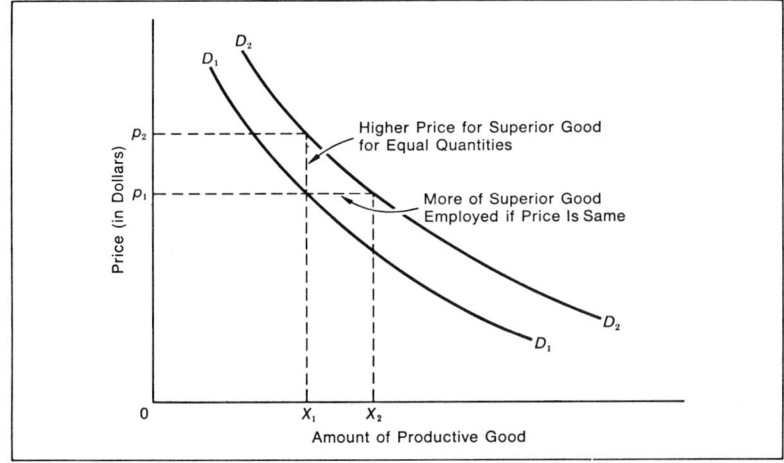

FIGURE 20–4. Demand for Inputs with the Marginal Productivities *Including* Marketable and Nonmarketable Marginal Products to Buyers

Curve D_2 shows demand for inputs that will do all that the inputs demanded according to line D_1 can do *plus* provide more desirable nonmarketable benefits to the demander. A beautiful secretary has a greater demand for her presence (as a secretary *and* a pleasing person) than an ugly one. The price paid for productive inputs reflects both the marketable productivity of the input plus the nonmarketable attributes as sources of utility to the buyer. Moral: Remember that nonpecuniary sources of utility are present in many inputs for productive use, as they are for consumption goods.

To prohibit or make it more difficult for one to keep and use profits raises the cost of increasing one's wealth. When the costs of obtaining pecuniary benefits are higher and the nonpecuniary are lower, one will increase his purchase of goods that are more heavily loaded with nonpecuniary sources of utility—good looks, racial and religious characteristics, friends, prestige, relaxation, etc. Nonpecuniary discrimination is cheaper and will be more common. Production will be less closely oriented to market demands and values. Market prices are also less likely to be high enough to clear the market—for reasons discussed in Chapter 10. The generalized marginal-productivity principle still stands, as long as one incorporates the various ways of "producing" utility—only one of which is wealth.

Our investigation of the selection of productive techniques and uses of productive resources is incomplete in that the *supply conditions of productive resources* were not investigated. The market for labor and for nonhuman resources will be investigated in the next four chapters.

29, 30, 31, 32, 33

The Circle Closed

Determination of prices of productive goods and rates of employment affects the wealth of their owners. From given wealth and preference patterns of people, which influence market demands for consumers' goods, we have gone via derived demands for inputs to the prices of resources and hence to income and wealth of those who provide or own the resources. Prices and outputs of consumers' goods, the wealth of individuals, and the allocation of productive goods have been analyzed primarily in the context of a market-exchange, private-property system—although we have occasionally considered these questions under other systems. If access to an open market is restricted, or if limitations are imposed on permissible bids or offers, the extent of adjustment of output to consumers' market demands is reduced; the efficient allocation of inputs is weakened, and the wealth of owners of productive goods is made less dependent upon satisfaction of consumers' market-revealed preferences.

Nothing in the analysis implies that such attenuation of efficiency in production or composition of output is undesirable. That depends upon whether or not one prefers the economic, cultural, and political implications of a free-market, private-property exchange system. Those who dislike that system (because they think they could achieve what they regard as a better way of life with a differently weighted mix of types of competition for resolving conflicts of interests in the presence of scarcity) will possibly try to reduce the scope of that system. For example, people with certain kinds of personalities may find "vote-getting," political competition, more favorable to them than market competition. They will expect to gain from extension of government activity. Socialists express that preference and intent. Some capitalists express a different preference; and yet some seek government limitation on their market competitors. By this stage of this book, it should be obvious that although some of the differences in cultural, political, and economic consequences of various economic systems are discernible with the aid of economic theory, economic theory cannot evaluate their propriety.

Fluctuations in Employment and Unemployment

The flow of services from households to firms is not always smooth, although there are powerful forces pushing the flow toward the full-employment rate for most resources. In general, the market economy has operated remarkably close to full-employment situations. In fact, from the preceding analysis one would be surprised if it did not do so. Our prior analysis suggested there were too many jobs to be performed and that the question was to decide which of the infinite range of scarcities one should strive to reduce. But unemployment and idle resources are with us persistently in varying degree. How can this be explained? Consideration of that is delayed until we complete analysis of resource-markets operation and the determination of individual incomes and wealth.

Summary

1 Substitutability among all productive inputs is pervasive.

2 Efficient, wealth-maximizing producers reveal a market-demand curve for inputs that is inversely related to the price of each input. The inverse (or negative) relationship with price of the input results from (a) substitutability among inputs, (b) diminishing marginal

value-productivity (which reflects both a decreasing marginal physical product and a lower price of the output as more is sold), (c) output expansion as consumers substitute cheaper for dearer goods.

3 A longer-period demand for inputs is more elastic. The effect of a price change will be less pronounced immediately than with the passing of some time.

4 An increased supply of any resource in the market implies a lower price, which induces a shift to techniques employing more of that now lower-priced input. The technique of production is revised toward more use of the now more plentiful and cheaper input—all without central direction or planning—provided, of course, that producers are not constrained by law to use inputs in proportions other than those which they choose in the light of market prices (that is, to the extent that there is open-market competition).

5 Since the income (or wealth) of any productive resource is determined by its selling price, the incomes of owners of various productive goods, be they labor or nonlabor forms of services, are determined in a free market by the forces of demand and supply. The demand for resources reflects their marginal productivities in highest-valued uses. For this reason, this analysis is often erroneously called the marginal-productivity theory of *pricing* of productive resources. More accurately, it is the marginal-productivity theory of demand for productive resources.

6 The marginal-productivity basis for demand applies to all types of economies. Economies based on different systems of property rights differ in the costs imposed on various types of decisions. This does not destroy the validity of the marginal-productivity theory of demand—whether it be demand for consumer goods or for pecuniary or nonpecuniary productive resources, in a capitalist or in a socialist economy. Nor does it have any bearing on how prices are set. They may be set by decree or custom. But the theory is invalid as an explanation of rates of use of inputs if the allocations are also controlled by decree or custom.

Questions

1 "Chicago, August 10, 1962. A federal judge blocked today the firing of thousands of workers on the nation's railroads pending final court ruling on the legality of the drastic economy. Prior to the decision five unions representing the men were ready to order a nationwide walkout. Today's U. S. District Court action, technically, granted the unions a court order barring the railroads from applying new work rules pending a union appeal to the U. S. Circuit Court of Appeals. Judge Perry said, 'I have preserved and protected the right of appeal,' adding that he felt an interim decision affecting both jobs and capital must be resolved in favor of jobs and men." In what sense can it be contended instead that the issue is one between jobs *and jobs,* rather than between jobs and capital?

2 Who is substituted for whom when a firm uses one typist, an electric typewriter, and a copying machine rather than two typists and two manual typewriters? This is called a substitution of capital for labor. Why is that misleading?

3 "The advent of the one-man bus involved more capital equipment: an automatically operated coin box and a door-control device—to name two of the capital goods that replaced the conductor."
  a. Is this a case of capital replacing labor? Where?
  b. Is it a case of labor replacing labor? Where?
  c. Is it a case of no substitution for labor at all, but instead a job revision with a greater total output? Where?

4 "Invention and the lower cost of power in the home have replaced the domestic servant by capital equipment. Without that machinery more people would be working in homes as 'servants.' But the replacement of domestic employees by capital has not led to the replacement of labor. The released labor is used elsewhere."
   a. Can you suggest where?
   b. What other goods are more plentiful because of the advent of domestic machinery?
   c. Who was aided and who was hurt by the use of the vacuum cleaner, washing machine, water heater, forced-air furnace, garbage disposal, automatic oven, electric mixer, and refrigerator?

5 The electric refrigerator replaced the iceman with capital. By eliminating (making other means cheaper) the job of the iceman, was the total number of jobs reduced? Explain.

6 "Automation does not mean there will be more people than jobs available. It does not mean fewer jobs for unskilled people—in fact a person can be less skilled if all he has to do is punch buttons, pull triggers, and turn steering wheels, compared to driving a team of horses, shooting a bow and arrow, or wielding a chisel." Do you agree? If so, why? If not, why not?

7 "A molecule of sugar is composed of a fixed ratio of atoms of hydrogen, carbon, and oxygen; it follows that there is no substitutability of inputs in the manufacture of sugar."
   a. Do you agree? Why?
   b. Is the reasoning in the preceding question applicable to every other kind of good that can be manufactured—whether or not the good is composed of a fixed ratio of components? For example, is the reasoning applicable to making gasoline, running a railroad, operating a bus, building a house, or selling groceries?

8 Why is economic efficiency a more general test than technical efficiency?

9 There are two kinds of economic efficiency—one of cost minimization and one of profit maximization.
   a. In what sense is profit maximization a more general criterion of efficiency?
   b. In what sense could it be considered a less desirable criterion?

10 A jet plane can fly across the United States three hours faster than a propeller plane. Which is the more efficient?

11 In Iowa the yield of wheat is 30 bushels per acre; in Washington it is 50 bushels per acre. Which is better?

12 Jet engines are given an efficiency rating according to the thrust generated per pound of engine weight. Explain why that is an inadequate measure of efficiency.

13 Steers can be bred with such superb qualities that they will sell for about 50 percent more per pound than the standard steers raised for meat. Which type should the farmer raise? Give the answer in terms of technological versus economic efficiency.

14 A high-fidelity stereo sound system is called efficient if it uses a low amount of electric power per decibel of sound generated. Why is that technical efficiency not an adequate efficiency criterion for choosing among sound systems, even if the quality of the sound were the same?

15 A water-storage dam is to be built, and engineers, asked for advice, propose a dam and attest to its efficiency.
   a. If they attest to its technical efficiency, does that still leave open the question of its economic efficiency? For example, if the value of the water stored is less than the cost of impounding and distributing it, is the dam, though it may be technically efficient, an economically efficient one?

b. This problem extends the notion of economic efficiency beyond the selection of the cheapest way of doing something. Economic efficiency is extended to include what?

16 The United States Federal Communication Commission says rights to use the radio-frequency spectrum should be assigned to permit maximum usage.
a. Explain why that statement as it stands is meaningless and useless.
b. Would it have been meaningful to say rights should be assigned to achieve efficient use? What would be the criterion of efficiency?

17 After adding 100 to all the output data in Table 20–1, recompute the marginal products of labor and the marginal products of capital. (This is not as hard and long a problem as it may at first seem.)

18 In Table 20-2, the data are *values* of output, where, for simplicity, each physical unit was assumed to be salable for $1. Suppose instead that the output can be sold for $2 each.
a. Recompute the "marginal value-products" for labor and for capital.
b. What is the effect of a rise in price of the product on the marginal-value productivity of inputs?

19 Use the data of Table 20–1 to answer the following questions:
a. Defining efficient production as the lowest-cost methods of production, which method is the efficient method for producing 277 units of X if the price of labor is $60 and if the price of capital is $70?
b. If the price of capital is $20 per unit and if labor is $10 per unit, which is the efficient way to produce 228 units of X: with 2 capital and 5 labor or with 5.1 capital and 1 labor?
c. Which is cheaper (that is, efficient) if the prices are $2 and $1 respectively?
d. $60 and $30 respectively?
e. So long as the prices bear the same ratios to each other, will the same method remain the cheaper method?

20 a. In Table 20–3, is the law of diminishing marginal returns illustrated by the decreasing values as one reads a row from left to right, or as one reads a column from bottom to top?
b. Explain the meaning of each method of reading the table.

21 The law of diminishing returns is a law of diminishing *marginal* returns. What is the difference between diminishing *total* returns and diminishing *marginal* returns?

22 You operate a factory and discover that some resource used obtains *increasing* marginal returns.
a. What would you do?
b. Does this suggest that we will never find any firm using an amount of resources involving increasing marginal returns?

23 "If the ratio of the prices of two resources differs from the ratio of their marginal products for the amount being employed, a change in the amounts employed can increase the total output without any increase in costs, or can reduce costs without reducing output." Explain why.

24 "If the ratio of the price of resource A to the price of resource B exceeds the ratio of the marginal value-products of A to B, it will be efficient to decrease the employment of A relative to B." Explain why.

25 Adjustments in the amount of resources used so as to equate the *absolute* prices of each resource with its marginal value productivity imply more than does the equality of the *ratios* of prices to the ratios of marginal productivities. What is the stronger implication?

26 "If a firm uses resources efficiently, a change in their prices will induce a change in the relative amounts employed." What will induce that change—some directive from a central planning agency, the social consciousness of the employer, or what?

27 "Even if only one combination of productive inputs could be used to produce some good, there would still be substitution among productive resources in response to changes in their prices." Explain what that substitution is and how it would be induced.

28 According to the analyses developed in this chapter, resources will be employed in open markets in amounts at which marginal value-product is not less than price. That also determines their earnings (price times the number of units employed).
   a. What ensures that the total earnings will not exceed the value of the total output?
   b. Who makes up the difference if payments exceed the value of output?
   c. If the payments are less than the total value of output, who gets the difference?
   d. In each case, what forces revise payments toward equality with value of output?

29 Suppose you operate a publicly owned factory in which profits cannot be retained.
   a. What would be your criterion of resource use in production?
   b. What would induce you to act in accord with that criterion?
   c. Would you have any incentive to adjust the use of resources to preserve the equality of the ratios of prices and marginal productivities—that is, to minimize the cost of the output? Explain.

30 "In a socialist state it is difficult for the state to own the producers' goods that are involved in artistic creativity—the human brain and body. Consequently musicians, artists, authors, and poets will be more able to behave in deviant, unorthodox, non-nationalistic ways than those whose earnings are more dependent upon state-owned resources—machines, factories, land, etc. In a capitalistic system this difference would not be present."
   a. What premises underlie the propositions?
   b. Would your preference for one system over another be influenced by the validity of those propositions? Why?

31 In Russia and China, two socialist states in which most producers' goods (goods with which you can earn a living) are owned by the government, targets are assigned to factories in terms of the total value of the output (not profits) they are supposed to produce. Plant managers are told to accomplish and overfulfill targets as much as possible. Prices are set by law.
   a. Is it desirable to have these targets overfulfilled?
   b. Is it more desirable to state a target in terms of total value of output or in terms of profits? What are the differences in performance that will be induced?
   c. Which criterion is more likely to provide a more effective incentive for the manager?

32 Assume that you are a member of a minority group in some country and have reason to doubt that your private-property rights would be enforced and respected in that community.
   a. In what forms of capital would you invest?
   b. What kinds of skills (as forms of accumulations of wealth) would you encourage for your children?
   c. Do you know of any evidence of such actual behavior by minority groups?

33 When Defense Secretary McNamara recommended against building nuclear rather than oil-fueled airplane carriers because the nuclear system was more expensive, Senator Pastore of Rhode Island is reported to have said that if we had looked at economics we would never have shifted from wooden sailing ships to steel, oil-fueled ships. Whatever the congressman may have said, is the asserted remark correct? Explain.

Wages and Employment in Open Markets

21

BEFORE inquiry into the determination of who does what tasks for what pay under what conditions of work—the main topic of this and the next chapter—note a few facts about the labor force. Of the nearly 90 million people in the labor force, most are in "service" industries—some 45 millions, compared to about 30 million in the "goods-producing" industries, with an even smaller number in agriculture. At the turn of the century, the order was probably reversed. Figure 21–1 is a projection made by the U. S. Bureau of Labor Statistics. Figure 21–2 shows the distribution of the labor force by the type of goods produced. Manufactured goods, both durable and nondurable (e.g., clothing, drugs, oil products, chemicals), are the dominant industries in number of employees. The distribution by type of skills or tasks is shown in Figure 21–3.

It is noteworthy that about 25 percent of the labor force received less than a full high school education, while over 25 percent received at least some college education. The former percentage is falling rapidly, and the latter is rising.

Roughly 50 of the 65 million males older than 15 years are employed (most of the remainder are in school), and of the 70 million women over 15 years about 30 million are employed while the rest are in school or are not seeking employment. (Incidentally, about 5 percent of the work force holds two jobs.)

Labor Service Is a Commodity

"Labor is not a commodity" is a battle cry of some labor groups. Whatever its emotional appeal, the assertion is misleading. Labor service is bought and sold daily.

What *is* different about labor is the absence of buying and selling of *people*: human

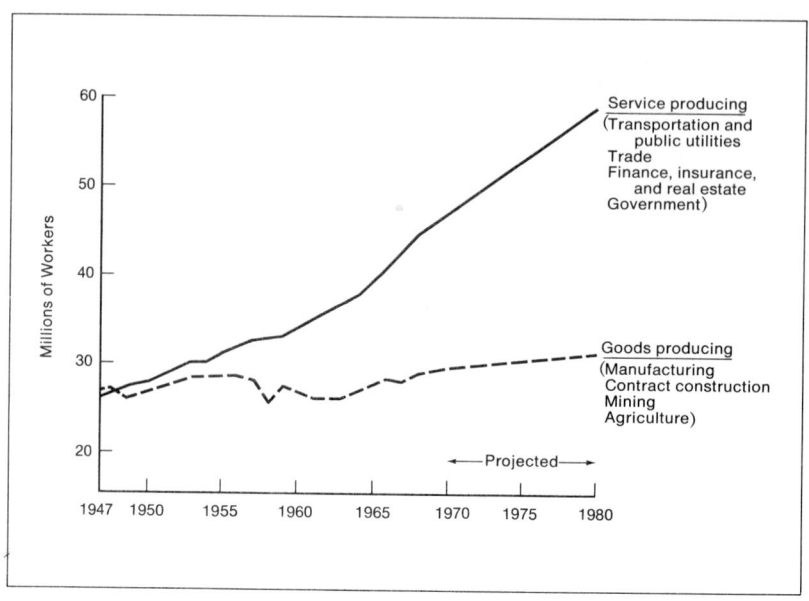

FIGURE 21-1

Employment trends in goods-producing and services-producing industries, 1947–1968 actual, and projected to 1980. (Wage and salary workers only, except in agriculture, which includes self-employed and unpaid family workers.)

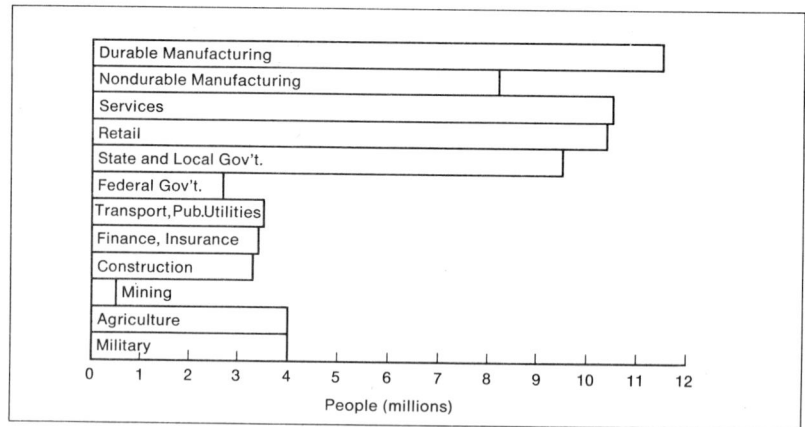

FIGURE 21-2. Number of People Working, by Industries (1968)

Service workers shown earlier, in Figure 21-1, are here reclassified into subcategories like retail work, finance and insurance, and government employees. The category here called "services" includes workers in amusement, entertainment, recreation, travel and hotels, education, health, etc. (In general, the term "services" is ambiguous and varied in its content among data sources.]
Source: U. S. Department of Labor, *Manpower Report,* 1969.

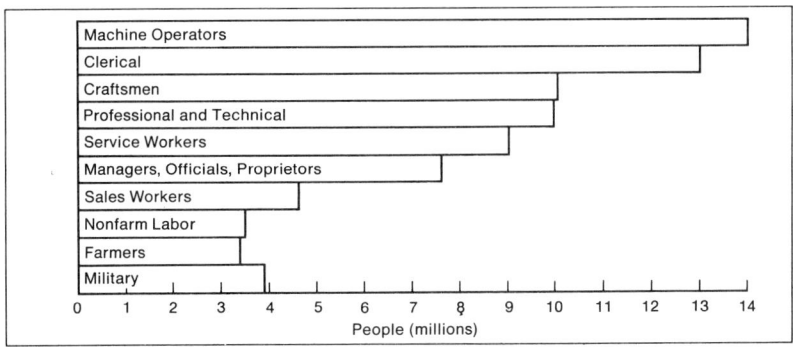

FIGURE 21-3. Number of People Working, by Skills (1968). Source: U. S. Department of Labor, *Manpower Report,* 1969

services are bought and sold.[1] In some countries, people are bought and sold by other people—or are "owned" by governments. Even where no one is a slave, private property in one's own labor is restricted if he is prohibited from selling his services to any other person at mutually satisfactory terms, or if he cannot migrate to another area to sell his labor services there. A few hundred years ago, Englishmen could not work where they pleased, for whom they pleased, on whatever terms they found mutually agreeable. Nor was entry into occupations unrestricted. And this is true today in many countries in varying degree, even in the United States. For example, I could not legally sell psychiatric, medical, or dental services to you. Laws often dictate qualifications, permissible wages, hours of work per day, and working conditions; other terms, although mutually agreeable between employer and employee, are not legal. These restrictions on market competition and sale of labor do not prevent labor services from being a marketable commodity.

Furthermore, the fact that labor services involve personalities and social relationships does not preclude market forces; they do, however, affect contracting and negotiating procedures. But before exploring that, we shall concentrate on the factors affecting wages and allocations of labor services via market competition—using again the analytic concepts of market demand and supply.

Economic analysis denies that, in the absence of legal protection for labor, employers would grind wages down to the minimum survival level. An analogy will suggest why. Why are rents on land not ground down by renters to zero? The demands by those who would use the land bid up the rents. Simple supply and demand are in operation. And so it is with labor. The alternative uses and values to which labor could be put are determined by all who compete for it. Potential employers, faced with the available supply, bid wages to whatever level enables them to get an amount of labor that can be put to profitable use. That may be a very high level, if labor is relatively scarce given its

---

[1] Fortunately, the ban against selling all one's future services for a single advance payment, as he could sell other things, does not prevent a person from converting some of his future earnings into present wealth values. If he has just obtained a higher salary, he can borrow more money now to buy a house and car and repay out of the greater future income. In this way, he has exchanged part of his future earnings and obtained goods. Without the right to borrow or to mortgage wealth as security or to buy on the installment plan, laborers would be at a greater disadvantage in adjusting consumption to present wealth value of future earnings.

productivity function. The price of labor, like that of every other good, depends upon demand and supply forces.

Demand for Labor

The basis of demand for any productive input was investigated in the preceding chapter, where we saw that market demand is derived from the anticipated marginal value-product of that input. The lower the price of the input, the greater the amount that will be demanded—this holds for labor services as well as for all other productive inputs. In this chapter we shall explore the supply of labor and then put demand and supply together to see what can be said about wage rates and the allocation of labor to various jobs.

Supply of Labor

In the United States, of 150 million able-bodied adults (over 16) nearly 90 million (or 60 percent) are in the labor force—i.e., employed or seeking employment. The labor-force participation rate has remained close to 60 percent since the turn of the century. Decreases in participation rates for teenagers and people over 65 were almost exactly offset by increases in female labor-force participation. Over 40 percent of women are in the labor force, almost twice that of 1900, probably reflecting increased education for women, ready-cooked and processed foods, appliances permitting more substitution of capital for household labor, and rise in wages from outside jobs for women relative to their productivity in the house.

America's wealth has been increasing, and so has its population. Over the years, the increase in wealth has been able to support a larger population. More recently, cheaper techniques of birth control seem to have destroyed the old generalization that poorer people have larger families, at least in the United States. With adjustments for education of the parents, their wealth, and agricultural versus city status, the evidence is that higher education and higher wealth are now associated with *higher* net reproduction rates. Agricultural areas (after adjustment for education and wealth) have a higher reproduction rate. Whether that relationship will change in some systematic way is still a question with no answer.

Immigration, which in the nineteenth and early twentieth centuries was a major source of population and labor-force growth, now has been reduced to a trickle, primarily because of laws restricting entry.

Whatever the population size, the proportion of the adult group seeking work will be a function of the reward for work. The size of the labor force may look like the line SS in Figure 21-4, showing more people entering the labor force or working longer hours as wage rates are higher. However, at some high rates, the employee's higher wealth or income provided by the higher wages decreases the amount of labor supplied as people seek jobs of shorter hours or as wives work less because their husbands earn more. Whether we have reached that level of wages is difficult to establish. Nevertheless, one component reducing the amount of labor supplied is the reduced number of hours people prefer to work in a week; it has fallen from 60 to 40 in the last hundred years.

In analyzing how the wage rate affects the amount of labor supplied, we should note two distinctions. The first is between a transient and a permanent rise in wage rates. A *temporary* increase, say for a weekend or for a couple of months, does not constitute as large an increase in the employee's *wealth* as would a permanently lasting wage increase.

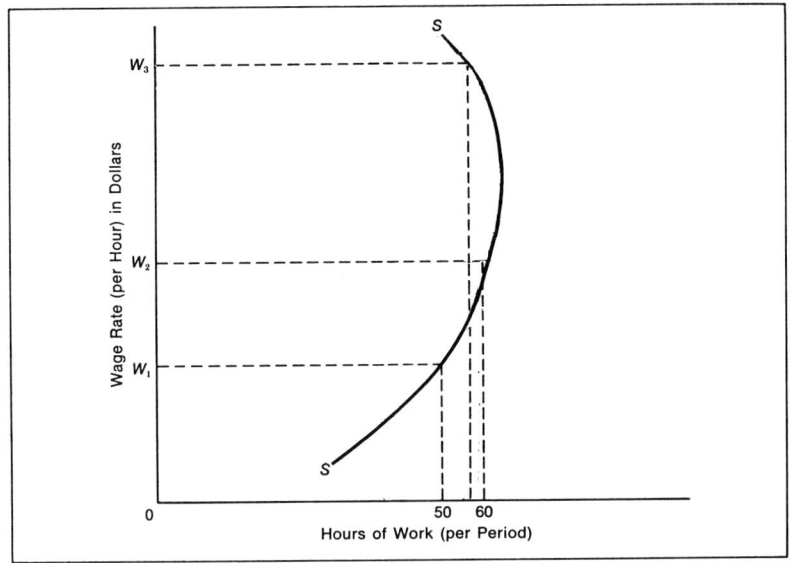

FIGURE 21-4. Possible Economy-Wide Supply Curve of Hours of Labor

To the economy as a whole the amount of labor available, the labor force, increases with higher wages, but at sufficiently high wages it is believed that the amount of labor decreases. The upward-rising portion can reflect more hours per week and more people seeking work. The backward ascending portion *may* reflect dominance of reduced hours offered per week (with higher wealth) over an increase in numbers seeking work. But the actual situation is not known.

(Remember the principles developed in Chapter 11 on the effect on wealth of a long-lasting increase in future receipts relative to a short-lived temporary increase.) A $1 increase per year for twenty years raises a person's "wealth" immediately by nearly $20 at ten percent rates of interest, whereas a rise lasting only one year increases wealth by only $1. Thus, wage changes that are believed to be transient do not have the same effect on behavior as changes that are believed to be long-lasting—because the effects on current wealth are not the same. Probably, a short-lived increase in wage rates would induce more labor services from a person, whereas a long-lived one could induce him to take more leisure and work fewer hours each week.

The second distinction is between the supply of labor to an individual employer or single industry and that to the economy as a whole. The amount supplied the total economy may decrease with permanently higher wages, yet the amount supplied will increase to any segment that raises its wage offers relative to other segments of the economy. Hence, to each segment the supply of labor is generally upward-sloping. It is in these various segments that the wage offers are negotiated and wages determined in competition against all other segments. See Figure 21-5.

1, 2, 3, 4

Open-Market Wage Rates

All the considerations in interpreting the demand and supply analysis of price and output effects are applicable to labor services, also, so they will not be repeated here in detail. Suffice it to say, demand-and-supply analysis of *open*-market determination of wages

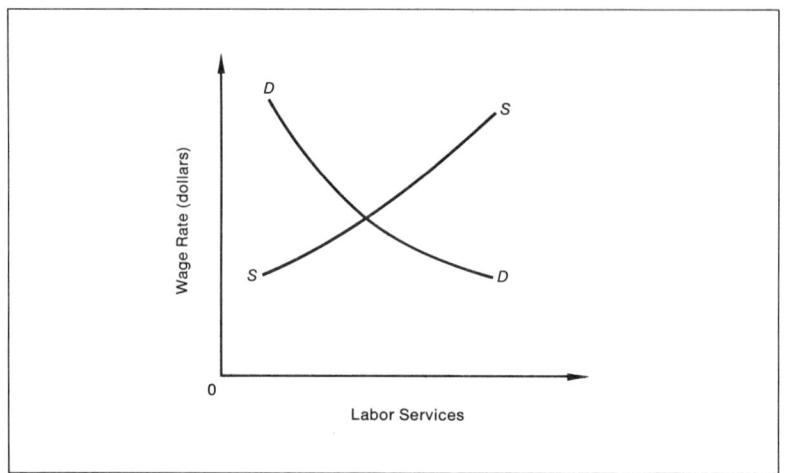

FIGURE 21-5. Demand and Supply of Labor to Segments of the Economy

For any segment of the economy, be it a firm or an industry, the supply-of-labor curve rises with higher wages, as labor is attracted from other segments or from the nonlabor-force portion of population into the labor force.

and employment is similar in principle to that for any other good. Underlying is the assumption that people are free agents and can quit or change jobs when they wish, and that at least some will change jobs when knowledge of more attractive openings is available. Employees who entertain offers to look for opportunities elsewhere also permit their current employers to make a counter-bid.

An employer, then, if he is to retain his employees, must detect and match offers of other employers. The employer who does so (through periodic wage and salary reviews and raises), without forcing his employees to seek offers and then ask for a raise, will have to pay no higher wages than if he waited for each employee to initiate negotiations. Job comparison is costly for employees; so the employer who is known to take the initiative in anticipating or matching market offers will find more employees willing to work for him than for one who tries to impose all the costs of job comparison on employees.

Because many employers periodically review wages and give raises without an employee's obtaining a competing offer, or because unions demand higher wages, it is sometimes alleged that wages are not set by market competition, but are adjusted simply because it is proper to do so or because of internal employee pressure. But market competition *is* present; the employer is meeting it by "rehiring" or keeping his existing employees from going elsewhere, as they would if he did not provide competitive wages. It is instructive to consider an example in which the supply of labor changes.

Suppose that the labor force in an occupation *decreases* because some laborers go to other jobs or communities. The smaller remaining supply will result in a rise in wage rates. Employers who lose employees will prefer to bid up wages to replace some of the employees, rather than continue with unfilled jobs (and less wealth). Competition among employers for employees will bid up wages. Employees need not move to get higher wages. Present employers will bid up wages to retain employees; otherwise they will lose workers and suffer some loss of business. And if employers do raise wages, they will demand fewer workers than at the old lower wages. In this way, the amount now demanded will be made equal to the smaller amount available. The higher wage rate induces substitution of other types of labor or inputs, according to the principles explained in the preceding chapter. For example, higher wages for carpenters will induce more standardization of types of woodwork, because standardization involves less carpentering service. The number of wood-paneled walls will decrease, and there will be more plaster and glass windows, with steel and aluminum window frames. There are thousands of ways to reduce the amount of carpenters' services by using other goods.

5, 6, 7

Wage Differences

We have been investigating open-market wages as if everyone were equal in ability and personal characteristics. But people are not, and it is time we examined some factors that make for differences in wages among occupations and among people within an occupation.

Some sense of proportion of differences in wages can easily be obtained from available data. First, however, Table 21–1 presents the distribution of the labor force by types of work. The largest category in 1963 was machine operatives, constituting about 18 percent of the work force. The fastest-growing category, professional and technical workers, was followed closely by clerical workers, with farm labor showing the greatest decline over the past several decades.

TABLE 21–1. Percentage Distribution of Civilian Employees in Various Tasks, 1963, Subclassified by Color

Major Occupation Group	Nonwhite	White
Professional, technical	6	13
Farmers and farm managers	3	4
Managers, proprietors	3	11
Clerical	7	16
Sales	2	7
Craftsmen	6	14
Machine operatives	20	18
Private-household services	15	2
Service workers, except household	15	9
Farm laborers	5	3
Laborers, nonfarm	13	4

Source: U. S. Department of Labor, *Monthly Bulletin of Labor Statistics*, 1963.

Table 21–2 gives annual wages of nonsupervisory employees in various industries in 1963. These are the *averages* of actual earnings, not the full-time equivalents. If people work on the average only about two-thirds of a full year in personal services work (as is the case), their full-time annual equivalent wages would be 50 percent larger.

An average wage does not indicate the *range* of wages in a given occupation. A substantial range of annual earnings is shown in Table 21–3 for employees in department stores, groceries, automobile dealers, and gasoline service stations. The range there

TABLE 21-2. Average of Annual Wages of Nonsupervisory Employees by Selected Industries, 1970

Personal services	$3600
Retail stores	3900
Apparel	4100
Textiles	4900
Assembly (toys, sporting goods, jewelry)	5200
Furniture	5300
Lumber	5500
Electrical	5900
All manufacturing	6800
Local bus	6700
Chemical	7400
Mining	8000
Motor vehicles	8800
Petroleum refining	8900
Bituminous coal	9000
College teachers (9 months)	9000
Contract construction	9100

Source: U. S. Department of Labor, *Monthly Bulletin of Labor Statistics*, 1970.

is basically dependent upon the differences in hours of work per week. Note, however, that the earnings of automobile salesmen, who are primarily on a commission earnings basis, do not conform as closely to hours of work.

TABLE 21-3. Percentage Distribution of Average Weekly Earnings of Nonsupervisory Employees in Selected Lines of Retail Business, 1961, by Hours

Hours per Week	Dept. Stores		Groceries		Motorcar Sales		Service Stations	
	Percent of Employees	$	Percent of Employees	$	Percent of Employees	$	Percent of Employees	$
1–14	8	12	9	12	1	14	8	11
15–34	21	32	26	33	4	47	20	29
35–39	13	53	6	59	4	76	3	49
40	43	67	25	83	16	100	11	61
41–48	13	73	23	78	45	100	18	70
Over 48	2	86	12	76	30	93	40	70

Source: U. S. Department of Labor, *Monthly Bulletin of Labor Statistics*, 1963.

Do not conclude that the range of wages in all occupations reflects just hours of work. Table 21-4 illustrates a range of wages reflecting incentive and skill, in this case for women sewing-machine operators in New York City. About 10 percent earn over $3.50 an hour, and almost 10 percent earn less than $1.50 an hour on a piecework pay system.

Even the size of the firm is a factor that affects wages. Larger firms pay more on the average than smaller ones. Employees may prefer small firms and therefore obtain higher wages in large firms as a pecuniary offset to the nonpecuniary advantages in a small firm.

TABLE 21-4. Percent Distribution of Incentive, Piecework Wages per Hour for Women Sewing-Machine Operators in New York City, 1963

Hourly Average Wage	Percent of Employees
Under $1.50	8
$1.50 and under $2.00	24
$2.00 and under $2.50	25
$2.50 and under $3.00	20
$3.00 and under $3.50	11
$3.50 and under $4.00	6
$4.00 and over	3

Source: U. S. Department of Labor, *Monthly Bulletin of Labor Statistics*, 1963.

Or possibly the large firm employs a higher general quality of labor. In retail trade, the average hourly earnings in 1963 for nonsupervisory employees were $1.74 for firms of over $1,000,000 in annual sales, $1.40 for firms with less than $250,000 in annual sales.

Table 21-5 shows the geographic distribution of hourly wage rates of nonsupervisory employees in retail trade in 1963. The percentage of employees earning less than $1.25, the 1963 legal minimum-wage rate, was 29 percent in the Northeast, 57 percent in the South, and 17 percent in the West. This does not mean that the West is more law abiding; the minimum-wage law exempted employees in several trades. However, the variation reflects productivity of employees and type of industry. Roughly half the employees at a given job have wage rates that differ by plus or minus 20 percent from the median in a given city.

If wages and incomes affect supply of labor, we ought to observe labor moving from lower-wage areas to higher-wage areas. And we do. Nationwide, the movement of people during the decade 1950-1960 was predominantly to areas with high income; gains in the total population of various counties through migration occurred only in the counties

TABLE 21-5. Hourly Wage Rates of Nonsupervisory Employees in Retail Trade, 1963, Cumulative in Regions

	Percent of Employees by Regions			
Wage Rates	Northeast	South	North Central	West
Under $ .75	1%	13%	3%	1%
" 1.00	3	31	12	3
" 1.25	29	57	34	17
" 1.50	49	72	54	35
" 2.00	74	88	77	60
" 2.50	88	94	89	77
Average	$1.74	$1.32	$1.65	$2.00

Eating and drinking places excluded. Source: U. S. Department of Labor, *Monthly Bulletin of Labor Statistics*, 1963.

with median family incomes (in 1959) of $6,000 or more, while all county groups with lower incomes had migration losses in both male and female and white and nonwhite populations. The counties with lowest median family incomes (under $5,000) had a net loss of over 28 percent of their population. Those in the $6,000 to $7,500 median family income group gained 11 percent. The migration was greater for younger people.[2] No doubt, labor is attracted by higher wages and repelled from the lower-wage areas.

Relative demand and supply. If first-class musical talent were widely available and the talent (strong back) to be a ditchdigger were relatively rare, some ditchdiggers would get a higher salary than fine musicians. The larger the supply, with given demand, the lower the wages; and for an equal amount of labor, the higher the demand, the higher the wages. For example, with ten window washers and ten doctors in a town of 5,000 people, the wages of doctors would be higher. The marginal product of a tenth doctor would probably be greater than of a tenth window washer. If the number of doctors were increased enough, their wages would fall below those of window washers.

Consequently, given the demand, wage differentials reflect the relative differences in supply of acceptable talent, resulting from heredity and training. If an extra dollar's worth of education and training increases a person's estimated productivity, it will pay him to buy the education, whether it be for a brain surgeon or for a cotton picker. The amount of training (investment in human capital) responds to its marginal cost relative to the increase it provides in productivity.

Suppose a person could borrow now against the clearly perceived higher future earnings he will be able to have as a result of education. Then a poor man, by borrowing against his prospective future earnings, could buy education as readily as a rich one. Notice, we do not say that the opportunity to buy education will equalize wealth among all people, but that all could exploit their potential talents by borrowing against their future, clearly perceived potential increase in earning power.

In fact, not everyone who wants to exploit his educational opportunities in this way can do so—for at least two reasons: (1) The future is uncertain. If I wanted to borrow $10,000 to buy an education, lenders would check into the evidence and form judgments of whether the education really would enhance my earning power and repayment probability. What will happen if the future earnings aren't as big as I expected? Will I repay and be poorer than if I had not borrowed so much money, or will I plead bankruptcy, or undue duress, when my creditor demands payment? (2) A large part of one's academic education is obtained before he reaches 21. Our legal system and courts will not enforce rigorously debts incurred before the age of 21. And since the courts are not inclined to enforce repayment out of earnings it is no wonder lenders are wary of educational loans to young people.

Specific versus general on-the-job training. Students are apt to overlook the very large amount of on-the-job training provided in business firms. Apprenticeships are one form of such education. Professional football and baseball players learn during their first couple of years of professional play. In fact, they are probably paid more in the initial years than their services are worth at that time. Why? Your instructor learned a lot in his

---

[2] Data reported by Gladys K. Bowles and James D. Tarver, "The Composition of New Migration among Counties in the United States, 1950–1960," *Agricultural Economics Research,* U. S. Dept. of Agriculture, January 1966.

first few years. Was he paid more than he was worth in those first years? It depends upon whether the on-the-job education is useful to him only as an employee for that one *specific* employer or whether it is useful in *general* for other employers. *Specific* training is useful only to the current employer, who is willing to pay for it, if the employee is not likely to quit as soon as he is trained and go to work elsewhere. The military service "gives" on-the-job training and some of it is useful for *general* civilian life. As you can expect, wages paid during training will be lower if the employee receives *general* training he can sell to *other* employers.

Employees with heavy specific training are less likely to quit or be laid off than untrained or generally trained employees. One implication of this is that we would expect to find more of the untrained or generally trained people in the group who most frequently change jobs and go through a period of unemployment while evaluating alternative job options.

Risk-bearing differentials. Some people are more willing to try new applications or techniques, giving up relatively sure prospective wages in the hope of getting a higher wage. An architect who gives up a secure job designing conventional buildings and risks coming up with desirable new designs may end up very much richer or poorer. Some choose the risk of ending up poorer for the prospect of being richer. In this sense, they prefer to have had the chance to be rich even though they may fail. And their choices produce a wide spread of *realized* life-time earnings.

Wage differences *within* many occupations are greater than among averages of occupations. The spread of actors' incomes within that profession is greater than the difference between the *averages* of doctors' and actors' incomes. Better a fine actor than an average doctor. Better a fine ball player than an average lawyer.

8, 9

Salary Differences Depend on Associated Wealth

Some people have been paid over a million dollars in one year for their personal services. Is there some force making personal earnings more different than the "inherent" abilities or skills? It has been argued as follows: "The president of General Products receives $500,000 a year. When he retires, someone now getting far less will take his place and will get that high salary. Surely the high salary is a function of the *position* rather than of some differences in abilities." But be careful to remember your economic principles. The marginal productivity of any resource or input affects its reward, and as we saw in the preceding chapter, the associated amount of capital affects marginal productivity. To see what differences in ability imply, when applied to control different amounts of wealth, consider two managers, one with ability to make correct decisions 5 percent more of the time than the other. Roughly speaking, that 5 percent superiority is worth about $50,000 in a $1,000,000 business, but only about $5,000 in a $100,000 business. The larger business will gain more with the superior man than would the small company. On the other hand two common labor employees that differed by 5 percent in their ability would not be making decisions that affect wealth as much as those of the top executives, and so the difference in their talents would not be so magnified. This implies that nonmanagerial skills will be paid about the same in *large and small* companies, whereas the salaries of top management will be correlated with the size of the company.

This is in fact what happens. Notice the explanation provided here is not that the big companies have more wealth and therefore the manager can get more. Rather it is that the bigger the company the greater is the marginal productivity difference between the managerial skills of any two potential managers.

Wage Differences and Nonpecuniary Factors

Employment conditions differ in nonpecuniary respects: employer personality, size of firm, safety, prestige, climate, type of work, location, congeniality of fellow workers. Higher pay to offset nonpecuniary disadvantages is called an "equalizing" wage difference; it helps equate labor's total rewards in different working conditions. These conditions can persist indefinitely if the cost of getting rid of them exceeds the "equalizing" difference in wages. For example, people may be willing to work in the heat only at premium wages; if the premium is less than the cost of air conditioning, pay differentials will continue.

Employees differ also. Better-looking, more courteous, pleasant, uncomplaining, cooperative, and congenial employees provide employers with nonpecuniary sources of utility. Both pecuniary and nonpecuniary products affect employers. Therefore, an employer discriminates among potential employees with respect to nonpecuniary attributes. If two stenographers have equal pecuniary productivity, but one is more beautiful, pleasant, well-dressed, with a better-modulated voice, then, at equal wages, she would be preferred. Her nonpecuniary qualities will get her a higher wage than the inferior (in a nonpecuniary sense) stenographer. Higher pay to the attractive stenographer is the same thing as lower pay for inferior people. And that lower pay enables inferior people to get jobs. "Equalizing wage differences," then, provide employment opportunities for inferior employees, just as equalizing wage differences induce people to work in inferior environmental conditions. However, although people recognize differences among employers in working conditions and environment as valid reasons for employees' discrimination in choice of employers, they resent such actions by employers on the basis of personal characteristics of employees. Federal laws declare employ*er* discrimination illegal, while employ*ees* may legally discriminate.

Preferences are revealed by "compensating" or "equalizing" wage and price differences, if markets are open to all types. Poor paintings sell for less than superb paintings; otherwise, the poor paintings would not be sold. Because Chevrolets sell for less than Cadillacs, Chevrolets can survive in competition against Cadillacs. At the same price, fewer would want Chevies.

Less attractive and homely people can offset their weaker appeal to other people to whom they desire to sell services by charging a lower price than that charged by beautiful people. You buy round steak rather than filet mignon only because the price of round steak is sufficiently lower, thus compensating you for the inferior tenderness and flavor of round steak, even though the food value of the two is the same.

People have preferences, and discrimination will occur *either* in wages paid or in extent and kinds of employment. At the same wage rate, the less preferred people will get less employment in good jobs. At lower wage rates, they can get more employment. But the less preferred will *not* receive *both* the same wage and the same amount or kind of employment—for the same reason that high-quality goods get a higher price or women of 35 get fewer jobs in a chorus line than girls of 25. The *customers* are discriminating.

So is an employer, even though he may be the only one who sees some of the employees. He discriminates among people in order to maintain morale, productivity, and cooperation of employees—that is, to satisfy the nontechnical aspects of employment. This interest in personal attributes explains why employees and employers both place so much reliance on personal channels of recruitment and job finding. It also helps to explain some marketing procedures for labor.

11, 12, 13, 14, 15, 16, 17

Effect of Technological Progress on Job Allocation and Wages

Although viewed with alarm and fought by various labor groups, automation (which has been progressing since man first learned to wield a stick) is a major source of increased wealth, new and easier jobs, and higher real incomes, and a larger population. The plow drawn by horses (rather than by people) was a great technological advance. What happened to the displaced people who lost their jobs in front of the plow? They turned to what were formerly less important tasks like collecting more wood and building more stone fences. And when the tractor replaced the horse and several plowmen, they went to work producing more of other things. With the advent of new machines, labor became less valuable *in the old* jobs than in jobs to which the workers then turned (and which formerly were too costly). Today, after millenniums of technological progress, people still worry about the mechanical, self-controlled machine because it induces labor re-allocation. And that is a valid reason for concern, though not of the kind most commonly talked about—lack of jobs.

Invention and Job Re-allocation

Automation or technological progress creates new jobs; but that really is irrelevant, despite overwhelming talk to the contrary. To see why, suppose *no* new jobs were created. Displaced workers must turn to jobs which formerly were left unfilled or unperformed because the cost of filling them was too high. That is, the sacrificed output would have been more valuable than that to be had from the unfilled jobs. But now the formerly unperformed jobs or unavailable output can be produced by those whose services are less valuable in the old jobs. Therefore, whether or not the new invention or technique increases the demand for workers in that industry, there still will be plenty of jobs—in fact, more than can *ever* be filled. There are not too few jobs, but *too many* jobs! The problem is deciding which jobs or tasks to perform and which jobs to leave unperformed. That is the persisting problem of labor allocation. Inventions, automation, and progress do not eliminate it. The more rapid the pace of invention, the more attention the problem requires. But it is *not* a problem of too few jobs, as many glib social observers contend.

The real cause of concern is that people whose services in their current jobs are outcompeted by new methods must shift to new jobs—presumably to jobs that pay less than the current jobs formerly did. We must therefore distinguish among three groups of people. Consider the invention of television. (1) Some get higher wages because they work with the new techniques or because they are demanded to produce the new equipment. Some people shifted from radio and movies to the manufacture of television programs and equipment and earned larger incomes. They benefit doubly—from the higher income and the lower prices of the increased output. (2) Some people experience no perceptible impact on their working conditions. They benefit from the lower costs of home entertainment, and they suffer no loss of income. (3) Some people find their old jobs being displaced by the new techniques. They must transfer to new jobs that pay less. This class can be further classified in three sub-categories: (a) Some nevertheless were better off on net, after considering the gains of their being able to use television as a consumer. (b) Of the remainder who did not reap a gain even after considering all the effects of this particular innovation, some were nevertheless better off than if they had been able to keep their old income but had to forsake *all* new progress since television. They gained through the general dispersal of improvements via lower prices and quality improvements to consumers—despite their income loss. (c) Some employees and owners of equipment suffered such severe reductions in demand for their services that, even after taking into account the gains from television and from all other technological improvements during the rest of their lives, they were still worse off. This category is more characteristic of older people than younger.

While it is preferable to be a member of group 1, the group in which a person finds himself depends upon the characteristics of new inventions and techniques. All of us fall in group 2 with respect to most inventions. Clearly we will resist inventions that place us in category 3; and we will complain and will be noticed more often than those in groups 1 and 2.

As yet, economic theory has been unable to tell in advance for any invention how many, let alone which, people will fall in each class. Even afterward it is often impossible to tell, because other changes impinge on the situation and obscure effects of earlier changes. For example, did the invention of the typewriter increase or decrease the demand for secretaries? The discovery of oil may have attracted labor from coal mines into oil-well drilling, refining, and pipeline work, so that the wages of coal miners increased despite the effect of oil on the demand for coal. New inventions not only affect the schedule of marginal value-productivity of workers in the affected jobs; they can also attract workers, thus raising wages elsewhere. Spectacular examples are the railroad and the automobile. They substantially lowered the costs of transport; as a result, transport increased, as did the demand for workers to provide materials for transportation. Canalmen, livery-stable operators, and buggy-whip makers shifted to better-paying jobs in the new transportation industry. It is true that the new machines sometimes reduce the cost of products so much that the increased amount demanded raises the demand for labor in that job; consequently, wages are raised.

Compensation Principle

Employees whose present wages or jobs are threatened have argued that the whole community ought, out of the net gain, to compensate re-allocated workers for any loss. This is logically an airtight possibility *in principle,* because the increased value of output exceeds the losses of the displaced factors. However, innovations are so extensive that it is impossible to identify each and to determine who loses how much. How would we know how much to pay a person who claims to be displaced by the introduction of electronic computers? How could we be sure that he has not taken some easy, low-paying job—in the expectation that he will be given a payment large enough to make up the difference? Only *if* people's incentives were not changed by the compensation principle, and *if* there were *no* costs in discovering who gained or lost how much, would that compensation system be feasible. Nevertheless, compensation is not ignored. Today people pay taxes for a program to retrain and to relocate workers.³

A more fundamental difficulty with the compensation proposal is that not only labor but also existing capital goods lose productive value. If one compensates labor, he should, in justice, also compensate owners of nonhuman assets. But if compensation is paid *out of taxes* for every change in value resulting from innovation, the *owners* of productive resources, human and nonhuman, do not bear the risks of unforeseeable future consequences; instead, the general public becomes the risk bearer according to the tax load and government services. The compensation principle conflicts with a basic purpose of a private-property society: to enable people to specialize in risk bearing—to escape common bearing of all risks of future values of all resources. If I don't want to bear the risks of the future value of some building, I simply choose not to be an owner of it; in that way I neither capture any gain nor suffer any loss of value. If I wish to bear the risk, I can buy a share of ownership in it or in like resources. Risk bearing is selective and adjustable. Suppose I were to agree to bear all the losses of value of my services, whatever the cause, and in exchange I obtain the right to keep whatever gains might occur in the value of my resources. That kind of agreement is implicitly made by a private-property owner. The compensation-by-taxing principle denies his making that agreement with the rest of society.

Adjustment to Change

The shift from a job where demand has fallen to a new job is a poignant problem of human adjustment. A move to a new area, a new job, a lower standard of living, and new colleagues and social circles can be a traumatic experience, especially for older people. Even if, in the overwhelming majority of cases, the job displacement caused by new innovations in technology shifted people to better and higher-paying jobs, the hardship for some is not avoided. These hardship cases are the ones most likely to be remembered.

Some adults never outgrow childhood fantasy; they believe scarcity is a result of some plot or failure to exploit our allegedly unlimited production potential. More people are alive today (probably about one in ten of all those who have ever lived to maturity) because we are not trying to survive with the technology of 1870 or 1770 or 1070. More are alive because they have knowledge and capital for a high marginal product. But there is no prospect that man will have all his wants fulfilled, with no jobs any longer worth doing. Until that unforeseeable day he must allocate his productive energies only to the most valuable jobs—an allocation that will change with new inventions, resources, and demands. And until that day, those experiencing a reduced market value of output of their current jobs (because others are outcompeting them in the market) can and will

---

³ This aid is proposed, however, not only for those whose incomes are cut by competition from new, more productive equipment, but for any laborer who lives in an area where there is general decline in demand for services—whatever the reason. A displaced worker in a prosperous *area* is not eligible.

The Trade Expansion Act of 1962 gives the President additional powers to negotiate for tariff reduction and provides for "trade adjustment assistance" for both business firms (through technical assistance, loans, tax relief) and workers (through special unemployment benefits, retraining, loans for moving to jobs in different communities) when injury from increased imports can be demonstrated.

resort to nonmarket-competitive behavior to try to offset market competition. Political competitive power may be directed toward changing the results of, or restricting, market competition. It is a very safe prediction that whenever one's wealth is being competed away in the market by new inventions, changing tastes, or new products, his attempts to restrict that market will increase.

18, 19, 20, 21

Summary

1 Labor service is a commodity, subject to the laws of demand and of supply like any other commodity.

2 The demand for labor is a negative function of the wage rate paid for labor. The supply function for labor services is one in which larger amounts of labor can be obtained by offering a higher payment for more services.

3 Differences in wage rates, like differences in prices of various goods, reflect relative demands and supplies of various kinds of labor. *Qualitative* differences in people's productive talents yield differences in relative supplies of those talents and hence in the wages paid. Differences in supplies of various talents reflect inequality in amounts of various *natural* talents, *costs* of training and developing talents, and *willingness* of suppliers of labor to engage in various kinds of work.

4 Differences in *monetary* wages sufficient to compensate for nonmonetary features of various jobs or of personal traits of employers or employees are called equalizing differences. These differences are sometimes called discriminatory wage differences, in that they discriminate or compensate for differences in the *nonmonetary* attributes of the job and the employer and employees.

5 Much education of people for productive work is on-the-job training. Some wage differences reflect compensation for on-the-job education, since the employee is willing to pay for this by accepting a lower wage. Employees receiving specific training do not thereby receive lower-than-competitive wages; instead they receive wages larger than their current marginal productivity to the employer and later receive wages less than their marginal productivity to this one employer.

6 Technological progress (currently called automation) does not reduce the number of work opportunities. It reduces the value of some jobs and induces people to shift to others formerly too expensive to perform—or formerly left unperformed because of lower value relative to other performed tasks. Not everyone gains from every technological advance. Some gain with higher demand for their services in the new activity. Some gain by lower costs of improved services from the new activity. Some owners of productive goods (labor as well as physical goods) lose wealth by being displaced to new tasks not paying as much as they formerly earned.

7 Compensation to people hurt by technological progress is in principle feasible, but because of exorbitant costs of determining accurately who is hurt and how much, either crude approximations are made by tax-financed compensation schemes or the risks of such effects are distributed via ownership arrangements.

8 Most public discussion of automation and technological advance suggests a "lump-of-labor" fallacy: that there is only so much work to be done, and that every task more efficiently performed with less labor means just so much less worthwhile work is thereby

left to be performed. This is identical to saying that currently society could produce all the goods and services it desires, so that any released effort has no other productive uses—an obviously false proposition.

Questions

1 Minors are not "free" individuals; for example, they cannot own property (a guardian oversees them) and they cannot make legally binding contracts. Their legal status is not far removed from temporary slavery. Because of the conflict of interest between parents and minors, such legal restrictions as compulsory education and prohibition of child employment (both of which are nineteenth-century developments) are imposed to increase the probability that the parent will make decisions of the kind the minor would presumably make if he were "of age and sensible." Is there an alternative and not necessarily incompatible force at work that would bring about an increase in academic education and a decrease in child employment even if no laws had been passed?

2 A 20-year-old with an earning expectancy of forty-five years (beginning at $3,000 per year and increasing annually at the rate of 6 percent to about $13,000 per year at the end of twenty years and then holding constant thereafter to retirement at 65) has a present capital value of his future earnings of about $100,000 at 6 percent rate of interest. If he expects continued salary increases after age 40, his present value will be even greater. It has been estimated, on the basis of projections of wage earnings of college graduates, that the "time-of-graduation capital value" of a college graduate's future income is on the average about $150,000 at 6 percent rate of interest. This means that if he could sell his future wages (and not affect his willingness to work!), he could "sell" himself for approximately $150,000 at graduation. A woman who marries him gets ownership of half his wages; by marrying him she "purchases" a wealth of about $75,000. Is there any other way "in effect" to sell off those future earnings? What method do most people use to spend now some of that capital value?

3 "Overtime premium wages are a device to restrain employers from working employees overtime." "Overtime premium wages are means whereby employers induce employees to work overtime more than they otherwise would." Which of these two propositions is correct? Explain.

4 "The birth rate is controlled by custom and emotion, not by economic calculations. Certainly, it is not reasonable to expect more children, the wealthier the parents." Yet the fact is that in communities with relatively widespread knowledge of contraceptive methods, there is a positive correlation between number of children and wealth of parents (after allowing for other factors like education, occupation, and location). For purposes of testing the above propositions, would you define "number of children" as number of pregnancies, of live births, of children surviving to age 1 month, or to 1 year, or to 6 years, or what?

5 Assume that wage rates of gardeners were to double, despite an unchanged demand.
   a. Would people go on hiring the same amount of gardener services and pay more?
   b. What would happen to gardens?
   c. What substitution for gardeners would occur?
   d. Where or from whom could you learn about the available substitution techniques?

6 "The higher the wage rate, the higher the wages." Explain the error in this statement.

7 "The population of Arizona is increasing at a record rate. Special effort must be made to create new jobs to provide employment for the increased labor force." Explain why this is wrong.

8 "Different workers receive different wages because the workers are different, the jobs are different, and workers can't move to other jobs easily." On the other hand, "Workers are different but get the same pay in many jobs; many different jobs pay the same wages; and it is just as 'easy' to move across the country as it is to move next door." Obviously one of these quoted statements is either wrong or ambiguous. Rewrite it to make it correct.

9 "My doctor charges me a high fee because he has to cover the high cost of his education and equipment. On the other hand, my golfing teacher also charges me a high fee, even though his education is practically absent." Is either one cheating or fooling me? Explain.

10 "Elizabeth Taylor was paid over $5,000,000 for making the film *Cleopatra*. Yet Audrey Hepburn could have taken her place for, say, $1,000,000. There must be something wrong with the movie industry. Certainly, Taylor is not worth that much more to 20th Century-Fox than Hepburn would be." Explain, using marginal-productivity theory, how it can be sensible to pay Taylor that much, even though Hepburn might have been available for one-fifth as much.

11 "A substantial number of relatively unskilled persons reported that they cannot find work. At the same time, there are many unfilled jobs for relatively skilled people. Apparently, the problem is that there are more unskilled people than unskilled jobs." What is wrong with the reasoning?

12 "The presidents of some big corporations are paid as much as $500,000 in one year. All they do is make the kinds of decisions that are made in thousands of other companies by much lower-paid people who are as intelligent, but who just haven't had a chance to get those fancy jobs and who aren't as well known or don't have the reputation. Clearly, salaries are based more on past experience, reputation, and pull. Therefore, marginal productivity—which is an academic, unrealistic abstraction of an imaginary world—is useless at best and false at worst." Explain why the last sentence is not implied by the preceding sentences.

13 In feudal England there was no unemployment—only work and leisure. Employment for wages was rare. Even rarer were market-negotiated wages. But the rise of the commercial system introduced markets for labor services and induced peasants to break away from their feudal ties and to sacrifice their feudal security for the hazards of private contractual employment and unemployment. By the sixteenth century employment for money wages was well established (but maximum permissible wage rates were set by government, and potential employers were exhorted not to offer more and were punished if caught).
a. What devices do you think developed as a means of circumventing the maximum-wage restrictions?
b. Why would the government impose *maximum* limits to wages whereas today *minimum* limits are commonly imposed?

14 America was founded partly on "slavery" of white men. In colonial days immigrants "indentured" themselves, pledging to work for the benefit of a master for seven (or some specified number of) years if the master would finance their way to America. Today, this is illegal.
a. Why?
b. Who gains and who loses if such contracts are prohibited?

15 "In the open market, wages are driven down to the subsistence level." That is the iron law of wages. What is meant by "the subsistence level"?

16 Why are the wages of the top managers of large companies generally higher than those of small companies? The answer is not that the larger companies have a greater ability to pay because they are richer (they do not pay more for their buildings or subordinate employees).

17 In what sense does the range of wealth and income of people reflect their own preferences?

18 A tape-recording machine displaces a telephone-answering girl. Who or what has displaced whom? Explain why the displacement of labor by capital reflects a displacement of labor by labor.

19 "Automation is destroying 300,000 jobs a month." Accepting this as a fact, explain why it does not mean that anyone will be left without a job.

20 "Automation, like any change in demand or supply of labor, leads to changes in jobs and wage rates—not to increased unemployables." Explain.

21 A candidate for the office of U. S. Senator proposed that employees be given time off with pay to promote political campaigns of their favored candidates. Tell under what circumstances you as an employer would not care if this were done. (Hint: Remember, there is more than the money pay that attracts employees to a job.)

Restrictions on Open Markets for Labor

22

BUYERS and sellers often restrict others from the market as competitors. And the buyers and sellers of labor services are no exception. Now labor markets will be analyzed in an effort to detect the constraints that work to change money wages from the open-market levels.

Employee-Employer Bargaining Power

First, we expose a fallacy. Restrictions on the market are often advocated to protect employees from the employer's superior bargaining power. Proponents say that individual workers are helpless against the powerful employer. An employee, acting alone, can readily be replaced if he asks for higher pay; his alternatives are limited. But, united, employees can prevent the employer from playing one against the other. To further protect the laborer minimum-wage, fair-employment, and working-condition laws are proposed.

Whatever one's impression about the plight of employees, the fact is that the price *anyone* can get is limited by the offers made to him by potential buyers. General Motors is also limited. What, for example, limits its ability to keep wages down? The answer is that if General Motors offers less pay than other employers, it will get fewer employees. Any employee can get a salary that is at least as high as his services are worth to some other employer. The authors are employees of the state of California. Any time we feel like it, we can quit and take jobs elsewhere. That is what "forces" the state to pay as much as it does. That it is willing to do so means that our services are worth at least that much to the purchaser. What "bargaining power" may mean, therefore, is simply the highest salary one can get from *other* jobs. If that is a great deal less than he is now getting, the employee will be reluctant to press for higher wages and may even accept some impositions or a wage cut rather than quit.

It may be said that the employer who loses an employee loses only one employee, while the employee loses his entire income. In fact, the employee does not lose his entire income; he loses the premium he was getting in his former job over the next best alternative adjusted for moving and job-exploration costs. Of course, if the employee quits, his losses can be greater than those imposed on the employer; but such a comparison is irrelevant. Employers hire employees because the employer gains by doing so, not because the employee gains less.

Do not mistake the purpose of the preceding remarks. They are not antiemployee, antiemployer, or antiunion; they are anticonfusion.

Labor Unions

"The high standard of wages of the American worker is a result of a strong labor-union movement." Would that it were true. The path to higher income for all workers in poor countries would be open: unionize and strike for high wages. However, neither economic reasoning nor factual evidence supports that prescription. The high marginal-productivity schedule of labor explains high wages and employment levels. If a community has abundant natural resources and capital equipment, high educational levels, skilled workers, and a system for organizing productive activity, then the marginal productivity of the existing supply of labor will be higher. The foundation of high wages and large incomes is there and no place else. What the spread of unions can do in that respect is help that system organize diverse talents more efficiently by smoothing grievance procedures, providing increased information about job opportunities, helping workers improve their skills, providing facilities for joint purchases, and monitoring payment of fringe benefits like insurance, retirement, etc.

By no means are these trivial. Anyone working in a large corporation under foremen knows that a disinterested and not-easily-intimidated agent to handle grievances helps working conditions. Unions can help provide valuable and hard-to-get information about alternative jobs. Joint purchases of insurance or loan services via credit unions are efficient, in that the union credit agency knows the member's work record and has a relatively quick means of assessing his credit worthiness and prospects of job and income continuance. These objectives deserve emphasis because some people think the only purpose of a union is to enable employees to strike effectively. That is, of course, the union's basic source of strength in improving wages and working conditions of *some union members* beyond those determined by open-market competition.

Labor unions enable employees to coordinate their actions and influence the employer's behavior by affecting the markets in which he buys labor or sells his products. Unions also influence legislation. Labor unions have existed for a long time, often despite their being held illegal as "criminal conspiracies." However, in 1842 the Massachusetts Supreme Court rendered a precedent-setting decision in *Commonwealth v. Hunt,* declaring unions to be legal. Presently in the United States about 16,000,000 employees (20–25 percent of the labor force) are in unions. Union membership is charted in Figure 22–1 along with the total civilian labor force. The *fraction* of the civilian labor force belonging to unions has fluctuated, as shown in Figure 22–2. The rise during the late 1930s has been attributed primarily to contemporary legislation compelling employers to negotiate with union agents for groups of employees, if a majority of the employees in those groups voted for a union (the Wagner Act of 1935).

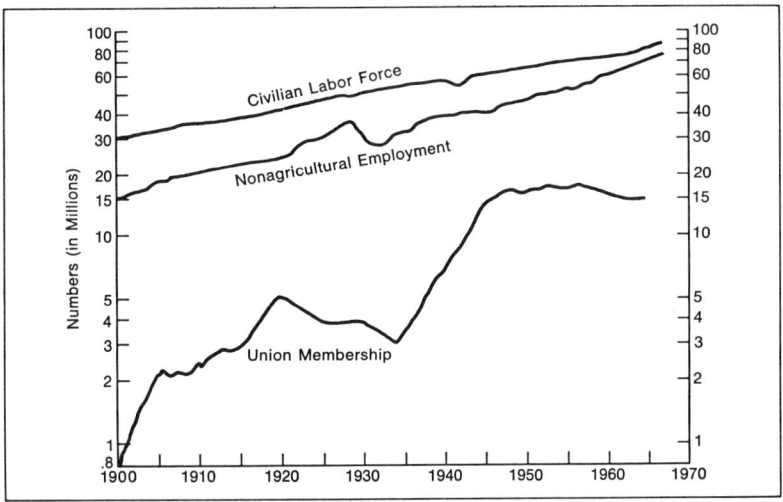

FIGURE 22–1. Civilian Labor Force, Employees in Nonagricultural Establishments, and Trade Union Membership, 1900–1965

Source: L. Troy, *Trade Union Membership, 1897–1962* (New York: National Bureau of Economic Research, 1965). Updated.

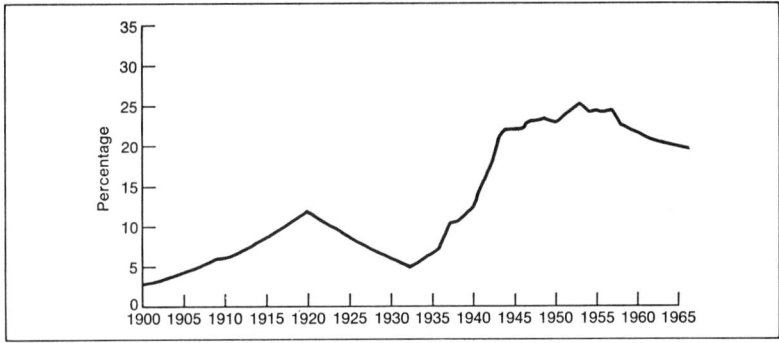

FIGURE 22–2. Percent of Union Membership in the Civilian Labor Force

Source: L. Troy, *Trade Union Membership, 1897–1962* (New York: National Bureau of Economic Research, 1965). Updated.

In some industries, virtually every employee is a union member (musicians, longshoremen, transport workers, construction workers) and in others, nearly none (chemists, typists, economists, farm workers). A few of the largest unions contain most of the members. For example, the ten largest contain almost half the total. (Teamsters with 1,500,000, Steel Workers with over 1,000,000, and on through Auto Workers, Hod Carriers, and Garment Workers, down to the Textile Workers with about 200,000.) The fraction of union members is larger in the northern and western states than in the southern states.

National unions are amalgamations of chartered "locals" to which employees belong. Although the national organization, or federation, has a constitution, the "local" usually has the basic power to apply membership rules and contract approval. For example, national federation constitutions assert that membership is open to all, regardless of race or creed, but the actual admission standards are determined by the local members, with much discrimination, especially in craft unions. Some craft unions have separate union locals for Negroes (e.g., musicians).

Craft union members are all skilled in the same craft; *industrial* union members all work in one industry regardless of particular skills. For example, the carpenters' union is a craft union, whereas the steel workers' union is an industrial union containing members with various skills. Most national craft unions are associated in a national *federation*, American Federation of Labor (AFL), while the Congress of Industrial Organizations (CIO) comprises mostly industrial unions. A few national unions (teamsters and coal miners) belong to neither. The AFL and the CIO have a top-level joint council called the "AFL-CIO." One of its purposes is to define jurisdiction of the national unions to reduce inter-union rivalry about, for example, whether an electrical fixture is to be installed by a carpenter or an electrical worker.

Local unions have officers (usually elected by the local membership) to maintain and expand coverage of union over more employers, to negotiate new contract terms, and to administer the routine affairs (pension funds, shop grievances). A "shop steward" is a union member and employee of the firm in which he helps to avoid or settle workers' grievances, much as an agent acts as an intermediary between two contracting parties. Safety rules, working hours, vacation interpretation, "goofing" on the job—these are a few of the perennial sources of misunderstanding and dispute that a shop steward can help to alleviate. The costs of union activity are financed by union membership initiation fees and monthly dues. Some initiation fees are hundreds of dollars, with monthly dues usually under $10.

Unions are recognized as the *sole* bargaining agent for a specified type of employee in any firm, if a majority of the voting employees so prefer under procedures established by the National Labor Relations Law, as administered by the National Labor Relations Board (NLRB). At the present time (and probably for many years in the future) one of the major disputes among employers, unions, and the NLRB concerns the Board's scope of authority.

A less ambiguous situation is the scope of union-membership requirement. Some employers have *closed shops,* meaning that only union members can *apply* for and retain jobs. Some have *union shops,* in which all employees must become union members or at least pay union fees, if they are to retain a job for more than one month (they need not be members when applying for a job). Open shops do not require union membership in any respect.[1]

In addition to modifying the negotiatory techniques for the sale of labor services, unions use methods of imposing severe costs on employers to induce agreement to union demands. A *boycott* is a *concerted* refusal by union members to buy the products of the employer being boycotted. Sometimes, other firms that do business with the boycotted firm will also be boycotted—a *secondary boycott*. The *strike*, which has proved to be a stronger weapon, consists of two parts: (1) incumbent employees stop work for their

---

[1] Current federal legislation (Section 14B of the Taft-Hartley Act) permits a state to prohibit union shops. This is called the "right-to-work" law, somewhat misleadingly. This law is under violent attack from unions, and almost every year attempts are made to repeal it in Congress by prohibiting any state from requiring open shops in all places of employment. About twenty states prohibit union and closed shops.

existing employer, *and* (2) other laborers are prevented from competing for those jobs on terms inferior to those sought by the striking incumbents. Without the ability to prevent other applicants from negotiating for these jobs, the strike would merely be a mass resignation. In fact, the union *as we know it today* would be practically destroyed. Since the strike involves closing the market to some sellers of labor, it is commonly associated with means of preventing those other people from entering the market. Initially violence or, later, its threat is required. We shall examine this in more detail in the next sections.

The Strike as a Basis of Union Power

It is a tribute to the intelligence and economic acumen of union leaders that they fought for the right to strike and that they insist that it is crucial to a strong and effective union. It is a tribute to their political skill that they concealed their real purposes behind the facade of "equating bargaining power" as a means of protecting the standard of "labor's" wages in America. It would not be a tribute to the intelligence of the reader to let that distinction pass unnoticed. Therefore, we shall apply economic analysis to the role of the union in affecting wages and employment allocation.

Legislation concerning unions and strikes. In England and in France, beginning with the French Revolution, labor or trade unions were prohibited as "conspiracies" to modify market negotiations. Union members threatened violence against other laborers who undercut desired higher wages. Although the threat of violence in the strike was basically what anticonspiracy laws aimed to stop, they tried to do it by abolishing the right to form a union—which is a very different thing from a strike. To unite voluntarily is defined as a right of free men, in most concepts of freedom. Hence, the anticonspiracy laws were opposed both by employees who had their sights on the right to strike and by people who had their sights on the ideal of freedom. By 1830, the English anticonspiracy laws had been repealed *and* the right to strike tacitly granted—with the forlorn hope that no violence or coercion would ensue.

The right to strike has had its subsequent ups and downs. At times, it was prohibited as an interference with a nonstriker's freedom of access to labor markets. Even when legalized, it has sometimes been tolerated only if strikers did not interfere with nonunion people who continued to work at less than the wages demanded by the strikers. Violence was almost inevitable if nonunion employees tried to cross the picket line. Police have at times permitted pickets to block entry and have refused to help nonunion employees cross the line, because that would mean a breach of the peace. At other times they have protected the nonstrikers.

Today some countries (Russia and Spain, to name but two) prohibit strikes; anyone can quit his job, or the whole group can quit. In other countries, tolerance ranges from legal restrictions against any interference with nonstriking employees and job seekers to legal support of the strikers by preventing strike breakers from working.

Congress, in the Clayton Act of 1914, intended to restrict judiciary power to use antimonopoly laws and "restraint-of-trade" injunctions against certain types of union activities, including the strike. In 1932, the Norris-LaGuardia Act more effectively restricted the judiciary's power to prevent unions from engaging in strikes, picketing, and certain types of boycotts. But subsequently, the Taft-Hartley Act of 1947 permitted the President to prohibit any strike that would create what he considers to be a "national emergency." Section 14-b of that act permitted states to ban union shops. Approximately twenty states have passed such so-called "right-to-work" (without joining a union) laws. Such laws do not, in logic, necessarily increase the workers' freedom or range of choice. For example, if some employer and all his employees want to have a union shop, the state "right-to-work" law would prevent it. On the other hand, one group of employees cannot force other employees to join a union if the employer or his other employees do not want a union shop.

Compulsory arbitration. To prevent strikes or settle grievances, the employer and union, if unable to resolve a dispute, sometimes hire an outsider to suggest terms that might be mutually acceptable, though neither party necessarily agrees to accept the terms. The outside mediator may be a private specialist, a government employee, or a disinterested person such as a university president. Presently, no law requires employers and unions to submit disputes to an arbitrator for a binding settlement, but about 90 percent of labor contracts provide for some kind of arbitration (though not necessarily compulsory) of grievances.

Some people favor compulsory arbitration in all union contracts. Whether the results would be more like those that would prevail in a situation with open markets for labor or would result in greater market restriction is impossible to say. Often it is thought that wage and work conditions can be most sensibly determined by the "ability" of an employer to pay—as judged by his income, the cost of living, or the change in productivity. None of these proposed forms of arbitration would reproduce the open market's wage and work conditions. But, of course, that is precisely what the union is trying to avoid by its threat to strike.

Maintenance of Effective Strike Power

Unions lose power as fewer of the existing employees join the union, for they may refuse to join in a strike. A way of overcoming this latent weakness is a "union shop," wherein all employees must become union members. Furthermore, all employees with a given skill should belong to but one union. If two unions represented, say, musicians, the two would try to dominate each other; and the employer could play one against the other—just as he lets one employee bid against another in the open market, and also just as each employee lets one potential employer bid against the other in open markets. The single bargaining agent and the union shop then become the "silent" rallying cry for unions.

Once the power to strike effectively is sanctioned, better working conditions can be sought for *some* members of the striking unions—better than if other people were free to compete in the same market. Higher wages, shorter hours, better working conditions, and increased job security are ways in which *some* union members can increase their wealth and utility.

However, the fact that union bargaining is associated with increases in wages is not conclusive evidence that it achieves higher wages than are obtained in an open market. Suppose, for instance, that a wage contract were signed two years ago for specified wage rates, and since that time wages in general have risen by 15 percent. The employer is ready to grant a pay raise of 15 percent. In fact, he may be eager to do so in order to retain, as well as improve, his work force in the face of better wages elsewhere. Union officials, however, might demand a 20 percent increase. After a ritual of negotiation and bargaining, the terms come out to be 15 percent; and the union claims it has raised wages. However, neither the employer nor the union sets the viable wage rate; instead, both accept, adopt, or adjust to wages in the open market—the employer offering that amount because he must in order to get employees, and the union negotiators accepting it unless they are prepared to face a loss of job opportunities from this employer. In the absence of a union, the wages would have risen anyway—maybe even earlier, since employer and employee had to wait for a formal union-contract negotiation.

Some people say that under present conditions the power of a union to strike effectively is tantamount to closing the market to competition, and that therefore the concept of free collective bargaining is misleading in the sense that it does not permit society a choice among alternative sources of production; nonunion labor is excluded and labor markets are restricted. Given the reduction of the competitive market, compulsory arbitration is viewed as a replacement of one form of closed market control by another form of closed market control—compulsory arbitration.

Unions and Wage Rates

Unions certainly have affected working conditions, insofar as a union bargaining agent will help settle grievances more efficiently than the industrial-relations officer for the company. As for wages, studies indicate large differences in effects among unions. Some unions have been able to raise hourly wage rates substantially above the open-market level (though not necessarily able to maintain the difference for more than a few years). Many appear to have had no effect on wage rates. The best estimates are that the effect of unionism on the average income of union workers compared with the average of nonunion workers has been at least 10 percent and probably not over 15 percent.[2] Some unions have had much greater effect—for example, the income of *employed* coal miners was estimated to be about 50 percent higher. Probably in the 1920s when unions were less widespread they may have increased wages as much as 20 percent. There is some evidence that since World War II the effect has diminished.

2, 3, 4, 5, 6, 7, 8

How to Raise Wage Rates

How can unions, or anyone else, raise wage *rates*? Our economic analysis (graphed in Figure 22-3) suggests three ways: (1) raise demand; (2) reduce supply; (3) raise wage rates directly.

1. While there have been cases of unions seeking to show employers how to use labor more efficiently and raise demand through lower product prices, there is little evidence of significant success.

2. Supply may be reduced by restricting entry to the labor market. As a result of a reduced supply in the market, wage rates are raised by competitive bidding among employers.

3. Wage rates may be arbitrarily raised as a result of strike threat, leaving the employer and union with the task of rationing out the jobs among applicants at the higher rates.

Some unions use one and some use all tactics. The coal miners used the last, and then had the problem of deciding which miners got the available jobs. The displaced had to take jobs which they formerly refused to accept.

Restricting entry to the labor market is a method used effectively by seamen, barbers,

---

[2] See H. G. Lewis, *Unions and Relative Wages in the United States* (Chicago: University of Chicago Press, 1963).

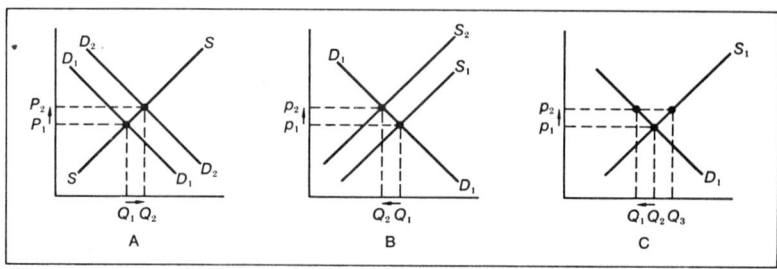

FIGURE 22–3. Alternative Means of Affecting Wage Rates and Employment

Panel A shows that an increase in demand will increase wage rates from p_1 to p_2 and employment from Q_1 to Q_2. Panel B shows that a decrease in supply will increase wage rates but not employment. Problem is how to exclude some people from the market, in order to reduce supply. Immigration restrictions, licensing, entry qualifications are some of the means utilized. Since those to be excluded will oppose restrictions, it's clever to reduce supply by restricting potential new entrants to this labor market. Panel C shows that an arbitrarily higher negotiated wage rate without a change in demand or supply will leave a group of displaced workers whose presence may be sufficiently strong to restrain possibility of pushing up wage rates. Problem is how to prevent new entrants and displaced workers from undercutting the agreed-upon wage rate. Jobs can be rationed or shared by spreading reduced work over all members, as the musicians' union does.

plumbers, teachers, electricians, projectionists, teamsters, linotypers, and butchers, to name a few. Apprenticeship limits or compulsory licensing are devices for restricting entry.

When unions are effective in controlling market competition so as to put wages higher than they would be in a free market, who gains and who loses? Usually it is claimed that the gains come out of the employers' income. But, according to economic analysis, the consequences are spread far more widely. Employers who cannot survive at the new higher costs sell their assets at correspondingly lower prices or take a write-down in the value of their assets. Output diminishes until supply is small enough to raise prices to cover the higher wage costs, or a growing industry does not grow quite so much. People who would have been employed had wages not been raised work elsewhere with smaller incomes. Output of products of the higher-wage labor is smaller, and output of other goods is larger. The labor transferred to the other industries would have produced a greater value of output in the first industry if labor could compete freely for highest-valued markets. Thus, in a fundamental sense, employees do not compete against employers; they compete against other labor. This is often concealed by slogans of "labor versus management."

Nonwage Rationing of Employment

When any group succeeds in getting a higher wage than the open-market level, the number of qualified job applicants will, by definition of an open market, exceed the number of jobs available at that wage rate.[3] The jobs must be rationed on some nonwage

---

[3] See footnote 5, page 439.

criterion. A common procedure is to use probationary union members for temporary and seasonal jobs; when demand falls, they will be the first to go. Apprentices and probationary members, whatever their other purposes, serve as an employment-rationing device protecting senior members. If the reduction in employment is particularly severe, so that some "seniority" men also are without jobs, work sharing often emerges, with limitations on the number of hours a week any one person can have. Compulsory attendance at frequent union meetings as a condition of good standing will help to reduce "excessive membership," because the hope of getting a job is less of an incentive to payment of dues and attendance at meetings than is keeping a present job. In time, some of the "hopefuls" will drop out, thus reducing unemployment in this union.

Jobs may be rationed through restriction on union membership (through larger initiation fees and more rigid standards: color, age, personality, sex, education, experience, probationary membership periods). "Unethical" job-seeking conduct prejudicial to the senior employed members of the union (whether it be the American Medical Association, the American Bar Association, the teamsters, or the longshoremen) can warrant expulsions; advertising or price cutting is unethical conduct. Probationary membership also helps to inculcate a sense of "proper" conduct and to weed out those prone to violating standards. It also restricts entry into the union. One publicized reason for these restrictions is protection of the employer and consumer from shoddy work.

Pervasive and creative of social conflict is control of entry to occupations on the basis of color. Today, a person who wants to become a carpenter, plumber, electrician, studio projectionist, mason, plasterer, to name a few examples, must first seek admission to the union as an apprentice. In some instances, he must first be nominated by three members in good standing, in the fashion of entry to a country club. Negroes have long been excluded from many unions. Even though a union charter states there is to be no discrimination, some criterion must be used to ration entrants as long as entry is not open to all who wish to join and work at existing wages.

Recent Negro protests and replies by union officials have elicited irrefutable evidence of union discrimination by color. National union officials have promised to try to change the situation. But union locals make their own decisions about admissions, and, as long as union membership is limited, discrimination is necessary in deciding who shall be admitted. The only question is what form of competition shall be weighted in granting membership—which returns us to the earlier discussion of principles of rationing when open-market pecuniary offers are not allowed as a competitive device to every potential employee and employer.

If the union is strong enough, it can impose work rules, known as "featherbedding," whereby an employer must employ laborers whether or not he wants them. Teachers decry the use of television; hod carriers once refused to carry premixed concrete; typesetters require newspapers to set duplicate type if preset type forms are submitted by advertisers; building codes specify unnecessarily expensive labor-using techniques; standby local musicians must be hired when touring orchestras perform locally. All are legal, and all rest on the monopoly power deriving from the power to strike effectively. The railroads have had perhaps the most publicized featherbedding provisions; and this should not be surprising, because the railroads were themselves in a *legal* monopoly position. The companies had a protected income; in effect, higher wages were paid out of the monopoly-rent potential. However, the growth of competition from trucks and airplanes has bankrupted several railroads. Threatened with complete loss of wealth, the railroad owners won court prohibition against the unions striking for such featherbedding contracts.

A serious employment impact of strong union contracts covering all workers in a given firm can occur from the reduced ability of each employee to renegotiate his own wage in the event of decreased demand for his services. If the demand for a firm's product should fall, some employees will be dropped unless wages can be cut sufficiently. The wage must not exceed the consumer's valuation of the employee's contribution to market supplies via the particular firm at which he is currently employed, for the employer will not be able to cover wage costs with the sales value of output. But the employee who is laid off cannot renegotiate a new lower wage if he is tied to a union scale. The union scale is agreed to apply to all employees; those who still are employed at the union scale will not want to see that scale cut just to permit continued employment for those who would be dropped. After all, not everyone is laid off. The extra rigidity imposed by a *group* wage scale that can be cut only with approval of a majority of the group will penalize the less senior or less able people who normally are just barely worth the particular scale imposed on the group. (Warning: there are no extensive studies of the degree to which this happens. Though the analysis is forceful and persuasive, we do not know how much this group uniformity and group control of wage rates, as distinct from market-negotiated wages between a single buyer and seller of labor services, increases the extent of unemployment.)

Closed-Market Monopoly-Rent Acquisition and Disposition

Restriction on entry into the union may be so severe that normal attrition by death and retirement will reduce membership. Entry might be completely closed for years (as with longshoremen's unions). If unions can maintain the restriction on entry, employers will bid up the wages of the remaining fewer union workers.

Limited membership in unions with higher than open-market wages permits "unusual" behavior. If the union agent or officer can keep wages *down*, though above the open-market rates, available workers must be rationed to the competing employers—who want more workers than are available. If the wage rate would have gone up to $5 an hour under the contrived scarcity, and if the agent can hold the wages to $4 an hour, then the employer would be prepared to pay an additional $1 per hour per worker to get more employees, perhaps to the person responsible for assigning workers to various jobs. The union agent can demand or accept payments from the favored employer. In effect, the cost is just as high to the employer, but it is paid not entirely in the form of wages to the workers. Reluctant employers can be penalized by not getting many employees.

Trustee controls imposed on banks have not been applied as strongly to union officers. An especially notorious form of monopoly reward to the union officers (for example, Teamsters Union officers) comes from their management of union funds for pensions, health, and recreation. These funds are invested and used to buy insurance policies. Frequently the officers make loans at lower than normal rates of interest; the borrower pays the difference to the union officers in the form of special salaries, commissions, or favors.

Considerations of equity and morality of the "sharing" by union officials are not simple. Union organizers claim they organized and accomplished the closed-market monopoly for the union. Why shouldn't they be rewarded with larger salaries, expense accounts, vacation resorts, and homes than the union members, who really had little to do with the development of the organization—in fact, no more than the employees of a successful businessman who builds a great enterprise? Economics gives no ethical criteria by which to judge this. It merely "explains."

Utilization of closed-monopoly power. Employers are quick to exploit opportunities inherent in the contrived labor monopoly. Some will propose to pay the union a special reward if it will withhold workers from competitor firms. The favored firm will be able to command higher prices for its services. (James Hoffa, the Teamsters Union president, used this tactic.) The "monopoly rent" (obtained by restricting market access to competitors) can be shared among owners of the protected firm, its workers, and union members, if adequate payment is made to the union. This form of agreement is known as a "sweetheart" contract. Whether first suggested by the employer or by the union official is immaterial; nor is it dependent on whether union officials or members get the monopoly rent.

Difficulty of maintaining long-lasting closed-market monopoly rent. The right to exclude competitors from the market does not give one unbridled economic power. Competition facing a union carpenter, for example, cannot be excluded merely by prohibiting nonunion carpenters from offering services to *his* employer. Other employers will hire nonunion carpenters and sell their products at lower prices. Even if all carpenters joined forces and forced all employers to hire only members of the carpenters' union, product competition would be effective. Plaster, steel, cement, glass, and other building materials can partially displace carpenters. Even doctors' attempts to raise fees are partly restrained by the availability of brand or proprietary drugs, advice of friends, Christian Science, do-it-yourself care, faith healers, etc. As any organization—be it a business firm, union, or professional group—acquires greater power to restrict competitors from the market and thus make effective the higher prices it wants for its services, the rest of the society is more likely to object to such use of power. Whether it is objecting primarily to higher prices or to denial of competition to others in the market or to interference with production during strikes is an open question.

Some people object to interference with rights of individuals to seek jobs in the open market. They believe participation in voluntary market transactions should not be prevented by anyone, let alone one's direct competitors. These critics do not object to unions as voluntary associations of employees for collective negotiation, but they do object to the strike as a coercive method of controlling access to the market. It is not clear whether these critics are aware to what extent a union would lose power if strikes were prohibited. Unions could still exist and negotiate with employers, but their power to get working conditions above the open-market level, by preventing access to the market for jobs, would be reduced. When the President of the United States says unions are basic institutions in a free society, the relevant question is still to be faced: "With what kinds of power over access to the market for jobs?" And on that issue reasonable, "humanitarian" men differ.

What is the difference between a labor union that prevents nonunion workers from working at wages less than those sought by the union, and a medical profession which prevents a free market for medical services? The differences are that the medical profession has *more successfully* defended its actions, in the name of higher quality of medical service. That it also enables doctors to get higher wages is obvious and not irrelevant. The second difference is that the medical profession does not have to rely on strikes and intimidation against competitors who would sell services at "substandard" prices; instead, it has obtained a licensing law, and, rather than strike against any seller or buyer of "substandard" service at "substandard" wages, it merely telephones the government to send a policeman and restrain the competitor. If labor unions could get laws prohibiting the sale of workers' services by anyone except a "licensed" (union) person, or prohibiting training except in approved schools, then the union could keep the supply small and wages higher.

Until unions can call upon the state to enforce the exclusion of nonunion members from the particular job market, they will probably continue with threats and intimidation of nonunion members. Were the public police force available, gangsters and hoodlums—the specialists in intimidation—would be of less value. Then union officials would all be as free of the "undesirable elements" and as respectable as are the officers of the medical and legal associations and public utilities, to name only a few.

Union monopoly versus employer monopoly. Union monopoly power is often said to be necessary to countervail the monopoly power of industry. This is a superficially plausible, but invalid, generalization. Consider the steel industry, which is often called a "monopoly." The steel industry is a group of independently owned firms—just as a union is a group of independent workers. Yet there is a fundamental difference in that access to the market is open to existing and to new steel companies. Under the law only *one* union can exist for any class of employees. Other unions may try to take its place, but only *one* is permitted to exist as the "exclusive" bargaining agent. In this one crucial difference lies the error of thinking that a group of price-searching employers constitutes a "monopoly," which requires a countervailing union monopoly. Not even for purposes of negotiating with a common "antagonist" is it possible for the steel companies to avoid open-market competition. The industry simply is an open monopoly. This bilateral-monopoly-bargaining thesis is empty unless the employer is a closed monopoly.

Public utilities are closed monopolies. When faced with union strikes, public utilities can, *at first,* more easily accede to union demands since they can draw on monopoly rent. The regulatory commission can allow the public utility to raise its restricted rate to offset higher wage costs. True, sales will be smaller with higher rates, but the wealth of the utility will not necessarily suffer, if the rates initially were below the wealth-maximizing level. The monopoly rent derived *via* the public utility's protected position is transferred to the utility employees.

11, 12,
13, 14,
15, 16,
17, 18,
19

Legal Restrictions on Open Markets for Labor

Minimum-Wage Laws

Minimum-wage laws prohibit employment at less than some stated wage per hour. Minimum legal wage rates vary among the several states that have such laws. Federal law specifies currently that the minimum wage shall be $1.60 an hour.[4] At the minimum

[4] Several exceptions are permitted. Among the major ones are motion-picture theater workers, highly seasonal amusement area workers, employees in small firms (less than $500,000 in annual sales), restaurant employees receiving a substantial portion of their income in tips, agricultural employees who would have a lower minimum ($1.00) and employees of educational institutions, and summer work by college students. It is a challenging problem to explain why these exceptions are granted if the effects of the law are desirable.

legal wage rate the quantity of labor demanded will be less than the quantity of labor services supplied—if the minimum wage is above the open-market wage level.[5]

Some of those who cannot get jobs at the legal minimum wage can and do resort to work as private, independent contractors to their former employer, taking a lower income by means of a low contract price rather than a reduced wage rate. For example, a person seeking a job as a taxi or a truck driver, at the stipulated rate of, say, $100 a week, could rent a vehicle from his employer and drive as an independent subcontractor, or independent driver. He can cut his wages below $100 by renting the taxi from his "employer" for a weekly fee of, say, $20 a week *above* the free-market car rentals (a sort of secret rebate).

Working conditions and other features of the job are not controlled by law. These will deteriorate, and employers can impose more spartan conditions as a partial offset to the

---

[5] Except allegedly in a "monopsonistic" market, in which the employer is such a significant part of the total demand that to increase employees he must offer higher wages for new *and* old employees. The graph shows a rising labor-supply curve, WW, to the firm. The marginal-wage-cost curve MWC, the height of which shows the increase in the *total wage bill* for one more employee, lies above the average-wage curve, WW, because the higher wage for the new employee must be paid also to all other employees. The intersection of the demand curve, DD, with the marginal-cost-of-labor curve, MWC, indicates the wealth-maximizing employment, E_0, at which the wages paid each person is W_0, indicated by the average wage curve, WW. To hire one more employee would increase total costs by the height of the MWC curve but would yield a marginal product indicated by the demand curve, DD.

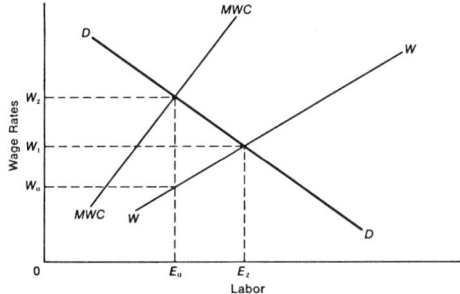

If now a minimum uniform wage is imposed at W_1, the employer would be able to hire as many employees as he wished at a *constant* wage rate out to the intersection of the horizontal line W_1 with the curve WW. Each extra employee (out to that limit) would increase his total wage bill only by the wages paid that new employee. In effect, line W_1 becomes the average-wage schedule. The marginal cost of more labor is therefore *equal* to the constant average uniform wage already paid each employee. It would pay the employer to hire out to where the horizontal wage line, W_1, intersected the demand for labor curve, DD. In the illustrated case, this employment rate at the higher constant wage W_1 is greater than with a rising wage for successive employees (which higher wage must also be paid to existing employees). Both the wage rate and the employment rate are made greater by imposing a *uniform,* constant wage.

So far so good. But there are three, often overlooked, factors to consider. First, the higher wage rate will raise total costs of operation for the firms; output will be reduced as price must be raised, and, with that, employment will be reduced. Second, employers faced with a rising supply curve for labor are often able to confine the higher wage only to the new employee: the old employee has no better option in any event, whether or not the new employee is hired; special fringe benefits or job classifications permit differential pricing without requiring uniform wages for all employees. Third, few employers are large enough relative to the market from which they draw labor to have significant long-time effects on wages by individually varying their rates of employment. Over a longer period, the flow of workers from other employers and areas makes this case of little significance.

higher money wages. Employees may get higher money wages and also lower-cost, less-attractive "fringe" working conditions. Whether or not he is better off is an open query.

Why do we have minimum-wage laws if they mean lower income to some workers? Because those who retain their jobs get higher incomes, and this is usually the majority (depending upon the elasticity of demand for that kind of labor). *If* they were formerly earning so little as to qualify for supplementary welfare payments, the number of supplementary payments will be reduced. In effect, the taxes used to pay for the welfare are now collected and distributed via the higher prices of the goods being produced. Although the minimum wage law may, if the above conditions are correct, have the effect of reducing the *number* of people on relief, it increases the *extent* of relief to those pushed into lower-paying alternatives. We wish we knew who are most likely to be disemployed. It has been contended that a majority of that group would be poorest Negroes and teenagers because of the relatively large proportion who have not acquired sufficient training to have sufficiently high productivity. If so, then our minimum wage law strikes hardest at the poorest Negroes and teenagers.[6]

Immigration Restrictions

Laborers can seek to limit competition by restricting immigration; this has been done in the United States since the late nineteenth century. While it is "impolitic" to admit a desire to create barriers against competition from one's fellow "Americans," it is ancient practice to bar entry to "foreigners." Currently, the favorite target is the Mexican agricultural migrant worker, who is either excluded or required to work at such high wages that fewer are demanded in the United States. Also many *products* of foreign workers have been excluded; the use of "pauper labor" abroad has been a persistent (but fallacious) argument of American high-tariff proponents (both employers and employees).[7]

Equal Pay for Equal Work

Wage differences exist among and even within occupations. In some instances, the differences reflect nonpecuniary factors. There are equalizing or compensating differences in wages. As we shall see, compensating differences are not always welcomed. One of the classic methods of trying to eliminate them is to advocate "equal pay for equal work"—on the presumption that equal work is easy to identify and that nonpecuniary differences among services of employees or employers should not count.

Proponents of imposed wage uniformities. Almost all employees seem to express dislike of wage differences based upon nonpecuniary differences—"equalizing differences." The "inferior" person dislikes being paid less for the "same" work, even though the wage

---

[6] To the extent this is true, it follows that since the minimum wage laws are not very effective for household help, a large portion of which is provided by Negro women, the law hits harder at Negro men than women, thereby making more difficult the task of preserving a strong paternal family head.

[7] This fallacy will be explained in Chapter 36.

difference enables him to offset his nonpecuniary "disadvantage." The source of his lower income is not the lower, difference-equalizing wage but other people's preferences about the traits that prompt it.

"Superior" people complain about the equalizing-difference because it allows "inferior" people to compete for jobs that would otherwise have yielded a still higher wage to superior people. In many jobs where both men and women might do equally well in a pecuniary sense, men usually are hired because of employer preference for male employees. But that preference is in part overcome with lower wages for women. Rather than try to prohibit women from access to these jobs in order to preserve the jobs for men, the men, cleverly, will advocate "equal pay for equal work"—at, of course, the wages now being paid to the men. Men can profess to be doing this for the benefit of women. Whatever the motivation, the effect is to protect men's jobs by reducing opportunity for women to replace men by taking a lower salary.

This analysis extends to geographical differences in pay. Wages for the same kind of labor are lower in the South than in the North. Also, wages are lower in Puerto Rico than in the United States. How can a northern employee protect his wage from the competition of lower-wage southern labor? And how can a laborer in the United States protect his job (and higher wage rate) from Puerto Rican labor? One device would be to advocate "equal pay for equal work" in the United States, *including* Puerto Rico, by legislating minimum wages higher than the prevailing level in the South and Puerto Rico. It should come as no surprise to learn that in the United States support for minimum-wage laws comes primarily from northerners who profess to be trying to help the poorer southern laborers.

Opponents of imposed wage uniformities. Who can object to equal pay for equal work? First, it is opposed by some people who are less productive in a *nonpecuniary sense* and who understand that their source of market power lies in their accepting a compensating wage difference. Second, employers and their customers might object; but if they do, they will be confessing to a "greedy" desire for more wealth as well as confessing to "prejudice" and discrimination in hiring. A third objection to these laws is that they interfere with "freedom of contract."

Fair-Employment Laws

If a uniform or minimum-wage law is effective in raising wages, discrimination will be transferred from wage rates to employee types. Fewer "inferior" people will get jobs. Therefore, pressure mounts for "fair-employment laws," prohibiting employers from choosing employees on the basis of any criterion ruled unethical—usually race, creed, age, and sex. These laws probably reduce the extent of observable discrimination among employers. But they are incredibly difficult to enforce. How can one tell whether an employer is hiring as many workers he and his customers consider "inferior" as he would if he really didn't think them "inferior"? Furthermore, the employer will be even more reluctant to observe the spirit of the law when he knows it will be more difficult to fire those whose services are unsatisfactory.

Fair-employment laws impose burdens on some employees. If Armenians prefer to work with Armenians, or Catholics with Catholics, or a Negro with Negroes, or a Mormon with Mormons, these laws make that illegal, for the employer would be susceptible to legal prosecution for *de facto* "discrimination" or segregation.

24, 25, 26, 27, 28, 29, 30, 31

Closed Monopsony: Buyers Close a Market to Other Buyers

Monopsony is analogous to monopoly, except that it describes the *buyer's* side of the market.[8] The preceding discussion in this chapter focused on means whereby labor *sellers* (employees) sought to close the market to their competitors. And in Chapter 19 the cases of collusion all involved sellers. But sellers are not alone in their efforts to restrict market competition. Buyers, particularly employers as buyers of labor, are anxious to close the market to other employers of labor to keep wages lower. They have had some spectacular successes, many of which have not been recognized for what they are. Some of the successes have been regarded as socially desirable! But most public attention is often drawn to the relatively ineffective cases of attempts to lower wages below open market rates.

For example, when asked to name cases in which employers "ganged up" on employees, people usually talk about "yellow-dog" contracts and "sweatshop operators," "child-labor" employers, and "company stores." A "yellow-dog" employment contract is one in which the employee had to agree not to enter a union. Sweatshops are businesses that pay low wages. (But lower than what? If lower than paid by other employers, why don't the employees work elsewhere?) Child labor is not very productive labor and will therefore get less. This does not imply that child labor is good. The general objection is that since children have low productivity, it pays to be in school learning to be more productive. The decrease in child labor in the past fifty years in the United States has been almost entirely a consequence of a shift from agricultural to industrial employment. The rate of child labor on farms has not decreased much. It's the decline in the amount of agricultural labor relative to nonagricultural employment that has produced the overall decrease in child labor in the population as a whole.

Company stores were owned by the employer, who sometimes paid employees in credit good only for purchases at a company store. The prices in the company store were higher than elsewhere, so the employee got a lower real wage. But why would anyone be his employee if the real wage was lower than that available elsewhere? Why wouldn't the employer simply pay lower wages and abandon this more expensive roundabout means of paying lower wages? Were both employers and employees stupid? The answer is simple. The *employee* knew what he was doing. He was cutting a *legal* minimum wage rate. For example, if the minimum payable wage is $1.60 an hour and if the open market wage is $1.00 for this type of labor, the laborer could agree to work for $1.60 on the condition that he spend his earnings at the company store, where he would pay high prices. In effect, he would net only about $1.00 an hour. Such was the reason for the payment of wages via credit at company stores. As those minimum wage laws gradually were abandoned and as wages in the open market gradually rose above the obsolete minimum wages, the company store wage system was abandoned.

We turn now to some cases of really effective collusive action by *employers* in restricting wages below open-market levels by closing the market to other employers. We call them important because they affect *over half* the young men in the entire labor force of the United States!

---

[8] A monopsonist is a buyer whose purchases or demand is sufficiently large to result in higher prices as he increases his amount demanded.

Hospital Interns

All the states require licensing by the American Medical Association or its members before a person is admitted to medical practice. Membership in a medical association is required if a doctor is to realize the greater income available from practice in a first-class hospital (other than at a medical school). Now suppose that the association were to restrain the hospitals from paying more than $600 a month for interns, whereas with open competition among hospitals the rate would be higher—say, $800 a month. Any hospital that violated the agreement could be punished by having its "class-A" certification withdrawn. The power to *enforce* the price agreement is now established. The gains from secret violation are small relative to the possible punishment, and violators will very likely be detected.

The hazards and obstacles have been conquered. All the buyers (class-A hospitals) of this service (interns) are forced into the agreement. The organization (the American Medical Association) wielding the power to enforce the price collusion was formed not simply to keep interns' wages down, but for other more valuable purposes, so that denial of membership as a doctor or surgeon means a greater loss of wealth than can be gained by violating the intern wage agreement.

One conclusion stands out: It is sufficient to get the power of the *law* on the side of the collusive organization so that persons who do not agree to abide by the price collusion can be *legally* prohibited from buying any of the "service" at any price. Without this *legal* constraint, secret violators could go their way, independently taking advantage of the price agreement by paying slightly more than the already low price and getting a larger share.

College Athletes and the NCAA

An effective collusion is that of colleges to hold down wages of college football players. Not long after intercollegiate football became a substantial source of income to colleges, the best football players received money inducements—hereafter called "wages" in our discussion. Some college administrators opposed all money payments to athletes, because that was professionalism. They believed amateurism had some inherent virtue or that a professional would attend college only to play football, basketball, or baseball. Other administrators, with an eye on the football income, were dismayed that the wage competition among schools was raising costs.

It is easy to see a strong inducement for college administrators to curtail wages of student football players. An agreement among the colleges to pay no wages was reached through the agency of the National Collegiate Athletic Association (NCAA). Not surprisingly, this collusion was violated as colleges switched to athletic fellowships, "free" room and board, travel to college, sinecures, jobs for relatives, clothes, etc. These methods of competition were later reduced under an agreement permitting wages up to $2 an hour. At identical offers, the most distinguished colleges would get the best football players. With identical money offers, the incentive was stronger for the less distinguished colleges *in metropolitan areas* (with large potential gate receipts) to resort to covert offers, and they did so—as evidenced by the frequency with which their violations were detected and punished. Choose from hundreds of examples; over a decade ago two California colleges, U.C.L.A. and U.S.C., were caught violating the NCAA code. They were assessed $100,000 fines and prohibited from playing in post-season (the most profitable) Bowl games. Even the tennis, basketball, track, and baseball teams—members of which had received no "unethical" payments—were banned from national tournaments. Currently, other state universities are under similar bans.

Why did the colleges agree to pay fines and accept the punishment? How could collusion to restrict wages survive in the face of the great advantages of "cheating," especially when colleges that stayed outside the agreement could offer just slightly higher wages than the rest were maintaining? After all, if television and radio networks tried to suppress performers' wages, other networks could profitably be organized to take advantage of the reduced wages. Somehow newcomers must be induced to agree to the terms of the collusive agreement as a condition of operating at all. The National Professional Football League tried to keep wages low but soon found itself faced with two other leagues that wouldn't abide by its pay scales. Similarly, the National Baseball League was faced with a new American League. Or, to put the question in analytic terms, what rewards of membership in the collusion are greater than the advantages obtainable by not belonging, so that the threat of membership cancellation can be effective in enforcing the agreement—on the assumption that violations can be detected without prohibitive detection costs? (The various athletic conferences—all members of the collusion—hire private detectives and investigators to spy on recruiting activities of students, coaches, and alumni.)

The answer lies in the fact that all the colleges belonged to the National Collegiate Athletic Association or to related associations, which supervised the rules of the games. The NCAA not only is the supreme authority in assessing fines and punishment, but, more important, it indicated that any college violating the athletic "code" could find its *academic* accreditation threatened. Any college placed on probation or expelled would find it much more expensive to recruit faculty, and students would be dissuaded from attending. Even Phi Beta Kappa refused to authorize chapters at colleges that gave "disproportionate" amounts of money to athletic scholarships, regardless of the academic qualities of the college. The survival of the college could be threatened.

But we can't stop here. Why don't some colleges that want to hire football players form their own accreditation group? Why does the present accreditation group have so much power that it can prevent formation of a new accreditation system? A very important reason is that colleges do not operate on a self-supporting basis. The profits from football are not enough to offset the losses from the low tuition fees at state or endowed colleges. A new college could not expect to survive from football profits if it had to charge competitive tuition to students. No new school could get subsidies from the state or major philanthropic foundations without recognition by the *present* accreditation group—which is powerful in influencing the government and the charitable foundations. We have finally arrived at the source of the value of membership in the NCAA and related organizations: subsidized education. Since the value of the subsidy exceeds the potential football profits, and since control over the subsidy lies partly in the hands of the NCAA, the wrath of the NCAA can mean some college's life or death. We emphasize that the NCAA was not created to restrict pay of football players. It was set up for other purposes, but once its greater value for these other purposes could be denied to a nonmember, it became an enforcement agency against certain kinds of competition.

Employers' Collusion for Professional Athletes

College athletics is small stuff compared to professional sports. The National Football League draft did not permit its team owners to bid against each other for players. Players were simply "drafted," and they had to play for whatever team wanted them.

With the rise of the vigorous American Football League to compete against the older National Football League, football players began to get their open-market price, which exceeds $1,000,000 for an outstanding athlete, who is paid almost nothing while in college. However, the football leagues have "combined," and those open competitive wages are now under "control."

For many years the two professional baseball leagues had a compact not to bid against each other for baseball players. The cozy arrangement was possible because entry of a new league was extraordinarily difficult. If a new league arose, any player who signed with it was permanently banned from the two older leagues. Clearly no young player would want to risk his future prospects. Yet even with all that collusive power, the teams, under enormous incentive to get better players, managed to offer side rewards to players, and thereby the system of bonuses developed. More recently the baseball teams returned to a *draft* system whereby the teams do not compete with each other in signing up new players.

There are (as of 1972) two professional basketball leagues competing for basketball players, and their salaries reflect it.

Military Draft

We have saved the most spectacular and "notorious" "collusion by buyers" for the climax—the military draft. The United States obtains the bulk of its enlisted men by a "draft." A draftee must work at wages set by Congress—unless he wants to lose valuable citizenship rights. Why does the United States require young men to work at less than market wages, when there is no law that requires them to do so as policemen, firemen, astronauts, garbage collectors, generals, admirals, or politicians? It is not true that mercenaries, or volunteers, are less able or less reliable. Nor is it true that the draft costs less. It lowers *only* the *explicitly* revealed money payments that pass through the government budget accounts. It is a "hidden" tax. The draft is a tax young people pay *in kind*, just as the old French kings drafted labor to build their palaces and roads. Since that tax is not included in the money payments of our defense budget, the wrong measure of cost is looked at. Under the draft, those who do not bear the tax *in kind* are those who are not drafted—the old, the smarter, the "physically handsome" who marry early and have children, and the women. One wonders if that is the intended basis for distributing our defense costs.

The fact is that the costs of the draft are *greater* than if the military forces were obtained without a draft, via explicit money taxes on all who should bear the burden of defense. Without the draft, all who serve would be obtained by market *money* bids for their services—just as airplanes, missiles, munitions and officers and politicians, policemen, firemen, and teachers are obtained. Not only would the true costs of the draft then be *revealed* but they would literally be *reduced* for any specified military capability. Remember what happened in our five-man economy if the wrong people were drafted into producing the various goods. The total possible output became smaller. And so it is with the draft. The explicit government-budget monetary tax bill could be larger, but the real cost would certainly be smaller.

If the cost of the military were measured by the budgeted expenditures, as it more fully would be without a forced draft, the military would have to pay more attention to the true costs of assignments and to means of providing services. Drastic shifts in combinations of inputs would occur, according to the principles outlined in Chapter 20. At the most obvious level, there would be more reliance on civilian employees to provide food and routine services. Custodial and sanitation work around military camps would be provided by labor cheaper than that of strong young men of greater value as soldiers. Less training in various trades would be given by the military. The turnover rate and new-enlistee training costs would be lower. In short, lower-cost methods would be forced into the open and the true cost thereby reduced. Claims that it is a person's duty to defend his country are beside the point. (Is it not a "duty" to pay taxes?) The question is what is the best way to defend ourselves. Everyone has an obligation to defend his country: but it does not follow that the obligation is to pay the tax *in kind,* which is what those who claim an obligation from *young men only* are really contending. Specialization in achieving military capability is just as sensible as it is for achieving our food, clothing, and domestic police protection.

If the military personnel were obtained by open-market competition, even the explicit money tax bill might *not* be larger. Recent studies made by the Defense Department suggest that higher wages would attract more efficient labor, would reduce enlistee training and replacement costs, and would also induce military leaders to substitute more efficient forms of capital for labor. But the military people strongly resist methods that would force them to change their way of life and modify their methods. They are not accustomed to principles of efficient allocation of labor—that is, a market-price system. Any change is difficult, especially if it results only in more efficient methods and provides no gain for those who must revise their way of life. And most politicians find it impossible to believe that the superficial costs they are concerned with—total *budgeted* costs—would be smaller.

Finally, lest it be thought the draft of military personnel is an unfortunate necessity and that the military is somehow so different that our economic theory doesn't apply, let it be noted that the Civil War Army of the North, in which we used a far greater proportion of our young men with higher fatality rates than in any subsequent war and in which the men fought with unexcelled valor, was *not* a draft army. It was purchased in the open market in the following way: men were "drafted" but every "draftee" had the right to hire someone to take his place, usually done by paying that other person a lump sum. In effect, the draft was a means of *assigning the tax* among the young men; once taxed, one could either pay the amount necessary to buy a substitute or he could work it out in the Army. The point is that those who served did so in the cold calculation of the amount of the tax and of the market value of services. Only the tax on young men was imposed by the draft, not the decision as to who would serve in the military.

32, 33, 34, 35

Summary

1 Bargaining power is a vacuous concept of little analytical substance.

2 Union membership increased from about 5 percent of the work force in the 1930s to about 20 percent at the end of World War II and has remained practically unchanged since then.

3 Unions affect the structure and procedure of wage and job negotiation. Wages will be affected insofar as the supply of labor is changed by modified conditions of labor entry to the labor markets. The union shop, the closed shop, strikes, control of entry to the union—all are means to affect the labor supply conditions for employers. Underlying all factors is the power to strike, without which the union would be a relatively ineffective instrument for influencing labor supply conditions.

4 The strike is a concerted action by a group of employees to prevent other people from working in specified jobs at wages less than demanded by the strikers. The union's right to strike effectively and close markets to competitors is protected by law and exempted from antimonopoly or unfair-trade laws.

5 Compulsory arbitration would prohibit some strikes and force an employer and a union to agree to terms set by government agencies.

6 The effect of unions on over-all wages is not definitely known. Estimates are that unions on the average have raised wages of their members about 5 to 15 percent above those of nonunion labor.

7 To the extent wages are set above the open-market clearing level, nonpecuniary productivity more strongly influences job allocation. People strong in desired features are not easily underbid by the people who are poorer in personal traits. "Discrimination" increases.

8 Wages set above the open-market clearing level yield a monopoly rent. Union leaders find their control over that rent enhanced to the extent that fringe benefits are utilized.

9 Union closed-market power appears "undesirable" because of the way it is enforced—usually by threatened or actual violence. Other professions with closed markets appear socially correct because laws authorize closing of markets with police force.

10 To the extent unions can close the market to competing labor the union is a closed monopolist. If the employer cannot close the market to *his* competitors he may be an open monopolist. The powers of the two types of monopolies are different.

11 Minimum-wage laws raise wages for some employees, while displaced employees must shift to lower-paying jobs not covered by the laws, or become unemployed. Beneficiaries are those who retain their jobs at the higher wage; higher-paid employees face less competition from services of the lower-cost labor.

12 Immigration restrictions limit labor supply and keep wages higher.

13 Equal-pay-for-equal-work laws help keep "inferior" producers (nonmonetary sense) from higher-paid jobs. Equalizing wage differences is prohibited.

14 Fair-employment laws make it illegal for an employer to choose employees on the basis of age, sex, color, race, religion (but do not prohibit employee's choice of employer according to these criteria).

15 Collusions among buyers have been most effective in the market for special types of labor.

16 The military draft, one of the most effective collusions against sellers, leads to inefficiency and a biased measure of the true cost of the military. It is an implicit tax on young, able-bodied, less educated males.

Questions

1 "A man's labor is perishable. If he isn't employed, he loses forever that potential earning. Therefore, labor has a special disadvantage compared to nonhuman goods, which can be stored and used later." Is that correct? (Hint: Suppose labor were storable. What do you suppose would be the effect?)

2 "Long ago we stated the reason for labor organizations. We said that they were organized out of the necessities of the situation; that a single employee was helpless in dealing with

an employer; that he was dependent ordinarily on his daily wage for the maintenance of himself and family; that if the employer refused to pay him the wages that he thought fair, he was nevertheless unable to leave the employer and resist arbitrary and unfair treatment; that a union was essential to give laborers opportunity to deal on an equality with their employer." (Charles Evans Hughes, Chief Justice, Supreme Court of the United States, from the decision in the case of the *United States v. Jones and Laughlin,* 1937.) Evaluate the above propositions for their meaning.

3 "The strike is an attempt to deny some people the ability to sell their services at open-market prices." Explain why this is a true statement. For which people?

4 "The union that utilizes or threatens to use the strike is a closed monopoly." If true, does that make unions bad?

5 A union strikes against some employer. The strike is unsuccessful if the employer is able to get sufficient other laborers. In order to prevent his successful operation with these other workers, the union initiates a "boycott," urging the public not to buy this employer's products. If that maneuver is successful, the employer will lose sales and close down, unless he is willing to hire only the union men at the wage they request. Thus, boycotts prevent the employer from profitably employing other workers than those on strike. Sometimes the union will also engage in a secondary strike—against anyone who buys that employer's products. Whether the union is refusing to work for the employer, picketing the employer as a means of urging customers to boycott products made by nonstrikers, or using secondary strikes against any producer who buys this employer's products, the tactics are designed to remove from the open market one particular group of people. Who? Explain.

6 In strike or labor-dispute negotiations, the government sometimes appoints an investigating panel composed of representatives from the union, the employers, and the consuming public. Which especially affected group is *not* represented on these panels? Can you explain why?

7 You are the leader of a strong, closed union that has obtained wages above the open-market rate for the union supply of employees.
a. At next contract negotiations, at which it is clear a still higher wage can be obtained in view of increased demand or reduced union supply relative to demand, what incentives are there for you, the union officer, to seek to get that higher wage not in the form of higher explicit money wages for the union members but instead in the form of fringe benefits—such as retirement pensions, medical insurance, vacation resorts, workers' uniforms—which are dispensed and controlled by the union?
b. Would a greater portion of the "wage" being diverted to the control of the union leaders increase the utility of the union leaders? How?
c. Does the income tax on *money* income also produce a "bias" toward nonmonetary fringe benefits?

8 Construct the analogue to the preceding problem for a situation in which the state, instead of paying money to students and letting them buy their education, pays the money to the schools and lets them give the education to the students. Does financing schools directly rather than giving money to students to spend for schooling increase the "utility" of school administrators and faculty relative to the students? Which schools? Which faculty members?

9 "In a society where there has not been an adjustment of wages to the savings of time afforded by the use of new techniques, and where such savings may result in an oversupply of labor, an agreement among laborers to prevent such conditions has a lawful

labor objective." (Decision by Superior Court Judge Martin Caughlin, San Bernardino, California, in case of *Orange Belt Chapter of Painting and Decorating Contractors v. AFL-CIO Painters District Council 48,* July 1958.) Suppose the introduction of spray and roller painting methods reduced the amount of man hours in painting a house to 50 percent of its former level.
a. Does the above decision mean that wages should be doubled? Or that the laborers can force the houseowner to hire as many hours of labor with the new technique as with the old?
b. What does it mean?

10 "The higher the legally constrained minimum-wage rate, the greater the amount of unemployment of unskilled workers." Is this correct? Explain.

11 "Technically speaking, any labor union is a monopoly in the limited sense that it eliminates competition between workingmen for the available jobs in a particular plant or industry. After all, all unions are combinations of workingmen to increase, by concerted economic action, their wages, i.e., the price at which the employer will be able to purchase their labor." (Arthur Goldberg, Justice, Supreme Court of the United States, and formerly Secretary of the Department of Labor and counsel for the United Steelworkers; quoted from *AFL-CIO: Labor United,* New York, McGraw-Hill, 1956, p. 157.) Why did he write "*technically speaking*" and "in the *limited* sense"? Is there some other mode of speaking and is there an unlimited sense of monopoly? Does a monopoly (closed or open?) eliminate competition? What does it eliminate and how?

12 "The steelworkers' union and the U. S. Steel Corporation are both monopolies." In terms of the closed and open monopoly distinction, is that correct?

13 You work for a television manufacturer as a welder, and two unions contend for recognition as the sole bargaining unit for welders. One, a "craft" union, would be composed only of welders; the other, an "industrial" union, would admit all employees who work for television manufacturers.
a. In which type of union do you think you will be able more effectively to raise your wages by imposing apprenticeship conditions and other devices to restrict the number of people who can seek jobs in competition with you?
b. Which union do you think will be more able to impose a wage-rate increase upon the employer without first restricting union membership? Explain why.

14 The National Association for the Advancement of Colored People contends that the building-trade craft unions (among others) discriminate against Negroes. The national-headquarter officials of each union reply that the local unions in each city are autonomous and determine membership. The charter provides that there will be no discrimination. The unions reply variously that no qualified Negroes have applied, that a new member must be nominated by three members in good standing, that they do have some Negroes, that they use a quota system to ensure that all groups are equally represented, and that the present time, when even the white members are unemployed, is not a feasible time to increase entry rates. Given that the craft union has the power to determine who and how many may join the union, some system of choice is necessary—if the number is to be restricted in order to maintain wages above the open-market level.
a. What criteria for selection do you think should be used and declared defensible? Explain why.
b. Would you recommend a quota system? Why?

15 "Plumbers' and steamfitters' union local 2 of New York has no Negroes, and 80–95 percent of the members are the sons of existing or former members." News story from *New York Times,* August 2, 1963. What explanation can you offer for this?

16 a. Labor groups were strong advocates of raising barriers to immigration in the nineteenth century. Employers objected. Why?
b. Labor groups were less enthusiastic for tariffs (taxes on imported goods), but some were in favor of them. Why?

17 Walter Reuther, former head of the auto workers' union, contended that automobile producers should lower their prices to benefit the public.
a. Why did he not propose that the current tax (tariff) of 12 percent on importation of foreign cars be abolished as a means of increasing domestic supply?
b. Why do you think Reuther wanted lower prices for products produced by members of his union?

18 Some employers welcome the growth of powerful unions that will be able to raise wages and control number of employees admitted to the union. Why? In answering, show why some employers would be hurt by the elimination of effective unions (even ignoring the conflict in trying to eliminate the union).

19 "Any craft union that has to resort to the strike to get higher wages is not being operated efficiently. It should instead concentrate on control of apprenticeship rules and admissions in order to assure high-quality, reliable, skilled union members. And it will incidentally thereby achieve its higher wages in a peaceful, democratic way." Explain what the speaker, a highly successful union leader, meant.

20 As a beginning lawyer, would you benefit if fees for the following were set by the bar association: drawing up someone's will, serving as an executor of an estate, arranging for a divorce?

21 A representative of the Congress of Racial Equality advocated raising the minimum legal wage to $2.50 an hour in order to help Negroes get higher wages.
a. Would Negroes benefit from a higher minimum wage?
b. Would it reduce or increase discriminatory hiring?

22 If in some town the minimum wage rate for taxi-driver employees were raised to $5 an hour, what would happen to the ratio of cabs driven by the owners to cabs driven by employees of cab owners? Why?

23 You are an immigrant. Would you prefer laws insisting on equal pay for equal work, minimum-wage laws, apprentice laws, or strong unions that have been effective in raising wages above the open-market level? Explain.

24 The federal government is taxing and paying for job retraining for those who lose a job.
a. Do you think it should provide an apartment-renovation service for people whose apartments become vacant?
b. What is the difference between the two forms of aid?
c. Why would you support one and not the other, if you would?

25 As a summer-job-seeking college student, are your chances of getting a job increased or decreased if the wages you can get in a cannery, summer resort, factory, etc., are set by a union comprised of current full-time employees? Why?

26 As a college-aged baby-sitter, would you benefit if an association of baby-sitters were organized and a minimum wage of $1.50 an hour enforced? Why?

27 A law is passed requiring each employer to provide hospitalization and premature retirement benefits for his employees who have "heart attacks."
a. Who will benefit by such a law?
b. Who will be hurt?

c. Who will pay the costs? (In answering, first consider the same questions if a law were passed requiring employers to pay for all the housing costs of redhaired employees. Explain why if you were a redhead you would be smart to dye your hair black. Similarly, if you had a heart condition, why would you try to keep it a secret? Does the employer pay for these services—in the sense that his wealth is lower as a consequence of the law? If he doesn't, who does?)

28 Some employment contracts provide the employee with the following: paid time off for jury duty, funerals of relatives, voting, sickness, and vacations; free parking space and work clothes; retirement; two weeks' severance pay; seniority rights over new employees; no discharge for union activities; no discharge if job is displaced by new machinery.
a. Suppose you were to offer to work for some employer who did not give any of these provisions and who insisted on the right to fire or discharge you at any time for any reason whatsoever. Would you consider working for him at the same take-home pay as for the other employer?
b. Would the employer be willing to pay you a higher take-home salary for an employment contract without all those provisions listed earlier?
c. In the light of your answers to the preceding questions, who do you think pays for those fringe benefits listed earlier?

29 The National Teachers Federation, a teachers' union, advocates a single salary scale—wherein every teacher, regardless of specialty, gets the same salary in his first year of teaching, with salary thereafter tied strictly to years of service. Who would benefit and who would suffer if that were made universal: Men or women? Negroes or whites? Superior or inferior teachers? Mathematics or physical-education teachers?

30 "If an enterprise cannot survive except by paying wages of 75 cents or $1 an hour, I am perfectly willing for it to go out of business. I do not believe that such an enterprise is worth saving at that price. It does more harm than good, socially and economically. It is not an asset; it is a liability. So if this kind of business is killed by a minimum wage of $1.25, I for one will not be sorry." (George Meany, Hearings before Subcommittee on Labor Standards, 86th Congress, 2nd Session, 1960, p. 36 of Part 1 of printed hearings.)
a. How does this statement differ from one that says, "Any person who cannot produce a product worth at least $1.25 an hour should not be allowed to work as an employee"?
b. Explain why Meany did not suggest that a business that paid wages of $5 an hour was an even greater liability to the community?

31 Laws have been passed designed to prohibit employers from discriminating among potential employees according to race, religion, and, in some instances, age. Why are there no laws prohibiting employees from similarly discriminating among employers for whom they choose to work?

32 Is the analysis of this chapter consistent with the fact of high unemployment rates among Negroes in the North? What is the explanation for high unemployment among male Negroes, Puerto Ricans, and Mexicans? (Do not answer "low education," "prejudice," or "immobility" since all of those would imply lower wages, not higher unemployment.)

33 "The National and American Football Leagues have finally gotten together and agreed to have a common draft of college players. The draft will eliminate those utterly ridiculous $600,000 bonuses that were paid to untried muscular meatballs from the college campuses. The peace pact will also put a stop to the alarming movement to tamper with the legal property of other clubs (i.e., bid players away from other leagues). The peace pact is welcome. If the cost is high, a continuation of the warfare would have been costlier." (Sportswriter Arthur Daley, *New York Times,* June 9, 1966.)
"Pete Gogolak, the star American Football League placekicker, said today he thought

player salaries would not suffer because of the merger of the two leagues. He said, 'The new players who stood to get big bonuses because of the competition between the two leagues may get hurt, but I think the salaries of the other, older players will remain high.' Gogolak had played out his option with the American League Buffalo Bills and then signed with National League Giants at a salary believed to be $32,000." (News item from *New York Times,* June 9, 1966.)

"The common draft, now agreed to by the two leagues, will drastically cut bonus payments and should appease the colleges who have railed against the in-season solicitation and premature signing of college players attributable to the scramble for talent." (Sportswriter J. M. Sheehan, *New York Times,* June 9, 1966.)

a. To which two of the three writers just quoted would you give a flunking grade in economics? Explain why.

b. If General Electric, Westinghouse, and other electrical companies could get together and have a common draft of graduating engineers, would engineers' salaries suffer? Why?

c. If General Electric, Westinghouse, and other electrical companies could get together and have a common draft of college students at a salary of $100 a month and could compel chosen students to work for them or face jail and loss of citizenship, do you think the draft would be regarded as defensible and in the social interest? Reconcile your answer with the existence of the Air Force, Army, and Navy common draft.

34 "An official Defense Department study reported that the elimination of the draft by raising wages to enlistees would cost about $5–$15 billions annually. Therefore the Defense Department in view of that prohibitive cost is recommending continuance of the draft." (News item from *New York Times,* June 1966.)

a. Explain why the first sentence is an incorrect assertion.

b. Would you be willing to assert that raising wages to abolish the draft would *reduce* costs? Why?

35 Minimum wage laws prevent relatively untrained people, especially teenagers and Negroes, from getting jobs. To overcome this the federal government is going to subsidize employers for hiring these less trained people. The rationale is that the workers hired at the minimum legal wage, though not that productive, will learn on the job and in time become productive enough to warrant that wage. In the meantime, the employer, receiving a subsidy of an amount equal to the difference between the worker's productivity and the wage paid the worker, is providing on-the-job education. Show how this amounts to facilitating a privately operated educational system, with choice by students of the private "school" they will attend.

36 At many colleges students are seeking membership on committees that appoint or fire faculty members. The faculty usually contends that employment is a matter best judged by qualified people like faculty members. Students contend that the faculty chosen affects their lives and hence they should have a say in the matter. (1) The authors say that neither faculty nor student should have the authority to hire or fire faculty. (2) Moreover, students already have more power than the faculty. Explain in what sense (2) is correct; then defend as best you can the preference expressed by the authors in sentence (1).

Interest, Saving, and Investing

23

AFTER man's fall from grace in the Garden of Eden he found he could obtain wealth by consuming less than his income. How much wealth he will get with his savings depends on the opportunities for converting present income to wealth. Wealth includes more than inanimate machinery, buildings, fertile land, sheltered harbors, rivers, and good climate. *People* are wealth, too; skills, talents, knowledge, initiative, manners, and customs are part of our capital. To know that the *non*human wealth of the United States has a market value of some three trillion dollars is to know only part of our wealth. Because people do not sell themselves like capital goods (even though they sell their services), market valuations of the wealth of people, as productive resources, are not readily available.

A person is an asset capable of producing future services, and his productive ability results partly from past investment in his training. Every student sacrifices current consumption for more production power (wealth). The knowledge and skills he acquires become embodied in him. A parent can spend current income for his child's education, or he can build a business for him. Either increases the child's capital goods.

Another segment of wealth is the stability of our government, reliability of the judicial process, and certainty of property rights. All have evolved from centuries of testing and adaptation and the past endeavors of man. Again, since these services are not marketed, we have no directly observable market values for them.

The accumulation of wealth is not a happenstance. We turn now to the many factors and forces upon which it depends. First we should see how current income (flow of services) can be converted to wealth (stock of productive resources).

Means of Converting Current Income into Wealth

A person can *save* in two ways: (1) He can *lend* current income for rights to future income (wealth). (2) He can buy fewer perishable goods and more durable goods. Neither of these changes the social totals. What one person gets, someone else gives up. But a third method does change the social total: (3) He can direct current output to *producing* goods for future marketable income rather than for near-term, present consumption—which is to say he *invests* in making "capital goods." Houses, steel, buildings, automobiles, lathes, bridges are usually considered "capital goods," while lettuce, fresh meat, pianos, shoes, and most commodities that are consumed are called "consumer goods." "Consumer goods" are, by definition, bought for *nonwealth-augmenting* purposes. It is apparent that a capital good can be a consumer good to one person and a wealth-producing good to another; for example, the pianist uses a piano to increase his wealth and another uses a piano for private pleasure. For some, a house is a consumer good, for others it is a source of monetary income.

1. Lending

Anyone can lend part of today's income for more future income. The lender usually gets a promissory note or a bond as evidence of his claim to future income. He has sold current income for future income.

The borrower may use the funds either to finance current consumption, perhaps a vacation, or to buy capital goods. Saving *and lending* do not necessarily result in production of wealth; they may result in consumption through a transfer of current income from one person to another. A positive rate of interest will exist if the portion of current income supplied to borrowers is less than the amount demanded at a zero interest rate—which is certainly the case in any normal society. (An "abnormal" one could be one in which the wealth of the world was expected to be reduced next year by some catastrophe.)

2. Buying and Selling Capital Goods

Anyone can exchange current income for wealth for himself by using part of his income to buy existing capital goods from someone else. These exchanges do not change the total social stock of resources.

Because people's circumstances are always changing, there is a constant buying and selling of capital goods. A person saves part of his income to buy some capital goods; at other times he sells some of his wealth for money to buy current consumption—that is, he dissaves. The parents of most college students saved and then sold assets to finance a college education.

The continuing redistribution of capital goods, money, and current services occurs in the retail markets (money is traded for consumption goods), bond markets (claims to future amounts of money are traded for money now), stock markets (claims to capital goods are traded for money now), and real estate markets (land and buildings are traded for money). All of these markets facilitate revision of asset holdings by exchange, and thereby will make a person more willing to accumulate any one kind of wealth. If I could never trade a house once I had built it, I would be less likely to build one.

Furthermore, prices in these markets reveal information about the relative values of producing various kinds of goods. The principles explained in the example of exchange between the Cuban and Hungarian and the exchange among the five people in our toy economy of Chapter 5 apply here too.

The interdependence of lending (bond) and the capital-goods (stock market) prices. Suppose the explicit interest rate in the *lending* market were 5 percent. Suppose also that in the stock market, some stock, expected to yield $10 a year for the indefinite future, were priced at $333, a yield of 3 percent. If you sold the stock and lent $333 at 5 percent in the loan market, you could get $16.65 a year instead of $10. The offer of this stock would lower its price (thereby raising the implicit yield rate in the capital-goods markets); and lending the money in the bond market would raise bond prices and lower the interest rate in the lending market. This "arbitrage" between markets by selling in one and lending (buying bonds) in another brings the yield rates nearer together.

Similar adjustments take place between countries. (1) A higher-interest-rate economy will borrow from a lower-interest-rate economy—as when the United States lends to South Americans. (2) The South American country will sell future-service-yielding goods to the lower-interest-rate country in exchange for current-consumption-yielding goods or resources.

Most often, changes in prices of common stocks reflect something other than a change in the interest rate. All companies have an uncertain future. For some, things get better and for others, worse. The anticipations about the future are reflected in stock prices. It is not always possible to separate factors causing deterioration in future income prospects from those causing a rise in the interest rate. Although the two are different in principle, they show their effects in similar ways—reduced prices of stocks. We usually, therefore, study interest rates by looking at bond markets, where the future payments are less variable and subject only to the possibility of default. If stock and bond prices fall at the same time, a rise in interest rates is probably the cause. If stock prices fall while bond prices stay steady or rise, the cause is usually believed to be a deterioration in future income prospects, rather than a rise in the interest rate. The "quality" of the capital goods represented by the common stocks is deteriorating. Regardless of the reason for a drop in stock prices, the effect on capital-goods production is quick.

3. Saving and Investing by Production

Production of wealth by diversion of present income from current consumption occurs in many ways. We convert fresh milk to cheese, apples to cider, pork to bacon, grain to whiskey, grapes to wine, olives to olive oil. The various goods produced differ in the length of time they can yield service. We can choose steel or wood, concrete or blacktop roads, diamond or metal-tipped record needles, pipelines or trucks.

Be careful of possible confusion. *Saving* means not consuming all of one's income. We can save by not consuming all currently produced consumption goods or by devoting part of present income *production* power to produce capital goods instead of current consumption. We hope the production of capital goods will be the amount that the public at large wishes to accumulate—a desire that will be revealed by their savings patterns. If they exactly match, then saving takes the form entirely of the accumulation of producers' capital goods. If they do not match, serious consequences may follow for the subsequent rate of production of such goods and for employment, depending upon the process of bringing demand and supply for more wealth via production of such goods into equilibrium. This phenomenon will in part be covered in the latter half of the book. Here we lay the preliminary groundwork for that analysis.

We have talked of saving *and* of investing. As a matter of fact, when a person saves he is accumulating wealth, i.e., he is "investing." Saving *is* investing, but the two words are used to emphasize different aspects of the process. Looking at it as not consuming, emphasizing the process of not consuming, we use the term "saving." But in looking at the particular kinds of goods that are accumulated or at the process of making goods to be accumulated as wealth rather than goods to be immediately consumed, we use the term "investing." Saving suggests the nonconsumption of income, whereas investing suggests what is done with the general income-producing power used to produce wealth goods. And so we use the two terms to indicate these general nuances, until further warning to the contrary.

Net Productivity of Investment Activity

For a dollar of current income used for investment rather than consumption, *more* than a dollar of income is often obtainable in the future. That miraculous *net* increase is called the *net marginal productivity of investment.* Plant a seed today and next year have more than one seed, after allowing for all other costs. This net productivity of investment is "economic" productivity. Profitable investment, directly or indirectly, converts energy, or material, to more desired forms. Capital goods usually require the intermediate step of making a tool or a good that is used later to produce consumption services; this is often called a "roundabout" or "indirect" method of production. Although we are accustomed to seeing future output increased by use of capital goods, we sometimes erroneously conclude that all durable goods or tools are productive of more future income than their current cost. It is easy to make durable goods that are worthless for future production. However, obviously wasteful production or investment is usually avoided, so that the capital goods we usually see are those that have proved productive.

A measure of the net productivity of investment. If we invest one unit of current income today and thereby get 1.15 units a year hence, the gain is .15 units. In general, for an amount, A, invested today, if we obtain a *year later* an amount $A(1+g)$, we define g to be the net productivity of investment per year. This is measured in units similar to rate of interest, as an *annual rate* of growth. However, the net productivity of investment (g) may be greater or less than the interest rate.

We never know in advance what g will be. But nevertheless, almost all of us make investments of one type or another—in education, buildings, cars, and business. We thereby "bet" (by sacrificing current consumption or going into debt to others who lend us current income) that the future product will be *sufficiently* greater than the present sacrifice; everyone who invests must gamble. His decisions are influenced in part by his estimates of the profitability of investments.

Profitable investment. Profitable investments are those that pay sufficiently more in the future, i.e., more than the rate of interest. If the interest rate a year ago had been 5 percent, and you invested $1 with a current payoff of $1.10—your investment would have been profitable.

An investment is profitable if it gives an increase of wealth at a rate, g, which exceeds the interest rate, i. In the example, the future wealth value was $1.10 with g of 10 percent exceeding the 5 percent interest rate. If that $1.10 were anticipated and discounted back one year, the good into which the $1 was earlier invested would then have been immediately revalued to $1.05. A profitable investment is one that (a) immediately raises one's *wealth* by more than the investment now or (b) results in a future wealth increment larger than the amount of investment compounded by the interest rate.[1]

Now we can see how crucial information is. You may be confident that your investment will in a year result in more than the present investment cost plus the interest even though no one else believes it. One way to test your belief is to make the investment. You may find that within two months other people also become persuaded, so they bid up the value of your asset above your cost, with allowance for interest. That excess is profit to you. How long you must wait for the value of an investment to be revealed cannot be foretold. It depends upon how quickly the rest of the community revises its market-expressed valuation—if ever.

Do not jump to the conclusion that it is desirable for an investor if the rest of market reacts quickly to his activity. The longer others fail to see what his activity is leading to, the more he can escape imitative competition from other people.

Higher rates of investment have smaller g. The net marginal productivity of investment, g, depends upon many factors. More wealth helps to increase productivity. Our legal institutions, property laws, security of peace, knowledge of laws of nature, availability of markets, and mental talents are also factors. But one that particularly affects the net marginal productivity is the amount of current income directed into investment, i.e., the *rate* of investment.

The higher the rate of investment, the lower is the net *marginal* productivity of investment, i.e., each increase in the investment rate will yield a smaller net product.

A decrease in *net marginal productivity* of investment at higher rates of current investment does *not* necessarily mean there are fewer ideas or ways to create more wealth. It means that less and less appropriate resources for investment must be diverted from current consumption to investment; the law of diminishing marginal returns is operating. The higher the current *rate* of investment, the more we resort to resources that are less efficient in investment activity. Recall from Chapter 12 on production that the higher the rate of production of Y, the higher the cost. Similarly, the cost will increase for successive increments in the rate of investment, which is a reverse way of saying that the net marginal gain will be lower at successively higher rates of current investment.

4, 5, 6, 7

Demand for Investment: The Most Profitable Rate of Investment

To explain some determinants of the rate of investment-saving that a person or economy is induced to undertake, we resort to the demand-and-supply relationships that relate the cost or price of an activity to the rate of the activity demanded and the rate supplied.

---

[1] When expressed as a ratio to the current increase of investment, this increase in future *income* (not wealth) consequent to a unit increase of current investment—$dY_{(t+1)}/dI_{(t)}$—is the marginal *efficiency* of investment.

The *demand*-for-investment activity relates (i) the net marginal productivity of investment, *g*, to (ii) the rate of investment activity. The investment demand schedule shows for any specified *g* the most profitable rates of investment feasible. That relationship has the characteristic that the higher the rate of investment activity the lower is the attainable marginal productivity of investment. Each extra dollar of current income devoted to investment activity yields a smaller increase in future income. If we think of this future income flow as the "yield," then the larger the rate of investment activity the smaller the yield; or the smaller the yield that one must obtain, the larger will be rate of investment activity that is feasible. This relationship is often called the investment-demand function, or, for short, investment demand.

In Figure 23–1, the investment demand curve *DD* shows, for each interest rate, the most profitable rate of investment: it indicates the largest rate of investment people think they can make while receiving on the *marginal* dollar of investment a rate of return, *g*, at least equal to the interest rate. The lower the interest rate the larger is the rate of investment that is most profitable.

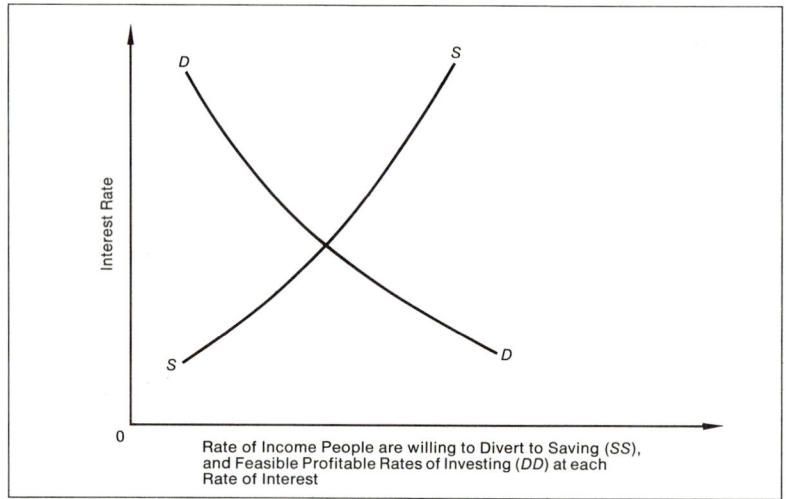

FIGURE 23–1. Demands for Investing and Supply of Savings Are Related to Interest Rate

The lower the interest rate of the economy, the greater the most profitable rate of investment that people believe is feasible, shown by the *DD* curve. The lower the interest rate, the lower the rate of saving that people are willing to incur, illustrated by the *SS* curve. The interest rate at which the most profitable feasible amount of investment would equal the amount of savings people would like to perform is brought about by adjustments in production, relative prices, and income (not graphed).

A lower interest rate should not be considered merely a reduction in interest payments when borrowing for some particular investment. Many people, noticing that interest costs of borrowed funds may be only a small portion of the total investment, jump to the erroneous conclusion that reducing the interest rate has little effect on costs and profitability and hence on the rate of investment. This ignores the fact that a lower *market* rate of interest *means that present values of capital goods rise relative to their current costs of production.* Usually, current services are used to produce longer-lived capital goods; hence *service prices do not rise as much as capital-goods prices when interest rates fall.* A higher rate of (or quicker) investment becomes profitable for a *wider* range of capital goods.

We can illustrate this principle quite easily. Suppose a concrete building costing about $750 would yield $100 a year net of all other costs for nine years. Its g is about 4 percent (see Table 11–3; $7.4 \times 100 = \$744$, a close approximation to $750, for 4 percent). Given a 5 percent interest rate in the market, the building would not be a profitable investment, for its present market *value* would be only $710. But if the interest rate were 3 percent the present value of the building would be about $780. The investment would be profitable. (Check our calculations by reference to the data of Table 11–3.) Since most people think of the interest rate as simply the rate at which they borrow or lend, *rather than also as a means of expressing current prices of capital goods relative to current service prices*, we can see why most of them would think it relatively trivial in affecting general investment activity. A failure to recognize this is often responsible for thinking that interest rates are simply the costs of borrowing, with trivial effect on investment.

Savings Supply

The *SS* curve in Figure 23–1 shows the rate of current income that people are *willing* to divert (save) from consumption to accumulation of wealth *if* they were offered the net rates of growth of wealth or future income (indicated on the vertical axis). The higher the rate or growth of wealth offered for a unit of saving, the more the savings supplied. People might be *willing* to save at the rate of $3,000 a year *if* they could get a growth of wealth of, say, 15 percent on the marginal dollar of saving. But there may be no way to get so high a rate of growth of wealth on the marginal dollar invested; hence the *DD* curve would lie to the left of the *SS* curve at 15 percent rate of interest.

Do not make the mistake of thinking that the distinction between the concepts of investment-demand schedule and savings-supply schedule is made *because* people who direct the investment are different from those who save. The basis for the distinction is not that they are made by different people; some people do both. However, having said this, we emphasize the importance of the fact that decisions about savings and investment are in large part made by different people. Therefore, markets or devices are required to coordinate the two—the (saving) lending and the (investing) capital-goods activities. If the savings or investment schedules shift, serious repercussions can follow for the total rate of income and aggregate employment, as we shall see later.

8, 9, 10, 11, 12, 13

Coordinating Investing and Saving Decisions

Every *person's* behavior is characterized by personal *DD* and *SS* curves, summarizing his investment yield beliefs and savings propensity. In Figure 23–1 the *community DD* and *SS* curves represent summations over all individuals. The interest rate is pushed toward that equilibrium at which the amount of income that people believe they can invest profitably is equated to the savings (that they are willing to provide). But it would be a mistake to think this adjustment occurs in just one special market for savings and investment, as such.

There is no market for "savings" or "investment." Instead, those activities are guided in several markets: the lending and borrowing markets, the capital-goods markets, and markets for current production. The effects of changes in (1) beliefs about feasible, profitable investment opportunities and (2) preference patterns for present consumption relative to more wealth (savings propensities) affects prices and activity in all these markets, i.e., in the entire economy.

The meaning of the response of investing and saving to changes in underlying preference patterns and productive investment possibilities can be investigated and, perhaps, better understood with a few examples.

A. Increase in Savings Propensity

If preferences should increase for future income (to more wealth relative to present consumption), this would imply an increase in the supply of saving, a shift in the *SS* curve to the right. (1) This would be manifested in markets by an increase in the supply of loanable funds. An increased willingness to save implies, in part, an increased demand for bonds—claims to future income. An increased demand for bonds raises the price of bonds, which means that the interest rate is lowered *in the bond market*. That change in price, or lower implicit interest rate, allocates the increased savings over the competing claimants—the same rationing problem investigated in earlier chapters. (2) Prices of existing assets will rise. Prices of steel and concrete buildings will rise relative to those of wood. Young, rapidly growing trees or animals will rise in value relative to older, slower-growing ones. Since a yearling steer grows at a faster percentage rate than an old steer, every pound of a yearling represents a greater increase of future beef than does that of older, slower-growing steers. The demand (and price) of yearlings will rise relative to steers, fewer yearlings will be slaughtered, the price of veal will rise relative to that of beef. Less veal and more beef will be supplied.

We can express these events in terms of interest rates. Recall that in the analysis of capital values and interest rates (Chapter 11), a rise in the price of long-lived goods relative to the price of short-lived goods (steel buildings relative to wooden ones) means the implicit interest rate has fallen. In fact, a change in the relative present values *is* a change in the interest rate *in the capital-goods markets*. For example, suppose the community initially places the value of $710 on each of two goods, one yielding $100 in each of nine years and the other yielding $200 annually for four years. This implies a 5 percent interest rate, which you can (and should!) check by using the data in Table 11–3. If the community's preference changes in favor of longer annuities, the nine-year annuity will be increased in value more than will the four-year annuity. If the present value of the nine-year $100-per-year sequence rises to $779 and the four-year stream to $743 (both up from $710), the interest rate will be 3 percent, down from 5 percent. (Check this, too!) Note also that production of the longer-lived goods will now be relatively more profitable. The interest rate has fallen in the production activity markets; i.e., prices of longer-lived assets will have risen relative to current service costs. House prices will have risen relative to rental rates for current housing services.

B. Increase in Productivity of Investment

Suppose there is an increase in the perceived *possibilities* of producing wealth profitably; new inventions enable us to get more future income; cheaper refrigeration, more durable and rust-resisting metals are examples of ways to create more future consumption per dollar of present investments. They will make more investment profitable.

The *DD* curve (of Figure 23-1) shifts to the right. The interest rate increases. In the lending and borrowing markets this appears as an increased demand to borrow current income—in the form of money. In terms of the demand and supply of bonds, the supply of bonds increases. The price of bonds falls—that is, the interest rate rises, facilitating rationing among the competing demanders of the presently available savings on the loan market. Failing a rise in the interest rate, more changes in nonprice rationing would occur. The allocation would be more heavily influenced by nonmarketable wealth-exchange offers—something we shall again investigate later in the context of specific lending markets.

C. Increased Stock of Capital Goods

What would happen if there were an increase in the stock of capital goods, possibly by a gift from a foreign country or by the accumulation of capital goods over the years? Don't jump to the conclusion that the interest rate will be lower just because the increased stock of capital goods means an increased potential future income. Once the increase in wealth is realized, present income is higher too. A larger stock of capital goods, *once it has been produced,* provides an increase in the *present and future* income. *If* the increase in wealth is heavily weighted by types of capital goods yielding greater future-service relative to the present than for prior existing goods, the interest rate would be higher than otherwise. Why? With a larger ratio of future consumption, relative to present, people are willing to pay more future income for present-consumption rights. The analogy of the person who learns he will in the future have more income than formerly expected is apt; he immediately borrows against his future. On the other hand, a reduced *proportion* of future, relative to present, consumption potentialities may be inherent in the increased stock of capital goods. The interest rate would be reduced. (Why?) Thus, we do not know whether a country that is rich in capital goods will have a higher or lower interest rate.

Prospects of Reduced Future Yields

Let's take a more difficult case. Suppose beliefs about future yields of existing producible assets deteriorate; the *DD* schedule shifts to the left. Those who first develop this belief will sell their common stocks or capital goods to others before the belief is confirmed by ensuing events. Their efforts to sell will depress stock prices (hereafter including prices of capital goods such as buildings and land). Lower stock prices make investment less profitable, so investment will be reduced. People will switch to assets whose future yields are not expected to deteriorate so much, for example, bonds or money. This will lower interest rates in the bond markets (raise bond prices).

The process is not pleasant. Investment-goods producers (and others) must shift to new jobs. Reduced employment means lower incomes which, in turn, make prospects look even worse as savings are reduced. So *both* the *DD* and the *SS* curves shift to the left, because both are affected by the wealth, or income, change. Firms, caught in a squeeze of falling asset prices and reduced income and the necessity of paying off debts, will seek to borrow money to refinance their debts and tide them over the "adjustment." As the interest rate in the loan markets is pushed up, stock prices keep falling. (Why?)

The point of this example is that determination of the interest rate pervades every market and exchange. Nor can a shift in the demand schedule for investment necessarily be treated as something that will not also shift the savings-supply schedule. Events that change the demand for investment and for capital goods or for more wealth have broad ramifications, which are not confined to one small market. The events are more important than a change in the demand for tires, wheat, or some other particular good. The interest rate reflects relative demands for *all* types of goods capable of rendering services in the future. And since rights to present and future income can be traded in many ways in many markets, the interest rate will be implicit or manifest in many markets.

Why the loanable funds market is a key market. Since almost all exchange occurs via the medium of money rather than between goods directly, people seek to revise the time profile of their income or consumption streams not by trading this good now for that good later, but by trading money now for money later. Hence, we can expect almost all revisions in investment prospects and savings willingness to affect borrowing and lending markets, where interest rates are most explicitly expressed. That is why factors affecting rates of interest and investment are often analyzed in terms of demand and supply for loanable funds.

The Meanings of the Interest Rate

When you reread this chapter you will note that the expression *interest rate* is associated with several different concepts. First is the net rate of increase in wealth from a dollar more of investment, also called the net marginal productivity of investment. Second is a personal subjective valuation of present consumption rights, measured in terms of the amount of future income that is equivalent to one dollar of consumption. Third is a market rate of return on loans, called a rate of interest on bonds, or promissory notes. If this third rate is greater than the second, people will reduce present consumption (save more). If the second is less than the first, investment will increase. Fourth, there is an implicit interest rate in the relationship between present prices of capital goods and their future income streams. All these rates—(1) the net marginal productivity of investment, (2) personal valuation of future income relative to current consumption, (3) return on bonds or loans, and (4) the interest rate implicit in relative prices of capital goods—are brought into equality by switching activity among the various markets and goods. When all are equal, the common value is the interest rate. If any are not equal, then adjustments will be induced in the various markets, pushing them all toward equality. Since the most easily perceived and measured rate is the rate in the market for secure bonds, we usually use the rate in that market to measure the interest rate.

You will note the interest rate is referred to variously as the price of "current consumption," the price of "savings," the price of "loans," the "rate of time-preference," the net rate of investment productivity, and the price of "money." It is, as we have seen, a measure of all these things.

Historical perspective is provided by Figure 23–2, which shows long-term interest rates (on 10–20 year bonds) during the past century. Some of the swings in that rate can be explained by long-term movements in the price level, by inflation anticipations, by governmental monetary policy, and by changes in business conditions. We shall explain later how these affect the rate of interest; for the moment, it is sufficient to note the rate seems to have averaged around 4–5 percent.

14, 15, 16, 17, 18, 19, 20, 21, 22, 23, 24, 25, 26

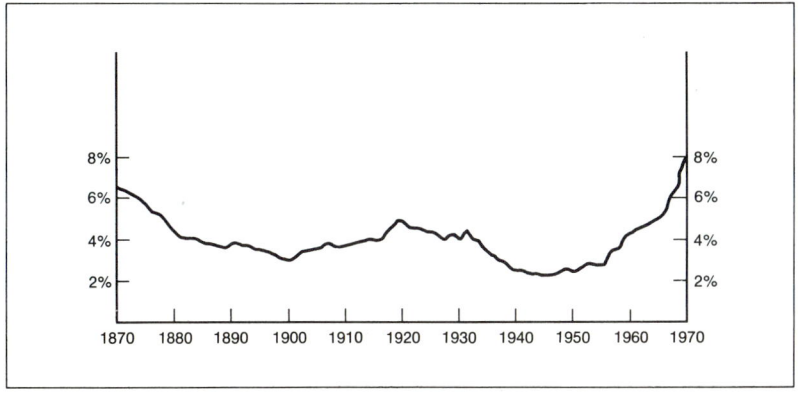

FIGURE 23-2. Long-Term (10-20 year) Corporate Bond Interest Rate (Highest Grade Bonds)

The long-term interest rate has slowly fluctuated over a wide range for various, not entirely explicable, reasons. We conjecture the recent rise to 8 percent is in anticipation of a rising price level in the future, thereby inducing lenders both to insist on a higher money rate and to be willing to pay more in money terms if prices are going to rise in the future. If inflation is curtailed, that recent rise should become a peak rather than a plateau. Source: National Bureau of Economic Research.

Stipulated Explicit Interest Rate and the Implied Effective Interest Yield

We learned in Chapter 11 many ways to express or measure the interest rate or yield on a loan. We know the interest rate stipulated in the loan as, say, 6 percent per year may not be the rate *effectively* promised. For example, if at the present moment you lend $900 for a promise of $1,000 in one year for a zero interest rate stipulated in the written terms of the loan, you will in fact, *if* the loan is repaid when due, have realized an interest rate of ($1,000 − $900)/900 = .111 or 11.1 percent per year. The implicit, effective *yield* is 11.1 percent per year at the time the loan is made (taking into account not only the stipulated rate of zero percent but also the initial present amount loaned and the amount due later). You can see that the implicit yield differs from the stipulated rate if either the present price or amount actually loaned differs from the amount to be repaid (excluding the explicit interest). In general, for any *one*-year loan, the *implicit* or *effective* yield, i, is given by the following formula:

$$i = [(Ar + A)/P] - 1$$

where r is the stipulated interest rate expressed in the loan agreement, A is both the principal amount on which the interest is to be paid and the amount to be paid as principal when the loan is due, and P is the present amount paid or loaned.

For example, suppose you buy an outstanding bond promising 5 percent interest per year on a principal amount of $1,000, due and payable in one year. The present price, or amount paid now, for that bond may be $900. The implicit yield is [($50 + $1,000)/$900] − 1 = .167, or 16.7 percent per year. If the present price had been $1,000, the implicit effective yield would be 5 percent.

In referring to an interest rate, we shall usually mean the implicit effective yield rather than the rate stipulated in the loan instrument. And if the loan is paid on schedule, the implicit effective yield will be the *realized* interest rate on that loan.

Default risk. Some debts have a very high assurance that the borrower will pay interest and principal promptly. Currently, U. S. government bonds are as high in quality as any available, but not because government officials are more honest or reliable than private individuals. Instead, the government can use the police to collect taxes.[2] (Also it can be shown it has the power to collect "taxes" by creating money.) Private bonds sometimes can be repaid only if the borrower is able to induce people to purchase his products. Bonds issued by private firms like General Motors, American Telephone and Telegraph, and Santa Fe Railroad are of very high quality because they are almost certain to be paid when due. Bonds of other strong firms promise an implicit yield of about 6 percent, with some running up to 10 percent. And then there is a vast range of riskier bonds that *promise* even higher yields.[3]

You will notice that we have referred to "promised yields" and not to the interest rate. Superficially, riskier bonds appear to pay a higher rate of interest. The promised yield includes a risk premium. For example, suppose a potential borrower offers to repay in one year with 5 percent interest per year, and you regard the chances of repayment as being only a half. To make that an attractive proposition, you could offer to lend him $50 for his promise to repay $105 in one year, if the stipulated interest rate is 5 percent. Under this arrangement you will get $105 with a probability of .5 and nothing with a probability of .5. *On the average* you would expect to get $52.50, which would be equivalent to 5 percent on your loan of $50. The promised yield on any one loan is 110 percent on a loan of $50.[4]

A test of the validity of this interpretation is provided by events in the bonds markets. If the risk premium accounts for the differences in promised yield, then when a business firm has increased earnings that improve its prospects of being able to meet its debt obligations promptly, the price of its outstanding bonds should rise. And they do.

Most of us are tempted to complain when lenders express doubts about our ability to repay. I may know I will repay a debt when due, but I cannot expect the lender to know it. Some people call the loan market imperfect because *they* cannot borrow at the same promised rate of interest as their neighbor; and some complain they cannot borrow at all. This is analogous to a seller of automobiles complaining that people are buying competitors' cars, when his are just as good. If they were just as good, he would sell his cars. But there is a difference in the eyes of the buyer.

The lender sees differences in the prospects that the borrower will repay promptly without extra costs being imposed on the lender. You should not expect a lender to tell you that your promises are too risky, especially if he can say it in a less offensive way. Thus, a banker says, in refusing to lend to you, "I'm sorry; we just don't have any funds to lend now." You should (we hope) wonder how the supply could be inadequate if the interest rate were really high enough to ration out the existing supply so that all who

---

[2] Evidence of the importance of the ability to collect taxes is that government bonds that are repayable only from receipts of particular projects (such as toll roads) are of lower quality than "general" tax-supported bonds.

[3] For example, Chilean government 3 percent bonds can be purchased for about $200, Boston and Maine Railroad 4½ percent bonds at about $400, and Estonian government 7 percent bonds for about $50. All promise to pay $1,000 at maturity.

[4] This is like reporting the yield on the *winning* ticket in a lottery.

want to borrow can do so. Actually, however, the banker is merely being tactful—and misleading. If he were tactless and completely honest he could have said, "We think the prospect of your repaying is not high enough. *We specialize* in loans to people with better credit prospects. To lend to you, we feel that we should ask 15 percent instead of 6 percent. And then we would have to be prepared to have a staff to take care of the collection problems and other activities involved in defaulted loans. We prefer not to engage in that kind of business. You should go to other lenders who specialize in higher risks and are prepared to handle your type of defaults."

Effect of Quantity of Money versus Effect of *Increasing* the Quantity of Money

Often it is said that the larger the quantity of money the lower the interest rate and the larger the rate of investment. However, a large quantity of money means high prices of wages and goods, land and stocks. At double the prices, everyone's wealth doubles, and people demand twice as many bonds to hold. The demand would push up bond prices—except that the supply of bonds will also increase, so that the net effect on bond prices and interest rates will be nil. There will be twice as much debt and twice as much wealth, income, savings, and investment in money terms—but no change in interest rates or in real quantities.

But, as we shall see later, there are interim effects of *changing*—say increasing—the quantity of money. There are long-run effects, too, from the *way the new money is created and initially spent*. Suppose that new money were created by a legal counterfeiter who proceeded to spend it on wine, women, and song—with the result that there was an interim increase in the demand and prices for wine, women, and song, without effect on interest rates. But suppose, instead, our dull fellow had used his new money to buy bonds. That would immediately push up the price of bonds, or, if you prefer, lower the interest rate. That creator of the money is a member of the community and he has shifted the *community's demand for future income* relative to present income by his expenditures of his newly acquired wealth.

It so happens, as will be explained later, that the usual process of legally increasing the quantity of money is almost always associated with the purchase of bonds and promissory notes. For this reason, low interest results not from creating and issuing money but from the purpose for which that new money is *initially spent*. The increase in the quantity of money and its initial expenditure increases the relative demand for bonds. This is why you will frequently read that *increased* money leads to lower *interim* interest rates—but only because of the institutional way in which the money is created and first spent for bonds. Insofar as increased money leads to anticipated inflation, money interest rates will be higher.

The Money and the Real Rates of Interest

This is a good place to explain the difference between the *money* rate and the *real* interest rate.

If the price level were expected to be twice as high next year as it is now, how much interest *in money* would you pay next year for a loan today, if the interest rate were 10 percent in money units *for a stable price level*? The amounts of $100 today and $200 next year will be equivalent in buying power at their respective times. A *real* interest rate of 10 percent would require that $220 be repaid next year for a loan of $100 now. This would require a *money* interest rate of 120 percent per year. On the other hand, if the price level were expected to be *halved*, an interest rate of −45 percent for a one-year loan would be equivalent to a 10 percent stable price level money interest rate.[5] Our discussion of the interest rate has been based on the assumption that the money-price level is stable. If it is not, and *if* the rate at which the price level is going to change is *foreseen*, then the money rate of interest on money loans will be higher, to give the lender the rate (real) that would have existed if there were no change in the price level. We shall analyze inflation later.

The *realized* rate in real terms can be ascertained only after the bond has matured and the past price level change known. If the price level rise of the preceding few years (e.g., in the 1960s) is used to estimate the future change, then the 5 to 6 percent per annum inflation of those years implies the rate of interest on a bond paying about 8 percent in money terms will be only about 3 percent in real terms. The real rate, measured in this way, has been between 3 and 4 percent for the past decade, while the nominal money rate has increased from 4 percent to 8 percent. We conjecture that a borrower today agreeing to pay 8 percent per year interest, as many well-known business firms are, is predicting that inflation will continue at 3 to 5 percent per year; a smaller rate of inflation will mean a substantial increase in his *real* rate of interest.

Specialization of Borrowers and Lenders

In the preceding sections, the roles of the rate of interest, savings, and investing were explained. Their effective interdependence depends upon the institutional situation within which decisions to save and invest are carried out. In the rest of this chapter, we explore some institutional features and their effects.

The loan market is a vast variety of institutions and marketplaces, because of gains from specialization and economics of collating information about borrowers, lenders, and proposed uses of funds.

People who save generally are not the people who direct productive investment activity. In our economy, savers rely on specialist producers of capital goods to produce those goods, while producers rely on others to save and provide the "funding" of current services for the investment activity. Connecting these groups—savers and investment-goods producers—is a broad variety of interrelated financial intermediaries (jargon for "middlemen") who channel savings from savers to investment-goods producers or to borrowers who utilize the "financing" made available by savers. We refer to "funds," "funding," or "financing," because in an economy using money as a medium of exchange and payment, people do not transfer services via barter. Savers simply save some income in the form of money and transfer the "funds" to others. Financial intermediaries are specialists in information about savers, sources of funds, and demanders of such funds, the investors and borrowers. Given the diversity of capital goods and producers, it is not surprising that there are specialists in knowledge about borrowers, their credit worthiness, and their likely demands for funds. Similarly, intermediaries specialize in catering to savers, using still other intermediaries to channel the flow of savings to investors and borrowers. Commercial banks, investment banks, savings and loans institutions, commercial credit and consumer loan companies, pension funds, insurance

---

[5] See footnote #8 on page 193.

companies (insurance premiums are composed partly of savings as well as payments for current risks), investment funds, bond markets, and stock exchanges with their host of brokerage houses are only a part of the financial intermediary structure.

Intermediaries intermediate in "bringing savers and lenders together," and they reconcile conflicting desires of savers, investors, borrowers, and lenders about the contract terms. If lenders want to lend on *short*-term, e.g., terms of less than one year, while borrowers want to borrow on *long*-term contracts or bonds, e.g., 10 years, the intermediaries act as adapters, borrowing on short-term from the savers-lenders and in turn lending the funds to the borrowers-investors on long-term contracts. They also provide the opposite arrangements where desired and profitable—usually by paying lower interest rates for the collected funds and receiving higher rates in order to cover their costs of intermediation. The savers who use the intermediaries get lower interest rates, but their costs are lower in not having to engage in expensive do-it-yourself search for the best borrowers and negotiation of attractive contracts. For example, a saving and loan institution permits its depositors (savers) to draw out funds with very short notice while it lends on long-term contracts. The owners of the institution anticipate, correctly, that the many savers will in their day-to-day offers and withdrawals of funds just about balance out with no large, unexpected net drain of funds, thereby permitting the institution to lend the funds on long-term bonds.

Another reason for the variety of borrowers can be illustrated by noting a few of the stages in making, selling, and using an automobile. A firm's employees and suppliers want to be paid so that they can consume now, but they are glad to make a car if someone else is willing to pay them now and wait for the future income from the car. If the owner of the business were to finance the work, i.e., pay now and collect later, he would have to defer some consumption. But he wants to specialize in production activity, not in saving. He seeks a lender to finance the current production by transferring current income rights to auto producers in exchange for later repayment.

Automobile manufacturers borrow by selling bonds to the public and to such institutions as insurance companies that channel public savings via investment brokers. They also borrow from commercial banks to carry them over seasonally active periods. Car retailers also rely on commercial banks. In addition, they borrow from finance companies and commercial credit companies. The ordinary consumer has little occasion to deal directly with some of these financial intermediaries. Yet, because they exist, the car dealer can carry a bigger inventory, allowing the consumer to inspect a larger variety of cars and get quicker delivery.

The typical consumer will borrow to pay for the car. He is likely to deal with a consumer credit company directly, or indirectly via the car dealer, who attends to details of the loan. The consumer may borrow from a credit union at his place of work, because the credit union is relatively well acquainted with his personal situation and prospects of repayment. He may borrow directly from a neighborhood bank or from an insurance company with which he has a policy. As goods pass along the line from producer to final consumer, a series of different lenders with special knowledge about successive participants finance each stage.

Negotiability of Bonds

Lenders who may not want to defer consumption until a bond is repaid could sell the bond to someone else, who will act as his substitute, deferring consumption rights. The right to sell an outstanding bond to someone else is known as "negotiability." The lender would then be willing to accept lower interest for the greater "liquidity."[6] However, a borrower may prefer not to have his debts transferable. The original lender, he feels, would be more considerate and lenient in pressing for legal action in the event of difficulty in repaying a debt. Because of the agreement not to sell the bond to someone else, nonnegotiable notes usually carry a slightly higher rate of interest.

Negotiability of bonds is facilitated by bond brokers and the New York Bond Exchange, a formal, privately owned marketplace where the bonds of well-known, strong American corporations can be bought (and sold)—not from the corporation itself but from people who lent money to the corporation, or from those who subsequently bought the bond from the original lender.[7] A large portion of bond resales takes place elsewhere via bond brokers or dealers—much in the fashion of used-car dealers. They maintain small inventories of bonds, but they know other dealers from whom any particular bond can be bought—at a price. These security brokers are known as "over-the-counter" security dealers, since they do not operate in a formal, physically compact exchange like the New York Bond Exchange. They rely on telephones and computers.

Because none of these bond-market transactions transfers money to the original borrower, some people erroneously think these markets serve no useful purpose to *original* borrowers or lenders. Used-bond markets are as important in the production and sale of new bonds (saving and lending) as the used-car market is for production and sale of new cars. How many people would buy cars if they could never sell them but had to keep them until they were junked? Because these markets facilitate the transfer of bonds, more people are willing to hold bonds. Negotiability of bonds also permits people to be more discriminating in their risk selections.

Legal Restraints on Access to Loan Market

The fact of a positive interest rate has been denied, condemned, and legally "prohibited." Aristotle asserted that money is "sterile," so no interest should be paid for money loans. Interest was paid long before Aristotle and continued thereafter—despite theology, protestations, and dogma. It was paid because the borrower offered to pay it rather than not get the loan. And he had to pay it because the demand for savings was greater than the supply at a zero price. Until about the sixteenth century Christian theology "officially" condemned interest as a venal sin. Christians conveniently borrowed from Jews, whose religion placed no severe ban on interest taking. In fact, however, the Papacy itself charged a positive interest—though under the name of "fees," "gratuities," or anything but "interest" or "usury." In medieval times, lords had claims to payments from users of land. Sometimes the lord wanted to sell to the church his rights to the future rents. Suppose an annuity of rents was expected to run for at least fifty years. For what price could it be sold? A fifty-year annuity of $1 a year would be sold to the church for less than $50—because the rate of interest was positive. In buying lands, the church was charging a positive rate of interest—unless it paid a price equal to the expected *undiscounted* sum of the future annuity payments. And it never did that, so far as we know.

---

[6] Most of our money is in the form of commercial bank debts, debts payable on demand. Holders of this kind of debt, because it is repayable immediately *on demand* at the option of the holder, will get a lower rate of interest *per year* than on a debt payable only after some time.

[7] Reports of prices and amounts of bonds exchanged on the major organized exchanges are given in the financial pages of major newspapers and in stock brokers' offices.

Interest rate ceilings. Economic facts of life have insidious ways of circumventing laws or decrees designed to ban them. With man's usual speedy perception, it took the church only about 1,000 years to lift the ban against interest on loans—but still, state governments decree "unreasonably" high (usurious) rates of interest are illegal. In most states, any rate over 10 or 15 percent is called usurious and illegal.

Lenders who make riskier loans at a higher rate of interest in the hope of averaging an acceptable return must resort to legal fictions. For example, pawn shops lend to strangers of dubious credit at a rate of 30 percent per year—not by a "loan," but by a purchase and repurchase agreement. You sell your camera to the pawnbroker for $100 (which is less than its market value) and simultaneously obtain the right to buy it back in one year for $130. Then when, and if, you buy it back, you have paid 30 percent to cover the risk and higher costs, under the facade of a capital gain to the lender.

An effective prohibition of high interest rates would prohibit borrowers with more dubious credit from borrowing at all. It would not lower the interest rate to the riskier borrower. Legal barriers, of course, are not necessarily undesirable. That depends upon one's attitudes toward the consequences of open contracting and open access to markets for lending. Restrictions on commercial banks' rights to make certain types of loans (long-term business loans, second mortgages, stock-exchange loans in excess of certain amounts) are alleged to prevent a bank owner from making "too risky" loans for their "own best interests" and the safety of their depositors' accounts. Also, they are legally restricted in the rates of interest they can offer to depositors or charge borrowers. However, a bank prevented from lending on certain *types* of loans can still make risky loans within the authorized class of business borrowers. A law restricting the class of borrowers to whom banks can lend, or the interest they can charge, does not prevent banks from competing with each other in other cost-incurring services in order to lend.

Furthermore, these restrictions compel many borrowers, especially the poor-risk borrowers, to resort to more expensive sources of funds. Rather than helping borrowers who would normally pay high rates to cover their low security status, laws that limit the interest rates that the better lenders can ask actually increase the costs of borrowing for poor people by forcing them to turn to less efficient sources of funds—or can prevent them from borrowing at all.

Limits on borrowing. Some restrictive laws are directed at the borrowers. For example, laws control consumers' installment purchases of furniture, appliances, cars, vacations. The principle behind these laws apparently is that since some consumers go "too far" into debt, everyone should be *prohibited* from going "too far" into debt. Furthermore, although it's all right to go into debt to buy a house, to meet doctor bills, or to buy business equipment—to go into debt "merely to enjoy consumption before one has earned all the costs" is bad. Thus a generation ago there was considerable publicity and legislation about the evil of consumer installment loans. But the convenience of earlier over later consumption, and of consuming while earning, dominated the virtue of consumption in one's old age. Today, despite many laws trying to limit the rate of interest and amount of borrowing, installment buying is an accepted modern convenience—which has brought the specialized loan market to the young man as well as to the older.

The U. S. government has a law that enables the Board of Governors of the Federal Reserve Banks to place limits on installment purchases. It once prohibited installment credit for more than 50 percent of the value of the item purchased. A 50 percent "down-payment requirement" is a prohibition against going into debt for more than 50 percent of the price of the item purchased. What is the purpose of this restriction? Three reasons have been advanced. First, as said earlier, it protects the consumer from "excessive" debt. A second reason is that the total amount of consumer credit is deemed too large for the "good of the economy," and must be curtailed to prevent "too rapid" an expansion of credit and "too vigorous" a growth of output of the items being purchased. A third reason alleged by *opponents* of the restriction was that the Federal Reserve Board, which is alert to the U. S. government's borrowing problems, wanted to channel more of the available savings to the government: by establishing borrowing limits for private consumers, the government was left with less competition for loans and could borrow at lower interest.

What are the effects? Do higher minimum down-payment regulations reduce the amount of installment debt? Yes. But they increase other kinds of debt. Frustrated consumers increase or maintain mortgaged debt on houses or land. The inconvenience and costs of increasing such debts often exceed the costs of installment loans. In addition, these loan restrictions have different impacts on people: the older, richer, and more informed are not restricted as much as the younger, poorer, and less informed about other sources of funds.

Individuals are prevented from "excessive" indebtedness not only as consumers but also as investors. The Federal Reserve Board can now limit the amount a person may borrow from a security dealer against the stocks and bonds he owns. Why? Not to protect him from loss of security if the stock should fall, but instead to prevent stock prices from being bid up higher—as they allegedly would be if people could buy shares with lower down payments. This power to control credit assumes the Federal Reserve Board is better able to judge what the general level of prices of stocks should be at any moment than are investors in an open market.

There are many ways to get around the debt limit. Borrow from your banker (instead of the security broker), using the stock as the pledged security. Your banker can lend more if he wants to, but not for the express purpose of buying stock. That restriction means very little, because the money you get from the banker can be used to pay some other bills, while the money you otherwise would have used to pay these bills is released for stock purchases. Money is fungible.

Most countries restrict access to security markets. Any person proposing to sell new bonds or new common stock who does not give out certain information or who attempts to market gleaming promises can be prevented from selling the securities via the mails or on security exchanges. If there are no controls on open-market solicitation and sale of investment securities, there will be more "suckers" in the get-rich quest. Some people will make bad investments. Established business firms will find it more difficult to borrow if new, unproved firms can compete for funds on those organized markets. Open markets do enable the market *testing* of investment options, but that requires actually making the investment. If it is believed that some people can select among investments better than can other people, and if these people can be identified in advance, then giving them power to control the kinds of investments for which funds can be solicited in the market may lead to less waste of resources.

The issue of the propriety of controls on the stock market cannot be settled by simply weighing their effects on the extent of profitable or unprofitable investments nor on the extent to which unethical security dealers are detected. It concerns also the question of whether a person ought to have a "right" to make whatever investment choice he would

Interest, Saving, and Investing

like to make, through whatever agency he chooses, as long as he pays for the resources used. Whether he invests foolishly or consumes too much chocolate cake is a decision he might consider his own. Who is right? It depends upon what you conceive to be the desirable basic rights of a person.

27, 28, 29, 30, 31, 32, 33

Personal Investment Principles

It is well and good to talk about wealth in general. But consider a widow who finds herself with a small fortune of, say, $100,000. In what form should she keep that wealth in order to provide herself with an income and perhaps a legacy for her children? What should a young father do to accumulate a fund for retirement? These appear to be two different questions. The first asks how to invest to achieve an income; the second asks how to invest to achieve wealth growth. They really are the same question but appear different because the first contemplates *consuming* income or growth in wealth, while the second proposes to *save* income and not consume any wealth growth. The same investment is best for both. Whichever yields the greatest income plus the greatest increase in capital value will provide the greater income or consumption power—whether it be consumed or saved. What differs is not how to invest but what one will do with what he gets.

What Variance-Risk?

For investment, a necessary choice is whether to invest in assets (we shall speak only of common stocks, as an example) that have a wider range of potential future values (up or down by perhaps 30 percent) in a year, or in assets that promise a smaller range (say, plus or minus 10 percent). The first are "volatile," and the second are "blue chips." Suppose you have purchased oil-well stock. If oil is discovered, the stock value will go up by a factor of ten; if not, it will fall to zero. But it almost certainly will not stay at its present price when the drilling is completed. That is a volatile stock. Or you could buy American Telephone and Telegraph and almost certainly at the end of a year your wealth in that stock will not be different by more than 10 percent. On the *average,* over *all* stocks, volatile or not, the net result a year later will be about the same no matter which you buy. Many different volatile stocks will yield on the *average* about what the very-small-variance stock will yield, say 8 to 10 percent a year. However, you cannot count on experiencing the *average* yield, so if you buy one volatile stock you will probably be farther from the average (above or below) at the end of the year than if you had bought the smaller-variance stock like AT&T. (For that extra risk of being farther above or below the average, it is widely believed but not proven, the riskier, larger-variance stocks yield on the *average* a slightly higher growth.)

Your choice must be the extent of variation (gain or loss) that you wish to expose your wealth to for some growth or income. You can achieve near certainty (zero variance) in your future wealth position by holding high-grade bonds or savings deposits. (However, while this gives you very high security about the *money* value of your wealth a year hence, it exposes you to a loss if inflation has not been accurately anticipated in the market, or a gain in real terms if unanticipated deflation occurs.) What size of *variance* of future growth (or loss) in wealth do you prefer? There is *no* way to avoid that decision—although you may refuse to recognize that you have in fact made such a choice.

Dividends or Capital Gain Stocks?

However, most people ask a different question—should they buy for dividend income or for capital-value appreciation? This question is (except for tax purposes) pointless. Why? Business firms, we hope, have net income which is used either to reinvest in the firm or to pay dividends to stockholders and thereby invest less in the business. Dividend-paying stocks mean that the companies do not *themselves* invest so much of their earnings, while nondividend-paying (capital growth) stocks mean the companies themselves invest all their earnings, if any. With either kind of stock you could consume the same amount. If the company pays dividends, you can buy more stocks and reinvest yourself. If they reinvest instead of paying dividends, you can sell some of your appreciated stock (reflecting the retained earnings) and consume as much as you would have if the dividends had been paid out and the stock had not risen to reflect the retained earnings.

For example, suppose you have 10,000 shares in a company that earns $1.00 per share annually. Assume the stock is now selling for $10 a share. If the company retains earnings, the stock will rise in value to $11 at year-end; if the company were paying dividends of $1.00, the stock price would not rise by that $1.00. If you hold dividend-paying stocks, you receive $10,000 annually as income which you can spend, and at year-end you have $100,000 in wealth. If you hold nonpaying stock with earnings (income) being retained by the corporation, you can sell 909 shares of the stock at year-end for $11 each and spend the $10,000 proceeds, and you will have 9,091 shares left worth $11 or $100,000 in total. In either case, the amount you can spend and the amount you have left is the same. Thus it makes no difference whether you own dividend-paying or capital-gain stocks: just sell some shares representing the retained earnings in one case, or use the dividends in the other.[8]

Random Selection, by Variance Class, Because of Stock-Exchange Efficiency

Except for taxes, do not be concerned about income stocks versus capital-gain stocks. Instead, be concerned only about the variance in future wealth position.

But once you have found a set of high- (or low-) variance stocks from inspection of past behavior of various stocks, which ones in that set should you buy? Pick at random! Shocking? It's correct, especially if you confine yourself to New York or American Stock Exchange stocks. This does not argue that innocence or ignorance is bliss. Rather, in big stock exchanges the flow of information about evaluations of various companies is quickly and openly revealed in the resultant stock prices, which reflect the best opinion of the market at large. Most stocks that *were* "good buys" have been bid up to where they are no better than previous "bad buys" whose prices have been allowed to fall until they are equally good buys. Competition in the open public market *with publicized prices* of actual trades provides stock *evaluation* at low cost to us innocents, for the best opinions of the insiders, professionals, and everyone else are revealed in the actual

---

[8] There *is* a difference for your income taxes. If you are in a tax bracket paying over 25 percent of the highest dollar earned, you would be well advised to hold nondividend-paying stocks and to realize the income in the form of capital-value proceeds by selling stocks. This is an idiosyncrasy of our tax laws which puts a lower maximum tax on capital gains.

transaction prices. The best opinion may be lousy, but unless you think you have access to (1) *better*, (2) *secret* information and can (3) *evaluate* it better than anyone else can, you had better accept the existing market price as an unbiased reflection of the relative worth of various stocks. The competitive process makes them all equally good buys on the *expectation* of future performance. All of your independent search and evaluation will merely replicate the market's, and if it doesn't, you have the horrendous task of wondering why your opinion differs from everyone else's. Unless you have inside information that no one else has yet had a chance to act on in the market, pick the stocks at random! The evidence supporting this contention is overwhelming.[9]

We are not praising ignorance. We praise and rely on the ability of the *stock exchanges* with their quickly published prices of all transactions to make almost instantly available to the public at large at extremely low cost the best information dug up by the myriads of stock analysts and investment counsellors. You must pay a commission to use the exchange, which in part reflects expenses of providing evaluations of the stocks in the stock prices as they move from moment to moment. But there is no point in paying for that information twice: once as commissions and again as a fee to an investment counsellor for advice over which you study and agonize, or to a mutual fund which will only reproduce that information and in fact does no better than the random sample procedure.[10]

Do not conclude that your stock broker or investment counselor is worthless. First, he is an agent who economizes costs of your use of the market for securities, and that is a significant function. Second, he can provide you with information to facilitate your *diversification* of risks so that with as few as 7 to 12 stocks you can reduce the variance of your portfolio to that of a very large portfolio—if you wish to reduce the variance. In the foregoing, we have not written about diversification and its principles, for that would take us beyond the scope of this book; but if we did, none of the principles exposited so far would be vitiated.

Picking stocks at random within variance classes is psychologically hard to accept. Consider the question: "If I took from the years 1926–1966 one year at random and then took one stock at random from the New York Stock Exchange, how much would my investment have changed in value during that one year?" We do know what the *average* of all such actions would have been: one dollar would have grown to $1.15, counting increased value of the stock plus any dividends paid out. You can be sure you would not experience exactly that average. What is the dispersion around that mean within which your experience would probably have fallen? In 90 percent of the cases your initial wealth of $1 would have been between $.46 and $2.00 at the end of the year. Half the time it would have been $.85 and $1.35, with the average of $1.15.

An easy means of expressing this range of potential loss or gain is Figure 23–3. The top section shows the wealth interval for .9 of all possible randomly selected *single* stock investments for *one* year. (The darker bars are for .5 of all results.) The probability is .9

---

[9] A myriad of performance tests have been conducted. See for a sample: E. F. Fama, "The Behavior of Stock Market Prices," *Journal of Business*, 38 (1965), 34–105; E. F. Fama, L. Fisher, M. C. Jensen, and R. Roll, "The Adjustment of Stock Prices to New Information," *International Economic Review*, February 1969. See also various issues of the *Journal of Finance* of 1970 and 1971.

[10] A weighty study showed that of all the mutual funds, those that did best spent the least amount for research and for commissions in changing stockholdings—thereby having the lowest expense ratio and hence the highest growth! W. F. Sharpe, "Mutual Fund Performance," *Journal of Business*, 39, Supplement, January 1966, 119–139.

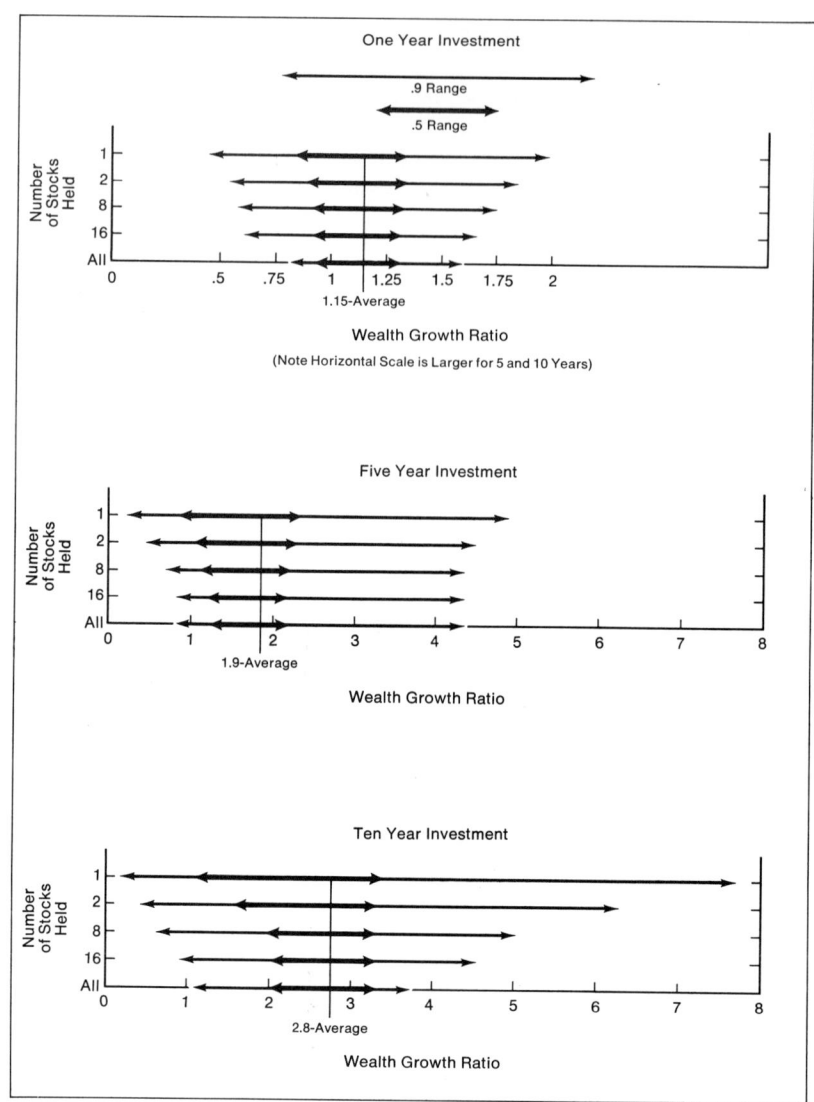

FIGURE 23–3. Investment Wealth Ranges for .9 and .5 Probabilities for Portfolios of 1, 2, 8, 16, or All Stocks on the New York Stock Exchange (1926–1966).

that the year-end value would be between .50 and 2.00 times the initial investment for a one-stock portfolio. Narrower intervals result if several randomly selected stocks are included in one's portfolio. The eight-stock portfolio range narrows to .6–1.7. And if every stock on the New York Stock Exchange were somehow held in your portfolio, the interval would be .65–1.6, which is pretty closely approximated with just eight stocks.[11]

---

[11] The data used for Figure 23–3 are taken from Lawrence Fisher and James H. Lorie, "Some Studies of Variability of Returns on Investments in Common Stocks," *Journal of Business,* April 1970, 99–134.

The intervals reported are for *one*-year investments. If the investment is maintained for 5 or 10 years, all on the basis of an initial random selection in the first year, what are the average wealth ratios and what are the widths of the .9 (and the .5) probability wealth-ratio intervals? The *average* wealth ratio for a 5 year investment was 1.9, and for 10 years 2.8.[12] The lower sections of Figure 23–3 give charts for 5 and 10 year investments and for portfolios of 1, 2, 8, and 16 stocks (and *all* stocks as a reference). The intervals are substantially greater for the longer investments, as one would expect. Increasing the number of stocks narrows the .9 interval substantially, whereas the .5 interval is narrowed only a minor extent. The greater number of stocks tends to avoid the extreme results, which is not surprising. That the intervals with only an 8 stock portfolio are nearly as narrow as for the whole market is surprising to most people.

Summary

1 Wealth consists of all goods, human and nonhuman. Some have readily measurable market values and some do not. Many of our institutions, such as laws, customs, and systems of property rights, are fundamental components of our social wealth.

2 Saving is the nonconsumption of current income. Investing and saving, under one popular definition of these two terms, are identical concepts.

3 An individual may save and accumulate wealth by trading his current saving for someone else's goods—wherein the other person thereby dissaves—with no change in the social total. A person can save and lend to someone else who thereby consumes more than his income and dissaves—again leaving the social total unchanged. A person may save and accumulate a larger total stock of wealth by production, rather than by exchange with someone else; the social total will increase.

4 Capital goods render (marketable) services in the future. A fall in the price of capital goods, *relative* to consumer goods prices, *is* a rise in the interest rate.

5 The interest rate is manifest in several markets: the lending and borrowing market, the capital-goods market, and production-activity market. All are interdependent; arbitrage among them will bring each to a common interest rate.

6 The net marginal productivity of investment is the net rate of increase of wealth per marginal unit of investment. The net marginal productivity of investment is a decreasing function of the rate of investment.

7 A lower interest rate affects investment *and* demand (in the sense of available profitable rates of investment) more than merely by lowering the interest costs on a loan. *The relationship of prices of capital and consumers goods—short-lived and longer-lived—changes*.

---

[12] A thorough student will notice that the *average* wealth-growth ratio for a ten-year investment is 2.8 instead of 4, which would be obtained by compounding the one-year average growth of 15 percent through 10 years. (See Table 13–2.) What is wrong? Nothing. You won't get the *average* growth rate in *every* year. The actual growth rate will be a random variable in some range around that average (which is what the range in the top of Figure 23–3 shows). When each year's growth is a *random variable* around some average, it is *not* correct to compute the average growth for a long-term investment by compounding each year at the one-year *average*-growth rate. The correct method must allow for the variations in a complicated way involving advanced probability theory. That is why we have presented graphs that are based on actual observed results.

8 Investment and saving are different concepts when used in the demand- and supply-schedule sense: saving represents the rate at which current income will be *willingly* diverted from current consumption to accumulation of wealth. That willing saving rate is a function of the interest rate. Investment is the current income that *can be profitably* diverted from consumption at a given rate of interest. In these senses, saving is a positive function of the interest rate, while investment is a negative function. The investment schedule is often called the demand for savings, while the savings schedule is called the supply of savings.

9 Saving and investing are equated not in a single market for saving and investment but in the loans markets, the capital-goods markets, and the production-activity market—all loosely called the saving-investment markets.

10 An increase in preference for distant income relative to present implies more current savings, an increase in the saving-supply schedule, and a lower rate of interest with more investment. An increase in investment demand consequent to an increase in perceived profitable investment opportunities results in a higher rate of investment and a higher interest rate.

11 Since both the supply and the demand schedules are explicit functions of the interest rate, it is tempting to think that the interest rate changes to equate the rate of investing with the rate of saving. But both saving and investing are dependent upon other variables also (wealth, income, expectations about the future), and these other variables also change to equate saving with investing.

12 An increased stock of wealth has effects on the rate of interest and rate of investment, depending upon the particular attributes of the increased stock of wealth.

13 The interest rate reflects the net marginal productivity of investment, the personal value of present consumption relative to wealth or future income (often called one's time preference), the rate of return on loans, and the relative prices of capital goods and consumers goods.

14 *Increasing* the quantity of money affects the interest rate because of the ways the increase is first spent. But the quantity of money will not in itself affect the interest rate; however, the price level is changed.

15 Our institutional mode of creating money is such that the increased money is spent in acquiring bonds; hence, the typical result is that increasing the quantity of money leads to lower interest rates during the increase.

16 The money interest rate is the real interest rate adjusted for the changes in the price level.

17 Interest yields are typically expressed inclusive of risk, so that riskier loans indicate a higher yield. The implicit interest yield on a one-year bond is $i = [(Ar + A)/P] - 1$, where r is the stipulated interest rate and A is the principal amount, both due at the end of the year, and P is the present price of that bond.

18 The capital market for lending and borrowing is a complex network of specialized intermediaries between savers and investors.

19 Negotiability is the legal right of the owner of a bond (creditor) to sell the bond to someone else. Bond exchanges facilitate negotiability; they also facilitate borrowing, because lenders regard negotiability of bonds as a desirable attribute.

20 Like many markets, the lending market is not entirely open and free of restrictions. Interest rates, extent of borrowing, and length of loans are commonly restricted by laws. These restrictions are supposed to protect borrowers and lenders from their own overoptimism. They do protect one class of borrowers or lenders from open-market competition of other borrowers and lenders.

Questions

1 A farmer who dries grapes to convert them to raisins is investing. Why is this investing, since it merely changes one form of consumption good to another form of consumption good?

2 Instead of playing bridge, a man works around the house painting and refinishing the walls. Explain why this is a form of investment.

3 Changes in the rate of interest are detectable in the changes in the structure of relative prices of various types of goods.
a. If the price of raisins (relative to grapes), of prunes (relative to plums), of whiskey (relative to corn), of cider (relative to apples) should rise, would that mean a change in the rate of interest? In what direction?
b. What effect would that have on the profitability of producing raisins, prunes, whiskey, etc?
c. Ultimately, what effect would the revised production have on the relative values (for example, of raisins and grapes)? What effect would that have on the rate of interest?

4 Suppose the world were going to last for just two years and you have wealth of $100.
a. If the interest rate is zero, what is the income available in each of the next two years?
b. If the interest rate is 10 percent, what is the income of each period (again assuming a two-year life to the world)?
c. If the interest rate is 10 percent but the world is going to last for an indefinitely long period, what is the maximum annual maintainable rate of consumption?
d. If the interest rate is 5 percent, what is the rate of income—assuming wealth is $100?
e. If your wealth unexpectedly increases from $100 to $120, what happens to income (with an interest rate of 5 percent)?
f. What was the amount of your profit when that wealth increase occurred?

5 Goods differ in their rate of yield of consumption services, or in their "durability." Pine lumber naturally deteriorates more rapidly than redwood. If demand for future consumption rights should *rise relative* to present consumption rights, would pine or redwood experience the greater rise in present price? Show why this is expressible as a fall in the rate of interest. (Hint: The interest rate is the exchange rate between present and future consumption rights.)

6 By giving up $100 of present income for $105 of consumption rights available in one year, a person gets what g?

7 "Roundabout, more capitalistic methods of production are always more productive than direct methods using less capital equipment. Therefore, any country that wants to develop should start increasing the amount of capital goods it has." Evaluate.

8 The interest rate is 10 percent per year. A person uses $100 of current wealth to make his wealth grow to $105 at the end of a year.
a. Has he maximized his wealth?
b. In what sense has he not even maintained his wealth, despite the fact that he has $105

at the end of the year compared to $100 at the beginning? (Hint: When his wealth was $100 at the beginning of the year, with an interest rate of 10 percent, how much could he consume during the year and still end up with $100? Could he not have consumed any amount up to $5 and still ended up with $105?)

9   A man plants a seed for a tree. Assume for simplicity that there are no subsequent expenses. The tree, if cut and converted to lumber at the end of any of the ages indicated in the table below, will yield lumber worth the amount indicated in the second column. The third column gives the *present* value of that future potential lumber, at 10 percent rate of interest. Some of the entries are not presented.

(1) Age	(2) Lumber Value	(3) Present Capital Value of Lumber	(4) Present Value of Costs	(5) Profit If Cut at Age Indicated
0	$ 0	$ 0	$5.00	$—5.00
5	1	0.62	5.70	—5.08
10	4	1.54	6.20	—4.66
15	11	2.63	6.50	—3.87
20	25.0	—	6.60	—
25	60.0	5.54	6.80	—1.26
30	140.0	—	6.82	—
35	260.0	—	6.95	—
40	450.0	10.00	6.96	+3.04
45	650.0	—	6.97	—
50	800.0	6.80	6.98	—0.18

a. Compute the missing values and find the age at which the tree should be cut to provide the maximum *present* value of that tree.
b. What is that maximum present value?
c. How much is a newly planted tree worth?
d. Suppose now that the rent for the land on which the seed is planted is 50 cents per year. Suppose that, in addition to that cost, there are other costs—spraying, watering, fire protection, taxes—to be paid over the years. The present value of those future costs for various lengths of time is indicated in column 4. Column 5 gives the present value net of these costs. Compute the missing data for that column.
e. Suppose that the value of the tree rises relative to current lumber prices. What would this imply about the rate of interest?
f. If no one owned the tree, and it could be cut by anyone who wanted to use the lumber, when would it be cut?

10 Some whiskies improve with age. The following table lists the consumption value of a barrel of whiskey at various ages. For example, if the whiskey is removed from its aging vat and sold now to consumers for current consumption, it will sell for $100. If sold in ten years, it will fetch $250 for *consumption*.
a. How much will the vat of whiskey be worth right now (at 10 percent) if it is to be held until the end of the second year before being bottled and sold?
b. For what length of time should one expect to keep the whiskey in the vat for a maximum present value? (Hint: How much is it worth paying for the whiskey now if it is to be held for five years? For ten years?)

c. If no one owned the vat of whiskey, how long would it remain unconsumed?
d. Suppose it were owned but could not be sold: how long would it be kept before consumption?

Consumption Date	Consumption Value	Consumption Date	Consumption Value
Now	$100		
1 year	120	6	205
2	140	7	220
3	160	8	230
4	175	9	240
5	190	10	250

11 "A rise in the profitability of constructing houses and buildings tends to push up the rate of interest." Why? Reconcile this statement with the preceding one. (Do so in terms of shifting demand or supply curves and movements along a curve.)

12 In a certain country the only productive goods are "rabbits." Either the rabbits are eaten, or the rabbits increase at the rate of 20 percent per year.
a. If there are 1,000,000 rabbits in the community at the first of the year, what is the income of the community (measuring the income in rabbit units)?
b. What will be the rate of interest in that community?
c. What is the maximum possible growth rate of the wealth of that country?

13 The propositions on costs in Chapter 15 imply that the demand curve for investment is negatively sloped with respect to the rate of interest—that is, that higher *rates* of investment will be less profitable. Why is this implied by the earlier propositions on behavior of costs?

14 "Debtors are exploited by creditors, because a person who has to borrow is usually in distress and is willing to pay a very high price to get the loan. Unless laws were passed controlling the rate of interest, debtors would be forced to pay unreasonable rates of interest." Is the analysis correct? Explain why.

15 "When interest rates rise, the profitability of constructing buildings falls relative to other kinds of productive activity." Why?

16 a. "If savings is defined as an increase in wealth and if investment is defined as an increase in wealth, then savings by definition is always equal to investment; for it is merely the same thing looked at from the point of view of two different people." Correct or incorrect?
b. Since the preceding statement is correct, how is it possible to speak of equilibrating the rate of investment and the rate of savings?

17 Define the demand for investment; define the supply of savings and do so in such a way that the two are not synonymous.

18 "The most important fact about saving and investment is that they are done by different people and for different reasons."
a. Is that why savings must be equilibrated to investment via a demand for investment and a supply for savings function? Why not?
b. Suppose that everyone who invested had to do his own saving and could not lend or borrow or buy capital goods from other people. Would that destroy the principles of demand-and-supply analysis for growth of wealth? Why?

19 If a person saves all his increase in wealth, how much does he save?

20 If the rate of interest is 10 percent in the New York bond markets and 5 percent in the Boston bond market, describe the adjustments you think will ensue.

21 "Where total investment is concerned, the economic system is in the lap of the gods." Do you agree? If so, why? If not, why not?

22 "Large corporations have so much of their own funds that they do not have to borrow in the capital-funds markets in order to make new investments. They are therefore immune to interest rates in the capital markets so that their investments are not screened as are those of investors seeking funds in the capital markets." Explain the error in that analysis.

23 You are a visitor in some underdeveloped country in which all lending and borrowing are effectively prohibited.
    a. Is there a rate of interest?
    b. If so, where could you get data to compute it?
    c. How could you tell when it changes?

24 Someone discovers how to reduce refrigeration costs to almost zero, and tells everyone about it.
    a. What will this new improved technology do to the rate of interest?
    b. What price shifts are implied?

25 If you received a gift of $10,000 in cash, in what forms would you hold your wealth? Suppose you decided to convert it to some intermediate kind of claim or goods (like bonds and savings-bank deposits) before finally holding more stocks and personal or business goods directly? Trace out the sequence of effects on the interest rate if you follow the sequence suggested in the preceding sentence.

26 The rate of interest helps to equilibrate investing and savings and the demand for borrowing and the supply of savings; it is the premium price of current consumption rights over future consumption rights; it is the price of money; and it equates the demand and supply of assets. Explain how it is all these things at once.

27 "Five states—Arkansas, California, Oklahoma, Tennessee, and Texas—have constitutional provisions restricting the maximum contract rate of interest. All other states, except Colorado, Maine, Massachusetts, and New Hampshire, have generally statutory restrictions upon the rate of interest that may be contracted for in the absence of special statutory authorization for higher rates. The most common maximum contract rates are 6 percent and 8 percent a year, but a few states permit contract rates as high as 12 percent. Loans to corporations are generally exempt." So says the *World-Telegram Almanac* of 1962.
    a. What is the difference between the "contract" rate and the rate paid?
    b. Who is helped and who is hurt by these laws if they are effective?
    c. Do you think they have any effect on the rate of interest?
    d. What effect do they have on borrowing activity?

28 You propose to buy a house for $20,000. You have $3,000 in cash now. So you seek to borrow $17,000 from a lender at 5 percent rate of interest. We say 5 percent because the government of the state in which you live has agreed to guarantee the loan on your house since you are a veteran. The law will guarantee your loan so long as the lender will lend at not over 5 percent. Unfortunately, no one will lend to you at that rate because 6 percent is available elsewhere. But you are clever enough to find a lender who will lend to you at 5 percent, *after* you make the following proposal: If he will lend you $17,000 at 5 percent (which is, let's say, 1 percent less than the 6 percent rate he could

get elsewhere—and thereby costs him $170 a year interest otherwise available; that is, 1 percent of $17,000 is $170 per year), you will buy from him insurance on the house and on your car and life. In doing this, you may or may not realize that you could have bought the same insurance at a lower rate or more conveniently elsewhere.
a. Why do you make this agreement with him?
b. Is he being "unfair" or "unscrupulous" or "unethical"? Are you?
c. Who is aided or hurt if such tie-in agreements are prohibited?
d. Do you think they can really be totally prohibited by laws? Why?

29 Diagnose and evaluate the following news story from the *New York Times* (February 7, 1959, p. 30): "Earl B. Schwulst, chairman of the Bowery Savings Bank, said he would be greatly distressed if other savings banks moved soon to increase their dividend rate to depositors. Most New York City institutions are paying 3¼ percent. There have been some rumors that some institutions would announce soon an increase to 3½ percent. Mr. Schwulst said that the Bowery, the largest savings bank in the nation, was as well qualified as any other institution to pay the higher rate. But, he said, the Bowery would not lead the way because of a number of reasons he described as 'in the long-run interest of our depositors.'"

30 The President of the United States, to prevent a loss of gold, decides to take governmental action to increase the rate of interest. If he can successfully do this, he believes foreigners will leave gold on loan in the United States for that higher interest rate rather than take the gold home. Suppose that belief is correct and suppose the interest rate is increased.
a. What do you think the effect will be on the rate of building and housing construction? Why?
b. Will the higher interest rate affect all kinds of business activity equally? Why?
c. Why do you think the businessmen are so concerned about the policy that may be taken by the President and Congress if those officials decide to try to prevent a further outflow of gold?

31 "Havana: October 15, 1961: All renters in the towns and cities of Cuba became property (building—not land) owners this morning when the Castro government approved a long-awaited reform law. However, renters must pay the Cuban government for their newly acquired property during the next five to twenty years at the same monthly rate as their present rents. In addition, they must pay the government the taxes formerly paid by the owners. The former owners will receive a "life monthly indemnity" of from 200 to 600 pesos without regard to the amount of property they owned. Heirs will receive nothing. Any buildings now in construction will be turned over to renters selected by the government. If the owner (up to today) refuses to complete the building, the state will seize the existing building with no compensation at all. Holders of mortgages on residences and apartment houses will receive 50 percent of the amount paid by the tenants to the state until the loan is paid, but no interest will be allowed." Why do people in many foreign countries "foolishly" hoard gold instead of using their wealth to develop the country?

32 The following is a quotation from the *Scientific American*, 1963: "Recently a number of steelmaking organizations in Western Europe and the U.S.S.R. have eliminated several costly steps in the manufacture of steel by advancing the technique known as continuous casting. U. S. steel firms, which account for about a third of the world output, were for the most part content to observe these developments. They were inhibited by a paradox of industrial supremacy: the huge sums already invested in established methods made experimentation with the new technique seem impractical. The smaller producers, whose competitive position might have been enhanced by continuous casting, could least afford to build the pilot plants."

Assume that the facts stated in the first sentence are correct. The second sentence describes the alleged behavior of U. S. steel firms in response to these facts; and the remaining sentences strive to explain that behavior. Do you agree that the last two sentences present an economically acceptable explanation of the events in the second sentence? Explain why they do not.

33 A further quote from the same article in the *Scientific American*: "The ideal time for a producer to consider the use of a continuous-casting machine is when he is building an entirely new steel mill, from melting furnace on through to milled products. In such a situation the mill can be designed around the known limitations of the continuous-casting process, and there will be no costly overlap between conventional and continuous equipment. Unfortunately, U. S. firms are not planning to build many new steel mills. Therefore, many U. S. producers are 'not ready' for continuous casting, whereas small producers in India, Venezuela, and Peru, for example, have already obtained plant designs. The producers in these countries will avoid the large cost of primary mills. If there is any solace in underdevelopment, it is this 'advantage.' "

Note that the writer did put the last word in quotation marks, as if to admit there really was no advantage as he seemed to suggest. Comment on the reasoning in the quotation; but first note whether or not the quotation says that *no* U. S. firms are now using continuous casting or merely that *not all* are; and whether *no* firms or *not all* firms plan to introduce it. In evaluating this quotation, consider: If you already have an old-model car, would you be more or less likely to buy a new-model car that *is* more economical than your "old" model?

Growth and Distribution
of Wealth

Sources of Greater Wealth

24

WHATEVER the wealth of a society, of greatest interest to each person is his own wealth and income. One can view the distribution of income and wealth as if it were established by dividing up a predetermined total, like dividing a cake among claimants. Or one can view the total amount of cake as the sum of each individual's contribution to the total. In either case there must be a procedure for determining who gets what part of the inheritance and who gets what portion of current product. Preceding chapters showed that economic analysis can explain who produces and who gets current product in various societies, although our predominant application was to the private-property, market-exchange system. Each generation inherits a legacy. The form, size, and division of that legacy among the heirs varies among societies. The amount a person will leave to the next generation certainly depends upon the rules of inheritance. No doubt, the legal right to endow one's children—rather than the next generation at large or only the "state"—is an incentive to accumulate wealth as a legacy. Furthermore, the form of the "wealth" is affected. Parents who wish to endow their children in ways that cannot be thwarted by other people would devote more to educating children in skills, knowledge, and developed abilities, and not primarily in buildings, land, or goods. Jewish emphasis on education and development of personal skills has been called a survival trait in the face of governments that confiscate nonhuman wealth—an experience in which the Jews have long suffered.

The sources of greater wealth are past and current saving, higher productivity, and efficient organization of human and nonhuman resources in exploiting profitable investment options. The existence of natural resources is not sufficient. Many countries (for example, a number in South America) are rich in natural resources but have been less than successful in exploiting them by efficiently organized or directed economic activity.

Natural resources have to be *converted* to useful form. In this country, the prairie was a forbidding area until man sweated over it with the plow. (With what incentive?) New England's soil is rocky, its winters severe and summers short. Natural resources are not free. They were available to the Indians for centuries, but still the Indians were poor. Resources must be worked with skill and energy. In other words, people are a part of the natural resources. America was fortunate in being populated by a biased sample of mankind. Those who came were harassed into leaving Europe because of unusual attributes. Many criminals "transported" to Georgia and Australia from England were guilty of strange crimes—disagreement with the crown, religious heresy, failure to pay debts, resort to black markets, and evasion of economic restrictions on open-market competition in England. Murderers were more likely to receive capital punishment—which is not to assert that none was transported. In general, those who came were escaping regimentation.

During the advance to the West, people who occupied and cleared the land could claim it as private property. They could sell it or borrow against it; they could profiteer; they didn't have to *stay* on it in order to obtain the value of its income, as one must today in many foreign countries that ban absentee landlords or land sale—for example, Mexico, Iran, Egypt, and India. They could "capitalize" and be directed by the profits from present market value of the future consequences of their present actions. The coordinating, incentive effects of a market-directed system were relatively strong. Prices, profits, and resource mobility were influenced by open-market competition—relative to many countries today in which property rights and markets are curtailed. Suppression of open-market competition and incentives by political competition for power over prices and production and by prohibitions on market exchanges reduces the scope of specialization in achieving growth of income and wealth. Despite these disadvantages, can the political authorities provide other, offsetting advantages? A definitive answer cannot be given. Adam Smith believed that restrained access to open markets suppressed growth. But others hold that a socialized economy can achieve a higher rate of growth by government control. Undoubtedly, a higher *proportion* of income can be saved by government action. The issue is whether a higher rate is desirable on those terms, and whether the higher proportion of diverted income will in fact be invested *successfully with as high a future yield*. The debate waxes eloquent and emotional, but the evidence is conclusive only to the adherents of each position.

The ever increasing flow of goods and services which provides economic betterment is not produced with an unlimited supply of resources. The overriding economic fact of scarcity calls for productive efficiency. And efficiency, in turn, requires that some resources be devoted to capital goods: factories, equipment, dams, harbors, roads, schools.

Assistance from abroad may be intended to help in the accumulation of capital. Capital accumulation doubtless is a *necessary* condition of economic development, but it is not a *sufficient* condition. And foreign aid is neither necessary nor sufficient for an appreciable degree of capital accumulation—a degree which, however, many will deem inadequate on various grounds. The benefit of outside aid to underdeveloped countries, while scarcely negligible, is basically limited, because (1) growth requires more than capital, and (2) "saving" must be done by the growing country itself.

We shall pursue only briefly the growth prerequisites other than capital—the "social," "psychological," and "political" as well as narrowly "economic." Are there enough literate and energetic workers? Are there enough experienced and imaginative entrepreneurs? Is there a favorable ratio of working force to other means of production? Are there adequate incentives for efficient work—and appropriate penalties for inefficiency? Is the government sufficiently stable, consistent, and honest to maintain economic, political, and civil order, to generate confidence in a future for which plans may be made, and probably to undertake certain production projects not attractive enough commercially to engage private enterprises? Are the mores, philosophy, and aspirations of the community cordial to "growth" activities? Are the people sufficiently flexible and mobile, geographically and occupationally? Can population increase be kept under control?

Note the words of a man who was for fourteen years in the "development business," first as a vice-president of the International Bank for Reconstruction and Development and then as president of the International Finance Corporation:

> Let us briefly examine some of the frequently cited causes of underdevelopment.
>
> It is often claimed that geography and natural resources are determining. They are of course important. . . . But resources lie inert and have no economic worth except as people bring them into use. It is easy to attribute the progress of the United States to its wide expanse and abundant physical resources. However, other areas—in Latin America, Africa, Asia—have comparable natural wealth, but most of it is still untouched. On the other hand, there are countries in Western Europe with limited fertile land and meager mineral deposits, yet they have achieved high levels of economic life. . . .
>
> Perhaps most often lack of capital is blamed. In the first place, there is in most developing countries more potential capital than is admitted. But large amounts are kept outside, because of political instability and depreciating currency at home. Or it is invested in often unproductive land, low priority buildings, or otherwise hoarded. . . . Over the postwar period immense sums have been made available to the developing areas. Some of these funds have been well applied and have produced sound results, others have not. . . . If [money] is applied to uneconomic purposes, or if good projects are poorly planned and executed, the results will be minus, not plus. The effective spending of large funds requires experience, competence, honesty and organization. Lacking any of these factors, large injections of capital into developing countries can cause more harm than good. The test of how much additional capital is required for development is how much a country can effectively apply within any given period, not how much others are willing to supply.
>
> It is popular in many quarters to charge colonialism with lack of development in territories which have been dependent. This argument seems less persuasive when we observe that a number of countries which have been their own masters for long periods are no further advanced.
>
> I am, therefore, forced to the conclusion that economic development or lack of it is primarily due to differences in people—in their attitudes, customs, traditions and the consequent differences in their political, social and religious institutions.[1]

---

[1] Robert L. Garner, International Finance Corporation, *Summary Proceedings, 1961 Annual Meeting of the Board of Governors*, September 21, 1961, pp. 4–6. "The slow rate of economic growth [in Asia and the Far East] after the war and in the early 1960's in spite of a general improvement in the rate of domestic saving and capital formation, including a large flow of foreign assistance in the form of grants, loans, and direct investment, indicates that capital resources alone are not enough for bringing about a satisfactory rate of growth. Countries have become more and more convinced that improvement in their human resources, in the form of more active participation of the masses in improving the social, economic, and political situation and structure, of sound planning and policy making, of better leadership, organization, and administration, of higher incentives in taking risks and introducing improved production methods, and of acquiring higher skills, is a necessary condition of achieving a sustained and accelerated economic development." From United Nations, *Economic Survey of Asia and the Far East, 1965* (Bangkok, 1966), p. 3.

Sources of Wealth

Having suggested that the world is a complicated place, we note the second reason why foreign aid cannot by itself ensure foreign growth: The would-be growers must, in a real sense, do their own saving.

Aside from receipts of gifts and investment from abroad, an economy can accumulate wealth only if it saves. There are two basic internal sources of wealth: (1) Some resources that are now producing for current consumption may shift into production of capital goods. (2) The total output of the economy may be increased, with the additional output (or some of it) being channeled into capital production. In either case, total output is greater than consumption; the excess requires an act of saving and constitutes investment.

Wealth accumulation, then, involves currently importing or producing more than is currently consumed. Current production in excess of current consumption makes it feasible to devote output to capital goods. But even if country Alpha consumes all of her own output, could she not build up her capital with gifts from abroad or with borrowing? Define "saving" as the gap between consumption and the *whole* of the community's available income, including that supplied by foreigners as well as from domestic production. Then outside aid will not contribute to Alphian capital accumulation if Alpha fails to save and instead uses the foreign resources simply for more current consumption.[2]

1, 2

Greater Availability of Wealth?

You hear about high-interest-rate versus low-interest-rate policies. (The former is also called "tight-money" policy.) Lower interest rates—i.e., higher prices of capital goods relative to prices of short-lived goods or to current consumption services—encourage a higher rate of investment (production of capital goods) by making it more profitable. The problem, however, is to reduce interest rates and get that shift in relative prices. We might encourage people to want to save and lend more. (How?) If successful, that would increase the supply of lending through the loan markets and also it would increase the demand for capital goods. That *alteration of preferences* would lower the market rate of interest and encourage a more rapid growth-rate for wealth.

A second way is to make investment more productive and profitable. (But how?)

A third way to encourage more investment is to make people less fearful of theft of the wealth they accumulate. An unwillingness or inability to strengthen property rights is one of the obstacles to rapid growth in many poorer, undeveloped countries of the world.

---

[2] And note this: "The earmarking of particular foreign loans or grants to specific investment projects may do something to ensure the productive use of funds, but is not by any means a basic remedy. Only where there is no domestic saving at all to start with can such earmarking be fully effective. The Austrian government, so the story goes, asked for the release of counterpart funds to reconstruct the Vienna opera. The E. C. A. [Economic Cooperation Administration, directing the Marshall Plan for postwar European reconstruction] is said to have replied that this would not be a productive investment and that the release could not be granted for this purpose. Then the Austrian government remembered that it was itself financing the construction of an electric power plant in the mountains. It went back to the E. C. A. and asked for a release of counterpart funds to pay for this piece of construction, to which the E. C. A. agreed. So all that happened was a switch: the wily Austrians, having got the E. C. A. to take over the financing of the power plant, now financed the reconstruction of the opera from their own resources." Ragnar Nurkse, *Problems of Capital Formation in Underdeveloped Countries* (Oxford: Basil Blackwell, 1953), pp. 95–96.

Some countries (for instance, Switzerland) have superb reputations for observing property rights, but some other countries (such as Brazil, Chile, Mexico, Iran, Egypt, Algeria, India, and Indonesia) have somewhat different reputations.

Fourth, private investment can be redirected by tax-financed government investment, on the belief that private wealth owners refuse to invest enough in "vital" projects. One way is to tax private wealth and use the proceeds for the kind of investment activity deemed more appropriate. One counter effect of this is to reduce saving out of the reduced after-tax private disposable income. Furthermore, individuals, to escape the tax, will invest in goods that yield more nonpecuniary income, since nonpecuniary income is rarely taxed as heavily as pecuniary income. (An example of this is evident in the United States, where homeowners are not taxed on the incomes from owning their own homes, whereas an investment in rental apartments or business tools yields a taxable money income.)

Fifth, the government may seek to increase investment in a particular kind of wealth —namely, education, research, or invention, i.e., public goods. Private investors in the discovery of new knowledge find that other people can use it at practically no cost— which reduces the incentive-reward value of the discovered knowledge to the initial discoverer. How much income should be diverted by governmental authority to research activity in the hope of discovering new principles and ideas that will enhance wealth (at a rate greater than the rate of interest)? If some investment in research seems to be wasted, the researcher can always claim that the real gains aren't perceived by the critic, that they are dispersed and not objectively measured. But the person footing the bill may just as honestly contend that the expenditure is really only consumption under the guise of research. There is as yet no generally accepted, objective test against which the value of more or less research can be assessed.

3, 4, 5, 6

Growth, Property Rights, Pollution, and Conservation

To maintain or increase our future wealth, it is often argued that we should restrict exploitation of many of our natural resources—for example, forests, fertile lands, and iron ore. But this argument fails to comprehend the meaning of capital values of resources and to recognize that "using" goods *can* mean converting them into even more valuable forms of wealth. If a tree is more valuable for the future than are the current goods that could be made with the lumber now, the present capital value of the live tree will exceed the value of the lumber in the felled tree. Consequently, the tree will not be cut now. All this would reflect the fact that capital goods made from current use of the lumber will give a smaller future income than the standing tree; otherwise, the tree would be cut. People can save and invest in trees, or they can save and invest by cutting trees and producing wealth with wooden products. Comparison of present values indicates which of the two will give the greater wealth. This explains why it is *not* true that the private-property system tends to cut trees "too" fast. It does "conserve" them by capitalizing the future lumber values to present market values to determine whether the live tree value is greater than the felled value.

But there are circumstances in which people will be induced to cut the trees even though the live value exceeds the lumber value. If no one owns a tree and the only way to capture the value of the tree is to cut it and take the wood, no one will have wealth incentives—or legal power—to preserve the tree from those who cut it now for lumber.

This is why the forests in many parts of England and China were prematurely cut. They were *community* goods—first come, first served. *Lack of well-defined, transferable property rights,* not personal greed, was responsible for this "wasteful" use of resources.

This same analysis can be applied to fish and wild game. Uncaught fish belong to no one. Everyone has an incentive to catch them, regardless of whether they may be worth more in the future. If someone had the right to prevent others from catching them, that owner would have an incentive to avoid premature or "over"fishing. In this way, fishing would be restrained, if it is "excessive," as is claimed for tuna, seals, whales, and salmon. As a substitute for property rights in "wild animals," governments have sometimes managed to reach agreements limiting fishing in order to prevent waste. Similarly, so long as no one owns the lakes or rivers or subterranean water in the United States, and so long as rights to present *and future* uses are owned by no one, everyone has less incentive to use water in its most valuable ways. First come, first served. Everyone dumps his garbage in the lake, since the loss of value of more polluted water is not thrust upon him or upon anyone with sufficient force to control pollution. But an owner would suffer that loss of value and would therefore prevent others from fouling the lake. Since most (but not all!) major lakes are not held as private property, lakes are polluted with garbage.[3] Water, beaches, and air provide examples. Water is today generally, though not universally, owned only by the person who "uses" it. Today people build aqueducts to sources of water, even though the water, if currently used, would not justify the present costs. Why build the aqueducts? The construction of the aqueduct and "using" the water now, often far in excess of currently economical amounts, is simply a (costly) way of establishing property rights to continued access to future flows of water. In the absence of property rights in the water, governments will ultimately intervene (1) to take action of the kind a private owner would take as a means of preventing uneconomic wastage of the fresh water or (2) to establish explicit and exchangeable property rights.

A similar threat once existed for petroleum. A form of solution was reached when subsurface oil rights were pro-rated to surface area owners. Now no one has an incentive to pump oil excessively in order to catch it first and get its value, as with the fish or non-owned goods. (This kind of ownership is *slowly* being developed for water.)

A specification of private-property rights in air is beyond our abilities. The fleeting nature of air is too great to do other than resort to nonmarket political controls, which are gradually developing.

Conservationist contentions. The conservationists have two contentions. First, the actual rate of saving of resources should be larger. One way is to force people to save by not letting the goods be used for consumption. Clearly, this contention assumes that people prefer more present consumption relative to future wealth than that which the conservationists think desirable. Second, people have the wrong idea about the most valuable *kinds* of goods to preserve for the future. Wildlife and natural-wilderness advocates want to close off certain areas from use as residences or as resort and ski areas. This has nothing to do with conservation or growth of *wealth.* It is instead an argument about which people should have which preferences satisfied. This is the issue with which this book started, the question of allocation of an existing stock of goods among competing claimants.

[3] One of the authors of this text owns land adjoining Lake Arrowhead and also land at Lake Tahoe. Arrowhead is owned by a private corporation; Tahoe, owned by no one, is divided between California and Nevada. At one lake he dumps his sewage in the lake, at the other he does not. Why is he an "irresponsible" person at one lake and not at the other?

Conservationists propose to control the rate of use with government planning boards. However, as we know, there is another kind of solution: to establish salable property rights in resources, rather than to let them be claimed by the first person who makes use of the resources. Then, like the tree, they will remain untouched until their use is economic. It is the *absence* of the private-property system that contributes to what appears to be a wasteful use of resources.

Personal Income and Wealth Differences

Age Differences

Assume every person will have an identical lifetime history of income, rising to a peak at about age 50 or 60. If the population is composed of people of *different* ages, then at any moment current incomes will be unequal, with the younger having the smaller earnings. Yet every person could have the same life history of earnings. All are equally wealthy, when adjusted to a lifetime basis or to a capital value at, say, age 18.

Investments and Income Dispersion

A source of income dispersion for people (of the same age) is differences in past investment. Some people will save at an early age and invest in property, personal knowledge, and skills. At an older age they will have higher incomes than people who earlier consumed more of their income. Those who saved earlier sacrificed the pleasure of earlier consumption for the sake of more income or wealth later. (Does a person who saves a larger fraction of his income in his youth for high consumption after retirement have a greater "life utility"?) The upshot is that savings when young can lead to greater wealth (property and personal) in older age. This will increase the *old* age dispersion of reported income. But it represents a voluntary temporal choice by each person and does not necessarily indicate unequal wealth or life-time earnings.

Medical doctors, college teachers, and scientists with a doctoral degree have larger wealth at age 30 because they invested more during college age. If a high school graduate were to go to work and save 75 percent of his income for about seven years he, too, would accumulate a respectable amount by age 25.[4]

For perspective, Figure 24–1 shows some differences in median salaries by occupation and sex. It shows also the temporal rise in median incomes by color and sex (expressed in 1968 dollar equivalents to remove the upward bias of inflation).

Change and Imperfect Foresight and Choice of Risk

Earnings over a lifetime do not have a gradually growing pattern. Chance makes for extra-high incomes in some years and lower ones in others and this too contributes to the

---

[4] If he earns $4,000 a year for seven years (and saves $3,000 each year) he will, at 8 percent, accumulate a wealth of about $27,000 in seven years. And this would yield him an annuity thereafter for thirty years of about $2,500 a year. In other words, at the end of seven years he would have a gross income from his labor *and* his accumulated wealth of $4,000 + $2,500 = $6,500 annually, ignoring the growth in his personal labor-earning power. Will your college education do as well for you? On the average, it is about a toss-up!

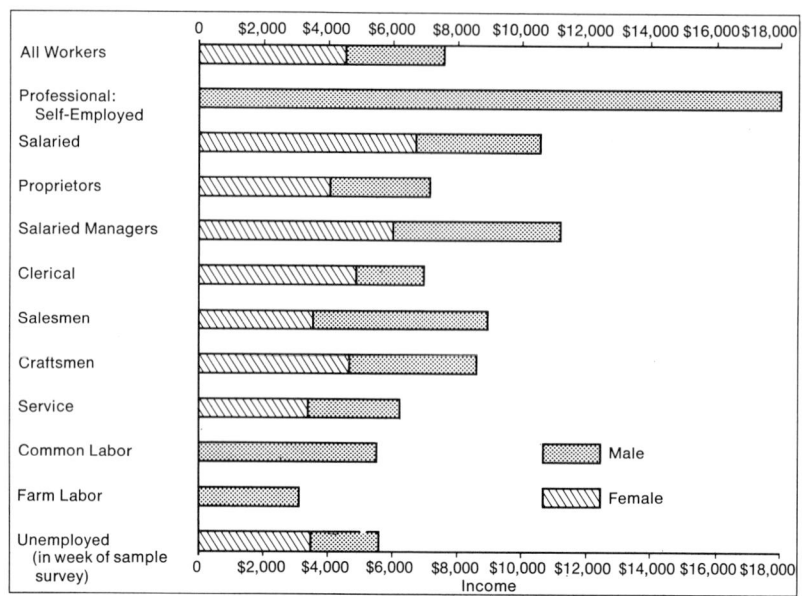

FIGURE 24–1. 1968 U. S. Median Year-Round Incomes

Differences in median incomes (income of the middle person in a class) are shown for female and male groups as well as by occupation. In some classes—self-employed, common-labor, and farm-labor—too few women were in the sample survey class to permit reliable estimates. The unemployed class is people unemployed in the particular week the sample survey was conducted but employed most of the rest of the year. Note that proprietors of businesses (but not those in professions—doctors, lawyers, dentists, architects, etc.) received lower incomes than salaried managers of similar businesses. We wonder how much a proprietor's status should reflect changes in value of the business, as distinct from his salary.

dispersion in the distribution of realized earnings at any time. Business earnings (industrial, commercial, and agricultural) are especially volatile compared to earnings of employees or salaried people. There is no way to avoid this volatility, given our imperfect foresight. The question is, "Who will bear it?" We can all share it and thus spread that volatility over everyone so that it contributes to each a smaller fraction of their total earnings volatility, or we can let some people escape it more fully by inducing others to bear a larger share. This is what is involved in the specialization of asset holdings by property owners and profit receivers. Those who choose a larger fraction of risky (volatile) earnings will show a greater dispersion of later incomes. Some businessmen are very wealthy and some are poor; self-employed lawyers have a greater dispersion of incomes over their lifetimes *and* in any year at any one age than do salaried lawyers. In part, this is the result of a choice of a *chance* for more income relative to greater probability of an intermediate income.

Obstacles exist to full exchange and specialization in risk bearing. To the extent that it is easier (cheaper) for people to negotiate exchanges of rights to various types of goods, this specialization is more effective. Investment in personal talents and skills is believed to be more difficult than in physical property. It is said that young people have a harder time borrowing for their own education than they do for housing or cars. However, in view of the subsidized college education for some young people, compared to their

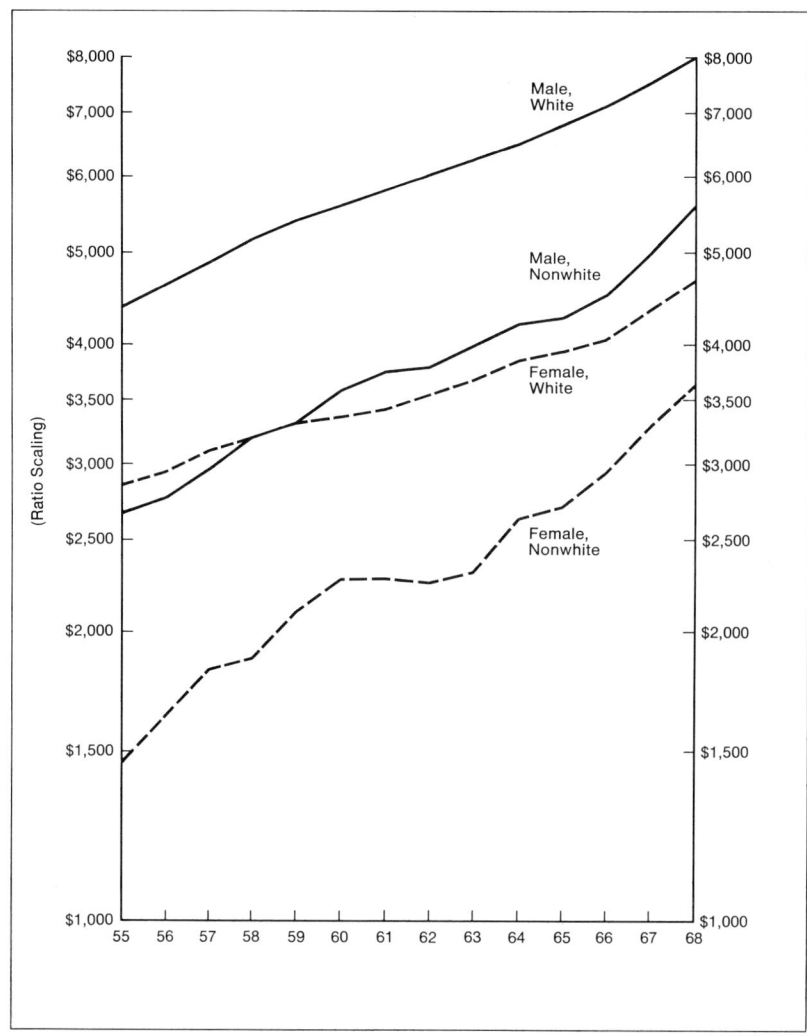

FIGURE 24-2. Median Incomes, U. S. Year-Round Full-Time Workers, 1954–1968

Incomes are in terms of 1968 dollar values. Price level was about 33 percent higher in 1968 than in 1955; therefore, figures shown for 1955 have been increased 33 percent above their 1955 nominal amounts so that upward trend reflects essentially the real income increase. (For each succeeding year since 1955, the upward adjustment is slightly less.)

ability to get "free" cars, land, or buildings, it is not clear whether investment (at the less educated taxpayers' expense) in personal skills suffers a net handicap.

In addition to age, investment, education, and change, there are other forces for inequality of reported annual, as well as life-time, earnings.

Market versus Nonmarket Income

Reported *money* earnings differ because people receive different portions of their earnings in nonmarketed goods (farmers versus city dwellers); although it is the same income, the money income flowing through the markets differs, thus giving another source of difference in personal money incomes.[5]

Although possessing the same present wealth potential, some people prefer to take life easier and enjoy more leisure rather than marketable purchases. The teacher who takes an easier life, with three months absence from teaching, has a smaller money income than if he worked all year. Money incomes will differ, because the "income" is taken in different proportions of marketed goods and services.

Housewives' services are never included in typical income measures. Yet, if the services of a housewife were to be purchased, they would usually run from $2,000 to at least $6,000 per year. Caring for children, cooking food, shopping, caring for the home, planning purchases—all these could be provided by paid servants, governesses, and housekeepers. If that were done, an explicit market measure would be available. As it is, the income value of those activities is never included. This understates the income of poorer families by a larger proportion than it does that of richer families. A husband earning $4,000 a year would probably have services costing close to $2,000 provided by his wife, equivalent to half his income. A person earning $40,000 a year would have services provided by his wife to the household at less than $20,000. Ignoring this makes money income distributions more unequal than real income distributions, because it is customary to classify money income recipients as "families," or as what are known as "spending units"—a group of related people who live together and pool their income.

Endowment Differences

Although all the preceding factors are sufficient to introduce a wide dispersion of earnings as of any moment, two of the most striking factors are differences in ability and endowments. In a sense these two are the same thing, for ability is an endowment received from our parents, just as is any physical wealth. The genetic skills and talents with which they endow us are not a result of their lifetime activities—it is just "natural"; but the propertied wealth and culture they bestow on us are more dependent on their conscious action.

Be careful of one common error. It is not the *inheritance* of property wealth that contributes to dispersion or inequality of wealth. It is the prior *accumulation* of wealth at different rates that contributes to the differences in wealth holdings. The inheritance merely continues it (and provides a convenient place to tax it away). The wealth of the Sinatra larynx, the Racquel Welch body, the Koufax arm, the von Neumann brain, the Kennedy personality were not taxed as an inheritance from their parents; but the Ford, Getty, and Sinatra endowment of propertied wealth to their children is heavily taxed—though not the Sinatra voice inherited by his children.

The Poor

"The poor will always be with us, by definition." But will the distressed? Even though the bottom 20 percent of income receivers in the United States may be enormously richer than most of the population in India, China, or Afghanistan, the concern for the local

---

[5] Doctors typically provide services for other doctors at "nominal" charges. The "real" income of the patient is larger than indicated by his money income, and services provided by doctors are larger.

poor or distressed will not thereby disappear. First, a few of the poorest in the United States, and they are very poor and few indeed, would not be much better off in absolute terms than in other, poorer countries. Second, even if our poorest were rich compared to other countries, there would still be reason to ask if the poorest here were being denied opportunities to realize their potential. And even at their potential, some (enfeebled or crippled) would have so low an income that the rest would be willing to do something to improve the lot of the poorest.

Deciding which families are in the "poverty" class requires, first, a choice of the standard of income that constitutes "poverty." This reflects one's beliefs about what could and should be the income of most people in the economy, and this will vary among places and times. In the United States, one criterion has been proposed by the Federal Social Security Administration, allowing for family size, ages, and locality. Table 24–1 shows its poverty-family income varying from about $1,100 for a single-person farm family to $5,400 for a seven-person urban family (about $800 a person). Without arguing the appropriate definition of poverty, let us inquire about factors affecting those who transiently fall in the poverty category in any given year and those who tend to remain there.

TABLE 24–1. Poverty Income Lines, 1967

Household Characteristic	Poverty Income Line Nonfarm Household	Farm Household
1 member	$1,635	$1,145
65 years and over	1,565	1,095
Under 65 years	1,685	1,195
2 members	2,115	1,475
Head 65 years and over	1,970	1,380
Head under 65 years	2,185	1,535
3 members	2,600	1,815
4 members	3,335	2,345
5 members	3,930	2,755
6 members	4,410	3,090
7 members or more	5,430	3,790

Note.—Poverty income standards are defined by the Social Security Administration; they take into account family size, composition, and place of residence. Source: Department of Health, Education, and Welfare.

The proportion of the population falling in this category has decreased since 1945 and almost certainly had long been decreasing before that (reliable data are not available). Figure 24–3 shows that the fraction has declined from about a third to a tenth. (Nominal income defining poverty has been adjusted over the interval.)

For at least three reasons, these data overstate the fraction that tends to remain in poverty. First, personal incomes fluctuate for transient reasons. In some years, the income of a family can fall into the poverty category, while in other years it will be sufficiently high to average above the poverty line.

Second, about one-third of the families in the poverty group are families of old people (head of the household over 65). Many are living off their income *and* consuming their

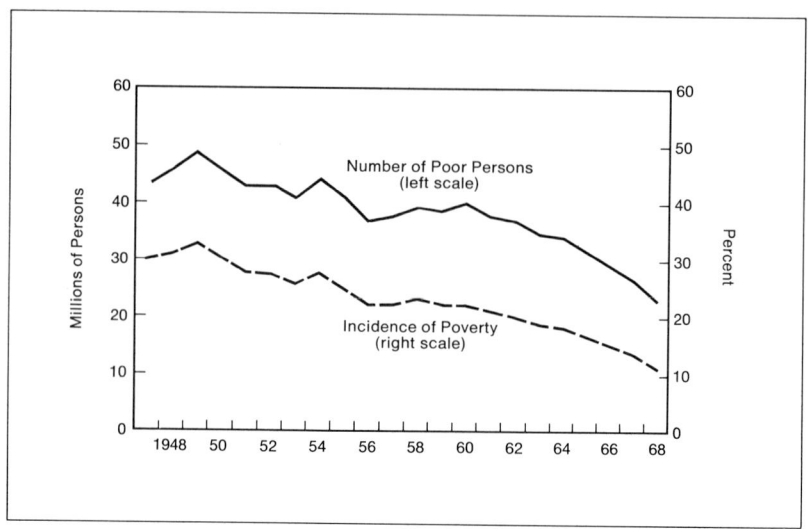

FIGURE 24-3. Number of Poor Persons and Incidence of Poverty

[1] Poor persons as percent of total noninstitutional population.
Note: Poverty is defined by the Social Security Administration poverty-income standard.
Sources: Department of Commerce, Department of Health, Education, and Welfare, Office of Economic Opportunity, and Council of Economic Advisers.

wealth, because of shorter life expectancy. This permits a higher standard of living than their income indicates.[6] Correcting for this bias would reduce the poverty group.

Third, immigrants (for example, Puerto Ricans) constitute disproportionately high membership in the poverty group—a characteristic of many immigrants in their initial years in the United States. This contributes toward a larger transient percentage of the population in the poverty group, until the immigrants rise to higher incomes. (While Puerto Ricans are about 8 percent of the New York City population, they represent about one-third of welfare recipients. No data exist to separate recent immigrants from longer-term residents.)

Who, then, tend to remain in the poverty group for many years?

Undoubtedly some of the poorest are incapable of producing a significantly greater income for themselves. Some with normal capacities lack the drive and responsibility to produce and save toward normal contingencies. Some were, in childhood, not given the kind of education that the rest of us received. Some are widowed, working mothers. Many of the poor are the very old, living off their wealth and relatives and reporting small incomes.[7] And students will also have noticed many young married couples (in college) with low *current* incomes.

---

[6] Some even give all their wealth to their children to qualify for welfare, relying upon their children to assure them of support for adequate consumption.

[7] A person with a life expectancy of five years and a wealth of $20,000 would report an income of perhaps one thousand dollars, although he could consume at the rate of about $6,000 a year for five years.

Families whose primary source of income is from a woman, an aged person, a farmer, a Negro, an immigrant, or a person lacking a high school education are more heavily represented in the poor. The immigrant status seems transitory; in a few years, once the language is well learned, their representation in the poor falls off.

One's responses to these varied situations differ. For some we are torn with sympathy and a willingness to help. For others we withhold aid. We do not look at just the current money income and conclude that for *every* low-income recipient the same corrective or alleviative actions are desirable. To analyze the problems of the poor or of the very poor is to analyze a variety of situations.

Family responsibility for relatives is a prime means of providing aid to the poor. The discrimination displayed in voluntary charitable aid reflects our judgments about the merits of each case. Social policy via government action cannot display such personal discrimination. When one is dispensing other people's money, extra care must be taken to ensure that the dispenser observes approved standards of discrimination. Tax-financed wealth transfers to revise the distribution of wealth are part of our social policy. The graduated income and inheritance taxes take a larger portion from the higher incomes. But other taxes, like the sales and property tax, seem to take larger proportions from the lower income groups. For example, it has been estimated that for families of under $2,000 income per year, federal and local taxes take over 40 percent of income, compared to about 25 percent for middle-income families and 40 percent for high-income families ($15,000 and over). But after allowing for transfers of tax proceeds back to families (social security payments, welfare, and unemployment compensation), the under-$2,000 families get a *net increase* of 80 percent of their pre-tax income. The near-poverty group, between $2,000 and $3,000, on *net* pays out about 15 percent of its income. And for higher-income groups the net outpayment percentage remains over 40 percent. The government's explicit tax and transfer system contributes a redistribution of wealth toward the very-low-income classes.

More direct aid to very-low-income groups has been proposed. One form, known as the reverse or negative income tax, would provide to those earning less than a specified amount a subsidy sufficient to bring them up to the standard, while those above that standard would, as now, pay taxes depending upon their income. This has been proposed as a substitute for the entire welfare system whereby each case is individually examined before giving aid. The negative income-tax plan would be less expensive to administer, but it would not be as discriminating, nor would it contain the purported remedial elements of the current welfare system. And it might have severe disincentive effects, although it is contended that few would sacrifice chances to rise *above* $2,000–$3,000 per year just to be *assured* $2,000–$3,000 without work by remaining poor. It may be that moves toward the negative income-tax system will be made—without abandoning the current welfare system.

To strike more directly at the causes of low income, better education at the elementary level for low-income-family children has been proposed, and federal programs to that end are being initiated. Typically, high school education has not provided sufficient vocational training to those not continuing to college; possibly more on-the-job training will be governmentally subsidized as an alternative to vocational training in the public schools.

To anyone having read this far, it is unnecessary to emphasize that aid to the lowest-income groups could be obtained also by reducing the extent to which jobs and markets are closed to potential entrants in various unions and businesses. This group-enforced closure to jobs is under heavy—whether or not effective—pressure. A comparison of the distribution of income after taxes with that before taxes usually shows a less unequal distribution, at least in the sense that the extremes are less disparate. Unfortunately that comparison is defective because it does not allow for the distribution of government services financed by the taxes. If the services are distributed even more heavily to the richer (than are the taxes) the richer would be aided and the poor hurt. Many government services are favorable to the richer income groups. Publicly subsidized golf courses, better schools, parks, and roads in richer residential areas suggest that, without more data than are now at hand, no clear answer can be given about the over-all effects of government tax and expenditure activities.

Government social welfare and poverty program activities are designed not merely to relieve the indigent by transferring wealth, but also to foster rehabilitation, training, or increase productive ability. There are some who argue that the poor, with relatively few exceptions, are poor because they have not worked as diligently and been as careful in saving and husbanding their income as have those who are not poor. Others have argued that the poor are poor for reasons not of their own making. "Poverty is the social by-product of a complex, highly interdependent, dynamic economy; therefore responsibility for alleviating this poverty rests primarily upon society." Both arguments, one placing blame on the individual and the other on the society, are defective. The first does not imply that nothing should be done for (or to?) those who are so irresponsible as to be poor. The second argument is defective in that the poor existed even when society was less complex, dependent, and dynamic; furthermore, everyone, rich and poor alike, lives in that kind of society, so should everyone be taken care of by everyone else? Neither argument gets us very far in deciding whether or not to give aid. More germane is the issue of what kind of aid to give—in what form, how much, and under what conditions? Should we take over their discretion and provide them with all the amenities as we do with institutionalized people and public schools?

Finally, poverty exists in socialist, communist, mercantilist, capitalist, and whatever kind of system has ever existed. All have extremes. A socialist state may not have as many millionaires (in market value) as a capitalist state, but in the socialist state the relative political power of the political authority over resources is greater. It has more "political millionaires." Taking into account *market* and *political* access to and control over economic resources, there is little basis to state in which society wealth is apportioned to greater extremes.

Group Differences in Income and Wealth

Explaining why personal incomes differ does not justify or evaluate the propriety of their differences. Nor should it be forgotten that differentiation is one thing and absolute income another. A rich society with large dispersion or a poor one with small may have entirely different connotations. A rich society with a wide dispersion may still leave the lowest 10 percent with more income and wealth than the middle 10 percent in a poorer society. The collected evidence of economies like that of the United States leaves no doubt that over the decades the rise in wealth and incomes has *not* been achieved by a small fraction getting wealthier while the masses stayed poor. The upward trend has moved up the lowest 10 percent by at least the same multiple that it has the top 10 percent. But using a worldwide reference, is it true that over the past century or two the worldwide distribution has seen the bottom quarter move up in the same proportion as the top? The common impression is that it has not. (But if we consider that a poorer person had a very short life expectancy a couple of centuries ago, then the increase in life length is a form of greater income and wealth that we must not overlook.)

Nothing so far said denies that discrimination and restrictions on opportunities are important factors contributing to *group* income and wealth inequalities, but they are only part of the contributing factors—which is not to suggest that they can therefore be regarded as unimportant and irreducible.

The poorer areas within a country are not necessarily a result of inefficiency or inadequate savings. Less habitable deserts or mountainous regions do not permit high productivity to anyone living there; to bring in resources like water or to exploit fertile soil by terracing is expensive. People shun those areas for others richer in natural resources. If people living in a naturally barren area are not allowed to emigrate to the geographically richer areas, they will have to use their resources as best they can, but they simply cannot expect to be as wealthy as people in the better areas. Only outside gifts permitting them to consume more could enable a higher rate of *consumption*—or invasion of the richer areas.

On the other hand, all areas have the potential for some development and would benefit from interregional trade. As specialization and local exchange permit higher incomes, so trade with people farther away or in other countries will bring the same result. For example, the ability of the United States and Puerto Rico to exchange goods with no taxes or imposed barriers has enriched many (but not all) Puerto Ricans and Americans. Capital goods move to Puerto Rico, and Puerto Ricans move to the United States. Mobility of human and nonhuman resources enables people to enhance their per-capita incomes, either by moving to more productive areas or by bringing in nonhuman capital goods to areas where it is profitable. Had that trade been prohibited, both would have been less rich. Artificial or imaginary lines on the earth demarking countries do not alter the consequences of specialization and exchange across those lines. As we have seen earlier, trade with new people helps some and sometimes hurts others who are displaced into other activities. Closing markets or areas to outsider entrants is one way to protect incumbent producers and enhance their wealth, though at a *greater* cost to the whole of society.

Much recent talk about black capitalism for the black ghettos reflects confusion. If black capitalism means that blacks are to rely only on black people for capital goods and resources, they will deny to themselves some cheaper sources of goods from white capitalists. If by that term they mean that blacks will patronize only black-owned stores, then black consumers will restrict themselves to a smaller set of competitors and are going to accept lower consumption (by paying higher prices). If black capitalism means that blacks will save and invest more in businesses that they *and* whites operate and will move more black labor to white areas, then the blacks will gain, and so will the whites, especially the white capitalists who save most and provide most of the loans and capital to blacks. On the other hand, black labor, now entering into competition more broadly and with less discrimination, will compete with white labor and, because of its greater availability as a close substitute for white labor, reduce the advance of white wages.[8]

As less-skilled white labor is disadvantaged by more open competition as blacks move into white labor markets, so black capitalists will suffer if white capitalists shift their

---

[8] This is one reason Northern whites propose *national* high minimum wage laws—to prevent black labor from access to employment markets at wage rates that would make it profitable to hire and employ blacks as competitors to higher-paid whites. See the discussion on pages 439–440. You will find no laws imposing a minimum interest rate or profit rate on capital goods before they are allowed to be used. Why not? Are white capitalists too social-minded, or are they unable to find a way to enforce such a law (because the profitability or realized rate of return cannot be determined in advance)?

capital to any areas dominated by black capitalists. One might anticipate that black savers and lenders (capitalists) would advocate black separatism, to restrict the competition of white capitalists, thereby enabling the black providers of capital to black people to get higher interest or profits on their investments. It is, however, extremely difficult to restrict the flow of savings and resources from one area to another, unless the areas are politically independent, and it is extremely difficult for a small group of black capitalists to get laws prohibiting entry of capital goods or savings from white people to black borrower-users—fortunately for black people as a whole.

Some Ghetto Economics

It has become common in popular journalism and speech-making to claim that ghetto merchants exploit customers. (Unfortunately, those making the charge generally avoid defining "exploitation" and do not substantiate their accusations.)

It is true that ghetto residents tend to pay more for their groceries, etc., than do those residing in middle-income communities. This is in part due to higher operating costs. Ghetto stores are more likely to be subjected to vandalism and theft; the employees are more likely to be subjected to injury than are nonghetto counterparts. This is true regardless of skin color of the employer or employees. The resulting higher insurance rates increase operating costs; premium pay to employees is necessitated by the greater physical danger; the self-employed merchant must be compensated for the additional danger in operating in the ghetto. When all firms are confronted with higher costs, there are higher prices and fewer firms, although each is receiving only normal competitive returns.

Interest rates charged by merchants in ghetto neighborhoods are higher than elsewhere. But competition among merchants selling "on time," as well as competition with other sources of borrowed funds (e.g., pawnbrokers) and with self-financing, drive interest rates down to a level equivalent to that which lenders could obtain elsewhere, given adjustments for operating costs and risk. Ghetto residents (except the Chinese!) are less likely to repay a debt than are those with greater wealth and more stable employment. In addition, poorer people are likely to give a smaller proportion of the total price as a down payment and are likely to make more frequent payments in smaller amounts. These factors increase the lender's risk and the cost of administering the loan. Thus, higher interest charges appear to reflect higher operating costs and greater risk, rather than monopoly or exploitation.

Neither merchant nor customer "exploits" the other. This does not imply that all prices will be uniform. For example, ghetto stores which are open nights and Sunday charge higher prices. From morning until early evening on Monday through Saturday, the high-priced store has little business. Late in the evening and on Sunday this store tends to have more patrons. Late hours are costly, since the merchant and his employees value their leisure. In addition, ghetto crime increases significantly after sundown. Patrons who purchase goods during the off-hours pay a premium for this costly service.

This analysis indicates that, in general, merchants are not exploiting customers. The merchants are responding to higher costs of operation, greater uncertainty as to collection of debts, and their consumers' preferences for lower-priced, lower-quality goods. It is dishonest ghetto residents who are increasing operating costs, and thereby prices, to honest ghetto residents.

The analysis does not imply that nothing can be done to reduce the costs of ghetto residence. On the contrary, it suggests several possibilities. Legal services to the poor could be expanded and combined with more stringent law enforcement to strengthen the market forces that discourage dishonesty on the part of merchants and customers. Greater efforts by coordinated local action groups to discourage vandalism, shop-lifting, and armed robbery could be very useful. Recent events in Los Angeles indicate that cooperating community groups can be effective.

National Differences in Per Capita Income and Growth

The "natural increase" of population equals the birth rate minus the death rate. Population changes slowly if both rates are nearly the same, as they are in most of Western Europe, North America, and Japan, where annual birth rates are generally around 17 to 25 per 1,000 population and death rates are around 8 to 12, giving a population increase of about 5 to 15 per 1,000—an average of about 1 percent annually. (The U. S. rate of population increase is approximately 1.1 percent per year.)

Both birth and death rates are high in the Far East and Asia (excluding Japan), Africa, and the Near East, with birth rates of 35 to 45 and death rates of 25 to 35. The rate of increase again is in the neighborhood of 1 percent. (India's rate is about 1.8 percent.)

An intermediate group, which continues to have high birth rates but has attained a lowered death rate and rapid population growth, includes Eastern Europe, Russia, and Latin America. Birth rates are, say, 30 to 45 and death rates are generally from 10 to 20, giving a rate of population growth of perhaps 2 percent, with a few rates as high as 3.5 to 4 percent.

The rate of change in national income minus the rate of population change approximately equals the rate of change in per capita income. Obviously, if national income increases at only 1 or even 2 percent per year, per capita income can hardly increase much, and it may even fall. Compare the U. S. and Mexico, the latter having a population increase of about 3.5 percent. If per capita income is to grow at 1 percent, U. S. income must grow by $1.0 + 1.1 = 2.1$ percent; but in Mexico the required income growth is $1.0 + 3.5 = 4.5$ percent. Or, to reverse the problem, if national income grows at 4 percent in both countries, U. S. per capita income grows at $4.0 - 1.1 = 2.9$ percent, while in Mexico it grows at only $4.0 - 3.5 = .5$ percent.

Americans, who are fabulously wealthy compared to most of the world's residents, should recognize that saving *may* be less attractive for the poor. The security of savings and the ability to invest as a shareholder in group enterprises are not as great in many countries as in the advanced Western nations. (With per capita income some ten or more times that of two-thirds of the world's people and a net saving rate of around 10 percent of national income, the average American saves each year more than the annual income of most of the inhabitants of the world.)

The Dismal Mathematics of Growth

An objective sometimes indicated, explicitly or implicitly, is that the tremendous absolute gap between per capita national incomes of richer and poorer areas should at least not increase and should even begin to decrease appreciably. One gathers from various statements that some time prior to Armageddon, the gap will—or must—be eliminated.

Pakistan representatives have asserted that the world looks for an early solution to the problem of "the slums of the world, which are otherwise called backward areas. A stable world order cannot be achieved with a growing disparity between the productivity and living standards of the underdeveloped and advanced countries."[9] We are warned that a "dual gap between the standards of life of the rich and the poor nations and between the political influence of the developing nations on the one hand and their economic opportunities on the other hand creates an explosive situation."[10] And Eugene R. Black, while president of the World Bank, agreed that we must not "be content to sit by and watch the gap widen between the standards of living. . . . Surely, if such a wide gap between standards of living . . . did not exist today—if during the last hundred years greater effort had been devoted towards improving conditions in the less developed areas of the world . . . —we might not today be witnessing so much social unrest. . . ."[11]

No one knows what tomorrow—much less the next century or two—holds. But it is suggestive to investigate the consequences of certain alternative and comparative reasonable rates of growth in per capita income. And the mathematics of income growth are not very comforting.

For our illustrative calculations, assume per capita annual income of the U. S. is $4,000 (in 1971, income per capita was about $3,800) and the income per person in country Alpha is $200. This ratio of 20:1 is probably representative of the income differential between the U. S. and many poor countries.[12]

---

[9] Ghulam Mohammed, International Monetary Fund, *Summary Proceedings, Fifth Annual Meeting,* 1950, p. 115; Mohamad Ali, International Bank of Reconstruction and Development, *Summary Proceedings, Annual Meeting of the Board of Governors,* Washington, D. C., 1953, p. 3. According to Tan Siew Sin, Minister of Finance, Malaya, ". . . the gap between the two groups tends to widen rather than to narrow . . . making industrialized countries richer and richer, and the developing countries poorer and poorer, comparatively speaking. It is clear, therefore, that our primary problem is to seek ways and means which would not only enable the developing countries to telescope into one generation what has taken the industrialized countries many decades and even centuries of economic endeavor to achieve but also to arrest the growing disparity between them." I.B.R.D., *Annual Meeting,* Washington, D. C., September 27, 1960, press release.

[10] David Horowitz, Governor, Bank of Israel, *Proceedings of the United Nations Conference on Trade and Development,* June 10, 1964, p. 502.

[11] I.B.R.D., *Summary Proceedings, Annual Meeting of the Board of Governors,* 1950, p. 9. Black also has stated: "I have noticed a tendency at times for development to be regarded as something which is due, as a right, from the more advanced nations to those less well developed. Whatever the rights and obligations of different nations may be, development is not something which can be imported from abroad. It is something which can only be won internally by acceptance of responsibility, hard work and sacrifice." *Ibid.,* p. 11.

[12] The 1961 *GNP* per head has been estimated at $70 for India, $84 for Nigeria, $111 for South Viet Nam, $120 for Iran, $179 for Peru, $188 for the Philippines, $240 for Portugal, and $268 for Brazil. See P. N. Rosenstein-Rodan, "International Aid for Underdeveloped Countries," *Review of Economics and Statistics,* Vol. 43 (May 1961), p. 126. ". . . in close to half the 80 [developing countries in the World Bank's membership], accounting for 50 percent of their population, income per head has risen by 1 percent or less. Even to keep abreast of recent high rates of population growth is not a negligible achievement, but it is far from sufficient. The average per capita income in this group is no more than $120 a year." George D. Woods, President, International Bank of Reconstruction and Development, *Summary Proceedings, Annual Meetings, 1965* (Washington, D. C., 1965), p. 9.

It is generally agreed that such income estimates substantially understate the incomes of other countries relative to that of the U. S.—the lower the income, typically, the greater the degree of understatement; a more accurate picture might be obtained by increasing the foregoing figures by some 50 to 100 percent. But even with such large adjustments, it is obvious that the international per capita income differences are very great.

Suppose we consider alternative U. S. annual growth rates for per capita income and ask what must be the corresponding rates of income growth in Alpha in order to maintain the initial *absolute gap* of $3,800 (= $4,000 − $200). The answer varies with the time period in question; the required rate of growth in Alpha becomes smaller as the time horizon lengthens. For example, if the U. S. per capita income grows at 2 percent (about the long-term average), the income of $4,000 would rise to $4,080 after one year, an increase of $80. To maintain the absolute gap, Alpha's income also must rise by $80, a 40 percent increase for Alpha. However, the absolute gap will be unchanged after ten years if Alpha grows at 18 percent. If we take a period of 100 years, the required Alphian growth rate is 5 percent.[13]

But this does not mean that the gap will be constant through all those years. On the contrary, at these constant respective rates of growth, the absolute size of the gap will grow larger for a time; at the end of half a century, it will be more than doubled, reaching a maximum of $10,155 after some seventy-four years. It will then decrease to $3,800 by the end of the hundredth year.[14] Thus, even if Alpha maintains the very impressive growth rate of 5 percent for a century, while the U. S. grows at 2 percent, the absolute gap at the end of 100 years will be as large as it was initially; and during most of that period, the gap will be much larger. (Incidentally, it would take some sixty-two years for Alpha's income to reach $4,000, equal to the initial U. S. income.)

It is not generally anticipated that the Alphas of the world will grow indefinitely at a per capita rate as high as 5 percent; by historical standards, such a growth rate over a prolonged period would be remarkable. Growth anticipations and objectives for per capita income very often are stated at around 2 or 2.5 percent. (For example, in 1961, the "Alliance for Progress" established as a "fundamental goal" for Latin America the achieving of a "substantial" growth rate "at the earliest possible date"; specifically, this means a minimum per capita rate of 2.5 percent to be attained "over the next ten years.") If the U. S. were to grow at a modest 1 percent, it would take over three centuries for Alpha's per capita income to catch up with America's if Alpha grows at 2 percent.

16, 17, 18, 19, 20

Epilogue and Preview

So far, we have presented principles and applied them to the analysis of (a) the prices and exchange of goods, (b) the particular mix of goods produced, (c) the demand for and supply of productive resources, and (d) the earnings and wages of the owners and

[13]

Required Percentage Rates of Foreign Growth to Maintain Absolute Gap of $3,800
(U. S. Initial Income: $4,000; Alpha Initial Income: $200)

Alternative U. S. Growth Rates	Years				
	1	10	25	50	100
1%	20	12	8	5	4
2%	40	18	11	7	5
3%	60	23	13	9	6
4%	80	27	15	10	7

[14]

U. S. and Alpha Incomes
(U. S. Grows at 2 Percent; Alpha Grows at 4.9542 Percent)

	0	1	10	25	50	74	100
U. S. income	4,000	4,080	4,876	6,562	10,766	17,317	28,978
Alpha income	200	210	324	670	2,244	7,162	25,178
U. S.–Alpha	3,800	3,870	4,552	5,892	8,522	10,155	3,800

suppliers of productive resources, i.e., their wealth and income. In actuality, the outcome within each of these depends upon all the others—yet we considered one at a time, assuming the others to be fixed. We used, in short, "partial-equilibrium" analysis to comprehend each problem without studying in detail how the solution of one would depend on or change the solutions to others.

A more rigorous and advanced formulation of the entire problem would explicitly indicate all interdependencies and would solve all these artificially segregated problems jointly and simultaneously. That is known as "general-equilibrium" analysis. When one turns to the general-equilibrium problem—involving *general*-equilibrium prices and outputs in all markets jointly—he discovers that the interdependencies imply that changes in one sector will cause, or be caused by, changes in other sectors. Suppose the prices of tires and potatoes do clear the markets for those goods—on the assumption that the incomes of tire and potato buyers are determined in a market for their productive services. But if the demand and supply for their productive services were *not* effectively matched and cleared, their incomes would fall and, in turn, reduce demands for potatoes and tires. Furthermore, the reduced demands for these consumer goods would change the derived demand for productive resources used to produce potatoes and tires; so the income of the producers of these goods would change, affecting their demands for other goods, and so on and on.

If all markets could be *independently* cleared, regardless of what was happening in other markets, the partial equilibrium analysis would be entirely reliable and usable for study of the operation of the economic system *as a whole*. The whole would be the sum of its independent parts. But the parts are not independent of incomes and prices in other markets and these adjustments in each market are not achieved costlessly and instantly. What happens in one affects what happens in others and the result may be swings in general income and production. Regardless of what any *one* person is doing, the whole of the economic cosmos reflects the speed and costs of ascertaining and moving toward those general equilibrating prices and outputs. Thus, recessions can occur in the economy as a whole.

In our exposition we implicitly assumed a monetary system that generated a supply of money in such a fashion as to avoid fluctuations in general demand and employment. Unfortunately, that is a false presumption: Occasionally (e.g., during the 1930s), the money system failed to do that. We have also implicitly and gratuitously assumed that sudden, large fluctuations in the portion of wealth the public demands to hold as money, in response to shifts in the anticipated profitability of investment, were absent or effectively offset by appropriate monetary and government policy. The other portion of the complete elementary course in economics investigates these factors affecting general income and employment in an endeavor to explain monetary activities and government expenditure and taxing policy (called "fiscal" policy).

The modern theory of national income fluctuation (associated with J. M. Keynes) has often been misinterpreted in oversimplifications which ignore its underlying relative-price, choice-theoretic structure. Such (incorrect) assumptions simplify the introductory analysis of current monetary and fiscal policy, but a full-blown analysis cannot make these gratuitous assumptions. While you may not in the next portion of the book observe an *emphasis* or *heavy* reliance on this relative-price foundation, do not make the mistake of thinking that the modern income determination theory rejects it or can exist without it.

Summary

1 The growth of wealth is increased if savings are cheaper (more plentiful), if property rights in wealth are more explicit and secure, and if profitable investments are more readily perceivable and exploitable by investors. Faster rate of growth of wealth is achieved not only by saving and investing more but by more profitable and effective institutions for *organizing,* coordinating, and directing productive activity.

2 Conservation, in the sense of preservation of resources in their initial form, is not necessarily a means of preserving or increasing wealth. Conversion of goods to other forms of wealth can be more productive of wealth. Incentive to conserve or convert goods to most valuable forms is aided by identifiable property rights in goods.

3 The distribution of income is partially a function of the age distribution of the population and the variations of a person's income with his age, life expectancy, investment in personal education and skills, savings, and investment in physical wealth. Even if everyone had an identical earnings potential, at any moment neither incomes nor wealth would be equal.

4 Chance and imperfect foresight of conjectural events lead to choices of risk bearing that result in differences of wealth of various people. Chance effects that cannot be sold to other people result in differences in income and wealth that do not reflect a choice of risk bearing.

5 Market, pecuniary income underestimates "real income" to spending units, because of self-production by, for example, farmers and housewives.

6 Preferences for monetary wealth relative to leisure and less difficult work contribute to increased differences in monetary income.

7 Different endowments occur both in personal abilities and in physical wealth. The accumulation of wealth, not the endowment, is a source of wealth differences.

8 Differences in productive ability are magnified by the correlation between superior abilities and the amount of capital resources submitted to the direction of superior talent.

9 The distribution of wealth, reflecting past savings and investment and future earnings of different life lengths (since people are not all the same age at any moment), is more unequal than the distribution of incomes.

10 Closed or restricted markets contribute to differences in wealth redistribution by permitting some people to acquire monopoly rents.

Questions

1 You are an unborn spirit; you are offered your choice of country in which to be born. In country A all land is owned by its users; absentee landlordism is forbidden by a progressive government. The land cannot be mortgaged by the owner or rented. Everyone is born with rights to use certain parcels of land and these cannot be taken away or contracted to others. In country B, absentee landlordism is common and legal. All land is privately owned and either used by the owner or rented to the highest-paying tenants. Land can be sold or mortgaged. Private-property rights are strictly enforced for everyone. Many people do not own land at all. Into which country will you request that you be born? Why?

2   If you were a Jew in an Arab country, or an Asian in Africa, or an Englishman in Indonesia, or an American in Argentina, or a Moslem in India, would you invest for your son in personal human capital or in physical capital? Why?

3   What is the connection between "saving," as usually defined, and "capital accumulation"? How is the connection altered by introducing the possibility of receiving foreign loans or gifts?

4   "Saving is necessary for investment. Investment is necessary for capital accumulation. Capital is necessary for maximum production. Production is the basis of economic welfare. Therefore, the necessary and sufficient condition for increasing welfare (that is, for economic development) is saving; and the larger is the rate of saving, the faster (proportionately) will be development." What do you think of that as a recipe for economic growth?

5   "A wealthy nation can do the saving for a poor nation: a nation receiving (sufficient) foreign aid can finance its economic development without itself doing any saving." Is this statement all right? Is it all wrong?

6   Mr. A. Brimmer of the Federal Reserve Board is reported (*Time,* July 1966) as saying that the rate of investment in the United States in 1966 was too high to be sustainable and that the damper should be put on the rate of investment. Evaluate that statement in the light of the following observations:
a. Which particular investments should be reduced?
b. A dean of a law school is reputed to have told his entering students that one out of three of them would flunk. Should he therefore have reduced enrollment by one third?
c. Fifty percent of new firms do not survive three years. Should half of new business be prohibited from being organized?
d. What does Mr. Brimmer know that individual investors do not know which, if they knew, would induce them to change their actions or which would be good for the community at large?

7   "Extending the three-mile limit now in force for American territorial waters out to 1,000 miles would help to conserve sea resources." Explain why. Why not extend the territorial claims out to half way across the ocean up to the territorial claims of other countries, as has been done in the North Sea for oil rights? What would that do to the doctrine of the "freedom of the seas"? What does the doctrine of freedom of the seas do to the efficient use of ocean resources?

8   If the State of Washington owned the water of the Columbia River, would that mean that Oregon could not get any of the water? Nor California? Or would Oregon and California be surer of getting water from the Columbia River? Why?

9   Distinguish between conservation of specific resources and the growth of wealth. Is conservation of specific resources an efficient way to increase the productive wealth of the community?

10 In a public park an apple tree yields excellent apples. These may be picked by the public, but not more than one apple per person at a time. When will apples be picked? Why?

11 If the American buffalo had been owned by someone, do you think the buffalo would now be so nearly exterminated? Why?

12 Do you think seals and whales would be faced with extinction if some person or group were able to buy, as private property, the right to catch whales and seals? Why?

13 A large lake is stocked with excellent fish, but no one owns the fish or the lake. Only by catching the fish can you acquire ownership in the fish.

a. What do you think will be the average age of fish caught as compared to the age of fish in a privately owned lake?

b. Which system will induce overfishing in the sense that more resources will be devoted to catching fish than the extra fish caught are worth? Why?

14. "Farmers' incomes are on the average lower than nonfarm income. Therefore farmers should be given special aid." If you agree, reconcile with the statement: "Teachers' incomes are on the average lower than those of businessmen. Therefore teachers should be given special aid." Why might the incomes of one group be lower without motivating a desire to help that group with special aid? Under what conditions would a lower income to some group be regarded as warranting tax-financed aid?

15. Ask your parents what your family's income was last year, before income taxes. Then compare the answer with the data in the following table, showing the 1967 distribution of money income received by each tenth of all spending units, by lowest income in each tenth:

Lowest Income within Tenth

Spending Units	1967
Lowest tenth	not available
Second "	$ 1,860
Third "	3,175
Fourth "	4,630
Fifth "	6,000
Sixth "	7,450
Seventh "	8,800
Eighth "	10,350
Ninth "	12,270
Highest "	15,400

a. Probably most of the students in your class come from families in the top half. Guess what fraction of total national income goes to the lowest tenth, to the fifth tenth, and to the highest tenth.

b. Do you think the dispersion of individual incomes is less than for spending units? It is. Why?

c. If after-income-tax incomes were recorded instead of pretax incomes, how do you think the numbers in the above table would be changed? What would be the effect on the percentage of post-tax income available to each tenth?

d. Why is the post-tax measure of income better than the pretax as a measure of incomes to each spending unit? Explain in what respects it is a worse measure than pretax income.

16. What is an "underdeveloped country," and what constitutes "economic development"? Evaluate the following statements by Jacob Viner, *International Trade and Economic Development* (Glencoe: The Free Press, 1952).

(a) An underdeveloped country is one "which has good potential prospects for using more capital or more labor or more available natural resources, or all of these, to support its present population on a higher level of living, or, if its per capita income level is already fairly high, to support a larger population on a not lower level of living. . . . On the basis of this definition, a country may be underdeveloped whether it is densely or sparsely populated, whether it is a capital-rich or a capital-poor country, whether it is a high-income per capita or low-income per capita country, or whether it is an industrialized or an agricultural country. . . . This definition, I am aware, would . . . be objectionable to those who want 'economic development' even at the cost of a lowering of per capita income levels provided it brings the filling up of empty spaces, or urbanization, or industrialization. Patriotic citizens may want their national economies to grow in size of aggregate income or of aggregate output because of prestige considerations or strategic considerations even if this involves a lowering of average living standards. To others, living standards may be a weighty consideration, but in terms of the living standards . . . of a particular class or a particular regional category of the population . . . a colonial power may be interested in the economic development of a possession as an incident to its becoming an enlarged market for the mother country's export products or an enlarged source of supply . . . without regard to the economic welfare of the colonial population" (pp. 125–126).

(b) "Let us suppose . . . that a country which has embarked on a program of economic development engages in periodic stock-taking of its progress, and finds not only that aggregate wealth, aggregate income, total population, total production, are all increasing, but that per capita wealth, income, production, are also increasing. All of these are favorable indices, but even in combination do they suffice to show that there has been 'economic progress,' an increase in economic 'welfare,' rather than retrogression? Suppose that someone should argue that the one great economic evil is the prevalence of a great mass of crushing poverty, and that it is a paradox to claim that a country is achieving economic progress as long as the absolute extent of such poverty prevailing in that country has not lessened or has even increased? Such a country, nevertheless, might be able to meet all the tests of economic development which I have just enumerated. If its population has undergone substantial increase, the numbers of those living at the margin of subsistence or below, illiterate, diseased, undernourished, may have grown steadily consistently with a rise in the average income of the population as a whole. Not only this, but if immigration is a significant factor, these statistical tests are consistent with no native having undergone an improvement in his economic status . . . Were I to insist, however, that the reduction of mass poverty be made a crucial test of the realization of economic development, I would be separating myself from the whole body of literature in this field" (pp. 126–127).

17 Very wealthy nations (the U. S.) and very poor nations (India) typically have relatively low rates of population increase (say, 2 percent or less); nations of "intermediate" wealth (Mexico, Venezuela) quite typically have high rates of population increase (3 percent or more). Isn't this a curious pattern? Why isn't there a better correlation between wealth and population increase—with wealthy nations having a low rate of population increase, moderately wealthy a higher population rate, and poor the highest rate?

18 Recently India proposed to build a steel mill, and she asked the United States government to finance the project. In defense of her request, an economist serving as American ambassador to India wrote: "Although it would be a large mill, there is no doubt that the steel is needed. While the plant would be costly, it would soon pay for itself in the imports that it would save. To import a million tons of steel products would cost the Indians about $200 million. The proposed mill with an annual capacity of 1 million tons would cost $513 million to build. Three years of operations would thus recover the dollar cost of the mill and more. Since India combines her pressing need for steel with an equally acute shortage of dollars, the economic attraction is obvious. She could not, in fact, afford to import the steel that the mill could supply." Explain why every sentence of that quotation —except the third and fourth—is wrong, nonsensical, or irrelevant.

19 Those who assume initial incomes and constant growth rates and then calculate "gaps" over two or three centuries are preoccupied with the implications of compound interest and indulge in misleading, wholly unrealistic predictions. Is that a fair indictment?

20 Having learned the lesson in Chapter 1 of this book on varieties of competition, you have just overthrown the existing government and established yourself as liberator of the people. If now you set out to establish conditions conducive to a growth of wealth and freedom for the people, without succumbing to the temptation to install devices that enhance your own wealth and political power instead, what kinds of laws and property rights would you enforce? Why?

Unemployment and Economic Fluctuations

25 THE preceding analysis did not account for recessions and unemployment. Earlier economists, among them John M. Keynes, tried to explain why such events occurred and what could be done about them. Downward swings of demand were observed to be associated with recessions and greater unemployment, while the reverse occurred during recoveries. Our preceding economic analysis suggests some reasons why downward sweeps of demand for products of individual firms do not induce price changes and job re-allocation with no unemployment or idle resources. It is easy to conclude that prices and wages are in fact not flexible enough immediately to bring about a clearing of market demands and supplies. The noninstantaneous adjustment of prices and wages results in "excess supplies." But this, of course, merely restates the issue. The question is: Why do sellers and buyers permit prices and wages to respond so as to result in *widespread* unemployment and idle resources in the face of decreased *general* demand? And why are there *swings* in *general* demand, i.e., for all goods at about the same time?

In this chapter we shall see why prices and wages do not adjust rapidly enough to maintain full output at market-clearing levels. In following chapters we shall explore factors inducing large swings or fluctuations in aggregate demand that cause swings in employment and output.

The Magnitude of Employment and Unemployment

The United States had almost 90,000,000 people with gainful employment of one kind or another in 1971. Almost 65,000,000 worked full time and over 25,000,000 worked part time. Approximately 10,000,000 changed jobs or took new jobs during the year. Every month approximately one in twenty employees quit, was laid off, or terminated a job for some reason; the same proportion took new jobs or returned to an old job. In this process, over 15,000,000 reported themselves as unemployed at some time during the year, although at any one time the number of unemployed averaged about 4,000,000. Of those 15,000,000, some 2,500,000 were employed all through the year; 1,500,000, from one to three months; and 3,000,000, from four months to more than six months. Over 5,000,000 had at least two spells of unemployment. There is a persistent and extensive flow of people from job to job and between jobs and unemployment, along with constant reassessment of old jobs and consideration of possible new occupations.

Unemployment

About 2 to 15 percent of the labor force is unemployed at any one moment, depending upon age, sex, color, and business conditions. The lowest unemployment percentage is in the "20 years of age and over, white male" group, running close to 1 to 2 percent normally.

What is the normal length of unemployment? Table 25–1 shows that over half the unemployed at any moment are without work for less than five weeks, and about a third experiencing up to three months, and less than 5 percent being unemployed over six months. As percentages of the total labor force, these convert to about 2 percent having been unemployed for less than one month, and about 1 percent of the labor force unemployed for over a month. However, in recessions those rates double or triple. They are higher for nonwhites, teenagers, and women. For teenagers of both sexes the normal unemployment rate runs at about 12 to 15 percent, with the white rate approximately half that of nonwhites; women normally experience an unemployment rate about 50 percent higher than men.

Why do unemployment rates differ by sex, age, and color? One answer—and not a good one—is that teenagers or women are not as well trained for the available jobs. Why is that a bad answer? Because there is an infinite number of jobs available—the tasks to be performed in a world of scarcity are unlimited. A common response to that assertion is "Why are not the unemployed working at the tasks they can do? Because they would rather not work than accept the wages in the best jobs open to them, or they have not yet decided what are the best jobs for them? Both may be correct. Some people are institutionalized and incompetent; they are not even counted in the labor force. Others may be sufficiently low in productivity even at the best possible job that they prefer not to work. But why do apparently sufficiently productive teenagers or nonwhites experience higher unemployment rates? One reason for teenagers is that they shift more than others from job to job as part of their search for the kind of work they will probably settle in as a career; taking a spell of nonemployment at each job shift to conduct the search is sensible. Another explanation is the minimum wage law, which restricts the abilities of younger, untested teenagers to induce employers to employ them as recruits and incur the job-training costs. Without these laws, employers would be more willing to hire untested teenagers or low-productivity people.

For nonwhites, an explanation lies in their higher migration. A larger fraction of blacks in a city are new migrants from the South; a larger fraction are engaged in job-opportunity search and evaluation, hence a larger fraction will show up as unemployed.

Statements about unskilled, untrained people or people with skills that do not correspond to job requirements are unacceptable. They would make sense only if wages had to be uniform for all workers in all jobs and if there were no scarcity of, or demand for, services that could be provided by low-skilled people. (Warning and disclaimer: Analysis and explanation should not be interpreted as implying that nothing should or can be done to alleviate the situation or that the existing situation is "desirable" or "proper." The doctor who explains the cause of your pain as an allergy is not saying that you deserve it or that nothing should or can be done to prevent or alleviate it.)

An analysis of unemployment must first more carefully consider the meaning of unemployment (of labor and of goods)—a term often applied indiscriminately to very different phenomena.

Some Sources and Kinds of Unemployment

One kind of unemployment is the excess of some resource, caused by a restraint on price or access to the market. For example, it is erroneous to call people "unemployable" because the value of their services is less than some maintained minimum wage. They are employable; but they are not employed because of the constraints placed on their employment in an open market. A similar group of "unemployed" are excluded from particular jobs because of apprenticeship or licensing laws. These people call themselves unemployed "electricians," "meat cutters," "projectionists," or "bricklayers" while taking less-desired jobs elsewhere on a temporary basis. If there are prices and wages below which sales and employment are illegal, some people will be prevented from selling their services at prices acceptable to buyers. If the wage rate is legally set at a minimum of $1, some less productive people who could do something worth, say, 80 cents, cannot be employed at that wage. We present a more detailed discussion of this later. Suffice it to note that some of these people will constitute members of the "unemployed" until they shift to "independent" owner-operator status. How many is not known.[1]

Another class of the "unemployed" are those who take employment only when demand for their services is high enough to warrant the higher wages that attracted them. Some housewives work during seasonally high demands at certain types of labor—in fruit-packing houses or dress shops during the Christmas season. The rest of the year, they prefer not to work at the lower available wages. People working in jobs that involve short-lived projects, like movies, plays, or construction, are commonly found in the ranks of the unemployed between projects—again, especially if they have qualified for unemployment benefits.

Sometimes it is asserted that there are not enough jobs available. This assertion is simply unacceptable if reality is to be recognized. Jobs are always available, but the wage offer may be unacceptably low in view of alternative job prospects or leisure. To ask a former steel-mill employee to work at 50 cents an hour as a gardener, handy-man, farm hand, clerk, or machine-tool operator is "ridiculous"—which means only that the steel-mill employee deems it preferable not to work at those jobs for those wages, perhaps because he believes he can get a better job by continued exploration of other job options. In other words, he believes the time spent seeking information is worth more than 50 cents an hour.

There are also people who would be happy to continue at their *old* job *at the old wage*

1, 2

---

[1] It is believed that this group is comprised primarily of the very young, the uneducated, Negroes, and women.

if *that* job were still available. But they will refuse to accept a wage cut sufficient to keep them at work in their former jobs, because they believe (sometimes correctly) that other job opportunities exist at approximately the same wages—or certainly at better terms than now available in the old job. After all, those other opportunities are what kept their wages up to the level at which they were in their recent jobs. Employees will therefore explore and compare these other opportunities—as long as the expected cost of discovering them is less than the loss of wealth from accepting a wage cut in the previous job.

When demand for a product falls, if the productive inputs immediately shifted to other tasks, there would be no unemployment and no "idle" resources. But such shifts are not possible at zero costs, because of the costs of finding the various buyers and sellers and bringing them together, so that each can realize his best trading opportunities. And this will explain a wide class of unemployment.

Frictional unemployment. Although it may seem paradoxical, "unemployment" is consistent with efficiency. Consider the costs that would be imposed on you if you were *never* allowed to be unemployed regardless of changing demand and supply conditions. Suppose you were dissatisfied with your present job and wanted another. You could not quit and spend a week or a month looking for a new one, because you would then be "unemployed." It is unlikely that you could find the *best* alternative job within an *instant* search of *no* cost or while working at the old job in order to avoid "unemployment." The activity in question is not *job* seeking, it is *job-information* seeking. Many jobs are available, but information is being sought about still other jobs in the belief that the other jobs may be superior. The currently known jobs do not pay enough to induce a person to stop looking for *better* job opportunities.

If an employer should experience a decrease in demand, so that he wants to employ fewer employees at the existing wage, he will drop employees. This is equivalent to the case in which a renter terminates his renting and leaves the apartment empty. Like the apartment owner, the employee now has the option of cutting his wages immediately by a relatively large amount to get a job quickly, or he can invest in a hunt for information about various alternative jobs. Like the apartment owner, he will not accept a cut in wages to whatever level is necessary to find another employer immediately. And if he believes that the sacrifices and costs he incurs in the search yield a greater increase in the present value of his wealth, then he will engage in some information hunting, an activity called job hunting.

New college graduates spend much time and other resources investigating alternative potential employers. No student knows everything about each potential employer, nor does each employer know everything about each potential college graduate. Wage offers differ among employers, in part reflecting nonpecuniary features that are in turn evaluated differently by various people. Offers obtained by college graduates even for the "same" kind of work will differ. Accepting the first offer reduces the probability of getting the highest-paid job and lowers one's *wealth* (present value of his future earnings) compared to what it would be if he took longer to find more offers. The more firms contacted, the greater will be the probability of finding higher wage offers or better jobs. The greater the difference among potential wage offers and working conditions, the greater the amount of search it would be profitable to perform. For teenage high school graduates, the problem of providing and getting information is evident in the fact that half the unemployed in 1969 were teenagers.

A person should search for and explore other wage offers until the expected marginal gain (in present value of anticipated future income) equals the incremental cost of continued search. The increment of *gain* from *extra* search time diminishes the longer the time devoted to information collecting. Hence, there is a limit to the length of search. Although few persons may make detailed calculations, their observed behavior conforms to this explanation.

Search by employees (and employers also) would eliminate all dispersion among offers *if* there were unchanging conditions of demand and supply and tastes of employers and employees. The greater the rate of change of tastes and demands and the greater the costs of movement, the greater will be the dispersion among job opportunities and the greater the gain in wealth by more extended search. Employment agencies, which specialize in obtaining and disseminating this kind of information, give concrete evidence of the cost of information.

A person engaged in acquiring information for better jobs is "frictionally unemployed." Frictional unemployment is applicable to labor, houses, capital goods, or any good whatsoever. It is the efficient way to adjust to unpredictable demand and supply changes. It might be called "frictional *use*" because the resources are being used to overcome "frictions" in the operation of an economic system.

Another facet of the frictional process is the presence of "unfilled" jobs. Some employers would like more employees, and, if information and transfer costs were zero, they would instantly hire the right people at the appropriate wage. But filling jobs immediately is more expensive, for it will take a higher wage to get the right person immediately; or, if the employer takes the first available person, he will have a smaller probability of getting the "best" person.

In many foreign countries, teenage unemployment is much lower than in the United States. In those countries, wage rates of teenagers are typically lower relative to wages of experienced workers than in the United States. Minimum wage laws are not uniform for all ages, and union wage structures are more varied. (Also, employers seem less reluctant to offer lower wages for teenagers, but we do not have a good explanation of why that difference in attitude exists, if indeed it does.) In the United States, highly unionized occupations have a smaller range of wages than in nonunionized occupations, thus making it more difficult for teenagers to be employed in unionized occupations. 3, 4, 5, 6, 7, 8

Structural Demand and Aggregate Demand Decreases

We explained why people and resources will become idle in the face of a fall in demand. However, there are two kinds of demand decreases: *structural demand* and *aggregate demand* decreases. They may occur simultaneously.

Structural Shifts

Structural *shifts* in relative demands for labor cause unemployment. Aggregate money demand over all goods may be steady or rising, but the demands for some goods fall while demands for others increase.[2] New techniques often change the relative values of

---

[2] Costs of acquiring information about alternative job operations and of moving, as explained in preceding sections, are present in each case.

each type of labor in various uses, and people whose services fall in value must either accept lower wages or shift to other jobs. Some people do not have other skills that would enable them to maintain their old wage, so they may accept the lower wage. Others who are upset by the changing patterns of consumer tastes or changing technology initiate a job-evaluation search (unemployment) rather than accept the lower wage.

An increase in supplies of new young labor, as at the beginning of each summer, introduces a shift in relative supplies. Again, the job evaluation process (as well as the potential employee comparison and evaluation by employers) yields the phenomenon known as unemployment.

Structural unemployment, based on *relative* demand or supply shifts, implies a shift in relative wages, incomes, and wealth. The sensible expectation of discerning a job that will avoid a wage cut initiates and extends the unemployment episode. Some people never find another job paying an acceptable wage. Old people whose services are outcompeted by new techniques may find it not worthwhile to incur moving costs to a new job for only a few remaining years. Unquestionably, jobs exist and are available, but at wages many regard as unacceptably low, as discussed earlier.

Shifts in relative demands and supplies may constitute a major portion of what we call frictional unemployment—although we are not sure about that. If these shifts in demands for various skills are complicated by minimum-wage laws or other restrictions, then the least-skilled labor (young, Negro, women, uneducated) will find employment opportunities closed off.

Fluctuations in Aggregate Demand

The unemployment of labor explainable by the information costs associated with changing (relative, but not *general*) demands for various products, changing tastes, new products, etc., seems to run about 2 to 4 percent of the labor force. However, at times the rate of unemployment (as evidenced by data taken from people eligible for unemployment pay or who report in labor force surveys that they are "out of work and seeking work") rises to substantially higher levels. In what we commonly call recessions, the rate runs between 5 and 10 percent. In the deep depression of the 1930s, it is believed to have reached 20 to 25 percent. But if the preceding analysis is valid, why should it ever go as high as 5 percent?

Possibly the demands for various goods shift so rapidly and greatly that many people will shift jobs, so job-information seeking increases accordingly. In fact, relative demand shifts do occur on a significant scale and contribute to unemployment. Some industries are expanding, and some are contracting; sometimes more are contracting than expanding. For example, Table 25–1 shows the *directions* of month-to-month changes in the value of new orders in manufacturing establishments over a representative interval. In the monthly change from June to July of 1966, new orders increased in six industries and decreased in eleven. Further, looking across the columns, each industry shows noticeable fluctuations. For example, iron and steel showed ten increases and nine decreases in the nineteen-month interval.

Within each industry a similar variety of behavior among firms comprising that industry would also be observable.

A more extensive index of the diffusion of productive activity is shown in Figure 25–1. The proportion of thirty industries experiencing an expansion in any given month

Unemployment and Economic Fluctuations

TABLE 25–1. Direction of Change in Value of Manufacturers' New Orders, Selected Industries

Industry	One-Month Spans 1969						
	Apr–May	May–June	June–July	July–Aug	Aug–Sep	Sep–Oct	Oct–Nov
Percent rising (36 industries)	46	40	60	40	81	37	29
Iron and steel	−	+	+	−	+	−	−
Primary nonferrous metals	−	−	+	+	−	+	−
Other primary metals	−	−	+	−	+	−	+
Electrical generator apparatus	−	+	−	−	+	+	−
Radio, television, and equipment	−	−	+	−	−	+	−
Other electrical equipment	−	+	−	+	+	−	−
Motor vehicles	−	−	+	+	+	−	−
Aircraft	+	−	+	−	+	−	−
Stone, clay, and glass products	−	−	−	+	+	−	−
Metalworking machinery	−	−	+	−	+	−	+
Special industrial machinery	−	+	−	0	+	−	−
General industrial machinery	+	+	−	+	−	−	−
Engines and turbines	−	+	−	+	+	−	−
Agricultural implements	+	−	+	−	+	+	−
Household appliances	+	−	+	−	−	+	−
Fabricated metal products	+	−	−	−	+	+	−

+ = rising; 0 = unchanged; − = falling. Series components are seasonally adjusted.
Source: U. S. Department of Commerce, Bureau of Census, *Business Cycle Developments*, August 1970.

is indicated. The curve fluctuates up and down, rarely reaching 100 percent or zero. In other words, not all industries are expanding at the same time, nor are all contracting at the same time. The curve usually oscillates within the limits of about 20 to 80 percent. *Industrial production* in various industries shows the same general pattern of diffusion of expansions and contractions.

If the line in Figure 25–1 were steady at about 50 percent, it would mean a relatively steady state of *aggregate national* demand, with offsetting shifts occurring among various goods. However, the diffusion index fluctuates over a wide span, suggesting that the

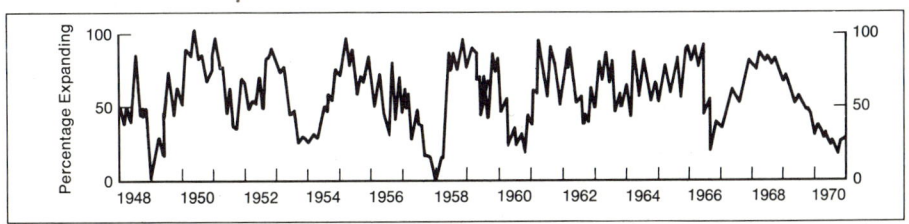

FIGURE 25–1. Proportion of Industries with Expanding Employment

This graph is based on thirty industries and month-to-month changes. Source: U. S. Department of Commerce, *Business Cycle Developments*, January 1970.

growths and declines in various industries are not exactly offsetting and are shifts of demand from product to product—by a large number of independent random deviations. Instead, an upward swing seems to indicate that most industries are expanding more than enough to offset contractions elsewhere; and at other times total demand summed over all goods seems to be decreasing. Fluctuations in *demand* for the products of various industries seem to be correlated rather than independent or mutually offsetting. As one would expect, when the curve runs along the bottom—most industries experiencing a contraction—a recession is indicated. If the general demand decline were replaced by an increase, unemployment would end even sooner. Much unemployment could be avoided by economic policies that prevent general decreases in demand. Some of the most severe decreases in general demand have been an unwitting result of extraordinarily inept and ignorant monetary policy. But that story is covered later.

Some unemployment is an inherent part of an open-market system of exchange, in which people are entitled to select their work and produce at their own volition at open-market prices rather than being tied to jobs as serfs or assigned them by dictators. In the military, everyone always has *a* job; however, it is not clear that this is more efficient or preferable to an "idle" search for other, *better* jobs. If less attention is paid to seeking over-all efficient assignments of workers, it is easier to keep everyone busy. Concealing or avoiding unemployment by arbitrary work assignments is called "disguised unemployment."

The explanation of unemployment suggests that after a decrease in demand with its increase in unemployment, there will be forces toward restoration of employment. Market forces push toward full employment. We should therefore expect to observe a complete recovery, with full employment after some depression. The bigger the recession, the greater the recovery. However, the reverse is *not* true—the extent of the prior rise to new highs of output and employment does not set the stage for some commensurate decrease in employment and output. The degree of recovery is not a random variable, being higher or lower according to some accident of fate without some built-in forces toward full employment, nor is any subsequent recession determined by the extent of a preceding "boom." As implied by economic analysis, recoveries are correlated with preceding recessions, but are not correlated with the preceding recoveries. Whatever the extent of some downswing, the economic system contains forces pushing output and employment back to full employment. It is the downward "shocks" that produce unemployment, not some inherent "what-goes-up-must-come-down" explanation. The bigger the downward "shock," the bigger the later upward recovery sweep. There is a powerful force toward full employment.

Fluctuations in employment and production define what are known as prosperities and depressions. In fact, depressions and prosperity are practically definable by total output and employment. Figure 25–2 shows an index of industrial production from 1948 through 1969, while Figures 25–3 and 25–4 show the number of employed and percentage of unemployment since 1948. There were recessions in 1949, 1954, 1958, 1961, and 1970.

General Aggregate Demand Decrease

We have seen some reasons why prices do not change instantly to maintain output in the face of transient demand fluctuations. For an individual good whose demand has fallen, output falls as resources refuse to continue to produce that good since they can transfer

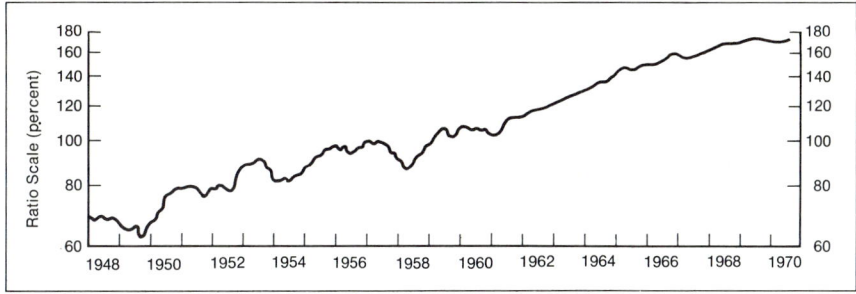

FIGURE 25-2. Industrial Production

Index is based on physical volume, adjusted for seasonal variation, 1957 = 100. Source: Board of Governors of the Federal Reserve System, *Monthly Bulletin.*

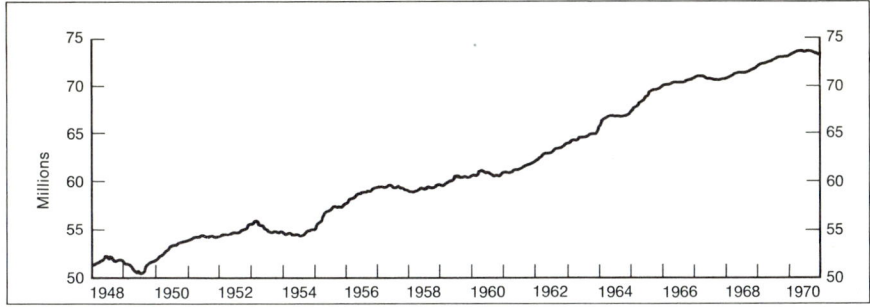

FIGURE 25-3. Total Nonagricultural Employment

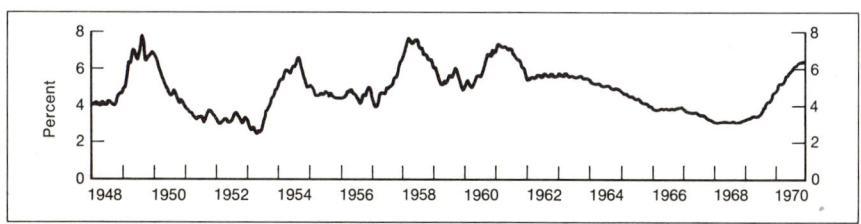

FIGURE 25-4. Unemployment Percentage (Nonagricultural Employees)

to other products. But if there is a decrease in demand *in general,* the situation is much more difficult.

You are an auto worker; demand for cars has fallen. You can retain your job only if you cut your wages to practically zero—unless all other inputs to autos also cut their prices at the same time by, say, 10 percent, in which case a 10 percent wage cut would suffice. Will prices of steel, tires, fabrics, copper, plastics, transport all immediately fall so as to permit you to retain your job with only a 10 percent wage cut? No. If your employer asked each of the other input suppliers to cut their prices, they would react as you did—unless all others cut theirs *and also* all those who sell services and goods to these suppliers of the auto industry. So steel workers' wages and the prices of all inputs in making steel, plus those in tires, copper, plastics, etc., must be cut; and, in turn, each supplier must do the same with all *its* inputs in an ever-widening network. There simply is no way for all that information to be simultaneously transmitted to every input, let alone to know *how much* each should be cut—since not all demands shift exactly the same amount, nor are all supply curves the same shape. And no one knows *how long* to expect continuation of the demand decrease which will affect what each is willing to accept as a price.

There is, indeed, some new set of prices for all the inputs of the economy which would, *if* it could be ascertained and made believable and acceptable to everyone, immediately restore full employment. It would take a miracle to reveal that instantly. No central brain or information network has even been conceived of—except in a formal, abstract, symbolic way—which would do so instantly or in a week. The collection and collation of the pressures of interlinked reduced sales necessitates a time lapse before there emerges a convergence toward a new equilibrating set of prices and assignments of inputs in new, most appropriate jobs. That is why general decreases in demand are accompanied by temporary (though not so temporary as to be insignificant!) increases in unemployment. Gradually, over a few months or a year, unemployment is reduced as the new prices and the best available new jobs at those prices are discerned and accepted.[3]

Recessions, Depressions, Fluctuations

In relation to business, the term "cycle" is better replaced by "fluctuations." There are no cycles in economy-wide economic activity (other than seasonal phenomena). Nor are periods of high prosperity or booms necessarily followed by depression or recession. It is not the case that booms breed "busts." A recession is identified as a reduction of economic activity; but whenever the recession occurs, it will *by definition* always have a prior peak. The boom of the late 1920s did *not* cause the depression of 1930.

As the characteristics of a recession—a decrease in the growth rate or an actual fall in the absolute level of activity—become more severe, the recession becomes a depression, with each person his own authority as to when to call it one or the other. Among the characteristics of central importance—and most are highly correlated in their pattern—are the money income of the economy, unemployment, output of goods in general, price levels, and wealth (as judged mostly by prices of corporate common stocks). Typically, any decrease in these variables lasting more than six months is likely to be called a recession, and certainly so if these magnitudes have not recovered in a year. Figures 25–2 and 25–3 show the degree of fluctuations that have prevailed in the past 20 years. (The picture is substantially the same for the past 150 years.) The biggest fluctuations in relative terms occur in unemployment rates and stock prices. If we speak of employment rather than *un*employment, the fluctuations are small, for a 2 percent decrease in

---

[3] We do not refer to "stickiness" or "inflexibility" of wage rates behind prices of other goods. We here assume that there is nothing to prevent any worker from immediately adjusting his offer price as low as he wants to: no custom or convention denies him perfect, instant flexibility. But his *conception* of what price he can get lags behind the facts; the cost of getting information makes his *state of knowledge* lag behind the actual equilibrating price which would restore employment. It is an *informational* lag. He chooses not to reduce the price of his services because he thinks the equilibrating price is higher than it actually is; or if it actually is as high as he thinks, the costs of search, and hence use of time, introduce a delay between the old and the new job. The lag must be understood to mean the time it takes people to discern what the new equilibrating price is.

employment from 97 to 95 percent is the same as a 66 percent increase in *unemployment* from 3 percent to 5 percent. To some, that record of keeping employment at about 95 to 97 percent of the labor force seems phenomenally good; to others, the unemployment rate of 3 to 5 percent seems too high.[4]

The cost of changing jobs *via unemployment* may equal quite a modest proportion of the present value of one's lifetime earnings stream. Suppose the present value of your lifetime earning stream is about $90,000 (equal to the present value, for example, of $8,000 per year for the next 30 years, at 8 percent rate of interest, as you can verify from Table 11–3 on page 183). If you refuse a wage cut at your present job and seek a new one paying the old rate, and if it takes two months to find that best alternative, you have sacrificed one-sixth of a year's pay, or $1,333. Hence, finding the best new job costs about 1.5 percent of the value of the resource moved. Compare the cost of transferring a car to a new user: its resale costs amount to nearly 20 percent. Or consider the costs of transferring a house from one *renter* to another; the *relative* normal costs of changing tenants (including the costs of time the quarters are vacant and the costs of finding new tenants) is about the same as for labor. The cost of transferring shares of common stock from one person to another via the New York Stock Exchange is about 2 percent of the value of the stock.

We introduce these facts, not to suggest that costs of unemployment search and transfer via unemployment are insignificant, but instead to give a sense of proportion about the costs of resource re-allocation, both absolutely and relative to transfer costs of other resources.

To be added to these costs of the *change of a job* are the losses (or gains) consequent to a *change in demand* for one's services in the economy at large, so that one's receipt-stream prospects have diminished (or increased). Recessions imply—indeed, mean—an interim reduction in demand for one's services relative to prior demand (and to future demand). That fall in income is not trivial and is the loss caused by whatever caused the recession. We should separate conceptually the two costs—changing a job and the interim, recession-reduced demand. Some measure of the recession effect can be obtained by examining stock market prices. Prices of common stock reflect the future-income expectations. If General Motors stockholders expected an annual stream of earnings of $5 per share and were capitalizing that at 10 percent, the market price would be $50. Now a recession sets in, and for the next year the earnings fall to a negative amount, say, −$3 per share, rising in the following year to $2 and back to $5 in the third year. The price of stock would fall from $50 to $41. (The change from $5 earnings to $3 loss is an $8 reduction in the earnings stream for the first year, and earnings in the second year are $3 smaller than formerly expected; all, when discounted to present values at 10 percent, implies a reduced present value of about $9.30.) As a matter of fact, when recessions set in, no one knows how long they will continue, so stock prices fall until it appears the end of the recession can be foreseen. Then stock prices will rise as people build up their expectations about the return of better times. So recessions are marked by

---

[4] Unemployment is desirable in that the *option* to be unemployed is better than the lack of an option to refuse to work at whatever wage a present employer would pay; it is undesirable in that information about alternative job options and knowledge about the equilibrating set of prices that would keep unemployment lower is so expensive. As we have seen, information about many, if not all, potential buying and selling opportunities of labor or any other services or goods is not free; it is expensive to collect and collate. The question is how well the economic institutions economize on those costs of facilitating re-allocations of input to best available jobs and in discerning best terms of trade.

early decreases in stock prices and recovery of stock prices when the end of the recession can be foreseen.⁵

The reductions in wage earnings, stockholder's earnings, and market prices are the reflections of reduced production during the recession. Thus we have economic money measures of the recession, such as stock values and national income received as wages and dividends; and we have physical indices, such as industrial production and employment. These all move in roughly similar patterns.

The view that evolves from our analysis is that the economy yields full employment except for those shifting from task to task as options and demands shift from one product to another and as productive possibilities alter. The constant readjustment of output capabilities to new demands and competing supplies brings a resource re-allocation process called "frictional" unemployment. While variations in employment occur, employment stays very close to full.

The historical record suggests that deviations in employment from a "full" rate of about 98–99 percent down to about 96 percent are an inherent part of the working of the economic nexus of Western societies with free enterprise and markets for privately owned resources. We have identified some reasons for variation, suggested why the employment rate tends to move back toward 98 or 99 percent. The impression is that of an employment rate bouncing along a ceiling like a helium-filled balloon.

But we add two modifications. First, the ceiling is not rigidly fixed: the number seeking to earn money income will vary. Women, the elderly, and the very young or the handicapped more likely will seek work during, say, a war, when social pressures to work increase. Women will vary in their participation in the labor force also depending upon education, marital status, number of children, income of husband, and the general status of female economic independence. Thus, unemployment will reflect not only those shifting from a past job to a new one, but also some who have recently decided to enter into search for the most rewarding job, to ascertain whether or not they will accept employment and at what task and on what terms.

The second modification in the conception of employment as being essentially "full" is the occurrence of depressions. So-called minor recessions, lasting a year or so and with unemployment rates going up to 5 to 6 percent, clearly *are* an inherent feature of the economic system as we have it. But deep depressions, lasting longer and more severe, are *not* inherent in the economic system. They have been caused by special events—perhaps misdirected monetary action by some political authority (as in the 1930s).

Having said that, we must remind ourselves that the demand shifts that cause only frictional unemployment as people adjust to new jobs can be very costly to *particular* industries and communities—textile mill towns, mining towns, Detroit when auto demands fall, Seattle when the Boeing plant experiences a decreased demand for jet planes, Orlando if the space program is reduced. These all fall within the rubric of frictional unemployment, which constitutes perhaps 1 to 3 percent of the labor force of the nation but may at times be a huge proportion of a particular community.

9, 10, 11

---

⁵ Of course, the recovery of stock prices does not mean stockholders have recovered their loss. For example, when GM stocks rise, a year or so later, back to $50, the stockholders are not back to where they would have been if no fall had occurred. The fall and its length reflects the loss of those interim earnings. Had earnings been maintained at $5 per year, stockholders would have had either more consumption or a greater wealth than $50 at the end of the recession.

Dispassionate Analysis and Compassionate Policy

Those who lose jobs see a world of reduced opportunities. It may seem that there are *no* jobs, certainly not of the kind they had been performing and at the former pay. To point out that there are other jobs, although not of the kind each person thinks it wise to accept, is not to say that people are foolish for not taking those jobs or that they deserve to suffer if they do not. Nor does an understanding of the reasons for massive unemployment constitute an excuse for it. Quite the contrary. It is not true that the rate of recovery from a recession is some natural rate that should not be affected by deliberate fiscal and monetary actions, about which we inquire in following chapters.

Determination of Aggregate Demand

What makes aggregate demand fluctuate instead of being constant with shifts from one product to another offsetting each other? What ties the demand for the products of various industries together? Expansions in one industry or sector set up forces for expansion in other sectors. Specialization in production means that some firms buy inputs from other firms. An increased output of final goods in one industry will increase the inputs bought from supplier industries. An increased demand for cars will increase the demand for steel and a host of other services, with some consequent feedback on the demand for cars. The web spreads throughout the economy. That several sectors would expand and contract in close step should not be surprising. But this does not explain why there occur large fluctuations in these mutually interrelated industries. Why should they experience large, persisting swings in demand for their products? It is these questions—the interconnection and size and duration of fluctuations in output and employment in the economy—that we treat for most of the remainder of the book.

Summary

1. Unemployment is not a sign that there are no jobs or work worth doing. It is, rather, a job-relocation process that involves search over other job opportunities to find the *best* one.

2. Contrary to what would be implied in a free-information-and-no-cost-of-quicker-adjustment world, reductions in demand do not imply that prices will be *immediately* reduced to market-clearing levels with sustained total employment and use of all productive resources. Instead, unemployment and idle productive resources are implied as modes of adjustment to changing demand and supply conditions.

3. Unemployment occurs for several reasons: (a) Restraints on markets (such as minimum-wage laws) that prevent some people from working at wages that reflect their marginal productivity. They shift to "noncovered" jobs or become self-employed "contractors." (b) Restraints on people working at jobs without a license or authorization (such as union membership or apprenticeship regulations). (c) The fact that some workers are willing to work only during seasonal peak demands when wages are high. (d) Shifting of relative demands or supplies that induce job shifting. This is called structural unemployment. (e) Falling *general* demand that requires reduced wages and prices. This is called "aggregate

demand deficiency" unemployment. (f) Resources often appear to be idle, or "unemployed," in order to economize on the costs of physical readjustments to unpredictable fluctuations in demand.

4 Unemployment of resources can be reduced by reducing the extent to which *general* demands fall. General demand decreases are a major source of the severe unemployment characteristic of depressions.

5 Major general recessions reflect "malfunctions" in the monetary and economic institutions, rather than decreases in general wants in any real sense.

Questions

1 In deciding who is an unemployed person, would you consider the following:
a. Is he now working for someone else as an employee? If his answer is "Yes," would you classify him as unemployed or as employed?
b. He answers "Yes" to the preceding question, but answers "No" to the question "Is your current job your usual kind of work?" He reports that he is working at a service station, while looking for a job as a lathe operator. Would you change the classification?
c. Next he is asked, "Are you willing to take an available job as a lathe operator at a wage of $2 an hour?" He answers, "No, I used to work for $6 an hour and I'm an experienced operator, not a novice." Is your classification of him still the same? Why?
d. If you do not call him unemployed in the preceding question, then how can you call anyone unemployed? For there are always jobs available at some sufficiently low wage—a wage he would call "ridiculous," "un-American," or "below standard."

2 The usual criterion of an unemployed person is "not employed by someone else and actively looking for a job." It says nothing about the range of jobs or wages he refuses to consider. What do you think the criterion implicitly assumes to avoid being completely useless?

3 "A man who loses his job through no fault of his own should not have to bear the losses of unemployment. The government must see to it that he does not." This is a quotation from a campaign speech of a major candidate for governor of California.
a. Is the candidate proposing that there be no unemployment or that anyone not currently employed should be given an income equivalent to what he was formerly getting?
b. How can either of these be accomplished?

4 Is a person who loses his job through no fault of his own also unemployed thereafter through no fault of his own? Explain.

5 "Unemployment is a wonderful privilege. Without it we would all be slaves to tyrants."
a. Can you interpret this "ridiculous" statement so as to make it not ridiculous. (Hint: There is no unemployment in the military. There is reputed to be none in Russia. Distinguish among the factors that shift demands, those that make job information costly, and the losses of wealth consequent to those demand shifts and costliness of job information.)
b. Would you prefer to live in a community in which unemployment is forbidden? Why? (Later we shall analyze ways of reducing unemployment without forbidding it.)

6 a. What different kinds of unemployment (with respect to why unemployment exists) do you think it is relevant to distinguish?
b. Why?

7 Suppose the daily sales of each of fifty firms are determined by a process simulated by the turn of a roulette wheel with numbers from 0 through 30. Further, suppose that the firm will on the next day seek to hire as many employees as the sales of the preceding day. Thus, if sales are 20 on the first day, the firm will seek to hire twenty people on the second day—given the wages of $25 per person per day. If there were fifty firms, the average number of employed people would be $50 \times 15 = 750$.

   a. Would that employment rate stay constant day after day despite the independent additive random process for determining the number of employees demanded at that wage rate?
   b. If those who were laid off by one employer took a day to select a new job, would there always be some unemployed?
   c. Would there always be some unfilled vacancies?
   d. Would these be equal to each other?
   e. What would happen to the number of job seekers and to the number of vacancies if the top five numbers on the roulette wheels were erased?
   f. What would happen if all the numbers had been increased by 5?
   g. The change from day to day in the totals of the fifty firms, with an unchanged roulette wheel, and the change from day to day when the roulette wheel is changed are two different kinds of changes. Which is consistent with the independent additive random fluctuations?
   h. Which would correspond to a correlated decrease in general aggregate market demand for goods?
   i. What could cause a general aggregate decrease?
   j. How quickly do you think a person would detect a general demand change?
   k. What does all this have to do with the real world?

8 On the average, the cost increment of each extra job investigated increases. Also, on the average, the gain in wages from another job investigated diminishes. If these two propositions are true, then what must be the relation between the increment of gain and the increment of cost in order to conclude that it will pay to take the first job investigated?

9 Employment agencies charge about 50–60 percent of one month's salary for their services for jobs paying about $400 per month. For jobs paying about $800, the fee is one month's salary. If this is paid to the employment agency by the employer, does it mean the employer bears the costs? Do you think this fee is too large? Why?

10 Is the analysis of this chapter consistent with the fact that unemployment among Negroes has become higher than among whites? Does it explain the level of employment at "full employment" or the massive changes in the unemployment rate?

11 When requesting a Congressional investigation into the methods, charges, and quality of services of private employment agencies, Mr. Abel, president of the United Steelworkers of America said, "A man or woman should not have to pay—often a large sum—for the privilege of obtaining a job." He also asserted that society and government had an obligation to make it possible for "every willing and able individual to work at or near his highest skill." Evaluate those remarks in the light of economic analysis.

National Income: Measurement and Meaning

26 GENERAL changes in demand are highly correlated with changes in national income and wealth. A higher national income induces an increase in aggregate demand; and a decrease in national income means a reduced aggregate demand, causing fluctuations in output and employment as well as in prices. What, precisely, is national income? How is it measured? What makes it fluctuate? What are the consequences of its fluctuations? What actions can be taken to prevent large fluctuations? These are some questions we shall investigate during the next several chapters.

National *money income* over a time period is the total *market value* of real (physical) national *product* created during that period. It is measured by and, indeed, consists of the aggregate of expenditures on *domestic current final products*.[1] Goods and services are produced and sold; payment is received by the sellers; and the money received is money income. The *real* income of the community consists of *real* products and is the basis of its "standard of living." But the production and exchange of the mass of variegated output is facilitated by and measured in *money flows*. And the circular flow of *spending* on products generates money income (see Figure 20–1).

Gross National Product (GNP)

Over a period of time, an economy produces a collection of goods and services. Whether or not each item is actually currently sold (some probably will be held in inventory at

---

[1] What is *generically* referred to here as "national income" is formally labeled "gross national product," and what is *officially* called "national income" is a measure which is a component of and smaller than gross national product.

the close of the period), everything produced can be assigned a market price, so we can measure the total flow of final products in dollar terms. The *market value of domestic current final output* is called *gross national product* (*GNP*).

Final Products

We are dealing with *production* of and *income* from final outputs, not with *all market transactions*. *All* transactions include inter-firm buying and selling of intermediate outputs (intermediate products are resold in some form to other firms). For example, most steel bought from U. S. Steel by General Motors is not at that time bought by the final user, for General Motors later resells the steel as an automobile. The purchase of the steel is, indeed, a market transaction, but it is not a "final" transaction. To add together the value of all transactions would mean counting the value of steel twice in measuring national output. The market value of General Motors' merchandise obviously is not attributable completely to the productive activity of General Motors, for some of the inputs utilized by General Motors were outputs of U. S. Steel and other suppliers. Similarly, U. S. Steel bought supplies from still other firms. Each firm along the line buys some inputs from others and adds to the value of those inputs. The national final production is, then, the *sum* of the *"values added"* by all of the firms.

Suppose a farmer produces wheat at a zero money cost and sells it to a miller for 5 cents; the miller works the wheat into flour, which he sells to a baker for 9 cents; the baker uses the flour to produce bread, which is sold to a customer for 15 cents. See Table 26–1. (1) The value of the final *output*, which is the sum of all the *values added* by the respective producers, is measured by the consumer's expenditure of 15 cents. (2) Also, 15 cents is the total of *incomes* earned by the producers: the farmer receives 5 cents; the miller receives $9 - 5 = 4$ cents; and the baker receives $15 - 9 = 6$ cents. Thus *final output equals income*. And while expenditure on the final output is 15 cents, expenditures in *all* transactions, including the buying and selling of "intermediate" products in inter-firm transactions, is $5 + 9 + 15 = 29$ cents.

Domestic Current Output

We are here interested in the *nation's* aggregate economic activity—income, output, employment; so we consider all spending on *domestic* final output. This includes purchasing by foreigners (exports) of our productions; by contrast, spending by domestic residents on foreign-produced goods (imports) is counted in foreign, not domestic, money income. (Does it follow that exports are "good" and imports are "bad"?) We

TABLE 26–1. Final Product Is Total of Value Added

	Value of Purchases of Intermediate Products from Other Firms	Value of Sales by Firms	Value Added
Farmer	0	5	5
Miller	5	9	4
Baker	9	15	6
	Total Value Added = National Final Product:		15

refer to "current" output simply to indicate that analyses of production, income generation, and income disposal encompass finite periods of time. The usual income-accounting period is one year, but no law precludes shorter or longer periods, and, indeed, data are commonly presented quarterly (i.e., every three months), although at an annual rate.

Exchanges of Existing Wealth

All market transactions also include buying and selling of wealth not currently produced. Perhaps the stock market provides the most obvious illustration. If you purchase a share of common stock of American Telephone and Telegraph, the transaction simply shifts ownership of *already existing* wealth from one person to another. Typically, the stock was issued by the corporation long ago, and A.T.&T. does not obtain funds from this current purchase. Even the purchase of stock directly from the corporation would not in itself contribute to *GNP;* the sale of stock for money is simply a "financial" transaction: A.T.&T. obtains a monetary asset, and the buyer obtains a corporate-ownership claim. Similarly, the buying and selling of land and of used cars are not constituents of national output,[2] even if both parties to the transaction have moved to preferred positions of asset holding. The transaction, although productive of utility, is a shifting of claims to *existing wealth*, not the *creation of income*.

1, 2, 3, 4

GNP and Changes in Quantities and Prices

GNP is the sum of the market values of the final goods produced by the nation's resources during the period in question. The value of each of the n-goods is given by quantity (q) multiplied by price (p). Thus, $GNP = p_1q_1 + p_2q_2 + \ldots + p_nq_n = PQ$, where P is an index of prices and Q is an index of output.[3] Obviously, *GNP* may change either because the physical collection of goods produced changes or because prices change. Actually, we can be sure that over any period both will change. The task of disentangling and measuring changes in quantities and prices gives difficult problems (and employment) to the keepers of the national income records.

Changes in the stream of physical output can take several forms. (1) Changes in the *proportionate* composition. Is basket A, consisting of 5 trucks, 40,000 haircuts, and 100,000 toothpicks, bigger or smaller than basket B, made up of 6 trucks, 1,000 haircuts, and 89,000 toothpicks? (2) Changes in the *constituent* composition. How does basket A or B compare with basket C, which contains radios instead of toothpicks? In both cases, we obviously have a problem of *weighting* the components, and there are alternative methods. (3) Changes in the *quality* composition, especially over longer and longer time periods. Compare basket A of 1954 with basket D of 1972. Both contain 5 trucks, 40,000 haircuts, and 100,000 toothpicks; but suppose 1972 trucks are better than 1954 trucks, 1972 haircuts are worse, and toothpicks stay the same. We can rely on the accountants and the statisticians in the back room to come up with *GNP* figures for 1954 and 1972. But what do the figures measure? When one component of the 1972

---

[2] There may be salesmen or lawyers or others who render services in connection with the transaction, and these services are part of the economy's output, their value contributing to *GNP*. But the value of the old asset itself is not included in current *GNP*.

[3] More specifically, P is the "implicit price index" (or "price deflator"), and Q is "*GNP* in constant dollars (prices)."

basket is worse than in the 1954 basket and another is better, we have a particularly difficult weighting problem. Even if prices are the same for all commodities in the two years, what would a larger figure for 1972 mean? That the 1972 basket is better or bigger? Hard-headed number-counters are likely to shy away from an evaluation smacking of subjectiveness.

Price Changes

In addition to quantitative and qualitative changes in the output stream, there are changes in prices. *GNP* is usually measured in terms of *current* dollar prices: 1954 output is measured in 1954 prices, and 1972 output is measured in 1972 prices. However, in order to estimate the change in real output, allowance is made for price changes by calculating *GNP* in terms of *constant* price dollars: *both* 1954 and 1972 outputs are multiplied by prices of a single year—which may be 1954, 1972, or some other. This device to eliminate the effect of price changes also has flaws, as does everything else this side of heaven. In particular, there is the problem of changes in quality. If the 1972 truck is better than the 1954 truck, then the use of 1954 prices to calculate 1972 *GNP* in constant dollars will underestimate 1972 output. But the biases and errors are not so large as completely to destroy the relevance of *GNP* measures.

We thus have two measures of *GNP* in any year: (1) *GNP* in *current*, or contemporary, dollars (GNP_{cur}); and (2) *GNP* in *constant* dollars (GNP_{con}) as a measure of real output.[4]

Further Difficulties in the GNP Measure

In addition to problems stemming from changes in quantities and prices, there are difficulties of coverage and conception. For example, the measurement of *GNP* does not include the value of services that are not exchanged in formal markets. The cooking services of a wife are not measured as part of national product, yet the same services bought in a restaurant are. Marriage of a bachelor to his maid will decrease the market-measured product, for he no longer pays her a salary—however much she may still contribute to his utility.

Furthermore, the definition of "final goods" is not perfect. Is a businessman's suit of clothes a final product or an intermediate good used in production? Both. Yet, in the

---

[4] Symbolically, with 1972 being the current year and 1954 the base year, $P^{72}Q^{72} = GNP^{72}_{cur}$, and $P^{54}Q^{72} = GNP^{72}_{con54}$. Dividing the first equation by the second:

$$\frac{P^{72}}{P^{54}} = \frac{GNP^{72}_{cur}}{GNP^{72}_{con54}}.$$

Letting the ratio of the current price index to the price index of the base period (which equals the ratio of current-dollar *GNP* to constant-dollar *GNP*) be *P*:

$$\frac{P^{72}}{P^{54}} = P = \frac{GNP^{72}_{cur}}{GNP^{72}_{con54}}.$$

The price ratio, *P*, is the "implicit price index," or "*GNP* price deflator." It follows that *GNP* in current dollars equals *GNP* in constant dollars multiplied by the price deflator.

measure of national product, the convention is adopted of counting the suit as a final good. Should the gasoline used to drive to work be counted as a final good or as an intermediate good? Again, probably both, but it is counted as a final product. This makes national output, which is the sum of final products, an overestimate of the income received from the national wealth. As a true measure of income, national product includes some items it should not and excludes others it should include.

The foregoing discussion of definition and measurement does not exhaust the difficulties in using *GNP* as a measure of the flow of final goods and services. But, inadequate though *GNP* is as a measure, one can reasonably suppose that, for example, a fall from $104,000,000,000 in 1929 to $56,000,000,000 in 1933 reflected an actual great decline—probably in the neighborhood of 50 percent—in aggregate spending on final output; and a fall, in the same period, from $104,000,000,000 to $74,000,000,000 in 1929 (constant) prices would scarcely be camouflage of an *increase* in the physical volume of output.

Absorption

Only by coincidence will *GNP* (current *national* output) be exactly equal to the goods and services currently *available* to and *used* by the national community for its own consumption and investment. The discrepancy between *domestic production* and *domestic utilization* of goods and services arises largely from participation by the economy in foreign trade.

Even if a country's foreign trade is balanced (money value of exports equal to money value of imports), international commerce makes possible a gain by more specialized use of resources. But with a given *GNP*, suppose that exports do *not* equal imports. If imports are greater than exports, on balance, the nation is receiving products from the rest of the world. This total of products available for domestic disposal is a broader measure than *GNP*; it is a measure of *world* production utilizable by the domestic economy. This measure of *total production available to the economy* is called *absorption* (A); it is the sum of *GNP* and the excess (which may be negative) of imports over exports: $A = GNP + (\text{imports} - \text{exports})$.

What is actually "absorbed" domestically is larger than *GNP* if the nation sells, lends, or gives less output to foreigners than it acquires from abroad; the net import of goods and services makes absorption greater than domestic production. Conversely, *net* export to foreigners makes A smaller than *GNP*. (Does this alter your view of the "goodness" and "badness" of imports and exports? Do you think that *net imports* should be labeled —as is frequently done—an "unfavorable" balance of trade?)[5]

5, 6

Net National Product

The difference between *gross* and *net* output is *capital consumption,* that is, depreciation. When production occurs, there is some wearing out and using up of equipment and plant. Presumably, part of the current output will be devoted to repairing and replacing

---

[5] In defining absorption as *GNP* plus the foreign trade balance, *inventory increases* were not mentioned, for they form a part of current output and are thereby included in *GNP*; that is, the community absorbs part of its current production by investing it in larger inventories. And we have implicitly treated *inventory decreases* as using up part of accumulated capital and thus as a component of capital consumption. Primarily because of problems of estimation and data collection, Department of Commerce national-income statisticians do *not* count inventory depletion as capital depreciation.

capital goods. But whatever is done, if anything, to replace and maintain the initial amount of capital, the depreciation itself means that net output is less than gross output. *Net national product (NNP) is equal to GNP minus capital consumption.* The two measures—*GNP* and *NNP*—are highly correlated.

National Income

National income *(NI)* consists of the total income to the *productive agents* of the economy: wages and salaries (some 70 percent of the total), profits (over 20 percent), rents, and interest. *NI* is smaller than *NNP*, for some of the spending counted in *NNP* is transferred to the government by "indirect business taxes," which are not considered a payment for any productive services by the government. The chief indirect business taxes are federal excise (especially liquor and tobacco) taxes, state sales (especially general and gasoline) taxes, and local property taxes. (Most conspicuously excluded are personal-income and corporate-profits taxes, for they are taxes on income and considered to be part of income, first disbursed to income recipients and then collected by government.) Thus *NNP* is national output valued in terms of *market prices,* for the prices include indirect taxes; *NI* is the same output valued in terms of *factor cost,* for the income payments to the owners of the inputs do not include indirect taxes.

Personal Income

Personal income *(PI)* is the portion of national income which goes to individuals (and to nonprofit institutions and private funds). Some portions of *NI* are not in *PI*: corporate income which is not distributed (corporate saving), corporate-income taxes, and social security taxes. However, *PI* includes some things which are not part of *NI*: net interest (paid by government and consumers) and government and business transfer payments (for example, veterans' benefits, which are *not* compensation for current productive activity).

Disposable Income

Not all of *PI* is available for private expenditure, for personal taxes must be paid. What remains of *PI* after payment of such taxes is disposable income *(DI)*—most of which is expended on personal consumption, with a little paid out as interest, and the remainder, by definition, saved.

Figure 26–1 summarizes these national accounting relationships as a circular flow of expenditures and income using approximate data for 1970.

Henceforth, we shall not distinguish between the different measures. A reference to national income will mean *GNP* or *NNP*, for the ratio, *NNP/GNP*, changes only minutely from year to year (ranging from .87 to .95 since 1929). Later, in connection with fiscal policy we shall refer to *disposable income* (national income minus tax collections). But we make no further mention of *NI* and *PI*; aside from expositional comprehensiveness, the only excuse for noting them at all is that they are sometimes referred to on financial pages of newspapers and the like.

7, 8, 9,
10, 11,
12, 13

National Income, Output, Employment, and Prices

National income, we have seen, is measurable as spending on current domestic final output. But more "basic" than mere *spending* is the real *output* itself and the *employ-*

National Income: Measurement and Meaning

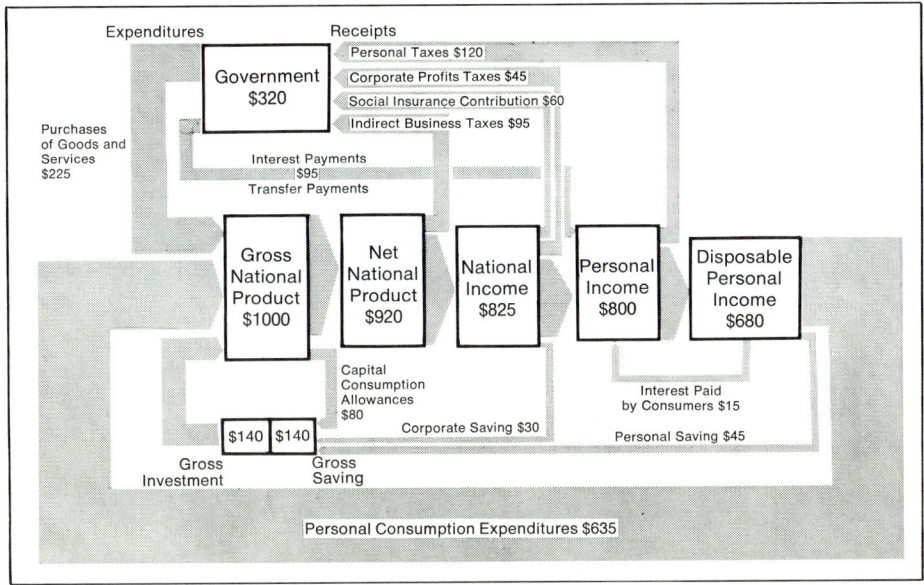

FIGURE 26-1. Flow of Income and Expenditures (Billions of Dollars), 1970

Gross national product was $977 billion in 1970 and can be measured as the sum of consumption expenditures ($617 billion), federal and state government purchases of goods and services ($221 billion), and gross investment ($139 billion), the latter including both gross private domestic investment ($136 billion) and net exports of goods and services ($3 billion). The difference between gross saving and gross investment reflects primarily a government deficit. Do not fret about inconsistencies of a billion dollars here or there. Data source: U. S. Department of Commerce.

ment of resources; also, changes in the *price level* may be of greater interest than just the dollar size of income. Over the past century the *secular* trend of national income has been upward at the average rate of about 4.6 percent annually, divided into 1 percent to higher prices, 1.6 percent to increased population and 2 percent to per capita growth in real income (although the major price-level rises have occurred sporadically, primarily because of inflationary means of financing wars). Figure 26-2 plots data for national income in actual dollar values, in real terms (adjusted for price-level changes), and the general price index. Also plotted are the labor force and the employed for the interval during which data are available. (Since 1950, half of the approximately 6,000,000 difference between the employed and the labor force is accounted for by military employment. The remaining 3,000,000 is the number of "unemployed" at any moment.)

Note the similarity of fluctuations in the series. As the labor force grows, employment grows with it. This is the answer to the people who ask, "Where will all these newcomers get jobs?" Each person will enter the market for specialized exchange of product and will produce goods and services and obtain claims to buy goods from other people. So long as scarcity exists, jobs will be available, whatever the size of the population.

It is apparent that these economic variables move together rather closely. For the period 1919-1970—over half a century encompassing peace and war, prosperity and depression, inflation and deflation—year-to-year changes in output, employment, and prices are in the *same direction* as changes in *GNP* between 85 and 90 percent of the time; similarly, employment and output move together about 90 percent of the time, and prices and output almost 80 percent of the time.

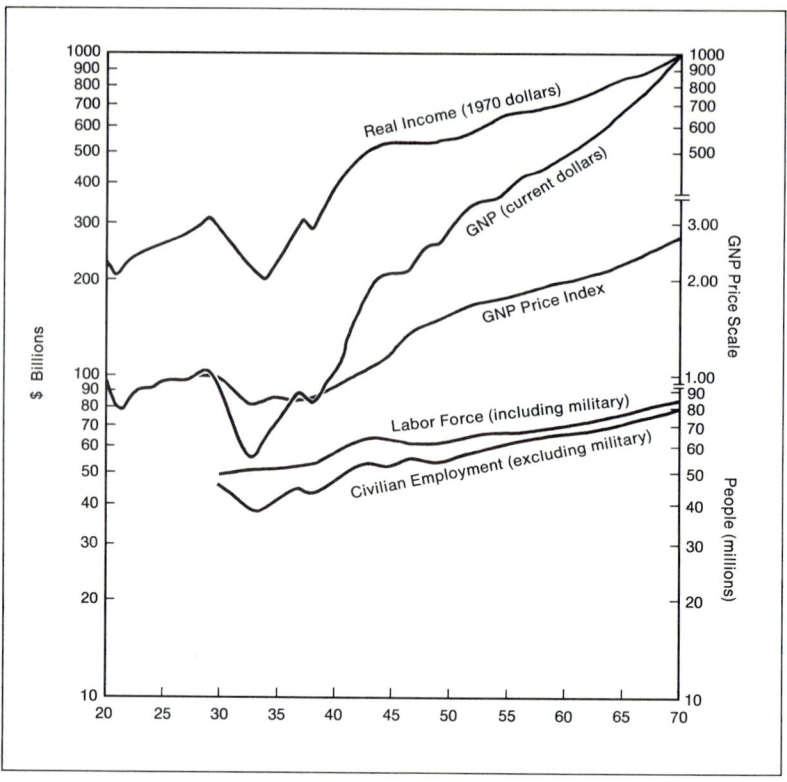

FIGURE 26–2. Gross National Product in Current and in 1970 Dollars, Price Index, Total Labor Force, and Civilian Employment

All lines are correlated. The *GNP* upward trend in constant (1970) dollars is steeper than civilian employment; this reflects an increasing stock of nonhuman capital wealth, and the increased productivity of human resources. Because *GNP* fluctuations are so highly correlated with those of other series, *GNP* changes are used as the single approximating index of general economic production. *GNP* in current dollars rises faster than real income (*GNP* in constant dollars is adjusted for price-level change) because the general price level has risen.

But even when two variables move in the same direction, the *proportions* of change may vary from period to period. If national income rises, P and Q usually rise also, but how much of the increase is comprised of changes in the one variable and how much in the other? And when income rises, employment also generally rises, but the percentage changes do not bear a constant relation to each other over time.

1933 was the bottom of the Great Depression. A large increase in *GNP* (63 percent from 1933–39) reflected a proportionately greater increase of output and employment than prices, partly because the unemployed were again taking jobs and partly because the average number of hours worked per week increased from the unusually low level of 1933. On the other hand, over a full-employment interval, income growth *could* be primarily in prices (if the money stock increased very rapidly relative to growth of population and productivity) or *could* be primarily in terms of output (reflecting the growth in per-capita productivity and resource and labor-force increase). Each episode has to be examined historically to see what happened. Of course, it is possible to *say* that if from a "full-employment" level *GNP* expands more than do per-capita productivity, resources, and the labor force, price rises will have accounted for some of the *GNP* rise. But that statement is not very helpful, unless we can assert that resources, productivity, and the labor force do not increase by more than some finely restricted rate. At the moment, about all we can say is that the combined effect of those factors gives a rise of between 2 to 5 percent per year.

National Income or Wealth

National income measurements are often used to determine whether a nation is becoming "better off." Sometimes the rate of growth of income is used to compare what is happening in two countries or two episodes in one country. We conjecture that more likely the amount of *wealth,* rather than income or growth of wealth, is the appropriate measure.

Concern about national rates of increase of wealth arises from a fear that one nation may use its wealth to acquire the wealth of the other. Whether that fear is well founded cannot be answered here. But it should be noted that a nation (or an individual) does not need to wait for superiority in either wealth or income, per capita or absolute, before muscle-flexing may be undertaken. Although the amount of wealth constitutes a constraint on what can be done in the aggregate, one activity can be increased by curtailing other activities. Devoting half of relatively meager resources to a selected endeavor (armaments) may carry the day over a competitor who commits only 10 percent of greater resources to that endeavor.

Although the foregoing considerations indicate a use for measurements of national wealth as well as of national income, there are few such measurements. The principal reason is that a major portion of our wealth is human, and people are not bought and sold. Only their *current flow* of services is sold. Hence, the only measure available is the current earnings from current use of human resources. Insofar as income flow measures are accurate, they provide an indirect measure of wealth via the interest-rate relationship between wealth and income.

National income changes do not accurately indicate changes in wealth. For example, if a building should be vacant for a year, the record would report no rental receipts even though the capital value of the building would not thereby have fallen to zero. Similarly, a person who reports no income for a period may still represent wealth value. Although real national income fell transiently by about 30 percent from 1929 to 1933, it does not follow that national wealth was 30 percent smaller in the latter year. And, therefore, when income rose by about 50 percent from 1933 to 1939, our stock of real wealth did not increase by that percentage. Only if the income decrease were permanent would wealth have fallen by the same percentage.[6]

---

[6] On the basis of one tabulation, national real (constant dollar) wealth—both "reproducible tangible" assets and "all" wealth, including nonreproducible assets—fell less than 5 percent from 1929 to 1933. For years 1933–39, reproducible tangible wealth increased about 5 percent and all wealth increase less than 1 percent. In 1929, the ratio of all wealth to *GNP*—the capital output ratio —was 4.2; it rose to 5.9 in 1933; and it fell back to 4.4 in 1939. Data from Raymond W. Goldsmith, *The National Wealth of the United States in the Postwar Period* (Princeton: Princeton University Press, 1962), tables, pp. 112, 114.

Summary

1   National money income over a period of time is the market value of real national product created during that time. This market value of domestic final output is termed the gross national product (*GNP*).

2   The aggregate value of final products is the sum of the values added by producing firms—not the total value of the output of each firm, which would entail double-counting of intermediate products sold by one firm to another.

3   Exchanges of existing wealth are not included in the national product.

4   Changes in *GNP* reflect changes in both the amounts of real goods produced and their prices. *GNP* can be calculated in *current* dollars or in *constant* dollars, using prices for some base period.

5   *GNP* only approximates real national income. It does not take into account services that do not pass through a formal market, the concept of the final product, and quality changes are ambiguities in the measurement.

6   Net national product (*NNP*) is *GNP* adjusted for depreciation of capital goods—*GNP* minus capital consumption. National income (*NI*) is *NNP* minus indirect business taxes paid to the government (and not available to anyone as income). Personal income (*PI*) is the national income which finds its way to individuals. Disposable income is that part of personal income remaining after payments of personal taxes.

7   In recent years, consumption has constituted about 65 percent of gross national product, investment about 15 percent, government purchases about 20 percent, and *net* exports about 1 percent. Long-run fluctuations in these proportions sometimes are substantial. Investment has varied from a low of 1 percent in 1932 to nearly 20 percent in 1950; government purchases have ranged from less than 10 percent in 1929 to nearly 50 percent in 1943 and 1944.

8   Wealth, rather than national income, measures the economic capabilities of an economy. Current national income is a measure of the current utilization of that capability.

Questions

1   Distinguish between *all* market transactions and so-called *final* transactions. Which is the better measure of the economy's "productive activity"? What is the relation between final transactions and the sum of values added?

2   Label each of the following statements true or false, and briefly defend your evaluation.
   a. "If we added the total amounts of goods and services sold by every individual and business firm in the United States in 1964, this sum would be *GNP* for 1964."
   b. "Inventory investment can never be negative, because purchases of goods for inventory cannot fall below zero."
   c. "Every money payment from one individual or firm to another increases *GNP*."
   d. "An increase in *GNP*, expressed in current prices, necessarily reflects a proportionately greater outflow of goods and services."

3 What are the inadequacies of *GNP* as a measure of aggregate productive activity? Distinguish between *GNP* in current dollars and *GNP* in constant dollars. Does the calculation of *GNP* in constant dollars resolve all of the deficiencies in the *GNP* measure?

4 The sales of General Motors are $20 billion annually; but its value added may be only $12 billion. Does that mean its profits are $8 billion? If not, what does the $8 billion measure?

5 "Gross National Product doubles in ten years." Interpret this if expressed in current dollars. In constant dollars. Which would you prefer?

6 What is the "*GNP* price deflator" or "implicit price index"? For what purpose is it used?

7 Seller sells an old house to buyer. Buyer says he has invested his savings in a house. Does that enter into the investment component of national income? Why?

8 Would you count the receipts of a gambling house in Las Vegas as part of the national income? Would you count any part of it as national income? Explain why.

9 Why does the government, or anyone for that matter, bother to collect data to estimate national income?

10 Should the costs of gasoline consumed in driving to work each day be counted as an expense of production, or as a person's consumption expenditure? Which procedure would make national income larger?

11 Figure 21-4 is a simplified version of Figure 26-2.
   a. Do you agree that if Figure 26-2 were turned upside down, it would show a flow of income in the same direction as Figure 21-4? In other words, do you agree that households are on the right-hand side and business firms on the left-hand side of Figure 26-2?
   b. What institution in Figure 26-2 is omitted from Figure 21-4?

12 "A transactions tax is levied on every market exchange of goods for money. It is the same as an income tax because it is a tax on money income, while nonmarket incomes (for example, owned homes rather than rented homes; housewives' services rather than maids' services) are untaxed." Evaluate.

13 Assume that economic activity of the economy in a given year consists of the following: (1) Steel producers fabricate $2.5 million of farm machinery, which is sold to farmers. (2) Farmers produce 4 million bushels of wheat, which is sold for $4 million to millers. The farm machinery depreciates $1 million. (3) Millers grind all the wheat into flour. Half of the flour is sold to bakers for $3 million; the remaining flour is kept in inventory and also valued at $3 million. (4) Bakers use the purchased flour to produce bread, which sells for $4 million. (5) The government spends $2 million in payrolls, of which $.5 million is financed by indirect business taxes.

   In addition to your final answers to the following questions, show your calculations; that is, indicate all of the additions and subtractions you make in arriving at the answers.
   a. What is the numerical value of Gross National Product?
   b. What is the value of Net National Product?
   c. What is the value of National Income?

14 Two cases of misplaced and misleading emphasis are (i) concentration on national money income rather than real income, and (ii) concentration on income rather than wealth. Defend *and* oppose this contention.

National-Income Theory:
The Basic Model

27 TO understand how various factors affect the value of national income, we require more than definitions of income and its components. An analytical structure showing the way each component is related to others is necessary. For this, we shall use the functional relationships of the simplified Keynesian model of income determination.[1] This model uses three relationships, one relating consumption demand to income and wealth, and another relating investment demand to income. They are called the consumption and investment functions. A third relationship states that the production of consumption goods and investment goods generates national income. Shifts in the positions of the two demand functions (like demand and supply schedules in a supply-and-demand diagram) affect income.

Income Creation and Income Disposal

National income can be categorized by the *kinds of goods and services* produced: private domestic consumer goods, private domestic investment-type goods, government

---

[1] John M. Keynes (1883–1946) was an English economist and government adviser. Since he dealt with crucial matters of economic policy, it was inevitable that he become controversial. Some have regarded him as a virtual messiah; in the eyes of others, he was—if not the devil himself—at least the first lieutenant of the fallen angel. Our purpose is not to discuss in detail the particular *policy* recommendations of Keynes; rather, we investigate a simple mode of income analysis that stems from his work, *The General Theory of Employment, Interest, and Money,* of 1936. In the sense that all economists use the language and functional relationships of that model, they are all Keynesians, but in the sense of agreement with the recommended policy, not all are Keynesians.

goods, and export goods. We call these consumption (C), and investment (I)—including accumulation of inventories, government (G), and exports (X). Thus, from the standpoint of creation of income, $Y = C + I + G + X$.

The (money) income received by productive factors is *disposed* of, or allocated, in various ways. If government and foreign trade were omitted from the picture, then there would be no G and X and no tax collections (T) and imports (M). In that case, money income is disposed of in two broad ways: some is spent on consumption (C), and the rest *not* spent on consumption is called savings (S)—whether it goes into the sugar bowl, the bank, or the purchase of investment goods.

Income not spent on consumption is called savings, not because it is not spent at all, but because it is used to increase one's wealth rather than to consume. The money income used for savings (increase of wealth) may be spent for investment-type capital goods or may simply not be spent, thereby increasing one's stock of money. Both are called savings—though the purchase of investment-type capital goods is usually called investment—even if one will hear of "investing" in a larger hoard of money.[2] When government and foreign trade are included, the definition of saving must be modified: saving (S) is that part of income *not spent* on domestic consumption (C) nor on taxes (T) nor on imports (M). Thus, from the standpoint of *income disposal*, $Y = C + S + T + M$.

In 1970, consumption accounted for almost 65 percent of gross national product; investment was approximately 15 percent of the total; government purchases were over 20 percent; and *net* exports ($X - M$) were .5 percent, though exports and imports both were about 6 percent. These proportions have remained highly stable since the early 1950s. In the period since 1929, consumption hit a peak of over 84 percent in 1932 as income fell in the Depression at a greater rate than did consumption, and consumption declined to a low of 52 percent of *GNP* in 1943 and 1944 during World War II. Investment has seen wide fluctuations, hitting bottom in 1932 with only 1.5 percent and reaching a high of nearly 18 percent in 1950. Government purchases, which were just over 8 percent of *GNP* in 1929, rose steadily during the 1930s, reached 46 percent during the war, and fell to a low of 12 percent in 1947 before leveling out at around 20 percent. *Net* exports typically are a minute proportion of *GNP*—its ratio does not reflect the total importance of the economy's foreign trade for our productive ability.

National income determination will be illustrated first for a pure-consumption economy, with no production of or demand for investment (capital) goods, i.e., with no saving. In this most simple case:

1. The consumption services *produced* generate national income, since all income is obtained by producing only consumption goods and services.

2. The amount of consumption goods *demanded* depends on (is a function of) that national income.

Income and consumption are such that both conditions are satisfied; that is, the rate of national income is such that it induces a rate of consumption demand exactly equal to that income itself.[3]

---

[2] If you suspect "investment" or "investing" are used in a variety of ways, you get the message. In reading general economic news, be aware of the ambiguity.

[3] Notice how similar this is to our early demand and supply analysis. There we had two relationships or conditions connecting *price* and quantity, rather than *income* and quantity. The two rela-

Simultaneous satisfaction of both conditions by the consistent values of consumption and income does not imply circularity. Rather, it is a matter of joint mutual determination. The *two* relationships between income and consumption are simultaneously satisfied. One relationship asserts that money income is what is spent on production or supplying of consumption goods.[4] This *first* condition can be expressed as:

$$(1) \quad Y = C.$$

Figure 27–1 presents the relationship graphically. Both the horizontal and vertical axes measure in terms of *money,* using the *same scale.* Therefore, a straight line from the origin, rising at an angle of 45 degrees, shows all points with equal coordinates. If

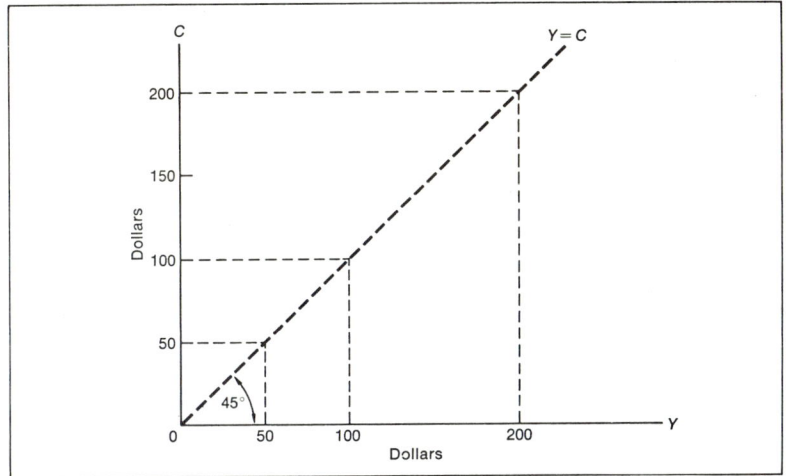

FIGURE 27–1. Income Equals Expenditure

Income (measured horizontally) must equal expenditures on goods and services (here only consumption, measured vertically): the economy must be *some* place on the 45-degree line. To know *where,* we must know more.

---

tionships—the demand function and the supply function—were separately identified by calling the quantity that satisfied the first relationship the quantity demanded, while the quantity in the other was the quantity supplied. The particular price and quantity that satisfied both conditions were an equilibrium, or consistent, price-quantity pair. Here, too, we have two relationships connecting the two variables, income and consumption. One relationship is called the consumption function (demand for consumption at each income) and the other is the income identity (rather than supply relationship). Unlike the demand and supply curves related to price, here we relate to income (and both are "positive" relationships between income and quantity, whereas with the price variable, demand was a negative function while supply was a positive function).

[4] Some modification is in order. For equilibrium, money income must be a manifestation of spending on *currently* produced output. Each component of income is not always spent on current output. For example, consumption expenditure is expenditure simply on consumption goods, whether produced currently *or* in the past. Suppose that the economy is producing nothing, and therefore no income is being generated; nevertheless, the community is consuming. Current consumption in the absence of current production is feasible only through reducing inventories, and a decrease of inventories is negative investment (or "disinvestment"); thus, the positive consumption is balanced by the negative investment, and income remains zero.

consumption (measured vertically) is $50, then income (measured horizontally) is $50, and the equal vertical and horizontal measurements locate a point on the 45-degree line.

We *must* be someplace on the 45-degree line. Where?

The Consumption Demand Function

Consumption demanded is a function of income. This is the *second* condition. The larger a person's income, the more he spends for consumption—food, clothing, medicine, housing, transportation, recreation. Also, the larger a person's income, the more he wants to save. (In the pure-consumption economy, he does not spend his savings on nonexistent investment goods, but wishes only to accumulate money.) The general relationship between income and consumption is described by the graph in Figure 27–2.

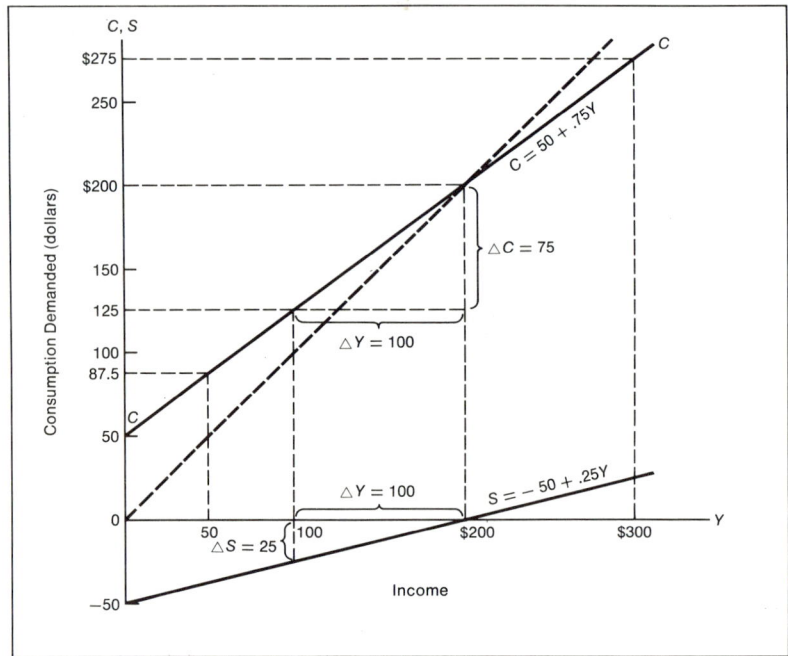

FIGURE 27–2. The Consumption and Saving Functions

Line C shows how larger income induces larger consumption expenditures, though the entire increment in income is not spent for consumption. The vertical distance between line C and the 45-degree line shows the rate of saving. At low incomes, consumption is larger than income, shown by C being above the 45-degree line. Line S shows directly the rate of saving. At income of $200, saving is zero: all income is spent for consumption. At incomes above $200, consumption is smaller than income, and saving is positive. The slope of line C, measured by the ratio of vertical change per unit of horizontal movement along the line, shows the marginal propensity to consume, in this case, .75. And the slope of line S, measured by $\Delta S/\Delta Y$, equals the marginal propensity to save, here .25. Knowing either the C line or the S line enables us to derive the other. The only consistent income is $200.

The solid line, C, indicates by its height the rate of consumption for any income; C thus depicts the consumption function.

Two features of line C must be noted. First, its slope, which is less than 45 degrees, has a value less than unity. This means that an increment of income, ΔY, is associated with a *smaller* increment of consumption, ΔC. An increase in income of $100 will increase consumption demanded by, say, $75; the remainder, $25, is not spent—and goes into saving. The *slope* of line C reflects the "marginal propensity to consume (MPC)"—the *ratio* of the increment in consumption demanded, ΔX, to the associated increment in income, ΔY. The ratio, $\Delta C/\Delta Y$, is the marginal propensity to consume; it is a measure of the slope of the consumption-demand line C and has a value of less than 1.00; in this example, .75.[5]

Second, for sufficiently small incomes, line C is above the 45-degree line. In that range, the person spends more than his current income; he dissaves. There is some larger income at which his consumption just equals income, while at still larger incomes he saves.

Shown in Figure 27–2 along the bottom is a graph of the demand for saving function, which is simply the difference between consumption and income. Its height equals the vertical distance at any income level between the C line and the 45-degree line.

TABLE 27–1. Marginal Propensities to Consume and to Save

Y	C	MPC = $\Delta C/\Delta Y$	S	MPS = $\Delta S/\Delta Y$ = 1 − MPC
0	50		−50	
		37.5/50 = .75		12.5/50 = .25
50	87.5		−37.5	
		37.5/50 = .75		12.5/50 = .25
100	125		−25	
		75/100 = .75		25/100 = .25
200	200		0	
		75/100 = .75		25/100 = .25
300	275		25	

In the *MPC* column, change in consumption is divided by the corresponding change in income. The increase in income from zero to $50 induces an increase in consumption from $50 to $87.5, a change of $37.5. The ratio of ΔC to ΔY is 37.5/50 = .75, which is the marginal propensity to consume. Of the $50 increase in income, $12.5 goes to saving (which is the remainder after consumption). *MPS* is .25; *MPC* + *MPS* = 1.0. Consistent (equilibrium) income is $200.

This proposition concerning the consumption-demand function is illustrated in Table 27–1. The first two columns show that for smaller incomes, consumption demanded exceeds income, but for larger incomes, consumption demanded is less than income, with saving being the difference ($S = Y - C$). The third column measures the marginal propensity to consume by computing the ratio of the increment of consumption to the associated increment of income. The rate of saving (or dissaving) is given in the S-

---

[5] The "slope" of a curve is defined as the vertical change divided by the corresponding horizontal change. In the 45-degree diagram (vertical change) ÷ (horizontal change) = (consumption change) ÷ (income change). Thus, slope of the consumption curve = $\Delta C/\Delta Y = MPC$.

column, and the marginal propensity to save ($MPS = \Delta S/\Delta Y$) is necessarily equal to the complement of MPC; $MPS = 1 - MPC$.[6]

Why does expenditure for consumption not rise equally with income? Reconsider remarks about the measurement of income *and* of wealth in the preceding chapter. We noted that the *measured* current income fluctuates more than wealth. If a real estate salesman does not sell any houses in one month, he does not assume that his income (or wealth) has fallen to zero. If a businessman's net receipts decline during some period, he does not conclude that they will necessarily stay as low in the future. A wage earner who loses his job does not suppose that his wealth and all future earning power have fallen to zero. Nor when he gets overtime pay does he assume his income will stay that high permanently. All receivers of income, as measured by sales value of *current* services, recognize that over short periods measured income from sales of services undergoes transient fluctuations. Therefore, people do not assume that their wealth—or permanent income—has changed proportionally with every fluctuation in current earnings. They do not gear their consumption rigidly to transient income. Instead, they relate it to long-run income or to wealth.[7]

A transient drop of $100 in income will induce a smaller drop in current consumption than if the drop were expected to last longer. Whereas a $100 decline in long-run income might have induced a decrease in consumption of $90 (and a drop in saving of $10), a decline of transient income would induce a decrease in consumption of, say, only $75. Conversely, if transient current income should increase $100, consumption would increase by, say, $75, whereas a $100 increase in permanent income would increase consumption by $90. Consumption may be a nearly constant proportion (perhaps .9) of the long-run average rate of income, so that rich and poor people alike may save about .1 of their expected permanent income. Thus, if people get richer over the decades, their rate of saving as a proportion of their permanent or average income may remain quite stable. This is, in fact, what seems to have happened in the United States.

If we relate consumption demanded to *transient* current income, rather than to permanent income (or to wealth), we find that consumption has fluctuated less than current money income. When transient money incomes fell, consumption fell by a smaller proportion. When transient money income rose, consumption rose by a smaller proportion.

Consumption demanded evidently is related basically to permanent income or wealth by a simple proportionality and is related indirectly to transient income in a slightly more complicated form. Nevertheless, we shall use the relationship of consumption to *transient* national income, for we are interested in transient variations in the production of goods and services—variations conventionally indicated by the current recorded monetary income.

It will be useful to give a numerical example of the relationship of consumption

---

[6] In this model, saving is income received but not consumed. A change in income would be disposed of partly through consumption and partly through saving: $\Delta Y = \Delta C + \Delta S$. If both sides of that income-disposal equation are divided by ΔY, we have: $1 = \Delta C/\Delta Y + \Delta S/\Delta Y$, or $1 = MPC + MPS$. It follows that $1 - MPC = MPS$.

[7] The distinction between transient changes and longer-period changes is similar to the distinction between cyclical and secular changes, the former referring to fluctuations of a short interval, say, a year or so, while the latter refers to movements lasting a decade or more. Our responses to short-lived, cyclical fluctuations in income—or prices or any other variable for that matter—are usually very different from our responses to the longer-lasting patterns of change.

demanded to transient current-money-income, as shown in Table 27–1. If $Y = 0$, then $C = 50$; if $Y = 50$, then $C = 87.5$. Thus, C increases from 50 to 87.5 as Y goes from 0 to 50; the ratio of the *change* in consumption demanded (37.5) to the *change* in transient income (50) is $\Delta C/\Delta Y = 37.5/50 = .75$. A little doodling with the data in the table will demonstrate that for any change in income, the ratio of the change of C to the change of Y is $\Delta C/\Delta Y = .75$. It follows that our consumption-demand function is:

$$(2)\ C = 50 + .75Y.$$

That is, consumption is equal to 50 plus three-fourths of whatever Y is. If, for example, $Y = 300$, then $C = 50 + .75(300) = 275$.[8]

Arithmetic-Tabular Determination of Income

The national income, Y, and the consumption, C, which jointly satisfy the two specified conditions are called the "equilibrium" values and can be ascertained by trying various values of income to see which one is associated with a rate of consumption sufficient exactly to absorb and maintain that income. In other words, what national income induces a consumption demand (condition 2) just large enough to sustain, or regenerate, that income (i.e., satisfy condition 1)? In Table 27–2, several incomes are listed, and

TABLE 27–2. Determination of Equilibrium National Income

(1) Actual (Received) Income	(2) Consumption	(3) (Saving)	(4) Implied (Generated) Income
0	50	(−50)	50
50	87.5	(−37.5)	87.5
100	125	(−25)	125
150	162.5	(−12.5)	162.5
200	200	(0)	200
250	237.5	(12.5)	237.5
300	275	(25)	275

With received national income of $200, all will be spent on consumption, and it will generate that same income. At smaller incomes (say, $100), consumption will be larger than received income and will generate a larger income (by $25), which is equal to the amount of dissaving. An income of $250 would not be an equilibrium income, for consumption purchases would not be sufficient to sustain that income, falling short by $12.5, the amount of saving.

with each is given the associated consumption (and saving, the amount not spent for consumption). At only one of the listed incomes, $200, is the associated consumption exactly large enough to match the income that induced that consumption. If income is $200, the community is induced to spend $200; and if the community then spends $200, income of $200 is again created.

At all hypothetical larger national incomes, for example, $250, consumption demand

---

[8] The numerical value of MPC (in this case, .75) is the value of the coefficient of the Y-variable. And since $C = 50 + .75Y$, the saving equation is: $S = -50 + .25Y$, with $MPS = .25$.

is less than income, and income is not recycled, as it were. Saving is accumulating as a sort of "leakage" from the flow cycle. And at all hypothetical incomes smaller than the $200 equilibrium, consumption would be larger than income. People would spend more for consumption goods than their income; *dis*saving occurs. Only the equilibrium national income of $200 is self-sustaining; only at that income does consumption exactly equal income, so that saving equals zero. (Remember that in this first step, we have assumed a zero-investment economy.)[9]

Graphic Determination of Income

We can show with a diagram this simultaneous satisfaction of the income generation and demand disposal conditions by some pair of values of Y and C. Examine Figure 27–3. The income generation condition states that the values of Y and of C must be someplace on the 45-degree line. The second (consumption function) condition states that they must be someplace on the C line. Obviously, both conditions are satisfied only at the point of intersection of both lines. In Figure 27–3, the lines intersect at $200. $Y = $200, and $C = $200. These are the *feasible, consistent* values of Y and C, the values *determined* by (1) the *income-generation* or supply *condition* and (2) the *consumption-function condition*—the two relationships comprising this income-determination model.[10]

Money and Income

This simplified economy produces one good (called consumption) and uses a second good, money. If money received by an income earner is not all spent on consumption goods, his money holding will increase. But the *total* money *stock* in existence remains constant (think of money for the moment as being just coins and paper money). The efforts of *individuals* to increase holdings of money by curtailing consumption means someone else must end up with less money. Not everyone can acquire more money, given the fixed total in the economy. As a result of the attempt to increase holdings of money, the money *flow* is diminished. National income falls, and given the unchanged amount of money, the ratio of the money stock to income increases—until incomes have fallen sufficiently to make people want to have just the quantity of money that actually exists. (In contrast to our earlier cases, in which prices change enough to induce the community to demand exactly the existing stock of a good, here it is their incomes that

---

[9] Our method of finding the equilibrium solution of national income can be improved by introducing the rule that if the trial income exceeds the expenditures on consumption so as to leave an amount of saving greater than the amount being invested (here assumed zero), then the next tentative trial income should be reduced; otherwise, increase the trial value. By successive trial and error, we will find the numerical solution.

[10] The solution for the feasible national income can be obtained also with grade-school algebra. Solution of the two conditions written as equations

$$(1)\ Y = C,$$
$$(2)\ C = 50 + .75Y,$$

will give the equilibrium values of income and of consumption (with equations representing simply the "conditions" between economic variables). By substitution, $Y = 50 + .75Y$, so $Y = 200$, and $C = 200$.

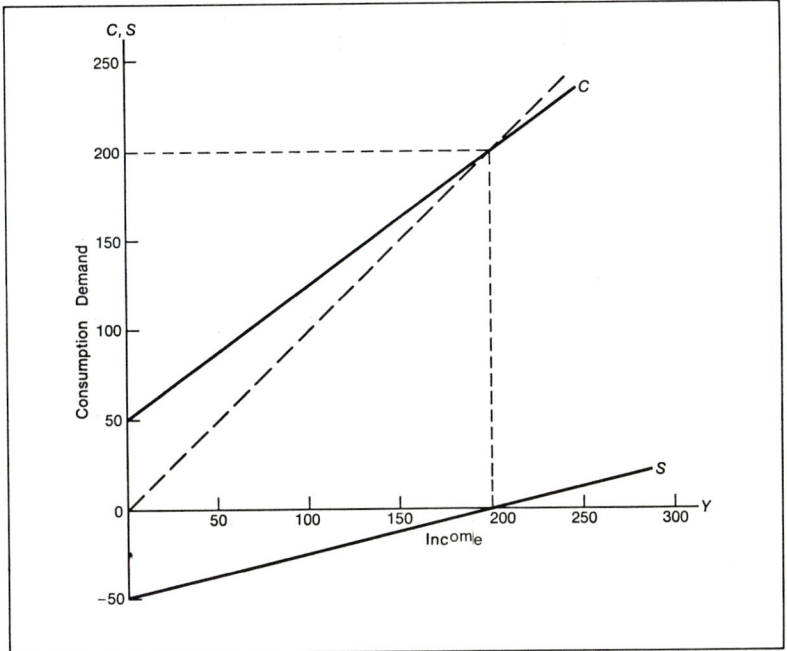

FIGURE 27-3. Determination of National Income

Intersection of C line and 45-degree line yields equilibrium national income. At all smaller incomes, total induced expenditures for consumption are larger than the generating income and thus give rise to a larger income. At all smaller incomes, total induced expenditures for consumption income and hence does not sustain the income. Same result can be obtained by using S line. At incomes less than intersection of S line with horizontal axis, dissaving occurs, indicating consumption in excess of income. At larger incomes, positive saving occurs, indicating consumption is less than income. We have assumed expenditures are solely for consumption, with investment zero.

change enough to bring about a demand for money just sufficient to match the amount of money available.)

Conversely, if consumption expenditures exceed income, some people must be spending out of their money stocks at a rate greater than their own money stocks are being replenished by receipt of money income. What one person spends, another must receive. So the attempt of each person (or most people) to reduce money holdings results in an increased flow of expenditure for goods—until national income becomes so large that people revise upward the amount of money they wish to keep on hand, i.e., the amount demanded.[11]

---

[11] This suggests that whether we work in terms of demand for consumption goods or in terms of demand and supply for money is purely an expositional choice in this simple model. Until now, we have let the demand and supply for money be implicitly adjusted with changes in consumption demand. We later examine the significance of the choice of which phenomenon to make explicit and which to leave in the background.

Income Determination in an Investment and Consumption Model

So far we have examined a model economy of pure consumption, with no growth of national wealth, all income consumed. Now we enlarge it to include investment activity.

The meaning of investment and saving, as used in income-determination analysis, should be made clear. In pages 457–460, investment was defined as production of investment-type goods that people undertake in the belief that it will be profitable. Investment goods (those not consumed currently) *can* be produced at a loss, especially if inefficient means are used or if the rate of production of such goods in any period is too high. If an investment is profitable, $1 of income diverted to it now will result in at least $1.06 of wealth a year later, assuming an interest rate of 6 percent. If the interest rate were 10 percent, we would have to end up with $1.10 of wealth. The rate at which it is feasible to invest, i.e., acquire capital goods, *profitably* depends upon several factors. One is the rate of interest, which we shall assume to remain constant.

There is some evidence that the (profitable) investment rate rises with the national income. There is even more evidence that the profitable investment rate is relatively unpredictable. But as a first approximation in our use of investment *as a determinant of national income*, we assume simply that there is some constant rate at which investment is demanded and that this rate persists despite changes in income. We shall assume that the community invests at a fixed rate of $50 and that our preceding consumption function remains the same. Condition 2 is now expanded into two conditions: output demanded is comprised of consumption demanded *plus* $50 of investment demanded: $C = 50 + .75Y$, and $I = 50$.

Recall that investment, I, is defined to be the amount of investment goods the public is willing to buy, given the prices and rates of return expected from those goods. Whatever the rate of demand for acquiring investment-type goods, will the public be willing to produce as much of investment-type goods as the public demands to acquire? (Since there is more than one person in the economy, there is no simple way to assure that the demands for such goods will be matched by their production at the existing income.) We shall assume that producers miraculously always adjust their production to match the amount demanded and do so profitably at the given prices of those capital goods. If we take those prices as given, it follows that the only thing which affects the demand for consumption output plus investment-goods output is national income. While national income here is assumed to have no effect on demand for investment-type goods, it does affect the demand for consumption-type goods. Thus we have to inquire into what is the level of national income which will generate a sum of consumption plus investment demand that will, in turn, induce production which generates income of the amount sufficient to sustain equivalent regenerative total demand.

Given the consumption demand function and the investment demand function, equilibrium national income can be determined. It is the income which induces a *sum* of (1) consumption demand and (2) investment demand equal to that income, i.e., $Y = C + I$, our first condition enlarged to allow for investment. We may call the sum of those two quantities of spending the *generated* income to suggest the circular flow of income: income is earned, goods are demanded, and the production again generates income. More rigorously, (1) the rate of consumption is indicated by the consumption function for any stipulated income; (2) the rate of investment is similarly indicated by the investment function; and (3) the sum of consumption and investment must equal the

National-Income Theory: The Basic Model

stipulated national income, if that income is to be the equilibrium income. Or to express the equilibrium requirement in terms of the saving and investment functions: (1) saving (derivable from the consumption function as that part of money income not spent for consumption) must equal (2) investment (indicated by the investment function) at the equilibrium income.

As with our earlier model, how these conditions determine equilibrium income can be illustrated by arithmetic, graphic, and algebraic modes of exposition.

Arithmetic-Tabular Determination of Equilibrium Income

In Table 27–3, investment-goods output demanded is assumed constant at $50 regardless of other conditions. (Column 4 has $50 for every income.) The income generated is the sum of consumption spending and investment spending: this sum is in column 5. The question is, what income in column 1 is equal to the sum of consumption and investment? That income will be consistent with our stipulated consumption and investment functions. In the present instance, the equilibrium income is $400. It induces consumption of $350 (and saving of $50); constant investment of $50 plus induced consumption of $350 is exactly sufficient to sustain that $400 income. And saving is entirely used for investment.

TABLE 27–3. Determination of Equilibrium National Income

(1) Received Income	(2) Consumption Demanded	(3) (Saving)	(4) Investment Demanded	(5) Generated Income
0	50	(—50)	50	100
50	87.5	(—37.5)	50	137.5
100	125	(—25)	50	175
150	162.5	(—12.5)	50	212.5
200	200	(0)	50	250
250	237.5	(12.5)	50	287.5
300	275	(25)	50	325
350	312.5	(37.5)	50	362.5
400	350	(50)	50	400
450	387.5	(62.5)	50	437.5

The consumption function is the same as in Table 27–2. An investment function has been introduced. The addition of a constant rate of investment of $50 increases the value of equilibrium income by $200 (from $200 to $400).

An income of $350 would be too small, because the induced consumption would be too large (even though smaller than if income were $400). The sum of consumption ($312.50) plus investment ($50) exceeds the initiating income ($350). An income of $450 is too large, for consumption is not enough ($387.50) to sum with investment ($50) to $450; the sum is only $437.50, so the initially received income is not maintained. An income above $400 would not have associated with it enough consumption plus investment to sustain that larger income. At incomes over $400, induced saving would be greater than scheduled investment. Goods would be produced at a rate higher than is profitable, and inventories would accumulate. The only income consistent with the given consumption and investment functions is $400.

Graphic Determination of Equilibrium Income

The presence of investment requires that a line denoting the rate of investment be added to the 45-degree diagram, as in Figure 27–4. The investment line is horizontal at $50, indicating a constant rate regardless of income (only by arbitrary assumption do the consumption and investment lines intersect on the vertical axis). Total expenditure (the $C + I$ line) is obtained by adding the consumption and investment lines. The $C + I$ line with the 45-degree line locates the equilibrium national income ($400). The portion consisting of consumption ($350) is indicated by the height of C, and the rate of investment ($50) is denoted by the distance from C to the $C + I$ line.

Also in Figure 27–4 we have the saving line. At the equilibrium level of income, the S and I curves cross; in other words, in equilibrium, $I = S$.[12]

Money versus Investment Goods versus Consumption Goods

We can interpret this in terms of the role of money. In the present analysis, we have three goods: consumption goods, investment goods, and money (ignoring labor). It is an old story now that received income which is not spent on consumption is saved. But saved money income may be either *spent* for investment or *held* as an increase in one's stock of money. The disposition of money *income* is between consumption and saving,

---

[12] The stipulated economic relationships can be expressed algebraically as follows:

(1) $Y = C + I$,
(2) $C = 50 + .75Y$,
(3) $I = 50$.

Equation (1) has been expanded to include the investment-spending component, which formerly was assumed to be zero. Equation (2) is unchanged from the earlier model. Equation (3) tells us that investment spending is 50 (instead of zero) regardless of income. By substituting (2) and (3) for C and I in (1), we can solve for the *equilibrium* values of income and consumption:

$Y = 50 + .75Y + 50$,
$.25Y = 100$,
$Y = 400$, and
$C = 350$.

Also, $S = Y - C = 50$, which is equal in equilibrium to the constant I. In general, the model used here is:

(1) $Y = C + I$ (income-sustaining condition),
(2) $C = a + cY$ (consumption function),
(3) $I = I_0$ (where I is a given constant for present purposes).

Combining equations and solving for Y yields:

(4) $Y = \dfrac{(a + I_0)}{(1 - c)}.$

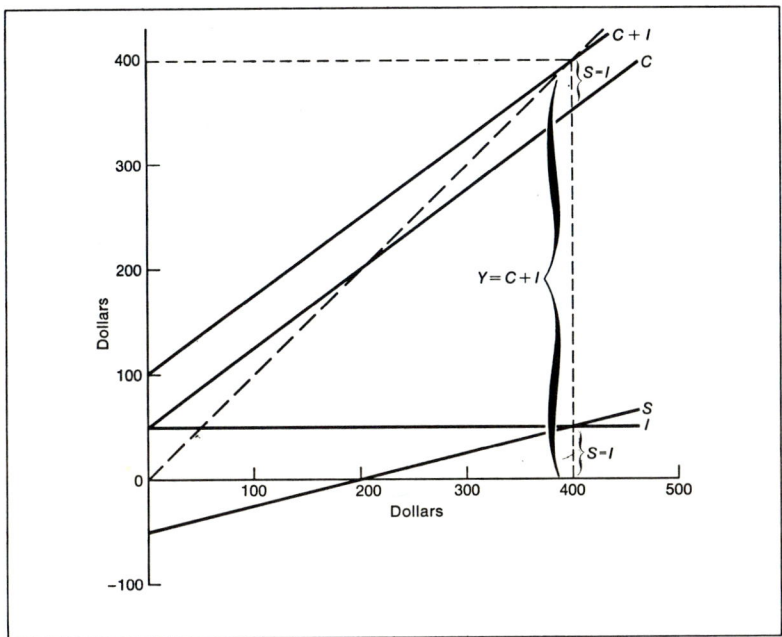

FIGURE 27–4. Determination of Equilibrium Income: Consumption and Investment Expenditure

The constant rate of investment is added to the consumption schedule. Equilibrium income is located by the intersection of the total expenditure line ($C + I$) with the 45-degree line: at equilibrium income, the community wishes to spend at a rate which maintains that income. Equilibrium income is located also by the intersection of the S and I lines: if income is maintained, the rate of leakage (saving) equals the rate of injection (investment).

and the disposition of *saving,* in turn, is between expenditure on investment and holding of more money.[13]

A person saving just as much as he is spending on investment goods does not change his stock of money. He already has as much money as he demands to hold, given his wealth and income flow; all his current money income is spent either for consumption or for investment goods. However, if his S is greater than his I, he is accumulating money and reducing his expenditures flow. This is picturesquely described as a "leakage" from income flows. (But some other person must be experiencing a decrease in his stock of money; he is "injecting" money.) Part of his saving is not spent for investment goods; it goes into his larger money balances. And conversely, if his S is smaller than his I, he is drawing down previously accumulated money balances.

We must not ignore differences between investment- and consumption-type goods.

---

[13] Certainly saved income can be spent on investment goods—either by the saver himself or by someone who borrows from the saver. But do not suppose that every dollar spent in investment must be a specific dollar previously saved. Commercial banks, we shall see, can "create money out of thin air," and an individual or a business firm or the United States Treasury may obtain for investment (or other kinds of) expenditure dollars which are newly created and were not saved by anyone.

Decisions to spend are not based solely on considerations to buy more goods *in general* versus spending less in order to retain more money. Decisions to buy investment goods reflect profit prospects. These prospects are relatively volatile compared to preferences for consumption goods. Hence, people make choices, not simply between goods generally and money, but among consumption goods, investment goods, and money. To ignore the distinction between consumption and investment (and money) is to ignore some of the reasons for changes in the rates at which currently received money incomes are respent for goods rather than to retain larger money balances.[14]

Changes in National Income

Now we are prepared to analyze *changes* in national income. For changes in income imply changes in employment, and our interest here is in fluctuations in employment and real and money national income, not in the value of income at any moment.

Autonomous Change in the Investment Function

Let the investment function shift down (from $50). This decrease in spending is *not induced* by a prior fall in income. Rather, it is an *autonomous* fall in the whole *I* curve. We are not here *moving along an I line in response to an income change*; instead, we *shift the entire demand curve* for investment-type goods. We shall call a change in a variable along this line in response to a change in income an *induced* change; any change that shifts the position of the line is a change in the whole investment-demand function and is called an *exogenous* or *autonomous* change. (In the earlier chapters analyzing price, we called it a change in *demand* as distinct from a change in *amount demanded* along the demand line.)

What event does a fall of the investment-demand schedule reflect? Anticipated profitability of investment has decreased. A few of the many possible reasons are: a tax on investment is increased; the laws of property are enforced less surely; there is greater fear that investment goods will be nationalized; interest rates have gone up; excessive stocks of investment goods have been accumulating.

Arithmetic-tabular determination of new equilibrium income. Table 27–4 is the same as Table 27–3 except that the investment function has decreased (an autonomous fall in investment) from $50 to $25. The new equilibrium income is $300, for that is the only income that yields consumption and investment whose sum gives a demand for production that regenerates that income. At smaller incomes, consumption and investment sum to more than the income; saving is less than investment; leakages from the income flow are less than injections; more production is induced with a resultant higher income. On the other hand, if income were larger than $300, the sum of consumption and invest-

---

[14] In the earlier, pure consumption-good model, there was no investment-type good. Money income received was spent either for consumption or not spent at all. That which was not spent was "saved," and all saving automatically went into accumulations of money stocks. But since the *whole* economy cannot accumulate money (when the total money stock is constant), the consequence of the attempt to accumulate money means that incomes fall until people demand only the amount of money that actually exists, whether or not there are investment-type goods.

TABLE 27-4. Determination of Equilibrium National Income

Actual (Received) Income	Consumption	Saving	Investment	Implied (Generated) Income
0	50	−50	25	75
50	87.5	−37.5	25	112.5
100	125	−25	25	150
150	162.5	−12.5	25	187.5
200	200	0	25	225
250	237.5	12.5	25	262.5
300	275	25	25	300
350	312.5	37.5	25	337.5
400	350	50	25	375

The consumption function is unchanged from Table 27-3, but investment is only $25 (rather than $50). This autonomous fall of investment reduces the value of equilibrium income by $100 (from $400 to $300).

ment would be less than that income, which, therefore, would not be maintained. The downward shift in the investment function has resulted in a decreased income, which induces smaller consumption *and* smaller saving. The reduction in income must be enough to reduce saving to the new investment. The *autonomous* drop in investment demand *induces* a drop in saving. The autonomous drop in investment (by $25) caused income to fall sufficiently (by $100) to induce a matching reduction in saving (for *MPS* = .25).[15]

Graphic determination of new equilibrium income. Figure 27-5 is the same as Figure 27-4 except that the *I* line is shifted down to show a lower investment demand at every income. With an unchanged consumption function, the *C* + *I* line is shifted downward, and the intersection with the 45-degree line slides down from $400 (the old equilibrium income) to $300 (the new income).

The new equilibrium income is indicated also by the intersection of the new *I* line with the old *S* line, which has not changed. By definition, and hence by construction, the intersection of the *C* + *I* line with the 45-degree line will always be at the same income as the intersection of the *S* and *I* lines.

Inspection of Figure 27-5 shows that so long as the *C* + *I* line slopes upward, any vertical drop in *C* + *I* will slide its *intersection* with the 45-degree line to the left by *more* than the vertical drop in the *C* + *I* line, and thus a change in investment has a "multiplier" effect on income. (Can you see that if the *C* + *I* line were horizontal, a

---

[15] With an unchanged consumption function and a smaller investment, we have a smaller I_0 in equation 4 of footnote 12.

$$Y = \frac{a + I_0}{1 - c} = \frac{50 + 25}{1 - .75} = 300.$$

When I_0 is $25 instead of $50, income is $100 smaller. The *autonomous* decrease in investment of $25 directly reduced income by that much, and the total fall in income *induced* a decrease in consumption of $75, the total decrease in spending (income) thus being $100. The autonomous $25 change in investment has resulted in a change in equilibrium income of $100, a ratio of investment change to income change of 1:4.

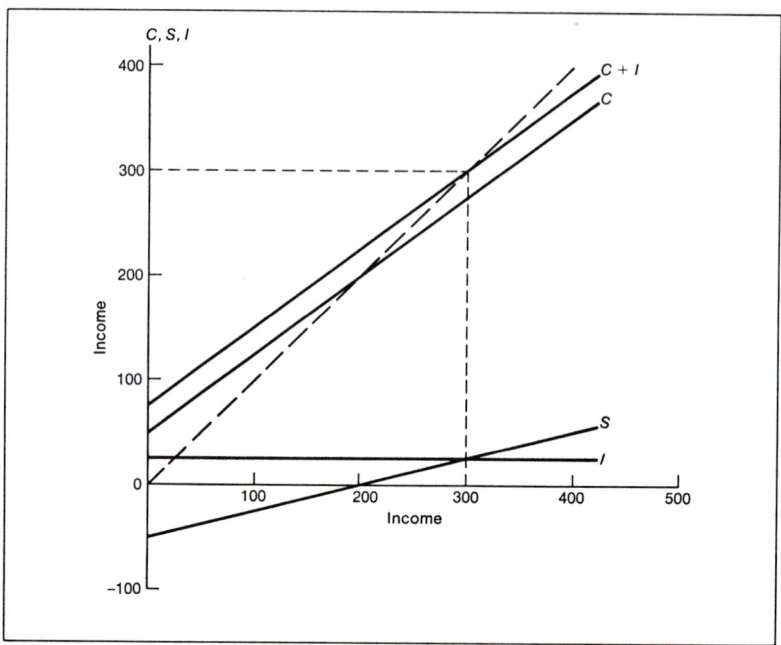

FIGURE 27-5. Determination of Equilibrium Income: Consumption and Investment Expenditure

The C and S lines are the same as in Figure 27-4; the I—and hence the $C + I$—lines are lower. The downward shift in the investment and total expenditure ($C + I$) by $25 reduces equilibrium income by $100. At the old equilibrium income ($400), total expenditure would not be great enough to maintain that income.

downward shift would make the intersection slide to the left by the *same* amount as the drop in the $C + I$ line? Can you see that a horizontal $C + I$ line would mean that, with a constant rate of investment, consumption also is constant regardless of transient income changes? If the rate of consumption is constant, is zero or one the numerical value of MPC?)

An Interpretation of the Process of Income Changes

How is income pushed down to $300? We can say from the preceding analysis that it does end up at a calculable lower equilibrium. But what are the economics of the *process* that the preceding graphic or tabular model represents? We give one interpretation. People do not know instantly how much their income is going to change, nor do they react instantaneously to perceived changes. True to the general principle that hastier action is more costly, people do not change their consumption (and saving) simultaneously with a change in income. A fall in income initiated by the original *autonomous* decrease of investment somewhat later *induces* a reduction in consumption. The delayed induced fall in consumption results in a smaller income, which, in turn, induces a further reduction in consumption.

National-Income Theory: The Basic Model

A lagged adjustment of consumption can be illustrated with the *special* assumptions of Table 27–5. For numerical simplicity, assume it takes one "period" for consumption and saving to respond to changes in income. Consumption and saving today are geared to income generated and received yesterday. Thus, income in a given period is determined by expenditure in that *same* period, and the money income thereby received in that period is disposed of in the *following* period. We continue the assumption that $MPC = .75$ and $MPS = .25$.

Periods 1 and 2 correspond to the same situation as in Figure 27–4. The community has consumption of $350 with investment (and saving) of $50, income being $400. This is an *equilibrium* level of income, which remains constant from one period to the next. The condition of equilibrium is that the consumption and investment demands equal the income that induces them. Or, in other terms, saving equals the rate of investment; in terms of the table, this means that $S = I$ in a given period.

The initiating autonomous change occurs in period 3; the investment function falls autonomously to $25. The situation is no longer one of equilibrium: S does not equal I in the current period. Income of $375 is generated in period 3—the sum of the consumption and investment spending of period 3. This fall in income from period 2 to period 3 induces a reduction of consumption from period 3 to period 4 (to $331.25), which, combined with the $25 investment, gives a total production demand in period 4 of $356.25. The resultant fall in generated income from period 3 to period 4 induces a still smaller consumption ($317.19) in period 5: combined with the continuing investment of $25, generated income of period 5 drops to $342.19. This induces a fall of consumption in period 6 to $306.64, which, added to investment of $25, determines a reduced creation of income of $331.64. Continuing downward through a sequence of such adjustments, income will reach $300 and stay there, with consumption thereafter being $275 and with saving and investment once again equal at a level of $25. The final equilibrium to which variables *converge* is given in the last line of Table 27–5.

The same process can be shown graphically. Figure 27–6 has the same C and $C + I$ lines as Figure 27–4. In this initial equilibrium, $C = \$350$, $I = \$50$, and $Y = \$400$ (point 1), which corresponds to the first two periods of Table 27–5. Now, as in period 3

TABLE 27–5. Income Change with Autonomous Decrease in Investment

Period	C	S	I	Y	
1	350	50	50	400	
2	350	50	50	400	$\Delta Y = -25$
3	350 } $\Delta C = -18.75$	50 } $\Delta S = -6.25$	25	375	
4	331.25	43.75	25	356.25	
5	317.19	39.06	25	342.19	
6	306.64	35.55	25	331.64	
	—	—	—	—	
*	—	—	—	—	
	275	25	25	300	

The autonomous fall of $25 in investment from period 2 to period 3 reduces income immediately by the same amount. $MPC = .75$, and $MPS = .25$. Therefore, the $25 reduction in income is reflected, with a one-period lag, in an $18.75 induced reduction in consumption and a $6.25 induced reduction in saving. A new equilibrium is attained when again $S = I$ (at a level of $25) in a given period. S is induced to fall a total of $25 by income being reduced $100; and the $100 reduction in income induces consumption to fall $75.

of the table, while consumption is still unchanged, investment falls autonomously by $25 at all income levels, dropping the total expenditure line to $C + I_1$. This appears to put us at point 2, when $C + I = \$375$ and $Y = \$400$. But if the community chooses to spend (in period 3) $375 when income received (in period 2) is $400, that expenditure induces a creation of income (in period 3) of $375—which puts us at point 3. However, point 3 is not an equilibrium situation, for income is $375, and the community spends only $356.25, which appears to locate point 4. The expenditure of $356.25 results in production and income of that amount, so the actual movement from point 3 is directly to point 5. And so it goes. Each new temporary income level induces an expenditure smaller than the income (for consumption falls although investment remains constant at its new level of $25), with our position sliding down the 45-degree line by successively smaller amounts to the new equilibrium, where $C = \$275, I = \$25$, and $Y = \$300$.

Beware! The step-by-step expository sequence of consumption and investment expenditure toward a new equilibrium national income is hypothetical. We are not saying that the economy moves literally in that fashion. But the sequence outlined here provides a reference framework for more detailed interpretation of the events summarized in the earlier analysis which compared one equilibrium solution with another. In more familiar terms, such as found in ordinary newspaper discussion, the adjustment could be characterized as follows: When the investment function shifts down, someone is left producing consumption- and investment-type goods at a rate higher than can be profitably sold. Therefore, producers incur losses; inventories accumulate or prices have to be cut

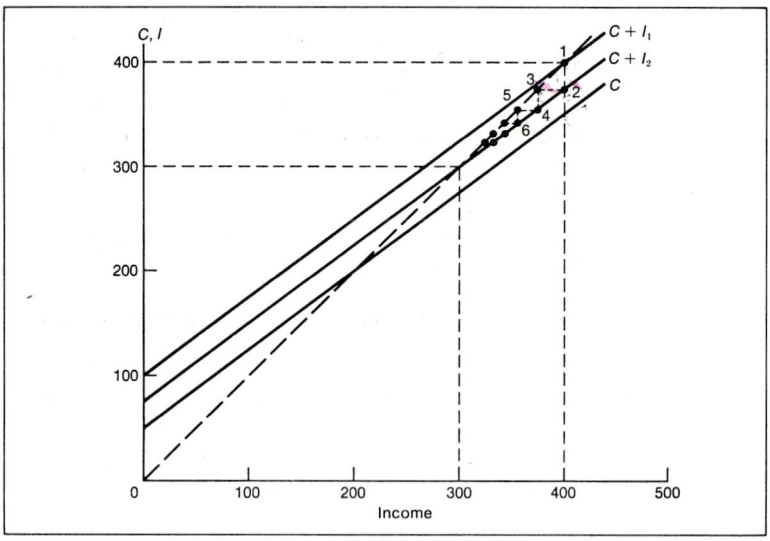

FIGURE 27–6. Decrease in Investment Function Results in Decrease in Equilibrium Income

The initial equilibrium is located by point 1. Investment autonomously falls, reducing the total expenditure line to $C + I_2$. With expenditure at the vertical level of point 2, income immediately falls to the level (both vertical and horizontal) of point 3 on the 45-degree line. Having arrived at point 3, lagged expenditure is at the vertical level of point 4, which reduces income to the level of point 5. In such stair-step fashion, we approach the new equilibrium where $C + I$ crosses the 45-degree line.

National-Income Theory: The Basic Model

or output is reduced. Income and employment fall until a new lower output is reached at which consumption and investment activity is self-sustaining (according to the new consumption and new investment functions).

Autonomous Change in Consumption Function: Alleged Paradox of Thrift

Let the community experience a decrease in the consumption function. This can be shown by shifting down the C line and shifting up the S line. (We confine ourselves to the graphic mode of analysis, leaving it to the reader to construct the tabular and algebraic interpretations.) Figure 27–7 shows a downward shift in the $C + I$ line consequent to a decrease in the consumption function, with investment held constant; the saving schedule is shown at a higher position (S_2) by exactly the amount of the drop in $(C + I)_1$ to $(C + I)_2$. Equilibrium income falls from Y_1 to Y_2. Consumption falls as a combined result of two factors: (1) the *autonomous* drop, shown by the vertical fall in the $C + I$ line, plus (2) the *induced* reduction as a result of the diminished equilibrium income. But saving is unchanged! Despite the increased thriftiness, saving has not increased. This is sometimes called a "paradox of thrift."

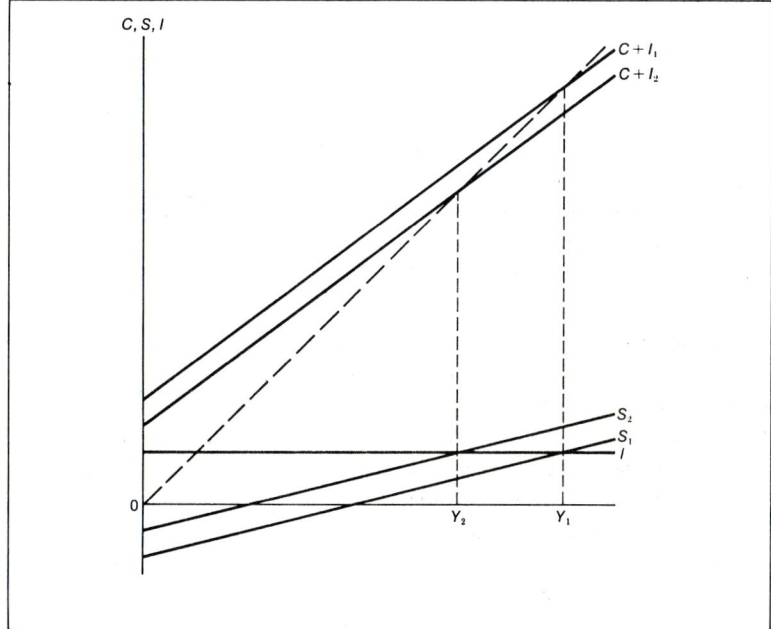

FIGURE 27–7. The Paradox of Thrift

The consumption schedule (not shown separately) falls, reducing the total spending curve from $C + I_1$ to $C + I_2$. At the same time, the saving schedule rises, as counterpart to the autonomous fall in consumption. The investment line is assumed to be unaffected. Equilibrium income falls, with the total spending curve sliding down the 45-degree line and the saving curve moving left on the investment line. The rate of saving at income Y_2 is equal to that at Y_1; a larger proportion of a smaller income is saved in the new equilibrium.

We may resolve the so-called paradox by recognizing that this decreased desire for consumption at all levels of income was associated with an *increased demand to accumulate money holdings.* The public reduced its demand for consumption but did not increase its demand for investment (for which there was no perceived increase in profitability) and instead increased its demand to accumulate money. With people trying to accumulate more money, but with a fixed money stock, a reduction in consumption would lead to lower income. People want to hold a larger ratio of money to income; the stock of money is unchanged, so the ratio is increased through a fall in income, as a result of a decrease in expenditure. There is no increase in investment to offset the reduction in consumption.

If people increase their desire to save and also *not spend that increase in saving on investment,* then—as shown in Figure 27–7—income falls sufficiently to induce people to save in the new equilibrium no more than originally despite the increased willingness to save at any given income. The paradox is created if we insist on thinking the increase in "thrift" (saving) must mean an equal increase in demand for investment. In that case, the increased propensity to save would be accompanied by an equal upward shift in the investment function, with income then unchanged and saving increased. Since an increase in thriftiness means only an increase in the desire not to spend for consumption, we must add a specification as to what happens to demand for money or for investment.

The Multiplier

We have illustrated several autonomous changes in total demand to spend—shifts upward and downward in both the consumption and investment schedules. These autonomous shifts upset the initial equilibrium and led to a new equilibrium, with the change in income from one equilibrium to the other being a *multiple* of the initiating autonomous expenditure change. For example, a $25 autonomous decrease in investment triggered a $100 decrease in income. Why the *larger* change in income than in investment?

To be sure, this result is a logical implication of the stipulated conditions. Given the general model and our specific values of the marginal propensities, it follows mathematically that the change in income from one equilibrium to another will be four times as large as the autonomous change in spending. But what is the intuitive, common-sense interpretation of the proposition that an *autonomous* expenditure change will lead to a change in income which is a multiple of the change?

Consider again the case of a reduction in the investment schedule, with the process of adjustment illustrated in Table 27–5. We may trace the multiplication of the impact of an autonomous investment change on income in alternative languages: (1) the saving-investment approach and (2) the spending-income approach.

1. We now know that income equilibrium is characterized by equality of saving and investment in a given period (see periods 1 and 2, and the last, of Table 27–5). When investment falls in period 3, saving is not yet changed; there is a gap of saving over investment. To reestablish equilibrium (at some level), the saving-investment gap must be closed by changing national income.

Saving and investment were initially $50; investment has now fallen to $25; income will not again be in equilibrium until saving also falls by $25. What will cause a fall in saving? A fall in income. How great a decrease in income is required to induce a fall in saving of $25? That depends upon the marginal propensity to save. In our illustration,

$MPS = .25$; in other words, saving will fall by $1 for every $4 that income goes down. For saving to fall $25, income must fall $100.

2. In the spending-income language, again there is a gap to be closed, namely the gap of income created in one period over consumption-plus-investment spending in the following period. In period 3, with the autonomous fall in investment, spending is $25 less than income in period 2, and this gap must be closed to re-establish equilibrium. Income immediately falls by $25 in period 3, but this induces a further fall in (consumption) spending of $18.75 in period 4; the fall in income has thus reduced the gap by $6.25. Since the gap is narrowed $1 for every $4 that income falls, the total fall in income must be $100 to close the entire initial gap of $25.

Whether we speak in the language of closing the gap in saving over investment or the gap of income over expenditure, income must fall by $100 to close a gap of $25 if marginal propensity to save is .25. This ratio of ΔY to ΔI, $\Delta Y/\Delta I = 4$, is called the "multiplier."[16]

The point can be easily illustrated in Figure 27–8. There are two alternative cases in the diagram, one with a sloping total spending line and the other with a horizontal line. In the *sloping* case, the original line is $C + I_1$, which then shifts by amount FH to $C + I_2$. Income falls from Y_1 to Y_2. The change in income, Y_1Y_2, is equal to distance GE,

---

[16] A little algebraic doodling will pinpoint how this is associated with the marginal propensity to consume or to save.

The relationship between an autonomous change in spending (represented by investment) and the resulting ultimate change in income is often expressed as a ratio, $\Delta Y/\Delta I$, and labeled the *multiplier* (k). Thus:

$$\text{multiplier} = \frac{\text{change in equilibrium income}}{\text{autonomous change in spending}},$$

$$k = \Delta Y/\Delta I.$$

Since $\Delta Y = \Delta C + \Delta I$ and therefore $\Delta I = \Delta Y - \Delta C$, we may substitute for ΔI:

$$k = \frac{\Delta Y}{\Delta Y - \Delta C}.$$

Dividing numerator and denominator by ΔY, we have:

$$k = \frac{1}{1 - \Delta C/\Delta Y},$$

$$= \frac{1}{1 - MPC},$$

$$= \frac{1}{MPS}.$$

So the multiplier (in this simple model which omits governmental and international transactions) equals the *reciprocal of the marginal propensity to save.*

Since $k = \Delta Y/\Delta I$, it follows that $k\Delta I = \Delta Y$. To apply this in our illustration, $k = \$100/\$25 = 4$; and $4(-\$25) = -\$100$. Or, to derive the value of the multiplier from the marginal propensities, $k = 1/(1 - .75) = 1/.25 = 4$.

It is apparent, since $k = 1/(1 - MPC) = 1/MPS$, that the larger is MPC (and thus the smaller is MPS), the larger is the multiplier. This is to be expected: the larger is the absolute response of consumption to given income changes, the greater will be the ultimate repercussion on income of an autonomous injection.

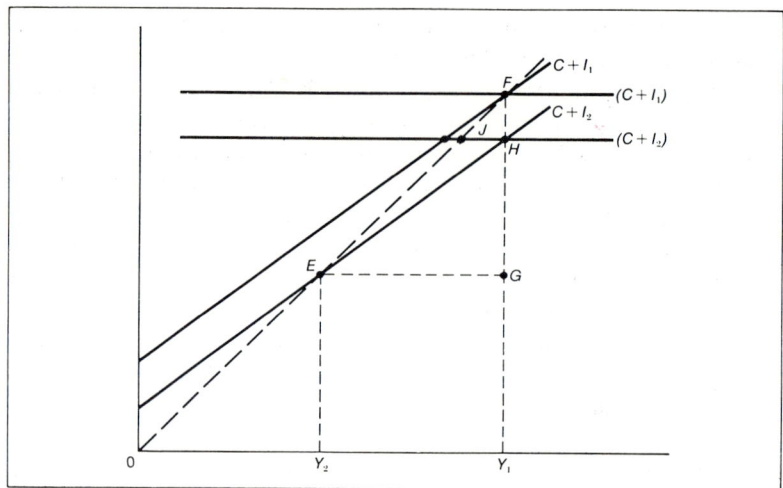

FIGURE 27-8. The Multiplier and MPC

If the *I* line is horizontal, the slope of the total expenditure curve equals the slope of the *C* line. With a shift in a positively sloping *C* + *I* line (*MPC* > 0), the multiplier is greater than unity: a shift of *FH* changes income by *FG*. With a shift in a horizontal *C* + *I* line (*MPC* = 0), the multiplier is unity: a shift of *FH* changes income by *FH*.

which equals *FG*. (Why?) Thus, the change in income is greater than the autonomous change in spending: the multiplier, *FG/FH*, is greater than unity and depends on the slope of the *C* + *I* lines. In the alternative case, let the total expenditure curve, marked $(C + I_1)$, be *horizontal*. Since the *I* line is horizontal, the slope of the total expenditure curve is equal to the slope of the *C* line, and in this instance *MPC* = 0. Again there is a downward shift by amount *FH*. Income falls by *HJ*, which equals *FH*: the multiplier is only unity.

Income or Interest Rate as Adjusting Variable

In Chapter 23, saving and investment rates were brought to equality solely by adjustments in the *interest rate* (reflected in the prices of longer-lived capital goods relative to consumption goods and wages); here, the equilibration is accomplished solely by changes in *national income*. In the earlier discussion, we were assuming in effect that income and all other variables which impinge upon saving and investment, except the interest rate, remained constant; the interest rate was the key variable. In the present analysis, we have been assuming that the interest rate and all other variables except income remain constant; income is the key variable. In fact, both adjust and reduce the extent to which income must change.

In the present context, which focuses on national income, we can suggest an integration of the two approaches by supposing that the positions of the *I* and *S* (and thus *C*) lines are determined by the interest rate. Starting from an initial situation, an increase in the interest rate would lower the *I* line and raise the *S* line (lower the *C* line). In turn, the interest rate would depend upon the saving and investment functions. A full, mutual

National-Income Theory: The Basic Model

determination could then be obtained in which *both* the interest rate and national income would change and by less than if interest rates were not to change.

To present a more complete model in one diagram, table, or set of equations is beyond the scope of this book. Instead, because we are here interested primarily in national income, we continue for a while *as if* the interest rate does not change and, given the consumption and investment functions, the rates of saving and investment are affected only by income.

Investment Volatility: The Accelerator

Throughout the preceding introduction to income-fluctuation analysis, we assumed the investment function was stable. Yet, one thing we can realistically be sure of: investment profitability is "nervous" and volatile. It reflects opinions, beliefs, and conjectures of people about profitability of investment-good acquisitions. The varying prices in the stock market are measures of changes in profit prospects of new investments. A speech from the Kremlin, Peking, Washington, or even Cairo, can shift the investment function. A suggestion of increased probabilities of higher (or lower) taxes will change it. The investment function can be shifted not only by influences outside the model—rumors of war or peace, elections, and all the manifestations of normal and abnormal mass psychology—but also by shifts of other functions within the model. Largely for technological reasons, shifts in the consumption function can induce shifts—sometimes in the same direction and sometimes in the opposite—in the investment function also. This sort of tie between shifts in consumption and in the investment function is called an *accelerator* effect and is illustrated in Table 27–6.

TABLE 27–6. Accelerator Effect

Year (1)	Shoe Sales (2)	Shoes per Machine (3)	Machines in Production of Shoes (4)	Depreciation (10 years, 10 percent) (5)	Replacement Demand (6)	Net Investment in New Machines (7)	Gross Investment in Machines (8)
20	100,000	5,000	20	2	2	0	2
21	110,000	5,000	22	2	2	2	4
22	130,000	5,000	26	2	2	4	6
23	150,000	5,000	30	2	2	4	6
24	155,000	5,000	31	2	2	1	3
25	155,000	5,000	31	2	2	0	2
26	145,000	5,000	29	2	0	0	0
27	140,000	5,000	28	2	1	0	1
28	140,000	5,000	28	2	2	0	2

Suppose that for some time the annual consumption and production of shoes has been 100,000, with 5,000 being produced per machine; twenty machines are used in making shoes; there are no idle machines to be put into operation if demand for shoes increases; the economic life of a machine is ten years; and the machines have been acquired and put into operation evenly in years gone by, so each year two machines (10 percent of twenty machines) wear out and are replaced. With consumption demand for shoes constant, the only investment demand for machines is to replace the two annually wearing out.

Now, in year 21, shoe demand rises 10 percent and with it the demand for new shoe machines. As usual, two machines are purchased for replacement of depreciating machines, and, in addition, two machines are required to meet the higher consumption demand for shoes. Thus, there is a *net* investment of two machines, to a total of 22. Four machines will be produced (two for replacement and two for net investment). And so it goes; the data of column 2 are assumed; column 3 is constant; column 4 equals 2 divided by 3; column 5 is given by the initial level of twenty machines and the 10 percent depreciation rate; column 6 reflects the sum of the total machinery replacement purchases with a ten-year lag and *decreases* in the current number of machines required (for example, in going from year 25 to year 26, required machines fall by two, and exactly two are wearing out, so none is replaced); column 7 equals an *increase* over the preceding year in desired machines; column 8 equals 6 plus 7.

The increase in consumption led to an increase in investment—shown in columns 7 and 8, depending on whether we think of net or gross investment. The investment function is shifted by the effects of a change in consumption. But notice: (1) The *percentage* effect on investment exceeds the initiating *percentage* change in consumption. Consumption increased 50 percent from year 20 to year 23, but gross investment tripled. Then from year 23 to 24, when consumption increased only about 3 percent, investment *decreased*. And from year 25 to 26, when consumption fell about 6 percent, investment fell 100 percent. The fluctuations in consumption are amplified in investment. And as the reader can verify with his own calculations, the more *durable* the machinery (the smaller the depreciation rate) the greater is the percentage movement in investment in connection with a given consumption change. (2) The *turning points* of investment *precede* those of consumption even though the line of causation runs from changes in consumption to investment. For example, investment reaches its peak in year 22 and starts down after year 23, while consumption continues to rise through year 24 and does not fall until year 26. Why? Increases or decreases of investment are determined by changes in the *rate* of growth of consumption, not simply by the *direction* of change. As long as consumption increased by larger annual amounts, investment rose. But when consumption failed to increase by *increased* amounts, investment fell. The same general relationship holds for downward changes in consumption.

The accelerator is not a rigid technological effect. Machines do not have to be purchased according to the inflexible assumptions in the illustration. Some machines are worked overtime, depreciation replacement is deferred, inventories are used as buffers to absorb demand fluctuations. A more general exposition would require advanced mathematical techniques and would yield a much greater variety in the fluctuation patterns of income, employment, and output. The basic result of a shift in consumption and consequent shifts in the investment function would still be present. We do not know at any given time how much a given shift in the consumption function will lead to a similar or opposite-direction shift in the investment function. We do know, however, that the relationship between the two is not always the same.

10, 11

Recessions: Changes in National Income, Employment, and Prices

A perceptive student will wonder why the discussion of price adjustments and the force of price as a resource director, in the earlier part of this book, is segregated from the present discussion of national income determination. National income is the summation

National-Income Theory: The Basic Model

of individual incomes, and individual incomes are dependent upon price adjustments. Then why is national income not dependent upon price adjustments? It is. There is no real segregation; there is only an expository segregation. We have been concentrating on the effects of income changes on demands for goods and, hence, on the further creation of income, without denying that prices play a role. We concentrate our attention on one thing at a time—here, on how aggregate demand shifts have an income effect, whereas formerly we inquired about the price effects of demand and supply shifts without inquiring into the repercussions those shifts would have on income.

Although an integrated analysis of price and income effects would take us far beyond the customary limits of an introductory inquiry, we can indicate some features of that analysis. In fact, we have already done so, to some extent. Recall the earlier discussion of the way production responds to changes in demand before prices change to readjust both the amounts demanded and supplied.[17] Recall also the discussion of employment and unemployment decisions about labor and capital goods.[18] Prices, although capable of being adjusted instantly, were kept predictably steady in the face of transient changes in demand, because that was preferred by buyers. And recall that employees would not immediately reduce prices in current activity to retain present employment; they prefer to seek opportunities elsewhere at unreduced prices, rather than cut prices as much as necessary to keep current jobs in the face of deteriorated demand.

All this means that a decrease (or possibly a reduced rate of growth) in national income will reduce employment and real output, for not all prices will *immediately* adjust *sufficiently*. In fact, prices will adjust so slowly that the adjustment and recession may last for several months before prices fall by the different necessary amounts. The downward fluctuation in national income brings lower income in terms of lower prices and also reduced employment and output. Detection of these changes in aggregate demand, discernment of appropriate reductions of various prices, and determination of consistent reshuffling of resources is not possible immediately or at zero cost. Information is not free. The readjustment brings a recession process. Recession may be associated with a decrease in employment of, say, 5 percent of the labor force; added to normal frictional number of people shifting about as *relative* demands shift, that would increase the unemployment rate to 8 percent from its "full employment" rate of about 3 percent—meaning that about 3 to 5 million more people will be unemployed for some interval during the recession.

The social and economic losses are sufficient to provoke search for means to attenuate recessions. There are factors that initiate a change in aggregate demand by shifting a consumption or an investment function. Can these initiating factors be prevented from occurring? Is there any action that can prevent national income from falling—or prevent the reduction in output, if initiating factors cannot be forestalled? Do these proposed social actions have significant undesirable side effects?

Two conspicuous sources of economic instability are changes in the money stock and in government expenditures. These sometimes, but not always, occur together as a result of the way government expenditures are financed. If large changes in government expenditures (not balanced by offsetting changes in the private sector) can be counterbalanced by appropriate policy by the monetary authorities, a major past source of severe recessions can be eliminated. In the next two chapters we examine how the money

---

[17] Pages 95–99.
[18] Pages 515–524.

stock affects national income and what affects the money stock. Then we examine governmental expenditure and tax policy (fiscal policy) and consider to what extent monetary and fiscal policies are interrelated.

Summary

1. National income determination is analyzed *via* Keynesian relationships: the consumption function and investment function.

2. The consumption function, relating consumption to income, specifies that consumption changes with income, but by less than the increment of income. The saving function (defined by the consumption function) specifies that saving changes with income, with the increment of income being divided into an increment of consumption and an increment of saving. Income in the consumption function that we have stressed is the transient income that fluctuates around a longer-run average.

3. The marginal propensity to consume is the ratio of (a) the increment of consumption induced by an increment of income to (b) the increment of income. The marginal propensity to save is the complement of the marginal propensity to consume: *MPC* and *MPS* are each less than, but together add up to, unity.

4. Investment is less clearly related to income and is believed to fluctuate more than consumption for any particular income. A major element in the downward or upward shocks affecting the national income seems to be the investment function. Since it is a reflection of *beliefs* and *predictions* about rates of investment that will be profitable, it is likely that over-optimism of profitability sometimes will lead to over-investment with ultimate discovery that too much of some types of goods have been produced. The resultant downward shift in the profitability of investment produces a recession.

5. A consistent (equilibrium) national income is one that induces a sum of consumption and investment equal to the inducing national income. Any smaller income would induce a larger sum of expenditure (and would increase the income); an income larger than equilibrium would induce a smaller sum and would tend to reduce the initial income.

6. A shift in the consumption or the investment function will induce a change in the equilibrium income that is a multiple of the initiating change in consumption or investment. The ratio of the ultimate change in income to the autonomous change in spending is called the multiplier; it is numerically equal to the reciprocal of the marginal propensity to save.

7. Shifts in the consumption (saving) function cannot always be made without also inducing a shift in the investment function. The accelerator effect refers to the process whereby a shift in the consumption function causes a temporary perturbation in the investment function with a still larger variation in resultant income. An autonomous shift in the consumption function might increase, decrease, or leave unchanged the investment function. We do not know enough about some sources of changes to be sure whether they shift both or just one of the functions. If they are shifted in opposite, offsetting directions, the analysis is less reliable for discerning implied directions of changes in national income and employment.

8. Associated with shifts in the investment and consumption (saving) schedules are changes in the demand for or supply of money. An initiating change in spending propensities requires adjustment in either the demand to hold money or the size of the money stock; and an initiating change in the demand for or supply of money will have repercussions on the positions of the spending schedules.

Questions

1. "Consumption is a function of income." But what kind of income: "transient" (measured money) income or "permanent" income (wealth)? What is the distinction between these two kinds of income? In our analysis of income determination, why do we generally relate consumption to one kind of income rather than the other?

2. How can consumption be both a *function* of income and a *determinant* of income? Isn't it inconsistent to posit a "line of causation" between C and Y running in *both* directions?

3. Distinguish between *autonomous* changes and *induced* changes in a variable (consumption). In the earlier discussion of supply and demand, was there an analogous distinction?

4. We have discussed two modes of determining equilibrium income or two approaches to characterizing the condition of equilibrium income: (a) the expenditure-income approach and (b) the saving-investment approach. Distinguish between these alternative expositions; illustrate them both in the 45-degree diagram and in the arithmetic period table. How is it that they necessarily give the same answer?

5. "In income equilibrium, $S = I$. Therefore, the larger S is, the larger will be I; and the larger I is, the larger is income. Therefore, an autonomous increase in S leads, through a larger I, to a greater income." Right?

6. "Of course, $MPC + MPS = 1$, whether MPI equals 0 or .05 or any other value." Why?

7. The theory of income presented in this chapter hinges on the shapes, positions, and changes in position of certain schedules (or functions). In particular, the analysis has run largely in terms of *savings* and *investment* schedules. In the first part of the book, we analyzed frequently in terms of *supply* and *demand* schedules. Are the (income) relationships between savings and investment at all analogous to the (price) relationships between supply and demand? If so, is the analogy perfect, or can you distinguish the two sets of relationships from each other?

8. Two eighteenth-century giants assure us that saving is splendid. Benjamin Franklin counsels that "a penny saved is a penny earned," and Adam Smith concludes that "every prodigal" is "a public enemy," while "every frugal man" is "a public benefactor." Does the "paradox of thrift" demolish this ancient wisdom—or turn it on its head?

9. Study the following figure.
   a. Carefully construct and draw in the implied line for the propensity to save. Label it S.
   b. Draw in the line for $C + I$.
   c. At what income does the $C + I$ line intersect the 45-degree line?
   d. What is the equilibrium national income?
   e. Do you get the same income for the intersection of the S and I lines? Should you?
   f. What is the consumption at that income?
   g. If investment, depicted by the I line, were to fall to zero, show by shifting the $C + I$ line what the new income would be.
   h. Is this fall in investment autonomous or induced?
   i. Is the income change autonomous or induced?
   j. How much does income change?
   k. By reading the graph, compute the marginal propensity to consume. (It is one of the following: 1, .8, .5, .2.)
   l. What is the multiplier value?
   m. Is the change in consumption autonomous or induced?

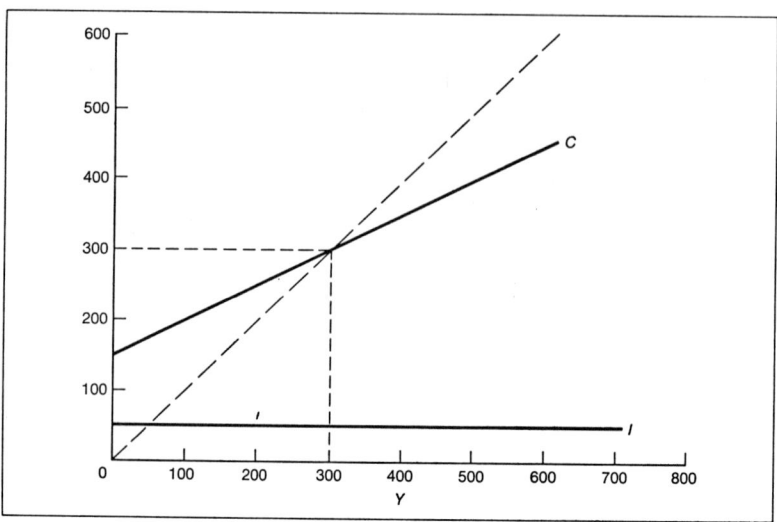

n. For the remaining questions, suppose the figure were redrawn, leaving the C line unchanged, but with the I line rotated around the point of 300 income and 50 investment, so that the left end of the I line goes through the origin. Define the marginal propensity to invest.

o. In this example, what portrays the marginal propensity to invest?

p. What is the numerical value of the *MPI*?

q. Now what are the values of income, consumption, and saving?

r. If the new I line were to be autonomously reduced by 50 at every point, what would be the new national income, consumption, saving?

10 In the theory of the accelerator, how can it be that the line of causation runs from changes in consumption to changes in investment and yet the turning points in investment precede the turning points in consumption? Is this not a case of the result preceding the cause?

11 Prepare two alternative versions of the table on page 563, in which the first four columns are the same as in the original table, but with the life of a machine being five years in one case and twenty years in the other. The original table, plus these two alternative versions, illustrates what characteristic of the accelerator?

Money and Income

28 Money

EVERYONE knows that money is what you use to buy things and pay debts. But we can usefully consider the nature and functions of money and the consequences of changes in the national stock of money in some detail—consequences which include repercussions on an aggregate price index, national income, employment, and output.

Functions of Money

Money is typically both (1) a *standard measure of value* or unit of account and (2) a *medium of exchange* or, more prosaically, a means of payment.[1] Life would go on, even if less opulently, without money, but money is so obviously useful that it is found in any society far enough advanced to spend most of its time out of the trees.

We earlier illustrated the productive advantage of having a monetary unit of account in which to express and compare exchange values. But even as a medium of exchange, money could be wholly intangible. Everyone could have a bank checking or credit card account, with payments made and revenues received solely by subtracting from or adding to one's account and with no specific, tangible items (engraved paper, stamped pieces of gold, or beads) being handled. In practice, money is comprised also of material means of payment, which facilitate small transactions. It is more convenient to buy a

---

[1] It is permissible to review pp. 55–57 on the role of money.

local bus ride with a coin or two than by writing a check; and even for many somewhat larger deals people often prefer peeling a paper bill from their wad to writing a check.[2]

Attributes of Money

Do not try to account for the general acceptability of money with the old wives' tale that money is "backed" by, or convertible into, gold. Gold coins have not circulated in the United States since 1933, when private ownership of gold was prohibited and made a government monopoly. There had been a fractional gold reserve requirement for the bulk of paper money (Federal Reserve notes), but recently Congress reduced the requirement to zero. Gold, then, does not give the dollar its value. However, the desire for gold is not based wholly on mysticism. People have sought, for good reason, to own gold and use it widely as money. It is portable, easily recognizable, readily divisible, and exceptionally durable. (Do you know anything that can match it in all those qualities?) In a world ridden with unstable governments and threats of confiscation of wealth or expulsion from a country, people find gold an attractive form of wealth. (Consider the problems of hiding and secretly transporting peanuts, cotton, leather, steel, or land.)

You accept money in exchange for valuable things only because you are confident that you, in turn, can pass on the money to others in payment for what you wish to buy. The first essential quality of money is confidence in its easy *marketability* to another holder. There are degrees of marketability, or "liquidity" as it is sometimes called. A good is more "liquid" the more predictable the price at which it can be resold and the closer that price is to the initial purchase price. More readily recognizable goods are likely to be more liquid. Goods that most people use are also generally easier to sell without a large difference in the buying and selling price. The most liquid of goods will be money. Money is very easily recognized and used by everyone, so it is readily exchanged again with other people at no discount from the price at which it was obtained. If you tried buying potatoes and then reselling them, you might find it inconvenient to locate a buyer and possibly difficult to get as high a price as you paid for them. Potatoes do not have great liquidity.

There is a long-standing myth (as far back as Aristotle) that money is sterile, yielding nothing to the person who holds it. But money avoids the higher transaction costs of barter in a world in which it is impossible to foresee one's future demands and those of others he may encounter while specializing and trading. Money performs the general kind of service we saw earlier provided by a fire extinguisher, stretcher, or eraser. While they stand available for potential use, would you say they were yielding no service, were of no value, and were contributing nothing to one's utility? You would say so only if you believe that people have perfect foresight. Money is a device that lowers costs of exchange and enlarges productivity via specialization.

Composition of Money in the United States

We follow most monetary analysts in designating money as: (1) currency and coins in the hands of the nonbank public—that is, outside the monetary authorities (the Federal

---

[2] It is commonly said that money performs two additional functions: (1) money is a "standard of deferred payments" (that is, contracts calling for payments in the future can be written in monetary terms); (2) money is a "store of value" (that is, wealth can be held in the form of monetary

Reserve banks and the United States Treasury) and outside commercial banks; and (2) the public's demand, or checking, balances in commercial banks.[3] Checking balances or accounts are known as *demand deposits*. Demand deposits are assets to the persons holding (owning) those claims or accounts against the bank; and they are "demand" liabilities of the commercial banks in which they exist. A $1,000 demand deposit can be readily (costlessly) converted into cash immediately on request at a one-for-one ratio. Rather than convert deposits, we can transfer them to others when making purchases: They *are* money.

Why not include time or savings deposits in the money category? These, too, are commercial-bank debts for stated amounts of money to the bank's customers. However, checks cannot be written directly on time deposits. Indeed, legally, time deposits cannot be converted immediately into currency or demand deposits, for the bank can require a warning period—although, in practice, time deposits can generally be withdrawn "on demand." We might label time deposits as "near money," in so far as the basic spending and saving decisions of most people are generally about the same whether they have dollars wholly in a demand account or, say, split half and half between demand and time accounts. Still, time deposits are rarely used as a medium of exchange.

In January 1971, the money supply was about $210,000,000,000, of which about $50,000,000,000 was cash and currency and $160,000,000,000 was demand deposits. Thus, about 80 percent of the money is in the form of demand deposits. The currency included about $4,000,000,000 in coins and $45,000,000,000 in paper money, more than nine-tenths of which were Federal Reserve notes, such as you have in your purse.[4]

Figure 28–1 plots the amount of money, along with real income, since 1920. Notice the general similarity in directions and even rates of change. Is there a cause and effect relation? Evidence of another type suggests (1) there is a strong *transient* effect of *changes* in the rate of growth of the money stock on real income *fluctuations*; (2) the long *secular trend* growth of real income probably does not depend heavily on the secular growth trend of the amount of money.

1, 2, 3, 4, 5, 6, 7

The Demand for Money

Common experience suggests the most convenient amount of money to hold depends in large part on one's income and wealth. *Different* people with the same incomes and wealths will hold different amounts of money; but a *given* person will generally hold more money at higher income and wealth. And the greater the aggregate wealth or national income, the greater the amount of money demanded.

The amount of money demanded by a person is *positively* related to (1) his money earnings or income, (2) the physical stock of goods he has, and (3) the prices of goods.

---

assets). But the first of these supplemental roles is subsumed under money as a unit of account, and the second is directly implied by money as a means of payment, for the means of payment at any given moment are being held (stored) by someone.

[3] Usual practice is misleading in suggesting the treasury and commercial banks do not *use* money in their business but just hold it passively to no purpose. Such balances should be counted in the national money stock—but we bow to convention.

[4] There are several other kinds of paper currency, which are quantitatively trivial and interesting mainly as historical curiosities. The only exception has been silver certificates, issued by the Treasury against silver—primarily because several western states have both silver and senators—but, on the basis of legislation in 1963, silver certificates are being eliminated.

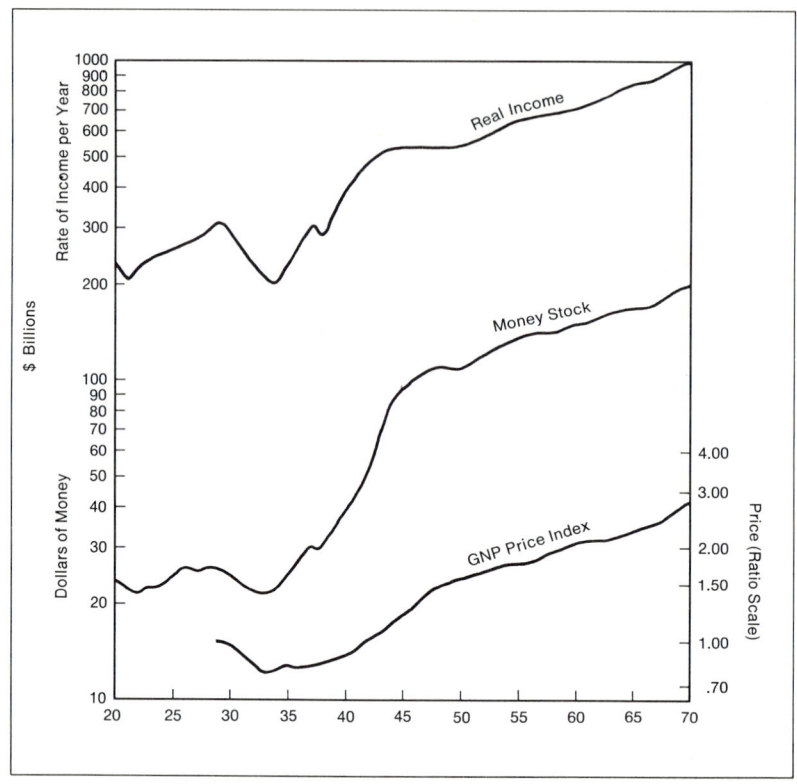

FIGURE 28-1. Money, Real Income, and Prices

The high correlation among directions of change in real income, money, and prices is evident. Cause and effect is suggested between changes in money stock and changes in price level. Evidence indicates that changes in real income are strongly influenced by changes in the rate of growth of the money stock, whereas the long-term upward growth of real income is not dependent upon secular trend rate of growth in money stock. Although money supply changes are an important factor in effecting changes in real income, they are not the only factor capable of inducing short-term fluctuations in real income. Rise in price level is explained by greater rate of growth of money stock than of real income. Why the money stock grew so fast is another story about which something is said in a later chapter on inflation.

(Wealth is the product of physical quantities and prices—that is, $W = PQ$, where P denotes the prices and Q the quantities.) And money demanded is *negatively* related to the rate of interest. The greater are one's income and one's wealth and the lower is the interest rate, the greater is the amount of money demanded. Having a bank balance or a stock of cash—"holding" money—involves a cost. One could have more goods for consumption or he could lend the money and get interest. But if he did, he would sacrifice some conveniences of holding some money and being able to buy goods at moments other than when he receives his income. The uses of money are (1) to hold it, which reduces future transactions costs, (2) to spend it now on consumption goods, and (3) to lend or invest it, which gives a growth in wealth equal to the interest rate. Any one of these can be increased at the expense of the other two. A person will adjust his holdings so that the marginal return in monetary *and* nonmonetary services for a dollar more is equal in all three uses.

If a person has *more* than his demanded amount of money, he will *spend* or *lend* more. And if he has less money than that, he will reduce his spending or will borrow until he accumulates a larger money balance. Consider a person with a $100-a-week income and total wealth of $5,000. If $4,000 of his wealth is in cash, he would probably spend more than his current income as he exchanged (spent) some of his money for other kinds of goods. But if he had only $10 in cash, he might reduce his expenditure rate relative to his money income until he had accumulated enough cash to facilitate his normal purchase rate.

8, 9, 10, 11, 12

Preview of Effects of Changes in Quantity of Money Supplied

With economic theory we can derive the effects of a reduction in the quantity of money supplied.[5] (Never mind now how the available quantity of money could decrease. Simply suppose that everyone lost 30 percent of his *money* in a fire or that the government taxes everyone 30 percent of his *money* and then destroys the money.) Everyone now has less wealth, but since the whole reduction in wealth was in money, the proportion of money to total wealth and income has fallen. Given that people formerly held the desired amounts of money, and given their remaining wealth, income, and interest rates, they now have *less* money than they want (despite their lower wealth). They attempt to recoup money balances by *spending less* of their income or by *selling* some of their other wealth and by *borrowing*. They will be buying less of current output and trying to sell some of their stocks, bonds, I.O.U.s, or other inventories in order to restore their money balances. But not *everyone* can do this, because people buy and sell to each other. Instead, as market demand falls, income, prices, and wealth fall.

As we know, if complete information about all market opportunities were free and instantly available, a decline in general demand could be accompanied by an immediate appropriate downward adjustment in prices, with no effect on real output or employment. In fact, however, unemployment of labor and equipment does increase during an episode of *decreasing* demand. And as long as demand is falling, as it will if the money stock is being reduced, unemployment will stay high, and the price level will decline (but too slowly to prevent unemployment). These effects can also be expressed with the analysis of the preceding chapter. Referring back to Figures 27–2 and 27–3, when the investment and the consumption functions are shifted downward in response to reduced money balances, a lower income is implied. We are now adding to the earlier analysis the *explicit* recognition that *the positions of these functions are affected by the quantity of and the demand for money*.

An *increase* in the stock of money leads to the opposite shifts and effects (see Figure 28–2). Suppose the government printed some new money and one night sprinkled it from the skies. Or suppose, as is essentially the case, it prints new money to finance its

---

[5] In this chapter we speak of a change in the *amount* of money. Strictly, we should always refer to a change in the *growth* of the money stock. Thus a decrease to a zero growth rate from an upward trend of 10 percent per year is to be treated as equivalent in its effects on employment to an actual 10 percent per annum decrease in the money stock.

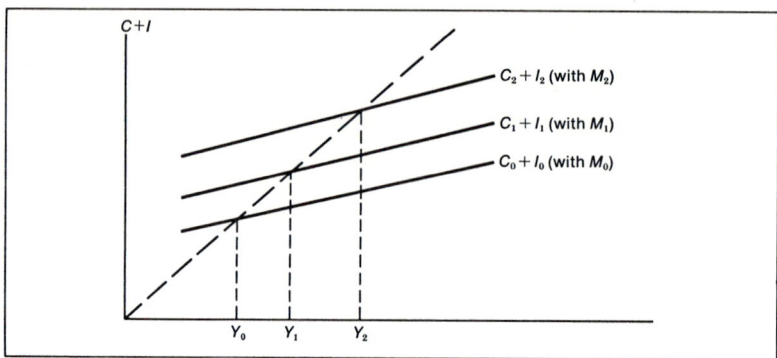

FIGURE 28-2. Effect of Amount of Money on National Income

Larger stocks of money imply larger rates of expenditures on consumption and investment: C and I functions are shifted up by larger money stock (M_2 denoting greater money stock than M_1 and M_1 greater than M_0). Shifts are the result of (1) direct incentive to spend more of money stock when it is excessive relative to income and (2) indirect attempts to reduce individual money holdings by lending more and depressing interest rates, which increases investment profitability. The rise in income increases amount of money people demand. And at a sufficiently higher income, there is no longer incentive to reduce still further the ratio of money held to income.

expenditures when these exceed its receipts. Or suppose that mysteriously every checking account were increased by 30 percent. With more money and no less of other goods, everyone has more money than he wants to hold (given his other wealth and income). People decide to buy some furniture, take a vacation, invest in stocks, lend more, or otherwise live it up. They increase spendings. The consumption and investment functions shift upward. Sales increase, inventories are drawn down, and manufacturers' orders are increased and they produce more. They seek more workers and resources. They have more "unfilled" jobs. Materials become "scarcer." As we saw in Chapter 24, employers do not instantly offer whatever wages are necessary to get new employees immediately, regardless of costs of moving or of additional appropriate workers. From the discussion of the price of meat in Chapter 8, remember how an increased demand operates to raise prices in some markets.

Income and wealth in dollar terms increase until at these higher dollar magnitudes the amount of money demanded is increased to the larger amount of money now existing in the community. Then the expansion in income and wealth stops; the new equilibrium national income is achieved. (To what extent output increases, temporarily or permanently, will be discussed later.)

Money versus Investment

It is usually disconcerting to learn there is some other way to analyze a problem, especially after learning one method. The approach via (1) the consumption and investment function to the determination of income at which saving and investment are equalized is logically equivalent to an approach through (2) the demand and supply of money. In our preceding analysis, we compressed all types of goods into just three broad categories—consumption goods, investment goods, and money. To say, in those circumstances, that the investment function has increased so that more investment goods are demanded is to say (assuming a balance of the consumption goods' demand and supply) that the public demands less money, so that with the given initial stock of money, the amount supplied is excessive. People are trying to switch from so much money to more investment goods. Thus an "excess of investment over savings" is cryptic language in which to say there is "an excess of the supply over the demand for money." The excess—no matter how expressed—is eliminated when income rises in nominal (dollar) terms.

The Quantity Equation and The Quantity Theorem

A definitional relationship among the money stock, the physical output, and the price level is often *summarized* in simple form by an equation,

$$v = \frac{PQ}{M},$$

where M denotes the amount of money in the community, P denotes the general price level, and Q the quantity of output, so that PQ is another way to express the annual national income. The term v, the ratio of national income to money, is usually called the income velocity of money. It is not an institutionally fixed value. It depends upon several factors—for example, costs of holding and using money, the rate of interest, extent of specialization in production, expectations about the rate of change of the price level. In the United States, gross national income is currently over one trillion dollars ($1,000,-000,000,000) per year, while the money stock is about $210 billion; therefore, v is close to 5.[6]

The usefulness of the equation $v = PQ/M$ as a means of deriving a theorem about the effects of a change in the quantity of money depends heavily on the presumption that (1) v is *relatively predictable,* whether or not the amount of money changes, and (2) if money does change in amount, it does not induce *unpredictable* changes in v. In fact, v has varied from about 2.5 to 5 in *slow* swings. It has *not* been greatly altered by changes in the quantity of money as an offset to those changes in the money stock. Now, if v is *sufficiently* stable, or predictably variable, when changes in M occur, we can by means of that fact express the strong quantity-theory proposition that a "substantial" increase in the quantity of money will induce a change in the same direction and in roughly the same proportion in national income. Speaking of "substantial" changes in the quantity of money is a way of recognizing that small changes in the stock of money (say, under 3 percent a year) will produce effects that are hard to detect above the random noise of all the other contemporaneous factors. If, however, the quantity of money should increase by, say 5 to 10 percent in one year, the impact on national income should be unmistakably detected.

Still to be settled is the question of how much of the change in national income is a

---

[6] As it stands, this is merely a definition of v. It cannot be "wrong." However, the equation can be used to express a special empirical proposition known as the quantity (of money) "theorem"—which is something different from the definitional quantity "equation."

change in *P* and how much a change in *Q*. The *equation* will not tell. Empirical evidence supports the proposition that the higher the preexisting unemployment, the more can an increase in national income (induced by an increase in the money stock) be in the form of increased output. And the lower the rate of unemployment, the more of the increase in national income that will be simply higher prices. If unemployment is less than about 2–4 percent, generally called "full" employment, an increase in the stock of money (beyond the rate required to match the secular growth in population and output, probably about 3 percent yearly) will result primarily in higher prices (inflation).

For example, from 1933 to 1939, a period starting with heavy unemployment, an 80 percent increase in the money stock was associated with an increase in real output of about 50 percent, while the price level rose approximately 10 percent. By contrast, 1943 through 1948 was a period of full employment. The money stock increased by about 75 percent, real output increased about 10 percent, and the price level rose about 50 percent. In both these periods, the money stock rose at an average of about 10 percent *per year*.

For other periods when the money stock rose by a smaller rate—less than 3 percent per year—the correlation was not detectable. For example, in 1923–29, a period of full employment, the money stock rose by about 20 percent (3 percent annually) with real output rising 33 percent (4 percent annually) and prices remaining almost constant (instead of falling, as would be implied if *v* were strictly constant). Again, in 1954–60, another period of full employment, the money stock rose 1.5 percent annually, while real output rose about 3 percent annually and the price level rose about 1.5 percent annually—instead of falling. The output increases are about equal to the secular growth of population and productivity.[7]

Clearly, the correlation between changes in the money stock and the changes in national income over a few years is poor for small rates of change in the money stock—that is, the demand to hold money will shift for reasons not made explicit in our present analysis. Nevertheless, the variations in the demand for money caused by unspecified factors are sufficiently small that changes in the supply of money of about 5 percent or more in a single year yield observable effects on the real output and price level, even without attempts to correct or adjust for the other concomitant factors. Furthermore, the cited periods illustrate the general proposition that money stock changes have a relatively greater effect on output than on prices in periods of unemployment.

We must avoid a possible misinterpretation. *Rising* prices are not necessary (or sufficient) to *maintain* full employment. We associate *rising* prices with increasing or full employment because we often achieve full employment by *restoring* it after a prior period of lower employment and prices. But once full employment is restored, it can be sufficient merely to prevent *declines* in the per capita stock of money. If that is done, advancing technology will result in lower costs of output and prices to consumers, with increased production. That kind of decrease in price—in response to lower costs and larger output—does not induce increases in the rate of unemployment. In United States history, there have been episodes when prices slowly fell while employment stayed high. In the 1880s and early 1890s, technology advanced, output grew, employment was high, and prices fell by about the amount that advancing technology would imply with the available money supply. Again, in the 1920s, output grew, employment was high, and

---

[7] In Chapter 33, where inflation is discussed in detail, and Figure 33–4 provide some evidence.

prices were stable or slightly falling. Similar intervals exist. If during those periods the money stock had increased more rapidly, prices would have risen (or fallen less). If decreases in the money stock never occurred, we could conveniently ignore their potential importance. However, there have been absolute decreases of large proportions in our money supply with traumatic and disastrous effects on output and employment.

We have seen that either the simplified consumption-investment model or the simple "quantity equation" can be used to derive effects of changes in the quantity of money. It may well be a matter of convenience whether we talk of decreases in the demand for consumption and investment goods rather than of increases in the demand for money (which leads to reduced expenditures for goods as a result of the attempt to increase one's stock of money to the amount demanded). An excess demand for money is synonymous with an excess supply of consumption and investment goods. It is only a matter of which variable you talk about.

If we are interested in emphasizing the difference between consumption and investment demand fluctuations, the money approach will be less helpful, because it compares money against everything else as a whole. If changes in the stock of money affect the demand for everything else in almost the same way, then the money demand, in which approach different goods are not distinguished from each other, may be more convenient. And if fluctuations in the stock of money, or in the demand for money, are important sources of fluctuations in general demand, concentration on money may be more convenient. But if money supply fluctuations are trivial compared to those in the investment or consumption functions, then we will find it convenient to express the analysis with the consumption and investment functions explicitly.

What are the facts? Clearly, changes in the stock of money have been closely associated with major fluctuations in national income. A change in the money supply caused, or at least was a major factor in, the Great Depression. Whether cause or effect in minor recessions, money changes *are* correlated with economic recessions and recovery. Similarly, fluctuations in investment have been strongly correlated with depressions and minor recessions; to what extent investment changes are cause or effect, or both, is still not established. But to ignore either money or investment is to ask for trouble. Usually a person who thinks money supply changes are more significant will use the explicit money approach, while one who investigates a problem in which the investment function seems to be the major factor of change tends to use the investment-consumption model. More modern analysts are using both approaches (with one of them really logically redundant) just to make sure that there is no unconscious associating of explicit analysis with empirical importance. But the exposition of these more inclusive theories would take us beyond the scope of an elementary exposition. And we must turn our attention first to the money-producing industry—the banks and the government—to see why changes in the quantity of money have been so great.

18, 19

Summary

1. Money serves as a standard measure of exchange (unit of account) and as a medium of exchange. Attributes of money include portability, recognizability, divisibility, and durability.

2. Money permits people to economize on the costs of exchange.

3   Liquidity is a good's capability of being readily resold at a price close to its purchase price. In this sense, money is the most liquid good.

4   Money is *not* sterile; it does provide utility.

5   The quantity of money demanded is positively related to the physical stock of goods and the price level (the product of which is wealth) and the current rate of income receipts, and negatively to the rate of interest.

6   The cost of holding money is (as for any other good) the income thereby forsaken.

7   If a person has an excessive amount of money, given his wealth, income, and interest rates, he will increase his expenditures until he holds just the amount of money he demands.

8   An increase (decrease) in the existing quantity of money will increase (decrease) expenditures by shifting up (down) the consumption and investment functions.

9   The quantity equation summarizes price and output effects of changes in the quantity of money on the assumption that there is no offsetting change in the demand function for money. "Velocity" is the ratio of national income to the stock of money. Changes in velocity are a means of expressing a change in the demand function for money (and, in other analytic terms, the consumption and investment functions). Changes (of more than 3–5 percent per year) in the quantity of money show a high correlation with the rate of unemployment, output, and prices. The correlation of money with prices becomes stronger at very low unemployment.

10 The simplified Keynesian consumption and investment expenditure model and the simplified quantity equation can be combined into a more general theory, including effects of changes in the quantity of money supplied and demanded as well as changes in the demand for investment goods relative to consumption goods, money, or bonds.

Questions

1   Which of the following would not serve as good money: tobacco, sugar, salt, cattle, nails, copper, grain, beads, tea, cowrie shell, fish hooks, chocolate, cigarettes, feathers, silver, gold, printed paper, stones, promissory notes, debt?

2   "Money is a medium of exchange. It is a common denominator or measure of value. It is a store of value. The first two are relatively unique to money, whereas the last is not." Explain what is meant by each sentence.

3   What are some desirable physical attributes for a commodity if it is to serve as money? For example, is its usefulness as money affected by its recognizability, portability, divisibility, durability, producibility? Why?

4   What is legal tender? A $10 Federal Reserve Note says, "This note is legal tender for all debts, public and private, and is redeemable in lawful money at the United States Treasury or at any Federal Reserve Bank." If you ask the Treasury to redeem that note for lawful money, what will you be given?

5   Does the value of money depend upon what it is made of or upon its quantity?

6   a. Do you think bus and subway tokens should be counted in the money supply? Why?
    b. Would you consider time deposits or savings accounts to be money? Why?
    c. Travelers checks?

7 How do we decide what to count as part of the money supply—that is, whether a given asset should rank as money? Choose the best criterion from the following and defend your choice:
(1) Does it have full gold backing—that is, is it convertible by the government into gold upon demand of an individual?
(2) Is it recognized by the community at large as spendable—that is, can it be freely and generally used to satisfy financial obligations?
(3) Is it a coin or paper currency (for in the last analysis these are the only things that can count as genuine money)?
(4) Has it been issued as lawful money by the federal government?

8 **a.** If the price of potatoes is 10 cents a pound, and a pound of butter is 50 cents, what is the "price of *getting* a dollar"?
b. If the interest rate is 6 percent per year, what is the cost of *holding* money? (Hint: Your answer should be consistent, in principle, with the answers to the following two analogous questions: What is the cost of *obtaining* ownership of a house whose price is $20,000? What is the cost of *owning* a house?)

9 "I never have too much money."
a. Are economic principles consistent with that assertion?
b. In what sense is that assertion incorrect?

10 What is meant by "the demand for money"? Money itself is not eaten, worn, or otherwise consumed; so, except for the miserly joy of running through it in one's bare feet, what gains can there be in *not* spending all money on consumption as soon as it is received?

11 Do you think the amount of money you would hold on the average would increase as much in response to a gift to you of $100 in wealth as for an increase in your wages of $10 per week? (Hint: What is the present value of an increase in wages of $10 per week? How does it compare with a gain of $100 in wealth?)

12 The ratio of the amount of coins, paper money, and checking-account money in the United States is about 1:10:50, or 1.6 percent coins, 16 percent paper, and 83 percent checking accounts.
a. Count your amounts of each; if your ratios differ, why are you so abnormal?
b. Which people do you think would have higher ratios of coins? Who have higher ratios of paper money? Who would have higher ratios of checking-account money? Explain.

13 a. Would you like to have twice as large a house as you do now? Would you object if other people were also as lucky as to have twice as large a house?
b. Then why should you be happy to wake up and find you have twice as much money, but not if other people also have that lucky experience?
c. Would you behave differently if you were the only one who luckily doubled his money stock than if everyone else also got twice as much overnight? Why?

14 Describe your behavior in terms of shifts in the Keynesian consumption and investment functions—in response to the following changes:
a. You wake up some morning and find that your income and wealth are the same, but someone has taken your car and left you ample cash payment in an envelope.
b. You wake up some morning and find the money in the envelope, but with nothing else changed.

15 Tonight the government prints twice as much money as there now is and sprinkles it from the skies as a sort of Fourth of July celebration and reward to all the people.
a. The next day, when the money is found, what do you think will happen to prices?

b. What will happen to the rate of interest? (Hint: How will the demand and supply of various goods be affected? How will the current demand for bonds be affected relative to the demand of other goods?)

c. Instead of sprinkling the money from the skies, suppose the government uses the money to buy up existing government or existing privately issued bonds. What will happen to the rate of interest?

d. Why does this give a different result, even though both involved an increase in the stock of money?

16 Indicate whether the following have any effect on the demand for money and in what direction: (a) total wealth; (b) interest rate on loans; (c) general price level; (d) day of the month (after payday); (e) month of year; (f) occupation; (g) in residence or traveling; (h) possession of a credit card; (i) fees for having less than a prescribed minimum balance in a checking account; (j) proportion of other assets held in stocks and bonds instead of in consumers' goods and business equipment; (k) rate at which you expect general price level to be rising (or falling); (l) kind of government; (m) cost of convertibility to money of other types or of other nations; (n) predictability of expenditure patterns in the near future; (o) one's credit standing in the community.

17 We have discussed "two complementary (and possibly competing) explanations for major fluctuations in rates of use of resources"—namely, the Keynesian and the quantity-of-money approaches. How, or in what senses, are these explanations complementary or competing? Is it possible that they are both?

18 Estimate your average amount of money held during last September. Estimate your earnings during the year. Form the ratio of the latter to the former; that is, put the annual earnings in the numerator. This is your personal v. Does your v have a seasonal pattern of variation? Why?

19 Quarterly data since World War II show the following "peaks" and "troughs" for fluctuations in the money supply and in *GNP* (in billions of dollars). "1947–IV" means the fourth quarter of 1947.

	Money Stock				**Gross National Product**		
Peak:	1947—IV	$110.6	− 1.9%	Peak:	1948—IV	$265.9	− 3.3%
Trough:	1949—IV	108.5	+16.3%	Trough:	1949—IV	257.0	+43.5%
Peak:	1953—II	126.1	+ .5%	Peak:	1953—II	368.8	− 2.7%
Trough:	1954—II		+ 6.2%	Trough:	1954—II	358.9	+24.9%
Peak:	1957—I	134.6	− .8%	Peak:	1957—III	448.3	− 3.4%
Trough:	1958—I	133.5	+ 5.5%	Trough:	1958—I	432.9	+16.4%
Peak:	1959—III	140.9	− 1.8%	Peak:	1960—II	504.1	− .7%
Trough:	1960—II	138.3	+23.7%	Trough:	1961—I	500.4	+48.0%
Peak:	1966—II	171.1		Peak:	1966—III	744.6	

From these figures, suggest possible generalizations concerning the correlation of money and income—relating, for example, to directions of changes, relative magnitudes of changes, and timing or sequence of changes of the two variables. Notice that the peaks and troughs do not coincide exactly.

Money Supply and Commercial Banks

29

WHILE some money is a creature of government edict or fiat (paper currency and token coins), some 80 percent of the money supply is comprised of commercial bank *demand* deposits. Despite being called "deposits," they are really *debts* of commercial banks. These bank liabilities are payable immediately and transferable on demand from person to person as *checking* accounts (and used for over 95 percent of the value of all purchases and sales). Although economics lacks a fully satisfactory theory of the supply of money for modern money systems, it does provide an understanding of the mechanism or institutional interconnections of that system. Since that system is subject to controls by *governmental authorities*, we can explain how their possible actions would affect the money supply. But the money supply is also determined, even if not consciously, by *commercial bankers* and by the *public*. In sum, the money creation process is a result of decisions taken by diverse units—government agents, bankers, and private individuals.

Our task is to investigate the legal and institutional arrangements for creating, transferring, and retiring demand deposits of commercial banks. And then we shall try to see what determines the amount of money in existence.

Commercial Bank Money: Supply Transactions

The simplest approach to understanding the meaning and means of creation of demand deposits in commercial banks is hypothetically to organize and operate our own bank.

1. Our first transaction is simply to pass the hat among us would-be owners (that is, stockholders) and obtain cash with which to start business.[1] (Despite the modest pro-

---

[1] Before we can do so legally, we must obtain a charter (permission) from the state banking commissioner and—if this is to be a "national" rather than a "state" bank—from the Federal Comptroller of the Currency. Prior to 1933, it was easier to get permission, and in the nineteenth century

tests of Alchian and Allen, the rest of you stockholders insist on naming our institution the A-and-A Bank.) We sell 10,000 shares of stock at $100 per share, total proceeds being $1,000,000. From the standpoint of the bank itself (rather than the owners of the bank), the cash acquired from the sale of stock is an asset, and, on the liability or equity side of the bank's accounts, we enter the same value as "capital stock." (From an owner's viewpoint, recorded in his personal balance sheet, one asset—cash—is reduced, and another asset—ownership claims in the bank, that is, stock—is increased.) The bank's balance sheet is thus:

A-and-A Bank

Assets		Liabilities and Equity	
Cash	$1,000,000	Cash	$1,000,000

2. We (bankers) have acquired cash. Now we must have a place of public business. So we construct a building and appropriately furnish it. Just as confidence is the sine qua non of the monetary system generally, so it is for our individual bank. To prompt people to trust us, we engender confidence by using much marble on the building and a massive vault (even if the door seems always to be wide open). Suppose that the building, fixtures, and equipment—designated "property," for short—cost $250,000 and that we pay for it with cash. The cash asset is reduced and the property asset increased by the same amount. (In all transactions, we shall designate with * the entries currently affected.)

Assets		Liabilities and Equity	
Cash	$750,000*	Capital stock	$1,000,000
Property	250,000*		

3. Dressed in our most conservative, confidence-inspiring garb, we deprecatingly open the doors of the bank to a public eager to "deposit" money with us. Happily, our customers thrust $400,000 in cash upon our tellers; of this total, $300,000 is placed in "demand" accounts and $100,000 in "time" (savings) accounts. How shall we record this in the bank's books? We dump the $400,000 in our vault, along with the other $750,000, and accordingly increase the cash item on the asset side. But our customers did not make us a gift of this cash. They have a claim on us for the whole amount. Indeed, as the word "demand" indicates, they can at any moment exercise that claim which is known as "demand" deposits. (A demand deposit claim has been created by an actual deposit of cash in the bank. This is called *primary* deposit creation. We shall see there is another very important way to create deposits, called *derivative* creation of demand deposits.) Legally, our bank can require several days' notice before "time" deposits are withdrawn, although in practice we will not require such warning—because

---

anyone could open a bank. As would be expected, the rate of bankruptcy or bank failure was about the same as for any other business. Since 1933, severe limits on entry into the business and strict supervision of bank activities, exercised by each of several government agencies, have reduced bank suspensions to fewer than ten a year. And if a bank takes out deposit insurance, depositors are guaranteed against loss of their deposits up to $20,000 for each account—and one person may have several such guaranteed accounts.

the competitor bank across the street does not. We are legally prohibited from paying interest to our customers on their demand deposits (indeed, we shall impose some "service charges" on them), but we will pay interest on the time accounts (the maximum rate being specified by law). Then why don't depositors put all of the money in time accounts? Because checks cannot be written on time accounts—they must first be transferred into demand deposits, and this nuisance makes time deposits somewhat less convenient for payment than demand deposits. People are willing to forego some interest to obtain some additional transactions convenience. The balance sheet is now:

Assets		Liabilities and Equity	
Cash	$1,150,000*	Demand deposits	$ 300,000*
Property	250,000	Time deposits	100,000*
		Capital stock (equity)	1,000,000

4. Whatever may have been the motivations of the rest of you stockholders, Alchian and Allen are in this business to get richer. And as of now, although the bank has total assets of $1,400,000, we have no "earning" assets. Except for the service charges we collect from our depositors, we are making no money. So let us invest some of our cash. We are legally restricted in the kinds of permissible investments, but a highly acceptable outlet for our funds is government bonds; so suppose we buy $1,000,000 worth. Thus:

Assets		Liabilities and Equity	
Cash	$ 150,000*	Demand deposits	$ 300,000
Government securities	1,000,000*	Time deposits	100,000
Property	250,000	Capital stock (equity)	1,000,000

5. Suppose our "commercial" bank is a member bank of the Federal Reserve System. Of approximately 14,000 commercial banks in the United States, about 6,000—a little less than half—belong to the System. However, these member banks have 80 percent of all commercial banks' loans and investments and hold a similar percentage of total demand deposits. The Federal Reserve Bank is the American "central bank"; along with the Treasury, it is the "monetary authority," with various methods at its disposal (which we shall explain later) to influence the money supply. There are twelve regional Federal Reserve banks (and a number of branches), which have substantial autonomy, particularly in their more routine activities, but which are supervised and coordinated by the Board of Governors in Washington, D.C. Despite the regional arrangement of the System, we shall be justified in generally discussing it as a monolithic institution under the direction of the Board of Governors.

Since our bank is a member of the System, it is required to hold at least a minimum of "reserves," the minimum being specified by the Board (within limits set by Congress). Two types of bank assets comprise legal reserves: deposits of the commercial bank at its Federal Reserve bank and cash in the bank's own vault.[2] We shall later discuss reserve

---

[2] The Federal Reserve Act was passed in 1913, and the System was organized in 1914. During most of the history of the System—from 1917 to late 1959—member-bank deposits in the Fed were the only form of legal reserves. During 1959–60, the definition of reserves was modified to include vault cash, i.e., cash in vaults of the commercial banks.

requirements and their connection with the Fed's monetary policies. Our attention here is directed to the role of member-bank deposits in the Fed in the more mundane, but highly useful, function of clearing checks, i.e., transferring demand deposits from one person to another. (Many banks also maintain deposits in the Fed for check-clearing purposes.)

Without pausing now to calculate the current legally required minimum reserve for our bank, let us simply establish a more than adequate $110,000 deposit in our regional Federal bank. As our customers brought cash to us and opened a demand deposit in our bank, so our bank can deposit cash in the Fed: the Federal Reserve Banks are banks for commercial banks. After we deposit $110,000 in the Fed, the bank's balance sheet is:

A-and-A Bank

Assets		Liabilities and Equity	
Cash	$ 40,000*	Demand deposits	$ 300,000
Deposit in FR	110,000*	Time deposits	100,000
Government securities	1,000,000	Capital stock (equity)	1,000,000
Property	250,000		

6. One of our customers with a demand deposit has to pay a bill of $5,000, and the person to be paid does his banking with the outfit across the street. Our customer is entitled to draw out $5,000 in cash. But he is unlikely to come to the bank to draw out the money and walk down the street with $5,000 in cash in his pocket. It is easier and safer to pay his bill by writing a check. A check is an *order to pay,* with the writer of the check ordering the bank to make payment to the beneficiary. The person receiving the check takes it to his own bank, the Bloated Trust Company, and deposits it in his demand account. The Trust Company, in turn, wants to collect on the check deposited in it. Instead of the check's being sent directly to the A-and-A Bank, on which it was written, it will be sent to the Fed, at which both banks have deposits. The Federal Reserve bank "clears" the check by adding its amount to the account of the Bloated Trust Company and deducting it from the account of the A-and-A Bank.

The net result is that demand deposits owed by the A-and-A Bank and the deposit in the Fed for the A-and-A Bank fall by $5,000 (and demand deposits and the deposit in the Fed for the Bloated Trust Company rise). The following balance sheet changes occur in the three banks:

A-and-A Bank

Assets		Liabilities	
Deposit in FR	—$5,000	Demand deposits	—$5,000

Bloated Trust Company

Assets		Liabilities	
Deposit in FR	+$5,000	Demand deposits	+$5,000

Federal Reserve Bank

Assets	Liabilities	
	Demand deposit of A-and-A	—$5,000
	Demand deposit of Trust	+$5,000

And the complete balance sheet of our bank is now:

Assets		Liabilities and Equity	
Cash	$ 40,000	Demand deposits	$ 295,000*
Deposit in FR	105,000*	Time deposits	100,000
Government securities	1,000,000	Capital stock (equity)	1,000,000
Property	250,000		

If one of our customers writes another check, but this time the beneficiary also is a customer of our bank, the aggregate balance sheet would not change, assuming that the beneficiary deposits the check he receives. To be sure, the writer of the check has his bank balance reduced, but the deposit of the beneficiary increases by the same amount, so total demand deposits are unaffected. Since the demand debt does not leave the bank, there are no clearings, either adverse (a loss of reserves) or favorable (an increase of reserves).

7. The public's demand for currency is a function of many variables, including interest rates, levels of income, prices, and employment, and anticipated directions and rates of change in such variables. Here consider a seasonable change in demand: the Christmas period is approaching; retail sales presumably will rise; and, consequently, we expect that our customers will soon start withdrawing some cash. It would be embarrassing to run out of cash, so let's increase our vault holdings. As customers of the A-and-A Bank can withdraw cash and thereby reduce their demand deposits, so the bank can draw down its deposit in the Fed by taking out cash in the form of Federal Reserve notes. The acquisition of, say, $10,000 in cash makes the balance sheet:

Assets		Liabilities and Equity	
Cash	$ 50,000*	Demand deposits	$ 295,000
Deposit in FR	95,000*	Time deposits	100,000
Government securities	1,000,000	Capital stock (equity)	1,000,000
Property	250,000		

Before taking up another transaction, let us calculate reserves. We are concerned with three reserve measures: actual reserves, legally required reserves, and excess reserves. So-called *actual* reserves are the assets owned by the A-and-A Bank which are legally designated as "reserves"; and, as we have seen, these actual reserves consist of vault cash plus deposit in the Fed—in this case, $50,000 + $95,000 = $145,000. *Legally required* reserves are calculated as a percentage of deposit liabilities; more specifically, the bank is required to hold actual reserves equal at least to a specified percentage of the demand deposits in the bank plus a (smaller) specified percentage of time deposits, the percentages being specified by the Board of Governors.[3] *Excess* reserves are simply the difference, if any, between the dollar volumes of actual reserves and of the required reserves. Normally, actual reserves are larger than required, but excess reserves can be and sometimes are negative.

Required reserves reflect a *legal* requirement imposed by Congress and administered by the Fed. But the amount of reserves that a bank feels it *should* keep may be in excess of the legally required reserves. Few people take precautionary action only to the extent specified by some law. Most of us apply our own standards of safety. And so it is with bankers, each sets his own standards of how much reserves to keep on hand per dollar of demand and time deposits. And they may choose to hold more (but normally will not hold less) than is legally required. If, therefore, we conventionally call the difference of actual over legally required reserves "excess" reserves, we must be aware that they are not excess in the banker's own judgment.

Suppose, quite realistically, that the designated required reserve percentage against demand deposits is 20 percent and that for time deposits it is 5 percent. Required reserves (RR) are thus: ($\$295{,}000 \times .2$) + ($\$100{,}000 \times .05$) = $\$64{,}000$. Actual reserves ($AR$) possessed by the bank are $\$145{,}000$; excess reserves ($ER$) = $AR - RR$ = $\$145{,}000 - \$64{,}000 = \$81{,}000$.[4]

8. Our expectations of a seasonal "cash drain" prove correct: customers with demand deposits withdraw $\$15{,}000$ in currency. The balance sheet becomes:

Assets		Liabilities and Equity	
Cash	$ 35,000*	Demand deposits	$ 280,000*
Deposit in FR	95,000	Time deposits	100,000
Government securities	1,000,000	Capital stock (equity)	1,000,000
Property	250,000		

What does the withdrawal of cash do to the bank's reserve situation? Before we calculate the exact numerical answers, note the *direction* of change in the reserve measures. Actual reserves fall, for cash is a component of actual reserves, and the other

---

[3] Until recently, there were three sets of required-reserve ratios, the set applicable to any given bank depending on whether the bank was in the classification of "central-reserve city" (generally only New York and Chicago), "reserve city," or "other" (commonly called "country"). The percentage requirements have been highest for the first classification and lowest for the third. In 1962, the central-reserve-city classification was abolished.

[4] Our calculations of required and excess reserves have been made with the required-reserve ratio against demand deposits (r_d) being 20 percent and the time-deposits ratio (r_t) being 5 percent. With a given balance sheet, required and excess reserves would have been different if the Fed had specified either higher or lower required ratios. The following figures illustrate reserve calculations for the current balance sheet with alternative required reserve ratios for demand deposits (although the required ratio for time deposits also could be varied):

I: $r_d = .2$; $r_t = .05$	II: $r_d = .25$; $r_t = .05$	III: $r_d = .15$; $r_t = .05$
$AR = \$145{,}000$	$AR = \$145{,}000$	$AR = \$145{,}000$
$RR = 64{,}000$	$RR = 78{,}750$	$RR = 49{,}250$
$ER = \$81{,}000$	$ER = \$66{,}250$	$ER = \$95{,}750$

component, deposit in the Fed, is unaffected. Required reserves fall, for the demand deposits against which reserves must be held are now smaller. Although both actual and required reserves are smaller, actual reserves fall by the full amount of the cash drain, while required reserves fall by only 20 percent of the drain. Consequently, excess reserves are diminished. Putting the data into the equation, $AR - RR = ER$, we have $130,000 - $61,000 = $69,000$. Excess reserves are reduced by $12,000—that is, from $81,000 to $69,000, equal to 80 percent of the cash outflow.

9. Customers who own time deposits in our bank anticipate writing checks; so they shift $50,000 from their time accounts into demand deposits:

Assets		Liabilities and Equity	
Cash	$ 35,000	Demand deposits	$ 330,000*
Deposits in FR	95,000	Time deposits	50,000*
Government securities	1,000,000	Capital stock (equity)	1,000,000
Property	250,000		

Actual reserves are unchanged, but required reserves rise as deposit liabilities are moved to a higher reserve-requirement category of deposits; consequently, excess reserves are reduced. Specifically, excess reserves = $130,000 - $68,500 = $61,500$.

10. Finally, and most important, suppose that someone comes to the bank in quest of a loan of $20,000. Along with making investments (for example, in government securities), *granting loans is our major way of making money.*[5] If the loan applicant is obviously enough a supplicant, we will reach deep into our resources and our mercy and—after extracting from the customer a detailed personal financial statement and possibly collateral consisting of his every available asset—give him the loan. Just what does this involve? Usually, the granting of the loan consists simply of two entries in the bank's balance sheet: "loans" now appear on the asset side (for the bank now owns an I.O.U. from the borrower), and demand deposits on the liability side increase (for the loan is taken in the form of a checking account). The balance sheet now is:[6]

Assets		Liabilities and Equity	
Cash	$ 35,000	Demand deposits	$ 350,000*
Deposit in FR	95,000	Time deposits	50,000
Government securities	1,000,000	Capital stock (equity)	1,000,000
Loans	20,000*		
Property	250,000		

[5] We shall quickly see that the reference to "making money" by granting loans has a double meaning.

[6] For bookkeeping simplicity, but certainly unrealistically, we have ignored interest on the loan. If the amount actually loaned is the full $20,000 and interest of, say, $250 is to be collected at the end of the loan period, the balance sheet is as shown in the text; when the loan is ultimately repaid and the interest is simultaneously paid (by a check on this same bank), then the loan item in the balance sheet falls $20,000, and demand deposits fall $20,250, with "undivided profits," on the liability side, increasing $250. Alternatively, if the bank gives a "discounted" loan, the $20,000 loan entry will be matched by an increase in demand deposits of only $19,750 plus "interest collected but not

This is the second ("derivative") way of creating demand deposits. The first ("primary") was by a deposit of cash in the bank. Although the two methods differ, the resultant demand deposits are indistinguishable. The bank has absolutely the same obligation, and there exists the same kind of asset to the person credited with the demand deposit. The "demand deposits" on the book of a bank are the sum of these two sources.[7]

Look at what has happened to the money supply. Our customer, in getting the loan, obtains a checking account of $20,000. Does that mean that now he really has $20,000 more money? Yes. Certainly, demand deposits are money, and demand deposits have been increased by the bank's granting a loan. Where did this new, additional money come from? Physically, it consists simply of notations in the accounts of the bank; so it came out of a fountain pen. Ignoring the grubby physical aspects, we can say that the money is a *debt*, a *special* form of debt owed by a *special* institution. This kind of debt by a commercial bank is a very efficient money—both in its use and in its production.

Bankers often deny—sometimes with both embarrassment and indignation—that a bank actually can "create money out of thin air." One objection is that the bank has done nothing more than "monetize" some nonmonetary asset of the customer; for, after all, the customer did give an I.O.U. (and possibly pledged collateral) to obtain the loan. True. But even though the borrower has legally committed himself to pay back the money, he *did* get money in the first place; he *did* have more money when he walked out of the bank than when he walked in. But, it may be asked, since he now has more money, doesn't someone else have less—with the aggregate money supply thus remaining constant? Who has less money now? No one! Demand deposits are $20,000 larger, and the stock of cash is no smaller. There *is* more money, because there is more commercial bank "demand" debt. Finally, do not contend that, even if the loan at first increases the money supply, repaying the loan in due course reduces the money supply and so, in some sense, it all later cancels out and doesn't really count. Isn't it better to say that bank lending creates money and repaying bank loans destroys money than just to deny the whole business?

One form of money, then, is a special kind of debt of commercial banks—convertible on demand to cash and transferable to third parties by written orders (checks). As we have shown, this kind of money is the result of a commercial bank's creating a demand debt against itself in exchange for someone's promissory note or debt. A private debt is obtained by the bank while the private party obtains in exchange the commercial bank's *demand debt* (which *is* money). To emphasize the written transferability or negotiability of the demand debt, it is called a *checking account*. But whatever the name, the crucial feature is that the major portion of our *money literally is debt*—the demand debt of commercial banks.[8]

1, 2, 3

---

earned" of $250; when the loan is repaid, the loan and the demand-deposit items both fall by $20,000, while a decrease in interest-collected-but-not-earned is offset by an increase in undivided profits of $250. You see, it really *is* simpler to assume zero interest.

[7] The granting of the loan by the creation of the demand deposit has not affected actual reserves, but required reserves have gone up $4,000 (equal to 20 percent of the increase in deposits); and excess reserves have fallen by the same amount, to a total of $57,500.

[8] An appendix to this chapter summarizes the direction of change in reserve and monetary variables for most of the transactions already discussed, and the reader will do well to extend the table to include further transactions as they are brought up. The table, it must be noted, refers to the effects of the respective transactions on the *entire* group or system of commercial banks, not to the effects on the A-and-A Bank alone.

Expansion of Demand Deposits in the Single Bank

The A-and-A Bank, let it not be forgotten, was organized and is operated in order to make profits. How does the bank earn income? It picks up a little through service charges, calculated in some esoteric way wholly incomprehensible to people not working for the bank. But the bulk of the income stems from two sources: dividends and interest on *investments* (for example, government securities) and interest on private *loans*. Our concern here is with the latter.

Since the bank's income is earned largely on loans, it would appear that the more loans, the better. Indeed, why not grant more and more loans without limit? A loan which will yield interest revenue in excess of the administrative expenses involved will enhance profits. And since the demand debt of the bank can be created by the bank out of thin air, it would seem that a bank is in a position to earn unlimited profits. But there *are* limits to how far a bank can go in granting additional loans. The limits are imposed in part by the Federal Reserve. As we have seen, a bank possesses a certain amount of actual reserves; it can calculate the amount of its excess reserves at any given time. For simplicity, we assume the *desired* amount of excess reserves is zero. The bank will "expand" (that is, grant additional loans and thereby create additional demand deposits) as long as it has excess reserves.

Given some initial amount of excess reserves, how big a loan can the bank make and still end up, after all checks are written and cleared, with exactly zero excess reserves? Examine Table 29–1.[9] There, with a required reserve ratio of .2 against demand de-

TABLE 29–1. Initial Situation
Bank A

Assets		Liabilities	
Deposit in FR	$1,000	Demand deposits	$1,000
	$1,000		$1,000

posits, excess reserves equal $1,000 − $200 = $800. Faced with this situation, a banker may claim that the maximum loan he can safely make is $800—that is, he can lend (create demand debts against his bank) an amount equal to his excess reserves. Let's see why that is a reasonable rule of thumb.

We can usefully break down the analysis into two stages, granting of the loan by the bank and spending of the loan by the borrower. In each step, excess reserves are reduced.

Table 29–2 gives the balance sheet after the loan is made but before it is used. Actual reserves are unchanged ($1,000), but required reserves have increased (from $200 to $360), for liabilities against which reserves must be held have increased; therefore, excess reserves have fallen (from $800 to $640). Evidently, even if borrowers never spend the proceeds of their loans—or if all checks written go to people in the same bank—there still would be a limit to the bank's granting of additional loans: demand deposits could be increased so much by loans that required reserves would absorb all actual reserves.

---

[9] To concentrate attention on the expansion process, we omit all other realistic details and record only the pertinent items.

TABLE 29–2. Stage 1: Loan is Granted
Bank A

Assets		Liabilities	
Deposit in FR	$1,000	Demand deposits	$1,800*
Loans	800*		
	$1,800		$1,800

But this is only half of the analysis, for presumably the borrower *will* write checks on his newly created demand deposit. At least some of those checks *will* go to people who hold their deposits in other banks. Assume that *all* of the loan has checks written on it and that *all* of the checks go outside this bank. We end up with the two balance sheets of Table 29–3—for Bank A and Bank B—on the assumption that all of the checks written on deposits in A are added to accounts in B.

TABLE 29–3. Stage II: Checks Are Written and Cleared
Bank A

Assets		Liabilities	
Deposit in FR	$ 200*	Demand deposits	$1,000
Loans	800		
	$1,000		$1,000

Bank B

Assets		Liabilities	
Deposit in FR	$800*	Demand deposits	$800*
	$800		$800

Naturally, demand deposits in Bank A fall back to $1,000 when the loan money is spent, and the check is cleared. Bank A's deposit in the Fed falls by $800. Required reserves are now back to their initial value ($200), and actual reserves are reduced to $200; therefore, excess reserves are zero. The net results are, then, that demand liabilities are unchanged while actual reserves are reduced to the point where there are no excess reserves in Bank A, and Bank B has reserves and deposits of $800. Banker A was right: on the assumption we have employed, he could safely lend no more than the amount of his initial excess reserves.[10]

---

[10] Although, as a first approximation, the single bank can grant new loans equal, at most, to its excess reserves, this conclusion rests on two rather severe assumptions: (1) *all* of the loans are utilized (that is, checks equal in value to the loans are written) and (2) *all* of these checks go outside the bank (that is, they are written to the orders of depositors holding accounts in other banks). If we were to relax either assumption, or both, the bank could lend something more than its initial excess reserves without ending up, when all checks have been cleared, with negative excess reserves. Still another assumption has been that the bank's customers are not, on balance, withdrawing cash. This matter of "cash drain" will be incorporated in our later analysis of expansion by the entire banking system.

Expansion of Demand Deposits in the Banking System

While, as a rule of thumb, the *individual* bank can grant a new loan no larger than its excess reserves, what of the *banking system* itself? If the system were simply the single bank writ large, then presumably the maximum expansion of the system would be equal to the total excess reserves of the system. This is an easy and obvious conclusion. It is also wrong.

If we confine ourselves to a "closed" economy (that is, one with no trade and financial transactions with the rest of the world), it becomes apparent that at least the mechanism of expansion is different for the system than for the single bank. Within one bank some customers will write checks that go to other banks, and, when these checks are cleared, reserves are lost. But other customers are depositing checks written on other banks, and clearing these checks increases reserves. A bank that grants loans readily, at a more rapid rate than the other banks, is likely to find that on balance its clearings are adverse. It thereby feels pressure to curtail its pace of expansion and to "get in step" with the average of other banks. However, the reserves lost by one bank are gained by another: *the banking system has no adverse* (or favorable) *clearings*. Thus, the major constraint on expansion by the *single* bank does not exist for the *system*.

If the system does not experience adverse clearings, what limits expansion of all banks together? First, there remains the constraint consisting of an increase in *required reserves* as demand deposits rise through additional loans. Second, we may incorporate the possibility of *cash withdrawal* from the bank system as deposits increase and the public wants more cash on hand.

Expansion of the system with no cash drain. At first, let us assume that the cash drain will be zero and concentrate solely on the first factor, the increase in required reserves.

We continue with our preceding illustration. There is a required-reserve ratio of 20 percent; initially, Bank A has excess reserves of $800, and all other banks have zero excess reserves. On the basis of our rule of thumb, Bank A grants a maximum loan equal to its excess reserves; the entire loan of $800 is spent by the borrower, and all of the checks he writes go outside the bank. Thus, when the checks are cleared, the borrower's deposit and reserves of Bank A are both reduced by $800.

Suppose that all of the checks written by the borrower are deposited in Bank B: deposits and reserves in B rise by $800—with required reserves increasing by $160 and excess reserves by $640. Assume that Bank B now lends $640 and that all of the loan is spent and leaves the bank. But, again, the deposits and reserves lost by one bank are gained by another, call it Bank C. Bank C thus has $512 in excess reserves, lends that much, and loses that much in deposits and reserves transferred to Bank D. So it goes, each bank in turn lending by the amount of its excess reserves; that amount, however, becomes progressively smaller as the action moves from bank to bank. Review this bank-by-bank expansion process with the aid of Table 29-4.

The table starts where Bank A has excess reserves of $800 (recorded in column 4). Bank A then increases deposits by $800 through lending (column 5) and promptly loses both reserves and deposits of $800 (column 6). But the $800 lost in column 6 for Bank A pops up in column 2 for Bank B. The process is repeated in Banks B and C.

How far does all this go? It is indicated in column 5 (and will be defended a little later) that the sum $800 + 640 + 512 + \ldots = 4{,}000$. A shrewd reader may deny

TABLE 29–4. Expansion of the Banking System

Bank (1)	Reserves and Deposits Gained (2)	Required Reserves (3)	Excess Reserves (4)	Loans: Deposits Created (5)	Reserves and Deposits Transferred (6)
A	—	—	$800	+$ 800	−$ 800
B	$ 800	$160	640	640	640
C	640	128	512	512	512
D	512	102.4	409.6	409.6	409.6
E	409.6	—	—	—	—
⋮	—	—	—	—	—
	$4,000	$800		$4,000	$4,000

that this sum indicates that the banking system can create a total of $4,000 in deposits, *all* of which are in existence at the *end* of the process; for what is created in column 5 at every step along the way is lost in column 6. But a still shrewder reader will note that what is lost (out of a given bank) in column 6 is found (in another bank) in column 2. That is, the entries in column 2 are *still on the books* of the respective banks. While Bank B, for example, loses $640 in deposits (that is, owes $640 less in the form of demand deposits), that is *not* a reduction of the *initial* $800 deposit in Bank B. Of course, the bank does lose $640 of the $800 in reserves that it initially picked up from Bank A, leaving $160 of these acquired reserves to serve as "required" against the $800 deposit still in the bank. The original $800 deposit still owed by Bank B plus the $640 deposit still owed by Bank C plus all the other still existing deposits listed in column 2 add up to $4,000.

Just as it is legitimate and instructive to add the entries in columns 2, 5, and 6, all of which measure the loans granted and the deposits created, so we may total the figures in column 3. The column of "required reserves" lists the actually existing reserves in the respective banks which must be held by them against the actually existing deposits listed in column 2. The sum of these required reserves, $800, equals the magnitude of the initial excess reserves of Bank A, which started the entire analysis and furnished the basis of the system's expansion. That is, the initial *excess* reserves are gradually distributed over the other banks and "absorbed" into the *required* category; when required reserves finally total $800 (column 3), no bank in the system has any excess reserves, and expansion has reached its limit. By that time, the lending activities of all these banks together have resulted in $4,000 in deposits, which do exist now but which were not in existence at the outset of the analysis.

It is now apparent that the system can grant loans in the aggregate which are several times greater than the initial excess reserves, although each single bank, in its turn, lends only the amount of its own excess reserves. How large is the system's expansion coefficient? In our illustration, the new loans ($4,000) are five times the initial excess reserves ($800). One's instinct suggests that the ratio 5:1, or its reciprocal 1:5, is determined by the proportionate required reserve (20 percent).

In this case, instinct is confirmed simply by noting certain definitional relations. Let:

ΔD = maximum change in deposits through lending;
E = excess reserves initially in the banking system;
r = required (minimum) ratio of reserves to deposits.

Money Supply and Commercial Banks

Given these definitions, it follows that $\Delta Dr = E$, and $\Delta D = E/r$. In our illustration, $r = .2$, and $E = \$800$, thus making $\Delta D = \$4,000$.[11]

Expansion of the system with cash drain. We have concluded that the banking system has a potential expansion of deposits equal to $1/r$ for each $1 of excess reserves—assuming that there is no withdrawal of cash. We may now modify the assumption. The amount of currency in circulation does change over time, and, unsurprisingly, it strongly tends to rise as the total money supply increases.

Table 29–5 is an elaboration of Table 29–4. The process begins as before, with Bank A possessing $800 of *excess* reserves and granting loans of that amount. Then, in column 6, it is assumed that the bank's customers, including the borrower, draw out cash equal to 15 percent of the new loans.[12] The "gross" deposits (D) of $800 created by the loan are thus reduced to "net" deposits (D_n) of $680 by the cash drain (C) of $120; that is, $D - C = D_n$. The remaining $680 of net deposits then are wholly spent, and all checks go outside the bank, that is, to Bank B. The procedure is followed, bank by bank, with the cash-drain ratio, $c = C/D$, remaining a constant 15 percent.[13]

TABLE 29–5. Expansion of the Banking System: Cash Drain

Bank (1)	Reserves and Deposits Gained (2)	Required Reserves (3)	Excess Reserves (4)	Loans Gross Deposits (D) (5)	Cash Drain (C) (6)	Net Deposits (D_n) (7)	Reserves and Deposits Transferred (8)
A	—	—	$800	$ 800	$120	$ 680	$ 680
B	$ 680	$136	544	544	81.6	462.4	462.4
C	462.4	92.48	369.92	369.92	55.49	314.43	314.43
D	314.43	62.89	251.54	251.54	37.73	213.81	213.81
E	213.81	—	—	—	—	—	—
—	—	—	—	—	—	—	—
	$2125	$425		$2500 =	$375 +	$2125	$2,125

Money held by public

The introduction of cash drain, or the cash-drain ratio, reduces the maximum lending of the system. Potential expansion stops when excess reserves are exhausted. The initial excess reserves are "absorbed" or "dissipated" in two ways. First, some of the original reserves are *lost* from the banking system through the cash drain to the public $(C = cD)$. Second, some wind up in the *required* category against the (net) loan-created deposits (rD_n). Thus, the original excess reserves are reduced to zero, partly through a

---

[11] Instead of speaking of the maximum *change* in deposits on the basis of initially existing *excess* reserves (and the given reserve requirement), we can note the maximum *total* deposits (D) which can be "supported" by *actual* reserves (A): $Dr = A$, and $D = A/r$.

[12] For the last twenty or so years, the ratio of total currency to the total money supply (currency plus demand deposits) has fluctuated between 19 and 22 percent. Of course, this "average" ratio of currency in circulation to all money is not necessarily equal to the "marginal" ratio (*change* in currency divided by *change* in money supply). The choice of 15 percent for the cash-drain ratio, while not obviously unreasonable, is thus largely arbitrary; it is assumed not to be 20 percent in order to avoid duplication of the value of the required-reserve ratio.

[13] The cash-drain ratio can be expressed as: $c = C/(C + D_n)$, which makes explicit that c is the currency proportion of all money held by the public.

reduction in actual reserves as the public drains cash out of the banks and partly through an increase in required reserves as demand deposits in the banks increase.[14]

Supply and Demand for Commercial Bank Money

A possibly surprising idea is that *debt is money*—provided that the debt is the particular kind owed by commercial banks, payable on demand and transferable by checks. Commercial bank demand deposits *are* money. They are created (1) by depositing cash or currency in a bank, and, more importantly, (2) by a bank's indebting itself in the form of demand liabilities in exchange for the private debts (promissory notes) of its customers.

It may seem that the economy runs on pretty thin ice, using debts (of commercial banks) as a medium of exchange. It does, indeed, in the sense that the quantity of that money can be rather quickly changed if bankers for some reason become less willing to extend debt against themselves. But in another sense it is very strong ice. The world relies heavily on credit and confidence in fulfilling one's debt obligations only where and when they *are* reliable. A society in which the sanctity of contract and enforcement of contract is cheaper and more reliable (in part, by appropriate government and social institutions) is a more stable one.

Do not confuse the weakness of formal means of *enforcement* with weakness of *credit* itself. Given appropriate and effective enforcement, credit can be very reliable. Do not think of enforcement as being solely that of courts and police. The web of *continuing* business relations and interest in present wealth values of one's future earning power imposes punishment on debtors who fail to honor their obligations. Even bankruptcy does not protect from that loss of credibility. Business and future exchange are withheld from those who renege, which is a potent threat, indeed. Similarly, any bank that fails to honor its debts will lose its business—a punishment far greater than the legal punishment to which it can be subjected for nonfulfillment of just present debts.

6, 7, 8, 9

Supply (Lending) and Demand (Borrowing) of Deposits

What do the commercial banks buy or get in return for the debt (demand deposits) issued against themselves? They get the interest-bearing debts of their customers. *Banks supply their demand deposits* in exchange for private debts of those who borrow from the banks. The *public demands money* from the banks and purchases it with their interest-paying debts to bankers. Figure 29–1 presents this as a demand-and-supply curve relationship.

[14] A bit of easy doodling yields the maximum value of loans by the banking system:

$$E = cD + rD_n,$$
$$= cD + rD(1 - c),$$
$$= D(c + r - rc),$$
$$D = \frac{E}{c + r - rc},$$
$$= 2{,}500 \text{ (if } E = 800,\, r = .2,\, \text{and } c = .15).$$

Thus, as reflected in Table 29–5, the initial $800 of excess reserves is wholly accounted for by the cash drain of $375 plus the absorption into required reserves of $425.

The introduction of cash drain has made a substantial difference in the maximum expansion of the system. If the cash-drain ratio (c) were zero, we would have $D = D_n = E/r = 4{,}000$. But with $c = .15$, loans are only about three-fifths of that value, and net deposits are just over one-half.

Money Supply and Commercial Banks 599

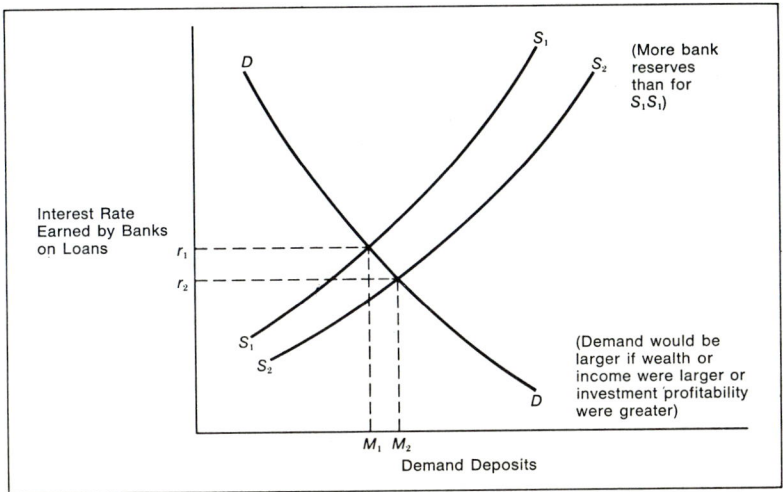

FIGURE 29-1. Demand and Supply of Commercial Bank Demand Deposits

S_1S_1 is supply schedule of commercial bank demand deposits with a quantity of reserves smaller than reserves available for S_2S_2. Increased reserves shift supply curve to the right; as banks acquire more debts from the public, by lending demand deposits, the interest rate is pushed down, and the quantity of money increases. Reduction in the interest rate is a result of the *way* in which demand deposits are created (in exchange for the public's debts) rather than of the mere *fact* of increased amount of demand deposits. If demand deposits were increased by bank purchases of paintings instead of debts, prices of pictures would be increased rather than interest rates reduced.

By lending more with a given quantity of reserves, the banks squeeze their actual reserve ratios (that is, the ratio of actual reserves to deposits) down toward the legally required (minimum) ratio. At higher interest rates, the profitability of creating demand deposits is increased, so bankers will be more willing to try to get by with smaller working reserve ratios. And at higher interest rates, bankers will be induced to seek more reserves in order to lend more; and they can get more reserves by borrowing from the Federal Reserve banks. An increase of reserves would be reflected in a *shift* of the supply curve of deposits to the right.

The *DD* curve shows the amounts of private debts offered by the public in exchange for demand deposits—a sort of demand to purchase demand deposits—as a function of the rate of interest they must pay on their private debt. The lower the interest rate (the less it costs the public to borrow), the more they will want to borrow. If the public's demand for money should increase, the *DD* curve would shift to the right. If the public were to become wealthier, it would want to hold a larger checking account, as a rich person holds a larger account than a poor person. Or if the price level doubled, everyone would want to hold more money in his checking account, since each dollar is now less useful.[15]

---

[15] Other factors can affect the position of the *DD* line—for example, interest rates on time deposits and in savings-and-loan associations, the ease of use of credit cards, the prevalence of over-draft privileges.

Typically, the borrower will want to get demand deposits to spend for other goods. Someone other than the initial borrower ends up holding the money. In turn, the investment and consumption functions of these sellers shift upward, either as their profitable production prospects have increased with the greater rate of sales or as their money balances increase. Recalling the analysis of the preceding chapters, the increase in the quantity of money leads to a higher national income and wealth.

At this higher wealth and national income, the demand to hold money will have increased enough to make people *want* to hold the increased quantity of money in existence.

Changes in Money Stock and the Interest Rate

The commercial banking system's process of creating demand deposits connects the quantity of money and the interest rate. If profitability of investment should appear improved, some parts of the public would be willing to borrow more funds for investing at any given interest rate. The *DD* curve for borrowing from banks would shift to the right.[16] The interest rate on debts to banks will go up as the intersection of the increased *DD* with the *SS* curve goes up. An increase in the *investment earnings rate,* by leading to an increase in demand for bank loans, results in a *higher bank lending rate*—and in a greater quantity of money as banks increase the amount of demand deposits supplied.

Suppose, alternatively, there is an increased amount of bank reserves or willingness to lend deposits (that is, to buy the public's debts), shifting the *SS* curve to the right. The quantity of bank lending increases; this time the interest rate *falls* as prices of private debts are bid up; the quantity of demand deposits increases. The increased amount of demand deposits (money) does not in itself contribute to a lower interest rate. Rather, the increased demand by banks for privately issued debts leads to a lower interest rate as well as to a larger quantity of demand deposits supplied. An increased amount of money can be obtained jointly with a rise *or* a fall in the interest rate depending on whether the demand for or supply of deposits increased.

Reductions in the Amount of Money

If investment prospects should worsen, willingness to borrow money from banks would decrease. The fall in the *DD* curve would reduce the quantity of money and the interest rate on new bank loans. The public would not renew expiring loans from the commercial banks and would repay some existing loans, since holding the demand deposits is not worth the interest rate being paid on the promissory notes to the commercial banks. The demand deposit debt of the bank to the public is canceled against the debt of the public to the bank: those who owe debts to the commercial banks write checks to the banks. The stock of money is reduced as bank debt is canceled in payment against private debt to the banks. The money disappears back into thin air.

On the supply side, the *SS* curve will shift to the left if the commercial banks lose reserves. The *SS* curve can shift to the left if the bankers suddenly fear that the public might try to drain out more cash than usual. The bankers will then want to keep more reserves for working purposes. In the Great Depression, bankers became more apprehensive about runs on banks and kept larger working reserves. The *SS* curve shifted to the

---

[16] Borrowing would increase from other sources as well. See Chapter 23.

left, and the money supply contracted. This can, we concluded earlier, plunge the economy into a recession or make a recession worse, as it did in 1929–32.

Conclusion

We have subjected the stock of money to economic analysis. A major component, commercial bank demand deposits, can be shown as determined by demand and supply relationships. The wealth-seeking motive of commercial banks gives the upward slope of the SS curve. Variations in the position of the SS curve can cause serious deflations or inflations. The DD curve can shift, also. If it shifts suddenly to the left, a reduction in money is the result, and a recession is upon us. Is the reduction of money that occurs with a recession caused by a leftward shift in the SS curve or in the DD curve? Or does the recession occur for *other* reasons and then *shift* the DD curve or SS curve to the left? Or do monetary or other factors shift the DD or SS curve to the left, thereby creating a recession? If we knew the answers to those questions, we would know more than any other economist.

For the major depressions in the United States of the past century (1871–75, 1891–94, and 1929–39, although there is much doubt about the first), the evidence indicates there was an autonomous decrease in the supply of money and that this played a major, if not dominant, role in the depth and length of the depression. In addition to these episodes, the economy has experienced minor recessions—or reduced rates of growth—on many occasions. Some have been caused by malfunctioning money-supply systems; e.g., the panic of 1907 and more recently the recessions of 1966 and 1970 were likely a result of sudden reductions in the rate of growth of the money supply permitted by monetary authorities.

Events occurring *independently* of depressions can induce shifts in the SS curve. The discovery of gold implies an increase in bank reserves and an increase in the SS curve. An increase in legal reserve requirements reduces supply—i.e., shifts the SS curve to the left. In the next chapter, we investigate some factors determining the position of the SS curve and some of the tactics and strategies available for consciously trying to control the SS schedule. We shall be concentrating on SS, not because DD is constant or because it moves only as a response to recession (and booms), but because SS is more subject to the control of monetary authorities.

Summary

1 Commercial bank demand deposits, the major form of money, are created by (a) depositing cash and currency in banks and by (b) bank exchange of its debts (demand deposits) for private debts.

2 Reserves of commercial banks consist of their vault cash plus deposits at the Federal Reserve banks. Commercial banks must, by law, maintain reserves equal to at least a specified minimum ratio of their demand (and time) deposits—the legal reserve requirement. Reserves in excess of legally required reserves are "excess" reserves, by definition, although the commercial bankers generally regard at least part of the "excess" as desired working reserves.

3 A single bank will create demand deposits against itself by lending to a customer. No one bank normally will lend more than the excess reserves it has.

4 The borrower from a bank writes a check against his new demand account, and the check typically is deposited in a second bank, creating a demand deposit in the second bank, canceling the demand deposit in the first bank when the check is cleared, and transferring reserves from the first to the second bank. In turn, the second bank lends on the basis of its increased reserves, transferring reserves to another bank as a check against the loaned deposit is cleared in favor of a third bank. Through such a sequence of deposits, loans, checks deposited in other banks, and transfers of reserves and deposits, a series of deposits is left behind in each bank; the sum of the series can be an amount greater than the initial excess (or working) reserves in the first bank.

5 If the public increases its holdings of cash and currency, that "cash drain" reduces bank reserves and thereby reduces potential bank expansion.

6 The amount of demand deposits supplied by commercial banks is an increasing function of the interest rate available from loans to private borrowers and of the available reserves. The willingness to borrow demand deposits from commercial banks is a negative function of the interest rate the borrowers must pay on their debt to the banks.

7 Because demand deposits are created by lending against private debts (rather than buying nondebt assets, say, Gauguin paintings), the interest rate is directly affected by bank creation of demand deposits (rather than affecting only the relative price of paintings).

8 Bank lending (exchange of bank debt for private debt) creates money; repayment of private debt to banks with demand deposits destroys money.

Appendix: Direction of Changes in Monetary Quantities Consequent to Monetary Transactions

Transactions	Actual Reserves of Commercial Banks	Required Reserves of Commercial Banks	Excess Reserves of Commercial Banks	Demand Deposits in Commercial Banks	Currency in Hands of Public	Money Supply
1. One bank buys government securities from other banks, financed by shifting the banks' deposits in the FR.	0	0	0	0	0	0
2. A bank buys government securities from a private dealer, financed by the dealer's accepting a check, which he deposits in a demand deposit.	0	+	−	+	0	+
3. Check is written on an account in a reserve city bank and deposited in a demand account in another reserve city bank, the check being cleared through the FR.	0	0	0	0	0	0
4. Check is written on an account in a reserve city bank and deposited in a demand account in a country bank, the check being cleared through the FR.	0	−	+	0	0	0
5. A bank increases its vault cash by withdrawing cash from its account in the FR.	0	0	0	0	0	0
6. Public withdraws cash from demand deposits.	−	−	−	−	+	0
7. Owners of time deposits shift their deposits into demand accounts.	0	+	−	+	0	+
8. Minimum reserve ratio required against demand deposits is increased.	0	+	−	0	0	0
9. Individual obtains a loan from a bank, proceeds of which are taken in the form of a demand deposit.	0	+	−	+	0	+

Questions

1 An initial balance sheet for a commercial bank is given in column 1. The balance sheets in columns 2 through 7 will be entirely *separate* from each other; each will be a modification of the *initial* balance sheet in column 1. In other words, this is *not* a cumulative program: begin with the initial balance sheet in recording each transaction.

In calculating required and excess reserves at the bottom of the balance sheets, assume a required reserve ratio against demand deposits of 25 percent. Finally, calculate the maximum new loans that can be granted by (a) the individual bank in a banking system and (b) the system as a whole, assuming that excess reserves initially are zero in all the other banks.

	(1)	(2)	(3)	(4)	(5)	(6)	(7)
Assets							
Cash	100	—	—	—	—	—	—
Deposit in FR	200	—	—	—	—	—	—
Loans	500	—	—	—	—	—	—
Government bonds	200	—	—	—	—	—	—
Liabilities							
Demand deposits	900	—	—	—	—	—	—
Capital	100	—	—	—	—	—	—
Required reserves	—	—	—	—	—	—	—
Excess reserves	—	—	—	—	—	—	—
New loans: single bank	—	—	—	—	—	—	—
New loans: entire system	—	—	—	—	—	—	—

(1) Complete column 1.

(2) A check for $50 is drawn by one of the bank's depositors, given to a person who deposits it in another bank, and the check is cleared through the Fed. (Record the new balance sheet in column 2.)

(3) A depositor withdraws $20 in cash from the bank, and the bank restores its vault cash by withdrawing cash from the Fed. (Record in column 3.)

(4) A check for $60 drawn on another bank is deposited in this bank and cleared through the Fed. (Record in column 4.)

(5) The bank sells $100 in government bonds to a bond dealer who pays with a check drawn on another bank. (Record in column 5.)

(6) The bank makes a loan of $10, the proceeds of which are taken in the form of a demand deposit. (Record in column 6.)

(7) The required reserve ratio against demand deposits is lowered to 20 percent. (Record in column 7.)

2 "Along with making investments (for example, in government securities), granting loans is a bank's major way of making money." Explain that the reference to "making money" by granting loans is a *double entendre*.

3 "A bank, through granting loans, can create money out of thin air. And air is a free good. Therefore, a bank can create loans (and thereby earn profits) without limit." Something is surely wrong in the quoted statement; straighten it out.

4 "Consider a single bank (one of many in the banking system); suppose that the required reserve ratio against demand deposits is 10 percent, and no excess reserves exist initially. Now, a customer adds to his demand deposit by depositing $1,000 in cash from his sugar bowl. As a result, without first-approximation assumptions concerning adverse clearings, the bank is *not* in a position to grant loans and thereby create deposits equal to ten times its (excess) reserves; rather, if it expands to the limit, it reduces reserves to one tenth the initial deposit." With the aid of T accounts, indicate step by step *what* happens and *why*.

5 The balance sheet of a single bank in a banking system is given. The legally required reserve ratio against demand deposits is 20 percent.

Cash	50	Demand deposits	5,000
Deposit in FR	1,000	Capital	1,100
Investments	2,050		
Loans	3,000		

a. As a conservative approximation, on the basis of the most severe assumptions we have used concerning adverse clearing balances, what is the maximum amount by which the bank can safely expand its loans?

b. How will the balance sheet appear some days after the loans in question (b) have been granted, that is, after all checks have been written and cleared?

6 "The banking system is made up of individual banks; the former is simply the sum of the latter. Therefore, it can scarcely be possible for the system to expand demand deposits by a multiple of initial excess reserves when any given bank can expand by (approximately) only the amount of its excess reserves." How could anyone disagree?

7 The banking system can expand as long as excess reserves exist; expansion stops when excess reserves are zero. But the banking system (as opposed to a single bank) does not lose reserves—assuming a closed economy and no cash drain. So where can the excess reserves go? Do we properly conclude that the system does not lose excess reserves and that consequently the system can expand without limit?

8 Using information given in question 5 and assuming no cash drain and no excess reserves in other banks at the outset of the problem, by how much can the *system* (including the bank that initiated the loan expansion) increase loans and deposits?

9 As an alternative to question 8, suppose there *is* a cash drain, with the cash-drain ratio being 10 percent of (gross) new loans. Then what is the maximum loan expansion of the banking system?

Money Supply: Determinants and Techniques of Control

30

THE money supply—more particularly, a *change* in the money supply—is crucial in analysis of income (both money and real) and employment. What are the immediate and some of the more remote determinants of the money supply? What powers do the monetary authorities have to affect the money stock, and how have they used their powers? Our discussion centers on (1) commercial bank reserves and (2) the monetary base, otherwise known as "high-powered money."

Bank Reserves and the Monetary Base

We have seen that (1) the great bulk of the money supply consists of demand deposits in commercial banks, (2) demand deposits change primarily with the lending activities of banks, and (3) lending activities are constrained by the reserve positions of banks. It is appropriate, therefore, to investigate the determinants of bank reserves.[1]

The potential *new* lending (money creating) by a bank or a banking system is limited by the amount of *excess* reserves—that is, the residual of actual reserves minus required reserves. Given the magnitude of deposit liabilities, excess reserves are determined by the absolute *amount* of actual reserves and the required-reserve *ratio*. This suggests that the basic rationale for requiring banks to hold reserves is that it provides the monetary

---

[1] There is reason to believe that, at least prior to 1970, Federal Reserve policy decisions have been made with respect, not to stock of money or to actual reserves or to excess reserves, but to excess reserves *minus* member-bank borrowings from the Fed, which equals "free reserves" if excess reserves are larger than borrowing and "net borrowed reserves" if borrowings are larger than reserves.

authorities with a means of controlling the supply of money. The Fed's authority operates, directly or indirectly, mainly on reserves, reserve ratio requirements, and to a minor extent directly on the money supply. The purpose of that control is to induce banks to follow desired lending (money-creating) activities. Control of the money supply is desired in the interest of "aggregate stabilization," interpreted as "full employment with a stable price level."

It has not always been understood that reserve requirements constitute essentially a tool of monetary management. Commonly, it has been suggested that banks are required to hold reserves in order to assure bank "liquidity" sufficient to protect the banks' depositors. Since depositors wish from time to time to withdraw cash, so the argument goes, banks should be required to hold a certain minimum amount of assets in the form of reserves—otherwise banks would be too recklessly seeking profits. Several remarks can be directed to the naive notion that legally required reserves are a device for protecting customers: (1) From 1917 to 1959 legal reserves consisted solely of member-bank deposits in the Fed and not at all of cash which could be readily paid out to customers. (2) Even now vault cash typically is seldom more than 4 percent of demand deposits; and all reserves, including deposits in the Fed, generally are no more than 25 percent of deposits in the bank, so that only a small portion of deposits could be simultaneously covered by cash taken out of reserves. (3) It would be impossible to maintain required reserves while paying out large reserve funds to customers. (4) Real protection of depositors is not in adequate reserves stashed away for a rainy day, but prevention of massive customer demands for cash; panic-inspired "bank runs" will scarcely materialize if the customers are confident that their deposits are safe. One method of generating such confidence is deposit insurance.[2]

We can widen the scope of the discussion and also the understanding of the determination of the money supply by introducing the *monetary base*. The monetary base, broader than commercial bank reserves, is used for bank reserves *plus* currency for the public. More fully, the monetary base is distributed among the following uses:

monetary base = vault cash held by commercial banks +
  commercial bank deposits in the Fed +
  currency in hands of public.[3]

---

[2] Depositors will not wish simultaneously to exercise their claims on banks unless they fear they could not get their money if they did decide to withdraw it. If word begins to get around that little money is available, the typical person will dash to the bank to get his before the bank runs out of cash. And after only a small proportion of deposits has been cashed in, the rumor is confirmed: sure enough, most of the money is not available! If the panic continues, the bank may well be forced to close its doors. But the Banking Act of 1933 established the Federal Deposit Insurance Corporation (F. D. I. C.), which guarantees payment on each account up to a certain amount, now $20,000. All members of the Fed plus some nonmember banks are covered by the F. D. I. C. With payment of deposits guaranteed, come what may, a giant, and perhaps wholly decisive, step has been taken to preclude massive runs on the banks.

[3] Purists would distinguish between nonmember and member banks of the Fed, for strictly speaking:
  monetary base = vault cash in all banks +
    Fed deposits of member banks +
    currency in hands of public.

However, the quantitative difference is easily ignored, for deposits of member banks in the Fed are some $24 billion, while deposits of nonmember banks are only about $600 million. So here and throughout the chapter, we suppose for convenience that all banks are members of the Federal Reserve System.

Therefore, about 70 percent of the monetary base (namely, currency held by the public) is itself part of the money supply, and the rest of the base consists of commercial bank reserves. That part of the base which is held by the public—over two-thirds of the total—is "diverted" from potential use as reserves of commercial banks. (Remember the "cash drain" of the preceding chapter?) Since bank reserves can "support" a *multiple* total of demand deposits, the monetary base has been dubbed high-powered money.

We may discern a three-tiered institutional pyramid, illustrated in Figure 30–1. (1) The monetary authorities issue coin and currency: Treasury currency (essentially metallic money) and Federal Reserve notes are monetary liabilities of the Treasury and the Fed. Another liability of the Fed is deposits owed to commercial banks. (2) The commercial bank deposits in the Fed plus some of the coin and currency (vault cash) constitute the reserves of the commercial banks. (3) The remainder—and much the larger part—of the coin and currency is a portion of the public's money stock, most of which consists of demand deposits in commercial banks.

The data in Figure 30–1 indicate that the money supply ($202 billion in mid-1970) was about 2.7 times as large as the monetary base ($75 billion) and some 7.2 times reserves ($28 billion). It would be analytically neat if these ratios were constant, for then a given change in the base or in reserves would always be associated with a definite change in the money supply. The monetary authorities, too, would find that very convenient. In fact, there *is* a strong historical correlation between the base and reserves, on the one hand, and the money supply, on the other, as is evident in Figure 30–2. For example, since 1917 the year-to-year changes in the base and the money supply have

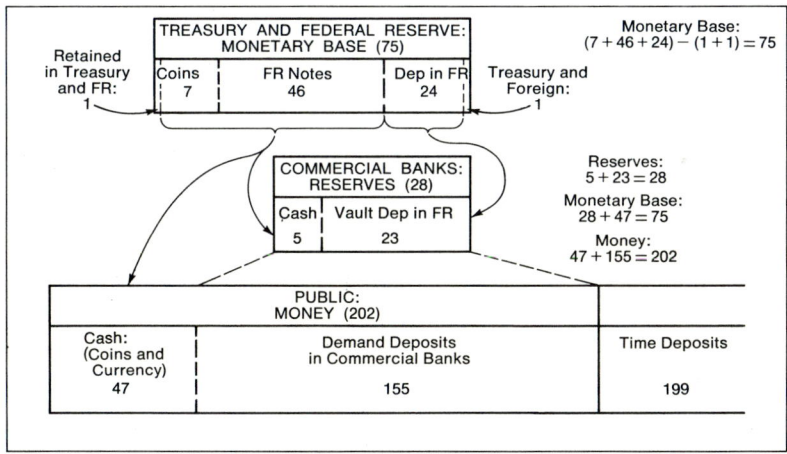

FIGURE 30–1. Institutional and Monetary Components of Money System (Approximate Data for Mid-1970 in Billions of Dollars)

Monetary authorities issue the monetary base. Commercial banks hold reserves. The public holds money. Coin and currency issued by the Treasury and the Fed are held primarily by the banks and the public, with smaller amounts held by the Treasury and the Fed. Currency in circulation (outside the Fed and the Treasury) plus commercial bank deposits in the Fed comprise the monetary base. Federal Reserve bank deposits, except for those in the name of the Treasury and foreign institutions, are commercial bank reserves. On the basis of reserves (vault cash plus deposits in the Fed), commercial banks owe demand deposits to the public.

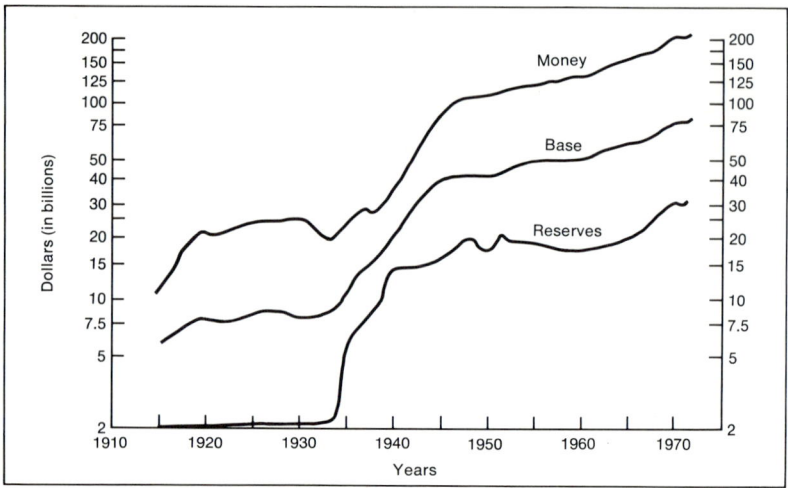

FIGURE 30–2. The Money Supply, the Monetary Base, and Commercial Bank Reserves, 1917–70

been in the *same direction* over three-fourths of the time; and reserves and the money supply have moved together annually some two-thirds of the time. Furthermore, the *ratios* of money to the base and of money to reserves have been generally stable over periods of a good many years; indeed, the ranges of fluctuations in both ratios have been very small throughout the post-World-War-II period. Still, the relations are not perfect—a fact indicating that changes in neither commercial bank reserves nor the monetary base wholly "account" for changes in the money supply.

Federal Reserve Bank Techniques for Control of Reserves

Having noted the considerable correlation of both bank reserves and the monetary base with the money stock, we should investigate the determinants of reserves and the base. Some of these determinants are subject to direct or indirect control by the Fed. A review of the Fed's chief tools of monetary control is a convenient and large first step in studying the general determination of bank reserves and the monetary base.

Reserve-Requirement Percentage

In the initial Federal Reserve legislation of 1913, the percentage legal requirements against demand and time deposits in the different categories of banks were specified. In 1933 (temporarily) and 1935 (permanently), Congress gave the Board of Governors authority to vary these requirements within a range. Table 30–1 gives the range and the specific requirements in effect in mid 1971.

Our earlier discussion of bank expansion makes clear the effect of a change in the reserve-requirement ratio on potential lending. From the standpoint of a *single* bank, reducing (or increasing) the ratio, other things remaining the same, directly increases (decreases) the *volume* of excess reserves. With a stroke of the pen, a change in the ratio

TABLE 30–1. Required-Reserve Ratios

	Demand Deposits		Time Deposits	
	Large-City Banks	Small-City Banks	Large-City Banks	Small-City Banks
Range of legal requirements (%):				
Minimum	10	7	3	3
Maximum	22	14	10	10
In effect May 1971	17.5(17)	13(12.5)	5(3)	5(3)

Figures in parentheses pertain—for reasons unknown to us—to banks with deposits of less than $5 billion.

changes required reserves; and, with given amounts of actual reserves, a change in required reserves will change excess reserves. For the banking *system,* altering the ratio has a double effect: not only is the *volume* of excess reserves affected, but, in addition, the *expansion coefficient* (the multiple by which a dollar of excess reserves may give rise to, or support, new deposits) is changed. Thus, if the Federal Reserve authorities diagnose the current situation as a "recession" and determine an expansionary policy, they can (within the prescribed limits) cut the required-reserve ratio, permitting a larger potential expansion of lending per dollar of reserves.

It would appear that changes in the required reserve ratio can be a powerful tool. (Currently in "reserve city" banks, demand deposits subject to reserve requirements total some $92 billion; a 1 percent change in the required-reserve ratio would thus change excess reserves by $920 million—compared to excess reserves now in reserve city banks of about zero and of $130 million for all member banks.) In practice, this tool has been used very gingerly. Changes in the ratio generally have been infrequent and small. To illustrate, consider the required-reserve ratio for demand deposits in reserve city banks. The original Federal Reserve law set this ratio at 10 percent. In 1936, it was raised to 15 percent; except for two changes of 2½ percent in 1937 and 1938 and one of 2 percent in 1948, all subsequent changes have been either 1 or ½ percent. In thirty-five years, there have been 21 changes, with the ratio varying between 15 and 22 percent from 1936 to 1971. Furthermore, most of these changes have come in several flurries; there were six successive decreases—from 22 percent to 18 percent—during four months in 1949.

Obviously, the reserve ratio is not used as a fine instrument, delicately modified from day to day or week to week. Indeed, it is necessarily an uneven instrument, for a change in the ratio for any given classification of banks will apply to all banks in that group, regardless of different reserve positions. An increase in the ratio which will reduce very large excess reserves for one bank will create negative reserves for another bank.

The general effect of a lower legal reserve requirement is suggested in Figure 30–3 by the shifting of the supply curve of demand deposits to the right. The *amount* of the shift induced by a reduction in the reserve requirement will vary with differing circumstances—including the amount of present excess reserves, predicted drains of cash by the public out of the banks, and feelings of business confidence regarding investment prospects and the safety of new loans. But the *direction* of shift in supply can be safely predicted: a larger amount of demand deposits will be offered at any stipulated rate of interest. A lower legal reserve requirement, therefore, increases the willingness (profitability) for bankers to supply demand deposits and pushes down interest rates on bank loans.

2, 3

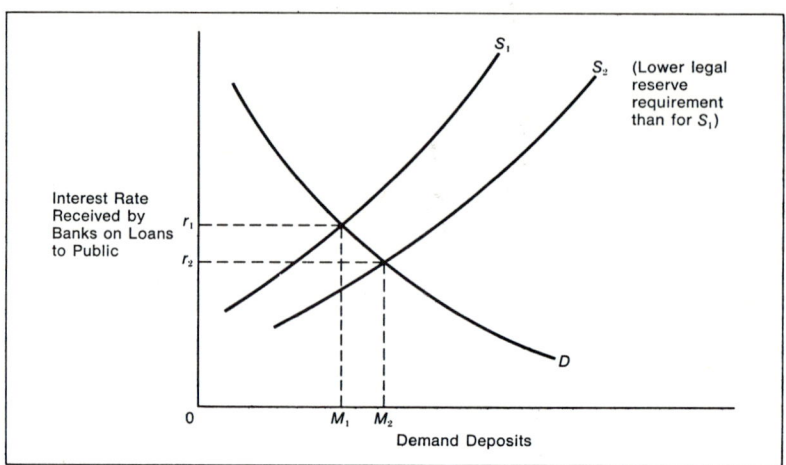

FIGURE 30-3. Reserves, Demand Deposits, and Bank Interest Rate

Reduced reserve requirement increases amount of demand deposits that can be outstanding with given reserves, so S curve shifts to right; quantity of demand deposits is larger and interest rate is lower. Reduced rediscount rate also shifts S curve to right. Open market purchases by Fed increase reserves and shift S curve to right.

Rediscount Rate

While changes in the legal required-reserve ratio directly change *required* reserves, changes in the "rediscount" rate may change the quantity of *actual* reserves.

The rediscount rate is the interest rate charged by the Federal Reserve banks on their loans to member banks. As a customer of a commercial bank pays interest on his borrowing, so does the bank when it borrows from the Fed.[4] And as a bank's customer will make his decision regarding how much he wishes to borrow partly in light of the interest rate, so the bank will be more inclined to borrow from the Fed at lower rediscount rates.

The rate is set at the discretion of the Fed. If member banks respond to a lower rate by borrowing more (or repaying less quickly), then member-bank reserves increase, for the loan is made in the form of a demand deposit in the Fed.[5] If the Fed wishes to

---

[4] Typically, when a customer borrows $1,000 from a commercial bank for one year (supposedly) at 5 percent, he does *not* receive $1,000 now and repay $1,050 a year later; rather, his I. O. U. is "discounted," and he receives $950 now and repays the face value of his note—$1,000—a year later. (Appreciate the infinite shrewdness of the banker: whereas 50/1,000 yields an interest rate of 5 percent, the actual rate is 50/950 = 5.051 percent, but the customer is not stupid: no one is fooled.) Now, the bank can use the I. O. U., known more grandly as "commercial paper," as collateral (security) for a loan from the Fed, and the Fed lends by discounting; since the same note is thus discounted a second time, it is rediscounted. However, the term "rediscount" rate applies also to the more common mode of bank borrowing from the Fed, in which the bank submits not already discounted commercial paper but a promissory note drawn on itself, with collateral generally but not always in the form of government securities.

[5] On the books of the borrowing bank, we would enter "deposit in Federal Reserve" on the asset side and "rediscounts and bills payable" on the liability side. Of course, paying off the loan involves canceling "rediscounts and bills payable" and correspondingly reducing the deposit in Federal Reserve.

pursue a more contractionary policy to combat inflation, it can increase the rediscount rate—inducing banks to borrow less than otherwise and thus preventing reserves from being increased as much. (For both expansionary and contractionary policies, in addition to changing the numerical *rate*, the Fed may change the *quality of collateral* required for a loan to a bank.) The effect of a lower rediscount rate, which increases reserves, can be indicated in Figure 30–3 by a shift to the right in the supply curve; an increase in the rediscount rate would reduce supply.

At the beginning of the Federal Reserve System, in 1914, the Reserve banks were expected to engage regularly and heavily in short-term rediscounting, and changes in the rediscount rate were to be *the* tool of credit control. Through the 1920s, this was the case; authority to change the required-reserve ratio did not yet exist, and use of open-market operations (discussed next) was slight. By the end of 1929, the rediscount rate of the Federal Reserve Bank of New York had been altered thirty times, within a range of 3 to 7 percent. It was changed another fifteen times from the beginning of 1930 to the spring of 1934, the range being 1 to 4 percent. But there was only one change during the next fourteen years, and except for the period 1955–60, when there were eighteen changes, the rediscount rate has not been very actively used for over thirty-five years.

Along with the relatively frequent changes in the rediscount rate in the 1920s, the volume of member borrowing from the Fed was relatively heavy; borrowings at the Fed were virtually zero from 1934 through 1943; during the past twenty years, average outstanding borrowings have approximated the volume of the mid-1920s—around $500 million; but this equaled something like one quarter of actual reserves in the 1920s, and it is only 2 or 3 percent of reserves now. Indeed, since the early years of the Fed, tradition has disfavored regular and substantial commercial bank borrowing from the Fed.[6]

Open-Market Operations

In general, the Fed's most important method of controlling bank reserves and the monetary base is through open-market operations. In such operations, the Fed buys or sells securities (but not gold), almost all of which are United States government debt instruments (bonds, notes, and bills) and comprise the largest portion of assets owned by the Federal Reserve banks.[7]

The transactions are conducted by the Fed with a few selected bond dealers who specialize in government securities. The Fed buys securities from them in the open market with checks drawn on the Fed. The dealers deposit the checks in commercial banks, thus increasing demand deposits in commercial banks (and the money stock).

---

[6] "The Federal Reserve policy of emphasizing to member banks that the use of its discount facilities should be temporary is reinforced in practice by a well-established tradition among this country's banks against operating on the basis of borrowed reserves—at least, for any extended period. This tradition does not mean that member banks feel reluctant to rely on Federal Reserve lending facilities to meet temporary or unusual cash drains. But it does mean that under normal conditions member banks manage their affairs so that they do not need to resort to Reserve Bank borrowing . . . and so that, once in debt, they seek to repay such debt promptly." *The Federal Reserve System—Purposes and Functions* (Washington, D. C.: Board of Governors of the Federal Reserve System, 1961), pp. 44–45.

[7] Decisions to buy and sell are made for the entire Federal Reserve System by the Federal Open Market Committee, which consists of all seven members of the Board of Governors plus five representatives elected by the reserve banks.

When the checks are cleared, commercial bank deposits in the Fed (bank reserves) also increase. Conversely, if the Fed sells securities in the open market, demand deposits in and reserves of commercial banks fall.[8] The dealers pay for the securities with checks drawn against their accounts in commercial banks. When these checks are delivered to the Fed and cleared, commercial bank demand deposits and commercial bank reserves decrease. The dealers also can replenish or reduce their inventories of government securities by trading in the market with other people and institutions (insurance companies, bankers, individuals, corporations, investment and pension funds, etc.). Indeed, the dealers, instead of buying or selling for their own account in dealing with the Fed, can be middlemen for others.

Again Figure 30–3 helps to identify the effects of a Federal Reserve policy on the quantity of demand deposits and bank-earning interest rates. An open-market purchase by the Fed increases reserves and shifts the supply curve to the right; a sale by the Fed moves the supply curve to the left.

How do open-market operations compare with changes in the required-reserve ratio and the rediscount rate? For one thing, open-market operations go on almost continuously, although not always on a massive scale; on the other hand, the other tools of control are employed only occasionally and may be unused for prolonged periods.

Next, there is a certainty of effect when the Fed acts in the open market—an effect that is characteristic also of changes in the required-reserve ratio but not of changes in the rediscount rate. When the Fed buys or sells in the government-securities market, bank reserves—actual, required, and excess—will be affected as soon as the buyer's check is cleared; and when the Fed raises or lowers the required-reserve ratio, required reserves (and excess reserves) change accordingly.

The final element of immediacy in the effect of open-market operations is not shared with either of the other tools of control. Buying and selling in the open market not only affect banks' reserves, but also directly and initially increase or decrease the money supply (demand deposits) by the amount of the transaction, whereas the other tools initially affect only reserves; any repercussion on the money supply involves a later lending reaction by the banks to the Fed's activity.

As suggested above, open-market operations were not dramatically consequential during the first part of the Fed's history. Throughout the 1920s, the Fed's holdings of government securities averaged around $200–300 million, rarely rising above $600 million. In 1932–1933, holdings of securities rose to about $2.5 billion and stayed there until 1942. The financing of World War II caused a tenfold increase to $25 billion; and, after a dip in the early post-war period, security holdings of the Fed have gradually risen to about $62 billion.

---

[8] Buying and selling activities, with the associated shifts in supply and demand, can change the prices of government securities. If, for example, the Fed is combatting recession by heavy purchasing of bonds, this increased demand for securities will tend to raise their prices. And an *increase in price* of a bond *reduces the interest rate*. For a bond paying an absolute dollar amount of interest, the reduction in the interest rate is an inevitable matter of arithmetic. (Remember Ch. 11?) If a bond pays $50 per year, the *rate* of interest is 5 percent if the price is $1,000 and 4.55 percent if the price is $1,100. Would such a decrease in the interest rate (if accompanied by a fall in rates generally) be supplemental to, or tend to offset, the basic anti-recession policy? If the general level of interest rates falls, one would suppose that the volume of borrowing would tend to increase; and thus the money supply and the amount of consumer and investment expenditures would be more than they otherwise would have been, which was what the expansionary open-market policy was trying to achieve.

Moral Suasion

The foregoing tools of credit control are tangible and direct. Less obvious is the Fed's moral suasion, or arm-twisting, in which the influence of the Fed partakes of a more subtle mother-hen aspect. Does the Fed believe that the economy is becoming rather too exuberant and that a little more monetary restraint (by a reduction in the money supply or smaller rate of increase) is in order? It may feel it is too early to use the obvious tools, but something should be done. So the Fed will tell the commercial banks that they might, in the light of the current situation, be just a bit more cautious in granting and extending loans. This message can be spread by such means as speeches and statements to Congressional committees by the chairman of the Board of Governors of the Fed; in addition, the numerous bank examiners can become a little stickier about the quality of collateral the banks accept when making loans. And when the word thus gets out, the banks may well fall into step, following the cadence of the Fed.

Summary

1. Commercial bank reserve controls of the Federal Reserve are primarily a means of controlling the supply of money.

2. The *monetary base* consists of (a) currency in the hands of the public plus (b) vault cash plus (c) commercial bank deposits in the Fed. The last two components comprise *reserves*.

3. Cash and currency held by the public plus commercial bank deposits (checking accounts) constitute the *money* stock.

4. The two prime monetary authorities are the U. S. Treasury and the Federal Reserve. They issue the monetary base. The Treasury issues currency and coins; the Fed issues (a) paper money known as Federal Reserve notes and (b) demand deposits against itself in favor of commercial banks.

5. The Fed sets legal reserve ratios expressing the minimum ratios of reserves to demand (and time) deposits which a commercial bank is normally required to maintain. Lowering the required reserve ratio decreases required reserves and thereby increases excess reserves. The Fed lends reserves to banks, charging them interest at a rate known as the "rediscount rate." The higher the rediscount rate relative to rates at which commercial banks can lend, the less incentive for a bank to borrow from the Fed. The Fed buys and sells securities (usually government debt) in the open market. Sales reduce commercial bank reserves; purchases increase commercial bank reserves.

Appendix: Sources and Forms of Reserves and the Monetary Base

We have given considerable attention to the *money supply*. Now we consider the monetary factors that directly determine the magnitude of reserves and how a minor rearrangement of terms will yield the monetary base as well.

Commercial Bank Reserves

Commercial bank reserves (vault cash plus deposits in the Fed) and the immediate determinants of the reserves are all entries in financial statements of the monetary authorities—the Federal Reserve and the Treasury.[9] We shall use the balance sheet for the twelve regional Federal Reserve banks consolidated with a "monetary account" of the Treasury; the cash and the deposits of commercial banks will be counterparts to liability entries in this consolidated Federal Reserve-Treasury account; thus, we may state commercial bank reserves as the algebraic sum of all of the other entries. It will be seen that only two or three of the remaining entries (determinants of reserves) dominate the picture.

Federal Reserve balance sheet. Table 30–2 presents a consolidated balance sheet for the Federal Reserve banks. Although it is incomplete, it presents the most important categories of our purposes.

TABLE 30–2. Federal Reserve Banks: Balance Sheet, March 1970 (Billions of Dollars)

Assets		Liabilities	
Federal Reserve bank credit	$61.4	Federal Reserve notes held by public and banks	$46.1
Gold certificates	11.0	Demand deposits of:	
Treasury currency	.2	Banks	22.5
	$72.6	Others (Treasury, foreign institutions)	1.4
		Other (net)	2.6
			$72.6

The term *Federal Reserve bank credit* is new here, but actually we have discussed it in connection with open-market operations and changes in the rediscount rate. Federal Reserve bank credit is a summary item that consists overwhelmingly of U.S. government securities; such securities held by the Fed in the spring of 1970 made up about $56 billion of the $61.4 billion total. A very small proportion of the total (about $.9 billion) consisted of "discounts and advances" to commercial banks.

While Federal Reserve bank credit is clearly the largest Federal Reserve asset, *gold certificates* also are substantial. Issued by the Treasury, they are "warehouse receipts" representing gold bullion bought by the Treasury. Gold certificates do not circulate but are issued only for Treasury deposit in the Fed. The Treasury has been committed to buy for $35 per ounce all gold brought to it. No one may keep gold in bulk; the law (since 1933) requires it to be sold to the U.S. government. The Treasury pays for the gold by writing a check on its deposit in the Federal Reserve banks. The seller deposits the check from the Treasury in his account in a commercial bank, which clears the check with the Fed. The Fed adds the amount to the bank's deposit in the Fed and correspondingly reduces the Treasury deposit. Finally, the Treasury almost always replenishes its deposit

---

[9] We continue the simplifying assumption that all commercial banks are members of the Federal Reserve.

in the Fed by issuing certificates with a face value equal to the value of the purchased gold and depositing the certificates in the Fed.

The balance sheets of the commercial bank and of the Federal Reserve record the net results of these transactions: (1) Demand deposits (of the seller of the gold) in the commercial bank are increased. (2) The deposit of the commercial bank in the Fed (the bank's reserve) is increased. (3) The Treasury deposit in the Fed first decreased (when the gold was bought) and then increased (when certificates were deposited in the Fed), ultimately being unchanged. (4) Federal Reserve assets in the form of gold certificates are increased. A gold sale by the Treasury results in changing the same balance-sheet entries, with opposite signs.

Treasury currency is largely silver money. Only a small part of the total ($.2 billion out of $6.9 billion) is held by the Fed. *Federal Reserve notes* held by the public and by commercial banks make up the largest liability in the Fed's balance sheet, and they constitute virtually all of our paper money. Almost all the rest of Federal Reserve debt is in *demand deposits*. The largest part of these deposits is owned by commercial banks and makes up some 85 percent of commercial bank reserves; relatively insignificant deposits are held by the Treasury ($1.2 billion) and foreign institutions ($.2 billion).

Treasury monetary account. Monetary institutional arrangements are based upon the Treasury as well as the Fed. The Treasury engages in money-holding as well as money-issuing, or money-creating. Here we are interested in only the latter activities. Therefore, rather than using an actual balance sheet for the Treasury, we will use one containing only certain monetary categories. The relevant data are in a "monetary account" shown in Table 30–3. The so-called Treasury monetary account is not an actual balance sheet; it is an artifice, an organizational device for the useful presentation of appropriate data—and different analysts may have somewhat different notions of just *what* data to include and even of precisely *how* to present them.

TABLE 30–3. Treasury Monetary Account, March 1970
(Billions of Dollars)

Assets		Liabilities	
Gold	$11.4	Gold certificates held by Federal Reserve	$11.0
Treasury currency outstanding	6.9	Treasury currency held by:	
	$18.3	Public and Commercial banks	6.6
		Federal Reserve banks	.2
		Other (net)	.5
			$18.3

The sources of commercial bank reserves and the monetary base provided by the Treasury are gold and Treasury currency. The nation's monetary gold stock is held by the Treasury at Fort Knox, and the *gold certificates* issued by the Treasury are held by the Fed. (The gold stock is slightly more than the aggregative value of the certificates, the excess being largely the "general fund" in gold.) *Treasury currency* outstanding (mainly coins) is held in small amount by the Fed (and the Treasury), but the bulk of it is in the hands of the public and commercial banks.

Federal Reserve–Treasury consolidated statement. Now, we consolidate the Federal Reserve and the Treasury statement into one account. Two sets of items cancel out: gold certificates held by the Fed and Treasury currency held by the Fed. We now have the "statement" in Table 30–4, which also defines the symbols used below.

TABLE 30–4. Federal Reserve and Treasury: Consolidated Statement, March 1966 (Billions of Dollars)

Assets (Sources of Reserves and Base)		Liabilities (Uses of Reserve and Base Funds)	
Federal Reserve bank credit (F)	$61.4	Federal Reserve notes and Treasury currency held by:	
Gold (G)	11.4	Public (C_p)	$48.0
Treasury currency outstanding (T)	6.9	Commercial banks (C_b)	4.7
	$79.7	Demand deposits in Federal Reserve of:	
		banks (D_b)	22.5
		others (D_o)	1.4
		Other (net) (O)	3.1
			$79.7

Reserves. We know that actual commercial bank reserves (A) consist of vault cash in commercial banks plus bank deposits in the Fed:

$$A = C_b + D_b$$
$$27.2 = 4.7 + 22.5.$$

Since total assets ($F + G + T$) equal total liabilities ($C_p + C_b + D_b + D_o + O$), we can express bank reserves as equal to the algebraic sum of the remaining entries:

$$A = F + G + T - (C_p + D_o + O)$$
$$27.2 = 61.4 + 11.4 + 6.9 - (48.0 + 1.4 + 3.1).$$

Thus, commercial bank reserves at any *given* moment equal the sum of Federal Reserve bank credit, gold, and Treasury currency minus currency held by the public and other deposits in the Fed (along with the residual item, O). It is conventional to call the first items (F, G, and T) "sources of (potential) reserves" and the latter items (C_p and D_o) "(alternative) *uses* of reserve funds." That is, were it not for C_p and D_o (and O), reserves would equal $F + G + T$; but, in actuality, a portion of these potential reserves is absorbed by, or diverted into, C_p and D_o. Reserves necessarily are equal to the total sources minus the alternative uses of potential reserve funds.

We also speak of "sources" and "uses" as *factors of increase* and *factors of decrease*. Over a *period* of time, the *change* in reserves accompanies an equal net *change* in the other items. An *increase* in F or G or T tends to *increase* reserves (and a decrease in these tends to decrease reserves); F, G, and T, then, are "factors of increase." Conversely, a *decrease* in C_p or D_o tends to *increase* reserves (and an increase tends to decrease reserves); C_p and D_o are "factors of decrease."

The Monetary Base

Like commercial bank reserves, the monetary base (B) consists of entries on the liability side of the consolidated Fed-Treasury statement. The base is simply the reserve components plus currency held by the public:

$$B = C_p + C_b + D_b$$
$$75.2 = 48.0 + 4.7 + 22.5.$$

Or, in terms of all the other items in the statement:

$$B = F + G + T - (D_o + O)$$
$$75.2 = 61.4 + 11.4 + 6.9 - (1.4 + 3.1).$$

As with reserves, F, G, and T are "sources" and "factors of increase" of the base. The only "use" or "factor of decrease" with respect to the base, other than the residual item, is D_o.

Approximate Determinants and Monetary Policy

It is apparent from the sources-uses equations that just two or three variables predominate at any time in determining the base and reserves and changes in them. As for the base, much the largest items are F and G. A moderately large item is T, but it is partially offset by D_o and O; furthermore, considering changes over a period, T is remarkably constant. It appears in Figure 30–4 that $(F + G)$ gives a good approximation of B and that it generally (over 90 percent of the time) moves in the same direction on a year-to-year basis.[10] Similarly, A is dominated by F, G, and C_p. It appears that $(F + G - C_p)$ moves together with A in annual changes nearly 90 percent of the time.

Over different periods, F, G, and C_p have differed in the relative importance of their respective changes. As shown in Table 30–5, the major influence on reserves and the monetary base in the latter part of the Great Depression was the tremendous increase in gold, which flowed in from Europe as World War II approached. During the war, government financing caused a great increase in the holdings of government securities by the Fed; while the base was thus swollen, reserves increased only moderately, mainly because of the absorption of potential reserves through an increase in currency in circulation. In the early post-war period, absolute changes in the "sources" and "uses" were of similar magnitudes. In the past twenty or so years, Federal Reserve bank credit again has been the major variable, but gold outflow also has been impressive.

To what extent can the Fed determine or change the magnitudes of reserves and the base? Gold and currency held by the public are not under the immediate control of the Fed, and only Federal Reserve bank credit can be determined "purely" on the initiative of the Fed. Many forces impinge upon the movement over time of G and C_p: interest rates and other prices both here and abroad; changes in technology and shifts in investment; international exchange rates and barriers to foreign trade and capital movements; the price of gold; anticipations of consumers, investors, and speculators. Some of these

---

[10] Prior to 1959, bank reserves consisted only of deposits in the Fed and not at all of vault cash. If reserves held in the Fed are designated A_f, then:

$$A_f = F + G + T - (C + D_o + O),$$

where $C = C_p + C_b$ and is labeled "currency in circulation." Here, C_b is a "factor of decrease" rather than a component of reserves. And it is then approximately:

$$A_f = F + G - C.$$

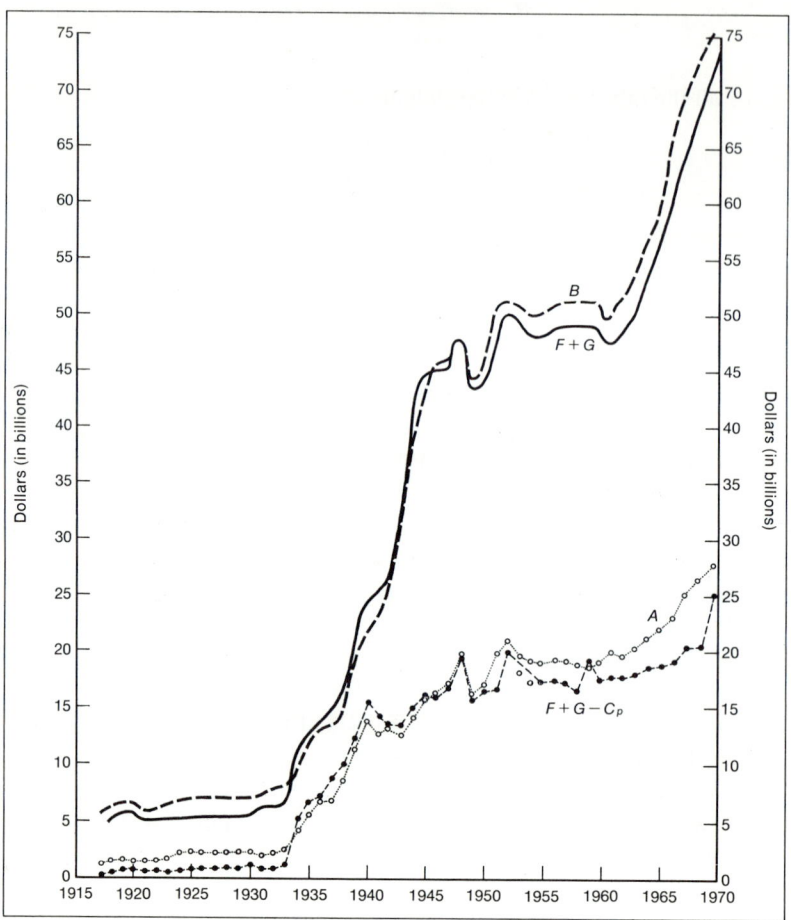

FIGURE 30–4. Commercial Bank Reserves (*A*), the Monetary Base (*B*), and Sources and Uses, 1917–1969

The base is approximated by the sum of Federal Reserve bank credit and gold. Reserves are approximated by the sum of Federal Reserve bank credit and gold minus currency held by the public (prior to 1959, currency in circulation).

factors themselves are shaped by actions of the Fed, but the influence of the Fed on G and C_p is not direct; it is at least one step removed.

The influence of the Fed on F is mainly direct, since F consists overwhelmingly of government securities held by the Fed. In making its open-market decisions, the Fed does have some constraints, and Fed officials may sometimes feel that they cannot utilize open-market operations aggressively enough to juggle reserves precisely. But, in principle, the Fed can (and probably does) employ such operations to keep reserves very close to the level it desires. Although there is no immediate linkage between the Fed and G and C_p, there *is* a close linkage between the Fed and *one* of the major determinants, F. For F can be used either to supplement or to counteract changes in G and C in such manner as to generate the size of A and B which the Fed wants.

TABLE 30–5. Factors of Increase and Decrease, Reserves, and Monetary Base, 1934–69 (Billions of Dollars)

	ΔF	ΔG	ΔC*	ΔA	ΔB
1934–40	−.2	13.7	3.1	10.0	13.1
1940–45	22.4	−1.9	19.8	2.0	21.7
1945–52	2.6	3.3	2.0	5.2	7.2
1952–69	38.3	−12.8	18.2	8.1	26.3

* In the first three periods, C is currency in circulation. During the last period, vault cash became a component of legal reserves, and the figure of $6.5 billion is the change from "currency in circulation" in 1952 to "currency held by the public" in 1969. See footnote 10.

Reserves, the Base, and the Money Supply

What would be accomplished if the Fed were to utilize its close linkage to F to control reserves or the base quite precisely? (Question: Is it inevitable that manipulation of F which yields the desired A or the desired B will yield *both*?) A matter of more ultimate concern than reserves or the base is the money stock. We saw earlier that the correlation between A and B and money supply, while generally high, is not perfect. Why the lack of perfect correlation?

First, we may look at the relation between reserves and money. To make the investigation very simple, we shall include only money in the form of demand deposits. The ratio of demand deposits to money supply rarely changes appreciably from year to year; it has shown only a slight downward trend since World War I. (In the 1920s, demand deposits made up about 85 percent of the money supply; in the 1930s, a little over 80 percent; and since World War II, slightly under 80 percent.)

Review the nature of reserves: $A = R + E$; that is, actual reserves equal required reserves plus excess reserves. Then, break down R into reserves required against demand deposits ($r_d D$) and reserves required against time deposits ($r_t T$). Then,

$$A = r_d D + r_t T + E.$$

It is apparent that the linkage between changes in A and in D is by no means purely mechanical, for three reasons. First, a change in A, on the left side of the equation, may be accompanied by a direct and equal change in E, on the right side, leaving D (and the money supply) wholly unaffected. Second, a change in A may be accompanied by an equivalent change in the reserves required against time deposits—the latter change, in turn, being determined by a change in either T or r_t, or both. Third, even if a change in A is matched by a change in the reserves required against demand deposits, the latter change may stem wholly from a change in r_d. Changes in r_d and r_t are made by the Fed, but changes in T and E stem essentially from decisions by the banks and the public. In light of all this, we should scarcely expect to find reserves and demand deposits invariably moving together. In the fifty-two year-to-year changes over the 1917–69 period, on six occasions either A or D did not change; in the forty-six remaining observations, A and D moved in the same direction thirty-two times and in opposite direction fourteen times.

Now let's look at the relation between the monetary base and money (M) given by:[11]

$$M = \frac{B}{\dfrac{C_p}{M} + \dfrac{A}{D} - \dfrac{A}{D}\dfrac{C_p}{M}}.$$

We may call C_p/M the "currency ratio," showing the proportion of the money supply which the public holds in currency. And A/D is the "desired reserve ratio," showing the ratio of reserves to demand deposits that commercial banks prefer to maintain. The currency component of the money supply, C_p/M, is about .2, the desired reserve ratio about .17. Since $.2 \times .17 = .034$ is quite small relative to C_p/M and A/D, it may conveniently be ignored for purposes of approximation, leaving:

$$M = \frac{B}{\dfrac{C_p}{M} + \dfrac{A}{D}}.$$

So the money supply varies *directly* with the monetary base (determined largely by the Fed) and *inversely* with the currency and desired reserve ratios (determined mainly by the public and the commercial banks).

The considerable correlation between M and B stems from the typical stability of the ratios, C_p/M and A/D. The currency ratio has hardly wavered from a value of .21 since 1949; similarly, it was highly stable from 1917–30 and fluctuated little from 1934–43; only during the Great Depression and, to a lesser extent, in World War II did it change markedly, rising quite sharply but briefly in both episodes. The story of the desired reserve ratio is similar: it has rarely strayed from a range of .17–.19 since 1944; it was remarkably stable from 1917–31; beginning in 1932, it rose steadily through 1940, as bankers chose to hold reserves far in excess of legal requirements.

---

[11] By definition:

$$(1) \quad B = C_p + A.$$

Dividing by M and D and also multiplying by D:

$$(2) \quad \frac{B}{M} = \frac{C_p}{M} + \frac{D}{M}\frac{A}{D}.$$

By definition:

$$M = C_p + D,$$

$$(3) \quad 1 - \frac{C_p}{M} = \frac{D}{M}.$$

Substituting (3) into (2):

$$(2a) \quad \frac{B}{M} = \frac{C_p}{M} + \frac{A}{D} - \frac{A}{D}\frac{C_p}{M},$$

$$\frac{M}{B} = \frac{1}{\dfrac{C_p}{M} + \dfrac{A}{D} - \dfrac{A}{D}\dfrac{C_p}{M}}.$$

Finally, M in terms of the other variables:

$$(4) \quad M = \frac{B}{\dfrac{C_p}{M} + \dfrac{A}{D} - \dfrac{A}{D}\dfrac{C_p}{M}}.$$

If we assume that $C_p/M = .15$ and $A/D = .2$, then the ratio of the money stock to the monetary base (M/B) is 3.125, which agrees with results of the preceding chapter (see Table 29–5).

In this context, what is the linkage of control from the Fed to the money supply? Given the currency and desired reserve ratios, an increase in the monetary base will increase the money supply. And the Fed can, in principle, determine the base by operations on Federal Reserve bank credit. Or, given the base, a decrease in either the public's currency ratio or the banks' desired reserve ratio will increase the money supply. The Fed can do little about the currency ratio; and if the public drains cash from commercial banks, reserves fall while the base and the money supply are not immediately affected. Also, commercial bankers do not always lend and thereby create deposits up to the legal limit set by their reserve holdings and the legal reserve ratio: they often prefer to have larger—occasionally much larger—"working reserves." Still, as Federal Reserve open-market operations affect B, changes in the required reserve ratio and in the rediscount rate can affect A/D. For lowering the required reserve ratio or the rediscount rate makes feasible, and tends strongly to result in, an increase in D, both absolutely and relative to A.

The Fed does not call its shots, so we cannot be sure how accurate it has been in adjusting the money supply to the level it desires. But it is reasonable to suppose that the Fed generally has come close to its chosen target. When the money supply has behaved inappropriately, it is because either the Fed chose its target badly or was not sufficiently bold in achieving it.

7, 8, 9, 10

Questions

1. Why are the forms of "money" constituting the monetary base called "high-powered money"? What kinds of money comprise the base, and who issues them?

2. "From the standpoint of the banking *system,* altering the required-reserve ratio has a double effect: not only is the *volume* of excess reserves affected, but, in addition, the *expansion coefficient* (the multiple by which a dollar of excess reserves may give rise to, or support, new deposits) is changed."
   a. Explain this double effect for the banking system.
   b. How is the effect of changing the required-reserve ratio different for a single bank?

3. "To rely upon a reserve requirement for the meeting of cash-withdrawal demands of banks' customers is analogous to trying to protect a community from fire by requiring that a large water tank be kept full at *all* times: the water is useless in case of emergency if it cannot be drawn from the tank." Is the analogy a useful one? Is it wholly and perfectly applicable?

4. Why is the rediscount rate called the "rediscount" rate?

5. Compare—in both principle and historical practice—open-market operations with changes in the required-reserve ratios and changes in the rediscount rate.

6. "High interest rates, known as tight money, are a result of the Federal reserve banks' not being willing to issue more credit. When less credit is supplied, according to the laws of demand and supply, interest rates will rise. That is why interest rates have risen during the past twenty years to their highest levels in fifty years." Evaluate.

7. Following are consolidated balance sheets of the Federal Reserve banks and the member banks.

Federal Reserve Banks

Assets		Liabilities	
Gold certificates	$15 billion	Federal Reserve notes	$31 billion
Government securities	32	Demand deposits	19
Other assets	5	Capital accounts	2
	$52		$52

Member Banks

Assets		Liabilities	
Cash	$ 3 billion	Demand deposits	$108 billion
Deposit in Fed	17	Time deposits	80
Investments	75	Capital accounts	20
Loans	120	Other liabilities	7
	$215		$215

a. If the required-reserve ratios for all member banks are 15 percent for demand deposits and 4 percent for time deposits, what is the numerical value of actual reserves? Required reserves? Excess reserves?

b. How much would the member banks have to borrow from the Fed in order to have excess reserves of $2 billion?

c. If the member banks were to borrow enough from the Fed to have excess reserves of $2 billion, what would be the maximum expansion of demand deposits (assuming that time deposits remain at $80 billion)?

d. If the member banks were to borrow enough to have excess reserves of $2 billion, what would be the maximum expansion of time deposits (assuming that demand deposits remain at $108 billion)?

e. Suppose member banks have previously borrowed from the Fed (with "discounts and advances" included in "other assets" of the Fed, and "rediscounts and bills payable" included in "other liabilities" of member banks). How large a repayment could member banks make without reducing excess reserves below zero?

f. The Open-Market Committee orders the Federal Reserve banks to buy $2 billion worth of government securities; the securities are sold by bond dealers out of inventories which are left depleted by the full amount of the transaction. Then what are actual reserves? Required reserves? Excess reserves?

g. To continue the preceding problem, suppose that the bond dealers replenish their inventories by buying $2 billion worth of securities from member banks. Then what are actual reserves? Required reserves? Excess reserves?

h. Reverting to the original balance sheets, would the Fed buy or sell in the open market in order to make excess reserves equal to zero? Buy or sell how much (assuming that the security dealers do not make a second transaction in order to offset the initial change in their inventories)?

i. If the Board of Governors lowers the required-reserve ratio against demand deposits to 10 percent, holding the time-deposit ratio at 4 percent, what is the value of actual reserves? Required reserves? Excess reserves?

j. If the required-reserve ratio against time deposits is 4 percent, how high would the required-reserve ratio against demand deposits have to be in order to wipe out all excess reserves?

k. If the required-reserve ratio against demand deposits is 15 percent, how high would the time-deposit ratio have to be in order to eliminate excess reserves?

Money Supply: Determinants and Techniques of Control

8 Below are approximate data (in millions of dollars for month of June) on the three major variables supplying and absorbing member-bank reserve funds.

	1929	1932	1941	1945	1970
Reserve bank credit	1,300	2,300	2,300	22,300	63,900
Gold	4,000	3,700	22,600	20,300	11,400
Currency in circulation	4,400	5,200	9,400	26,600	53,300

a. From 1929 to 1932, did the change in currency in circulation add to, or subtract from, member-bank reserves?
b. From 1929 to 1932, did the change in gold add to, or subtract from, member-bank reserves?
c. From 1929 to 1932, on the basis of the data given, what was the change in member-bank reserves (plus or minus how much)?
d. From 1932 to 1941, what was the change in member-bank reserves?
e. From 1932 to 1941, did the change in gold add to, or subtract from, member-bank reserves?
f. From 1932 to 1941, the major change was in which variable? From 1941 to 1945, the major change was in which variable?
g. From 1941 to 1945, did the change in Reserve bank credit add to, or subtract from, member-bank reserves?
h. From 1945 to 1970, was the largest change in the variables expansionary or contractionary?
i. What was the total of member-bank reserves in 1970? Were reserves in 1970 more or less than in 1945?
j. Normally, over which of these three variables do the monetary authorities have the greatest power of direct manipulation?
k. Is currency in circulation a "factor of increase" or a "factor of decrease"?

9 Figure 30–1 will help answer the following two questions:
a. For each of the following, tell whether the monetary base would be increased and why.
(1) Production of more gold in the U. S.
(2) Increase in the amount of Federal Reserve notes issued.
(3) Export of gold.
(4) Open-market purchases of bonds by the Fed. (Would it make any difference from whom the bonds were bought?)
(5) Increase in the amount of currency in circulation.
(6) Increase in treasury deposits.
(7) Issuance of new treasury currency.
b. For each of the items in question 7, tell how bank reserves would be affected.

10 "The linkage between member-bank reserves and demand deposits in member banks is not definite and purely mechanical. Thus it is not surprising that reserves of member banks and deposits in member banks do not always move closely together." Explain the nature of the "linkage" and how it permits the relation between reserves and deposits to be loose.

Government Finances

31 GOVERNMENT is socialism, by definition. As such, we could devote much space to the economics of socialism, i.e., the economics of government activity. This would involve specification of the behavior and constraints in socialism and the resultant processes of producing and allocating governmentally provided goods and services. How does that system operate without market-determined prices as guides to values of different goods in alternative uses and to various people? What determines the goods and their qualities to be produced, and who gets them? How are incomes determined? How are jobs distributed among potential claimants? All the questions and problems we have studied so far could be repeated for a strictly socialist system—one in which all productive resources are controlled by government agents.

In fact, we have in several places already illustrated how such questions are settled in sectors not characterized by private property and open markets. The applications presented were selected for two reasons: First, our economic system is predominantly, but not exclusively, a private-property, market-exchange system. Had our economy been primarily socialistic, we would have devoted more analysis to behavior in a socialist economy. Second, the theory and analysis of socialist systems is not as well worked out as that for private-property, market systems; therefore, less can be said about how such systems do operate and adapt to changing circumstances. Because we know so well the attributes of a private-property, market system, and because we deem some of them undesirable, it is tempting to jump to the assertion that the evils can be avoided by a different system, say, a socialist one. That may or may not be justified. As yet there is no clear knowledge as to what "evils" of a capitalist private-property, market system would be alleviated or increased by a move toward socialist organizations. Whether socialized schools, medicine, housing, steel production, airlines, radio and television, recreational parks, postal services, etc., avoid the perceived weaknesses or flaws of such activities conducted nonsocialistically is open to grave doubt, at least. In some instances, as we have suggested earlier, things seem to be "worse" under socialism, if we may interpose *our* evaluation. In others, things seem to be improved, e.g., national defense. Until a clearer, more powerful theory of socialist activity is available (and by theory we mean an engine of positive analysis, not formalization of goals and hopes), little can be said with scientific value.

There is, however, one activity about which information and analysis is becoming available. Government spending, taxing, and borrowing (i.e., fiscal activities) affect national income. Fiscal activity encompasses spending and financing but not regulatory activities, such as minimum wage rates, transportation, food and drugs, securities exchanges, television, and contractual liability conditions. Government financial operations can have significant effects on the national economy, whereas few private businesses are individually significant enough to require our consideration of their separate activities on the economy's national income.[1]

Without government, a system of private property and market-oriented exchange and production would be impossible on any significant scale. To judge simply from examples of government supported closures of markets to new competitors and of other restrictions on the role of business competitors in the open market, one might suspect that government would undermine that system. But government, as such (meaning police power and spending and taxing power), can be used for various purposes, depending upon who has influence in the uses of government power. It can benefit a few (domestic oil producers) or many (aged welfare recipients). It can hurt a few (drafted young men) or a large group (consumers who must pay more for clothing because cheaper, imported clothing is restricted). Governmental power is exercised by masses and by small groups. The large majority can be as dictatorial as a military dictator; and a king can be as careful of civil rights and official judicial processes as a democracy. We cannot categorically state that governments *as such* extend or restrict the working of a private-property, open-market system—or even of a socialist system, for the government ruling group may move away from a socialist system, as is suggested at times in Yugoslavia.

What we can do is inquire into and describe the activities of a particular government at a particular time. Inquiry can be aided by economic analysis, though it will not in its own right tell us what activities are good or bad. In this chapter we list the span of economic activities engaged in by government and the means of financing them. Contrary to the usual case in the private sector, wherein consumers are the payers for the services, for government services the *users* or *beneficiaries* are much less likely to be the *payers* (free college education, for example)—which is not necessarily a condemnation, for the desire to separate the users from the payers and controllers of the type of product may be the reason the service is produced or allocated by government agencies.

Or this separation may have occurred because the users wanted, and were cleverly able to make, someone else to pay part of the costs (municipal golf courses are invariably subsidized by taxpayers), or because much of the public wanted to contribute to indigents (welfare), or because it is believed by a sufficient number of those with political influence that the users or beneficiaries of some service are so diffused and expensive to find and individually collect from, relative to doing so via general taxes, that

---

[1] How that significant effect of government policy occurs and what principles should guide Congress and the President is the primary issue of the next chapter.

Government Finances

government action is more efficient in determining the amount of service and assignment of costs to beneficiaries (national defense and roads are assumed to be examples).

In each case, since consumers are not those who pay, it is easy to allege that the beneficiaries are using political power to have access to the taxing power and the public purse. But the real facts and motives are not so easy to establish. Therefore, in this chapter we identify some of the principal government activities, the amounts of expenditures, and the sources of government revenue. Then, in the next chapter, we inquire how the expenditure and revenue collection can influence national income and induce or alleviate economic recessions.

Government Expenditures and Receipts

Government Expenditures

The magnitude of government expenditures and receipts gives some idea of the scope and significance of government activity. Figures 31–1 and 31–2 show the relative historical expenditures for activities, while Tables 31–1 and 31–2 present detailed data. National defense, roads, and education comprise the bulk of expenditures, with the last two being predominantly state and local matters. What the data do not reveal is the variety among states and localities; some states have per capita (state plus local) expenditures about twice as high as the over-all average for all states, while some run to

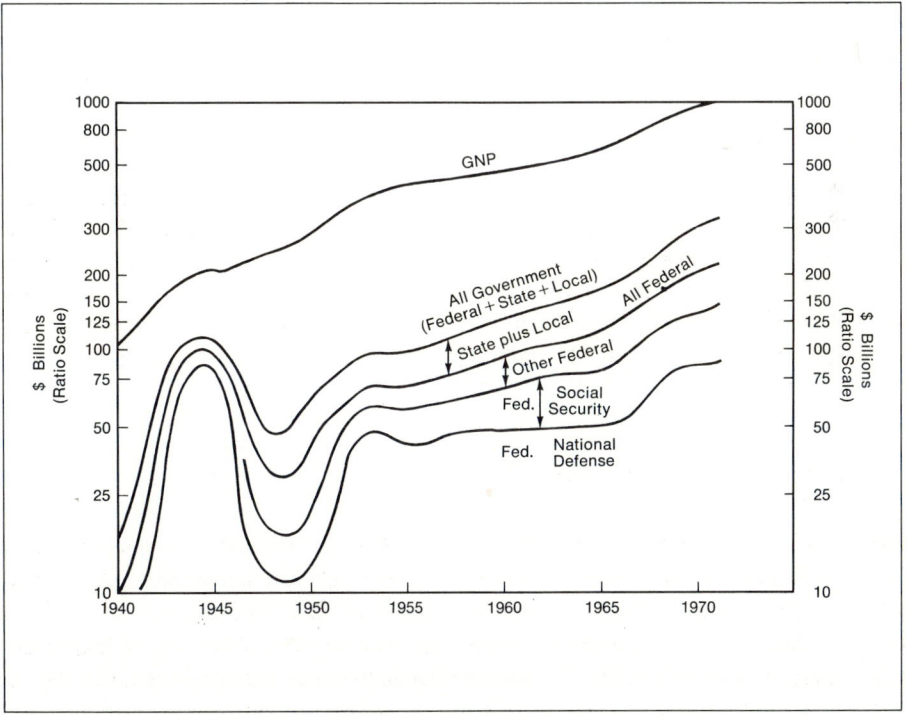

FIGURE 31–1. Government Expenditures and GNP—Federal, by Purpose, and State plus Local

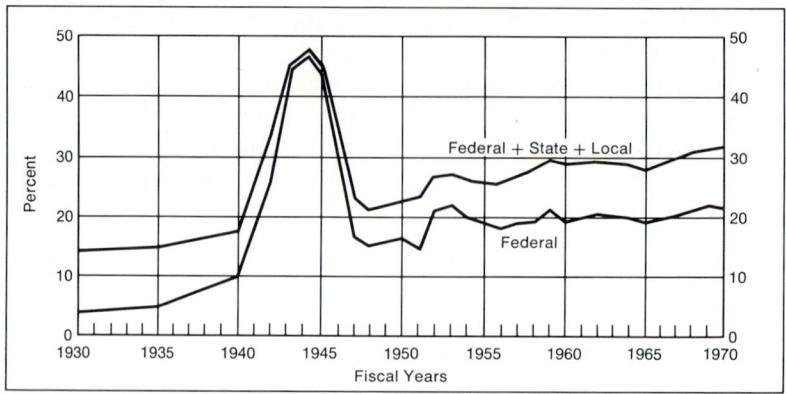

FIGURE 31-2. Government Payments as a Percent of Gross National Product

about half that level. No state is uniformly high in every category, though there is a strong consistency in relative ranking.

Be cautious in interpreting expenditure figures. The economic significance of an activity cannot be judged solely from the expenditures devoted to it. The marginal productivity of an extra dollar in a given activity may fall very rapidly so that relatively little may be spent in some important activity. Some activity may be very cheap—for example, restricting the market or enforcing licensing may be great in its economic impact but not involve large governmental expenditures. The expenditure for a fatal dose of poison is very small compared to that for a bottle of champagne. Would you judge the significance of drinking each by the purchase price?

Government Receipts

Summary information about federal taxes is shown in Table 31-1. The prime reliance is on the personal and corporation income tax, social security payroll taxes, and commodity and service taxes (called excise taxes). Table 31-2 shows similar data for state, county, and city governments. Figure 31-3 shows the recent major tax receipts of state and local governments, which rely primarily on income, property, and sales taxes and increasingly on transfers from the federal government. And in turn local governments are relying more on transfers from state collected taxes.

Federal Individual Income Taxes

Table 31-3 shows, for the federal personal income tax, the total taxable income and income taxes paid in various income classes, along with the percentage of the taxable income each represents. The total *taxable* personal national income, shown at the bottom, is about half of total personal national income. The difference is explained by the fact that, in defining taxable income, personal national income is reduced by social security payments, income in kind and nonpecuniary imputed income, capital gains reported as income but not taxable, nonreporting of taxable income, income of nontaxable individuals, allowable deductions, personal exemptions, and miscellaneous minor

TABLE 31–1. Federal Government Receipts from and Payments to the Public

(Estimated)

	1971 Total (Billions)	1971 Per Capita
Receipts		
Individual income taxes	$ 91.0	$ 455
Employment taxes (Social Security)	49.0	245
Corporation income taxes	35.0	175
Excise taxes (alcohol, transport, telephone, customs, etc.)	17.1	89
Estate and gift taxes	3.6	36
Customs	2.3	12
Other receipts	3.6	18
Total receipts	$202	$1,000
Payments		
National defense	$ 73.6	$ 368
Social Security	50.3	252
Interest	17.8	89
Health, labor, and welfare	15.0	75
Commerce and transportation	8.8	44
Veterans' benefits and services	8.5	42
Education	8.1	41
Agriculture and agricultural resources	5.4	27
Housing and community development	3.8	19
General government	3.6	18
International affairs and finance	3.6	18
Space research and technology	3.4	17
Natural resources	2.5	12
Total payments	$201	$1,000
Excess of receipts from (+) or payments to (−) the public	−1	

Source: Budget Message of the President, 1970.

items. Nearly two-thirds of the exclusion is accounted for by personal exemptions, allowable deductions, nonreporting, and transfer payments. The percentage-of-taxable-income taxes rise with income. The tax on each successive increment of taxable income rises even more rapidly. Data for 1971 personal income tax rates are shown in Table 31–3.

Despite the rapidly increasing tax rate on higher taxable incomes, Table 31–4 shows in 1963 only about 10 percent came from people with more than $15,000 in taxable income (or $30,000 for married couples). If *all* the income of people receiving more than $30,000 per married couple were taxed away, total tax receipts would increase only about $3 billions, or about 6 percent (ignoring the inevitable effect on incentive to obtain income). On the other hand, if the minimum tax rate of 14 percent were raised to about 22 percent and kept constant over all income classes, the same amount of income tax (as now) would be collected (again ignoring incentive effects).

TABLE 31–2. State and Local Government Expenditures and Receipts, 1968

	Total (Billions)	Per Capita
Expenditures		
Education	$ 41.2	$206
Roads	14.4	72
Public assistance	9.9	49
Hospitals	7.5	38
Police	3.5	17
Fire	1.6	8
Sewage, sanitation	2.7	12
Parks, recreation	1.4	7
Natural resources	2.5	12
Housing	1.6	8
Airports	.5	2
Water transportation	.4	2
Penal	1.3	6
Libraries	.6	3
Administration	3.6	18
Interest	3.3	16
Other	6.4	32
Total expenditures	$102.4	$512
Receipts		
Individual income tax	$ 7.3	$ 37
Corporation income	2.5	13
Sales taxes	22.9	138
Property tax	26.5	109
Fees, licenses	16.5	
Utility revenue	6.6	33
Liquor store revenue	3.0	15
Unemployment compensation	8.8	44
Transfers from federal government	16.5	86
Increase in debt	7.0	35
Total receipts	$117.6	$586

Source: U. S. Department of Commerce, Bureau of Census, *Governmental Finances,* Aug., 1969.

Corporation Income Tax

The second largest source of federal income is the corporation income tax, which takes 30 percent of the first $25,000 of net income and 52 percent of income over that amount. Dividends paid from the remainder are taxable under the personal income tax.

The tax on the corporation depends each year upon its earnings. But on the whole, roughly half of earnings are taxed away. Who pays the tax?—by which we mean, Whose wealth is reduced by the present value of the taxes to be collected? The tax is on the corporate form of business organization and is therefore paid (in the sense that the

TABLE 31–3. Married Taxpayers' Federal Income Tax for 1971

If the taxable income is:		the tax is
Not over $1,000 .... 14%		
Over —	But not over —	of excess over —
$1,000	— $2,000	$140, plus 15% — $1,000
$2,000	— $3,000	$290, plus 16% — $2,000
$3,000	— $4,000	$450, plus 17% — $3,000
$4,000	— $8,000	$620, plus 19% — $4,000
$8,000	— $12,000	$1,380, plus 22% — $8,000
$12,000	— $16,000	$2,260, plus 25% — $12,000
$16,000	— $20,000	$3,260, plus 28% — $16,000
$20,000	— $24,000	$4,380, plus 32% — $20,000
$24,000	— $28,000	$5,660, plus 36% — $24,000
$28,000	— $32,000	$7,100, plus 39% — $28,000
$32,000	— $36,000	$8,660, plus 42% — $32,000
$36,000	— $40,000	$10,340, plus 45% — $36,000
$40,000	— $44,000	$12,140, plus 48% — $40,000
$44,000	— $52,000	$14,060, plus 50% — $44,000
$52,000	— $64,000	$18,060, plus 53% — $52,000
$64,000	— $76,000	$24,420, plus 55% — $64,000
$76,000	— $88,000	$31,020, plus 58% — $76,000
$88,000	— $100,000	$37,980, plus 60% — $88,000
$100,000	— $120,000	$45,180, plus 62% — $100,000
$120,000	— $140,000	$57,580, plus 64% — $120,000
$140,000	— $160,000	$70,380, plus 66% — $140,000
$160,000	— $180,000	$83,580, plus 68% — $160,000
$180,000	— $200,000	$97,180, plus 69% — $180,000
$200,000		$110,980, plus 70% — $200,000

Of the first $1,000 of income (after allowance of about $1,600 for personal exemptions and standard deductions) the tax on a married couple is $140 or 14 percent. On the next $1,000 of income, the tax is 15 percent, or $150 more for a total of $290. On the next $1,000 it is 16 percent. The percentage tax of each increment of income continues to rise, to a maximum of 70 percent. A married couple with $200,000 taxable could keep about $90,000. If Willie Mays earns $100,000 a year, he keeps about $50,000 after taxes.[2]

corporation sends the money to the government) by the corporation. But the corporation is the property of the stockholders, and it is their wealth that would be smaller by an amount equivalent to the present capital value of the future tax stream of payments to the government. We said "would be smaller" because the tax on the corporate form of business is a cost of doing business as a corporation and must be covered from receipts, as are labor and material costs. The sales receipts to each corporation cannot be arbitrarily raised to whatever extent is required to cover those costs. As shown earlier (pages

---

[2] Prior to the Internal Revenue Act of 1964, the (marginal) tax rates in the various brackets of taxable income—that is, the rates which apply only to those parts of income falling within the respective brackets—ranged from 20 to 91 percent. Now, the range of rates is from 14 to 70 percent. The *average* tax rate for people with income beyond the lowest tax bracket is naturally smaller than the marginal, for the marginal rises from the outset. In addition to the rate being higher in each succeeding income bracket, other features depress the average well below the marginal, including the

TABLE 31–4. Distribution of Taxable Income and Federal Personal Income Tax by Taxable Income Classes,* 1963
(In Billions of Dollars)

Taxable Income Class	Total		Cumulated from Smallest Income		
	Taxable Income	Tax	Taxable Income	Tax	Proportion of Total Tax
0 to $1,000	$ 76.7	$15.3	$ 76.7	$15.3	.32
$1,000 to $2,000	52.7	10.5	129.3	25.9	.54
$2,000 to $4,000	42.2	9.3	171.6	35.2	.73
$4,000 to $6,000	13.2	3.4	184.8	38.6	.81
$6,000 to $8,000	6.9	2.1	191.7	40.7	.85
$8,000 to $10,000	3.9	1.3	195.6	42.0	.88
$10,000 to $12,000	2.5	1.0	198.2	43.0	.90
$12,000 to $14,000	1.9	.8	200.0	43.8	.92
$14,000 to $16,000	1.4	.7	201.5	44.5	.925
$16,000 to $18,000	1.1	.6	202.6	45.0	.94
$18,000 to $20,000	.7	.4	203.3	45.4	.95
$20,000 to $50,000	2.9	1.8	206.2	47.2	.985
$50,000 to $100,000	.55	.44	206.8	47.6	.995
$100,000 and over	.34	.31	207.1	47.9	1.00
	$207.1	$47.9			

* Taxable Income is about $1,000 less than gross personal income (before allowances for personal exemptions and standard deductions) in low-income brackets.

324–328), any increased costs, whether from taxes or higher material costs, will reduce the corporate output or the number of corporations sufficiently to permit a higher price per unit of product of the corporate form of business. The higher product price will, *in*

filing of joint returns by married couples and the relatively low maximum rate applied to capital gains. The *average* effective rates for joint returns in 1956 were as follows:

Returns with adjusted gross income of:	Actual tax as percent of adjusted gross income:
$ 600– 2,500	4
2,500– 5,000	7
5,000– 10,000	11
10,000– 15,000	15
15,000– 20,000	17
20,000– 25,000	20
25,000– 50,000	25
50,000– 100,000	35
100,000– 150,000	41
150,000– 200,000	44
200,000– 500,000	47
500,000–1,000,000	49
1,000,000 or more	49

Source: Richard A. Musgrave, "How Progressive Is the Income Tax?" *Tax Revision Compendium* (Washington, U. S. House Committee on Ways and Means, 1959), p. 2226.

part, mean the consumers of corporate products are paying more and, *in part,* the owners of the corporate resources (removed from the corporate sector to less valuable uses) have lost the value of those resources.

Do not fall into the trap of thinking a tax on corporations is borne by an inanimate corporation. Some person's private wealth is smaller than it otherwise would be—consumers and capital-goods owners. Like every tax, the corporation tax is a tax on people—the particular assignment of the tax differs. No definitive studies have been possible showing exactly which people pay how much of the corporation tax. But one thing is known: It is in some degree paid by everyone who lives in an economy of corporations or whose wealth is in any way dependent upon the value of corporate assets. (Be careful: If the tax on corporations did not exist, you would still be paying taxes, but in some other form with a different interpersonal distribution of the taxes.)

Social Security and Insurance Taxes

Payroll taxes of about $17 billions are collected under the Old Age, Survivors, and Disability and Health Insurance system (OASDHI). This tax rate in 1971 is 10.4 percent (5.2 percent paid directly by employer without formally appearing in employee's pay and 5.2 percent withheld from employee's formally stated wages) of salary under $7,800 per year, but is scheduled to increase to 11.8 percent by 1987. (We conjecture the rate will increase faster and to higher rates than currently scheduled as more contingencies or risks are covered—if we project from past events.)

Differences among the state and local governments' revenue structures are substantial. Some states have no income taxes, while others have heavy ones. Similar variations exist for sales taxes. All use the property tax extensively. However, both state and local governments are moving toward greater reliance on income taxes, usually collected by the state and distributed to local governments. Also, there is a trend towards grants to states from the federal government.

To complete this description of government expenditures and receipts, one should see the relationship between receipts and services. But there is no known way to do this. In the first place, taxes generally are not earmarked for some specified service. And if every tax were so identified, there would still be room for argument about whether the benefits received by each individual matched the taxes he paid for that activity. There also is the fact that some taxes are used to redistribute wealth.

What Kind of Taxes?

It is impossible to define what is meant by an ideal system. We run the risk of confusing effects with purposes when we attempt to rationalize all government activity on the grounds that government exists to provide uninduced external effects, to maintain law and order, to regulate the economic activity of people, and to redistribute the wealth.

It is as futile to prescribe a proper scope of government activity as it is to prescribe the proper mix of goods and activities provided by the capitalist system. We can only say what happens under different systems of competition for use of political power. And it isn't justifiable to say that the result is "right" (or, for that matter, "wrong") just because it is produced by the government, or by the capitalist system.

Conspicuously absent here has been any extensive discussion of the proper kind of taxes that ought to be levied to support government activity (other than for external benefit). However, criteria for good and bad types of taxes have been suggested. The tax should be certain, not too expensive to collect, equitable, related to the service to be financed, should not have unintended effects. These criteria, insofar as they have any content, overlook the rules and operation of the system of political competition and striving for political power. What might appear as a good tax from the point of view of its direct economic effects may be a terrible tax from the point of view of the political viability of the existing authorities. From the political point of view, it has been said that taxes used should be those that lose the least number of votes or political power. They "should" be of that type in the sense that "should" refers to the kinds of taxes we should *expect to see* most commonly used. Politics, like economics, has analytical value as a science explaining what *does* happen, how systems *do* operate—not how they *ought* to operate.

Efficiency of Government Services

Although government power can be used to ensure that more of certain services are provided, it cannot solve the problem of efficient production of those services. Socialists may have no qualms in decreeing how much of some good they think ought to be provided for society, but they have not solved the problem of devising an *incentive and control* system to induce public administrators to direct production efficiently. Under government ownership, the administrator does not lose wealth equivalent to any higher costs of more wasteful techniques nor is he as responsible to any agent who does bear them. No system yet devised is as effective as private property in inducing the administrator to act in accord with costs as reflected in potential marketable values. On the other hand, not all costs are revealed in market values, because some people who bear costs of other peoples' actions cannot economically identify the responsible parties. Though the government action may be less influenced by the noticeable marketable value, it may be more responsive to the broader range of effects that are not reflected in the marketable value, because of weak property rights or high transactions costs.[3]

In government operation, efficiency is not the sole criterion. Worrying about efficiency has been humorously compared with worrying about the cost of a plane ticket without first thinking about where one is going. Such comparisons are more misleading than informative. And it is equally obstructive to contend that those who deprecate the efficiency argument are interested only in the announced destination rather than in whether and how they will get there. We ought to understand that all our choices between "*this or that*" *depend upon both* what the good is *and* how much it costs.

National Defense

National defense from external threats to the security and interests of the United States is the largest portion of federal activity in terms of costs and persons involved. As a fraction of national income of government budgeted expenditures, it responds, of course, to the perceived potential aggression against the interests of the United States, however

---

[3] It is not the case that market prices ignore "noneconomic" effects. Rather, the market values do not reflect those effects that no one has incentive to insist on being reduced or increased (if desired) because of the absence of enforceable, transferable property rights. As a result, excessive (or even insufficient!) pollution occurs. Recall pages 240–245.

they are conceived by the Congress and the President. Extremely expensive capital goods (planes, rockets, electronic gear, submarines, ships, and atomic bombs) involve several years of development, so government expenditures for national defense are usually budgeted in terms of five-year programs, rather than annual or indefinitely persisting programs. Such planning, programming, and budgeting of activities is fraught with intensive debate as to type of items, time of development, and desirability of alternative defense strategies. Given the poor information about intentions of other governments and technological discoveries, it is easy to see why differences of recommendations can be so hard to resolve. We can indicate, however, the elements of inquiry that proponents of any program should observe.

1. The cost of any program should be estimated—not in terms of this year's outlay but in terms of the (present capital value of) *future sequence* of expenditures under a proposed program lasting, say, five or ten years. Too often, the "foot in the door" trick is used; a proponent will look only at the first-year expenditure as the index of the cost, either out of ignorance or an attempt to make his proposal look cheaper.

2. There is the sunk-cost fallacy of looking at *past* costs and arguing that if the program is not continued all those past expenditures will be wasted. True, the avoidance of waste may depend upon what is done next; but the past expenditures are irrelevant as a measure of the cost of what one does next. All that counts is what *more* will one get if *more* money is spent in the future.

3. Still another fallacy in costing government activity is the very common one of ignoring some of the costs of a program because they are not paid for via *explicit* taxes paid to the government and counted in the budget. Rather, the activity is financed by concealed, indirect subsidies financed and operated by private firms for the government. (For example, airlines charge higher fares for transcontinental long routes and use the proceeds to subsidize the noncost-covering local air routes between Congressman Pork's home village and the nearest major city.) Those hidden taxes do not appear in the government budget. This can occur any time the government allows an industry to regulate itself and with the closed-monopoly profits subsidize or produce special goods or activities not otherwise supported by individual consumers' purchases. (Can you see how this occurs in radio and TV programming, state liquor licensing, taxi franchises, and all public utilities given exclusive franchise rights?)

A prime example of concealed costs has been the military draft, which is a tax on the drafted young man, who pays a tax equivalent to the difference between the military pay that would have induced him to serve voluntarily and the pay he actually receives, a tax currently estimated to be about 50 percent of the potential civilian income of draftees. Not only is that tax deceptively concealed but it is also inefficient and *greater* than implicit taxes would have to be if they were openly obtained and the military were obtained by sufficiently high pay. It is inefficient in that many current draftees could instead work at higher-paying civilian jobs while releasing others to work in the military at pay rates that are sufficient to attract them voluntarily. (Review the efficiency effects of restricted job assignments for Mr. C and E on pages 221–222, for a reminder of the analysis.)

Social Security

Bulking larger and larger in the proportion (15 to 20 percent) of federal receipts and expenditures is social security. Receipts come from current taxes on wages. These funds are not invested to yield a return in the future that will pay back to the survivors their social security benefits, although the idea of accumulating such an investment fund was once contemplated. Instead the social security benefits are paid from current general tax receipts including the social security taxes. The coverage of social security has increased both in scope of employees covered and in terms of events in old age for which payments will be made—retirement payments, death insurance, disability, medical care, and some unemployment (under a provision wherein states may receive some of the funds for state unemployment payments).

Why is the social security system based on nearly universal compulsory membership rather than voluntary or privately managed insurance schemes? This question admits of no definite answer. (1) The initiation of the program brought benefits to the initial beneficiaries (the then aged) without their having paid an earlier contribution. Whether this was sufficient to introduce the system is arguable. Certainly it pays older generations to obtain immediate expansion of benefits, and expansions have frequently occurred, benefiting the older generation beyond what they had paid earlier. This can occur so long as the economy is growing. (2) Others have said that people would not provide adequately for their old age or take out health insurance unless compelled to do so. Many people say this applies to them, and who can disprove it?

It would also be possible to provide for old age if each generation had in its younger days contributed savings toward investment in more capital and wealth, and then upon retirement had consumed the accumulated wealth. The difference between that system and the existing one is that there has been no accumulated stock of wealth. The older are paid from incomes of the younger. To the extent that the payments to social security would otherwise have been devoted by individuals to a private-investment-for-age program, social security has contributed to lower investment and growth of wealth.

Again we ask, Who pays the tax? Whose income stream will be smaller after taxes by the amount of the taxes collected by the government (ignoring the question of who will benefit from the expenditures)? Does the employer pay half? Or is he just a middleman who transmits half the tax payment while in reality the employees' post-tax wages are smaller by the combined amount of the employer's and employee's contribution? Or, at the other extreme, maybe, the whole cost is borne by the employer and consumers—with wages being no smaller than they would have been had there been no social security tax.

If every dollar paid now to social security is regarded by the employee as just as desirable as each dollar of current take-home pay, the employee is "paying" the entire tax. (The employee is attracted to work not only by his take-home pay but equivalently by the value of the social security taxes as claims to benefits and to that extent is just as willing to work for a lower take-home wage now if he is also paid in claims to future retirement benefits.) If, on the other hand, the employee regards every dollar now contributed toward social security as less valuable than a current dollar paid as take-home wages, part of the social security benefits to employees will be paid for by consumers of the products and by owners of resources in the covered types of employment industries. Why? Because the inferior (social security) form of wage payment to the employee reduces his willingness to work and raises the costs of production with consequences exactly similar to those of an arbitrary tax on the product of that industry (see pages 325–328). If, as we suppose in an extreme supposition, the social security payments are regarded as completely worthless by all employees, social security claims will not be acceptable as even a partial compensation. Therefore, the supply of employees at the old take-home wage is not changed. But the social security costs must be paid. The costs of hiring employees are increased by the full amount of the social security taxes. This raises costs to employers, so that employment and output will be reduced, with consumers paying a higher price, and other resources used in production having a lower value. It is highly unlikely that either this extreme zero evaluation of social security benefits, or the former complete equivalence with wages is the dominant force. Something in between is conjectured to be the actual case—but we can cite no overwhelming evidence for our conjecture.

Redistribution of Wealth and Income

An important government activity is the redistribution of wealth—usually imagined to be from the richer to the poorer. Examples are relief, unemployment payments, social security, farm subsidies and price supports, public parks, housing, public works, and higher education. These activities are financed by taxing larger incomes proportionately higher, but unless those who pay less use proportionally more of the provided services, there is no redistribution from richer to poorer. Farm subsidies and crop-price supports, subsidized college, public parks, and subsidies of the arts in fact represent aid to the richer people. A strong argument can be made that government activity has redistributed wealth more to the rich than to the poor, particularly if one considers government restrictions on entry to many markets—the effect of which is to maintain higher prices for consumers and closed-monopoly rents for the favored groups. On the other hand, some studies suggest that on balance the redistribution probably has been from the richer to the poorer, or from both extremes to the middle.

Deficits and Debt

Larger expenditures by the government must be matched by receipts, if the government is to spend. Where does it get the money receipts? From taxes. If taxes are less than expenditures, a *deficit* (or a surplus) is said to occur. And any time the explicit taxes or fees for services are insufficient a deficit exists (or a surplus, if taxes exceed expenditures) with a year being the conventional interval over which the totals are compared. Expenditures can exceed tax receipts if the deficit is covered (i.e., financed) by other sources—and there are four: the government can (1) *borrow* money, obtained by the sale of government bonds or notes, just as any person can spend more than his income if he borrows the difference; (2) print the money, something of a legal counterfeiter, and as we shall see this is done in a roundabout way and has been utilized by every major government throughout recorded history; (3) deplete its money holdings and try to get along with smaller stocks of money; (4) sell some of its property and spend the proceeds. (We shall see later that printing new money *is* a tax on holders of money.)

Increasing taxes or borrowing to cover the deficit of higher spending tends to offset the aggregate-demand increasing effects of government spending. This is so because control of spending is transferred from the private to the government sector. The impacts need not be exactly offsetting; possibly the government-spending increase may not reduce private spending by exactly the amount of the taxes or borrowing. It is usually presumed that the private sector will reduce its demand by less than the income transferred away from it by taxes or loaned to the government. In that case an increase in government spending matched by taxes or borrowing from the private sector would result in a net increase in aggregate community demand (as we shall see in the next chapter). Any increase in debt to finance a deficit will almost surely never be reduced later by repayment of debt at a more rapid rate than new borrowing. Usually a new loan is made to replace the one coming due; one bond replaces another as a result the government's debt increases. Where will it all end? And furthermore, won't interest payments increase until they eventually absorb the entire national income, so that we end up taxing away our national income and transferring it back as interest payments in accord with bond holdings? In which case, why work?[4]

The contravening fact is that though the national debt has increased—and primarily as a result of financing deficits in time of war—it has not increased relative to our national wealth or income. In fact, although in 1970 it was smaller (45 percent) relative to our income than it was before World War II, in 1940 (50 percent), it was larger than in the 1920s when it was about 15 percent of gross national product. Figure 31–3 shows

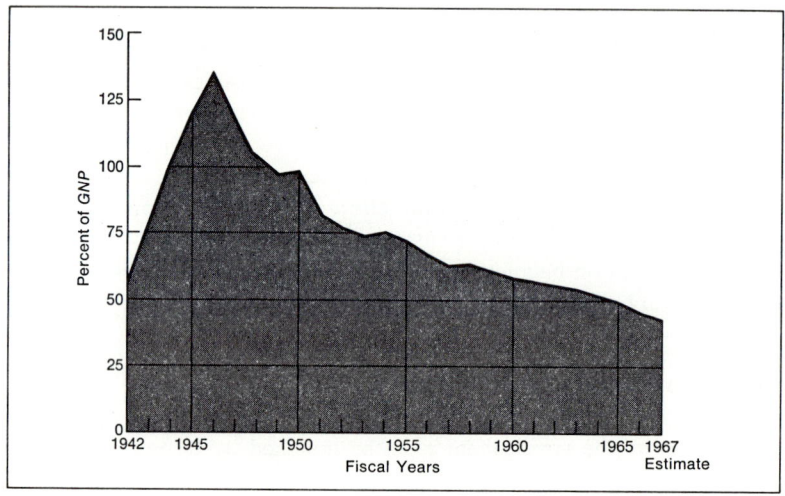

FIGURE 31–3. Federal Government Debt as a Percent of Gross National Product

Federal debt has grown relative to gross national product during wars and has decreased during peacetime. However, the recent higher interest rate suggests that interest on the national government debt will show an increasing ratio to GNP.

its relative size since 1929. If both national income and government debt grow at the same rate, the ratio will be unchanged, and the interest payments will remain substantially the same fraction of national income, but with variations depending upon the changes in the interest rate.

National government debt has increased less rapidly than *private* debt since 1945, though it increased much more during World War II.

The situation is really not much different from that for private debt. We buy with private credit, and as we pay off old debts we incur new ones in a never-ending sequence

---

[4] Thus, imposing a tax simply to take from a person what we give back to him will reduce his incentive to work, with no net gain. The cost of income relative to leisure is raised. Since it pays everyone to respond to the disincentive effect, the main effect of the transfer is reduced national income from the disincentive effect of the tax.

(or for as long as we live). As we get richer, the amount of credit we have used (debts we have incurred and are outstanding) increases. There is nothing ominous in this. At death, heirs inherit our debts *and our assets* and continue the pattern. So it is with government. (The main differences are that governments can tax to obtain revenue—but this is true whether they borrow or not; and they can create new money for themselves—and this too they can do whether they borrow or not.) So government debt is in principle much like private debt. Not even the statement that we owe the national debt to ourselves makes it different from private debt, for that too we owe to ourselves as a national group. In both cases the amounts owed by us are not the same as the amounts owed to us. Some of us have small holdings of national debt and of private debt, and some of us owe big taxes and have big private debts against ourselves. Not much advance in analysis or understanding is evoked by the saying "We owe it to ourselves."

Not even if the debt is held by foreigners does it change fundamentals much. Some people have argued that if a debt is incurred by borrowing from foreigners, then when the debt is being paid, with taxes on "us," we aren't paying ourselves, so there is a burden to us. (We ignore the chauvinistic conception of "us" as being just people who live in our country, as if people of other countries were in some sense less worthy of consideration. After all, why is a payment to some other American more of a humanitarian offset than a payment to some resident of a foreign country?) Well, suppose the debt is held by foreigners; income is then transferred from this community of people when the interest and principle are repaid. Do you think, therefore, it would have been better had the debt been held by a person within the nation?

A source of confusion that popular writers like to introduce is called the "burden of the debt." What that means is not clear. In one sense, if schools or roads or welfare are financed by borrowing (just as a private individual can finance his tuition, car, or consumption by borrowing), sacrificed alternative output is forsaken no matter how the purchase is financed. Whatever is bought with the borrowed funds (or out of current income without borrowing!) involves a current cost—the sacrifice of other potential goods or services. The method of financing those purchases does not change that fact. A purchaser may regard borrowing as preferable to delaying purchase until he has saved enough in an interim to purchase some good—such as a car or a house. The purchaser-borrower can use the car *while* he is saving and repaying the debt, instead of having to sacrifice consumption *prior* to the purchase. And the lender prefers to lend because the later interest payment to him more than compensates for his deferral of consumption. So no one bears any burden by incurring a debt; both lender and borrower are better off than if no debt had been incurred. There is no burden of debt in this fundamental sense.

Of course, if one borrows and uses the funds for wasteful purposes because he is mistaken about the advantages of some purchase or investment, then he bears the burden of paying off his debt. That is not a burden of a debt but of making a bad investment or bad purchase, which could have been done without borrowing. Do not call the *loss* of a bad purchase or investment a burden or cost of borrowing to make that purchase—unless you want to obstruct accurate analysis.

Reminder

Excluded from this chapter are two major classes of government activity: (a) the production of public or collective goods where these are deemed to be inadequately provided in the private sector and (b) the protection of rights to resources of one person from the actions of other people, where rights are absent in communal resources. Governments can institute those rights (as, for example, the federal government did when it converted communal rights in land in the United States to privately owned land via Land Grant Acts), or can assert control over the use of the resources (as it did in establishing the Federal Communications Commission to control the radio-frequency spectrum), or can encourage and aid the states to enter into compacts to control uses of water in interstate rivers and lakes. These two general classes of actions—political action to produce certain goods, and establishment of a structure of rights to resources in order to aid their efficient use—were not explored in this chapter because they were extensively discussed at more appropriate places in earlier parts of this book. Do not erroneously infer by their absence from this chapter that they are less significant activities of governments.

Summary

1. In the past half century the fraction of gross national product allocated by the governmental sector has increased from about 10–15 percent to over 30 percent; a major portion of the increase has been at the federal level.

2. Individual and corporation income taxes and social security taxes are the major sources of federal governmental receipts; for states and localities, the sales and property tax, and more recently the individual income tax, are the major sources of receipts.

3. National defense, social insurance, and welfare are the major components of federal expenditures. At the nonfederal level, education, roads, and welfare payments are the major avenues of expenditures.

4. Intergovernmental transfers from the federal to the state to the local level have been increasing.

5. Individual income tax rates are progressive (higher fraction of tax on larger incomes), but the over-all tax structure is much less progressive and more nearly proportional except at the very low income strata.

6. Those whose wealth or income is reduced by a tax cannot be identified from the name of the tax nor from the particular item being taxed, nor is the person making the payment to the government.

7. The exact extent of taxing and subsidizing cannot be ascertained from the *budget* receipts and expenditures, for some pass indirectly via the private sector and some are implicit in kind (military draft).

8. Fluctuations in the aggregate spending and taxing by governments affect the gross national income of the economy. Government taxing and spending policy (fiscal policy) is therefore attentive to its national income effects.

9. Some major functions of government are: to provide services for which external effects are not sufficiently "internalized;" to prohibit uses of goods for which external harmful effects are not sufficiently internalized on the decision maker; and to provide public goods where there is no superior alternative; to restrict market competition; and to redistribute wealth.

10. A federal debt increasing in absolute size does not necessarily imply an increasing debt transfer cost relative to national income.

11 Debt owed to foreigners is *not* a less advantageous debt than one held by domestics, despite payment of interest and principal to foreigners. To think it is disadvantageous is to ignore gains from the ability to borrow resources.

Questions

1 a. "Police activity is one kind that must be operated by the government." Do you agree? If so, how do you explain the fact that there are thousands of private policemen in London, and that many U. S. residential areas have private police service?
   b. "Judicial activity is one kind of activity that must be handled by the government." Do you agree? If so, how do you explain the existence of private arbitration for adjudicating contract-term disputes between employees and employers?
   c. "Lawmaking activity is one that must be handled by the government." Do you agree? If so, then how do you explain the creation of labor-employee relations law by contract negotiation, custom and common-law development from precedents of arbitration, and social custom and its enforcement via ostracism?
   d. "Defense of the community is one activity that must be handled by the government." Do you agree? If so, then how do you explain the existence of private armies in past history—armies to defend cities, paid by private citizens? How do you explain the papal army prior to the time of the papal state?
   e. "There is no function that must be exclusively reserved to the government." Do you agree? If so, why? If not, which function refutes the assertion?

2 "Property taxes are taxes on physical goods, but income taxes are taxes on people." Evaluate.

3 If you use the proportion of government expenditures as a guide to the significance of government economic activity, you can be seriously misled. What types of government activity have a far greater impact than indicated by the costs of such activity?

4 To subsidize the cultural arts, new taxes are proposed. It is proposed to levy taxes according to ability to pay. One group proposes to levy heavier taxes on rich people in an absolute sense, but to make the proportion of wealth taxed increase for the wealthier. Another group argues that such progressive or graduated rates are more than in accord with ability to pay, and advocates instead a constant proportional tax. Another group argues that even a constant proportion is too much and that it is more in accord with ability if the rich person just pays a greater absolute amount, although possibly a smaller proportion of his wealth. Another argues that old people should be taxed more heavily since they haven't so long to live and have more ability to pay taxes. What do you think is the meaning of ability to pay?

Fiscal Policy Impacts on Income

32

GOVERNMENT expenditure and taxation account for almost one-quarter of gross national product. These fiscal activities encompass a vast array of purposes and projects—defense, law enforcement, road construction, education, redistribution of wealth, and on and on. Inevitably, those actions affect income, employment, and prices whether or not there is a conscious and coherent *policy* of avoiding destabilization. And over the past third of a century, economists, government officials, and editorial writers have given more and more attention to the possibilities of deliberately using governmental spending, taxing, and borrowing—in short, "fiscal policy"—for stabilization. Fiscal policy can, indeed, be a potent factor—although how effectively it has been and will be used is another question.

Analysis of effects of fiscal activities on national income requires inclusion of government spending (G) and tax collections (T) in the income model of Chapter 27. Government spending, like investment, can be interpreted as an "injection" into the income flow, expanding the income-creation equation to: $Y = C + I + G$; and taxes, like saving, can be interpreted as a "leakage" from the income flow, making the income-disposal equation: $Y = C + C + S + T$. These two factors, G and T, are subject to *discretionary* manipulation by government agencies. In the awesome machinery of government—and the emphasis here is on the federal government—it is impossible to point to a particular person or even to a department or agency exercising sole spending or taxing discretion. Nor can government spokesmen foretell precisely just what will be the dollar values of government spending and taxing over the next year or two.

Since changes in fiscal actions often involve changes in monetary actions, the consequences of each change on national income are often confounded. Protagonists have accused each other of fantasies—e.g., only money matters or only fiscal actions matter.

Evidence leaves no doubt that neither of those positions is correct. A couple of decades ago there was a "lapse" into the position that money doesn't matter or matters hardly at all; now, as before that lapse, the importance of money is recognized. What is not clear is exactly how much and how fast it affects income. Similarly, whereas before the 1930s fiscal effects on national income were given little formal analytical attention, now they have much.

In this chapter we present a few combinations of changes in government spending and tax structure to illustrate how fiscal actions can affect national income, either intentionally or as a by-product (when government expenditures or taxes are *changed* for other reasons, e.g., wars, education, welfare, etc.). In each case, we leave open the specification of the implicit monetary actions. Our purpose is not to derive the optimal combination of fiscal and monetary policy, if such a thing exists, but instead to indicate the national-income perturbation effects of fiscal actions and how they are affected by monetary factors.

Is fiscal action a desirable avenue to alleviating recessions, or should monetary factors be used? In actuality, it is not possible to separate them so definitely. Suppose it were decided to use monetary means, i.e., to increase the stock of money. To whom should the new money be made available and for what should it be spent? That is a fiscal question. Sprinkled from the sky? Given to the government? Sold to the government in exchange for its bonds? At what price (interest rate) to the government? And for what should the government spend this money (part of which will find its way into the reserves of the commercial banks)? Everyone claims he knows best how to spend that new money. In all probability, the federal government will get it first and will use it to finance its activities. (Lest you think this is a marvelous way to finance government without taxes, be warned that any increase in the stock of money that leads to higher prices is a tax on holders of currency—as we shall explain more fully in Chapter 33.)

Despite the interdependence of fiscal and monetary actions, we shall start with an exposition of the way in which government spending and taxing is postulated to affect national income. Because we want to focus on fiscal activities, the implicit monetary adjustments will be indicated only *en passant*, deferring a more complete discussion to later parts of the chapter.

Equilibrium Income with Government Spending and Taxing

The income effects of government expenditures and taxes can be easily shown with the model of Chapter 27. Suppose they are absent and the consumption function is such that people consume .8 of whatever is their income. Also, investment is constant at $180. In Figure 32–1, line $C_1 + I$ is the sum of the consumption and the investment functions. Equilibrium income is $900 (where the $C_1 + I$ line intersects the 45-degree line), and consumption is $720. Now suppose government expenditure is $100 ($G = 100), financed by a *fixed* tax, $T = 100, regardless of what national income may be. The introduction of tax collections calls for a slight change in the consumption function, if we assume the income on which consumption depends is *disposable* income, D, that is, income disposable after paying the $100 tax: $D = Y - T$. With consumption equal to .8 of *disposable* income, consumption would be smaller by $80, since disposable income is reduced by the levy of the $100 tax.

Graphically, the (pre-tax) $C_1 + I$ line is shifted downward by $80 (horizontally to

Fiscal Policy Impacts on Income

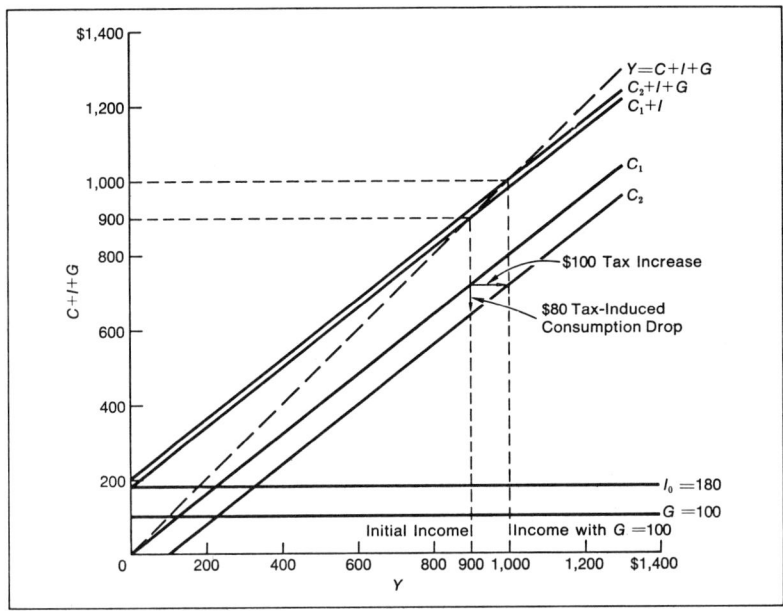

FIGURE 32–1. Change in Equilibrium Income with Addition of Equal Taxes and Government Expenditure

The initial consumption and investment line, with no government expenditure, is $C_1 + I$; equilibrium income is then $900. Now, both taxes and government spending are raised from zero to $100. (1) Tax collections reduce C to new line C_2, $80 lower; (2) the government expenditure of $100 is added to $C_2 + I$, making the total expenditure $C_2 + I + G$ and determining a new equilibrium income of $1,000.

the right by $100).[1] This gives a lower $C_2 + I$ line after the levy of the tax. But do not forget government expenditure G. This must be added to the $C_2 + I$ line, so a new line, $C_2 + I + G$, appears above the old. $C_2 + I + G$ is exactly $100 higher than the $C_2 + I$ line and above the old pretax consumption-plus-investment line by $20. Not all the $100 tax is paid by reducing consumption. Part ($20) is paid by reducing saving. (Only at the higher national income of $1,000 would saving again match the given constant investment rate.)

Arithmetic-Tabular Determination of Equilibrium Income

The preceding description of income determination can be traced arithmetically in Table 32–1.[2] The top line shows the equilibrium situation prior to the inclusion of government

---

[1] A shift to the right of $100 means that whatever a person consumed before (the height of the line) at a given income he would now consume only at an income $100 larger (to compensate for the tax).

[2] Students with some familiarity with algebra will find it helpful to study the chapter Appendix where there is an algebraic exposition of all the cases of fiscal policy given here.

TABLE 32–1. Equilibrium Income with and without Government Spending and Taxing

	Received Y	T	D	C	S	I	G	Generated C+I+G	
$G = T = 0$	900	0	900	720	180	180	0	900	
$G = T = 100$	950	100	850	680	170	180	100	960	Disequilibrium
	975	100	875	700	175	180	100	980	
	1,000	100	900	720	180	180	100	1,000	Equilibrium
	1,100	100	1,000	800	200	180	100	1,080	Disequilibrium
	1,200	100	1,100	880	220	180	100	1,160	

spending and taxing ($G = T = 0$). The next five lines give some alternative incomes with government spending and taxing of $100. In the middle line, with income of $1,000 in the first column and tax collections of $100 in the second, disposable income is $900 ($Y - T$). Of this, $720 is spent for consumption, leaving $180 as saving ($D = C + S$). Investment is assumed to be a fixed $180. Government spends $100. The sum of income-generating expenditures ($C + I + G$) is $1,000, exactly what was initially received. This is, then, a self-sustaining, equilibrium national income. Leakages (T as well as S) equal injections (G as well as I).

At incomes smaller than $1,000, $C + I + G$ would exceed the initially received income. For those incomes, leakages from the income flow would be less than injections, and income would have to rise. At incomes larger than $1,000, the reverse would occur.

In the initial equilibrium, before introducing the government sector, equilibrium income was $900; with government spending and taxing of $100 now added, equilibrium income rises to $1,000. In the new equilibrium, however, the private sector's disposable income is still $900, despite the increase in taxes (which tends to decrease disposable income) and despite the increase in income (which tends to increase disposable income). Of course, the summary explanation of the lack of increase in D is that the entire increase of $100 in Y is "consumed" by government: Y has increased because G has increased, with C and I unchanged. But T also rose $100. Why didn't the T leakage exactly offset the G injection, thereby maintaining Y at the old level of $900? Through taxation, private consumption fell. For example, in the initial situation, C was $720 when Y was at the equilibrium level of $900; with tax collections, C would be only $640 if Y were still at the old (now disequilibrium) level of $900 because disposable income (D) is $100 lower. C has fallen $80 at every possible Y. But the downward shift in C ($80), which tends to decrease Y, is more than offset by the increase in G ($100), which tends to increase Y. Tax collections were taken from people who would have spent only 80 percent of the income taxed away. (D falls by the full amount that T rises, but C falls by only .8 of the fall in D.) The government spends *all* of the tax receipts ($G = T$). That is, of the $100 tax, only $80 reflects a reduction in consumption (and $20 is the reduction in saving), while the entire $100 collected in taxes is spent by the government. With C reduced $80 and G raised by $100, the total expenditure function ($C + I + G$) rises a net of $20. Thus, the government-plus-consumption function has shifted up, with investment constant, and Y has therefore been increased.

Why does the $20-higher rate of spending raise income by a multiple of five? Starting with the initial equilibrium, autonomously increase G and T by $100. Throughout, by our assumption, I remains at $180; however, the increase in T from reducing D lowers S to $160, i.e., $20 below investment. Adjustment to a new income equilibrium, when G continues to equal T, requires closing the gap of I over S. With $MPS = .2$, income must rise $100 (to $1,000) to induce S to increase by $20, back up to $180. The income rise of $100 also slides people up the consumption line, from a rate of $640 to $720, leaving C (like S and D) at its initial level.[3]

This remarkable increase in income may provoke two queries. First, is it odd to assume that investment spending remains constant despite reduction in disposable income subsequent to the tax? We might argue, persuasively or not, that investment is affected primarily by prospects of profitability and that a reduction in current disposable income should not induce one to abandon investment ventures. But if investment were *reduced,* then the equilibrium income would be *smaller.* (See why by shifting downward the investment line in Figure 32–1.) Or if you think that the increase in G and T will *increase* the investment rate, then shift the investment line upward and observe the resultant *increase* in income. Assuming an unchanged investment simplifies the exposition of the effects of a matching increase in G and T, as a practical matter the effect of an increase in G and T on investment demand would be highly relevant.

Since you have learned your lessons on money, a second, more profound doubt arises in your mind. Is the same old stock of money sufficient to meet the increased demand for money that will be associated with the larger national income?

The amount of money demanded by people depends upon their income—and income is up. Where did the extra money come from with which to satisfy the increased demand? Or what persuaded people to make do with the same money stock? Simply assume that the Federal Reserve Board, with infinite wisdom and foresight, managed to sprinkle just the right amount of extra money in the right places to accommodate the increased demand. This is a powerful assumption, which may conceal an important unresolved issue. Some economists would say the increase in national income would not occur unless the money stock increased: no matter what the size of government spending and no matter what the size of any deficit or any balanced budget, the increase in the money stock is a necessary and a sufficient condition for the rise in national income. The government-spending increase was just a concomitant event which would induce no increase in national income unless the money stock had increased at the same time.

That is an allegedly extreme position, but is it *valid*? Evidently, there is more than a grain of truth in the proposition that the change in the money stock is *sufficient,* even if not *necessary,* for income changes. To say it is necessary is to say no change in national income could occur without a change in the money stock, and that is not entirely correct. The supply of money is *not* all that matters—demand for money could change. But if the size of government spending and taxing were to change, would that alone, without any accommodating or initiating change in the stock of money, change national income? The available evidence suggests that it could induce significant changes. But the evidence is not yet conclusive. In the meantime, monetary and fiscal authorities are taking actions on one or the other premise—and sometimes, apparently, on no premise

---

[3] Can you see that the new equilibrium income would have been $1,100 if we had assumed G and T to be $200? And if G and T had been $300, income would have been $1,200? (Do your own doodling to verify this.) We conclude that an excess of government spending over tax receipts, i.e., a budget deficit, is *not* necessary to increase income: With our assumptions, an increase in government spending balanced by equal tax receipts gives an increase in income—one equal to the increase in G and T.

at all! Of course, you could advocate both increased government spending and increased money supply simultaneously and hope to have the best of both worlds—along with the worst of both—and the monetary and fiscal authorities in Congress, in the President's office, and in the Federal Reserve System act as if that were their policy.

Fiscal Policy and Variations on a Theme

Having introduced the government sector into the income model, we can investigate the effects of discretionary fiscal activities on national income (and thereby employment and the price level, as well). We shall go through a series of alternative cases—and it is important to appreciate that there *are* alternatives—each with a different combination of government spending and taxing designed to achieve some specified income. In each case, we shall start with the same initial situation taken from the results of the preceding example:

C	S	I	G	Y	T	D
720	180	180	100	1,000	100	900

That is, consumption, investment, and government functions give expenditures $(C + I + G)$ that determine income (Y) of \$1,000; subtraction of income-tax collections (T) of \$100 from Y gives disposable income (D) of \$900, where $T = rY$ and r here is both the marginal and the average tax rate $(r = T/Y = 100/1,000 = \Delta T/\Delta Y)$; and MPC (otherwise designated c) $= \Delta C/\Delta D = .8$ and MPS $= \Delta S/\Delta C = .2$. Income is \$1,000, an equilibrium level as evidenced by the equality of $(C + I + G)$ with $(C + S + T)$. Although income is at an "equilibrium" level, at prevailing prices and wage rates it may not be at a *full-employment* level (where "full employment" is consistent with "frictional unemployment," as discussed in Chapter 25).

Imagine that government officials (perhaps the President, with the compliance of Congressional leaders, on the advice of a few economists and many lawyers scattered through various departments) decide to raise income to \$1,200, an increase of \$200. Why? If a recession had set in, perhaps because investment prospects deteriorated, prices of capital goods would have fallen. In other words, prices of common stock (ownership claims to businesses which are conglomerations of capital goods and managerial talent) have fallen and with them the demand prices of buildings, factories, etc. To restore full employment, wages and input costs can be reduced if profitability of production is to be restored. But that involves an unpleasantly and unnecessarily long period of wage and cost deflation and depression. There is nothing about the prices of capital goods so sacrosanct that all other wages and prices must adjust to them. Instead, let the depressed prices be raised again. One way to accomplish this is to expand national income: The resultant increased demand can restore the profitability of investment without such a great portion of the price readjustment being thrown onto a decrease in wages and general input costs, with the unemployment involved in the process.

So it is decided to try to raise national income to \$1,200, an increase of \$200. How was the figure of \$1,200 determined? There are a number of infallible guides, including a wetted finger to the breeze and a Ouija board. Now, some recalcitrants may deny the infallibility of such sources: some suggest an increase of \$93 and others an increase of \$469; some want an expansionary policy but prefer to rely wholly on monetary policy, leaving government spending and tax rates unchanged; others desire some judicious mixture of monetary and fiscal policy; and a few even deny that expansion is the right *direction* in which to move. The fact is, of course, that even if all of the government advisers and officials decide that (1) an expansionary policy is desirable and (2) reliance is to be placed on fiscal policy, no one *knows* just how big a change in income is required for full employment—or just how much production will increase if full employment is achieved. And (3) even if all agree on an increase of $200 in income through fiscal policy, no one *knows* just how big a change in government spending and/or tax rates is required to achieve the desired income increase. Finally, (4) there will be considerable heartburn over the question of relative emphasis on the two tools of fiscal policy, with some favoring a tax cut (which taxes?) and others an increase in government expenditures (on what goods?).

Still other things are unknown (for example, how much price inflation, if any, would be generated by increasing income by $200). But enough has been said to warn the reader that the world is neither so easily predictable nor so readily described as the following mechanical discussion might suggest. Still, the mechanics are useful.

To return to our illustration, the *objective* is to raise national income from $1,000 to $1,200; and there are two fiscal *tools* available, to be used either singly or together: government spending (*G*) and the tax rate (*r*). Investment spending is assumed to remain constant at $180, and there will be no *autonomous* changes in consumption spending or the consumption function (all changes in *C* being induced by changes in disposable income). A number of combinations of changes in government spending, *G*, and in the tax rate, *r*, can meet the income objective:

1. Increase *G*; *r* unchanged.
2. *G* unchanged; *r* reduced.
3. Increase *G*; *r* reduced.
4. Increase *G* and increase *r* with budget balanced.
5.   "   "   "   "   "   "   "   deficit.
6.   "   "   "   "   "   "   "   surplus.
7. Decrease *G* and decrease *r* with budget deficit.

In other words, to expand income, we can *increase G* with a deficit, a surplus, or a balanced budget, but if *G* is *decreased* (Route 7), there must be a deficit for an expansionary effect.

Route 1: Increase Government Spending with Constant Tax Rate

The first policy to raise income from $1,000 to $1,200—by increasing government spending while holding the tax *rate* (not tax *collections*) constant at 10 percent of income—is illustrated in Table 32–2. The autonomous increase in *G*, shown in the second row of the table, triggers the multiplier process. If government spending is raised to $156, income rises to $1,200 which is the only income consistent with the new conditions: income of $1,200 is associated with $C + I + G$ expenditure of $1,200, and $C + I + G$ is again equated to $C + S + T$.

Arithmetic Determination of Income

To see why the new, larger national income is the only one consistent with the new conditions, it can be instructive to follow through a step-by-step testing of incomes successively closer to the new equilibrium. In Table 32–2, let *G* be autonomously

TABLE 32–2. Government Spending Increased, Tax Rate Unchanged

$(\Delta G = 56; \Delta r = 0; r = .1)$

C	S	I	G	Y	T	D
720	180	180	100	1,000	100	900
720	180	180	156	1,056	105.600	950.400
760.320	190.080	180	156	1,096.320	109.632	986.688
789.350	197.338	180	156	1,125.350	112.535	1,012.815
810.252	202.563	180	156	1,146.252	114.625	1,031.627
.	.	.	.	.	.	.
.	.	.	.	.	.	.
.	.	.	.	.	.	.
864	216	180	156	1,200	120	1,080

increased from $100 to $156. Income is thereby increased by $56 and disposable income by $50.40. With marginal propensity to consume for disposable income being .8, C rises by $40.32. Continuing with this sequence of responses of consumption (and saving) to disposable income, the variables converge to the equilibrium values shown in the bottom row.

We can easily verify that the desired income, $1,200, requires that G rise by $56 to $156. Examine the bottom (equilibrium) row. We know the value of Y ($1,200), for that is the specified objective. Since there is no change in the tax rate ($\Delta r = 0; r = .1$), we can immediately calculate $T(.1Y = \$120)$ and then $D(\$1,200 - \$120 = \$1,080)$. With the value of D (and thus ΔD), we can determine C and S by means of the marginal propensities: $c\Delta D = \Delta C = \$144$, so the new $C = \$864$. And S is $1,080 − $864 = $216. Investment is assumed constant. Since $Y = C + I + G$ and we now know the value of Y, C, and I, we infer that $G = \$156$ and $\Delta G = \$56$.

2a, 2g

Graphic Analysis

The consequence on income of the increase in government expenditure with the tax rate constant is portrayed in Figure 32–2. The initial total expenditure line $C + I + G_1$ cuts the 45-degree line at income of $1,000. The autonomous increase of $56 in G raises the total expenditure line by that amount to $C + I + G_2$, which locates the new equilibrium income of $1,200.

In the original equilibrium, $I = S$, and $G = T$. In the new equilibrium, *total* injections again equal *total* leakages: $I + G = S + T$; but now $I < S$, and $G > T$. The government is running a deficit, and there is a counterbalancing, or compensating, excess of private saving over investment by the same amount. The government deficit matches the private surplus.[4] How is the government deficit financed?

Suppose the government *prints money*, and, as the government spends it, the money stock rises. Or the government could *borrow new money* from the Federal Reserve or commercial banks, and, again, as the government spends, the money stock increases. Money would continue to increase as long as there is a deficit to finance. The rise in the

---

[4] A private sector is said to have a surplus at some income if its spending rate $(C + I)$ at that income is *less* than its disposable income, D. Since $C + S$ is always, by definition, equal to D, it follows that, if $C + I < D$, then $I < S$.

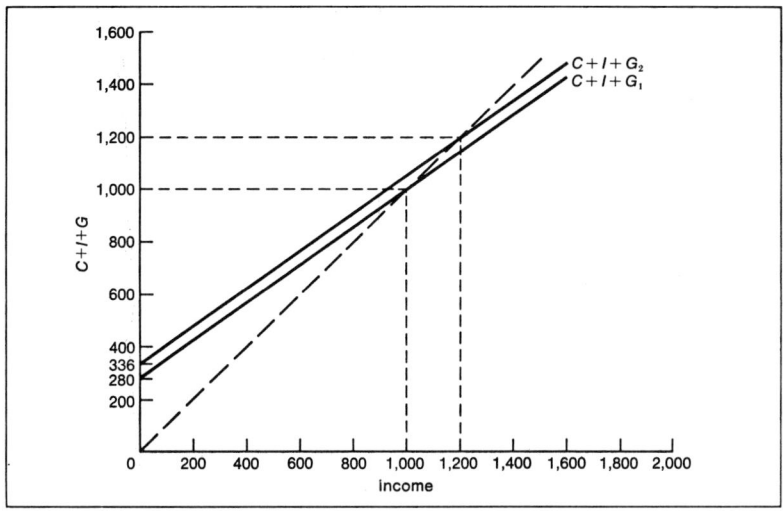

FIGURE 32-2. Increase in Income from Increase in Government Spending

The consumption and investment schedules are unchanged, so $C + I + G$ rises by the amount of the increase in the government expenditure schedule. The new total expenditure line is higher than the initial line by $56 at every level of income, and as a result the equilibrium level of income is raised by $200.

money stock increases the public's ratio of money holdings to income, leading the public to try to lower the money/income ratio by an increased rate of spending on goods and services.[5] In a different type of financing, the government sells bonds to the public: The government *borrows existing money* and spends it, with the public accumulating I.O.U.s of the Treasury and—after the government expenditure—holding as much money as before. As long as the deficit continues, the public's holding of bonds rises, with the public attempting to transfer assets from the form of bonds to other goods. In both instances—trying to reduce the ratio of money to income and trying to reduce the ratio of bonds to other assets and income—the public is increasing consumption and investment spending until the deficit is eliminated, thereby raising income even further than is indicated in the multiplier mechanism illustrated in Table 32-2.

A deficit is financed, then, in some combination of two basic ways: creating new money or borrowing existing money. And it is apparent that fiscal policy involves monetary policy; one cannot be unambiguously defined without specifying the other.

Route 2: Unchanged Government Expenditure with Reduced Tax Rate

Return to the initial equilibrium situation, and now to raise income, we reduce the tax rate, r. The autonomous fall in tax collections in row 2 of Table 32-3, as a result of the

---

[5] The consumption and investment functions are pushed up until income rises to the level at which the deficit is eliminated. What is that income? In our example, the tax rate is .1, so taxes increase by 10 percent of the income increase. Since the initially created deficit was $56, taxes must increase $56, and this requires income to increase $560. Thus, Y must rise, not just to $1,200, but to $1,560.

TABLE 32–3. **Government Spending Unchanged, Tax Rate Reduced**

($\Delta G = 0$; $\Delta r = -.05833$, $r = .04167$)

C	S	I	G	Y	T	D
720	180	180	100	1,000	100	900
720	180	180	100	1,000	41.667	958.333
766.666	191.667	180	100	1,046.666	43.615	1,003.051
802.441	200.610	180	100	1,082.441	45.105	1,037.336
829.869	207.467	180	100	1,109.869	46.248	1,063.621
.	.	.	.	.	.	.
.	.	.	.	.	.	.
.	.	.	.		.	.
920	230	180	100	1,200	50	1,150

lower tax rate, starts the multiplier process. But how large must be the change in r? We know, by assumption of the objective, that $Y = \$1,200$; and we know, by assumption, that $I = \$180$ and $G = \$100$. Since C must equal $Y - (I + G)$, then $C = \$920$. Since ΔC is $\$200$, it follows that ΔD must be $\$250$. (Why?) And since taxes are equal to $Y - D$, $T = \$1,200 - \$1,150 = \$50$. Finally, $r = T/Y = \$50/\$1,200 = .04167$, that is, .05833 less than the initial rate of .1. Having thereby found r, we can fill in the entire table, with the autonomous decrease in tax collections in the second row being $\$58.333$ ($= \$100 - \$41.667$), compared to an autonomous increase in government spending of $\$56$ in Route 1.

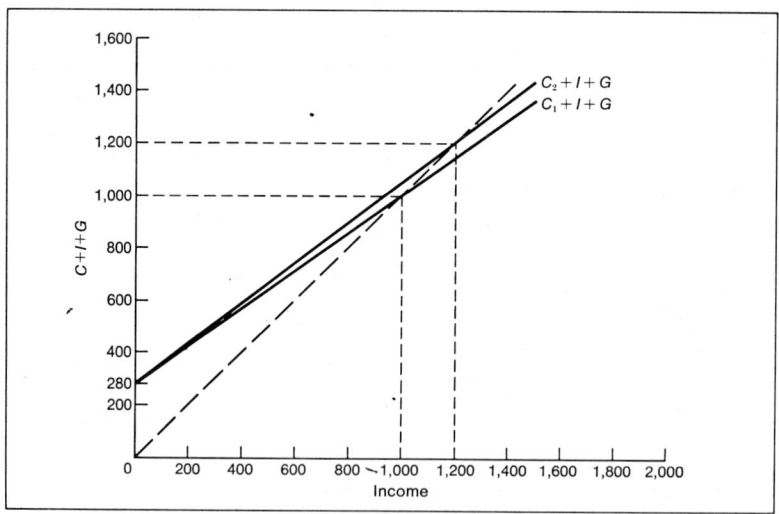

FIGURE 32–3. Reduction in Income Tax Rate

As less of income is taxed away and *disposable* income (D) is thereby made larger, consumption out of any *national* income (Y) is increased. The C line shifts upward as its slope increases slightly. The new $C_2 + I + G$ line is higher and steeper, with the same intercept on the vertical axis as the original total expenditure line and intersection with the 45-degree line at a larger national income.

Within the context of Table 32–3, $1,200 is, indeed, an equilibrium income: that income is associated with C, I, and G expenditures of $1,200, and injections equal leakages. But again we have a government deficit in the new equilibrium. Once more this must be financed by the government's creation of new money or by borrowing private savings. And, as before, the accumulation of money or bonds by the public will shift the consumption and investment functions so as to lead to a national income higher than $1,200.

2b, 3, 4

TABLE 32–4. Government Spending Increased, Tax Rate Reduced

($\Delta G = 50$; $\Delta r = -.00625$; $r = .09375$)

C	S	I	G	Y	T	D
720	180	180	100	1,000	100	900
720	180	180	150	1,050	98.438	951.562
761.250	190.312	180	150	1,091.250	102.305	988.945
791.156	197.789	180	150	1,121.156	105.108	1,016.048
812.838	203.210	180	150	1,142.838	107.141	1,035.697
.	.	.	.	.	.	.
.	.	.	.	.	.	.
.	.	.	.	.	.	.
870	217.500	180	150	1,200	112.500	1,087.500

Route 3: Increase Government Spending and Reduce Tax Rate

We can "combine" the first two routes, increasing G by less than $56 and reducing r by less than .05833. If we decide arbitrarily on a new value for either of these variables, the value of the other is implied. If, on the one hand, we designate that $\Delta G = \$50$, we can (as in Route 2) immediately determine the new equilibrium value of C, and this implies the new D and then the new T and r. On the other hand, if we decide that $\Delta r = -.00625$ and therefore that the new $r = .09375$, we can calculate T and therefore D; the change in D implies the change in C and thus the necessary value of G.

The effects of the rise in government expenditures and a fall in the tax rate are portrayed graphically by shifting up the consumption-plus-investment-plus-government-expenditure line, and by minutely increasing its slope. This is illustrated in Figure 32–4, with the new and old equilibrium incomes shown by the intersections of the new and old expenditure lines with the 45-degree line. (Again the *ultimate* outcome, which we do not show here, depends on the method of financing the deficit.)

2c

Route 4: Increase Government Spending and Tax Rate with Budget Balanced

In each of the preceding alternatives, a budget deficit ($G > T$) was created with the inception of the policy, and a deficit (of smaller magnitude) still existed even when the new equilibrium income was attained. It might be supposed that *any* income-expansionary policy *must* be characterized by a deficit. After all, how could it be expansionary for the government to relieve the community of as many dollars through collecting taxes as

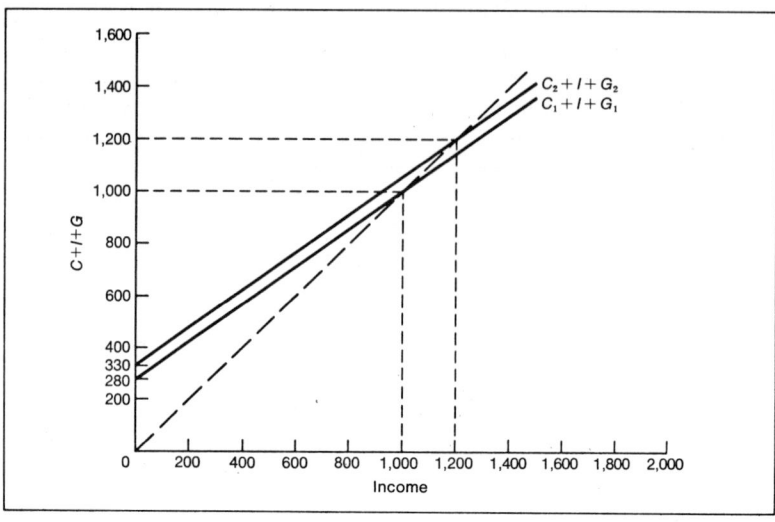

FIGURE 32-4. Effect of an Increase in G and Reduction in the Tax Rate

The increase in G and the reduction in taxes (which raises C for any national income) push up the total expenditure line and increase the C-line slope (from $720/1,000 = .72$ to $870/1,200 = .725$).

it pumps into the income stream through spending? And yet, as Table 32-5 illustrates, even though the budget was balanced initially and is balanced in the new equilibrium (at a higher level of spending and taxing), income has again increased to $1,200 when *both* G and T are autonomously increased by $200.[6]

Income rises by $200 simply because the *spending* components which constitute income have increased in the aggregate by $200. The important point with respect to income creation is *not* the government deficit (or, more generally, the government budget) *per se*; rather, it is the matter of *aggregate spending*. In our illustration, investment spending is assumed, as before, to be unchanged; consumption spending is unchanged (actually lower during the transition) by the curtailment of disposable income as a result of the increased tax rate and consequently the increased tax collection; so income rises, dollar for dollar, by the increase in government spending. (Indeed, income increases by the increase in aggregate spending even if the government has a budget *surplus*—as we shall see in Route 6, below.) With the balanced-budget case there would seem to be no money supply change or any bond supply effect. As we shall see later, this case does imply a reduced ratio of money to national income—that is, a reduced demand to hold money.

---

[6] The source of the expansionary effects does *not* lie in the fact that a deficit exists throughout the transition from the initial equilibrium to the new, beginning with the third period. For, as the reader can verify with his own table, it would be possible to maintain a budget *surplus* all through the transition, either by increasing G only gradually to $300 instead of jumping directly to that figure or by initially raising r to more than .25 then gradually reducing it .25. As a third variant on the "balanced-budget route," we could eliminate the transition entirely, by increasing G to $300 in the *same* period as r is increased to .25 instead of increasing G in the *following* period, as in the table.

Fiscal Policy Impacts on Income

TABLE 32–5. Increased Government Spending and Tax Rate, Budget Balanced (G = T)
($\Delta G = 200$; $\Delta r = .15$; $r = 25$)

C	S	I	G	Y	T	D
720	180	180	100	1,000	100	900
720	180	180	100	1,000	250	750
600	150	180	300	1,080	270	810
648	162	180	300	1,128	282	846
676.8	169.2	180	300	1,156.8	289.2	867.6
.	.	.	.	.	.	.
.	.	.	.	.	.	.
720	180	180	300	1,200	300	900

It may be objected that if disposable income is not increased (and even is decreased during the transition), this balanced-budget policy is scarcely worthwhile. The objection seems to gain force if the increase in money income is accompanied by increased employment; for if a given disposable income is divided among more employees, the *average* disposable income per *employed* worker actually falls. While a previously unemployed person who now has a job is better off (that is, some income is better than none), those who already had jobs and who now have a lower income are worse off. What can we say about the "goodness" of this policy? Two types of evaluation can be suggested. First, while aggregate disposable income is not increased from $900, total output may well be larger. If there has been no price inflation, the entire increase in money income represents an equivalent increase in real income. (Of course, if there *is* some degree of inflation, one consequence is that *real* disposable income is actually *less* as a result of the fiscal policy.) With disposable income unchanged, the entire increase in real output (income) goes to, and is disposed of by, the government. This enlarged "communal" income can take the forms of, say, more parks and missiles. So those (previously employed) workers who now have smaller incomes may be mollified by the availability of more public parks, where they can sit in the evenings and happily contemplate the nation's growing military strength.[7]

This favorable evaluation of the balanced-budget policy may appear unconvincing. But consider a second evaluative approach, one in which it is considered actually *desirable* to *curtail* disposable income. Suppose it to be 1939 or 1940. There is a substantial amount of unemployed resources; there is also a growing threat of war. Therefore, we have a twofold objective: (1) increase national income to $1,200 and (2)

---

[7] Some workers, however, may feel that their emjoyment of the communal income does not fully compensate them for their loss of private income. And if some members of the community are hurt by a policy, even though others gain, it is not clear that the policy has increased over-all "social welfare." At least in abstract principle, there is a possible solution to this "welfare" problem. When you give *no* private income to the newly employed and continue to split up the unchanged aggregate disposable income among the originally employed, the originally employed have as much private (money) income as before, in addition to greater communal income; also, the newly employed have no less private income than before, but they do gain in communal income. With the aid of some supporting—and perhaps heroic—assumptions (notably, that the utility of increased communal income to the newly employed is greater than the disutility of work and the disutility of receiving no private income when others are being paid), we can conclude that social welfare is unambiguously increased: *everyone* is better off!

prevent private consumption (and investment) from rising, thereby permitting all of the increased output of the economy to flow to the government for the war effort. Route 4 meets both conditions (and Route 6 gains the first objective while actually *reducing* the consumption "absorption" of the national output).

In the graph of Figure 32–5, the G component of the $C + I + G$ line is increased; but the increase in the tax rate shifts down the C component (by less than the taxes collected). Since the tax is all spent by the government, the G line shifts up by more than the drop in the C line. The new $C + I + G$ line is higher but less steep; national income is higher.

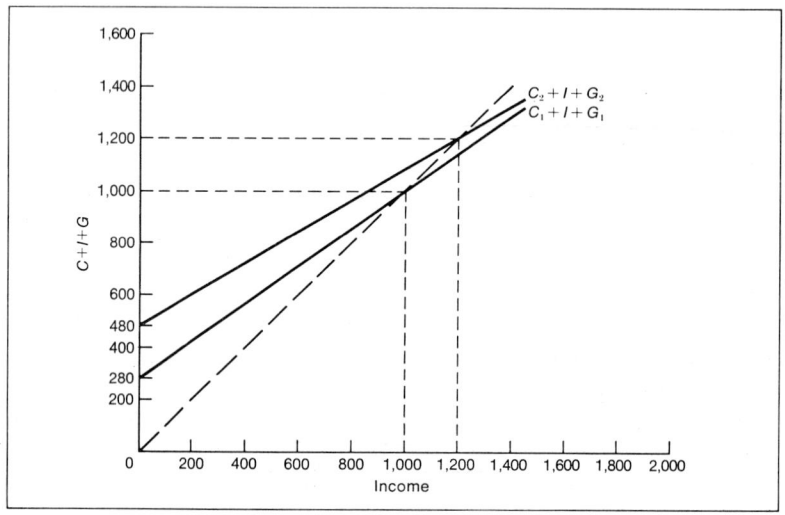

FIGURE 32–5. Income Effects of an Increase in G with a Balanced Budget

The increase in G shifts up the expenditure line, and the increase in the tax rate reduces its slope to .6.

Once more consider the monetary situation affected behind the scenes. The amount of money the public wants to hold rises with national income and wealth and falls with the interest rate. If the interest rate is considered for the moment to be constant, the increase in income will induce efforts to build up larger holdings of money, the new higher income can be maintained. But suppose the money stock is not increased: the public is then faced with using an unchanged stock of money to accommodate a larger income. People *try* to accumulate more money as income rises. With a constant stock, not everyone can succeed, but the effort involves a reduction in the rate of expenditure on goods and services and also on bonds (the latter resulting in a fall in bond prices and a rise in interest rates, which further discourages investment purchases). The curtailing of spending reduces the consumption and investment functions, thereby reducing income from its new level of $1,200—tending to drop it all the way back to the original $1,000. Monetary policy in this case—with unchanged money supply—negated the effects of fiscal actions.

In the first three policies, the supply of money (or bonds) increased as a result of financing a deficit; consequently, income rose some additional amount beyond the seeming equilibrium levels deduced in the pure fiscal policy tables. In those cases, the deficit fiscal policy was affected by an expansionary monetary adjustment, with both fiscal and monetary effects on income working in the same direction. But in the balanced-budget fiscal policy, there is no government deficit (except possibly in a transition from the original income equilibrium to the new equilibrium). Without a deficit to finance, the monetary authorities have no immediate incentive to increase the money stock. And without an increase in the money stock, the new income equilibrium can be maintained only if the public's demand for money happens to fall (in the face of a rise in income) to the level which can be satisfied by the unchanged money stock. In short, in this balanced-budget case, monetary policy may not be geared to making fiscal policy effective, with the latter thereby being largely frustrated in its expansionary purpose. In all cases, maintenance of an increased income calls for either (1) increase in the stock of money or (2) autonomous reduction in the demand to hold money.

Route 5: Increase Government Spending and Tax Rate with Budget Deficit

An *equal* increase in both government expenditures and tax collection will, in the context of the present model, yield a larger national income. Here, a rise in income to $1,200 is obtained by increasing G *more than* T. In Route 1, taxes were not raised while G was increased; the increase in G had to be only $56. But if taxes are raised, then the increase in G must be bigger than $56. In Route 4, an equal increase in taxes required that G increase by $200. This suggests that if taxes are raised less than the increase in G, the required increase in G will be *less* than $200 (since less of a reduction in C, consequent to the tax increase, must be offset) and *more* than $56 (since some reduction of C must offset). For each possible increase in G greater than $56, there is some increase in the tax rate which will yield the desired $200 increase in national income.

We choose G of $100 arbitrarily and ask what increase in r will prevent income from rising above $1,200. Table 32–6 is based on arbitrarily chosen $G = \$100$. Since I is assumed constant at $180, $I + G = \$380$. Thus C must be $820 in order that $C + I + G$ be $1,200. Since .8 of disposable income is consumed, we can compute the necessary D as $1,025 ($= 820/.8$). Finally, if national income is $1,200 and disposable income is $1,025, then taxes must be $175, or .14583 of $1,200. G is $200 and T is $175, giving a deficit of $25. (For brevity, only the initial and the new equilibrium data are given in Table 32–6, ignoring monetary factors involved in covering the deficit.)

TABLE 32–6. Increased Government Spending and Tax Rate, Budget Deficit ($G > T$)
($\Delta G = 100$; $\Delta r = .04583$; $r = .14583$)

C	S	I	G	Y	T	D
720	180	180	100	1,000	100	900
820	205	180	200	1,200	175	1,025

Route 6: Increase Government Spending and Tax Rate with Budget Surplus

We have seen in Route 4 that a deficit is not required for an expansionary fiscal policy. And a slightly overbalanced, or surplus, budget with still greater G also can be expansionary. Table 32–7 shows an increase in national income from $1,000 to $1,200, this

TABLE 32–7. Increased Government Spending and Tax Rate, Budget Surplus (G < T)
($\Delta G = 300$; $\Delta r = .25417$; $r = .35417$)

C	S	I	G	Y	T	D
720	180	180	100	1,000	100	900
620	155	180	400	1,200	425	775

time with a budget surplus. There is a variety of possibilities, depending upon how large we make G. With an increase of $300 (which can be large enough, since $200 would suffice with a balanced budget) and keeping I at $180, we have $I + G$ equal to $580. For $C + I + G$ to equal $1,200, C must equal $620. Disposable income must be $620/.8 = \$775$. In turn, taxes must equal $1,200 - \$775 = \$425$. Thus, a policy of greater G and r with a budget surplus (and a corresponding private sector deficit of I over S) calls for increasing both policy variables by more than they were raised in the balanced-budget Route 4.

Route 7: Decrease Government Spending and Tax Rate with Budget Deficit

If the income objective is to be attained by reducing both G and r (necessarily with a budget deficit), r must fall by more than in Route 2, where G was kept constant. Table 32–8 gives an illustration.

TABLE 32–8. Decreased Government Spending and Tax Rate, Budget Deficit
($\Delta G = -20$; $\Delta r = -.07917$; $r = .02083$)

C	S	G	I	Y	T	D
720	180	100	180	1,000	100	900
940	235	80	180	1,200	25	1,175

Which Route?

There are, then, these seven types of combinations of ΔG and Δr, each of which results in a ΔY of $200; and each type has variations of one sort or another. Which of the infinity of alternatives is best? Or, since each can affect income by the same amount, are they all equally good? What are some of the possible criteria that may be used in evaluating the alternative routes?

Size of taxes. First, almost everyone would agree that the smaller the tax collections, the better. Even if one desires certain consequences of greater taxes (for example, to curtail disposable income, as in Routes 4 and 6), few people rejoice in higher taxes.

Size of government. A smaller tax can be achieved by making a larger deficit through a larger G. So a second criterion relates to the size of government. Some would be pleased to have G larger within a broad and indefinite limit in order for government better to fulfill its "obligations." They speak of the benefits of socialism, with public ownership of resources in order to satisfy "unmet social needs"; of a more equal distribution of wealth; of the inability of the individual to make efficient decisions in a complex world. Others refer to greater satisfaction of "unmet private needs"; of less redistribution of wealth by government and more by voluntary aid; of the right of the individual to make decisions for himself; of a preference for greater individuality and personal responsibility and for market-type behavior and competition relative to political competition.

Size of disposable income. Whereas one might expect a great majority of the community to prefer a greater D to a smaller, at times (as in girding for war) a smaller D is preferred. And as some may prefer a larger G on grounds, say, that government uses resources more "efficiently" and "equitably" than do households and business firms, so a reduction in private income may be desired.

Nature of the budget. One might feel that the smaller the deficit or the larger the surplus, the better. Or perhaps a balanced budget is judged to be ideal, but perhaps with a surplus being less undesirable than a deficit. Deficits may be disliked because they imply a larger government debt and a larger stock of money, with a likelihood of inflation.

Even this brief and incomplete review indicates that there are various criteria and that no route is best according to all criteria. Table 32–9 ranks the seven routes according to these several criteria. All the routes rank alike according to the criteria of smaller taxes, smaller government spending, and larger disposable income. But when ranking by size of budget deficit, the order is exactly reversed. It appears that an income-expansion policy best designed to satisfy a person desirous of smaller government spending and taxing would choose a fiscal policy that gave larger deficits. And those desirous of larger government activity and larger taxes with smaller disposable income would prefer policies associated with budget surpluses. We can agree on how each fiscal policy increases income while differing strongly on the desirability of various other consequences.

TABLE 32–9. Summary Evaluation of Alternative Fiscal Policies with Alternative Criteria

Rank	Smallness of Taxes		Smallness of Government Spending		Largeness of Disposable Income		Budget Balance	
	Route	(Size)	Route	(Size)	Route	(Size)	Route	(Size)
1	7	(25)	7	(80)	7	(1,175)	6	(25)
2	2	(50)	2	(100)	2	(1,150)	4	(0)
3	3	(112)	3	(150)	3	(1,087)	5	(−25)
4	1	(120)	1	(156)	1	(1,080)	1	(−36)
5	5	(175)	5	(200)	5	(1,025)	3	(−37)
6	4	(300)	4	(300)	4	(900)	2	(−50)
7	6	(425)	6	(400)	6	(775)	7	(−55)

Limits to Expansion of Income

Suppose larger G and T can increase national income while maintaining a balanced budget, and that income will rise by the same amount that G and T are increased (Route 4). Why not expand income without limit? An increasing degree of socialization of consumption and investment activity (the government may engage in both) may be deemed undesirable because of the kinds of goods produced, the modes of rationing used, and the relative increase in importance of the political competitive process. Thus the potential contribution of government spending to national income may be restrained.

But arbitrarily setting aside this important, largely psychological, ideological, and cultural consideration, we certainly shall come up against one insurmountable obstacle: limits of the economy's production capacities. The higher the rate of current services drawn from our resources, the higher the costs of getting still higher rates; ultimately each resource would reach a finite limit of services it could or would provide. Diverting people from leisure and nonmarket earnings activities, for example, becomes more and more expensive at higher rates of uses of their services. If increased government expenditure then takes place and if new money is created to accommodate the increased demand to hold money at higher incomes, the increase in national money income will result in higher prices—inflation. And a number of spectacular inflations have occurred as governments attempted to obtain a larger fraction of national product. Not only may real income (production of goods and services) not increase as prices skyrocket, but an extraordinary inflation may be so disruptive of specialization and exchange activities that real income actually falls as money GNP rapidly rises—as we shall see in Chapter 33.

A Different Problem: Revised Allocation of Income to Guns or Butter

If we started from a position of unemployed resources and wanted more guns, all *increased* income could be directed to the government. But suppose there are no substantial idle resources, so real income cannot be appreciably increased. The only way for the government to acquire more of the total output is to curtail the output going to the rest of the economy. One way to do this is to raise taxes and thereby reduce disposable income, thus inducing a fall in consumption. (*Some* forms of investment also may be curtailed, but while fewer bowling alleys are built, Ford will build a new factory to produce bombers. Aggregate investment could well increase, even though its composition is changed.) For convenience, in Table 32–10, we continue the assumption that I remains constant.

TABLE 32–10. Government Spending Increased with Income Constant
($\Delta G = 200$; $\Delta r = .25$; $r = .35$)

C	S	I	G	Y	T	D
720	180	180	100	1,000	100	900
520	130	180	300	1,000	350	650

Suppose that G is increased to $300. With I held at $180 and with the stipulation that Y remains $1,000 (for, with full employment, an increase in money income is a reflection of higher prices, not of increased output), it follows that C must be cut to $520. The fall of $200 in C will occur if D is reduced by $250 (to $650). Thus T is raised to $350 $(= \$1,000 - \$650)$, giving a new $r = \$350/\$1,000 = .35$.

If an increase in money income is to be avoided, it is not sufficient to raise T merely by the amount of raising G. It is not enough to "pay our way" by matching government

Fiscal Policy Impacts on Income

spending with tax collections, keeping the budget balanced. That would be simply our Route 4, and income would rise by the amount of the budget. To avoid inflation, taxes must be raised by *more* than government spending: we must generate a *surplus*.[8]

On this criterion, the U. S. record of war financing is not very good, but improving. In the Civil War period, 1861–65, federal government receipts (other than receipts from borrowing) were equal to only 24 percent of expenditures, and the consumer price index rose at an annual rate of about 15 percent. In the World War I period, 1917–19, receipts were 30 percent of expenditures, and the price level rose at a rate of almost 18 percent per year. For World War II, 1941–46, receipts were 45 percent of expenditures, and prices rose at an annual rate of 8 percent. And for the Korean War, 1950–53, receipts were 94 percent of expenditures, with prices rising at about 2 percent. But progress has been made: the percentage gets bigger with each war. After a few more tries, we'll get the hang of it, if it's not too late.

Summary

1. "Fiscal policy" encompasses the use of government spending and taxing (and borrowing) for deliberately affecting national income, employment, and prices.

2. We have illustrated several *types* of combinations of government spending and tax rates which can be used to increase income. They illustrate that income can be raised by deficit government budgets, balanced budgets, and surplus budgets. None is "best" on all obvious criteria.

3. When income is at an equilibrium, total injections $(I + G)$ equal total leakages $(S + T)$. Thus if the government budget is in deficit $(G > T)$, the private sector is in surplus $(I < S)$; conversely, a government surplus is matched by a private deficit.

4. We have noted certain *monetary* consequences and prerequisites of *fiscal* policy.
   a. If the government is running a *deficit*, it must soon obtain financing through borrowing "old" money or creating "new" money. The resulting increase in the public's holdings of government bonds and/or money will tend to raise the consumption and investment schedules, resulting in an equilibrium income greater than that implied by the initial fiscal policy alone.
   b. If there is no deficit (the *balanced*-budget route), there is less likelihood that monetary and fiscal policy will be complementary. A policy of holding the money supply constant could, for good or ill, negate the expansionary effects of fiscal policy.
   c. If there is a government *surplus*, we would still normally associate maintenance of a new, higher level of income with an increase in the money stock. But the government is collecting more in taxes than it is spending, and, unless the surplus is used to retire government securities held by the public or an expansionary monetary policy is adopted, the public is in the unacceptable position of having a larger income while the money stock is actually falling.
   In the deficit cases, necessary financing of the deficits increased the money supply, and demand for money was correspondingly raised by the rising income, income being in-

---

[8] If there is initially a sufficiently large deficit in the new equilibrium the budget must be *balanced*. (For example, if tax collections in the first period of Table 32–10 had been only $50, giving a deficit of $100 - 50 = 50, G could be raised from $100 to $300 without raising the equilibrium level of income if the budget is balanced in the final equilibrium—that is, if T is raised from $50 to $300. Try it.) But in any case, it is necessary that $\Delta T > \Delta G$.

creased both by the initial fiscal policy impact and by the following increase in the money stock. In the balanced-budget and surplus cases, demand for money was raised by increasing income through fiscal policy, and the higher income would be thereafter sustainable only by the increased money stock.

5 Fiscal policy may be used for purposes other than raising income. For example, we have reviewed the problem of increasing government spending while keeping income constant. If we start with a balanced budget, achieving these dual goals requires generation of a budget surplus.

Appendix: Algebra in the Analysis of Income Determination

A little algebra can go a long way toward clarifying the analysis of income effects of pure fiscal activity (*ignoring the monetary factors*—and this is a sterilizing over-simplification of a potentially useful analysis of practical policy). The income-determination model of Chapter 27 could be summarized in three simple equations:

$Y = C + I$ the income equilibrium condition,
$C = a + cY$ the consumption function, with c being the marginal propensity to consume,
$I = I_0$ investment is an autonomous constant.

These three equations, solved simultaneously, yield $Y = (I_0 + a)/(1 - c)$, where $1/(1 - c)$ is the multiplier. We have seen how changes in I_0 and in a and in c would change national income, Y. In this chapter we introduced two new variables, taxes, T, and government expenditures, G. Taxes are treated as income taxes, and government expenditures as a governmentally determined variable, that is, an autonomous variable. This gives five equations:

(1) $Y = C + I + G$ income equilibrium condition,
(2) $C = a + c(Y - T)$ for now consumption depends on income disposable after taxes,
(3) $I = I_0$ autonomous constant,
(4) $G = G_0$ autonomous variable,
(5) $T = t + rY$ tax-collection function, with r being the marginal rate of taxation and t being the amount of taxes that is not dependent upon income.

Substitution for terms in Equation (1) gives
(6) $Y = a + c(Y - T) + I_0 + G_0$.
Substitution from (5) in (6) gives
(7) $Y = a + c(Y - t - rY) + I_0 + G_0$.
Solving (7) for Y gives
(8) $Y = \dfrac{I_0 + G_0 + a - ct}{(1 - c + cr)}$.

Here $1/(1 - c + cr)$ is the new multiplier to be applied to increases in I_0 or G_0 or a or t. Knowing directions and magnitudes of changes in I_0, G_0, a, t, or the tax rate, r, will from Equation (8) tell what happens to Y—if somehow money demand were appropriately accommodated.

The first example in the text in this chapter started with $I_0 = 180$, $c = .80$, $a = 0$, $t = 0$, $r = 0$, and $G = 0$. Y was therefore $900. Government activity was then set at $G = 100$ and $t = 100$. Y increased to $1,000.

In the discussion of fiscal policy, the various routes all started with an initial situation in which $c = .8$, $I_0 = 180$, $G_0 = 100$, $t = 0$ and $r = .1$. This yields $Y = 1,000$. *Route 1* involved an autonomous increase in G from $G_0 = 100$ to $G_0 = 156$. This yields an increase of Y from 1,000 to 1,200. The problem, as put in the text, was to find the change in G_0 required to change Y from 1,000 to 1,200. Solving Equation (1) for G_0 yields

$$G_0 = Y(1 - c + cr) - (a + I_0 - ct)$$
$$= 1,200 (1 - .8 + .08) - (180 - 0) = 156.$$

Route 2 used an unchanged G and a reduced r, in order to increase Y from 1,000 to 1,200. Solving Equation (7) for r gives $r = .0417$, so the reduction, $\Delta r = .1 - .0417 = .0583$.

Route 3 seeks a lower r *and* a higher G that will give a Y of 1,200. Putting in all terms except r and G in Equation (7) enables one to see there is an infinite number of pairs of r and G that will satisfy that equation. Arbitrarily setting G at 150 gives $r = .09375$.

Route 4, the balanced-budget route, adds a condition, namely that $G = T$. Since $T = t + rY$ (and $t = 0$), this means $G = T = rY$. Substituting T, or rY, for G in Equation (6) or (7) yields T (and hence G) $= 300$, which implies that $r = .25$ (since for a balanced budget $G = T = rY$).

Route 5 uses a budget deficit associated with *increased* government spending (rather than a reduced tax rate, which was Route 2). We remember that in Route 2, G increased by 56 with no change in r, so that a deficit appeared. But here in Route 5 we want to increase G and T. So any increase in G to above 156 will require some increase in r to prevent Y from rising above 1,200. Arbitrarily increasing G from 100 to 200 will, from Equation (8), yield the requisite $r = .1458$, an increase of .0458 or 45.8 percent in the income tax rate.

Route 6 requires that T be larger than G so as to have a budget surplus. Going back to Equation (6), which contains both G and T, we solve for T and G: $G = Y(1 - c) - a - I_0 + cT$. Inserting specified values of Y, c, a, and I_0 gives $G = 60 + .8T$, or $T = -75 + 1.25G$. All combinations of G and T satisfying this equation will yield an income of 1,200. Some combinations will have G greater than T and some will have G less than T, with one combination having G equal to T, namely $G = T = 300$.

Route 4 had $G = T$, a balanced budget, $G = T = 300$. Route 6, $T = 425$ and $G = 400$. Route 7, involving a deficit and sufficiently large G to obtain Y of 1,200, $G = 80$, and $T = 25$.

Finally, one stern warning. This model is useful only as an illustration of some of the relationships among some of the relevant economic variables in our economic system. A far more elaborate model using more variables (for example, three more are money, interest rates, and wage rates) and more relationships among the variables is required for real assessment of alternative policies.

Questions

1 Assume the following equilibrium values:

$$Y = 1{,}600 \qquad I = 380$$
$$C = 1{,}000 \qquad G = 220$$
$$S = 310 \qquad T = \ ?$$

Assume further that investment remains constant at 380 throughout the analysis; finally, assume that *MPC* (with respect to disposable income) is .8.

a. What is the level of government tax collections?
b. Is the government running a surplus or a deficit? Of how much?
c. What is the level of disposable income (D)?
d. What is the numerical value of the multiplier?
e. Suppose that the government now balances the budget by adjusting its *expenditures* while still collecting the same number of dollars in taxes. What will then be the new equilibrium values of: Y, D, C, S, I, and G?

2 Following are seven separate problems pertaining to fiscal policy—adjustments (increase or decrease) in G (government spending) and in r (marginal and average tax rate). In *each* of the seven cases, assume the following initial situation:

C	S	I	G	Y	T	D
700	100	100	200	1,000	200	800

In each case, assume $c = \Delta C/\Delta D = .9$. There are no induced changes in G and none in I except in the last case. Now, your job is to compute the *final equilibrium* situation for each case—with one or two or three of the figures already filled in.

a. Adjust G; r constant

C	S	I	G	Y	T	D
		100		1,250		

b. G constant; adjust r.

C	S	I	G	Y	T	D
		100	200	1,250		

c. $G = 250$; adjust r.

C	S	I	G	Y	T	D
		100	250	1,000		

d. $G = 250$; adjust r.

C	S	I	G	Y	T	D
		100	250	900		

e. Adjust G; adjust r.

C	S	I	G	Y	T	D
		100	250	1,250		

f. Consumption initially falls autonomously by 50; adjust G; r constant.

C	S	I	G	Y	T	D
		100		1,250		

g. Adjust G; r constant; $i = \Delta I/\Delta Y = .05$.

C	S	I	G	Y	T	D
				1,250		

Fiscal Policy Impacts on Income

3. Go back to question 1 and its original situation. Suppose that the government again balances the budget, this time by adjusting the amount of *taxes collected* while leaving its expenditures unchanged.
   a. The change in tax collections initially (autonomously) changes D by how much and in what direction?
   b. As a result of this change in D, the initial change in C is how much and in what direction?
   c. As a result of this initial change in C, the change in Y eventually (when the multiplier has fully worked itself out) is how much?
   d. What will be the new equilibrium values of Y, D, C, S, I, and T?

4. a. Begin with the situation depicted below; it is assumed that $MPC = .8$ and $MPS = .2$ with respect to disposable income. Is income at an equilibrium level? Is the government budget balanced? Is there a necessary connection between the answers of those two questions?

C	S	I	G	Y	T	D
720	180	180	100	1,000	100	900

Initially, the average and marginal tax rates are both .1. Now, suppose that the objective is to increase national income to an equilibrium level of 1,200, by means of a cut in the *average* tax rate, leaving the marginal rate unchanged, with the government budget balanced at a level of 100 in the new income equilibrium. Let there be a marginal propensity to invest (defined as $\Delta I/\Delta Y$) of appropriate size. Fill in the table for the first several periods and for the new equilibrium values. What is the relation between the numerical values of the marginal propensity to save and the marginal propensity to invest?

b. Next, alter the initial situation, with tax collections smaller than before and saving and disposable income correspondingly larger.

C	S	I	G	Y	T	D
720	190	180	100	1,000	90	910

The objective—raising income to 1,200 with a reduced average tax rate and with an ultimately balanced budget at 100—remains the same. Again fill in the table. And now what is the relation between MPS and MPI?

c. Finally, go back and fill in the tables again for each of the two alternative initial situations, keeping the objective unchanged, but let there be one difference from the earlier cases: while there is to be a cut in the average tax rate in period 2, as before, there is also an autonomous increase in investment in period 3 equal to 9 (an increase equal to 5 percent of the original level throughout the investment schedule). Again, in these two new solutions, what is the relation between MPS and MPI?

5. "Money counts, and it matters significantly—not only in *monetary* policy, but also in *fiscal* policy." Persuasively concur.

6. a. In Route 6, we raised income to 1,200 by increasing both G and r, with a budget surplus in the new (higher) equilibrium. Can you work out an analogous case, beginning with the same initial situation, in which equilibrium income is *lowered* to 950 by *decreasing* both G and r, with a budget surplus in the new equilibrium?
   b. In Route 7, G and r are reduced, and a deficit obtains in the new (higher) equilibrium. Can you *lower* income to 950 by *increasing* G and r in such fashion that a deficit exists in the new equilibrium?

7. Evaluate the following quoted statements.
   a. "A disadvantage of using public works as a counter-cyclical policy is that tax collections would have to be raised in depressions in order to finance the government expenditures."

b. In 1947, a year of "full" employment, President Truman vetoed a tax-reduction bill, and a financial columnist commented: "Perhaps the most curious argument in the tax message [of the President] was that when business is active and employment high, it is unwise to reduce taxes. In other words, we must not cut taxes when there is a lot of money coming into the Treasury, but we must wait for a depression, when tax revenues fall, to cut taxes. Whoever wrote this tax-veto message would have a tough time getting a passing mark in a course in freshman economics."

c. "Inflation, by definition, is a situation in which prices are rising, which is to say that the purchasing power of the dollar is falling. Since the value of each dollar is being reduced, it is in the interest of each person to retain command over as many of his dollars as possible; and thus it is appropriate in a period of inflation to cut taxes."

Inflation

33 INFLATION, like death and taxes, appears inevitable. We know of no nation that has escaped it. Inflation is a tax—of a special kind—on money. Perhaps because it is such an easy tax to impose, governments have used it. In addition, other features "commend" it: it usually is not thought of as a tax, it redistributes wealth from creditors to debtors, and it often results from "good" causes, like attempts to keep employment from falling every time the growth-rate of employment slackens. In this chapter we explain what inflation is, why it occurs, what are its sufficient conditions, what kinds of actions designed to stop it are fallacious, and how one can increase his chances of avoiding or reducing the tax imposed by inflation.

What Is Inflation?

Inflation is a rise in the general level of prices of assets and services. If the prices of eggs, butter, and shoes rise, while those of clothing, gasoline, and fruits fall, the lower prices of one set of goods can offset the rise of the others. The question is: "Can people purchase the same level of utility—not necessarily the same pattern of goods and services—at the same total cost?" If the money cost has risen, there has been inflation.

We must know whether the new pattern gives the same utility, and this is almost always an impossible empirical task. When relative prices change, people use more of the relatively lower-priced good and less of the other good. But we don't actually know just how much substitution of cheaper items for more expensive items is required to leave people as well off as before. Hence, we can't compute the costs of the new unknown combinations.

There is the further complication of changes in quality. If people switch from black and white to color television at three times the price, has the cost of living risen? Quality changes have been so extensive that what appears to be a rising price level may in fact be a rising utility level, with a *falling* price level for the *old* level of utility.

Can we never know, then, whether inflation has really occurred? Some evidence is provided if we observe the costs of fixed patterns of consumption from month to month, on the assumption that changes in quality or relative prices have been *relatively* insignificant. The U. S. Bureau of Labor Statistics each month publishes a Consumer Price Index as an approximation to the cost of living of the ordinary-employee-class family income. The course of that index over the past 140 years is shown in Figure 33–1. Because of sampling, quality changes, and purchase-pattern shifts, to name a few factors, a change of 2 to 4 percent in one year in that index could occur if there really were no change in the general cost of living; this leeway of 2 or 3 percent reflects the margin of error or range of effects of fluctuations of the other pertinent elements. A change of some 90 percent within a few years, as happened from 1941 to 1947 in the United States, certainly is not the result of sampling deviations, changes in quality, or changes in purchase patterns. The major swings in that index are taken to be a reliable indicator of inflation or deflation.[1]

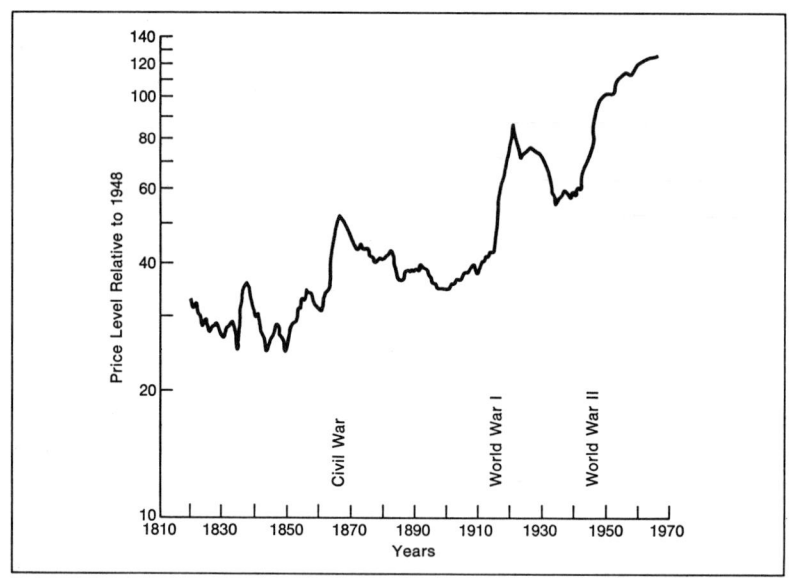

FIGURE 33–1. Consumer goods price index, 1820–1970. Source: U. S. Department of Labor, *Monthly Bulletin*.

More pronounced, more spectacular, and faster have been the inflations in several other countries. For example, since World War II several countries show the rises graphed in Figure 33–2.

1, 2, 3, 4

[1] The major inflations and deflations have been great enough that their dates can be fairly well noted by any of several closely related measures of price levels—we hope. In addition, the index does not include prices of capital goods (it covers primarily prices of current services). The severity of bias or degree of error resulting from this omission has not yet been determined. Nevertheless, we will use the conventional, though incomplete, measure.

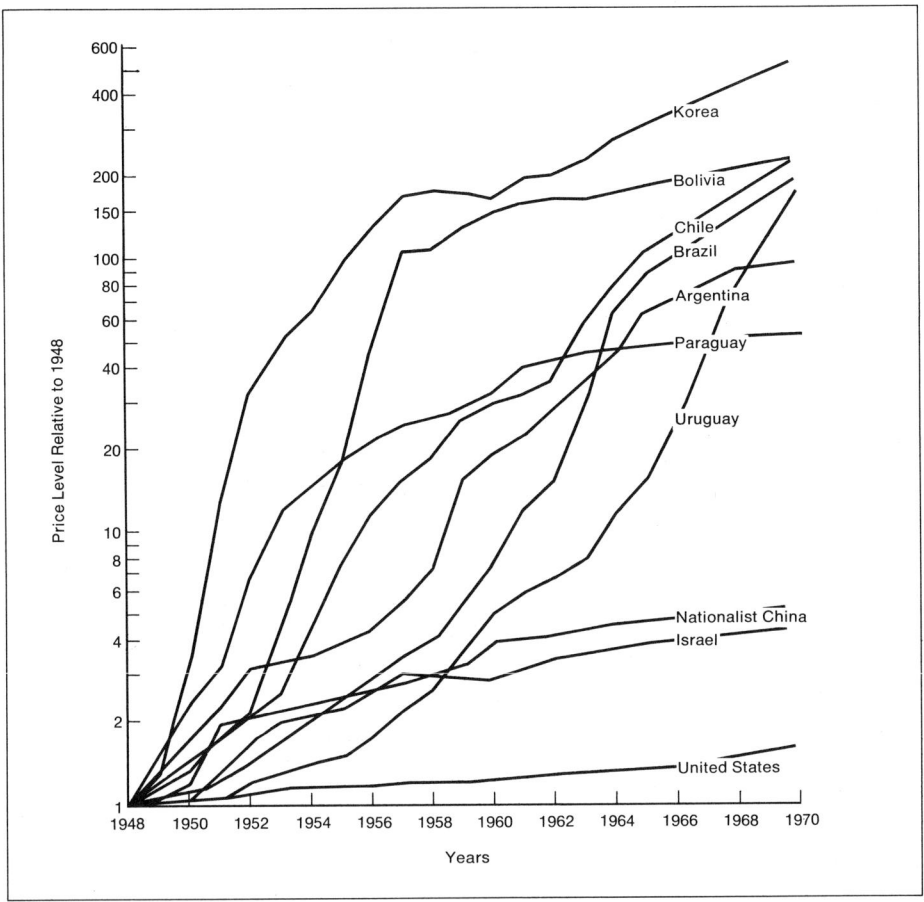

FIGURE 33–2. Recent inflations. Source: United Nations Bulletin of International Financial Statistics.

The Meaning of the Effects of Inflation

Regardless of the reasons for inflation, there are known verified effects of the rise in the general level of prices. There is a wealth loss to holders of money. And it is tempting to add that inflation always implies a transfer of wealth from creditors to debtors. That, however, is *not* logically implied for all types of inflations. To see why, a distinction is necessary between two kinds of inflations.

It has become popular to give names to inflation: creeping, galloping, runaway, hyper, repressed, wage-push, and demand-pull. Some of these designate inflations by causes; some designate the kind of responsive action taken by the government; and some define the rate or extent of inflation. None of these is relevant for identification of effects. The analytically critical distinction is between *unanticipated* and *anticipated* inflation.

Anticipated inflations are those for which people foresee the timing and extent of the inflation, and they plan and act accordingly. If people believe there is going to be a rise in the general price level of, say, 10 percent during the coming six months, their market actions will be different, immediately and during that six-month period, than if they had not foreseen the impending inflation. Inflations in which people inaccurately forecast (usually underestimate) the extent of the inflation are unanticipated inflations. An anticipated inflation can be at a slow rate of, say, 2 percent a year or a hyperinflation of 2,000,000 percent per year. And the same is true for unanticipated inflations.

Wealth-Transfer Effects of Unanticipated Inflation

Two Types of Assets

During *un*anticipated inflation, wealth is transferred from owners of monetary assets to those who have monetary liabilities. The economic logic which implies that debtors gain from *un*anticipated inflation, but not from a correctly anticipated one, rests on the fact that there are two types of assets—monetary and real. Monetary assets are legal claims or rights to fixed amounts of money now or in the future (and usually carrying an explicit interest if they are claims to future amounts). The amount of the money claim in any contractual right is independent of subsequent changes in prices of other commodities or services; it is therefore independent of inflation or deflation.[2] Examples of monetary assets are money, time deposits, mortgages, bonds, promissory notes, pension plans promising a *fixed* number of dollars per year, and accounts receivable. On the opposite side of these contracts is the debtor against whom these claims exist. To every monetary asset there is a monetary liability—the two sides of the same contract. "Real"—or nonmonetary—assets are not claims to fixed amounts of money. The thing claimed—house, car, pair of shoes, hour of labor—can change in money value. A real liability is an obligation to deliver some good whose money price can change.

Net Monetary Debtor Status and Inflation

To cut straight to the heart of wealth transfer, start with the definition of equity or net wealth:

(1) Equity = Assets − Liabilities.

Classify assets and liabilities into real and monetary items:

(2) Equity = (real assets + monetary assets) −
    (real liabilities + monetary liabilities)
  = (real assets − real liabilities) +
    (monetary assets − monetary liabilities)
  = net real assets + net monetary assets.

If the price level rises by a ratio P, real assets and liabilities rise by P; so we have:

(3) New equity = P (net real assets) + (net monetary assets).[3]

For equity to rise at all, as P rises, there must be positive net real assets. For it to rise as much as the price level, net real assets must equal equity (net monetary assets must be

---

[2] We do not assert that the current *price* of a monetary asset cannot change. The *price* of a bond, which is not the amount of the claim, can change; but not the amount claimed. A bond is a monetary asset.

[3] $P = 2$ if the price level doubles.

zero). For it to rise more, net real assets must exceed equity (there must be net monetary liabilities).

If net real assets are less than equity (if there are net monetary assets), equity will rise less than in proportion to the rise in prices unless the monetary assets bear a high enough rate of interest to compensate for the rising prices. We give illustrative examples of the arithmetic. Before inflation, the balance sheet of an economic unit may be:

Before Unanticipated Inflation

Assets		Liabilities	
Cash	$10	Debt	$ 6
Inventory	4	Equity	8
	$14		$14

If the price level doubles, the result is:

After Unanticipated Inflation

Assets		Liabilities	
Cash	$10	Debt	$ 6
Inventory	8	Equity	12
	$18		$18

This economic entity is a net monetary creditor to the extent of $4; its monetary assets ($10) exceed its monetary liabilities ($6). Equity has increased only 50 percent, whereas the price level has increased by 100 percent. And "real" wealth is lost when prices rise by 100 percent while equity rises only 50 percent. Real wealth is reduced from $8 to $12/2 = $6 (in pre-inflation prices).[4]

In the following example, the entity is neutral; that is, its monetary assets equal its monetary liabilities (its net real assets equal its equity).

Before Unanticipated Inflation

Assets		Liabilities	
Cash	$ 6	Debt	$ 6
Inventory	4	Equity	4
	$10		$10

[4] Notice how this example is consistent with equation (3) on page 674. Thus:

$$\text{New equity} = P \text{ (net real assets)} + \text{(net monetary assets)}.$$
$$\$12 \quad = 2(\$4) \quad\quad + \quad (\$10 - \$6).$$

The increase in prices, P, increases equity (assuming net real assets are positive) in money terms, but if the ratio of new equity to initial equity is less than P (as it will be if net monetary assets are positive), the real value of new equity is less than that of initial equity.

After an unanticipated doubling of prices, we have:

After Unanticipated Inflation

Assets		Liabilities	
Cash	$ 6	Debt	$ 6
Inventory	8	Equity	8
	$14		$14

Equity doubles to $8 when the price level doubles. Evidently, equity can increase proportionally to the general level of prices only if equity is equal to net real assets (if there are *zero net monetary* assets).

The only way the entity can experience a rise in equity by a proportion greater than the rise in the price level is by being a net monetary debtor—that is, by owing more money than it has plus what is owed to it. For example, if our economic entity owes $6 and has $4 in money, it is a net monetary debtor to the extent of $2.

Before Unanticipated Inflation

Assets		Liabilities	
Cash	$ 4	Debt	$ 6
Inventory	10	Equity	8
	$14		$14

After Unanticipated Inflation

Assets		Liabilities	
Cash	$ 4	Debt	$ 6
Inventory	20	Equity	18
	$24		$24

Equity has more than doubled, from $8 to $18.

One can obtain an increase of equity greater than the percentage change in the price level only by being in a *net monetary liability status*. Merely holding some monetary debts is not sufficient; such debts must exceed monetary assets. In the example, net monetary *debts* were $2 (cash of $4 minus monetary debt of $6 = − $2).[5]

---

[5] Let R and M be net real and net monetary assets, respectively, and E, the initial equity. Thus: $E = R + M$. If E' is the new equity when prices rise by proportion P, then: $E' = PR + M$. Finally, let Q be the proportionate increase in the money value of the equity: $Q = E'/E$. Now, substituting and rearranging:

$$Q = \frac{PR + M}{E}$$
$$= P\left(\frac{R}{E}\right) + \frac{M}{E}$$
$$= P\left(\frac{E - M}{E}\right) + \frac{M}{E}$$
$$= P - (P - 1)\frac{M}{E}.$$

These examples illustrate that the gain in equity which is proportionately greater than the rise in prices is a result *not* of holding some real goods, but of owing more money than is owed to one.[6]

One of the commonest ways to be a net monetary debtor is to buy a house with a large mortgage. If a person can buy a $20,000 house and offset it with a monetary debt of $20,000, the following two balance sheets show his equity before and after an unanticipated doubling of the price level. (He holds $20,000 of real assets and has an equity of only $100.)

Before Inflation

Assets		Liabilities	
Cash	$ 100	Debt	$20,000
House	20,000	Equity	100
	$20,100		$20,100

After Inflation
(Doubling of Price Level)

Assets		Liabilities	
Cash	$ 100	Debt	$20,000
House	40,000	Equity	20,100
	$40,100		$40,100

His equity increased from $100 to $20,100, giving him an increase in real wealth of $9,950 (in pre-inflation price-level units).

Folklore that old people (widows, orphans, and teachers) suffer as a result of inflation must presume that all (or a majority?) of them are net monetary creditors. There is evidence that more older people tend to have a net monetary *asset* position and hence will lose; but not all older people are net monetary creditors. Categorizing economic units according to such characteristics as age, sex, occupation, marital status, or degree of wealth is deceptive in detecting who gains or loses from the wealth-transfer effect from inflation. Only the net monetary status is relevant, for each of the categories identified has some in each monetary class.

5, 6, 7,
8, 9,
10

Tax on Money

Money is an important form of monetary assets; furthermore, it rarely bears interest. Inflation will therefore impose a loss of wealth on its holder, and a gain to the economic agent whose debts or promises constitute the money. As we saw earlier, the economy's

---

For example, in the third illustration, $Q = 2 - (2 - 1)(-2/8) = 2\frac{1}{4}$; and, to be sure, $18/8 = 2\frac{1}{4}$.

Whether Q is larger than, equal to, or smaller than P (assumed bigger than 1) is determined by whether $(P - 1)(M/E)$ is smaller than, equal to, or larger than zero; and that, in turn, hinges on whether M is negative, zero, or positive. In our first illustration, M was positive ($10 - 6 = 4$), so Q was smaller than P ($1\frac{1}{2} < 2$); in the second, M was zero, so Q equaled P; and in the third, M was negative, so Q was larger than P.

[6] Which means also that he has net real assets in excess of his equity. The excess is possible only by being a net monetary debtor. These are two ways to express the same situation.

money stock is composed principally of (1) demand deposits, which are debts of the commercial banks, and (2) legal-tender money issued by the government and Federal Reserve banks. Unanticipated inflation imposes a wealth loss on commercial banks because, strange as it seems, they are invariably net monetary creditors.[7] Commercial banks are, in effect, intermediaries in a wealth-transfer process. During an unanticipated inflation, they obtain wealth from the people to whom they owe the demand deposits (as the real value of those deposits declines), but they lose even more to the people who are indebted to the bank. In this way, the inflation imposes a "private tax" (or wealth redistribution) on holders of money and monetary assets.

The second biggest item of money in the United States is currency and coins issued by the government or the Federal Reserve banks. Federal Reserve money is a debt of the Federal Reserve banks. An inflation imposes a loss on holders of this money. The gains of the Federal Reserve banks are distributed to those who owe them money (their monetary debtors). The primary debtor of the Reserve banks is the U. S. government, for the Reserve banks hold primarily U. S. government bonds.

Inflation imposes a tax on money holders in proportion to the amount of money (not general wealth) that they hold, with the gains going to those whose debts constitute that money. A major beneficiary of unanticipated inflation, therefore, is the government, since it is typically a net monetary debtor to the rest of the community. It gains from its monetary liabilities, which serve as money, and also from its monetary debts (bonds and notes), which are held by the public.

What is meant by saying that the "government" gains wealth? The government is not *a* person; everyone is somehow involved. Strictly speaking, the government is part of the wealth structure of every person. People gain from inflation to the extent that their taxes are smaller and that they are beneficiaries of however the government uses the increase

---

[7] A typical balance sheet is presented in the table below. Almost all of its assets are monetary. These exceed its monetary liabilities by $5,838,000. If the price level were to double, the bank would lose half the real value of that net monetary credit. *Every* bank is a net monetary creditor.

City National Bank (December 31, 1970)

Assets	$ (000)	
Cash and due from banks	$ 17,360	
U. S. government bonds	15,957	
State and municipal banks	7,259	Monetary Assets = $96,278
Private bonds and notes	55,290	
Federal Reserve bank stock	412	
Bank premises and equipment	6,641	
	$102,919	
Liabilities	$ (000)	
Deposits	$ 88,240	Monetary Liabilities = $90,440
Other liabilities	2,200	
	$ 90,440	
Ownership-Equity	$ (000)	
Capital stock	$ 3,820	
Surplus	8,659	
	$102,919	

in its wealth. Even though no one may include his latent tax obligations in a balance sheet of his wealth, an inflation reduces the "real" value of the amount of future taxes that must be collected to pay interest on existing bonds; it benefits payers of explicit, conventional taxes.

General Applications and Illustrations of Inflation-Induced Wealth Redistribution

Many monetary assets (and liabilities) consist of more than money. Some are bonds, notes, accounts receivable, life-insurance policies, retirement pensions, and long-term leases. Substantial evidence has been collected from inflation of the past fifty years in the United States to establish that the inflations were unanticipated or incompletely anticipated, so that a transfer of wealth occurred from net monetary creditors to net monetary debtors. Strong evidence is provided by the experience of business firms whose stocks are owned by the public. Annual balance-sheet reports show which firms are net monetary creditors and which are net monetary debtors. The former have a larger total of cash and accounts receivable than they owe in accounts payable and bonds (to mention only the major monetary assets and liabilities), while the latter have the opposite balance.[8]

During an inflation, as well as any other time, a host of factors affect the fortunes of every business firm—new products, changes in demands, new management, fires, inventions, etc. Nevertheless, one steady differentiating factor contributing to a gain for all the net-monetary-debtor firms is the wealth-redistribution process just outlined. On the average, the price of a share of common stock (share of ownership in the equity of the corporation) in firms that are net monetary debtors should rise *relatively* to those of net monetary creditors during unanticipated or incompletely anticipated inflations.

---

[8] An example of a net monetary debtor is Reynolds Metals Corporation. As of December 31, 1970, it possessed monetary assets totaling about $270 million (cash, government securities and loans to others, and accounts receivables); and it owed in monetary liabilities about $1,131 million (bonds, preferred stocks, and notes and accounts payable). On net, Reynolds was a net monetary debtor to the extent of $861 millions. With 16.6 millions shares of common stock outstanding, each one bore a net monetary debt of about $85. You could buy a share of common stock at that time for about $25, becoming a net monetary debtor to the extent of about $60, over twice your equity. In effect, you had claims to about $110 of real nonmonetary goods, offset in part by the monetary debt of $85, leaving you an equity of $25. It is as if you had bought a $110 good by paying $25 down and borrowing the remaining $85. If the price level rises 10 percent, your equity would increase by $11, which is a 44 percent increase relative to your $25 equity. Thus a 10 percent rise in the general price level would result in your wealth increasing by 44 percent, giving you a net gain in real wealth of 35 percent (the net gain of 44 percent in monetary terms adjusted for the rise in the price level). Inflation would increase your real wealth if you held Reynolds common stock *unless* other people had anticipated the inflation gain and had already bid up the price of Reynolds common stock—in which case you would neither gain nor lose if the inflation did occur.

An example of a net monetary creditor is Filtrol Corporation, which on December 31, 1970, was a net monetary creditor to the extent of $22 millions ($24 millions in monetary assets minus $2 millions in monetary debts). With 2.2 millions common shares outstanding, this is $8.5 a share, one-third of the $25 price of the common stock. In effect the owners had paid $25 for $16.5 of real goods and $8.5 of monetary assets (equivalent to cash). In the event of an inflation, only the $16.5 in goods would increase in value, giving one a smaller percentage increase in his $25 equity. An unanticipated inflation would hurt the stockholders of Filtrol. If the inflation were correctly anticipated, then the stock price of Filtrol would be lower initially and one who bought after the inflation was anticipated would not lose from the inflation.

Since almost half of the business firms on the major stock exchanges are net monetary creditors while the other half are net monetary debtors, we can test for that wealth-transfer effect. Data of stock prices and assets and liabilities for thousands of firms over the period 1914–52 have been collected and bear out the analysis. Figure 33–3 presents the evidence. In every instance, net monetary debtors did better than net monetary creditors, as can be seen in the upper portion of that figure. The opposite effect is observed during deflations. Finally, as is implied by economic theory, during the episodes of stable prices there was no significant difference between the two classes.

The distinction between unanticipated and anticipated inflation can now be made clear. Anticipated inflations are those in which the rise in prices is foreseen, so that borrowers and lenders will have made loans with sufficient adjustments in interest rates,

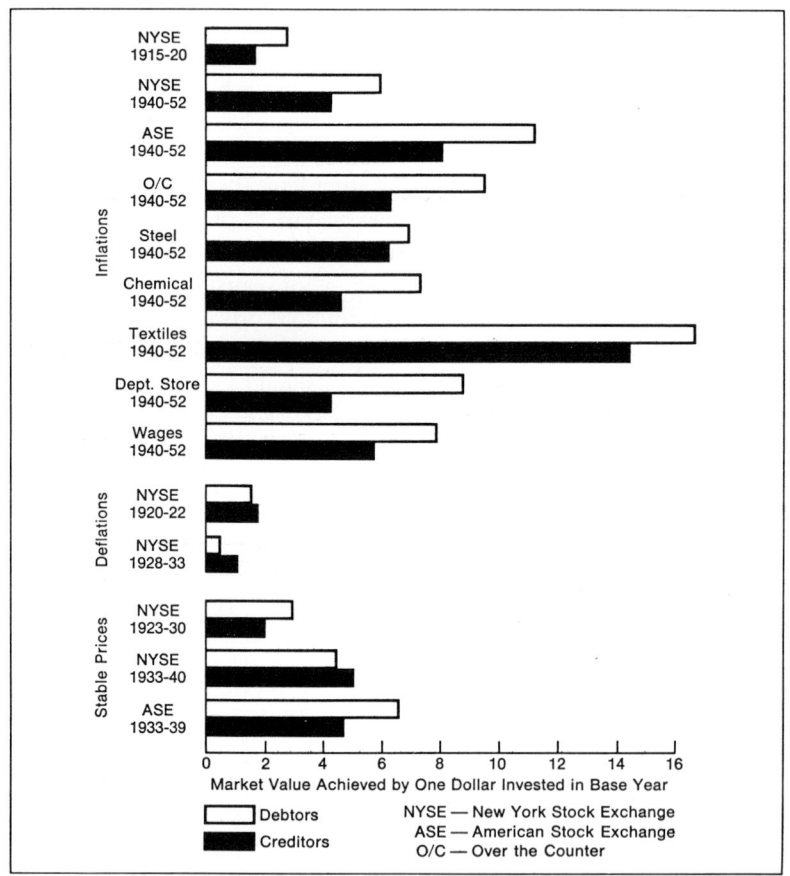

FIGURE 33–3. Effect of Inflation on Market Value of Equity for Net Monetary Debtor and Creditor Business Firms

During every inflation, net monetary debtors experienced an increase in the value of their equity more than did net monetary creditors. During deflations, the opposite effect occurred. During periods of stable prices, no dominance by either debtors or creditors was evident. Source: A. Alchian and R. Kessel, "Redistribution of Wealth through Inflation," *Science,* Vol. 130, No. 3375 (September 4, 1959), p. 538.

or amount to be repaid, to allow for the depreciation in the value of the unit of money. Unanticipated inflations are those not perfectly foreseen and for which such advance adjustments were not made. If net real assets exceed equity, an unanticipated inflation will increase equity more than in proportion to the rise in the price level, because net real assets can exceed equity only if net monetary assets are *negative*—which is to say that the monetary liabilities exceed the monetary assets. A rise in prices will reduce the "real" or "price-level-adjusted" value of one's liabilities. The principle can be summarized: an unanticipated inflation transfers wealth from net monetary creditors to net monetary debtors. A person will gain wealth (in price-level-adjusted units) from unanticipated inflation if he is a net monetary debtor and will lose if he is a net monetary creditor. We explore the distinction between unanticipated and anticipated more fully a bit later.

The Wage-Lag Doctrine: An Exercise in Debunking

One of the most common fallacies about inflation is that wage rates typically, if not always, lag behind prices. Exhaustive examination of available historical evidence gives it no support. During some inflations there was indeed a fall in "real" wages (money wages adjusted for price-level changes), but there were also some in which real wages rose.

What explains the persistent, erroneous belief that wages lag behind prices during inflations? First, anyone whose wages do not rise as much as other people's—whatever the reason—will seek some scapegoat. If there is concurrently an inflation, there is the excuse. (During that same time, people whose wages are rising more rapidly will attribute the rise not to inflation but to their own superiority.)

Second, everyone—whether he is selling labor, pencils, or automobiles—will notice that the price of what he sells lags behind the level of other prices most of the time. His prices change sporadically, whereas the *average* of all other prices, being an average of a host of sporadically changing prices, will change more smoothly and steadily. Although his price is not rising, the average is rising. Of course, at the moment his is adjusted, it "leads" the general rise. The *average* of actual wages does *not* lag behind the average of all prices.

Third, inflations often occur when governments shift demand—for example, from peacetime goods to armaments or from consumer goods to space vehicles. The shift in demand toward certain goods increases prices and wages of those goods (armaments and wages of armament workers) relative to other prices and wages. These are the normal responses to shifts in relative demands. Yet, if demand shifts are accompanied by the creation of money, inflation also will occur. As demand shifts away from retail clerks, teachers, etc., to welders, machinists, and associated armament producers, it is easy to see why the relative decline in wages of teachers could be considered a result of inflation rather than of the revised demand. The government, during the last two world wars, accomplished that revision in demand by creating new money to spend for the newly desired goods.

Fourth, although wage rates in a given job may not change much, workers will change jobs in response to revised demands. Even if there were no change in wage rates in each job, relocation of employees from lower- to higher-paying jobs would mean an increase in *realized* wages. Concentration of attention on particular wage rates rather than the earning of employees can mislead one into thinking wages lag behind prices.

Fifth, because wages are paid for production of goods, which are sold later, it is often believed that a rise in the demand for some good will affect the wages of the producers only after the price of the product has increased. This error is based on the assumption that the economy is a simple sequence of production steps from raw materials to final products. In fact, some goods are inputs for earlier and for later stages, with feedbacks so that one cannot tell whether some good is at an earlier or later stage in a production process. Furthermore, even in a simple one-directional flow of services, the price response is not necessarily from consumer goods to labor-input wages. If you recall the example of the rise of the price of meat to consumers in response to demand increases (in Chapter 6), you will remember that a demand increase does not necessarily invoke a series of price rises starting at the *consumers'* end of the distribution process.

Sixth, the wage-lag belief has been fostered in part by fallacious economic reasoning. "Inflation increases the resources at the command of the government or the agency creating the new money; it follows that there is less left for the remaining segments of the economy. But the remaining segments of the economy also are experiencing increases of money incomes. If they are to consume less, and they must since there is less for them, the prices at which they buy must rise relative to their incomes. This means a decrease in the ratio of their money incomes relative to the cost of living." Where is the flaw in this analysis? It ignores the *wealth* transfer. Net monetary creditors will lose *wealth* and will consume less; their wage *incomes* do not lag. For example, if a thief stole half the wealth of the public, the public would have to consume less. But this would not mean that its income from wages must fall relative to prices of goods it buys. Instead, it means solely that their wealth has decreased. The wealth owned by the net monetary creditors falls relative to the total wealth of the community. Inflation is a wealth transfer from monetary asset holders, *not* a tax on wage income. Money-wage incomes rise with the price level. Holders of monetary assets issued by the government (currency and government bonds) lose wealth to the government.

An adjunct of the inflation wage-lag doctrine is the "forced-savings" doctrine. This widely asserted doctrine contends that the "lost income" from the alleged "wage lag" goes to profit receivers in businesses, who invest it in new equipment. People have gone so far as to contend that it brought about the industrial revolution of Western Europe. During World Wars I and II this doctrine served as a justification for special taxes on business profits, which allegedly were unwarranted gains from "forced savings" imposed on employees by a lag of wages behind prices. Yet, neither economic analysis nor empirical evidence supports such a notion. On the contrary, it is denied by both.

16, 17, 18, 19

The Causes of Inflation

Deliberately, the causes of inflation have been ignored in order to isolate the effects. Examination of the "causes" can center on the following: (1) the *fact* of an increase in the supply of money relative to demand; (2) an explanation of the *ways* in which the quantity of money was increased relative to other economic goods, or the demand for it reduced; (3) an explanation of *why* the quantity of money was increased or why the demand for it was reduced. Each qualifies as an answer to a reasonable interpretation of the "cause" of inflation. We shall discuss each.

Inflation occurs because the supply of money increases *relative* to the amount of money that people want to hold, given their existing wealth and income. If each of us awoke and found we had twice as much money as on the previous day and no less of any other goods or services, we would prefer to spend some of the money and reduce the proportion of our wealth in money. But not *everyone* can reduce his holdings of money by spending it, since that merely transfers it from person to person. As a result, the increased desire for other goods relative to money constitutes an increase in demand for other goods; and their prices are driven up. Everyone finds himself getting wealthier in dollar terms, some at a faster rate than others (depending upon net-monetary-asset status). Prices will rise until every person's wealth and income is so large that he will *want* to hold as much money as he *has*. On the average, people will hold bank balances and pocket money aggregating to twice the amount formerly held, while prices, wealth, and income are about twice as high.

Very often it is not the quantity of money that changes but the physical stock of other goods. In a predominantly agricultural society, if the annual harvest is unusually small, prices of goods will be higher than usual. A historically significant case occurred during the Black Death in England in the fourteenth century. The plague killed a substantial fraction of the population, with no corresponding decrease in money. Wage rates rose spectacularly; the prices of other goods also rose, but not nearly so much, since their supply had not decreased as much relative to money. Money wages rose more than the price level, so that the survivors experienced a substantial increase in real income. This change in wages relative to other prices was a result of the change in relative amounts of labor and other goods—not of the inflation.

In the first of the two preceding examples, the population experienced a *decrease* of real wealth and income because it had a smaller agricultural crop to eat. It then experienced an inflation. Which is the cause? Which the effect? Common sense would suggest that the reduced crop (without a corresponding decline in money) induced the inflation of prices. But exactly this kind of situation has been carelessly called an example of an *inflation's* effect in reducing the real income of the community. In the other example, the inflation associated with the decrease in population relative to the money stock was accompanied by a *rise* in living standards for the survivors. This has misled some people to deduce that inflation leads to increases in wealth.

Aside from changes in the stock of nonmoney goods, which change the demand for money, the nominal quantity of money may change. But why would the quantity of money increase? If the money system enables people to increase the quantity of money by printing more or by issuing short-weighted gold and silver coins, then the temptation to print and issue "light-weight" money is overwhelmingly strong. The government authorities, regardless of the form of the government, under pressures from various people, find it expedient to print money, rather than levy *explicit* taxes, to exert claims to a greater share of the wealth in the nation. This may be done to prosecute a war; to reach the moon; to give aid to the poorer people, to farmers, to businessmen, to education; to prevent or reduce unemployment; or to aid the politically powerful people directly.

If the government spends more than it receives from taxes or loans from the public, it can finance the remainder of its deficit by printing new money. Some governments simply start the printing presses, while others use more complicated procedures. In the United States, the federal government may "persuade" the Federal Reserve banks to buy U. S. bonds. According to current law, a Federal Reserve bank can print new money or "reserves" if it has an equivalent of U. S. bonds in its possession as "backing" for that new money. Bluntly put, this is known as monetizing the public debt; it is a roundabout way of creating money, but the result is the same. New money is created by a "central bank" instead of by the government's treasury itself. Thus deficit financing, *if* it is accompanied by money creation, becomes a source of inflation.

Currently, in every country experiencing substantial inflation, the cause is the government's creation of new money to finance its activities—which in no way implies that the government should not be undertaking those activities or engaging in inflationary finance.⁹ That depends upon the alternatives.

In sum, one thing is true beyond doubt. Never has an inflation happened without an increase in the money stock relative to other goods, and never has such an increase in the money supply happened without an inflation. No other factor is so associated with inflation. Everything else alleged to result in inflation at one time or another has at other times not yielded inflation. It is the disproportionate growth in the money supply that is the necessary and sufficient condition.

You will at one time or another undoubtedly hear that foreign aid, agricultural-support programs, social security, and our space, military, education, or unemployment-relief programs are inflationary. All of these activities involve expenditures. Whether or not they will "cause" inflation depends upon how they are financed, in particular whether or not it is done by increasing the quantity of money. Whether the program itself or the increase in the quantity of money with which the program is financed is to be called the cause of the inflation depends upon how one chooses to construe the meaning of "cause."

Especially current in public discussion is the contention that action by the government to maintain full employment is resulting in a "wage-push" or "administered" price inflation. The argument contends that some wages and prices are arbitrarily increased because of some "market power" in the hands of "key" people and that all other people must adjust to these key or "bellwether" prices. Steel prices or union wage rates are often cited as examples. In fact and in theory, there are no key commodities to whose prices the prices of other goods adjust. It is easy to *say* that if the price of steel or wages of some group increase, then other prices must rise to reflect the cost of these components. However, even though an imposed rise in the price of steel will raise the costs of products using steel, it will also reduce the rate of output. Resources will be released to other goods, whose prices will fall as their supply is increased. The *average* price of all output remains unchanged. No inflation occurs; there is only a rise in the price of some goods and a fall in others. However, inflation *will* occur *if the released (unemployed) resources consequent to the higher imposed price are able to induce the community to engage in a policy of inflation by increasing the quantity of money*. The unemployed resources might succeed in persuading the political authorities to create new money with which to increase the demand for the products of the unemployed in their old jobs. (We examine this more in the next chapter.) The way in which the new money is spent will affect relative prices momentarily, but soon the increased quantity of money will raise all prices. Prices will rise to the former levels they had *relative* to the prices of the good whose prices were arbitrarily raised. This inflation restores the former relative price structure.

If the bulk of newly created money is first spent for the particular commodity whose price was arbitrarily raised, there is a transient increase in the relative demand for "steel" and then an inflation.

The causing of inflation by the increase in the quantity of money must be kept distinct from the *motivation* for the increased quantity of money. In our example, the motive was to permit an increase in demand for particular goods to restore employment to certain resources in their *former* activities at the new higher imposed prices. If the government keeps its eye on the rate of unemployment in the steel industry, it is easy to see that steel could be called a "key" industry. If the government keeps its eye on some

---

⁹ With the exception of the massive gold and silver discoveries, history records no major inflations in the absence of money creation by governments.

other industry or block of employees, they, too, could be called the "key" group—regardless of whether they be teachers, janitors, or actors.

Personal Protection from Inflation

If you want to bet that inflation will occur and want to gain from it, be a net monetary debtor. If you want to gamble that there will be deflation, then be a net monetary creditor. But if you want to avoid that gamble, be a net monetary "neutral." One relatively easy way to do this is by appropriate investment in common stock. The ownership of common stock in a corporation also affects one's monetary wealth structure. If the corporation in which common stock is purchased is a net monetary debtor, then the stockholder is a monetary debtor. For example, a purchase of one share of Reynolds Metals would increase one's monetary indebtedness by about $85 (see footnote 8). On the other hand, a purchase of common stock in Filtrol Corporation would change his monetary-debtor status toward a net monetary neutral or creditor by $8.5. Appropriate purchase of common stocks can alter substantially one's net-monetary asset or liability status.

Remember, however, no one common stock will move along exactly with the price level. But a person can own a mixture of goods or stocks, so that on the average the gains and losses come closer to balancing. This averaging of risks explains part of the advantage of the corporate form of ownership. A person distributing his wealth among several corporations in various lines of production can achieve a relatively well-balanced portfolio of risks against the wealth redistribution from monetary creditors to debtors in unanticipated inflation.

Inflation Does Not Destroy the Value of Savings

A common erroneous allegation is that inflation destroys the incentive to save by destroying the value of savings. The error in this arises from a confusion between savings (increases in wealth by not consuming income) and the form in which one holds his wealth. Wealth (past savings) held as nonmonetary assets is not transferred away by inflation. Only wealth held as monetary assets is transferred by higher prices to the debtor of that monetary asset. The classic example of the transfer of wealth from savers is the case in which the saver holds his wealth in the form of monetary assets—bonds, pensions, and life insurance, which are almost always claims to *fixed amounts* of money in the future. However, there is no reason why a person cannot hold his wealth in nonmonetary form, by investing in common stocks with a neutral net monetary status, investing in "variable annuity" pensions that are not claims to fixed amounts of money but instead are claims to equities.

Quantity of Money and Inflation: Some Historical Episodes

In measuring the amount of inflation, we can use either the rate of inflation (some percentage rate of rise of prices per month) or the rise over some long episode. In the first case a low rate may continue for a long period and thereby yield a large change over several years. Or a high rate may last for only a few months. In some countries inflations have continued at a rate of only a few percent a month for several decades. In other countries there have been short, spectacular inflations.

Explosive inflations have occurred during catastrophes such as invasions or revolutions. During such events normal productive activity is obstructed; also, the government finds its normal administrative taxing power diminished. Sometimes a new government has seized power and has not arranged its administrative procedures. Creating more money remains as one easy means of financing government activity.

The proposition that larger quantities of money, relative to other goods, implies inflation does not say that a 1 percent increase in the stock of money relative to goods will increase the price level 1 percent. Many factors besides a change in the stock of money affect the price level. Changes in demand for money may occur, for example. But changes in other factors are rarely big enough to induce a change in the price level of more than a few percent. Exactly how much change in money stocks must occur in, say, one month or six months in order to raise prices in general is not specifiable; however, in almost every instance of a change of money of, say, 5 percent within a month, a change in the price level is detectable within six months. And certainly a 20 or 50 percent increase within a year will be accompanied by a rise in the price level of similar magnitude. Figure 33–4 shows the correlation between the average annual rate of increase in the quantity of money and in prices for each of sixty-five countries for the period 1948–65. The relationship is striking. The picture would be even more spectacular

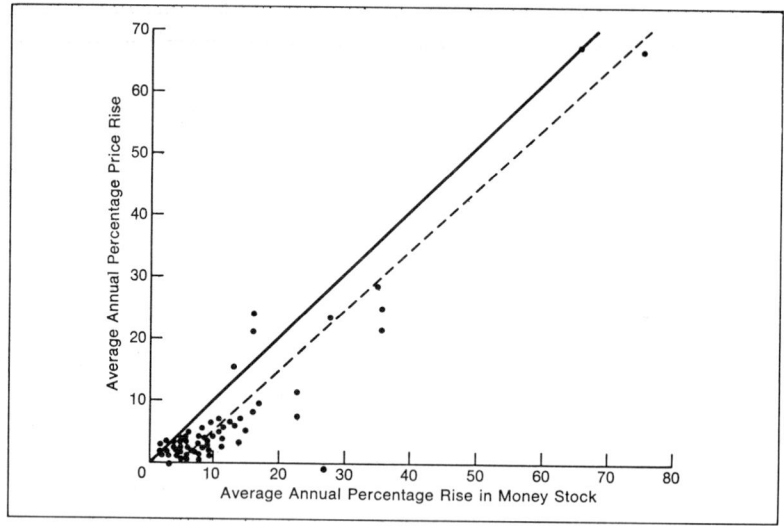

FIGURE 33–4. Money-Supply Increase and Price-Level Rise (Average Annual Percentage) for Sixty-Four Countries, 1948–65

The general correlation between increases in money and the rise in the price level is vividly illustrated by this chart. The straight-dashed slanting line is the line of equal proportional changes in prices and quantity of money after allowance for a 4 percent annual growth of physical stock of goods. (Notice the unbelievable reported price fall for one country—Tunisia—despite a 28 percent per year increase of money. This is probably an index based on "legal" controlled prices only.) Source: *International Financial Statistics,* 1963–64 Supplement, International Monetary Fund, 1966.

and impressive if it also showed experiences from extreme inflations such as occurred in Germany in 1923, when prices rose by a factor of about 100 billion in one year, while the amount of money increased by a factor of 10 billion. This is equivalent to a doubling of prices every two weeks. Similar episodes occurred in Greece in 1944, in Poland in 1923, in Russia in 1921–23, and in Hungary in 1923 and again in 1946, to mention only a few. The Hungarian inflation of 1946 saw prices doubling on the average every two or three days to a factor of about 10 with 26 zeros after it, in about one year. Plotting these experiences would require an enormous graph, but, as expected, the plotted points would be in the far upper right.[10]

Anticipated Inflation

Each person's demand for money balances, given his wealth and income, depends upon his beliefs about future prices. If he expects prices to be higher tomorrow, he will seek to spend more of his money today. His demand to hold money will fall. (If he expects prices to *fall* tomorrow, his demand for money will increase; he will defer spending.) Formerly, with anticipations of stable prices, the cost of holding money was the forsaken use derivable from other goods that could have been owned instead. Now, with money *known in advance* to be depreciating in value (i.e., more expensive to hold), people will strive to hold fewer dollars in order to avoid some of those increased costs, just as they would with any good that has become more expensive to hold. Prices will rise as people attempt to get into goods and out of so much money before prices rise. But this attempt makes prices jump now.

People will not abandon the use of money, for that would impose an even greater cost than the loss from holding some of the deteriorating money. The advantages from holding and using money as a medium of exchange are so great that people will continue to use some money even though they expect the price level to rise at, say, a rate of 25 percent per week (equal to a value loss of 20 percent per week).[11] Prices will rise higher than in proportion to the increase in nominal money. This is often expressed as a reduction in the *real* stock of money—despite any increasing nominal amount of money. This fall in the real value of money balances is a result of the efforts of people to economize on the use of resources that have become dearer to hold.[12]

One means of economizing on the use of money is to hold a smaller proportion of one's wealth as money, with the attendant reduced convenience of using the market. Specialization is facilitated by efficient, low-cost markets; and anticipated inflation increases the costs of using the market as people resort to shorter intervals between purchases and payments. Shopping costs and the time devoted to it increase. People will

---

[10] Inspection of Figure 33–4 shows that, on the average, prices do not rise in proportion to the increase in the amount of money. If they did, the points would cluster around a 45-degree line out of the lower left corner. Instead, most points lie below it. If, however, we experience a growth of population and nonmoney goods of about 3 or 4 percent a year, the price level will rise about 3 or 4 percent a year less than the rate of change in the amount of money. This implies that the points should lie around the dashed line drawn on the figure, and they do.

[11] Twenty-five percent per week would raise prices by a factor of about 100,000 in one year.

[12] People will want to hold an amount of money equal to say, four weeks' income rather than five. If they try to do so, prices will rise by 25 percent so that at the higher incomes the old stock of money now matches only four weeks' instead of five weeks' income.

shift more to barter and to nonmarket arrangements; therefore, the anticipated inflation will result in reduced output consequent to less specialization. The higher costs of using the market with a smaller amount of "real" money are willingly borne in order to avoid the still higher costs of holding larger amounts of deteriorating money. In sum, *anticipated* inflation, depending upon its rate, imposes a cost in the form of a "destruction" of part of the money capital of the community. An analogy is illuminating. A tax on windows would collect wealth for the taxing agency, but at the cost of people's shifting to houses with smaller or fewer windows; thus, the cost of the tax is not merely the pecuniary wealth transferred to the taxing agency but also the reduced level of well-ventilated or -lighted houses. And so it is with anticipated inflation. Aside from the wealth transfer, real wealth and income are reduced by the higher costs of using money in the money-exchange system.

The greater inconveniences are superficially ascribed to a "shortage" of money. Yet, as we have seen, the reduced amount of "real" money is the result of each person's response to more costly money. The way to reduce that cost is to stop the inflation and thus remove the anticipation of further inflation. Strangely enough, some people contend that the way to alleviate the "shortage" of money is to print money even more rapidly—which would, of course, increase the rate of anticipated inflation and increase the shortage even more. The way to eliminate the shortage of money is to stop increasing the nominal amount of money so as to eliminate or reduce the anticipations of inflation—a solution that is paradoxical only to those who forget the difference between relative and absolute amounts of money (or, in other words, real and nominal amounts of money).

Once people begin to suspect a change from relatively stable price levels to rising price levels consequent to an impending expansionary monetary policy, anticipated inflation will set in. Prices will immediately rise in anticipation of the coming inflation.

The rise in prices and in nominal (though not necessarily in real) interest rates will provoke much public discussion, complaint, and search for a scapegoat. (See page 468 for why nominal interest rates will rise.) Politicians blame greedy labor unions and business leaders, who in turn will blame it on higher costs (remember pages 95–99 ?). The Federal Reserve Board "can," in a technical sense, stop the inflation by simply not letting the money stock grow disproportionately rapidly. But to do so would put the Fed up against the Congress and Treasury and President, all of whom "could" have avoided the inflation if they had reduced spending or raised taxes to avoid a deficit or if they had offered high enough interest on the new bonds to induce savers to buy them and thus eliminate the political necessity of the Fed's financing the deficit by buying the bonds with new money. The problem is simple technically but not politically.

The episode of 1970 is instructive. From 1962 to 1969, an increasing rate of expansion of the money supply, exceeding the growth in per capita output, resulted in prices rising as much as 6 percent per year by 1969. The only way to stop that price rise was to curtail the money-stock growth for a sufficiently long time. What is sufficiently long? Long enough to convince people that the lower growth rate of the money stock would *persist*. And that belief depends upon the strength of people's anticipations (based on past experience) about the surety of the government's intentions and future performance. It may take a couple of years to yield convincing evidence that the government will not continue its inflationary monetary increases.

In the meantime, as a result of reduction in the rate of growth of the money stock, demand for services and goods at existing prices will fall with a transitional reduction in employment and output, as in 1970. Immediately the cries for alleviatory, demand-increasing action—almost invariably involving a restoration of the greater rate of expansion of the money stock—may thwart the resolve to stop the inflation. If the government undertakes to live up to prior assurances that it will prevent any *transitional* recession or pockets of unemployment in various areas, crafts, or industries, it has no alternative but to resume rapid inflation of the money stock. Do not confuse this proposition with a similar, but false, proposition that inflation is necessary for high employment. It is not: full employment can and does occur without inflation. The assurance of continued full employment at all times or with little lag, *at whatever wages or prices people want* or for whatever reason unemployment occurs, does imply a policy of monetary expansion and inflation. It is the strength of the assurance that no recession or unemployment will be tolerated that leads to an inflationary monetary policy. It is not the general case that a high average rate of employment requires inflation.

28, 29

Price Controls versus Open Inflation

An almost visceral political response to inflation is the imposition of wage and price controls (recently being called euphemistically an "income policy"). Price increases are called "excessive and unjustified." We hardly need say that "excessive" and "unjustified" are unhelpful adjectives. Their use may stem from the mistaken belief that inflation is caused by greedy businessmen and labor unions seeking to get higher prices and wages. The proposed controls are often clothed under the sham of "voluntary" controls.

Price controls, in so far as they have effect, destroy some of the value of money—and do so in two ways.

1. It is a delusion to think that controlled prices below those that would exist in open markets have the same significance and influence as uncontrolled prices. Controlled prices are not prices at which people can buy as much as they demand at those prices. The resulting inevitable shortages are reductions in the power of money to command goods in exchange. Other sources of exchange power must be used in an effort to compensate for the reduced exchange value of a dollar: status, personal characteristics, standing-in-line, obsequiousness, political power are examples—as explained earlier in Chapter 9.

2. Market prices must be allowed to change in response to market demand and supply forces if they are to direct and induce people to make revised productive and allocative decisions. If prices are restricted from doing so, the market price system loses power as an economical transmitter of information about relative values of resources and goods to different people in different uses. Other types of communication and evaluation will be emphasized—political and personal influence, for example. Less economical means of communication and exchange are used; consumers perform more distribution and transportation services themselves. Specialization is reduced and total output thereby reduced. The usefulness of both money and market prices as institutions for communication and control is reduced because they are, in part, outlawed.

The irony is that price controls which were presumed to preserve the value of the dollar in fact reduce the value of the dollar by making the dollar price less relevant for exchange *and* also reduce the roles of market prices and money as institutions in the economy. Which is better for determining the extent of trade, allocation, and specialization of production: a low but less influential price, or a higher but more powerful price? The fact is that price controls, rather than protecting the dollar, reduce the exchange value of a unit of money, increase the role of other factors in allocation decisions, and reduce the role of market prices in the economy. Open inflation does only the first; while it reveals reduced exchange value of an individual unit of money, it does not at the same time reduce the power of money and market prices in the economy.

In Germany, three years after World War II, price controls were removed; and the economy responded with great increases in production. Japan and Italy had similar experiences. These increases could not be attributed to recovery from war damage, but instead were sufficiently isolated and abrupt to reveal how severely market-price constraints reduce the economic efficiency of the market as an informative, allocative, incentive system.

Whatever may be our preferences, it is a fact that in all countries inflation is accompanied by political control of wages and prices. We know of few cases in which substantial rates (say, over 10 percent in one year) of inflation have been allowed without imposing price and wage controls. To judge by the relative frequency of "suppressed or distorted" inflation, we have to conclude that most countries "prefer" political control of wages and prices to open inflation.

We conjecture that those who believe they can exercise a disproportionate extent of political power will clamor for price controls. They expect their greater political power will more than offset their loss of competitive market power. Many economists who propose price controls find themselves (not unexpectedly) employed as price controllers. Many politicians who disapprove of relative competitive power of unions or other groups propose price controls to increase the influence of their political status. Again, we warn, this should not be taken as condemnation. Who is to say what is the best form of competitive power for allocating resources and goods? That the various forms operate differently with different effects on total productive potential does not prove one of them necessarily the desirable one, whatever may be your own preferences.

The Case for, and Against, Anti-Inflation "Guidelines"

Price and wage guidelines were invoked by the Kennedy, Johnson, and Nixon Administrations. The guidelines say people should ask only for wages or prices that would mean no inflation. If productivity of inputs in real terms is increasing at the rate of 3.2 percent per year, then input prices could rise 3.2 percent per year on the average without increasing the costs of final output.

We have seen that a necessary and sufficient condition for inflation to occur is an increase in the quantity of money relative to the amount demanded—which, at existing prices, is correlated with the supply of other goods. If the supply of money does not increase, higher prices will not be sustainable with the same rate of sales. Hence, it would be unnecessary to exhort people not to raise prices. Price raisers would only find themselves priced out of the market and forced to lower prices. Why bother to "jawbone" them if the inexorable forces of demand make higher prices nonsustainable? On the other hand, if the stock of money does increase, all the talk in the world will not stop prices from rising. Why then all the desire for "guidelines" about noninflationary price increases? There is a good reason! To see it, we must (1) distinguish between anticipated and unanticipated inflation, (2) recognize the power of a monetary authority to determine the quantity of money, and (3) assume that there is a government policy of sustaining full employment regardless of any resultant rate of inflation.

Suppose some members of the society agree to long-term contracts, say, labor union wage contracts for the next three years. Suppose further that these employees and employers in anticipation of inflation during those future years now agree to *future* wages that increase by an agreed-on anticipated rate of inflation. Assume also that later changes in these contract prices are difficult to negotiate. A severe disappointment in sales would be required to induce an attempt to reduce them, a lengthy process that might take six months to a year. It would take time to convince people that the anticipated inflation had not *and* is not going to occur. Under these conditions, it is easy to see why the monetary authorities will have to choose between (a) increasing the quantity of money enough to sustain those high, previously contracted prices at full employment and (b) failing to increase the money-supply to sustain full employment at those excessively high prices. The monetary authorities are in a bind. If people anticipate there will be an inflation and if the monetary authorities are prepared to increase the quantity of money sufficiently to validate those expectations and the agreed-upon future prices, then the inflation will occur and the anticipations will have been validated. With a commitment always to increase the money supply sufficiently to avoid increase in unemployment, there is no way to stop that inflation from occurring—unless the *future prices* contracted for can be kept at present levels. This requires convincing people that there will be no future inflation, making them anticipate that negotiation of high future-price commitments will entail a consequent rise in unemployment. They must be convinced that the government will not increase the money supply sufficiently to permit the anticipated inflation under which high future-price commitments would be consistent with full employment.

What do announced guidelines try to do? They try to convince people that the future price level which "really" will exist will be little, if at all, higher than the present. Note carefully that the guidelines are guidelines for *future* prices, agreed to now, not for present prices of present goods and services. It is too late to do anything about *present* full employment prices.

It is the *future* contracted prices that are, it is hoped, being influenced. *If* the public could be convinced the guidelines are really valid predictions of the full-employment future prices, then long-term contract prices would not be set so high and the consequent necessity of increasing the money supply in order to make those future prices full-employment prices can be avoided.

Guidelines are essentially announcements of the degree of inflation that the monetary and government authorities are prepared to permit—if you are willing to believe their word. And that is the catch. The government may of course announce guidelines indicating what prices would be noninflationary in the future. But if people did believe them, what assurance would there be that in fact there would be no inflation and therefore that contracts for future wages could be made on that basis? Regrettably, not much! The record is notable for the unreliability of such pronouncements. Every government has inflated the money stock for reasons in addition to sustaining full employment demand at higher prices.

The money supply is essentially controlled by the Federal Reserve authorities, who are subject to severe political pressures from Congress and the President, who in turn are subject to forces of the public who want more spending and less taxing. It is easy to see why money-supply increases at inflationary rates are commonplace. (Remember, inflation is a tax on money, and it also taxes away some real value of the public's holdings of government bonds. Also, by raising nominal incomes, inflation puts people in higher income tax brackets without new tax legislation.) Finally, once anticipations of inflation are verified (as they have been in the last decade in the U. S.), it is not easy to change people's beliefs by saying one thing while continuing to do another, by announcing noninflationary "guidelines" while holding to a money-supply policy of sustaining full employment at whatever price commitments have been made. You have only to look at the complaints about sacrificing employment to stop inflation anticipation in 1970 to see how hard it is politically to take the steps that will convince people that future contract prices should not be increased because in fact there will be no future inflation.

In sum, *if* (a) guidelines were to contribute to convincing people not to make long-term contracts with *future* prices higher than would occur simply for reasons of increased productivity and *if* (b) governments did not renege on their implicit promise not to inflate the money stock to finance government expenditures greater than tax collections, then they would contribute to reducing the extent of future inflation. Those are very substantial "ifs."

Anti-Inflation Monetary Reforms

One other form of fighting inflation is sometimes observed. Some countries have abandoned repressed inflation because it heavily impairs productive and allocative efficiency; often they have turned to "monetary reform" prior to removing price and wage controls. The monetary reform consists of confiscating much of the public's money and leaving only enough so that prices will not rise once wage and price controls are lifted. Usually paper money and bank accounts are heavily "taxed" and the proceeds simply canceled. Obviously, those who hold more of their wealth in monetary forms will suffer the greater loss of wealth. But contrary to an open inflation there will be no transfer of wealth to private net debtors, which may be the reason the monetary reform is used, as it was in Germany (1948), the Confederacy (1864), and Belgium (1949). Whether monetary reforms of this type are desirable (they are certainly not necessary) prior to abandoning wage and price controls is highly debatable, as one can see from the following analysis.

Once the stock of money has increased relative to the stock of goods and services, *nothing* can be done to prevent a wealth transfer—unless everyone happened to be a net monetary neutral, which is certainly not the case. Only four policies are available, once the money stock has increased. (1) Attempts to suppress prices will mean that people can't spend their money and get what they want at freely negotiable prices. Price controls preventing the free negotiation of mutually acceptable prices reduce the rights of people to exchange money for other goods. Money as a medium of exchange loses some of its competitive rationing power; money holders lose "wealth." Other systems of competition will be relied upon more for rationing. (2) If prices are allowed to rise freely, in response to increased money supplies, as in an open inflation, the higher prices will reduce the real wealth value of the money, again imposing the wealth loss on money holders. But the role of exchange competition relative to other forms of competition (political competition) in rationing goods will not be changed. (3) A third alternative is to engage in a monetary reform in which a portion of the money is simply canceled. (4) The fourth alternative is to impose a special tax on nonmoney wealth with which to buy up and cancel some of the money. This would avoid the inflation wealth-loss of money holders. But, then, if this kind of tax could have been imposed, it would probably have been used instead of creating money. History records no instances of a special tax for this purpose.

Thus, whether prices are allowed to rise freely, or are suppressed, or the money supply is arbitrarily cut, money holders lose wealth.

We should remember that almost all taxes involve a redistribution of wealth and that inflation is a tax—on money. Therefore, the redistribution of wealth *per se* does not make an inflation unusual; what makes it unusual is the particular classes between whom wealth is transferred. Most taxes also have an efficiency effect; and inflation, by taxing the medium of exchange raises the costs of exchange with money.

The question of whether inflation is good or bad cannot be answered simply by looking at consequences. Also relevant is the situation that otherwise would have existed without the inflationary method of financing. Since alternatives are idiosyncratic to each situation, they cannot be subjected here to general analysis.

Summary

1 Inflation is a rise in the general level of prices of consumer goods. Measurement difficulties arise because of quality changes, substitutions among consumer goods in response to relative price shifts, ascertainment of actual prices, and determination of unchanged levels of utility at which to compute costs.

2 Effects of inflation should be distinguished from effects of factors causing inflation.

3 Anticipated inflations are those for which people correctly foresee the extent and timing. Incompletely anticipated or unanticipated inflations are those in which the anticipated rate of inflation is less than that which actually occurs. The effects of inflation are different, depending upon whether or not inflations are anticipated.

4 Monetary assets are claims to fixed amounts of money; monetary debts are obligations to pay fixed amounts of money.

5 If one has more monetary debts than monetary assets, he will get a wealth gain from an incompletely anticipated inflation at the expense of net monetary creditors (those who hold more monetary assets than monetary liabilities).

6 Money, being a monetary asset, is taxed by inflation; holders of money lose wealth during an inflation (of any kind—so long as interest is not paid on money) to those whose credit constitutes the money or to those who issue token or fiat money (governments).

7 The government, being a very large net monetary debtor, gains from incompletely anticipated inflation. About half of American business corporations are net monetary debtors and half are net monetary creditors. It cannot therefore be said that businessmen gain from inflation or that they lose.

8 A common fallacy is that wage rates typically, if not always, lag behind consumer goods prices. Extensive evidence lends no support to that proposition, nor does economic theory imply it. The illusion or allegation arises, we conjecture, because (a) specific wages are erroneously compared with averages of consumer goods, (b) demand shifts under circumstances that induce an inflationary policy, (c) job ratings and job changes are ignored, (d) it is erroneously believed that prices of consumer goods always rise before the prices of components, and (e) because of the fallacious belief that if the government gets more of the community's wealth and income by issuing money and raising prices, there must be less left for the community (which is true) and that therefore real wages must have fallen (which is false—the transfer comes from the *wealth* transfer, not from a shift in wages relative to consumers goods).

9   Inflation does *not* reduce the value of saving. It reduces the value of monetary wealth, and savings need not be held as monetary wealth.

10 Inflation occurs because the supply of money increases *relative* to the amount of money that people demand to hold, given their existing wealth and income. The absolute supply may increase or the demand may decrease, possibly because of loss of wealth from plague, drought, or disaster.

11 Causes of inflation usually refer to reasons for an absolute increase in the stock of money which is also an increase relative to existing stocks of physical wealth. Thus the technique of causing an inflation must be kept separate from the motive for using that technique.

12 Inflations are not caused by cost-push or administered prices. Saying so confuses the *motives* for resorting to inflationary increases in the quantity of money with the *increase* in the quantity of money. The former alone will not cause an inflation. The latter will, regardless of the motive for the increase in the stock of money. Every significant inflation (over 10 percent in one year) has been caused by an absolute increase in the quantity of money. Reductions in real wealth are usually of relatively minor significance.

13 If fully anticipated, an inflation avoids the wealth transfer from net monetary creditors to debtors because the interest rate on such debt was fully adjusted to allow for the price level rise. But to the extent an inflation is anticipated, it leads to resource distortion in that people try to reduce the "real" amount of money wealth, giving rise to the phenomenon of a "money shortage" and making exchange more difficult (expensive), thereby sacrificing some of the gains from fuller specialization in production and exchange. This effect does not occur in an open and unanticipated inflation, but the wealth transfer does.

14 Repressing inflation of prices by wage and price controls does not reduce the transfer of wealth from net monetary creditors to debtors, because the exchange value of money is reduced by restricting the *ability or right* to offer it for exchange in the market; open inflation achieves a similar effect by direct increases in prices. Repressing price changes leads to reduced use of the exchange market and to reduced efficiency of market-directed specialization and exchange. Repressed inflation enhances the politically oriented criteria of resource use and allocation.

15 Anti-inflation monetary reforms are confiscation or taxation of money forms of wealth. No transfer of wealth to net monetary debtors is involved, which would occur in an open inflation.

Questions

1   If every price rises, can you be sure there has been an inflation? (Hint: What about changes in quality of goods?)

2   You spend one fourth of your income on good *A* as $1 per unit. And you spend three fourths on *B* at $1 per unit. Now the price of *B* doubles while the price of *A* falls to 80 cents. If these are the only two goods available, has there been a rise in the price level (counting money as a third good)?

3   The reported indices of price levels have an upward bias in their measure of the change in the price level. Thus, a reported rise of 3 percent in one year may be consistent with an actual decrease in the cost of obtaining a former level of utility—not to mention im-

proved quality of goods. Almost all consumer price indices for the U. S. report a rise of about 5 to 10 percent over the price level of about ten years ago.

a. To test your belief in that, would you rather—given an annual income of, say, $5,000—do all your purchasing from a 1960 Sears (or Ward's) mail-order catalogue or from a current one? (If you are tempted to pick the current one because of changes in styles of clothes, suppose the styles were to be altered at no cost.) Which year's catalogue would you choose?

b. Remember, if you choose the current one, you are expressing disbelief in all the measures of the cost of living! How do you reconcile your position—if you choose the current one?

4   You are trying to compute a price index. The price of some good is reported as $100. However, the amount available in the shops is less than the amount demanded.
a. Do you think $100 is a meaningful price?
b. Suppose I offered to sell you a 1964 Cadillac for $1,000 when I have one in stock. I don't have one available now, nor is it likely I shall ever have one. Would you record that price as a relevant price?
c. How does this differ from the preceding case of the $100 good?
d. Suppose that apartments are subjected to rent controls and, at present rents, twice as many people as can get it want more housing at that price. How relevant is the controlled price as a measure of the rental costs?

5   Is a monetary asset one whose price is fixed or is it one that represents a claim to a fixed value in money terms? Give an example of a good that satisfies the latter condition but not the former.

6   a. Is a one-year lease on an apartment a monetary or nonmonetary asset of the tenant?
b. Is it a monetary or a nonmonetary liability of the apartment owner?
c. Is a life-insurance policy a monetary or a nonmonetary asset?

7   Which of the following are monetary? Are they assets or liabilities? (a) Money: checking accounts; (b) charge account at department store; (c) prepaid subscription to *New York Times*; (d) long-term lease for land; (e) rental arrangement whereby tenant pays 1 percent of monthly sales as rental to the building owner; (f) U. S. bonds; (g) a share of General Motors common stock; (h) house; (i) social-security benefit rights; (j) pension rights in a retirement fund; (k) teacher's salary.

8   If, during an inflation, you held all your wealth in cash, would you gain or lose wealth relative to the change in the price level? (Hint: Not sufficient information.)

9   If, during an inflation, you held all your wealth in the form of real goods would you gain or lose wealth relative to the price level? (Hint: What else must you know?)

10   Is there any evidence that schoolteachers are net monetary creditors as a class?

11   Refer back to page 633. Show how an inflation that doubles the price level will bring to the government more than twice as much in income taxes. (Hint: Estimate the taxes for a person earning $4,000 a year before the inflation and $8,000 after the inflation.)

12   Today schoolteachers compare their income status after taxes with the 1940 status after taxes. Because taxes have increased substantially more than in proportion to income, the teachers can show that their real income after taxes is smaller. As a legislator, tell why you would not shed tears for the plight of the teachers using this argument.

13   Explain how bank owners as a class suffer from inflation.

14

The AZ Company
Balance Sheet of June 30, 1971

Assets		Liabilities	
Cash	$ 20,000	*Current*	
U. S. bonds	50,000	Accounts payable	$ 25,000
Accounts receivable	30,000	Notes payable	80,000
Inventories	100,000	Prepaid orders	5,000
Building and equipment	90,000	Accrued taxes	4,000
Goodwill	100		$114,000
		Long-term	
		Notes	$ 40,000
		Bonds	100,000
			$140,000
		Equity	
		Common stock	$30,000
		Surplus	6,100
			$ 36,100
	$290,100		$290,100

Is the AZ Company a net monetary creditor or debtor? By how much? Each of the 30,000 shares of common stock has *market* value of $40 (despite the initial value of $1 per share recorded in the balance sheet); if you buy one share, how many dollars of net monetary debtor or creditor status will you acquire?

15 a. In your college library, refer to Moody's *Industrials* as a source of balance sheets for American industrial corporations. Inspect the latest balance sheet for United Nuclear Corporation and indicate whether it is a net monetary debtor or net monetary creditor. An alternative source is Standard and Poor's *Statistical Reports*. The librarian should be able to guide you to these volumes.
b. Try to find a corporation that is a net monetary creditor. Check on the following to see which are net monetary creditors.

(1) Standard Oil Company (New Jersey).
(2) Ford Motor Company.
(3) International Chemical and Nuclear.
(4) New Park Mining Company.
(5) Metromedia.
(6) Piper Aircraft Company.
(7) American Greeting Card Company.
(8) McCloud River Lumber Company.
(9) Oxford Paper Company.
(10) Laboratory for Electronics, Inc.

16 To test whether average wages lag behind prices, someone examines the record for thirty years of price-level increases. He finds that half the time the wage rates rose less than the price level, while in the other half they rose more. He concludes that the wage-lag effect was present half the time. What would you have concluded? (Hint: If someone said a roulette wheel gave odd rather than even numbers and then on 100 trials he found that half the numbers were odd, would you say his assertion was correct half the time or that his assertion was simply wrong? Is this comparable to the wage-lag assertion?)

17 "Wages must lag behind prices simply because demand first affects selling prices and then filters down to the prices of productive inputs." Evaluate.

18 "If government increases its share of national income, there simply has to be less left for the private sector. With a smaller real income available to the private sector, and with the same wages, real wages must be smaller simply because available real income is smaller." Even if it is true that the real income left for the private economy is smaller, there is an error in that reasoning. What is it? Who loses the income obtained by the government?

19 **a.** Referring to footnote 9 for information about Reynolds Metals Corporation, to how high would the price have been bid in anticipation of a 10 percent inflation in one year (assuming the initial $50 price were the price with no inflation anticipated and the rate of interest were 5 percent)?
b. Under similar circumstances to what price would Filtrol common shares have fallen?

20 If you were asked for the cause of the inflation in Brazil, how would you revise the question?

21 Suppose that all colleges were forced to pay professors a minimum salary of $25,000 per year in order to preserve the dignity of professors. Many professors will soon find themselves without jobs. Being of great influence in government, the professors tell the politicians that their demands are reasonable and that the basic trouble is insufficient demand. To increase demand the government can increase its expenditures to colleges to enable them to hire all the professors at $25,000. If it finances this by taxes, demand will fall elsewhere and unemployment will result until wages and prices fall to keep resources employed. The fall in prices elsewhere simply offsets the rise in professors' wages. Or the government could embark on a program of general-demand expansion by spending more and taxing less, and meeting the deficit with money creation. If the government assures college professors that they will have full-employment demand conditions without wage cuts and without causing unemployment elsewhere, is inflation the inevitable policy? Why?

22 "The progressive deterioration in the value of money throughout history is not an accident, and has behind it two great driving forces—the impecuniosity of governments and the superior political influence of the debtor class. . . . The power of taxation by currency depreciation is one which has been inherent in the State. . . . The creation of legal tender has been and is a government's ultimate reserve; and no state or government is likely to decree its own downfall, so long as this instrument still lies at hand unused" (J. M. Keynes, *A Tract on Monetary Reform,* London: Macmillan and Co., Ltd., 1923, p. 9). Explain in more detail what Keynes meant.

23 "Inflation causes price distortions because not all prices are equally responsive to changes in demand. Therefore, a period of rapid inflation causes inefficiencies in the economic system. Evidence of the distortion is clear if one looks at the fact that, during inflations, relative prices change." Would you consider that as evidence for the proposition that inflation causes a change in relative prices? Is there some other reason why you would expect the beginning of an inflation to be associated with greater relative changes in prices more than during the subsequent inflation or during periods when price levels are constant? (Hint: Why did the inflation occur? That is, what events caused the increase in money stock relative to demand for money?)

24 "Inflation is caused by excessive government spending." Expose the fallacy of that statement.

25 It was asserted that if producers of molybdenum responded to increased demand by raising their prices, the effect would be inflationary. Can you spot a fallacy in that argument? (Hint: Remember the discussion of the way meat prices might rise in response to a rise in demand? Suppose that cattle raisers had not asked for a higher price in response to an increased demand. Would that have meant that meat prices to consumers would not have increased?)

26 Young movie stars under the age of 21 are ordered by judges to save a fraction of their weekly earnings and buy U. S. government bonds. They are not allowed to invest that savings in stocks.
a. If you were a young movie star, would you regard that as good advice?
b. If you were a judge, would you regard that advice as good?
c. Can you give any reasons why jurists and the legal system are prone to advise investments in U. S. government bonds?

27 a. If in drawing up your will you were arranging for advice to your widow about investing your life insurance, would you recommend that the funds be invested in bonds or in stocks?
b. How do the risks differ in each case?

28 a. If you knew that every price was going to rise at the rate of 10 percent a week, would you try to hold larger or smaller amounts of money relative to your wealth and income?
b. Would you resort to barter to save 10 percent of your money wealth every week?
c. In 52 weeks how much higher would the price level be? (Use tables from Chapter 10 to compute the answer.) Are you therefore not surprised to see why people will still use money even when they know the price level will rise by that amount in one year?
d. Are you convinced that even at an anticipated 100 percent per *week* rise in prices, people would still use money?
e. If people reduce their money balances relative to their wealth and income from say one-fourth of their annual income to one-tenth (in order to avoid so large a loss of wealth from the decreasing value of the money), approximately how much would prices jump immediately?

29 "Higher interest rates are higher prices and therefore are an element of inflation." Expose the error of that assertion.

30 Emperor Julian exhorted the merchants of Antioch to practice self-restraint in pricing their wares. Today government leaders exhort businessmen and labor leaders to exercise statesmenlike self-restraint. Tomorrow the story will be the same. Why is such exhortation worse than useless?

31 In countries where the money supply has increased while wages and prices were legally controlled, an attempt sometimes is made to prevent all wages and prices from rising by "reforming" the money system. A portion of the money stocks are simply canceled out by government decree; thereby prices are kept from rising. Does that tactic avoid a wealth redistribution? Explain.

32 The Federal Reserve board contends it is helping to prevent inflation by restricting credit (and at the same time it is increasing the monetary base at a record rate for peacetime). Is the Fed helping to restrain inflation?

Stabilization or Destabilization Policy?

34

WITH influence over the monetary base (or high-powered money) and government expenditures and taxes, governmental fiscal and monetary authorities can and do affect national income. Until about 1930, authorities acted with little recognition of that fact. The disastrous monetary policy causing the Great Depression has taught some people to be aware of that power and of the importance of using it wisely.

For exposition, it has been convenient, though not wholly accurate, to divide government actions into fiscal and monetary categories. Fiscal actions pertain to taxing, spending, borrowing, and lending by government. Monetary are those *directly* affecting the money supply—*directly,* because in an indirect way fiscal policy, too, affects money supplies, and, in turn, monetary supply actions affect fiscal actions. A *policy* requires evaluation of alternative consequences, and that opens debate and disagreement about the *relative desirability* of alternative consequences.

Finally, beware of the assumption that mere recognition of the importance of fiscal and monetary policy will avoid catastrophe. Despite recognition of monetary policy and power delegated to the Federal Reserve System, we suffered the severe depression of the 1930s, in no small part because our monetary authorities concentrated on avoiding higher interest rates and higher prices (while prices were falling!), and on preserving a balanced budget. The Federal Reserve Act transferred monetary power from the commercial bankers to the Federal Reserve board, but the Fed acted inadequately, partly because it misunderstood its power and partly because its immediate objectives are now seen to have been inappropriate.

What are the announced policy objectives about which there can be dispute? And the alternative activities about which there can be differing evaluations? In the Employment Act of 1946, Congress recognized the relevance of fiscal and monetary policy by creating a Council of Economic Advisers to recommend fiscal and monetary activities. Note the generality of the Act's declaration:

> The Congress declares that it is the continuing policy and responsibility of the Federal Government to use all practical means consistent with its needs and obligations and other essential considerations of national policy, with the assistance and cooperation of industry, agriculture, labor, and State and local governments, to coordinate and utilize its plans, functions and resources for the purposes of creating and maintaining, in a manner calculated to foster and promote free competitive enterprises and the general welfare, conditions under which there will be afforded useful employment opportunities, including self-employment, for those able, willing, and seeking to work, and to promote maximum employment, production and purchasing power.

Even a communist would agree, for communists believe in free competitive enterprise, as *they* interpret those words, when they exhort factory managers to introduce products more acceptable to consumers. But the significant fact is the attention to effects on employment and production. The Act is called a "living document, adaptable to changing circumstances," undoubtedly because its generalities mean all things to all people. We cannot expect to find in it explicit criteria for choice among policies, except insofar as an action may make more employment and production available with no less of any other goods or goals. But few significant actions present so simple a choice.

Inflation, Low Employment, and Wage and Price Controls

The fiscal and monetary policy goals of (1) price-level stability, (2) *assured* employment, and (3) free markets have trade-offs among them. More of one goal can be achieved at the cost of some others. A first area of dispute about policy arises from the common but mistaken belief that low unemployment, maintained by fiscal and monetary policy, implies inflation. However, some are impressed with evidence that simply a prevention of aggregate demand *decreases* will maintain a sufficiently low incidence of unemployment. Others suggest that if *assurance* were not given that people could count on government action to provide employment despite the "high" wages and prices asked, the threat of unemployment or lost sales would prevent price increases that result in unemployment or production cutbacks; and price cuts and wage decreases would be more common. In part the dispute hinges upon what is believed to be (1) a sufficiently low incidence of unemployment to sustain political viability of a given monetary and fiscal policy and (2) judgments about the significance of the bad effects of inflation relative to (3) the merits of *assured* employment.

Structural Unemployment Reductions

Though aggregate demand were maintained constant to avoid unemployment, there might be extensive *relative* demand shifts among various products and skills as well as shifts in relative supplies of productive inputs. An increased shifting of relative demands and supplies will induce so-called *structural* unemployment. Should fiscal and monetary action be taken to reduce structural unemployment? Aggregate demand could be expanded to reduce the time between abandoning one job and acceptance of another. An inflationary policy in this connection would make demand increases more noticeable in absolute dollar terms. So attempts to reduce the amount of unemployment consequent to shifting relative demands and supplies could lead fiscal and monetary authorities to adopt inflationary policies. Giving aid, whether by increasing the demand for certain resources, or by financing their relocation or geographic mobility, raises the question of who is to pay for the aid. To what degree should the tax system be used to aid particular individuals suffering from shifting demands and supplies? If a businessman claims bankruptcy because of a shift in demand to a new product, should he along with his employees be paid to continue in their old, less useful work? Paid to move elsewhere? Will that reduce a person's incentive? What is the "right" combination of government tax-supported welfare aid and private responsibility? Since we can only indicate the sources of disagreement about employment maintenance policy, not resolve them, we go on to other questions.

Counterdeflationary Policy

With falling aggregate demand, fiscal and monetary actions are usually taken to restore aggregate demand. This keeps prices from falling as they otherwise would in restoring employment and production. And a policy simply of counteracting aggregate demand-decreasing forces may maintain low enough unemployment to be politically viable. This kind of stabilizing fiscal and monetary activity could keep employment low without increasing prices in general.

Cost-Push, or *Assured* Low Unemployment

If the belief spreads that political authorities will initiate all fiscal and monetary activity necessary in any circumstance to assure no lasting unemployment, then some labor groups or industries may believe they can set higher wages or prices with impunity. When their sales fall, the authorities will, with sufficient speed, increase the demand for their products to offset the higher prices. *Other* prices, too, will be increased in the process. However, inflation is a result not simply of setting higher prices and wages but of increasing supplies of money to *increase* aggregate demand sufficiently to restore employment at the higher announced prices and wages. An inflationary, general demand-increasing monetary policy is adopted to restore employment and output where prices were initially raised by their sellers. *Relative* prices may be returned to their original ratios, but *absolute* prices are higher. This is often called a cost-push, or sellers', inflation, to indicate the *motive* for expansionary monetary policies. Without the expanded monetary supplies resulting from the expansionary fiscal and monetary policy, the inflation would not have occurred. Instead, some prices would have been higher, while those who lost their jobs or suffered output reductions at the announced higher prices would have to settle for "zero" prices (no sales) or be shifted to other jobs with lower prices.

A more concentrated direct means of restoring employment and production in areas where wages and prices have been arbitrarily raised is to increase the demand initially in *just those particular* areas of unemployment. For example, in Chapter 19 the wheat and cotton farmers induced the government authorities to set higher prices *and* to increase government demands for wheat and cotton (via crop "loans"). The increased demand for the wheat and cotton was financed by higher taxes (reducing demands for other goods) or by government deficits *financed with new money creation*. The former is noninflationary, while the latter is inflationary and raises other prices.

Alternatively, the government could deny any intention of rescuing those who ask wages or prices higher than would permit their present employment or sales. The "discipline" of unemployment or reduced sales could control wages and prices, if the money supply were not increased. But that is not politically viable, for it is difficult to know whether unemployment is a result of increases of particular wages and prices too great to permit full employment, or is a result of general reductions in demand. A governmental assurance that it will quickly relieve unemployment due to general recessions will almost surely lead to expansion in the money supply. This inflationary bias in employment "stabilization" policy is the reason we hear of a dilemma between inflation and full employment. It is *not* the case that full employment can occur only by an inflationary policy. Rather, the political *promises* that *no* increase in unemployment—whatever the cause—will be tolerated will involve inflationary money expansions, if the promises are kept.

So long as *assurance* of employment-maintaining policies is given, it will pay large groups (say, unions) to ask for higher group-controlled wages. A majority of the group will retain employment at the higher wages, while those who do not will provide enough complaint to the government to motivate it to do something. The wages are set *for the group,* so the unemployed cannot cut their own wages to keep their jobs. And the disparity of interest between those who do manage to sell their services and those who do not at the higher prices does not inhibit the majority from asking for higher wages and prices. Those who believe they can avoid this inflationary motivation by exhorting people not to increase their asking prices "inordinately" are spitting into the wind.

To be sure, the government, rather than letting sellers face unemployment when consumers refuse to pay new asked prices for the former quantities purchased, may try to intimidate sellers to continue old prices. If "guidelines" or "voluntary" price and wage controls miraculously dissuade people from asking for higher prices, the government will have less cause to resort to inflationary money increases. But such "jawboning" tactics have never succeeded without turning into outright wage and price controls.

Advocates of the use of discretionary fiscal policy to affect national income believe it desirable and feasible, when recessions threaten, to adapt fiscal actions to alleviate the recession—*if* one can be *sufficiently* sure he knows what is impending. But if knowledge of special circumstances that imply an impending recession is not sufficiently reliable and if there are delays in implementing fiscal actions (which must go through Congress and the President), the results can be *destabilizing.* A signal of an impending recession can be misread, and the fiscal response will be inappropriate—or so lagged that it overdoes the recovery. We are not asserting that more knowledge and use of available means in special circumstances to alleviate or prevent fluctuations is undesirable. We are asserting that we may not have the ability or knowledge that we hope we have, so that acting on misdiagnoses can aggravate fluctuations.

What special information is available to guide policy authorities in trying to dampen fluctuations in aggregate national demand? Efforts to find economic indicators that forecast, or lead, changes in aggregate demand have so far been to little avail. Figure 34–1 shows some charts of economic series that are leading indicators. Can we watch the leading series and know when to embark on expansion policies and when to restrict the rate of growth? Alas, leading indicators don't forecast reliably. Consider the series in Figure 34–1. Imagine you are at mid-1951; you are to predict whether a downturn has or is about to set in. If you think a downturn is signaled, you are mistaken, for that

Stabilization or Destabilization Policy?

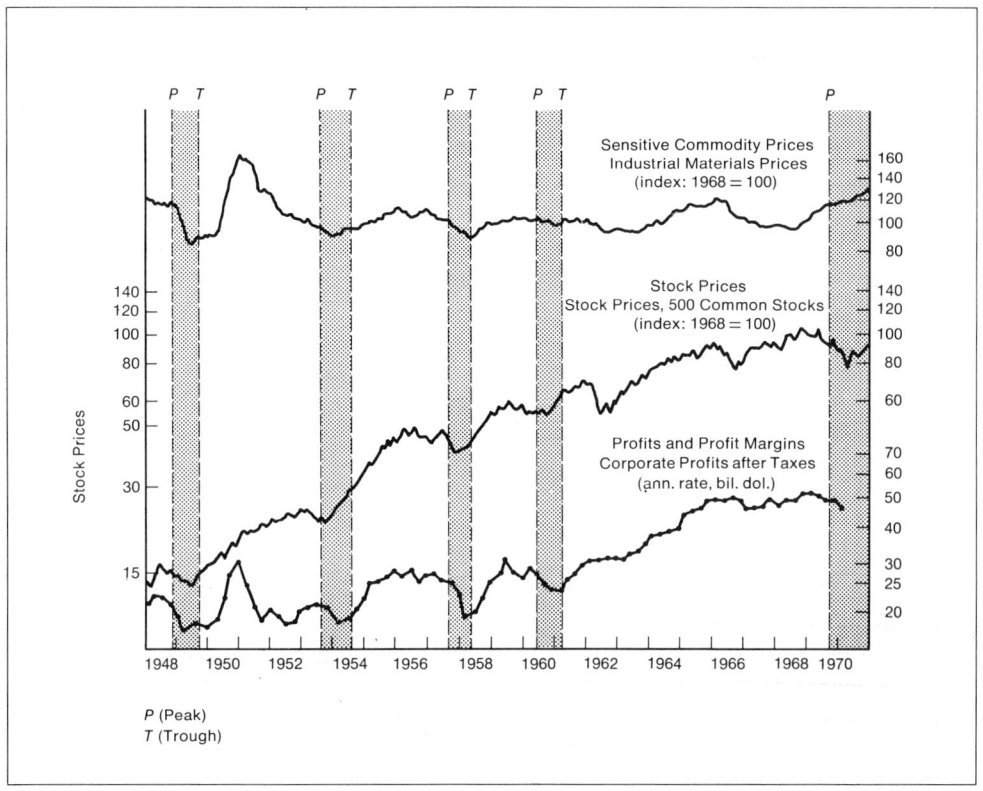

FIGURE 34–1. Leading Cyclical Indicators: Prices and Profits (1948–1970)

Shaded zones indicate episodes called recessions, starting at peak and ending at trough. Recovery starts at the trough. Debate exists as to whether the episode of slower growth and higher than normal unemployment in 1966 should be called a recession and be shaded. What will be the ultimate decision on 1969–70? In any event, "leading indicators" are not very reliable indicators of downturns—too many false signals are shown.

downturn you see in the indicators is just a transient wiggle of the kind that all indicators manifest even when there is no downturn coming. Try the same test in 1956 and in 1966. It is easy to look back at *confirmed* downturns and see that leading indicators signaled those properly, but the question is how many times did a leading indicator signal a downturn falsely, i.e., when none did occur? And that is the difficulty facing the policy makers. Do the leading indicators cry "wolf" so that by the time policy makers discover it was a false signal they have already set in motion the wrong forces? There appears to be no leading indicator that does not cry "wolf" too often to be worth the costs of its false cries. With present knowledge, there can be no guarantee that discretionary policy to control national income will reduce rather than aggravate fluctuations. In fact, to many who have carefully examined the record, the evidence strongly suggests that unintended destabilizing results have been more frequent. Yet even those who are sceptical of discretionary policy will agree that fiscal actions have effects that should be contemplated when taking fiscal actions for *other* purposes, so as to avoid undesirable effects on national income. Adjustment of fiscal and monetary activities in the realization of potential destabilizing effects on national income is not the same thing as adoption of a discretionary policy designed to alleviate fluctuations every time they are believed to be impending. Automatic stabilizers (discussed later) are consistent with the former but not necessarily with the latter.

Political and Economic Problems in Discretionary Policy

Fiscal activity adopted with intent to affect national income is largely thought of as discretionary fiscal policy. Public-works programs for flood control, roads, education, space exploration involve expenditures for employment of resources in one form or another and, in principle, could be initiated (or increased) and terminated (or decreased) at times appropriate for income stabilization.

The question of discretionary fiscal policy involves more than stabilization. A President who wants greater discretionary power to lower or raise taxes or to spend more or less as a stabilizing force is asking for powers which have been historically assigned to Congress for "good" reasons. The President might use such powers for political purposes not wholly consistent with stabilization—or so many Congressmen believe. It is not a muddleheaded disbelief in fiscal policy which restrains Congress from granting the President the power to change taxes or expenditures independently and with his own discretion. Discretionary stabilization policy clashes with political expediency and with the principle of division and balance of powers between Congress and the President. Success in stabilization is only one of the criteria in judging the institutional arrangements of government.

But aside from these political issues, the various economic difficulties facing those who conduct discretionary policy are enough to arouse sympathy for them and fear of the possible consequences. Consider the difficulties and the American record of monetary stabilization policy.

There is, first, the problem of accurately diagnosing the illness in time to take action before the situation changes. There is a double lag involved here: it takes time also for the prescribed medicine to take effect. In a cyclical swing of moderate length, we could very well find anti-recession policies becoming effective at about the time the upswing begins and anti-inflation policies taking hold at about the beginning of a downswing with a resultant exacerbation rather than alleviation of economic fluctuation.

Second, there are the matters of (1) understanding the monetary system well enough to appreciate the available modes for controlling the money supply, (2) choosing which tools to employ, if not all of them, (3) deciding the vigor with which the tools should be employed (should $150 million worth of securities be in the open market, or $412.8 million?), and (4) coordinating all actions so that one does not cancel out another.

Third, there is the matter of community relations. Some people will benefit from an expansionary policy regardless of the level of employment. Enlargement of the money supply by Fed open-market purchases will lead to a lower interest rate, and this will make production of capital goods more profitable. Construction industries and construction trade unions will always be favorable to further expansion, especially if associated with lower interest rates.[1]

---

[1] It is important to keep in mind one way in which *increases* in money affect interest rates. A persisting lower interest rate occurs initially if the Fed first buys bonds with the new money, rather than sprinkling the money from the skies. That increased demand for bonds lowers the interest rate

Generally few people will argue to curtail expansion, although some will deplore inflation. The consequences of overexpansion (inflation) are usually treated as less weighty than those of underexpansion (less employment). The Fed will find itself bucking strong pressures if it acts in a nonexpansionary way, especially now that its powers and the consequences of using them are becoming more widely appreciated.

Fourth, objectives other than stabilization can play a powerful role in determining monetary actions. Three times the Federal Reserve board has yielded to pressure from Congress and the President to pursue an alternative goal—the avoidance of higher explicit taxes to finance wars. In both World Wars and in the Korean War, the Fed "accommodated" by standing ready to purchase (or lend against) *any quantity* of government securities *at par*. This action made the securities virtually indistinguishable from money and ensured their sale by the Treasury. The public, notably including commercial banks, was encouraged to buy government bonds (that is, lend to the government), for it knew that the bonds could be converted into money at a guaranteed price at any time. During World War II the Fed printed money and also issued Federal Reserve deposit credit against itself in order to buy directly from the Treasury nearly a third of the bonds issued by the government to fill the gap between expenditures and tax collections. Resulting increases in the quantity of money, which doubled in the four years of World War II, produced a large inflation. Even during the Vietnam war, it has similarly aided the Treasury.

It is to be emphasized that government deficits, as such, neither increase the quantity of money nor cause inflation. The effects on the stock of money and also on (excess) reserves of commercial banks depend upon the *method of financing* the deficit—that is, upon who is the buyer of government bonds: (1) if the deficit is financed by the Treasury selling bonds to the Fed, both the money supply and excess reserves are increased as the Treasury spends the proceeds;[2] (2) if the bonds are sold to commercial banks (in exchange for demand deposits), the money supply is increased, and excess reserves are reduced; and (3) if the bonds go to the nonbank public, their sale affects neither the money supply nor excess reserves.[3]

---

below what it otherwise would be. If the Fed bought bricks or Gauguin paintings, only the price of bricks or paintings would be changed—not interest rates. But when the new money, however it is created, is placed in commercial bank reserves, the commercial bankers will increase their purchase of private debt from customers, thereby pushing up prices of private bonds and notes (equivalent to a lower rate of interest). With lower interest rates, people will, in equating the yields of their various assets on the margin, shift from bonds to other long-lived goods (sliding back up along the demand curve for bonds). This raises long-lived capital-goods prices relative to wage and short-lived goods prices, thereby making long-lived investment more profitable and shifting up the *I* function in the income theory presented in Chapter 27. The interest-rate effect occurs, then, because commercial banks increase their demand deposits by obtaining private *bonds and notes* (i.e., by lending). If commercial banks had issued demand deposits against themselves in exchange for houses or textbooks, instead of private debt, the interest rate would not have changed.

[2] It is not entirely clear why the Treasury does not print and issue "greenbacks" instead of paying interest on bonds. That is the technique used by many governments and by our government during the Civil War. Perhaps the indirect avenue is used to obscure what is taking place, or perhaps the direct way is too conducive to government deficits.

[3] Go through these cases—and those that follow—step-by-step, noting changes in the *T* accounts of the Treasury, the Fed, and the commercial banks. Always assume, realistically, that expenditures by the Treasury are out of its demand account in the Fed: while the Treasury keeps the great bulk of its operating balances in commercial banks, it does not spend directly out of such balances; it first transfers these funds to its account in the Fed, against which it then writes checks.

However, *if* any holder (commercial bank or the public) can costlessly shift government bonds to the Fed, these distinctions lose force. It makes little difference who is the initial purchaser of the Treasury bonds if they can readily be sold again at par to the Fed: (1) if the bonds are initially sold to the Fed and the newly created deposit of the Treasury is spent, the money quickly finds its way into the commercial banks, increasing bank reserves as well as the money stock; (2) if the bonds are sold to commercial banks and then resold by the banks to the Fed, bank reserves are increased, and expenditure by the Treasury of the proceeds of the initial sale will increase the money supply; and (3) if, say, insurance companies first bought the bonds and resold them to the Fed, the proceeds would be deposited in commercial banks, with both the money supply and bank reserves increased. All these "monetize" the public debt in the sense that the government debt is used to increase reserves.

During World War II when the Fed was a willing "buyer of last resort" at a pegged price, the government bond market was—as the euphemistic expressions went—"stabilized" and "orderly." With bond prices supported, interest rates were held down, which pleased the Treasury, because borrowing costs were thereby kept low. The Fed continued its bond-support policy for a half-dozen years after the war. One consequence of the policy was largely to nullify the effectiveness of the Fed's money controls. The policy removed most of the discretionary power of the Fed over open-market operations: the Fed bought whatever bonds were presented, even if such purchases were undesirable in the interest of full employment with a stable price level. Furthermore, the other controls lost much of their effectiveness. If a bank found its reserve position growing tight, it could increase its reserves by simply selling some of its government bonds to the Fed (in late 1945 commercial banks had accumulated a total of over $90 billion in bonds, which was much more than their existing demand deposits).[4]

Monetizing the public debt has, indeed, been one of the Fed's main activities. But there is conflict between the two missions of central banks—namely, (1) to control the

---

[4] Analogous to the accommodation of a government's desire to sell bonds at low interest rates is the ancient but fallacious theory—which was central in the advocacy of a Federal Reserve System prior to 1914—that banks should provide the amount of money required for "legitimate business purposes." This is called the "real-bills doctrine" or "commercial loan theory." The idea is that commercial banks should confine loans to businessmen to finance "normal" business operations (inventories, investments in buildings, prepayments to labor, etc.) in which sales proceeds will enable repayment of the loan. Supposedly, as long as banks follow this "productive-purpose" loan policy, they will issue just the proper *quantity* of loans; the money stock will *vary* with the "needs of trade" as (only) "bona fide" activities are accommodated; and the banks themselves will remain "sound" by holding only "self-liquidating" commercial I. O. U.s. The validity of the real-bills doctrine hinges upon many conditions, including the following: (1) The only productive, economic activity warranting bank financing is conducted by business firms. (2) All business financing is done only by bank borrowing. (3) The money created by the loan is spent only once, just on the project for which the loan was granted—to maintain a constant relation between the money stock and national output. (4) The system as a whole follows the rules and maintains the flow of financing, for outstanding loans will not be self-liquidating if would-be commodity buyers cannot obtain expected bank loans. (5) Price levels do not change even though the stock of money increases.

In short, following the doctrine would not avoid an inflationary increase (or deflationary decrease) in the quantity of money. Yet, even today, businessmen are urged against investments that are not for "legitimate" purposes; they are urged not to expand their plants for the "speculative" purpose of increasing capacity—as if investment *per se* were inflationary. It is not. Those who fear that investment increase will cause increased amounts of money should note that *any* expansion of demand deposits will be inflationary; during relatively full employment, it is the *increase* in the quantity of money that is inflationary, not the *purpose* for which the money is created.

quantity of money in the interest of full employment and a steady price level and (2) to create money for the government when the government wants it. One can judge the behavior of the Fed appropriately only by considering which of these missions is most significant at any given time. During the war, the Fed fulfilled its money-creation function effectively at the sacrifice of steady prices. Its performance in controlling the money supply to avoid cyclical fluctuations in prices and employment has been less impressive.

The Stabilization Record of the Federal Reserve

A split-second survey of the use of the three major credit controls since World War I suggests the following picture. The heyday of the rediscount rate was the 1920s (and into the early 1930s), when changes in the rate were more frequent and bank borrowing from the Fed was relatively heavier than in later periods. Open-market operations appeared to dominate after the 1940s as the Fed holdings of government securities rose to impressive levels and were subject to appreciable changes in short periods of time; however, in the middle and late 1950s there was a small flurry of activity with the rediscount rate. There has been no lengthy period when manipulation of the required-reserve ratio was conspicuous. From the early 1930s to the early 1950s, all of the Fed's tools were generally unused—except for its acquisition of securities during World War II.

Although the Fed has tended most of the time to be essentially passive and quiescent, it is appropriate to ask about the *quality* of the Fed's actions. Have the tools been used at the right times and in the right directions? (One could ask also whether they have been used in appropriate quantity, but this is even more difficult to answer than the questions on timing and direction.)

In order to have some standard of reference in evaluating Federal Reserve policies, consider first an idealized "business cycle" and the timing and direction of the Fed's actions to dampen the cycle.[5] We may envisage a cycle of economic activity (measured by some conglomerate index) fluctuating about a rising trend, and we assume that the Fed wishes to restrain both inflation of price levels and recessions. As anti-recession moves, the Fed would (1) lower the required-reserve ratio, (2) lower the rediscount rate, and (3) buy government securities. Anti-inflation policies would be the opposite. How closely has Fed activity resembled this pattern?

Figures 34-2 and 34-3 will serve our summary purposes. They present two indicators of economic activity: consumer prices and industrial production. The *magnitudes* of the fluctuations in these curves are not to be compared, for the measures are indices plotted on different scales. Our main concern here is with the *turning points,* and the two measures—along with the stock of money—move together quite closely, generally changing in the same direction.

---

[5] Despite the books, articles, and college courses devoted to "business cycles," there is reason to use the label with caution. Presumably, the idea of a "cycle" embodies automaticity, regularity, and self-generation—that is, a system or mechanism such that swings in economic activity will lead with some precision to a turning point which reverses the direction of the swing. That there have been *fluctuations* in economic activity is apparent; that these fluctuations have been sufficiently neat and coherent to warrant the label of "cycle" is not so apparent.

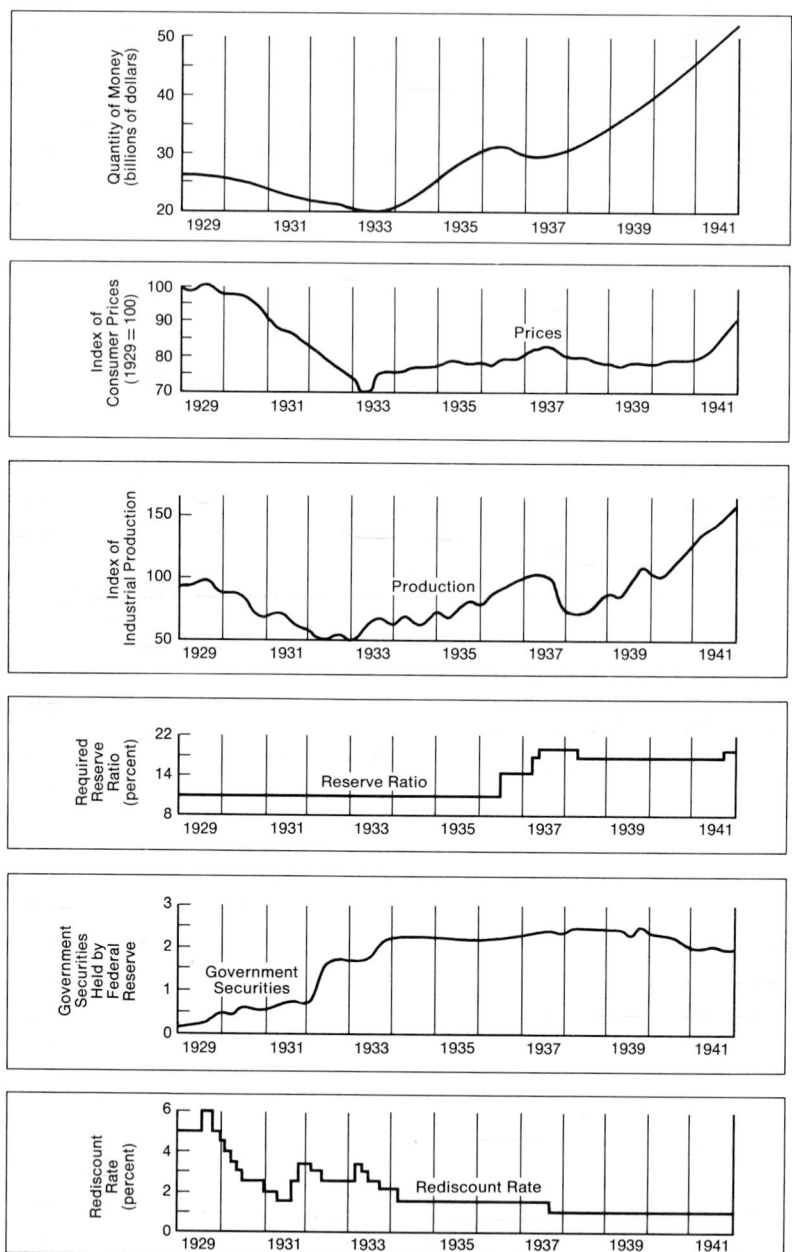

FIGURE 34-2

Money, prices, production, and income related to Federal Reserve actions, 1929–41. Source: *Federal Reserve Bulletin.*

Stabilization or Destabilization Policy?

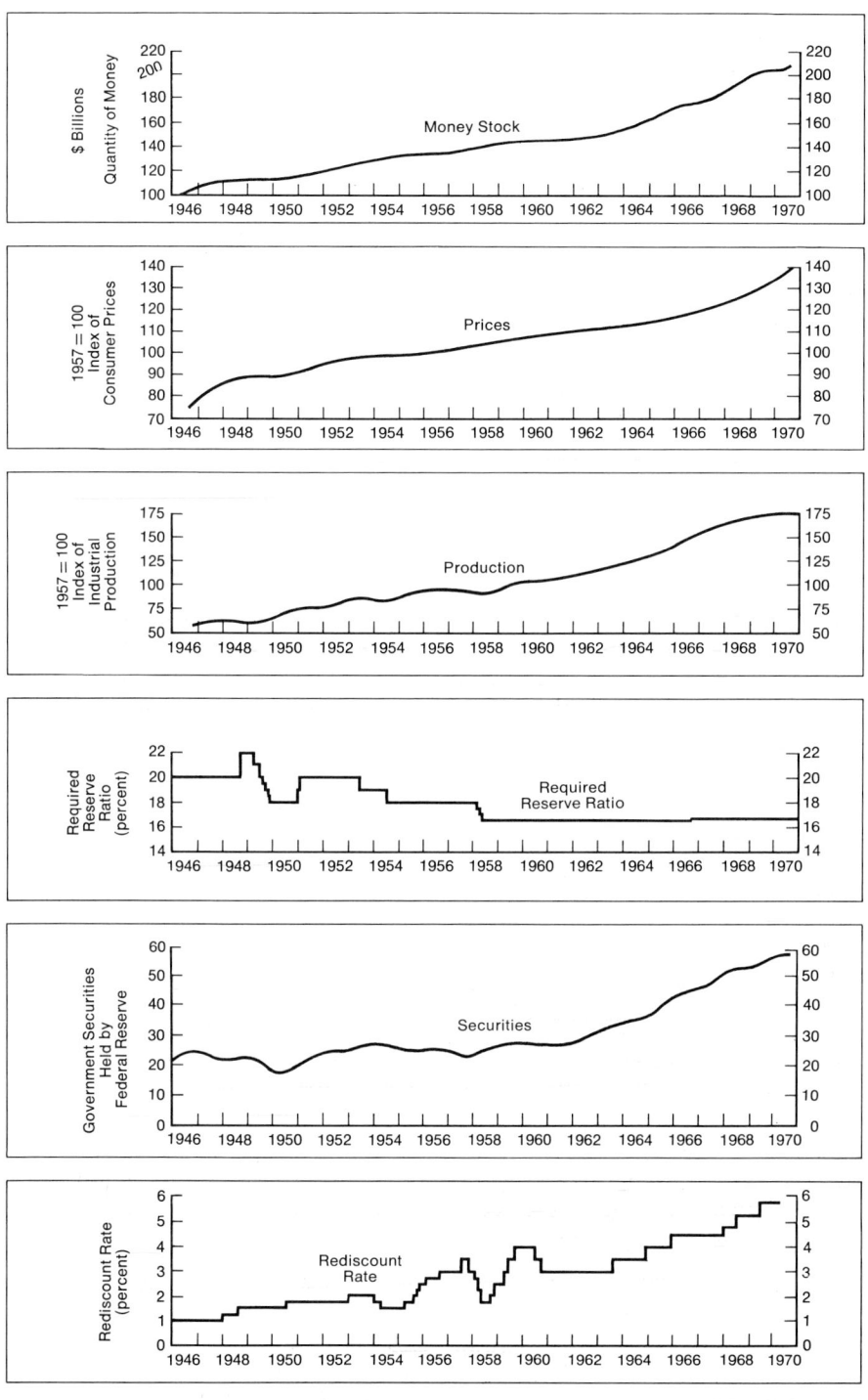

FIGURE 34-3

Prices, production, and income related to Federal Reserve actions, 1945–65. Source: *Federal Reserve Bulletin.*

The fourth quarter of 1929 was the beginning of what came to be known as the Great Depression, which hit bottom around the first quarter of 1933. What was the response of the Fed? From 1929 to 1933, the required-reserve ratio remained constant by statutory provision; there was no significant change in holdings of government securities until mid-1932, and, even then, the increase was very modest in light of the magnitude of the problem, however bold it might have appeared by earlier standards. More attention was given to the rediscount rate.[6] After a full percentage-point increase in July 1929, it was progressively lowered until late 1931, when (for balance-of-international-payments purposes rather than domestic policy) it was sharply increased—long before the depression reached its lowest point. Then, after some backing and filling for two years, it settled down at a level maintained until well after World War II.

Do not pass over this experience lightly. The money stock contracted from over $25 billion in 1929 to less than $20 billion in 1933. By contrast the losses of money and wealth through bank failures was only $.2 billion, only 1 percent of the money stock. Although individually serious, that was a trivial loss to the economy. The catastrophic event was the 25 percent contraction in the stock of money even in banks that didn't fail. (Once before, 1920–21, the money stock fell at an even greater rate—over 12 percent in one year.) Such an enormous decrease in the stock of money is bound to have severe effects on the state of general demand, prices, and employment. What was responsible? Several factors, but one fact stands out boldly. The Federal Reserve, designed to stabilize the quantity of money, failed in a primary mission. While the money stock was falling and banks were failing, the Fed persisted in looking primarily at interest rates. It largely eschewed open-market purchases of government bonds and private debt. Its administrators did not comprehend or did not accept their primary function: to control the total quantity of money and not to act like private bankers. Had they acted correctly and more strongly within their powers, the decrease in the money supply could have been avoided and the depression prevented or reduced in severity and length. Possibly they did not believe that changes in the quantity of money had anything to do with the level of unemployment, or maybe they thought that only the interest rate counted or that the money supply automatically adjusted to the "needs" of business or that some inflation would occur if they acted to increase bank reserves—and that at a time when deflation was taking place.

From about the beginning of 1934, open-market operations and the rediscount rate were virtually moribund. Perversely, the required-reserve ratio was doubled from 10 percent to 20 percent for reserve city banks in 1936–37—just in time to help create the severe setback of 1937–38.[7]

However the charitable observer may account for these actions, it seems that, with the possible exception of handling the rediscount rate from late 1929 to late 1931, the record of the Fed in the 1930s is, at best, one of too little and too late, involving even some dubious decisions as to direction of action.

Is its record after World War II more impressive? Look at Figure 34–3.

---

[6] Each of the twelve Federal Reserve banks has its own rediscount rate. They do not always move simultaneously, and they do not always all settle at precisely the same level; but the changes and the levels do not greatly diverge. For expositional convenience, we here consider the rate of only the Federal Reserve Bank of New York.

[7] As with rediscount rates, we choose one of several reserve-requirement ratios as representative, there being three (central reserve city, reserve city, and country) until mid-1962, when the central-reserve-city classification was dropped.

If one considers the counter-recession policies in the recessions of 1948–49, 1953–54, 1957–58, and 1960–61, the record is no better than mixed; and on balance it is not conducive to great confidence. For instance, take the first post-war recession, although the story would be similar for any of the others. We may date the beginning of the downturn as the fourth quarter of 1948 and the beginning of the upturn as the first quarter of 1950. What happened to the three controls? (1) The required-reserve ratio was *raised* in September 1948 and held constant until May 1949, although the index of industrial production fell steadily beginning in September 1948. Then, in the second half of the downswing, the ratio was lowered several times. (2) The rediscount rate was held *constant* all through the downswing. (3) The Fed's holdings of government securities *decreased* (and hence reduced reserves), rather than increased, so as to stimulate economic activity; except for an increase in the fourth quarter of 1948, they fell precipitously all through the downswing.

The sustained expansion from 1961 to early 1966 was marked by persistent, large annual increases in the money stock, the monetary base, and the reserves—at a rate greater than the percentage increase in population and physical output and in excess of the rate of increase and duration in any other peacetime interval, except that of the recovery from the depression (1934–39). Large open-market purchases of government securities by the Fed permitted or induced that increase. Those years were marked by prosperity, low unemployment, and rising prices. Had the Board of Governors of the Fed (with its changing membership) finally adopted a policy of steady expansion of the monetary base and reserves in order to prevent decreases or fluctuations in the money stock? Had the Fed's evaluation of the consequences of more inflation relative to a higher sustained output and employment put more weight on avoiding unemployment and less on avoiding inflation? Belief that it had was destroyed by its performance in 1966 and in 1969 when it *sharply reduced* the money growth rate to zero. It is possible that, aside from price levels, quantity of money, or employment, still a different criterion was being used—low interest rates. A government deficit financed by selling new bonds would push down bond prices, thereby raising interest rates. If the Fed thinks that interest rates should be kept relatively stable or low, it will buy bonds to keep their price from falling. Such open-market purchases will, of course, increase reserves and the monetary base. There has, in fact, been a high correlation between the increase in government debt and open-market purchases by the Fed. But at least up to 1970 the Federal Reserve Board has been sufficiently divided and ambiguous in official pronouncements to confuse analysts seeking to discern the criterion, if any, of the Fed's action. A distinguished economist, Arthur F. Burns, joined the Board as Chairman in 1970. Whether he will direct a clear policy is yet to be seen.

4, 5

Discretionary Monetary Policy and Stabilization Possibilities

We have said that the Fed has techniques enabling it to change reserves and the supply of demand deposits offered by commercial banks. But how accurately or reliably can it control the amount of money actually in existence—determined by the intersection of the demand and supply schedule? If the demand for money should shift violently, how rapidly will the Fed respond? And by how much? And in what direction? These questions take us to the frontier of, or beyond, economic analysis and knowledge.

Even if the monetary authorities do control the stock of money, they face a difficult problem. The public has *expectations* about future prices. If they expect inflation, evidently only an increase in the supply of money *larger* than enough to sustain the public's expectations will increase real output and employment. The increase of the money supply that will not disappoint anticipations and will not induce a recession is one that must match the public's anticipations about future prices. But the monetary authorities do not precisely know those anticipations of the public. For example, in early 1970 the question was, "What is the state of inflationary anticipations, and how can it be changed by monetary actions to convince the public that their anticipations about higher future prices (at, say, the recently observed 7 percent per annum increase) are *not* going to be sustained?" To change that anticipation may require a reduction, or reduced rate of growth, of the stock of money of such large magnitude (if done in one year) as to provoke a severe recession. If not stopped in one year, the inflation will have to be permitted to last longer and be more gradually brought down. But not enough is known now about what reduced rate of growth of the money supply will gradually induce revised anticipations without initiating a recession.

Since the anticipations of inflation reflect in part (it is believed by economists!) past high rates of growth of the money stock, some economists have proposed that a steady growth in the money supply be announced and held to steadfastly. And the Federal Reserve Board has stated, through its chairman, that a steady growth rate of between 2 to 6 percent will be sought, instead of fluctuating between rates as high as 10 percent per annum or as low as zero or negative rates.

Steady Money Growth

Evidence suggests the Fed has the technical capability of controlling the position of the supply function and the quantity of demand deposits actually supplied (the intersection of the demand and supply curves in Figure 30–3), but evidence of unreliability of its anticipatory foresight, the tardiness of its policy responses, and lags in ultimate effects is not reassuring.[8] Still, some believe that now we have a better understanding of the effects of changes in the quantity of money and of means of controlling the money supply; we should therefore rely on discretionary "fine-tuning" control by the Federal Reserve Board to increase the money stock more rapidly when recession appears and reduce the growth of money when prices begin to rise too rapidly. Others believe that the Federal Reserve Board, no matter who its members are, cannot have enough foresight to engage in such "fine-tuning," and they doubt that the timing and the magnitude of the effects of money control are so invariant as to permit benefits from such attempts. Given present ability to forecast and the variations in the effects of monetary (or any other) policy, they believe such discretionary action too often will reinforce recessions and inflations. The issue is not the importance of money supply changes; rather, the question is what is best to do precisely because of the importance of shifts in the demand and supply of money. Some propose an alternative to predominantly discretionary fiscal and monetary policy (and notice that the alternative is to the *discretionary* element—not to monetary and fiscal policy). They propose to lock the monetary mechanism to a goal of a steady increase in the money stock of, say, 3 percent per year (one close to the long-

---

[8] The depressions and recessions beginning in 1921, 1929, 1937, 1964, 1966, and 1969 all can be persuasively ascribed to discretionary monetary policy, in part reflecting misdiagnoses of special circumstances and plain bad forecasting.

term rate of growth of population and full employment output potential in order to get price-level stability). The exact rate is not crucial; more important is the constancy and reliability of the rate of expansion of the money stock. In this way the monetary authorities would have to take whatever action is required to prevent absolute declines in the money stock, such as occurred in the past great depressions, and to prevent decreases in the rate of the expansion of the money stock such as have occurred in the past several recessions. Advocates of this policy believe that the steady growth of the money stock will avoid severe depressions. And they have much evidence in their favor.

It is no reply to assert that with discretionary policy we could accept the policy of steady money growth as a first principle but adapt or improve it by use of knowledge of unusual conditions that justify departure in the interest of full employment, stable prices, and real growth. That contention begs the key question of whether we can in fact identify sufficiently in advance such "unusual justifiable conditions" so that discretionary authorities will not wrongly act prematurely or overreact too late and on balance make recessions more frequent and greater, inflation more severe, and real growth slower. It may be that in the past steady money growth would have been the best policy recommendation, whereas it may be wrong for the future. There is evidence against the advisability of discretionary actions—but faith in one's ability to take into account special circumstances, even though the past record is dismaying, is hard to cast aside.[9]

Gold Standard

Some have advocated going to a gold standard and letting the quantity of money be determined strictly by the amount of gold. These advocates recognize the evils of prolonged recessions, but they are very fearful of governmental power and of the fluctuation which they think will flow from discretionary fiscal and monetary policy. There has been an increase in inflation in most countries, with a rise in governmental power with fiscal and monetary policy, but the direction of the cause and effect relationship is not so clear. Nevertheless these advocates are not out of touch with the times, nor are they crackpots. None of the advocates of these various policies can be considered to be economically illiterate, inhumane, or insensitive to the ills of depressions, inflations, and consequences of greater political power of the society. They have a different evaluation of the prospects for discretionary money-supply controls, even when looking at the same historical evidence, and they could be right, even though their program seems to have no chance of adoption.[10]

---

[9] Even aside from diagnostic ability, political forces are ever-powerful. The monetary authorities in the Fed can assert an intention to maintain a fixed money supply or one that grows at a fixed rate come what may. But the government might embark on an expenditure program with a deficit which must be financed with borrowing from the private sector—with no money-increasing special purchases of bonds by the Fed, because the Fed is sticking with its rule. The result will be higher interest rates and lower prices of long-lived capital goods like houses, buildings, machine tools, and stocks. Could the Fed long maintain its policy in the face of complaints about high interest rates and depression in the construction industry? (The apparent futility of attempts to limit discretionary action is illustrated by the Congressional limit on the national government's debt. Subsequently, every time the limit was approached, it was conveniently raised—almost annually during the past decade.)

[10] But, in another sense, a gold *foreign policy* has been adopted. As we shall see in Chapter 38, political authorities display an obsessive opposition to gold flows out of a country. When our imports of foreign goods or services exceed exports to such an extent that foreigners want the difference covered by gold shipment to them, our political authorities tend to panic and seek to prohibit out-

Automatic Stabilizers

In Chapter 32, we investigated alternative *discretionary fiscal policies* for affecting national income. In addition to deliberate changing of government spending and the tax rate, the *fiscal system* itself "automatically" acts to modify fluctuations in income. So-called automatic, or built-in, stabilizers cannot hold the income level constant (indeed, the stabilizers operate only as income varies), but they act to dampen the income effects of autonomous changes in spending components.

Of the several stabilizers, the most obvious is the income tax. The existence of a tax rate (and thus of tax collections) in the income model we have used "stabilized" income—that is, reduced the size of income fluctuations—even though we employed a "proportional" rate, and a "progressive" or graduated rate would have been even more effective.[11] Reduced tax collections have an expansionary effect on national income. The *automatic* or induced reduction in tax receipts consequent to a reduction in income automatically moderates the fall in income. The larger is the tax rate applied to incomes, the greater will be the automatic stabilizing, or moderating, effect.

In Table 34–1 we have three alternative cases involving an autonomous fall of investment by $30. Basically, all cases begin with the same equilibrium situation—although, in the first case, in which there is no taxation leakage, saving is correspondingly higher. In Case B, the marginal tax rate equals the average, so that Y and T move together proportionately. The result is that income falls substantially less than in Case A. The autonomous change in investment is the same in both instances, but introducing the (proportionate) tax rate reduces the repercussion on income. We now have a second leakage, taxes, to supplement saving, so a relatively small change in income will bring leakages and injection back into equality.

In Case C, beginning with the same average tax rate ($100/$1,000 = .1) as in Case B, the marginal rate ($r = .15$) is greater. As income falls, the tax leakage falls more rapidly than in Case B, thereby reducing $(S + T)$ to the new level of $(G + I)$ before income has been reduced so far. Other things the same, the more responsive is T to changes in Y, that is, the greater is the marginal tax rate, the smaller need be the change in income in order to equate leakage with injections.

---

flows, as if gold were blood. Restrictions are placed on rights of Americans to import goods, travel or invest abroad, and even to own gold. We make ourselves prisoners of our own country. Such results of a gold-mentality standard are the opposite of what is implied by a gold *monetary* standard.

[11] With a "proportional" tax, collections change with income by the same percentage, and "progressive" tax collections change by a larger percentage. To put the distinction differently, with a proportional tax, the marginal tax rate $(\Delta T/\Delta Y)$ equals the average rate (T/Y): $T = rY$, and the schedule of tax collections is a straight line through the origin of the 45-degree diagram; with a progressive tax, the marginal rate *exceeds* the average rate: $T = a + rY$, where a is the (negative) vertical-axis intercept of the tax-collection schedule. In the figure, T_1 reflects a proportional tax and

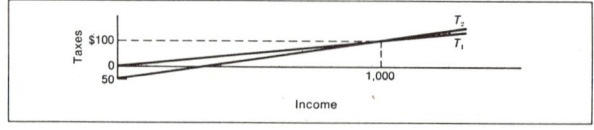

T_2 a progressive tax ($a = -\$50$), with $100 collected under each alternative at the assumed initial income level of $1,000. Obviously, the marginal tax rate, measured by the slope of the T curve, is greater with T_2 than with T_1 (with the slope of T_1 measuring also the average rate in both cases at the initial income level): $r_1 = .1$, and $r_2 = .15$.

Stabilization or Destabilization Policy?

TABLE 34–1. Income Effects of Autonomous Fall in Investment with Alternative Tax Arrangements

(A) Autonomous fall in investment with no tax

C	S	I	G	Y
720	280	180	100	1,000
720	280	150	100	970
696	274	150	100	946
.	.	.	.	.
.	.	.	.	.
.	.	.	.	.
600	250	150	100	850

(B) Autonomous fall in investment with proportional taxation ($r = .1$)

C	S	I	G	Y	T	D
720	180	180	100	1,000	100	900
720	180	150	100	970	97	873
698.4	174.6	150	100	948.4	94.84	853.56
.	.	.	.	.	.	.
.	.	.	.	.	.	.
.	.	.	.	.	.	.
642.857	160.714	150	100	892.857	89.286	803.571

(C) Autonomous fall in investment with progressive taxation ($r = .15$)

C	S	I	G	Y	T	D
720	180	180	100	1,000	100	900
720	180	150	100	970	95.5	874.5
699.6	174.9	150	100	949.6	92.44	857.16
.	.	.	.	.	.	.
.	.	.	.	.	.	.
656.250	164.062	150	100	906.250	85.938	820.312

Taxes—in particular, the personal income tax—are not the only stabilizer. We have directed attention to the tax rate and the *multiplier*. But stabilizers can involve also the *multiplicand* (autonomous injections that are multiplied). All automatic government-transfer payments and nondiscretionary government expenditures which "run counter" to income fluctuations and thus modify those changes can be classed as stabilizers. Such, for example, are unemployment-compensation payments to beneficiaries: as income falls and unemployment rises, payments would increase (and tax collections for the program would fall), thus tending to support disposable income and spending. Social security payments to the aged also are relatively independent of the current national income and are, therefore, a stabilizing element in the fiscal structure. (Unemployment-compensation payments act as a stronger stabilizer per dollar because they *increase* when national income falls, rather than merely remaining constant.) While our discussion and illustrations have been related to modifying decreases in income, the stabilizers tend also to dampen increases in income—although the symmetry of operation of the stabilizers is not always matched by the attitudes of observers; for some people, while rejoicing in the alleviation of recessions, take a dimmer view of restraints on expansions. (What is "stabilizing" in dampening a recession is a "drag" on a recovery. What's in a name?)

The quantitative importance of automatic stabilizers is not trivial: in the first four postwar recessions, the federal government's budget moved in the direction of bigger deficits or smaller surpluses for "automatic" reasons by an average of about $6.5 billion, and in the recoveries, the change in the budget toward larger surpluses or smaller deficits was over $11 billion. Indeed, generally and on the average, the magnitudes of automatic budget changes were much larger than those of discretionary changes. Furthermore, the automatic changes were always countercyclical, whereas discretionary fiscal changes sometimes aggravated the fluctuations in national income.

Full-Employment Income Budget Balance

A test of the extent to which fiscal actions have been stabilizing or destabilizing can be made by asking to what extent and at what times governmental spending plans and tax-collection structures have changed. Speaking loosely, the fiscal changes are expansionary if the deficit increases, and restrictive if the deficit diminishes or a surplus increases. But the deficit or surplus changes with national income itself. A larger national income increases tax revenue and thereby reduces a deficit or increases a surplus. If a larger deficit occurs, it may be either because tax rates or spending plans changed or because national income fell. To eliminate the effect of national income on our deficit-surplus indicator of expansionary or restrictive fiscal-policy changes, we compute what tax receipts and spending *would* be at a given, say full employment, income. Then changes in those tax receipts would no longer reflect changes in national income but only changes in the tax and spending laws, i.e., in fiscal *policy*. If in some year tax rates were raised (restrictive effect on national income) but national income had been smaller than in the prior year, the tax *revenues* could be smaller (because the reduced-income effect dominated the higher tax-rate effect). Using our *adjusted* tax receipt and spending estimates, we would call this a fiscal-policy change toward restriction—even though actual tax receipts had fallen. If we calculate estimates of what budget deficits and surpluses would have been at full-employment income (so as to eliminate national income effects), (1) we can see whether the existing fiscal policy was restrictive or expansionary (budget surplus or deficit at full employment income), and (2) by comparing changes from period to period in that projected budget at full employment, we can see whether the fiscal policy *changed* toward *more* expansion or restriction.

For example, it might be that over past years the budget would consistently have been exactly in balance *at full-employment income* (though deficits or surpluses actually occurred, because national income differed from the full-employment income). We would consider that a stabilizing fiscal policy, or at least not a destabilizing one. What does the actual record look like? Figure 34–4 shows that the estimated, hypothetical full-employment-budget surpluses or deficits have varied from year to year. (This does not show the *actual* surplus or deficit.) We see that at times tax laws and spending programs have changed to be more expansionary policies (1964) and at other times have changed to more restrictive (1968). Could these changes be interpreted as a discretionary fiscal policy, a resort to a more expansionary policy when national income is low and to a less expansionary or more restrictive policy when it is "too" high? (After all, taxes and expenditures reflect other considerations, too.) The changes were *not* generally in the income-stabilizing direction when they did occur. In other words, the projected adjusted

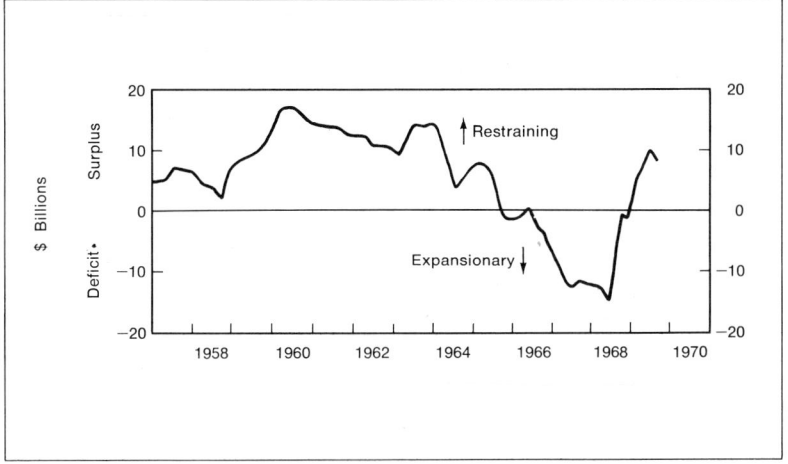

FIGURE 34-4. Budget Surplus or Deficit that Would Exist at High Employment

Changes in tax laws and spending programs move the calculated budget line up and down. An upward sweep of the line indicates government policy actions which imply a less expansionary effect of fiscal policy, for an upward slope implies a smaller deficit or a larger surplus at full employment. Typically, the full-employment budget has been "appreciably" out of balance. Note the "restraining" shift of some $25 billion from mid-1968 to mid-1969. Exactly how much effect on national income these changes in fiscal policy have is an unresolved issue: No highly reliable test or measure of the effects has been deduced.

full-employment budget was not typically on the expansionary (deficit) side at times of abnormally low national income and the reverse when income was abnormally high. Perhaps in a few more decades the brief record may look better.

Summary

1 Income-and-employment-stabilization policy has many specific goals, with potential conflicts among the objectives of full employment, nonincreasing prices, and open markets without price and wage controls. Policy disputes involve choices among the extents to which the various goals are to be attained.

2 Stabilization policy includes deliberate government fiscal or monetary activities. Those more fearful of government political power lean toward monetary activities, for that usually involves less expansion of overt governmental authority.

3 The amount of reserves provided the commercial banking system by the Fed has responded to desires to help the government sell its bonds to finance its debts, to sustain a growing economy (via increased stocks of money and also lower interest rates), and at times to avoid inflation. Anti-inflation policy can include reducing commercial bank reserves, making reserves more costly to obtain, and raising reserve requirements.

4 The objectives of Fed policy to accommodate the government's sale of bonds, to sustain a growing economy with high employment, and to avoid inflation are not mutually achievable in full. A trade-off of more of one and less of another is involved.

5 The Fed has not been spectacularly successful in maintaining money stocks appropriate for sustained growth and for anti-recessionary policy. Its record gives evidence that it misunderstands its powers and purposes and has difficulty predicting the most appropriate actions, even when there is agreement on goals.

6 Attempts to restrict discretionary power of political authorities have led to the suggestion that the money supply be increased *regularly* at a rate commensurate to population and productivity increase, thereby avoiding swings in money supply. In the same category are proposals that (a) federal expenditures and revenues be regulated by the rule that they balance only at full employment and/or (b) the gold standard be adopted, eliminating discretionary control over the money stock. All such proposals face the difficulty that it is impossible to force people to abide by rules they make but will later abandon if they think they can do better.

7 Stabilizing fiscal activities may be "automatic" rather than discretionary. The income tax, unemployment compensation, and social security payments dampen fluctuations in income, supporting a falling income and curtailing a rising income.

Questions

1 Why are stable price levels, full employment, and free markets regarded as inconsistent goals? In what sense, if any, are these goals more, or less, inconsistent with each other than any other goals one may have?

2 Explain why "cost-push inflation" is not a kind of inflation but is instead a reference to an aspect of inflation.

3 We have considered alternative means of financing a government budget deficit, noting in each instance the effect of the financing on (i) the money supply and (ii) excess reserves of commercial banks. Now, suppose that we have a budget surplus, with tax receipts greater than expenditures; suppose further that the surplus is to be used to reduce the government debt—the Treasury is to use the surplus tax collections to buy back (retire) government bonds. The first step is the collecting of taxes from the public, which reduces the public's demand deposits and increases the Treasury's demand deposits in commercial banks.

a. Analyze the use of the Treasury's deposit, after it has been transferred to the Fed, to buy bonds alternatively from (i) the Federal Reserve, (ii) commercial banks, and (iii) the public; record these alternative transactions in the T accounts of the Treasury, the Fed, and the commercial banks.

b. In each of the alternative bond purchases, note the effect on the money supply and on excess reserves; and determine the best seller of bonds if the purpose of the Treasury is to reduce the debt in an expansionary (or at least noncontractionary) manner or, alternatively, in a contractionary (or nonexpansionary) manner with respect to the money supply and excess reserves.

4 "As long as commercial banks extend credit (and increase demand deposits) only to finance production and distribution of inventories, the stock of money will be appropriate for the national income." This is known as the "real bills doctrine." It is fallacious. Can you explain why?

5 The Federal Reserve is the designated primary agency for the determination and conduct of monetary policy. On its record, indict the Fed for poor performance. Conversely, defend the Fed. Do you think it unjustified or in any relevant sense unfair to charge that "in the years 1930–32, the Fed exercised its responsibility for monetary policy so ineptly as to convert what otherwise would have been a moderate contraction into a major catastrophe"?

6 One monetary specialist emphasizes the importance of active monetary policy. "Walter Bagehot said, 'Money will not manage itself.' If there must be management, there is need for machinery and operators who will manage it adequately and effectively" (E. A. Goldenweiser, *Monetary Management,* New York: McGraw-Hill Book Co., Inc., 1949, p. 6).

Another has little confidence in the monetary managers. "Both history and an examination of human nature suggest that we cannot rely upon men vested with discretionary monetay powers to act promptly and wisely. The undue anxiety of central bankers about the future and their tenacious and misguided hope that they can predict developments lead them to ignore present difficulties much too often. . . . We need not weapons to combat developed booms or depressions but stable monetary conditions maintained in accordance with some one, announced rule of action" (Lloyd W. Mints, "Monetary Policy and Stabilization," *American Economic Review,* Vol. 41, May 1951, pp. 191, 193).

A third suggests a rule stated "in terms of the behavior of the stock of money . . . a legislated rule instructing the monetary authority to achieve a specified rate of growth in the stock of money . . . an annual rate of X percent, where X is some number between 3 and 5. . . . While this rule would drastically curtail the discretionary power of the monetary authorities, it would still leave an undesirable amount of discretion in the hands of Federal Reserve and Treasury authorities with respect to how to achieve the specified rate of growth in the money stock, debt management, banking supervision, and the like" (Milton Friedman, *Capitalism and Freedom,* Chicago: University of Chicago Press, 1962, p. 54).

Compare these three positions. To what extent can they be reconciled? On the basis of your assiduous study of income and money, what is your reaction to the Friedman statement?

7 Do you comprehend the following statement in a book review? Explain it: "The authors [A. M. Okun and N. M. Teeters] reaffirm the usefulness of the hypothetical calculation of the federal budget surplus at full employment as a general measure of budgetary impact on the economy. They emphasize the shortcomings of the actual federal surplus (or deficit) as an indicator of fiscal policy when the economy is either booming or slack. During the present economic slowdown, for instance, federal revenues are curtailed by the sluggish growth of incomes; this pushes the budget into deficit and makes fiscal policy appear to be stimulative. But the erosion of revenues should be recognized as an automatic stabilizer rather than a stimulus: the fiscal furnace starts working because it is colder outside, not because the thermostat is turned up."—*Brookings Bulletin,* VII (Spring 1970), p. 2.

Imports and the "Gain from Trade"

35 MUCH of the first part of this book was devoted to the *bases* (or *prerequisites*) of mutually beneficial exchange, the *pattern* (or *direction*) of the trade, the *terms* (prices) on which the trade was conducted, and the *gain* from the trade. The discussion was couched in terms of *individuals*—the Cuban and the Hungarian. But to a very large extent, what was said about trade between two individuals can be said also about the aggregate trade between whole regions and nations.

Individuals, we concluded, can trade to their mutual advantage if (1) they differ from each other in their (marginal) personal valuations of two or more commodities; (2) each person sells (exports) articles he values less than the things he acquires (imports); (3) the terms of trade (the price of exports relative to the price of imports) lie within limits, and the limits consist of the initial (pre-trade) respective personal (marginal) valuations of the two traders. Each person sacrifices the things he exports, but each values still higher the things he imports; so trade has allowed each person to move to a preferred consumption situation.

If we were to replace the names "Cuban" and "Hungarian" with "Cuba" and "Hungary" or "England" and "America," the same conclusions would hold. To be sure, some *additional* things should be said about international trade. Trade between *multi*-person economies presents issues of distribution of gains and costs not found in trade between *single*-person "economies"; people in one country use the same monetary unit, whereas two currencies are involved in English-American trade; uncoordinated policies of autonomous governments, different financial institutions, different customs and laws all add complications to international trade. But basically the gains from productive specialization and subsequent exchange are to be found in foreign as well as domestic trade. The gain from trade is the gain from trade, whether or not the traders reside in the same country.

And yet, the community in general applauds domestic commerce but holds foreign trade suspect. At least, *imports* are suspect, if not condemned outright; *exports*, it is typically felt, are permissible and probably even to be encouraged, for they relieve the economy of "burdensome surpluses" and perhaps bring in gold. And, of course, nothing else is really quite as good as gold.[1]

Does the "gain from trade" really emanate most directly from *exports*? Is economic welfare actually enhanced if the outward flow of goods and services to the rest of the world is increased and the inward flow reduced? Economic well-being rests on the consumable and investable things that are possessed and can be utilized. One of our fundamental axioms has been that *more* (of economic goods) is *better* than less. How does foreign trade enable a community to obtain the most for its own use? Scarcely by giving to foreigners as much as possible of the fruits of domestic production and taking nothing in return. *Exports are a cost,* draining domestically produced output from the country; *the gain from trade stems from imports,* which add to the domestically available supply of goods and services.

If this is so, why export at all? Aside from sheer ignorance, on what ground can England, for example, adopt the slogan "Export or Die"? England bears the cost of exports in order to obtain imports—just as an individual is willing to hand over (export) a $10 bill in order to obtain (import) a sack of groceries, because he values the meat and potatoes more than the $10. But note that the gain from the transaction does not lie in paying out the $10; it lies in getting the merchandise, to the extent that he values it more than the money. If the same sack of merchandise could be obtained for less than $10 or if $10 would fetch a bigger bundle of goods—that is, if the *price* of groceries were lower (or the "*terms of trade*" were better)—the gain from the transaction would be even greater.

The lower the price of things one buys, the better. A zero price—making the "purchase" a gift—is best (assuming that we rule out negative prices, with the seller paying the buyer to take the stuff). But since the price of imports normally will be greater than zero, there is a limit to the amount of imports residents of a country can "conveniently" *obtain*—even if there is no limit in sight to the amount they *desire*. An individual can live too high off the hog and run into financial embarrassment; so can a country. As we shall see in more detail later, a nation that persists in "living far beyond its currently earned means" is courting a "balance-of-payments crisis."

Because imports normally are not free, we should modify our initial conclusion that imports are good, and the more imports the better: *imports are good, and the more the better*—to the extent that they can be "conveniently" financed.

1, 2, 3, 4, 5

The Gold Bug, Foreign Aid, and National Income

A rather long period some centuries ago—from about 1500 to 1800—has been labeled the age of "mercantilism." Mercantilists, generally businessmen and government officials,

---

[1] Whatever the typical American attitudes toward international trade, (a) the United States—with exports and imports of goods and services at annual levels of well over $50 billion—is absolutely the biggest world trader by a large margin; and (b) foreign commerce represents a relatively modest proportion of its national income. Total U. S. trade (exports plus imports) is roughly twice that of England and of West Germany, and it is more than three times that of France and of Canada. However, the U. S. average propensity to import (commodity imports relative to national income) is about .04, while it is .2 or greater (sometimes much greater) for many major commercial countries (Belgium, Canada, Denmark, Netherlands, Sweden, West Germany).

were concerned with economic policies that might enhance the wealth and power of their respective emerging national states. Much of their attention was focused on foreign-trade policy, and they were motivated by fear of most imports and generally a passion for exports; if the exports of goods and services exceeded the imports, the balance would be received in gold.

Despite their great attention to international commerce, the mercantilists failed to comprehend the economic rationale of international specialization of production and of free exchange. Especially conspicuous among the doctrines of modern (and ancient) mercantilists is the following: Foreign trade is suspect unless a country has an export surplus, and the major reason for an export surplus is to stimulate national income and employment. This was the most pervasive Congressional argument presented in support of the Reciprocal Trade Agreements Act in 1934 (and in the debates on the periodic extensions of the act); it has bulked large in debates on other measures of foreign economic policy, including the Marshall Plan in the late 1940s and the Trade Expansion Act of 1962, the successor of the Trade Agreements Act.[2]

In order to put into reasonable perspective the mercantilistic proclivity for *export* balances in the interest of supporting national income, imagine that there evolved an unusual insect, which we shall call the gold bug. The gold bug has the ability and the desire to burrow into the vaults of Fort Knox, grasp a piece of gold, tunnel beneath the Atlantic Ocean, and leave the gold where it will be found by some European peasant.

The peasant is overjoyed, for he can get domestic currency—marks, francs, lire—from his monetary authorities in exchange for the gold.

The foreign monetary authorities are elated, for with gold they can acquire dollars from the United States Treasury, and with dollars they can buy American (and other) merchandise.

The Treasury presumably is delighted, for it has long stood ready to buy unlimited quantities of gold at a fixed price—and then put the gold into Fort Knox.

Finally, the American producers (and their employees) who now get purchase orders from abroad—orders which are paid in dollars—are highly pleased.

It appears that the antics of the gold bug have started a sequence of events in which everyone is happy. (Apparently no one pauses to wonder how a nation is enriched by transactions which, in the aggregate, involve giving up more goods and services than the nation receives in return.) There is, in fact, a circular flow of gold; but, since the gold bug's activity goes unnoted, there *seems* to be only a movement of gold into the United

---

[2] The Trade Agreements Act instituted a program of bilateral (two-country) executive commercial agreements to achieve reciprocal reductions in tariff duties and other trade restrictions. It was enacted "for the purpose of expanding foreign markets for the products of the United States," mainly in the interests of combating "the present economic depression." In order "that foreign markets will be made available," it was deemed necessary to afford "corresponding market opportunities for foreign products in the United States," but "the admission of foreign goods . . . [must be] in accordance with the characteristics and needs of various branches of American production."

The Trade Expansion Act broadens still further the authority of the President to enter into trade agreements, increasing the allowable percentage reductions in tariffs and permitting negotiated reductions by broad categories of goods rather than being restricted to item-by-item alterations. The act was largely a response to the European Common Market (the European Economic Community), which became effective January 1, 1958, and is intended progressively to eliminate trade barriers among the members (France, West Germany, Italy, Belgium, the Netherlands, and Luxembourg), while maintaining a common tariff vis-à-vis the rest of the world. In submitting the bill to Congress, President Kennedy contended: "Our bargaining authority" must be "increased in both flexibility and extent" in order "to empower our negotiators with sufficient authority to induce the EEC to grant wider access to our goods. . . ."

States, matched by United States exports of merchandise. No mercantilist could ask for anything more.

This supposedly happy process could continue indefinitely, as long as no one took inventory at Fort Knox. Of course, if some snoop did check up (and people have been elected to Congress partly on the promise that they would audit our gold holdings) and find that the gold stock was not increasing as it should, there likely would be unbounded consternation in the United States—some of the nation's "wealth" had evaporated (or been stolen by the opposition party)!

If this gold-bug theory seems too farfetched to be enlightening, note that foreign aid achieves substantially the same results. With an American foreign-aid program, instead of obtaining dollars from selling gold-bug gold back to the Treasury, foreign governments receive the dollars as a gift from the United States government—which can create as many dollars as it pleases (and sometimes more than is desirable). The American producers are just as happy to get these dollars for their merchandise as they were in the gold-bug case.

But while we all like to see American producers busy, for this maintains national income and employment, some are dubious about giving goods to foreigners. Perhaps we could have the best of all possible worlds (promote exports that foreigners never receive) if (1) the government, as under a foreign-aid program, creates dollars; (2) the government spends the dollars to buy domestically produced goods; (3) the goods, as before, are put on ships and set sail; and (4) the Air Force sinks the ships in mid-ocean. Not only can this stimulate domestic employment, but the Air Force gets some bombing practice.

However, eventually even some of the mercantilists may perceive that this is rather expensive target practice. Instead of "exporting" merchandise to the kingdom of Davy Jones, why not have it distributed in some way to American consumers? This does, indeed, appear reasonable. We thereby continue to maintain employment but avoid the waste of destroying goods.

Thus, *we have maintained employment without exports.* Full employment can be achieved through domestic (monetary and fiscal) measures, as we have previously discussed; we need not rely on foreign aid and trade policy to achieve that goal. Therefore, foreign economic policy well can, and presumably should, be determined on criteria other than probable repercussions (which in themselves might or might not be welcome) on domestic income and employment. In any case, foreign commercial policy as a means of attaining domestic, or internal, objectives is likely to be relatively ineffective; for some countries, including notably the United States, foreign transactions are a relatively small component of *GNP* and, by their nature, are not under the unilateral control of any one of the participating countries. Also, such use of commercial policy may well be disruptive of cordial international relations; attempts by one country to grab a bigger share of the current world-trade total by subsidizing exports and curtailing imports may inspire retaliation and then counter-retaliation. That foreign economic policy should be determined in its own right rather than employed as a tool of domestic income stabilization is the positive conclusion of our line of thought.

On the other hand, we should emphasize two points *not* implied by our analysis. First, we are not implying that foreign economic aid is inevitably useless or undesirable. To pass judgment on this issue requires consideration of many elements not included in this discussion. But we do conclude that the aid program is unnecessary for the specific purpose of keeping U. S. income high. Second, and even more fundamental, we certainly are not suggesting that there are no gains to be derived from international trade. But, contrary to the mercantilists, dead and alive, the gains from trade do not stem from a persistent export surplus.

International Payments and Exchange Arbitrage

The purpose of including here a brief discussion of some mechanics of "international finance" is not to explain how to run the foreign-exchange department of a New York bank. Rather, surveying how international payments are made and how rates of exchange are "equalized" through arbitrage will help understanding of other important matters: the determination of exchange rates, the balance of payments, and even international-trade theory.

Making International Payments

Conversion of currencies. The most conspicuous problem associated with making international payments stems from the existence of more than one currency. When an American sells goods to an Englishman, the American normally wishes to receive payment in dollars, while it serves the convenience of the Englishman to make payment in pounds sterling. It is feasible for the buyer to pay one currency and the seller to obtain another through the intermediary of foreign-exchange dealers (banks holding inventories of foreign monies in the form of demand deposits in banks abroad) who are willing to buy and sell one kind of currency against another. The "conversion of currencies" is the primary function of the foreign-exchange market.

Provision of credit. Foreign-exchange dealers simultaneously provide "credit." Not only does the exporter in an international transaction wish to receive payment in a currency different from that in which the importer wishes to remit, but he may want the payment immediately, while the importer may want to delay at least until the goods are received and sometimes for several additional months. Both parties can be satisfied if a foreign-exchange dealer takes over the exporter's claim on the importer, reimbursing the former right away and extending a loan to—and receiving interest from—the latter.

Financing an export. Suppose that International Harvester, an American firm, contracts to sell a tractor to an Englishman for $2,100, and suppose further that International Harvester prefers to receive immediate payment while the buyer desires ninety-day credit. The exporter wants *dollars immediately,* and the importer wants to pay *pounds later.* We can trace a possible financing procedure with the help of Figure 35–1.

The exporter sends the tractor to a shipping firm. Among the various documents involved is a *bill of lading* (B/L), drawn by the shipping company and given to International Harvester as (a) a receipt and serving also as (b) a claim to the tractor when presented by a *bona fide* holder (step 1). As the goods are sent on their way, International Harvester draws a "draft" on the importer. The draft—otherwise known as a *bill of exchange* (B/E)—is a written order by International Harvester, directing the importer to pay a certain sum (in pounds) in ninety days to an appropriate third party. (An ordinary check used in domestic commerce, also being an order to pay, is a form of

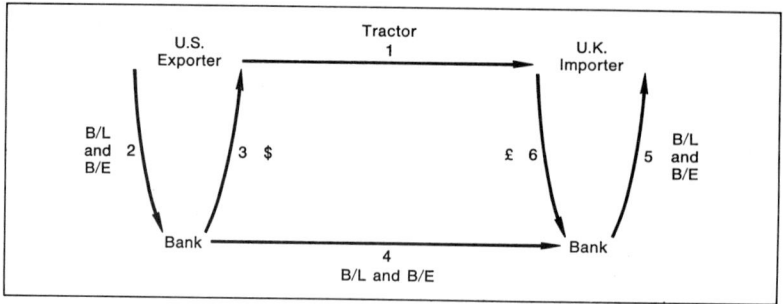

FIGURE 35-1. Financing an Export

Foreign-exchange dealers both (1) convert currencies (pay the U. S. exporter in dollars and receive payment from the U. K. importer in pounds) and (2) provide credit (the exporter is paid immediately while the importer makes payment later). The U. S. export of merchandise is financed by a U. S. capital outflow (an increase in U. S. claims on the U. K.).

bill of exchange.) The number of pounds equivalent to $2,100 is determined by the rate of exchange, or exchange rate. An *exchange rate* is the price of one currency in terms of another. If, for example, $3 = £1 (or £.333 = $1), then $2,100 is equal to £700. The face value of the draft includes the interest to be paid on the ninety-day loan.

International Harvester does not send the "order to pay" directly to the Englishman. Instead, it takes the B/E, along with the B/L and other attached documents, to a New York bank (step 2). The B/E is "discounted"; that is, International Harvester sells the draft to the bank for the face value minus the interest to be accumulated. The draft itself is denominated in pounds, but International Harvester receives dollars (step 3). In the normal course of events, this is the end of the transaction for International Harvester: it has produced, sold, and shipped a tractor and received immediate payment in dollars.

The U. S. bank that purchased the draft on the Englishman does not collect from him directly. Instead, it works through an English bank, which may be a branch of the U. S. institution or a "correspondent" bank with which the American bank has a working arrangement. The draft and documents are sent to the U. K. (United Kingdom) bank (step 4). The U. K. bank presents the B/L to the importer after the importer "accepts" the draft—that is, acknowledges his indebtedness by signing the draft (step 5). With the B/L thus acquired, the importer can go to the dock and claim the tractor. At the time of maturity of the draft, the importer pays pounds to the U. K. bank (step 6).

The pounds paid by the importer belong to the U. S. bank, which owned the draft on the importer, and are put in a demand deposit held by the U. S. bank in the English institution. The U. S. economy (through International Harvester) *supplied* a tractor to the rest of the world (and International Harvester was rewarded with dollars); the U. S. economy (through the New York bank) *received* a checking account in an English bank. Thus, the U. S. has *exported merchandise* and *imported a claim* on foreign goods and services.

The tractor transaction could be financed in an alternative manner. Instead of International Harvester's drawing a sterling draft and discounting it with a U. S. bank, the draft could be drawn in dollars and sent directly to the importer. The importer then must acquire dollars in order to meet his obligation. He does so by buying dollars from a U. K. bank holding a demand deposit in a U. S. bank. The importer pays pounds to his bank and acquires command of dollars; these dollars are then paid to International Harvester;

and, of course, the U. K.-owned demand deposit in the U. S. bank is thereby reduced. In this case, the *U. S. merchandise export* is paid for, not by the U. S.'s importing (increasing) a claim on England, but by *reduction of a U. K. claim on the U. S.*

Whether the U. S. export is financed by increasing U. S. claims on foreigners or by decreasing foreign claims on the U. S., the U. S. has supplied merchandise "on credit." The U. S. has *not* received goods and services or gold in return, nor has the U. S. given away the merchandise; the economy *per se* (not International Harvester) must, therefore, have granted a loan; that is, there was a "capital movement" from the U. S. to the U. K.

Exchange Arbitrage

In the foregoing illustration, International Harvester received dollars, and the importer paid pounds. With two currencies involved, obviously a "link" or an "equivalence" must exist between them—namely, a rate of exchange. We assumed that $3 = £1$. Is this the ratio of exchange between dollars and pounds in the New York or in the London foreign-exchange market? Both. As a result of a market procedure or operation known as "arbitrage," the New York dollar-price of the pound becomes 3, and simultaneously the London pound-price of the dollar is ⅓. The New York and London rates on the respective foreign currencies are "consistent"; that is, 3 and ⅓ are reciprocals.

Suppose that in fact there is a discrepancy in the rates, as indicated:

In New York: $3.00 = £1$ or $1.00 = £.333$
In London: $2.97 = £1$ or $1.00 = £.337$

With two prices existing for the same article, there surely must be a way to cash in, if you are not legally prevented from buying and selling as you please in foreign-exchange markets. But what to buy and what to sell?

There are profit-making possibilities in buying low and selling high. An American arbitrageur may think: *given* the fact that the actual price of $1 in London is £.337, the dollar-price of the pound *should* be $2.97, but actually in New York it is $3, so the *New York dollar-price of the pound is too high.* And *given* the fact that $1 = £.333$ in New York, the price of the pound in London *should* be $3, so the *London dollar-price of the pound* ($2.97) *is too low.*

Similarly, an Englishman concludes that the *London pound-price of the dollar is too high* (£.337 instead of £.333), and the *New York pound-price of the dollar is too low* (£.333 instead of £.337).

Both the American and the Englishman capitalize on the inconsistent rates by *selling pounds and buying dollars in New York* and simultaneously *buying pounds and selling dollars in London*. The American, starting with dollars, can buy £1,000 in London for an outlay of $2,970 and sell £1,000 in New York for receipts of $3,000, netting a profit of $30. The Englishman can pay £1,000 for $3,000 in New York and sell $3,000 in London for £1,010.1, yielding a gain of £10.1.

But arbitrage activity itself alters exchange rates in such fashion as to eliminate the basis of further arbitrage. The increased supply of pounds lowers the price of pounds in terms of dollars, and the increased demand for dollars raises the price of the dollar; and the increased supply of dollars lowers the pound value of the dollar, and the increased demand for pounds raises the value of the pound. With high prices falling and low prices rising, the price discrepancies are eliminated. The final result might be about $2.99 = £1$ (or $1 = £.334$) in both New York and London.

7, 8, 9

Questions

1 On the basis of the analysis of this chapter, evaluate and compare the following statements on the immediate source of the "gain from trade" by an eighteenth-century economist and by a nineteenth-century economist:

". . . foreign trade . . . carries out that surplus part of the produce of their land and labour for which there is no demand among them, and brings back in return for it something else for which there is a demand. It gives a value to their superfluities, by exchanging them for something else, which may satisfy a part of their wants, and increase their enjoyments."—Adam Smith, *An Inquiry into the Nature and Causes of the Wealth of Nations* (1776), ed. E. Cannan (New York: Random House, Inc., 1937), p. 415.

"The only direct advantage of foreign commerce consists in the imports. A country obtains things which it either could not have produced at all, or which it must have produced at a greater expense. . . . Adam Smith's theory . . . was that it afforded an outlet for the surplus produce of a country. . . . The expression, surplus produce, seems to imply that a country is under some kind of necessity of producing the corn or cloth which it exports; so that the portion which it does not itself consume, if not wanted and consumed elsewhere, would either be produced in sheer waste, or if it were not produced, the corresponding portion of capital would remain idle. . . . Exportation ceasing, importation to an equal value would cease also, and all that part of the income of the country which had been expended in imported commodities, would be ready to expend itself on the same things produced at home, or on others instead of them."—John Stuart Mill, *Principles of Political Economy* (1848), ed. W. J. Ashley (London and New York: Longmans, Green & Co., 1929), p. 578.

2 Now what do you think of the following Congressional arguments of the late nineteenth century in favor of high tariffs? (Suggestion: Return to these quotations after studying later chapters and see if your evaluation is then different.)

"The protectionist theory is to discriminate by duties in favor of every article which can be grown or manufactured in the protected country in sufficient quantities for the use of the people, and everything which can not be grown or manufactured in sufficient quantities . . . should be placed upon the free [zero-tariff] list."—Senator Henry C. Lodge, *Congressional Record,* Vol. 26 (April 10, 1894), p. 3617.

"Free trade . . . makes trade of the first importance as a condition of natural wealth and prosperity. . . . The true and lasting source of wealth is production, and trade, even though it enhances the value of the product, is at the same time a tax upon production, on account of the cost of transportation. A nation without trade may be permanently rich and prosperous, but a nation without production and dependent solely on trade holds riches and prosperity by a frail tenure."—Senator Lodge, *op. cit.,* p. 3620.

"Every additional yard of goods thus brought into our market will displace a yard of American-made goods. . . . It is certain that the consumption of goods will not materially increase, and certain that the American production must be curtailed practically in the proportion of the increased imports . . . a large part of the money that is annually paid to American employees will be paid to the foreign laborers."—House Report 234, minority, to accompany H. R. 4864, 53rd Congress, 2nd session, December 19, 1893, pp. 53, 57.

3 "If imports are really desirable and exports are really a cost, it would seem ideal to have a situation in which we exported nothing at all and the rest of the world flooded us with their own goods and services." Do you accept this?

4 "The theory of international trade tells us that *imports* are good and the more the better. But typical international financial and commercial policy consists in trying to promote

exports and perhaps discourage imports. Obviously, since we cannot have an import balance and an export balance at the same time, trade theory and economic foreign policy are in conflict. Perhaps the theory is bad or perhaps the policy makers have not taken a course in economics." On the basis of your study thus far, do you agree that there exists an irreconcilable dichotomy between theory and policy?

5 It has been argued in this chapter that the gain from trade stems most immediately from imports and that exports are a cost. The United States has had an export balance of merchandise in virtually every year since 1873 and an export balance of goods and services in literally every year since 1895. Does it follow that over this considerable period the United States has been worse off as a result of foreign trade?

6 "Exports are an 'injection' into the domestic income stream, along with investment and government spending. Imports are a 'leakage' out of the income stream, along with saving and taxes. Since a bigger national income is preferable to a smaller, it follows that exports should be larger than imports." Right?

7 Review how "the foreign-exchange market" makes the following possible.
a. An international seller of merchandise is paid in one currency while the buyer makes payment in a different currency.
b. The seller receives payment immediately while the buyer makes payment at the end of a credit period.

8 "With inconsistent exchange rates between two currencies, it appears in *each* of the countries that the domestic-currency price of foreign exchange is too high—or too low." In the illustration in the text, which case is it? I.e., in *both* New York and London, is the price of foreign money too high or too low? Can you alter the data in such fashion as to yield the alternative case?

9 Arbitrage can involve three currencies; if there are consistent "cross rates" between any pair of currencies, an arbitrageur could spend some of his initial money for either of the other currencies, then convert the second money into the third, and then convert the third into as many units of the first as he spent at the outset. Suppose that the rate of exchange between currencies X and Y is $1X = 2Y$, and between currencies X and Z it is $.25X = 1Z$.
a. What is the consistent cross rate between Y and Z?
b. Suppose that you own some of currency X and that the actual cross rate is $1Y = 3Z$. As an arbitrageur, what currencies would you buy and sell in sequence?
c. In light of arbitrage activity, specify carefully what happens to the demand for and supply of each currency.
d. In what directions do the three sets of exchange rates move?

International Trade Theory

36 THE preceding chapter stated that the analysis of production specialization and exchange is the same whether persons are in the same country or in different countries. Domestic trade and gains from it are not basically different from international commerce and its gains. In both instances, acquisitions of goods and services can be maximized for given costs or costs can be minimized for given returns. And in both domestic and foreign trade, the gains stem most immediately from "imports" (what is acquired) rather than from "exports" (what is paid). But while the fundamental analysis of all trade is essentially the same, there are some considerations of international commercial activities—in their nature, largely institutional—and issues of governmental policy which warrant separate discussion.

It is convenient to investigate the theory of international trade by successive steps of elaboration. We shall suppose first that our only information is output (commodity) prices. Then we shall introduce data on a *single* input assumed to produce the commodities. Finally, the analysis will consider production by *two* inputs which can be used in variable proportions.

The Output-Price Theory

Suppose that the world contains only two countries, the U. S. and the U. K., and only two commodities, textiles and steel. Each country has its own monetary unit for stating prices: the dollar and the pound sterling.

TABLE 36–1. Prices of Textiles and Steel in the U. S. and the U. K.
(Equal Price Ratios: No Basis for Two-way Trade)

	Textiles	Steel
U. S.	$5	$10
U. K.	£2	£4

"Equal" Advantage

Given the price information in Table 36–1, our initial question is: Does the situation present a basis for *mutually beneficial, two-way* trade? Is it feasible for the U. S. to underprice the U. K. in one commodity (and thus be able to export it) and for the U. K. to underprice the U. S. in the other?

Is the U. S. price of $5 for a unit of textiles more or less than the English price of £2? To answer, we must have an exchange rate between the two currencies, in order to convert the U. K. pound-price of textiles into dollars—or convert the U. S. dollar-price into pounds. If the exchange rate is $2.50 = £1, then $5 is the equivalent of £2, and textiles would be the same price in both countries. At any higher dollar-price of the pound, the pound-price of textiles in the U. K. would be the equivalent of more than $5; in that case (and in the absence of trade barriers), the U. S. could profitably export textiles to the U. K. And if the price of the pound is less than $2.50, the U. K. could underprice the U. S. in textiles.

It happens—since the ratio 5/2 equals the ratio 10/4—that we have precisely the same results with steel: the U. S. will export steel if the dollar price of the pound is more than 2.5, and it will import steel if the rate is less.

It follows that the total situation of Table 36–1 does not allow *two*-way trade. Since the ratio of textile prices equals the steel price ratio, any exchange rate that allows the U. S. to export textiles (e.g., $3 = £1 or $1 = £.333) will also allow the U. S. to export steel; and any rate leading the U. S. to import either commodity (e.g., $2 = £1 or $1 = £.5) will induce importing the other as well.

One-way trade, with one country exporting both commodities and importing neither, *is* possible. If $3 = £1, the U. S. will export both goods, and U. S. banks (exchange dealers) will accumulate demand deposits in English banks or U. K. deposits in American banks will be depleted, as we illustrated earlier in discussing international payments. But as U. S. banks continue to pile up pounds in English banks, they will be willing to buy still more pounds only at a lower price; that is, they will give fewer dollars to U. S. exporters for a pound, and the exchange rate thus changes, with the dollar price of the pound falling (the pound "depreciates" relative to dollars). And as the dollar holdings of U. K. banks are persistently reduced, they will charge U. K. importers higher and higher pound prices for a dollar. In a market where the exchange rate is free to move far enough, the rate will continue to fall until it reaches $2.50 = £1 ($1 = £4). But at that rate, textiles will be equally priced in both countries, as will steel. There is then no basis for even one-way trade. Similarly, if initially the dollar price of the pound were less than 2.5, the U. S. would import both commodities, and the dollar price of the pound would be bid up to 2.5.

We conclude that *when the price ratios are equal*—that is, 5/2 = 10/4 (textile and steel price ratios) or, alternatively, 5/10 = 2/4 (U. S. and U. K. price ratios)—*there is no basis for two-way trade* or even, in a foreign-exchange market in which exchange rates are free to move, for prolonged one-way trade. With equal commodity price ratios, any exchange rate between the national currencies which permits any trade will induce only *one*-way trade, and such trade puts pressure on the exchange rate, tending to move it to a value which eliminates the basis of *all* trade.[1]

"Comparative" Advantage

In Table 36–2, the U. K. price of steel is £8, rather than £4, as in Table 36–1. The commodity price *ratios* now are *different*—5/2 ≠ 10/8 (and 5/10 ≠ 2/8); consequently, there should exist the possibility *of two-way trade to the advantage of each country*. (This is directly analogous to saying, in earlier discussions, that there is a basis for mutually beneficial exchange between the Cuban and the Hungarian when their subjective valuations for two commodities differ.)

TABLE 36–2. Prices of Textiles and Steel in the U. S. and the U. K.
(Unequal Price Ratios: Basis for Two-way Trade)

	Textiles	Steel
U. S.	$5	$10
U. K.	£2	£8

As before, we must have an exchange rate in order to make the U. S. and U. K. money prices comparable. If the rate is $5 = £2 ($2.5 = £1), neither country can underprice the other in *textiles;* if the rate is $10 = £8 ($1.25 = £1), neither can underprice the other in *steel*. If the actual rate falls within these *limits* (if the dollar price of the pound is

---

[1] The foregoing discussion assumes that the rate *is* free to move. But gold movements or other pegging devices may limit movement of the rate. Under either the "classic" (pre-1914) gold standard or the post-World War II International Monetary Fund (I.M.F.), a "par" rate of exchange is defined on the basis of the prices of gold in the respective currencies.

If, for example, the dollar price of gold is $30 per ounce and the pound price is £10 per ounce, then $30 = £10, or $3 = £1. It might cost 2 cents to ship between the U. S. and the U. K. the amount of gold that sells for £1 (1/10 ounce). Therefore, if the rate in the foreign-exchange market moves to $2.98 = £1, an English importer is indifferent between buying dollars directly (obtaining $2.98 for £1) and buying gold for £1 in the U. K. (selling it for $3 in the U. S. and paying 2 cents in shipping costs). The dollar price of the pound would not fall below 2.98, for, with the option of shipping gold to the U. S., the Englishman (or anyone with pounds) would not accept less than $2.98 for £1. Thus, $2.98 = £1 is the U. K. "gold export point" (and the U. S. gold import point); similarly, $3.02 = £1 is the upper dollar price of the pound and is known as the U. K. gold import, or U. S. gold export, point.

The situation is analogous under the I.M.F., except that gold may (and does) flow before the market exchange rate hits the specified limits. If, in our illustration of a U. K. import balance from the U. S., English exchange dealers begin to run short of dollars, they can replenish their inventories by buying dollars with pounds from the Bank of England. If the Bank, in turn, is short of dollars, it can purchase more with gold sold in the U. S. Finally, if the Bank runs short of both dollars and gold, it may be able to purchase (borrow) dollars with pounds at the I.M.F.

While the exchange rate may be pegged for a time at a level which allows the trade imbalance to persist, there are limits on the necessary "ammunition"—foreign exchange, gold, and borrowing power. As we shall see later, if the pegging ammunition lasts long enough, the trade imbalance may be eliminated by means other than a change in the exchange rate.

less than 2.5 and more than 1.25), we can have two-way trade. Suppose that the rate is $2 = £1$ (or $1 = £.5$). We can then convert all prices of Table 36–2 into either dollars or pounds, as seen in Table 36–3. Stated in terms of either currency, textiles are cheaper in the U. K., and steel is cheaper in the U. S. Therefore, the U. S. will produce steel, consume some of it, and export the remainder in return for some English textiles; and the U. K. will specialize in textiles, export some of its output, and import U. S. steel.

TABLE 36–3. Comparable Dollar and Pound Prices ($2 = £1$)

	Dollar Prices		Pound Prices	
	Textiles	Steel	Textiles	Steel
U. S.	$5	$10	£2.5	£5
U. K.	$4	$16	£2	£8

The Gains from Trade

In what sense are both the U. S. and the U. K. better off as a result of the specialization and exchange? The most obvious answer is that buyers prefer a lower price to a higher price: Americans prefer buying textiles at $4 (the price of U. K. textiles) to buying at $5 (the U. S. price), and Englishmen prefer paying only £5 for steel (the price of U. S. steel) to £8 (the U. K. price).

In the U. S., before foreign trade began, both textiles and steel were produced, because there was a demand to consume both. What was the *domestic market-exchange ratio* between textiles and steel? With textiles priced at $5 and steel at $10, two units of textiles in the U. S. had the same market value as one of steel: $2t = 1s$. However, in the U. K., the exchange ratio domestically was different, with four units of textiles at £2 equaling one of steel at £8: $4t = 1s$.

Money may always be used in the actual buying and selling of textiles and steel, rather than bartering one commodity directly against the other, but the purchase of one unit of steel in, say, the U. S. requires an expenditure which could have bought two units of textiles. The consumer has foregone the potential of two textiles in order to acquire the steel. Thus, even in a money economy, it is meaningful to say that the textile price of steel was 2 and that the steel price of textiles was .5.

An American would be better off if, with foreign trade, he could buy steel for less than the equivalent of two textiles or if he could sell steel for more than two textiles; or if he could buy textiles at a price of less than .5 steel or sell textiles at more than .5 steel. And an Englishman would be pleased to be able to buy steel for a sacrifice of less than four textiles or give up steel in exchange for more than four textiles; or buy textiles at less than .25 steel or sell textiles at more than .25 steel. These alternatives, in terms of textile prices of steel (the amount of textiles per unit of steel) are summarized in Table 36–4.

An individual, then, gains from foreign trade, for with trade he can acquire the import commodity at a lower price (in terms of the export commodity) or sell the export commodity at a higher price (in terms of the import commodity) than would be possible with only domestic exchange. In short, with appropriate international specialization in production, *the terms of international trade are better for residents of both countries than the respective domestic exchange ratios before foreign trade commenced.*

International Trade Theory

TABLE 36–4. Domestic Exchange Ratios and Terms of International Trade

	U. S.	U. K.
Domestically (in the absence of foreign trade):	$2t = 1s$	$4t = 1s$
With foreign trade, import textiles and export steel if:	$(2+)t = 1s$*	$(4+)t = 1s$
With foreign trade, import steel and export textiles if:	$(2-)t = 1s$	$(4-)t = 1s$*

* Asterisks indicate the feasible foreign-trade terms of trade: the U. S. wishes to import textiles and export steel if the terms of trade are *more* than *two* textiles for one steel, and the U. K. is willing to export textiles for steel if she must yield *less* than *four* textiles in exchange for one steel.

The $2t = 1s$ domestic *exchange* ratio in the U. S. prior to foreign trade is a reflection, we may suppose, of a $2t = 1s$ (marginal) *production* ratio. That is, a given bundle of resources could produce $2t$ or $1s$. The economy can produce an additional $2t$ by putting a minimum additional quantity of resources into the textile industry. Assuming full employment of resources, these additional resources would have to be transferred out of the steel industry. And the amount of resources required to expand textile output by two units would have produced one unit of steel. The steel *cost* of $2t$ is 1, just as is the initial domestic steel *price* of $2t$.[2]

Suppose that the terms of *international* trade are $3.5t = 1s$. The U. S. can sacrifice (export) $1s$ and obtain (import) $3.5t$, whereas without foreign trade the sacrifice of $1s$ would have yielded (by shifting resources from steel production to textile production) only $2t$. The U. S. thus can obtain textiles more cheaply in real terms via international trade by specializing its production in steel and then exporting some steel for textiles than by producing textiles directly with its own resources. Similarly, the U. K. can import $1s$ by exporting only $3.5t$, whereas by domestic production alone one more steel would have meant a cost of $4t$.

With foreign trade, each country obtains *more* for a *given* cost, or, alternatively, each obtains a *given* bundle of commodities for a *smaller* cost. As long as aggregate resources of an economy are constant and employment is full, the maximum "production possibilities" are unchanged, and, in the absence of foreign trade, the "consumption boundary" is the same as the "production boundary"; but the introduction of foreign trade extends the consumption boundary. With given resources, more goods and services are available with foreign trade than without foreign trade. That is the "gain from trade."[3]

Finally, we may elaborate the meaning of such a statement as, "The U. S. specializes

---

[2] Strictly, we should say that the *exchange* ratio equals the *production* (or *physical transformation*) ratio in *long-run equilibrium* in a price-takers' market. To envisage the market mechanism by which the exchange ratio is equated with the production ratio, suppose that initially the trading ratio differs from the technological ratio of $2t = 1s$: perhaps trades are actually taking place at a ratio of $3t = 1s$. In such a case, what wise entrepreneur would use his resources to produce textiles? The market is "undervaluing" textiles and "overvaluing" steel: the entrepreneur can devote himself to producing steel (at a cost of forgoing *two* textiles for each steel produced) and then swapping the steel for textiles (obtaining *three* textiles for each steel sold). But as this realization spreads through the economy, more and more resources are drawn out of the textile industry into the steel industry, and the ever growing supply of steel and demand for textiles reduces the textile price of steel (raises the steel price of textiles) until the equilibrium rate of $2t = 1s$ is attained.

[3] We emphasize again that the analysis is exactly the same as that in Chapter 12, with two people replaced by two "countries."

its production in, and exports, steel, because it is more efficient in steel production, and similarly the U. K. is better in textile production." How are we to interpret "more efficient" and "better"? In physical (technological) input-output terms, is the U. S. "absolutely" superior to the U. K. in producing steel? That is, with given real inputs (labor and other resources), can the U. S. produce more steel than can the U. K. with the same amount of inputs? With just the information given, we cannot tell. Table 36–3 gives only the *money* prices of outputs. We can tell what the domestic exchange ratio in the U. S. would be in the absence of foreign trade; for example, the *textile* price of one steel is 2. But neither the *money* price of steel nor the *textile* price of steel alone tells us whether the *input-expenditure* price of steel in the U.S. is more or less than the cost of steel in the U. K.

The U. S. may be physically superior in producing both commodities (it may be able to produce more of each commodity *per unit* of resources); it may be inferior in both; it may be superior in steel production and inferior in textile production (but it may *not* be inferior in steel production and superior in textile production). It does not matter for present purposes. For two-way, mutually beneficial trade, it is necessary only that domestic exchange ratios (relative costs) in the two countries be different. Graphically, these domestic production-exchange ratios reflect the *slopes* of the production-possibility curves, in equilibrium with price-takers' markets. But, in the absence of physical input-output data, we cannot establish the *positions* of the production lines (see Figure 36–1). *Comparative*, not *absolute*, advantage in production is the essential principle underlying gains from specialization and trade among peoples of different countries—as it does among people within a country.

The Terms of Trade and the Exchange Rate

We saw that, (1) if there is to be two-way international trade, the terms of *commodity* trade (textiles for steel) between the two countries must lie within the limits set by the respective domestic commodity exchange ratios: $2t = 1s$ (the U. S. ratio) and $4t = 1s$ (the U. K. ratio).[4] (2) Also, we saw that the *currency* exchange rate between dollars and pounds must lie within limits set by the ratios of dollar- and pound-prices of each of the commodities: $\$2.5 = \pounds 1$ (the textile ratio), and $\$1.25 = \pounds 1$ (the steel ratio). Finally, (3) we can relate the terms of commodity trade and the currency exchange rate, since knowledge (or assumption) of one implies a necessary value of the other.

Assume, as before, that the exchange rate is $\$2 = \pounds 1$. As seen in Table 36–3, the dollar-price of U. K. textiles is 4. How many imported units of textiles at $4 each will equal in value one steel in the U. S. at $10? Answer: $2.5t = 1s$—which, of course, falls within the limits set by the domestic exchange ratios, given in Table 36–4.

Alternatively, given the terms of trade, we can deduce the exchange rate. If the terms are $2.5t = 1s$ and if the price of steel in the U. S. is $10, it follows that the U. K. textile price is $4, for $\$4 \times 2.5 = \$10$. Then, if the price of textiles in the U. K. is £2, it follows that the exchange rate will be $\$4 = \pounds 2$, or $\$2 = \pounds 1$.

---

[4] If there were *three* goods, the problem of setting limits would be complicated but solvable. Confining the illustration to two goods considerably simplifies the discussion and still gives the essentials of the analysis.

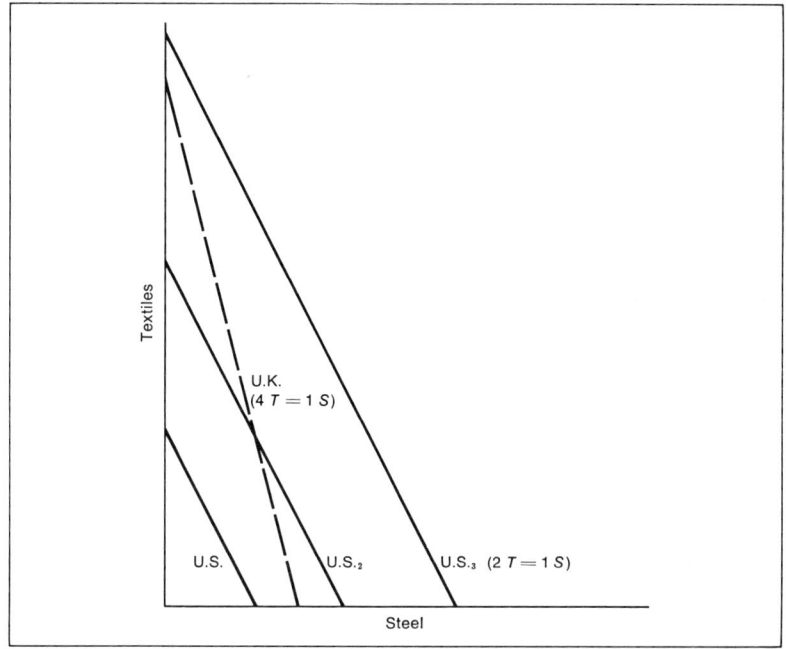

FIGURE 36-1. Comparative Advantage: Alternative Production-Possibility Curves

The price data of Table 36-2 indicate that the *slope* of the U. S. production-possibility curve, showing maximum textile production with a given steel output (or maximum steel production with a given textile output) is 2:1; and the U. K. production curve has a slope of 4:1. But such data do not establish *where* (as opposed to *how steep*) to plot the curve of either country. Given the arbitrarily placed U. K. curve, the maximum outputs of both commodities are smaller in the U. S. if its curve is U. S.$_1$; the U. S. could produce more of both with curve U. S.$_3$; and with curve U. S.$_2$, the U. S. might produce less of both or more of both or the same amount of both or more of one and less of the other. In *each* of the three cases, the U. S. has a *comparative* advantage in producing steel, and the U. K. has a *comparative* advantage in producing textiles. (Suppose we knew that the correct *output* curves were U. S.$_3$ and U. K. but that we did not know the total amounts of *inputs* utilized in the respective countries. Could we then say anything about *absolute* advantage?)

Equalization of Commodity Prices

Our discussion has been based on an initial (pre-foreign trade) disparity in domestic exchange ratios. Therefore, when commodity prices of each country were expressed in a common currency, at least one commodity (in our illustration, both commodities) had different money prices in the two countries. But free (unrestricted) international trade combines the geographically separate markets of the U. S. and the U. K. into a single economic market, and in a single market a common price will exist in equilibrium (abstracting from transport and transactions costs). Thus, one result of trade is to *equalize domestic* (U. S. and U. K.) *prices of a given good*.

The establishment of a uniform price of a good in the international market is illustrated in Figure 36–2. In the left half of the figure, we have the U. S. demand for and supply of the commodity in question; on the right are the U. K. demand and supply schedules for the same commodity.[5] If there were no foreign trade of this good, the U. S.

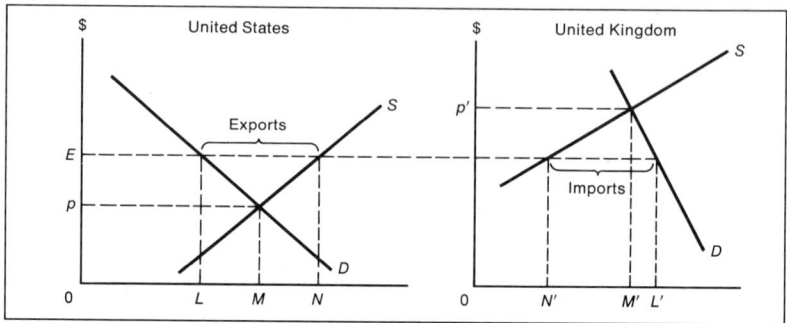

FIGURE 36–2. Intercountry Equalization of a Commodity Price

A single world price of *OE* is established for this commodity, with total quantity demanded equal to total quantity supplied and the quantity of U. S. exports equal to the quantity of U. K. imports.

equilibrium price would be *OP*, with quantity *OM* exchanged; and in the U. K., equilibrium price would be *OP'* and quantity *OM'*. But if there is trade—with neither costs of transportation nor tariffs or other restrictions on trade—then the U. S. and the U. K. become a consolidated market. In this larger single market, there is an equilibrium price, at which total (U. S. plus U. K.) quantity demanded is equal to total quantity supplied.[6]

The equilibrium price with international trade is *OE*. At that price, quantity demanded (*OL* by the U. S. plus *OL'* by the U. K.) is equal to quantity supplied (*ON* plus *ON'*). The U. S. alone supplies a greater quantity than it demands ($ON - OL = LN$), and the U. K. has a surplus of quantity demanded over quantity supplied ($OL' - ON' = N'L'$).

---

[5] We here assume upward-sloping supply curves which yield the result that, in trade equilibrium, both countries supply some quantity of the good. In the next chapter, for a different problem, we shall assume horizontal supply curves. Both types are consistent with the price data tables.

[6] Note that prices in *both* countries are in terms of dollars: the U. K. prices, expressed domestically in pounds, have been translated into dollars on the basis of the going exchange rate. If the exchange rate were to alter, the U. K. supply and demand curves in the figure would rise (if the dollar-price of the pound increases) or fall (if the pound depreciates in terms of the dollar) by the same proportion as the change in the rate. And *if* the rate is free to move and *if* the commodity here being analyzed is a significant part of the total U. S.-U. K. trade, the exchange rate would tend to change as international trade in this commodity is introduced and the price of the commodity moves toward an equilibrium level.

Suppose that initially this commodity is not yet invented and the foreign exchange market is in equilibrium (at the existing exchange rate, the quantity of dollars supplied is equal to the quantity demanded). Now, the commodity is brought into existence, and the respective domestic prices at first are *OP* and *OP'*, as in the figure. The U. S. will export the good, and the U. K. will demand dollars to pay for it. With this increase in the total U. K. demand for dollars, the pound-price of the dollar is bid up (the dollar-price of the pound falls); and the U. K. supply and demand curves, assumed to remain *unchanged* in terms of *pounds*, thus *fall* in terms of *dollars*. But in a real-world situation of many commodities (and services and I.O.U.'s and gold and gifts), this effect on the exchange rate is likely to be minute.

The U. S. gap of "excess" supply (LN) is exported, and the U. K. gap of "excess" demand ($N'L'$) is imported. Since the world market is cleared at price OE, U. S. exports equal U. K. imports; alternatively, since desired U. S. exports do equal desired U. K. imports, it follows that the world market is cleared. (Question: If trade is based on a price difference and if trade establishes a common price, does trade *eliminate* trade? In the figure, when a world price of OE is reached, does foreign trade *cease*?)

Three Countries and Three Commodities

Obviously, a two-country, two-commodity model is a very simple schema. The world economy actually consists of dozens of countries exchanging hundreds of commodities—and also exchanging claims (I.O.U.s) and gold and making gifts, which for the time we ignore. We can briefly illustrate by introducing a third country and a third commodity, say, France and wine.

After making the dollar, pound, and franc prices of the three goods in the three countries comparable by means of a set of consistent exchange rates, we may reasonably suppose that *each* country is cheapest in selling *one* of these commodities. So each country will export one commodity and import the other two in "triangular" (multilateral) trade, as pictured in Figure 36–3. Each country can import two of the three commodities more cheaply than those commodities could be purchased at home, and exports of its production specialty pay for the imports.[7]

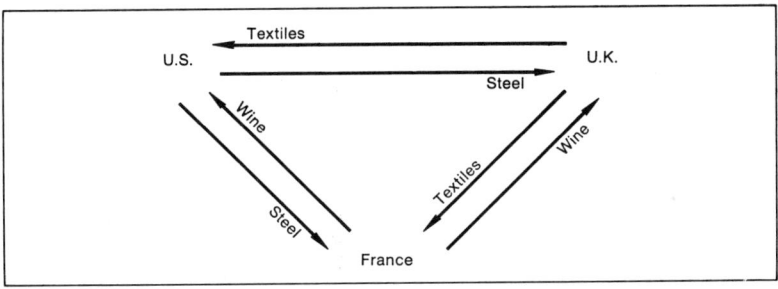

FIGURE 36–3. Triangular Trade

Each country has a comparative advantage in, and exports, one commodity and imports the other two commodities.

1, 2, 3

The Single-Input Theory

In the preceding discussion, we started with domestic *output prices*. Although reference was made to the implied "physical transformation" *ratio* in shifting resources from one industry to another (see in particular footnote 2 and Figure 36–1), no information was

---

[7] It is neither required nor inevitable that each country have balanced trade (export value equal to import value) with *each* of the other two countries. France might have an import balance in trade with the U. S. and an equal export balance with the U. K.; and U. K. would finance its import balance with France through an export balance with the U. S.; and net imports of the U. S. from the U. K. would equal net exports from the U. S. to France. This would mean that each country has balanced trade with *all* the rest of the world, and the net movement of trade is counterclockwise: net exports from France to the U. K., from the U. K. to the U. S., and from the U. S. to France.

given on the *absolute* amounts of resources used in producing the commodities. Now we introduce *input* data, first a single type of input, "labor." This permits a distinction between absolute advantage and comparative advantage, and it also clarifies certain common fallacies about productivity and wages in trade.

Absolute Advantage

In a two-country, two-commodity, single-input world, a general situation of absolute advantage exists when *each* country is productively superior (greater output per unit of input) in only *one* of the commodities (and thus inferior in the other).

In Table 36–5, the U. S. economy has 300 workers, and the U. K. has a labor force of 90. (We do *not* need economies of the same size to have mutually advantageous trade.) In the U. S., 300 man-days of labor can produce *either* 12 units of steel *or* 30 of textiles; and in the U. K., 90 man-days can produce 1.5 units of steel or 15 textiles. Dividing labor expenditure by the commodity outputs yields the labor input per unit of output (in U. S. production of steel, 300 labor can produce 12 units or 1 steel requires $300/12 = 25$ labor).[8] In long-run equilibrium, then, the U. S. domestic exchange ratio in the absence of foreign trade is $2.5t = 1s$, for the labor input of 2.5 textiles is equal to the labor input of 1 steel. Similarly, with the given input-output data of the U. K., the domestic exchange ratio there is $10t = 1s$.

TABLE 36–5. Two Countries, Two Commodities, Labor Input: Absolute Advantage

		Output		Man-days per Unit		Domestic Exchange Ratio
	Man-Days	Steel	Textiles	Steel	Textiles	
U. S.	300	12	30	25	10	$2.5t = 1s$
U. K.	90	1.5	15	60	6	$10t = 1s$

Finally, the difference in initial domestic exchange ratios provides a basis of trade. The U. S. produces steel relatively inexpensively, for the U. S. commodity (barter) cost of 1 steel is 2.5 textiles, while the U. K. commodity cost of 1 steel is 10 textiles; and if the textile-price of steel is *lower* in the U. S. than in the U. K., it follows that the steel-price of textiles is *higher*. Thus, the U. S. exports (the U. K. imports) steel, and the U. S. imports (the U. K. exports) textiles. The original domestic ratios of $2.5t = 1s$ and $10t = 1s$ provide the limits within which the terms of trade must fall.

Let us add *money* data to the "real" input-output data, by having a daily money wage rate. If the U. S. wage rate is $30, the daily wage payments for 300 workers is $300 \times \$30 = \$9,000$; with an assumed U. K. wage of £10, the expenditure is $90 \times £10 = £900$. Next, the money costs (in the respective domestic currencies) per unit of output are calculated by dividing total money cost by the number of units of the commodity (if the U. S. spends $9,000 to produce 12 steel, the unit cost is $9,000/12 = \$750$).[9] The

---

[8] This is sometimes called "cost." But *cost* is *forsaken opportunity*—not the *amount of some input*. Remember the lesson of Chapter 13.

[9] This *is* cost, since the dollar figure measures the value of the resource in the highest-valued output use.

introduction of money has not altered the domestic exchange ratios, as seen in Table 36–6.

If there is to be two-way trade, the U. S. will export steel, and the U. K. will export textiles. This requires that $750 (the U. S. steel price) be less than—nor no more than—£600 (the U. K. steel price), and £60 (the U. K. price of textiles) must be no more than $300 (the U. S. textile price). To compare a dollar-price with a pound-price requires an exchange rate. To take the limiting cases, if the exchange rate is $1.25 = £1 (taken from the steel data: $750 = £600), then the U. K. price of steel in dollars is 600 × 1.25 = 750; and if the rate were $5 = £1 ($300 = £60), both countries would have the same price of textiles. So, given the input-output data and the wage rates, it follows that the exchange rate must lie within $1.25 = £1 and $5 = £1, if two-way trade is to occur.

TABLE 36–6. Two Countries, Two Commodities, Labor Input, Money Wages: Absolute Advantage

	Man-Days	Output		Man-Days per Unit		Wage Rate	Total Wages	Domestic Currency Cost per Unit		Domestic Exchange Ratio
		Steel	Textiles	Steel	Textiles			Steel	Textiles	
U. S.	300	12	30	25	10	$30	$9,000	$750	$300	2.5t = 1s
U. K.	90	1.5	15	60	6	£10	£900	£600	£60	10t = 1s

In Table 36–6, we have wage rates of $30 in the U. S. and £10 in the U. K. Which country has the higher wage? If the exchange rate is at the limiting level of $1.25 = £1, then the U. K. wage of £10 is equal to $12.50, less than the U. S. figure; at $3 = 1, the wage rates of the two countries are equal. Thus, if the dollar-price of the pound is in the range of $1.25 up to $3, then U. S. wages are higher. A dollar-price of the pound from anything more than $3 up to the limiting $5 (which would make U. K. wages equal to $50) yields a higher wage rate for U. K. A characteristic of the situation of *absolute* advantage is that *the wage rate may be higher in either country*.

Take another look at the limiting ratios of wage rates. One ratio is 30/12.5, or 2.4; the other is 30/50, or .6. That is, the U. S. wage may be as much as 2.4 times as large as the U. K. wage, and it must not be less than .6 of the U. K. wage. We determined these ratios by use of the *money costs* of the commodities and the exchange rates they implied. But they can be deduced more directly from the *labor inputs* of the commodities. In steel, the U. S. uses only 25/60 as much labor as does the U. K.; that is, U. S. labor is 60/25, or 2.4, times as productive as U. K. labor in steel. Therefore, U. S. labor can be paid up to 2.4 times as much as U. K. labor and still allow the U. S. to have a lower money cost in steel. To put it differently, if U. S. wages are exactly 2.4 times U. K. wages, then *money* payments to U. S. workers exactly offset the U. S. *physical* (productivity) superiority, so steel would have the same money costs in both countries. But in the other commodity, textiles, the U. K. is physically (technologically) superior; the U. K. absolute advantage in textiles is in the ratio of 10/6; therefore, the U. K. wage can be 1.67 as large as the U. S. wage, which is to say that the U. S. wage must be at least .6 of the U. K. wage.

We can easily summarize the relation between *relative wages* and the *exchange rate*. Let w_{us} be the *dollar* wage rate in the U. S. and w_{uk} be the *pound* wage rate in the U. K. To express the U. K. wage rate in dollars, we multiply by the exchange rate (dollar-price of the pound), $/£. Thus, U. K. wages in dollars are w_{uk} ($/£). We know that the ratio of U. S. wages to U. K. wages lies within the limits of 2.4 and .6:

$$\frac{w_{us}}{w_{uk}(\$/£)} = \frac{w_{us}}{w_{uk}}\left(\frac{£}{\$}\right) = 2.4, \text{ and } \frac{w_{us}}{w_{uk}}\left(\frac{£}{\$}\right) = .6.$$

Given the labor-input data, if we assume the value either of relative wages or of the exchange rate, the limiting values of the other are implied. If we take wages to be $30 and £10, that is, $w_{us}/w_{uk} = 3$, as in Table 36–6, then $3(£/\$) = 2.4$, and $£/\$ = .8$ (or $\$/£ = 1.25$); and $£/\$ = 6/3 = .2$ (or $\$/£ = 5$).

Finally, if we take *both* wages and the exchange rate as given, we imply the *terms of trade*. Suppose that wages are $30 and £10 in the respective countries and that the exchange rate is $3 = £1$. With those wages, we have previously deduced that the price of steel produced in the U. S. would be $750 and that the price of U. K. textiles would be £60, and, with that exchange rate, the textile price would be the equivalent of $180. Since we have assumed that only steel and textiles are traded, the dollar value of U. S. exports (steel) at $750 per unit must equal the dollar value of U. S. imports (textiles) at $180 per unit. Therefore, $750/180 = 4.167$ textiles will trade for 1 steel. Note that these terms fall within the initial domestic exchange ratios of $2.5t = 1s$ and $10t = 1s$.

Comparative Advantage

In a two-goods case of comparative advantage, *one* country is absolutely superior in *both* commodities (or one country is superior in one commodity and of exactly equal proficiency in the other)—with the *degree* of superiority different in the two commodities. In Table 36–7, the U. S. has a lower labor input per unit than the U. K. in both goods, but the U. S. productivity superiority is $60/25 = 2.4$ in steel and only $15/10 = 1.5$ in textiles. The U. S. is *absolutely* superior (has an *absolute* advantage) in both commodities, but the over-all situation, encompassing both goods, is one of *comparative* advantage. Specifically, the U. S. has a comparative (as well as absolute) advantage in steel and a comparative disadvantage (although an absolute advantage) in textiles. The U. S. has an absolute advantage in both products, but, by the nature of the notion, it can have comparative advantage in only one.

TABLE 36–7. Two Countries, Two Commodities, Labor Input, Money Wages: Comparative Advantage

		Output		Man-Days per Unit		Wage Rate	Total Wages	Domestic Currency Cost per Unit		Domestic Exchange Ratio
	Man-days	Steel	Textiles	Steel	Textiles			Steel	Textiles	
U. S.	300	12	30	25	10	$30	$9,000	$750	$300	$2.5t = 1s$
U. K.	90	1.5	6	60	15	£10	£900	£600	£150	$4t = 1s$

In the absolute advantage situation, we saw that *either* country could have a higher wage rate than the other (within limits), because *each* country had an absolute advantage in one commodity. But in the comparative advantage situation, where one country is superior in *both* productions, the country of superiority must have a higher wage. Again there are limits to the relative wages, determined by the data on relative labor inputs. Since the U. S. is 2.4 times as productive in steel, the U. S. wage can be as much as 2.4 times as high; and since the U. S. is 1.5 times as productive in textiles, the U. S. wage *must* be at least 1.5 times as high.

In comparing wages, we are expressing—as we did before—both wages in terms of a common currency, so again the exchange rate is involved. Since we have:

$$\frac{w_{us}}{w_{uk}}\left(\frac{£}{\$}\right) = 2.4, \text{ and } \frac{w_{us}}{w_{uk}}\left(\frac{£}{\$}\right) = 1.5,$$

then if we assume wages of $30 and £10, as in Table 36-7, it follows that the exchange rate has limiting values of $£/\$ = 2.4/3 = .8$ (or $\$/£ = 1.25$) and $£/\$ = 1.5/3 = .5$ (or $\$/£ = 2$).

To complete the picture, if we assume an exchange rate of $1.50 = £1$, then U. K. textiles, priced at £150, will be the equivalent of $225. Since the U. S. exports steel at a price of $750, then $750/225 = 3.333$ textiles trade for 1 steel.

The theory of comparative advantage is sufficiently subtle to warrant special discussion of several additional points.

1. The theory makes clear that *both* parties (here the U. S. and the U. K.) can gain from specialization in production and exchange even if one of them has an absolute advantage in both commodities. Trade can be based on a situation of *absolute* advantage, with each party selling (exporting) a good he can produce with less physical input per unit of output than can his trading partner. But in a situation of *comparative* advantage, one party is buying (importing) a good which he himself can produce more cheaply in physical terms, as when the U. S. imports textiles in our illustration—and many an editorial writer has had trouble grasping the rationale of buying a product from a foreigner technologically inferior to (but *economically* cheaper than) domestic producers.

2. A common argument in American public tariff debates has been the "pauper labor" case for protection. In its crudest and most popular form, the argument is that domestic producers cannot survive in free trade with countries of much lower wages: with very low wages, foreigners will surely be able to underprice us in everything. And yet, our analysis of the comparative advantage case indicates that not only *can* the U. S. underprice its trading partner when U. S. wages are higher, American wages *must* be higher by some minimum proportion (in our illustration, they must be at least 50 percent higher than in the U. K.) if American producers are not to undersell the British in both goods.[10]

---

[10] The would-be and erstwhile U. S. textile manufacturers claim that tariff protection is appropriate in light of lower U. K. wages. But all that is desired is that a tariff rate be "scientifically" determined. And a "scientific" tariff "equalizes costs of production." Then producers in the U. S. and U. K. can start the race for survival at the same place, so to speak, and may the better man win this fair competition!

Even the English steel producers can agitate for such a scientific tariff. U. K. wages are, indeed, lower than those in the U. S. But *somehow* the U. S. costs of steel production still are lower—and this is unfair.

So, still assuming that average total cost per unit equals price, Americans should levy an import tax on each unit of textiles of $300—£150($/£), and the English tariff on steel should be £600—$750 (£/$). These tariffs equalize costs and prices—and, therefore, *they eliminate the basis of trade.*

The "scientific" tariff criterion of cost-equalization was advocated in the Republican platform first in 1904; the Democratic platform did not explicitly reflect this degree of "enlightenment" until 1928, but many Democrats joined Republicans in their support prior to World War I. The notion is embodied in the Tariff Act of 1922 and is retained in the Smoot-Hawley Act of 1930.

3. What is the basis of higher American wages? It has often been argued that tariffs and other barriers to imports are required in order to "protect the American worker's standard of living." But obviously tariffs were not the basis of higher U. S. wages in our illustration: until now, free trade was presumed. U. S. wages were higher, not because trade restrictions curtailed American purchases of lower-priced foreign commodities, but because U. S. *productivity* was higher. The U. S. produced more per man, and so it had more goods (real wages) per man.

4, 5, 6, 7, 8

The Multiple-Input, Factor-Endowment Theory

We continue to speak of two countries (the U. S. and the U. K.) and two commodities (steel and textiles).[11] But now let there be two inputs, "labor" and "capital." Suppose that both inputs are of equal quality in both countries. Furthermore, assume that a given commodity has the same input-output relation (production function) in both countries. Specifically, let a unit of steel be producible in both the U. S. and the U. K. by any of the combinations of labor and capital shown in Table 36–8a (or by any other smoothly interpolated combinations between those listed); and a unit of textiles can be produced in both countries in the alternative input combinations in Table 36–8b. An additional assumption is that for two units of a commodity, both inputs are to be doubled; for three units of output, triple both inputs; and so forth. In short, the *physical conditions of production are identical* in the two countries: (1) the inputs are qualitatively "homogeneous," and (2) the production functions are internationally uniform, with "constant returns to scale."

TABLE 36–8. Illustrative Combinations of Labor and Capital Required in Both the U. S. and the U. K. to Produce One Unit of:

8a Steel		8b Textiles	
Labor	Capital	Labor	Capital
3	17.75	7	14.25
4	13	8	9.5
5	10	9	6
6	8	10	4
7	6.75	11	2.5
8	6	12	1.75

The immediate basis of trade is differences in relative money prices of the commodities. And, if we assume price-takers' markets, the equilibrium price of a commodity will equal its cost of production. The cost of production equals the sum of payments to factors of production. Finally, the payment to factors equals the number of units of labor used multiplied by the price per unit of labor plus the number of units of capital multiplied by the price of capital.

---

[11] Although we are still dealing with two countries and two commodities of the preceding pages, the numerical data in this section are not related to previous illustrations.

Which of the combinations of labor and capital that *can* be used to produce a unit of steel or of textiles actually *will* be used? And will the same combination of inputs be used in both countries to produce a given commodity? We have seen before (Chapter 20) that the particular combination of inputs cheapest in producing a given output is determined by the relative prices of the factors. Starting with the pair of inputs which is least expensive in producing a certain output, if the price of capital were to rise relative to the price of labor, that output can now be most cheaply produced by utilizing less capital and substituting additional labor.

Given the technological production function, then, relative factor prices determine the least-cost combination of inputs. What, in turn, determines relative factor prices? While both demand for and supply of factors will affect prices in price-takers' input markets, it is generally presumed that supply conditions vary more than demand from region to region and predominate in establishing equilibrium prices. If country A has "a lot" of capital and "not much" labor *compared* to country B, then the presumption is that the price of capital relative to the price of labor will be lower in country A than in country B in the absence of foreign trade. Indeed, in our two-country model, we shall *define* the (relatively) "capital-abundant" country as the country in which the ratio, (price of labor)/(price of capital), initially is higher; and, necessarily, the other country is "labor abundant," with a lower ratio of labor price to capital price.

Now, countries do differ in their relative endowments and accumulations of factors, so we would expect relative factor prices to differ from one country to another before foreign trade is begun. And if relative prices differ internationally, so will the combinations of factors used to produce a given commodity.

In Table 36–9, we put together certain hypothetical data in order to illustrate the line of argument. In the initial situation, before international trade begins, the prices of steel in the U. S. and the U. K. are $87 and £34, respectively, and the prices of textiles are $124.5 and £38. To determine if each country is cheaper in one commodity (and thus more expensive in the other), we can note, first, the *domestic relative prices*—that is, the steel-textile exchange ratio in the U. S. and the ratio in the U. K. In the U. S., price of steel = $87, and price of textiles = $124.5; therefore, it requires $124.5/87 = 1.431$ units of steel to equal (have the same market value as) one unit of textiles—or $1.431s = 1t$. In the U. K., the domestic exchange ratio is $1.118s = 1t$. As we saw in the first part of the chapter, if the pre-trade domestic exchange ratios differ, international trade can be

TABLE 36–9. Pre-trade and Trade Factor Prices and Combinations, Costs, and Exchange Ratios

	Factor Prices		Steel (One Unit)				Textiles (One Unit)				
			Amount of Factor		Total Cost		Amount of Factor		Total Cost		
	U. S.	U. K.	U. S.	U. K.	U. S.	U. K.	U. S.	U. K.	U. S.	U. K.	Exchange Ratio
Initial (pre-foreign trade) situation											
Labor	$12	£3	4	6	$48	£18	8	10	$ 96	£30	U. S.: $1.431s = 1t$
Capital	$ 3	£2	13	8	$39	£16	9.5	4	$ 28.5	£ 8	U. K.: $1.118s = 1t$
					$87	£34			$124.5	£38	
Foreign trade situation											
Labor	$10	£4	5	5	$50	£20	9	9	$ 90	£36	
Capital	$ 4	£1.6	10	10	$40	£16	6	6	$ 24	£ 9.6	World: $1.267s = 1t$
					$90	£36			$114	£45.6	

mutually advantageous at terms within the domestic ratios. In this instance, textiles are cheaper (in terms of steel) in the U. K., and the U. K. will export textiles, if it exports anything; and steel, being cheaper (in terms of textiles) in the U. S., is the potential export commodity of the U. S.

We have seen further that the exchange rate between the two currencies must lie within limits in order to have two-way trade. These limits are the rates which would equalize the prices of one good or the other in both countries. Thus, the exchange rate must lie between $87 = £34$, or $2.559 = £1$, and $124.5 = £38$, or $3.276 = £1$. If, for example, the rate is $3 = £1$, then U. K. textiles are priced at the equivalent of $(38 \times 3 =) \$114$; and with steel in the U. S. at $87, the terms of trade will be $114/87 = 1.310$ steel per unit of textiles.

These deductions are precisely the sort of thing we have done before. Our new problem is to look at what determined the prices (costs) of steel and textiles in each of the countries.

Initially, a "unit" of labor is four times as expensive as a "unit" of capital in the U. S. ($12 compared to $3) and only one-and-one-half times as expensive in the U. K. (£3 compared to £2).[12] The ratio of labor price to capital price in the U. S.—$(P_L/P_C)_{us}$—is greater than that ratio in the U. K.—$(P_L/P_C)_{uk}$. By definition, since $(P_L/P_C)_{us} > (P_L/P_C)_{uk}$, the U. S. is (relatively) capital abundant, and the U. K. is (relatively) labor abundant.

We must look not only at relative factor *endowments* of the two *countries* (and thus their relative *factor prices*), but also at the relative factor *requirements* of the two *commodities*. With the initial ratios of factor prices, steel is (relatively) "capital intensive," and textiles are (relatively) "labor intensive." That is, the ratio of the amount of capital used to labor used in making a unit of steel is greater than the capital/labor ratio in producing textiles. This is the case in both countries (in the U. S., $13/4 > 9.5/8$, and in the U. K., $8/6 > 4/10$). Although steel is capital intensive in both the U. S. and the U. K., one unit of steel is produced with different combinations of capital and labor in the two countries because of the difference in relative factor prices: since capital is relatively cheap in the U. S., the U. S. uses a larger ratio of capital to labor in both goods than does the U. K. But while the particular input combinations vary as relative input prices vary, steel will be capital intensive in *both* countries with *every* ratio of factor prices. And the capital intensive commodity (steel) can be produced more cheaply in the country that is capital abundant (U. S.).

We are now in a position to summarize this theory of the basis of trade:

1. The immediate basis is a difference in the respective *domestic exchange ratios* ($1.431s = 1t$ is different from $1.118s = 1t$).

2. A domestic exchange ratio is determined by *domestic prices* of the commodities ($124.5/87 = 1.431$, and $38/34 = 1.118$).

3. The price of a commodity equals its *cost*, which equals the quantities of the utilized inputs multiplied by their respective prices (for example, for steel production in the U. S., $12 \times 4 + 3 \times 13 = 87$).

---

[12] The sizes of these units of inputs can be arbitrarily specified, and, of course, with different sizes used in the calculations, the numerical results will be different. But in this connection, all that is crucial is that we use the *same* unit of labor and the *same* unit of capital in *both countries*.

4. A country will be a relatively low-cost producer and exporter of the commodity *produced with relatively large amounts of its relatively abundant (cheap) factor* (the U. S. is capital abundant, with capital relatively cheap, and is lower-priced in producing steel, which is capital intensive; and the U. K. which has relatively cheap labor, will export the labor-intensive commodity, textiles).

So much for the *basis* of trade. Now consider certain *results* of trade.

The originally disparate domestic exchange ratios merge into the single terms of international trade. In Table 36–9, $114/90 = 45.6/36 = 1.267$. Any resident of the U. S. or U. K. can exchange steel and cloth at $1.267s = 1t$, either with a resident of his own country or with a foreigner.

Have we here concluded that the *money price* of a commodity is made uniform in the world market or that the *barter ratio* is made uniform? Certainly the barter ratio is equalized: with foreign trade, $1.267s = 1t$ in both countries. But it must be true also that a given commodity has a uniform money price in both countries (when the prices are converted by the exchange rate into a single currency). The exchange rate is $\$90 = £36$, or $\$114 = £45.6$, both of which are equal to $\$2.5 = £1$. In short, the establishment of a single barter ratio ($114/90 = 45.6/36 = 1.267$) necessarily implies an exchange rate ($90/36 = 114/45.6 = 2.5$) which yields a single money price for a particular commodity.

In Table 36–9, not only are relative *commodity* prices in the two countries equated with each other through foreign trade (a predicted result not unique to the multiple-input, or factor-endowment, theory), but also the relative *factor* prices are equated: $P_L/P_C = \$10/\$4 = £4/£1.6$. And the establishment of equal factor-price ratios—along with our assumptions concerning the nature of the factors and of the production functions—means that a unit of either good will be produced in both countries with the same input combination.

To equalize—or to move in the direction of equalizing—factor-price ratios in the U. S., the price of labor (the relatively scarce factor in that country) will fall compared with the price of capital, and, in the U. K., the price of capital (the relatively scarce factor there) will fall compared to the price of labor. Why, in both countries, does the price of the "scarce" factor fall and the price of the "abundant" factor rise when the total quantities of labor and of capital remain constant in each country? Our discussion will focus on the U. S. market adjustments; analogous results obtain in the U. K.

We have seen that, given the data of the initial (pre-trade) situation, the U. S. will export steel and import textiles when trade is begun: the demand for American steel increases, and the U. S. demand for domestically produced textiles decreases. The U. S. output of steel will increase, and its output of textiles will be curtailed, with some resources (labor and capital) shifting out of the textile industry into steel production. But resources evidently are not released from textiles in the *same proportion* as they are absorbed in steel: reducing textile output by one unit cuts the use of labor by 8 units and capital by 9.5 ($L/C = 8/9.5 = .842$), while increasing steel output by one unit requires 4 more units of labor and 13 of capital ($L/C = 4/13 = .308$). If the steel industry hires all of the labor released by the textile industry, capital will be in short supply; or if the steel industry demands exactly all of the released capital, some of the available labor will not be rehired. However stated, the contraction of the labor-intensive industry and the expansion of the capital-intensive industry will bid up the price of capital relative to labor: the ratio, P_C/P_L, will increase.

There is a common price of labor and a common price of capital throughout the economy. Since capital has become more expensive and labor cheaper for *both* the steel and textile industries, *both* industries will find it advantageous to change their input combinations, using more labor and less capital than before. But is it possible for *both* industries to use a larger ratio of labor to capital when the total amounts of labor and of capital in the economy remain constant? In Table 36–10, we assume that the U. S. initially produces 80 units of steel and 120 of textiles, which requires a total of 1,280 labor and 2,180 capital. Now, if labor and capital are transferred out of textiles into steel at a labor-capital ratio of *more* than .308 and *less* than .842, the labor-capital ratio will rise in both industries. Suppose we shift to 675 labor and 950 capital—that is, at a labor-capital ratio of $675/950 = .711$. We still have a total of 1,280 labor and 2,180 capital in the economy (and, at the new factor prices, all labor and all capital are still employed), but the labor-capital ratio is now higher in both industries (.500 compared to .308 in steel and 1.500 compared to .842 in textiles). Production of steel is now increased to 199, and textile output is reduced to 31.667.[13]

TABLE 36–10. U. S. Production of Steel and Textiles and Allocation of Labor and Capital before and with Foreign Trade

	Before Trade				With Trade			
	Units of Commodity	Labor	Capital	L/C	Units of Commodity	Labor	Capital	L/C
Steel	80	320	1,040	.308	199	995	1,990	.500
Textiles	120	960	1,140	.842	31.667	285	190	1.500
		1,280	2,180			1,280	2,180	

[13] The new (with-trade) ouputs of steel and textiles are determined subject to constraints: since the price of labor has fallen, more labor is to be used in producing a unit of either commodity, and since the price of capital has risen, less capital is used in both products, and, finally, we are to continue to use all 1,280 labor and 2,180 capital.

Total labor (1,280L) will equal five units of labor (5L) multiplied by the number of units of steel produced (S) plus nine units (9L) multiplied by the number of units of textiles (T); that is:

$$5LS + 9LT = 1{,}280L.$$

Similarly, total capital (2,180C) is equal to the amount of capital used in steel and textiles:

$$10CS + 6CT = 2{,}180C.$$

Rearranging:

$$L(5S + 9T) = 1{,}280L,$$
$$C(10S + 6T) = 2{,}180C.$$

Or:

$$5S + 9T = 1{,}280,$$
$$10S + 6T = 2{,}180.$$

Now, dividing the first of these equations by 5 and the second by 10, we have:

$$S + 1.8T = 256,$$
$$S + .6T = 218.$$

Subtracting the second from the first: $1.2T = 38$; and thus: $T = 31.667$.

Since each unit of T requires 9 labor and 6 capital, it follows that the industry will use a total of 285 labor and 190 capital. (You can now easily determine the output of steel and the inputs employed, can't you?)

Finally, the fact that the labor-capital ratio rises in both industries means that, throughout the economy, the physical *marginal productivity* of labor falls and the marginal productivity of capital rises, for the marginal productivity of either of the factors is a function of the *ratio* at which it is combined with the other. So the money price and the marginal product of labor fall, and the price and marginal product of capital rise.

Thus, in this model of multiple-factor inputs and zero costs of transportation, unrestricted access to international markets has joined geographically separate markets into a single economic (world) market in all respects: commodity prices have been equalized, factor prices have been equalized, and one unit of any given product is produced everywhere with the same input combination.

One way to emphasize the result of creating a "single market" is to note that *international trade in commodities has substituted for international movement of factors.* Instead of labor and capital moving freely among regions to where their prices are highest, thereby eliminating factor-price differentials, the factors are assumed to remain "at home," organize their production in accordance with their comparative advantages, and then exchange portions of their products. In our illustration, U. K. labor does not migrate to the U. S., but rather the U. K. exports labor-intensive textiles; and U. S. capital does not move to the U. K., but the capital-intensive product of steel moves.

Although all possibilities of production specialization and exchange are thus exploited, not every person is pleased, for there has been an income redistribution that hurt some while benefiting others. Not only has the price of capital risen relative to the price of labor in the U. S.—thereby giving capital a *proportionately* larger share of the national absorption of goods—but the increased physical marginal productivity of capital has increased the *real, absolute* payment to capital, while the fall in the marginal productivity of labor means a reduction in the real income per unit of labor. Trade results in capital-intensive exports and makes capital, the comparatively abundant factor, better off, both relatively and absolutely; but trade here hurts labor, the relatively scarce factor, so workers have an incentive to restrict trade.

We have illustrated a case of complete factor-price equalization consistent with our assumptions. But we would never satisfy *all* of the assumptions required to achieve *full* factor-price equalization—and in some instances none of them—in the real world. These assumptions include:

1. There are only two productive factors, labor and capital, each of which is "homogeneous" throughout the world.
2. A given commodity has a single production function.
3. There are only two commodities, both produced with constant returns to scale.
4. One commodity is labor intensive and the other is capital intensive at all relative factor prices.
5. Production specialization is partial rather than complete: in equilibrium, each country continues to produce some of both commodities.
6. For both buyers and sellers, there are price-takers' markets.
7. There are no costs of transportation.
8. There are no imposed barriers to trade.

9, 10

Summary

1. We may deal with a model containing only money prices of commodities and no input data. With two countries and two commodities, a situation of "equal" advantage—in which price ratios are uniform—does not provide a basis for two-way trade. If price ratios differ, the situation may be considered one of "comparative" advantage, and mutually beneficial trade is feasible; the terms of international trade are more favorable for both countries than their respective domestic exchange ratios in the absence of foreign trade. Such trade is beneficial because it pushes the "consumption boundary" beyond the constant "production boundary."

2. The domestic exchange ratios in the two countries will be the limits of the terms of international trade. The exchange-rate limits will be the ratios of the prices of the commodities in the two countries. With only two commodities entering trade, either the terms of trade or the exchange rate implies the other.

3. Unrestricted trade results in a single world price for a commodity, after allowance for transportation costs.

4. A model including a single input ("labor") makes possible a distinction between "absolute" and "comparative" advantage.[14] With two countries and two commodities, an absolute advantage situation exists when each country is technologically superior in the production of one commodity; in a comparative advantage situation, one country is superior in both commodities, but the degrees of superiority are different.

5. In an absolute advantage situation, the money price of the input (wage rate) *can* be higher in either country within limits determined by the international productivity ratios in the two commodities. In a comparative advantage situation, the wage rate *must* be higher in the productively superior country, again within a range determined by productivity ratios.

6. Introduction of a second input ("capital" along with "labor") makes it feasible to analyze (a) resource allocation within as well as among industries (to discover the least-cost combination of inputs for a given amount of a commodity and the combination of commodities in the national output) and (b) the effects of trade on the distribution of income.[15]

7. In the multiple-input, factor-endowment theory, there are two immediate determinants of the basis of trade: (a) regions differ in relative amounts of factors and thus have different relative factor prices, and (b) commodities differ in relative factor requirements. Therefore, a country can export the commodity which requires relatively large amounts of the factor it has in relative abundance and import the commodity that is factor-intensive in a factor that is relatively scarce domestically.

8. Trade tends to result in equalization of relative factor prices throughout the world.

---

[14] The single-input approach was characteristic of the "classical" and "neoclassical" economists, including the Englishmen David Ricardo (1772–1823) and John Stuart Mill (1806–73) and the American Frank William Taussig (1859–1940).

[15] Associated with the early development of the factor-endowment theory are Eli F. Heckscher (1879–1952) and Bertil G. Ohlin (1899–   ) of Sweden.

Questions

1. Assume the following price data in the U. S. and the U. K. in their respective domestic currencies:

	U. K.	U. S.
Shoes	£4	$15
Coats	£5	$ 6

   a. In general terms, what is the evidence that there exists a basis for mutually beneficial, two-way trade?
   b. The U. S. has a comparative advantage in which commodity? Which commodity will the U. K. export?
   c. Define "rate of exchange." In this example, what are the limits to the possible rates of exchange which would provide a basis for long-run trade?
   d. Define "terms of trade." What are the limits to the possible terms of trade in this illustration?
   e. What relation do the terms of trade have to the concept of "opportunity (or alternative) cost"? What is the opportunity (alternative) cost of imports?
   f. If the exchange rate is $2 = £1$, what are the terms of trade?
   g. If the terms of trade are $2c = 1s$, what is the exchange rate?

2. We have discussed situations of two countries and two commodities. Now consider a case of more commodities than countries, with the set of prices being:

	U. S.	U. K.
Hats	$ 5	£ 2
Coats	$10	£ 8
Shoes	$15	£10

   a. In the absence of foreign trade, what are the equilibrium hat-coat, hat-shoe, and coat-shoe exchange values (ratios) in the U. S.? In the U. K.?
   b. Measuring the cost (price) of one commodity in terms of the others, which country is the cheaper producer of coats? Of hats? Of shoes?
   c. If now foreign trade is introduced—with each country exporting at least one commodity and importing at least one—what is the pattern of trade (what does each country import and export)? Is there more than one possible pattern of trade?
   d. So that each country can export at least one commodity, what are the upper and lower limits to the dollar-pound exchange rate? So that each can export only one commodity (thereby omitting the third commodity from international trade), what must be the exchange rate?
   e. If the exchange rate is $2 = £1$, what are the hat-coat, hat-shoe, and coat-shoe terms of trade?
   f. If the hat-coat terms of trade is $3.6h = 1c$ (or $1h = .278c$), what is the exchange rate?

3. "Nothing useful can be deduced about patterns of production specialization and exchange or the gains from trade or the terms of trade from only price data—especially

price data expressed in different national currencies. Money prices are not sufficient. We must have information on *physical* input-output relations." If that statement is correct, the first part of this chapter has been a big mistake. Salvage it.

4 "Suspicious as we may well be of dealing with foreigners, there may be some sense in buying things abroad when they can be produced there absolutely more efficiently (i.e., with greater output per unit of input). But it can make no sense at all to spend good dollars to buy an article abroad when it can be produced more efficiently (i.e., with fewer resources) here." Right?

5 "Unfettered world trade would tend powerfully to reduce all workers (and other resource owners) to the world's lowest level. For a nation with lower wages—and all nations do have wages lower than those in the U. S.—could then undersell us, not only in 'third' markets, but right here in our own country. Thus, American producers would be ruined; or, in order for us to be able to sell and thus to survive, our wages would have to be cut to the lowest level of our competitors. It would be ridiculous to expose our high standard of living to the ruinous competition of the poorer rest of the world." How could you dispute this?

6 What is the so-called "scientific" tariff?

7 Assume that labor is the only input. In Abyssinia, five units of labor produce either 20 bushels of wheat or 20 yards of linen; in Brazil, five units of labor produce either 30 bushels of wheat or 45 yards of linen.
a. In the absence of foreign trade, what would be the equilibrium ratio of exchange between wheat and linen in Brazil?
b. If trade opens between the two countries (and neither trades with any third nation), which nation will export wheat?
c. The terms of trade must lie between what ratios of linen and wheat, assuming two-way trade?
d. Explain how, or in what sense, each nation gains from trade if the terms of trade are 10 wheat = 13 linen.
e. In order to allow mutually beneficial, two-way trade, must the wage rate be higher in one country or may it be higher in either? What are the limits of the ratio of the two wage rates?
f. If the Brazilian wage rate were 10.7 times as large as that in Abyssinia, could there be any foreign trade between the two countries? If so, what would be the pattern of trade? Would there be any economic forces tending to change the ratio of wages?

8 In country A, one laborer can produce two units of Y or two of X; in country B, one laborer can produce two of Y or six of X. Each country has 100 laborers. After trade opens, each country specializes production completely in one commodity.
a. If A produces nothing but X, how many units can it produce? If A produces nothing but Y, how many units can it produce?
b. A has a comparative advantage in which commodity?
c. Assume terms of trade of $2X = 1Y$. If A now consumes 100 units of X, it will consume how much Y?
d. If A consumes $100X$, how much Y will B consume?
e. How many units of X will B consume?
f. Suppose that *before* trade began, A was producing and consuming $100X$. How much Y was it producing and consuming?
g. Suppose that *before* trade, B was producing and consuming $100Y$. How much X?
h. Therefore, *before* trade, A and B together were producing and consuming a total of how many units of X and how many of Y? *After* trade begins, they produce and consume how much X and how much Y?

9   The two proximate conditions of trade in the multiple-input, factor-endowment theory have been reviewed: "The prerequisites of initiating trade may thus be summarized as *different relative scarcities, i.e., different relative prices of factors of production in the exchanging countries,* as well as *different proportions between the factors of production in different commodities.*"—Eli Heckscher, "The Effect of Foreign Trade on the Distribution of Income," *Ekonomisk Tidskrift* (1919), translated by Professor and Mrs. Svend Laursen and reprinted in H. S. Ellis and L. A. Metzler, eds., *Readings in the Theory of International Trade* (Philadelphia: The Blakiston Co., 1949; now published by Richard D. Irwin, Inc.), p. 278; emphases in the original. Using the format of Table 36–9 (including factor prices in two countries and factor requirements of two commodities), illustrate that *both* of these conditions must be satisfied in order for two-way trade to exist.

10 What is the basic role or function of the multiple-input, factor-endowment (Heckscher-Ohlin) approach to trade theory? That is, what does it contribute to trade theory that is missing from the single-input (classical) version? Are the two approaches inconsistent with each other?

Resource Allocation, Terms of Trade, and Tariffs

37 THE preceding chapter provides the crux of trade theory, and here we review and extend some of the earlier discussion. Specifically, we shall (1) elaborate the analysis of the effects of trade on resource allocation, (2) introduce demand elements to round out the prior trade model, which was based on differences in costs, and provide a means of determining the equilibrium terms of trade, (3) use the expanded model to investigate the theory of tariffs imposed by a single country, (4) evaluate different measures of the terms of trade, and (5) broaden the theory of tariffs to encompass customs unions.

Trade and Resource Allocation

With quite simple diagrams, we can illustrate for two countries and two commodities the patterns of consumption and production (both before and with foreign trade), the quantities and terms of trade, and the gain from trade. This will be a slight generalization of the analysis applied to exchange between two people with specialization in production, given in Chapters 12–13.

Figure 37–1 shows the production possibilities of the U. S. and the U. K. Suppose that the U. S. has available a fixed quantity of resources which, for convenience, we call "labor." If *all* of the labor produced nothing but textiles, the maximum textile output per time period would be OY_1; alternatively, if the U. S. specialized completely in steel, OX_1 of steel could be produced. Since line Y_1X_1 gives all the possible combinations of textiles and steel, it may be labeled the *production-possibility* line. Moving down the line to the right indicates that it is possible to produce more and more steel at the (alternative) cost of foregoing production of more and more textiles; and moving up the line to

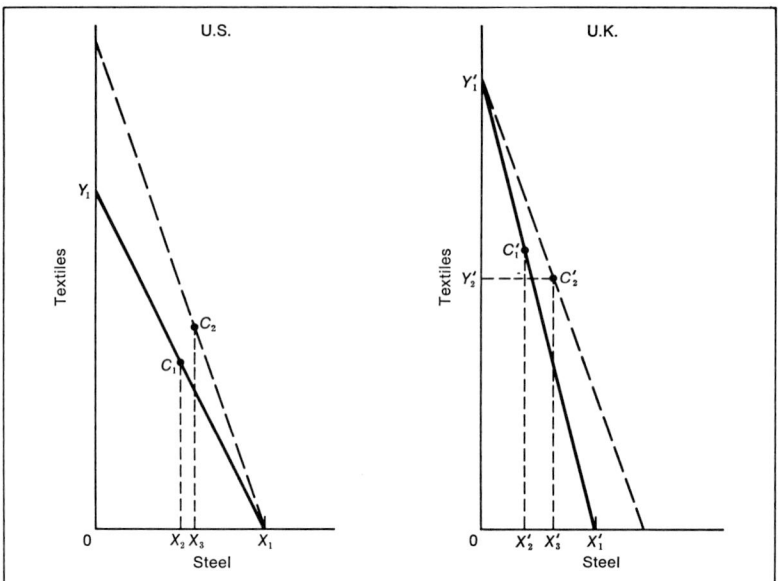

FIGURE 37–1. Two Countries: Conditions of Trade, Production Specialization, and Imports and Exports

The slopes of the respective production-possibility lines differ, giving rise to different domestic exchange ratios in the absence of foreign trade. With trade, assume complete production specialization on the basis of comparative advantage. The U. S., instead of producing and consuming at point C_1, now produces at X_1 and consumes at C_2; as a result of specialization and trade, the U. K. moves from C_1' to producing at Y_1' and consuming at C_2'. The new consumption points, C_2 and C_2', are on the (parallel) terms-of-trade lines. U. S. exports (and U. K. imports) are X_1X_3 ($=OX_3'$) of steel; U. S. imports (U. K. exports) are X_3C_2 ($=Y_1'Y_2'$) of textiles.

the left shows the steel cost of producing more textiles. The *straightness* of the line manifests the *constancy* of marginal cost: no matter where we are on the line, the cost of producing one more steel is, say, two textiles, and the cost of one more unit of textiles is one-half unit of steel. Similarly, the slope of the U. K. production-possibility line reflects a marginal production cost of four textiles for one steel and one-fourth steel for one textile.

Before the introduction of foreign trade, each country presumably will wish to produce and consume some of both commodities: C_1 could be the production-consumption point, with the combination of OX_2 steel and X_2C_1 textiles for the U. S. and similarly for the U. K. Before trade, then, lines Y_1X_1 and $Y_1'X_1'$ are the respective "production boundaries," and, since an isolated economy cannot consume more than it produces, those lines are also the "consumption boundaries."

Since the domestic exchange ratios in the two countries (equal to the production-substitution ratios and measured by the slopes of the production-possibility lines) *are different, there is a basis of trade.* The U. S. has a comparative advantage in steel and the U. K. in textiles. It is reasonable (although not literally necessary) to suppose that both countries specialize completely in production: the U. S. will produce OX_1 steel and no textiles, the *production* point then being X_1, and the U. K. production point is Y_1'. The *consumption* point of a country is to be found on its terms-of-trade line (that is, on its consumption boundary with foreign trade). From each country's production point, we trace out a straight dashed line, the slope of which lies within the slopes of the U. S. and U. K. production-possibility lines and measures the terms of international trade. Since each of the trading partners is faced with the same terms of trade, the two dashed lines—which are steeper than the U. S. production-possibility curve and less steep than the U. K. curve—are parallel. Suppose that C_2 and C_2' are the new consumption points.

To summarize: *Before* trade, the U. S. both produces and consumes at C_1; *with* trade, she produces at X_1 and consumes at C_2. If the U. S. is now producing OX_1 steel and consuming only OX_3, the remainder, X_3X_1, is *exported*; and if she is consuming X_3C_2 textiles while producing none, she is *importing* X_3C_2. Similarly for the U. K., with $X_3X_1 = OX_3'$ (U. S. exports = U. K. imports), and with $X_3C_2 = Y_1'Y_2'$ (U. S. imports = U. K. exports).

Both countries have succeeded, through production specialization and trade, in pushing their respective consumption boundaries (the terms-of-trade line) out beyond the production boundary (the production-possibility line). The production-possibility lines have not been affected in all this, and yet the U. S. at point C_2 is consuming more of both commodities than she had been at C_1. The U. K., although now consuming more steel than initially, has less textiles. While it appears clear that the U. S., with more of both goods, is better off, is there unambiguous gain for the U. K., with more of one commodity but less of the other? We have already indicated a commonsensical answer: the terms-of-trade line is the "consumption boundary," and foreign trade has pushed out this boundary, making larger the alternative consumption combinations now potentially feasible. The residents of a nation are not obliged to trade—if the community prefers a consumption point on the production-possibility line (say, C_1') to the point on the terms-of-trade line consistent with trade equilibrium, it will not trade; therefore, the existence of trade presumably reflects some gain, with the U. K. preferring to consume at C_2' rather than at the initial C_1'.

[1,2]

Reciprocal Demand and the Terms of Trade

The nature of the trade equilibrium—the quantities of imports and exports and the terms of trade—can be more fully appreciated by explicitly including demand (more particularly, *reciprocal* demand) schedules. For up to this point, we have arbitrarily chosen the slope of the terms-of-trade line any place between the slopes of two production-possibility curves, and we have arbitrarily selected the consumption point on the terms-of-trade line.

Assuming no transactions in other commodities or in services or in gold or in I.O.U.s (capital movements) and international gifts (unilateral transfers), the value of U. S. exports of steel must equal the value of U. K. textile exports. To continue an earlier illustration, the U. S. and the U. K. prices of steel and textiles are given in Table 37–1. Since these prices are given without reference to quantities produced or sold, it can (but need not) be supposed that they hold for all quantities. If we assume that the price of a unit of U. S. steel is $10 irrespective of quantity, the *supply* curve of U. S. steel would be horizontal at a price of $10. But Table 37–1 gives no information on the U. S. and U. K. *demand* schedules.

Since we are analyzing international trade, and since the U. S. is importing textiles and the U. K. is importing steel, we wish to know the U. S. demand for textiles and the U. K. demand for steel. Assume that they are as given in Table 37–2.

TABLE 37–1. Unequal Domestic Price Ratios

	Textiles	Steel
U. S.	$5	$10
U. K.	£2	£8

TABLE 37–2. Demands for Imported Commodities

U. S. Textile Demand		U. K. Steel Demand	
Dollar Price	U. S. Quantity Demanded	Pound Price	U. K. Quantity Demanded
6	0	10	0
5	1,000	9	200
4	2,000	8	400
3	3,000	7	600
2	4,000	6	800
1	5,000	5	1,000
0	6,000	4	1,200
		3	1,400
		2	1,600
		1	1,800
		0	2,000

Each country is both a supplier (exporter) and a demander (importer) internationally. It will be convenient, in considering the determination of the "quantity" terms of trade, to merge the U. S. data on supply of steel and demand for textiles into a single schedule and similarly to calculate a single schedule of U. K. textile supply and steel demand.

Consider point I in Figure 37–2(A): at a price of £10, U. K. residents will demand a zero quantity of steel; therefore, *total* expenditure (price multiplied by quantity) is zero. Since the pound value of imports equals the pound value of exports, receipts from textile exports also are zero, which means that the quantity of textiles supplied, in Figure 37–2(B), must be zero. Thus point I in the demand diagram corresponds to point I' in the supply diagram. And any other point on the U. K. demand curve has a corresponding point on the U. K. supply curve, since export and import values must be equal. To take another example, at price £9, U. K. quantity of steel demanded is 200, and the value of imports is £9 × 200 = £1,800; the value of textile exports also is £1,800, and, at a price of £2, the quantity supplied is 1,800/2 = 900: point II corresponds to point II'. (Why do the points on the supply curve move to the right, as the points on the demand curve are lower, through point IV' and then begin to move to the left, as with points V' and VI'?)

Now, we may plot against each other the total *quantities* imported and exported, ignoring hereafter the *monetary* data. Thus, we plot 0 steel with 0 textiles (point I in Figure 37–3), 200 steel with 900 textiles (point II), and so forth. Connecting such points gives the U. K. "reciprocal demand" curve of Figure 37–3, showing the total

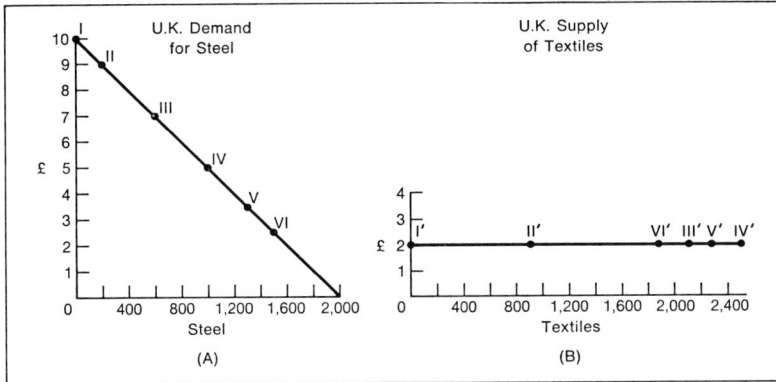

FIGURE 37-2. Corresponding Points on U. K. Steel Demand and U. K. Textile Supply

Assume (1) U. K. demand for steel to be given, (2) U. K. supply of textiles to be horizontal at price of £2, and (3) value of U. K. steel imports to be equal to value of U. K. textile exports. Any point on the U. K. demand curve has a corresponding point on the U. K. supply schedule. For a given point on the demand curve, total expenditure on steel imports equals price times quantity; total expenditure on steel equals total receipts from textile exports; total receipts divided by price equals quantity of textiles.

quantity of textiles the U. K. is willing to supply or pay (export) for any given quantity of steel demanded (imported). In analogous fashion, we obtain the U. S. "reciprocal demand" (steel supply and textile demand) schedule in Figure 37-4.[1] Note that both curves at the origin have positive slopes and ultimately can bend "backward." As we move up the U. S. curve, the ratio of steel to textiles (the steel-price of textiles) decreases; the quantity of textiles demanded increases; and the steel expenditure on textile imports first rises, reaches a maximum, and then falls. (Can you translate this into *elasticity*?)

Finally, in Figure 37-5, we plot the reciprocal demand curves together. The U. S. export (and U. K. import) product is measured horizontally, and the U. S. import (U. K. export) product is measured vertically. At the equilibrium terms of trade, the markets for both products are "cleared": the quantity of steel (textiles) demanded equals the quantity of steel (textiles) supplied. In our illustration, the terms of trade are about 2.82 textiles = 1 steel, with approximately 2,460 textiles exchanging for 871 steel. The terms of trade are measured by the slope of a line drawn through the origin: the steeper the

---

[1] The straight lines radiating out of the origins of the two figures represent the respective domestic exchange (production) ratios in the absence of foreign trade. In the initial U. K. situation, 4 textiles = 1 steel, and the line in Figure 37-3 has a slope of 4; in the pre-trade U. S. situation 2 textiles = 1 steel, so the line in the reciprocal demand diagram of Figure 37-4 has a slope of 2. Since no one in the U. K. will pay more than (the equivalent of) 4 textiles for 1 steel, the segment of the straight line which "cuts through" the curvilinear schedule we have constructed is part of the U. K. reciprocal demand curve. While we remain on the straight-line segment, the terms of *international* trade equal the initial *domestic* ratio $(4t = 1s)$, and it would be a matter of indifference to U. K. residents whether or not there is foreign trade. Similarly, the U. S. reciprocal demand curve follows the straight line from the origin to the combination of 500-steel-and-1,000-textiles (for no one in the U. S. will accept less than 2 textiles for 1 steel) and then bends upward for higher textile-prices of steel.

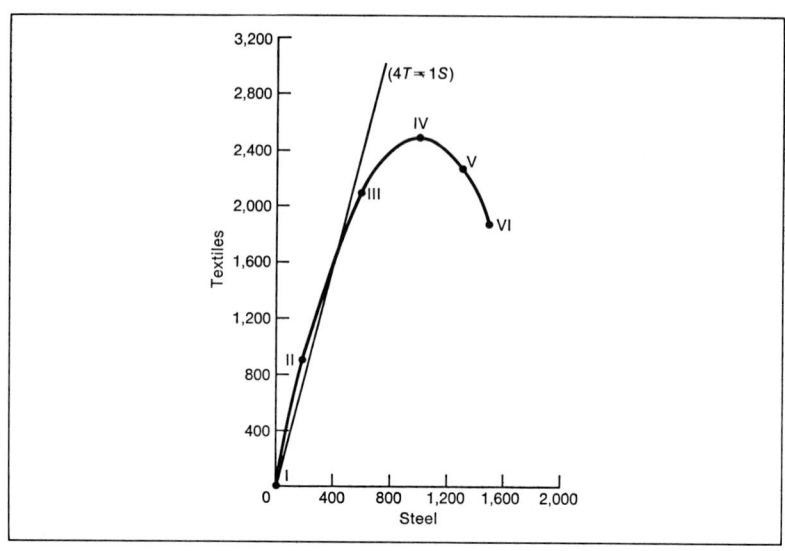

FIGURE 37-3. Construction of U. K. Reciprocal Demand Curve

The corresponding total quantities of steel imports and textile exports in Figure 37-2 are plotted. A line from the origin, rising at a slope of $4t = 1s$ and cutting through a portion of the plotted curve, reflects the U. K. production-possibility line. The U. K. reciprocal demand curve begins at the origin and follows the straight-line (production-possibility) curve until it cuts the plotted curve (at 400 steel, 1,600 textiles) and then continues along the plotted curve.

slope, the greater the ratio of textiles to steel (and the smaller the ratio of steel to textiles).

Any other terms—for example, 3.5 textiles = 1 steel—would be a disequilibrium price (ratio). We can put the matter in terms of the price and the quantities demanded and supplied of either commodity, for each reciprocal demand curve is both a demand schedule and a supply schedule. With respect to steel, at terms of 3.5 textiles = 1 steel, the U. S. quantity supplied is greater than the U. K. quantity demanded, and the textile-price of steel would be bid down; also the U. S. quantity of textiles demanded is greater than the U. K. quantity supplied, so the steel-price of textiles would be bid up. Whichever way stated, the terms-of-trade line would rotate clockwise until it reached the intersection of the U. S. and U. K. reciprocal demand curves. Where the curves cross, the terms-of-trade line has a slope of 2.82 (2.82 textiles = 1 steel), and quantity demanded equals quantity supplied for both commodities.

Suppose that one of the reciprocal demand curves shifts—for example, in Figure 37-6, the *U. K.* curve "falls" to *U. K.'*. With curve *U. K.'*, at any given terms of trade, England is demanding less steel and supplying fewer textiles than she was with the original curve. The point of intersection of curves *U. S.* and *U. K.'* determines a new terms-of-trade line (*OT'*). Compared to the steeper *OT*, *OT'* represents fewer textiles per steel (or more steel per textiles). Since the U. K. is buying steel and selling textiles, she is pleased to have a lower price of imports: the terms of trade have improved from the U. K. point of view. And the terms from the U. S. point of view have worsened.

Note that a change in the *terms* of trade is one criterion for determining the welfare

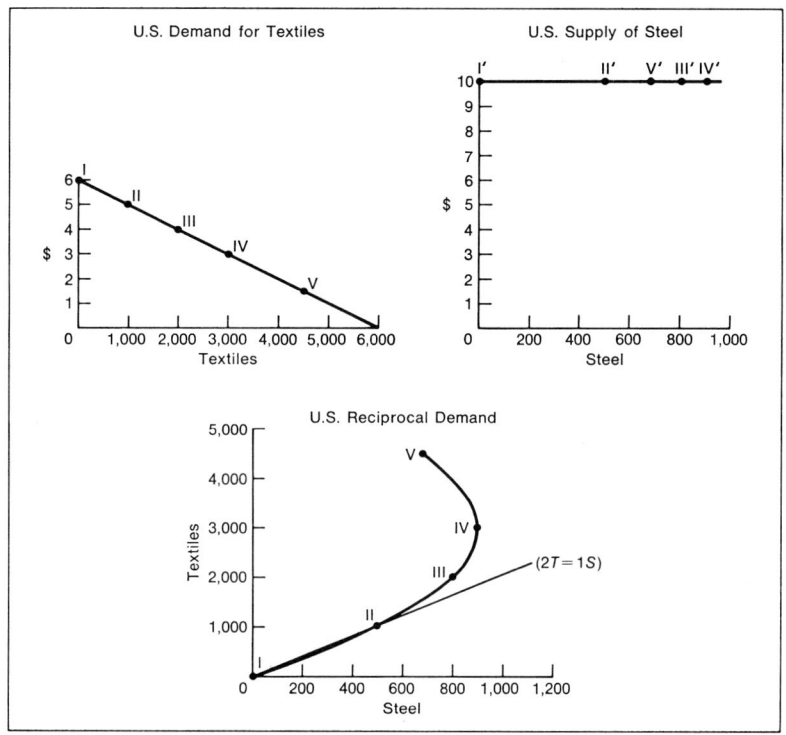

FIGURE 37–4. Derivation of U. S. Reciprocal Demand Curve

As in Figures 37–2 and 37–3, we are given demand for the imported commodity (textiles) and supply of the exported commodity (steel). Pairs of corresponding points on the demand and supply curves are plotted to form the reciprocal demand curve.

effects of the shift in the U. K. reciprocal demand, but there are other criteria—notably, change in the *volume* of trade. At the new equilibrium, the U. K. is suffering a smaller drain of exports. And, in the illustration of Figure 37–6, where the $U.K.$ and $U.K.'$ curves intersect the $U.S.$ curve in the range where the latter is "bending backward," England now obtains more imports. But in what seems empirically the more plausible case of Figure 37–5, if we had lowered the $U.K.$ curve, which intersects the $U.S.$ curve in a positively sloping range, the volume of imports would have diminished.

Why, or how, would the $U.K.$ curve shift to $U.K.'$? One possibility is a fall in English national income, which reduces English demand for steel. If the $U.K.$ demand curve in Figure 37–2 were lowered, the calculated reciprocal demand schedule would shift from the original $U.K.$ toward $U.K.'$. There would be the same sort of shift if the supply of textiles in Figure 37–2 were reduced.

Tariffs and Trade

Let us pursue in more detail a particularly important case of reducing the U. K. reciprocal demand. Suppose that the British government levies a tariff on steel imports equal to

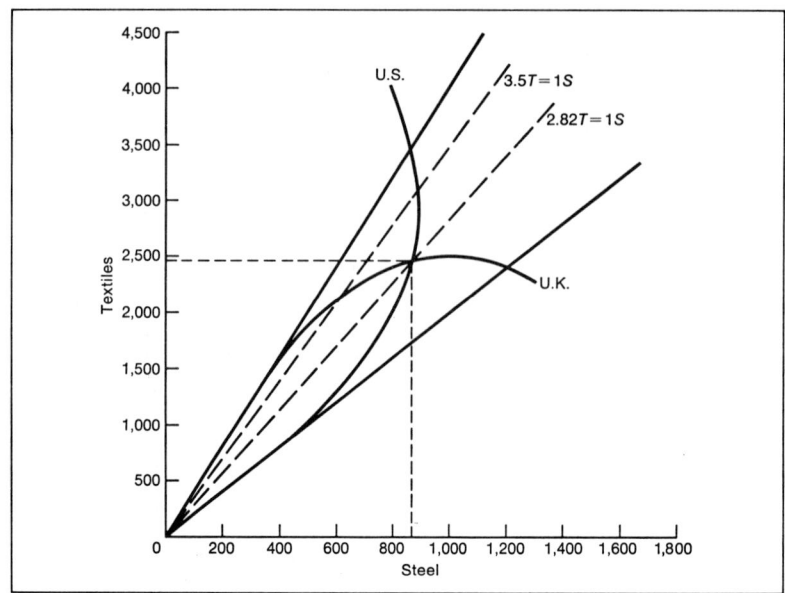

FIGURE 37–5. Reciprocal Demand and Determination of Terms of Trade

The U. K. and U. S. reciprocal demand curves of Figures 37–3 and 37–4 are plotted in the same diagram. The intersection of the curves locates the equilibrium terms of trade, $2.82t = 1s$, where quantity of steel demanded (by the U. K.) equals quantity of steel supplied (by the U. S.) and where quantity of textiles demanded (by the U. S.) equals quantity of textiles supplied (by the U. K.). At a textile-price of steel greater (steel-price of textiles smaller) than equilibrium, $3.5t = 1s$, the quantity of steel supplied is greater than the quantity demanded, and the quantity of textiles demanded is greater than the quantity supplied, thereby tending to shift the terms of trade toward the equilibrium level.

25 percent of the "gross" price, *inclusive* of the tariff (33⅓ percent of the "net" price, *exclusive* of the tariff). In itself, the tariff does not affect the U. K. demand schedule *as seen by residents of the U. K.* Before the tariff, people in the U. K. demanded 400 units of steel at £8 each; after the tariff, they are *still* willing to buy 400 units at £8. However, the price *received* by the U. S. seller is only £6, for the U. K. government collects £2 as tax (£2 being 25 percent of the "gross" price and 33⅓ percent of the "net" price). To put it a bit differently, the U. K. buyer is confronted by a "domestic" price of £8, and he is indifferent that part of his outlay goes to the government, leaving the U. S. exporter with only £6.

In Figure 37–7 (top left), the original U. K. demand is repeated from Figure 37–2; that is now the "gross" demand, inclusive of the tariff. Below the "gross" demand curve is the "net" curve, which is exclusive of the tariff: any point on the "net" curve is 25 percent lower than the point directly above it on the "gross" curve. We find points on the U. K. supply curve (top right) corresponding to selected points on the "net" demand curve. Plotting these pairs of points (below) gives the U. K. reciprocal demand curve, labeled *U. K.'*; the original curve, *U. K.*, is included for comparison.

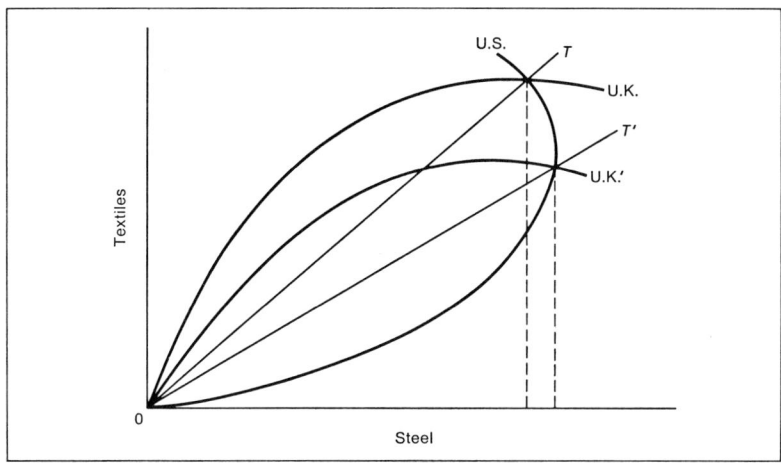

FIGURE 37-6. The Terms of Trade and the Volume of Trade

If the English reciprocal demand shifts (falls, decreases) from *U. K.* to *U. K.'*, the equilibrium terms of trade move from *OT* to *OT'*, a reduction in the textile-price of steel (an increase in the steel-price of textiles). English exports of textiles are reduced. English imports of steel increase in this illustration, but if curve U. S. were vertical or positively sloping in the segment bounded by the two points of intersection, English imports would remain unchanged or be reduced.

Thus, the U. K. improves her terms of trade—moving the terms-of-trade line from the pre-tariff *OT* to *OT'* (in Figure 37–6)—and U. K. imports may decrease or increase, depending on whether the *U. K.* and *U. K.'* curves cross the *U. S.* curve where the latter is sloping up to the right or to the left.[2] But these effects of the U. K. tariff are contingent on an absence of foreign retaliation. In Figure 37–8, we begin with initial reciprocal demand curves, $U.S._1$ and $U.K._1$, which intersect at point 1. Now, England levies a tariff, moving her reciprocal demand to $U.K._2$ and the intersection to point 2. This position represents an improvement in the U. K.'s terms of trade: U. K. exports fall, and U. K. imports rise. But suppose that the U. S. retaliates with her own tariff, moving her reciprocal demand to $U.S._2$; in the move from intersection point 2 to point 3, the terms are worsened for the U. K. (improved for the U. S.), and exports fall for both countries.

---

[2] What is a desirable import volume? It depends upon one's criteria or perspective. We earlier concluded that the "gain from trade" lies in the imports, to the extent that they can be conveniently financed; so, from the viewpoint of the economy as a whole, more imports presumably are desirable. But perhaps the immediate motivation for the tariff was, for good or ill, to protect U. K. steel producers from foreign competition. If so, it would be a bit awkward for a tariff to *increase* steel imports.

The terms-of-trade argument for tariffs is relatively subtle, and one would hardly expect it to play a conspicuous role in public debates. The *quantity* of trade has received the bulk of attention. In Congressional tariff debates, the "infant industry" argument was often used prior to World War I. According to this argument—which has some respectability as theory—a country might have a future comparative advantage in some undeveloped industries if these industries could be protected during establishment and maturation. A more enduring plea for protection in Congressional discussions, before and after World War I, was the "pauper labor" argument urging protection of American workers from low-wage competition abroad—an argument of very little respectability.

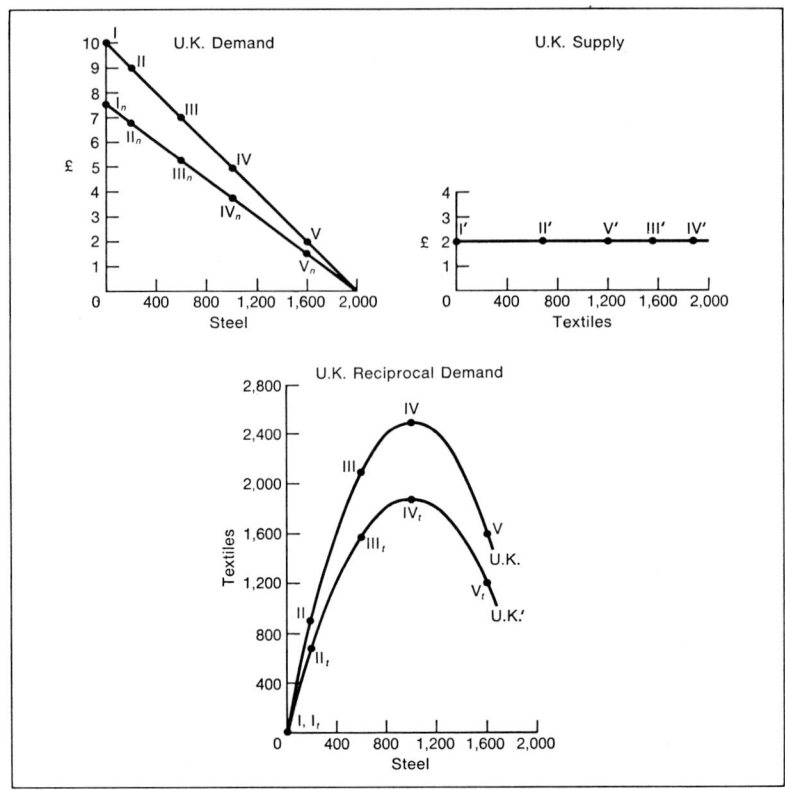

FIGURE 37–7. Effect of Tariff on Reciprocal Demand

A tariff of 25 percent of the "gross" price lowers by 25 percent any point on the initial demand curve (inclusive of tariff) to the new demand curve (net of tariff)—is 25 percent lower than in the demand diagram. Corresponding to any point on the "net" demand curve is a point on the supply curve—point I' corresponds to point I_n. By plotting pairs of corresponding points on the demand and supply curves, we trace out the reciprocal demand curve. Curve *U. K.* is based on the initial ("gross") demand, and *U. K.'* is based on the new ("net") demand.

Then England can counter-retaliate with a higher tariff ($U. K.^3$), followed again by the U. S., and so on. In any given situation, regardless of how many retaliations there have been, and with a small probability of foreigners' future retaliation, a country may well anticipate improved terms of trade from levying or increasing a tariff. But when the smoke from tariff warfare has cleared away, the terms of trade probably will not be greatly changed from the original OT, and almost certainly both countries will have suffered a great decline in the volume of trade.

To summarize: in the absence of retaliation, imposition of a tariff

(1) improves the terms of trade for the tariff-levying country;
(2) reduces exports of the tariff-levying country, which
   (a) is good from the aggregate standpoint of decreasing the drain of goods and services out of the country;

Resource Allocation, Terms of Trade, and Tariffs

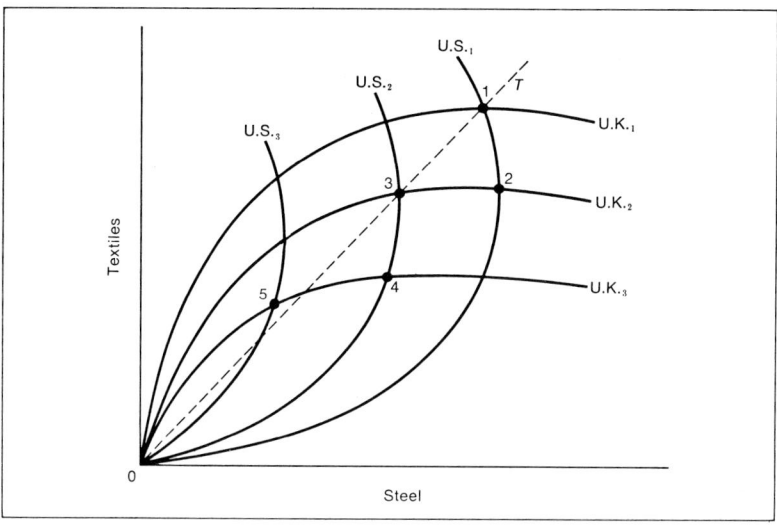

FIGURE 37–8. Tariff Retaliation and Counter-Retaliation

Each country in turn raises its tariff, the intersection points of the reciprocal demand curves moving from 1 to 2 to 3. . . . When a country raises its tariff, it improves its terms of trade. But a sequence of changes by both countries tends to make the net change in the terms small and to reduce greatly the volume of trade.

    (b) is bad from the standpoint of individual firms and industries whose sales are heavily oriented to foreign markets;
    (c) tends to reduce money national income—which is good or bad, depending on whether the general setting is inflation or deflation;
(3) may increase, decrease, or leave unchanged the volume of imports, an increase being desirable from the aggregate standpoint of increasing total goods and services available to the community but being undesirable for individual firms and industries competing with those foreign-made products.

If there is retaliation, and especially if there is initiated a process of counter-retaliation, the terms of trade can either worsen or improve, but may change very little, for a given country; and both imports and exports probably will be reduced, perhaps greatly.

Various criteria should be used to evaluate tariffs; a given policy may well be "good" according to some criteria and "bad" according to others. Interference in the market may help the entire economy as a unit (as when a tariff both improves the terms of trade and increases imports while reducing exports) but hurt parts of the economy (domestic producers of goods which are being imported in increasing volume).

What Do the Terms of Trade Measure?

The terms of trade can be stated in various ways. Thus far we have used "price" terms (the ratio of export price P_x to import price P_m and "quantity" terms (the ratio of import quantity Q_m to export quantity Q_x). In the special case of international transactions consisting only of commercial exports and imports, the "price" and "quantity" terms necessarily give the same result. For if the value of exports equals the value of imports, we have $P_xQ_x = P_mQ_m$, and this can be rearranged: $P_x/P_m = Q_m/Q_x$. The price ratio rises and falls in the same proportion as the quantity ratio. An *increase* in P_x/P_m and in Q_m/Q_x signifies an *improvement* in the terms: they are different ways of saying that the country is obtaining more imports per unit of exports (or is giving fewer exports per unit of imports).

But real-world international transactions are more complicated: generally the value of exports does *not* equal the value of imports. Some of a country's exports may be financed by "credit"—that is, an import of an I.O.U., or by an import of gold, or by making foreigners a gift and thereby importing nothing. In such cases, the "quantity" and the "price" terms of trade give different results.

Suppose that initially we have the following situation of balanced trade:

Exports	Imports
600 units at $4 = $2,400	800 units at $3 = $2,400

Then the "price" terms of trade are $4/3 = 1.333$, and the "quantity" terms are $800/600 = 1.333$. But now increase exports of merchandise by 400 units, financed by receipt of some kind of I.O.U. (claims on foreigners):

Exports	Imports
1,000 units at $4 = $4,000	800 units at $3 = $2,400
	I.O.U.'s received = 1,600

The "price" terms remain $4/3 = 1.333$, but the "quantity" terms are now $800/1,000 = .8$. If the use of a terms-of-trade measure is to indicate the exchange ratio between exports and imports of goods and services (the export cost of a unit of imports or the import receipts per unit of export expenditure), the "price" terms remain valid. But the "quantity" terms now are not very useful. The "quantity" terms, derived from *aggregate* exports and imports, have worsened, but in any *individual* transaction, with money prices unchanged, one unit of exports can still purchase 1.333 units of imports. Furthermore, it would not be a matter of indifference how the increase in exports is financed—whether by receipt of I.O.U.s (perhaps demand deposits in foreign banks) or of gold or by making a gift.

Presumably, we are interested in the terms of trade as some sort of indicator of "welfare." One criterion of "betterment" is surely the international exchange ratio. But perhaps more basic than the ratio of imports to *exports* is the ratio of imports to required *productive resources* embodied in exports. Said a bit differently, the *expenditure* per unit of imports one wishes to minimize is not simply exports but, more ultimately, inputs. We may call the terms-of-trade measure, imports/inputs, the "factoral" terms and define it as $(P_x/P_m)Z$, where P_x and P_m are *indices* of export and import prices, respectively, and Z is an *index* of productivity in the industries making export goods.

Go back to the original case in which we export 600 units at $4 per unit and import 800 at $3. This is the "base" period situation, so we may assign index values of 100 to each of the prices (if, for example, the export price rose 10 percent, to $4.40, the index of the export price would rise to 110). And suppose that it requires 50 "man-years" to produce the 600 units of exports: 12 units of output per man-year is 100 in the productivity index. Thus, in the base period, the "factoral" terms of trade are: $(P_x/P_m) Z = (100/100) \, 100 = 100$.

In a later period, 600 units of exports can be produced with only 40 man-years: output per unit rises to 15 and the productivity index to 125. If prices of exports and imports have remained unchanged, the "price" terms are unchanged, but the "factoral" terms have improved to $(100/100) \, 125 = 125$. One man-year of input now acquires (through production and trade) 25 percent more imports than in the base period.

This is not to say that the "price" terms are irrelevant. With a given productivity change, the factoral terms would have improved even more if the ratio, P_x/P_m, had risen, and they would have improved less if the "price" terms had deteriorated—indeed, P_x/P_m could fall enough to overbalance the rise in Z, with the "factoral" terms thereby worsening.

Still other definitions of "terms of trade" could be considered. Where does all this leave us? First, one should exercise care in speaking of "the" terms of trade and should require others to make clear which of the definitions they are using at any given time. Second, the general notion of "terms of trade" certainly has substance, and in well-specified circumstances it can serve as an indicator (not "the" indicator) of some sorts of changes in "well-being"—at least in principle, although actual statistical measurement, especially over long periods, is notoriously difficult (the nature and quality of both commodities and data are likely to change). But applications of the notion are to be made gingerly, and the results should not have to bear excessive weight. There are those who grandly evaluate whole commercial policies and historical developments of broad consequence, not only of individual countries but of whole groups of countries (sometimes "wealthy" nations versus "underdeveloped" nations), primarily on the basis of what "the" terms of trade are and how they have been changing. Beware of misplaced boldness.

8, 9

Customs Unions and Trade

Our discussion of tariffs has pertained to individual countries unilaterally imposing taxes on their imports. However, countries can act with some kind of *common* tariff procedure or policy. Several (perhaps many) countries may meet in a tariff conference at which each country negotiates tariff rates and other conditions of trade with the other members of the conference. While the actual negotiations are carried on bilaterally between pairs of nations, the tariff and trade "concessions" are "generalized" to apply to all participants, so the negotiations are, in effect, multilateral.[3] This procedure has been used at several large conferences since World War II under the auspices of the General Agreement on Trade and Tariffs (GATT).[4]

---

[3] The "generalizing" provision of the trade agreements is the *most-favored-nation* (MFN) clause. In the "unconditional" form typically used, any tariff rate imposed on a type of import from a particular country will be imposed on such imports from *any* country. If country A puts a certain tax on bananas from country B, under the MFN clause it puts that same tax on bananas from every other country: discrimination is avoided by treating *every* country as "the most favored nation."

[4] GATT has had a strange evolution. Post-war plans included an International Trade Organization (ITO) to provide a code of commercial relations and to reduce various specific trade barriers through negotiations. Agreement on a charter for ITO was reached in 1948—but the United States has never ratified the charter, and the organization thus died aborning. But even before agreement on the charter,

Another type of concerted tariff policy occurs when several countries form a "free-trade area," removing legal barriers to movement of goods and services among the members of the group, but with each country following its own policies toward countries outside the group.[5] Or countries may form a "customs union," with free trade within the union and a *common* tariff on imports into the group. A "common market" (see footnote 2, p. 765) goes a step still further toward "economic integration": in addition to internal free trade and a common external tariff, there can be free movement of labor and capital and other forms of economic cooperation and standardization of economic procedures.

We can illustrate some of the consequences and possibilities of a limited form of economic integration. Let the trading world consist of three countries, and consider production and trade among them of a given commodity under alternative tariff conditions, culminating in a customs union.

First, in Figure 37–9, if *free trade* (along with zero transportation costs) prevails, the world price common to all countries is OP. For at price OP, the imports of country H plus the imports of country L (measured by the sum of the gaps of quantity demanded over quantity supplied) equal the exports of country F (the excess of its quantity supplied over quantity demanded). (This is the same geometric representation used in Figure 36–2 with two countries.)

Now, let countries H and L impose *different specific tariffs* (a tax of fixed amount per unit regardless of price), with the tariff of country H being larger than that of country L (and country F continues its free-trade policy). The high tariff of country H is measured by distance T_H, and the low tariff of L is T_L. Given the amounts of the tariffs, the new price levels in the three countries are located so that the quantity of total world exports continues to equal total imports (but at a reduced amount). The prices in H and L are then greater, and the price in F is less, than in the free-trade situation.

Finally, let countries H and L join into a customs union, with free trade between them and a *common external tariff* on imports from country F. The common tariff means a common price in H and L. And let the post-union common tariff (T) be within the limits T_H and T_L. What are the price, trade, and production effects?

1. The post-union price in H and L cannot be as high as the pre-union price (with individual tariffs) in H. For if it were, H's imports would be unchanged, L's imports would fall (perhaps, as in our geometric illustration, becoming exports), and since $T < T_H$, F's exports would rise. In short, world imports would fall, and world exports would rise, destroying the equality between them. So the post-union price in H must be lower than it was initially, and H increases imports and decreases home production.

---

in 1947, upon the proposal of the United States, twenty-three nations concluded the General Agreement, which was to be an interim measure pending adoption of the ITO charter. No special authority was required by the U. S. executive to participate in GATT, for the negotiations were carried out under the Trade Agreements Act of 1934. The General Agreement goes a considerable distance in providing the "code of good conduct" in the abortive ITO charter; the major provisions include unconditional MFN treatment, general elimination of quantitative restrictions, general nondiscrimination in application of allowable restrictions, and obligation to negotiate for tariff reductions upon request of another member.

[5] The European Free Trade Association (EFTA) was inaugurated in 1960 by Britain, Norway, Sweden, Denmark, Austria, Switzerland, and Portugal. Evidently it was organized largely for bargaining with the European Economic Community (EEC, commonly called the Common Market) established by 1957 treaty. The EFTA, a simpler organization than the EEC, is characterized by scheduled reductions of internal trade barriers but no common external tariff.

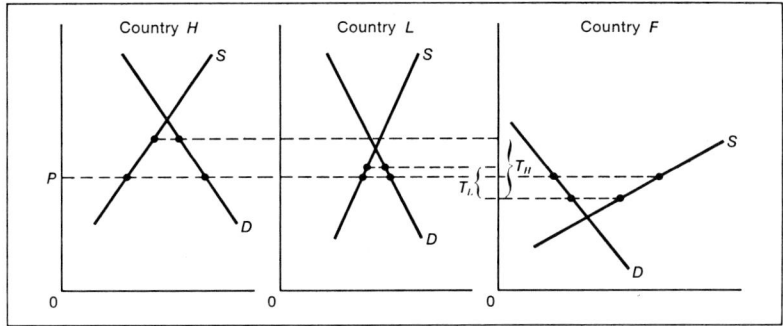

FIGURE 37-9. Prices, Outputs, and Trade under Different Tariff Conditions

Trade equilibrium requires that world exports of the commodity equal world imports. (1) With universal free trade, the common world price is OP, with countries H and L importing the good and country F exporting it. (2) If H has specific tariff T_H and L has T_L, prices diverge from country to country, increasing in H and L (decreasing their imports) and decreasing in F (decreasing her exports). (3) If H and L then adopt a common tariff smaller than T_H and larger than T_L, price falls and imports rise in H, price rises and imports fall in L, and price and import changes are in general indeterminate in F. For world trade to increase as a result of adopting the customs union tariff, H's imports must increase more than L's imports decrease, with F's exports increasing.

2. The post-union price in H and L cannot be as low as the pre-union price in L. If it were, L's imports would be unchanged, H's imports would rise, and since $T > T_L$, F's exports would fall. So the post-union price, while lower than initially in H, is higher in L, decreasing L's imports (perhaps becoming exports) and increasing L's production.

3. The post-union price in F may be higher or lower or unchanged compared to the pre-union price. (a) As the price falls in H and rises in L, if H's imports increase as much as L's imports decrease, then F's price, exports, and production are unchanged; (b) if H's imports increase more than L's decrease, then the price in F and F's production and exports increase; and (c) if H's imports increase less than L's decrease, then L's price, production, and exports decrease.

Has the association of H and L in a customs union created additional world trade—that is, is the volume of trade in this commodity now greater than it was under the tariff system prior to formation of the union?

A situation of trade creation, or trade expansion, is one represented by alternative 3(b) above—that is, an increase in F's exports, associated with H's imports increasing more than L's imports decrease. We can conveniently specify the condition of trade creation in terms of (1) price changes in H and L resulting immediately from imposition of the union tariff and (2) the arithmetic sums of the slopes (or their reciprocals) of the supply and demand curves of H and L.

Consider again in Figure 37–9 the pre-union tariff situation, with tariffs T_H and T_L and with the world imports (by H and L) equal to world exports (by F). And now there is adopted a union tariff, T, which is larger than T_L and smaller than T_H. The increase in H's imports, as a result of adopting the (lower) union tariff, is $(T - T_H)S_H$, where

S_H is the arithmetic sum of the reciprocals of the supply and demand slopes of H.[6] Similarly, the decrease in L's imports is equal to the price change multiplied by the sum of the reciprocals of the supply and demand slopes in L: $(T - T_L)S_L$.

If $(T - T_H)S_H > (T - T_L)S_L$, or $(T - T_H)/(T - T_L) > S_L/S_H$, then the import balance of H increases more than the import balance of L falls, and the export balance of F increases.[7] Thus, for trade creation, a relatively small price change in H (that is, a relatively small difference between H's pre-union tariff and the union tariff) must be accompanied by relatively small slopes in H. Put differently, trade creation is associated with a relatively low union tariff and relatively great absolute response of quantities demanded and supplied to price changes in H compared to L.

10, 11

Summary

1 With straight-line (constant-marginal-cost) production-possibility schedules for each of two countries, it is reasonable to assume complete production specialization. Each country exports part of what it produces; all of what it consumes of the other commodity is imported. The terms-of-trade line is the "consumption boundary" and lies beyond the "production boundary" (production-possibility line) of each country.

2 For each country, a "reciprocal demand" curve shows both the quantities exported (supplied) and the quantities imported (demanded) at alternative terms of trade. Intersection of the reciprocal demand curves of two countries locates the equilibrium terms of trade and thereby determines the specific quantities of goods traded.

3 A country lowers its reciprocal demand curve by imposing a tariff. The terms of trade are thereby improved for the tariff-levying country (with the reciprocal demand of the other country a straight line through the origin, the terms would remain unchanged), and the quantity of imports might increase, decrease, or be unchanged. A sequence of retaliatory tariffs probably would reduce the volume of trade and might have little net effect on the terms.

4 There are several measures of the terms of trade. We have talked mainly about the "price terms" (P_x/P_m) and the "quantity terms" (Q_m/Q_x), which give the same results only if value of exports equals value of imports. An interesting measure is the "factoral terms" $(P_x/P_m)Z$, which gives the ratio of imports to inputs embodied in exports. In all these measures, an increase in the value of the ratio signifies an "improvement" in the terms.

5 Tariffs can also be levied by "customs unions" composed of several countries. A customs union has free trade within the union—which, in itself, tends to increase world trade—but it has a common tariff on imports from outside the union—which, like tariffs generally, tends to reduce trade. Replacing the pre-union tariffs of individual countries with the common union tariff and free intra-union trade may or may not increase trade.

---

[6] Ignoring signs and speaking arithmetically, in H price falls initially by amount $(T - T_H)$; quantity demanded (Q_d) increases by $(T - T_H)$ multiplied by the reciprocal of the slope of the demand curve (S_d) in H; quantity supplied (Q_s) decreases by $(T - T_H)$ multiplied by the reciprocal of the slope of the supply curve (S_s). The increase in H's imports is $\Delta Q_d + \Delta Q_s = (T - T_H)(1/S_d) + (T - T_H)(1/S_s) = (T - T_H)(1/S_d + 1/S_s) = (T - T_H)S_H$. S_H, the sum of the reciprocals of the slopes (not to be confused with the reciprocal of the sum of the slopes) is $(1/S_d) + (1/S_s) = (S_s + S_d) / S_d S_s$.

[7] As a special case, if the union tariff is exactly midway between the pre-union tariffs of H and L, that is, $(T - T_H)/(T - T_L) = 1$, then the condition of trade creation is $1 > S_L/S_H$, or $S_H > S_L$; if the sum of the *reciprocals* of the slopes in H is *larger* than that in L, the sum of the *slopes* is *smaller* in H. As another special case, suppose that the union tariff is identical to T_L; that is, $T - T_L = 0$. Then the situation is necessarily one of trade creation.

Questions

1 "If foreign trade increases the domestic consumption of *both* commodities (in a two-commodity case), we can reasonably say that trade is beneficial to that country. But the with-trade consumption combination may include *less* of one of the commodities than the before-trade combination; and in that situation it is ambiguous whether there is a gain from the trade, and we can say nothing about the matter." Can't we say *anything* about the possible gain in this situation?

2 The consumption points of the U. S. and the U. K. with trade (i.e., points C_2 and C_2' in Figure 37–1) have much in common: The amount of steel exported by the U. S. (X_3X_1) equals the amount imported by the U. K. (OX_3'), and U. K. textile exports ($Y_2'Y_1'$) equal U. S. imports (X_3C_2). Does this mean that the two countries share *equally* the gains from trade? If not, which country obtains a *greater* share?

3 Explain why, or in what sense, a "reciprocal demand curve" is *both* a demand curve and a supply curve.

4 At any given point on a reciprocal demand curve, we can measure a desired quantity of imports demanded, the maximum quantity of exports which will be supplied for those imports, and the corresponding export price of imports (the terms of trade); the import and export quantities are measured by *distances* along the vertical and horizontal axes, and the terms of trade are indicated by the *slope* of a line through the origin. Now, could you plot this same information—imports, exports, price—in the sort of diagram used earlier in the book, in which quantity demanded is measured horizontally, price is measured vertically, and the demand curve slopes downward to the right?

5 A reciprocal demand curve can "bend backward." For example, in Figure 37–4, the U. S. curve first rises from left to right, then becomes vertical, and finally rises with a negative slope. This means that as the export price of imports falls, the quantity of imports demanded increases—which reflects the basic law of demand; but it means also that the total quantity of exports offered first reaches a maximum and then diminishes. Doesn't it seem a little odd that, beyond certain terms of trade, a country can import a larger and larger quantity while giving up less and less exports? Is this a manifestation of any concept discussed earlier in the book?

6 "A tariff normally improves the terms of trade of the tariff-levying country. A tariff may increase or decrease the quantity of imports. The improvement in the terms will be greater, the smaller is the decrease or the larger is the increase in imports. Speaking generally, a large improvement in the terms is accompanied by a large increase in imports." Demonstrate the foregoing geometrically. Is it "good" and "desirable" that the greater the improvement in the terms, the greater the value of imports? From what perspective: the economy "as a whole," or domestic producers competing with imports? Is it good from the viewpoint of a nation trying to protect domestic "infant" industries?

7 A common sophomore complaint runs something like this: "Economics is so frustratingly inconclusive. Take the matter of tariffs. Surely the economist should be in a position to pass final judgment. Are tariffs good or are they not? Instead, he agonizingly (a) spells out *various* criteria in judging tariffs and (b) points out that, with respect to a *given* criterion, tariffs may be either good or bad, depending on one's objective or perspective. We have run into similar inconclusiveness in other areas (for example, in comparing alternative expansionary fiscal policies). Such subtleties may amuse the economists, but red-blooded youths want *answers*. And in many other social science courses, we *do* get

answers: by the end of the semester we are sure that we *know* things; and the questions in these other, noneconomics courses are every bit as vital and grandiose as the topics in this course." Come to the defense of the beleaguered economics teacher. What reply can he reasonably give to the complaining student?

8   What is the relationship between the terms of trade and the gains from trade? Is any measure of the terms a wholly adequate indicator of the gains? Is any measure of the terms useful at all as a welfare indicator?

9   The text speaks of "factoral" terms of trade, where the "price" terms are modified (multiplied) by an index of productivity in export industries. The factoral terms indicate the ratio of imports to inputs. Commonly, this measure is called the *single* factoral terms, for productivity in only this country's export industries is taken into account. But another measure is the so-called *double* factoral terms. What do you suppose the double factoral terms of trade are? Would that measure be a better indicator of welfare than the single factoral terms?

10 What is the distinction between a "free-trade area" and a "customs union"? Which form of association is more consistent with, or contributes more toward achieving, free trade among all countries of the world?

11 What happens to the most-favored-nation principle under a customs union? Are the principle and the organization consistent? In general, is establishment of a customs union a step toward—or away from—freer international trade and less discriminatory trade policies?

The Balance of Payments and Its Interpretation

38

The "gain" from trade, we have seen, stems most immediately from imports, not exports. Therefore, the more imports, the better—*to the extent that they can be "conveniently" financed*. A nation or any other economic unit living beyond its currently earned means is faced with a balance-of-payments problem. It is time to take a look at the balance of *international* payments to see how it may help in evaluating the international financial situation of an economy.

Balance-of-Payments Accounting

The balance of payments of a nation is a double-entry accounting statement of the international economic transactions, commonly over a year, of the residents (individuals, business firms, government units) of the country. There are two sides of the balance, generally labeled "credits" and "debits," or "receipts" and "payments," or simply "plus" and "minus." The credits or receipts or plus side is basically the *export* side. Listed there, in money value, are the country's exports of merchandise, services, claims, and gold— sales or transfers of things to foreigners: sales are "credited," and sales establish a claim to "receipts." And the debits or payments or minus side is the *import* side: purchases are "debited" and give rise to "payments."

Consider a series of international transactions of the U. S. and how they are recorded.

1. A U. S. firm sells a tractor to an Englishman for $2,100, the sale being financed by an increase in U. S.-owned demand deposits in a London bank. (You may review pp. 727–729 on technicalities of making international payments.) The value of the tractor *export* is listed on the *credit* side in the *merchandise* account. The increase in the

demand deposit held abroad constitutes an *import* of a claim (for demand deposits are money, and money is generalized command over goods and services) and is listed on the *debit* side under *short-term capital*.[1]

2. The preceding transaction was financed by a "time" bill of exchange, giving the importer ninety days in which to pay, the interest charged the importer being the pound equivalent of $10. The receipt of the interest by the U. S. bank is listed as *investment income* on the *credit* side. The interest payment of $10 by the importer is entered under the *short-term capital* account on the *debit* side.

3. In accordance with the contract between the exporter and the importer, the exporter pays for shipping the tractor. A French ship is used, and payment of $150 is made, which the Frenchman leaves on deposit in a U. S. bank. The increase of foreign claims on the U. S. is a *credit* in the *short-term capital* account. And the U. S. has bought (imported) shipping services, the value of which is listed as a *debit* in the *services* account.

4. American residents purchase British linen for $450, paying for it by drawing down U. S.-held demand deposits in the U. K., which were accumulated in earlier transactions. The reduction in these U. S. claims is a *short-term capital* entry on the *credit* side; the *merchandise* import is a *debit*.

5. American investors spend $600 for Canadian corporate bonds, making payment by drawing down previously accumulated balances in Canadian banks. The reduction of U. S. demand deposits held abroad is a *credit* in the *short-term capital* account; the import of the bonds is a *debit* of *long-term capital*.

6. The American government gives $700 worth of wheat to Pakistan. The wheat export, like the tractor export in the first transaction, is a *credit* in the *merchandise* account. But how is it financed; what does the U. S. receive that can be listed on the debit side? Since the wheat is a gift, nothing is received. But the books are balanced by inserting among the *debits* an account called *unilateral transfers*, "unilateral" denoting the one-way aspect of the transaction.

7. The Bank of France uses $300 previously accumulated in the Federal Reserve Bank of New York to buy gold from the U. S. Treasury.[2] The export of gold is a *credit* in the *gold* account, and the reduction of foreign demand deposits in the U. S. is a *debit* under *short-term capital*.

---

[1] Conventionally the dividing line between short-term and long-term capital is one year. Demand deposits, payable on demand, are clearly short term.

Remember that an increase in U. S. claims on foreigners (or a reduction of foreign claims on the U. S.) amounts to "giving credit," "granting a loan," or "investment" by the U. S. Or, as the expression goes, it constitutes a "capital movement" from the U. S. to the U. K. This may be a confusing expression, for this capital "export" or "outflow" is listed on the debit (import) side of the balance of payments. But a so-called "capital export" refers to an *import of a claim* (either an initial import of a foreign I.O.U.—increasing U. S. demand deposits held abroad—or a repatriation of an old American I.O.U. held by foreigners—decreasing foreign-held demand deposits in the U. S.), and imports of claims against foreigners are debits, just as are imports of goods and services.

[2] Only foreign monetary authorities—central banks and treasuries, not private persons and business firms—may buy gold from the Treasury. From 1961–68, the U. S. participated with several other countries in a "gold pool" which intervened in the London gold market, as a sometimes seller or buyer, to dampen fluctuations in the unofficial (unpegged) gold price. Private parties (but not U. S. citizens), along with official institutions, were among the market traders. But in March 1968, the gold pool terminated: the former members, joined by other major commercial nations, agreed henceforth to buy and sell gold only among themselves (at the official price of $35 an ounce) and to cease trading in all private markets (where prices free to fluctuate would prevail).

8. The British Treasury sells bonds to American investors for $400 and puts the proceeds on deposit in a New York bank. The increase in foreign-owned deposits is a *credit* under *short-term capital,* and the U. S. purchase of bonds is a *debit* in the *long-term capital* account.

Now, let us list all eight transactions together in the U. S. balance of payments:

	Credits	Debits
Merchandise	2,100 + 700 = 2,800	450
Services		150
Investment income	10	
Long-term capital		600 + 400 = 1,000
Unilateral transfers		700
Short-term capital	150 + 450 + 600 + 400 = 1,600	2,100 + 10 + 300 = 2,410
Gold	300	
	4,710	4,710

Aggregate balance is inevitable, for each *individual* transaction, recorded in double-entry manner, balanced.[3] To make use of the balance of payments, we must concentrate on the balances (or imbalances) of appropriately chosen subcategories or groups within the total statement. One such group is the *current account*, comprised of the merchandise, services, and investment-income entries.[4] In our illustration, the current account balance is $(2,800 + 10) - (450 + 150) = 2,210$. This is variously known as a "surplus" balance, an "export" balance, a "positive" balance, a "favorable" balance, or an "active" balance (where balance clearly means "difference," not "equality").

It is common, also, to group all entries constituting change in international claims (a change in the international creditor-debtor status of a country) into a *capital* account. (Payments and receipts of investment income have been included in the current, not the capital, account. The transfer of interest and dividends does not in itself involve change in the principal of international indebtedness.) For some purposes, it is advisable to segregate long-term from short-term capital, but the total account in our illustration is $1,200 - (600 + 2,410) = -1,810$. The minus value indicates a net outward flow of capital—a net increase in the U. S. creditor (or decrease in the U. S. debtor) position.

While we must divide the total statement into at least these current and capital accounts, it is useful to note two more accounts: gold and unilateral transfers. The *gold account* is generally segregated, for gold is an asset constituting "money" in the world economy. As indicated earlier, the *unilateral-transfer account* reflects "one-way" transactions; when a gift is made or received, there is no counter-movement.

1, 2, 3

---

[3] The balance of payments *must* balance, not only in principle but also in practice. To ensure balance, the statisticians insert, if need be, an entry of appropriate size on the appropriate side of the statement; the entry is called "errors and omissions."

[4] We may call the balance of merchandise alone the "balance of trade," here equal to $2,800 - 450 = 2,350$. The balance of trade is thus part of the balance on current account.

Interpretations of "Imbalance"

Now that we have recorded transactions in the balance of payments and grouped the entire statement into a number of categories, what do we do with the information? The record of past transactions can be instructive only within limits. How best to *define* "balance-of-payments equilibrium," much less how to *measure* "disequilibrium," is still a topic of discussion—sometimes heated, sometimes subtle, never conclusive. Indeed, in a fine show of humility, analysts frequently avoid the terms "equilibrium" and "disequilibrium" and speak simply of "shortage" or "gap" or "deficit" or "imbalance."

It will be helpful to review two general approaches to balance-of-payments analysis, illustrated by two recent periods in U. S. data: 1946–49 and 1958–69.

U. S. surplus: "dollar shortage." Table 38–1 covers the four-year period after World War II, a period characterized by so-called "dollar shortage," or "dollar gap." Many a fine-spun theory was advanced to explain why the dollar shortage existed. We shall not get entangled with them. Our problem is to determine *what* the dollar shortage was, as measured by the balance of payments.

TABLE 38–1. United States Balance of Payments, 1946–49
(Net Annual Average in Millions of Dollars)

Current account		8,172 ⎫
Goods and services	7,287	⎬ Surplus = 5,200
Investment income	885	⎭
Long-term capital		−2,972
Unilateral transfers		−4,118
Short-term capital		− 561
Gold		−1,292
Errors and omissions		771

Source: U. S. Department of Commerce, *Balance of Payments, Statistical Supplement, Revised Edition.*

The U. S. had a net export balance on current account "financed" by net gifts, net long-term capital outflow (U. S. investment abroad and foreign disinvestment in the U. S.), net short-term capital outflow, and net import of gold. Of course, the aggregate financing (net debits) balanced the current U. S. surplus (net credits). But did it matter *how* the financing was done? Table 38–1 would indicate a dollar shortage only if we believed either that (1) *no* way to finance the current account surplus (U. S. export balance) can be deemed commercially "proper" or "legitimate" or "acceptable" or "normal"—the *total* imbalance of the current account must equal the dollar shortage; or that (2) *some* ways of financing are "proper," but some are not—the dollar shortage is equal to that *part* of the current account imbalance not covered by "proper" forms of financing.

Consider the net debit ("financing") entries individually. The persistent and conspicuous presence of unilateral transfers in the accounts may be considered a signal that all is not well. It is straining the concept to say that a balance of payments is in "equilibrium" when it contains a large volume of unilateral transfers—however wise, under the existing circumstances, the giving or receiving of the gifts may be. Presumably, the U. S. made net annual gifts in excess of $4 billion precisely because it was believed that the rest of the world (or a large part of it) was not in a healthy financial position and that, in the absence of the gifts, the rest of the world would be undesirably (from America's point of view) "short" of dollars.

Heavy and persistent reliance on short-term capital and gold also may indicate international financial trouble. Short-term claims on foreigners and gold together make up the "international reserves," or "liquidity," of a country. Within ill-defined limits, a nation may draw upon its reserves, as an individual may spend some of his cash, without a balance-of-payments crisis. But a financing procedure appropriate in small, occasional doses is cause for alarm if pressed too far—for either a country or an individual. The gold holdings of the rest of the world could eventually be drained away entirely, as could previously accumulated foreign balances in U. S. banks and other foreign-owned short-term dollar assets. There is no such obvious physical limit on foreign short-term borrowing from the U. S. (which, like the reduction of foreign-held balances in the U. S., is a debit in the U. S. balance of payments), but monetary officials abroad may well wonder how far, and on what terms, they can go on borrowing in the U. S.

Large U. S. debit balances on unilateral transfers, short-term capital, and gold, then, suggest that the rest of the world has bought too much (relative to how much it has sold) on current account and has thus been forced to fall back excessively on means of financing that indicate market imbalance. If there is an appropriate way for the rest of the world to pay for its current purchases other than through current sales (thus not requiring a zero balance on current account), it appears to be by U. S. purchases of long-term foreign assets. It may be that the residents of a nation can prudently obtain financing for their international purchases by selling long-term bonds and stocks to foreigners. In the nineteenth century, for example, U. S. railroads were built with considerable British capital; and few would suggest that this long-term capital inflow into the U. S. was evidence of a decades-long balance-of-payments crisis. Long-term loans are not necessarily wise, for either lender or borrower, just because they are long-term; but such financing is not likely to reflect the immediate financial pressures and panic associated with a forced scramble to scrape up large amounts of "international cash" (short-term capital and gold). Long-term financing may make feasible the initiation of well-planned investment activity over a substantial future period; massive reliance on short-term capital and gold is likely to be the consequence of past and current disasters and imprudence.

According to this line of thought, the dollar shortage is the absolute (arithmetic) difference between the U. S. current-account surplus and the U. S. long-term capital outflow—that is, $8{,}172 - 2{,}972 = 5{,}200$. But since total credits equal total debits, the imbalance of these two categories must be matched by an equal-sized imbalance (of opposite sign) of all the other categories. Thus, we can measure the absolute size of the dollar shortage alternatively: $4{,}118 + 561 + 1{,}292 - 771 = 5{,}200$.

An alternative version, sometimes used in official statistics, places unilateral transfers with the current and long-term capital account. This so-called "basic" balance approach segregates these three accounts—for supposedly they are relatively "persistent" and "stable" in the short run, changing only in trends and in response to broad, pervasive economic forces—from the remainder of the balance of payments, which is more volatile and erratic and more responsive to monetary policy measures. Then the shortage is: $8{,}172 - 2{,}972 - 4{,}118 = 1{,}082 = 561 + 1{,}292 - 771$.

A major warning is in order. Do not suppose that *first* the "shortage" sprang full grown out of nowhere and *now* the existing "shortage" must be financed, or the "gap" must be filled. The imbalance of the current and long-term capital accounts could exist only because net financing of $5,200 in the aggregate was available. With less financing available, the shortage would have been smaller. Indeed, if the U. S. had made no net gifts and no short-term loans and if the rest of the world had not drawn down short-term claims on the U. S. or shipped gold to the U. S., there could have been no shortage.

This point is of particular interest with respect to unilateral transfers, which closely approached the size of the shortage. Some have suggested that the role of U. S. gifts was to fill a balance-of-payments deficit which already had come into existence, and that a bigger gap would have "required" still more aid. What would have happened to the balance of payments if unilateral transfers had been eliminated? In principle, the dollar shortage could have remained the same, with larger gold and short-term capital movements taking up all the slack: a given shortage does not "necessitate" a given amount of aid or, indeed, any aid at all. At the other extreme, as a consequence of eliminating U. S. gifts, foreign purchases on current account in the U. S. might be equally reduced: With all the balance of payments other than unilateral transfers and current account remaining the same, the dollar shortage would be reduced by the amount of the decrease in U. S. gifts. In actuality, probably the U. S. current-account surplus would have fallen somewhat if unilateral transfers had been eliminated, but by a lesser amount. It thus appears that, instead of the size of U. S. gifts being "dictated" by the size of an existing gap, the gap is itself a function of the magnitude of the gifts. The greater or smaller the amount of U. S. aid, the greater or smaller the dollar shortage.

U. S. deficit: "dollar-glut." Based on comparing the current and the long-term capital accounts, in 1946–49, the rest of the world had a "dollar shortage"—that is, the U. S. balance of payments was in *surplus* disequilibrium—of $5.2 billion on a yearly average. Now the balance of payments, it is widely concluded, has shown since 1957 an average annual *deficit* of nearly $2.9 billion. However, the commonly used measure of the recent deficit is not the previously used measure of the surplus. (Table 38–2 indicates that, according to the old measure, the U. S. still had a surplus of over $2.7 billion in 1958–69.)

TABLE 38–2. United States Balance of Payments, 1958–69
(Net Annual Averages in Millions of Dollars)

Current account		5,748
Goods and services	2,212	
Investment income	3,536	
Long-term capital		—3,003
Unilateral transfers		—4,137
U. S. short-term capital		— 813
Foreign short-term capital		2,250
Gold and other U.S. reserves*		609 } Deficit = 2,859
Errors and omissions		— 654

* In 1958–60, monetary gold alone; beginning 1961, includes convertible currencies held by U. S. monetary authorities; beginning 1962, includes International Monetary Fund position ("essentially automatic" drawing, i.e., borrowing, right of U. S.).
Source: U. S. Department of Commerce, *Balance of Payments, Statistical Supplement, Revised Edition* and *Survey of Current Business.*

This new measure of the imbalance is used because of the great change in "liquid" international assets held by U. S. monetary authorities and in "liquid" international liabilities of U. S. monetary authorities. The assets in question consist primarily of *gold,* and the liabilities are *short-term claims on the U. S.* held by foreigners—claim which, directly or indirectly, can be exchanged for U. S. gold.[5] In this measure of actual plus potential gold outflow, the short-term capital account has been divided into two components: foreign investments in the U. S. and U. S. investments abroad. In the specification of the deficit, only the former—the change in foreign short-term claims on the U. S.—is used. This measure is to reflect the "international liquidity" position of the country *from the viewpoint of U. S. monetary authorities,* who are concerned with maintaining the pegged dollar-price of gold: whereas these foreign claims can be liquidated to buy U. S. gold, the private U. S. claims on foreigners are not at the disposal of the U. S. monetary authorities and do not constitute an offset to foreign claims on the U. S.[6]

Some analysts prefer a modification of the "liquidity" measure. They hold that, as the liquid assets in question are held by (domestic) monetary authorities, the relevant liquid liabilities, too, should pertain only to (foreign) monetary authorities rather than to all foreigners: it is only foreign authorities, not private parties, who can directly buy U. S. gold. Thus the U. S. deficit in the "official settlements" measure consists of loss of U. S. gold and other reserves (as in the "liquidity" measure) plus increase in liquid (and some nonliquid) claims on the U. S. held by foreign monetary authorities.

Generally, the two approaches, "liquidity" and "official settlements," have given results of the same order of magnitude, with the deficit figure being somewhat larger with the "liquidity" approach. But the supposed measure of the change in U. S. liquidity and the supposed measure of balance of payments disequilibrium as reflected in official reserve transactions[7] can give very different messages: in 1969, the "liquidity" approach yielded a *deficit* of $7.1 billion, and the "official settlements" approach indicated a *surplus* of $2.7 billion.

4, 5, 6, 7, 8, 9, 10

---

[5] In 1946–49, there was an annual average *inflow* of gold equal to nearly $1.3 billion and a net short-term capital *outflow* (increase in U. S. claims on foreigners and decrease in foreign claims on the U. S.) of over $.5 billion. But since 1957, the U. S. has *sold* gold at an annual rate of over $.6 billion, and foreign short-term claims on the U. S. (otherwise known as "liquid dollar assets") have *risen* at a rate of over $2.2 billion.

[6] One consequence of using only the foreign component of the short-term capital account in measuring the deficit is a certain asymmetry of effect on the deficit from alternative ways of financing a given transaction. Suppose the U. S. imports an article from England. It may be financed, we have seen, either by (1) reducing U. S. deposits in an English bank or (2) increasing an English deposit in an American bank. In either case, we credit the over-all short-term capital account. But under alternative (1), which involves a movement of U. S. capital out of England, the balance-of-payments deficit is not affected, whereas under alternative (2), which is a movement of foreign capital into the U. S., the deficit is increased.

[7] The "official settlements" version stems from work of a governmentally appointed committee chaired by E. M. Berstein. The committee gives its general orientation: ". . . the main purpose of a summary indicator of the balance of payments position should be to indicate the extent of any *disequilibrium* that may exist in the country's international transactions. We wish, essentially, to *measure the gap* between the *normal* supply of and demand for foreign exchange—a gap which the monetary *authorities,* here and abroad, must fill by adding to, or drawing down, their reserve assets if exchange rates are to be held stable. . . . The side of these transactions in international reserves provides the best available measure of the *market intervention* that has been necessary, of the *gaps* that have had to be filled, and hence of payments disequilibria" (italics added). *The Balance of Payments Statistics of the U. S., Report of the Review Committee* (Bureau of the Budget, April 1965), pp. 109–10.

The Dollar, the Deficit, and International Liquidity

Especially since World War II, the dollar has been very widely used as a medium of international payment. In the later 1940s, the U. S. held almost three-fourths of the (noncommunist) world gold stock, and the dollar-price of gold presumably was firmly fixed. Many nations came to look upon the dollar as the equivalent of gold in computing and managing their "international reserves," making the dollar a "reserve currency" and the U. S. a "world banker." As major commercial nations gained in financial strength in the 1950s, they were happy to build up their liquid dollar assets. (Table 38–3 indicates that international reserves in the form of foreign exchange tripled between 1949 and 1969. In 1969, most of this foreign exchange held as reserves consisted of U. S. dollars and English pounds, with dollars being 52 percent of the total and pounds being 29 percent.[8] But gold has not gone out of fashion; foreign monetary authorities tripled their gold reserves in this period, partly through gold production and even more importantly through importing gold from the U. S.) As long as the world considers the dollar "as good as gold," there is little likelihood of a massive "run on the dollar"—that is, a general move by foreigners to cash in their dollar assets for gold. However, if the feeling developed that the U. S. was on the verge of curtailing the freedom of foreign monetary authorities to buy gold or that the dollar was soon to be devalued (the dollar price of gold raised), then there would be a scramble for U. S. gold.

TABLE 38–3. World Trade and Reserves, 1949–69
(Monetary Data in Billions of Dollars)

	World Trade (Exports f.o.b.)	Reserves						Gold Reserves as Percentage of World Trade	Gold Reserves as Percentage of World Trade
			Gold			Foreign Exchange	I.M.F. Position*		
		Total	Total	U. S.	Other				
1949	53.9	45.5	33.5	24.6	8.9	10.4	1.7	84	62
1951	74.8	49.4	33.9	22.9	11.0	13.7	1.7	66	45
1953	73.4	51.8	34.3	22.1	12.2	15.6	1.9	71	47
1955	83.0	54.3	35.4	21.8	13.6	17.0	1.9	65	43
1957	99.1	56.6	37.3	22.9	14.4	17.0	2.3	56	38
1959	100.3	57.7	37.9	19.5	18.4	16.5	3.3	58	38
1961	118.6	62.6	38.9	16.9	22.0	19.6	4.2	53	33
1963	136.1	66.6	40.2	15.6	24.6	22.4	3.9	49	30
1965	165.4	70.7	41.9	14.1	27.8	23.4	5.4	43	25
1967	190.6	73.9	39.5	12.1	27.4	28.6	5.7	39	21
1969	243.0	76.9	39.1	11.9	27.2	31.1	6.7	32	16

* The amount a member may draw (borrow) "essentially automatically" from the International Monetary Fund.
Source: International Monetary Fund, *International Financial Statistics*.

Thus far, there have been only a few serious signs of a panicky demand for U. S. gold. Of the total "deficit" since 1957, some 80 percent (a larger proportion in recent years) has taken the form of increased foreign holdings of liquid dollar claims. Still, the remaining 20 percent has included a substantial gold outflow. Most or all of the gold

---

[8] However, the relative attractiveness of the dollar as a reserve currency has diminished: In 1965, dollars and pounds comprised virtually all of foreign exchange reserves, with dollars being 70 percent of the total.

outflow—reducing the U. S. monetary gold stock from over 70 percent of the world total (with the exception of Russia and China) to about 30 percent—may have been a desirable world redistribution. But a prolonged continuance of such outflow might cramp American foreign trade and investment and unsettle much of the world's commerce—based, as it is, on the dollar as the major "reserve currency" and with exchange rates held essentially stable by pegging operations in the foreign exchange market.

The gold outflow would be reduced if the total "deficit" were reduced and if the 80–20 ratio of foreign short-term capital and gold were maintained. Probably, if the total "deficit" were substantially reduced (and thus confidence in the dollar enhanced), even the proportion of the deficit represented by U. S. gold sales would fall: the gold outflow would be a smaller part of a smaller total. Put in these terms, the solution to the U. S. liquidity (gold) problem is to "adjust" the balance of payments and thereby to reduce or eliminate the "deficit."

But we are here faced with something of a dilemma. (1) On the one hand, monetary authorities in both the U. S. and elsewhere (primarily Europe) have expressed concern with the continuing U. S. "deficit." For the deficit increases the actual and/or potential outflow of gold, and fear may develop that the U. S. will soon be unable to meet all anticipated demands for gold at a fixed dollar price, and such fear itself would tend to accelerate the drain of gold. In turn, breaking the fixed tie between the dollar and gold—leaving the dollar not really as good as gold, after all—would have severe psychological consequences in eminent financial circles. And, for good or ill, the dollar might then no longer be considered a reliable reserve currency, the U. S. might no longer be used as the major world banker, and the entire arrangement of pegged exchange rates would be endangered—for good or ill. (2) On the other hand, if the U. S. *does* succeed in eliminating its balance-of-payments "deficit" (if the U. S. were no longer to supply the rest of the world with dollars and gold), where will other countries obtain increasing quantities of "liquidity"? As Table 38–3 indicates, from 1949 to 1969 world trade increased almost five-fold while total reserves increased by only 70 percent; total reserves and gold reserves both have fallen sharply as percentages of trade.[9] Many fear that trade cannot continue to increase if additions to reserves keep lagging behind. And elimination of the American deficit would greatly increase the lag.[10]

In short, the present international monetary arrangement may collapse from panic and the draining of gold from the world's banker if the U. S. "deficit" long continues, and it may be stifled by lack of liquidity to support an appropriately expanding world trade if the U. S. "deficit" is long corrected. Much of this will become clearer if we appraise the major methods of possible balance-of-payments adjustment, and that is the subject of the following chapter.

---

[9] The great decline in the ratio of reserves (or of gold) to trade does not by itself say that the world is moving from or toward an *optimal* ratio. Indeed, the value of the optimal ratio varies with different circumstances pertaining to balance of payments policies. Reserves are to finance, not the *total volume* of trade, but only *residual imbalances*. And trade imbalances which call for financing with reserves are not inevitably correlated positively with trade volume.

[10] When the present two-price (sometimes called two-tier) system of gold was adopted in 1968 (see footnote 2), the aggregate amount of monetary gold supposedly was virtually frozen. This was deemed acceptable in anticipation of early usage of Special Drawing Rights (SDRs). The first of three allocations of SDRs were made to members of the International Monetary Fund in January 1970 and January 1971, with a subsequent allocation scheduled for 1972, the total of these distributions to be $9.5 billion. SDRs are a supplemental international reserve asset *created by,* not simply *deposited in,* the I.M.F.

Summary

1 The balance of international payments of a country records its exports and imports of goods, services, claims, and gifts over some accounting period. The *credit* side lists exports, which (except for gifts) provide claims on (or receipts from) foreigners; imports, listed on the *debit* side, create obligations to make payments.

2 While total credits must equal total debits, subcategories of the balance of payments may be in imbalance. The major subcategories include the current account, unilateral transfers, the capital (short-term and long-term) account, and the gold account.

3 One way to measure balance-of-payments imbalance is to compare the current account with the long-term capital account. In the late 1940s, the U. S. current export balance was larger than its long-term capital outflow, and the difference was called a "dollar shortage." A variant measure is the "basic" balance, in which unilateral transfers are added to the current and the long-term capital accounts.

4 Especially since 1957, the U. S. has had a balance-of-payments "deficit," measured—in the "liquidity" approach—by gold (reserves) outflow plus increase in short-term dollar claims held by *all* foreigners. In the alternative "official settlements" approach, "disequilibrium" is measured by gold (reserves) outflow plus increase in short-term claims held by foreign *official institutions*.

5 The dollar is the major "reserve currency" used by countries to settle imbalances in their current and capital accounts. A continued deficit in the U. S. balance of payments may shake confidence in the convertibility of dollars into gold at a fixed rate. But if the deficit is corrected, the supply of that significant component of international "liquidity" will be sharply curtailed.

Questions

1 The credits (or receipts) side of the balance of payments is the *export* side; for example, the export of merchandise is recorded on the credits side. But we also put *capital imports* (or *inflows*) on the credit side. Aside from utter confusion on the part of the compilers of the international records, on what basis can you account for this inconsistency?

2 "The U. S. balance of payments always shows some unilateral transfers (otherwise known as donations), and beginning in 1941 they have bulked very large. But the balance of payments is compiled on a *double*-entry basis; that is, each transaction involves both a credit entry (in general, what we export) and a debit entry (what we import). And since we import nothing when we make a gift and export nothing when we receive a gift (a unilateral transfer is a *one*-way 'transaction'), the recording of unilateral transfers necessarily unbalances the international accounts, leaving total credits not equal to total debits." Really?

3 Suppose we were to have zero unilateral transfers and zero gold movements, so that the balance of payments would consist solely of the current account and the capital account. On the basis of what criterion may we distinguish between the current and capital accounts; that is, what is the basis on which a given entry is included in one account instead of the other?

4 Following are the balances of payments of four countries:

	I		II		III		IV	
	Credits	Debits	Credits	Debits	Credits	Debits	Credits	Debits
A. Merchandise	900	1,100	2,000	1,770	1,930	1,210	1,000	1,700
B. Services	100	350	230	300	195	190	100	150
C. Interest	200	275	390	190	75	40	250	125
D. Unilateral	10	0	30	375	10	440	50	50
E. Short capital	550	150	200	185	125	150	70	60
F. Long capital	90	120	170	350	150	300	690	150
G. Gold	195	50	305	155	20	175	125	50

a. What is the magnitude of the balance of trade of Country I?
b. What is the balance of trade of Country II?
c. Is the balance of trade of Country III an import or an export balance?
d. What is the balance of payments on current account of Country III?
e. What is the balance of payments on current account of Country IV?
f. Does Country I have a "favorable" or an "unfavorable" balance on current account?
g. On balance, is Country II selling or buying services?
h. Is Country IV receiving net interest payments from abroad or making payments?
i. Is Country II receiving or making net unilateral transfers?
j. Is Country II exporting or importing net long-term capital?
k. Is Country I experiencing a gold inflow or a gold outflow?
l. In its general configuration, which country best represents the U. S. in the late 1940s? Explain.
m. In its general configuration, which best represents the U. S. since 1957?
n. Of the remaining two countries, one seems more nearly in long-run "equilibrium" than the other. Which one? What is your evidence?

5 Person *A* claims: "The only straightforward way to consider the status of the balance of payments is to concentrate on the current account. There is no really 'satisfactory' way to finance an imbalance in the current account. Something is wrong, and it is a sign of financial misfortune or weakness to have to use any capital movements—long or short— or gold movements or gifts to balance the current account." Person *B* contends: "It is ridiculous to identify financial health with a balanced current account. Net capital movements (borrowing and lending) on either long or short term are as reasonable (and as inevitable) for a nation as for the individuals and businesses who largely make up the nation. There is only one thing to worry about: gold movements. To evaluate the status of the balance of payments, we need concern ourselves only with the gold account." Defend each of these persons in turn. Rebut each in turn. Which do you think has the stronger position? Do you fully accept either argument?

6 "The size of the so-called 'dollar gap' or 'shortage' in the late 1940s was, in large measure, a function of United States aid. Odd as it may seem, the 'dollar gap' would have been smaller with less aid and larger with more aid." Explain the line of thought behind that statement.

7 Since 1957, the U. S., it is said, has "suffered" a large balance-of-payments "deficit." How has this "deficit" been measured? Why has it been measured that way (what is the rationale of the measure)? Who cares about the "deficit" (who is worse off and in what sense is he worse off because of the "deficit")? What would be the nature of the cost, if any, if the "deficit" were to double in size?

8 The method most commonly used to measure the U. S. deficit—U. S. gold outflow plus inflow of foreign short-term capital—is defended by Walther Lederer, chief of the Bal-

ance of Payments Division of the Department of Commerce: "The definition of surplus or deficit is a matter of analysis, and analysis may vary with the purpose for which it is made. . . . The analysis which I believe to be [most] useful is designed to meet essentially a practical purpose: to measure the changes in our capability to defend the exchange value of the dollar. This defense is the responsibility of our monetary authorities, and their capability depends upon their liquid resources and the liquid claims which can be exercised against these resources" ("Measuring the Balance of Payments," in *Factors Affecting the United States Balance of Payments* [Joint Economic Committee, 87th Congress, 2nd session, 1962], pp. 81–82). Lederer suggests alternative purposes and types of analyses. Can you suggest others? Must the emphasis of balance-of-payments interpretation be on the provision of guides and indicators to monetary authorities? How about the approach we applied to the data of the late 1940s; does it have any relevance for today's analysis?

9   We have discussed four approaches to balance of payments interpretation, four ways of measuring deficits and surpluses: an unnamed balance, the "basic" balance, the "liquidity" balance, and the "official settlements" balance. Using the data in the eight transactions reviewed in the first part of the chapter, calculate the numerical value of deficit or surplus for each of these approaches.

10 A commonly ascribed characteristic of "equilibrium" is *sustainability*; if a given value of a variable or a given configuration of a set of variables is *non*sustainable, it is then deemed to be a state of disequilibrium. Now, suppose that officials of country Beta are relying heavily on receipt of unilateral transfers—and are confident that Beta will indefinitely continue to receive unilateral transfers. Can we reasonably conclude that this situation is consistent with a state of equilibrium?

11 "The present international monetary system is based largely on 'reserve currencies,' i.e., the dollar and the pound, which provide much of the 'international money' used to finance foreign commerce. For some years, both the U. S. and the U. K. have had persistent balance-of-payments deficits. The system seems 'damned if it does and damned if it does not' experience an end of the deficits of the reserve countries." Why?

Balance-of-Payments Adjustment

39

WHILE there is broad room for discussion on the *meaning* and empirical *measurement* of balance-of-payments disequilibrium, balance-of-payments problems do exist. How are such problems solved or eased? What are the "balance-of-payments adjustment mechanisms" provided by the market?

The focal point of an adjustment mechanism is the current account. To be sure, gold and especially capital movements also will be affected *directly* by those variables—interest rate, exchange rate, commodity prices, national income—that impinge upon the current account. But our emphasis is on the *indirect* effects of such market variables on international reserves (mainly gold and short-term international assets) through altering the current account. The basic objective, then, is to induce such a balance in the current account that there is no net movement of international reserves.[1]

Market variables may be permitted by institutional arrangements to interact in such fashion as to yield an automatic adjustment *mechanism*. Or these variables may be utilized by monetary and fiscal authorities to provide a chosen adjustment *process*. Or

---

[1] To specify the *meaning* of "balance-of-payments adjustment mechanism" in terms of the *objective* of adjustment again raises questions of defining balance-of-payments balance or equilibrium. For example, assuming that long-term assets are not considered part of international reserves, the condition of zero net movement of reserves does not require a zero net balance on current account: a surplus or a deficit could be accompanied by an equal-sized long-term capital outflow or inflow, respectively, and this, we have indicated earlier, has sometimes been used as the characteristic of balance-of-payments "equilibrium." Or suppose that the current account imbalance is matched by unilateral transfers; there would still be no movement of reserves, but this could scarcely be called a situation of market "equilibrium." Or suppose that the current account is balanced (or that the imbalance is matched by long-term capital); despite this seeming "equilibrium," there could be a drain (or gain) of reserves because of granting (or receiving) unilateral transfers.

market channels may be employed in a dual approach, with an impersonal mechanism of adjustment supplemented with discretionary policy. But some discretionary policies consist of direct interferences with trade and payments and thus circumvent the market. Such interferences affect the current account generally by reducing the *volume* of trade, by altering the commodity *composition* of trade, and by redirecting the geographic *pattern* of trade. They include import quotas, export subsidies, and foreign-exchange rationing schemes. All such devices, particularly so-called "quantitative restrictions" and "exchange controls," are discriminatory in some sense to some degree—often deliberately so.

To illustrate, a country faced with a dwindling gold supply and exhaustion of previously accumulated foreign-exchange holdings may curtail the purchase of foreign goods, services, and securities with a system of licenses. A would-be importer seeking foreign exchange must not only spend domestic money to acquire it; he must also obtain an import license from the government. By limiting the number of licenses, the government can limit the value of imports. The government may be relatively liberal in granting licenses for the purchase of foreign tractors but permit the importation of few Cadillacs—perhaps just enough to supply the government officials. And the tractor-import licenses may—for economic or political-military reasons—permit purchase of tractors from Country A but not from Country B. With discretionary decisions required from the bureaucratic Mt. Olympus on *how much* of *which* goods from *what* countries will be imported by *whom*, the possibilities of economic inefficiency—not to mention the sordid possibilities of moral corruption—are awe-inspiring. What are the *market* variables that constitute an adjustment mechanism?

Adjustment and Absorption

What an economy *produces* in a year and what it has available for *domestic use* (*absorbs*) may be different magnitudes, as noted in Chapter 26. Let Y represent income (the measure of output) and A represent absorption of goods and services by the domestic economy. Not all of the domestically produced output is available for use in the home economy, for some of it is exported to other countries; and some things available in the home economy were not produced there, for they were imported. If the money value of exports equaled the money value of imports, then (with Y being gross national product and assuming no net reduction in inventories) there would be no discrepancy between Y and A. (Does it follow that there is necessarily no gain from "balanced" trade—that is, $X = M$? Anyone who answers "yes" must write "comparative advantage" 578 times.)

The nation's standard of living rests on the goods and services actually available, rather than on output as such. Some output is drained away in exports, whereas imports contribute to absorption. With a given Y, A becomes larger as X decreases and M increases. We can write: $A = Y - X + M$, and $Y - A = X - M$: the difference between income and absorption is equal to the current account balance. And it follows that $A > Y$ if $M > X$, and the trade balance can be improved (X increased relative to M) only if Y is increased relative to A.[2]

[2] M is one component of A. What are the others? We have:
$$A = Y - X + M,$$
and
$$Y = C + I + G + X.$$
Therefore, by substituting:
$$A = (C + I + G + X) - X + M$$
$$= C + I + G + M.$$

The relation of Y and A is relevant to balance-of-payments adjustment, to the extent that adjustment involves altering X and M (the current account). In light of the U. S. loss of gold and the increase in foreign-owned liquid dollar assets, some urge that U. S. *exports* be *increased*: if foreigners spend more of their purchasing power in this country on goods and services, they will have less to spend on gold and liquid assets. Others urge that U. S. *imports* be *reduced*: curtailed purchases abroad by Americans will supply less purchasing power to foreigners, who will thus find it expedient to cut back on acquiring U. S. gold and liquid assets. The first method tends to reduce absorption by draining away additional domestic production, leaving less of a given Y for C, I, and G; the second method reduces absorption directly by reducing one of its components.

Thus with a *given* income, adjustment of a balance-of-payments deficit hurts, for it involves a cut in absorption. Adjustment is feasible with unchanged or even increased absorption *if* income rises and absorption rises by a smaller amount; but this—producing more but not absorbing all of the increase—hurts, too.

The Adjustment Alternatives

The Price–Specie-Flow Mechanism

In the eighteenth century, David Hume formulated a theory of balance-of-payments adjustment based on gold flows and price changes. The essence of Hume's theory is simple: an export balance in Country Alpha will be financed by an inflow of gold, which raises domestic prices and lowers foreign prices (and, incidentally, raises the foreign-currency price of domestic currency), thereby reducing Alpha's exports and increasing Alpha's imports; similarly, an import balance generates a gold outflow, which alters relative domestic price levels and eliminates the imbalance.

A number of elaborations are in order. For one thing, the development of fractional-reserve banking and the expanding role of central bank action complicate the monetary mechanics, sometimes intensifying the basic process envisaged by Hume and sometimes dampening it. Also, Hume's model can be well supplemented by modern income theory, and his meager reference to exchange rates should be expanded.

The Money Supply

In our investigation of the balance of payments, eight illustrative transactions were specified (pp. 777–779). Table 39-1 lists these transactions and notes whether they increase (+), decrease (−), or leave unchanged (0) the U. S. money supply and excess reserves of U. S. commercial banks. The money supply here includes demand deposits in commercial banks and currency in the hands of the public (although these transactions presumably will not directly affect currency holdings).

In five of the eight transactions, neither the money supply nor excess reserves are changed. Transaction 6 is a unilateral transfer of merchandise, and no monetary variables are involved. In transaction 2, the U. S. bank presents its bill of exchange, including interest charged as well as principal, and receives a U. K. demand deposit: the bank gives up one asset and gains another, but neither deposits in U. S. banks nor excess reserves of U. S. banks are affected. Transaction is a case of shifting ownership of deposits in U. S. banks from domestic ownership to foreign, but total deposits remain the same; therefore, excess reserves also are unchanged. Transaction 7 may be surprising, for here a gold

TABLE 39–1. International Transactions, the Money Supply, and Reserves

	Money Supply			Excess Reserves in Commercial Banks
	Domestically Held	Foreign Held	Total	
1. U. S. export of merchandise, financed by increase in U. S. deposits held abroad	+	0	+	−
2. Receipt of interest by U. S. bank in form of deposit held abroad	0	0	0	0
3. U. S. import of services, financed by increase in foreign deposits in U. S.	−	+	0	0
4. U. S. import of merchandise, financed by decrease in U. S. deposits held abroad	−	0	−	+
5. U. S. import of corporate bonds, financed by decrease in U. S. deposits held abroad	−	0	−	+
6. U. S. gift of merchandise	0	0	0	0
7. U. S. export of gold, financed by decrease in foreign deposits in Federal Reserve	0	0	0	0
8. U. S. import of government bonds, financed by increase in foreign-owned deposits	−	+	0	0

outflow has no monetary effects, in contrast to the gold movements that were discussed earlier. But whereas before we had assumed that the purchaser of gold from the U. S. Treasury paid for it with a deposit in a *commercial* bank, here payment is made from a deposit in a *Federal Reserve* bank.[3]

In transaction 1, it is implied that the U. S. exporter drew a draft on the importer and sold it to a domestic bank, and the bank, in turn, collected pounds from the U. K. importer. The balance sheet of the U. S. bank shows an increase in domestically held demand deposits (liability) and an increase in demand claims on foreigners (asset). With increased demand liabilities and no change in reserves, excess reserves are lower.

Transactions 4 and 5 are similar. An American importer (of merchandise or securities) meets his obligation by buying, with dollars, foreign currency owned by a U. S. bank. This reduction in demand deposits, with no change in actual reserves, increases excess reserves.

These sample transactions indicate considerable slippage in the linkage between international transactions and the money supply. Exports do not always increase the money supply; imports do not always reduce it. Even gold movements do not necessarily affect the money supply.

Even if there were normally an *automatic* relation between foreign trade and the money supply à la Hume, the connection could be affected by *discretionary* action by the monetary authorities. The central bank might follow "the rules of the game" by supporting and intensifying the normal effects on the money supply—for example, raising the rediscount rate when a balance-of-payments deficit appears; this was international financial protocol under the pre-1914 gold standard. But, in the interests of domestic stability, the central bank might deliberately try to counterbalance the foreign-

---

[3] In terms of sources and uses of member-bank reserve funds (see Chapter 29), a decrease in a "factor of increase" (gold) is offset by a decrease in a "factor of decrease" (other—foreign—deposits in the Fed), with the Treasury deposit in the Fed (another "factor of decrease") first rising with the proceeds of the gold sale, and then falling as gold certificates are retired.

trade effects on the money supply, particularly when a balance-of-payments deficit exists and the money supply may therefore normally tend to fall.

National Income

We have seen earlier that "exports" (X) and "imports" (M)—the current account of the balance of payments—can be incorporated into the basic income equations. Exports, representing expenditure on domestic output, are a variable in the income-creation equation:

$$Y = C + I + G + X.$$

Imports also represent spending—but on foreign, not domestic, output; imports are, therefore, a form of income disposal:

$$Y = C + S + T + M.$$

Imports, like consumption and saving, are a function of disposable income (D), and we can refer to the marginal propensity to import—defined, analogously to other marginal propensities, as $m = \Delta M/\Delta D$. The income received in one period is disposed of in the following period as consumption, saving, and imports; therefore, in our expanded model, $c + s + m = 1$.

Suppose that investment and government spending remain unchanged ($\Delta I = 0$ and $\Delta G = 0$) while the initial income equilibrium is upset by an autonomous increase in exports, perhaps because foreigners reduced their tariffs on American goods. Table 39–2 is an elaboration of tables employed in Chapter 27, to include columns for imports, exports, and the trade balance ($X - M$); the marginal propensities are indicated.

TABLE 39–2. Foreign Trade and Income with Autonomous Increase in Exports
$c = .6;\ s = .3;\ m = .1;\ r = .1$

C	S	M	G	I	X	X—M	Y	T	D
700	150	50	100	150	50	0	1,000	100	900
700	150	50	100	150	70	20	1,020	102	918
710.8	155.4	51.8	100	150	70	18.2	1,030.8	103.08	927.72
716.632	158.316	52.772	100	150	70	17.228	1,036.632	103.663	932.969
719.781	159.261	53.705	100	150	70	16.195	1,039.781	103.978	035.803
.	.	.	.	.	.	.	.	.	.
.	.	.	.	.	.	.	.	.	.
723.478	161.739	53.913	100	150	70	16.087	1,043.478	104.348	939.130

In the first period, there is an equilibrium level of income (as well as a zero trade balance), evidenced by the fact that total leakages ($S + T + M$) equal total injections ($I + G + X$). In the second period, exports rise autonomously by 20 and stay at that new level. This, in itself, constitutes an increase in income and gives rise to an increase in disposable income in that same period, the increase in disposable income inducing increases in consumption, saving, and imports in the following period ($D_1 = C_2 + S_2 +$

M_2). The sum of spending on domestic output in any period creates income in that period ($Y_1 = C_1 + I_1 + G_1 + X_1$). Income rises at a decreasing rate and ultimately levels out at a new equilibrium value, the increase in income (43.478) being a multiple of the autonomous injection (20).[4] Of course, in the new income equilibrium, total leakages again equal total injections. And in the process of reaching the new equilibrium, the export balance is reduced from 20 to a bit over 16: the rise in (disposable) income has induced additional imports and thereby reduced, but not eliminated, the foreign-trade surplus.[5]

For further illustration of the relation of national income and the trade balance, consider the problem posed in the first period of Table 39–3. Income equilibrium exists,

TABLE 39–3. Foreign Trade and Income with Autonomous Fall in Government Spending
$c = .6$; $s = .3$; $m = .1$; $r = .1$

C	S	M	G	I	X	X—M	Y	T	D
700	140	60	100	150	50	−10	1,000	100	900
700	140	60	48.889	150	50	−10	948.889	94.889	854
672.4	126.2	55.4	48.889	150	50	−5.4	921.289	92.129	829.16
657.496	118.748	52.916	48.889	150	50	−2.916	906.385	90.639	815.746
649.448	114.724	51.575	48.889	150	50	−1.574	898.337	89.834	808.503
.	.	.	.	.	.	.	.	.	.
.	.	.	.	.	.	.	.	.	.
.	.	.	.	.	.	.	.	.	.
640	110	50	48.889	150	50	0	888.889	88.889	800

but there is an import balance of 10. Suppose that the objective is to reduce the balance-of-payments deficit to zero by *cutting government spending* sufficiently to reduce imports—assuming that exports remain constant—through a fall in disposable income.

---

[4] We can derive a ΔY equation in the same manner as earlier, except that here the autonomous change in spending is ΔX instead of ΔG:

$$\Delta Y = \frac{\Delta Y}{1 - c + cr},$$

$$= \frac{20}{1 - .6 + (.6)(.1)} = 43.478.$$

[5] As in Chapter 27, multiplier theory is inadequate without reference to monetary variables which may shift the spending schedules. In transaction 1 of Table 39–1, an export raises the money supply. A continuing excess of exports over imports will continue to increase the stock of money. As money balances rise, we cannot expect income to remain at its current, supposedly equilibrium level: spending will increase as people try to bring back down the ratio of money they hold to other assets and to income. The increase in spending both raises income and increases imports. In a "true" income equilibrium, there will be no trade balance to change the money stock.

The substance of this adjustment is not changed if foreigners finance their net purchases from the U. S., not by increasing deposits of Americans in foreign banks, but by reducing their own deposits in American banks through transferring them to American exporters. The same flow of U. S. exports is maintained and the same increase in domestically held money in the U. S., with consequent repercussions on spending, income, and imports, results with either manner of financing the net exports.

Instead of asking about the effect of autonomous changes in trade on national income, we here analyze the effect of autonomous changes in income components on trade. What must be the new value of G such that a reduced D will exactly equate a diminished M with the unchanged X?

The table illustrates that the new G must be 48.889. In the equilibrium row of the table, we can immediately insert the values for I and for X, for they are assumed to be unchanged. Also, we know that $M = 50$, for that is the assumed objective, and thus $(X - M) = 0$. But if $\Delta M = -10$ and if $m = .1$, it follows that $\Delta D = -100$, and thus $D = 800$. Knowing that $\Delta D = -100$ and the values of c and of s, we can easily calculate the new equilibrium values of C and of S. Also, since $\Delta D = (1 - r)\Delta Y$ and $\Delta D/(1 - r) = \Delta Y$, it is apparent that $\Delta Y = -100/.9 = -111.111$, and $Y = 888.889$. Finally, since $Y = C + I + G + X$, and we now know all these values except G, it follows that $G = 48.889$.[6]

The Exchange Rate

Consider once again a two-country case, with each country exporting one commodity to the other. Suppose that we are given the U. S. demand for U. K. goods and the U. S. (perfectly elastic) supply of goods to the U. K., both the U. S. demand and supply prices stated in dollars; also, we know the U. K. demand for imports from the U. S. and the U. K. (perfectly elastic) supply of exports, with prices stated in pounds. Assume that initially the rate of exchange is $\$4 = £1$ and then the pound is devalued (the dollar is appreciated) to $\$3.20 = £1$. The given and the derived data are represented in Table 39–4 and plotted in Figure 39–1.

All of the supply and demand schedules of the two countries remain unchanged in terms of "domestic" currency. That is, the U. S. curves are constant in *dollar* prices, and the U. K. curves are constant in *pound* prices. But when the pound is devalued with respect to the dollar, the U. K. curves measured in *dollar* prices *fall* at every quantity by the proportion of devaluation; and when the dollar is appreciated with respect to the pound, the U. S. curves measured in *pound* prices *rise* at every quantity by the proportion of appreciation.

As a result of the change in the exchange rate, what happens to the balance of payments of, say, the U. K.? In *quantity*, clearly U. K. imports are reduced, and U. K. exports are increased. But we are interested in the change in the *value* of exports relative

---

[6] We have seen earlier that $\Delta Y = \Delta G/(1 - c + cr)$. Since $\Delta D = (1 - r)\Delta Y$ and $\Delta M = m\Delta D$, we can write:

$$\Delta D = \frac{(1-r)\Delta G}{1-c+cr}, \quad \Delta M = \frac{m(1-r)\Delta G}{1-c+cr},$$

and thus:

$$\Delta G = \frac{\Delta M(1-c+cr)}{m(1-r)},$$

$$= \frac{-10(1-.6+.06)}{.1(1-.1)} = -51.111.$$

TABLE 39–4. Supplies and Demands with Alternative Exchange Rates

U. S. Demand for Imports from U. K.

Quantity	Given Dollar Price	Derived ($4 = £1) Pound Price	Derived ($3.2 = £1) Pound Price
0	$16.339	£4.085	£5.106
1.58	14	3.5	4.375
2.94	12	3	3.750
4.29	10	2.5	3.125
5.65	8	2	2.500
7	6	1.5	1.875
8.35	4	1	1.250
9.71	2	.5	.625
11.06	0	0	.000

U. S. Supply of Exports to U. K.

Quantity	Given Dollar Price	Derived ($4 = £1) Pound Price	Derived ($3.2 = £1) Pound Price
All amounts	$3	£.75	£.9375

U. K. Demand for Imports from U. S.

Quantity	Given Pound Price	Derived ($4 = £1) Dollar Price	Derived ($3.2 = £1) Dollar Price
0	£2.5	$10	$8
4	2	8	6.4
8	1.5	6	4.8
12	1	4	3.2
16	.5	2	1.6
20	0	0	0

U. K. Supply of Exports to U. S.

Quantity	Given Pound Price	Derived ($4 = £1) Dollar Price	Derived ($3.2 = £1) Dollar Price
All amounts	£1.5	$6	$4.8

to imports; and if the focus of the analysis is the international (rather than domestic) situation of the country, we would do well to make our measurements in foreign currency (the dollar, from England's point of view).

U. K. import value in dollars definitely falls: a smaller quantity is imported (12.5 units compared to the original 14) at an unchanged price. What happens to U. K. export value is not so obvious: a greater quantity is exported (7.8125 compared to 7), but price is lower ($4.8 compared to $6). In this case, export value is reduced, for in the price range of $4.8 to $6, U. S. demand is inelastic.

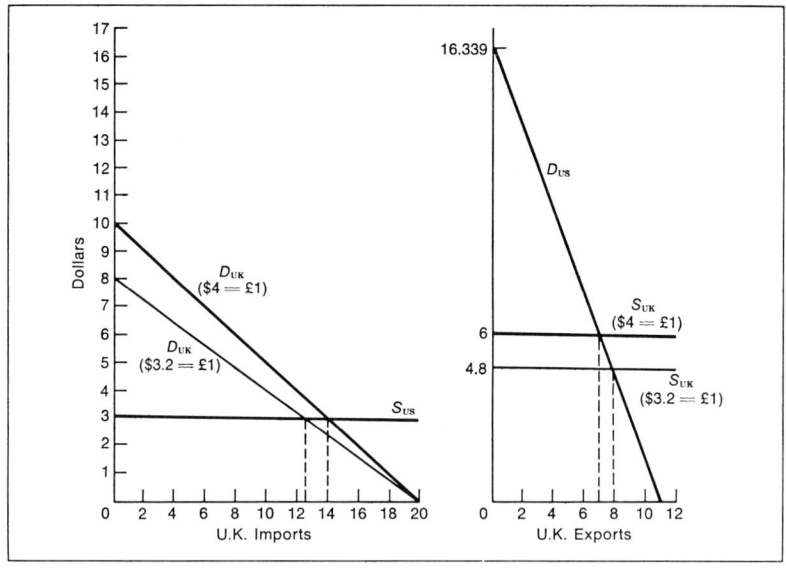

FIGURE 39-1. Foreign Trade Supplies and Demands with Devaluation: Dollar Prices

It is assumed that all supply and demand schedules remain unchanged in the respective domestic currencies. Since we here measure prices in dollars, the U. S. curves are unaffected by altering the exchange rate. But the U. K. curves (import demand and export supply), which are constant in terms of pound-prices, fall in terms of dollars by the proportion of devaluation of the pound. Since the pound is reduced from $4 to $3.2, every point on a U. K. curve falls by 20 percent. With a horizontal U. S. supply curve, the dollar-price of U. K. imports is unchanged, and the quantity of imports falls; the dollar-price of U. K. exports falls, and the quantity of exports increases.

We can summarize the effects of pound devaluation as follows:

	U. K. Imports	U. K. Exports	Trade Balance
	Price × quantity = value	Price × quantity = value	X — M = balance
Initially	$3 × 14 = $42	$6 × 7 = $42	$42 — $42 = 0
Devaluation	$3 × 12.5 = $37.5	$4.8 × 7.8125 = $37.5	$37.5 — $37.5 = 0

We began with balanced trade, and after devaluation trade is still balanced. (Although the *balance* of trade is unaffected, the *volume—quantity—*of trade has changed, with fewer imports and more exports. Is that good or bad?) An unchanged balance is not a general result. In other circumstances, devaluation could raise export value relative to import value (even if export value absolutely fell); and export value could fall more than import value, thus creating an import balance of trade. In this case of horizontal supply curves, the crucial consideration—determining whether devaluation leaves the trade balance unchanged at zero or creates an export balance or an import balance—is the *sum of the elasticities* of U. S. and U. K. *demand*.

Elasticity at a point can be measured by OP/PT, where O is the origin, P is the price, and T is the vertical-axis intercept.[7] Thus, at a price of $3, the elasticity of the initial (pre-devaluation) U. K. demand is $OP/PT = 3/7 = .4286$; and, at the same price, the elasticity of the new (post-devaluation) schedule is $3/5 = .6$. We shall take the average, $(.4286 + .6)/2 = .5143$, as *the* elasticity. Similarly, the elasticity of U. S. demand at $6 is $6/10.339 = .5803$, and at $4.8 it is $4.8/11.539 = .4160$, the average being .4982. The sum of these averages is $.5143 + .4982 = 1.0125$; for an approximation, we may say that the sum is *unity*.

We conclude that in a situation of (1) horizontal supply curves and (2) initially balanced trade, *devaluation does not change the trade balance if the sum of the demand elasticities of the two countries is unity*. But if either demand curve were flatter, still going through the point of initial intersection with the supply curve, the elasticity of the demand curve in question would be greater at any price; and the value of imports would fall more, or the value of exports would fall less (or even increase): *When the sum of demand elasticities is greater than unity, devaluation improves the trade balance*. And if either demand curve were steeper than in Figure 39–1, still going through the same initial equilibrium point, then import value would be reduced less by devaluation, or export value would fall more: *If the sum of demand elasticities is less than unity, devaluation worsens the balance of payments*. There is substantial evidence indicating that, in actuality, demand elasticities are sufficiently large that devaluation will increase export value relative to import value.

We can put the analysis in terms of pounds, the domestic money, and it is appropriate to do so if we wish to note the effects of devaluation on national income. Income (and price-level) effects are important not only in their own right, but also because of their possible repercussions on the balance of payments.

Recall our income-creation and income-disposal equations:

$$Y = C + I + G + X,$$
$$Y = C + S + T + M.$$

It appears in Figure 39–2 that the pound-value of U. K. exports rises: more physical units are sold at an unchanged pound price. (Import value may rise, fall, or remain the same, depending on the elasticity of U. K. demand in the relevant price range.) If the other expenditure components (C, I, G) do not fall, income will be increased—a desirable result, even if awkwardly attained, if a depression initially existed. But since World War II, the common setting for devaluation has been full employment and

---

[7] It will be recalled that elasticity measures the proportionate change in quantity divided by the corresponding proportionate change in price, it may be designated $e = (\Delta Q/Q)/(\Delta P/P)$. Thus elasticity of demand curve TT' at point P' is equal to $(MM'/OM) \div (RP'/MP')$. By substituting and rearranging, we have $e = (RP''/PP') \cdot (OP/RP') = (RP''/RP') \cdot (OP/PP') = (PP'/PT) \cdot (OP/PP') = (OP/PT)$.

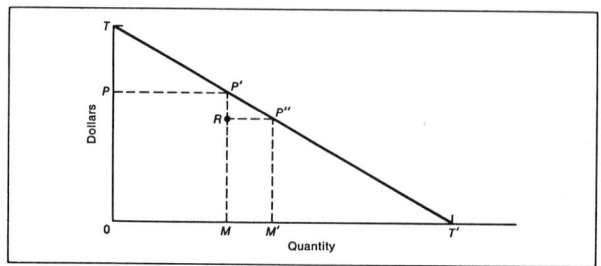

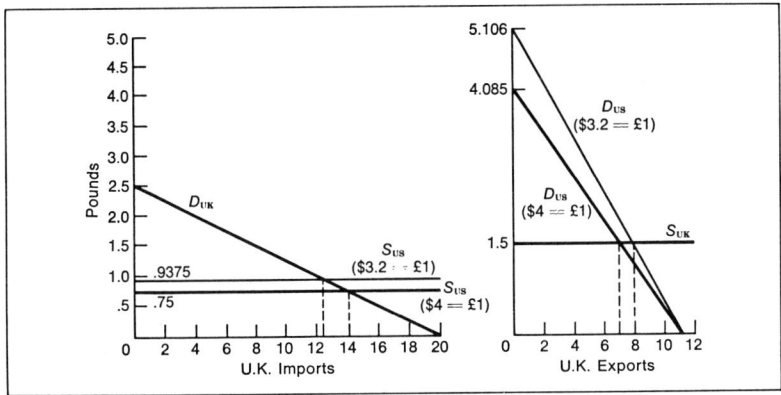

FIGURE 39–2. Foreign Trade Supplies and Demands with Devaluation: Pound Prices

As in Figure 39–1, each country's curves remain constant in terms of its own currency. Since here prices are in pounds, the U. K. curves are not shifted. But the U. S. curves move upward by the proportion of appreciation of the dollar (equivalent to depreciation of the pound), the pound-price of the dollar increasing from $1 = £.25 to $1 = £.3125. As a result of the upward shifts in the U. S. curves, the pound-price of U. K. imports rises, and the quantity falls; the pound-price of U. K. exports is unchanged, and the quantity increases.

inflation: the income-objective while devaluing has been to avoid an increase in Y. But if X rises, Y will remain unchanged only if $C + I + G$ falls by the amount of increase in X. If M also rises, we might expect some reduction in C, for at least part of the increased expenditure on imports might represent a shift of spending from domestic goods; and if C does fall, the requisite decrease in $I + G$ is that much smaller. However, if C should rise, perhaps because of a fall in M, then $I + G$ must fall enough to offset the greater C as well as the greater X. Finally, if devaluation results in an export decline[8] while income is held constant, then absorption $(C + I + G + M)$ has been reduced: $C + I + G$ fell by the amount that X rose, and M, if it increased at all, could not rise as much as did X.

Pegged versus Freely Fluctuating Rates

We have been analyzing the consequences of a change in the exchange rate. If the rate is permitted freely to fluctuate, it will be determined by market forces of supply and demand. For example, envisage an increase in English demand for American goods: U. K. imports (and U. S. exports) rise, while U. K. exports (U. S. imports) remain unchanged. The U. K. trade deficit is financed, we may suppose, by a combination of reducing U. K.-owned demand deposits in New York and of increasing U. S.-owned demand deposits in London. The increase in demand for dollars and supply of pounds, resulting in lowering the dollar inventories and increasing the pound inventories of

---

[8] Starting with balanced trade, the creation of an export balance stated in dollars must mean also the creation of an export balance stated in pounds.

foreign exchange dealers, will bid up the pound-price of the dollar and bid down the dollar-price of the pound.

By contrast, the institutional arrangement may be such, as under the International Monetary Fund, that the rate is maintained ("pegged") within narrow limits for indefinitely long periods (see p. 791, n. 1). A change beyond the limits will involve a discretionary act by monetary authorities.

Opinion is not unanimous on whether a system of freely fluctuating exchange rates or an I.M.F. system of pegged but infrequently adjustable rates is preferable—but impressive support has developed for increasing the degree of permitted rate flexibility.[9] The case for flexible rates includes the following considerations. (1) If the exchange rate is held virtually constant for prolonged periods, the balance of payments must be adjusted through other means. These alternative methods of adjustment—essentially, variations in domestic incomes and prices—require unsettling the internal economy, which is too high a price to pay to avoid movements in the exchange rate. And if neither the exchange rate nor the domestic income and price levels are to be allowed to induce balance-of-payments adjustment, reliance must be placed eventually on trade-reducing and trade-distorting direct controls over foreign commerce and payments. (2) If there is to be neither a process of continuous adjusting nor suppression of certain manifestations of disequilibrium through direct controls, very large international reserves must be available. To preclude adjustment indefinitely in an otherwise free market is to run the risk of having to finance a balance-of-payments deficit for an indefinite period. Even if it be anticipated that the fat years of surplus (that is, financially fat, but with a net drain from the economy of goods and services) ultimately will balance the lean years of deficit, the deficits can greatly strain or exhaust a country's reserves of international liquidity. (3) Even if a rate is pegged at what is initially an equilibrium level, as circumstances change, the equilibrium value of the rate is likely to diverge further and further from the actual value. As the balance-of-payments strain accumulates, policy decisions must be made. When should the rate be changed? By how much? (4) In anticipation of the alteration of the rate, speculation will be encouraged,[10] and, when the change finally is made, it probably will be sizable. By contrast, a freely fluctuating rate would provide a constant adjustment, avoiding unsettling speculation and a reserve crisis, finally forcing a largely arbitrary and uncertain act of discretion by the monetary authorities.

Powerful as the case for freely fluctuating rates appears to be, many find it less than wholly convincing. If the rate is perfectly free to move, it will move, and the movements create problems. The swings in the rate may be very wide, it is feared, because of cumulative speculation. If, for example, it is thought that the dollar-price of the pound is likely to rise, dollars are spent in demand for pounds; and if there is no institutional ceiling on the dollar-price of the pound, the sky supposedly is the limit.

---

[9] There have been suggested a number of "compromises" between a system of pegging rates within very narrow limits and a system of rates which are perfectly free to fluctuate—"compromises" which do not necessarily embody the best of both worlds and may have unique disadvantages.

[10] Suppose a rumor begins that the pound is likely to be devalued compared with the dollar. Then those with pounds will begin to sell them for dollars at, say, $4 = £1, in the hope of being able later to repurchase pounds at less than $4 per £1. If the rumor proves false, nothing will have been lost (unless the interest return in the U.S. money market is substantially lower than the rate in the U.K.); if the rumor is well founded, a gain of perhaps 30 or 40 percent will be obtained. And even if the rumor initially was not well founded, the act of speculation tends to be self-fulfilling, for a large movement out of pounds into dollars will tend to bring about (or to aggravate) a drain of foreign-exchange reserves and gold, which will make devaluation more likely.

Even modest movements in the exchange rate can be disturbing to foreign trade and investment. Unless the transaction is hedged against adverse changes in the rate, an American exporter selling a tractor for £1,000 will be chagrined to convert his proceeds into dollars at $2 = £1 when he had anticipated a rate of $2.50 = £1, and an American importer will be discouraged to find that he must pay $2.50 = £1 when the rate was $2 = £1 at the time he ordered the English linen. However, it is possible to hedge transactions in major currencies for periods of several months through the facilities of the "forward" foreign-exchange market. If the U. S. exporter contracts with the Englishman to deliver a tractor in three months at a price of £1,000, he can protect himself against a fall in the dollar-price of the pound (but also will forego any windfall gain from an appreciation of the pound) by entering into a second contract. This additional contract is with a foreign-exchange dealer, calling for the dealer *three months from now* to supply dollars against the exporter's pounds at an exchange rate agreed upon *now*. This future, or forward, rate may not be the same as the current, or "spot," rate of $2.50 = £1, but it normally will not deviate far. Similarly, the U. S. importer, who contracts to pay £1,000 in, say, six months, can contract *now* with an exchange dealer to acquire the pounds for dollars at that *future* time.

Even if forward facilities are available to hedge all trading and some investing transactions,[11] there still might be undesirable consequences from constant fluctuations in the exchange rate. For a substantial change in the rate could induce a shift in resource allocation, encouraging the expansion (or initial creation) of this industry and leading to the curtailment (or elimination) of that industry; then, once production plans were changed and perhaps were being implemented in their new form, the rate might change in the opposite direction, upsetting all schemes again.

Neither abstract analysis nor economic history indicates that freedom of the exchange rate to move would typically have such unhappy consequences. But there must inevitably be *some* method of balance-of-payments adjustment or means to make balance-of-payments disequilibrium sustainable. Either adjustment or the camouflaging of disequilibrium will be costly. The question is: Are the costs increased or reduced by heavy reliance on movements in the rate of exchange?

4, 5, 6, 7, 8, 9, 10, 11, 12, 13

Adjustment and the I.M.F.

We have several times referred to the International Monetary Fund, a post-World War II institution, which (1) provides the bulk of the noncommunist world with a system of pegged exchange rates and (2) can supply member nations with short-term (say, three- to five-year) loans to help finance temporary balance-of-payments deficits. But merely *financing* deficits is not necessarily to *eliminate* them; indeed, too ready financing of an essentially nontemporary deficit (and who can reasonably say at the outset just how temporary an incipient deficit will turn out to be?) can undesirably increase and prolong the deficit by delaying the application of necessary correctives. Presumably, the major role of the I.M.F. is to contribute to balance-of-payments adjustments. Does the Fund furnish an "automatic mechanism" of adjustment?

---

[11] While the facilities of the forward market do not provide protection from rate fluctuations for long-term investment, the risk for the investor may be no greater under a system of freely moving rates than under the I.M.F. system. For it is apparent that over periods of five or ten or twenty years, rates can be moved under the I.M.F., and presumably it is a matter of indifference to the investor whether they move continuously and gradually or by big jumps at irregular intervals.

One potential adjustment variable is the rate of exchange, which, under the Fund arrangement, is free to move only within very narrow limits. The Fund has vigorously defended its system of indefinitely pegged rates. It asserts, quite correctly, that "stability" of rates over substantial periods need not and should not mean absolute "rigidity" of rates throughout all eternity.[12] Rates are to be "realistic" as well as stabilized, and they may be altered if they "have lost touch with economic realities."[13] But the condemnation of fluctuating rates is strong, and the Fund's attitude toward the possibility of occasional rate changes is cautious and restricted.[14] *If,* for good or ill, a system of stable rates is to prevail, perhaps they should be very stable. But the Fund sometimes may wrongly conceive that arguments for infrequent and grudging changes in pegged rates are also arguments for a system of pegged rates in the first place.

Devaluation is inevitable, the Fund feels, in the "exceptional circumstances" of persistent and strong inflation.[15] But the Fund—considering devaluation a *cause,* as well as a *consequence,* of inflation—believes it must be handled very gingerly. To be effective, devaluation must be supported by restrictive domestic policies—policies which, the Fund seems to suggest, come close to being a *substitute* for devaluation.

Direct trade and exchange controls are possible means of achieving nominal payments equilibrium. But the Fund is intended to promote nondiscrimination and multilateralism. Its support of these objectives, often powerfully stated, has been tempered by a reasonable (and sometimes perhaps unreasonable) regard for the difficulties in making haste in dismantling controls adopted in the 1930s and 1940s.

The Fund apparently relies heavily on two remaining adjustment possibilities. First, simply wait—perhaps with the aid of borrowed Fund resources—and hope that the trouble will go away. Second, if the balance-of-payments deficit is too persistent, then domestic measures are in order. While inflation is strongly condemned, little suggestion has been made that a country actually deflate. All this is scarcely a neat answer—running in terms of a discernible and quasi-automatic market mechanism—to the question of which domestic variables to alter, to what degree, within what limits, in which direction, and in response to what proximate stimuli. However, the Fund has established close consultative relations with member nations, based on analyses and advice of broad scope and backed by considerable, although not massive, lending resources. This emphasis on domestic policies suggests the gold-standard mechanism, but the discipline of the gold standard has been considerably modified.

The Fund may be establishing itself as an influential force in behalf of "responsible" domestic and foreign-exchange policies and international financial cooperation. Still, aside from the limited provision of additional exchange resources, the prospect of occasional rate adjustments in accordance with uncertain criteria, and the urging by the

---

[12] International Monetary Fund, *Annual Report, 1949,* p. 21.

[13] *Annual Report, 1948,* p. 21.

[14] The Fund agrees that a change in the rate may be preferable to the alternatives of a violent contraction in domestic economic activity and of direct controls. "A fixed exchange rate is desirable as long as a country is able to adjust its economy to changes in its real international economic position. But when the adjustments needed in face of a *radical* change in a country's international economic position cannot be made through home prices and costs, it *may* be necessary to change the exchange rate. . . . It *may* be preferable for a country to change an unsuitable exchange rate . . . rather than to subject its economy to the risks of *serious* deflation and unemployment or to impose restrictions that keep imports so low as to *endanger its well-being and efficiency." Annual Report, 1949,* pp. 21–22 (emphases added).

[15] *Annual Report, 1948,* p. 26.

Fund of "proper" economic behavior, it is not apparent that the Fund provides, or can provide, a perceptible *mechanism* for either cyclical adjustments or more basic and long-term corrections.

Summary

1 A balance-of-payments *disequilibrium* or *imbalance* is a state of accounting entries that "normally" cannot persist (without direct administrative controls over commercial and financial transactions and operations). A *market mechanism* of balance-of-payments adjustment refers to some set of variables and functional relationships that will reconstitute the recorded transactions into a relative state that can, in the absence of outside shocks, persist indefinitely. A *mechanism* of adjustment suggests an element of automaticity, even if supplemented by discretionary policy, a distinguishable system of correcting pressures and repercussions that can induce a persistent tendency toward equilibrium.

2 The current account $(X - M)$ equals the difference between income and absorption $(Y - A)$. If a current account deficit is to be reduced, absorption must be reduced *relative to* income.

3 The "market variables" that can provide an adjustment mechanism include: national price levels, national incomes, and exchange rates. Domestic deflation tends to encourage exports and discourage imports, and inflation can increase a balance-of-payments deficit. The price level, in turn, can be influenced by changes in the money stock, but not all international transactions alter the money supply. There may be discretionary monetary policy, sometimes supplementing and sometimes dampening the effects of the trade balance and of prices and incomes on each other.

4 There can be a foreign trade (export) multiplier, analogous to consumption, investment, and government-spending multipliers. In a nominal income equilibrium, total injections of $I + G + X$ will equal total leakages of $S + T + M$. But if in this nominal equilibrium, X does not equal M, we may generally expect the money stock held by domestic residents (if not the total money stock) to change. And a change in money held will tend to change spending and thereby to change income and imports.

5 A market-induced change in the exchange rate or a repegging by monetary authorities of the rate at a new level can strongly affect the current account. A rise in the domestic-currency price of foreign currency (a depreciation or devaluation of the domestic currency) could worsen rather than improve the current account. But if, as we should expect, the sum of domestic and foreign demand elasticities is greater than unity, devaluation will improve the balance of payments.

6 There remains controversy on whether the exchange rate should be free to fluctuate or should be pegged within very narrow limits by monetary authorities. Freely fluctuating exchange rates would resolve balance-of-payments imbalances without heavy reliance on fluctuations in price levels and incomes, direct controls over international transactions, or massive reserves to finance large or persistent deficits. But many believe the exchange rate should not perform an equilibrating function; they fear that large fluctuations in the rate might inhibit international trade and finance as well as unsettle some portions of the domestic economy.

7 The International Monetary Fund is characterized by pegged exchange rates. But it provides no genuine adjustment mechanism in lieu of fluctuating exchange rates.

Questions

1 "Correction of a balance-of-payments deficit is perfectly simple—if only we deal with it directly and straightforwardly. A deficit means that we are spending more than we are receiving, buying more than we are selling. Well, then, if we are serious about eliminating the deficit, why pussy-foot around trying to *induce* people to buy less by juggling interest rates, tax rates, exchange rates, and the like? Why not just *forbid* buying too much? Go right to the heart of the problem: a little exchange control will effectively ration our foreign spending to keep payments down to receipts. Such imposed restrictions (determined and administered by public servants in the national interest) are quick and certain, and we practical people like that." Are you, too, a practical person?

2 Should we include *tariffs* with import quotas and other restrictions as a type of discretionary balance-of-payments policy which "circumvents the market"?

3 The "absorption" approach to analysis of balance-of-payments adjustment tells us that elimination of an import balance requires that the economy pull in its belt and absorb fewer goods and services. Correct?

4 In an essay of 1752, David Hume wrote: "Suppose four-fifths of all the money in Great Britain to be annihilated in one night, . . . what would be the consequence? Must not the price of all labour and commodities sink in proportion . . . ? What nation could then dispute with us in any foreign market . . . ? In how little time, therefore, must this bring back the money which we had lost, and raise us to the level of all the neighbouring nations? Where, after we have arrived, we immediately lose the advantage of the cheapness of labour and commodities; and the farther flowing in of money is stopped by our fulness and repletion.

"Again, suppose that all the money of Great Britain were multiplied fivefold in a night, must not the contrary effect follow? Must not all labour and commodities rise to such an exorbitant height, that no neighbouring nations could afford to buy from us; while their commodities, on the other hand, became comparatively so cheap, that, in spite of all the laws which could be formed, they would be run in upon us, and our money flow out; till we fall to a level with foreigners, and lose that great superiority of riches, which had laid us under such disadvantages?"

Does this theory of balance-of-payments adjustment have any applicability to today's world? Is it at all deficient? If it can be salvaged but still requires modification or elaboration, what changes would you make in it?

5 With the introduction of foreign trade (or, more specifically, the current account) into the income model, we concluded that in equilibrium total injections—I, G, and X—equal total leakages—S, T, and M. But how or why do we include exports among the injections, and imports among the leakages? Is there no difference between X, on the one hand, and I and G, on the other; and between M and S and T? In particular, we earlier spoke of S and T as forms of nonconsumption, but M certainly may (and does) consist largely of consumption goods.

6 The income-creation and income-disposal equations have expanded to:

$$Y = C + I + G + X.$$
$$Y = C + S + T + M.$$

Now, suppose that (a) $M > X$—we have an import balance; (b) Y is stipulated to remain constant, perhaps because we already have "full employment" and we wish to avoid inflation; and (c) the "adjustment" policy is to reduce M to the level of X by direct controls. When M is thus reduced, what are the repercussions on $C, S, T, I,$ and G? Does the imposition of direct controls over imports obviate the use of fiscal and monetary policies?

7 *Why,* or *how,* is it that, in Table 39–2, the change in income did not completely eliminate the trade imbalance?

8 In the text, we discussed eliminating an import balance by an autonomous decrease in government spending, which reduced disposable income and thereby induced a fall in imports. Now, starting again with the first period and the marginal propensities in Table 39–3, reduce the current-account deficit to zero by autonomously changing the tax-collection schedule (but not changing the *marginal* tax rate), holding G (along with I and X) constant at the initial level.

9 Defend or demolish the following statement: "As long as foreign transactions are out of equilibrium, home income cannot be in equilibrium either. Theories of incomplete external adjustment that assumed fixed 'propensities' to import, to consume domestic goods, and to save miss the point that such propensities simply cannot remain fixed indefinitely in the face of persistent change in the money supply."—Leland B. Yeager, *International Monetary Relations* (New York: Harper & Row, Publishers, 1966), pp. 76–77.

10 Explain whether you agree or disagree with the following summary statement: "With normally shaped export and import supply-and-demand schedules, devaluation of its currency by a country will increase the volume (i.e., quantity) of its exports and decrease the volume of its imports, and thus it must improve the balance of payments."

11 Demonstrate with the aid of diagrams the following proposition: It is sufficient, for devaluation to improve the balance of payments, that *either* one (and not necessarily both) of the export supply curves be vertical—assuming that the import demand curves are not vertical.

12 We have noted that, starting with balanced trade and devaluing the pound from, say, $\$3 = £1$ to $\$2 = £1$, the creation of an export balance measured in dollars ($B_\$$) will create an export balance expressed also in pounds ($B_£$). For example:

Exchange Rate	$X_\$ - M_\$ = B_\$$	$X_£ - M_£ = B_£$
$\$3 = £1$	90 − 90 = 0	30 − 30 = 0
$\$2 = £1$	80 − 50 = 30	40 − 25 = 15

What generalizations can you make from the following cases of pound devaluation with an initial dollar deficit?

	Exchange Rate	$X_\$ - M_\$ = B_\$$	$X_£ - M_£ = B_£$
(1)	$\$3 = £1$	60 − 90 = −30	20 − 30 = −10
	$\$2 = £1$	60 − 60 = 0	20 − 30 = 0
(2)	$\$3 = £1$	60 − 90 = −30	20 − 30 = −10
	$\$2 = £1$	74 − 64 = 10	37 − 32 = 5
(3)	$\$3 = £1$	60 − 90 = −30	20 − 30 = −10
	$\$2 = £1$	42 − 58 = −16	21 − 29 = − 8
(4)	$\$3 = £1$	60 − 90 = −30	20 − 30 = −10
	$\$2 = £1$	56 − 76 = −20	28 − 38 = −10
(5)	$\$3 = £1$	60 − 90 = −30	20 − 30 = −10
	$\$2 = £1$	42 − 68 = −26	21 − 34 = −13
(6)	$\$3 = £1$	60 − 90 = −30	20 − 30 = −10
	$\$2 = £1$	50 − 80 = −30	21 − 34 = −13

13 A good deal of the debate on pegged versus freely fluctuating exchange rates has turned on the issue of "speculation." The proponents of each of the alternative systems of rates have urged that their system would minimize the problem of speculation. What is the problem of speculation? Indeed, what is exchange-rate speculation itself?

14 What is the "balance-of-payments adjustment mechanism" under the International Monetary Fund?

15 In Chapter 33, we offered the conclusion that "foreign economic policy should be determined in its own right rather than employed as a tool of domestic income stabilization." What do you think of the converse proposition, viz., domestic income policy should be determined in its own right rather than employed as a tool of balance-of-payments equilibration?

Answers

Chapter 1

1 You are not expected to be able to answer this now. But upon finishing this course, you should be able to show why the concluding sentences are wrong. As for the first sentence, economic science has not trapped us—scarcity has.

5 This question will be answered much later in the book and is designed to provoke a little independent thought on a term commonly used in economics.

9 A theory is logically valid if all its elements are *logically* consistent with each other or with some broader theory with which it is associated. It is empirically valid if its implications about observable phenomena agree with the observed phenomena. Neither implies the other.

Chapter 2

1 False. It is because people are reasonable and, therefore, act in accord with their interest that there are economic problems and wars.

2 **a.** Yes.
   b. We know of no institution with dominant power of coercive violence that is not the government in any country. Government is an institution for enforcing certain admissible rules and procedures for resolving interpersonal conflicts of interest. The making and enforcement of laws and the judicial settlement of disputes are events that support the propositions. (Note that the statements say that government is *an* agency, not the only agency. For example, many social disputes are resolved by social ostracism, and by agreement to use an arbitrator.) Do not assume that government should not have that coercive monopoly.

3 G. Washington; F. Franco; T. Mao.

5 **a.** Until you know what "socially preferred" means, you cannot answer this question.
   b. We do not know what socially preferred means. For example, does it mean that a majority prefer it, or that the most important people prefer it, or that everyone prefers it, or that the speaker thinks everyone should prefer it, or that he prefers it? Beware of any expression referring to the preference of a group.

6 **a.** You should first want to know the behavioral consequences of each kind. More than that, we can't say now.
   b. The only kind of competition made illegal by a price ceiling is that of offering more money (and all that can be bought with it) than the legal limit as means of offsetting weaknesses in other attributes in competing for goods. Fair-employment laws (prohibiting choice of employees by color, creed, or age) prohibit competition in terms of specifically offering an employer the personal attributes he may prefer. Pure food and drug laws prohibit offers of inferior food at lower prices or of new and possibly better but untested (according to government tests) foods and drugs. Private-property rights prohibit competition by violence and involuntary dispossession of goods deemed to be private property. Socialism prohibits competition in terms of offers of types of services and goods that individuals privately prefer, without having to obtain authorization of government officials for propriety of producing the services. These are merely examples of types of competition that are ruled out—not a complete chronicle, and certainly not an evaluation of the desirability of the various types.

8 **a.** Promises to raise or lower taxes (affect other people's wealth) in order to benefit those who vote for you. But the politician can't offer to sell services as a businessman can.
   b. Will letters of recommendation help you get a better grade in this course? Does your past record influence the teacher of this course in making grades? Does wealth of parents?
   c. Employees can offer to work for lower salary to get a job with favored employer in preferred town. Will this work in fraternities? How about candidate's ability to increase wealth of fraternity?

15 **a.** They are different—because these all involve social, interpersonal interactions. As such, one person's behavior with respect to these characteristics or attributes will affect other people, and

their response to his behavior will vary accordingly. Their response and their ability to influence his actions will depend upon whether or not there is private property—for reasons we shall see as we progress through the book.

b. Nothing like this question to kill a discussion! (Remember, evidence does not consist of one's idiosyncratic memories or *ad hoc* examples.)

16 All societies use force and compulsion. The pertinent issue is what kinds of coercion and force do various economic, political, and social systems use. The capitalist system uses the force of self-interest; it is coldly impersonal in its market effects; it is a severe and unforgiving taskmaster. He who produces at a loss is forced out of business, perhaps with less compassion than under a socialist dictator, who could spread the loss over other people. More relevant than the question of which system uses less force is the question of the various kinds of forces (incentives, rewards, signals, orders, and penalties)—in terms of the resultant effects on the economic, cultural, and political behavior. For example, how are freedom of speech, job mobility, social fluidity, individual dignity, religious worship, search for the truth, etc., affected? The effects on all the various goals of a person must be considered.

Not even reference to the use of the rule of law versus the rule of arbitrary dictators is a basis for ultimate judgment. Here too the question is what law and what rules will be enforced by the ruling law: the rule of private-property rights, the rule of socialism, or some other?

Differences are implied about the kinds of opportunities or "freedoms" provided to individuals living under each system. The implications are that an open-market system gives individuals a greater range of consumption patterns or goods from which to choose. Whether it is "good" that individuals should have such a range of options to explore is a question that economic theory cannot answer. A greater range of choice can be regarded as a greater range of temptation, risk, error, regret, and deviant behavior. Just as a parent restrains his children's choices for their own good, we may prefer to restrain the choices of adults because everyone retains some childlike impulses.

Whether you wish to regard one system or the other as giving more freedom depends upon your meaning of "freedom." In one sense, freedom can include protection from the costs of resisting temptation and from making unfortunate choices; and, in another sense, freedom might include the right to bear those costs and to make those choices and explore tempting alternatives. Whatever your interpretation, the implications derived from economic theory about the factual consequences of different allocative systems will be helpful in forming a judgment.

Chapter 3

2 Individuals, not abstract things called "colleges," make decisions.

7 Free speech means a right to speak or communicate with others who are willing to listen, free of government intervention or prohibition. It is not a right to take resources of other people for purposes of communication with other people. To use college property without the permission of the college authorities for speech is not a right of free speech; it is simply appropriation of property as if the property were free for the taking. Nor is it a denial of free speech if a college or anyone else denies the use of resources under its or his control which others would like to use for the purposes of communication; it is instead a denial to others of resources to use in ways they would like. This does not mean that colleges ought to refuse to allow use of its resources for communication of popular or unpopular ideas; it is simply a clarification of the difference between free speech and the proposition that resources are "free" to anyone for the taking so long as they will be used for communication.

9 It is.

12 **c.** Postulates 3 and 2 together.
  d. Yes.
  e. Postulate 3.
  f. Postulate 4.

16 **a.** Economics does not use the concept of satisfaction. It refers only to choices among available options. Remember "utility" is merely a name for an index for ordering choices.
  b. Ditto.

17 By drawing another curve above this one (or to the right of it) with similar properties (slope and curvature).

18 The first statement contains no implication about any thought process. It would also apply to rocks and water obeying the law of gravity. The second statement suggests some mental calculation and choice among alternative possible actions. Neither statement has the slightest dependence on the concept of free will or independence of behavior; both are red herrings to the present problem. Economics does *not* have to assume the second statement as a basis for its theory, despite common arguments that it does.

19 The first statement means that more of one goal is achieved at the cost of having less of another. The second statement means that goals do not exclude each other.

21 **a.** Yes.
    b. We don't know that any of them do.

29 *No* to all questions.

Chapter 4

1   **a.** Between .25 and .33 meat for one unit of vegetable. Or, saying the same thing in reverse, between 3 and 4 vegetables for one unit of meat.
    c. Linus values vegetables higher in terms of meat than does Charlie. But Charlie values meat in terms of vegetables more than does Linus. So we could say that Linus, instead of valuing vegetables higher, values meat less than does Charlie. Implication is that values of any one good are expressed and measured in terms of some other good. Hence, both are involved in valuation, and we cannot tell which *one* is being valued; each is being valued in terms of the other.
    e. Consumption-substitution ratios must differ between two people, at their present situations, if exchange is to be mutually acceptable.

3   No. They do not imply what is good, bad, better, or worse. They imply what will be observed in the real world.

5   **a.** If it is supposed to mean that one area had more of some good than it wanted (could possibly use at all), the statement is dead wrong. And we can't think of anything else it might mean.
    b. We propose that the relative supplies were different so that relative values were different—leading to mutually preferred exchange and re-allocation of goods among Mediterranean and Baltic people, à la Charlie and Linus.

7   No, it does not. It is the theory and its structure that conform to laws of logic and rationality. The predictable regularities of response of people to changes in their environment do not require they be "rational" any more than the response of water to a slope requires rationality by each molecule of water.

8   **a.** Yes. It is true for all goods.
    b. We have yet to find one.

11 Middlemen facilitate exchange and specialization, while "do-it-yourself" is a reduction of specialization and exchange.

12 It assumes that the middleman performs no service to consumers or producers in facilitating exchange and that therefore he can be eliminated without someone else's having to perform the service in which he specialized. Eliminating the middleman is a form of do-it-yourself and as such is not necessarily more economical.

13 All are denials of open markets.

Chapter 5

1   Recognizability, portability, storability, divisibility—all of which go to make the price of the good relative to any other goods susceptible to variation among people. Possibility of producibility would induce production until value of one unit of the money would equal cost of production—unless quantity is limited by law or controlled by government.

2   Borrow one pair of shoes; sell the pair for four shirts; sell the four shirts for eight pairs of socks; then sell the six pairs of socks for one pair of shoes—leaving you with two pairs of socks. Repeat the operation, each time picking up a net gain of two pairs of socks.

3 Exchange rates among goods are prices, whether or not money be one of the goods exchanged. Prices are not bids.

4 Rate of 18,250 gallons a year.

6 70 gallons, because he will consume 140 gallons in the week rather than 70 gallons.

7 It is a fall in the price of candy in ice-cream units. Candy is cheaper relative to ice cream than formerly.

9 **a.** No.
b. The negative functional relationship between price and amount demanded. The explicit numbers serve merely to illustrate explicitly the meaning of the negative relationship.

13 **a.** Incorrect. Ratio (ignoring the algebraic sign) is greater than one.
b. Correct.
c. It is conventional to call this an increase in amount demanded, not an increase in demand—which refers to a shift in the whole demand relationship.

15 He who purchases seven per week, for that is the same as a rate of 365 per year, and he does it at a higher price.

20 Demands a and b have the same elasticity at any considered price. But the elasticities of a and b decrease at lower prices. Demand c has a lower elasticity at any price than demands a or b, and its elasticity decreases at lower prices. (Hint of reason: The slope of b is greater than for a, but the quantity at any price is proportionally greater also. Demand c has the same slope as b but its quantities are larger at any price. Hence for any small price cut, the change in the amount demanded on line c and b is the same, but for c, the increase in amount demanded is smaller *relative* to the amount demanded at that price.)

21 **a.** Economic theory says they would. Compare cars in countries with higher gasoline prices. How about extent to which automatic transmissions would be used?
b. Increases gas use.
c. Effects would be more extensive in three years than in three months.

22 All except last one. (Why?)

23 Nonsense expressions. Presumably, these terms mean only that someone wants more of something than he now has.

24 **a.** No such thing as basic need. We could use more and we could also get by with less security. It's a matter of what price we are willing to pay.
b. We "need" more of everything that is not free. The amount of any economic good we choose to have is a function of its price. To say our children need more schools ignores what we propose to give up to get more schools.
c. It depends upon the price, whether it is good enough to have at the price. If this says simply that more is better than less, O.K. Otherwise, it seems to deny relevance of alternatives.

28 If this happened with *equal* prices for slums and for high-quality spacious apartments, we would be stumped. In fact, however, we find that the prices of the high-quality dwellings are higher, which reduces the amount of the high-quality apartments demanded. Given the law of demand, we see that with a higher price of higher quality apartments, it is possible to reduce the amount people want or demand so that it does not exceed the amount available. Just why the price of slums should be so low as to induce more slums to be wanted than are available is something we shall take up later. For the moment we are interested in showing the implications of the law of demand.

29 What does invaluable mean? We are reminded of a caption in *Life* magazine describing a pearl necklace: "This priceless four-strand necklace is now in the possession of Mrs. Lovely, who bought it for $85,000." Rarely do we find such an incongruous juxtaposition of obvious inconsistencies. However, in fairness to those who often use the term "priceless," we suspect they usually mean that the priceless good is not reproducible. Thus, a Grecian urn or an original Dufy cannot be replaced at any price if destroyed. At the same time, one should be careful not to think it can't be bought at a finite price, or that a nonreproducible item is necessarily valuable.

Chapter 6

1. **a.** 0, 1, 2, 4, 6, 8, 9, 11, 13, 15 for prices from 10 through 1.
   b. 4 to *A* and 2 to *B*.
   c. Shortage.
   d. Surplus.
   e. All depends upon where price is.

3. **b.** No. He values a sixth one at $5.

7. True.

9. First is rate; second and third are stocks.

Chapter 7

2. You should disagree. A higher price permits a re-allocation of existing goods—a re-allocation that would not occur in the absence of higher prices. Immorality is a gratuitous judgment. That the profits to those who own the goods when prices rise are "unwarranted" is also a gratuitous judgment. The point is to note that higher prices do have a consequence—re-allocation—and that personal preferences should not blind one to that fact.

5. Holding down the wholesale price of cattle to the meat processors increases the spread between purchase price and selling price for the processors. The price to consumers would rise anyway because of the increased demand for meat. The wealth that would have been available to cattle growers is instead given to the cattle processors.

6. Yes, for it does advance the argument (analysis?) to grasp the meaning of scarcity and to understand that economics says nothing about which goods ought to be allocated via the exchange-market form of competition. We leave it to you to try to figure out why the "degree of scarcity" should affect the form of competition that should determine how a scarce resource is allocated among alternative uses and users. We can't.

7. The belief that money or market-exchange value is the sole criterion of allocation is so widespread, deeply ingrained, and incorrect that it is worth spending some time in examining it. Money is not the only criterion; that much has already been established with our analysis. (That it ought to be or ought not to be is not the issue.) When I dine in a restaurant, I select my dinner according not only to prices but also according to what the item is. I never tell the waitress to bring me the cheapest items only. The taste, nutrition, and looks of the item are considered. Similarly, when buying a suit, I take into account the style, feel, looks, and fit, as well as the price. For national security, we don't buy the cheapest weapon regardless of what it will do, nor the most modern, expensive weapon simply because it is the most expensive or modern—but not as effective as three units of a cheaper weapon (for example, one B-70 as compared to three missiles).

   Only if the options are equivalent in *all* other respects do money costs become the *sole* criterion, simply because cost is the only one that, in this case, makes any difference. On the other hand, if money costs were equal, then only the other attributes would be relevant.

   Suppose that I own some land next door to where I live. Of two people who apply to buy the land, one—an ordinary man who offers $1,000; the other, a beautiful woman who offers at most only $995—I will sell to the woman. Her presence as a neighbor is worth more than $5 to me. The man could overcome his handicap if he offered $100 more. Money (exchange value) does count, but it is not the sole nor even the dominant (whatever that means) criterion.

   A related criticism of the capitalist system says it relies on *market*—revealed money demands rather than intrinsic or humanitarian needs. By now there is no "need" to discuss the nonsense of "needs." But why do *market* demands count so much? The reason market demands are so effective is simply that exchange is a way to increase utility. Every person is free to reject the market demand and to exchange his wealth with "more deserving" people who offer less attractive market bids. But the market demand for exchange is heeded because people prefer to gain by exchange—not because they are perverted by capitalism or a desire for money.

If private-property rights did not exist, people would not be able to make such extensive market offers, because they would have nothing legally to buy or sell. In a university, the faculty does not have private-property rights in offices and classrooms; therefore, there is no marketplace where classrooms and offices are so easily exchanged. In a socialist system, market money demands are less effective simply because there is relatively less exchangeable property.

8 According to this criticism, a person is so influenced by his interest in his economic wealth that other criteria are dominated. However, the exchanging of goods does not make it difficult for anyone to be influenced by the artistic, social, humanitarian, or cultural uses to which he can put his goods and services.

Playwrights complain that the financial "backer" invokes his crass monetary standards. Artists complain that businessmen want mere display copy, not true art. The architect complains because builders do not want the artistic designs he proposes. What they really are objecting to are other people's tastes and preferences. But the issue is rarely put in so embarrassing a way.

Saying that only lowbrow products sell well seems to suggest that this is a result of the money-value system. But that system effectively reveals and enforces the "lowbrow" tastes and desires of the public. The actors and writers wish the public valued such quality more than it does. Hence, actors and artists are frustrated because other people don't want as much "quality" as the artists would like to provide at the prices they would like to get. Or putting it "selfishly," the artists must admit that the income they can get from "low-quality" work is so high that they prefer to produce low-quality plays and get a big income rather than produce high-quality plays and live with a lower income. In this case, it is also the artists' and actors' own tastes for more wealth, not merely that of the public's, that precludes quality.

9 Both. Choice is an act of discrimination.

10 All.

11 True.

12 Price controls do not increase probability that lower-income groups will get more housing. They may get less (and over time with effect on production of housing, housing quality and quantity will deteriorate). Outcome depends more upon possession of nonpecuniary attributes that now play a greater weight in allocative decision.

15 Open-market prices would encourage (force) consumers to use other goods. Restaurant customers will take other foods, of course; but then this means households use more rice than if they too had to pay higher price. Greater revision in food habits occurs for those who eat in restaurants rather than at home. Continues apparition of "shortage."

Chapter 8

1 **a.** At $2 per bushel, I could not affect price by withholding my stocks of wheat. Best price I could get is the market price of $2, whether I sell 1 or 1,000 bushels.
   b. No.
   c. Horizontal straight line.

2 **a.** Yes; 4,000 bushels; 2,000 bushels; none.
   b. No.
   c. Yes.

3 Yes. Because higher rate of sales is available without a lower price, hence increase in revenue for each higher rate is equal to the price of the unit of the higher rate.

5 Constant.

6 Yes, although in strict terms we assume that there is no rise in price as a result of withholding one's offers. This analytical classification yields implications that are for all practical purposes equivalent to those of a less extreme, discrete classification. For example, in this instance, it would not pay anyone to reduce sales for a higher price. The trivial effects are, for all intents and purposes, equivalent to no effects at all. Hence, in all the discussion it must be understood that we are using an extreme assumption simply because it makes the analysis so much easier without changing any of the pertinent implications. Marginal revenue is about 61⅜ per share; total revenue difference is ($61,500 − $30,812.50 =) $30,687.50 for 500 shares change in sales. This is $61.37 per share.

8 a.

Price	Quantity	Revenue Total	Revenue Marginal	Revenue Average
20	2	40		20
			17	
19	3	57		19
			15	
18	4	72		18
			13	
17	5	85		17
			11	
16	6	96		16
			9	
15	7	105		15
			7	
14	8	112		14
			5	
13	9	117		13
			3	
12	10	120		12
			1	
11	11	121		11
			−1	
10	12	120		10
			−3	
9	13	117		9

  b. It goes to purchasers as a lower price. For example, between a price of $18 and $19 with sales of four and three units, respectively, the marginal revenue, $15, is less than the average revenue, $18, by $3. This amount is distributed to buyers of the three units by a price that is $1 lower than formerly.
  c. Seven units.
  d. $15.
  e. Yes. See (f).
  f. Having smaller profits than if price were set at $16.

9 a. He is searching for the wealth-maximizing price.
  b. He is likely to find himself losing money as others enter business and reduce the price-cost spread.

11 a. Either $5 or $6.
  b. $7.
  c. None. It is the wealth-maximizing price.

13 a. Yes.
  b. Two more, for a total of eight trees.
  c. No. Remember, an eighth tree is worth at most $3. What you paid for "earlier" trees is irrelevant except insofar as it affects your remaining income and thus your demand for everything else. But this effect is spread over all your purchases, and we assume here it is a trivial amount compared to your total income.
  d. Eight.
  e. Yes.
  f. Marginal price is same under each circumstance, and we adjust to price of extra units.

18 A higher price of tickets would have reduced the amount demanded; *but* if the demand were inelastic the proceeds would have been greater, even with seats unsold for every performance. In any event, the sell-out indicates the price was too low and should be raised; the producer has less revenue than he could have had.

Chapter 9

1 Law of demand relates purchase-rate to price. Law of demand and supply states price is at intersection of supply and demand. The former holds generally. The latter does not.

3 a. Yes.
  b. Yes, and it pays not to cut rent to get an immediate occupant (because the cost of his moving soon is greater than wage cut would be worth).
  c. No.

6 Yes, this could be so. While it is not possible to know what is necessarily better, it is true that the total cost of providing parking space could be cheaper if it were not policed as carefully as a park-for-pay lot. A free lot would impose the costs on those who purchase from the persons who provide the free parking lot, but not on those who use the lot without doing any business with the providers of the parking space.

7 Seats are allocated first come, first served, rather than sold to worshipers—except in some churches, where a person donates a large sum and is given a special pew as a token of appreciation.

9 False.

10 **a.** Camp sites are not privately owned.
b. Less space per person.

12 Tendency to price public parks and services at less than a market-clearing price is explanation. Motels, priced higher than facilities in parks, rely on the law of demand to keep amount demanded in line with facilities available.

13 The market-exchange system characteristic of private property (capitalism) has been the dominant institutional context of the preceding chapters. The economic theory used in the analysis is applicable to any system of competition (capitalist, communist, or what have you) for resolving conflicts of interest among people arising from the fact of scarcity. In fact, the analysis of allocation with prices at less than the free-market price is an application of economics to a socialist society in which free-market prices are not used. Think of the actual money price as being zero, or at some level below the free-market price. Then how will goods be allocated among the competing claimants? (Review Chapter 8.) The relatively greater nonpecuniary "discrimination" should come as no surprise.

Many communist systems rely on money prices and private property to ration existing stocks of some consumer goods. In Russia, many goods are sold for money, and individuals get money income from wages and salaries—*but not* from ownership of productive physical capital goods and instruments and land. Given a person's money income, he is allowed to choose among a variety of consumption patterns by voluntary exchanges with other people via controlled (as distinct from open) market prices.

The postulates are not idiosyncratic to capitalist systems. They hold for all known societies. The laws of demand and production hold also, whether or not exchange of resources *via* a private-property exchange system is used. We illustrated the use of these laws under noncapitalist situations where private property and open markets were not the ruling institutions for the particular goods and services investigated.

What we are striving to emphasize is the distinction between economic theory and analysis on the one hand and, on the other hand, the institutional (legal and political) circumstances or conditions to which they are applied.

14 (c) is correct.

17 False; it is the consumption of the good that is referred to in the definition of a public good.

20 True.

22 As many as people want to use or create. No other objective test of the right number.

23 Depends upon extent to which you want to give parents authority to determine allocation of funds to family members.

25 Building and nonfaculty purposes gain and faculty also gains to extent faculty salaries are raised more than they otherwise would have been raised. Money that would be spent for faculty salary increases can be spent for other purposes.

26 **a.** $500 release of money for other purposes, plus a better education, which you deem worth $400 more than the one you otherwise would have purchased.
b. Parents gain a cash release of $500 (and you get an education worth $400 more to you).

32 **a.** Price of stock fell.
c. National and Eastern gained wealth value of the airline route. Taxpayers lost the value of those rights, which otherwise could have been kept by government when it sold those rights—as it sells timber and gas-prospecting rights on federal lands.

Chapter 10

1 **a.** May through September.
b. May price is lower than March price, suggesting new crop is appearing. Lower prices for July

suggest new crop is still being harvested and stocks are increasing, permitting higher consumption rates at lower prices.

c. One or two cents a bushel—estimated by differences between prices during interval when no wheat is being added to stocks.

2 Primarily for profit.

3 Perishable. Increase in new supplies will be greater relative to carryovers, enabling greater increase in rate of consumption and lower prices. High storage costs (high perishability) implies lower future supplies (and larger present consumption).

5 Spot.

7 It usually protects against large losses, without giving up rights to large gains.

9 If we assume the price of the futures contract falls by the same amount as the spot price, he will be able to buy back his futures contract at 35 cents per 100 pounds less than the price at which he sold it. The profit on his futures contract (ignoring contracting costs of about $30) is $175 (35 cents per 100 pounds for 50,000). This will offset his loss on the processed soybeans—if the two prices move together by exactly the same amount.

13 In the sense of having a greater range of potential future positions with greater probability of having a different wealth than now, I have the greater risk.

15 a. I bet on Mets and you bet on Dodgers.
b. We have shared some risk and reduced range of our resultant wealths; in that sense we have reduced risk. I buy some (half) rights to your parking lot and you buy (half) rights to mine for the World Series days. Neither of us expects actually to help the other operate the parking lot. Instead, we just buy out the contracts later. He who lives in the winning team's town simply pays half his parking revenue (zero, since there are no games in his town). Each gets half the receipts regardless of which team wins the playoff game.

16 No. Speculation also exists where future is uncertain. Futures markets permit re-allocation of speculative burden.

17 You should disagree. Open futures markets reveal information for all at a lower cost. Those with superior knowledge could benefit from abolition of futures markets because they could then more readily keep their information secret.

19 Ask those who consider it immoral. Some people say "Selling what you haven't already got is immoral." A contractor who bids on a building at a fixed price sells what he doesn't yet have. He has sold a promise or commitment. Short sellers do the same thing.

20 a. We couldn't think of any method. Can you?

21 To $50.

24 a. No. It means there is less exchange and re-allocation of risks.
b. Processors, growers, middlemen, and some consumers.

Chapter 11

1 ($370 − $350)/$350 = .057.

2 $250(1 + .07)^3 = 306.25. Would double in about 10 years (72/7 = 10.3).

3 Refer to Table 13–1, present value of $1. At 10 percent the present value of $1 deferred one year is now $.9091. Therefore, the present value of $220 deferred one year is $220 × .9091 = $200.

7 5.075 × $50 = $253.75.

8 Annuity of five years with present value of $1,000 at 6 percent rate of interest is $1,000/4.21 = $237.53.

10 a. They fall relative to costs.
b. Reduce profitability.

12 Yes. With higher rate of interest you still buy other resources equivalent to your house, but with fire you can buy only half a house or equivalent type of resource. In both cases you do suffer a loss relative to some other resources, but loss is more general in case of fire.

16 $5,000.

17 $1,000 and it will stay at that value.

Chapter 12

1 a. Usually production is used to refer only to activity that is not illegal. We wish we knew of a better answer. The question helps to reveal the hidden normative content of concepts which at first seem to be objective and free of ethical presuppositions.

2 a. 7 and .6; 6 and .8; 5 and 1; etc.
  b. .2 bushels soybeans for 1 bushel of oats.
  c. 5 bushels of oats per soybeans.
  d. Yes.
  h. Does it refer to weight, volume, value, calories? Without some rule for converting to equivalent common units, there is no way to assign meaning to question. As it is now, one has more soybeans, the other more oats.

3 d. 1.67 of each for Smith; 1.50 of each for Black.
  f. Nonsense question. (i) is 6.5 oats and 2.5 soybeans while (ii) is 3.17 of each.
  g. Still meaningless.
  h. No, for reasons we shall see later.

4 b. Different set.

5 a. Smith grows oats and Black grows soybeans.
  b. Switch to oats.
  c. If the price of oats is less than one-fifth the price of a bushel of soybeans, Smith should switch to soybeans.

6 (1) Production is efficient if the output of one of the possible products is maximized for stated amounts of the other products. (2) Production is efficient if an increase in output of one of the products can be achieved only by reducing the output of some other product.

9 Private property and observance of contracts.

12 a. Large.
  b. Greater variety of relative talents and training so that differences between people's relative abilities are more common. Further, the larger market enables a person to sell more of his special output at profitable prices.
  c. Greater concentration of time on same repeated subtasks. For example, hair-shearing for poodles only; specialists in color-TV only; architects specializing only in certain types of buildings; greater number of specialty shops.

13 Suggests I shall be poorer and engage more in "do-it-yourself." Reduced opportunity to trade limits extent to which gains from trade can be achieved.

Chapter 13

2 Costs are not undesirable consequences of an act; they are the highest value of the forsaken output—the opportunity forsaken.

3 a. Highest valued.
  b. Expressed in a common denominator or measure of value.
  c. In general, no. Not if more than one thing could have been produced—including leisure.

4 Disagree. Lower cost is measure of substitution ratios between outputs, not a measure of the maximum amount of a good that can be produced.

5 The slope is the ratio of the change in output of one good to the implied change in the other, along an efficient possibility curve. This ratio of substitution in production possibilities is called marginal costs.

8 a. GOODS

X		Y	
8	and	0	
7	"	1.5	A produces 1.5
6	"	2.9	A produces 2.9
5	"	3.9	B produces $1Y$; A produces $2.9Y$ (and $3X$)
4	"	4.9	B produces $2Y$; A produces $2.9Y$ (and $3X$)
3	"	5.9	B produces $3Y$; A produces $2.9Y$ (and $3X$)
2	"	6.8	B produces $3Y$; A produces $3.8Y$
1	"	7.5	B produces $3Y$; A produces $4.5Y$
0	"	8	B produces $3Y$; A produces $5Y$

Increments of Y per successive units of X sacrificed are 1.5, 1.4, 1.1, 1, .9, .7, .5. These diminishing increments of Y for unit sacrifices of X mean that marginal costs of Y increase for higher rates of output of Y. Thus, marginal costs of Y increase from $.67X$, to $.71X$, to $1X$ and on to $2X$, and then to infinite costs, since no more than $8Y$ can be produced per day.
b. Mr. A would be first; Mr. B would be last.
c. Mr. A would be first.

9 a. Yes. Larger.
b. We have assumed independent additive outputs from each person, as if they were lifting boxes separately. If they work jointly, two might do more than twice the work of each. We should then denote a team of workers as A, and another team as B. Similarly we could denote a team as a business firm, and the same principles would be applicable to firms. Joint interdependencies do not affect allocative principle but do make the exposition and analysis more complicated. At the present level of exposition, the simplification employed here is permissible.

10 A, B, C, D lose compared to what they would have been able to purchase with their income had C been able to produce Y and sell to A, B, and D. E gains in wealth compared to what he would have had with open access to markets. C loses wealth also. That C lives on an island across the Pacific rather than on the American continent does not change effects.

14 a. B.
b. A.

15 a. C and E produce Y; A and D produce X. B can produce either.
b. Yes.
c. All except A produce Y.
d. Yes.

16 a. Output of Y would increase to eight units.
b. Appears here as increased demand for Y. But relatively there is no difference.

17 a. Rates of output, say per day—not measures of total output of X and Y over time.
b. No. It means that if demand changed at noon, 7.5 units would have been produced that morning at a rate of 15 per day.

22 No. It merely assumes that existing knowledge can be used and subjected to performance tests. Assumes no restrictions on rights to purchase or exchange knowledge. Knowledge is a valuable (economic) resource. To assume it is free is, for example, to deny that schools exist and that teachers perform a useful desired service. A substantial fraction of our wealth is devoted to gathering information of one kind or another. Do not assume that ignorance is irrational, ridiculous, or the result of inefficiency or wastefulness or deliberate lying.

Chapter 14

2 All costs of a decision are borne by the decision maker.

4 If you define access to sunlight as an aspect of land ownership, then it is a strengthening of private-property rights.

5 b. No, it shouldn't.
c. In some cases damages have been awarded, but this is rare.

7 A is suing for property rights to uncongested streets. Under current law this kind of right seems not to be recognized. Presume we would rule against him. What do you say?

11 Nonsense. Property rights are the rights of people to do things with goods and services. They are human rights. Usually objection is made to the way a person uses his property, which means that the conflict usually is between one set of human rights and another set of human rights—not between human rights and property rights.

14 e. Nothing is implied about that.

19 Nader ignores the social gains provided by activities that produce smog and pollution as a by-product. Just as automobiles and airplanes produce death, just as travel takes up land for roads, just as making sheet-steel involves less of other desirable things like leisure, quiet, and rest, just as oil wells create some smell in the neighborhood—so all productive activity involves some undesirable by-products. All of these "pollutions" of our environment are part of the costs of production and could be avoided if we were willing to have a less convenient, more Spartan life. We should not look only at costs and think that something is wrong with those economic activities that involve the largest costs, for they, in general, may also yield the greatest benefits. Relieving one's self in the river contributes little to social welfare. The pollution of rivers by industries permits larger industrial output. Similarly, smoggers are producing other services in the process, whereas muggers produce no social service.

The complaint that Nader should develop is that governments and courts have not introduced a system of making people pay for the right to pollute—a system which would induce people to pollute less *if* the gains obtained from activity that yield pollution are worth less than the pollution damage. Just as we could make cars and planes safer but more expensive with less travel, and just as we could produce less oil or less paper by having less pollution of air and streams, there is a trade-off between "pollution" and greater output. Efforts to expose that trade-off rate and to induce the pollution costs to be taken into account by a system of prices for the right to pollute (by fines) rather than with zero prices or absolute prohibitions (infinitely high prices) are what Nader might more usefully be recommending.

Chapter 15

1 True, by definition.

2 Because they include future foreseeable sacrifices of present actions.

4 a. $3,000 (to nearest dollar) $= 20,000 - .909 \times (19,000 - 300)$.
b. $4,482.
d. Two-year annuity with present value of $4,482 is $2,591 per year.
f. $1,183 per year.

5 a. $5,000 - ($3,000 \times .909) = $2,273.
c. $2,273. See answer to (a).
e. ($6,000 \times .909) plus $2,273 = $7,727.
f. ($6,000 \times .909) plus ($6,000 \times .909^2$) plus $3,761 = $14,171.
g. $f - e = $6,444.
h. $1,000.

6 The renter of the car pays for the depreciation as part of his rental charges. He avoids tying up capital funds only in the sense that the leasing company is lending him the car and charging him for its rental, whereas he could have borrowed money, bought a car, and then paid rental on the borrowed money (as interest). The rise of leasing services is primarily a consequence of business tax laws too detailed to go into here. But the point is that renting or borrowing money or paying out of your already accumulated wealth doesn't change the costs at all—aside from idiosyncracies of the business tax laws.

7 Cost increases less than in proportion to volume. (What did you assume about rate of output?)

8 Rate and the total amount planned for production.

10 4,000,000 units.

14 It decreases.

16 It decreases.

18 Yes.

21 Public prefers lower cost more than greater variety of models.

23 Price will be greater for quick delivery of completed product.

26 The latter—regardless of the relationship between output and cost.

28 The ad writers have mixed up rate and volume effects on costs. A greater supply—volume—implies a lower unit cost and also a lower price. Bigger volume demand yields lower price because it evokes a greater supply (in volume sense). But in the *rate* (or speed of production) sense, higher demand yields a higher price. When demand increases in both the volume demanded and the speed at which that volume is demanded, price may fall (in response to volume effect) but it will be higher than otherwise in order to increase the rate of production. What advertising can do is to affect the volume demanded, but if it also increases the rate at which the good is demanded, it leads to higher prices.

29 Old firms are not burdened by old equipment. They too can switch to new goods. That they don't simply means they can compete by using old equipment, whose value is recapitalized to whatever level will enable it to continue to be used—unless its value must be zero, in which case it will certainly be retired. First sentence is typical of a very common error—an error that ignores market's valuation process of existing goods.

30 **a.** Impossible to divide costs between these two uses.
b. Not answerable. Divide it half and half if you wish. But what difference does it make for any real problem? None.

33 **a.** None. That they will not far exceed it for long is a result of open markets.
b. None.

34 Output of other products, of which gasoline is one, increases. Since gasoline, unlike oil, must be stored in very expensive tanks, refineries induce service stations to buy more gasoline and store more in station storage tanks. These retailers, presented with lower prices, keep their tanks more nearly full—and is evidenced by retailers' increased frequency of smaller than usual orders. In other words, retail service stations keep their storage tanks more fully loaded, maintaining a higher average load during low-price periods. In turn, motorists are induced to keep their tanks more nearly full.

Chapter 16

3 Yes. Also salable without permission of other owners.

4 Convenient way to assemble capital. No one owner has to put all his wealth in one company in order for company to be large. Easy salability of ownership also enhances attraction of investment. In other words, it is an efficient form of property risk bearing.

5 No to all questions.

7 The "boss" is able to tell people what to do because he pays them. Turning it around, the employee tells the boss what to do—that is, to pay the employee some money. Obviously, neither tells the other what to do. Each agrees to do something if the other will do something. If it be said an employer can fire an employee, so can an employee fire his boss by changing jobs.

8 **a.** No. In ordinary circumstances we would expect stability.
b. Should the typical voter or minority groups be able to turn out the governor of their state? It is precisely in order to prevent every single person from making his own will count that voting systems are utilized.
c. It means a majority controls through the medium of a minority of the stockholders to whom a majority gives its votes, as the Congress represents a minority of the American public, being only some 537 people representing 200,000,000.

9 **a.** Wealth constraints are different in the two classes of cases.
b. The former, because of reduced possibility of personally capturing capitalized value of improvements of new management—as can be done in private-property corporations via purchase and sale of common stock.

10 **a.** Present value of receipts is $19,662. Subtracting present value of costs of two-year ownership and operation (from question 5f, Chapter 14), $14,171, the difference $5,491 is the imputed profit.

12 Both—you first had a profit of $50; then, by continuing to hold that wealth, you incurred a loss of $25 during the second month. Whether or not you convert it to cash has nothing whatever to do with the fact of your change in wealth—that is, of profits or losses. Only the income-tax people use the conversion-to-money principle, for computing taxes.

13 Depends upon what you mean by "very few." Annually many corporations show decreases in the value of their common stock. Approximately 30 to 40 percent of all corporations report losses for

the year, although the firms reporting losses are not always the same. Since 1916 the percentage has always been above 20 percent and has been over 50 percent in several years. For all reporting corporations the aggregate earnings (after taxes) normally run about five times that of the losses. For more details consult *Statistics of Income*: U. S. Treasury, issued annually.

20 Sentence is correct. By selective purchase of assets of personal wealth holdings, people can vary their mixtures to suit their risk-bearing preferences.

21 Socialism does not permit selective, discretionary, optional selection of wealth holdings by each individual. Profits and losses are borne in accord with taxes, rights to use government resources, and powers of political office.

22 Former facilitates or permits the latter to be revised in accord with personal preferences.

26 A loss was realized when the stock price fell. If the price rises, the old loss is now fortunately offset by a new profit. You can't hide from losses by burying your head in the sand or by not converting your wealth from one form to another. You merely throw away options with that kind of reasoning. Don't make the logical and economic error of thinking you can escape a loss by not selling while the price is lower than it used to be, or even lower than what you paid for it. That kind of thinking does not engender strong survival traits for your wealth.

27 They perform selective risk-bearing function, whether they know it or not. In prospecting for oil, some will lose and some may win. And some of us do not have to commit our wealth to that risky venture. Still, if we want more oil, the "lucky" investors who bear the risks relieve us of that risk. For that function they are allowed, under private-property system, to obtain profits. As for taxing them away, that depends upon your desire to have risks borne selectively, voluntarily, upon your willingness not to renege on general agreement to let lucky ones keep wealth, and upon attitudes toward differences in wealth among people.

29 a. All. Some by patent rights, some by licensing which limits entry, some by limiting access to open markets for competitors, and one (Sinatra) by natural superiority.

Chapter 17

1 No.

2 Output program is 15 if price is $1.50; $6.20 profit; output program, if price is $5, is 24.

4 a. To produce more would involve costs that exceed the value of the extra amount produced. Resources could be used elsewhere in higher-valued uses—as reflected in their costs.

7 Marginal costs along with marginal revenue indicate maximum wealth output, while average costs in relation to price indicate whether the profits are positive or negative.

9 b. $1.40.
c. 1,400 per year.
f. Buyers or sellers who want to buy or sell more than they can at the existing price.
m. Under our assumption that all firms are identical, yes; all would survive up until total output reached 2,100. If more enter, losses will occur and some will have to leave or continue to lose wealth.
o. Profits will be capitalized into costs; and costs, recognizing value of all the resources used by the firm, will equal revenue.

11 Resources will be increased in production of X until extra value of output of X falls to $5.

12 Suppose only the president of the company knew the secret and also owned some shares. He would be less willing to sell at the old price and would be willing to buy more shares. In other words, his demand to hold shares increases and thus affects market demand. Certainly several people in the company knew the secret and several also owned stock in the company. Price would rise because their own demand to hold the stock had increased in the light of the secret developments.

13 Not "consumer sovereignty" but "individual sovereignty" is more accurate. Individuals make choices as consumers (buyers) and as producers (sellers). An individual expresses choices about working conditions as much as about consumption goods. If mining is unpleasant compared to cutting timber, so that individuals are more willing to work at the latter rather than the former, the amount of lumber relative to coal will be larger than if individual preferences as producers were reversed.

Because there are so many other people, each of us is usually powerless to affect output or market demand in a significant way. This does not mean we cannot choose among alternative purchases or products to produce. Nevertheless, because we cannot significantly change the range of offers made to us, each open-market producer thinks the consumer (a personification of the market) is sovereign, while the consumer erroneously thinks that producers (personification of supply) decide what consumers can have.

14 **a.** Reduce the output.
    b. At first, if output is not reduced but taxes are paid, the wealth of peanut growers will fall. Higher marginal costs indicate a lower output as the new wealth-maximizing output. Or some who formerly made profit or broke even will now have a loss and be induced to abandon or reduce peanut production.
    c. Reduced supply, shown by shift of supply curve to left, implies higher price.
    d. Land will fall in value only to extent it was worth more for peanut growing than for next-best use.
    h. Peanut consumers.

Chapter 18

2 Price-takers' demand curve is horizontal at highest price at which seller can sell any of his product, while in price-searchers' market his demand curve is a negatively sloped function.

7 **a.** Same as before; $2.70 price and output of 14.

8 **a.** Raise it by 30 cents.

9 **a.** Price-searcher; an open-market monopolist.

10 In the sense that it indicates the amounts of the good that the productive resources would be willing to provide through the intermediary of the businessman. But it does not present the supply schedule of the amounts actually forthcoming at each potential selling price of the good, because the intermediary businessman is heeding marginal revenue rather than price (average revenue).

11 **a.** Yes.

13 Price that maximizes their wealth depends on demand, not on their own desire for more wealth. Prices three times as high would, in opinion of sellers, yield smaller wealth or profits.

14 **a.** Yes.
    b. The government is not a monolithic agency of just one person. It often does conflicting things at the same time, in response to different pressures.

16 **a.**

		Revenue	
Price	Quantity	Total	Marginal
$4.00	0	0	0
3.90	0	0	0
3.80	0	0	0
3.70	0	0	0
3.60	0	0	0
3.50	0	0	0
3.40	1	3.40	3.40
3.30	2	6.60	3.20
3.20	3	9.60	3.00
3.10	4	12.40	2.80
3.00	5	15.00	2.60
2.90	6	17.40	2.40
2.80	7	19.60	2.20
2.70	8	21.60	2.00
2.60	9	23.40	1.80
2.50	10	25.00	1.60

  b. Output is 18.

17 Sales price, if goods were available at that price at time of sale. Price means exchange prices, not hoped-for price.

19 Yes, because extent of exchange and specialization is reduced, with consequent smaller wealth.

22   b. Yes.
    c. It is, when I do it. How about you?

Chapter 19

1   a. Slightly more than 10 cents. (Call it 10 cents for subsequent computations.)
    b. Between 65 and 67 cents. Call it 67 cents for subsequent computations.
    c. Each would sell ten units at 67 cents each, for $6.70 daily.
    d. Formerly received (10 cents × 20 units) $2 daily. Each gets $4.70 more.

4   Government agencies enforcing laws against collusions concentrate on collusions against government. Second, government uses system of sealed bid, publicly opened. This is ideal for preventing secret price cutting or evasion of collusion by colluding firms.

5   a. Team owners are able to sign new players at lower wages, since other owners agree not to compete for these players. The team owner's problem is to pay just enough to induce the newcomer to play; he does not have to compete against other owners. The competition is transferred to that of determining the initial assignments of newcomers to each team—by giving the lowest-standing team first choice of the newcomers (high school graduates) and the next-lowest team the next choice. This is the "draft." Although this assignment system is alleged to help equalize team abilities, it does not; players are subsequently sold to other teams, at prices far in excess of that paid the newcomers. The draft is simply a device to pay players less than they would get in open markets, while the resale of the players to other teams at higher prices is a scheme of wealth redistribution among the teamowners. (If the two football leagues reach an effective agreement, as seemed to be happening as this book went to press, they must beware of the Canadian Football League, which, being "left out," will be able to get new players more cheaply than otherwise.)

    The better athletes suffer. Since it is impossible to know in advance precisely how good an athlete will be, the initial sign-up price will be lower to reflect that uncertainty. There is a stipulation in all contracts that wages cannot be cut "rapidly," so those who turn out to be poorer than expected will be overpaid for a substantial time. Those who turn out better than expected will be underpaid thereafter, because other team owners will not bid for their services by offering the player the higher wage, but will instead pay the team owner to get that player.
    b. Perhaps this explains why we call these "sports" rather than "businesses." No business could do this. It is a much tougher, and still unsolved, task to explain why other businesses cannot do what sports can do. The existence of laws restricting business firms does not solve the problem.

7   Collusion connotes elements of deception in seeking to negotiate exchanges in the pretense that the sellers are acting as independent competitors. Buyers are misled into presuming sellers are acting independently. If buyers knew sellers were in agreement, buyers would be alerted to incentive of each seller not to bid as he otherwise would. Without element of secrecy, buyers are aware of lack of inter-seller conflict of interest—as, for example, among the two salesmen of the same firm. The pretense of competing with respect to prices and quality is designed to induce buyer to think he is already obtaining advantages of inter-seller competition.

    With open collusion, such as mergers, there is no pretense. Buyers are not deceived and can then obtain offers from other independent sellers. Open agreements not to compete are not deceptive and consequently are much less effective in open markets. Partnerships being open are not deceptive, hence do not connote elements of collusion. Element of deception is undesirable.

    Competition connotes elements of method of resolving who will get what of existing resources, while cooperation connotes joint action to increase total stock of wealth to be distributed. Some actions do both at the same time. Thus, exchange with specialization is both competitive and cooperative in increasing wealth as well as in allocating it.

10   b. Yes, because it permits discrimination among customers according to their demand.

12   Each can judge what is best for himself, we suppose. As for us, we would prefer formal exchanges not to shut off trading in particular securities, thereby reducing exchange opportunities. Under present system, presumption is built up that stock-exchange officials are good judges of

what price changes are justified or what news ought not to be allowed to affect decisions of individual investors—a presumption which not even the stock-exchange officials will defend. Rationale for restrictive practice is that wide price swings resulting from news that turns out to be incomplete or exaggerated are often blamed on the stock market, with suggestion that stock-market officials were responsible or that they ought to have prevented such unjustified (with hindsight) swings. In fact, these wide swings are the result of incomplete information, which no one can improve on at the time. On the other hand, if the stock exchange closes trading at such uncertain times, and if the news is verified and does bring a persisting change in demand and supply conditions, the exchange can say that the new price truly reflects the situation. What this ignores is that stopping trading during those times locks existing owners into continuing ownership even though they would prefer to shed the uncertainty by selling to others who are more willing to bear it. Bad news is made more damaging for existing holders in that they cannot sell out as early at the suggestion of worsening conditions. Consequently, it is not correct to say that closing down the exchanges at the arrival of big news (assassination of president, outbreak of war), or suspension of trading in particular stocks, is a good thing.

13 **a.** We think students can discriminate as ably as any other group you would suggest. To the argument that students are prone to take snap, popular, "theatrical" courses, we ask, "What is bad about popular, theatrical courses if the course is nevertheless good?" To say that students select snap courses (meaning courses that are easy—not because teaching is good but because course content is trivial) is to provoke question as to why students do that. To say they are lazy is to presume that they should not be lazy or that only hard-working students should attend a class—a rather presumptive judgment. More germane is question of why students who are able and motivated to go to college should nevertheless sacrifice "good" courses for sake of an easy grade. Does it suggest something about the criteria imposed on the students by the college administrators? What?

14 **a.** The best—by definition, since the students can select from the entire world, rather than just within one state.

15 **a.** No. We know only of more economical goods driving out less economical goods. Ignoring price or costs, we can cite examples in each direction—an irrelevant exercise.

16 **b.** As any of these groups, we would oppose the development proposed.

18 That capitalist money-seeking activity cultivates deceitful advertising, false claims, and dishonesty is so serenely believed by some people that it's a shame to waken them. The fact is that dishonesty and deceit often do pay. Therefore, it is sometimes said that free and open competition in the market gives a seller an incentive to lie in order to get customers from his competitors. Yet politicians also lie and don't tell the whole truth when campaigning or making speeches. They are not more honest than commercial advertisers. The socialist governments are not distinguished for their devotion to the truth. Surely there are good grounds for doubting that capitalism is more conducive to dishonesty than other systems. Nevertheless, it is worth considering the questions "Does capitalism reward one more for cheating than does any alternative system? Is the cheater likely to be discovered in the capitalist system and punished as effectively as in a different system? Is the public more likely to be deceived?"

That everyone has an incentive to lie and cheat is not denied. But is the ability to get away with it affected by the ease of competitors' making counterclaims? The question has only to be posed to be answered. A newspaper will be more careful with the truth if it knows that other news media can challenge its veracity. Politicians are more cautious if they know opponents can challenge their statements. A witness in court is more careful with the statements of facts if he knows he is going to be cross examined by the opposition. The easier it is for all to enter the market of ideas, the more counterclaims and different interpretations of events will be offered. In open-market capitalism, the incentives to disprove the claims and to submit counterclaims are increased. That is why it is a good rule to talk to a Ford salesman if you want to detect the truth about Chevrolets, and conversely.

22 **a.** Owners of high-cost stations and stations already in existence would benefit. Low-cost stations and those who might enter business are hurt.
b. Your guess is as good as ours. How about men with the prettiest wives?

23 **a.** Longer-run consequences are, insofar as foreseen, discounted into present capital value of the enterprise and are hence borne by the present owner.

25 **a.** We don't know the answer to this question. But it shows the difficulty of deducing collusion from overt behavior.
b. Newspapers are privately owned and use privately owned resources. Their right to publish is not controlled by government agency.

Chapter 20

1 Jobs of workers on railroad engines and jobs the displaced workers will accept elsewhere; also, jobs of workers on railroad engines and jobs of workers making equipment that will be used if railroads can revise their work rules and assignments.

3 a. Yes. Equipment on the bus for a laborer on the bus.
b. Yes. Labor off the bus for labor on the bus.
c. Yes. Total labor is re-allocated in its tasks. No labor is released from work force, since that labor is used to produce more of other goods—except to the extent that some now choose a bit more leisure (as total output is larger).

5 No. Unlimited number of jobs available; only those are filled which are highest-value jobs, given present knowledge and resources. New inventions induce labor to move to other unfilled jobs. Each time the labor moves to a less valuable job, relative to old job. But at the same time the total wealth of the community is increased. The displaced person, as explained in the text, has no assurance of realizing a net gain from the particular innovation which displaces his most profitable job opportunities; but he does gain from most other innovations that do not displace his job.

7 a. Fixity of ratios of kinds of inputs in the final product says absolutely nothing about the ratios in which those inputs will be used to produce the good.

8 There are many alternative ways of doing something, all of which can be technically efficient. But, of these, only one minimizes the value of forsaken opportunities; that is the economically efficient one.

10 It is impossible to tell from that information. Costs are unknown.

13 Can't tell. This tells us nothing about cost. We presume new method is technologically or technically efficient, in that no more could be obtained as output for given amount of specified inputs. But this doesn't tell us output is worth the input.

15 b. To include exchange efficiency. Values of outputs are being included as judged by what people will pay in an exchange system. Thus, efficiency is broadened to include deciding what to produce, rather than merely the cheapest way to produce an arbitrary output.

16 a. Suppose you had one piece of paper and were told to maximize your use of that paper. What would you do? Is it clear now that the expression has no meaning or that it means anything you want it to mean? Usage is not something you maximize; for usage is not measurable in a single-dimensional sense. In international radio-communications conferences, the statement sounded good to many radio and electronic engineers working for the Federal Communications Commission and for the State Department—precisely because it lets them interpret radio uses however they wish to. It's like having your parents tell you to maximize the use of your time at college.

18 a. All now twice as large.
b. Increases them proportionally to rise in price.

19 a. Three labor and 4 capital, but if we interpolate we can do still better by using a little less than 4 capital and a little more than 3 labor—but not as much as 4 labor and 3 capital, which costs more than using 3 labor and 4 capital.
b. 2 capital and 5 labor.
c. Same one is cheaper. Relative prices of inputs did not change.

21 Decrease in total versus decrease in increments.

22 a. Increase the amount of that resource used relative to other resources.

23 Explained in text on pages 452–453.

24 See text, pages 452–453.

26 The desire for greater wealth and the competition among actual and potential employers for those resources that give greater rather than less wealth.

29 a. Same as before: maximize utility. But, now less profit or net value of output can be retained or taken out by the owner; hence, less attention to profits as a source of utility.
c. Possibly some, but not as strongly as if enterprise privately owned. Would let it depart from ratio if thereby obtained more utility from other uses of resources rather than for profits or higher pecuniary exchange value.

32 **b.** Invest in personal intellectual skills, since these are not as easy for the state to appropriate as physical wealth.

Chapter 21

3   Both can be correct—as explained in text.

4   Depends upon infant mortality rate. If half of all children died in first year, and .2 survived to age 10, and if desire for children reflects desire for "grown-up" children, and if these mortality rates were lower for higher wealth and education of parents, we would expect higher number of births for poorer parents and fewer for richer; but in number of children in family at age 10, we could find more for richer than for poorer. The point is that in comparing countries, if one uses the same definition of "children," he can be misled about effects of wealth and education and population growth.

7   An unlimited number of jobs are available in a world of scarcity. If productivity in those jobs or tasks that people can perform in Arizona is not as great as elsewhere, population increase will fall off as people move elsewhere.

8   People differ in their productive abilities, and their costs of acquiring skills. The cost of acquiring skills (costs referring to all factors that restrain one person's ability to duplicate that of another) are such that wage differentials can exist. These wage differentials will be smaller than the costs of acquiring skills that would enable lower-paid workers to do work of higher-paid people. Except for fortuitous matching of demands and supplies at wages equal in all tasks, differences in wages will persist, but they will be less than costs of acquiring skills of higher-paying jobs and/or any other transfer costs.

10 Movie producers do believe that receipts from picture will be at least that much larger if they have Taylor rather than Hepburn. In other words, last sentence of quoted statement is challenged. Whether or not she is worth that much more is a judgment that producer has to make; and his actions reveal that if Hepburn could have been obtained for only $1,000,000, the marginal product of Taylor is, in his opinion, greater by at least $4,000,000.

Marginal product in demand for resources is reflected in estimates of what marginal product will be when the resources are employed. On what basis would you as an employer estimate product of various resources? Would you ignore past record of various people? Would you as a football coach pay no attention to high school athletic performance when recruiting athletes, or would you look only at their physical appearance? Undoubtedly there are many talented people who could do just as well—if you only knew who they were. Marginal-productivity theory does not say that marginal product of every person in every possible job is known to all people. It says instead that demand for any resources is based on employer's estimates of marginal product of any given resource to him. It also says demand is a negative function of price of resource. Whether the theory is useless or false depends upon how well its implications agree with facts of economic life (compared with other theories). On that score it is far and away the best available theory of the demand for productive resources.

11 An infinite number of "unskilled jobs" exists. Most pay less than people are willing to accept, because they can get more money elsewhere. Whatever the reason for the unemployed, it is not that there are fewer unskilled jobs than unskilled workers. (We discuss some reasons for unemployed later.)

14 **a.** Induced higher rate of immigration. Perhaps labor already in U. S. wanted to restrict entry of new laborers from Europe. Ask your history teacher. (Note that today you can import a foreigner if you will guarantee him a job or guarantee that he will not be a public-welfare recipient for a year.)

15 We don't know.

16 The superiority of one manager over another in making good decisions is worth more to a bigger firm, since the value of wealth affected by his decision is greater in big than in smaller firms. Firms will bid against each other for that superior skill—up to the value of the gain to them of that superiority, or, in other words, up to the marginal productivity to the firm of the superior managers.

19 It means that 300,000 workers in jobs now refuse to cut wages enough to compete with new techniques in present jobs and prefer to accept jobs elsewhere at not so great a cut in wages. Of course, they prefer not to shift to a new job at all at a wage cut. Automation is revising the relative demands for labor on various jobs, lowering some and raising some. Only those that are

lowered are noticed in this statement that is being evaluated. (We do not hold the number 300,000 as valid other than for purposes of discussion.)

Chapter 22

2 All the statements are empty, wrong, or irrelevant. This question is designed not as a device to evaluate unions but rather as a device to evaluate sentences written about unions. That many sentences written about unions are empty, wrong, or irrelevant in no way implies that unions are useless, wrong, or misunderstood.

4 True, but not necessarily bad.

6 Those people who would be willing to work at open-market wages and who do not belong to unions. You explain why.

8 Too embarrassing for us to answer.

9 **a.** Ask the judge.
   b. Ditto.

10 Those who cannot provide services worth as much as the minimum-wage rate will have to work as self-employed or commission-basis employees. Thus, in saying that a higher minimum wage reduces employment, we meant employment for wages—not productive work as self-employed or commission-basis employees.

12 Yes, except for important fact that union is not open-market monopoly and U. S. Steel is. (With respect to world open markets, both are closed-market monopolists as a result of immigration laws and tariff and taxes on imports.)

22 Increase. Self-employment is a way of evading wage regulation.

25 Decreased. Union will set wages higher to keep only full-time employees at work, with less interest in casual, seasonal laborers.

27 **a.** It will aid people who already are employed and who are going to have heart attacks and who either do not plan to shift to new jobs or who appear not prone to heart attacks.
   b. It will make job shifting more difficult. Will hurt those who reveal a higher probability of heart attacks insofar as they want to change jobs. Will help them as long as they stay with *current* employer (with employer at time of passage of law).
   c. All new employees will bear some of costs since heart attack is not perfectly predictable. People with record of attack will bear heaviest cost, since they will not be able to get jobs at as high a wage as formerly.

30 **a.** Doesn't differ except in degree to which it reveals implications of what is said.
   b. At $5, reduction in number of employees would be too great. Self-employed do not join unions. Meany depends upon unions.

31 We don't know. We conjecture that employee discrimination is regarded as acceptable, and would be incapable of being prohibited by any law, in any event.

34 **a.** Correct form of statement would be that it would raise the *payments* the federal government would have to record in its budget. Real costs are being paid already by those who are drafted. The income they are sacrificing is the cost and this would be reduced if the draft were eliminated and military personnel were obtained by paying adequate wages to attract men.
   b. You should, since it will. By better assignment of people to jobs in this country—which would be a result of using adequate wages for military personnel—the total productive efficiency and output would be increased, which means that our sacrificed output would be smaller. Draft conceals costs—by making federal expenditures lower through device of compulsory service—just as police-department costs could be made to appear lower if police were drafted.

Chapter 23

2 It increases the marketable pecuniary value of wealth because it increases the future available consumption.

3 **a.** Yes. A fall in the rate of interest.
   b. Increase the profitability.
   c. Reduce the ratio of the price of raisins to grapes. Raise interest.

4 **a.** $50 per year.
   c. $10 per year.
   e. Increases from $5 to $6 per year.

7 False. Remember, only the more productive roundabout methods are employed. Those that are less productive are shunned. Important thing is to get right kind of capital goods—not *any* capital goods.

8 **a.** No.
   b. In the sense that he could have even more wealth if he used his wealth differently. To say the interest rate is 10 percent means he could have used his wealth to have $110 at the end of one year. If he actually made it grow to $110 (regardless of what he then consumed), he did the best expected. If instead he managed to have it grow only to $105, his poor management has cost him $5 in consumption. We can say his poor management is equivalent to a $5 consumption activity, except that we doubt he regarded the joys of poor management as a sort of consumption activity. But then again, who knows; maybe he did—by hiring pretty girls as congenial employees rather than pecuniarily efficient ones.

10 **a.** $115.60.
   b. Three years.

12 **a.** About 200,000 rabbits.

13 Higher rate of investment means a higher rate of production of some goods, and this implies a higher cost per unit of those goods.

16 **a.** Correct.
   b. A different definition than that given in this question is used. (See next question.)

17 Investment is defined as that rate of conversion (of present income) to wealth which can be profitable. The function relating these rates to the rate of interest is the investment-demand function. Saving is defined as that rate of conversion of present income to wealth that the community wants to engage in. This desired rate, or rate at which the community is willing to divert income from current income to wealth accumulation, is a function of the rate of interest (among other things); and this relationship between the saving rate and rate of interest is the supply-of-savings function.

22 Corporation managers do not have to invest all funds within the corporation. They can invest in other companies; they can lend the money. So long as they consider possible alternative investments, they will use funds within the firm only if that looks more profitable, as would be the case if the funds were to be borrowed from the market.

25 Ignoring the effects arising from the adjustments of the person from whom you got the money, and looking at only your own impact, the effect of the sequence of actions would be to push down interest rates in the bond market as you purchased bonds—but later to be reversed as we sell the bonds preparatory to purchase of other goods. If we assume the money received was new money issued by the government, then, in addition to the above transient effect, the general price level would be pushed up as the demand for goods experiences a net increase. (Admittedly, $10,000 is a drop in the bucket for the whole economy, but even drops have their ripples; and sensitive devices can measure fractions of drops.)

27 **a.** Contract rate refers to stated, not effective rate. See question 1 of Chapter 13.
   b. Among those hurt are people whose credit is so poor that they are unable to borrow at these low rates. Among those helped are the better-credit borrowers, since some funds that would have gone to high-risk borrowers are now diverted to the safer borrowers with a consequent lower interest rate to them.

Chapter 24

2 Personal human capital. Less subject to expropriation. If I were absolutely sure there would be no expropriation, I would invest in nonpersonal capital; for the buyer of the services of such goods does not associate them with the owner's personal characteristics as much as he would if buying personal services.

4 One can hardly quarrel with the contention that saving (in some relevant sense) is a *necessary* condition for development, but it is clear also that saving is not a *sufficient* condition. Saving

makes resources available for production and accumulation of "productive" capital. But much investment contributes little to output-increasing capacity and instead finds its way, for example, into private accumulations of gold and deposits in foreign banks and into industrial monuments (steel mills and airlines) for which there is no comparative advantage.

8 No. Oregon and California could buy water, just as they buy lumber and canned fish from Washington. Whether state ownership and sale of *water* are more difficult than exchange among individuals is a fine debatable question, about which not enough is known to justify any statements.

10 Soon as someone thinks an apple is ripe enough to eat with more satisfaction than not eating one at all (contrasted to eating it when it is riper and better). Apples will be eaten greener than they would be if privately owned.

13 a. Fish will be younger and smaller, for the same reason that apples don't ripen in a public park.
b. When no one owns all the fish in the lake, the extra value of fish taken will be judged by each separate fisherman according to *his* catch rather than by the total catch in the lake. Absence of property rights in fish causes competition to acquire *property rights* in fish.

15 b. Higher-income spending units have a larger number of individuals in the unit; spending units are defined as groups of "all persons living in the same dwelling and belonging to the same family, who pool their incomes to meet their major expenses."
c. Graduated income tax is heavier proportionately on higher incomes, hence after-income-tax picture should show smaller dispersion. But many other taxes (for example, sales, gasoline) take larger proportion from lower-income groups. Best evidence seems to be that gross tax effect is to lower very largest incomes relative to lowest, thus reducing degree of dispersion, lowering proportion of total income in top tenth, and raising it in lowest—though not by spectacular amounts.
d. Post-tax measure indicates income available for spending at discretion of income unit. But to look at post-tax measure exclusively is to ignore the purposes to which taxes are put. Larger taxes provide more government services and income transfers; hence, income in fullest sense to any person is not correctly measured by his post-tax income alone.

17 Natural population change is a function of both the birth rate and the death rate. Population does not rise rapidly if the birth rate is only a little greater than the death rate, whether both rates are large (India) or small (U. S.). Typically, in the early stages of economic development, the death rate falls sooner and faster than the birth rate, giving rise to a rapid increase in population.

18 Any statement based on asserted "needs" is suspect at the outset; the suspicion is compounded by references to what can be "afforded"; and reliance on a supposed "shortage of dollars" calls for very careful treatment. But there is more wrong here than a sloppy choosing of words; basically, the inadequacy stems from failure to utilize the principle of comparative advantage. Virtually any commodity can be made in any country, and thus foreign purchasing power (i.e., gold and foreign currencies) could be "saved" by curtailing or eliminating imports of a particular good and producing it at home. And, of course, in three years or some other number of years, the value of the import "savings" would be equal to the immediate cost of putting up the mill or the plant or the farm in question. If this were all that is involved in the investment "paying for itself"—if there were really no other costs than initial construction of plant, no costs of maintenance, repair, and updating the plant and no costs of materials and labor for operation of the plant—then there would be no rationality in any international trade at all. Certainly, India *can* produce steel; but can she thereby acquire steel with smaller expenditure of (scarce) resources than by producing some other commodity and trading (exporting) it for foreign-produced steel? Adam Smith observed that "By means of glasses, hotbeds, and hotwalls, very good grapes can be raised in Scotland, and very good wine too can be made of them—at about thirty times the expense for which at least equally good can be brought from foreign countries" (*Wealth of Nations,* p. 425). The Ambassador to India strangely fails to distinguish between feasibility and desirability.

Chapter 25

2 A person should be able to get a job at a salary close to his last salary without a significant cost of finding such a job.

4 No. He chooses not to accept best alternative job he has so far discovered and is instead looking at more jobs—which is not to say that he is lazy or deserves to be poorer.

7 **a.** No. The sum of a random variable, summed over trials (one for each firm), will still be a random variable. Random deviations do not cancel each other exactly.
   b. Almost certainly. Very rare that every firm would have bigger sales on following day.
   c. Almost certainly. Very rare that every firm would experience a decrease in sales.

Chapter 26

1 *All* transactions include exchanges of intermediate products and of previously produced assets; they give a total value, for which many types of output are counted more than once. *Final* transactions yield Gross National Product, which counts each item of current output only once and thus gives a better measure of the economy's production. The total of final transactions equals the total of values added by all the producing units.

2 **a.** False. The value of the total amounts sold by individual units of the economy is much greater than the values added by the respective units, for the total amounts include a "double-count" of input, or intermediate, products.
   b. False. While a negative value of inventory has no meaning, we can speak of a negative *change* (*decrease*) in inventory—which is called "disinvestment."
   c. False. Only payments for *currently* produced *final* outputs produced *domestically* form a part of Gross National Product.
   d. False. The dollar value of *GNP* in *current* prices may rise while real output increases, decreases, or remains constant. Calculation of *GNP* in *constant* prices is intended to obviate the effects of price changes.

8 Not the receipts, but the "value added" would be counted. Suppose receipts were $100, payouts to gamblers were $80, purchases of materials and rents were $5, and wages were $6. The value added would be $15.

12 Not the same. The transactions tax is on *all* exchanges and taxes more than the value added or income element that may arise in an exchange. Also, the income tax has exemptions and differential rates depending upon size of income.

13 **a.** In terms of "final products," under the headings of *C, I,* and *G,* the economy produced *C* (bread) of 4.0, *I* (machinery and flour inventory) of 2.5 + 3.0, and *G* of 2.0. This is a total of 11.5 for *GNP*. In terms of "valued added," we have 2.5 in machinery production, 7.0 in production of bread and flour inventory (4.0 by farmers, 2.0 by millers, and 1.0 by bakers), and 2.0 in provision of government services.
   b. If $GNP = 11.5$, then $NNP = 11.5 - 1.0 = 10.5$.
   c. If $NNP = 10.5$, then $NI = 10.5 - .5 = 10$.

Chapter 27

2 There is no circular reasoning: it is a case of mutual determination of income and consumption. In the income-creation equation, *C* in a *given* period is *a determinant* of income in that *same* period; in the income-disposal equation, *C* in a *given* period is a *function* of income. Mutual dependence is not an inconsistency.

3 An autonomous change is a *shift* in an entire schedule. For example, consumption expenditure is now different from initial values at all income levels; or quantity demanded of a good is now different at each alternative price. An induced change involves moving *along* a constant schedule. As the term is used in the present context, the movement along the curve is *induced* by a change in income, which is analogous to moving along a demand curve as a result of a change in price.

5 Starting with an equilibrium income at which $S = I$, an autonomous increase in saving will, indeed, upset the equilibrium, and equilibrium will not be re-established until again $S = I$. But what closes the gap of S over I? Unless we conveniently assume an autonomous increase in I to match that in S, then S will be equated to I by a *fall* in income. Income will fall enough to induce the community to save no more per period than is being invested.

6 The fact that $MPC + MPC = 1$ derives from the income-*disposal* equation: since $\Delta Y = \Delta C = \Delta S$, then $\Delta Y/\Delta Y = \Delta C/\Delta Y + \Delta S/\Delta Y$, or $1 = MPC + MPS$. All this has nothing to do with investment, which is a variable in the income-*creation* equation.

11

Year (1)	Shoe Demand (2)	Shoes per Machine (3)	Number of Machines (4)	Depreciation Rate (5 Yr.; 20%) (5)	Replacement Demand (6)	Expansion Demand (7)	Total Demand (8)
20	100,000	5,000	20	4	4	0	4
21	110,000	5,000	22	4	4	2	6
22	130,000	5,000	26	4	4	4	8
23	150,000	5,000	30	4	4	4	8
24	155,000	5,000	31	4	4	1	5
25	155,000	5,000	31	4	4	0	4
26	145,000	5,000	29	6	4	0	4
27	140,000	5,000	28	8	7	0	7
28	140,000	5,000	28	8	8	0	8

Year (1)	Shoe Demand (2)	Shoes per Machine (3)	Number of Machines (4)	Depreciation Rate (20 Yr.; 5%) (5)	Replacement Demand (6)	Expansion Demand (7)	Total Demand (8)
20	100,000	5,000	20	1	1	0	1
21	110,000	5,000	22	1	1	2	3
22	130,000	5,000	26	1	1	4	5
23	150,000	5,000	30	1	1	4	5
24	155,000	5,000	31	1	1	1	2
25	155,000	5,000	31	1	1	0	1
26	145,000	5,000	29	1	0	0	0
27	140,000	5,000	28	1	0	0	0
28	140,000	5,000	28	1	0	0	0

The point to be emphasized here is that the more durable is the machine (the lower the depreciation), the greater is the degree (percentage) of fluctuation in total machinery demand: the increase in column 8 from one machine to five is a greater proportionate change than the increase from four to eight.

In addition, the tables contain other complications. In the first table, note the larger depreciation figures (column 5) in years 26–28, reflecting a five-year lag behind acquisitions in years 21–23. In the second table, replacement demand (column 6) in years 26–28 reflects the creation of excess productive capacity (because machine requirements fell faster than machines wore out) in year 26.

Chapter 28

1 All have served as money at one time or another in various countries.

2 Most exchanges involve money as one of the goods, and the exchange rates are expressed in terms of money. But many goods have value that persists over time.

6 a. No. They are used only for exchange for a particular good. They are receipts for prepayment for a special kind of service to be rendered you.
b. We would not, because they are not used generally for purchases; instead, they are first converted to currency or checking accounts. But they are so readily transferred to money that for some problems it may prove more useful to consider them as money.
c. Yes.

Chapter 29   833

7   Question (2) is the most fundamental one. However important gold and government decree may be *institutionally*, the key characteristic of the *nature* of money is its general acceptability in discharge of obligations. Whether only coin and currency should be included in the money supply or whether money subsumes also demand deposits or time deposits or still other assets is a pragmatic matter of usefulness in empirical research. Most analysts include demand deposits, along with currency, under "money."

8   **a.** Ten pounds of potatoes or 2 pounds of butter.
    b. The cost of holding a dollar of money (aside from the costs of keeping it secure) is 6 percent per year, just as it is for any other good.

11 More for the increase in wages.

17 Historically—particularly in the 1940s and into the 1950s—the Keynesian "income-expenditure" approach and the "quantity of money" approach have been considered alternative ways to elucidate and predict the economy's aggregative behavior. In their simplest forms, the two approaches often have been made to appear almost wholly unique and distinct from each other. The "income" theory is then couched in terms of expenditure and leakage schedules, with fiscal measures dominating policy proposals, with money and monetary processes entering the picture only marginally, if at all, and with little or no attention given to the level of prices. And the "money" theory places emphasis well nigh solely on the money stock and its variations, relating the money source to bank activity and to actions of monetary authorities. Fiscal activities are of interest primarily only in the way that the government budget is financed and the government debt is managed; attention is directed at least as strongly to the general price level as it is to the national income level. Without denying—or necessarily decrying—that the "income" theory and the "money" theory provide, or encourage, somewhat different orientations and emphases, we have indicated that the analyst is better equipped with both approaches than with either one alone.

In simplest summary, the various schedules of the 45-degree diagram and their slopes and shiftings provide a highly convenient expository framework in which to consider the determination of equilibrium income, but the analysis is much fuller and more complete if the position or shift in a spending or leakage schedule is related to the quantity, and changes in the quantity, of money. In a significant sense, the quantity of money "lies behind" the configuration in the 45-degree diagram; for example, consumption is better considered a function of income *and* of money supply, rather than of income alone. The consumption curve is plotted higher (consumption is larger at any given income level), the greater the money stock. And with both approaches at our disposal, we more naturally and readily incorporate income *and* prices, fiscal *and* monetary policy, in our analysis.

Chapter 29

1   Blanks should be filled in as follows:

	(1)	(2)	(3)	(4)	(5)	(6)	(7)
Cash	100	100	100	100	100	100	100
Deposit in FR	200	150	180	260	300	200	200
Loans	500	500	500	500	500	510	500
Government bonds	200	200	200	200	100	200	200
Demand deposits	900	850	880	960	900	910	900
Capital	100	100	100	100	100	100	100
Required reserves	225	212.5	220	240	225	227.5	180
Excess reserves	75	37.5	60	120	175	72.5	120
New loans: single bank	75	37.5	60	120	175	72.5	120
New loans: entire system	300	300	240	300	400	290	*

* Can't say because it depends upon amount of existing demand deposits at all other banks.

3 Of course, there are legal limits to loan expansion. The limits take the form of minimum-reserve requirements. But even in the absence of legal limits, there would still be the constraining influence of adverse clearing balances for a given bank that expand much more rapidly than banks in general. If all banks were to expand together, with no substantial problem of adverse clearings, they could expand farther—but they still would be subject to cash drain to the public.

4 (1) The cash is deposited:

Cash	1,000	Demand deposit of depositor	1,000
Required reserves	100		
Excess reserves	900		

(2) A loan equal to initial excess reserves is granted:

Cash	1,000	Demand deposit of depositor	1,000
Required reserves	190	Demand deposit of borrower	900
Excess reserves	810		
Loans	900		

(3) The loan is spent, and all checks go outside the bank:

Cash	1,000	Demand deposit of depositor	1,000
Deposit in Fed	−900		
Required reserves	100		
Excess reserves	0		
Loans	900		

Thus, the loan is equal just to the excess reserves (not ten times those reserves) existing at the time. But, on our assumptions, there is an adverse clearing equal to the loan, which reduces actual reserves by that amount, thereby eliminating excess reserves.

5 **a.** 50.
   b.

Cash	50	Demand deposits	5,000
Deposit in FR	950	Capital	1,100
Investments	2,050		
Loans	3,050		

7 The reserves that were initially "excess" do not "go" any place. But they do shift from the "excess" category to "required" as the banks' demand liabilities increase—and when all of the actual reserves are required, expansion is halted.

8 250.

9
$$\frac{50}{.2 - .1(.2 - 1)} = 178.57.$$

Chapter 30

1 High-powered money (cash, currency, and deposits in the Fed) owned by commercial banks enables them to issue demand debts (deposits) against themselves, and these demand deposits are a form of money. Creation of demand deposits in amounts *greater* than the available high-powered money held as reserves suggests the term "high-powered." High-powered money, or the

monetary base, is comprised of (a) currency and cash issued by the Treasury and the Fed and held by the public and commercial banks plus (b) deposits held by commercial banks in the Fed.

2 **a.** Excess reserves = actual reserves − required reserves. Lowering the required-reserve ratio reduces required reserves and thereby increases excess reserves; raising the ratio decreases excess reserves. The change in excess reserves divided by the required-reserve proportion gives the possible or necessary change in deposits; the lower (higher) is the reserve ratio, the larger (smaller) is deposit expansion.
b. Changing the ratio changes the volume of excess reserves for each bank. But the expansion of a given bank will still be (approximately) confined to whatever excess reserves are: the expansion coefficient for the single bank is still (approximately) unity.

4 The rediscount rate is the interest rate charged by the Fed on loans to commercial banks. The collateral for those loans may be I.O.U.'s the banks have already discounted in making loans to their own customers. If now these I.O.U.'s are discounted a second time, we can speak of the rate of "rediscount." (But, more commonly, the collateral for loans from the Fed are new I.O.U.'s drawn by banks on themselves.)

7 **a.** Actual reserves = 20; required reserves = 19.4; excess reserves = .6.
   b. 1.4.
   c. 13.333.
   d. 50.
   e. 6.
   f. Actual reserves = 22; required reserves = 19.7; excess reserves = 2.3.
   g. Actual reserves = 22; required reserves = 19.4; excess reserves = 2.6.
   h. Sell .706.
   i. Actual reserves = 20; required reserves = 14; excess reserves = 6.
   j. 15.556.
   k. 4.75.

8 **a.** Subtract.
   b. Subtract.
   c. −100.
   d. 14,700.
   e. Add.
   f. 1932–41: gold. 1941–45: Reserve-bank credit.
   g. Add.
   h. Expansionary.
   i. 22,000. More.
   j. Reserve-bank credit.
   k. Factor of decrease.

9 (1) Increase; gold is sold to Treasury via Federal Reserve banks in exchange for new Fed deposits.
(2) Increase, since Federal Reserve notes are money.
(6) Unchanged. This transfers some Federal Reserve credit from commercial banks to Treasury. However, reserves are reduced, since only that part of Fed credit held by commercial banks or public is counted in reserves.

Chapter 31

2 Property taxes are based on a person's physical wealth, while income taxes are based on his income from personal services as well as from nonhuman wealth. Both taxes, whatever the basis for the amount to be paid, are levied against people.

3 The laws and regulations have an impact far beyond the cost of implementing them. For example, restricting use of markets to all but those with licenses can be considered a greater role than building a dam, which may cost more.

Chapter 32

1. **a.** 290.
   b. Surplus of 70.
   c. 1,310.
   d. 5.
   e. $Y = 1,950; D = 1,660; C = 1,280; S = 380; I = 380; G = 290$.

2.

	C	S	I	G	Y	T	D
a.	880	120	100	270	1,250	250	1,000
b.	950	127.778	100	200	1,250	172.222	1,077.778
c.	650	94.444	100	250	1,000	255.556	744.444
d.	550	83.333	100	250	900	266.667	633.333
e.	900	122.222	100	250	1,250	227.778	1,022.222
f.	830	170	100	320	1,250	250	1,000
g.	880	120	112.5	257.5	1,250	250	1,000

3. **a.** Increase 70.
   b. Increase 56.
   c. 280.
   d. $Y = 1,880; D = 1,660; C = 1,280; S = 380; I = 380; T = 220$.

4. **a.** Income is at an equilibrium level, for total injections $(G + I)$ equal total leakages $(S + T)$. It happens that the budget is balanced $(G = T)$. There is no necessary connection between the two: it can be the case that $G + I = S + T$ whether or not $G = T$.

C	S	G	I	Y	T	D
720	180	100	180	1,000	100	900
720	180	100	180	1,000	80	920
736	184	100	180	1,016	81.6	934.4
747.52	186.88	100	183.2	1,030.72	83.072	947.648
*880	220	100	220	1,200	100	1,100

$MPS = .2 = MPI$. Since $G = T$ in both the initial equilibrium and the new equilibrium, then $\Delta S = \Delta I$. And since in this illustration $\Delta Y = \Delta D$, it follows that $\Delta S/\Delta D = \Delta I/\Delta Y$.

b.

C	S	G	I	Y	T	D
720	190	100	180	1,000	90	910
720	190	100	180	1,000	80	920
728	192	100	180	1,008	80.8	927.2
733.76	193.44	100	181.92	1,015.68	81.568	934.112
*872	228	100	228	1,200	100	1,100

$.2 = MPS < MPI = 48/200 = .24$.

c.

C	S	G	I	Y	T	D
720	180	100	180	1,000	100	900
720	180	100	180	1,000	80	920
736	184	100	189	1,025	82.5	942.5
754	188.5	100	192.875	1,046.875	84.688	962.187
*880	220	100	220	1,200	100	1,100

$.2 = MPS > MPI = 31/200 = .155$.

C	S	G	I	Y	T	D
720	190	100	180	1,000	90	910
720	190	100	180	1,000	80	920
728	192	100	189	1,017	81.7	935.3
740.24	195.06	100	192.315	1,032.555	83.256	949.299
*872	228	100	228	1,200	100	1,100

$.2 = MPS > MPI = 39/200 = .195$.

6 a. We can lower equilibrium income by decreasing G and r with any type of budget: balanced, surplus, or deficit—which are analogues of Routes IV, V, and VI. In the surplus case, reduce G by anything less than 50 (the fall in income). One possibility is:

C	S	G	I	Y	T	D
720	180	100	180	1,000	100	900
710	177.5	60	180	950	62.5	887.5

b. As in Route VII, in which there must be a deficit if income is to rise with decreases in G and r, there can be only a surplus if income is to fall with increases in G and r.

Chapter 33

2 The average price has risen from $1 to ($2 + $.80)/2 = 1.40. On the other hand, you will rightly contend that we should weight them by their importance—weighting the price of good A by ¼ and that of B by ¾. Then the average is $(¼ \times 2.00 + ¾ \times .80)/1 = .50 + .60 = 1.10$, indicating a rise of 10 percent. But, on second thought, you will remember the law of demand and take account of the fact that people will now choose to buy more of the relatively cheaper good. Therefore, suppose that, after the price change, the proportion of one's income spent on good A falls to .1, while that on good B rises to .9. Now new prices weighted by the new proportions give $(.1 \times 2.00) + (.9 \times .80) = .92$. Clearly, we can't tell whether or not there has been an inflation. Some prices have risen and some have fallen, and the average depends upon which prices we consider more important (the weight we assign to each).

5 Claim to a fixed amount of money. A bond is a claim to a fixed amount of money, but its selling price fluctuates.

6 a. A lease is a real asset to the leaseholder, the lessee; he has a claim to use of the building.
b. The owner of the building, the lessor, has a monetary asset—a claim to a fixed series of money receipts.
c. Life insurance is a monetary asset.

8   Must know what my liabilities are. If I owe more monetary liabilities than I hold as money, I would gain from an inflation.

10 No.

13 They are net monetary creditors. Part of their equity or net wealth, represented by this amount of net monetary assets, does not rise in proportion to the price level.

14 The AZ Company is a net monetary debtor to the extent of $154,000 (= $254,000 − $100,000). Each share has a $5.13 net monetary debt ($154,000/30,000). Given the $40 purchase price, this is about 12 percent net monetary debt per dollar of equity.

16 The wage-lag assertion usually refers to a systematic force and not to random events, so lag should be apparent more than half the time. All evidence refutes the existence of a lag.

18 Acquisition of a greater share of resources and services is a wealth acquisition. Rest of economy is poorer, and this effect is a wealth effect—revealed and made effective by the reduced value of money—not by a decrease in the real wages. Suppose a thief stole half of your money and gave it to the government; your income from wages would be no smaller, although your total income would be smaller simply because you have lost wealth, not because prices at which you buy have increased relative to prices (wages) at which you sell your services.

19 **a.** Using the formula in footnote 5 of this chapter, we have $Q = 1.10 − (1.10 − 1)(−23/50) = 1.146$, where Q is the percentage rise in the value of the stock. Price rises from $50 to $57.30, or 14.6 percent.
    b. Using same formula, we have $Q = 1.10 − (1.10 − 1)(18/50) = 106.40$, so price would fall to $50 × 106.4 = $53.20.

21 Yes. Reason detailed in body of question shows why inflation is the only method of fulfilling that assurance.

23 The desire to revise the pattern of demand is often a reason for resorting to a policy of money creation. The inflation does not therefore cause the revised price pattern; instead, the revised demand brought about by the new money causes the relative price changes. At least this interpretation is consistent with facts about sources of inflations and observed changes in relative price patterns. The statement that inflation in and of itself causes a dispersion of prices because of price rigidities is not entirely false if regard is given to prices that are fixed by law and can be changed only by appeal to a regulatory agency (as with public-utility prices). But assertion usually is made in a more sweeping context, and for that there is no supporting evidence.

26 **a.** I would not.
    b. Yes, because legal ethics and principles are concerned only with the nominal absolute value of the funds and not with their real value (relative to price-level changes).
    c. Our legal system seems to be premised on non-inflation as a fact of life—so that nominal value of investment is all that has to be protected by a prudent trustee of your investments.

30 Directs attention away from source of inflation and will restrain extent of trade—which you may consider undesirable.

Chapter 34

3   **a.** (i) The Treasury buys bonds from the Fed:

Treasury		Federal Reserve	
Deposits in FR	decrease	Bonds	decrease
Bonds in FR	decrease	Treasury deposits	decrease

(ii) The Treasury buys from commercial banks:

Treasury		Federal Reserve	
Deposits in FR	decrease	Treasury deposits	decrease
Bonds in commercial banks	decrease	Commercial bank deposits	increase
Commercial Banks			
Bonds	decrease	Deposits in FR	increase

(iii) The Treasury buys from the public:

Treasury		Federal Reserve	
Deposit in FR	decrease	Treasury deposits	decrease
Bonds held by public	decrease	Commercial bank deposits	increase
		Commercial Banks	
Deposits in FR	increase	Public deposits	increase

b. In (i), neither the money supply nor excess reserves are affected; in (ii), the money supply is again unchanged, but excess reserves rise; in (iii), both the money supply and excess reserves increase. If expansion is desired, the Treasury should buy bonds from the public; if contraction, or non-expansion, is desired, the Treasury should buy from the Fed.

5 In making your evaluation, review the difficulties of conducting discretionary "stabilization" policy. But just how much is to be excused? Milton Friedman, the author of the statement quoted in the question, goes on to say that "there is nothing in the economic situation as it stood in, say, September or October, 1930, that made the continued and drastic decline of the following years inevitable or even highly probable. In retrospect, it is clear that the Reserve System should already have been behaving differently than it did, that it should not have allowed the money to decline by nearly 3 percent from August 1929 to October 1930—a larger decline than during the whole of all but the most severe prior contractions. Though this was a mistake, it was perhaps excusable, and certainly not critical." But in late 1930 there began a series of depositor "runs" on banks, resulting in numerous bank failures and drastic fall in the money supply. ". . . one of the major reasons for establishing the Federal Reserve System was to deal with such a situation. It was given the power to create more cash if a widespread demand should arise on the part of the public for currency instead of deposits, and was given the means to make the cash available to banks on the security of the bank's assets. . . . The first need for these powers . . . came in November and December 1930. . . . The Reserve System failed the test miserably. It did little or nothing to provide the banking system with liquidity, apparently regarding the bank closings as calling for no special action. It is worth emphasizing, however, that the System's failure was a failure of will, not of power. . . . Had the money stock been kept from declining, as it clearly could and should have been, the contraction would have been both shorter and far milder. It might still have been relatively severe by historical standards. But it is literally inconceivable that money income could have declined by over one-half and prices by over one-third in the course of four years if there had been no decline in the stock of money. I know of no severe depression in any country or any time that was not accompanied by a sharp decline in the stock of money and equally of no sharp decline in the stock of money that was not accompanied by a severe depression." *Capitalism and Freedom* (Chicago: University of Chicago Press, 1962), pp. 46–50.

Chapter 35

4 Whether or not policy is typically formulated with conscious attention to, and desire to act consistently with, formal theory, it is not necessarily irrational or naive for policy makers to be concerned with maintaining or promoting exports. Exports in general finance imports. While the gains from trade derive immediately from imports, imports will not be obtainable without exports.

7 The essence of the matter is that a foreign-exchange dealer, or bank, acts as a third party, or intermediary, between the importer and the exporter.
  a. The dealer pays off the exporter in one currency and collects payment from the importer in the other currency.
  b. The paying of the exporter and the collecting from the importer need not occur simultaneously; a credit period may elapse before the importer meets his obligation.

9 **a.** $1X = 2Y$, and $1X = 4Z$; therefore, $2Y = 4Z$ or $1Y = 2Z$.
  b. Since Y is overvalued in terms of Z (and Z is undervalued in terms of Y), use X to buy Y, then use Y to buy Z, and finally use Z to buy X.
  c. The X demand for Y (the supply of X in exchange for Y) increases, and the Y demand for X (supply of Y for X) decreases; the Y demand for Z (supply of Y for Z) increases, and the Z demand for Y (supply of Z for Y) decreases; and the Z demand for X (supply of Z for X) increases, and the X demand for Z (supply of X for Z) decreases.
  d. The X price of Y, the Y price of Z, and the Z price of X all go up—which is to say that the Y price of X, the Z price of Y, and the X price of Z all go down.

Chapter 36

1 **a.** The price ratios differ: $15/6 \neq 5/4$.
  b. U. S. has comparative advantage in coats. U. K. export shoes.
  c. Rate of exchange: price of one currency in terms of another. Limits: $\$3 = £1$ and $\$1.5 = £1$.
  d. Terms of trade: international-exchange ratio, the price of exports in terms of imports. Limits: $2.5c = 1s$ and $1.25c = 1s$.
  e. The terms of trade indicate the export cost of imports. The most immediate opportunity cost of imports is the exports with which the imports are purchased.
  f. $1.67c = 1s$.
  g. $\$2.4 = £1$.

2 **a.** In the U. S.:
$$1h = .5c = .333s$$
$$1c = 2h = .667s$$
$$1s = 3h = 1.5c$$
  In the U. K.:
$$1h = .25c = .2s$$
$$1c = 4h = .8s$$
$$1s = 5h = 1.25c$$
  b. The U. K. is cheapest in hats; the U. S. is cheapest in coats; the U. K. is cheapest in shoes with respect to the coat price, but the U. S. is cheapest in shoes with respect to the hat price.
  c. The U. K. exports at least hats, and the U. S. exports at least coats. If $\$1.5 = £1$, shoes do not enter foreign trade; at higher dollar prices of the pound, the U. S. exports shoes; at lower rates, the U. K. export shoes.
  d. $\$5 = £2$ (i.e., $\$2.5 = £1$), and $\$10 = £8$ (i.e., $\$1.25 = £1$).
  e. $2.5h = 1c$; $3.75h = 1s$; $1.5c = 1s$.
  f. $\$1.39 = £1$.

4 Except for people who believe that they obtain status from importing just because the imports are foreign-made, it would make no sense to buy things abroad at a *money* price higher than that charged domestically. But an article may have a lower *money* price abroad although its *input* price (cost) is higher there than domestically. And if the foreign money price is lower, it is sensible to buy the commodity there regardless of the relative international physical input-output efficiencies.

7 **a.** 1.5 linen = 1 wheat.
  b. Abyssinia.
  c. 1 linen = 1 wheat and 1.5 linen = 1 wheat.
  d. Abyssinia obtains (imports) 1.3 linen for each 1 wheat given up (exported) rather than only 1 linen for 1 wheat without foreign trade; Brazil must give up only 1.3 linen to obtain 1 wheat rather than 1.5 linen.
  e. The wage rate must be higher in Brazil, which has an absolute productive superiority in both commodities; the limits of the wage-rate ratio are 1.5/1 and 2.25/1.
  f. There would be only *one*-way trade, with both commodities moving from Abyssinia to Brazil and being financed by either gold or I.O.U.'s moving in the opposite direction. The great demand for goods of Abyssinia and the zero demand for goods of Brazil would increase wages in the former country relative to wages in the latter.

8 **a.** $200X$; $200Y$.
  b. Y.
  c. 150.
  d. 50.
  e. 500.
  f. 100.
  g. 300.
  h. Before trade: $400X$ and $200Y$; after trade: $600X$ and $200Y$.

Chapter 37

1 Without foreign trade, the "consumption" point is the same as the "production" point, and, with full and efficient employment, that point is some place on the production-possibility curve. With foreign trade, the production point will still be on the production-possibility curve (generally at an axis intercept, reflecting complete production specialization), but the consumption point will be on the terms-of-trade line, which lies beyond the production boundary. Thus (a) the consumption boundary has been extended outward, and (b) the terms of international trade imply a lower price of the imported commodity than would prevail in the absence of foreign trade. But the consumption point, while presumably indicating greater consumption of what is now the *imported* commodity, may well reflect smaller consumption of what is now the *exported* commodity. For as we sweep out alternative terms-of-trade lines, rotating around the production point and showing lower and lower export prices of imports, the quantity of imports demanded will increase; but the quantity of export expenditure also will increase within a range—specifically, the range of elastic demand for imports—and thereby leave less of domestic production of that good for domestic use. We are assuming that the trade is not coerced: the members of the community *prefer* to forego some of the export commodity (comparing the trade and pre-trade situations) in order to obtain more of the import commodity. (In Figure 35–1, compare the initial and the new U. K. consumption points, C_1' and C_2'. Note that a line connecting the two points not only is flatter than the production-possibility line, the slope of which measures the exchange ratio before foreign trade, but also is flatter than the terms-of-trade line. In short, the "effective" exchange ratio between C_1' and C_2' implies a relatively low textile-price of steel—sufficiently low that the U. K. residents are willing to pay it.)

2   The fact that the two countries have a "common" consumption point is an inevitability—U. S. exports of steel equal U. K. imports, and U. S. imports of textiles equal U. K. exports—and says nothing about how the gain is divided. And, in general, we do well to avoid trying to measure the *relative shares* of gain. What could it mean to say that the U. S. gains more (or less) in moving from C_1 to C_2 than does the U. K. in moving from C_1' to C_2'? We *can* say that both the U. S. and the U. K. have gained, and, if the terms of trade change over time, we can say that the terms improve for one country and worsen for the other. But to note *directions* of change is not to compare the respective *amounts* of gain at a given time.

4   The same type of information is found in each sort of diagram. (a) The reciprocal demand diagram presents the quantity demanded (imported) as a distance along an axis, as does the usual diagram. (b) The reciprocal demand diagram presents the quantity supplied of the exported good (expenditure) as a distance along the other axis; in the usual diagram, expenditure (in the form of money rather than of another commodity) is an area of price times quantity. (c) In the reciprocal demand diagram, price (terms of trade) is indicated by the slope of a line through the origin; in the usual diagram, price is a distance along an axis.

5   The question relates to elasticity of demand. Where elasticity is arithmetically greater than 1 (the schedule is elastic), a fall in price yields an increase in total expenditure by the buyer; expenditure reaches a maximum at the price where elasticity is unity; and in a range of demand where elasticity is less than 1 (inelastic), a lower price is accompanied by smaller expenditure. In the reciprocal demand case, expenditure takes the force of exports. Thus changes in export expenditure, as the terms of trade change, reflect varying elasticity along the reciprocal demand schedule.

Chapter 38

1   There is no "inconsistency" when the chosen phraseology puts emphasis on the direction of movement of the *asset* rather than on the direction of the *financing* of the transaction. This is the convention when the asset in question is merchandise or services. But when the asset is an I.O.U. (for example, a bond or a bank account), it is customary to emphasize the movement of the financing rather than of the asset itself. Thus, if the U. S. *exports* a bond (a foreigner buys a U. S. bond), the value of the bond sale is listed on the *credit* side of the U. S. balance of payments—as would be the export of merchandise. But the commonly used phraseology labels this I.O.U. export a "capital import," which does indicate the direction of the international investment—from the rest of the world to the U. S.

4   a. −200.
    b. 230.
    c. Export.
    d. 760.
    e. −625.
    f. "Unfavorable."
    g. Buying.
    h. Receiving.
    i. Making.
    j. Exporting.
    k. Outflow.
    l. Country III. Large current-account surplus is financed primarily by making unilateral transfers, exporting long-term capital, and importing gold.

m. Country II. Still sizable current-account surplus and debit balances on unilateral transfer and long-term capital accounts, but with a large gold outflow.

n. Country IV would seem to be in the better position. Both countries, I and IV, have import balances on current account. But the current deficit is financed primarily by long-term capital inflow by Country IV and by short-term capital inflow by Country I. Also Country I has a greater gold outflow, and long-term capital adds to—rather than helping to finance—Country I's deficit.

6   We may refer to the "dollar gap" as the excess of net foreign purchases from the U. S. on current account over net inflow of U. S. long-term capital into the rest of the world. The excess had to be "financed" somehow; the necessity of "financing" is reflected in the inevitable equality of total U. S. credits and debits. One form of "financing" was by U. S. gifts. By giving dollars and goods to the rest of the world, the U. S. made feasible a larger net credit balance on current account; and a larger current surplus with a given long-term capital outflow constitutes a larger "dollar gap."

11   The statement is, in part, from Robert G. Hawkins and Sidney E. Rolfe, *A Critical Survey of Plans for International Monetary Reform* (New York University, C. J. Devine Institute of Finance, Bulletin 36, November 1965), p. 8. The pamphlet explains: ". . . the international monetary system is inevitably crisis-prone. If the deficits of the reserve currency countries, especially the U. S., should be permanently eliminated under the present system, a shortage of world liquidity and reserves would soon develop. With inadequate world reserves, trade and investment would be retarded; a reversion to direct controls, competitive currency devaluations, and other beggar-my-neighbor devices to accomplish balance-of-payments equilibrium would likely occur. But if, on the other hand, the deficit-reserve currency countries cannot stop their deficits, confidence in the continued convertibility between their currencies and gold will be lost and runs on these currencies could force devaluation or crisis application of exchange restrictions, gold embargoes, or other autarchic measures."

Chapter 39

3   Elimination of an import balance does not necessarily require an *absolute* fall in absorption. Rather, it requires a fall in absorption *relative* to income. If income rises, reduction of an import balance is consistent with an *increase* in absorption. Since $Y - A = X - M$, an increase in X relative to M is accompanied by an increase in Y relative to A, but the size of A itself may increase or remain unchanged (if Y increases) as well as decrease.

5   Certainly there are differences between X, on the one hand, and I and G, on the other; indeed, there are differences between I and G. It is hardly a matter of indifference in all respects whether production goes into goods and services bought by foreigners, by private investors, or by government. But X, I, and G have one thing in common: each represents a portion of currently produced, final, domestic output; and spending on these components of output—whether the buyers are foreigners or domestic residents—contributes to money national income.

Similarly, M, S, and T differ in various ways, but each is a disposition of income that does not constitute spending on domestic output. Imports consist largely of (foreign) consumption goods, but imports—like saving and taxes—do not involve consumption of domestic goods.

6   If M is autonomously reduced while Y is held constant, then $C + S + T$ must rise by the amount that M falls. If C remains constant—so that $S + T$ alone offsets the change in M—the income-creation equation is not affected. If monetary and fiscal policies do not succeed in channeling all of the increase into S and T, then C rises—in both equations. In the income-creation equation, a larger C requires a smaller $I + G + X$: if we hold X constant (in order to retain a zero trade balance), then $I + G$ alone must offset C; and a reduction of I and G again calls for monetary and fiscal policies.

8

C	S	M	G	I	X	X − M	Y	T	D
700	140	60	100	150	50	−10	1,000	100	900
700	140	60	100	150	50	−10	1,000	146	854
672.4	126.2	55.4	100	150	50	− 5.4	972.4	143.24	829.16
640	110	50	100	150	50	0	940	140	800

12 Case 1: If a dollar deficit is eliminated, the pound deficit is eliminated. Case 2: If a dollar deficit is converted into a surplus, the pound deficit becomes a surplus. Cases 3, 4, 5: If a dollar deficit is reduced but not eliminated, the accompanying pound deficit may decrease, remain constant, or increase. Case 6: If a dollar deficit is not reduced, the pound deficit rises.

Index

Abel, Mr., of United Steelworkers, 527
Absorption, 533
Abu-Lughad, Janet, 65
Accelerator, 563–66
Accounting, 290–91
   typical balance sheet, 299–305
Acquisition costs, 256, 276
Advertising
   excessive, 347–48
   restrictions on, 367–68
Aggregate demand, and fiscal policy, 702–6
Agricultural surpluses, control of, 369–72
Ali, Mohamed, 504 n 9
Allocation
   of consumable goods, 161–69
   of property rights, 241–43
Annuities
   present capital value, 182–85
   and retirement, 186
Antitrust laws, 358–59
Aquinas, St. Thomas, 16
Arbitrage, 457, 729, 731
Aristotle, 16
Assets
   corporate, 300–1
   monetary, and inflation, 674–77
   real, and inflation, 674–77
   types of, 674
Automation and job re-allocation, 419–22

Bagehot, Walter, 721
Bain, J. S., 345 n 9
Balance of payments
   accounting procedures, 777–79
   adjustment and absorption, 792–93
   adjustment mechanisms, 793–803
   balance or equilibrium, 791 n
   deficit measurement, 782–83
   demand elasticities, 799–800, 800 n
   devaluation of currency, 798–801, 804
   "dollar glut," 782–83
   the dollar as medium of payment, 784–85
   "dollar shortage," 780–82
   exchange rate, 797–803, 804
   "imbalance," 780–83
   international liquidity, 785
   International Monetary Fund's role in adjustment of, 802, 803 n, 803–5
   money supply transactions in adjustment, 793–95
   national income, relation to adjustment, 795–97
   price–gold-flow theory of adjustment, 793
   U.S. deficit, 784–85, 786, 787–88
Balance sheet, typical, 299–305
Bank reserves, 587–88, 589–90, 601, 607–10, 616–18
   and demand deposits, 608 n 2
   determinants, 619–20
   excess reserves, 607
   Federal Reserve balance sheet, 616–17
   Federal Reserve control techniques, 610–15
   "free reserves," 607 n
   and the monetary base, 607–10
   "net borrowed reserves," 607 n
   relation to money supply, 621
   reserve requirements, 608
   reserve-requirement ratio, 610
   Treasury monetary account, 617
Banks
   bank panic, 608 n 2
   cash-drain ratio, 597, 597 n 13
   changes in monetary quantities after monetary transactions, 602
   changes in money stock and interest rate, 600
   charters, 585 n
   demand deposits, 573, 585, 586–87, 593–98
   earning assets, 587
   expansion with and without cash drain, 595–98
   Federal Reserve deposits, 608 n 3
   in Federal Reserve System, 587–88
   interest on loans, 593–94
   lending and borrowing of deposits, 598–601
   liquidity, 608
   loans, 591–92, 598 n
   ratio of total currency to total money supply, 597 n 12
   rediscount rate, 612–13, 712, 712 n
   reductions in amount of money, 600–1
   supply and demand for money, 598
   supply transactions, 585–92
Berstein, E. M., 783 n 7
Black capitalism, 501–2
Black, Eugene R., 504, 504 n 11

Blough, Roger, 345–46
"Blue sky" laws, 292 n
Bonds, negotiability, 469–70
Borrowing, 192
   installment buying, 471–72
   limits on, 471–73
Bowles, Gladys K., 416 n
Brand names, 120
Brimmer, Andrew, 508
Brozen, Y., 345 n 9
Buffer stocks, 139–40
Burns, Arthur F., 713
Burns, E. M., 16
Business firms, 281–99
   accounting practice, 290–91, 299–305
   assets, 300–1
   balance sheet, 299–305
   corporations, 283–87
   equity, 302–5
   legal structure, 283
   liabilities, 301–2
   and new firms, 318–19
   partnerships, 283
   profits, 287–98
   proprietorships, 283
   resource values and resource uses, 320–22
   retained earnings, 303
   see also Corporations; Industry(ies)

Capital
   accumulation, 284
   gain or loss, 288 n, 289
   as resource, 387–88
Capital consumption, 533; *see also* Depreciation
Capital goods
   buying and selling, 456–57
   increased stock, 463
Capital value, 175–76, 190–91
   of humans, 191–93
Capitalization principles, applications, 185–89
Cartel, *see* Collusion
Cary, Mr., of SEC, 366 n
Cash-drain ratio, 597, 597 n 13
Caughlin, Judge Martin, 448–49
Charity, economics of, 148–49
Child labor, 442
Chinese Communist economic doctrines, 250–51
Clayton Act, 359, 431
Closed markets, inefficiency, 251–53
Collusion, 42, 354–56
   closed monopsony, 442–46
   by employees, 359–60
   ethics of, 357–58

   laws regulating, 358–59
   sealed bids to government, 355
   self-regulation in, 356
Commercial banks, *see* Banks
"Commercial loan theory," 708 n
Commodity markets, 161–69; *see also* Speculation
Commodity prices, equalization of, 739–41
Competition, 11–15
   collusion, 354–56, 357–60
   consumer protection, 364–68
   forms of, 11–13
   mergers, 356–57
   monopoly rents, 374–75
   patents and copyrights, 360–63
   predatory tactics, 353–54
   price-cutting, 353–54
   price discrimination, 363–64
   producer protection, 368–72
   public utilities, 372–74
   suppression of new ideas, 361
   trademarks and trade names, 360
   see also Constraints, market
Conservation vs. future wealth, 491–93
Constraints, market
   collusion, 42, 354–56
   compulsory licensing and self-regulation, 42
   control of business hours, 41
   franchise fees, 43
   merger, 42
   see also Competition
Consumer Price Index, 672
Consumer protection, 364–68
   advertising restrictions, 367–68
   quality protection, 365–66
   sanitation standards, 364–65
   unethical sellers, 367
   working hours of employees, 366–67
Consumption, 542–44
   consumption demand function, 544–47, 559–60
   subjective marginal consumption-substitution ratio, 21–22
Copyrights and patents, 360–63
Corporations, 283–87
   continuity of, 284
   limited liability, 284
   ownership and control, 284–87
   see also Business firms; Industry(ies)
Cost effects
   and date of output, 258, 265–68
   of increases in rate and volume, 262–65
   of rate or speed of production, 258, 260–62
Cost of living, lower, 209–10
Cost-push inflation, 95–97, 703

Index

Costs
  acquisition costs, 256, 276
  common, of joint products, 269–70
  of continuing possession, 256, 277
  cost curves, 314–15
  cost-recovery period, 298
  depreciation and obsolescence, 256, 271
  fixed and variable, 257, 314
  of information, 137–41
  long-run and short-run, 265–68, 312–13
  marginal, 315–16
  money measures of, 219–20
  operating costs, 256, 277–78
  passing on higher costs, 326–28
  per-unit-of-service measures, 257–58, 259
  production costs, 312–15
  of resources, 271, 320–22
  of shut-down decisions, 268–69
  and volume, 258–60
Credit, 185–86
  in international trade, 727
Currencies, conversion of, 727
Customs unions, 769–72
Cycles, 522–24

Daley, Arthur, 451
Deficit financing, 707–9
Demand
  adjustment to changes in, 84–85
  aggregate, and fiscal policies, 702–6
  allocation and equilibrium price, 79–81
  anticipated, response to, 340–43
  changes in amount vs. shift in, 58–59
  derived, 394–97
  effect on output, 311–24
  exogenous and endogenous factors, 86 n
  fluctuations in employment and unemployment, 400
  and income, 71–73
  vs. need, 67
  and prices, interdependence, 86–88
  reciprocal, and terms of trade, 759–63
  substitution, 87, 394–96
Demand analysis, applications to market pricing and allocation, 95–107
Demand curve, 57–60
  shift in, 86–87
Demand deposits, 573, 585, 586–87
  expansion of, 593–98
Demand elasticities, 61–64
  in balance of payments, 799–800, 800 n
Demand fluctuations, 338
  effect on price predictability and stability, 140–41
  and production, 311–12, 316–17
Demand function, 57–58, 71–73

Demand, laws of, 60–66
  exceptions to, 67–68
  illustrations of laws, 64–66
  price effects on income and substitution, 68–70
  validity, 70–71
Demand schedule, 57–60
Demand and supply
  analysis, 542 n 3
  reservation demand, 88–90
  see also Supply and demand
Depreciation, 277, 277 n 1, 533–34
  costs of, 256, 271
Depressions, 522–24
  and decrease in money stock, 601
  Federal Reserve response to Great Depression, 712
Discount, 185–86
Discretionary monetary policy
  political and economic problems in, 706–9
  and stabilization, 713–15

Earnings, forms of distribution, 386–87
Economic behavior
  behavioral postulates, 20–23
  preference maps, 27–29
  preference postulates, 20–23
  rational analysis of, 24
  self-interest, 24–25
  utility curves, 27–29
  utility-maximizing, 25
Economic development, 488–89, 509–10
Economic doctrines, Chinese Communist, 250–51
Economic efficiency, 389–90; see also Production efficiency
Economic good, 20
Economic indicators, 704–6
Economic rent, 105–6
Economic theory, 6–7
Economics, functional analysis, 6–7, 25–26
Edgeworth Exchange Box, 47–49
Edgeworth, Francis Ysidro, 47
Efficiency, see Production efficiency
Einstein, Albert, 235
Elasticity
  of demand, 61–64
  mathematical definition of, 61 n 2
Employment
  and recessions, 565
  statistics, 513–14
  see also Unemployment
Employment Act of 1946, 701–2
Equilibrium income
  arithmetic, tabular determination of, 647–50

Equilibrium income (*cont.*)
  with government spending and taxing, 646–50
Equilibrium national income, *see* National equilibrium income
Equilibrium price and distribution, example of, 79–81
Equity, 674–77
  corporate, 302–5
European Economic Community (EEC) (European Common Market), 725 n, 770 n 5
European Free Trade Association (EFTA), 770 n 5
Exchange, 35–49
  achieving efficient production by, 208–10
  common medium of, 55–56
  costs, 41, 137–42
  economic analysis of, 45–46
  as form of competition, 12
  personal values of goods, 43–44
  price controls, 100–4
  production and, 200–1
  productivity, 44
  reasons for, 44
  see also Trade
Exchange rate
  and balance of payments adjustment, 797–803, 804
  devaluation of currency, 798–801, 804
  and gold prices, 735 n
  pegged vs. freely fluctuating, 801–3
  and terms of trade, 738
  and wage rates, 743–44
Exchange ratio, 736–38; *see also* Gains from trade
Exports, 724; *see also* International finance; International trade
Expropriation, risk of, 186
External benefits, 243–44
  exclusion of nonpayers, 244–45
  internalizing of, 244–45

Fair-employment laws, 441
Fama, E. F., 475 n 9
Farm surpluses, control of, 369–72
"Featherbedding," 435
Federal Communications Commission, 642
Federal Deposit Insurance Corporation (F.D.I.C.), 608 n 2
Federal Reserve Act, 587 n
Federal Reserve System, 587 n, 587–88
  bank credit, 616
  and commercial bank reserves, 616–21
  Federal Open Market Committee, 613 n 6
  during Great Depression, 712
  legislation, 610, 611
  limits on installment buying, 471–72
  and monetary base, 618–23
  money-creation function, 707–9
  notes, 617
  open-market operations, 613–14
  rediscount rates, 612–13, 712 n
  reserve-requirement ratio, 610
  stabilization record, 709–13
  steady money growth policy, 714–15
  and Treasury, consolidated reserves, 618
  and war financing, 707–9
Federal Trade Commission, 359
Federal Trade Commission Act, 359
Finances, government, *see* Fiscal policy; Government finances; Monetary stabilization
Fiscal policy
  algebraic analysis of income effects, 664–65
  allocation of national income, 662–63
  assured low unemployment, 703–6
  balanced-budget policy, 655–59
  cost-push inflation, 703
  counterdeflationary policy, 703
  determinants of, 619–20
  discretionary, political and economic problems, 706–9
  economic indicators, 704–6
  evaluation criteria, 660–61
  evaluation of management, 721
  goals, 702
  impacts on national income, 645–65
  during inflation, 689–93
  limits to income expansion, 661–62
  monetary stabilization, 701–20
  policies varying government spending and tax rate, 646–61
  reduction in structural unemployment, 702–3
  wage and price controls, 703–6
Fisher, Lawrence, 475 n 9, 476 n
Fluctuations, 522–24
Foreign aid, 151–52, 726–27
Foreign trade, *see* International finance; International trade
Franchise fees, 43
Franklin, Benjamin, 567
Free goods, 20
Free-market system benefits, 52
Friedman, Milton, 721, 839
Futures prices market, 163–67
  allocation of risks, 167–68
  see also Speculation

Gain from trade, 210–11, 723–24, 730, 736–37
Garner, Robert L., 489, 489 n

General Agreement on Trade and Tariffs (GATT), 769, 769 n 4
"General-equilibrium" analysis, 506
Ghetto economics, 502–3
Gifts
  for employees, 150–51
  foreign aid, 151–52
  free school transportation, 152
  income tax deductions for, 149 n
  intentional or unintentional, 149–50, 152–53
  nontransferable, 154
  philanthropy, 148–49
Gogolak, Pete, 451–52
Gold
  and exchange rate, 735 n
  international gold reserves, 784–85
  in international trade, 715 n 10, 725–26
  Special Drawing Rights, 785
  stock of, 617
Gold certificates, 616–17
Gold standard, 715
Goldberg, Arthur, 449
Goldenweiser, E. A., 721
Goldsmith, Raymond W., 537 n
Goods
  free and economic, 20
  preference postulates, 20–23
  scarcity, 21
  substitutability postulate, 21–23
  utility, 20–21
Government finances, 627–43
  corporation income tax, 632–35
  deficits and debts, 639–41, 707–9
  expenditures, 629–30
  fiscal policy, impacts on national income, 645–65
  government services, 636–39
  national defense, 636–37
  personal income taxes, 630–31
  receipts, 630–36
  redistribution of wealth and income, 639
  securities, changes in prices of, 614 n
  social security taxes, 635, 637–39
  and unanticipated inflation, 677–79
  see also Fiscal policy; Income, national
Great Depression, Federal Reserve response to, 712
Gross national product (GNP), 529–30
  and absorption, 533
  and changes in quantities and prices, 531–33
  measurement of, 532–33

Hawkins, Robert G., 842
Heckscher, Eli F., 752 n 15, 755
Horowitz, David, 504
Hudson, H. E., 65

Hughes, Chief Justice Charles Evans, 447–48
Hume, David, 793, 806

Imports, 723–24
Income
  as adjusting variable, 562–63
  change process, 556–62
  converting to wealth, 456–58
  current- and future-earnings, 191–93
  and demand, 71–73
  equilibrium, 646–50
  fluctuations, 546
  multiplier, 560–62
  standard, 189
  transient current income, 546–47
  ways of saving, 456–58
  see also Wealth
Income effect of price changes, 68–70
Income elasticity, 71–73
Income, national, 487–93, 496–506, 529, 534
  and adjustment of balance of payments, 795–97
  arithmetic-tabular determination of, 547–48, 551–52, 554–55, 651–52
  categories, 541–42
  changes in, 554–56
  consumption, 542–44
  consumption demand function, 544–47
  creation and disposal, 541–44
  disposable, 534
  domestic current output, 530–31
  and foreign aid, 726–27
  and gold, 725–26
  graphic determination of, 548, 552, 555–56, 652–53
  gross national product, 529–30, 531–33
  and growth, 503–6
  inventory increases and decreases, 533 n
  investment and consumption model of determination, 550–51
  and money, 548–49
  money, investment goods, consumption goods relationships, 552–54
  money stock, output, and price level relationships, 577–79
  national income growth, 503–5
  and national wealth, 537
  net national product, 533–34
  personal incomes, 534
  and recessions, 564–66
  relation to output, employment, and prices, 534–37
  savings, 542
Income, personal
  age differences, 493
  endowment differences, 496

Income (*cont.*)
  group differences in, 500–3
  income dispersion, 493
  market vs. nonmarket, 495–96
  and money, 548–49
  national differences in per capita income and growth, 503–5
  by occupation, 413–14, 493
  poverty class, 496–500
  variation in lifetime earnings, 493–95
Income tax(es)
  corporation, 632–35
  negative income tax, 499
  personal, 630–31
  of poverty class, 499
  proportional tax, 716 n
  as stabilizer, 716
Industry(ies)
  "fly-by-night," 319
  market supply, 316–17
  response to entry of new firms, 318–19
  "sick" industries, 319–20
  see also Business firms; Corporations
Inflation
  anticipated, 673, 687–89
  anti-inflation measures, 690–93
  causes, 682–85
  cost-push, 703
  effects of, 673–74
  and interest rates, 193–94
  and investments, 685
  measuring amount of, 685–86
  and net monetary debtor status, 674–77
  price controls in, 104 n 3 and 4, 105, 689–90
  and savings, 685
  unanticipated, 674–81
  wage-lag doctrine, 681–82, 693
  wealth redistribution, 679–81
Installment buying, 471–72
Insurance, 294–96
Interest
  and annuities, 182–85
  biasing rate of, 187
  compound, 180–82
  computing future amounts, 180–82
  historic attitudes toward, 470
  illustrative applications, 185–89
  and loans to college students, 187
  and pension funds, 187–88
  present-value factor, 179–80
  as the price of money, 179
  and profits, 190
  "rule of 72," 181 n
  and savings, 189–90
  and standard income, 189
  and wealth, 189

Interest rate, 176–77, 464
  as adjusting variable, 562–63
  ceilings on, 471
  changes in, 600
  default risk on loans, 466–67
  high, 490, 623
  high vs. low, 490
  and inflation, 193–94
  and investment and savings decisions, 461–64
  legal restrictions on, 482
  on loans, 465–67
  methods of expressing or measuring rate, 177–78
  and quantity of money, 467, 706 n
  real interest rate and money rate, 467–68
  "real" vs. nominal market, 193, 193 n
  and social security, 188–89
  stipulated rate vs. implied effective yield, 465–67
  "tight-money" policy, 490, 623
International finance
  conversion of currencies, 727
  exchange arbitrage, 729
  financing an export, 727–29
  making international payments, 727–29
  provision of credit, 727
International Monetary Fund (I.M.F.), 785 n 10, 802, 803 n, 803–5
International trade, 723–24, 724 n, 733–52
  balance of payments, 777–86, 791–805
  basis of, 746–49
  customs unions and trade agreements, 769–72
  gains from trade, 723–24, 730, 736–37
  labor-capital ratio, 746–51
  multiple-input, factor-endowment theory, 746–51, 755
  output-price theory, 733–41
  "pauper labor," 745, 765 n
  reciprocal demand and terms of trade, 759–63
  resource allocation, effects of trade on, 757–59
  results, 749–51
  single-input theory, 741–46
  tariffs, 730, 745, 745 n, 763–67, 765 n, 769, 769 n 4, 773
  terms of trade, 759–63, 765–69
  see also International finance
International Trade Organization (ITO), 769 n 4
Interstate Commerce Commission, regulation of public utilities, 373–74
Inventories and market pricing, 95–97, 139–40

Investment, 457–58
  average wealth-growth ratios, 477, 477 n
  bonds, negotiability of, 469–70
  demand for, 459–61
  for dividends vs. capital gain, 474
  vs. money, 576–77
  net marginal productivity, 458–59
  personal considerations, 473–77
  profitable, 458–59, 462–63
  random selection of stocks within classes, 474–77
  reduced future yields, 463–64
  and savings, coordination, 461–64
  U.S. government bonds, 466
  variance-risk, 473
  volatility, 563–66
Investment function accelerator, 563–66

Jensen, M. C., 475 n 9
Job displacement effects, 419–22

Kennedy, President John F., 52, 725 n
Keynes, John M., 541 n, 697
Keynesian model of income determination, 541

Labor
  child labor, 442
  demand for, 410
  effect of technology on, 419–22
  equal pay for equal work, 440–41
  fair-employment laws, 441
  labor services as a commodity, 407–10
  legal restrictions on open markets for, 438–41
  minimum-wage laws, 438–40
  occupational wage differences, 413–14, 493
  profits of, 293–94, 413–14, 493–95
  as resource, 387–88
  right-to-work laws, 432
  size of labor force, 407, 410–11
  "yellow-dog" contract, 442
Labor restrictions, open market, 427–47
  closed monopsony, 442–46
  employee-employer bargaining power, 427–28
  immigration restrictions, 440
  labor unions, 428–34
Labor unions, 428–34
  boycott, 430
  closed shops, 430
  craft and industrial unions, 430
  discrimination in membership, 435, 449
  job rationing, 434–35
  as monopoly, 449
  and monopoly rent, 436–38
  national, 429–30

  open shops, 430
  strike legislation, 431–32
  strikes, 430–33
  union bargaining and wage rates, 432–34
  union officials, monetary rewards, 436–37
  union shop, 430, 432
  union wage scale and unemployment, 436
  work rules ("featherbedding"), 435
Laissez-faire, 210
Land Grant Acts, 642
Land rent, 106–7
Land-use rights, 240
Lederer, Walther, 787–88
Lending, 456; *see also* Loans
Lewis, H. G., 433 n
Liability
  corporate, 301–2
  limited, 284
Licensing, compulsory, 42
Loan market, legal restraints on access to, 470–73
Loans, 591–92
  default risk, 466–67
  interest-free or low-interest, 187
  interest rates on, 465–67, 471
  intermediaries in, 468–69
  limits on borrowing, 471–73
Lodge, Senator Henry C., 730
Lorie, James H., 476 n

McGee, J., 354 n 2
McNamara, Robert, 404
Marginal product schedule, 394
Marginal-productivity theory, 389–93
  evaluation of, 397–99
Marginal value-product, 394, 396
Market(s), 56–57
  closed, 251–53
  constraints on, 41–43
  futures prices market, 163–67
  gains from market size, 210–11
  information-collecting function, 81–82
  monopsonistic, 439 n
  open, 41
  "orderly markets," 368–69
  price-takers' and price-searchers', 111–29
"Market-clearing" situation, 80–81
Market competition, *see* Competition
Market-entry restrictions, *see* Competition; Constraints, market
"Market power," 344–45
Market prices
  buffer stocks and inventories, 139–40
  of common stocks, 99–100

Market prices (*cont.*)
  cost-push illusion, 95–97
  costs of enforcing property rights, 141–44
  costs of negotiating exchange, 141–42
  nonclearing, 137–55
  nonprofit institutions, 144–47
  predictability, 139–41
  price controls, 100–5
  of public goods, 147–54
  in rentals and allocation, 97–99
  see also Pricing
Market restrictions, 237–39; *see also* Competition; Constraints, market
Marx, Karl, 213
Meany, George, 451
Mercantilism, 724–25
Mergers, 42, 356–57
  antitrust laws, 358–59
Middlemen, role in trade, 35–40
Mill, John Stuart, 730, 752 n 14
Mints, Lloyd W., 721
Mohammed, Ghulam, 504
Monetary assets, 674
  and inflation, 674–77
Monetary base, 618
  and bank reserves, 607–10
  components, 608–10
  determinants, 619–20
  relation to money supply, 622–23
Monetary debtors and creditors, 679–81
Monetary policy, *see* Fiscal policy; Monetary stabilization
Monetary stabilization, 701–20
  assured low unemployment, 703–6
  automatic stabilizer, 716–18
  discretionary fiscal policy, 706–9, 713–15
  Federal Reserve record of, 709–13
  full-employment income budget balance, 718–19
  goals, 702
  gold standard, 715
  reduction in structural unemployment, 702–3
  steady money growth, 714–15
  wage and price controls, 703–6
Money, 55–56, 572
  as buffer, 56 n
  demand for, 573–75
  functions, 571–72, 572 n
  gold standard, 715
  vs. investment, 576–77
  and investment goods vs. consumption goods, 552–54
  liquidity, 572
  as measure of value, 56
  as medium of exchange, 55–56
  money-price quantity demand function, 57
  quantity of, 467, 600–1
  quantity equation and quantity theorem, 577–79
  relationship between money stock, output, and price level, 577–79
  steady money growth, 714–15
  tax on, 677–79
  "tight" money, 623
  in the United States, 572–73
  see also Money supply
Money rate and real interest rate, 467–68
Money supply
  in adjustment of balance of payments, 793–95
  bank reserves, 607–10
  changes in, 575–76, 600
  and commercial banks, 585–603
  determinants and control techniques, 607–23
  and government deficits, 707
  relation between monetary base and money, 622–23
  relation between reserves and money, 621
Monopoly(ies), 121–22
  antitrust laws, 358–59
  closed monopoly, 333–34
  labor unions, 449
  open monopoly, 334
  patents and copyrights, 360–63
  public utilities, 372–73, 438
Monopoly rents, 29, 374–76
  and labor unions, 436–38
"Monopsonistic" market, 439 n
Monopsony, 442–46
  examples of, 443–46
Multiple-input, factor-endowment theory, 746–51, 755
Multiplier, 560–62
Musgrave, Richard A., 634 n

Nader, Ralph, 251, 820
National equilibrium income
  arithmetic-tabular determination, 551–52, 554–55
  graphic determination, 552, 555–56
National income, *see* Income, national
Needs vs. demands, 67
New York Bond Exchange, 470
Nonclearing market prices, 137–55; *see also* Market prices
Nonprofit institutions, 144–47
Norris-LaGuardia Act, 431
Nurkse, Ragnal, 490 n

Obsolescence costs, 271
Ohlin, Bertil G., 75 n 15
Okun, A. M., 721
Old Age, Survivors, and Disability and Health Insurance (OASDHI), 188–89, 635, 637–39
Oligopoly, 120–21, 345
Open-market operations of Federal Reserve, 613–14
Open-market system, production controls under, 223–28
Open markets, 41
Output
  effect of taxes on, 324–28
  "joint and variable," 269
  programs, 258–62
  response to demand, 311–24
  timing, 323
  wealth maximizing, 315, 322–23
  see also Production; Production efficiency
Output-price theory
  "comparative" advantage, 735–36
  "equal" advantage, 734–35
  equalization of commodity prices, 739–41
  gains from trade, 736–37
  terms of trade and exchange rate, 738

Palmer, Arnold, 11
"Paradox of thrift," 559–60
Partnerships, 283
Pastore, Congressman, 404
Patents and copyrights, 360–63
"Pauper labor," 745, 765 n
Pension funds, and interest, 187–88
Perry, Judge, 401
Personal income, *see* Income, personal
Pollution
  airport noise, 242
  vs. future wealth, 492
  smog, 243
Poverty level, 496–500
Preference patterns, 23
Preference postulates, 20–23
Price(s)
  in absence of price competition, 345
  administered or wage-push, 684, 694
  and demand, interdependence, 86–88
  equilibrium, 79–81, 316–17
  information costs, 137–41
  predictability, 139–41
  price-cutting, 353–54
  price rigidity, 346–47
  price-setting vs. price search, 344–45
  and recessions, 565
  spot prices, 163
  stability, 338
  wholesale and retail, differences between, 297–98
  see also Market prices
Price controls, 100–5, 703–6
  discrimination in, 103–4
  and inflation, 104 n 3 and 4, 105, 689–92
  rationing, 104
  rent controls, 105
  wealth transfer in, 101–2
Price discrimination, 125–27, 362–64
Price effects, validity, 70–71
Price searchers
  in closed markets, 252–53
  market behavior, 118
  as monopolists, 121–22, 296–97
  multipart pricing, 123–25
  as oligopoly, 120–21
  output control with, 226–28
  price changes, justifying, 345–46
  price discrimination, 125–27
  pricing behavior, 117–18
  wealth maximization, 343
Price-searchers' markets, 114–20, 333–49
  advertising, excessive, 347–48
  anticipated demand, 340–43
  brand names, 120
  comparisons with price-takers' markets, 116–18
  determination of price and output program, 335–38
  elasticity of demand, 116
  entry of new firms, 339–40
  marginal revenue, 115–16
  price rigidity, 346–47
  price-setting, 343–45
  product differentiation, 119–20
  profits and concentration of industry, 345–47
  reactions to new products, 341–42
Price-takers' markets, 111–14
  adjustments to increased demand, 322–24
  control of production rate, 225–26
  demand and output, 311–16
  effects of taxes, 324–28
  elasticity of demand, 116
  market-equilibrium price, 113–14
  market supply, 316–17
  pricing and market behavior, 118
  supply response to new firms, 318–19
Pricing, 343–45
  and discrimination, 100
  economic rent, 105–6
  inventories in, 95–97
  land rent, 106–7
  multipart, 123–25
  in price-searchers' markets, 333–49

Pricing (*cont.*)
  price-takers vs. price searchers, 117–18
  producer vs. consumer in, 126
  quasi-rent, 106
  wealth vs. utility maximization, 127–28
  see also Market prices
Private property, 199
  creation vs. operation, 243
  induced external benefits, 243–45
Producers
  of agricultural surpluses, 369–72
  and orderly markets, 368–69
  protection of, 368–72
  reactions to new products, 341–42
  response to anticipated demand, 340–43
Production
  and costs, 255–72, 311–15
  decision to shut down or continue, 315–16
  and demand changes, 311–12
  and exchange, 200–1
  incentives, 223–25
  marginal-productivity theory, 389–93, 397–99
  possibilities in foreign trade, 757–59
  in price-searchers' markets, 333–49
  in price-takers' markets, 311–29
  production flow, 90 n
  substitution effect, 394–97
  under various market conditions, 219–33
  wealth-maximization output, 315, 322–23
Production control
  control of rate with price-takers, 225–26
  with price-searchers, 226–28
  under private-property, open-market system, 223–28
  and production rules, 207–8
Production efficiency
  achievement by market exchanges, 208–10
  evaluation, 213
  incentives to, 223–25
  inefficiency, 237–39, 343, 343 n 4
  intensive margins, 393 n 4
  law of diminishing marginal returns, 391–93
  production and exchange, 204–5
  production-possibility boundary and set, 201–3
  productive and utility efficiencies, 230–32
  and relative input prices, 390–91
  and specialization, 201–8
  techniques, 388–91
  technological, 389
  and wealth maximization, 228–30

Production possibility, 759
Production-possibility boundary, 4–5, 201–3
  as supply schedule, 220–23
Production-possibility set, 201–3
Productivity, *see* Output; Production efficiency
Products
  interdependence, 342–43
  marginal product, 391–93
  new, reactions to, 341–42
  product differentiation, 119–20
Profit-sharing, 191
Profits, 209–10, 287–98, 313
  accounting records, 290–91
  concentration in few firms, 345–47
  cost-recovery period, 298
  definitions of, 287, 297–98
  differences between wholesale and retail prices, 297–98
  expected current losses, 298
  future net earnings, 291–92
  and insurance, 294–96
  and interest rates, 190
  of labor, 293–94, 413–14
  measures of, 288–92
  and monopoly, 296–97
  and ownership and management, 293
  reduction in, 41
  and revenues, 287–88
  sources of, 292–93
  before taxes, 298
  see also Wealth maximization
Property costs, 239–45
Property rights, 190–91
  allocative effects, 241–43
  costs of defining and exchanging, 240
  costs of enforcing, 141–42
  costs of safeguarding, 239
  exclusivity of, 142–44
  and future wealth, 491–92
  and noise and air pollution, 242–43
  radio and television, 242
  trademarks and trade names, 360
  transactions costs, 55–56, 240–41
  transferability, 142
  usufruct rights, 249
  water, 242
Proprietorships, 283, 286
Public goods attributes, 147–54
Public goods production, 245–47
Public utilities, 372–73
  as closed monopolies, 438
  and Interstate Commerce Commission, 373–74

Quasi-rent, 106

Radio
  advertising, 347
  property rights, 242
Rationing, 104
Real assets and inflation, 674–77
"Real bills doctrine," 708 n
Real interest rate and money rate, 467–68
Recessions, 522–24
  and employment, 565
  Federal Reserve response to, 713
  fiscal policy in, 704–6
  and national income, 564–66
  and prices, 565
Reciprocal Trade Agreements Act, 725
Rediscount rate, 612–13, 712, 712 n
Rent controls, 105
Reserve requirements, 608
  reserve-requirement ratio, 610
Reserves, bank, *see* Bank reserves
Resource allocation, effects of foreign trade on, 757–59
Resource values and resource uses, 320–22
Resources, productive
  derived demand for, 394–97
  labor and capital as, 387–88
Retirement, and annuities, 186
Reuther, Walter, 450
Revenues and profits, 287–88
Ricardo, David, 752 n 14
"Right-to-work" laws, 432
Rights, exclusivity of, 142–44
Risk, *see* Speculation
Risk-taker in commodity markets, 161–68
Robertson, D. H., 282
Robinson-Patman law, 363
Rolfe, Sidney E., 842
Roll, R., 475 n 9
Rosenstein-Rodan, P. N., 504 n 12

Salaries, *see* Wages
Savings
  and interest, 189–90
  and investment coordination, 461–64
Scarcity, 3–5, 11–15, 21
Schwulst, Earl B., 483
Scitovsky, T., 113 n
Sealed bids, 355
Sharpe, W. F., 475 n 10
Sheehan, J. M., 452
Sherman Antitrust Act, 358
Sin, Tan Siew, 504 n 9
Single-input theory, 741–46
  absolute advantage, 742–44
  comparative advantage, 744–46
Smith, Adam, 12, 200, 200 n, 212, 274, 488, 567, 730
Smoot-Hawley Act, 745 n

Social security, 635, 637–39
  and interest rates, 188–89
Socialism, 199
  vs. capitalist private-property market system, 627–29
  and output based on wealth maximizing, 322–23
  and specialization, 213–14
  team production in, 282
Specialization
  disadvantages, 212–13
  efficiency, 201–8
  evaluation of, 211–14
  Marxism and socialism, 213–14
Speculation
  allocation of risks, 167–68
  under different economic systems, 168–69
  future prices markets, 163–67
  rate of consumption, 163
  the risk-taker, 161–68
  spot prices, 163
Speculator, 161–68
Stabilization, *see* Monetary stabilization
Stabilizers, automatic
  government-transfer payments and nondiscretionary government expenditures, 717
  income tax, 716
Stigler, George J., 345 n 9, 347
Stock(s)
  "callable," 303
  common, 302–3
  convertible, 302
  for dividends vs. capital gain, 474
  income tax considerations, 474 n
  preferred, 302–3
  prices during recessions, 523–24
  purchase price, 303–5
  random selection within classes, 474–77
  stock-exchange information on, 474–77
  stockholders, 284–86
  stock-option systems, 191
  suspension of trading in, 379
  "watered," 292
Stock market
  arbitrage, 457
  interdependence of lending and capital-goods prices, 457
  see also Speculation
Strikes, 430–33
  compulsory arbitration, 432
  legislation on, 431–32
Substitutability postulate, 21–23
Substitution
  indifference rate, 21–22
  inter-firm, 395–96

Substitution (*cont.*)
  personal substitution values, 22–24, 36–37
  speed of, 397
  substitution value, 22–23
Substitution effect, 68–70, 394
Sullivan, Representative Leonor K., 171
Supply and demand
  adjustment to changes in supply, 83–84
  concepts, 86–88
  market illustration of, 82–86
  use of intermediaries, 85–86

Taft-Hartley Act, 430 n, 431–32
Tariff Act (1922), 745 n
Tariffs, 763–67, 765 n, 773
  General Agreement on Trade and Tariffs (GATT), 769, 769 n 4
  high, 730
  rates, 745, 745 n
Tarver, James D., 416 n
Taussig, Frank William, 752 n 14
Taxes
  corporation, 632–35
  criteria for, 635–36
  effect on output, 324–28
  hidden, 637
  on money, 677–79
  personal income, 630–31
  social security and insurance, 635
  wealth effect, 325–26
Teeters, N. M., 721
Television
  advertising, 347
  property rights, 242
Terms of trade, 767–69
  and reciprocal demand, 759–63
  and tariffs, 765–67
"Tight money," 490, 623
Torrens, Robert, 200 n
Trade
  as basis of exchange, 35–49, 758
  in capitalist vs. socialist cultures, 45
  ethics of free trade, 44–45
  foreign, *see* International finance; International trade
  gains from, 210–11
  international, *see* International finance; International trade
  the middleman, 35–39
  principles of trade, explained with Edgeworth Exchange Box, 47–49
  reasons for, 44
  see also Exchange
Trade agreements, 769–72
  "most-favored-nation" clause, 769 n 3
Trade Agreements Act, 725, 725 n 2, 769 n 4

Trade Expansion Act, 421 n, 725, 725 n
Trading stamps, 126 n
Transactions costs, 55–56, 240–241
Treasury bonds, 707–8
Treasury currency, 617
Truman, President H. S, 668

Underdeveloped countries, 488–89, 509–10
Unemployment, 514–15
  assured low, as fiscal policy, 703–6
  costs of job research, 516–17, 523
  demand fluctuations, 517–25
  frictional, 516–17
  kinds of, 515–17
  reasons for, 514–17, 525–26
  statistics, 514
  structural, 702–3
  teenage, 517
Unions, *see* Labor unions
"Unseen Hand," 210
U.S. Bureau of Labor Statistics, Consumer Price Index, 672
Usufruct rights, 249

Values
  common measure of, 56
  input vs. output values, 23–24
  personal, diminishing, 39
  personal substitution, 22–24, 36–37
Viner, Jacob, 509–10

Wage-lag doctrine, 681–82, 693
Wage and price controls, 690–92, 703–6
Wage rates and exchange rates, 743–44
Wages
  and demand and supply, 416
  effect of job re-allocation on, 419–21
  equalizing-difference wage, 440–41
  imposed wage uniformities, 440–41
  on-the-job training, 416–17
  minimum-wage laws, 438–40
  occupational differences in, 413–14, 493
  open-market, 411–13
  risk-bearing differentials, 417
  wage differences, factors in, 413–19
Wagner Act, 428
Water, property rights, 242
Wealth, 189, 455
  black capitalism, 501–2
  from buying and selling capital goods, 456–57
  future net earnings, 291–92
  group differences in, 500–3
  growth and distribution of, 487–507
  from investing, 457–61, 461–64
  from lending, 456
  measures of changes in, 288–90
  natural resources, 488

Wealth (*cont.*)
  net wealth (equity), 674–77
  personal income differences, 493–500
  vs. property rights, 491–93
  redistribution during inflation, 679–81
  from saving, 456, 457, 461–64
  in underdeveloped countries, 488
  see also Income; Wealth maximization
Wealth maximization, 313–14, 315, 455–79
  means of, 189–90, 487–91
  in price-searchers' markets, 335–38
  in price-takers' markets, 315, 322–23
  and productive efficiency, 228–30
  see also Profits
Wealth, national, *see* Income, national
Wheeler-Lea Act, 359
Woods, George D., 504 n 12

Yeager, Leland B., 807
"Yellow-dog" contract, 442